III. DEFINITIONS OF FINANCIAL VARIABLES

C_0, C_1, C_t Individual's level of consumption in t

CAR_t Cumulative average residual as of t

F_{it} Face value of security i in period t

F_{ht} Value of factor h in period t

G Average annual geometric rate of return

g, g_n, g_s Growth rate of earnings or dividends (n is normal, s is supernormal)

I_{it} Net investment outlays by firm i in period t

n_{it} Number of shares of security i outstanding in t

N_{it} Accounting depreciation of firm i in period t

P_{it} Price of security i in period t

R_f Risk-free interest rate

R_{it} Holding period return on i in t

R_{It} Holding period return on the market index in t

R_{mt} Holding period return on the market portfolio in t

R_y Yield to maturity

R_t^* Return on corporate real capital investment in t

INVESTMENTS

INVESTMENTS

Nancy L. Jacob
University of Washington

R. Richardson Pettit
University of Houston

Second Edition
1988

Homewood, Illinois 60430

Acquisitions editor: Gary L. Nelson
Project editor: Susan Trentacosti
Production manager: Irene H. Sotiroff
Artist: Jay Bensen, The Artforce
Compositor: J.M. Post Graphics, Corp.
Typeface: 10/12 Times Roman
Printer: Arcata Graphics/Halliday

ISBN 0-256-05831-8

Library of Congress Catalog Card No. 87–82521

Printed in the United States of America

1 2 3 4 5 6 7 8 9 0 H 5 4 3 2 1 0 9 8

To
Barney, Randy,
Caroline, Scot,
and Erin

Preface

This book describes the theory and practice of investment decision making. It is designed for instructional use in upper-division undergraduate and graduate (M.B.A. or M.S.) courses in investments. A unique feature is the book's consistent reliance on a basic set of financial and economic principles for discussion of both the *theory* and the *practice* of investment decision making. This feature plays an important role in closing the many potential gaps between theoretical concepts and evidence from actual financial markets—gaps that can frustrate learning. One such gap, for example, is in the relationship between individuals' portfolio selection decisions based on their evaluation of a security, and the establishment of equilibrium prices in the capital asset market. In attempting to fill this gap and others, this book integrates the broad subject area of investments, thus avoiding the considerable "handwaving" present in most other investments texts.

This edition of the book has been extensively rewritten with a view toward the elimination of extraneous material, the simplification of many concepts and ideas, and the development of a more concise method of presentation. The net effect is a book that is about 20 percent shorter than the first edition with the same comprehensive coverage of the subject of investments.

Content of the Book

We believe that any financial issue can be analyzed in terms of the interactions among the four basic components of financial decisions: financial market opportunities, market prices, individual preferences, and wealth levels. These components, or building blocks for investment decisions, provide the basis for the three theoretical frameworks that form the basis for the book's analytical approach. The first is the **theory of choice under uncertainty** which leads to the proposition that consumer-investors, given their current wealth levels, make decisions to maximize personal utility. In later chapters, use of this theory allows a better understanding of why, for example, investors diversify, why perceptions of risk influence security values, and why portfolio managers with different stated objectives should be evaluated according to different performance standards.

The second theoretical framework is that of **efficient capital markets,** whereby security prices fully reflect all publicly available information relevant to security valuation. The validity of this theory is questioned, tested, and analyzed throughout the book. It is used as a frame of reference for assessing the value of various types of investment information. Further, the theory is used to test the potential for superior performance that underlies various investment strategies in different securities markets.

The third framework we use extensively is that of **modern portfolio theory** and the **capital-asset pricing model.** Based originally on the principles of portfolio theory, the CAPM allows us to develop specific equilibrium valuation models for both common stocks and fixed-income securities. These models are applied to investment decision making and to understanding the financial relationships that exist in actual securities markets.

These basic theories enrich our understanding of events in real securities markets and enable investors to discriminate between truth and illusion, thus helping them avoid potentially costly mistakes. To ensure clarity of presentation, each theory is developed as a logical extension of the others over the course of a number of chapters. The basics of the theory of choice are first presented in Chapters 1 and 2. The concept of efficient financial markets is developed in Chapter 6 as a logical extension of the investor's search for a preferred investment decision. Portfolio theory and the capital-asset pricing model are developed in Chapters 7 and 8.

Other models, theories, and concepts are also discussed. These include the concepts of **no arbitage profits** and the **law of one price.** We use these ideas to increase our understanding of the valuation of debt and equity securities, futures and forward contracts, and put and call options.

Where reality departs from theory, we do not hesitate to consider the theory's potential shortcomings in explaining the observed phenomena. Thus, we discuss security analysis and portfolio management in terms of potential disequilibrium (or undervalued and overvalued) prices for securities. Moreover, we use reality to emphasize the evolutionary state of modern financial theory. At present, for example, there is no satisfactory model to explain how Japanese common stocks should be priced relative to Australian stocks in imperfect world capital markets. Neither do we know how to explain why *Value Line Investment Survey* has historically produced superior forecasts for individual stocks, while tests reveal that many mutual fund managers have tended to underperform the market over long periods of time. Reference to existing theories, however, can help us determine where our knowledge is inadequate and what we need to study in the future.

Design and Layout of the Book

This book has a number of new design and format features that have been developed jointly by the authors and the publisher as a way to make difficult material easier to comprehend. These include:

1. The interspersion of institutional and conceptual material throughout the book to aid in integrating theory with practice.
2. The presentation of new concepts or ideas verbally, graphically, and, where necessary, mathematically. One approach reinforces the other and gives the student multiple perspectives on the subject matter.
3. The labeling of mathematical terms and equations at the time they are introduced to reinforce the connection between the mathematical statement represented in equation form and the meaning of the concept being developed. Moreover, where we think it is most important, a direct verbal interpretation of an equation is set immediately below that equation.
4. The use of relatively large graphs for easy interpretation of detail. In addition, where it can add to understanding of the conclusion developed in the text, a verbal interpretation of the graph is presented within the graph itself.
5. The use of consistent mathematical notation throughout.

The net effect of these features is page design that provides for ease of reading with a greater level of comprehension and more enjoyment.

Chapter Questions and Problems

End-of-chapter questions and problems for this edition are new. There are a large number of problems that address the issues related to applied investment analysis. Most important, there are questions at the end of each chapter that have been selected from past examinations given by the Institute of Chartered Financial Analysts (they are marked with a CFA designation when they appear). We gratefully acknowledge the assistance of the Institute in allowing us to use these excellent questions.

On the Use of Software

A number of portfolio choice and present value software programs can be used in conjunction with the book to supply students with an understanding of how the concepts can be applied to actual securities markets. We have used the program MPS Optimizer (by *Modern Portfolio Strategies Inc.*, P.O. Box 3230, Ann Arbor, MI 48106) with the book very successfully in the past two years. This program, written by Stan Kon at the University of Michigan, illustrates the use of portfolio theory and integrates it with the capital-asset pricing model, index futures trading, and options strategies. The user is able to determine the sensitivity of portfolio weights to different levels of risk aversion and different parameter input values for the individual securities analyzed. The program accepts raw price data "downloaded" from a text file or from a database service such as Dow Jones News Retrieval, and data fed in manually by the user. Optimal portfolio weights (efficient sets) can be constructed for more than 40 individual securities—with and without short sales constraints.

Course Design

The book may be used either in a quarter system (10 weeks) or a semester system (15 weeks). We have found it easy to cover Parts I through IV in one long semester. However, at the instructor's discretion and depending on the backgrounds of students, the chapter coverage can be altered to provide more in-depth treatment of some topics. Thus, while the book attempts to integrate the various theories and concepts of finance for the student, the method of presentation and writing style are developed to allow the chapter material to be covered in a different order than the one presented in the book. Instructors have, variously, covered performance measurement and valuation earlier than they are presented in the book and have presented the efficiency of financial markets and arbitage pricing theory later than they are presented in the book.

The authors have also used the book in quarter system classes. This has been accomplished, for example, by not covering, or covering selectively, the material on the theory of choice (in Chapters 1 and 2), on arbitage pricing (Chapter 10), on security analysis and forecasting (Chapters 15, 16, and 17), and on futures, options, and applied portfolio management (Chapters 17–22). This leaves approximately 11 or 12 chapters to cover in a 10-week quarter. Often in quarter systems the omitted material is presented in other courses, and the subjects are developed here with that in mind.

Acknowledgments

A number of people have contributed significantly to this book. In some cases the contributions have spanned a number of years and two editions. We realize now that it would have been desirable to maintain an ongoing file of contributors to ensure that no one's assistance would be overlooked. No such list could possibly ignore, however, the important help we received from the following colleagues: Robert Klemkosky, Indiana University; Donald Puglisi, University of Delaware; Steve Figlewski, New York University; Richard Castanias, University of California–Davis; Gary Schlarbaum, Miller, Sherrand; Jim Morris and Jean-Claude Bosch, University of Colorado–Denver; A. J. Senchak, University of Texas; Stanley Kon, University of Michigan; John Crockett, George Mason University; Patrick Shen, Michigan Technological University; Leonard Rosenthal, Bentley College; Mike Hopewell, University of Oregon; Steve Wyatt, University of Cincinnati; and Alfred C. Morley, Institute of Chartered Financial Analysts. We also wish to thank Charles D'Ambrosio and Avi Kamara from the University of Washington and, from the University of Houston, Shalom Hochman, Ron Singer, Ramon Rabinovitch, P. C. Venkatesh, and Kean-Pang Song. Comments from Theodore Day, Vanderbilt University; John Glascock, Louisiana Tech University; Richard Hanson, University of California–Irvine; Robert Korajczk, Northwestern University; Susan Malley, Fordham University–Lincoln Center; Gregory Niehaus, University of Michigan–Ann Arbor; George Racette, University of Oregon–Eugene; and James Savarino, University of Washington–Seattle, aided us in our work on this edition.

A special thanks goes to those responsible for typing a major portion of the manuscript—Cheryl Redmond and Millie Dooris.

Nancy L. Jacob
R. Richardson Pettit

Contents

Part I: The Savings and Investment Decision   1

1. Investment Decisions   3

Finance and Economics. The Organization of This Book. Applying Economic Theory to Investment Decision Making. The Theory of Choice: *Available Opportunities. Market Prices. Wealth. Preferences. The Choice. Changing Conditions and Changing Decisions.* Investment Decisions. Market Equilibrium. Three Points in Time and Arbitrage: *Equal Rate of Return. Arbitrage.* Present Values in a Multiperiod World.

2. Uncertainty and Decision Making   26

Uncertain Outcomes. Random Variables and Probability Distributions. Summary Measures of Probability Distributions: *Expected Value. Standard Deviation. Skewness and Peakedness.* Decisions under Uncertainty: *The Level of Utility. The Implications of Diminishing Marginal Utility for Risk Aversion. Justifying the Use of Expected Utility. Monetarizing the Aversion to Uncertainty. Utility Comparisons. How Can the Level of Risk and Reward Be Summarized?* Willingness to Trade Off between Risk and Wealth: *Changing the Units from Dollars to Rates of Return.* Introduction to Valuation under Uncertainty. Summary Measures of Joint Probability Distributions: *Covariance. Correlation. Regression. Multiple Regression. Financial Applications of Regression: An Example.* Manipulation of Random Variables: *Rules for Calculating Expected Values. Rules for Calculating Standard Deviations. Rules for Calculating Covariances.*

Part II: Market Structure   55

3. Investment Opportunities   57

The Purpose of Investing. Business Firms and the Investment Opportunities They Create. The Firm and Its Contracts: *To Open or Close.* The Costs and Benefits of Financial Contracts: *Contract Clarity. Costs of Monitoring. Divisibility. Marketability. Maturity or Longevity of the Contract. Risk of the Contract. Summary of Costs and Benefits of Open Incorporation.* Types of Security Contracts: *Common Stock. Bonds and Fixed Income Securities. Debt/Equity Combinations. Third-Party Financial Contracts.* Financial Investment and the Wealth of Society. The Operating Efficiency of Markets for the Exchange of Securities: *Marketability. Marketability and Efficiency.* How Many Types of Financial Instruments?

4. *Securities Markets*   77

Primary Securities Markets: *Financial Institutions. Investment Bankers. Mortgage Bankers.* Secondary Securities Markets. Types of Securities Traded. The Organized Securities Exchanges: *History and Organization of the Exchanges. Exchange Membership. Listing Requirements.* The Trading Process on Exchanges: *Description of Orders. How Trades Are Consummated. Exchange Automation. Marketability. Settlement. Margin Transactions. Foreign Securities and Foreigner's Investments in Listed Securities. The Composite Ticker Tape. Block Transactions.* The Over-the-Counter Market: *Negotiated Markets. Securities Traded in the OTC Market. Brokers and Dealers. NASDAQ and Price Quotations. Consolidated Quotations. NASDAQ Listing Requirements.* Regulation of Securities Markets: *Securities Act of 1933. Securities Exchange Act of 1934. Securities Investor Protection Act of 1970. Securities Act Amendments of 1975.* Market Indicators: *Dow Jones Averages. Standard & Poor's Indexes. NYSE Composite Index. NASDAQ OTC Index. Wilshire 500 Equity Index.*

5. *Investment Returns*   115

The Calculation of Rates of Return. The Historical Record: Common Stock and Bond Indexes: *Multiperiod Returns and the Geometric Mean Return. Comparison of Multiperiod Stock and Bond Returns. Wealth Distributions Implied by Stock and Bond Investments. Index Construction.* The Historical Record: Other Investment Alternatives: *Government Bonds and Short-Term Bills. Foreign Common Stocks. Collectibles and Objects of Art. Real Estate. Commodity Futures. The Value of the Aggregate World Market Wealth Portfolio.* Inflation and Investment Returns. Return and Risk—A Summary.

6. *Market Efficiency*   145

Introduction. The Pricing Process: *Factors Affecting Supply and Demand. An Ideal Market. Price Adjustments in Ideal Markets. Efficient Market Hypothesis.* Testing the Efficient Market Hypothesis: *Indirect Tests of Market Efficiency. Direct Tests for Dependencies.* The Use of Technical and Fundamental Analyses. Oh, Yes. What about the Top 20?

Part III: Portfolio Choice and Equilibrium Market Returns   181

7. *Portfolio Choice*   183

Risk Management. The Insurance Principle. Risk Reduction in Stock Portfolios. Empirics of Risk Reduction: *Measures of the Comovement of Returns. When Diversification Pays.* The Effect of Diversification on Risks and Returns: *Two-Security Diversification. Risk Reduction and Diversification Applied to Six Securities. The N Security Case.* Efficient Portfolios and Optimal Diversification: *The Efficient Frontier.* Portfolio Choice: *Risk-Free Borrowing and Lending. The Separation Theorem.* Short Selling and the Efficient Set. An Efficient Set for the Dow Jones Securities. Portfolio Revision. Errors in Estimation.

8. *Capital Asset Pricing*   223

Market Equilibrium: *The Complexity of the Problem. A Definition of Equilibrium.* The Capital-Asset Pricing Model: *The Market Portfolio. The Capital Market Line.* Security Risk and Return:

Security A's Contribution to Market Portfolio Return. Security A's Contribution to Market Portfolio Standard Deviation of Return. Security Market Line. Beta and the Security Market Line. Over- and Undervalued Securities. Portfolios. Equilibrium Prices. Appendix: Relaxing the Assumptions of the Capital-Asset Pricing Model.

9. *Capital Asset Pricing: Evidence*   255

The Market Model: *Security Characteristic Lines. The Market Portfolio Revisited. Beta and the Components of Risk. Examples of Calculated βs. Alpha and Equilibrium Valuation. Portfolio Characteristic Lines. Application to the Value Line Contest.* The Market Model and Empirical Estimates of the CAPM. Testing the Accuracy of the CAPM. Implications of the CAPM. Testing the Model's Postulates: *Ex Ante and Ex Post Data Problems. Estimating Betas and Returns. Time Series Tests of the CAPM. Cross-Sectional Tests of the CAPM.* Problems with the CAPM: How Serious? *Is the Theory Testable at All? How Far Off Is the CAPM?* Appendix: The Difference between *m* and *I*—Resolving the Roll Controversy.

10. *Arbitrage Pricing*   292

The Law of One Price. Multiple Factors Affecting Returns. Portfolios of Securities. The Arbitrage Pricing Model. Similarities between the APT and the CAPM. Tests of Arbitrage Pricing Theory. Do the Coefficients on the Factors Explain the Differences between Securities' Returns? What Are These Factors? The APT and a Multifactor CAPM.

Part IV: Valuation   305

11. *Introduction to Valuation*   307

The Basic Concept. Three Concepts of Value: *Personal Value. Market Value (Price). Underlying Equilibrium Value.* Single-Period Valuation: *Evaluating the Cash Flows. Evaluating the Discount Rate.* Equilibrium and Disequilibrium. Putting It All Together: The Components of Equilibrium Value. Multiperiod Valuation: *The Problem. The Multiperiod Solution. Stability Over Time.* Personal Value: The Multiperiod Case. Risk and Value: *Business Risk. Financial Risk. Interest Rate Risk.* Appendix: The Certainty Equivalent Approach to Valuation.

12. *Valuation of Fixed-Income Securities*   332

Contracts and Claims: *Definition of Fixed-Income Securities. Distribution of Cash Flows.* Valuation of Fixed-Income Securities. Rates of Return on Fixed-Income Securities: *Securities Free of Default Risk. Securities with Default Risk. Yield to Maturity. Current Yield.* Risk of Fixed-Income Securities: *Nondiversifiable Default Risk. Nondiversifiable Interest Rate Risk. Duration. Bond Betas. Estimating Bond Betas. Risk Management.* Maturity and Returns: The Term Structure of Interest Rates: *Market Risk Preferences. Anticipated Future Supply and Demand.* Inflation and Fixed-Income Securities: *Real and Nominal Returns. Inflation and Default-Free Securities. Inflation and Securities with Default Risk. Inflation and the Value of Other Economic Variables. Inflation and After-Tax Returns.* Appendix: Improving the Precision of Rate of Return Calculations.

13. Fixed-Income Securities Markets   372

Federal Government Securities: *Treasury Bills. Treasury Bonds and Notes.* Federal Agency Securities. State and Local Government Securities: *General Obligation Bonds. Revenue Bonds.* Deposits at Financial Institutions. Corporate Securities: *Money Market Securities of Corporations. Corporate Bonds and Preferred Stock. Risk. Specialized Corporate Debt Securities.* Bond Ratings. Private Individual Issues.

14. Valuation of Equity Securities   405

Stockholder Claims. Distribution of Cash Flows. Valuation of Common Stock: *The Role of Earnings in Valuation. The Role of the Firm's Investment Opportunities in Valuation. Growth and the Dividend Capitalization Model. The Growth of Earnings and Dividends. Nondividend-Paying Growth Stocks and Value. Growth and Stockholder Returns.* Rates of Return on Common Stock. Risk of Common Stocks: *Nondiversifiable Cash Flow Risk. Nondiversifiable Interest Rate Risk. Empirical Estimates of the Relationship between β_i and Firms' Characteristics.* The Price/Earnings Ratio. Valuation of Common Stock: Empirical Evidence: *Hypotheses to Be Tested. A Regression Study of Price/Earnings Ratios. Event Studies of Security Value.* Are Stock Prices Too Volatile to Be Explained by Earnings or Dividend Expectations? Integration of Valuation Theory with Portfolio Choice.

15. Security Analysis   442

The Production of Private Information. Security Analysis and the Production of Private Information: *Analyst's Valuation. Analyst's Expected (Disequilibrium) Return. GAF Illustration. DEC Illustration.* How Large Can the $\hat{R}_i$ Values Be? Security Analysis. Dividends and Earnings: *Determinants of Earnings. Normalized Earnings. Properties of Earnings and Dividends.* Risk or Beta. Security Market Line. Standard Deviations and Covariances. Analysis of Aggregate Market Returns: Timing: *How Valuable Is a Good Forecasting Technique?*

16. Forecasting Returns   475

Myths and Realities. Valuation, Analysis, and Forecasting. Requirements of a Forecasting Model. Forecasting Earnings: *Statistical Extrapolations. Forecasts Using Other Predictor Variables. Managers' Forecasts. Analysts' Forecasts.* Forecasting $\hat{\beta}$: *Historical. Blume Adjusted. Merrill-Lynch Adjusted. BARRA Adjusted. Summary of Forecasting Schemes.* Can Analysts Forecast Individual Security Returns? Insider Information and Return Predictions. Forecasting Returns on the Market Portfolio: *Forecasting Interest Rates. Forecasting Aggregate Market Earnings. Forecasting Market Returns.* Forecasting with "Technical Analysis."

17. Management Decisions and Value   508

The Managerial Decision Nexus. Investment Decisions and Value: *Anticipated and Unanticipated Investment Opportunities. The Real Effects on Price.* Mergers and Value: *Mergers and Valuation: An Example. Mergers and Valuation: The Empirics.* Financing Decisions and Value: *Debt and Returns to Shareholders. Debt and Risk. Debt and Value. Other Incentives for the Use of Debt.* Dividend Policy and Value: *The Ex-Dividend Behavior of Stocks. Preferences for Dividends. Dividend Signaling: The Informational Content of Dividend Announcements.* Share Repurchase and Value: *Open Market Purchases. Tender Offer Repurchases.* Stock Dividends, Stock Splits, and Value.

18. *Futures and Forward Markets*   540

Futures and Forward Contracts: *Definitions of Important Terms. Forward Contracts. Futures Contracts.* Profit and Losses: *The Purpose of Futures and Forward Contracts. Which Commodities Will Have Forward or Futures Markets?* Institutional Arrangements and Trading Procedures: *Commodity Exchanges: Futures Trading. Transactions on Futures Markets. Commodity Futures Trading Commission. Price Limits. Margin.* Valuing Futures and Forward Contracts: *Arbitrage and the Expected Future Spot Price. Carrying Costs. The Expectations Hypothesis. Normal Backwardation and Contango: The Demand for Hedging and Futures Prices. Supply and Demand. Supply, Demand, and Commodity Spreads.* Financial Futures Markets: *Why Futures in Financial Securities Were Created. Hedging and Speculating with Interest Rate Futures. Hedging Transactions with Interest Rate Futures. Expanding Interest Rate Futures. Stock Market Futures. Hedging Transactions with Stock Index Futures. Foreign Exchange Futures. Valuation of Foreign Exchange Futures.*

19. *Options*   573

Introduction: *The Option as a Financial Instrument.* Kinds of Options: *Call Options. Put Options. Warrants. Rights. Options on Futures Contracts. Employee Stock Purchase Options. Corporate Call on Bonds. Convertible Bonds and Convertible Preferred Stock. Extendable and Redeemable Bonds. The Equity Option.* Profits in Options: *Options Returns: An Illustration.* Why Do Options Exist? Trading Options on Exchanges. Trading Over-the-Counter. Option Valuation: Calls. Option Pricing: Black, Scholes, and Merton: *Example: How Does Price Vary as Terms Change? Dividends and Value.* Valuing Puts: *Put–Call Parity.* Strategies for Using Options to Affect Portfolio Characteristics. Options Have Betas. Valuing Warrants. Valuing Convertible Securities. Valuing Other Option-Type Instruments. Empirical Evidence on the Pricing of Options. Taxation of Options.

20. *International Securities*   617

International Investing. The Size and Nature of Foreign Investment Opportunities. Historical Returns on Foreign Financial Opportunities. Foreign Exchange Markets and Exchange Risk: *American Depository Receipts. Foreign Exchange Risk. Foreign Exchange Prices, Inflation, and Interest Rates. Foreign Exchange Prices and Diversification.* Forward Market for Foreign Exchange: *Interest Rate Parity. Eliminating Foreign Exchange Risk.* Efficiency of Foreign Exchange Markets. International Portfolios and Diversification: *Diversification and Transaction Costs.* Beta Coefficients on Foreign Securities. Diversification, Using Multinational Firms. Valuation of Foreign Securities. Success at Investing Internationally: An Example.

Part V: Managing the Investment Process   643

21. *Investment Portfolio Management*   645

The "Financial Planning Model" Developed So Far. Applying the Model. The Active/Passive Management Question: *Passive Management. Active Management. Active/Passive Combinations. Variants of the Active/Passive Strategy.* The Revision Question. The Diversification Question. The Contraints Question: *Cash Flows. Portfolio Proportionate Holdings. Eligible Securities.*

Portfolio Time Horizon. The Manager Question. Types of Professionally Managed Funds: *Open-End Mutual Funds*. *Money Market Funds*. *Closed-End Mutual Funds*. *Real Estate Investment Trusts*. *Bank Commingled Funds*. *Pension Funds*.

22. *Performance Measurement*   *668*

Control. Performance. The Performance Standard. Ex Post Security Selection Ability. Ex Post Market Timing. Total Performance. Performance Measurement: An Example. Diversification Performance. An Application of Performance Measurement Techniques. Single Parameter Performance over Many Periods. Historical Performance of Professionally Managed Portfolios: *Can Some Funds Outperform the Market Consistently? Other Performance Characteristics*. The Performance of Self-Managed Portfolios.

Appendix: Selected Investment Information Sources   *691*

Author Index   *701*

Subject Index   *703*

P A R T

I

THE SAVINGS AND INVESTMENT DECISION

CHAPTER

1

Investment Decisions

Finance and Economics

This book describes and explains the economic activity of investment decision making. Economics is primarily concerned with the study of markets: It attempts to describe and explain how people make choices among various goods and services, how firms and governments make production decisions, and how these choices interact in the marketplace to generate prices. Being concerned with investments, this book focuses on economic behavior in markets for financial instruments or assets that have a potential for yielding monetary rewards in some future period. Thus, it attempts to characterize the supply of and demand for securities and explain how they come together in the financial marketplace to determine market prices.

Not surprisingly, the economic theory that is useful for understanding the markets for goods and services is also useful for understanding investment markets. How, in particular, does that theory apply to investment decision making? Principally in two ways. First, the theory is useful in studying how people *should* make choices between current consumption and savings. This application of theory is the *normative* side of economics, and it can produce useful guidelines for managing investment portfolios. Second, it is necessary to know how individuals *may* act in investment markets to have an understanding of the operation of those markets. This application is part of *positive* economics: the study of actual relationships between prices and other characteristics of investment opportunities (e.g., the firm's earning power). With these relationships we can examine the prices of various securities or other assets in which we may be tempted to invest, and learn why prices are what they are and how they might change as circumstances change.

Successful operation in these markets (as a money manager, financial planner, broker, analyst, market maker, or investor) requires the understanding of both normative and positive elements of the theory and practice of investment. As we describe in this chapter, not only is an understanding the market environment required, but also an awareness of the relationships among our preferences, our objectives, and the ultimate decisions we make. More generally, a sound conceptual framework for understanding the subject of investments is what this book intends to provide.

The Organization of This Book

This book is organized into five parts. Part I is devoted to a brief introduction to the basic components of choices involving consumption and savings. We focus on how individual preferences and objectives should be taken into account when making actual investment decisions. First we concentrate on the essence of the decision process in a world of certainty. Then, after describing the nature of uncertainty, we reconsider how desired objectives can be achieved by choosing among investment alternatives offering different distributions of possible returns (i.e., offering different kinds or levels of uncertainty).

Part II is a positive study of the investment environment and the part it plays in successful decision making. This section is mainly institutional and descriptive as our primary goal is to attain a better understanding of the characteristics of investment assets (securities) and the markets in which they are traded. We summarize the general nature of financial instruments and how the markets for them operate. We also develop summary measures of the returns these investment alternatives have generated in the past.

Part III develops an integrative theory of optimal investment decision making and shows how prices are formed in competitive financial markets in a way that reflects the expectations and preferences of all market participants. This is capital market theory. It models how rational investors should make decisions in a complex and uncertain environment, and it traces the effect of these decisions through to their ultimate impact on an investment's risk and return. This material leads directly into Part IV, which considers the subject of valuation. It describes how one ought to go about valuing different financial instruments, such as stocks, bonds, and options, and suggests those particular factors or characteristics that are likely to determine the value of a security. Part V considers explicitly the way in which the investment function should be managed, either by an individual or professional management firm.

In Parts IV and V we use what we have learned in the first three parts to develop an approach to realistic decision making. This material might best be thought of as answering the question: How can we *apply* these concepts to actual markets? In other words, given our preferences and what we believe to be true about the environment in which we must operate, how can we make successful investment decisions in practice? For a complete answer, we must take three steps: (1) make forecasts about the future prospects for securities, (2) apply an appropriate decision rule to those forecasts so as to choose a portfolio (or collection) of securities to hold, and (3) assess our decision after the fact to determine if we achieved our objectives. We might call these three stages, respectively,

forecasting, financial planning and portfolio choice, and **performance measurement.** Each step is of vital importance to achieving success in applied investing. And when you have finished the book, you will (we hope) be able to evaluate your chances of successfully operating in one capacity or another in financial markets.

Applying Economic Theory to Investment Decision Making

Throughout the book, economic theory serves as a basis for our conceptual discussions. It will not, however, limit us. Often, theory is regarded as not particularly helpful in making practical decisions. Since it is often highly abstract, we may feel that it simply doesn't mirror the real world. It is true that there is much more to decision making than the mere application of theory. It is equally true that theory often proceeds from assumptions abstracted from real-world situations. In some ways, however, the lack of "complete realism" in theory is a virtue. It allows us to focus on the more important aspects of the decision process without involving ourselves in unnecessary complexities. On the other hand, the more realistic a theory is, the more useful it will be when we ultimately make decisions. But increased realism is not without its price: a lessened ability to concentrate on fundamentals.

If theory is to be useful we must be able to apply it. However, there are many aspects of actual investing that existing theories do not address. As a result, we need to recognize the limitations of theory as well as its strengths. Theory cannot solve all the problems in investment decision making. Thus, we should not be limited by it, and neither you nor we should hesitate to depart from it to explore the investment world in more detail.

For the remainder of this chapter, we shall discuss the basic components of the **Theory of Choice** and how these components can be used to describe individuals' decisions regarding current consumption and savings (investment). We shall then use these components to build an overview of the investment decision process as it will be presented throughout the rest of the book. Our initial statement of finance theory will concentrate on how individuals behave (micro theory). Later, we describe how this behavior leads to theories of market prices.

The Theory of Choice

To study investing from the vantage point of the Theory of Choice, we shall begin with one of the more basic of people's personal attributes: their wants (or desires). In any person's experience or imagination, there is a tremendous variety of desirable kinds of things which he or she would like to own or use. It does not matter whether the things are bicycles, haircuts, college degrees, or time spent at the beach. The wants we are referring to relate to anything which gives the person **utility**, or satisfaction. Unfortunately, if you are at all like we are, the list of things wanted *exceeds resources available to obtain them*. Thus, since we are unable to have everything we desire up to the point of complete satiation, we must make *choices*.

But how do we decide? Is it better to purchase a new suit or season football tickets, to buy a car or a sailboat? Normative economic theory can help answer this question. It assumes that each of us wishes to maximize the utility (satisfaction) we derive from consumption goods, given the contraint imposed on us by our wealth in relation to prices. If we are willing to accept this, the theory can tell us how to choose among alternative bundles of goods. Very simply, in choices where absolute certainty as to the outcome prevails, economics says there are four basic components of rational choice. These are the set of available **opportunities** (goods and services, including financial services), **market prices, wealth,** and **preferences.** All economic decisions (including financial decisions) involve these, and only these, four components.

Available Opportunities

This first component defines the **bundles of goods or services that are available.** Virtually everything that it is possible to produce or acquire through a market falls into the category of available opportunities. Here, only nature or restrictions on certain types of markets may constrain our list of opportunities. Some products one might wish to obtain, for example, are clearly impossible given the laws of nature or the laws of society, e.g., a perpetual motion machine or U.S. dollars (in 1982) if you were a Mexican bank.

Also important from our standpoint are opportunities which are unavailable due to the lack of markets for them. For example, have you ever tried to arrange *now* for a loan to be available at the time of your retirement? Moreover, there is no way to purchase the U.S. Army (though there may be a market for the Bonneville Power Administration), or many other goods that are collectively consumed. There simply may be no market for some goods and services; hence, we can usually exclude these from the set of available opportunities.[1]

Importantly, for the usefulness of the model, the opportunities generally need to be defined in terms of bundles of goods and services. You and I make decisions based on more than the comparisons of single items. We choose from among a number of different bundles of goods and services. The desirability of a computer may well depend on the software available to go with it, for example.

Market Prices

The second component of rational choice is **the set of market prices that prevail** at the time you make your decision. Prices are essential in making choices. They tell us how much of one thing we have to give up to get one unit of another thing. Even if you preferred the suit to the football tickets (holding constant everything else in the consumption bundle) you may still buy the tickets if the cost comparison substantially favors that opportunity. Moreover, there is some level of relative prices at which you would be indifferent to purchasing either. At this set of prices, the amount of the suit you would have to give up to purchase the tickets would just be equal to the worth you place on the one or the other. The same relationship holds true for investment services. If you are

---

[1]The market for goods and services has expanded rapidly in the past two decades as collective goods and services have come under increasing competitive pressure from private markets. Corporate police forces, private postal services, and private pensions that substitute for social security are but a few examples.

indifferent between spending $10,000 for a $100-a-month annuity or spending $8,000 for a car, the price ratio (or 10:8) implies the relative worth of each good to you.

Wealth

The third component is your wealth. Wealth is the total market value of all the assets (goods and services, including investment services) you own. In other words, **wealth represents your total potential for consumption.**

Your wealth always imposes a constraint on consumption as long as added consumption increases your utility. For example, suppose you feel committed to saving for future contingencies but you have $200 of immediately spendable wealth. Purchasing a $200 suit not only precludes you from enjoying the benefits of $150 football tickets, but also prevents you from enjoying the increased utility associated with the "purchase" of a $50 savings account. Clearly, you would have to search your soul to decide from among the available alternative bundles. All economic and financial decisions involve opportunities that are forgone as choices are made.

Preferences

The final component is simply a description of how strongly you feel about the **relative desirability of the various bundles of goods and services** under consideration. If you were deciding between the suit and the combination of tickets and a savings account, it would be reasonable to represent the thought process as one of comparing the total satisfaction derived from the alternatives. In short, given all the factors you hold to be important, which would you rather have? And, as mentioned before, your preference ordering may depend upon the availability of other goods and services.

If these preferences are well defined, it should be possible for you to develop your own preference ordering over all possible bundles of goods and services. Such an ordering is a list of things ranked from "most desired" to "least desired." In theory, your preference ordering can be applied to all things, even if you never have occasion to make many of the choices implied. Importantly, we do not wish to constrain your choices in any way. Instead, we will use your ordering to help you assess your likes and dislikes.

Making a Choice

How do you put the four components together to make a choice? Start with your preference ordering over all available opportunities or bundles. Go down that list until you encounter a bundle whose price reaches the limit imposed by your wealth constraint.

This procedure is oversimplified, and would be inefficient if employed in actual decision making. But it is the basis for understanding the process used by a real decision maker who attempts to maximize the utility of consumption subject to a constraint on wealth.

Determining Market Prices

If enough people prefer bundles that include some goods (say the suit) but not others (the tickets), the supply of those goods in demand may be exhausted quickly. Free markets adjust to this pressure in the short run by an increase in price of those goods in demand relative to those not in demand. Such an increase in price has two effects. First, some consumers may decide to select a new bundle of goods and services. Second, the higher price serves to signal to producers that it is advantageous for them to produce more of the goods for which the excessive demand exists. This, in turn, results in a shift of productive resources (labor, management, and capital) from the less- to the more-desired goods. The interaction of consumer choices, in other words, serves to set market prices, which in turn affect both the choices of consumers and the decisions of managers. The price mechanism is the force that drives the allocation of scarce goods and services.

This process of choice that culminates in the determination of prices is a very simple and uncluttered version of the Theory of Choice. Moreover, since the process is essentially the same in financial markets as in the markets for current consumption goods, the theory provides a starting point for a discussion of the decision to save.

The Decision to Save

Suppose now the objects of choice directly involve "current" and "future" consumption. Thus, an individual can consider not only the relative merits of consuming a car or boat but also alternative time patterns for their consumption. The difference is that in this case we are concerned with opportunities, prices, wealth, and preferences defined **over time.** The choice of waiting until next year to purchase a car, without any change in the consumption of other goods and services, involves a decision to save in this period. The choice will depend on the price of cars and other goods in this period and next, on wealth, and on how we feel about waiting until next period to enjoy the benefits of the car. This type of decision—involving a trade-off between "now" and "later"—is precisely what **saving** is all about. In fact, virtually all savings decisions are made for one of the following three reasons (all of which are related to opportunities, prices, wealth, and preferences):

- To achieve a pattern of consumption over time which is preferred to that offered by the current situation (**redistribution motive**).
- To ensure against unexpected events causing a disparity between desired consumption levels and income (**precautionary motive**).
- To take advantage of opportunities to enhance the overall level of available and consumable wealth (**investment motive**).

As you might suspect, the first reason is based on conditions of certainty, whereas the second is based on uncertainty. In the first case, people save because they *know* their future incomes are different in different time periods, and they generally want to avoid drastic lifestyle changes each time the variations occur. This is, of course, why many individuals save for retirement: They anticipate that their income will be reduced after age 65, and they would like to consume more than their income at that time would allow. It is a fact of human nature, perhaps, that people generally seek to redistribute consumption over time so that it is more level or "smooth" than their income flows.

In the second case, people are assumed to save because of *unexpected* decreases in income or increases in consumption. "What will happen if I lose my job?" "Suppose I don't sell any textbooks next month?" Uncertainty provides a powerful incentive to save, because many individuals do not like to face the possibility of severely curtailing expenditures to make ends meet. Whenever an individual expects that the future may bring adversity of some sort or another, it is often desirable to save to ensure against the possibility of adverse events. The acquisition of insurance policies is one of the most obvious methods of saving used by individuals hedging against the possibility of the unexpected. Moreover, the precautionary motive varies considerably among decision makers.

The third motive relates to the encouragement that may exist through opportunities to increase one's overall level of wealth. A 50 percent rate of return, and the anticipated larger level of future consumption that might be afforded with its use, may be sufficient to encourage some to delay current consumption.

Saving means giving up current consumption in favor of future consumption. In the choice of how much to save for the future, we have the same four components—opportunities, prices, wealth, and preferences—that we discussed above.

Opportunities

The opportunities we consider here are merely bundles of goods and services available for consumption at different points in time. These points in time can be thought of as periodic "chunks" of time, successively numbered from now (time 0) to some distant point (t). One consumption bundle is represented in the diagram below. Each entry in the diagram, $\tilde{C}_{it}$, measures the consumption of good i (the rows) in period of time t (the columns):

		Period				
		0	*1*	*2*	$\cdots$	*t*
	Good$_1$	C_{10}	$\tilde{C}_{11}$	$\tilde{C}_{12}$	$\cdots$	$\tilde{C}_{1t}$
	Good$_2$	C_{20}	$\tilde{C}_{21}$	$\tilde{C}_{22}$	$\cdots$	$\tilde{C}_{2t}$
	Good$_3$	C_{30}	$\tilde{C}_{31}$	$\tilde{C}_{32}$	$\cdots$	$\tilde{C}_{3t}$
Bundle $\tilde{C}$	$\vdots$	$\vdots$				
	Good$_i$	C_{i0}	$\tilde{C}_{i1}$	$\cdots$		$\tilde{C}_{it}$
	Security$_1$	S_{10}	$\tilde{S}_{11}$	$\cdots$		$\tilde{S}_{1t}$
	Security$_2$	S_{20}	$\tilde{S}_{21}$	$\cdots$		$\tilde{S}_{2t}$
	$\vdots$	$\vdots$	$\vdots$			$\vdots$
	Security$_h$	S_{h0}	$\tilde{S}_{h1}$	$\cdots$		$\tilde{S}_{ht}$

Each row represents the pattern of consumption of a good or service (say season football tickets) over time. Each column represents a pattern of consumption for the specified period. Income available in each period has to be allocated to each consumption good. If the economy were a hypothetically simple one in which there is no saving mechanism then the only allocations to be made would be those involving choices among goods and services *within* points in time. It would be impossible for an individual to make allocations over time. The original distribution of income over time could not be altered. In this case there would be no savings, and, in fact, no subject of finance.

The world can be made more realistic if goods themselves can be saved. Buying a boat that provides services over two or more periods is an act of saving. Moreover, ancient economies that herded domestic animals "saved" by definition, as did those who first decided to retain grain seed for next year's planting.

In theory, the market determines prices for each of these goods and services, even for those to be consumed in future periods. "Futures prices" or "forward prices" are just the prices for future goods and services. While futures and forward prices do not exist for all goods and services in practice, they do exist for a surprisingly large number of commodities. Wheat, silver, plywood, oil, home mortgages, football talent, and U.S. Treasury securities are but a few examples where futures prices exist.

Now consider an explicit new category of savings services. Each represents a mechanism for saving, or a *financial security*. They are labeled $\tilde{S}_{ht}$ in the diagram, for security type h in period t. With these securities, consumption opportunities *over time* are expanded considerably. Wealth not consumed in period 0 would be allocated to one or more securities. When the security "matures" in period t the value of the security at that time is available for use in purchasing goods and services for period t's consumption.

Thus, if your entire wealth consisted of $50,000 in the current period, and you consumed $40,000, $10,000 would be allocated to the various financial securities available to you. In the next period the maturity value of the securities (say $10,500, if maturity is in one year with a 5 percent interest rate) can be used to acquire goods and services, including securities. A useful characteristic of some securities is that they may allow you to draw on future wealth to increase the level of current consumption, i.e., you can *borrow* on your future wealth. Essentially, with the financial services we call securities, wealth can be easily transferred between periods—perhaps to even out consumption, or to take advantage of some of today's bargains.[2]

To see how this works, consider a simple economy in which:

- There is only "today" and "next year" (periods 0 and 1) during which consumption takes place.
- There is no uncertainty surrounding future events that would affect wealth available for consumption.
- Because of the above conditions there is only one security—a savings and borrowing account in a bank.
- All goods and services available are adequately summarized by a "claim" on consumption, and are called $.

In this simple world all opportunities available to our consumer can be described once we know the consumer's wealth and characteristics of the security that permits our consumer to transfer wealth between the two periods. Suppose the Robinson family income is $20,000 a year to be paid in a lump sum at the beginning of each period. In addition, the Robinsons have accumulated other assets that are currently worth $30,000. Thus,

---

[2]During the inflationary period of 1978–80, federal analysts were perplexed when they observed many households borrowing at an extraordinary rate at the same time interest rates were at an all-time high. What was happening, of course, was that the high interest rates were considered a real borrowing bargain when the prices of the goods households wished to consume were rising faster than the interest rate. Even at high interest rates the level of savings was low.

This anecdote should serve to illustrate how hard it is to control a modern economy with monetary policy alone.

FIGURE 1–1   **Two-Period Opportunity Set**

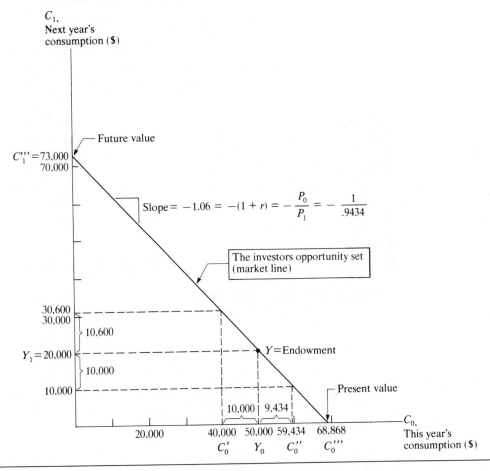

their current "endowment" is $50,000 and is represented in Figure 1–1 by Y_0. Their future endowment, Y_1, is $20,000. This, of course, is one of the bundles of opportunities available to them.

Market Prices

The Robinsons can change this foreordained pattern of consumption if they have access to a financial security. Suppose the security allows them to exchange $1 currently for $1.06 in the future by saving (lending), or exchange a future $ for $.9434 currently by dissaving, or borrowing from the future. The latter value is the "price of saving." Thus, you can "buy" a savings account for $9,434 now. In return you will receive $10,000 in one year to supplement future consumption. Alternatively, you can "sell" a savings account by receiving $9,434 now with the obligation to return $10,000 in one year. Long centuries of development have resulted in the conventional quotation of this price as the inverse of this figure—less one, or the market rate of interest; as follows:

$$\begin{pmatrix} \text{Market} \\ 1 + \text{interest} \\ \text{rate} \end{pmatrix} = \frac{1}{\text{Price of savings}}$$

$$1 + .06 = \frac{1.00}{1/(1 + .06)} = \frac{1}{.9434}$$

With knowledge of this price and of the endowed quantities of Y_0 and Y_1, the market opportunities available to the Robinson family are described graphically in Figure 1–1. Here the horizontal axis (C_0) measures this year's generalized claims to consumption (this year's $), and the vertical axis (C_1) measures next year's claims. The endowed position is represented by the point (Y_0, Y_1) in the graph. The opportunities available to the Robinsons to change the time pattern of their consumption from their endowed position are represented by the line through Y having a slope of -1.06. Each point along this line represents a pattern of consumption over time that can be created by using the available security to exchange current $ for future ones or future $ for current ones. Thus, for example, transferring $10,000 of current endowment to next year can be accomplished by saving $10,000 (buying the security and, as a result, moving from Y_0 to C_0'). This enables the Robinsons to increase future consumption, C_1', by $10,600 to $30,600— generating a new pattern of consumption over time. Moreover, by borrowing $10,000 from their future endowment they can increase current consumption (since they have sold the security) by $9,434, to a level of $59,434, at the price of $10,000 of future claims.

The line itself represents the set of opportunities that are available to the family when the financial market opportunity to borrow and lend at 6 percent exists—it is the **market line.** In the absence of this opportunity the Robinsons would be constrained by the time pattern of consumption imposed by their endowment. With this opportunity, constraints on their time pattern of consumption are less severe. This conclusion holds in a broader context as well—the greater in number and variety are the financial market opportunities available to consumers, the greater their opportunities to find the time pattern of consumption that is most desirable to them.

Wealth

In the timeless world we discussed in introducing the Theory of Choice, wealth was simply the sum of the market values of the goods and services you have claim to. In a multiperiod world the current value of your claims to consumption in future periods also are included. Precisely how the market values those future claims is the subject that we treat in great detail throughout this book. It *is* finance. For the abstract world of the Robinsons, however, the computation is easy. Since the current price per $ of future claims is $.9434, the Robinson's **current wealth level** is $50,000 + ($20,000) (.9434) = $68,868. Graphically, this amount is represented by the point where the opportunity set strikes the horizontal axis.

This amount represents the **present value** of the Robinson's endowment, or, in fact, the present value of any of the opportunities on the market line that might be selected. To generalize:

- The concept of "present value," or wealth, is *derived* from market opportunities, not vice versa. Thus, present value or wealth can be represented as

$$\text{Wealth} = P_0(C_0) + P_1(C_1) = C_0 + (C_1)(1/[1 + r])$$
$$= \$50,000 + \$20,000(1/1.06) = \$68,868$$

$$\text{Wealth} = (\textit{price of current \$})(\textit{amount of current \$})$$
$$+ (\textit{price of future \$})(\textit{amount of future \$})$$
$$= (\textit{amount of current \$}) + (\textit{current value of future \$})$$

- Only *market* prices (market interest rates) should be used in assessing the present value of future cash flows.
- Without the market opportunity set, the individual would be constrained to holding the original endowment. Thus, the existence of market opportunities provides a mechanism to allow individuals to move wealth between time periods.

These points will hold throughout the book. In the savings decision problem it is wealth which imposes the ultimate constraint on our choices, rather than our income or pattern of endowment.

Preferences

Just as in the case of the timeless economy considered earlier, each consumer must rank all the bundles of time-dependent opportunities available in order of their desirability. This ranking helps to *reveal* the preferences of the decision maker. If bundles with low or negative amounts committed to savings instruments are ranked high, the individual is expressing a high **marginal rate of time preference** for consumption. Consumption now is relatively more preferred than consumption later—a classical hedonist, if you will. The marginal rate of time preference simply states the number of units of future consumption that would willingly be given up by our consumer in order to obtain one unit of current consumption. For the individual consumer or family unit the *willingness* to give up future consumption for current consumption is solely a function of their desires, and is independent of the *ability* to exchange future for current consumption that comes from the prices for financial services in the marketplace. Moreover, the subject of finance places few constraints on individual preferences. It is sufficient for us that the decision maker can uniquely rank the bundles. We will not criticize the ranking or maintain that a different ranking of the bundles will make the decision maker happier.[3]

Not surprisingly, financial theory has a way of summarizing an individual's preferences. This is done with **indifference curves,** each of which identifies different bundles of goods and services that give rise to the same level of satisfaction or utility. One such set of indifference curves, the ones relevant to describing the preferences of the Robinsons, is superimposed on the opportunity set and is depicted in Figure 1–2. The curves do not cross (as that would imply the same bundle supplies two different levels of satisfaction)

---

[3]The *typical* marginal rate of time preference of members of a society is revealed only by their actions over time. It probably differs from society to society by the level of wealth, by political conditions, by the availability of consumer goods (saving is high in Russia), and by a myriad of other factors. Whatever the rate, this is one of the pressures that helps to determine the interest rate in an economy.

FIGURE 1–2   The Optimal Level of Savings and Consumption

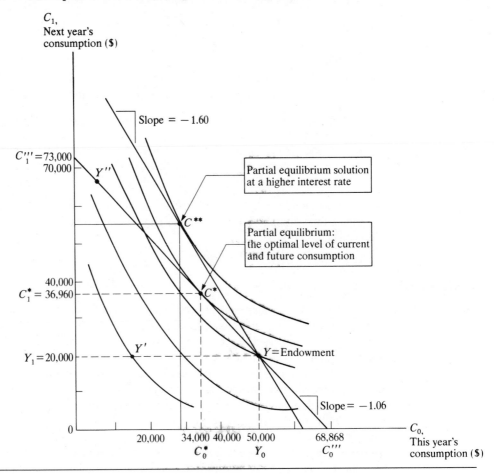

and are concave from above (to assure nonspecialization of consumption in one period, thereby affording the opportunity to "exist" in both periods), but do not suggest that specific levels of utility are associated with each curve (we only know that a higher curve implies more satisfaction, not X percent more). The slope of the curves at any point on the graph imply the consumer's marginal willingness to exchange current consumption for future consumption. As such, the curves represent the decision maker's marginal rate of time preference, and summarize how bundles of C_0 and C_1 would be ranked.

The Choice

While its possible to think of the consumer ranking all bundles of time dependent claims and finding the highest ranked bundle that doesn't violate the wealth constraint, the fundamental nature of the choice can best be understood with reference to Figure

1–2. If the Robinsons attempt to make themselves best off, they must find the *point* on the opportunity set (market line) that places them on the *highest* indifference curve. Any other point would unnecessarily restrict the total level of satisfaction from consumption through time. Graphically, the solution occurs at the point of tangency between the opportunity set and the indifference set. This is called the **partial equilibrium solution** to the consumption/saving problem. For the Robinsons the solution is at C^*, which calls on the family to consume $34,000 this year and save $16,000.[4] This permits them to consume $20,000 plus $16,000 (1 + .06), or $36,960, in the next period. At this point the marginal *ability* to exchange C_0 for C_1 (the slope of the opportunity set, -1.06) equals the marginal *willingness* to exchange C_0 for C_1 (the slope of the indifference set).

(1–1)   *Condition for Optimal Choice*

$$\text{Marginal ability} = \text{Marginal willingness}$$
$$\text{to exchange} \qquad \text{to exchange}$$
$$C_0 \text{ for } C_1 \qquad C_0 \text{ for } C_1$$

At any other point, the slopes are not equal and it's possible for the family to improve their position by either saving more (if the marginal ability to exchange C_0 for C_1 is exceeded by the marginal willingness to do so, as at point Y in Figure 1–2) or saving less.[5]

Changing Conditions and Changing Decisions

As inputs change consumers' decisions about the time pattern of consumption will also change. A change in preferences, endowed wealth, or the rate of interest may cause consumers to devote more or less to savings in the current period. An individual with a greater rate of time preference will have more steeply sloped indifference curves, causing him to save less or, if C^* falls below Y on the opportunity set, to borrow.

In addition, as the level of endowed wealth changes so will the solution. Consumers faced with a sudden decrease in their current endowment will unambiguously change their optimal pattern of consumption since their wealth has changed. The most probable effect of this change will be for the consumer to save less, as you can see in Figure 1–2 with a shift from point Y to point Y'. The propensity to save will decline with a fall in the *current* endowment. A fall in the level of the *future* endowment generally will tend to increase the propensity to save.

On the other hand, if the endowments were at Y'', with the 6 percent interest rate, the eventual solution to the Robinsons' problem would not be different. The optimal choices, C_0^* and C_1^*, would be the same, although the actions to achieve that point would be different. Point Y'' is located on the same market opportunity line as Y at the 6 percent interest rate and has, therefore, the same present value.

A change in the interest rate also will affect an individual's decision, for the simple reason that a change in the price of future $ affects the demand for those $. This situation is explicitly considered in Figure 1–2. As the interest rate is allowed to change from 6

---

[4]Throughout the book an asterisk is used to indicate optimal values of any decision variable.

[5]For instance, if the slope of the indifference curve at point Y is -0.5 and the slope of the market line is -1.06, then since $-1.06 < -0.5$, the decision maker is relatively more willing to reduce C_0 in favor of C_1.

percent to 60 percent the **opportunity set** available to the Robinsons becomes more steeply sloped—reflecting the lower price of future $. There are two effects associated with this rotation of the opportunity set. First, as long as our consumers have any future endowment, Y_1, their current wealth will decline. An increase in the interest rate, other things constant, will bring about a decrease in current wealth or the present value of the claims. This occurs because the market price of future $ has declined.

Second, our consumer will select new values for current consumption and savings, conditional on the new opportunity set and the consumer's preferences. For the Robinsons this new equilibrium occurs at C^{**} in Figure 1–2. This new optimum implies more savings (it looks like they would consume about $28,000 of goods and services this period and save $22,000 for next period) than when the interest rate was at 6 percent. In general though, the new optimum point could imply more or less savings, depending on the decision makers' preferences. A higher interest rate may mean more emphasis on future consumption (the substitution of C_1 for C_0, called the "**substitution effect**") or more emphasis on current consumption (an increase in C_0 as well, an "**income effect**").

Importantly, whether a particular consumer/saver is considered better off or worse off with the higher interest rate depends on preferences and endowments. In general, a family with much of its endowed wealth available only in the future (say at Y'') would find that an increase in the rate of interest reduces the opportunity set in the relevant range of the family's preferences. They would be worse off. Thus, if younger wage earners (students for example) count on their future income-generating ability as a means for supplementing their current consumption (i.e., they tend to borrow), an increase in the rate of interest affects them more adversely than it affects the general population.[6] Contrarily, high interest rates benefit the retired and those with significant accumulations of current claims to consumption, C_0.

Investment Decisions

To this point we have assumed that only one mechanism allows consumers to transfer wealth between periods. For the Robinsons this was a savings (or borrowing) account with a 6 percent interest rate. However, as more opportunities appear, the consumer must deal with the *investment motive* for savings mentioned on page 8. That is, the decision maker must choose a portfolio, or collection of investment opportunities, in which to hold nonconsumed wealth. Doing so may allow him to improve his well-being beyond that available from a single savings opportunity. In the real world these investment opportunities include savings accounts, bonds, stocks, and other assets that provide a flow of income or capital gains over time.

We will illustrate this problem at this early stage with two additional opportunities

---

[6]In fact, the immediate consumption effect of an increase in the rate of interest across all elements of the economy would be zero, since for every borrower there is a lender. Changes in the interest rate will *not* affect the entire economy unless and until it affects the level of investment in real productive activities such as the size of the labor force or the investment in real capital equipment. Thus, an increase in interest rates would tend to reallocate wealth to those with more of their wealth in current dollars and away from those with more of their wealth in the form of future claims. This was the problem faced by young families during the high interest rate periods of the late 1970s and early 1980s—a point that was obvious to those attempting to borrow money to purchase a house for the first time.

FIGURE 1–3   **The Choice with Productive Investment Opportunities**

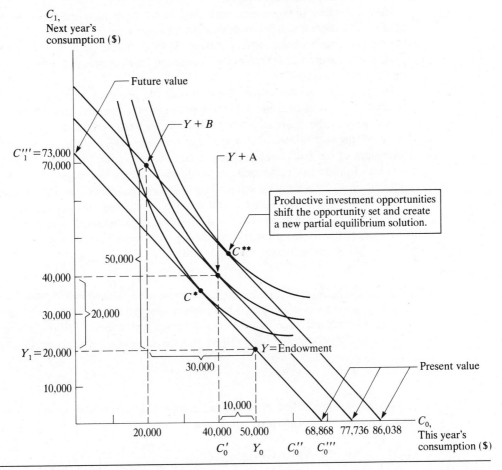

available to the Robinson family. The first is the opportunity to "invest" $10,000 now in tuition and books in return for increased income in the amount of $20,000 next period. The second involves the investment of $30,000 now in productive equipment that will increase future income by $50,000. Neither is a financial market opportunity of the kind previously available to the family, and they must be accepted or rejected in whole. Thus, only $10,000 can be invested in the first of these opportunities. Which opportunity, if either, should be selected can be solved by employing the same model used by the Robinsons to determine how much to save or borrow.

These opportunities are represented graphically by points $Y + A$ and $Y + B$ in Figure 1–3. Ultimately, of course, the issue for the Robinsons is to determine which, if either, of the options will permit them to position themselves on a higher indifference curve. However, since the use of the financial security is not precluded by the selection of one of these investment opportunities, the solution to this problem requires drawing three market lines to represent all opportunities available from Y, $Y + A$, and $Y + B$. Each market line has a slope of -1.06 to represent the ability of the Robinsons to lend or borrow in the financial marketplace.

Since the market opportunities associated with $Y + B$ allow the family to achieve the highest market line, it also positions them on the highest indifference curve. Consequently, B is the investment opportunity to choose. Then, from the point $Y + B$ the Robinsons would borrow about $22,000 from their enhanced future claims to select the consumption bundle represented by C^{**}.

The perceptive reader might also note that the optimal selection of A or B or the rejection of both can be made *without* appealing to the decision maker's preferences. In fact, as long as the financial market opportunities exist, productive investment opportunities of the sort illustrated A and B can be made *independently* of the consumption preferences of the individual decision maker. In effect, all families, if faced with the same set of productive opportunities, would make the same choices. They would differ only in their use of borrowing and lending to achieve the desired pattern of consumption.

This **separation** of productive investment decisions from consumption decisions plays a central role in the valuation of any and all assets. In particular, as long as this separation holds, calculation of the present value of the cash flows from the opportunities will be sufficient for deciding among the opportunities.

> The **separation principle,** which shows why productive decisions can be evaluated without reference to the decision maker's preferences, holds as long as financial market opportunities exist to provide means for securing the desired consumption bundle.

For the two productive opportunities considered, the present value calculations (or what is termed the **net present value**) are

$$(1-2) \qquad NPV_A = -\$10,000 + \frac{\$20,000}{(1 + .06)} = \$8,868,$$

and

$$NPV_B = -\$30,000 + \frac{\$50,000}{(1 + .06)} = \$17,170.$$

These values can be located in Figure 1–3 on the horizontal axis as the difference between the initial present wealth of $68,868 and the wealth positions corresponding to the points $Y + A$ and $Y + B$ of $77,736 and $86,038, respectively.[7]

These points emphasize two of the primary benefits conferred by the existence of

---

[7]The point is always made in basic courses in finance that the corporation can make decisions regarding which assets to purchase (capital budgeting) by applying a present value rule *without* having to account for its individual shareholder preferences. The reason is the same as that presented here. As long as financial markets exist that allow the individual the opportunity to transform wealth in accordance with preferences, the only thing the decision maker need be concerned with is the "market value" or "present value" of the opportunity. This principle holds whether the decision maker is Robinson acting on behalf of his family or the corporation acting on behalf of its current shareholders.

financial markets where securities can by bought and sold. First, they permit individuals to make utility-maximizing consumption decisions without being constrained to consumption patterns dictated purely by productive investment alternatives. ($Y + B$ is less desirable than $Y + A$ if the financial market opportunities did not exist.) As a result all individual consumers can make themselves better off. Second, with market opportunities available, it is more likely that individuals will engage in productive investment activities (B will be accepted) leading to enhanced economic growth and an improvement in the well-being of society in general.

Market Equilibrium

To this juncture, the interest rate has been taken by the Robinsons as given. This is realistic. The Robinson family itself would have no monopolistic power over the market for savings and would act as if the interest rate were determined exogenously (beyond the Robinson's ability to affect it either directly or indirectly). But in addition to the Robinsons, there are a large number of other households making similar saving-investment decisions. The collective impact of all of these other decision-making units will affect the rate of interest, just as the collective impact of all potential consumers and producers of other goods and services will have an impact on the price of those commodities.

If, at the current interest rate, the sum total of all household savings exceeded the sum total of all household borrowings, there would be an excess supply of savings. This excess supply would tend to exert downward pressure on the interest rate. At the lower interest rate fewer households will save and more households will borrow, thus relieving some of the pressure on the rate. Interest rates will continue to drop until there is no longer an excess supply of savings.

If, in the economy, there is greater borrowing than saving, the pressure will tend to force up the market interest rate. This will relieve some of the pressure by persuading some households to reduce their borrowing and some to increase their savings. Once again, the pressure will continue until there is no longer an excess demand for savings.

Where will it all stop? Changes in the rate of interest will no longer occur when the excess demand and excess supply are zero. Consequently, **market equilibrium** is defined as that rate of interest where the quantity of savings supplied equals the quantity demanded. There is only one such rate in a world of certainty.

The graphic presentations presented before show that pressures for an upward change in the market equilibrium rate of interest would exist if consumers in the aggregate (1) have preferences that lean heavily to a high level of current consumption given the present (disequilibrium) rate, or (2) have endowments that supply much more future than present consumable wealth. In either case, the large demand for borrowing and the small supply of savings would cause rates to rise above 6 percent.

We can use this introduction to market equilibrium to say some things about equilibrium interest rates in an economy that have a very practical and applied interpretation. For example,

- An agrarian economy, wracked by drought this year but with adequate capital and labor to replant for next year, would find the one-period interest rate this year to be high, since "endowment" this year is low and the populace attempts to draw on the future endowment, i.e., Y_1 is large relative to Y_0.

- An economy with higher current output but with an aging or outdated means of production (Rome near the fall) would have a low interest rate, since savings would be high as people attempt to shift consumption to the future.
- An economy with sudden technological advances that raise the rate of return to productive investment (as seemed to coincide with the digital computer) will see an increase in its future wealth. As the populace draws on that wealth, interest rates will rise.
- A society with a strong incentive to help future generations and with an inclination toward thrift will have a low interest rate.
- A society with a strong inclination toward current consumption will have high interest rates.

The concept of market equilibrium is central to the study of financial markets. We use it throughout the book as a method for describing the workings of financial markets, for analyzing the impact of items that might change supply and demand, and for assessing situations in which markets may be in disequilibrium.

Three Points in Time and Arbitrage

It's easy to relax our initial limitation of a two-period world. By so doing we can develop the **Equal Rate of Return Principle,** and define the term **arbitrage.**

Equal Rate of Return

Suppose there are three points at which *consumption* can take place: now in period 0, one year from now at 1, and two years from now at 2. In this economy there will be three securities created to allow consumers to *transfer* $ between time periods. If r indicates the rate of interest, the first security transfers funds between periods 0 and 1 at the rate $1 + {}_0r_1$. Another transfers funds between periods 1 and 2 at the rate $1 + {}_1r_2$. This second security is actually a forward contract—it's an arrangement made *now* for an exchange (of money for a security) to be consummated in one year. The third security is a two-period instrument for making direct transfers between period 0 and 2. The rate at which these transfers are made is $1 + {}_0r_2$.

Note that in this economy there are two paths by which funds can be moved between now and period 2. One path uses two securities of one period each, while the other path uses the two-period security. Since the paths are otherwise equivalent they would have to provide the same future $ from a given commitment of current $ through savings. If they did not, then some enterprising consumers, noting the discrepancy, would buy the high-return path securities and sell the low-return path securities. This would lead to an excess demand for the high-return securities, an increase in their price, and a reduction in the interest rate they offer. For consumers to be indifferent between the two paths the following relationship must hold:

(1–3)   *Different Equivalent Paths Must Yield the Same Reward*

$$(1 + {}_0r_2) = (1 + {}_0r_1)(1 + {}_1r_2).$$

This relationship—whereby **two equivalent savings opportunities must offer the same rewards**—is called the equal rate of return principle. More generally, the equal rate of return principle is a market equilibrium condition that says that all *equivalent* investment or savings opportunities must offer the same return.[8] It is a special case of the strong economic principle of the "law of one price," which says that two equivalent goods must sell at the same price on the market. Since $_0r_2$ or $_0r_1$ and $_1r_2$ provide equivalent paths to period-2 dollars, the above relationship must hold.

Arbitrage

Arbitrage is a mechanism used to take advantage of any violations of the equal rate of return principle. Suppose, in the three-period case,

$$_0r_1 = .10 \qquad _1r_2 = .12 \qquad _0r_2 = .30$$

An arbitrager could borrow \$10,000 period-2 dollars at 12 percent, returning \$8,928 (\$10,000/1.12) to period 1; borrow \$8,928 period-1 dollars at 10 percent, returning \$8,116 (\$8,928/1.10) to period 0; and then lend \$8,116 in period 0 to period 2, yielding \$10,550 (that is, \$8,116[1.30]). Using \$10,000 of this amount to pay off his borrowing, he reaps a reward for his arbitrage activity of \$550 in period 2. Pressures brought about by this activity will eventually change market rates. One set of rates consistent with the equal rate of return principle would be

$$_0r_1 = .106 \qquad _1r_2 = .13 \qquad _0r_2 = .25$$

but there would be many others as well. Which configuration of rates "wins out" would depend on the relative pressures of the market, just as in the two-period case.

It is arbitrage schemes like this that help to move markets toward equilibrium. Formally, **arbitrage is a riskless activity, requiring no investment, that attempts to capitalize on disequilibrium market prices for securities.**

Present Values in a Multiperiod World

How would productive investment opportunities *A* and *B* discussed earlier be evaluated if the cash flows were received in period 2 instead of period 1? The answer must reflect the market opportunities that exist in the three-period world. Thus, the net present value of each (using the no-arbitrage rates above) is

$$\textbf{(1-4)} \quad NPV_A = -\$10,000 + \frac{\$20,000}{(1 + _0r_2)} = -\$10,000 + \frac{\$20,000}{(1 + _0r_1)(1 + _1r_2)}$$

$$= -\$10,000 + \frac{\$20,000}{(1 + .25)} = -\$10,000 + \frac{\$20,000}{(1 + .106)(1 + .13)}$$

$$= \$6,000$$

---

[8]Suppose the government said that forward transactions were illegal and could not be made, and also suppose that the one-period interest rate that *will exist* between periods 1 and 2 is unknown now (a case of uncertainty). Then, the relationship posited in the text may not hold. The value of $_1r_2$ is not known for sure and hence the $(1 + _0r_1)(1 + _1r_2)$ path is more uncertain. If some savers and borrowers are averse to this uncertainty, the structure of rates may begin to reflect their attitudes toward the uncertainty.

$$NPV_B = -\$30,000 + \frac{\$50,000}{(1 + .25)} = -\$30,000 + \frac{\$50,000}{(1 + .106)(1 + .13)}$$

$$= \$10,000$$

With these rates, opportunity B is still preferred (once again, regardless of preferences). However, any value of $_0r_2$ above 50 percent would result in a preference for opportunity A.

In more general terms, any productive opportunity that promises the series of cash flows of $C_0, C_1, C_2, \ldots , C_t$ would have a value of

(1–5)
$$\text{Value} = C_0 + \frac{C_1}{(1 + {}_0r_1)} + \frac{C_2}{(1 + {}_0r_1)(1 + {}_1r_2)} +$$
$$\ldots + \frac{C_t}{(1 + {}_0r_1)(1 + {}_1r_2) \cdots (1 + {}_{t-1}r_t)}$$

In each case, the cash attributable to the asset in each period is discounted by the relevant market interest rate to calculate its value in terms of current dollars. If the interest rate is the same in each period the expression for present value simplifies to

(1–6)   ***Present Value of Cash Flows***

$$\text{Value} = C_0 + \frac{C_1}{(1 + r)} + \frac{C_2}{(1 + r)^2} + \ldots + \frac{C_t}{(1 + r)^t}$$

Value = The sum of the present values of each of the cash flows.

Thus, if a security promises cash flows of $10, $15, and $20 in periods 1, 5, and 7, respectively, its value in terms of the current period or its present value at an 8 percent interest rate is

$$\text{Value} = \frac{\$10}{(1 + .08)^1} + \frac{\$15}{(1 + .08)^5} + \frac{\$20}{(1 + .08)^7} = \$31.138$$

It would have to be this value because that amount, at an 8 percent interest rate, would enable the investor to *generate* cash flows of $10 in year 1, $15 in year 5, and $20 in year 7, with nothing left over. In other words,

$$(\$31.138)(1.08)^1 = \$33.629$$
$$\text{Less} \qquad 10.00$$
$$\overline{\qquad\qquad\qquad} \$23.629 \text{ at end of year 1}$$
$$(\$23.629)(1.08)^4 = \$32.147$$
$$\text{Less} \qquad 15.00$$
$$\overline{\qquad\qquad\qquad} \$17.147 \text{ at end of year 5}$$
$$(\$17.147)(1.08)^2 = \$20.00$$
$$\text{Less} \qquad 20.00$$
$$\overline{\qquad\qquad\qquad} \$ 0.00 \text{ at end of year 7}$$

Summary

So far, we have attempted to provide a foundation for analysis of the savings and investment decision processes. The starting point in this analysis lies in the economic theory of choice applied to the very basic question: "How much of my wealth or income should I consume now and how much should I save for later?" This is the savings decision. The answer to this question lies in the relationship among our opportunities, prices, wealth and preferences. Each of these components must be considered in the savings decision, if our choices are to be both feasible and desirable.

The set of available **opportunities** defines two things. One is the allowable transactions in which individuals can engage in the securities market—which in our simple world are borrowing and saving. The other is the collection of productive investment opportunities which are open to the individual.

Market prices of the available opportunities enter into the decision by determining the feasible consumption combinations available for individuals. The most immediately important of these prices is defined by the market rate of interest, r. It determines the slope of the market line by specifying the rate of exchange between dollars today and dollars in the future.

An individual's **endowed wealth,** in conjunction with the market rate of interest, serves to locate his market line. Thus, the feasible opportunities for consumption now and in the future are constrained by that person's initial endowment or wealth. Opportunities, market prices, and the endowment determine the *ability* of the consumer/saver to exchange current consumption for future consumption.

Preferences enter into savings decisions by indicating the *desirability* of various alternative time patterns of consumption afforded by the particular market line upon which an individual finds himself. By specifying these preferences in the form of indifference curves, the most preferred allocation of wealth between current and future consumption can readily be found. Preferences indicate the willingness of decision makers to exchange current consumption for future consumption.

The goal of the productive decision, in contrast, is to choose from among available capital assets those that will cause the individual's wealth to expand by the largest increment. By making use of the market line that expands the opportunity set to the largest extent possible, an individual can increase his consumption and achieve the greatest satisfaction. The productive decision takes into account only the present value of the various investment opportunities open to the individual. It may be considered independently of the savings decision (the separation principle), which requires knowledge of the more personal characteristics of preferences and endowments.

As a point of departure and an introduction into the next chapter, it is useful to distinguish the subject of finance from the basic theory of choice that provides the foundation for modern microeconomics. Finance expands on or considers additional complexities by introducing into the realities of decision making (1) consumption over many periods of time, (2) uncertainty associated with time, and (3) the variety of financial devices that exist to deal with the uncertainty. Finance, in other words, is the study of the allocation of wealth over an uncertain future among a variety of investment opportunities. We think it is these realities that make the subject of finance and investment both important and interesting.

References

Brealy, Richard, and Myers, Stewart. [1984] *Principles of Corporate Finance,* 2nd ed. New York: McGraw-Hill, chap. 1.

Copeland, Thomas E., and Weston, J. Fred. [1983] *Financial Theory and Corporate Policy.* 2nd ed. Reading, Pa.: Addison-Wesley Publishing.

Elton, Edwin J., and Gruber, Martin J. [1981] *Modern Portfolio Theory and Investment Analysis.* New York: John Wiley & Sons, chap. 1.

Fama, Eugene F., and Miller, Merton H. [1972] *The Theory of Finance.* New York: Holt, Rinehart and Winston, chap. 1.

Fisher, Irving. [1965] *The Theory of Interest: Reprints of Economic Classics.* New York: Augustus M. Kelly.

Graham, Benjamin; Dodd, David L.; and Cottle, Sidney. [1962] *Security Analysis Principles and Techniques.* 4th ed. New York: McGraw-Hill, chap. 4.

Hirshleifer, Jack. [1970] *Investment, Interest and Capital.* Englewood Cliffs, N.J.: Prentice-Hall, chap. 2.

Homer, Sidney. [1977] *A History of Interest Rates.* 2nd ed. New Brunswick, N.J.: Rutgers University Press.

Questions and Problems

1. What four things must be taken into account in the decision to save or borrow?

2. The reasons for saving or borrowing include the redistributive, precautionary, and investment motives. In terms of your own situation, describe the role each has played in the financial decisions you have made since you decided to attend school.

3. Several advertisements for luxury automobiles talk about the purchase of an automobile as an investment. May such a purchase be viewed as an investment? If so, how?

4. Explain how the following events would effect your level of savings and why:

   a. You receive a promotion and a raise in pay.

   b. Your automobile has started making strange noises in the night.

   c. You see a destitute old man on the subway who held your job at the bank prior to his retirement.

   d. There has been a change in the interest paid on your savings account.

5. The decision to save or borrow involves considering the effects of opportunities, endowments, prices, and preferences on your well-being or utility. Suppose you have a decision to make regarding how much to save for next year and how much to consume now. Your endowment is $40,000 currently and $70,000 for next year. The current market rate of interest is 10 percent, and you can borrow or lend at that rate. Answer the following:

   a. Describe the opportunity set graphically to scale.

   b. Superimpose on this opportunity set your indifference curves, representing your relative willingness to exchange consumption levels between the periods. Identify the level of savings or borrowing that gives you the greatest utility.

   c. Calculate the present value of your endowments, and your optimal level of consumption over time after your savings decision is made. Are these values dependent on your relative willingness to exchange this period's consumption for next period's consumption?

   d. Now allow the interest rate to change to 30 percent. How much more or less would you borrow or save? What is your new present value of wealth? Are you worse or better off?

6. In the graph developed in the prior problem, analyze whether it is advantageous for you to invest in a productive opportunity that costs $25,000 now and returns $30,000 in one year? Does your answer depend on whether a 10 percent or 30 percent interest rate is available in the market?

7. Suppose you go to your banker and ask him "What is the current price of a deposit account that will give me $10,000 in one year?" What should his answer be if the market rate of interest is 10 percent?

8. A $10,000 Treasury bill, which is risk-free in our economy, and matures in 270 days, is priced at $9,450. What is the going interest rate on a nine-month basis? What is the equivalent annual rate of interest? (Assume 30-day months.)

9. The present value of $100 to be received one year from now, assuming an annual discount rate of 15 percent equals ————.

    CFA

10. Assuming a discount rate of 10 percent, an asset that generates cash flows of $10 in year 1, $12 in year 2, negative $10 in year 3, and is sold for $175 at the end of year 4 has as present value of

    ————.

    CFA

11. The owner of a Midwestern farm has signed a contract to sell his farm in one year for $1 million. However, the holder of the contract has just come to him with an offer to close the deal today for a price of $900,000. If the interest rate is 10 percent, and the land would simply lie fallow at no cost to either party during the year, should the farmer sell now or wait?

12. Suppose in Problem 11 the farmer had the opportunity to work the land for the year if he doesn't sell it now. Doing so allows him to increase his income in the future by $150,000. Of course, this plan entails some out of pocket current expenses, amounting to $75,000. Now what should he do?

13. Currently you have a mortgage on your house (i.e., you have borrowed by issuing a mortgage), that pays an interest rate of 11 percent. The remaining principal balance is $75,000 and there are 20 years remaining to maturity. The other day your local savings and loan quoted you the following refinancing options, all for 30-year loans:

    a. A 9 percent loan for which you "pay" three points (.03 times the principal borrowed) at the time the loan is taken out.

    b. A 9 1/2 percent loan for which you pay one point.

    c. A 10 percent loan with no points.

    Including the option of doing nothing, analyze the relative benefits of these four options. Of course, make your "relative value" computations and state why your computation is sufficient for making a decision.

14. The J. C. Penney Company has just announced a plan to its Board of Directors to open 10 stores in the USSR. This investment project is so extensive that Penney's has indicated to you, a major stockholder and member of the board, that it will have to cut this year's dividend to zero. Not only will this upset your plans for consumption this year, but you fear it will have the same effect on many other shareholders as well. Assuming the project is riskless (maybe it is insured by the World Bank), how should this project be analyzed?

15. Suppose the numbers in the Penney case above are as follows: Total current expenditures are $150 million. Cash flows net of all expenses, taxes, and future required investments are $25 million in years 1 through 5, and $35 million in years 6 through 12. After year 12, the USSR takes over the facilities and Penney's can recoup nothing on its original investment of $150 million. Should the project be undertaken, (i.e., will the stockholders benefit)? Use an interest rate of 10 percent.

2

Uncertainty and Decision Making

Uncertain Outcomes

In the preceding chapter, we examined the investment and savings decisions people make when the future is known with perfect certainty. Since there is no ambiguity in the funds available next year, there is no need to be concerned with allocating funds to savings for precautionary or speculative motives. Savings is simply a by-product of the decision about how to consume over time. Yet, most economic decisions involve a confrontation between costs and benefits that are conjectural at the time the decision must be made. Since the world is "uncertain," decisions have to be made before the outcome of an action is resolved. This uncertainty influences the way we make decisions.

Some decisions are intrinsically involved with uncertain outcomes. They simply cannot be depended upon to yield the same result every time. In deciding among alternative educational strategies you may not be able to anticipate completely the level or stability of the future income streams provided by each. Moreover, chances are that such uncertainties are material to the choices you make; that is, you are not indifferent as to the extent of the uncertainties you confront. Would you rather have a job that offers a relatively stable future income or one in which future income is *expected* to be the same but which is highly unpredictable (e.g., a self-employed financial consultant)? If you have a preference for one of these alternatives you rationally would want to take uncertainty into account in making your occupational choice.

Savings decisions also are frequently made under conditions of uncertainty. If you purchase common stocks with your savings, there is always the possibility that stock market prices will rise (or fall) much faster or farther than you had anticipated. If this happens, you will end up with considerably more (or less) consumption in the future than you had planned at the time you made your decision.

With reference to the bundles of opportunities described in Chapter 1, uncertainty renders the future level of consumption of goods and services unknown at the time the decision must be made. In general, this will affect the preference ordering of the bundles and, thereby, the consumer's choice. The presence of uncertainty also will give rise to a demand by consumers for a variety of different financial instruments that may allow them to manage uncertainty in a way that increases their overall level of well-being.

In the first part of this chapter we develop measures to summarize the individual opportunities available to the decision maker when they offer uncertain outcomes. The second part of the chapter develops a framework for understanding the *effect* of uncertainty on savings and investment decisions.

Random Variables and Probability Distributions

Uncertain opportunities are characterized by possible alternative events, or outcomes, that can arise subsequent to the decision maker's action. If only one event can logically occur, then the outcome of the action is known with certainty. But if two, three, several, or an infinite number of events are possible, then we say that the situation is one of uncertainty.

The degree of uncertainty inherent in a situation may be characterized by probabilities associated with the various possible events or outcomes. **A probability is a number that measures the degree of likelihood of a given event.**

For the material dealt with in this book we have chosen to interpret probabilities in the subjective sense; i.e., as *beliefs* an individual may hold concerning the degree of likelihood of various events. I may, for instance, be convinced that the probability of rain on any given day is .75, while you—being more optimistic—assume it is only .4. Who is right? In many cases, it may not matter, since the *true* underlying probabilities may not be observable—and thus are not relevant. Especially in the social sciences, knowledge of the true likelihood of an event is generally unobtainable. What is the chance of war? How likely is it that IBM's stock price will be 1 percent higher next month?

What is important is what we *believe* the probabilities to be, since belief ultimately forms the basis of action. Of course, each of us wants his own beliefs to be as informed as possible; hence, it is appropriate to gather pertinent data concerning the events we are attempting to forecast. However, there is no guarantee that, even if we had all the information it is possible to acquire, the probabilities we would assign would be the "correct" ones in an objective sense. This is precisely why we view the assignment of probabilities to events as basically a subjective process.

Of course, there are incentives for rational individuals to uncover the probabilities that will most closely represent what would happen on average if the "event game" were played many times. Consider the example of two fans competing with each other to determine how many football games U.C.L.A. will win this fall. For pride or money it may pay each of these individuals to secure information on the likelihood of a six- or seven- or eight-win season. In this case (we hope) the actual probabilities both are unknown and cannot be influenced by our two fans. Yet, subjective probabilities can be rationally formulated (based on talent, past history, coaching changes, etc.) and would form the basis for the "best guess" by each.

Investment and savings markets are similar; however, it is earnings, dividends, capital investment opportunities, and other economic factors that are important in assessing the likelihood of future outcomes. In both markets incentives exist for the rational formation of expectations. Indeed much of finance relies on the belief that those operating in financial markets do not make decisions capriciously or arbitrarily, but rather form expectations rationally, based on information they have determined is in their best interest to use.

The various outcomes possible in uncertain situations may be thought of as corresponding to specific values of a **random variable.** The market value of an ounce of gold two years from today is a random variable. It can take on a value of $400, $800, or any one of a large number of other values. The exchange rate prevailing between U.S. dollars and Mexican pesos on July 12, 1989, is also a random variable (prior to that date at least). In the case of gold, the random variable is expressed in dollars; in the case of

---

FIGURE 2–1   Estimated Probabilities of Two Stocks

(a) Probability distribution of $\tilde{P}_{XON}$

(b) Probability distribution of $\tilde{P}P_{DD}$

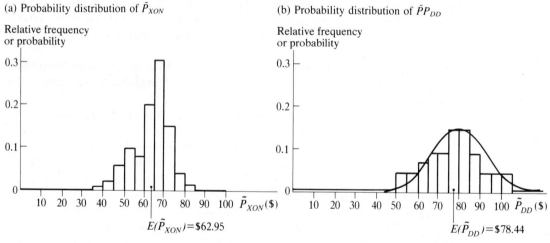

$E(\tilde{P}_{XON})=\$62.95$

$E(\tilde{P}_{DD})=\$78.44$

Price per Share Interval	Probability	Price per Share Interval	Probability
0–$30	.005	0–$50	.03
$30.125–$35	.005	$50.125–$55	.05
$35.125–$40	.01	$55.125–$60	.05
$40.125–$45	.03	$60.125–$65	.07
$45.125–$50	.06	$65.125–$70	.10
$50.125–$55	.10	$70.125–$75	.10
$55.125–$60	.085	$75.125–$80	.15
$60.125–$65	.20	$80.125–$85	.15
$65.125–$70	.30	$85.125–$90	.10
$70.125–$75	.15	$90.125–$95	.05
$75.125–$80	.04	$95.125–$100	.05
$80.125–$85	.01	$100.125–$105	.05
$85.125–$100	.005	$105.125–$150	.05
Total	1.000	Total	1.00

exchange rates, it is a ratio (of dollars to pesos). Some random variables may not have numerical values; e.g., the outcome of three aces in a poker hand.

To provide a fairly typical illustration of the use of random variables in financial decision making, we have assigned probabilities to various possible prices one year from today for two well-known common stocks: Exxon and Du Pont. Our probabilities are conditioned by the fact that Exxon was priced at $62 and Du Pont at $80 at the time of our calculations and by other economic information that might logically be used to forecast one year into the future.

These subjective probabilities are summarized in a series of nonoverlapping price intervals of $5 for each stock, and are presented in tabular form and graphically in Figure 2–1. Thus, for example, and according to our subjective estimates, there is a 10 percent chance that the price of Exxon will be above $50 but less than or equal to $55 per share. According to these estimates there is little likelihood that the price of Exxon will exceed $85.125 or be less than $35 in one year. The set of probabilities over all possible outcomes is called the **probability distribution** or **frequency distribution** of the random variable. To clarify our discussion we use a tilde (˜) to signify that the value the variable can take on is unknown. Thus, $\tilde{P}_{XON}$ and $\tilde{P}_{DD}$ are random variables representing next year's price for Exxon and Du Pont stock (XON and DD are the New York Stock Exchange ticker symbols for the firms). Each random variable has a probability distribution showing the relative frequency of occurance of particular values of the variable.

One type of probability distribution, a "normal," or Gaussian, distribution, plays a particularly important part in the social sciences. A normal distribution is superimposed on the probability distribution of Du Pont's stock price in Figure 2–1(b). If the normal distribution is a reasonable approximation to Du Pont's distribution, we may be able to use it to characterize Du Pont's common stock. Much is known about normal distributions so this knowledge may be useful in evaluating the worth of an investment in Du Pont.

Summary Measures of Probability Distributions

Since much of our work in finance will involve a comparison of different random variables and their frequency distributions, it is often useful to summarize the main characteristics of the distributions as a means of describing the random variable. Thus, we might be interested in knowing if the random variable tends to take on some values relatively more frequently than others, tends to be dispersed (or spread) over a wide range of values, tends to be symmetric, or tends to be more peaked. A number of the most often used summary measures are defined and discussed below.

Expected Value

The **expected value,** or mean, of a random variable is a measure of location or central tendency. Its calculation is given by the weighted sum of each of the possible values that the random variable can have. The weights associated with each value are given by the probability with which that value can occur. Using $\tilde{P}_i$ to represent the random variable that is the future price of security i, P_{ij} to represent the jth price, (or price range; such as $50.125 to $55) out of n possible prices, and π_j to indicate the probability of occurrence of a specific P_{ij}, then the expression for the expected value of the random variable $\tilde{P}_i$ is the weighted summation,

$$\textbf{(2–1)} \qquad E(\tilde{P}_i) = \pi_1 P_{i1} + \pi_2 P_{i2} + \pi_3 P_{i3} + \ldots + \pi_n P_{in}$$

For the price of Exxon's common stock the expected value calculation would be

$$
\begin{aligned}
\textbf{(2–2)} \qquad E(\tilde{P}_{XON}) &= \pi_1 P_{XON,1} + \pi_2 P_{XON,2} + \pi_3 P_{XON,3} + \ldots \pi_{13} P_{XON,13} \\
&= .005(15) + .005(\$32.5625) \\
&\quad + .01(\$37.5625) + \ldots + .005(\$92.5625) \\
&= \$62.95
\end{aligned}
$$

For Exxon the midpoints of the class intervals were used to indicate the values that the security's price could take on. Du Pont's expected value is $78.44.

Expression (2–1) can be written in more compact summation notation as

(2–3)   *Expected Value*

$$E(\tilde{P}_i) = \sum_{j=1}^{n} \pi_j P_{ij}$$

$$
\begin{array}{rcl}
\textit{The expected value of} & & \textit{The summation } (\Sigma) \textit{ of the products} \\
\textit{the random variable, } \tilde{P}_i & = & \textit{of the jth probability } (\pi_j) \textit{ and the} \\
 & & \textit{jth value } (P_{ij}) \textit{ of the random} \\
 & & \textit{variable } (\tilde{P}_i) \textit{ for j equals 1 to n.}
\end{array}
$$

Note that any *given* value, such as P_{i2}, is not a random variable. Neither is the expected value a random variable. Each of these is a scalar value. That is, a value that takes on only *one* amount. If all values of a random variable are equally likely, then all probabilities, π_j, are equal to $1/n$, and Expression (2–3) becomes the same as the familiar arithmetic average, or equally-weighted summation,

$$\textbf{(2–4)} \qquad E(\tilde{P}_i) = 1/n \sum_{j=1}^{n} P_{ij}$$

Conceptually, the expected value of a random variable tells you the value that is expected, *on average,* from a large number of sample points "selected" or "drawn" from the frequency distribution for the random variable. That is, if we were to randomly draw observations from an urn containing balls marked with each of the 13 intervals in Figure 2–1(a), and placed in the urn according to the frequency of occurrence of each of the intervals, the average of the drawn balls would tend toward the expected value of the random variable—$62.95. The larger the number of *independent* draws (that is, each draw is unrelated to all prior draws), the closer the actual average price of the draws should come to the expected value. This is the **Law of Large Numbers.** Its practical significance lies in the fact that since the average of a set of observations tends toward the expected value, we can use the set of observations as experiments in developing a picture of the frequency distribution that characterizes the random variable.[1] Geometrically, 50 percent of the area under the frequency distribution curve lies on either side of the expected value of the random variable.

---

[1]For notational convenience we use $E(\tilde{P}_i)$ to represent both the expected value of the random variable and the sample average of a finite set of drawings from the probability distribution.

Standard Deviation

The expected value of a random variable provides only one piece of information useful in summarizing the nature of a random variable. An investor in common stocks or commodity futures may be quite concerned with the variations from the expected value that may occur. For these types of random variables, there is always the distinct *possibility* that the actual future value of one's investment will turn out to be considerably above or below the value that is "expected." It is important to know in advance if a very low or high value is a *likely* prospect!

The dispersion of the frequency distribution is one way of characterizing this possibility, and the **standard deviation** is a calculation that defines one measure of the degree of dispersion of the probability distribution of a random variable. Its definition is

Standard Deviation

(2–5)

$$\sigma(\tilde{P}_i) = \sqrt{\sum_{j=1}^{n} \pi_j [P_{ij} - E(\tilde{P}_i)]^2}$$

$$= \left[\sum_{j=1}^{n} \pi_j [P_{ij} - E(\tilde{P}_i)]^2 \right]^{1/2}$$

Standard deviation = *The square root of the sum, from j equals 1 to n, of the probability of the occurrence of the jth value of the random variable times the square of the difference between the jth value and the expected value.*

For Exxon the standard deviation is

$$\sigma(\tilde{P}_{XON}) = [\pi_1 (P_{XON,1} - E(\tilde{P}_{XON}))^2 + \pi_2 (P_{XON,2} - E(\tilde{P}_{XON}))^2 + \dots]^{1/2}$$

$$= [.005(15 - 63.3253)^2 + .005 (32.5625 - 63.2353)^2 + \dots]^{1/2}$$

$$= \$10.$$

The standard deviation is in the same units as the expected value. Thus, if $\tilde{P}_i$ is the $ price of the common stock of firm i, $\sigma(\tilde{P}_i)$ is the $ standard deviation of the probability distribution of the price. The "variance" is the square of the standard deviation,

Variance

$$[\sigma(\tilde{P}_i)]^2$$

The standard deviation, along with the expected value, completely characterizes the shape and location of a random variable that is formally described by a Gaussian, or "normal," distribution. Thus, if earnings reports or stock returns are normally distributed, it would be possible to completely compare two or more distributions with knowledge of their expected values and standard deviations only. No other characteristic of the distribution would be relevant, since no other characteristic would differ between the two. One standard deviation on either side of the expected value encompasses about 68 percent of the total area under the curve or about two thirds of the relative frequency of values of the variable. This is true of all normal distributions, regardless of how disperse they are. Thus, using the **normal distribution** as an approximation[2] for Du Pont's distribution, and a standard deviation computed with Equation (2–5) of $19.4, there is a two thirds chance that Du Pont's price will be in the range of $59 to $98 next year.

Clearly, the standard deviation gives potential investors information that can be extremely important in making the investment decision. Indeed a measure of dispersion may be as important to the investment decision as the expected value. For example, how would you rank the following opportunities if you could invest your $2,000 savings in only one of them?

Opportunity	Expected Value in one Year	Standard Deviation
1	$2,200	$ 500
2	2,400	600
3	2,800	1,200
4	2,200	300
5	2,400	400
6	2,800	800

For some investors at least, the ranking based on expected value alone will be much different from the ranking that included consideration of the relative dispersion of the random variables about their expected values. The standard deviation is only one measure of dispersion, but it's a fairly descriptive one and one that is precise for normally distributed random variables that seem to approximately characterize many financial values.

Skewness and Peakedness

Skewness is a term used to measure the extent to which a probability distribution has a right-hand (positive) or left-hand (negative) elongated tail. That is, it measures the departure of a distribution from symmetry. In finance, some important random variables can be skewed by the way they are constructed. For example, corporate bonds pay interest in a specified (coupon) amount, set in the contract between bondholders and the firm, unless the corporation is unable to pay and defaults. If there is some small possibility of the corporation defaulting, then the probability distribution of the interest payment will be skewed to the left. Figure 2–2(a) plots a hypothetical distribution for the interest payment on a corporate bond with an annual coupon of $80 (8 percent per $1,000 par value bond).

An option on a common stock is an instrument that normally contains positive skewness. It is a security that pays off handsomely if the stock price goes up, and loses everything for the investor if stock price falls. Given the possibilities of the stock price rising, the probability distribution of the dollar payoff of an option may look like that in

---

[2]The normal distribution is of particular importance to finance since the probability distribution formed from a number of different events that may impact on a firm has a *sampling* distribution that is likely to be normal. For example, suppose, on any given day, there are 10 things that happen that affect the price of a common stock. One might be a change in the price of a competitor's product. Another might be the firm's dividend announcement. If each piece of news causes the market to react in such a way that the price of the firm's stock moves either up or down by one eighth point, depending on whether the news is good or bad, then the distribution of daily stock price changes—which is the collective effect of the 10 news items—will tend to be *normally* distributed. This is an application of the Central Limit Theorem of statistics.

FIGURE 2–2   **Skewness**

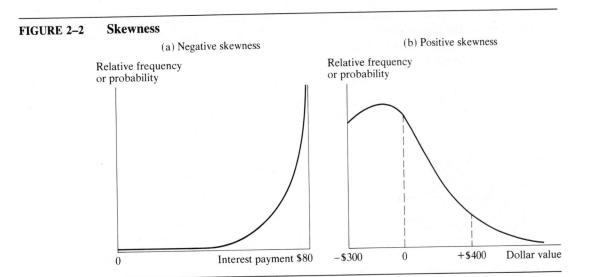

Figure 2–2(b). Here, $300 is the cost of the option—and is the maximum amount the investor could lose.

Skewness is usually defined as the sum of the cubes of the difference between the value of the random variable and its expected value, weighted by the probability of occurrence of the variable, and then divided by the cube of the standard deviation. Cubing the values, of course, allows a large influence of those values a great distance from the expected values, and this is the way asymmetry influences the calculation. For purposes of this book, it is not necessary that explicit values for skewness be considered, only that the student have an intuitive grasp of the direction and magnitude of the skewness of a distribution.

The **peakedness,** or **kurtosis,** of a probability distribution refers to the extent to which the distribution tends to have a relatively larger proportion (than the normal distribution) of frequencies around the center and in the tails of a distribution. This characteristic of a probability distribution is important only because some financial variables seem to have a greater than normal percentage of extreme values. Thus, for example, there is some evidence from historical data that the rates of return on common stocks show a tendency for more returns in the extreme tails of the distribution. As you might guess, this may be reflected in individuals' choices of investment types to the extent that extreme positive or negative returns could prove quite beneficial or costly to the decision maker.

Decisions under Uncertainty

The probability distributions of the common stock prices of Exxon and Du Pont point out the obvious: uncertainty is a two-edged sword. Its existence creates the possibility of gain from profitable outcomes, but it is acquired only with the possibility of some loss. When you buy a share of Exxon at $62, for example, you have acquired the rights to the probability distribution depicted in Figure 2–1. That distribution offers you a chance that the value in one year will be above the current $62 price. But it also includes the possibility that in one year it will be below $62.

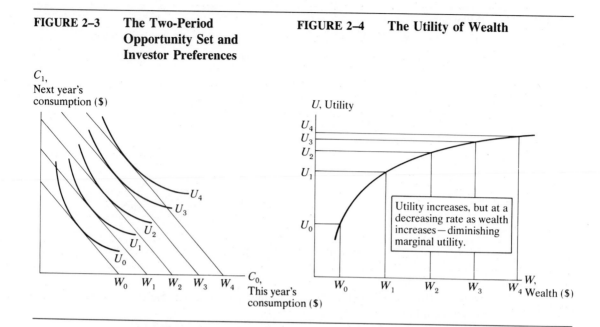

FIGURE 2–3   **The Two-Period Opportunity Set and Investor Preferences**

FIGURE 2–4   **The Utility of Wealth**

Utility increases, but at a decreasing rate as wealth increases—diminishing marginal utility.

In this section we consider how uncertainty affects decision making. We demonstrate that considering the effects of uncertainty is just as important as considering the expected return from an opportunity. Expected return and uncertainty of return must be jointly considered in making investment decisions.

In addition, we will use the term **risk** to characterize the level of uncertainty inherent in a financial opportunity. In this book, as in finance generally, we do *not* adopt the statistical convention of refering to risk as a description of a known or objective probability distribution—primarily because all the distributions we will be dealing with are subjective in nature. There are no securities for which the probability distribution is known and agreed upon by all.

The Level of Utility

To determine the investor's attitude toward uncertainty we need to know something about how his **utility** (i.e., happiness) increases or decreases with changes in his wealth. Consider Figure 2–3 for example, which is identical in concept to those developed in Chapter 1. There is a level of utility, U_i, associated with each **indifference curve** and a level of wealth, W_i, associated with each market line that is tangent to that indifference curve. To describe how utility and wealth are related for this investor we need only plot the pairs of U_i and W_i values. The result of this is Figure 2–4, and the line itself is called a **utility curve.**

We have drawn the curve to be everywhere increasing, and increasing at a decreasing rate. This particular shape to the utility curve could not be inferred from Figure 2–3 itself. In fact, to arrive at this general shape we have used two assumptions that finance and economics accept as characteristic of human behavior. The first is that individuals or family units get some satisfaction out of additional levels of wealth. They are never completely satiated with W. The second is that as more and more units of wealth are conferred on the decision maker, it is likely that each subsequent unit will bring smaller and smaller increases in satisfaction. These assumptions are the basis of the doctrine that individuals express **diminishing marginal utility for wealth.** And that, of course, is what the concave curve in Figure 2–4 represents.[3]

The utility function serves as a device for assessing the total satisfaction from some given level of wealth. We can use the function to analyze and compare the decisions of individuals faced with investment opportunities that have uncertain outcomes.

The Implications of Diminishing Marginal Utility for Risk Aversion

Using the utility function described in Figure 2–4, we can analyze the investor's response to uncertain investment opportunities. In particular, suppose our investor begins with the level of wealth designated by W_2 in Figure 2–5, and is faced with an opportunity to participate in an investment involving the outcome of a bankruptcy proceeding. There are only two outcomes possible in his view. One outcome (bankruptcy) costs him $10,000 and leaves him with wealth of W_1 (or $W_2 - \$10,000$). The other outcome (profitability) leaves him with W_3, which represents a gain of $10,000. The investor views each outcome as equally likely, so the investment is one that offers the rights to a simple probability distribution with a .5 probability of gaining or losing $10,000. This distribution is drawn at the bottom of Figure 2–5. If the investor decides not to participate in this opportunity he does nothing, and, as a result, with perfect certainty, remains in his current wealth level, W_2.

The relevant question is how the individual would compare the uncertain option with the opportunity to remain at W_2. One (not very good) option is to ignore the vertical axis and make the decision by calculating the expected monetary outcome or expected value of each opportunity. For the option of doing nothing the monetary outcome clearly is W_2. For the risky investment in the bankruptcy proceeding the calculation follows from the **expected value calculation** in Equation 2–3. The exact expression is

$$E(\tilde{W}_{Bank}) = .5(W_2 + 10,000) + .5(W_2 - 10,000) = W_2$$

In this case both the opportunities have the same expected value: W_2. If expected value is the decision criterion, the investor will appear to be indifferent between the two options. The problem is that this gives equal weight to the $+\$10,000$ and $-\$10,000$ outcomes. The implication is that the investor loses as much satisfaction from a dollar lost as he gains in satisfaction from a dollar gained, and a loss of $10,000 carries precisely 10 times the loss in satisfaction as the loss of $1,000.

---

[3]We don't need to assign unique numbers to the vertical axis in Figure 2–4, and, in fact, any numbering scheme will do that maintains the relative distance between points on that axis.

FIGURE 2–5   Uncertainty and Expected Utility

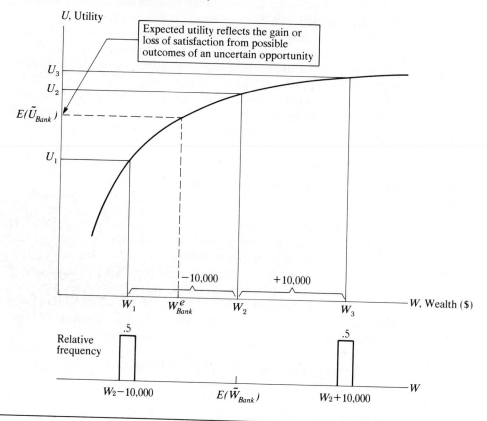

While it is possible that some investors under some circumstances would regard these outcomes as beneficial as they are harmful, we know this is not true for the investor whose utility function is represented in Figure 2–5. In fact, in terms of overall satisfaction or happiness, our investor gains less from an addition to wealth of $+\$10,000$ than he loses from a $\$10,000$ loss. Quantitatively, from the graph,

$$U_3 - U_2 < U_2 - U_1$$

What criteria might be employed to overcome the obvious deficiency of decisions that are based on expected value? One that is obvious from Figure 2–5 is to calculate **expected utility.** That is, we might use the values on the vertical axis, rather than on the horizontal axis, to calculate the expected benefit of the alternatives. These numbers have the advantage of representing the individual's "attitude" toward the outcomes of the opportunities. They can account for the individual's loss of satisfaction from the negative outcome and the gain in satisfaction from the positive outcome.

The expected utility, $E(\tilde{U})$, follows directly from Equation (2–3) as the sum of the utilities associated with each potential outcome, weighted by their probability of occurrence, or

(2–6)   *Expected Utility*

$$E(\tilde{U}) = \sum_{i=1}^{n} \pi_i U_i$$

Each uncertain opportunity has a unique expected utility which expresses the relative desirability of that investment opportunity to the investor. The criterion involves selecting the alternative that has the highest expected utility. The opportunities considered in Figure 2–5 involve a comparison of U_2, the utility associated with wealth W_2 when the investor does nothing, with the expected utility of the bankruptcy proceeding option. That amount is

$$E(\tilde{U}_{Bank}) = .5(U_1) + .5(U_3)$$

Clearly in this case U_2 exceeds $E(U_{Bank})$, and it would be best for the investor to forego participating in this risky venture, as long as the expected value of the two alternatives is the same. The reason is simple. Our decision maker feels there is more to lose, in terms of units of satisfaction, than to gain from a fair risk involving the gain or loss of $10,000. And it is this, and nothing more, that makes individuals averse to risk. Risk aversion, in other words, means the investor has a "preference" for relative certainty when the expected value of the outcomes is the same.

Experimentation with different investment opportunities in the framework summarized in Figure 2–5 yields additional insights into investor behavior. For example, it seems clear that if the bankruptcy opportunity offered equally likely cash flows of −$5,000 or $15,000 (essentially shifting the probability distribution to the right on the wealth scale), the expected reward of +$5,000 might sufficiently increase expected utility to cause the investor to forego the certainty of doing nothing and accept the risky investment. Moreover, a change in the probabilities so that the positive outcome is more likely might have the same effect on expected utility.

Finally, an increase in the size of the risk (say by increasing the magnitude of the negative and positive outcomes), given diminishing marginal utility, would reduce the expected utility of the opportunity. Thus, as the risk increases the aversion to the opportunity grows.

Justifying the Use of Expected Utility

There is more to the selection of the expected utility criterion than is apparent from the rationale presented above. There are detailed and formal proofs suggesting what conditions have to exist before **maximizing expected utility** can be unambiguously chosen as *the* criteria to employ with a risky investment. While we (thankfully) will not develop the arguments here, we will summarize the aspects of human behavior that cause expected utility to be the best criteria for investors. Basically: (1) investors must be able to rank all bundles of goods and services available to them (i.e., they aren't confused by choices);

(2) the ranking must be transitive; and (3) gambles involving combinations of the ranked bundles themselves can be ranked (e.g., if bundle C_1 is preferred to bundle C_2 is preferred to bundle C_3, then a gamble involving the bundles C_1 and C_3 can be compared directly with C_2).

If investors behave in accordance with these principles, then they are best off making choices on the basis of expected utility. Of course, these statements of behavior are limited to the economic choices we deal with in finance. We are not suggesting that noneconomic decisions (to the extent there are any) would employ similar criteria.[4]

Monetarizing the Aversion to Uncertainty

An important concept in the decision rule of maximizing expected utility is that the degree of an investor's aversion to risk can be expressed as a dollar equivalent. The investor facing the $+\$10,000$ or $-\$10,000$ opportunity in Figure 2–5 has an expected utility for the opportunity of $E(\tilde{U}_{Bank})$. This utility level is the same as would be enjoyed if the individual had the wealth level W^e_{Bank}. We call this amount the **certainty equivalent wealth** since, received with certainty, it would offer the same satisfaction or level of utility offered by the opportunity with a .5 chance of gaining or losing $10,000 and an **expected value** of W_2.

The difference between W_2 and W^e_{Bank} is the amount the individual would be willing to pay to avoid the uncertain situation. That is, he is just as well off in terms of utility to pay $W_2 - W^e_{Bank}$ and move to W^e_{Bank} on the horizontal axis as he is to participate in the risky bankruptcy proceeding option. The distance between W_2 and W^e_{Bank} is then a monetary measure of the individual's aversion to the uncertainty of the situation. In general, for any uncertain situation the aversion to uncertainty as measured by this distance will be greater the more dispersed the possible outcomes and the more concave the utility function (i.e., the faster marginal utility diminishes).

Utility Comparisons

The aim of our analysis is to be able to say something about the kinds of decisions a person will make when confronted with opportunities having uncertain outcomes. Comparison of utility functions between individuals must be limited to an expression of relative

---

[4]Perhaps we should make our statement even weaker. A well-known student of how people make decisions, Howard Raiffa, notes "No one claims that most people *do* behave as they *ought* to behave. Indeed, the primary reason for the adoption of a prescriptive or normative theory (that is, an 'ought to do' theory) for choice behavior is the observation than when decision making is left solely to unguided judgment, choices are often made in an internally inconsistent fashion and this indicates that perhaps the decision maker could do better than he is doing. If people always behaved as this prescriptive theory (maximization of expected utility) says they ought to, then there would be no reason to make a fuss about prescriptive theory. We could just tell people, 'do what comes naturally.' " (See Raiffa, [1968], pp. 81–82.)

preference. We can compare individuals' attitudes by showing that one would reject an opportunity that another would accept. But the analysis cannot be extended to concluding that one individual is happier than another or that a profitable investment opportunity would provide more satisfaction to one investor than to another. Certainty equivalent values can be compared, of course, since they have been converted to dollar amounts. Thus, it is possible to compare the amounts that two investors would expend to rid themselves of the same risk (e.g., the $-\$10,000$ or $+\$10,000$ risk described).

How Can the Level of Risk and Reward Be Summarized?

We have limited the number of possible outcomes from an uncertain opportunity to present the expected utility analysis graphically. But how could the opportunity be summarized if complete enumeration of the possible outcomes were impractical or impossible? The answer lies in our adoption of two parameters of the probability distribution of outcomes from the opportunity, mentioned in the first half of this chapter. The first is the **expected value** of the possible outcomes. It measures the general tendency of the opportunity to affect the wealth of the investor. The second is the **standard deviation** of the outcomes. It is a measure of dispersion that *best* summarizes the extent to which the probability distribution offers outcomes that, were they to occur, would significantly affect the utility of the investor.

Thus, we might summarize the probability distribution for Du Pont's price next year with its expected value of $78.44 and standard deviation of $19.40. Similarly, the expected value and standard deviation of the bankruptcy venture, as you can see by applying Equations (2–3) and (2–5), are W_2 and $10,000.

This is *not* meant to imply that these two parameters completely summarize all of the important elements of the distribution. Yet studies of investor behavior and outcomes from investments in stocks and bonds seem to suggest that the use of the expected value and standard deviation of the opportunity adequately accounts for what is important in making choices among investment opportunities. Of course, if the distribution is normal, these two parameters would completely describe the opportunity.

Willingness to Trade Off between Risk and Wealth

As you have seen, utility provides a mechanism for describing individual aversion to uncertain opportunities. The bankruptcy option with an uncertain expected outcome of $E(\tilde{W}_{Bank}) = W_2$ and a standard deviation of $10,000 was the equivalent (in utility terms) of receiving a certain amount W^e_{Bank}. In Figure 2–5 the axes measured $ wealth or value (the horizontal) and utility (the vertical). Standard deviation was incorporated in determining the relationship between expected wealth and expected utility. However, to get more insight into the trade-offs that investors need to be concerned with, let's plot the information contained in Figure 2–5 onto a new set of axes.

FIGURE 2–6   **Using Indifference Curves to Show Risk Aversion**

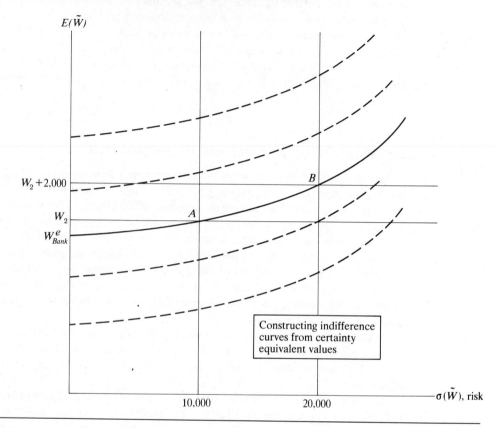

Figure 2–6 has risk or standard deviation on the horizontal axis and expected wealth on the vertical. Point *A* represents the bankruptcy opportunity with its expected value of W_2 and standard deviation of $10,000. Point W_{Bank}^e represents the certainty equivalent of this opportunity. By definition these two points must lie on the same indifference curve (since, in the view of the investor, they are combinations of expected wealth and risk that give rise to the same level of expected utility).

Of course, there are many other combinations of $E(\tilde{W})$ and $\sigma(\tilde{W})$ that generate the same level of utility as the two combinations we have analyzed. For example, as risk is doubled to $20,000, the investor needs to be compensated by an increase in the expectation of wealth to $E(\tilde{W}_2 + \$2,000)$ at point *B*.

The line through these three points (*A*, *B*, and W_{Bank}^e) is an **indifference curve,** and it summarizes the relative willingness of the investor to trade off between greater risk and greater expected wealth. Moreover, there are other indifference curves corresponding to different levels of expected wealth at a given risk level. As a set, the curves deliver information regarding the investor's tolerance for risk, and suggest relative preferences for combinations of expected wealth and the risk to which that wealth is exposed.

Changing the Units from Dollars to Rates of Return

Indifference curves defined in terms of dollars of expected wealth and standard deviation are cumbersome. Consequently, we will normalize the curves that represent the investor's willingness to exchange risk for expected wealth by dividing both sides, $E(\tilde{W})$ and $\sigma(\tilde{W})$, by the initial amount that must be paid for the opportunity, the cost of investment, I. The result is

Expected Rate of Return and Standard Deviation of Return

(2–7)
$$\frac{E(\tilde{W})}{I} = E(\tilde{R}) + 1$$

and

(2–8)
$$\frac{\sigma(\tilde{W})}{I} = \sigma(\tilde{R})$$

which simply puts the numbers in terms of a **rate of return expected,** $E(\tilde{R})$, and a **standard deviation of the rate of return,** $\sigma(\tilde{R})$. The shape of the curves will not change. However, we are now in a position to analyze investment opportunities in terms of their impact on investor well-being in a standardized framework, or in terms of the rate at which the investor's wealth—and thus utility—might be affected. Such a graph is presented in Figure 2–7, where the indifference curves are shown as having the same general shape and location as on Figure 2–6. In essence, this adjustment allows us to depict preferences over investment opportunities in terms of their rate of return and standard deviation of the rate of return.

In fact, suppose the investor formed expectations about the expected return and standard deviation of return as follows:

	$E(\tilde{R})$	$\sigma(\tilde{R})$
American Telephone & Telegraph (T)	12%	14%
Eastman Kodak (EK)	20	29
Standard Oil of California (SD)	15	23
Exxon (XON)	14	19
Texaco (TX)	15	20
USX (X)	18	29

Where would he put his money? If each of these securities was to be held individually, the location of each opportunity using expected return and standard deviation coordinates is given in Figure 2–7. It is apparent from these hypothetical figures that:

a. Kodak dominates USX (they have the same standard deviation but Kodak offers a higher return).

b. Texaco dominates Standard Oil of California (they have the same return but Texaco has a lower variance).

Also, our investor's willingness to exchange risk for return (the relatively flat set of curves) is such that his preference would be to invest in Eastman Kodak. This selection

---

FIGURE 2–7   Preferences and Opportunities: The Optimal Choice

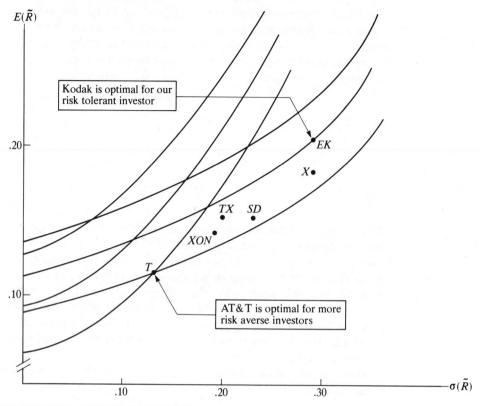

will place him on the highest achievable indifference curve, i.e., the highest level of utility. In his view the combination of standard deviation and expected return offered by Kodak dominates those offered by the remaining opportunities.[5] Alternatively, AT&T may be optimal for an investor who is less tolerant of risk and, therefore, has more steeply sloped curves.

Introduction to Valuation under Uncertainty

Faced with a set of uncertain situations, an individual may express strong preferences among the choices. How will this be reflected in that individual's assessment of the value of an asset that offers an uncertain set of cash flows? The answer, of course, is the subject of the remaining chapters, though it will be useful to indicate at this point the nature of some key relationships.

---

[5]We were careful to construct this example as a choice among individual securities. Combinations of securities were ruled out in this analysis. However, the possibility of combining securities into a portfolio will significantly change the set available, and as we show in Chapter 7, will create new opportunities that can be expected to dominate these individual security offerings.

1. The value of an asset will have to incorporate the expected value of the uncertain cash flows.
2. The present value of the expected cash flows would have to define the future period in which the flows are to be received, and, given the risk, the appropriate return that is required by the market to correctly compensate for the risk of those flows.

As in the case of the value of an asset in a certain world, the rate of return used to discount the expected future flows of an uncertain asset is a market rate. Thus, if in the financial marketplace assets or securities with a given risk level must offer a return of 16 percent, then that is the rate of interest to be applied to the cash flows to determine their present value.

If an asset offers uncertain cash flows with expected values of $10, $15, and $20 in years 1, 5, and 7, and securities with the same amount of risk offer returns in equilibrium of 16 percent, then the value of the asset is calculated as

$$(2\text{--}9) \qquad \text{Value} = \frac{\$10}{(1 + .16)^1} + \frac{\$15}{(1 + .16)^5} + \frac{\$20}{(1 + .16)^7} = \$22.84$$

Its value would be $22.84 since, with this amount, the investor would be *expected* to be able to generate these cash flows by investing in equivalent risk securities with expected returns of 16 percent. In other words,

$$(\$22.84)(1.16)^1 = \$26.46$$
$$\text{less} \qquad \underline{10}$$
$$\$16.46 \text{ at end of year 1}$$

$$(\$16.46)(1.16)^4 = \$29.79$$
$$\text{less} \qquad \underline{15}$$
$$\$14.79 \text{ at end of year 5}$$

$$(14.79)(1.16)^2 = \$20$$
$$\text{less} \qquad \underline{20}$$
$$0 \qquad \text{at end of year 7}$$

Of course, in an uncertain world these values may not be achieved. But such is the nature of uncertainty, and the requirement that the asset be valued to offer a 16 percent return is to make up for that risk. A general expression for value then, where $E(\tilde{R})$ represents the market rate of return, is

$(2\text{--}10)$ ***Present Value***

$$\text{Value} = E(\tilde{C}_0) + \frac{E(\tilde{C}_1)}{(1 + E(\tilde{R}))^1} + \frac{E(\tilde{C}_2)}{(1 + E(\tilde{R}))^2} + \ldots + \frac{E(\tilde{C}_t)}{(1 + E(\tilde{R}))^n}$$

Value = The sum of the present values of the expected cash flows.

The present value of each term reflects the risk of the asset, the time period in which it is to be received, and the returns available in the market from other assets with that risk level.

Summary Measures of Joint Probability Distributions

To this point we have only considered the probability distribution of a random variable as a distinct separate uncertain characteristic. This ignores a good deal of what is interesting and important in finance. It may be useful to know that Exxon's stock price next year is uncertain (in part) because of the uncertainty surrounding the firm's ability to generate profits from its operations. However, it also may be important to know how closely connected is the price of Exxon with the price of an index representing the value of many common stocks. In large part, in fact, finance studies the relationships among financial random variables. Representing these relationships is an important task that requires statistical sophistication going beyond that summarized in expected value and standard deviation to the consideration of **covariance, correlation,** and **regression.**

Covariance

The covariance measures the tendency for the value of one random variable to be above or below its expected value when the value of another random variable is above or below its expected value. The calculation is given by

(2–11)   *Covariance*

$$Cov(\tilde{P}, \tilde{R}) = \sum_{j=1}^{n} \pi_j[(P_j - E(\tilde{P}))(R_j - E(\tilde{R}))]$$

where $\tilde{P}$ and $\tilde{R}$ are two random variables and π_j is the joint probability of the occurrence of P_j and R_j. If P_j and R_j tend to be high together, the product of $[P_j - E(\tilde{P})]$ and $[R_j - E(\tilde{R})]$ will be large. If P_j and R_j tend to be low together the product will also be large. This relationship between $\tilde{P}$ and $\tilde{R}$ will tend to give a high value for the covariance. That is, $\tilde{P}$ and $\tilde{R}$ tend to show "comovement."

If, when P_j is large, R_j tends to be neither large nor small, and when P_j is small, R_j tends to be neither large nor small, the covariance will be small. If the two variables move completely independently of one another, the covariance will be zero.

The covariance, or degree of comovement, will be large and positive when $\tilde{P}$ and $\tilde{R}$ tend to move in concert with each other, and large and negative when $\tilde{P}$ and $\tilde{R}$ tend to move in opposite directions. Also, comovement or covariance can be defined only with reference to pairs of random variables. $\tilde{P}$ can be related to $\tilde{R}$, and $\tilde{R}$ and $\tilde{P}$ together can be related to another variable, $\tilde{S}$, but it makes no sense to talk in terms of the comovement of $\tilde{P}$, $\tilde{R}$, and $\tilde{S}$ together. The units of the covariance are the products of the units of the variables. For example, the covariance between the price of apples and bushels of wheat produced would yield units of dollar-bushels—a measure that some would find difficult to interpret! Nevertheless, the greater the unit number, the greater the comovement of the price of apples and bushels of wheat. The covariance of two prices would produce a covariance in dollars squared.

For example, Table 2–1 has the calculated expected values, $E(\tilde{P}_i)$, and standard deviations, $\sigma(\tilde{P}_i)$, for the prices of three common stocks (General Mills, Allegis—the parent of United Airlines, and Exxon) based on historical data for 1985 and 1986. Also calculated are the covariances of the prices of each pair of stocks. The covariance between

TABLE 2–1 **Sample Computations of Statistics for Random Variables and for Combinations of Random Variables**

Prices

Date	General Mills $\tilde{P}_{GIS}$	UAL $\tilde{P}_{UAL}$	Exxon $\tilde{P}_{XON}$	$\tilde{P}_{GIS} + \tilde{P}_{UAL}$	$\tilde{P}_{GIS} + \tilde{P}_{UAL} + \tilde{P}_{XON}$
J 1985	$55.125	$ 45	$ 48	$ 93	$148.125
F	55.125	48	47.5	95.5	150.625
M	58.125	46.25	50.25	96.5	154.625
A	52.75	40.25	51.5	91.75	144.5
M	60	53.625	54	107.625	167.625
J	63.625	53.625	53.875	107.5	171.125
J	56.75	55	52.5	107.5	164.25
A	56.875	55	52.75	107.75	164.625
S	61.5	47.25	51.875	99.125	160.625
O	61.75	47.75	55	102.75	164.5
N	59.5	48.75	53.375	102.125	161.625
D	61.125	49.75	55.125	104.875	166
J 1986	61.75	53.75	51.75	105.5	167.25
F	69.25	58.875	52.25	111.125	180.375
M	74.25	58.25	55.75	114	188.25
A	69.875	62.125	56.625	118.75	188.625
M	77.5	59.75	59.875	119.625	197.125
J	83	54.875	60.875	115.75	198.75
J	87	52.25	60.75	113	199
$E(\tilde{P}_i)$	64.4	52.1	53.9	106.0	170.4
$\sigma(\tilde{P}_i)$	9.4	5.5	3.7	8.1	16.6

$$Cov(\tilde{P}_{GIS}, \tilde{P}_{UAL}) = 30.3 \qquad \rho(\tilde{P}_{GIS}, \tilde{P}_{UAL}) = .59$$
$$Cov(\tilde{P}_{GIS}, \tilde{P}_{XON}) = 30.1 \qquad \rho(\tilde{P}_{GIS}, \tilde{P}_{XON}) = .88$$
$$Cov(\tilde{P}_{UAL} + \tilde{P}_{XON}) = 10.8 \qquad \rho(\tilde{P}_{UAL}, P_{XON}) = .53$$
$$Cov[\tilde{P}_{GIS}, (\tilde{P}_{UAL} + \tilde{P}_{XON})] = 60.4$$

$$c = 10 \text{ is a constant}$$
$$\sigma(c\tilde{P}_{GIS}) = 10 (9.4)$$
$$Cov(c\tilde{P}_{GIS}, \tilde{P}_{XON}) = 10 (30.1)$$

General Mills and Allegis using equal probabilities for each of the 19 observations, is given by

(2–12) $\quad Cov(\tilde{P}_{GIS}, \tilde{P}_{UAL}) = \displaystyle\sum_{j=1}^{n} \pi_j \{[P_{GIS,j} - E(\tilde{P}_{GIS})] [P_{UAL,j} - E(\tilde{P}_{UAL})]\}$

$$= \frac{1}{19}\{[55\frac{1}{8} - 64.4][45 - 53.9]\}$$

$$+ \frac{1}{19}\{55\frac{1}{8} - 64.4][48 - 53.9]\} + \cdots = 30.3$$

The covariance between Allegis and Exxon, on the other hand, is a much smaller 10.8. This figure undoubtedly reflects the similar effects on both firms of general business conditions and the different effects on them attributable to the cost of oil (Exxon was damaged by falling oil prices during this period, whereas airlines benefited). Note there is a covariance for each pair of random variables.

Correlation

The units in the covariance calculation can be avoided by dividing the covariance by the product of the standard deviations of the two variables, which yields the correlation coefficient (ρ). This yields a "unitless" or normalized covariance,

(2–13)   *Correlation*

$$\rho(\tilde{P}_{GIS}, \tilde{P}_{UAL}) = \frac{Cov(\tilde{P}_{GIS}, \tilde{P}_{UAL})}{\sigma(\tilde{P}_{GIS})\sigma(\tilde{P}_{UAL})} = .59$$

The unitless value varies between $+1.0$ and -1.0. Both the covariance and the correlation coefficients are measures of the comovement of two random variables. The correlations between each pair of common stocks in Table 2–1 are all positive—reflecting the positive comovement of the prices of these securities. UAL has about the same level of correlation with General Mills, .59, as with Exxon, .53.

Regression

The relationship that describes how one random variable, say $\tilde{P}$, tends to move in response to the movement of another random variable, $\tilde{R}$, can be expressed in the functional form $E(\tilde{P}_j \mid R_j) = a + bR_j$. In this expression the expected value of P_j is conditional on R_j (the vertical line represents "conditional on") and is functionally related through the coefficients a and b. In this case the relationship is linear. In the more general case, the functional form may be a more complex nonlinear relationship. Often it is desirable, with some a priori knowledge or theory, to attempt to statistically determine the relationship between two (or more) random variables by estimating the coefficients a and b. A common and generally statistically sound way of doing this is to "regress" the dependent random variable, $\tilde{P}$, on the independent, exogenous, or determining variable, $\tilde{R}$.

Regression analysis assumes that an additive "error term," $\tilde{u}$, exists in the description of the relationship between the two random variables. Thus, for any particular observation of the random variables (say the value of the variables in June 1987 or the value of the variables for a particular firm) the equation

(2–14)   *Regression*

$$P_j = a + bR_j + u_j$$

holds. The relationship between $\tilde{P}$ and $\tilde{R}$ is stronger if u_j is smaller. If, across all observations ($j = 1, \ldots n$), the value of u_j is small, then there is a very close causal relationship between $\tilde{P}$ and $\tilde{R}$. In particular, $\tilde{R}$ would be a major factor determining $\tilde{P}$. Empirically, of course, $\tilde{u}$ may tend to be large or small depending on the random variables being studied. For example, there may be a fairly close connection between a firm's earnings and its stock price. The connection between a firm's sales and stock price may be much weaker.

Regression analysis is employed to identify relationships between two or more random variables by estimating the values of a and b that minimize the sum over the n-valued sample of the squared values of the error term:

FIGURE 2–8   **Regression Analysis**

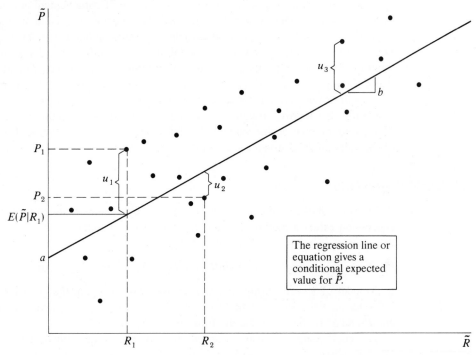

The regression line or equation gives a conditional expected value for $\tilde{P}$.

$$(2\text{–}15) \qquad \underset{\{a,\,b\}}{MIN} \sum_{j=1}^{n} u_j^2 = MIN \sum_{j=1}^{n} [P_j - (a + bR_j)]^2$$

That is, regression involves an optimization. Fortunately, efficient routines exist that easily solve the optimization problem, even for complex problems, so that the use of this statistical procedure has become an integral part of the study of economic and financial relationships. For a simple regression of one variable on another the slope and intercepts defined by the minimization are

$$(2\text{–}16) \qquad b = \frac{Cov(\tilde{P}, \tilde{R})}{[\sigma(\tilde{R})]^2} = \rho(\tilde{P}, \tilde{R}) \frac{\sigma(\tilde{P})}{\sigma(\tilde{R})}$$

$$a = E(\tilde{P}) - bE(\tilde{R})$$

The slope is, thus, the ratio of the covariance between the variables and the variance of the independent variable.

The regression problem is set forth graphically in Figure 2–8. Each point on the graph represents a measured value for the two random variables for each observation. The intercept, a, and the slope coefficient, b, are selected via the minimization to create a line of "best fit." For example, if $\tilde{R}$ is the price of feed and $\tilde{P}$ is the price of cattle, then the relationship in Equation (2–15) is solved for and depicted graphically by a linear relationship between these two random variables. Clearly, from Equation (2–16) the slope of the regression is closely dependent on the degree of comovement among the random variables. There is one important difference. The method of calculating the coefficients depends on an assumption of the independent, or right-hand-side variable ($\tilde{R}$ in this case), *causing* to some extent the value of the left-hand-side variable, $\tilde{P}$. Thus, the assumption would be that the price of feed in some way influences or affects, in part, the price of cattle. In any case, the presence of a slope coefficient b implies some degree of positive (if $b > 0$) or negative (if $b < 0$) comovement of these two variables.[6]

Finally, the regression equation can be interpreted as a conditional expected value. That is, conditional on the value of R_j taking on some specified value, the *best* estimate of the value of P_j is given by $a + bR_j$.

Multiple Regression

The price of cattle, of course, may be affected by more than the price of feed. **Multiple regression** offers a method for defining how a set of independent variables influences the value of one dependent variable. Thus,

$$(2\text{–}17) \qquad P_j = a + b_1R_j + b_2S_j + u_j \qquad j = 1, \ldots n$$

is a model of a relationship that shows how two "independent" variables, R_j and S_j, influence the value of P_j. Here the degree of comovement is between $\tilde{P}$, on the one hand, and $\tilde{R}$ and $\tilde{S}$, on the other (in the form $a + b_1R_j + b_2S_j$).

The coefficients are also estimated by minimizing the sum of the squared errors, $\Sigma_{j=1}^n u_j^2$, where

$$(2\text{–}18) \qquad u_j = P_j - [a + b_1R_j + b_2S_j]$$

The regression will depict the relationship between one random variable and a *set* of other influencing random variables. Thus, it is often a useful way to picture financial relationships. For example, it may be possible to use a regression equation to specify the functional relationships between the prices of common stocks and the earnings, dividends, and uncertainty of firms that have issued the stock.

Financial Applications of Regression: An Example

One widely used application of regression analysis is in relating the rate of return on one security to the rate of return on a broad-based index of all security returns. Thus,

---

[6]For regression estimates to be "best and unbiased," a series of conditions have to hold. While it does some damage to precision in econometrics, the essence of the conditions are that:

1. The mean of $u, E(\tilde{u})$, must be zero for all values the independent variables can take.
2. The standard deviation of u must be the same for the entire range of values for the independent variable.
3. The values of the independent variables must be completely free of the influence of values of the dependent variables. Thus, the direction of causation must run from the right-hand-side variables to the left-hand-side variable.

One additional requirement exists for this method to supply an accurate and unbiased view of the true relationship between the dependent variable and the set of two or more independent variables. It is that the set of independent variables are not themselves causally related to one another.

when the monthly rate of return on UAL, $\tilde{R}_{UAL,t}$, from 1980 to 1985 is regressed on the monthly rate of return on the New York Stock Exchange Index, the slope and intercept is

(2–19)
$$\tilde{R}_{UAL} = -.01 + 1.32\,(\tilde{R}_{NYSE})$$

Over this period, if the NYSE index return was 6 percent in period t, the return on UAL "tended" to be 6.9 percent in period t, or

$$R_{UAL,t} = -.01 + 1.32(.06) = .0692$$

If the market return was a negative 5 percent, the value for UAL would tend to

$$R_{UAL} = -.01 + 1.32(-.05) = -.076$$

If this relationship is stable over time, it clearly supplies some insights into understanding the movement of UAL's stock.

Manipulation of Random Variables

Thus far, our discussion has focused on one random variable, or the relationship between two or more random variables. But random variables, like any other numbers, can be added, subtracted, multiplied, or divided. Indeed, it should be obvious that many important financial random variables are dependent on some combination of other random variables. Total revenues of a firm are the result of multiplying together two other random variables—the price of the product and the number of units of the product sold. Earnings are the result of the difference between one random variable—total revenues—and another—total costs of operations. A collection of securities into a portfolio combines many different random variables—the rates of returns on the individual securities—into one random variable—the return on the portfolio. In view of these effects, it is essential for you to understand the algebraic rules for performing manipulations on random variables. Fortunately, the process is simple enough that only three rules need to be introduced. These rules define the expected values, standard deviations, and covariances of combinations of random variables.

Rules for Calculating Expected Values

The expected value of a *sum* of two or more random variables is equal to the sum of the expected values of each variable. Thus,

(2–20)   ***Expected Value of a Sum of Random Variables***
$$E(\tilde{P} + \tilde{R} + \tilde{S}) = E(\tilde{P}) + E(\tilde{R}) + E(\tilde{S})$$

For the three stocks in Table 2–1,

$$E(\tilde{P}_{GIS} + \tilde{P}_{UAL} + \tilde{P}_{XON}) = 64.4 + 52.1 + 53.9 = 170.4$$

This rule holds regardless of the shape of the probability distribution of each of the three variables. There is an equivalent rule for the *difference* between two random variables. Just use the usual rules of algebra, or

(2–21) $E(\tilde{P}_{GIS} - \tilde{P}_{UAL}) = E(\tilde{P}_{GIS}) - E(\tilde{P}_{UAL}) = 64.4 - 52.1 = 12.3$

Finally, the expected value of any constant, *c*, times a random variable is the constant times the expected value of a random variable. The appropriate expression is

(2–22)
$$E(c\tilde{P}_{GIS}) = c[E(\tilde{P}_{GIS})]$$

Thus, if you multiplied General Mills 19 prices times 10 shares and found the expected value of the new random variables $10\,\tilde{P}_{GIS}$, it would be

$$E(10\tilde{P}_{GIS}) = 10(64.4) = 644$$

Rules for Calculating Standard Deviations

The standard deviation of a sum of random variables involves a more complex calculation than that for the expected value. Consideration must be given to how the random variables comove with each other. Think of two simple bell-shaped probability distributions, both with expected values equal to zero. If the values drawn from one distribution are closely correlated with those drawn from the other, then the selection of a high value from one would tend to be associated with the selection of a high value from the other, resulting in a very high value (the sum of two high values). This tendency for comovement would give rise to a probability distribution that is quite disperse—that is, it would have a large standard deviation.

However, if the two distributions being summed were negatively correlated, then a large positive value selected from one would tend to be combined with a large negative value from the other. The summed value would be close to zero. Whatever the value drawn from one distribution, the value selected from the other would tend to offset it, leading to a set of summed values that have little dispersion and, therefore, a low standard deviation.

The expression defining this relationship is as follows:

(2–23)   *Standard Deviation of a Sum of Random Variables*

$$\sigma(\tilde{P} + \tilde{R} + \tilde{S}) = \{[\sigma(\tilde{P})]^2 + [\sigma(\tilde{R})]^2 + [\sigma(\tilde{S})]^2$$
$$+ Cov(\tilde{P}, \tilde{R}) + Cov(\tilde{R}, \tilde{S}) + Cov(\tilde{P}, \tilde{S})$$
$$+ Cov(\tilde{R}, \tilde{P}) + Cov(\tilde{S}, \tilde{R}) + Cov(\tilde{S}, \tilde{P})\}^{1/2}$$

$$\begin{matrix} \text{Standard deviation of a} \\ \text{sum of random variables} \end{matrix} = \begin{matrix} \textit{Square root of the sum of the variances} \\ \textit{(square of the standard deviation) plus the} \\ \textit{sum of all covariances between each pair} \\ \textit{of random variables.} \end{matrix}$$

$$\sigma(\tilde{P}_{GIS} + \tilde{P}_{UAL} + \tilde{P}_{XON}) = [(9.4)^2 + (5.5)^2 + (3.7)^2 + 30.3 + 30.1$$
$$+ 10.8 + 30.3 + 30.1 + 10.8]^{1/2} = 16.6$$

The covariance of $\tilde{P}_{GIS}$ with $\tilde{P}_{UAL}$ is the same as the covariance of $\tilde{P}_{UAL}$ with $\tilde{P}_{GIS}$, as you can establish by looking back to the definition of the covariance in Equation (2–11). If any covariances were negative, they would simply be introduced as negative values within the brackets. While the equation looks messy, it consists of only two types of terms, variances and covariances, terms with which you are already familiar.

The standard deviation of a difference between two random variables is given by

(2–24)

$$\sigma(\tilde{P} - \tilde{R}) = [[\sigma(\tilde{P})]^2 + [\sigma(\tilde{R})]^2 - 2Cov(\tilde{P}, \tilde{R})]^{1/2}$$

$$\alpha(\tilde{P}_{GIS} - \tilde{P}_{UAL}) = [(9.4)^2 + (5.5)^2 - 2(30.3)]^{1/2} = 7.1$$

Note the sign change. That is, the variances are still added, but the covariance is *subtracted*. If you *subtract* one random variable from another, and those variables are *positively* related, then the effect is to reduce the level of dispersion and the resulting standard deviation.[7]

Finally, the standard deviation of a constant times a random variable is equal to the constant times the standard deviation of the random variable, or

(2–25)
$$\sigma(c\tilde{P}) = c\sigma(\tilde{P})$$

For General Mills the multiplication of each of the 19 prices by 10 shares would lead to a standard deviation for that new random variable, $c\tilde{P}$, equal to 10 times 9.4, or 94.

Rules for Calculating Covariances

Like expected values, covariances are additive. Thus, the covariance of one random variable with the sum of two others is equal to the sum of the separate covariances. Simply:

(2–26)

$$Cov(\tilde{P}, \tilde{R} + \tilde{S}) = Cov(\tilde{P}, \tilde{R}) + Cov(\tilde{P}, \tilde{S})$$

To ensure that the importance of this to financial relationships doesn't escape you, consider the case of a firm currently selling flat-rolled steel sheets, S, and railroad rails, R, that is considering adding steel pipe, P, to its product line. One factor important to its decision is how the new product's demand (the random variable $\tilde{P}$) is likely to affect the use of its current plant. If there is some independence of demand for pipe, $\tilde{P}$, with the demand for its existing product line, $\tilde{R} + \tilde{S}$, then better utilization of plant and equipment may be the end result. On the other hand, if the comovement is high, then when the output of steel sheets and rails is high, the demand for pipe is also high, and plant capacity may be unable to satisfy the demand. In this case, there may be little to gain by adding P to its product line. Quite clearly, the decision may hinge, in part, on the covariance in demand between $\tilde{P}$ on the one hand and $\tilde{R} + \tilde{S}$ on the other.

Similarly, if you held Allegis and Exxon in your portfolio and wished to know how *your portfolio* comoves with General Mills, simply calculate

$$Cov[\tilde{P}_{GIS}, (\tilde{P}_{UAL} + \tilde{P}_{XON})] = 30.3 + 30.1 = 60.4$$

---

[7]Suppose total firm revenues and total costs had equal standard deviations and a perfect positive comovement. In that case profits would have no deviation. There would be no uncertainty to profits. This relationship can be constructed with "cost-plus" arrangements which characterize some contracts.

Finally, the covariance of a constant times a random variable with another random variable is equal to the constant times the covariance between the random variables, or

(2–27) $$Cov(c\tilde{P}, \tilde{R}) = cCov(\tilde{P}, \tilde{R})$$

If c is 10, then for General Mills and Exxon,

$$Cov(10\tilde{P}_{GIS}, \tilde{P}_{XON}) = 10(30.1) = 301$$

Summary

We have suggested in this chapter that the world in which real financial decisions are made is, for all practical purposes, one of uncertainty. We cannot know beforehand the outcomes of the decisions we make.

To measure the degree of uncertainty inherent in a situation, probabilities are assigned to each of the possible events or outcomes that can occur. The probabilities assess the degree of likelihood assigned to the corresponding events. These outcomes may be thought of as values of a *random variable*.

The set of probabilities that correspond to the possible outcomes of a random variable are referred to collectively as a *probability distribution*. Frequently, it is useful to summarize the shape of such distributions as a means of summarizing certain characteristics of random variables. The three measures used extensively in finance and investments are the mean or expected value, the standard deviation, and the covariance of one random variable with another.

The introduction of uncertainty into the savings–investment decision requires a marked increase in the complexity of the trade-offs involved in making decisions. To handle this problem finance introduces the concept of utility to represent the well-being associated with the different outcomes from an uncertain event.

With the concept of utility, and the assumption that individuals express diminishing marginal utility for wealth, it is easy to show that investors dislike uncertainty and are averse to risk. Moreover, the maximization of expected utility provides the best basis for selecting from among a set of alternative uncertain investment opportunities. Finally, the expected utility of an opportunity can be used to describe the decision maker's monetary certainty equivalent of an uncertain opportunity. These results allow us to describe individual preferences for uncertain opportunities with a set of indifference curves—with each opportunity being described by its expected outcome (expected value or expected rate of return) and the standard deviation of the outcomes (standard deviation of value or standard deviation of return).

References

Alchian, A. A. [1953] "The Meaning of Utility Measurement." *American Economic Review*.

Amihud, Yakov. [1980] "General Risk Aversion and an Attitude towards Risk." *Journal of Finance* (June).

Arrow, K. J. [1971] *Essays in the Theory of Risk Bearing*. Amsterdam: North Holland Press.

Borch, Karl. [1969] "A Note on Uncertainty and Indifferences Curves," *Review of Economic Studies* (January).

Fogler, Russell, and Ganapathy, Sundaram. [1982] *Financial Econometrics*. Englewood Cliffs, N.J.: Prentice Hall.

Hadar, J., and Russell, W. R. [1969] "Rules for Ordering Uncertain Prospects." *American Economic Review* (March).

Katz, David A. [1982] *Econometric Theory and Applications*. Englewood Cliffs, N.J.: Prentice-Hall.

Luce, R. Duncan, and Raiffa, Howard. [1957] *Games and Decisions: Introduction and Critical Survey*. New York: John Wiley & Sons.

Mossin, Jan. [1973] *The Theory of Financial Markets*. Englewood Cliffs, N.J.: Prentice-Hall.

Pratt, John W. [1964] "Risk Aversion in the Large and in the Small," *Econometrica* (January/April).

Raiffa, Howard. [1968] *Decision Analysis: Introductory Lectures on Choices under Uncertainty*. Reading, Mass.: Addison-Wesley Publishing.

Sharpe, William F. [1970] *Portfolio Theory and Capital Markets*. New York: McGraw-Hill.

von Neumann, John, and Morgenstern, Oscar. [1947] *Theory of Games and Economic Behavior*. 2nd. Princeton, N.J.: Princeton University Press.

Williams, J. T. [1977] "A Note on Indifference Curves in the Mean-Variance Model." *Journal of Financial and Quantitative Analysis* (March).

Questions and Problems

1. Name three assets you own that are important to your financial well-being. Are they random variables? If so, explain why their values are uncertain. Is it reasonable to assume their dollar values are characterized by normal distributions? Why?

2. Compute the expected value of the price of one share of stock in the firm of Minnesota Mittens and Mufflers, given the following probabilities for different price levels:

Probability	Price Level
.2	$29.50
.3	$30.90
.4	$32.00
.1	$33.50

3. Calculate the standard deviation for Minnesota Mittens and Mufflers' prices as given in Problem 2.

4. What is the mean and standard deviation of the dollar payoff of a $100 bet on a football game where the team you are betting on has a 0.4 chance of winning and no chance of a tie? Graph the distribution.

5. Calculate the expected dollar payoff and the standard deviation of the dollar outcomes for the following investment that costs $10,000:

Value in One Year	Probability
$7,500	.05
$8,200	.07
$8,900	.09
$9,400	.12
$9,800	.10
$10,300	.07
$10,700	.05
$11,200	.10
$11,500	.05
$12,000	.05
$12,200	.08
$13,000	.10
$13,500	.02
$14,200	.02
$15,000	.03
	1.00

6. If you observe an individual who refuses to pay $10 for a lottery ticket in which he has an equal probability of winning or losing an additional $50, what can you conclude about his utility curve? Explain.

7. What can you say about the risk aversion of investors A, B, and C if their indifference curves are as depicted below? Why? Assume $U_3 > U_2 > U_1$.

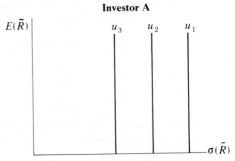

Investor A

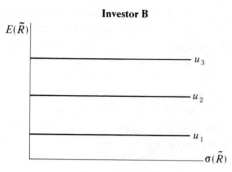

Investor B

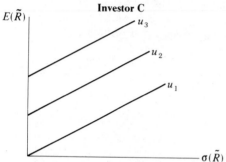

Investor C

$P_{SP,0}$	$P_{SP,1}$	$P_{SP,2}$	$P_{SP,3}$
267.8	266.5	267.0	268.3
$P_{SP,4}$	$P_{SP,5}$	$P_{SP,6}$	$P_{SP,7}$
266.6	265.4	265.7	268.1
$P_{SP,8}$	$P_{SP,9}$	$P_{SP,10}$	
270.2	272.3	274.4	

Calculate the rates of return on the Index and the covariance between these returns and those on the Eastman Kodak call option. Also calculate the correlation coefficient between the two.

12. For the rates of return on the S&P Index and the Eastman Kodak call options, plot the return coordinates for each on a graph with the rate of return on the S&P Index on the horizontal axis. Draw a visual line of best fit between these points and indicate its slope and intercept.

13. What is the expected future wealth of a portfolio of four securities with expected returns of 8 percent, 10 percent, 12 percent, and 26 percent, if the dollar amounts invested in each are $20,000, $6,000, $10,000, and $14,000, respectively?

14. If the covariance between the rates of return and two stocks is negative, is it possible for the two stocks to have a positive correlation coefficient? Explain your answer.

15. If an investment strategy has an expected annual return of 15 percent and an annual standard deviation of 15 percent, and investment returns are normally distributed, in any one year there is:

   a. About a 68 percent chance that the actual return will fall within the range of −15 percent to +15 percent.

   b. About a 68 percent chance that the actual return will fall within the range of 0 percent to +30 percent.

   c. About a 32 percent chance that the actual return will exceed 30 percent.

   d. None of the above.

   CFA

8. If it were possible to find an individual with increasing marginal utility of wealth, what would this imply about his attitude toward risk? What would the person's indifference curves in risk-return space look like?

9. Consider an investment opportunity promising a set of future cash flows. A change in one of the future cash flows: (a) will have greater impact the earlier they occur, (b) will have greater impact the later they occur, (c) is the same regardless of their timing, (d) is negligible because they are the same dollar amount.

   CFA

10. Calculate the expected return and standard deviation of returns from these daily prices for an Eastman Kodak call option. Note that you must calculate rates of return, since these are prices. Your purchase price is the first price given, $P_{EK,0}$.

$P_{EK,0}$	$P_{EK,1}$	$P_{EK,2}$	$P_{EK,3}$
2 1/8	2 1/8	2	2 1/4
$P_{EK,4}$	$P_{EK,5}$	$P_{EK,6}$	$P_{EK,7}$
2 3/8	2 1/8	2 1/2	2 3/8
$P_{EK,8}$	$P_{EK,9}$	$P_{EK,10}$	
2 5/8	2 3/4	2 7/8	

11. During the same period as in Problem 10, the Standard & Poor's Index of 500 common stocks were priced as follows:

16. What is the expected return for stocks, bonds, and T-bills in the following situation?

Economic Scenario	Probability	Scenario Returns		
		Stocks	Bonds	T-bills
A	.5	+18%	+14%	+11%
B	.3	−15%	+35%	+7%
C	.2	+10%	−8%	+12%

CFA

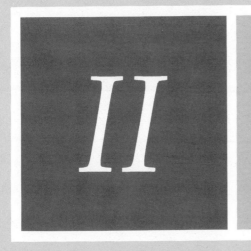

P A R T

II

MARKET STRUCTURE

CHAPTER

3

Investment Opportunities

The Purpose of Investing

In the first two chapters we discuss a world in which consumers often find it in their best interests to use financial or productive investment opportunities to improve their well-being. The improvement is achieved through investments that allocate wealth over time to a desired pattern of consumption or to desired risks and returns to supplement future consumption. We now begin a discussion that will take you through an in-depth look at the nature of the investment opportunities that are actually available for these purposes.

An investment is anything which is expected to change the consumer's risk position or time pattern of consumption in future periods. An individual may purchase a bond for $1,000 today in hopes of having $1,100 available for consumption a year from now. The purchase constitutes an investment since it reduces current consumption by $1,000 and increases expected future consumption by $1,100. The purchase of an automobile (at least a model expected to last over more than one period) has its investment characteristics as well. For example, if the car's value at the end of one year is expected to be $6,500, you can think of this portion of the $8,000 purchase as being an "investment." In effect, investing $6,500 now enables the consumer–investor to consume at a higher rate in those future periods. Thus, the purchase has all the characteristics of an investment. Indeed, in comparing alternative investments the individual should consider other uses for the $6,500 "invested" in the car.

Business Firms and the Investment Opportunities They Create

Firms and governments exist because they aid in the production of goods and services that are desired by individuals. Some of these business firms are very small: consisting, perhaps, of one individual with skill and a few assets sufficient to make a decent standard of living. Others are very large, populated by thousands of employees and managers whose connections with the firms owners are tenuous at best. The form and size of organization that survives the rigors of the marketplace is the one that delivers the goods and services demanded at the lowest cost.

In the world economy, of course, both types of firms exist. Apparently, in some economic activities small firms produce more efficiently than large firms do. In other activities the opposite is the case. In fact, in the United States between 30 and 40 percent of all private productive activity is performed by firms with less than 100 employees.

To produce, these firms need to acquire financial capital to obtain capital equipment and to meet the financial commitments made to other factors of production (employees, suppliers, credit to customers). It is in the process of acquiring financial capital that these firms create the various investment opportunities that are available to you. This chapter concentrates on these opportunities and the factors central to their creation.

The Firm and Its Contracts

Any firm, large or small, can be thought of simply as a set of contracts. Some of these are explicit contracts such as those with union labor, and some are implicit contracts that exist as a result of the laws or mores of society. Thus, there are contracts that exist between the firm and its customers, its suppliers, its employees, the government, its managers, and, of course, those who invest financial capital in the firm. For example, employee contracts cover the terms of employment, pension benefits, and implied occupational safety. Management contracts cover the terms of employment, stock option and pension plans, and an implied contract that effectively bars management from making deceptive statements about the operations of the firm. These contracts are enforced by law and legal remedies as well as by penalties that are built into the contracts or are enforced upon violation of their terms, e.g., managers can be fired in ways that affect their future employment value.

Figure 3–1 identifies the basic contractual structure of the firm. In total, these contracts define the "rules of the game," or system for dividing up the wealth of the firm.

The most commonly employed **financial contracts** include common stock and debt contracts. The common stock contract is evidence of ownership of equity in the firm. The holder of this contract has a residual claim on the value of the firm. That is, in theory at least, the common stockholder is entitled to the residual value of the enterprise after all other contractual obligations have been satisfied. An individual owner's share of the residual value is proportional to the number of ownership units held. According to the contract, all shareholders of the same type of equity claim have the same rights.

Debt contracts are evidence of a creditor claim on the firm. Each debt contract specifies the financial obligation of the firm, and may include specific provisions for the firm to

FIGURE 3–1   The Firm as a Set of Contracts

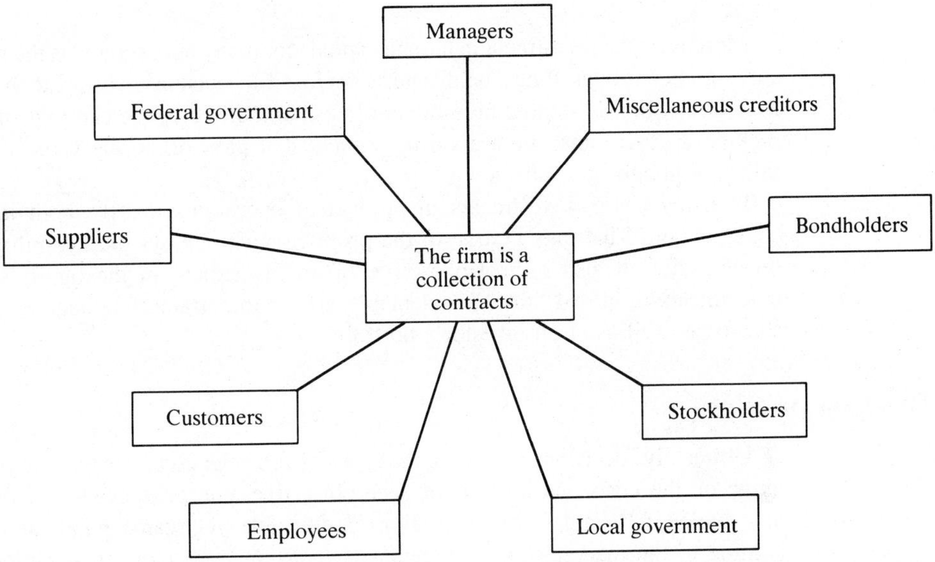

```
                        Managers

   Federal government                    Miscellaneous creditors

                                                    Bondholders
   Suppliers              The firm is a
                          collection of
                          contracts

   Customers                                        Stockholders


             Employees              Local government
```

follow. As the provisions vary so does the nature of the debt contract. Consequently, firms ordinarily have outstanding at any one time a number of different debt contracts that are used to finance their operations.

While it is the financial contracts of the sort illustrated by stocks and bonds that provide opportunities to investors, it is important to realize that the value of these contracts depends heavily on the nature of the contracts the firm has with others. The value of a "loan" to a firm depends on the value of the labor contract. The value of an equity investment depends on the ability of the management contract to provide the incentive for managers to act in the best interests of the owners.

As a gross generalization of the real complexity of our world, we will differentiate between firms on the basis of whether they are **"open" to financial investment** from outside, or **"closed" to outside investment.** Open firms are most often corporations that have issued a set of financial contracts that can be purchased by a wide variety of outside investors. Typically, these contracts include publicly traded bonds and common stock. Typically, also, there is a distinct line of separation between manager and investor. The contract details this separation and specifies the rights and obligations of each party to the contract.

Closed firms are proprietorships, partnerships, or corporations that have financial contracts that generally are not held by outside investors. Often the distinction between manager and investor is blurred. There is little separation of the decision-making function from the risk-bearing function. In many cases the financial contract is simply an understanding that the profit of the firm (after the firm has met all of its other obligations) accrues to the owner. Examples of arrangements where these financial contracts dominate include virtually any small business, a McDonald's franchise, a tractor-trailer rig, a farm in Idaho, or a writer's pro rata share of the proceeds from a widely selling finance textbook.

Moreover, the investment in human capital, for many households, is the most important and significant opportunity held, and it is closed to outside investment. Nevertheless, it is clear that the substantial investment of cash and the foregone earnings of an individual seeking an MBA may be a good *investment* if it pays off in the form of higher future salary or greater job satisfaction.

In many cases, investments in productive operations involve both investment and consumption. That may be true of the proprietor who enjoys the flexibility of "working for himself." It also ordinarily is true of an investment in the family's house. Such investments in closed "firms" undeniably are an important component of the wealth of society as well as of an investor's portfolio.

To Open or Close

Ultimately, decisions regarding the types of financial contracts that are issued by firms hinge on the costs and benefits of each. In a free enterprise economy, the function of any market is to aid in the allocation of desirable yet scarce goods and services. By coming to the market with their demands, consumers disclose their preferences. Firms use the information contained in market prices to organize production. The markets themselves provide a mechanism for the distribution of the goods and services produced.

The process is the same whether the markets are for goods or services or for investment opportunities. Potential investors register their preferences in the form of demands for different varieties of investment opportunities. Open firms, reading those demands, produce the opportunities that investors are willing to hold. Those willing to pay the highest price (accept the lowest return) will be able to purchase the opportunities as they desire. As a result of this process the firms are able to acquire capital in financial markets for use in the production process, and can do so at the lowest possible cost.

The operation of the market for investment opportunities provides some obvious benefits to consumer–investors as well. The availability of such opportunities may help the investor allocate wealth over time in a manner that brings the greatest satisfaction from consumption of that wealth. That is, as described in Chapter 1, the financial market is a mechanism for transferring wealth between time periods in a way that will enhance the individual's total level of happiness or utility.

Moreover, the availability of different risk opportunities (perhaps with higher risk being associated with higher return) permits the investor to achieve a package of risk and return that is consistent with his preferences. In some cases, investors can reduce or even eliminate some risks by shifting the risk to those who are more willing to accept it. While it may cost something to do this, the opportunities for adjusting one's risk exposure allows investors to achieve more highly desired positions. This was the crux of Chapter 2.

The process whereby open firms register their financial capital needs on financial markets, and potential investors view those alternatives with an eye toward their effects on utility, is summarized in Figure 3–2. As suggested by the diagram, the two groups get together in financial markets and exchange money for securities. If everything works

---

FIGURE 3–2   Financial Markets and the Objectives of Firms and Investors

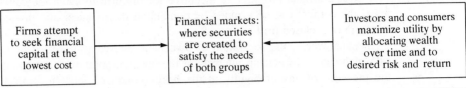

---

correctly, both groups are able to satisfy their objectives. Much of what we will talk about in this chapter and the rest of the book is concerned with how competition within and between these groups results in the creation of particular securities with particular risk and return attributes.

The decisions of firms to "open" themselves and issue securities present three immediate questions of interest to us:

- What causes some firms to become open corporations that issue financial contracts offering investment opportunities to a broad spectrum of investors, while others choose the closed corporate form?
- What kinds of financial contracts tend to be issued by open corporations to finance their operations?
- How do such contracts contribute to the wealth and well-being of society?

The Costs and Benefits of Financial Contracts

To answer the above questions we must analyze the costs and benefits associated with different financial contracts. For some firms, creating financial contracts in the form of securities for sale to outside investors (and, thereby, to become an open corporation) will be the easiest and least expensive method for acquiring needed financing. The costs and benefits of such a strategy require assessment of six factors:

1. The clarity or precision with which the security contract can be written.
2. The cost of monitoring for compliance with the terms of the contract.
3. The divisibility of the contract units.
4. The marketability or liquidity of the contract units.
5. The maturity characteristics of the contract.
6. The risk characteristics of the contract.

We hope a brief discussion of these factors will help you understand why some firms become open corporations and why they tend to issue certain types of financial contracts.

Contract Clarity

Decisions in the open corporation are in the hands of managers whose interests are not identical to those of the firm's investors. If it is difficult or costly for the firm to write a clear set of contracts with investors and managers that specifies the rights and obligations of each party, the value of the contract to investors will be less. This increases the firm's cost of capital, and provides an incentive for the firm to avoid the conflict. In part, at least, the conflict can be avoided by combining the manager and investor functions in the form of a closed firm.

In other words, the separation of ownership and control created by the widespread sale of financial ownership interests in the open corporation (e.g., common stock), in the presence of any ambiguity in the firm's contracts, leads to problems. The most important of these problems are related to the agency relationship that investors have with managers. The key question, central in understanding corporate behavior, is whether managers have been or can be imbued with a set of incentives that cause them to act in ways consistent with the best interests of common stockholders, bondholders, or others who hold the firm's financial contracts. In fact, the problems created out of the separation of manager and investor functions are called **agency costs.** The greater are the agency costs of open incorporation, the less it is likely that a given firm will choose to issue financial contracts for outside investors.

An example may help to emphasize the importance of this point. Investors traditionally have assumed at least two things about the common stock contract issued by open corporations. One is that they will share pro rata in the residual value of the firm. A second is that if the firm's obligations to other contractors exceeds the firm's value, the firm is bankrupt and, as residual claim holders, the value of the investors' position is zero. Neither of these is always true. In the 1980s there have been more than 30 cases of managers of large publicly traded firms using the firm's money to buy out the common stock positions of a *selected group* of stockholders at a price that exceeded the market price at the time of the transaction. Such **greenmail,** as it is termed, ensures that the remaining stockholders' position is diluted. Simply, they have not received their pro rata share of the distribution. Ordinarily, courts have allowed this type of activity to proceed because the common stock contract implicitly allows managers to make "business judgments" regarding what is beneficial for shareholders. Unfortunately, this creates ambiguity in the contract, and greater costs to open corporations.

Ambiguity is also present in interpreting the claims in bankruptcies. It is not uncommon to observe firms exiting from bankruptcy with bondholders and other contractors receiving less than what the firm was obligated to pay, at the same time that stockholders are receiving more than zero. The obvious conclusion is that even straightforward common stock and bond contracts are ambiguous to a degree. The more ambiguity, the more costly these contracts are to issue.[1]

---

[1]Some financial contracts are inherently ambiguous. As an example consider the fate of income bonds. These bonds were issued originally in the 1930s and 40s as a straight bond that participated in a share of the firm's net income from operations. Unfortunately (for income bond owners) there was sufficient leeway in the definition of *income* to allow management to drive the income component of the bond's return to near zero. Stockholders, of course, had the incentive to persuade management to do this, effectively shifting wealth from the income bondholders to themselves. In other words, the contract establishing the rights of the bondholders and the obligations of other parties was not sufficiently well defined to protect the bondholders' financial position. Because of the "increasing cost" the security soon disappeared from the marketplace.

Costs of Monitoring

Even if a clear and unambiguous set of contracts can be written by the firm, there are obvious problems of ensuring compliance with the terms of the contract. Courts are awash with a variety of securities cases where firms have told investors they would do one thing, and then did another. For this reason investors monitor the firm's activities (through audits or analysts' reports for example). Firms participate in this process (by publishing important information, such as financial results) by attempting to persuade investors of their intention to comply with the contract in order to reduce the cost of capital. The cost of monitoring is larger the greater the separation of managers from investors. If the costs become too high, firms will find it in their best interests to remain closed to outside investment.

Both bond and stock contracts specify to some extent the monitoring procedures that are required of the firm and its managers. In addition, as a method of cultivating investor goodwill, open corporations will signal their successes and failures to the financial markets. Doing so assures investors that there are not enormous differences between their expectations for the corporation and the facts. In effect, competitive pressures in the financial markets cause most firms' managers to release information publicly. If they don't, the investors, being less able to monitor the firms activities, will be less willing to purchase firms' securities. It follows that if some firms decide it is very costly to release such information, they will remain closed corporations with no public ownership.

For similar reasons you usually do not find publicly issued financial contracts prevalent in firms that rely extensively on entrepreneurial talent or the dedication of their work force. These important assets are hard to monitor and can be easily absconded with, to the detriment of the outside security holder. Thus, while there are a number of very large and very profitable law firms, accounting firms, and advertising firms, they only infrequently "go public."

Offsetting the obvious disadvantages for open corporations stemming from the difficulty of writing clear contracts and monitoring them, the next four points lean in the direction of *favoring* issuance of financial contracts to outside investors.

Divisibility

At little cost, financial contracts issued to outside investors can be made almost perfectly divisible. An individual unit of a common stock or a bond can be made arbitrarily small. As long as there is a provision in the contract that all holders of the contract share pro rata in the returns from an investment there is no loss from the divisibility.

Divisibility of the contract into a large number of contract units overcomes the enormous problem that firms and investors would have in assembling sufficient capital to build an efficient-sized steel mill, for example. Basically, a high level of divisibility allows the firm to acquire large indivisible factors of production by issuing securities to a large number of investors, each of whom contributes only a small portion of the cost. In this way, a great many more individuals can afford to invest in business firms than would otherwise be the case.

Moreover, with divisibility, investor diversification is possible. With common stock split into small units, individuals can hold ownership claims to several kinds of productive activities simultaneously. The uncertainties associated with the income offered by any one security thus hold less influence than they would if each security were held by itself. This, in turn, makes people who are risk-averse generally more willing to invest in securities. Hence, capital formation is aided in this way, too.

Financial contracts issued by open corporations are not perfectly divisible, however. You can't invest $100 in IBM or any corporate bond. Moreover, some certificates of deposit cannot be purchased in units of less than $100,000. Mortgage-backed bonds issued by the Government National Mortgage Corporation (Ginnie Mae) have a minimum denomination of $25,000. If you wish to invest in the U.S. government and have at least $10,000, you can buy U.S. Treasury bills, but if you have only $500, you're limited to series HH bonds.

Nevertheless, as you will see in the coming chapters, the trend in most financial markets has been toward increasing divisibility. For example, you can buy a mutual fund that invests in Ginnie Mae securities with a minimum investment of $500. More recently, brokerage houses have begun buying large-denomination certificates of deposit (originally issued by banks or savings institutions) and splitting them into smaller units for resale to their customers.

Marketability

If a financial contract can be sold to others outside the firm the investor can reacquire cash in the amount of the current value of the contract. This ability to liquidate an investment gives the individual the flexibility to adjust consumption or risk to the desired level. Thus, as circumstances change and it becomes necessary for an investor to reduce risk or reduce the amount of wealth devoted to investment opportunities, marketability offers something of value. The ability to liquidate an investment in a closed corporation is limited, typically, to the investor's ability to find another individual that has the money, inclination, and support of the other owners of the firm. An investment in an open corporation can be liquidated as long as the financial contract contains terms that appeal broadly to many investors. Because of its key role in understanding the operation of financial markets that specialize in the exchange of securities between investors, the marketability of an investment will be defined in detail later in the chapter.

Maturity or Longevity of the Contract

In *closed* firms, where there is little exchange of financial contracts between investors, the required commitment by investors extends to the maturity of the firm or the equipment the firm purchases. Each investor has to search for opportunities whose life corresponds fairly closely to his needs. Someone attempting to shift wealth two or three years into the future would find it difficult to justify an investment in a McDonald's franchise or other small business. There is not a close match between the timing of the returns on such an investment and the cash flow needs of the investor.

Financial contracts of *open* corporations overcome this problem. First, regardless of the expected pattern of cash flows or the "maturity" of the firm, financial contracts can be developed to divide up this term to correspond to the demands of investors. A production process that is expected to last 20 years can be financed with a series of debt contracts of shorter term if the cost comparison favors that strategy. Or the firm might plan to use debt to finance a major portion of the cost of the equipment and pay that debt off well before the end of the equipment's life. In this case, the equity holders would have a smaller investment in the early years of operation that is increased as equity is substituted for debt later on. In sum, indirect investment through securities provides the flexibility in setting contract terms to correspond to investors' desires to allocate wealth over time in an optimal manner.

Second, the term specified in a security contract can be shortened if a secondary market exists for trading in the security. Specifically, a bond with a 20-year term to maturity can be turned into one with a much shorter maturity at the discretion of the investor simply by selling the bond. This flexibility allows the investor to adjust the distribution of his wealth over time as the situation warrants, and is a key item in understanding the advantages and widespread issuance of publicly held financial contracts by open corporations.

Risk of the Contract

Finally, open and closed firms differ in their ability to allocate the risk inherent in a firm or its capital equipment. As the *open* corporation issues various financial contracts or securities it allocates the risk of the firm to the holders of those contracts (and away from manager/owners). That is, securities created by open firms provide a means for convenient allocation of the risk to investors that are willing to accept it—at least at the right price. In particular, the firm's issuance of secured debt, debt subordinated to other debt issues, preferred stock, and common stock causes the risk (as well as the returns, of course) to be divided up among these security holders according to the terms of the contract the firm has with each holder. Thus, secured debtholders who invest $1,000 in a firm face only a small fraction of the risk that is accepted by those investors who purchase $1,000 of the common stock. Investors who are very averse to risk will hold the bonds, while those less averse to risk will invest in the stock.

Financial contract terms can be developed to allocate the risk and expected return in any manner desired by investors. The result is that investors are willing to pay more for the securities than they would if risk could not easily be allocated among different buyers. Basically, open corporations are able to appeal to the *different* risk-averting proclivities of investors, just as auto manufacturers are able to produce different types of cars to appeal to the different preferences of consumers.

Summary of Costs and Benefits of Open Incorporation

Where needs will lead is not always clear. While it is easy to gain the impression that open corporations like IBM and General Motors dominate our modern industrial economy, it is generally not the case. Small businesses exercise control over nearly *half* of the productive capital in the United States. Moreover, there are well over 100 firms that are privately held that have sales of over $1 billion.

Nevertheless, it is clear that a large number of corporations issue financial contracts to the public. In these cases the costs and benefits that accrue from the six factors listed above result in the firm being able to acquire financial capital conveniently at the lowest possible cost. For the costs to be low the contracts must confer substantial benefits to outside investors. That is, the securities that are issued must offer investors a convenient means for allocating wealth in accordance with their preferences.

The process can be summarized as follows:

> Firms, governments, and individuals attempt to issue securities to acquire financial capital that can be used for the acquisition of real capital, labor, and management talent. Individual consumer investors need to be persuaded to purchase these securities. To the extent that individuals view financial contracts as offering the substantial benefits referred to above, they will be persuaded to purchase the securities offered at a higher price than if those benefits were not present. In turn, the higher the price of the security the more the firms, governments, and individuals will have to invest in productive assets. Those that enjoy more profitable real investment alternatives will be able to acquire more financial capital, and there will be a tendency for savings to flow to its best productive use. Capital investment will be encouraged where demand for securities is greater, and the output of the economy will be greater.

The success of this process is evident in today's financial marketplace. There are an incredible number of securities with different contract terms issued and outstanding in the world. We will first briefly summarize the major types of contracts that exist, and in the remainder of the chapter suggest why there is such a great demand for these securities.

Types of Security Contracts

Common Stock

The nature of the common stock contract is defined in the corporate charter filed in the state of incorporation according to state laws. An example of the certificate evidencing the stock contract of Dow Jones & Company is presented in Figure 3–3. Normally, we tend to think of the stock simply as: (1) giving the owner the right to receive his share of the residual value of the firm after all other obligations have been satisfied, (2) having the right to the pro rata share of the earnings of the firm paid out in the form of dividends, and (3) having the right to sell it to another investor. However, there is more to it than this. For example, the contract ordinarily specifies the types of corporate decisions for which votes of shareholders are required. Often, but not always, this means shareholders elect the board of directors and are called upon to vote for or against major changes in the capitalization of the firm (such as in a merger, in the decision to change the state of incorporation, or in the decision to change the charter itself).

FIGURE 3–3   Stock Certificate

In fact, it is a misnomer to think of common stock contracts as uniform and without variation from one firm to another. The list that follows indicates some important differences between common stock contracts. Common stock may:

- Be voting or nonvoting.
- Be issued with or without permission of existing shareholders.
- Be repurchased or not repurchased from selective shareholders.
- Permit or not permit shareholders to accumulate their shares for purposes of voting.
- Restrict or not restrict the proportion of the stock that can be held by one investor.

Many of these differences have been shown to affect the value of the security. In sum, it is important for investors to understand that there are substantitive differences among these contracts, and knowledge of the specific contract terms is useful to understanding the investment value of the security. These issues are raised in more detail when stock contracts are valued in Chapters 14, 15, 16, and 17.

Bonds and Fixed Income Securities

These contracts ordinarily specify the financial obligations the issuer has to the "creditor" that holds the contract. Most require the issuer to pay interest and principal in specified amounts at specified future dates.[2] There is a great deal of variation in how these obligations are to be satisfied. For example, the normal corporate bond contract requires interest only payments on a regular basis, with principal repayments taking place infrequently and possibly only at the maturity of the contract. Standard mortgages, on the other hand, require periodic interest and principal payments throughout the life of the contract.

In recent years there has been an increase in the variety of such contracts issued publicly. Corporations now issue such securities as: term loans, lines of credit, commercial paper, debentures, subordinated debentures, collateral trust certificates, variable rate bonds, zero coupon bonds, puttable bonds, convertible bonds, and preferred stock, to name but a few. Moreover, unlike common stock, other productive agents in our economy issue fixed-income contracts. State and local governments issue financial contracts in the form of revenue bonds and general obligation bonds. The U.S. government and foreign national governments issue bonds, bills, Eurobonds, Eurobills, and a variety of federal agency securities. Individuals, of course, also issue fixed-income securities in the form of mortgages, consumer loans, and home equity loans. There are, perhaps, hundreds of thousands of *different* fixed-income securities outstanding. Many of them have common contract terms, but hundreds of substantive differences exist between these contracts. Chapters 12 and 13 discuss some of the major contract types, and how they should be valued.

Debt/Equity Combinations

Financial contracts also may be combinations of debt and equity securities. Warrants may be attached to each bond as part of a bond issue of a corporation. These warrants are financial instruments entitling the bondholder to purchase a specified number of shares of common stock of the firm at a specified price. The bondholder may hold this option to purchase for a specific period of time. The warrant may have some value and, thus, it constitutes an investment if there is some possibility of the common stock price exceeding the price specified in the warrant. You can think of the warrant as an investment alternative whose value is *contingent* on the price of the common stock. The payoff, being conditional on the price of the common stock exceeding the purchase price contained in the warrant, is different than the payoff pattern of either the bonds or the common stock of the firm. It is a financial asset nonetheless. Covertible and callable bonds are also contingent contracts that are combined debt and equity securities issued by firms.

Some partnership agreements can be traded publicly, and many of them have contract terms that define and limit the risk taking of some partners. In these cases there is no neat separation of the equity and debt components of the financing arrangement. For example, in many real estate partnerships there is a single "general" partner and a number

---

[2]Common stocks and most bonds are not "bearer" instruments. They are registered and cannot be sold by anyone but the registered owner. Thus, possession of the certificate is not evidence of ownership. Most firms issuing securities hire a trustee agent to keep track of ownership as trading takes place.

of "limited" partners. Not infrequently, the limited partners are promised specific financial rewards (e.g., tax shelters, or a floor on the price at which the limited partner can sell his unit to the general partner) that have some of the aspects of a debt contract. In any case, the risk-sharing attributes of these contracts are different from those for standard stocks and bonds. Limited partnership arrangements have been widely used in real estate and in the production of commodities such as cattle and oil.

Third-Party Financial Contracts

Bonds, common stock, warrants, and partnerships are contracts between the issuer of the security (the corporation, for example) and the purchaser. The contract specifies the rights and obligations of both parties, and the success or failure of the purchaser's investment depends upon the performance of the issuer. If the corporate issuer generates value at a rate greater than that expected, the return to the purchaser will be high. If not, the return will be low.

Contracts between two parties, the payoffs of which are conditional on the performance of a *third party,* also constitute investments. These are third-party financial contracts, and have been the most rapidly growing segment of the financial marketplace over the last 20 years.[3]

Options. Suppose you and I enter into a contract specifying that you have an option to purchase from me 100 shares of common stock of General Mills Corporation for a price and period specified in the contract. Our contract is, in fact, a financial asset. The contract clearly has the potential for changing your current consumption by the costs of the contract, and can change mine in some future period by the gain (or loss) from your exercising the right specified in the contract. The fact that you or I have nothing to do with the operation of General Mills Corporation in no way invalidates the contract or its investment characteristics. Such contractual arrangements are called **call options,** and their recent growth as an investment alternative has been nothing short of phenomenal. Options as investment alternatives offer a wide variety of financial arrangements, and to some extent can be tailored to the needs of the individual. There are options to either buy or sell shares of common stock, or options to do both. There are also options on real capital investments such as on land or in lease-purchase arrangements. Figure 3–4 depicts a call option contract. These contracts are discussed in detail in Chapter 19.

Futures Contracts. Futures contracts are a second type of third-party arrangement. They are similar to options in the sense that the contract involves two parties and the payoffs usually depend on the price of a third item such as a commodity, a metal, another financial instrument, or another currency. A futures contract in wheat, for example, may specify that 12 months from the date of the contract, you promise to deliver to me 1,000 bushels of No. 1 Kansas City Winter Wheat. In return, I promise to pay you $3.25 per bushel.

Clearly, since the future wealth of both of us is dependent on the price of wheat in a

---

[3]See Miller [1986] for an explanation of why the growth rate of third-party contracts has been so large.

FIGURE 3–4 Call Option

> This contract must be presented to the cashier of the firm it is endorsed by, before the expiration of the exact time limit. IT WILL NOT BE ACCEPTED AFTER IT HAS EXPIRED AND CANNOT BE EXERCISED BY TELEPHONE.
>
> New York, _____ 19____
>
> **For Value Received,** the bearer may CALL on the endorser upon presentation hereof for
>
> _____ ONE HUNDRED _____ (100) shares of the _____ stock of the
>
> _____ at _____
>
> ($_____) dollars per share at anytime within _____ from this date.
> DURING THE LIFE OF THIS OPTION, THE CONTRACT PRICE HEREOF SHALL BE REDUCED BY THE VALUE OF ANY PAID DIVIDENDS AFTER THE STOCK GOES EX-DIVIDEND. IN THE EVENT OF STOCK SPLITS OR STOCK DIVIDENDS, THIS OPTION BECOMES AN OPTION FOR THE EQUIVALENT IN NEW SECURITIES AND THE CONTRACT PRICE WILL NOT BE REDUCED.
>
> Expires_____ 19___ at _____ AM
>   PM
>
> THE UNDERSIGNED ACTS AS INTERMEDIARY ONLY, WITHOUT OBLIGATION TO THE HOLDER HEREOF, WHO ACCEPTS THIS OPTION UPON SUCH UNDERSTANDING.
>
> DELIVERY & SETTLEMENT ACCORDING TO CUSTOMS OF
> THE NEW YORK STOCK EXCHANGE
>
> **CALL OPTION**

year, the contract is a financial asset. Also, the nature of the contract makes this an investment alternative that differs from an investment in a bond or stock in the sense that there is no limit to your liability, although you could seek to modify your risk position by making arrangements to deliver the promised item (by growing wheat, for example). Moreover, there is no current exchange of money and, thus, no principal invested. As the seller, you will be better off if the price goes down, whereas, as the buyer, I will be better off if the price goes up. Characteristically, the individuals who are party to the contract have no way of influencing the price of the commodity that will ultimately determine the value of the contract, although, of course they may produce or use the commodity itself. Chapter 18 discusses futures contracts in detail.

Financial Investment and the Wealth of Society

For the economy as a whole, financial securities cancel out. That means that for every borrower there is a lender, and for every stockholder there is an equity issuer. If you put your money in a savings account, you have in effect purchased a financial security having a market value equal to the amount of your deposit. The bank from which you "purchased" it records the account as a liability. A liability, however, is just a financial security of which one holds a "negative" amount (a net borrower). The positive amount of the security which you hold and record as an asset is just equal to the negative amount the bank holds and records as a liability. Hence, the net amount outstanding is always zero. In our two-period certainty world of Chapter 1, the sum of borrowing equaled the sum of savings in equilibrium.

In contrast, the net investment in "real" productive assets (such as plant and equipment) is positive. We can distinguish, therefore, between those transactions which **increase an**

economy's productive capacity and those which merely **redistribute claims to that capacity** among individuals. Real investment increases the potential supply of goods and services in the economy by creating a capital asset and, therefore, contributes to aggregate wealth. The purchase of financial securities by itself does not increase aggregate wealth; it only serves to redistribute the ownership of capital assets among individuals. It is easy to see this: If I deposit money in a savings account or buy a bond, I am not directly causing any increase in production through my purchase of this financial security. But if I "create" a capital asset (such as by investing in my human resources), I am adding to the existing stock of productive assets in the economy.

This obvious distinction between financial and real assets has been a point of contention for some elements of society who conclude that financial markets, having no direct effects on capital assets, serve few purposes. Some groups, in fact, have argued that severe restrictions should be placed on the types of transactions that can be conducted in financial markets because they appear to provide nothing more than an outlet for people's risk-taking propensities.[4] That this argument is false should be now be self-evident. An analysis of the costs and benefits of issuing securities suggests a strong relationship between the existence of securities and the wealth and well-being of society. Financial contracts offer indispensible benefits to real capital formation by encouraging savings and reducing the cost of financing expenditures on real productive resources.

The Operating Efficiency of Markets for the Exchange of Securities

Our discussion to this point has indicated that investors and issuers of securities get together to decide on terms that are appropriate to the objectives of both. Only brief mention has been made of the importance of the contract allowing the investor to sell the security to another. In fact, the marketability of the contract is an indispensable part of the investor's demand for it. Consequently, we will now define the marketability of an investment opportunity. In Chapter 4 we discuss the means and methods used by the New York Stock Exchange, the National Association of Securities Dealers, and others to facilitate the marketability of securities.

Marketability

A security is marketable if it offers the following traits:

1. **Liquidity**—including that: (*a*) there are continuously existing offers to buy (bid price) or sell (ask price) the security; (*b*) the difference between the bid and ask

---

[4]This argument has ancient roots, even predating currencies, to the use of goats, silver, and wheat as mediums of exchange. Church doctrine in the first 1,200 years A.D. generally held interest of any sort as an immoral payment. Pope Leo the Great considered the taking of interest to be "shameful gain" (Homer [1977], p. 70). In the 13th century, St. Thomas Aquinas held that money was inherently sterile, and concluded that the "breeding of money from money is unnatural and justly hated" (Homer, p. 71).

Even today certain societies formally prohibit charging interest. Islamic banks do not charge "interest," but rather lend money and charge a "fee" to be paid back over time (which one might have trouble differentiating from interest).

price is small and there are few other costs to transacting; (*c*) a significantly large number of units of the security can be traded at the same price per unit as can a small number of units of the security.

2. **Price Continuity**—implying that the market price is set by the interaction of underlying supply and demand, rather than temporary supply and demand imbalances.

3. **Fairness**—implying that the price at which an investor is willing to trade and the timing of his entry onto the market alone govern whether a trade will take place.

If the price of an opportunity changes depending on the number of units being bought or sold, then the security is traded in a "thin" market and liquidity is not high. Moreover, if the market is not in continuous operation, or is not made up of traders who continuously offer bid or ask prices, then liquidity is not high.[5] Markets for residential homes, commercial property, quality art, and antiques generally offer less than complete liquidity (try getting rid of 1.5 million square feet of prime office space in Houston, or 100 antique oak straightback chairs).

Moreover, the market for some opportunities may be so spotty that investors have to spend a good deal of time, effort, and money to find a buyer for their investment. That would certainly characterize the market for a small business in Luling, Texas, for example.

On the other hand, the market for U.S. Treasury securities and most New York Stock Exchange common stocks is quite liquid. Virtually any trader in these markets (even the Federal Reserve itself) is an "atomistic" competitor, who has no monopolistic or oligopolistic power. There is no problem in selling $50 million of Treasury securities on an instant's notice, and, since the market is worldwide, it could be accomplished at any hour of the day. There is little problem in getting rid of $50 million of IBM's stock (at least while the exchanges that trade the security are open).[6] Other stocks and bonds generally have reasonably high liquidity, as do most options and futures contracts.

Price continuity refers to the need for the market price at any point in time to reflect only the underlying, or permanent, supply and demand for the opportunity. Temporary trading imbalances that may be created simply by the random arrival of traders will not affect market price, if the market offers price continuity. How some markets attempt to achieve this objective is considered in Chapter 4.

Fairness refers to the absence of discrimination. Thus, it doesn't matter who you are or whom you represent, if your treatment in the market depends solely on the price you are willing to pay or receive or the timing of entrance onto the market, the market is fair. Most markets for the exchange of securities are fair. The reason is a simple one: it is in the interests of everyone concerned to see that the "best" price is secured. That best

---

[5]Walter Dolde [1978] offers explicit estimates of how much different lifetime consumption plans would be for the average consumer in perfectly operating financial markets versus markets that place restrictions on borrowing rates and the amount borrowed—both of which are a form of liquidity constraint.

[6]There are occasions when the market for a particular NYSE stock is closed for a few minutes or hours. Typically, this occurs when there is an impending disclosure of some particularly important piece of information, such as a surprising earnings report or corporate disclosure. However, these disclosures are relatively few and far between. During a 16-month period in 1974 and 1975, for example, there was an average of three to four suspensions a day on the 2,000 or so stocks on the exchange. See Michael Hopewell [1978].

price will always be the lowest ask price or the highest bid price. Whether the markets for all investment opportunities are fair is not clear. If markets are fragmented or separated it may be that a higher "offer to buy" exists, but can't be observed by the investor.

Marketability and Efficiency

Markets that are liquid, price-continuous, and fair are those where marketability is high. They allow investors to adjust their investment positions almost instantaneously to the desired level with the desired combination of risk and return. This increases utility and encourages saving and economic growth. When marketability is high the operating efficiency of the market is high. In financial markets at least, **the terms** *marketability* **and** *operating efficiency* **can be used almost interchangeably.** Any increase in the operating efficiency of the New York or Tokyo stock exchanges will also have positive effects on the level of marketability of the securities traded on those markets.

How Many Types of Financial Instruments?

We have discussed some of the types of securities that are currently available, and alluded to the periodic creation of new ones. When will it all end? When will investors be satisfied with the types of securities in existence? The answer is "not very soon." In fact, we might expect new securities to be created at an increasing rate in the future, simply because people's needs for shifting risk or shifting funds change over time. There is a direct relationship between the variety of financial assets available and the economic well-being of society.

Actually, Nobel Prize winner Kenneth Arrow [1964] suggested the answer in a classic paper he wrote two decades ago. He showed that the incentives to create new and different securities would end only when the number of different securities equaled the number of possible alternative economic outcomes (states of nature). By "different" securities, he meant that each security must offer a set of futures payoffs that is not duplicable by purchasing existing securities or combinations of securities. In this respect, we would expect GM's stock to be different from Ford's, and that an option to purchase Johnson & Johnson's stock would be different from J&J's common stock. By outcomes, or "states of nature," Arrow meant the virtually infinite number of configurations of economic events which could occur at any given future date. Thus, in one possible state of nature on January 17, 1993, for example, GM may earn $12.50 per share of common stock and Ford $7.50, while the unemployment rate is exactly 6.8 percent. In still another possible state of nature on the same date, the figures might be $12.25, $8.0, and 6.8 percent.[7]

In the last few years a number of new financial securities have been invented or have gained wider acceptance. Among these are exchange-traded stock options, futures markets in U.S. Treasury securities and in stock market indexes, zero coupon corporate bonds,

---

[7]Nils Hakansson [1976] has formulated a financial instrument in a way that attempts to make Arrow's ideas directly applicable—by the security paying off if a single (well-defined) outcome occurs and paying nothing otherwise. Hakansson shows that such an instrument can be used to eliminate the risk of changes in the purchasing power of the dollar.

options on futures contracts, options on residential real estate, graduated payment mortgages, variable interest rate debt instruments and mortgages, money market mutual funds, and a host of others. Stock market index futures contracts, for example, began trading in March, 1982, with options on these futures contracts beginning to trade early in 1983. A few securities have for the most part disappeared, including income bonds.

Summary

Hundreds of thousands of different types of investment opportunities exist in the world. Each one is "created" out of a contract that exists between the issuer (such as a business firm, a government, or an individual) and the investor. A large number of these financial contracts are issued by open corporations (or governments or individuals) to investors that have no direct tie to the operations of the issuer. Whether an issuer chooses to sell the financial contracts it creates to outside investors, to become an "open" corporation, depends on six factors that influence the costs and benefits of doing so. These factors are: (1) the clarity of the contract, (2) the ease and cost of monitoring for compliance with the terms of the contract, (3) the divisibility of the contract into small units, (4) the marketability of the contract, the ease with which it can be sold to others, (5) the desirability of the maturity terms of the contract, and (6) the desirability of the risk attributes of the contract.

By issuing financial contracts publicly the issuers may be able to acquire funds for use in purchasing factors of production at a low cost. Investors benefit by being able to shift their wealth over time and to risk levels consistent with their preferences. This increases the propensity to save and invest, and fosters economic growth and efficiency.

There are a wide variety of financial contracts or types of securities that have been issued in the world economy. These include common stocks, bonds, warrants, partnerships, and third-party financial contracts such as options and futures contracts—all of which are discussed in detail later in the book.

A key component of an investor's willingness to hold a security depends on the security's marketability. Marketability depends on the liquidity, price continuity, and fairness of the market on which the security is traded. As you will see in Chapter 4, various security exchanges and other marketplaces are measured in terms of their ability to supply these characteristics. Marketability is their measure of the efficiency with which they are able to facilitate the exchange of securities between investors.

References

Arrow, Kenneth. [1964] "The Role of Securities in the Optimal Allocation of Risk-Bearing." *Review of Economic Studies* (April).

Black, Fisher, and Scholes, Myron. [1974] "From Theory to a New Financial Product." *Journal of Finance* (May).

Crockett, John H. [1986] "Financial Contracting in the Venture Capital Market." Working Paper, George Mason University (July).

Dolde, Walter. [1978] "Capital Markets and the Short-Run Behavior of Life Cycle Savers." *Journal of Finance* (May).

Fama, Eugene F., and Jensen, Michael C. [1983] "Agency Problems and Residual Claims," *Journal of Law and Economics* (June).

Fama, Eugene F., and Jensen, Michael C. [1983] "Separation of Ownership and Control." *Journal of Law and Economics* (June).

Hakansson, Nils H. [1976] "The Purchasing Power Fund: A New Kind of Financial Intermediary." *Financial Analysts Journal* (November/December).

Homer, Sidney. [1977] *A History of Interest Rates.* 2nd ed. New Brunswick: Rutgers University Press.

Hopewell, Michael, and Schwartz, Arthur. [1978] "Temporary Trading Suspensions in Individual NYSE Securities." *Journal of Finance* (December).

Miller, Merton. [1986] "Financial Innovation: The Last Twenty Years and the Next." *Journal of Financial and Quantitative Analysis* (December).

Partch, M. Megan. [1985] "The Issuance of Limited Voting Common Stock and Shareholder Wealth." Working Paper, University of Oregon (January).

Russell, T. [1974] "The Effects of Improvements in the Consumer Loan Market." *Journal of Economic Theory* (November).

Teweles, Richard J., and Bradley, Edward S. [1982] *The Stock Market* 4th ed. New York: John Wiley & Sons.

Questions and Problems

1. We have emphasized that financial contracts may be ambiguous. In a current issue of *The Wall Street Journal* carefully examine for instances of conflict between the interests of the stockholders and the interests of management, e.g., management rejects a merger proposal that seems to be in the best interests of shareholders. Note that you probably will not be able to determine if there is, in fact, a conflict.

2. Do the same thing as in Question 1 for potential conflicts between the stockholders of a firm and the firm's creditors or debtholders.

3. What characteristics would indicate an efficient financial marketplace?

4. Open corporations apparently have decided that it is in their best interests to issue financial contracts to the public. What factors should be considered in making this decision?

5. During the 1980s a number of very large open corporations (e.g., Safeway and Beatrice) closed their ownership to the public by engaging in leveraged buyouts. (The common stock of the firm was purchased by a few individuals who borrowed heavily to finance the acquisition.) What possible advantages exist to "going private"? Select such a case and explore newspaper accounts of the transaction for reasons for the decision. Use *The Wall Street Journal Index* to locate articles about the firm.

6. Liquidity is an extremely important measure of the operating efficiency of a financial marketplace. Define liquidity, and rank the following markets by your view of the liquidity offered by each. Briefly explain your rankings.

   a. Certificates of deposit at a local bank.

   b. Residential housing units in a large city.

   c. The stock you receive from the small firm you work for.

   d. The common stock of IBM.

   e. A 1965 Mercedes Benz convertible.

7. Thumb through the second section of any *Wall Street Journal* and list the different types of third-party financial contracts you can find.

8. What kinds of benefits to individuals and to society in general are created by the existence of viable financial markets for securities? After all, the flow of money between individuals does nothing to directly expand the set of goods and services available for consumption.

9. In the decade between 1970 and 1980 U.S. government statisticians estimated that assets held in large firms (in excess of $10 million of assets) grew at twice the rate of assets held in small firms. If large firms tend to be characterized by open and public ownership (evidenced by securities issued to finance the asset purchases) and

small firms tend to be characterized by closed ownership of the assets, explain the factors that may have contributed to this differential in growth rate.

10. Which statement is *true?*

    a. Capital markets enhance economic development because they bring borrowers and savers together

    b. Secondary markets are economically unimportant, because issuing firms only are concerned with primary markets

    c. Money market instruments typically possess lower liquidity/marketability than comparable long-term securities

    d. All of the above.

                                                    CFA

CHAPTER

4

Securities Markets

Trading securities is a big business worldwide. On a typical business day, more than 150 million shares of common stock, issued by 2,000 firms and worth nearly $4 billion, change hands on the New York Stock Exchange. On the Tokyo Stock Exchange, almost 20 hours ahead of New York's trading day, 500 million shares of common stock worth about 200 billion yen (or $3 billion in the United States) are traded. Add this to the volume of trading on other exchanges in the United States and around the world, and you can see why the institutions that exist to facilitate trading in these securities are so economically significant.

Most of us assume that the organized stock exchanges such as the NYSE *are* the securities markets. This is not surprising. Stock exchanges are the most highly centralized and visible institutions involved in the trading of financial securities. Newspapers the world over provide daily listings of trading-price ranges for securities listed on these exchanges.

Actually, organized stock exchanges are only a part of the institutional framework of the world's financial markets. With today's communication technology, financial markets are no longer properly thought of as physical locations. In fact, most of the world's financial transactions need no central place where the securities buyer personally faces the seller and closes a deal.

This chapter looks at the institutional framework and operation of the world's financial markets. We begin with a discussion of the differences between primary and secondary securities markets, since this distinction is crucial to understanding the different functions performed in the securities markets.

Primary Securities Markets

Primary securities markets are those in which capital is raised by business, government, and individuals for consumption or for the financing of productive investment opportunities.

Transactions in the primary markets occur when a borrower (such as a corporation or the U.S. government) issues bonds or other debt instruments, or when a corporation issues common or preferred stock. For example, on June 25, 1986, the Crazy Eddie Corporation issued $72,000,000 in 6 percent convertible subordinated debentures due to mature in the year 2011. Similarly, on the same day, Newmont Gold Company issued 5 million shares of common stock priced at $9.50 per share. Both transactions were effected in the primary market. The primary market is also the forum for first-time issuance of new series of U.S. Treasury bills, notes, and bonds, U.S. government agency securities, municipal bonds, CDs, and a wide variety of other instruments which we introduced in Chapter 3.

The primary market is important because it allows the issuer to acquire financial capital to be invested, directly or indirectly, in productive assets. Without primary securities markets, and a supply of investors willing to purchase the securities issued in it, society's ability to allocate resources to production, and thus to enhance its standard of living over time, would be greatly hampered.

The success of the primary market system is evident by its sheer size. U.S. corporations alone issued more than $500 billion of registered debt and common and preferred stock to the public, not including private placements, in the first half of the 1980s. Figure 4–1 shows the dollar value of SEC-registered public offerings by U.S. corporations of bonds and common and preferred stock month by month for the years 1982–85. These figures do not include the debt issued by the U.S. government or by municipalities, nor the extensive volume of mortgages, negotiable certificates of deposit, and many other primary securities placed privately. All told, the U.S. primary market is a very active one.

A number of middlemen operate in the primary market. Their principal role is to assist in the creation of securities that will appeal to both issuers and investors, and to act as brokers in pooling and distributing funds so that buyers and sellers can consummate their desired transactions. The major types of middlemen include: financial institutions and investment and mortgage bankers.

Financial Institutions

Financial institutions such as commercial banks, savings banks, credit unions, and some insurance companies, take money from individual or business savers and distribute the funds to individuals or businesses who need funds to operate their households or firms. In the process, they convert one type of financial security—a savings account, for example—into another—say a mortgage or a business loan. In the process they have

FIGURE 4–1   Public Offerings in the United States by Months

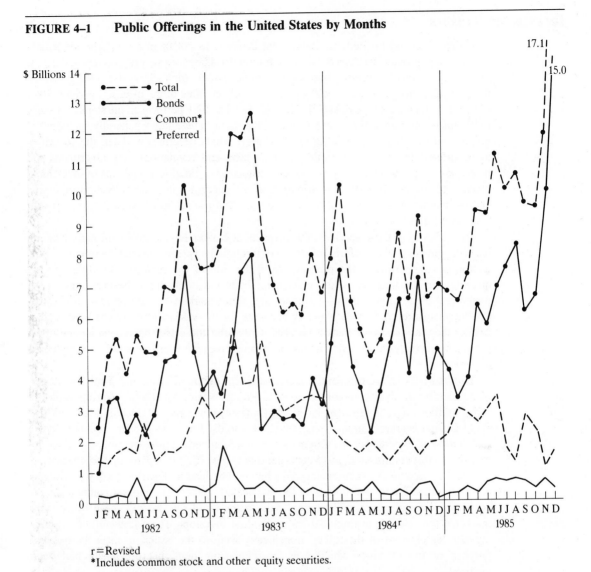

r=Revised
*Includes common stock and other equity securities.

Source: U.S. Securities and Exchange Commission *Monthly Statistical Review*, vol. 45, no. 2 (February 1986), p. 25.

exchanged a relatively illiquid, indivisible instrument with unique qualities (which limit its appeal to prospective investors) into a very liquid, almost totally divisible and fungible security with few risks. By serving as *intermediaries* in this market, these institutions have provided services to both savers and borrowers that simultaneously increase the desirability of saving and lower the cost of borrowing. This leads to a larger pool of loanable funds and a lower rate of interest for investment in production than would be the case otherwise.

Investment Bankers

Unlike financial institutions, investment bankers do not themselves issue securities. Instead, they provide services to facilitate transactions between security issuers and investors. They do this by offering two services to the issuer. First, they advise the issuer on the type of security to create and the proposed market value of the offering, given market conditions and the issuer's financial situation. Second, they perform all the steps necessary to complete the transaction, once it is decided upon. These steps generally include: (1) preparing the prospectus (or offering brochure), which describes in detail the securities to be offered in compliance with securities laws and regulations; (2) advertising and marketing the proposed issue to potential investors; (3) arranging a syndicate of investment bankers to manage the actual distribution of the securities and the collection of funds; and (4) maintaining an "after market" to ensure that trading in the security gets off to a reasonable start.

For performing these services, the investment banker is paid either through a fixed-fee arrangement (a "best efforts" offering) or through the spread between the remuneration it promises the firm and the proceeds from the sale of the securities (a "fixed price" offering). In the latter case, the investment banker actually buys the securities being issued and then markets them—he hopes at a retail markup—to the ultimate investors. This retail marketing service typically accounts for the vast majority of the total underwriting fee the investment banker charges. Only after these fees have been agreed upon is the issue actually marketed. The issuer then receives the "net," or wholesale, value as his proceeds.

To illustrate this arrangement, consider a recent public offering of 3.5 million shares of an electric utility's common stock at $13^5/_8$ per share, for a total offering value of $47.7 million. The investment banking syndicate, consisting of Merrill Lynch White Weld Capital Markets Group, Dean Witter Reynolds, Inc., and Kidder, Peabody & Co took a total of 50 cents per share in markup, for a total underwriting commission of $1.75 million. Of this commission, just 5 cents per share, or $175,000, represented compensation for their underwriting expenses and risks borne. The lead underwriter took 9 additional cents per share for its role in putting the syndicate together. The biggest component, 36 cents per share or $1.26 million, was paid to the retail salesmen of these firms, who marketed the issue to institutional and individual investors. The $45.9 million remaining after assessment of these fees immediately went to the issuer, to meet the original purpose of the offering, which was for refinancing debt that previously had been incurred.

Mortgage Bankers

Mortgage bankers provide precisely the same sort of services that investment bankers do, except that the *security issuers* are typically a group of homeowners, and the *security purchasers* are typically financial institutions or other institutional investors. Savings banks, insurance companies, and the Federal National Mortgage Association are examples of investors which hold the securities created through the mortgage banking function.

Secondary Securities Markets

Secondary markets are those in which financial securities already outstanding are exchanged among investors. Unlike transactions in the primary markets, the proceeds of such trades do not end up in the hands of the issuer of the security. That is, secondary market transactions involve the exchange of securities that are already issued and in the hands of investors. If you purchase 500 shares of IBM stock on the New York Stock Exchange, you are doing so in the secondary market. If Washington Mutual Savings Bank sells a package of mortgages to a large life insurance company, that transaction also takes place in the secondary market. Similarly, if Fidelity Fund (a mutual fund) purchases a large block of common stock from the Teamster's Pension Fund, this also will take place in the secondary market.

In the United States, there is a continuing evolution toward the creation of a nationwide market system for secondary market trading. As noted earlier, this is made possible through technology and the advent of high-speed computing and telecommunications suitable for data transmission. It is also being actively encouraged by the Securities and Exchange Commission, the nation's chief regulator of securities markets and of the brokers and dealers who operate in them, and by Congress, which has passed legislation in recent years to extend the SEC's regulatory powers to facilitate the formation of the single, nationwide market.

One of the greatest strides in the creation of the nationwide market was made with the advent of the consolidated transactions tape and the Intermarket Trading System (ITS). The ITS is a body of trading policies and rules governing the manner in which orders are executed by the organized exchanges and by brokers and dealers acting in the over-the-counter markets. An Intermarket Surveillance Group is responsible for making and periodically reviewing the effectiveness of these policies, which are designed to ensure that the public's orders are executed at the best available prices in whatever market the prices are quoted. The consolidated tape provides market-makers in each exchange and in the OTC market with current information about prices quoted and the prices of the most recent trades in all other markets. It does this on a real-time basis, making it possible for market-makers to operate in the context of a nationally competitive market.

For the most part, our discussion concentrates on secondary markets for common stock. We do this not only because of the importance and magnitude of the market, but because most of the essential features of the common stock market are present in the markets for all types of debt securities, options, and futures, whether primary or secondary in nature. Of course, some difficulties *do* exist (in the bidding process for Treasury bills, for example), and we discuss those market structures specifically in later chapters.

Types of Securities Traded

Within the primary and secondary security markets, the various securities traded differ according to their maturity and the nature of the security. Three major market subdivisions based on the distinctions among securities are: money markets, long-term securities markets, and options and futures markets. The first two subdivisions exist within both the primary and secondary markets; the latter is typically viewed as part of the secondary market only.

TABLE 4–1   U.S. Securities Debt and Equity Securities Listed on U.S. Securities Exchanges

Type of Security*

Exchange Registered	Common		Preferred		Bonds		Total Securities	
	Number	*Market Value ($ millions)*	*Number*	*Market Value ($ millions)*	*Number*	*Market Value ($ millions)*	*Number*	*Market Value ($ millions)*
American	769	$ 59,865	113	$ 3,371	342	$ 17,577	1,224	$ 80,813
Boston	95	$ 1,439	0	0	3	19	98	1,458
Cincinnati	4	141	3	50	6	48	13	239
Midwest	16	1,024	6	14	0	0	22	1,038
New York	1,449	1,830,548	791	52,119	3,746	1,328,951	5,986	3,211,618
Pacific	47	1,157	17	628	80	1,347	144	3,132
Philadelphia	17	357	21	1,091	38	1	76	1,449
Intermountain	n/a	n/a	0	0	0	0	n/a	n/a
Spokane	26	8	0	0	0	0	26	8
Chicago Board Options Exchange (CBOE)†	0	0	0	0	0	0	0	0
Total	2,423	$1,894,539	951	$57,273	4,215	$1,347,943	7,589	$3,299,755
Includes Foreign Stocks:								
New York	54	$67,550	4	$114	110	$10,347	168	$ 78,011
American	48	22,521	3	123	5	78	56	22,722
Pacific	4	32	0	0	2	5	6	37
Total	106	$90,103	7	$237	117	$10,430	230	$100,770

*Excluding securities which were suspended from trading at the end of the year, and securities which because of inactivity had no available quotes.
†The Chicago Board Options Exchange lists only equity and nonequity options.
n/a = not available.
Source: *SEC Monthly Statistical Review*, vol. 45, no. 5 (May 1986).

Money markets are those markets in which short-term securities are issued (if in the primary market) and traded (if in the secondary market). Short-term securities, by convention, have an original maturity (or life) of one year or less, and include commercial paper, bankers' acceptances, negotiable certificates of deposit, and U.S. Treasury bills. Options and futures contracts, which also may have short maturities, are not viewed as money market instruments, however.

Long-term securities markets are those in which original maturities of over one year are exchanged. These securities include common stocks, preferred stocks, and government and corporate bonds. Mortgages issued by individual homeowners also would be included.

Options and futures markets are those in which short- or intermediate-term option contracts and futures contracts are traded. These securities are unusual in a very important sense. The aggregate amount of them that exists at any one time is zero. My "long" position in IBM call options, for example, must equal some other investors' "short" position in the same options. Since there is only an investor "issuer," and since all positions in these securities net out across all investors, the distinction between primary and secondary market operations tends to disappear.

TABLE 4–2   Trading Volume of Stocks and Options on U.S. Securities Exchanges, 1985 ($000)

Exchange	Preferred and Common Stock	Equity Options	Nonequity Options	Total Volume
American Stock Exchange (AMEX)	$ 26,332,151	$ 8,600,805	$ 2,967,329	$ 37,900,285
Boston Stock Exchange	14,419,101	0	0	14,419,101
Cincinnati Stock Exchange	2,104,862	0	0	2,104,862
Chicago Board Options Exchange (CBOE)	0	15,801,516	22,629,031	38,430,547
Midwest Stock Exchange	79,068,763	0	0	79,068,763
New York Stock Exchange (NYSE)	1,023,202,389	43,306	660,664	1,023,906,359
Pacific Stock Exchange	36,752,467	3,103,341	20,918	39,876,726
Philadelphia Stock Exchange	17,894,497	2,403,771	2,840,540	23,138,808
Intermountain Stock Exchange	295	0	0	295
Spokane Stock Exchange	11,609	0	0	11,609
Totals	$1,199,786,134	$29,952,739	$29,118,482	$1,258,857,355

Source: *SEC Monthly Statistical Review*, vol. 45, no. 3 (March 1986).

The Organized Securities Exchanges

In 1987 there were 10 organized securities exchanges in the United States and 6 in Canada. The U.S. exchanges are listed in Table 4–1, along with the **market value** of the stocks and bonds listed on each as of December 31, 1985. Table 4–2 displays the **trading volume** for stocks and options on each of these exchanges for 1985. The two largest exchanges, the NYSE and the AMEX, are usually referred to as the *national* exchanges, with the other seven being referred to as *regionals*. The Canadian exchanges include three large and active exchanges in Montreal, Toronto, and Vancouver, as well as three smaller regional exchanges.

Numerous stock exchanges also exist outside the United States and Canada. The best known is the Tokyo Stock Exchange. It is the biggest of Japan's eight stock exchanges (accounting for over 80 percent of trading volume on all Japanese stock exchanges) and, after the NYSE, the world's second largest stock exchange. Hong Kong also has a major stock exchange, the Stock Exchange of Hong Kong, which represents the consolidation of four older stock exchanges. Then, there is the Stock Exchange of Singapore Limited, the London Stock Exchange, the Paris Stock Exchange, the Johannesburg Stock Exchange, and many others. Some of these foreign exchanges, most notably the Tokyo Stock Exchange, have trading procedures and listing requirements that closely resemble those of the NYSE, principally because the NYSE, being one of the world's oldest exchanges, has often served as a model. Recent market value and trading volume comparisons of two of these exchanges with the NYSE are displayed in Table 4–3.

Even though most domestic exchanges have the word "stock" in their titles, Table 4–1 indicates that, for the most part, the exchanges make markets in other types of securities

TABLE 4–3   Comparison of Three World Stock Exchanges (December 31, 1984)

	Tokyo	New York	U.K.
Number of stock-listed companies			
Domestic	1,444	1,490	2,171
Foreign	11	53	582
Number of listed issues			
Stocks			
Domestic	1,450	2,266	1,857
Foreign	11	53	504
Bonds			
Domestic	536	3,549	3,179
Foreign	200	202	1,520
Total market value (U.S. $ billion)			
Stocks	$644	1,529	236.3
Bonds	$371.1	1,021.8	240.9
Trading value (U.S. $ billion)			
Stocks	$271.1	764.7	240.9
Bonds	$150.6	7.0	42.3
Number of member firms	83	628	216

Source: *Japan 1986: An International Comparison,* Keizai Kobo Center, September 30, 1986.

too. Besides equities, the NYSE the AMEX, the Pacific Stock Exchange, and the Philadelphia Stock Exchange also feature trading in corporate bonds, common stock warrants, and stock purchase rights. The AMEX, NYSE, Pacific Stock Exchange, Philadelphia Stock Exchange, and of course, the Chicago Board Options Exchange also feature trading in stock options. In spite of this diversity in the types of securities traded, common stock transactions provide the mainstay of business for most of these exchanges.

As is obvious from the tables, the NYSE dominates the trading in listed equities, with the AMEX and Midwest exchanges the distant second and third.

History and Organization of the Exchanges

The New York Stock Exchange is the oldest of the organized securities exchanges. It was founded in 1792 by a group of 24 securities brokers who formed an agreement called the Corres Hotel Pact. Later, this agreement became popularly known as the Buttonwood Agreement, for it allegedly was consummated under a buttonwood tree on the streets of New York City.

The agreement these gentlemen signed had several interesting provisions, the spirit of some of which have lasted for nearly 200 years. It specified that they would treat each other preferentially, and simultaneously discourage outside competition in the trading of securities. They also expressed an intent to charge investors a fixed, noncompetitive fee (commission) for all stock transactions which they executed. It was, in other words, a classic cartel. Not until 1975 was the fixed commission structure done away with on the NYSE, and until then the NYSE exerted a powerful monopoly influence over stock market trading.

Within 30 years of signing the agreement, the Buttonwood group had taken business away from exchanges in Philadelphia and Boston, and by 1850 it had emerged as the central marketplace for common stocks. At that time it began to charge its new members a $1,000 initiation fee for a "seat" on the exchange. In the late 1870s trading in NYSE "seats" began (originally, these were literally armchairs). Brokers who became members were entitled to sit in armchairs while trading in listed stocks was conducted. In 1875 the price of such a seat on the NYSE reached $6,800. Prices progressed steadily, though irregularly, upward until they reached $625,000, in 1929. Prices dropped during the recession and war years, but even the excellent markets in the late 1960s revived the price only to an average of $515,000. In 1985 the average price was about $400,000.[1]

Just before the turn of the century, a rival exchange threatened to take business away from the NYSE. Known as the New York Curb Market Association (NYCMA), it offered customers active trading in stocks at competitive commission rates. Later, in 1910, the NYSE and the NYCMA entered into an agreement whereby the latter exchange would concentrate in the trading of stocks of relatively small or new firms, while the former would concentrate in trading the stocks of older, more established firms. Thus, since neither would trade in the securities offered by the other, they effectively agreed to share the monopolized market for exchange services. In 1953 the name of the NYCMA was changed to—you guessed it—the American Stock Exchange (AMEX).

Exchange Membership

On both the NYSE and AMEX, there are several types of members who have access to the trading floor. The most important of these are the *commission brokers* and the *specialists*. Most are involved in executing orders transmitted to them by individual or institutional investors.

Commission Brokers. A brokerage firm, or stockbroker, accepts investors' orders to purchase and sell securities and is paid a commission for transmitting these orders to the appropriate exchange for execution. There are two principal types of brokerage firms— retail houses, whose clients are typically individual investors, and wholesale houses, which deal with institutional investors. Some firms have both individual and institutional customers. They include most of the well-known firms such as Merrill, Lynch, Pierce, Fenner & Smith, Inc., or Prudential-Bache Securities, Inc. Others, such as Salomon Brothers, however, accept only institutional investors as clients. As soon as an order is placed with a brokerage house, it is relayed by high-speed lines to the exchange floor. There it is received by a commission broker, the brokerage firm's representative on the floor of the exchange. These are the members of the exchange who actually see that customer orders get executed according to his or her instructions.

Specialists. Specialists and their employees are key members of any exchange. They have two functions: (1) to execute orders which are entrusted to them by other members of the exchange (most commonly, commission brokers) and (2) to maintain a fair and orderly market in the particular securities for which they are responsible. In this capacity their economic function is to provide **liquidity** (sales and purchases of securities can take

---

[1]New York Stock Exchange, *1986 Fact Book.*

place instantly without having the transaction affect market price), **price continuity** (as trading occurs over time, the price adjusts appropriately to underlying changes in supply and demand), and **fairness** (only price and time of order are considered in executing security transactions). These functions, which together ensure the **marketability** of the security, were specifically defined in Chapter 3.

Rules established under the Intermarket Trading System referred to earlier also require that, under normal circumstances, the specialist execute customer orders at the best prices quoted at the time the orders reach the exchange floor, whether or not the quotes originate on the same or on different stock exchange floors. For example, if a NYSE specialist receives a sell order for a stock that is also traded on the Pacific Coast Stock Exchange (PCSE), and the latter exchange is currently quoting a higher bid price for that stock, the specialist is required under ITS rules to direct the order to the PCSE for execution, provided it is for more than 100 shares. To do otherwise is referred to as "trading through the market," which is strictly prohibited under ITS rules and is subject to redress by the exchange quoting the better price.

A related concept of fairness, for which the specialist is also held responsible under ITS rules, is that he cannot "lock the market." This means, for example, that if a NYSE specialist, in executing an order, notices that the PCSE is quoting a price of 20-1/8 for the particular stock in question, the specialist cannot execute the order on the NYSE floor at the same price of 20-1/8. If the specialist cannot offer a better price on the NYSE, he must send the order to the PCSE. Rules such as this endeavor to ensure that the customer's interests are kept paramount while at the same time competition among exchanges is promoted.

A specialist earns income from two sources—from commissions received by executing orders requested by other exchange members, and where permitted, from profits obtained by buying and selling shares for his own account. In the first case, the specialist is compensated for acting as a broker; i.e., filling public orders on his book with shares made available from other public orders. This activity is called "crossing orders," and, typically, it is his principal activity. In the second case, the specialist is compensated for risks he incurs from maintaining an inventory of the security (to be used in filling customer orders) and thus providing price continuity—whenever there may be a temporary imbalance of buy or sell orders coming to the floor. New York Stock Exchange specialists are permitted to trade for their own accounts, and thus earn this second source of income. On the Tokyo Stock Exchange, however, the saitori members (which are the Japanese counterpart of our specialists) are not permitted to trade for their own accounts. This would appear to be a major constraint on Japanese specialists when compared to NYSE specialists, who in 1985 bought and sold 5.9 billion shares for their own accounts.[2]

In 1986 the NYSE had 65 specialist units. Each of these specialist units specializes, or "makes a market" in one or more stocks, with the average being about 25. Many specialist units have only one or two stocks, whereas others may have 50 or more. A unit is usually a business corporation or partnership of several individuals which is authorized to maintain a continuous auction market in the securities in which the unit makes markets. In a continuous auction, unlike the usual call auctions conducted to sell antiques or oriental rugs, trading in all items is conducted for the duration of the auction.

---

[2]Ibid.

The auctioneer acts as a market maker standing ready to buy or sell specific quantities as orders arrive. This is usually accomplished through maintenance of an inventory, or buffer stock, which offsets temporary trading imbalances that may arise from time to time.

Listing Requirements

The securities traded on the floor of the exchange are those that have been **listed.** Firms with securities that have met a particular exchange's listing requirements and have chosen to apply for listing are officially accorded the right to be traded on the floor of that exchange. In general, exchanges have listing requirements to ensure that there is a reasonably active market for the security. There are considerable fixed costs to instituting a market for trading in a given stock, and if trading is active, the costs can be offset to allow the specialist to earn a "reasonable" return for his labor services and the risks he bears.

The NYSE has more stringent criteria for listing than any other U.S. exchange. The requirements for initial listing are concerned with specifying minimum levels for a company's recent earnings, its total assets, the market value of its publicly held shares, the extent to which the shares are publicly held, and the number of shareholders.[3] With respect to earnings requirements, the criteria require that the company have earnings of either $2.5 million before federal income taxes for the most recent year and $2 million before-tax earnings for each of the preceding two years, or an aggregate for the last three fiscal years of $6.5 million with a minimum required in the most recent fiscal year of $4.5 million. All three years must be profitable in either case. With respect to assets, the requirements specify net tangible assets of $18 million. The minimum market value of publicly-held shares as of December 31, 1985 was also $18 million, though this figure fluctuates with the NYSE Index of Common Stock Prices. The company must also have a total of 1.1 million common shares that are publicly held by at least either 2,000 holders of 100 shares or more, or 2,200 total shareholders and average monthly trading volume for the most recent six months of 100,000 shares. Modifications of these listing requirements apply to foreign companies.[4]

To continue being listed, a company should maintain more than 1,200 shareholders of 100 shares or more, with at least 600,000 shares held publicly. It should also maintain an aggregate market value of its publicly-held shares of at least $5 million. If a company fails to meet these standards on an ongoing basis, the NYSE may at any time de-list, or suspend the company from trading on the exchange. And, of course, if a company is acquired or goes private, it will disappear from the exchange.

Another interesting, and increasingly controversial, listing requirement involves the NYSE's historical position opposing the listing of nonvoting common stock. That is, all common shares traded must bestow full voting rights to the purchaser. As corporations have begun to look for creative ways to obtain the benefits of equity offerings without losing the control enjoyed by existing shareholders, nonvoting or limited-voting classes of common stock have become more common. General Motors, Hershey Foods, Alberto-

---

[3]Ibid.
[4]Ibid.

Culver Co., and 19 other NYSE-listed companies have more than one class of common stock with differential voting rights. Because of this, the NYSE has found itself under increasing pressure to relax its policy. In 1986, after two years of debate, the NYSE agreed to a rules change which will permit these companies to list more than one class of common stock with the exchange.[5]

In 1985 the NYSE added 97 common stock issues to its list of traded securities, at the same time de-listing 105 other common stock issues. As of year end, a total of 1,503 firms had securities listed on the NYSE.[6] Because of the relatively stringent listing requirements, these companies tend to be among the oldest and largest in the nation. Included are such "blue chips" as American Telephone & Telegraph, Exxon, General Electric, Ford Motor Company, and General Mills. In fact, a majority of the Fortune 500 companies have securities listed on the NYSE. During 1985 the most actively traded of these companies were American Telephone & Telegraph, International Business Machines, and Phillips Petroleum, the share volume for each topping 200 million for the year.

In addition to common stocks, the NYSE also listed 3,856 different bond issues from 1,010 issuers, mostly U.S. corporations.[7] To have a bond listed, the company must meet listing requirements applicable to its common stock. Twenty-two different warrant issues were listed for 19 companies whose common shares were traded on the NYSE.

The AMEX and the regional exchanges in the United States have less restrictive listing requirements than the NYSE. To qualify for initial listing of its common stock on the AMEX, a firm must have, for example, $400,000 net after-tax earnings in the most recent fiscal year.[8] Both the NYSE and the AMEX require that each listed firm publicly disclose quarterly sales and earnings figures and make certain that other financial information is publicly available so investors may better evaluate the securities.

As noted above, some stocks listed on the NYSE or AMEX are also traded on the regionals. A few NYSE stocks occasionally are also traded on the AMEX. Stocks which are traded on either or both of the national exchanges and also on one or more of the regionals are said to be "dually listed." A large number of stocks fit this category; however for most NYSE and AMEX issues the vast bulk of trading occurs on the floor of the AMEX or NYSE. For example, in 1985, 83.4 percent of all trading volume in dually-listed NYSE-listed stocks originated on the NYSE floor.[9] Some dually-listed issues include USX (formerly U.S. Steel), Nabisco, and Merrill, Lynch (these are listed on the NYSE, the Midwest Stock Exchange, and the Pacific Stock Exchange). The AMEX and the regionals also engage in "unlisted trading," wherein shares which are not formally listed on a particular exchange are traded there anyway. In this case, the issuing firm need not meet that exchange's listing or financial reporting requirements. The Securities and Exchange Commission must approve admission of a stock to unlisted trading on an exchange. The shares of USX, for example, are also traded, though unlisted, on the Boston, Cincinnati, and Philadelphia Stock Exchanges.

[5]"Big Board Agrees to Let Companies List More Than One Class of Common Stock," *The Wall Street Journal*, July 7, 1986.

[6]New York Stock Exchange, *1986 Fact Book*.

[7]Ibid.

[8]American Stock Exchange, *1986 Fact Book*.

[9]New York Stock Exchange, *1986 Fact Book*.

The Trading Process on Exchanges

The price at which a security trades in the secondary market is partially controlled by the corporation through the number of shares that it has issued in the primary market. Thus, if a privately-held corporation having equity value of $100 million goes public by issuing 1 million shares, the shares should trade initially at a price of $100. An identical corporation issuing 4 million shares would set the price initially at $25 per share. The corporation can always change this ratio by effectively retiring old shares and issuing new ones through a stock split—say, on a two-for-one basis. Changing the capitalization in this manner would cause the first security's price to fall to $50.

After the number of shares outstanding is set, the price will change on the stock exchange as supply and demand conditions change. By custom—and for no other reason—trading on U.S. stock exchanges takes place in most securities at one eighth (dollar) intervals. Thus, trading may take place at $25^1/_8$, but not at $25^1/_3$ or $25^1/_{10}$.[10] This convention differs around the world. On the Tokyo Stock Exchange, for example, trading takes place in one yen increments (about $.006 in the United States).

Securities exchanges do not directly buy or sell securities. Rather, they provide trading floors on which a continuous auction market is conducted. To transact business on the trading floor of an exchange an individual must be a member; that is, a seat on the exchange must be purchased. Individual or institutional investors who place orders to buy or sell the securities listed on an exchange are not allowed to be present when their orders are executed. Rather, they must transmit their orders through their brokerage house to an exchange member, usually a commission broker—who sees that they are carried out.

Description of Orders

The kinds of orders which can be executed on a securities exchange can be grouped roughly as follow:

1. Order types—buy, sell, sell short.
2. Order sizes—round lot, odd lot.
3. Limit orders—price limit, time limit.
4. Special orders—stop orders, large block orders.

Order Types.   There are three types of orders which can be executed. The first two are self-explanatory: orders to **buy** and orders to **sell** a specified quantity of a financial security. The third, an order to **sell short,** is a sell order initiated by an investor who does not own the security being sold. In the stock market, it is perfectly legal to sell something you do not own. *Short sales,* as they are called, simply involve your borrowing the specified quantity of the stock, bonds, or other security from someone who actually owns them and is willing to allow this borrowing to take place.[11] Most often, your broker has

---

[10]A few stocks trade at one sixteenth point intervals, and options and "penny" stocks on some regional exchanges may trade even narrower intervals. Also by custom, stock prices, when quoted in one eighths, are not labeled as a dollar amount. Thus, 25 1/8 or $25.125 represents the same dollar figure per share.

[11]The transaction is the same as might be taken by a car dealer in selling you a car he doesn't have, shopping from other dealers' inventories to borrow a car to deliver to you, and replacing the borrowed car at a later date when one becomes available from the manufacturer.

other clients who own the security and are willing to do this. Upon borrowing the shares and selling them on the exchange, you are committed—at a later date—to returning an identical quantity of the security to your broker. This reverse transaction is called covering a short position, but it really involves your initiating a simple buy order.

As you might expect, the outcome of a short sale is exactly the opposite of that of a purchase. You would be wise to undertake a short sale only when you expect that the security's price is going to fall in the near future. Exchange rules permit short sales to be executed only after a positive 1/8 movement in the security's price; that is, after "an uptick." This prevents short sellers from overwhelming a stock's trading and causing the price to engage in a self-reinforcing downward spiral.

An important part of the short sale mechanism is that you do *not* get to keep the proceeds of the short sale order at the time the trade is executed. In a regular sell order of 100 shares of IBM, for example, the investor would receive 100 times the share price at which the trade was executed, less the broker's commission, within five business days of the trade. In a short sale, this money is held by your brokerage firm, essentially in escrow, until the short is covered, at some time in the future. In addition, to ensure that you can cover your short position, your broker will demand that collateral be posted. As you might imagine, brokerage companies don't discourage short sales, since they get to keep the interest earned on both the collateral money and the proceeds from the sale, which are invested in short-term money market securities while your short position is in effect. The profits generated can be substantial, especially if you don't cover your short position for some time.

Interestingly, on the NYSE, almost 40 percent of all short selling involves specialists trading for their own accounts in their attempt to maintain orderly markets. When a large number of public buy orders come in, the specialist often has to sell short to fill these orders on a short-term basis.

When any of the three order types is initiated, and is unaccompanied by additional instructions, it is treated as a **market order.** A market order is simply an offer to buy, sell, or short sell a security at the current market price. Thus, an order to buy (sell) 100 shares of Xerox stock with no further instructions means that the broker will execute the trade immediately at the lowest (highest) price available at the instant the order is brought to the exchange floor. The broker will not wait for the price to change from its present level before executing the order.

Order Sizes. Every order must specify the number of shares or trading units of a particular security which are to be bought or sold. A **round-lot order** in most common stocks listed on the U.S. exchanges is 100 shares; a few stocks, however, are traded in round lots of 10 shares. These are usually inactive stocks or stocks whose share prices are unusually high. For bonds, a round lot is a multiple of $1,000 in par value.

Odd lots normally are orders for less than 100 shares, or for that portion of an order which represents the excess over a multiple of round lots. An order to sell 440 shares of General Motors is composed of four round lots and one odd lot of 40 shares. The distinction between the two is necessary only because of the peculiar manner in which securities exchanges operate; round lots and odd lots historically have always been executed separately.

Although specialists execute odd-lot transactions just as they do round-lot transactions that are brought to them, such orders are not always brought to the specialist. Sometimes the brokerage firm will fill the order itself in an attempt to provide better service to the customer or to gain additional profits. And, sometimes—but not always—there is a markup on odd-lot purchases and a markdown on odd-lot sales. This penalty is known as the **odd-lot differential** and typically is 1/8 point for stocks selling below $40 and $^1/_4$ point for stocks selling above $40. The differential is justified on the grounds that the specialist (or broker) in executing such transactions is acting as a dealer, rather than as a broker, and uses the differential to offset the added costs of his dealer activities. The distinction is that, to fill odd-lot orders promptly, inventories must be maintained. If the specialist were to wait for an offsetting odd-lot order to come in with which to fill your current odd-lot order, you might have to wait longer than you care to.

Limit Orders. There are two types of **limit orders:** those which specify a **price limit** and those which specify a **time limit.** Of the two, price limit orders are the more common.

A price limit order to buy (sell) is accompanied by instructions specifying the highest (lowest) price the buyer (seller) is willing to pay (accept) for each unit of the security. Price limit orders, when they reach the floor of the exchange, are held "on the books" of the specialist until trading in the particular security results in a price at which they can be executed. Depending on the particular price limit specified, such orders could—theoretically, at least—remain on the books for an hour, a day, a week, or longer. If Exxon is selling at $70^3/_4$ and an investor enters an order to "sell 100 shares of Exxon at $72^1/_2$ limit," the order will not be executed until the stock's price rises by at least $1^3/_4$ points.

Alternatively, orders might specify a particular time limit, after which they are to be canceled. Although infrequently used, time limit orders can be quite useful for specific purposes. An investor who is planning to leave town and does not want the order executed in his absence might wish to enter a day, week, or month order. Day orders expire at the close of the trading day on which they were initiated. More popular, however, is the open or good-till-canceled order, which remains in force until canceled by the customer or for six months, whichever comes first. Time limits can be used in conjunction with all types of price-limit orders, but they make little sense with market orders, since the latter are always executed when placed. Only the specialist (and his clerical assistants) have access to the set of limit orders that have been placed for execution and entered on the specialist's book. Quite clearly that is valuable information since it represents a partial demand and supply schedule for shares of that firm.

Special Orders. The best-known type of special order is the **stop order.** It is an order to buy or sell a specified number of shares of stock or other security and it converts into a market order as soon as the security's price reaches a specified level. Stop orders may be used to initiate transactions at critical market levels, or, more commonly, to protect paper profits or (partially) ensure against large losses in the event of a major change in a security's price. If an investor originally purchased 100 shares of Primerica at $65, and it is now selling at $75, the investor might wish to protect a portion of his $10-a-share profit in the event of a sudden decline by initiating an order to "sell 100 shares of Primerica at 70 stop." If and when the price per share dipped to $70, this order would become a market order to sell at the best possible price. If the share price never dropped this far, however, the sale would not be effected. The disadvantage, of course, is that the price can drop well below the "stop" price of $70 before the transaction is executed.

One way of getting around this potential disadvantage is to use a stop order in conjunction with a price-limit order. The result, called a **stop limit order,** sets a specific limit on the price a buyer or seller will accept in the event the security reaches the stop price. In the example above, if the investor wanted to obtain at least $70 per share for the Primerica stock, a stop limit order might be constructed to say "sell 100 shares of Primerica at 71 stop, limit 70." This instructs the broker to activate the sell order when the stock's price dropped to 71 or below, but in any case to sell at a price no lower than 70.

Large-block orders are also special orders, since they often involve use of special procedures at the exchange. Large blocks usually involve the purchase or sale of thousands of shares of a particular security and/or have dollar values in the millions. It sometimes takes days to accomplish transactions of this magnitude. Before the exchanges will accept orders for large blocks, therefore, they may require advance notification.

How Trades Are Consummated

In executing round-lot orders, a typical scenario involves the commission broker on the floor of the exchange taking the order to the specialist of the security involved. The specialist maintains a "book" for each stock his specialist unit is responsible for. Each "page" of this book represents a dollar price; buy orders are listed on one side of the page and sell orders on the other. All orders entered in the book are price-limit orders. A sample of the traditional specialist's book is shown in Figure 4–2. In the left column

FIGURE 4–2   Specialist's Book

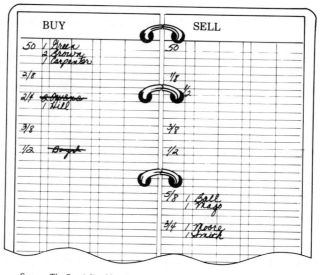

Source: *The Specialist,* New York Stock Exchange, March 1, 1973.

FIGURE 4–3 **Video Display Unit from NYSE**

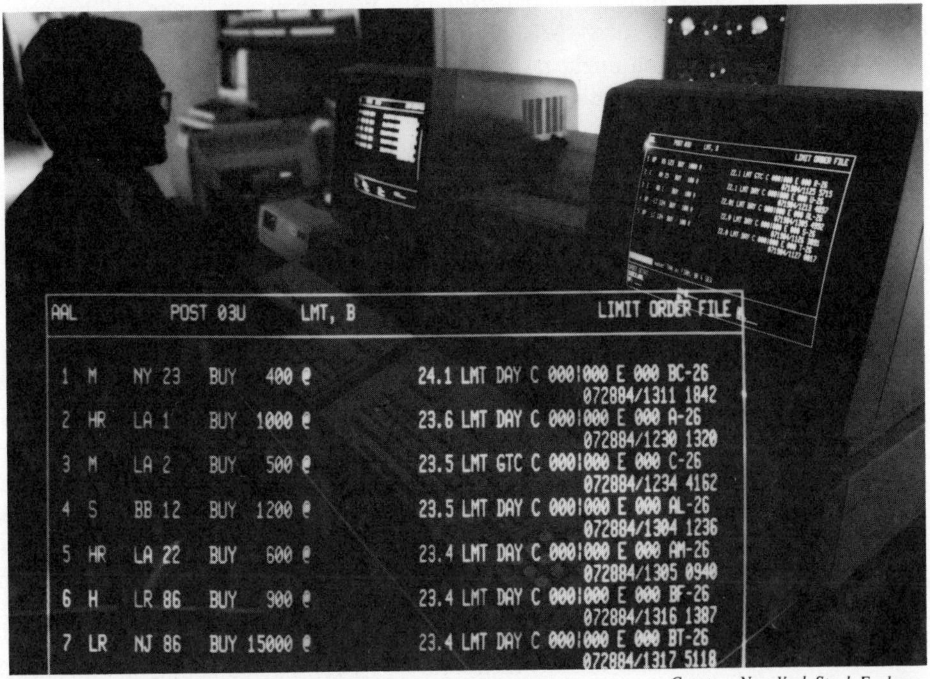

AAL		POST 03U		LMT, B		LIMIT ORDER FILE
1	M	NY 23	BUY	400 @	24.1 LMT DAY C 0001000 E 000 BC-26 072884/1311 1842
2	HR	LA 1	BUY	1000 @	23.6 LMT DAY C 0001000 E 000 A-26 072884/1230 1320
3	M	LA 2	BUY	500 @	23.5 LMT GTC C 0001000 E 000 C-26 072884/1234 4162
4	S	BB 12	BUY	1200 @	23.5 LMT DAY C 0001000 E 000 AL-26 072884/1304 1236
5	HR	LA 22	BUY	600 @	23.4 LMT DAY C 0001000 E 000 AM-26 072884/1305 0940
6	H	LR 86	BUY	900 @	23.4 LMT DAY C 0001000 E 000 BF-26 072884/1316 1387
7	LR	NJ 86	BUY	15000 @	23.4 LMT DAY C 0001000 E 000 BT-26 072884/1317 5118

Courtesy New York Stock Exchange

of the "buy" page is the price limit for each order on the book. The numbers in the next column over indicate the number of round lots at that price. The names are those of the brokers who entered each order. Orders where names are scratched out are those already executed or canceled. In this figure the buy order at $50\frac{1}{2}$ has been executed.

Increasingly, as the floor of the NYSE has been automated, the traditional specialist's book has been replaced by an **Electronic Display Book System,** which contains the same information as the old handwritten book, but has the advantage of reducing paperwork and speeding up executions. At the end of 1985, there were 24 electronic screens at specialist posts on the floor of the NYSE. A picture of such a video display unit is shown in Figure 4–3.

The specialist's book records bid and ask limit order prices for each stock on a continuous basis. The specialist quotes his own bid and ask price based on the information contained in the book. The specialist's **bid** price is the price at which he offers to purchase shares of stock, whereas the specialist's **ask** price is the price at which the specialist offers to sell shares. The bid price will be the higher of the highest limit order on the book, the bid price prevailing in another market (if a better price is quoted there), or the price at which the specialist stands ready to buy for his own account. The ask price will be the lower of the lowest limit order on the book, the ask price prevailing in another market, or the price at which the specialist stands ready to sell for his own account. At any given price, transactions from the book must have precedence over specialist transactions for inventory.

To illustrate how an order might be executed on the floor of the exchanges, suppose you have just placed a market order to sell 300 shares of Fuqua Industries common stock. Suppose further that the specialist's book shown in Figure 4–2 pertains to Fuqua stock, and that it shows existing buy limit and sell limit orders on the stock. The following conversation might take place between the Fuqua specialist and the commission broker who is representing you:[12]

> "FQA." (The **commission broker** calls out the ticker symbol, FQA, for Fuqua's stock. Notice he does not disclose the side of the market he is on).
>
> "FQA fifty and two eighths bid, offered five eighths." (This means that the **specialist** is quoting a price of fifty and two eighths to those who wish to sell and a price of fifty and five eighths to those who wish to buy.)
>
> "Three hundred at fifty and two eighths." (The **broker** finally reveals that he wishes to sell.)
>
> "I'll take three hundred at fifty and two eighths, one of them here, two of them at Tompane" (The **specialist's clerk.**)

In the course of this conversation, the broker has indicated a desire to sell 300 shares of Fuqua common at the bid price on the specialist's book, $50.25. The specialist's clerk then indicates that only 100 of these will be purchased to fill a buy limit order on the specialist's book (note the buy order for 100 shares by a broker named "Hill"). The other 200 will be purchased for the specialist's own account (i.e., not to fill a public order). A. B. Tompane & Company is the name of the specialist unit making a market in Fuqua Industries stock.

The broker could have responded "300 at a half," indicating an attempt to sell three hundred shares at $50^1/_2$ instead of $50^1/_4$. He may be hoping to do better than the current market for his customer. The specialist (or anyone else in the vicinity) has the option of accepting or rejecting this proposal. These two examples serve to illustrate the double-auction nature of the exchange floor.

The broker may also encounter another broker at the specialist's post who also has a customer order to buy or sell the same stock. If one wishes to buy and the other to sell, the two can simply trade the shares at an agreed-upon price. This transaction must take place in front of the specialist, and clearly must occur at a price which is at least as favorable to the customers involved as the bid/ask prices quoted by the specialist. It is most likely, however, that the broker will not be able immediately to "cross" his order with that of another broker. Instead of waiting around for another broker to arrive, he can execute the order on the spot with the specialist—as the above example illustrates.

Exchange Automation

As the NYSE has become increasingly automated, as noted above, more of the procedures illustrated in the example are now being conducted by computer and electronic transmission. For example, commission brokers may now place pre-opening market orders of up to 5,099 shares on a computer system that automatically and continuously pairs buy and sell orders and informs the specialist of the imbalance as of the opening of trading on the exchange, so that he can better determine the appropriate opening price. This system is called **Opening Automated Report Service** (OARS).

---

[12]Example patterned after a similar one appearing in *The Wall Street Journal*, September 18, 1973.

A service similar to OARS is provided for post-opening market orders of up to 2,099 shares. This service is called SuperDOT, the last three letters of which stand for **Designated Order Turnaround.** SuperDOT is an electronic order-routing system through which NYSE member firms may bypass the commission broker on the floor and route their orders directly to the specialist. In most cases, the speed with which SuperDOT can transmit orders to the floor is such that most orders can be executed and an execution report issued back to the member firm in just two minutes from the time the order is placed on the system. This reduces the brokerage firm's costs, probably improves service to the customer, and reduces errors over the traditional execution process.

Marketability

As has been discussed, the specialist, while executing transactions, is charged with maintaining a "fair and orderly" market in the securities for which he is responsible. By acting as a dealer standing ready to buy or sell shares for inventory, the specialist is expected to maintain a degree of liquidity, price continuity, and fairness. When there is a temporary imbalance between buy and sell orders, the specialist may be required to buy or sell for his own account in order to reduce the variability of the security's price between successive transactions. Each exchange has rules which govern the specialist's activity in this regard; and, as noted, some exchanges forbid specialists trading for their own account. These issues will be discussed again in the section of this chapter entitled Regulation of Securities Markets.

Settlement

When an order is placed with a brokerage house and is executed on the exchange floor, it must be "settled" within five working days. This means that the investor placing the order must deliver, within this time period, the cash (for a purchase) or security certificates (for a sale) to his broker. Frequently, two brokerage firms—the seller's broker and the buyer's broker—are involved in a transaction. To execute such a transaction, the seller's broker must deliver the securities to the buyer's broker in return for cash payment. All of this must be accomplished within five full business days following the date of trade on the exchange. Currently, much of the process takes place through a clearing mechanism that nets out positions to member firms.

Exceptions to the five-day settlement rule occur when a security is traded on a *when issued* basis. In this case, delivery is due on the date specified by the exchange. This occurs principally with new issues, for which issuance by the company has been fixed at some future date.

Margin Transactions

Securities purchases need not be cash transactions; that is, financing typically is available. The amount of money the purchaser must provide is known as **margin.** Margin is combined with borrowed money to meet the full purchase price of the securities involved in a transaction.

Most common stocks and bonds listed on U.S. exchanges can be purchased on margin. The securities purchased or other securities held by the investor are used as collateral for the loan. In this case the securities must be held in **street name;** that is, they are registered in the name of the brokerage firm acting as custodian for the client. Regulation T of the Federal Reserve Board governs the minimum initial margin requirements. Since January 1974 these requirements have been 50 percent for the purchase of common stocks and convertible bonds, 5 percent of the principal amount for U.S. government securities, and 25 percent of the market value of listed and qualified corporate bonds and other nonequity securities. This means that the customer's initial down payment must equal at least 50 percent of the market value of equity securities purchased.

Many exchanges impose their own requirements for margin in addition to Regulation T's minimum initial margin. For instance, the NYSE requires that to open a margin account with any of its member brokers a person must deposit at least $2,000 (or its equivalent in the market value of securities). The NYSE also sets requirements for the maintenance of customer margin over time. According to the exchange's rules, the amount of a customer's margin may at no time be less than 25 percent of the market value of the securities being used as collateral. Let's see how this works:

An investor purchases $10,000 of common stock, putting up $5,000 of his own money to do so. The initial amount of margin is thus $5,000, or 50 percent of the market value of the stock, in conformance with Regulation T. Later on, however, the market value of the common stock declines to $8,000. The amount of margin (or equity) in the customer's account would now be worth only $3,000, or the $8,000 in market value less the $5,000 in borrowed funds. Margin would now constitute only 37.5 percent of the market value of the stock. If the value of the stock declines below $6,666, the margin would constitute less than 25 percent of that value. At this point, the broker would be required—under NYSE rules—to request that the customer put more cash into the account to restore a 25 percent maintenance margin.

Some brokers require more than the minimum NYSE-imposed 25 percent maintenance margin. Thus a **margin call** to the customer might be initiated when the percentage margin drops to 30 percent, or even 40 percent. Typically, margin calls must be covered by the end of the business day or the securities will be sold, but there is some flexibility in the system as a result of the policy of the customer's brokerage house. On average, during 1985, there was approximately $28.3 billion in margin debt outstanding for margin customers of NYSE member firms.[13]

Foreign Securities and Foreigner's Investments in Listed Securities

As of 1985, there were 168 foreign securities listed on the NYSE stock and bond markets. Thus, it is easy for U.S. investors to hold investments in firms domiciled in other parts of the world. Many of the firms which have their stocks traded on the NYSE, such as British Petroleum, Ltd. of Great Britain and Kyocera Corporation of Japan, have

---

[13]New York Stock Exchange, *1986 Fact Book.*

international operations. They have discovered that U.S. trading of their securities facilitates the tapping of U.S. primary capital markets for needed cash. The foreign securities listed on U.S. securities markets are called **American depository receipts,** or ADRs. Shares of these securities, when bought and sold in U.S. markets, are held by a custodian outside the United States. ADRs are either sponsored or unsponsored. If an ADR is sponsored—as are all the ADRs traded on the NYSE and AMEX—the foreign issuer agrees to comply with all SEC reporting requirements. Unsponsored ADRs, by contrast, are usually issued by banks in response to investor demand, and the bank registers the ADR with the SEC. For this reason, less financial information may be available for an unsponsored ADR.

Foreign investors are also large holders of U.S. securities. In 1985 foreigners participated in transactions in $157 billion of U.S. stocks, with a net capital flow to the United States of $4.9 billion. This market has some obvious importance to the management of the U.S. balance of payments. A sudden reversal one way or the other can significantly increase or decrease the excess supply of dollars in foreign hands.

The Composite Ticker Tape

The stock ticker tape is a familiar feature of brokerage firms' boardrooms throughout the country. Each trading day, a live report of transactions in common stocks which have taken place on the NYSE, AMEX, the regional exchange floors, and in two over-the-counter markets (the latter are NASD and Instinet, which are discussed in a later section of this chapter) is transmitted electronically to brokerage houses. Investors see this for NYSE stocks in the form of a continuous electronic display presented for all to see. On an average day, the composite ticker might show a display like this one:[14]

$$\text{CLX} \quad \text{FQA} \quad \text{T} \quad \text{EK}$$
$$57^7/_8 \quad 50^5/_8 \quad 24\text{s } 25^1/_8 \ 5\text{s}3^3/_8 \quad 58$$

On the top line appear stock symbols, which may consist of one, two, or three letters. The numerals on the bottom line indicate volume and price for each transaction reported. When a transaction involves a single round lot, no volume figure is indicated. When more than one round lot is included in a single trade, the volume is shown as "2s" (for 200 shares), "3s" (for 300 shares), etc., to the left of the price. (The notation "24s" means 2,400 shares, or 24 round lots). When block transactions of 10,000 shares or more are traded, the volume is specified in the actual number of shares traded, such as "25, 800s", which refers to a trade involving 25,800 shares. The following is a translation of the ticker tape shown above:

Name of Stock	Number of Shares	Price
Clorox (CLX)	100	$57^7/_8$
Fuqua Industries (FQA)	100	$50^5/_8$
AT&T (T)	2,400	$25^1/_8$
AT&T (T)	500	$25^3/_8$
Eastman Kodak (EK)	100	58

---

[14]Stocks chosen for the example are from Orline D. Foster, *The Art of Tape Reading: Ticker Technique,* 1965.

Some investors believe that watching the ticker's electronic display as it spews out price and volume figures all day enables them to get a "feel for the market." Indeed, it may be informative to study the pattern of trading that evolves on particular days; for example, when news items are released that have selective impact on particular firms, there may be sudden increases in volume of trading or sharp price moves in the associated stock. Also, some believe that watching the ticker during the first half hour or so of trading after the market opens may reveal the overall "mood" prevailing in the market that day. The real value of such activities will be partially revealed in subsequent discussions in this book.

Block Transactions

The continuous auction market in which the specialist has a dominant role works most effectively when there are a large number of relatively small orders being processed during a short period of time. When this is the case, the specialist is able to "cross" a good many orders with each other and to buy and sell stock out of his own inventory without tying up a great deal of his own capital. Institutional investors, however, frequently trade blocks of several thousand shares of stock at once. This sometimes creates problems for the specialist and the exchange.

Suppose a sell order for 50,000 shares of Colgate Palmolive arrives at the specialist's post. If he is unable to find a buyer for this block of stock, what happens? The specialist might use several million of his own funds to purchase the stock and, until a buyer is found, hold this stock in inventory. But, since specialists are prohibited from soliciting business directly from institutional investors, the Colgate Palmolive specialist would be unable actively to seek out a buyer. Understandably, specialists are reluctant to accept orders involving large blocks.

Commission brokers who accept institutional brokerage accounts solve this problem to a great extent. In order to handle the large orders placed with them by their institutional clients, these brokerage houses maintain direct communication lines with various institutions for the purpose of locating potential buyers or sellers. If, for example, an institutional client wishes to sell 50,000 shares of Colgate Palmolive stock at any price above $42 per share, a wholesale "block house" would attempt to locate a potential buyer of the 50,000 shares. If the house is unable to find a buyer without lowering the price below $42, he will either purchase all or part of the block for the brokerage house's own account or inform the institution that it must accept a lower price for the shares. Usually the brokerage house, which is a member of one or more exchanges, is in frequent contact with its commission brokers on the exchange floor in order to determine whether the specialist unit in that stock may have sellers for the stock or may be willing to purchase a portion directly. Once a buyer, or group of buyers, has been located and the terms of the trade agreed upon, the block is sent to the exchange floor for execution. In such transactions, the specialist plays a relatively minor role. Large-block transactions account for a significant portion of the share volume on an average day.

A computerized system for large-block positioning was introduced in 1969 under the name AutEx. The subscribers to this system include block brokerage houses and institutional investors. AutEx's function is to reduce brokers' expenditure of time in doing telephone canvassing to solicit buying-and-selling interest among its institutional clients. If a large block of stock needs positioning, a broker may key-in an "interest message" on a computer terminal and request that it be directed (through a central computer) to one specific institutional subscriber, to AutEx, to several, or to all institutional subscribers. An institution, seeing the interest message, may then use the system to direct an inquiry to the broker to negotiate terms of the trade. This automated communications system reduces the time and effort necessary to effect institutional-sized transactions.

The Over-the-Counter Market

As we have discussed, the organized securities exchanges have the following basic characteristics:

1. They have centralized trading floors where all orders are processed.
2. They maintain continuous auction markets in corporate securities; i.e., common stocks, bonds, options, and warrants.
3. They limit trading privileges to exchange members.
4. They impose stringent requirements for an exchange listing.

The exchange markets are thus limited-access, institutionalized auction markets where a restricted set of corporate securities are bought and sold.

In contrast to the structured, well-organized securities exchanges, the over-the-counter market seems, at first inspection, disorganized and chaotic. For example:

1. It is decentralized and widely dispersed geographically.
2. It uses negotiated rather than auction markets.
3. It permits trading by brokerage firms meeting minimal requirements.
4. It conducts trading in virtually any security registered for public trading.

Negotiated Markets

In a negotiated market, buying and selling transactions are accomplished through dealers. The number of dealers making a market in a particular issue varies, depending on the size and popularity of the issue. Each dealer maintains an inventory of that security, purchasing from prospective sellers at a bid price while selling to buyers at a higher ask price. Profit for the dealer derives from the spread, or difference, in these prices.

A person who wishes to buy or sell in the negotiated market usually approaches a broker who acts as agent in locating the dealer who offers the best price. Usually some "shopping" must be done to accomplish this, since there may be variations in the bid-ask quotes of different dealers. For their services in finding the most favorable dealer price, the broker is usually paid a commission by the buyer or seller.

It is also obvious from this discussion that a negotiated market need not have a centralized location or trading floor where all orders are processed. Dealers can be geographically disperse and, as long as there is rapid communication between buyers and sellers and their brokers and between brokers and the various dealers, this market can operate just as effectively as a continuous auction market.

Securities Traded in the OTC Market

All publicly held securities which are not listed on the organized securities exchanges are traded in the OTC market. The types of securities which can be traded over the counter include common and preferred stocks, corporate bonds, U.S. government securities, municipal bonds, options and warrants, and foreign securities. There are a variety of reasons why some securities are not listed on the organized exchanges. Some are securities issued by smaller companies or companies with limited geographical appeal which cannot meet the exchanges' listing requirements. And, many of these securities are **unseasoned issues.** These are securities which have been traded in the secondary markets for only a short time, and, thus, investors are not as aware of their general characteristics. Usually issued by firms that have never before publicly issued securities and have not yet had sufficient time to qualify for exchange listings, unseasoned new issues typically must be traded in the OTC market.

In other cases, securities traded in the OTC market have been issued by firms qualified for, but resistant to, exchange listing. It is estimated that there are about 600 OTC-traded companies which are eligible for NYSE listing, and another 1,600 eligible for AMEX listing, that remain traded in the OTC market. Sometimes this is because the managements of those companies prefer the negotiated market, with its multiple market makers, to the specialist-type auction market offered by the organized exchanges. In other cases, companies may wish to avoid the financial disclosure and reporting requirements imposed by the exchanges. Until about 1964, most banks and insurance companies chose to have their securities traded OTC, primarily to avoid the disclosure requirements of the exchanges. Even today many large financial institutions are not listed on exchanges. Finally, some exchange-qualified companies which have issued multiple classes of common stock chose, until recently, to be traded in the OTC market due to the NYSE's previous rule that it would not list more than one class of common for a given company.

All government-issued securities are traded over the counter, and still other securities are traded both on exchanges and OTC.

Brokers and Dealers

Each broker and dealer registered with the SEC to make markets in OTC securities may act as a broker in many security issues, a dealer in one or more securities, and as both a broker and a dealer in some of those issues. An OTC broker may also be a member of one or more exchanges; OTC brokers and dealers and the brokerage houses discussed earlier are generally the same group of people.

A dealer in a particular security issue must maintain firm bid and offering prices and must stand ready to buy or sell (for his own account) a given number of units at quoted prices. Usually, the minimum quantity for which a given bid or ask quote is assumed to be valid is based on the security's normal trading unit. For stocks, this is 100 shares, and for bonds it is equivalent to five $1,000-par bonds. For some very actively traded issues, one or two dozen dealers may aggressively compete with one another, whereas for securities which are inactively and erratically traded, only one or two dealers may exist.

Dealer bid-ask quotes are viewed as wholesale, or interdealer, prices. When, however, an OTC broker or dealer receives a customer order for a security in which it does not normally maintain a market, the customer will pay a retail price, which includes a markup over the wholesale price. To accomplish the transaction, the broker normally consults a NASDAQ (which stands for "National Association of Securities Dealers Automatic Quotation") computer terminal. NASDAQ lists, at any point in time, all the dealers who make markets in particular stocks and their respective bid-ask quotes. The next step involves contacting the dealer listed by NASDAQ as offering the best quote for the transaction. The customer who placed the order then pays the wholesale price quoted by the dealer plus the retail commission to the broker.

Obviously, when an OTC broker receives an order for a security in which a market is maintained, the firm may act as both broker and dealer in executing the trade. However, this does not eliminate the obligation to obtain the best price for the customer.

There are two principal OTC markets in the United States. We have already mentioned one: the NASDAQ system, which was developed and is maintained by the National Association of Securities Dealers. The other is called Instinet, which is a computerized trading mechanism in which institutional investors may interact directly with one another. NASDAQ is by far the more economically important of the two OTC markets, and it accounted for 16 percent of the dollar volume of all stock trading in the United States in 1985.[15] Because of its importance, our discussion focuses on the NASDAQ system.

NASDAQ and Price Quotations

Prior to 1971, all OTC quotations were published on "pink sheets" that were compiled daily by the National Quotation Bureau in a laborious, manual process which was instituted in 1911 and had remained largely unchanged through the years. OTC brokers and dealers subscribed to this system as the only central means of communication concerning which stocks were being traded at what prices and by which dealers.

In 1971 the National Association of Securities Dealers (NASD)—an association of OTC brokers and dealers—began providing automated quotations through its NASDAQ system. This system electronically displays bid and ask quotations to the brokers and dealers who operate in this market. As of the close of 1985, there were 500 registered market makers in the NASDAQ market, taking positions in almost 4,784 NASDAQ securities.[16]

In 1982 the NASD introduced the NASDAQ National Market System (NMS), which by 1986 included approximately 2,700 of the companies listed by NASDAQ. The NMS is a major effort to provide the OTC market with trading characteristics of liquidity and operating efficiency that many thought were only achievable in a centralized exchange, like the NYSE. This attempt is concentrated in two areas. The first is to provide comprehensive, continuous information on market bid-ask prices quoted by member firms standing ready to buy and sell securities in which they make a market. The second is to provide current transactions information electronically on OTC-traded common stocks similar to that provided by the ticker tape on the organized securities exchanges. Prior

---

[15]NASDAQ, *1986 Fact Book.*
[16]Ibid.

to the advent of NMS, NASDAQ only provided representative dealers' bid and ask quotations for all of the companies it lists. For those companies included in NMS, summaries of daily trading volume and high, low, and closing transactions prices are available, both during the trading day and at its close.

The Securities and Exchange Commission has mandated that the NMS include all OTC-traded stocks whose issuing company has tangible assets of $2 million or more, stockholder's equity (book value) of $1 million or more, at least 500,000 shares held publicly by at least 300 shareholders and which are worth at least $5 million in market value, a share price of $10 or more, an average of 600,000 shares traded over a six-month period, and at least four market makers. Additionally, NMS may encompass a number of voluntary inclusions, which the SEC allows to meet somewhat lower requirements.

Today, whether or not an OTC stock is part of the NMS or not, each of the nearly 5,000 securities included in the NASDAQ system and the more than 400 market makers operating in the OTC market are included in NASDAQ's Consolidated Quotations Service (CQS).

Trading on the NASDAQ system is heavy. NASDAQ boasts a dollar trading volume level which makes it the third largest secondary securities market in the world, after the NYSE and the Tokyo Stock Exchange. In 1985, securities worth $230 billion were traded through NASDAQ.

The Small Order Execution System (SOES) is a NASD innovation that provides a means for small transactions in NASDAQ securities to be automatically executed at the best available price via NASD computers. The system further reduces the cost of trading in small lots of 500 shares or less by reducing the necessary "shopping," thus significantly improving the efficiency of the trading process for small investors. NASDAQ also has developed an agreement with the London Stock Exchange (the fourth largest stock exchange in the world) to share quotations in 600 "world class" stocks. The step seems to enhance the integration of secondary security markets.

Consolidated Quotations

As noted earlier, some companies which are listed on the NYSE are also traded on other exchanges and/or in the OTC market, though they are not quoted and traded through NASDAQ. In 1977 the Consolidated Quotation Service (CQS) of the NASD was instituted for the purpose of providing online bid and ask quotes for NYSE stocks which are traded in more than one of these markets. Without such a system, a broker who wishes to have an order for an NYSE-listed stock executed has to shop—usually by telephone—for the best price. By consolidating the bid and ask quotes of all specialists on all exchanges, as well as those of OTC dealers, the ITS (Intermarket Trading System) rules referred to earlier can be enforced and competition among markets promoted. It is worth emphasizing, however, that currently no NASDAQ listed stocks are traded on *any* of the organized exchanges, so competition in these securities is limited to that within the OTC market.

NASDAQ Listing Requirements

NASDAQ, like the organized securities exchanges, also has listing requirements. For initial NASDAQ inclusion, domestic common stocks must be issued by companies with a minimum book value of $2 million in assets and $1 million in stockholder's equity, there must be 100,000 shares publicly held by at least 300 stockholders, and at least two dealers making a market in the shares. To maintain its NASDAQ status, a company must have at least $750,000 in the book value of total assets, at least $375,000 in stockholder's equity, must maintain the initial inclusion standards for shares publicly held and the number of stockholders, and must keep at least one market maker. Securities other than domestic common stocks have different listing requirements.[17]

Some foreign common stocks, in the form of American Depository Receipts (ADRs), and other foreign securities are listed on NASDAQ. As of the end of 1985, about 300 ADRs and 216 foreign securities were traded in the NASDAQ market. The top volume leaders in this market included such well-known international companies as Glaxo Holdings of Great Britain, Fuji Photo Film of Japan, and De Beers Consolidated Mines of South Africa.

Regulation of Securities Markets

Over the years, a number of federal laws have been enacted to protect the public interest where the operations of the nation's securities markets are concerned. These laws collectively deal with virtually every aspect of both the primary and secondary markets, from the registration of new securities issues to the regulation of broker-dealers and organized securities exchanges. While it is impossible to list all of the various laws that pertain to the operation of the securities markets, we do discuss the more important ones.

Securities Act of 1933

The Securities Act of 1933 provides for the registration of securities issued for the first time on primary security markets and for full disclosure of relevant information concerning such issues to prospective purchasers.

Under the provisions of the 1933 Act, any nonexempt new security which is sold publicly through the mails or in interstate commerce must be accompanied by a prospectus which contains information concerning the financial status of the issuer. Only a few security issues are exempt from these provisions: securities issued by the U.S. government and its agencies, securities of state and local governments, and securities for which the aggregate amount of the public offering is less than $500,000 (termed a Regulation A offering). Although the government, in requiring registration of new issues, makes no attempt to assess their merits, it will nevertheless refuse to allow public sale of securities when information in the prospectus is found to be misleading, incorrect, or incomplete.

Securities Exchange Act of 1934

The Securities Exchange Act of 1934 provides for regulation of the primary and secondary markets, predominantly through registration of exchanges and broker-dealers.

The 1934 Act established the Securities and Exchange Commission (SEC) as an independent agency of the federal government and authorized it to oversee the registration of security issues and the disclosure of information pursuant to the 1933 Act. The 1934

---

[17]Ibid.

legislation also authorized the SEC to require periodic disclosure of financial information from companies whose shares may be listed on an organized exchange or whose total shares are broadly traded in over-the-counter markets. It also empowered the agency to regulate trading in the firm's securities by the firm's directors or employees (insiders), to register and regulate organized securities exchanges, to oversee all secondary market trading in both the OTC and the exchange markets, and to register and regulate broker-dealers. In short, the 1934 act endowed the newly created SEC with broad regulatory powers over the securities industry. This act provides the basis for the current spate of lawsuits relating to insider trading in securities and misrepresentation in the information given to security owners.

Securities Investor Protection Act of 1970

A third and more recent piece of legislation was the Securities Investor Protection Act of 1970. It established the Securities Investor Protection Corporation (SIPC) to protect individual investors from financial losses as a result of brokerage-house failures. SIPC provides roughly the same service for stock and bond investors as does the FDIC for bank depositors. Currently, the limits of protection are $500,000 per customer, except that claims for cash are limited to $100,000 per customer.[18]

All persons who are now registered as brokers or dealers under the Securities Exchange Act of 1934, and all persons who are members of organized stock exchanges in the United States are also members of SIPC. As of December 1985, total membership stood at 11,004. SIPC charges each of its 11,000 members a $100 uniform annual assessment. SIPC may also borrow from commercial banks, if needed, to meet disbursements. The SIPC fund, consisting of the aggregate of cash and investments in U.S. government securities, amounted to $327 million on December 31, 1985.

Protection provided by the SIPC ensures that the investor *will receive* the securities held by the troubled brokerage firm (although SIPC does not guarantee *when*). Also, SIPC does not ensure the market value of the securities. Since 1970, SIPC has undertaken 189 customer protection proceedings against member firms, of which 130 had been completed as of year end 1985. During this period, SIPC satisfied more than 200,000 claims requiring disbursements from the SIPC fund.

Securities Act Amendments of 1975

By far the most significant and sweeping piece of federal legislation to appear in recent years was the Securities Act Amendments of 1975. It provided the impetus for a fundamental reform of the economic and regulatory structure of the securities markets. It specifically expanded the power and authority of the SEC to develop a truly nationwide market system which would replace the then existing fragmented markets and offer a more vigorous, efficient, and competitive mechanism for trading securities.

---

[18]*Annual Report* [1985] Securities Investor Protection Corporation.

A nationwide market system or, even better, an international market system is desirable because it provides assurances that:

1. Economically efficient mechanisms for executing securities transactions exist.
2. Information is freely available with respect to quotations for, and transactions in, individual securities.
3. There is fair competition among brokers and dealers and among the various exchanges and the OTC markets.
4. The execution of a customer's order takes place at the most favorable price available at the time the order is placed.

Unfortunately, the existing market structure does not yet provide for all these features. For instance, it is not always possible to guarantee that any given customer order is executed at the best price available, due to the fragmentation of trading between the organized exchanges and other markets. A closely related difficulty is that there is, as yet, no completely comprehensive, consolidated quotation system that provides up-to-the-minute information on bid and ask prices, though great strides toward the development of such a system have been made in recent years. Another problem with the existing market system relates to the role of the specialist in an auction market. As we discussed, the specialist is supposed to maintain liquidity, price continuity, and fairness. The specialist assumes an immense responsibility to fulfill these roles adequately. First, to step in and act as a dealer when required frequently requires more capital than is currently available. Second, the specialist's behavior and motives must be beyond reproach. There is a conflict of interest present whenever the specialist acts as both a dealer for his own account and as an agent. It is not unheard of for specialists to neglect their duties to the public in order to profit from their own trading opportunities. Further, because they alone have access to the book of limit orders, specialists are in a position to take advantage of unique knowledge of supply and demand. Thus, in investigations conducted by the Senate Committee on Banking, Housing and Urban Affairs prior to the enactment of the 1975 law, it was found that "a single specialist, regardless of the regulation to which he is subject, often is unable to provide adequate liquidity and continuity to the market for a security." The existing illiquidity in the system became apparent on October 19, 1987, when the "Black Monday crash" involving equities worldwide led to a one day 22 percent fall in value (a loss of about $.5 trillion to investors in NYSE securities alone). A major contributing factor in the decline was the inability or unwillingness of specialists and other market makers to maintain markets in securities in the face of a sudden increase in supply.

One of the purposes underlying the nationwide market trading system outlined in the Securities Act Amendments of 1975 is to enhance the competitive structure of the securities markets by specifying that many specialists or other dealers should make simultaneous markets in given securities. This should, in theory, create free market incentives to increase efficiency, liquidity, and fairness. To the extent that one specialist did not offer these services, the customer would have the opportunity to go elsewhere. Such a system would require a composite limit-order book to which all market makers would have access, so that buy and sell orders would be protected as to price priority.

Other provisions of the 1975 act set uniform trading rules and procedures for all market makers. Similarly, it fostered the implementation of a composite transactions tape and a composite quotation system, broadened the SEC's regulatory powers, moved toward elimination of the stock certificate, and established regulations governing the operation of brokers, dealers, and banks trading in municipal securities. It seems certain that the 1975 act fostered an environment that has allowed NASDAQ to compete effectively with the exchanges, providing better, lower cost service to all investors.

Market Indicators

Stock market indicators are useful gauges of the extent to which political, business, and economic events affect the prices of common stocks on average. Watching these indicators over a period of time provides investors with a summary measure of the manner in which the investment community interprets major news events (e.g., outbreak of war in the Mideast, an increase in the Federal Reserve discount rate, or a Presidential election) and draws implications affecting the investment outlook.

When it comes to the measurement of the general level of stock prices, there are two major types of indicators: averages and true indexes. The first type, typified by the Dow Jones Averages, is computed by summing individual stock prices and then dividing the result by a particular number. In the truest sense of the word, the end product is an "average" price level. Indexes, on the other hand, are based on more sophisticated statistical measures. Their purpose is to establish the current level of stock prices relative to the level which prevailed during a particular "base period." Examples of true indexes include the NYSE Composite Stock Index, the Standard & Poor's 500 Composite Stock Index, the Wilshire 5000 Index, and NASDAQ's OTC Composite Index.

Dow Jones Averages

The Dow Jones Industrial Average (DJIA), which is the best-known and most widely quoted stock market average in existence, has a long history. It was first computed on May 26, 1896, well before any other market indicators were introduced. Although it was originally computed as the average of the prices of 20 common stocks, in 1928 the number of component stocks was increased to 30. The 30 stocks which now make up the DJIA are the shares of giant, "blue-chip" corporations.

As a stock-price average, the Dow Jones Industrials is denominated in dollars per share. The manner in which it is computed is as follows: The share prices of the 30 stocks constituting the average are totaled and divided by a number which varies over time. Originally, when the index was started with 20 stocks, the divisor was set at 20. When this was the case, the average simply relfected the mean price per share of those 20 stocks. Over time, however, various changes necessitated alterations in the divisor. Some stocks were deleted from the DJIA and others added, due to mergers, acquisitions, bankruptcies, and other events. Other stocks experienced splits. To avoid having these nonmarket events affect the level of the average, the divisor was adjusted. That practice continues today, with the divisor being adjusted each time one of these events occurs. Currently, the divisor (as of December 1986) stands at 0.889.

Dow Jones & Company computes and publishes three other stock price averages: the Transportation Average, consisting of 20 stocks drawn from the airline, trucking, and railroad industries; the Public Utility Average, consisting of 15 electric and natural gas utilities; and a 65-Stock Composite Average which combines all stocks into one average.

FIGURE 4–4

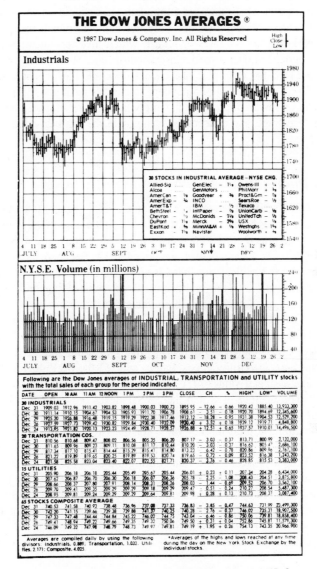

Figure 4-4 shows information about the DJIA as it appears daily in *The Wall Street Journal.* As the figure shows, high, low, and closing figures are charted for each day during the previous five months. The 30 securities currently in the average are given as well. Also given are hourly, high, low and close figures for each of the four averages during the previous four days. The current values of the divisor for each index are supplied in a footnote.

Each of the three stock averages is computed in the same fashion and, because of the manner in which they are computed, each should be very carefully interpreted. Changes in these averages over time are not numbers which measure representative changes in market value (or rates of return) which investors in the component stocks would have experienced over a particular period of time. When the level of the DJIA goes from 2000 to 2100, for example, one cannot conclude that the percentage change in the average market values of the component stocks has been about 5 percent. As long as the divisor changes over time, there is simply no fixed relationship between percentage changes in the average and percentage changes in the market value of the stocks making up the average.

Standard & Poor's Indexes

One of the shortcomings of a stock-price average is that components with the highest share prices have the greatest influence on the level of the composite average. For instance, a stock priced at $100 per share would have considerably more effect on the level of the Dow Jones Averages than one priced at $25 per share even if the issuing companies were otherwise identical. An index is an attempt to overcome this problem by weighting prices in proportion to the number of shares outstanding and measuring changes over time relative to an unchanging base value.

The Standard & Poor's Indexes are weighted, true indexes. There are five such indexes: (1) the S&P 500 Stock Index (also called the Composite Index), (2) the S&P 400 Stock Index (also called the Industrials Index), (3) the S&P 20 Transportation Stock Index, (4) the S&P 40 Utility Stock Index, and (5) the S&P 40 Financial Stock Index. All have been assigned values of 10 for the base period 1941–43.

The manner in which the S&P Indexes are computed is as follows: The share price of each stock in the index is multiplied by the number of shares outstanding, thereby obtaining a total market value for that stock issue. The aggregate market value of the index is then computed by summing these individual market values. The result is divided by the average market value during the base period of 1941–43 and then multiplied by the base value of 10. Use of this procedure avoids having to make adjustments for stock splits, since splits simultaneously increase the number of shares outstanding and decrease share values in the same proportion, leaving the index unchanged. Some adjustments are necessary, however, for mergers and substitutions in the list of shares making up the index.

NYSE Composite Index

In 1966 the NYSE began publishing a composite index of all common stocks listed on the exchange. Like the S&P indexes, this is a proper index, and provides a value-weighted measure of stock price levels relative to those prevailing in a base period. A procedure analogous to that for the S&P indexes is followed in calculating the NYSE Composite Index, except that the base date is taken as December 31, 1965, on which the base value was set at 50. (On that date, the weighted average price of a share on the NYSE was about $50.)

Movements in the NYSE Composite Index give a different picture of average price changes in the index than do either the Dow Jones Industrials Average or the S&P Composite Index. Since all stocks listed on the exchange are included, this index is theoretically more representative than the other two. And, since the stocks are included in proportion to their aggregate market values, those issues properly having the most influence on market movements are those of the firms with the largest capitalization.

The NYSE also publishes group indexes for industrials, utilities, transportation, and financial stocks. These are computed in the same way as the Composite Index, although for a smaller number of issues.

The American Stock Exchange Market Value Index is computed in roughly the same manner as the NYSE Index. Its base value has been set at 50, which is based on the close of trading on August 31, 1973, when that index was introduced.

NASDAQ OTC Index

The OTC Index supplied to NASDAQ subscribers has become increasingly important in recent years, due to the burgeoning interest in OTC trading. This measure is a composite index of all domestic common stocks listed by the NASDAQ system. Also available through NASDAQ are specialized group indexes for industrials, banks, insurance, transportation, utilities, and miscellaneous financial firms. They are updated at five-minute intervals throughout the day and are reported as of the end of each trading day in newspapers throughout the country.

Wilshire 5000 Equity Index

In recent years, as the nationwide market system has evolved there has been an increasing need for a truly nationwide market index which reflects overall market performance across the organized exchanges and the OTC markets. The Wilshire 5000, first introduced in 1974, meets this need.

The Wilshire 5000 Equity Index is a market-value-weighted index of about 6,000 of the largest U.S. common stocks, ranked in terms of the market value of the equity capitalization of the issuing firms. Currently, the capitalization of the index is about 86 percent NYSE-listed stocks, 3 percent AMEX stocks, and 11 percent OTC stocks.

The Wilshire Index is calculated in much the same way as the S&P 500 and the NYSE Composite Indexes. Its base value was at 1404.595 on December 31, 1980. As of January 30, 1987, the value was 2742.996, representing a 95 percent increase in the value of the stocks represented during the six-year period. This reflects *only* capital gains. Additionally, a Total Performance Index is calculated by Wilshire Associates that reflects the reinvestment of all cash dividends on the stocks included in the index at the end of each month. Thus, on December 31, 1980, the value of the Total Performance Index stood at 2.53589, while on January 30, 1987, it stood at 6.39986. This reflects a 152 percent increase in wealth, including dividends.

Figure 4–5 displays the information *The Wall Street Journal* provides daily on the S&P indexes, the NYSE Composite Indexes, the various NASDAQ indexes, and others.

FIGURE 4–5 Major Stock Market Index Information

STOCK MARKET DATA BANK							Dec. 31, 1986	
Major Indexes								
HIGH	LOW (12 MOS)		CLOSE	NET CH	% CH	12 MO CH	%	FROM 12/31 %
DOW JONES AVERAGES								
1955.57	1502.29	30 Industrials	1895.95	− 12.66	− 0.66	Closed	......	+ 349.28 + 22.58
866.74	686.97	20 Transportation	807.17	− 3.03	− 0.37	Closed	......	+ 98.96 + 13.97
219.15	169.47	15 Utilities	206.01	+ 0.23	+ 0.11	Closed	......	+ 31.20 + 17.85
767.89	602.83	65 Composite	736.83	− 3.45	− 0.47	Closed	......	+ 120.30 + 19.51
NEW YORK STOCK EXCHANGE								
145.75	117.75	Composite	138.58	− 0.54	− 0.39	Closed	......	+ 17.00 + 13.98
167.70	134.22	Industrials	160.11	− 0.70	− 0.44	Closed	......	+ 20.84 + 14.96
80.85	61.35	Utilities	73.77	− 0.26	− 0.35	Closed	......	+ 10.54 + 16.74
132.54	105.58	Transportation	117.65	− 0.03	− 0.03	Closed	......	+ 3.68 + 3.23
159.45	129.78	Finance	140.05	− 0.28	− 0.20	Closed	......	+ 8.76 + 6.67
STANDARD & POOR'S INDEXES								
254.00	203.49	500 Index	242.17	− 1.20	− 0.49	Closed	......	+ 30.89 + 14.62
282.77	224.88	400 Industrials	269.93	− 1.38	− 0.51	Closed	......	+ 35.37 + 15.08
217.28	176.16	20 Transportation	197.27	− 0.12	− 0.06	Closed	......	+ 8.55 + 4.53
123.74	90.33	40 Utilities	112.29	− 0.47	− 0.42	Closed	......	+ 19.12 + 20.52
31.13	25.19	40 Financials	26.92	− 0.17	− 0.63	Closed	......	+ 11.20 + 43.55
NASDAQ								
411.16	323.01	OTC Composite	348.83	+ 1.51	+ 0.43	Closed	......	+ 23.90 + 7.36
414.15	326.56	Industrials	349.33	+ 1.75	+ 0.50	Closed	......	+ 19.16 + 5.80
467.05	381.59	Insurance	404.14	+ 4.91	+ 1.23	Closed	......	+ 22.07 + 5.78
457.59	349.08	Banks	412.53	+ 0.68	+ 0.17	Closed	......	+ 63.17 + 18.08
174.84	137.20	Nat. Mkt. Comp.	149.04	+ 0.57	+ 0.38	Closed	......	+ 10.78 + 7.80
155.55	122.51	Nat. Mkt. Indus.	132.57	+ 0.57	+ 0.43	Closed	......	+ 8.44 + 6.80
OTHERS								
285.19	241.81	AMEX	263.27	+ 1.73	+ 0.66	Closed	......	+ 17.14 + 6.96
1425.9	1094.3	Fin. Times Indus.	1313.9	+ 5.3	+ 0.41	Closed	......	+ 182.5 + 16.13
18936.24	12881.50	Nikkei Stock Avg.	Closed	......		......	......	......
246.80	210.84	Value-Line	225.62	− 0.17	+ 0.08	Closed	......	+ 10.76 + 5.01
2598.03	2115.49	Wilshire 5000	2434.94	− 6.36	− 0.26	Closed	......	+ 270.25 + 12.48

Source: Reprinted from *The Wall Street Journal*, January 2, 1987. © Dow Jones & Company, Inc., 1987. ALL RIGHTS RESERVED.

Summary

This chapter has discussed the operation of the securities markets, with emphasis on secondary markets like the New York Stock Exchange, American Stock Exchange, various foreign and regional exchanges, and the over-the-counter market. On organized exchanges, trading is conducted on a continuous auction basis most often by specialists who act as agents in executing public orders and as dealers who trade for their own accounts. Orders are placed with brokers who own memberships on the exchange. They may be full-service brokers, who provide investment advice and other services in addition to order execution, or discount brokers, who generally provide only the latter. The ticker tape provides an automated, up-to-the-minute record of transactions that take place each day in securities listed on one or more exchanges. Each exchange has listing requirements for the securities it authorizes for trading; usually these requirements are related to factors that render a security of interest to a broad cross section of investors.

The over-the-counter market, in contrast to the exchanges, is not organized on an auction basis and does not offer a centralized location for trading. Rather, it is a loose network of broker-dealers interconnected by a communications network. Securities traded in the OTC market include common and preferred stocks; corporate bonds; the securities of federal, state, and local governments; options and warrants; and foreign securities. In 1971, the National Association of Securities Dealers began providing automated quotations on OTC stocks through its NASDAQ system. Today, NASDAQ provides current dealer quotes on over 4,000 securities. NASDAQ has its own listing requirements, not unlike those of the exchanges, but they are considerably less restrictive.

A number of federal laws regulate the operation of the securities markets. Among the more significant are the Securities Act of 1933 and the Securities Exchange Act of 1934. These laws provide for the registration of new security issues, for disclosure of relevant information concerning such issues, and for the establishment of the Securities and Exchange Commission to oversee the securities industry and to regulate the organized securities exchanges and broker-dealers. A third law, the Securities Investor Protection Act of 1970, established the Securities Investor Protection Corporation (SIPC) for the purpose of insuring individual security accounts on deposit with brokers. Perhaps the most sweeping legislation is that provided in the Securities Act Amendments of 1975, which call for a number of reforms of the economic and regulatory structure of the securities markets in order to develop a competitive national market system.

Several stock market indicators are regularly published in the newspaper. These aid the investor in gauging the extent to which political, business, and economic events affect the prices of common stocks in general. These indicators are of two types (*a*) averages, such as the Dow Jones Industrial Averages and (*b*) true indexes, such as the Standard & Poor's 500 Stock Index or the New York Stock Exchange Composite Index.

References

Annual Report, National Association of Security Dealers, published annually.

Annual Report, The New York Stock Exchange, published annually.

Barnea, Amir. [1974] "Performance Evaluation of New York Stock Exchange Specialists." *Journal of Financial and Quantitative Analysis.* (September).

Barnea, Amir, and Logue, Dennis. [1975] "The Effect of Risk on the Market Maker's Spread." *Financial Analysts Journal* (November–December).

Beatty, Randolph O., and Ritter, Jay R. [1986] "Investment Banking, Reputation, and the Underpricing of Initial Public Offerings." *Journal of Financial Economics* (February).

Benston, George. [1973] "Required Disclosure and the Stock Market: An Evaluation of the Securities Exchange Act of 1934." *American Economic Review* (March).

Benston, George, and Hagerman, Robert. [1974] "Determinants of Bid-Ask Spreads in the Over-the-Counter Market." *Journal of Financial Economics* (December).

Black, Fischer. [1971] "Toward a Fully Automated Exchange." *Financial Analysts Journal* (July–August) and (November–December).

Bloch, Ernest, and Sametz, Arnold. [1977] *A Modest Proposal for a National Securities Market System and Its Governance.* New York: New York University.

Building A Better Future: Economic Choices for the 1980s. The New York Stock Exchange.

Carey, Kenneth. [1977] "Nonrandom Price Changes in Association with Trading in Large Blocks: Evidence of Market Efficiency in Behavior of Investor Returns." *Journal of Business* (October), pp. 407–14.

Cohen, Kalman; Maier, Steven; Ness, Walter; Okuda, Hitoshi; Schwartz, Robert; and Whitcomb, David. [1977] "The Impact of Designated Market Makers on Security Prices." *Journal of Banking and Finance* (November).

Cohen, Kalman; Maier, Steven; Schwartz, Robert; and Whitcomb, David. [1978] "Limit Orders, Market Structure, and the Return Generation Process." *Journal of Finance* (June).

Cohen, Kalman; Maier, Steven; Schwartz, Robert; and Whitcomb, David. [1979] "Market Makers and the Market Spread: A Review of Recent Literature." *Journal of Financial and Quantitative Analysis* (November).

Cohen, Kalman; Maier, Steven; Schwartz, Robert; and Whitcomb, David. [1978a] "The Returns Generation Process, Returns Variance, and the Effect of Thinness in Securities Markets." *Journal of Finance* (March).

Cohen, Kalman; Maier, Steven; Schwartz, Robert; and Whitcomb, David. [1981] "Transaction Costs, Order Placement Strategy, and Existence of the Bid-Ask Spread," *Journal of Political Economy* (April).

Cuneo, Larry, and Wagner, Wayne. [1975] "Reducing the Cost of Stock Trading." *Financial Analysis Journal* (November–December).

Garbade, Kenneth. [1978a] "Electronic Quotation Systems and the Market for Government Securities." Federal Reserve Bank of New York *Quarterly Review* 3 (Summer).

Garbade, Kenneth, and Silber, William. [1978] "Technology, Communication and the Performance of Financial Markets: 1840–1975." *Journal of Finance* (June).

Glosten, Lawrence R., and Milgrom, Paul R. [1985] "Bid, Ask and Transaction Prices in a Specialist Market with Heterogeneously Informed Traders." *Journal of Financial Economics* (March).

Hakansson, Nils H.; Beja, Avraham; and Kale, Jivendra. [1985] "On the Feasibility of Automated Market Making by a Programmed Specialist." *Journal of Finance* (March).

Hamilton, James. [1978] "Marketplace Organization and Marketability: NASDAQ, the Stock Exchange, and the National Market System." *Journal of Finance* (May).

Handbook of Securities of the United States Government and Federal Agencies. Boston: First Boston Corp., published annually.

Ho, Thomas S. Y., and Stoll, Hans R. [1983] "The Dynamics of Dealer Market under Competition." *Journal of Finance* (September).

Kraus, Alan, and Stoll, Hans. [1972] "Price Impacts of Block Trading on the New York Stock Exchange." *Journal of Finance* (July).

McCurdy, Christopher. [1977–78] "The Dealer Market for United States Government Securities." Federal Reserve Bank of New York *Quarterly Review* 2 (Winter).

Rock, Kevin. [1986] "Why New Issues Are Underpriced." *Journal of Financial Economics* (February).

Roscow, James P. [1986] "Three Wise Men." *O-T-C Review* (March).

Sanger, Gary C., and McConnell, John J. [1986] "Stock Exchange Listings, Firm Value and Security Market Efficiency: The Impact of NASDAQ." *Journal of Financial and Quantitative Analysis* (March).

Santomero, Anthony. [1974] "The Economic Effects of NASDAQ: Some Preliminary Results." *Journal of Financial and Quantitative Analysis* (January).

Smith, Clifford W., Jr. [1986] "Investment Banking and the Capital Acquisition Process." *Journal of Financial Economics* (February).

Stigler, George. [1964] "Public Regulation of the Securities Markets." *Journal of Business* (April).

Stoll, Hans. [1976] "Dealer Inventory Behavior: An Empirical Investigation of NASDAQ Stocks." *Journal of Financial and Quantitative Analysis* (September).

Stoll, Hans. [1978] "The Supply of Dealer Services in Securities Markets." *Journal of Finance* (September).

Tinic, Seha, and West, Richard. [1972] "Competition and the Pricing of Dealer Service in the Over-the-Counter Stock Market." *Journal of Financial and Quantitative Analysis* (June).

Tinic, Seha, and West, Richard. [1974] "Marketability of Common Stocks in Canada and the U.S.A.: A Comparison of Agent versus Dealer Dominated Markets." *Journal of Finance* (June).

U.S. Securities and Exchange Commission. [1978] "Staff Report on the Securities Industry in 1977." *Directorate of Economic and Policy Research* (May).

West, Richard. [1971] "Institutional Trading and the Changing Stock Market." *Financial Analysts Journal* (May–June).

Wolfson, Nicholas, and Russo, Thomas. [1970] "The Stock Exchange Specialist: An Economic and Legal Analysis," *Duke Law Journal*.

Questions and Problems

1. Define the difference between primary securities markets and secondary markets. List all the transactions you think would constitute primary market transactions.

2. Define the difference between money markets and other types of securities markets. What is the major characteristic of money market instruments?

3. In your opinion, why has the New York Stock Exchange grown to be a dominant force in the secondary market for common stocks? Why **not** in the secondary market for corporate bonds?

4. What are the potential costs associated with a **market order** used to purchase or sell securities on the New York Stock Exchange? Of a **limit order** to buy or sell these same securities?

5. What checks and balances are used by the New York Stock Exchange to help ensure that the investor can buy at the lowest available price or sell at the highest available price?

6. Why do the NYSE and AMEX have minimum listing requirements? Why would firms that qualify for listing be willing to pay a listing fee and be subject to the exchange's disclosure requirements?

7. What is the purpose behind a "short" sale of a security? Define the margin required for a short sale. Who receives and can use these funds until the short sale is covered? Why do brokerage houses consider short sales to be a particularly profitable transaction?

8. A Dutch auction starts from a very high price which drops until someone purchases the good or service. It is similar to a sealed-bid auction. An English auction is one where bidders start from a low value and work the price higher until no higher bids are forthcoming. The specialist system of the floor of the New York Stock Exchange is a double auction that is more or less continuously made during the exchange's open hours. Would it make any difference what type of auction process was used for transacting in securities on the floor of an exchange? That is, do you believe that investors might be better off

or worse off as a result of some form of Dutch or English auction as opposed to the currently used double auction? In which type of auction would one be most dependent upon the characteristics and abilities of the auctioneer?

9. How are odd-lot orders currently handled on the floor of the NYSE?

10. Currently, the margin requirement is 50 percent. With $10,000 to invest, how large a portfolio can be constructed if all of the margin available is used by the investor? How far would the stock be allowed to drop in value before the brokerage house would be required to place a margin call on the account?

11. Describe the function of the specialist on the floor of the New York Stock Exchange. What are the objectives of the specialist system and what kinds of problems can occur in such a system?

12. What kinds of protection exist to ensure that the specialist does an adequate job of market making? In particular, how might the ability of the specialist to trade into and out of his inventory of shares affect the prices at which transactions are made?

13. What is the composite ticker tape and why do many in the industry feel that it improves the efficiency of security markets?

14. In your opinion, how has the formation of the National Association of Security Dealers Automated Quotation Service (NASDAQ) affected the efficiency of security markets?

15. Describe the differences in the transacting process of over-the-counter markets and of the New York Stock Exchange.

16. In your opinion, how has legislation changed the nature of security markets in the United States? What benefits have occurred? What costs?

17. Describe the functions performed by the NYSE in the large (i.e., its contribution to and relationship with the real-goods sector of the economy) and in the small (i.e., its contributions to investors attempting to make investment decisions to achieve a high level of utility of present and future consumption).

18. How can the development of the Intermarket Trading System help make the market more efficient?

19. Secondary security markets, by offering liquidity and price continuity, offer services to investors. Define liquidity and price continuity.

20. Specialists on the NYSE do all of the following *except:*

    a. Act as dealers for their own accounts.

    b. Execute limit orders.

    c. Help provide liquidity to the marketplace.

    d. Act as odd-lot dealers.

    CFA

21. If you place a stop order to sell 100 shares of stock at $55 when the current price is $62, how much will you receive for each share if the price drops to $50? Can you determine that from the information given? What if you placed a stop limit order with a limit of $53?

    CFA

22. You wish to sell short 100 shares of XYZ Corporation stock. If the last two transactions were at $34^{1}/_{8}$ followed by $34^{1}/_{4}$, you only can sell short on the next transaction at a price of:

    a. $34^{1}/_{8}$ or higher.

    b. $34^{1}/_{4}$ or higher.

    c. $34^{1}/_{4}$ or lower.

    d. $34^{1}/_{8}$ or lower.

    CFA

23. Why might an investment in ADRs be appealing to an American investor who wishes to internationalize his portfolio holdings, if the alternative is to invest directly in the foreign stock market?

24. As a measure of returns on broadly diversified portfolios of NYSE-listed common stock over time, which stock market indicator is preferable, and why: The Dow Jones Industrial Average or the Standard & Poor's 500 Stock Index?

25. Why might either of the market indicators in Problem 24 be inaccurate when used as a measure of how all U.S. equity investments have fared over time?

26. Why might an investor use a full-service (retail) broker instead of a discount broker? What types of investors would you expect use discount brokers?

27. The Dow Jones Industrial Average has all these characteristics as a stock market index *except:*

    a. It is price weighted.

    b. It is dominated by just a few companies.

    c. Companies having stock splits are weighted less heavily.

    d. It has more systematic risk than the S&P 500 Index.

    CFA

CHAPTER

5

Investment Returns

The study of history is important to success in any human endeavor to which experience adds insight. Indeed, as the saying goes, those who fail to understand the lessons of history are doomed to repeat them. By carefully studying the past, we can learn to anticipate some of the changes the future may bring and also avoid repeating others' costly mistakes. This chapter examines the historical records of rates of return earned on a variety of financial assets.

Studying the historical record of investment opportunities will help us assess the relative risks and returns various financial assets offer the investor. Simply, the returns observed for these assets in the past can help us assess the probability distribution of returns we acquire when we buy securities in the future. Moreover, if there is any underlying stability in economic relationships, an historical analysis helps to reveal some of the factors that most heavily influence the level of, and variation in, rates of return. Then, when we endeavor to develop more accurate forecasts of future returns, we at least know on what factors to base our forecasts.

We must keep in mind, however, that the lessons of history, though perhaps indispensable to the successful investor, are not fully revealing. Future distributions of returns are affected by changes in the financial services offered to investors and by the evolution of the economy.

The Calculation of Rates of Return

Chapter 1 emphasized the fact that individuals make consumption and investment decisions based on four factors: the opportunities available, the market prices of those opportunities, their personal preferences or utility, and the wealth available for allocation across the opportunity set. Since, in the remainder of this book, we are concerned only with *investment* opportunities and the decisions of investors to purchase them, we shall ignore any aspects of the available opportunities that have *consumption* value to the individual. That is, investments are undertaken in order to alter the time sequence and uncertainty surrounding one's future consumption. The fact that real estate, gold, Picasso paintings, or Tiffany lamps are physical assets that can be touched, felt, and appreciated for their beauty or their functionality is irrelevant to their investment properties. Picasso paintings, to our narrow minds in this chapter, are strictly investment opportunities by virtue of the cash they generate upon their sale.[1]

To facilitate our comparison of the alternative historical returns of various assets, it is necessary to express the benefits to the investor in a common unit of measure over the life, or holding period, of each investment. The unit of measure we use is the investment's **rate of return.** The dollar price of an investment opportunity, taken together with its forecasted pattern of dollar cash flows over time, uniquely determines its rate of return, or:

$$\frac{\text{Rate of}}{\text{return}} = \frac{\text{End of period price} + \text{Cash payment} - \text{Beginning period price}}{\text{Beginning period price}}$$

Note that the investment's beginning period price is inversely related to its rate of return, given the future cash flows afforded by that investment. An increase in the asset's beginning period price causes a decrease in its rate of return, if all future cash flows are left unchanged.

An asset's **holding period return** is the rate of return actually earned on an investment over a specified period of time. Suppose, for simplicity, we think of the holding period as "one unit of time" or "one period." Assume that an investor purchased a share of the common stock of PACCAR, Inc., on date $t - 1$ and sold it on date t. The rate of return over that period is:

(5-1)   *The One-Period Rate of Return*

$$R_{it} = \frac{P_{it} + D_{it} - P_{it-1}}{P_{it-1}} = \frac{P_{it} + D_{it}}{P_{it-1}} - 1.0$$

---

[1] Some investments such as gold, real estate, and artwork, of course have value as consumption goods as well as value as investments. Certainly, gold has been in demand for centuries for its visual appeal. We would not argue that it should be otherwise. We are, however, saying that one must be prepared to talk purely about the investment value of such opportunities if one is interested in making accurate comparisons of their returns with those of other investments (such as stocks and bonds), which do not have such appeal. Stated more precisely, from an investment perspective, a ton of perfectly preserved steer manure that costs the investor the same and yields precisely the same probability distribution of future cash flows as a specific quantity of gold should be valued equally by all investors.

In this equation, P_{it} is security i's price observed on date t, D_{it} is the cash flow (if any) received on date t, and P_{it-1} is asset i's price at date $t - 1$.[2] The equation simply measures the wealth increment per dollar of investment. Since it represents the rate of return to the investor who made the purchase at a per unit price of P_{it-1} and who sells it one "period" later at P_{it}, it is also termed the holding period return.

For example, the investor who purchased 100 shares of PACCAR, Inc., common stock on April 17, 1985, at a price of $45.25 per share, sold these shares at $55.75 on February 13, 1987, and received a dividend during the holding period of $2.97 had a holding period return of:

$$R_{PAC,t} = \frac{\$55.75 + \$2.97 - \$45.25}{\$45.25} = .2976,$$

or a 29.76 percent return. The 29.76 percent, as you are aware, is *not* an annualized return, so—strictly speaking—it cannot be compared to annual returns earned by other assets. While this example used a $21^1/_2$-month "holding" period, more generally, holding periods may span calendar periods as long as many years and as short as to the next transaction in the security.

For purposes of comparison, most of the holding period returns presented in this chapter are calculated over a standardized period of time; such as a month, a year, or several years. Moreover, as in the example above, all of the calculations include both cash flows paid to the owner by the issuer (sometimes called the current yield), and capital gains received upon sale of the security (either realized or unrealized—sometimes called the capital gains yield). The sum of these two yields represents the total return on the investment opportunity.

The Historical Record: Common Stock and Bond Indexes

Table 5–1 presents a listing of the rates of return on investments in common stocks over annual holding periods during the period 1926 through 1986. The figures in the body of the table represent the experience of a hypothetical investor who purchased a portfolio of common stocks at the end of one calendar year and held them until the end of the next year. The actual annual returns shown are those generated from "investing" in Standard & Poor's Composite Index of 500 Common Stocks.

How would this hypothetical investor have fared? Suppose the Standard & Poor's Index portfolio had been purchased at the end of 1925 and been held through the end of 1926, with all dividends being reinvested in additional "shares" of the index as received. In this case, the investor would have realized an 11.6 percent **holding period return.** Alternatively, had the portfolio been purchased at the end of 1926 and held for one year,

---

[2]The calculation assumes the cash flow, D_{it}, is received at the end of the period. Equation (5–1) would not be strictly correct for cash flows received before the end of the period and would be more incorrect the earlier in the period the cash flows are received. But as long as the period is defined to be short enough and D_{it} is small enough, Equation (5–1) will be sufficiently accurate for our current purpose. It is easy to account explicitly for intraperiod cash flows, but this inherently makes a multiperiod calculation necessary; i.e., a present value calculation.

TABLE 5–1   Historical Returns on Investments in Standard & Poor's Index of 500 Common Stocks

Year	Return (percent)	Year	Return (percent)	Year	Return (percent)	Year	Return (percent)
1926	11.6	1941	− 11.6	1956	6.6	1971	14.3
1927	37.5	1942	20.3	1957	− 10.8	1972	19.0
1928	43.6	1943	25.9	1958	43.4	1973	− 14.7
1929	− 8.4	1944	19.8	1959	12.0	1974	− 26.5
1930	− 24.9	1945	36.4	1960	0.5	1975	37.2
1931	− 43.3	1946	− 8.1	1961	26.9	1976	23.8
1932	− 8.2	1947	5.7	1962	− 8.7	1977	− 7.2
1933	54.0	1948	5.5	1963	22.8	1978	6.6
1934	− 1.4	1949	18.8	1964	16.5	1979	18.4
1935	47.7	1950	31.7	1965	12.5	1980	32.4
1936	33.9	1951	24.0	1966	− 10.1	1981	− 4.9
1937	− 35.0	1952	18.4	1967	24.0	1982	21.4
1938	31.1	1953	− 1.0	1968	11.1	1983	22.5
1939	− 0.4	1954	52.6	1969	− 8.5	1984	6.3
1940	− 9.8	1955	31.6	1970	4.0	1985	31.7
						1986	18.3

Source: Ibbotson Associates [1986].

the holding period return would have been 37.5 percent. Looking over the entire table and examining all possible annual total returns, the highest would have been earned in 1933, when the total return was 54.0 percent, while the lowest would have been earned in 1931, when it was a negative 43.3 percent.

Revealing as these figures are, they do not show the precise effect of such investment returns on wealth. The table has been constructed assuming there are no income taxes and no transactions costs deducted from total returns. To construct a realistic portfolio that precisely mimics the returns on the S&P 500 Index would involve considerable transactions costs. Moreover, the portfolio strategy employed (buy and hold) assumes no intrayear purchases or sales of selected stocks within the index, except when the index itself changes composition and some stocks are added or deleted.[3] In spite of these limitations, the figures do provide some basic information about the returns that could have been secured from a naive investment in these widely held NYSE securities.

Figure 5–1 graphically depicts the series of one-year holding period total returns that appeared in Table 5–1. Three significant facts can be deduced:

1.   The average annual total return over this 61-year period was positive. In fact, it averaged about 12.0 percent.
2.   In about two years out of three, common stocks earned positive rates of return. In 19 of the one-year holding periods, the rate of return was negative; in the remaining 42 years, it was positive.

---

[3]Surely, we ask rhetorically, wouldn't we have been able to achieve higher returns than are shown in the table if we "cut our gains" on the stocks that rose by more than 25 percent during the year and let our "losses ride"? Or conversely, perhaps we could have improved our returns if we "cut our losses" and "let our profits ride"?

FIGURE 5–1   Year-by-Year Total Returns on Common Stocks

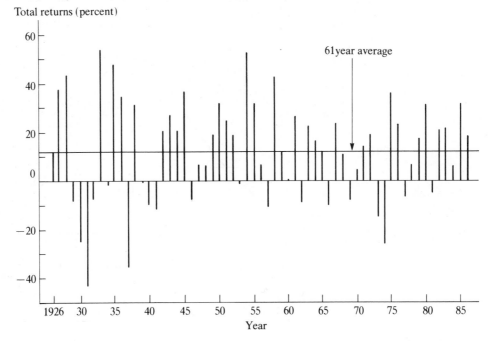

Total returns (percent)

Source: Ibbotson Associates [1986].

3. The average annual returns on common stocks in the decades represented has been variable. In some 10-year periods, such as the 1950s, the average total return was considerably higher than for other 10-year periods, such as the 1970s.[4] Thus, it would appear that using periods as short as one decade to assess long-run average stock market returns is hazardous at best.

Figure 5–2 is a smoothed histogram, or probability distribution, of the returns depicted in Figure 5–1. It is a picture of the annual returns that an investment in the S&P 500 Index would have generated, calibrated by their historical frequency of occurrence. Under the assumption that some stability is present in this distribution, Figure 5–2 may approximate the frequency distribution of returns from which the values in Table 5–1 were drawn or may be drawn in the future. The expected return of this frequency distribution is 12.0 percent. It has a standard deviation of 21.2 percent, and is slightly skewed to the right.

---

[4]There is a revealing explanation for this phenomenon. During the 1970s, fundamental changes in the rate of inflation in the economy took place, due primarily to the shock of higher oil prices as a result of the 1973 "energy crisis." As investors demanded higher returns to compensate for the decline in the future expected purchasing power of the dollar, the prices of existing securities were held below the levels that would have been generated with lower inflation, thus generating low ex post (but not necessarily ex ante) returns. Precisely how this effect on value takes place is explained in Chapters 11, 12, and 14.

FIGURE 5–2   Relative Frequency of Return Values: Standard & Poor's Index, 1926–1986

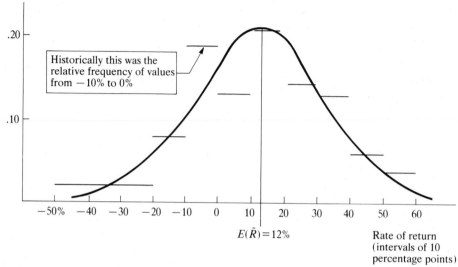

Source: Computed from Table 5–1.

Many investors, of course, contemplate holding their investments for more than one year. Thus, our assumption that the holding period is a single year may not represent a realistic investment strategy. Consequently, we now explore the relationship between one-year total returns and actual increases in wealth experienced by investors who hold their investments over different, multiyear holding periods.

Multiperiod Returns and the Geometric Mean Return

As long as uncertainty exists, we can never take future returns for granted. Think of future rates of return as random drawings from a particular probability distribution representing the prospects offered by a specific investment opportunity, say a share of Boeing common stock. Figure 5–3 is an example of such a distribution. It is similar to the one shown in Figure 5–2, but it is symmetric, with an expected value of 14.1 percent. It represents the distribution of possible (uncertain) future rates of return on this stock (as you might perceive these possibilities today for the coming year).

The actual return generated during the next year (period t) will be a random "drawing" from this distribution. In this case, the value most likely to be drawn is the expected return of 14.1 percent. But other values may also be drawn, according to the probability of their occurrence as specified on the vertical axis. If the distribution is expected to remain constant over the planned investment period (e.g., 2 years or 20 years), and if

FIGURE 5–3 **A Hypothetical Probability Distribution of Return on Boeing Stock for Period *t***

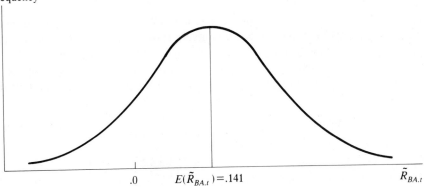

$R_{BA.t}$ = the annual return in period t on stock BA (Boeing Company)

$E(\tilde{R}_{BA.t})$ = the expected value of the distribution of $\tilde{R}_{BA.t}$

all dividends are reinvested in the purchase of additional shares of Boeing stock, your wealth, W, will accumulate in a geometric series of the general form:

(5–2) *Wealth Accumulation*

$$\frac{\tilde{W}_I}{W_O} = \prod_{t=1}^{T} (1 + \tilde{R}_{BA,t})$$

Accumulated wealth *Product of one plus*
per dollar of initial = *all periodic holding*
invested wealth *period returns*

To see how this relationship works, suppose you were to invest $1,000 in shares of Boeing stock for a period of three years. If the three annual rates of return actually drawn are − 12.0 percent, + 26.2 percent, and + 28.1 percent, your final (accumulated) wealth per dollar committed to this investment would be:

$$(0.880)(1.262)(1.281) = 1.423,$$

for a 42.3 percent increase in value. Your total dollar wealth at the end of the three years would be $1,423. In this case, the average of the three returns drawn is equal to the mean of the probability distribution of 14.1 percent. Yet the accumulation of wealth is not the same value that would have resulted if you had earned the stock's **expected return,** 14.1 percent, in each of the three years. That value is:

$$(1.141)(1.141)(1.141) = 1.485,$$

which represents a 48.5 percent increase in value.

The existence of uncertainty as reflected in a distribution of possible values makes the **expected value,** or arithmetic average rate of return, a misleading and biased representation of the wealth increments which will be generated from multiperiod investment opportunities.

The average *annual* rate of wealth accumulation over the investment period, termed the **average annual geometric rate of return,** correctly measures the average annual accumulation to wealth when multiple periods are involved. For an investment held for T periods, the average annual geometric return is found by taking the Tth root of the compound returns and subtracting 1.0 from the result. This calculation can be expressed as:

(5–3)   *Average Annual Geometric Return*

$$\tilde{G} = \left[\prod_{t=1}^{T} (1 + \tilde{R}_{it}) \right]^{1/T} - 1.0$$

where G is the average annual geometric rate of return. This figure is the return which, if earned over each and every period in the investment horizon, would have generated the same final wealth as the actual pattern of annual returns generated. For the above example involving Boeing stock,

$$G = [(0.880)(1.262)(1.281)]^{1/3} - 1.0 = .125$$

or 12.5 percent average annual geometric return. In contrast, the average annual geometric return that would be earned if the expected value were generated in each period would be, of course,

$$G = [(1.141)(1.141)(1.141)]^{1/3} - 1.0 = .141,$$

or 14.1 percent.

The average annual geometric rate of return (the geometric mean return, for short) is lower than the expected return (the arithmetic mean return) for any investment characterized by uncertain returns. And, the difference between the two measures of return is greater the *larger* the dispersion of the probability distribution of returns.

To appreciate the relevance of geometric mean return for investment purposes, consider an example. You plan to spend $1 on a lottery ticket promising equal chances of returning you $1.50 if you win or $.50 if you lose. Under this assumption, a win gives you a +50 percent return and a loss gives you a −50 percent return on your initial dollar invested. The arithmetic mean return is $(1/2) (+.50) + (1/2) (-.50)$, which is just 0.0, or break-even. The geometric mean return, however, is given by:

$$G = [(1.50) (.50)]^{1/2} - 1.0 = -.134$$

This tells you that you are sure to lose money if you use this strategy long enough, since your wealth "accumulates" at the rate of −13.4 percent each time you play. While you could continue to play forever, since the lottery always returns part of your "investment" to you, your wealth declines geometrically. This is true even through the gamble itself offers a "fair game" expected return of zero. The difference between G in this case and the gamble's expected return is $-.134$, or -13.4 percentage points—an amount that would drive you toward bankruptcy very quickly.

This example suggests that the geometric mean return is an appropriate measure of the investor's annual return over multiyear holding periods in which, at the end of each single period, accumulated investment returns are reinvested and thus compound themselves. Applying the concept of the geometric mean returns to multiyear holding periods for the S&P 500 as shown in Table 5–1 is now straightforward.

Comparison of Multiperiod Stock and Bond Returns

Ibbotson Associates [1986] constructs geometric mean returns for all possible continuous annual periods. These data are given in the interior of Table 5–2 for the S&P Index from 1926 through 1986. In this table, the row headings indicate the year in which the investment period of interest ended, while the column headings indicate the year in which the period began. Thus, the **average annual rate of wealth accumulation** over the seven years starting in January 1926 and ending in December 1932 was -3.3 percent, and over the 30-year period beginning in January 1955 and ending December 1986 was 10.4 percent.

The table suggests, not surprisingly, that the profitability of a well-diversified stock portfolio has historically depended greatly on the holding period selected. Note that the geometric mean return on the S&P 500 Index, assuming all dividends were reinvested when received over the 61-year period, was 9.9 percent. This compares to the arithmetic mean return of 12.0 percent over this period.

Table 5–3 shows comparable values constructed for a long-term corporate bond portfolio. Each rate of return shown approximates the actual rate of return earned on a portfolio in which equal dollar investments were made in each of 17 representative bonds comprising the Salomon Brothers' High Grade Long-Term Corporate Bond Index, and in which all the periodic interest payments were reinvested in the portfolio when received. Over the entire 61-year period, the arithmetic mean return on this portfolio was 5.3 percent per year, while the geometric mean was 5.0 percent per year.

As you can see, over time on average, an investment in bonds has been generally less profitable than an investment in stocks, though there are some significant periods of time when the relationship was reversed (e.g., compare the values in each table near the diagonal). Generally speaking, however, stock market investors have earned returns that were higher than those earned by bond market investors. Why, then, would anybody purchase bonds? The data suggest the answer: there were only 14 years in which investors actually lost money throughout the entire 61-year period shown. And, in those years, when investors did lose money, they never lost more then 8.1 percent of their investment (1969). In contrast, during the best year for bonds, the maximum gain was 30.9 percent (1985). This makes the maximum range of historical annual rates of return less than 40 percentage points for bonds over the entire period, compared to almost 100 percentage points for stocks.

Clearly, bonds appear to offer both smaller risks and smaller returns than stocks. Not only are their annual average returns smaller than for stocks, both the maximum annual

TABLE 5–2 Common Stocks: Total Returns (rates of return for all yearly holding periods from 1926 to 1986; percent per annum compounded annually)

From the beginning of

To the end of	*1926*	*1927*	*1928*	*1929*	*1930*	*1931*	*1932*	*1933*	*1934*	*1935*	*1936*	*1937*	*1938*	*1939*	*1940*	*1941*	*1942*	*1943*	*1944*	*1945*	*1946*	*1947*	*1948*	*1949*	*1950*	*1951*	*1952*	*1953*	*1954*	*1955*
1926	11.6																													
1927	23.9	37.5																												
1928	30.1	40.5	43.6																											
1929	19.2	21.8	14.7	−8.4																										
1930	8.7	8.0	−0.4	−17.1	−24.9																									
1931	−2.5	−5.1	−13.5	−27.0	−34.8	−43.3																								
1932	−3.3	−5.6	−12.5	−22.7	−26.9	−27.9	−8.2																							
1933	2.5	1.2	−3.8	−11.2	−11.9	−7.1	18.9	54.0																						
1934	2.0	0.9	−3.5	−9.7	−9.9	−5.7	11.7	23.2	−1.4																					
1935	5.9	5.2	1.8	−3.1	−2.2	3.1	19.8	30.9	20.6	47.7																				
1936	8.1	7.8	4.9	0.9	2.3	7.7	22.5	31.6	24.9	40.6	33.9																			
1937	3.7	3.0	0.0	−3.9	−3.3	0.2	10.2	14.3	6.1	8.7	−6.7	−35.0																		
1938	5.5	5.1	2.5	−0.9	−0.0	3.6	13.0	16.9	10.7	13.9	4.5	−7.7	31.1																	
1939	5.1	4.6	2.3	−0.8	−0.1	3.2	11.2	14.3	8.7	10.9	3.2	−5.3	14.3	−0.4																
1940	4.0	3.5	1.3	−1.6	−1.0	1.8	8.6	11.0	5.9	7.2	0.5	−6.5	5.6	−5.2	−9.8															
1941	3.0	2.4	0.3	−2.4	−1.9	0.5	6.4	8.2	3.5	4.3	−1.6	−7.5	1.0	−7.4	−10.7	−11.6														
1942	3.9	3.5	1.5	−1.0	−0.4	2.0	7.6	9.3	5.3	6.1	1.2	−3.4	4.6	−1.1	−1.4	3.1	20.3													
1943	5.0	4.7	2.9	0.6	1.3	3.7	9.0	10.8	7.2	8.2	4.0	0.4	7.9	3.8	4.8	10.2	23.1	25.9												
1944	5.8	5.5	3.8	1.7	2.5	4.8	9.8	11.5	8.3	9.3	5.7	2.6	9.5	6.3	7.7	12.5	22.0	22.8	19.8											
1945	7.1	6.9	5.4	3.5	4.3	6.6	11.5	13.2	10.4	11.5	8.4	5.9	12.6	10.1	12.0	17.0	25.4	27.2	27.8	36.4										
1946	6.4	6.1	4.7	2.8	3.5	5.6	10.1	11.6	8.8	9.7	6.8	4.4	10.1	7.7	8.9	12.4	17.9	17.3	14.5	12.0	−8.1									
1947	6.3	6.1	4.7	3.0	3.7	5.6	9.8	11.2	8.6	9.4	6.7	4.5	9.6	7.5	8.5	11.4	15.8	14.9	12.3	9.9	−1.4	5.7								
1948	6.3	6.1	4.7	3.1	3.8	5.6	9.6	10.8	8.4	9.1	6.6	4.6	9.2	7.3	8.2	10.6	14.2	13.2	10.9	8.8	0.8	5.6	5.5							
1949	6.8	6.6	5.3	3.8	4.5	6.3	10.1	11.2	9.0	9.7	7.4	5.6	10.0	8.3	9.2	11.5	14.8	14.0	12.2	10.7	5.1	9.8	11.9	18.8						
1950	7.7	7.5	6.4	4.9	5.6	7.4	11.1	12.3	10.2	11.0	8.9	7.3	11.5	10.0	11.0	13.4	16.6	16.1	14.8	13.9	9.9	14.9	18.2	25.1	31.7					
1951	8.3	8.1	7.1	5.7	6.4	8.2	11.7	12.9	11.0	11.7	9.8	8.4	12.4	11.1	12.1	14.3	17.3	16.9	15.9	15.3	12.1	16.7	19.6	24.7	27.8	24.0				
1952	8.6	8.5	7.5	6.2	6.9	8.6	12.0	13.2	11.3	12.1	10.3	9.0	12.8	11.6	12.5	14.6	17.4	17.1	16.1	15.7	13.0	17.0	19.4	23.1	24.6	21.2	18.4			
1953	8.3	8.1	7.2	5.9	6.5	8.2	11.4	12.4	10.7	11.4	9.6	8.3	11.9	10.7	11.5	13.4	15.7	15.3	14.3	13.7	11.2	14.2	15.7	17.9	17.6	13.3	8.3	−1.0		
1954	9.6	9.5	8.6	7.4	8.1	9.7	12.9	14.0	12.4	13.1	11.6	10.4	13.9	12.9	13.9	15.8	18.2	18.0	17.4	17.1	15.1	18.4	20.4	23.0	23.9	22.0	21.4	22.9	52.6	
1955	10.2	10.2	9.3	8.2	8.9	10.5	13.7	14.7	13.2	13.9	12.5	11.4	14.8	13.9	14.9	16.8	19.1	19.0	18.5	18.4	16.7	19.8	21.7	24.2	25.2	23.9	23.9	25.7	41.7	31.6
1956	10.1	10.1	9.2	8.2	8.8	10.4	13.4	14.4	12.9	13.6	12.2	11.2	14.4	13.5	14.4	16.1	18.2	18.1	17.5	17.3	15.7	18.4	19.9	21.9	22.3	20.8	20.2	20.6	28.9	18.4
1957	9.4	9.3	8.5	7.4	8.1	9.5	12.3	13.2	11.8	12.4	11.0	10.0	13.0	12.1	12.8	14.3	16.2	15.9	15.2	14.9	13.2	15.4	16.4	17.7	17.6	15.7	14.4	13.6	17.5	7.7
1958	10.3	10.2	9.5	8.5	9.1	10.6	13.3	14.3	12.9	13.6	12.3	11.4	14.3	13.5	14.3	15.8	17.6	17.5	16.9	16.7	15.3	17.5	18.7	20.1	20.2	18.8	18.1	18.1	22.3	15.7
1959	10.3	10.3	9.5	8.6	9.2	10.6	13.3	14.2	12.9	13.5	12.3	11.4	14.2	13.4	14.1	15.6	17.3	17.1	16.6	16.4	15.1	17.1	18.1	19.3	19.4	18.1	17.3	17.2	20.5	15.0
1960	10.0	10.0	9.3	8.3	8.9	10.3	12.8	13.7	12.4	13.0	11.8	10.9	13.5	12.8	13.5	14.8	16.4	16.1	15.6	15.3	14.0	15.8	16.6	17.6	17.5	16.2	15.3	14.9	17.4	12.4
1961	10.5	10.4	9.7	8.8	9.4	10.8	13.3	14.1	12.9	13.4	12.3	11.5	14.1	13.4	14.0	15.3	16.9	16.7	16.2	16.0	14.8	16.5	17.3	18.3	18.3	17.1	16.4	16.2	18.6	14.4
1962	9.9	9.9	9.2	8.3	8.8	10.1	12.5	13.2	12.1	12.6	11.4	10.7	13.0	12.3	12.9	14.1	15.5	15.3	14.7	14.4	13.3	14.8	15.4	16.1	15.9	14.7	13.9	13.4	15.2	11.2
1963	10.2	10.2	9.5	8.7	9.2	10.5	12.8	13.5	12.4	12.9	11.8	11.1	13.4	12.7	13.3	14.5	15.8	15.6	15.1	14.9	13.8	15.2	15.8	16.6	16.4	15.3	14.6	14.3	15.9	12.4
1964	10.4	10.4	9.7	8.9	9.4	10.6	12.9	13.6	12.5	13.0	12.0	11.3	13.5	12.9	13.5	14.5	15.8	15.6	15.2	14.9	13.9	15.3	15.9	16.6	16.4	15.4	14.7	14.4	16.0	12.8
1965	10.4	10.4	9.8	9.0	9.5	10.7	12.9	13.6	12.5	13.0	12.0	11.3	13.5	12.9	13.4	14.5	15.7	15.5	15.0	14.8	13.8	15.1	15.7	16.3	16.2	15.2	14.6	14.3	15.7	12.8
1966	9.9	9.8	9.2	8.4	8.9	10.1	12.2	12.8	11.8	12.2	11.2	10.5	12.6	12.0	12.4	13.4	14.5	14.3	13.8	13.6	12.6	13.7	14.2	14.7	14.4	13.4	12.7	12.4	13.4	10.7
1967	10.2	10.2	9.6	8.8	9.3	10.4	12.5	13.1	12.1	12.5	11.6	10.9	12.9	12.4	12.8	13.8	14.9	14.7	14.2	14.0	13.1	14.2	14.6	15.1	14.9	14.0	13.4	13.1	14.2	11.6
1968	10.2	10.2	9.6	8.9	9.3	10.4	12.4	13.1	12.1	12.5	11.6	10.9	12.9	12.3	12.8	13.7	14.7	14.5	14.1	13.9	13.0	14.0	14.5	14.9	14.7	13.8	13.3	13.0	14.0	11.6
1969	9.8	9.7	9.1	8.4	8.9	9.9	11.8	12.4	11.4	11.8	10.9	10.3	12.1	11.6	12.0	12.8	13.8	13.6	13.1	12.9	12.0	13.0	13.3	13.7	13.4	12.5	11.9	11.6	12.4	10.1
1970	9.6	9.6	9.0	8.3	8.7	9.7	11.6	12.2	11.2	11.6	10.7	10.1	11.9	11.3	11.7	12.5	13.5	13.2	12.8	12.5	11.7	12.6	12.9	13.2	13.0	12.1	11.5	11.1	11.9	9.7
1971	9.7	9.7	9.1	8.4	8.9	9.9	11.7	12.2	11.3	11.7	10.8	10.2	11.9	11.4	11.8	12.6	13.5	13.3	12.8	12.6	11.8	12.6	12.9	13.3	13.0	12.2	11.6	11.3	12.0	10.0
1972	9.9	9.9	9.3	8.7	9.1	10.1	11.9	12.4	11.5	11.9	11.0	10.5	12.1	11.6	12.0	12.8	13.7	13.5	13.0	12.8	12.0	12.9	13.2	13.5	13.3	12.5	12.0	11.7	12.4	10.5
1973	9.3	9.3	8.7	8.1	8.5	9.4	11.1	11.7	10.8	11.1	10.3	9.7	11.3	10.8	11.1	11.8	12.7	12.4	12.0	11.7	10.9	11.7	11.9	12.2	11.9	11.2	10.6	10.3	10.8	9.0
1974	8.5	8.4	7.8	7.2	7.5	8.4	10.1	10.6	9.7	10.0	9.1	8.5	10.1	9.5	9.8	10.5	11.2	10.9	10.5	10.2	9.4	10.1	10.2	10.4	10.1	9.3	8.7	8.2	8.7	6.9
1975	9.0	8.9	8.4	7.7	8.1	9.0	10.6	11.1	10.2	10.6	9.8	9.2	10.7	10.2	10.5	11.1	11.9	11.6	11.2	11.0	10.2	10.9	11.1	11.3	11.0	10.3	9.7	9.4	9.9	8.2
1976	9.2	9.2	8.7	8.0	8.4	9.3	10.9	11.4	10.5	10.9	10.1	9.5	11.0	10.5	10.8	11.5	12.2	12.0	11.6	11.3	10.6	11.3	11.5	11.7	11.5	10.8	10.3	9.9	10.4	8.8
1977	8.9	8.8	8.3	7.7	8.1	8.9	10.5	10.9	10.1	10.4	9.6	9.1	10.5	10.0	10.3	10.9	11.6	11.4	11.0	10.7	10.0	10.7	10.8	11.0	10.7	10.0	9.5	9.2	9.6	8.1
1978	8.9	8.8	8.3	7.7	8.0	8.9	10.4	10.8	10.0	10.3	9.6	9.0	10.4	9.9	10.2	10.8	11.5	11.3	10.9	10.6	9.9	10.5	10.7	10.9	10.6	9.9	9.4	9.1	9.5	8.0
1979	9.0	9.0	8.5	7.9	8.2	9.1	10.6	11.0	10.2	10.5	9.8	9.2	10.6	10.1	10.4	11.0	11.7	11.4	11.1	10.8	10.2	10.8	10.9	11.1	10.8	10.2	9.7	9.4	9.8	8.4
1980	9.4	9.4	8.9	8.3	8.7	9.5	11.0	11.4	10.6	10.9	10.2	9.7	11.1	10.6	10.9	11.5	12.2	11.9	11.6	11.4	10.7	11.3	11.5	11.7	11.5	10.9	10.4	10.2	10.6	9.2
1981	9.1	9.1	8.6	8.1	8.4	9.2	10.6	11.0	10.3	10.6	9.9	9.4	10.7	10.2	10.5	11.1	11.7	11.5	11.1	10.9	10.3	10.8	11.0	11.2	10.9	10.3	9.9	9.6	10.0	8.7
1982	9.3	9.3	8.8	8.3	8.6	9.4	10.8	11.2	10.5	10.8	10.1	9.6	10.9	10.5	10.8	11.3	11.9	11.7	11.4	11.2	10.6	11.1	11.3	11.5	11.2	10.7	10.2	10.0	10.4	9.1
1983	9.6	9.5	9.1	8.5	8.9	9.6	11.0	11.5	10.7	11.0	10.3	9.9	11.1	10.7	11.0	11.5	12.2	12.0	11.6	11.4	10.9	11.4	11.6	11.8	11.6	11.0	10.6	10.4	10.8	9.6
1984	9.5	9.5	9.0	8.5	8.8	9.6	10.9	11.3	10.6	10.9	10.3	9.8	11.0	10.6	10.9	11.4	12.0	11.8	11.5	11.3	10.7	11.3	11.4	11.6	11.4	10.9	10.5	10.2	10.6	9.4
1985	9.8	9.8	9.4	8.9	9.2	9.9	11.3	11.7	11.0	11.3	10.7	10.2	11.4	11.1	11.3	11.8	12.4	12.3	12.0	11.8	11.2	11.8	11.9	12.1	11.9	11.4	11.1	10.8	11.2	10.1
1986	9.9	9.9	9.5	9.1	9.4	10.0	11.4	11.8	11.1	11.4	10.8	10.4	11.5	11.2	11.4	11.9	12.5	12.4	12.1	12.0	11.4	12.0	12.1	12.3	12.1	11.6	11.3	11.0	11.4	10.4

From the beginning of

To the end of	*1956*	*1957*	*1958*	*1959*	*1960*	*1961*	*1962*	*1963*	*1964*	*1965*	*1966*	*1967*	*1968*	*1969*	*1970*	*1971*	*1972*	*1973*	*1974*	*1975*	*1976*	*1977*	*1978*	*1979*	*1980*	*1981*	*1982*	*1983*	*1984*	*1985*	*1986*
1956	6.6																														
1957	−2.5	−10.8																													
1958	10.9	13.1	43.4																												
1959	11.1	12.7	26.7	12.0																											
1960	8.9	9.5	17.3	6.1	0.5																										
1961	11.7	12.8	19.6	12.6	12.9	26.9																									
1962	8.5	8.9	13.3	6.8	5.2	7.6	−8.7																								
1963	10.2	10.8	14.8	9.9	9.3	12.5	5.9	22.8																							
1964	10.9	11.5	15.1	10.9	10.7	13.5	9.3	19.6	16.5																						
1965	11.1	11.6	14.7	11.1	11.0	13.2	10.1	17.2	14.4	12.5																					
1966	9.0	9.2	11.7	8.2	7.7	9.0	5.7	9.7	5.6	0.6	−10.1																				
1967	10.1	10.5	12.8	9.9	9.6	11.0	8.6	12.4	9.9	7.8	5.6	24.0																			
1968	10.2	10.5	12.7	10.0	9.8	11.0	8.9	12.2	10.2	8.6	7.4	17.3	11.1																		
1969	8.7	8.9	10.7	8.2	7.8	8.7	6.6	9.0	6.8	5.0	3.2	8.0	0.8	−8.5																	
1970	8.4	8.6	10.2	7.8	7.5	8.2	6.3	8.3	6.4	4.8	3.3	7.0	1.9	−2.4	4.0																
1971	8.8	8.9	10.5	8.3	8.0	8.7	7.1	9.0	7.4	6.1	5.1	8.4	4.8	2.8	9.0	14.3															
1972	9.4	9.5	11.0	9.0	8.8	9.5	8.1	9.9	8.6	7.6	7.0	10.1	7.5	6.7	12.3	16.6	19.0														
1973	7.9	7.9	9.2	7.3	6.9	7.5	6.0	7.4	6.0	4.9	4.0	6.2	3.5	2.0	4.8	5.1	0.8	−14.7													
1974	5.7	5.7	6.7	4.8	4.3	4.6	3.0	4.1	2.5	1.2	0.1	1.4	−1.5	−3.4	−2.4	−3.9	−9.3	−20.8	−26.5												
1975	7.1	7.1	8.2	6.4	6.1	6.5	5.2	6.3	5.1	4.1	3.3	4.9	2.7	1.6	3.3	3.2	0.6	−4.9	0.4	37.2											
1976	7.8	7.9	9.0	7.3	7.1	7.5	6.3	7.5	6.4	5.6	5.0	6.6	4.9	4.1	6.0	6.4	4.9	1.6	7.7	30.4	23.8										
1977	7.1	7.1	8.1	6.5	6.2	6.6	5.4	6.4	5.4	4.6	3.9	5.3	3.6	2.8	4.3	4.3	2.8	−0.2	3.8	16.4	7.2	−7.2									
1978	7.1	7.1	8.0	6.5	6.2	6.6	5.5	6.5	5.4	4.7	4.1	5.4	3.9	3.2	4.5	4.6	3.3	0.9	4.3	13.9	7.0	−0.5	6.6								
1979	7.5	7.6	8.5	7.1	6.8	7.2	6.2	7.1	6.2	5.6	5.1	6.3	5.0	4.5	5.9	6.1	5.1	3.2	6.6	14.8	9.7	5.4	12.3	18.4							
1980	8.4	8.5	9.4	8.1	7.9	8.3	7.4	8.4	7.6	7.1	6.7	8.0	6.9	6.5	8.0	8.4	7.8	6.5	9.9	17.5	13.9	11.6	18.7	25.2	32.4						
1981	7.9	7.9	8.8	7.5	7.3	7.6	6.8	7.6	6.9	6.3	5.9	7.1	6.0	5.6	6.9	7.2	6.5	5.2	7.9	14.0	10.6	8.1	12.3	14.3	12.2	−4.9					
1982	8.4	8.4	9.3	8.1	7.9	8.2	7.4	8.3	7.6	7.1	6.8	8.0	7.0	6.7	7.9	8.3	7.7	6.7	9.4	14.9	12.1	10.2	14.0	16.0	15.2	7.4	21.4				
1983	8.8	8.9	9.8	8.6	8.5	8.8	8.1	8.9	8.3	7.9	7.6	8.8	7.9	7.7	8.9	9.3	8.9	8.0	10.6	15.7	13.3	11.9	15.4	17.3	17.0	12.3	22.0	22.5			
1984	8.7	8.8	9.6	8.5	8.4	8.7	8.0	8.8	8.2	7.8	7.5	8.6	7.8	7.6	8.7	9.1	8.7	7.9	10.2	14.8	12.5	11.2	14.1	15.4	14.8	10.7	16.5	14.1	6.3		
1985	9.5	9.6	10.4	9.3	9.2	9.6	8.9	9.7	9.2	8.8	8.7	9.7	9.0	8.9	10.1	10.5	10.2	9.6	11.9	16.2	14.3	13.3	16.2	17.6	17.5	14.7	20.2	19.8	18.5	32.2	
1986	9.8	9.9	10.7	9.6	9.3	9.9	9.3	10.1	9.6	9.2	9.2	10.1	9.5	9.4	10.6	11.0	10.8	10.2	12.4	16.4	14.7	13.8	16.5	17.7	17.6	15.4	19.7	19.3	18.4	25.1	18.3

Source: Ibbotson Associates [1986], with the 1986 figures computed by the authors.

TABLE 5–3 Long-Term Corporate Bonds: Total Returns (rates of return for all yearly holding periods from 1926 to 1986; percent per annum compounded annually)

To the end of	*From the beginning of*																													
	1926	*1927*	*1928*	*1929*	*1930*	*1931*	*1932*	*1933*	*1934*	*1935*	*1936*	*1937*	*1938*	*1939*	*1940*	*1941*	*1942*	*1943*	*1944*	*1945*	*1946*	*1947*	*1948*	*1949*	*1950*	*1951*	*1952*	*1953*	*1954*	*1955*
1926	7.4																													
1927	7.4	7.4																												
1928	5.9	5.1	2.8																											
1929	5.2	4.5	3.1	3.3																										
1930	5.8	5.4	4.7	5.6	8.0																									
1931	4.4	3.9	3.0	3.1	2.9	−1.9																								
1932	5.3	5.0	4.5	4.9	5.5	4.3	10.8																							
1933	6.0	5.8	5.5	6.0	6.7	6.3	10.6	10.4																						
1934	6.8	6.7	6.6	7.3	8.1	8.1	11.7	12.1	13.8																					
1935	7.1	7.0	7.0	7.6	8.3	8.4	11.2	11.3	11.7	9.6																				
1936	7.1	7.0	7.0	7.5	8.1	8.1	10.3	10.1	10.0	8.2	6.7																			
1937	6.7	6.6	6.5	7.0	7.4	7.4	9.0	8.6	8.2	6.3	4.7	2.7																		
1938	6.6	6.6	6.5	6.9	7.3	7.2	8.6	8.2	7.8	6.3	5.2	4.4	6.1																	
1939	6.4	6.4	6.3	6.6	6.9	6.8	8.0	7.6	7.1	5.8	4.9	4.3	5.0	4.0																
1940	6.2	6.2	6.1	6.3	6.6	6.5	7.5	7.0	6.6	5.4	4.6	4.1	4.5	3.7	3.4															
1941	6.0	5.9	5.8	6.1	6.3	6.1	7.0	6.6	6.1	5.0	4.3	3.8	4.0	3.4	3.1	2.7														
1942	5.8	5.7	5.6	5.8	6.0	5.8	6.6	6.2	5.7	4.7	4.0	3.6	3.8	3.2	2.9	2.7	2.6													
1943	5.6	5.5	5.4	5.6	5.8	5.6	6.3	5.8	5.4	4.5	3.9	3.5	3.6	3.1	2.9	2.7	2.7	2.8												
1944	5.6	5.5	5.4	5.5	5.7	5.5	6.1	5.8	5.3	4.5	4.0	3.6	3.8	3.4	3.3	3.2	3.4	3.8	4.7											
1945	5.5	5.4	5.3	5.5	5.6	5.4	6.0	5.6	5.2	4.5	4.0	3.7	3.8	3.5	3.4	3.4	3.6	3.9	4.4	4.1										
1946	5.3	5.2	5.1	5.3	5.4	5.2	5.7	5.3	5.0	4.3	3.8	3.5	3.6	3.3	3.2	3.1	3.2	3.3	3.5	2.9	1.7									
1947	5.0	4.9	4.7	4.8	4.9	4.7	5.2	4.8	4.4	3.7	3.3	2.9	3.0	2.6	2.4	2.3	2.2	2.2	2.0	1.1	−0.3	−2.3								
1948	4.9	4.8	4.7	4.8	4.9	4.7	5.1	4.8	4.4	3.8	3.3	3.0	3.1	2.8	2.6	2.5	2.5	2.5	2.4	1.9	1.1	0.8	4.1							
1949	4.9	4.8	4.6	4.7	4.8	4.6	5.0	4.7	4.3	3.7	3.3	3.1	3.1	2.8	2.7	2.6	2.6	2.6	2.6	2.2	1.7	1.7	3.7	3.3						
1950	4.8	4.7	4.5	4.6	4.7	4.5	4.9	4.5	4.2	3.6	3.2	3.0	3.0	2.8	2.6	2.6	2.6	2.6	2.5	2.1	1.8	1.8	3.2	2.7	2.1					
	4.5	4.3	4.2	4.3	4.3	4.2	4.5	4.1	3.8	3.2	2.9	2.6	2.6	2.3	2.2	2.1	2.0	2.0	1.8	1.4	1.0	0.9	1.7	0.9	−0.3	−2.7				
1952	4.4	4.3	4.2	4.2	4.3	4.1	4.4	4.1	3.8	3.3	2.9	2.7	2.7	2.4	2.3	2.2	2.2	2.1	2.0	1.7	1.4	1.3	2.0	1.5	0.9	0.4	3.5			
1953	4.4	4.3	4.2	4.2	4.3	4.1	4.4	4.1	3.8	3.3	2.9	2.7	2.7	2.5	2.4	2.3	2.3	2.2	2.2	1.9	1.6	1.6	2.3	1.9	1.6	1.4	3.5	3.4		
1954	4.4	4.3	4.2	4.3	4.3	4.2	4.4	4.1	3.8	3.4	3.1	2.9	2.9	2.7	2.6	2.5	2.5	2.5	2.5	2.2	2.0	2.1	2.7	2.5	2.3	2.4	4.1	4.4	5.4	
1955	4.3	4.2	4.1	4.1	4.2	4.0	4.3	4.0	3.7	3.2	2.9	2.7	2.7	2.5	2.4	2.4	2.4	2.3	2.3	2.1	1.9	1.9	2.4	2.2	2.0	2.0	3.2	3.1	2.9	0.5
1956	3.9	3.8	3.7	3.7	3.7	3.6	3.8	3.5	3.2	2.8	2.4	2.2	2.2	2.0	1.9	1.8	1.7	1.6	1.6	1.3	1.1	1.0	1.4	1.0	0.7	0.5	1.1	0.5	−0.4	−3.2
1957	4.1	4.0	3.8	3.9	3.9	3.7	4.0	3.7	3.4	3.0	2.7	2.5	2.5	2.3	2.2	2.2	2.1	2.1	2.1	1.9	1.7	1.7	2.1	1.8	1.7	1.6	2.3	2.1	1.8	0.6
1958	3.9	3.8	3.6	3.7	3.7	3.5	3.7	3.5	3.2	2.8	2.5	2.3	2.3	2.1	2.0	1.9	1.9	1.8	1.8	1.6	1.4	1.3	1.7	1.4	1.2	1.1	1.7	1.4	1.0	−0.1
1959	3.7	3.6	3.5	3.5	3.5	3.4	3.6	3.3	3.0	2.6	2.3	2.2	2.1	1.9	1.8	1.8	1.7	1.7	1.6	1.4	1.2	1.2	1.5	1.3	1.0	0.9	1.3	1.0	0.6	−0.3
1960	3.9	3.8	3.7	3.7	3.7	3.6	3.7	3.5	3.3	2.9	2.6	2.4	2.4	2.3	2.2	2.1	2.1	2.1	2.0	1.8	1.7	1.7	2.0	1.8	1.7	1.7	2.2	2.0	1.8	1.2
1961	3.9	3.8	3.7	3.7	3.7	3.6	3.8	3.5	3.3	2.9	2.7	2.5	2.5	2.4	2.3	2.2	2.2	2.2	2.2	2.0	1.9	1.9	2.2	2.1	2.0	2.0	2.4	2.3	2.2	1.7
1962	4.0	3.9	3.8	3.8	3.9	3.7	3.9	3.7	3.5	3.1	2.9	2.7	2.7	2.6	2.5	2.5	2.5	2.5	2.5	2.3	2.2	2.3	2.6	2.5	2.4	2.4	2.9	2.9	2.8	2.5
1963	4.0	3.9	3.8	3.8	3.8	3.7	3.9	3.6	3.4	3.1	2.9	2.7	2.7	2.6	2.5	2.5	2.5	2.5	2.5	2.3	2.2	2.3	2.6	2.5	2.4	2.4	2.9	2.8	2.7	2.4
1964	4.0	3.9	3.8	3.8	3.8	3.7	3.9	3.7	3.5	3.1	2.9	2.8	2.8	2.7	2.6	2.6	2.6	2.6	2.6	2.5	2.4	2.4	2.7	2.6	2.6	2.6	3.0	3.0	2.9	2.7
1965	3.9	3.8	3.7	3.7	3.7	3.6	3.8	3.6	3.3	3.0	2.8	2.7	2.7	2.5	2.5	2.5	2.4	2.4	2.4	2.3	2.2	2.3	2.5	2.4	2.4	2.4	2.8	2.7	2.6	2.4
1966	3.8	3.7	3.6	3.6	3.6	3.5	3.7	3.5	3.2	2.9	2.7	2.6	2.6	2.5	2.4	2.4	2.4	2.3	2.3	2.2	2.1	2.1	2.4	2.3	2.2	2.2	2.6	2.5	2.4	2.2
1967	3.6	3.5	3.4	3.4	3.4	3.3	3.4	3.2	3.0	2.7	2.5	2.3	2.3	2.2	2.1	2.1	2.1	2.0	2.0	1.9	1.8	1.8	2.0	1.9	1.8	1.8	2.1	2.0	1.9	1.6
1968	3.5	3.4	3.3	3.4	3.4	3.2	3.4	3.2	3.0	2.7	2.5	2.3	2.3	2.2	2.2	2.1	2.1	2.1	2.0	1.9	1.8	1.8	2.0	1.9	1.9	1.8	2.1	2.0	1.9	1.7
1969	3.3	3.2	3.1	3.1	3.1	2.9	3.1	2.9	2.7	2.4	2.2	2.0	2.0	1.9	1.8	1.7	1.7	1.7	1.6	1.5	1.4	1.4	1.6	1.4	1.3	1.3	1.5	1.4	1.3	1.0
1970	3.6	3.5	3.4	3.4	3.4	3.3	3.4	3.2	3.1	2.8	2.6	2.5	2.5	2.3	2.3	2.3	2.2	2.2	2.2	2.1	2.0	2.0	2.2	2.1	2.1	2.1	2.3	2.3	2.2	2.0
1971	3.7	3.6	3.6	3.6	3.6	3.5	3.6	3.4	3.3	3.0	2.8	2.7	2.7	2.6	2.6	2.5	2.5	2.5	2.5	2.4	2.4	2.4	2.6	2.5	2.5	2.5	2.8	2.7	2.7	2.5
1972	3.8	3.7	3.6	3.7	3.7	3.6	3.7	3.5	3.4	3.1	2.9	2.8	2.8	2.7	2.7	2.7	2.7	2.7	2.7	2.6	2.5	2.6	2.8	2.7	2.7	2.7	3.0	2.9	2.9	2.8
1973	3.7	3.7	3.6	3.6	3.6	3.5	3.6	3.5	3.3	3.0	2.9	2.8	2.8	2.7	2.6	2.6	2.6	2.6	2.6	2.5	2.5	2.5	2.7	2.6	2.6	2.6	2.9	2.9	2.8	2.7
1974	3.6	3.5	3.4	3.4	3.5	3.4	3.5	3.3	3.1	2.9	2.7	2.6	2.6	2.5	2.5	2.4	2.4	2.4	2.4	2.3	2.3	2.3	2.5	2.4	2.4	2.4	2.6	2.6	2.5	2.4
1975	3.8	3.7	3.7	3.7	3.7	3.6	3.7	3.6	3.4	3.2	3.0	2.9	2.9	2.8	2.8	2.8	2.8	2.8	2.8	2.7	2.7	2.7	2.9	2.9	2.8	2.9	3.1	3.1	3.1	3.0
1976	4.1	4.0	3.9	4.0	4.0	3.9	4.0	3.9	3.7	3.5	3.4	3.3	3.3	3.2	3.2	3.2	3.2	3.2	3.2	3.2	3.2	3.2	3.4	3.4	3.4	3.4	3.7	3.7	3.7	3.6
1977	4.0	4.0	3.9	3.9	3.9	3.9	4.0	3.8	3.7	3.5	3.3	3.2	3.2	3.2	3.2	3.1	3.2	3.2	3.2	3.1	3.1	3.2	3.3	3.3	3.3	3.4	3.6	3.6	3.6	3.5
1978	4.0	3.9	3.8	3.8	3.9	3.8	3.9	3.7	3.6	3.4	3.2	3.2	3.2	3.1	3.1	3.1	3.1	3.1	3.1	3.0	3.0	3.1	3.2	3.2	3.2	3.2	3.5	3.5	3.5	3.4
1979	3.8	3.7	3.7	3.7	3.7	3.6	3.7	3.6	3.4	3.2	3.1	3.0	3.0	2.9	2.9	2.9	2.9	2.9	2.9	2.8	2.8	2.6	3.0	3.0	2.9	3.0	3.2	3.2	3.2	3.1
1980	3.7	3.6	3.5	3.6	3.6	3.5	3.6	3.4	3.3	3.1	2.9	2.8	2.9	2.8	2.7	2.7	2.7	2.7	2.7	2.7	2.6	2.7	2.8	2.8	2.8	2.8	3.0	3.0	2.9	2.8
1981	3.6	3.5	3.5	3.5	3.5	3.4	3.5	3.3	3.2	3.0	2.8	2.8	2.8	2.7	2.7	2.6	2.6	2.6	2.6	2.6	2.5	2.6	2.7	2.7	2.6	2.7	2.8	2.8	2.8	2.7
1982	4.2	4.1	4.1	4.1	4.1	4.0	4.2	4.0	3.9	3.7	3.6	3.5	3.5	3.5	3.5	3.5	3.5	3.5	3.5	3.5	3.5	3.5	3.7	3.7	3.7	3.7	4.0	4.0	4.0	3.9
1983	4.2	4.1	4.1	4.1	4.1	4.1	4.2	4.0	3.9	3.7	3.6	3.5	3.6	3.5	3.5	3.5	3.5	3.5	3.6	3.5	3.5	3.6	3.7	3.7	3.7	3.8	4.0	4.0	4.0	4.0
1984	4.4	4.3	4.3	4.3	4.3	4.3	4.4	4.3	4.2	4.0	3.9	3.8	3.8	3.8	3.8	3.8	3.8	3.8	3.8	3.8	3.8	3.9	4.0	4.0	4.1	4.1	4.3	4.4	4.4	4.4
1985	4.8	4.7	4.7	4.7	4.8	4.7	4.8	4.7	4.6	4.4	4.3	4.3	4.3	4.3	4.3	4.3	4.3	4.4	4.4	4.4	4.4	4.5	4.7	4.7	4.7	4.8	5.0	5.1	5.1	5.1
1986	5.0	4.9	4.9	4.9	5.0	4.9	5.0	5.0	4.9	4.7	4.6	4.6	4.6	4.6	4.6	4.6	4.6	4.7	4.7	4.7	4.7	4.8	5.1	5.1	5.1	5.2	5.4	5.5	5.5	5.5

To the end of	*From the beginning of*																														
	1956	*1957*	*1958*	*1959*	*1960*	*1961*	*1962*	*1963*	*1964*	*1965*	*1966*	*1967*	*1968*	*1969*	*1970*	*1971*	*1972*	*1973*	*1974*	*1975*	*1976*	*1977*	*1978*	*1979*	*1980*	*1981*	*1982*	*1983*	*1984*	*1985*	*1986*
1956	−6.8																														
1957	0.7	8.7																													
1958	−0.3	3.1	−2.2																												
1959	−0.5	1.7	−1.6	−1.0																											
1960	1.4	3.5	1.8	3.9	9.1																										
1961	1.9	3.8	2.6	4.2	6.9	4.8																									
1962	2.8	4.5	3.6	5.1	7.3	6.4	7.9																								
1963	2.7	4.1	3.4	4.5	6.0	5.0	5.0	2.2																							
1964	2.9	4.2	3.6	4.6	5.7	4.9	4.9	3.5	4.8																						
1965	2.6	3.7	3.1	3.8	4.7	3.6	3.6	2.1	2.1	−0.5																					
1966	2.4	3.3	2.7	3.4	4.0	3.2	2.9	1.7	1.5	−0.1	0.2																				
1967	1.7	2.5	1.9	2.4	2.9	2.0	1.5	0.3	−0.2	−1.8	−2.4	−5.0																			
1968	1.8	2.5	2.0	2.4	2.8	2.1	1.7	0.7	0.4	−0.7	−0.8	−1.3	2.6																		
1969	1.1	1.7	1.1	1.4	1.7	0.9	0.4	−0.6	−1.1	−2.2	−2.7	−3.6	−2.9	−8.1																	
1970	2.1	2.8	2.4	2.7	3.1	2.5	2.3	1.6	1.5	0.9	1.2	1.5	3.7	4.3	18.4																
1971	2.7	3.3	3.0	3.4	3.7	3.3	3.1	2.6	2.6	2.3	2.8	3.3	5.5	6.5	14.6	11.0															
1972	2.9	3.6	3.2	3.6	4.0	3.6	3.5	3.0	3.1	2.9	3.4	4.0	5.8	6.7	12.1	9.1	7.3														
1973	2.8	3.4	3.1	3.5	3.8	3.4	3.3	2.9	2.9	2.7	3.1	3.6	5.0	5.6	9.3	6.4	4.2	1.1													
1974	2.5	3.1	2.7	3.0	3.3	2.9	2.8	2.4	2.4	2.1	2.4	2.7	3.9	4.1	6.7	3.9	1.7	−1.0	−3.1												
1975	3.1	3.6	3.4	3.7	4.0	3.7	3.6	3.3	3.3	3.2	3.6	4.0	5.1	5.5	8.0	6.0	4.8	4.0	5.4	14.6											
1976	3.8	4.3	4.1	4.5	4.8	4.5	4.5	4.3	4.4	4.4	4.9	5.4	6.6	7.1	9.4	8.0	7.4	7.5	9.7	16.6	18.6										
1977	3.7	4.2	4.0	4.3	4.6	4.4	4.3	4.1	4.2	4.2	4.6	5.0	6.1	6.5	8.4	7.1	6.4	6.3	7.6	11.4	9.9	1.7									
1978	3.5	4.0	3.8	4.1	4.4	4.1	4.1	3.8	4.0	3.9	4.2	4.6	5.5	5.8	7.5	6.2	5.5	5.2	6.0	8.4	6.4	0.8	−0.1								
1979	3.2	3.6	3.4	3.7	3.9	3.7	3.6	3.4	3.4	3.3	3.6	3.9	4.7	4.8	6.2	5.0	4.2	3.8	4.3	5.8	3.7	−0.9	−2.1	−4.2							
1980	2.9	3.4	3.1	3.4	3.6	3.3	3.3	3.0	3.1	3.0	3.2	3.4	4.1	4.2	5.4	4.2	3.4	3.0	3.2	4.3	2.4	−1.3	−2.3	−3.4	−2.6						
1981	2.8	3.2	3.0	3.2	3.4	3.1	3.1	2.8	2.8	2.7	2.9	3.1	3.7	3.8	4.9	3.7	3.0	2.5	2.7	3.6	1.8	−1.2	−2.0	−2.6	−1.8	−1.0					
1982	4.1	4.5	4.4	4.6	4.9	4.7	4.7	4.5	4.7	4.7	5.0	5.3	6.0	6.2	7.4	6.6	6.2	6.1	6.6	7.9	7.0	5.1	5.8	7.4	11.5	19.3	43.8				
1983	4.1	4.5	4.4	4.6	4.9	4.7	4.7	4.5	4.7	4.7	5.0	5.2	5.9	6.1	7.2	6.4	6.0	5.9	6.4	7.5	6.7	5.1	5.6	6.8	9.8	14.2	22.7	4.7			
1984	4.5	4.9	4.8	5.1	5.3	5.2	5.2	5.1	5.2	5.2	5.5	5.8	6.5	6.7	7.8	7.1	6.8	6.8	7.3	8.4	7.7	6.4	7.1	8.4	11.1	14.8	20.6	10.4	16.4		
1985	5.3	5.7	5.6	5.9	6.2	6.1	6.1	6.1	6.2	6.3	6.7	7.0	7.7	8.0	9.1	8.5	8.4	8.5	9.1	10.3	9.8	8.9	9.8	11.3	14.1	17.8	23.1	16.8	23.4	30.9	
1986	5.7	6.1	6.0	6.3	6.7	6.6	6.6	6.6	6.7	6.8	7.3	7.6	8.3	8.6	9.7	9.1	9.1	9.2	9.8	11.0	10.6	9.9	10.8	12.2	14.8	18.0	20.4	17.4	21.9	24.9	19.1

Source: Ibbotson Associates [1986], with the 1986 figures computed by the authors.

loss and the maximum annual gain on bonds have been much less than those for stocks for over a half a century of experience. Hence, for some risk-averse investors, bonds are more attractive than stocks.[5]

Wealth Distributions Implied by Stock and Bond Investments

Table 5–4 displays the results of simulated stock and bond investments based on the individual single year return values given in the diagonal elements of Tables 5–2 and 5–3.

In each case annual returns were drawn randomly from the tables to simulate investment performance over the length of time the investment was assumed to be held. The table summarizes returns and wealth accumulations for holding periods of 10, 20, and 30 years, assuming an original investment of $1,000.

Table 5–4(a) shows that in approximately 10 percent of all cases, the investor who invests $1,000 in the S&P 500 and holds this investment, reinvesting all dividends, for 20 years will end up with less than $2,565. The average annual geometric mean return for this level of final wealth is just 4.82 percent. But on the more optimistic side, about half the time, after 30 years of buying and holding the S&P 500, an investor would have accumulated more than $19,879, corresponding to a geometric return of 10.48 percent. Notice that the longer the holding period, the narrower the range of geometric mean returns between the 10th and the 90th percentiles, though the wider the range of final dollar wealth levels. The equivalent simulations for the returns on long-term corporate bonds are displayed in Table 5–4(b).

One word of caution is in order. The figures in the table are valid only if we assume no transactions costs and that the investor "bought and held" the securities composing the index with no intermediate trading—except to reflect changes in the composition of the index or to reinvest dividends and interest income. These assumptions may not be realistic; on the other hand, we have learned a very basic lesson about the profitability of a truly "unmanaged" portfolio. To earn the returns shown, under our assumptions, would have required no skill, no brains beyond the average, no insider information or "hot tips," and no forecasting ability. And, by ignoring income taxes and transactions costs, we have concentrated on assessing the actual returns on stocks and bonds without having to know the investor's tax bracket, number of dependents, or risk preferences.

This discussion of geometric returns and wealth accumulations gives us a chance to correct a misperception that is common in the financial planning field. Too often the following ill-informed logic is employed by those attempting to sell their financial services: "During the past 10 years our fund has generated annual returns that have averaged 20 percent. An investor who invests $10,000 with us for 20 years, assuming the same return, could expect to accumulate $383,000 after 20 years." The statement is wrong because it compounds the average arithmetic return, $E(R) = .20$, over 20 years rather than the

---

[5]A legitimate question is: Why are bond returns less disperse than stock returns? The general answer was given in Chapter 3 where we noted that the rules for dividing up corporate wealth include a provision whereby the issuing corporation is required to allocate cash flows to bondholders (coupon interest payments and principal repayments) in the prescribed amount prior to paying stockholders. By this rule, the stock of a corporation would have to be more risky than the bonds of the same corporation.

TABLE 5–4 **Wealth Accumulations from Simulated Investments in Stock and Bond Portfolios**
($1,000 initial investment)

Percentile Ranking	Final Wealth for Investment Period of:			Geometric Return for Investment Period of:		
	10 yrs.	*20 yrs.*	*30 yrs.*	*10 yrs.*	*20 yrs.*	*30 yrs.*
(a) Stock Portfolios						
10	$1,327	$ 2,565	$ 5,194	2.87%	4.82%	5.64%
20	1,797	3,707	8,028	6.04	6.77	7.19
30	2,142	4,966	11,614	7.92	8.34	8.52
40	2,490	6,034	15,244	9.55	9.40	9.51
50	2,867	7,394	19,879	11.10	10.52	10.48
60	3,225	8,926	25,279	12.42	11.56	11.37
70	3,705	10,699	30,998	13.99	12.58	12.13
80	4,322	13,247	42,092	15.76	13.79	13.27
90	5,558	18,031	61,279	18.71	15.55	14.70
(b) Corporate Bond Portfolios						
10	$1,212	$1,757	$2,497	1.94%	2.86%	3.10%
20	1,329	1,965	2,931	2.89	3.43	3.65
30	1,410	2,170	3,265	3.50	3.95	4.02
40	1,485	2,338	3,619	4.04	4.34	4.38
50	1,559	2,524	3,999	4.54	4.74	4.73
60	1,662	2,737	4,472	5.21	5.16	5.12
70	1,766	2,988	4,953	5.85	5.62	5.48
80	1,910	3,313	5,720	6.69	6.17	5.98
90	2,131	3,899	6,932	7.86	7.04	6.66

average geometric return. Actually, if this portfolio was invested in stocks with a standard deviation equal to that of the S&P 500 index, the accumulation of wealth would be more on the order of $220,000. The difference between $220,000 and $383,000, to an investor planning for retirement, needless to say, is substantial.

Index Construction

It is instructive to know just how the returns on stock market indexes are calculated if we are going to use and interpret the resulting figures. The return on the S&P 500 Index, for example, is constructed by weighting each security's observed return by its total value (the number of shares outstanding times the price per share) relative to the total value of all stocks in the index. This calculation can be written algebraically as:

$$R_{S\&P,t} = \sum_{i=1}^{500} w_{it-1} R_{it}$$

where

$$w_{it-1} = \frac{P_{it-1} n_{it-1}}{\sum_{i=1}^{500} P_{it-1} n_{it-1}}$$

and where P_{it} is the price of the ith security in period t, and n_{it} is the number of shares of the ith security outstanding in period t.

This particular means for representing the general movement of the market is, of course, arbitrary. Alternative market indexes, some of which we discussed in Chapter 4, can be constructed by using a different set of securities or by altering the weights (the w's) used to collect the returns together. For example, the Dow Jones Industrial Average uses 30 common stocks instead of 500 and it weights them, not by total market value, but exclusively on the basis of price per share. In Table 5–5, returns for the Wilshire 5000 Index, calculated using market value weights and alternatively using equal weights for the component stocks are compared to the S&P 500 returns given originally in Table 5–1. Not surprisingly, the returns generated from these different broad-based indexes are quite different. In this case, it reflects variations both in the weighting schemes used as well as in the stocks included. The equally weighted Wilshire Index, however, differs from the value-weighted Wilshire Index only in the weights. The former gives more weight to the returns generated by the stocks of smaller firms than the latter. As you can see, an investor who chose a portfolio with greater representation in smaller firms would have fared quite well in the 1970s and early 1980s.

In 1981 the return observed on the Wilshire 5000 equal-weighted index was *positive*, while the returns observed on the other two indexes were *negative*. This means that the

TABLE 5–5   Historical Returns on Equal-Weighted and Value-Weighted Portfolios

		Wilshire 5000 Total Performance Index	
Year	S&P 500 Index (percent)	Value-Weighted (percent)	Equal-Weighted (percent)
1971	14.3	17.7	26.9
1972	19.0	18.0	9.4
1973	−14.7	− 8.1	−17.8
1974	−26.5	−36.5	−42.1
1975	37.2	35.6	66.8
1976	23.8	29.3	59.5
1977	− 7.2	− 2.6	31.5
1978	6.6	9.3	27.7
1979	18.4	25.6	40.0
1980	32.4	33.7	33.8
1981	− 4.9	− 3.7	5.6
1982	21.4	18.7	36.9
1983	22.5	23.5	49.5
1984	6.3	3.0	− 2.1
1985	31.7	32.6	44.0
1986	18.3	16.1	23.0
Average return, $E(R)$	12.4	13.3	24.5
Standard deviation of return, $\sigma(R)$	17.9	19.1	28.4

Source: Wilshire Associates, Santa Monica, Calif. The Total Performance Index assumes all cash dividends are reinvested in the Wilshire 5000 Equity Index at the end of each month.

stocks of very large companies such as General Motors, IBM, and Boeing, performed relatively poorly compared to the stocks of smaller companies such as Airborne Express, Sunstar Foods, Tandem Computers, University Genetics Corporation, and U.S. Bankcorp. Some simple comparisons of "good" and "bad" years in the stock market reveal a tendency for the Wilshire equal-weighted index to be more volatile than the S&P 500. This, as can be seen from the methods of calculation in the bottom of Table 5–5, suggests a tendency for so-called large capitalization firms (those with relatively large values of $n_{it}P_{it}$) to supply less volatile year-to-year returns than so-called small capitalization firms.

Maintaining an investment in a securities portfolio which tracks an index that is anything other than value-weighted requires active trading.[6] Securities which experience price increases must be sold, with the proceeds reinvested in securities experiencing price declines. To emulate exactly an equal-weighted index, one would have to engage in such "portfolio rebalancing" on a continuous basis. From a practical standpoint, however, this may be unnecessary. Weekly or monthly rebalancing may get one "close enough" to the index.

As straightforward as these returns seem, buying and holding a stock market index cannot produce returns that are *fully* representative of the returns on *all* common stock investments. Each investor's holding period returns will depend crucially on which particular stocks are owned, and in what amounts. And, since some investors may be better at picking stocks than others, one would expect to find considerable variation in the range of actual experience with common stock portfolios. In Chapter 6 we will explore more fully whether or not there are obvious ways to use investment strategies to enhance one's holding period returns over those discussed in this section.

The Historical Record: Other Investment Alternatives

Figures 5–4 and 5–5 display historical mean returns and standard deviations for an array of investment opportunities. Figure 5–4 supplies estimates of 10- and 5-year geometric mean returns for periods ending in 1981 on everything from bonds to Chinese ceramics. Figure 5–5 displays annual arithmetic mean returns and standard deviations of returns measured over the period 1960 to 1984 on different financial securities. Some of these investment types are discussed further below.

Government Bonds and Short-Term Bills

The annual returns on U.S. Treasury securities are given in Figure 5–6 and are compared with corporate bond returns. U.S. Treasury bills are short-term securities, typically having one- to three-month maturities, but in no case having maturities longer than one year. The returns on these securities have shifted fundamentally since they became active instruments of federal monetary policy around the time of the Korean War. Prior to this, the returns offered by these securities were affected by nonmarket factors,

---

[6]Maintaining an investment in a value-weighted index also involves some trading, to the extent that some securities are "delisted" and others added over time, or whenever certain securities disappear (as can happen with mergers, acquisitions, and bankruptcies).

FIGURE 5–4   Returns on Investment Opportunities (average annual geometric; period ending June 1, 1981)

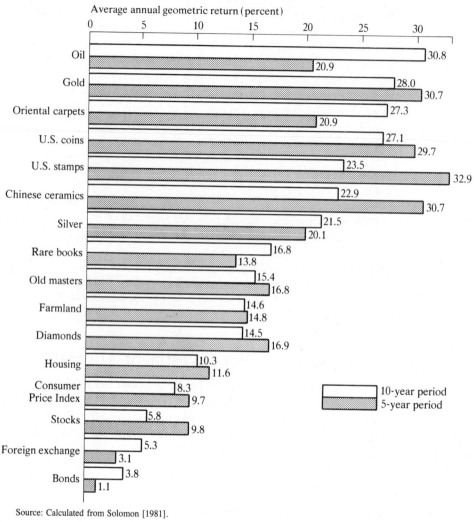

Source: Calculated from Solomon [1981].

including a "pegging" system for interest rates which was used to hold down the cost of government financing. The close-to-zero returns observed during the 1933 to 1942 period reflected demand and supply factors induced by the Depression years, including: excess industrial capacity, low levels of inflation (even deflation), and an apparent low level of investor time preference.

The long-term U.S. Treasury series is made up of bonds with 20-year maturities (which are somewhat longer than those for the Corporate Bond Index presented earlier). Holding

FIGURE 5–5   **Returns and Standard Deviations on Financial Market Opportunities (1960–1984)**

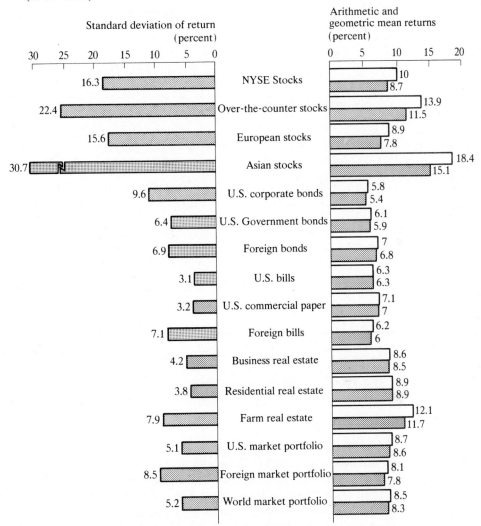

period returns on these issues vary markedly as a result of changes in interest rates inducing changes in the prices of the longer-term bonds. Note that the arithmetic mean return on Treasury bonds was 4.4 percent over the 60-year period, compared to 5.1 percent for corporate bonds, 3.5 percent for the shorter-term Treasury bills, and 12 percent for the S&P index of common stocks. In general, these differences in ex post returns are matched by differences in the ex post variability of the returns as measured by the standard deviation.

FIGURE 5–6   Historical Returns on Investments in Bonds and Stocks (1926–1985)

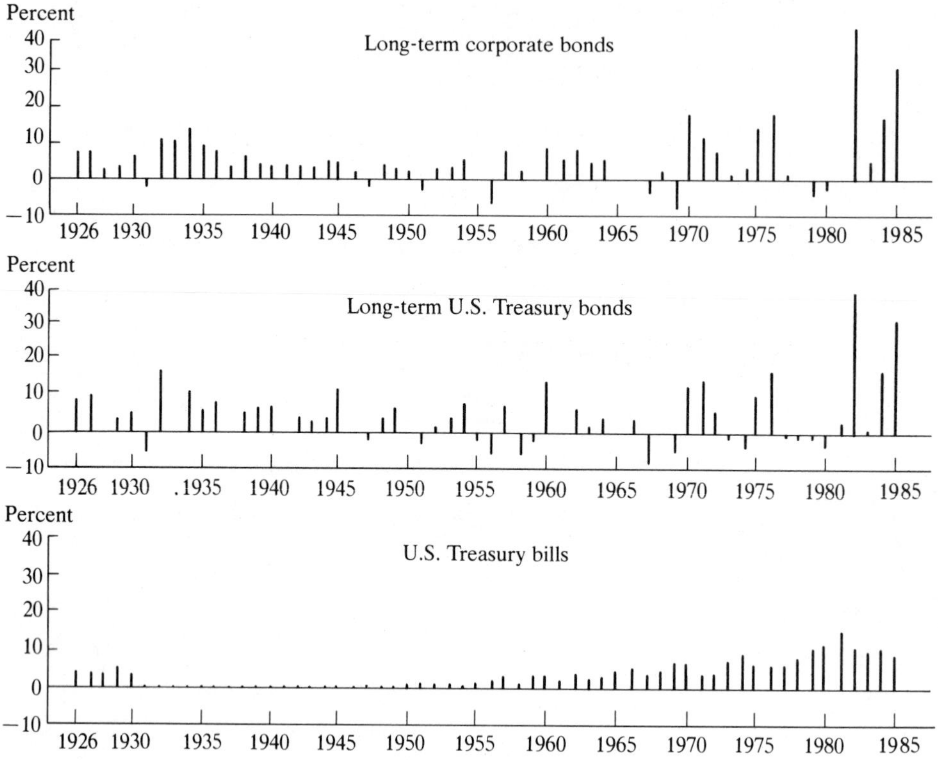

Source: Calculated from Ibbotson Associates [1986].

Foreign Common Stocks

Historical returns on the common stocks of various countries (to U.S. dollar investors) are estimated in Figure 5–7 along with their respective standard deviations. The figures suggest that foreign national stock markets have returns which tend to differ from one another. High returns to Japan, Hong Kong, and Singapore equities generally were not matched by returns in other areas of the world during this period. The highly negative return on Mexican equities was attributable to the precipitous fall of the peso in this period. EAFE is an index composed of European, Australian, and Far Eastern common stocks. These numbers are important to our later analysis of **international investment opportunities** in Chapter 20.

Collectibles and Objects of Art

Would it be useful to you to know that an Egyptian black schist ushebti figure, purchased in 1972 for £347, sold in May 1974 for £3675? Or that a John Herring "Study of Coach Horses Waiting a Change on a Great North Road," purchased in 1968 for $14,000, sold in October 1973 for $170,000? While such figures are interesting, they do

FIGURE 5–7   **Returns and Standard Deviations to U.S. Investors on Stocks in 21 Countries (1970–1985)**

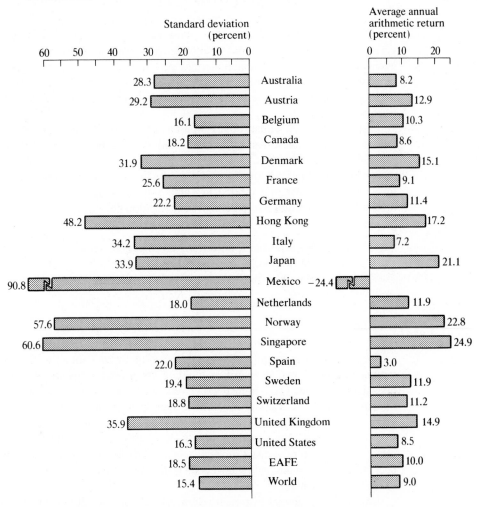

Source: Calculated from *Capital International Perspective,* various dates.

not provide appropriate comparisons to other opportunities since, though we tend to hear of the great profits made in art transactions, we don't tend to hear much about the losers.

Without an ability to study returns from art investments that is not contaminated by such **selection bias,** it's impossible to assess the average returns to investments in art. Generalizing from the particular is a hazardous approach, especially when data are unavailable to confirm or deny the particulars. Even apparently general statements can be misleading. One article on the subject[7] summarizes an index prepared by *"The London*

---

[7]James O. Winjun and Joanne T. Winjun, "The Art Investment Market," *Michigan Business Review,* November 1974.

Times and one of London's leading auction houses" that, while mutual funds increased 8-fold over the 20-year period 1950–70, "Old Master prints increased 37-fold, modern art increased 29-fold, and Old Master drawings 22-fold. . . ." While these figures *may* reflect the true nature of the art market over that period, one must be alert to obvious potential biases in the figures. Thus, those paintings that declined in value during the period (say, to near zero) undoubtedly were less likely to have been sold and may have even disappeared from circulation (into private collections for personal consumption purposes). Since such paintings would tend to reappear less frequently "on one of London's leading auction houses" the *average returns* would tend to reflect only those objects that increased in value.[8]

In spite of this disclaimer, objects of art and other collectibles, such as antiques, coins, and stamps, are investment opportunities which may provide substantial returns (and probably substantial risks). Data that may give reasonable clues as to the ex post returns generated in past periods from a portfolio containing a representative collection of these investments is reluctantly offered in Table 5–6. As long as you remember the lesson offered by the selection bias potentially contained in the numbers, some comparisons can be made:

1. Like common stocks, during any given period, some art and collectibles do well and some do poorly.
2. The variation in price over time is impossible to determine since any given art object does not generally trade regularly.

Real Estate

We all have a stake in real estate, either directly or indirectly. Clearly, if you are buying a house or own an apartment building, the impact of the return on your real estate investment is direct and immediate. Even if you are renting, however, you will be influenced by the real estate investment market. Rents are affected by the returns that owners demand for investments in properties and the net cash flows they expect to receive from continued operation of the property. Knowledge of the influence of returns on real estate may, therefore, impact on a consumer's decision to rent or buy, as well as on the decision to invest in the real estate market instead of (or in conjunction with) an investment in the securities market.

Unfortunately, actual historical return distributions are difficult to construct for real estate due to the selection bias problem mentioned earlier. Nevertheless, some attempts have been made to measure historical returns from real estate holdings. For example, a study of 463 industrial properties that exchanged hands between 1973 and 1978 was carried out by Hoag [1980]. The value-weighted arithmetic mean return over the period was about 13.5 percent with a standard deviation of about 30 percent per year, quite comparable to the figures for individual common stocks presented earlier.

---

[8]To a much lesser extent, similar biases exist for our stock market indexes. In particular, stocks that are eliminated from the exchange because of financial trouble are not included in the return calculations for that period because end-of-period prices will not exist (unless they are collected separately).

TABLE 5–6   The Rates of Return to Art and Coins

(a) American Paintings Sold at Sotheby's, New York, 1979–1980

Item	Date of Purchase	Purchase Price	Date of Most Recent Sale	Most Recent Price	Annual Geometric Return, G
The Plains Country West Texas, Benton	1961	$ 2,500	1979	$ 11,000	8.6%
On the Swing, Brown	1966	1,100	1980	43,000	30.1
The Sidewalk Dance, Brown	1914	730	1980	105,000	7.8
Street Musician, Brown	1938	100	1980	15,000	12.8
The Parade, Burchfield	1972	15,000	1979	40,000	15.0
Centerport Series, Dove	1973	2,700	1979	3,500	4.0
The Beach at Cohasset, Gifford	1968	2,200	1980	47,500	29.2
Sea Widow Summer #2, Hartley	1944	1,500	1980	42,000	9.7
Still Life with Calla, Hartley	1974	2,000	1980	7,500	23.5

(b) Impressionist and Modern Paintings Sold at Sotheby's and Christie's in New York, May 1980

Item	Year of Purchase	Purchase Price	Sale Price	Annual Growth Rate
Peasant in a Blue Blouse, Cézanne	1959	$406,000	$3,900,000	10.7%
Nude Study, Dégas	1962	197,700	660,000	6.9
Tahitian Women under the Palms, Gauguin	1960	38,000	1,800,000	15.6
Argenteuil, Monet	1948	8,500	570,000	14.0

(c) Price Performance of 20 Modern Coins 1950–1980

	Grade	1950	1955	1960	1965	1970	1975	1980
1878 One Cent	Unc	$ 7	$ 13	$ 29	$ 100	$ 88	$ 95	$ 135
1909 SVDB One Cent	Unc	13	30	98	350	200	275	400
1914-D One Cent	Unc	20	80	275	775	560	675	750
1883 NC Five Cents	Unc	1	2	4	8	11	40	50
1926-S Five Cents	Unc	70	100	175	400	440	470	625
1910 Dime	Proof	4	8	44	80	100	185	600
1911-D Dime	Unc	4	5	15	19	23	75	275
1916-D Dime	Unc	10	150	360	750	675	950	2,500
1942 Dime	Proof	1	3	5	23	20	55	425
1895 Quarter	Proof	7	12	43	75	100	350	600
1897-O Quarter	Unc	16	50	100	145	125	325	1,500
1917-Type I Quarter	Unc	3	6	10	36	48	175	275
1930 Quarter	Unc	3	5	8	23	33	75	150
1932-D Quarter	Unc	33	45	90	240	250	425	3,000
1936-D Quarter	Unc	9	25	25	265	245	270	900
1892 Fifty Cents	Unc	4	9	20	60	100	400	800
1915 Fifty Cents	Proof	30	250	500	575	550	625	1,200
1916 Fifty Cents	Unc	6	18	25	55	110	210	400
1936 Fifty Cents	Proof	16	45	118	350	265	475	2,400
1949-S Fifty Cents	Unc	1	2	5	27	24	38	250
Total		$348	$858	$1,999	$4,316	$3,967	$6,188	$17,235

Source: (a) and (b): J. Patrick Cooney, "Paintings" in Marshall Blume and Jack Friedman (Eds.), *Encyclopedia of Investments* (New York: Warren, Gorham, and Lamont, 1982). (c): R.S. Yeoman, *A Guide Book of the United States Coins*, 4th through 34th editions, 1951–81 (Racine, Wis.: Western Publishing Co.).

FIGURE 5–8   **Rates of Return to Investment in Real Estate (1960–1984)**

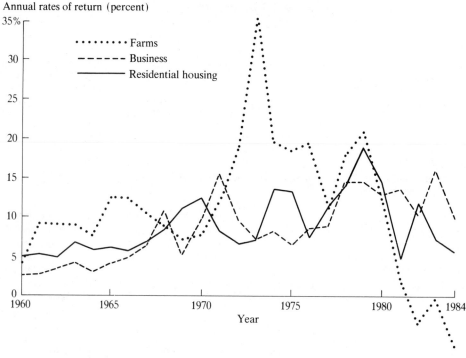

Source: Calculated from Ibbotson, Seigel, and Love [1985].

Other evidence comes from Ibbotson, Seigel, and Love [1985] and is presented in Figure 5–8. The arithmetic mean returns are 12.1 percent for farm real estate, 8.9 percent for residential housing, and 8.6 percent for business real estate over the period from 1960 to 1984. Note that the figures for the 1970s, unlike those for common stocks and long-term bonds, are quite high. The value of farm property during this period rose rather rapidly, but fell back sharply after 1980.

Commodity Futures

The rates of return to commodity future contracts (which are financial instruments based on a contract for the exchange of a commodity for money at some future date) also have been the subject of study. Over the period 1950 to 1976, Bodie and Rosansky [1980] found that the average rates of return for an index of between 10 and 20 commodity futures matched fairly closely the average overall return earned on common stocks during that period. These results are presented in Table 5–7. In addition to offering rates of return that were slightly in excess of the average rates of return offered by common stocks during the period, commodity futures showed year-to-year variability that was actually quite close to that displayed by common stocks. This seemed to be true in spite of the fact that there was little correlation in the annual returns of the common stock and

TABLE 5–7   Rates of Return on Commodity Futures (1950–1976)

(a) Annual Rates of Return

Year	Common Stocks	Commodity Futures	Rate of Inflation
1950	31.7%	−52.6%	5.8%
1951	24.0	26.7	5.9
1952	18.4	−1.2	0.9
1953	1.0	−6.3	0.6
1954	56.6	14.9	−0.5
1955	31.6	−4.8	0.4
1956	6.6	14.8	2.9
1957	−10.8	−2.3	3.0
1958	43.4	−1.3	1.8
1959	11.9	0.5	1.5
1960	0.5	−0.1	1.5
1961	26.9	1.6	0.7
1962	−8.7	0.9	1.2
1963	22.8	22.8	1.7
1964	16.5	12.1	1.2
1965	12.5	10.6	1.9
1966	−10.1	14.7	3.4
1967	24.0	4.1	3.0
1968	11.1	1.2	4.7
1969	−8.5	20.8	6.1
1970	4.0	12.0	5.5
1971	14.3	3.3	3.4
1972	19.0	33.7	3.4
1973	−14.7	101.5	8.8
1974	−26.5	32.0	12.2
1975	37.2	−4.0	7.0
1976	23.9	12.8	4.8

Source: Bodie and Rosansky [1980].

(b) Average Returns by Commodity

Commodity	Arithmetic Mean Return	Standard Deviation of Return
Wheat	3.2%	30.8%
Corn	2.1	26.3
Oats	1.7	19.5
Soybeans	13.6	32.3
Soybean oil	25.8	57.7
Soybean meal	11.9	35.6
Broilers	13.1	39.2
Plywood	18.0	40.0
Potatoes	6.9	42.1
Platinum	0.6	25.2
Wool	7.4	37.0
Cotton	8.9	36.2
Orange juice	2.5	31.8
Propane	68.3	202.1
Cocoa	15.7	54.6
Silver	3.6	25.6
Copper	19.8	47.2
Cattle	7.4	21.6
Hogs	13.3	36.6
Pork bellies	16.1	39.3
Egg	−4.8	27.9
Lumber	13.1	34.7
Sugar	25.4	116.2

commodity futures index. For example, the historical correlation between the commodity futures and common stocks was − .24. As one might expect, however, the correlation over this period of time between commodity futures and the level of inflation was quite high, .60.[9]

The variability in the average returns and the standard deviations that were apparent over this period varied substantially from commodity to commodity. For example, the arithmetic mean rate of return on potato futures was around 7 percent per year with a standard deviation of over 40 percent. The rate of return to propane futures was 68 percent and the standard deviation somewhat over 200 percent. Historically, the largest returns

---

[9]Inflation may explain the negative correlation between returns on stocks and commodity futures. Inflation, reflecting the increasing price of commodities, also serves to increase the price of money—the interst rate. As interest rates increase, the price of bonds and stocks tend to fall since the future cash flows from these securities are discounted at a higher rate. Unless the cash flows on the securities expand proportionally with inflation, there will be a negative correlation between ex post inflation and ex post stock returns. Thus, commodity prices and stocks will be negatively correlated when the main driving force is inflation. In noninflationary times the relationship may not be present.

seem to have been offered by investments in sugar (but more recently the prices of sugar have fallen drastically), soybean oil, propane, and plywood. The lowest returns seem to have been associated with platinum, silver, and the various grains. Egg futures seem to be the only ones that offered a negative rate of return during the period. Precisely what can be gained by an analysis of the rates of return of the individual commodity is not very clear. Even the averages supply limited insight. From 1976 (when their study ended) through the mid 1980s most commodities offered returns that were well below those offered on common stocks and bonds. For example, between the end of 1976 and the end of 1985, the Commodity Research Bureau "Futures Price Index" generated an average annual geometric return that was near zero! Even over the longer two-decade period between 1967 and 1986, the average geometric return was only about 4 percent.

The Value of the Aggregate World Market Wealth Portfolio

The **aggregate world market wealth portfolio,** or the portfolio made up of all assets, will be a key to the development and analysis of concepts of risk, return, and valuation in financial markets. Consequently, we close this section by summarizing the nature of the rates of return that have been offered in the past by this aggregate portfolio. Clearly, this portfolio would have to be made up of common stocks, fixed-income corporate securities, real estate, and government securities, at the very least. Obviously, it would be useful to include such things as the value of antiques and other collectibles, and the value of unincorporated businesses whose equity or partnership interests are not generally traded, and for which no secondary market immediately exists.

In spite of the difficulties associated with constructing an aggregate world market portfolio, an attempt has been made by Ibbotson, Seigel, and Love [1985] to construct measures of the aggregate value of all corporate securities, all real estate, and all government-issued securities. Thus, for example, the market value of all common stocks listed on the NYSE in 1947 was about $60 billion. By the end of 1978, this figure had risen to a value of $790 billion, and by 1984 to almost $1,600 billion. Alternatively, the quantity of long-term U.S. corporate bonds outstanding stood at $36 billion in 1947, and $1,773 billion by 1984. Considering these and other estimates of the returns offered on financial instruments and on real estate, the study arrived at the estimates given in Table 5–8. The world's total investible wealth (excluding commodities, metals, and foreign real estate, in these calculations) in 1984 was estimated at about $13 trillion! Common stocks made up about 23 percent of the total in 1984, and bonds and short-term securities made up about 47 percent. Between 1959 and 1984 the proportion of total wealth in equities (stocks) fell somewhat, while that of other securities rose. For the most part this reflects an increasing reliance on fixed-income securities for financing government and business expenditures over the period.

Inflation and Investment Returns

All of the return figures thus far presented have ignored the influence of inflation on the value of the investor's future wealth. To take actual inflation into account requires only that nominal annual returns be converted into "real" returns by dividing one plus the nominal returns by one plus the observed rate of inflation, or

TABLE 5–8   Value of Aggregate World Market Investment Opportunities (1959 and 1984)

Investment Opportunity	Wealth (in billions)		Proportion of Aggregate Wealth (1984)
	1959	*1984*	
NYSE stocks	309	1,587	12.2%
Over-the-counter stocks	24	207	1.6
European stocks	103	489	3.8
Asian stocks	14	670	5.1
U.S. corporate bonds	196	1,773	13.6
U.S. Treasury bonds	125	1,410	10.8
Foreign bonds	329	2,284	17.5
U.S. Treasury bills	33	374	2.9
U.S. commercial paper	3	223	1.7
Foreign bills	14	103	.8
Business real estate	59	652	5.0
Residential real estate	459	3,631	27.9
Farm real estate	137	690	5.3
U.S. market portfolio	1,241	9,282	71.3
Foreign market portfolio	484	3,740	28.7
World market portfolio	1,725	13,022	100.0

Source: Ibbotson, Seigel, and Love [1985].

(5–4)   ***Real (Adjusted for Inflation) Returns***

$$R_{it}^{\text{real}} = \frac{1 + R_{it}}{1 + \Omega_t} - 1.0$$

where Ω_t is the rate of inflation and R_{it}^{real} is the computed real rate of return. With inflation of 6 percent and a return of 15 percent on the investment the real return is

$$R_{it}^{\text{real}} = \frac{1 + .15}{1 + .06} - 1 = .085 \text{ or } 8.5\%$$

Historical annual rates of inflation are given for 1950–1985 in Table 5–9. Real rates of return are presented in the table for common stocks, Treasury bonds, and Treasury bills. As one would expect, the inflation-adjusted returns are considerably lower than nominal returns. Moreover, the standard deviation of Treasury bond real returns is larger than the standard deviation of nominal returns (by about 1.5 percentage points) reflecting the negative correlation of inflation with holding-period returns on bonds.

These figures suggest an interesting question: Does the obvious importance of inflation to an investor's well-being require that returns to investment alternatives be expressed in terms of their real values rather than their nominal values (as we have done thus far)? The answer is "No." A decline in the purchasing power of the dollar affects all investment alternatives equally by a factor of $1/(1 + \Omega_t)$ during a given investment period. Thus, comparisons can be made equally well between real or nominal returns.

Changes in ex ante, or expected, inflation may influence different investments in different ways, however. If the nominal return earned by a security in period t, R_{it}, is affected by the level of inflation anticipated for future periods, then the impact of inflation is much more complex. This relationship is part of the discussion on the influence of

TABLE 5–9　　**Real Rates of Return** (adjusted for the rate of inflation)

Year	Rate of Inflation	Real Rates of Return		
		Common Stocks	Long-Term Treasury Bonds	Treasury Bills
1950	5.8%	24.5%	− 5.4%	−4.3%
1951	5.9	17.1	− 9.3	−4.1
1952	0.9	17.3	0.4	0.9
1953	0.6	−1.6	3.0	1.2
1954	−0.5	53.5	7.7	1.4
1955	0.4	31.2	0.9	1.2
1956	2.9	3.6	− 8.2	−0.5
1957	3.0	−13.4	4.3	0.2
1958	1.8	40.9	− 7.7	−0.2
1959	1.5	10.3	− 3.7	1.4
1960	1.5	− 1.0	12.1	1.2
1961	0.7	26.0	0.3	1.4
1962	1.2	− 9.8	5.6	1.6
1963	1.7	20.8	− 0.4	1.4
1964	1.2	15.1	2.3	2.3
1965	1.9	10.3	− 1.3	2.1
1966	3.3	−13.0	0.4	1.4
1967	3.0	20.3	−11.9	1.1
1968	4.7	6.0	− 4.8	0.6
1969	6.1	−13.8	−10.6	0.4
1970	5.5	− 1.4	6.4	1.1
1971	3.6	10.6	9.5	1.0
1972	3.4	15.1	2.2	0.4
1973	8.8	−21.6	− 9.1	−1.7
1974	12.2	−34.6	− 7.0	−3.7
1975	7.0	28.2	2.0	−1.1
1976	4.8	18.2	11.5	0.4
1977	6.7	−13.0	− 6.9	−1.5
1978	9.0	− 2.2	− 9.3	−1.7
1979	13.3	4.5	−12.9	−2.6
1980	12.4	17.8	−14.7	−1.0
1981	8.9	−12.8	− 6.7	5.3
1982	3.9	16.8	35.1	6.4
1983	3.8	18.1	− 3.0	4.8
1984	4.0	2.2	11.1	5.7
1985	3.8	27.4	26.3	3.8
Arithmetic mean return	4.4%	8.7%	0.4%	0.8%
Standard deviation of returns	3.6	18.9	9.2	2.2

Source: Ibbotson and Sinquefield [1982a].

economic conditions on value, summarized in Chapters 12 and 14 on bond and stock valuation.

Return and Risk—A Summary

Perhaps the most appropriate summary of the figures we have looked at in this chapter can be made by comparing the historical average arithmetic returns on a variety of

FIGURE 5–9   **Risk and Return of Portfolios** (of different types of securities; 1960–1984)

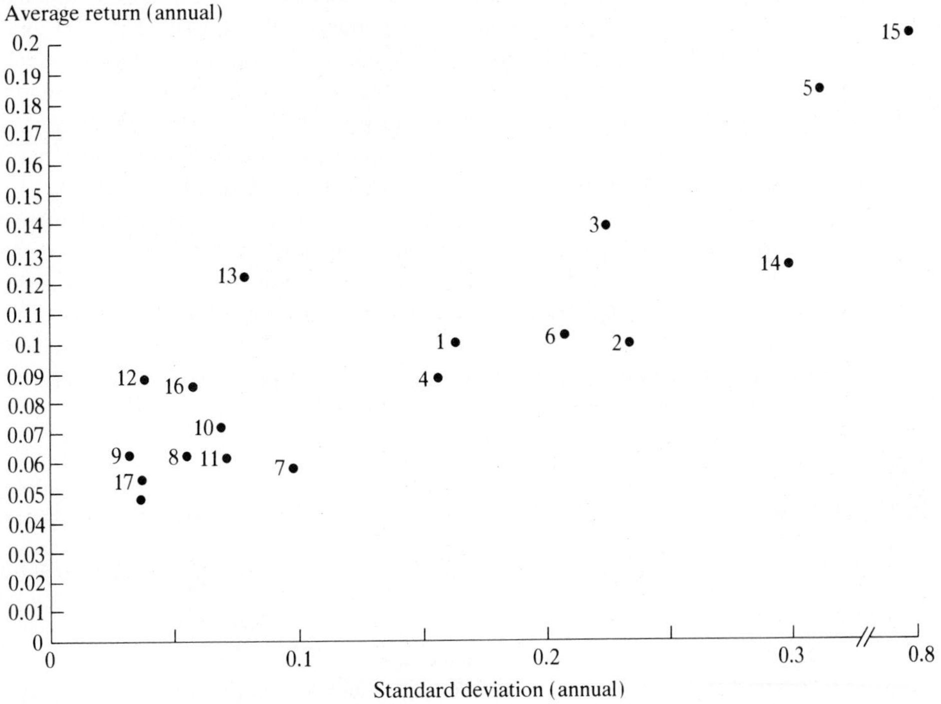

Average return (annual)

Key	Stocks	Key	Bonds	Key	Real estate and commodities
1	NYSE	7	U.S. corporate bonds	12	Residential
2	AMEX	8	U.S. Treasury bonds	13	Farms
3	OTC	9	U.S. Treasury bills	14	Gold
4	European	10	Foreign bills	15	Silver
5	Asian	11	Foreign bills	16	World
6	Other			17	U.S. inflation

Source: Computed from Ibbotson, Seigel, and Love [1985].

opportunities with the risks of those opportunities. This is done in Figure 5–9, which plots the historical relationship observed over the last 25 years, using the standard deviation as a measure of the risk associated with these investment portfolios. That there is a distinct upward slope to the set of points probably comes as no surprise. The chapters that follow will explain why this relationship exists and what should be done to allow the investor to make the most of it.

Summary

Are historical returns indicative of future returns? Only time will tell, of course, but some knowledge of past returns is useful for characterizing the kinds of investment opportunities available. Historically the most widely traded common stocks have offered annual returns in the neighborhood of 12 percent. Government and corporate bonds have generated returns that were substantially lower than this, on average. Commodities and real estate generally have offered returns between those of stocks and bonds, although the available data represent investor experience beginning with the 1950s only. Of course, investment returns have been generated in other widely divergent opportunities, such as diamonds, collectibles, coins, and artwork. Yet biases in computations prevent an exact comparison historically with the more widely traded stocks, bonds, and futures contracts. While this ex post selection bias plays havoc with historical comparisons, such numbers as can be computed are necessary for comparing investment alternatives ex ante.

In addition to substantial differences in returns, the investment alternatives summarized in this chapter differ in another important respect. Different investment opportunities carry substantially different risks. The standard deviation of the time series of returns on stocks was nearly seven times as large as that for corporate bonds over the six-decade period we looked at. The year-to-year variation of other opportunities also was substantial and serves to emphasize the attention we must pay to both return *and* risk in the course of our developments in following chapters.

References

Bodie, Zvi, and Rosansky, Victor. [1980] "Risk and Return in Commodity Futures." *Financial Analysts Journal* (May–June).

Bowers, R. David. [1982] "Coins." In Marshall Blume and Jack Friedman (Eds.), *Encyclopedia of Investments*. New York: Warren, Gorham and Lamont.

Cooney, J. Patrick. [1982] "Paintings." In Marshall Blume and Jack Friedman (Eds.), *Encyclopedia of Investments*. New York: Warren, Gorham and Lamont.

Fisher, L. [1966] "Some New Stock Market Indexes." *Journal of Business* (January).

Fisher, Lawrence, and Lorie, James. [1968] "Rates of Return on Investments in Common Stock: The Year by Year Record, 1926–65." *Journal of Business* (July).

Fisher, Lawrence, and Lorie, James. [1970] "Some Studies of Variability of Returns on Investments in Common Stocks." *Journal of Business* (April).

Hoag, James W. [1980] "Toward Indices of Real Estate Value and Return." *Journal of Finance* (May).

Ibbotson Associates. [1986] *Stocks, Bonds, Bills, and Inflation: 1986 Yearbook.* Chicago: Ibbotson Associates Capital Management Research Center.

Ibbotson, Roger G. [1980] *International Equity Study.* Chicago: R. G. Ibbotson & Co.

Ibbotson, Roger G., and Fall, Carol L. [1979] "The United States Market Wealth Portfolio." *Journal of Portfolio Management* (Fall).

Ibbotson, Roger G., and Sinquefield, Rex A. [1982a] *Stocks, Bonds, Bills and Inflation: The Past and the Future.* Charlottesville, Va.: Financial Analyst's Research Foundation.

Ibbotson, Roger G.; Siegel, Lawrence B.; and Love, Kathryn S. [1985] "World Wealth: Market Values and Returns," *Journal of Portfolio Management* (Fall).

Ibbotson, Roger G.; Sinquefield, Rex A.; and Siegel, Lawrence B. [1982b] "Historical Returns on Principal Types of Investments." In Marshall Blume and Jack Friedman (eds.), *Encyclopedia of Investments.* New York: Warren, Gorham and Lamont.

Nelson, C. R. [1976]. "Inflation and Rates of Return on Common Stocks." *Journal of Finance* (May).

Soldofsky, Robert M. [1984] "Risk and Return for Long-Term Securities: 1971–1982," *Journal of Portfolio Management* (Fall).

Solomon, Robert S., Jr. [1981]. "Bonds and Foreign Exchange May Be the Only Bargains Left," *Stock Research Investment Policy.* New York: Salomon, Brothers.

Stoll, Hans, and Whaley, John. [1983] "Transactions Costs and the Small Firm Effect." *Journal of Financial Economics* (in press).

Winjun, James O., and Winjun, Joanne T. [1974] "The Art Investment Market." *Michigan Business Review* (November).

Questions and Problems

1. An investor carefully plotted the historical annual returns on IBM's common stock over the past 30 years. The average return was 13 percent and the standard deviation of return was 18 percent. He concluded that the expected future accumulation of wealth on an investment in IBM would be at the rate of 13 percent per annum. What two mistakes has he made?

2. Money managers typically construct portfolios of securities for each client, then use the performance of these portfolios as a base for measuring how well they have performed their function. One money manager wrote this assessment: "Clients who have stayed with us for the duration of the decade have experienced average annual returns of 20 percent and standard deviations of returns of 22 percent. This compares favorably with the S&P index values of 17 percent and 16 percent." While not trying to determine if the manager's performance compares favorably with the index, why is the comparison subject to error, misstatement, and possible bias?

3. The money manager in Question 2 went on to argue, "If we continue this level of performance for the next 20 years, each client's dollar will grow to a level of $(1 + .20)^{20}$, or $15.40, by the end of the period through the 'miracle' of compound returns." What's the problem with the manager's computation?

4. Summarize how returns and risks on stock investments in different countries have differed over the past 20 years.

5. The figures below represent the monthly historical rates of return on a series of sequential investments in 30-day Treasury bills:

.004	.006	.005	.005
.004	.004	.005	.004
.003	.004	.005	.004

What annual return has been earned by an investor in these bills? Since the particular months of these returns have not been specified is the problem ambiguous? That is, does the order of the returns matter?

6. Indicate your opinion of the nature and size of the ex post selection-bias problem in measuring the average return and standard deviation of return to these investment alternatives:

   a. Luxury sailboats.

   b. Condominiums at ski resorts.

   c. "Penny" stocks on the Calcutta Exchange.

   d. Picasso originals.

   e. Indian head pennies.

   f. Office buildings in Manhattan.

7. Of all the investment alternatives mentioned in this chapter rank them in terms of historical average returns, rank them again in terms of historical average standard deviations.

8. Below are prices for a series of one-year T-bills issued at the beginning of each indicated year, and each maturing at the end of the year at a price of $100. Calculate the holding period return for each year, the 10-year average return, the average annual geometric return, and explain or interpret each of these figures.

   Year, and price at the beginning of the year

1978 . . . . $92	1981 . . . . $88	1985 . . . . $94
1979 88	1982 90	1986 93
1980 87	1983 92	1987 93
	1984 91	

9. Below are price and end-of-year dividend figures for Occidental Petroleum. Calculate the average annual holding period return and the average annual geometric return on the assumption that the dividends are reinvested in the stock when they are received (assumed to be at year's end).

	Price	Dividend
1976	20	1.00
1977	27	1.19
1978	25	1.25
1979	27	1.31
1980	40	1.92
1981	23	2.42
1982	19	2.50
1983	25	2.50
1984	28	2.50
1985	33	2.50

10. General Motors pays dividends of $1.20 per share at evenly spaced intervals four times a year. Assuming you bought the stock at $80, just after a dividend payment, reinvest your dividends (at the same risk as your investment in GM) to earn 12

percent per year, and sold your stock after one year at $75, what return did you earn on your investment?

11. You are a stock analyst for the auto industry and decide to construct an index to represent the returns to investments in that industry. You've collected the following figures for two years.

End of Year 1

	Price	Number of Shares
GM	$80	200 million
Ford	60	150 million
Chrysler	30	140 million

End of Year 2

	Price	Number of Shares	Dividend
GM	$75	200 million	$4.50
Ford	68	150 million	2.80
Chrysler	34	150 million	1.20

Compute the rate of return on an equally-weighted index and on a value-weighted index from the data, assuming the dividends were received at the end of the year.

CHAPTER

6

Market Efficiency

Introduction

While the historical return distributions for different financial assets summarized in Chapter 5 give a good deal of information about the nature of returns to investment, it will be useful to begin a preliminary investigation into how those returns are generated and how they tend to vary over time. This is not a new or novel inquiry, of course. The incentives to understand how security prices change from one time period to another have been sufficient to encourage in-depth investigations for a long time. Sometimes such studies were concerned with the relationship between the price changes and earnings, management decisions, or the growth of the economy. Many times, however, the inquiry was directed at attempts to see if *past prices* could be used to *predict* future ones. Clearly, these issues are important. Investors who understand how security prices move within a trading day or week have a substantial advantage over those who do not.

Figure 6–1, for example, lists the names of and returns on the top 20 return-generating securities from the Fortune 500 over the decade from the end of 1971 through 1981. The average return on investments in these stocks was about 26 percent—well above the 8.5 percent return on Standard & Poor's index during the period. How would you expect these securities to perform after 1981? Would these securities tend to continue outperforming the market? Or would they tend to generate low returns to compensate for the extraordinarly high returns generated in the past? Toward the end of this chapter you *should* have formed expectations about the post-1981 behavior of these firms. At that time we will disclose their actual performance to emphasize our conclusions.

FIGURE 6–1   **Top 20 Performers, 1971–1981** (Fortune 500 common stocks)

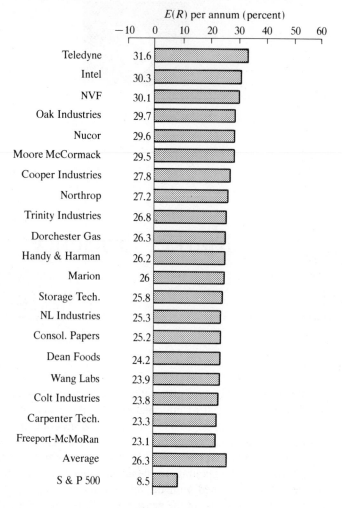

Source: Constructed from information given in *Fortune*, May 2, 1982.

In more general terms, the material in this chapter is directed to supplying insight into how security prices or rates of return behave over time. In exploring this issue, we employ some fundamental economic principles to suggest how returns ought to behave under a given set of institutional and market conditions. We then raise the question of how closely actual markets conform to the given conditions, and finish by briefly looking at a number of empirical studies that summarize the behavior of investment returns over time.

The Pricing Process

The price of a security, like the price of any commodity in a competitive market, is generated through the interaction of supply and demand. If a sufficient number of investors *increase their demand* for a security at the current market price (or expected return offered), the total quantity of the security demanded will exceed the quantity supplied. In a freely competitive market, this excess demand is eliminated through an increase in the price of the security. The increase in price will cause more of the security to be supplied and less of it to be demanded. The process continues (that is, price will continue to adjust) until a price is achieved that causes the quantity demanded and supplied to be equal. This price is termed the **equilibrium price.** At this price there will be no further tendency for any price changes to occur, and excess demand and excess supply are zero.

Precisely the same effect occurs if there is an increase in supply, although the effect on the equilibrium price is in the opposite direction. Thus, an increase in the quantity of the security supplied by some investors desiring to liquidate their investment positions creates an excess supply at the current market price, forcing the price down to a new equilibrium level.

Factors Affecting Supply and Demand

An overly simplistic and preliminary view of those factors that lead to a security being demanded or supplied by investors is summarized in Figure 6–2. Here potential investors receive information signals from a number of different sources and use that information as a basis for forming expectations about the firm's future prospects. These expectations are translated into forecasts of the return that can be had from investing in the security, as well as the risks that accompany the investment. Exactly how the signals lead to expectations of return and risk is not important at this stage but is a subject we treat throughout much of the rest of this book.

FIGURE 6–2   Information Signals and the Supply and Demand for Securities

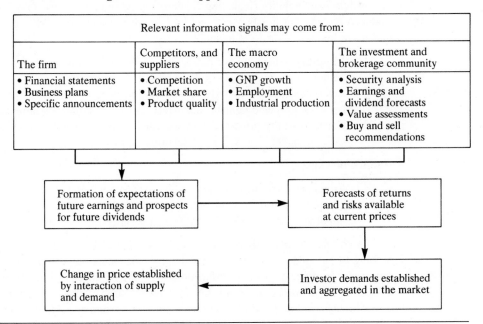

In this illustration the sources of information are divided into four groups that offer firm-specific, industrywide, and economywide information. The investment and brokerage community's part in all this is to collect information from the other three sources and analyze it with an eye to helping investors make their choices. With this information investors form expectations of future cash flows they would receive and use these expectations to form forecasts of the rate of return and risk inherent in investing in the security.

With the forecasts of return and risk, investors set their demands and supplies for securities and go to the market with these schedules. If expected returns are large, demand for the security will be great. If returns are low, the investor may choose to forego investing in that security in favor of another or in favor of increased consumption. In the market the supplies and demands of all investors are added, and the market maker (a specialist, for example) establishes a market-clearing price. Thus, if an important piece of information is presented to the market that causes many investors to revise their demand upward, the price of the security will rise from one equilibrium level before the information is disclosed to another equilibrium level after it is disclosed.

While all this is going on, individuals holding the security over the period of time that prices are changing are generating returns. The returns may be negative if the price falls or positive if the price rises as a result of the changes in demand or supply. In fact, price changes of this sort (plus cash flows in the form of interest or dividends) generated the historical returns that were scrutinized in the prior chapter.

An Ideal Market

A convenient abstraction for studying how prices are generated and behave over time is the concept of an **ideal market.** An ideal market is characterized by the assumption of absolute marketability (including liquidity, price continuity, and fairness), as we introduced the concept in Chapter 5 and by one other assumption. Thus, the assumptions that make up an ideal market include:

1. **Liquidity**—there are no transactions costs, and all investors are atomistic competitors (or price takers) in the market.
2. **Price continuity**—underlying supply and demand determine price, and temporary supply and demand imbalances have no extraneous influence on price.
3. **Fairness**—only price and time are used to discriminate between different prospective buyers and sellers of securities.

And the new one:

4. **Equal access to information**—all market participants have equal access to freely available information, including current and past price information, which is important for assessing the value of a security.

The absence of transaction costs is to be thought of broadly. Not only does it cost nothing to buy and sell securities, but the investor incurs no personal costs in terms of time spent in processing or recordkeeping that may be devoted to other productive activities. If all investors and firms are price takers, no participant has enough wealth to affect in any way the price of a security, and all investors are atomistic competitors.

The second assumption simply ensures that the market does its job of putting supply and demand together. This is not to suggest that supply and demand respond in a particular way, for this is precisely the point that needs to be considered. Rather, given the way supply and demand are affected, the price adjusts in immediate response to them.

The new assumption regarding equal and free access to information is the key to understanding how equilibrium market-clearing prices are formed in an ideal market. Literally, the assumption requires that information produced by the agents mentioned in Figure 6–2 be available to all investors simultaneously. The assumption does not require that all investors draw the same implications from the information, so *homogeneous expectations* formed from the information is *not* part of the model.

Price Adjustments in Ideal Markets

With transactions costs being zero in our ideal market, individual investors will continuously search the market for investment opportunities that allow the investor to attain the highest utility. Consistent with our discussion in Chapter 2, these are opportunities that provide returns that tend to be larger or risks that tend to be smaller than those available from alternative opportunities. Discovery of such a "profitable" opportunity would cause the individual to increase his demand for the security. The new level of demand by the investor will be influenced by the risk and the size of the returns that can be generated, as well as the investor's wealth and preferences.

In a market in which many such investors participate, all would be playing the same game. Competition for these opportunities would be great. Each individual's attempt to purchase the security offering high returns would be met with an uncountable number of other investors attempting to secure the same profit. Consequently, each would bid slightly more for the purchase of the security than the other, and this competitive pressure would drive up the security's price.

The new, higher price for the security will create a new, lower return to those who purchase the security after the adjustment process takes place. In a world in which transactions costs are zero, competition for profits will continue (with the pressure on price) until the return offered on the security no longer exceeds the return offered on other opportunities (until the "profits" are zero). At this point, excess demand for the security is zero; the quantity supplied and quantity demanded are equal; and the security price is, once again, in equilibrium at a new higher level.

The case in which investors view the security as being overpriced is equivalent in principle. As investors reassess their estimates of security value, they will enter the market with excess supplies of the security and collectively drive the market price down. In an ideal market, there is nothing to prevent them from selling securities they don't have (selling short). Consequently, the supply pressure potentially comes from everyone in the market and not just from those investors who originally held the security in their portfolios.

Since any change in the set of information will be expected to change the configuration of supply and demand, any new information signal will change price. From assumption (4), all investors will have equal access to the information set. From assumption (1), there is no cost to acting on beliefs about the value of a security generated from the information available so **the investor response to changes in the information set will be instantaneous.** Because investor response is instantaneous in this ideal market, the price of the security will adjust from its original equilibrium value (derived from the original information set) to its new equilibrium value (with use of the new information set) instantly. In other words, given the assumptions of an ideal market, the movement from one price generated by the interaction of supply and demand to another, with different supply and demand functions, takes place faster than one can say "efficient markets."

A reasonable and frequently asked question in response to this analysis is: What prevents investors from over- or underreacting to the information, causing the new price to be only a *temporary* new equilibrium position? Undoubtedly, investor forecasts with the use of the information set are imperfect. Consequently, individual investors will tend to under- or overreact. Yet, in the absence of a herd instinct (or a market psychology, either conservative or daring, that is not related to influences on the prediction of return and risk) these "mistakes" on the part of investors will not take the form of a collective systematic under- or overreaction to a particular kind of information. In this sense, the new equilibrium price would be an *unbiased* market response to the change in the information set that has been made publicly available. Thus, **in an ideal market, price responses would be** *instantaneous* **and would** *unbiasedly* **represent the new equilibrium price.**

The new price is not necessarily the price that would be generated if the market had "full information" about the prospects for the firm or the economy. After all, the information set available under our assumptions is the one that has been presented publicly to the market. Nothing in our analysis so far suggests that the price would not be different if some important privately held piece of information was disclosed. Certainly managers have a wealth of private information. A manager might logically form different expectations for the firm than would investors. In other words, the **price at any point in time reflects instantly and unbiasedly the** *market consensus expectations* **based on the information that has been** *publicly disclosed.*

However, this price is not necessarily the "correct" one, since a market price more representative of the true underlying value of the security could be generated if *private information* were used to supplement that publicly available. The difference between the price that reflects the market concensus expectations based on publicly available information, and the price that might be generated if more information were available is set forth in detail in Part IV of the book.

The implications of this theory for the movement of security returns over time is straightforward.

As new information flows into the market, competition among investors will move security prices instantaneously from one equilibrium position to another. Because returns are generated by the change in price and cash flows, the returns will be generated by the market response to the new information. Moreover, since price adjustments are instantaneous and unbiased, new information will have an effect on price that is *completely independent* of the effect of all prior information. Consequently, returns generated over time, while being created through perfectly reasonable market responses to items of information, will be *independent* from one to the next.

Due to this independence, the return (or price change) in some prior period, being greater or less than expected, implies nothing about whether the return in the current period will be greater or less. In this kind of market, returns observed over time would appear as random drawings from some probability distribution or, as it has come to be called, a **random walk** through time.[1]

Efficient Market Hypothesis

The ideas presented in the prior section have led to the development of a theory of price responses to the publication of information that is directly relevant to the valuation of securities. This theory is developed in the paragraphs that follow.[2]

By definition, the rate of return on security i in period $t + 1$ (as in equation 5–1) is

$$(6\text{–}1) \qquad \tilde{R}_{it+1} = \frac{\tilde{P}_{it+1} + \tilde{D}_{it+1} - P_{it}}{P_{it}}$$

The rate of return is a random variable because future price, $\tilde{P}_{it+1}$, and the dividend or interest, $\tilde{D}_{it+1}$, are random variables. Investors have an incentive to uncover information that would allow them to form rational predictions of $\tilde{P}_{it+1}$ and $\tilde{D}_{it+1}$. Thus, each investor would develop views regarding the likelihood that $\tilde{P}_{it+1}$ would be high, low, or somewhere in between. That is, each investor would develop a subjective probability distribution for $\tilde{P}_{it+1}$ and $\tilde{D}_{it+1}$. If investor preferences depend on the expected value and standard deviation of returns, then each investor would calculate:

$$(6\text{–}2) \qquad E(\tilde{R}_{it+1} \mid \phi_t) = \frac{E[(\tilde{P}_{it+1} + \tilde{D}_{it+1}) \mid \phi_t] - P_{it}}{P_{it}}$$

where ϕ_t is used to represent all available information useful to valuing securities in t. This expression states the expected return as *conditional* (the $\mid$ line) on the information set, ϕ_t, available to the investor when expectations were formed in period t.

If new information is published in t, investors will revise their expectations. If expectations are revised sufficiently to cause enough investors to change their demand for this ith security, then the price will change from its current level to a new level. Thus, if ϕ_t is revised to ϕ_{t+1}, the price will change from one equilibrium price, where demand and supply are equal, P_{it}^e, to another, P_{it+1}^e. Obviously, P_{it+1}^e may differ from the price that was expected $E(\tilde{P}_{it+1} \mid \phi_t)$ because of the revision in the information set. The rate of return actually generated from t to $t + 1$ or $\tilde{R}_{it+1}$, thereby, may be different from the rate of return expected $E(\tilde{R}_{it+1} \mid \phi_t)$. Such is the nature of risk and uncertainty in financial markets.

Everything that may hold relevance to the investor is included in the information set. It may include micro information on the firm's management or earnings, macro information on productivity or unemployment, and all the past prices of the security. At this point we wouldn't even throw out the possibility that some investors use information

---

[1]Considerable confusion was originally created by the use of the term *random walk* to describe this process. Some read it as an attempt by academicians to suggest the market had no logic or economic basis. Nothing could be further from the truth. The random walk is created precisely as a result of rational and immediate market responses to information that has relevance to valuing a security.

[2]Eugene Fama [1976], p. 135 provides the most complete and precise theoretical statement of the adjustment of prices to information. Much of our discussion is based on his approach.

contained in horoscopes. Moreover, the information set includes what is known about the relationships among these variables (e.g., an increase in the money supply increases commodity prices for an economy at capacity), and "whatever is knowable about the process that describes the evolution of the state of the world through time" (e.g., technology always moves forward). As a practical matter, the information set changes continuously. Thus, the time interval between t and $t + 1$ may be very short or quite long (in which case the difference between ϕ_t and ϕ_{t+1} may be quite large).

To summarize all this,

> Market participants, acting in their own self-interest, use available information to attempt to secure more desirable (higher return) portfolio positions. In doing so they collectively ensure that price movements in response to new information are instantaneous and unbiased and will "fully reflect" all relevant information. Competition will drive security prices from one equilibrium level to another so that the change in price in response to new information (and the return generated from the change in price) will be independent of the prior change in price. Price changes and returns will be a random walk in response to the information.[3]

A market so characterized is termed an **efficient market.**

There is a final theoretical issue that should be mentioned—the probability distributions of price changes may themselves have various characteristics. They may be symmetric or skewed, or bell-shaped or uniform in nature. Moreover, they may be constant from period to period, or change over time to reflect different expected values or different standard deviations.[4] It would not be surprising to find that new information would change both the expected value and the standard deviation of these price changes.

Testing the Efficient Market Hypothesis

The basic empirical issue associated with the efficient market hypothesis is, simply, whether the information set, ϕ_t, used by the market includes all available information. If it does, market efficiency is established. If it does not, then some dependency in security prices exists, knowledge of which would allow one to ferret out profitable investment

---

[3]This proposition holds precisely only if the expected returns, $E(\bar{R}_{it})$, are constant over time for security i. This does not hold true for all securities for all periods. Institutional arrangements in security markets and the nature of some securities themselves may make one or the other of these propositions technically incorrect. For example, as a security approaches its dividend payment data its price rises in expectation of the dividend payment. On the date the security goes "ex-dividend" its price drops, usually by the amount of the dividend paid. This institutional arrangement for paying dividends (as opposed to one where dividends are paid out continuously by the firm) creates a peculiar nonlinear correlation—but one of low magnitude.

[4]The formal terms *submartingale* and *random walk* are statistical descriptions of random variables in a series. A variable is a random walk if it has a constant expected value and standard derivation, yet values of the variable occur independently over time. A submartingale is not so restricted. Which one is an appropriate description of the securities markets is relevant because it has implications for the statistical procedures used to analyze security return series. Although the differences between the two will not be of much concern here, the reader with an interest is directed to Fama [1976], for a discussion of the relevance of these concepts to finance.

opportunities with the existing information set. To put the issue differently: Since actual securities markets (especially ones where trading may be infrequent or "thin") are not characterized by all of the assumptions of the ideal market, how far distant from this instantaneous adjustment process are actual markets? It is true, for example, that the cost of transacting may be 1 to 2 percent of the value of the transaction on the NYSE, and may reach 5 or even 10 percent for over-the-counter securities and real estate. It is also true that information is sometimes costly (consider the search for real estate or collectibles), as is the analysis that one performs with it. Moreover, relevant information may not be available to all market participants on an equal basis (although the SEC considers this to be one of its major objectives).

There are two general approaches to evaluating what is contained in ϕ_t to determine the extent to which markets may diverge from being efficient. The first is to observe a piece of information (or what someone thinks may be a piece of information) and observe price changes or returns generated in response to the information to see if the pattern confirms what we expect from an efficient market. These are **direct tests** of the efficiency of markets (also called "semistrong form" tests). The second is to measure the statistical dependencies that exist in a security price series. These are **indirect tests** of the efficiency of markets (also called "weak form" tests). The importance of this issue is undeniable. Knowledge of how prices respond empirically over time will be of fundamental importance in developing an optimal investment program and avoiding investment pitfalls.

The remainder of the chapter is devoted to summarizing the results of some of these empirical investigations. The studies explicitly discussed in the text were selected both because of their breadth of coverage and because of the appropriateness of the empirical methodology employed. The idea is to consider market efficiency from a number of different perspectives.

Indirect Tests of Market Efficiency

Indirect investigations of market efficiency look for statistical dependencies in returns generated over time. But, since there are a large number of reasonable forms that the dependency could take, proving the existence of efficient or inefficient financial markets is obtained only as more and more evidence accumulates. The evidence we will look at includes: (1) short- and long-run serial correlations of price changes, (2) the extent to which price changes from transaction to transaction in one direction tend to be followed by price changes in the same or opposite direction, and (3) the "seasonality" of returns.

Serial Correlation. Security price dynamics have been most extensively studied through the use of serial correlation coefficients. Serial correlation or auto correlation, in this context, measures the general tendency for the price change of a security in one period to be associated with the price change in some prior period. Thus, if positive price changes in one period seem to be associated with positive price changes in the next, then positive serial correlation exists. Finding that serial correlations are neither statistically nor economically different from zero would be evidence that supports the efficiency of financial markets, since it suggests that security returns move independently over time.

Some years ago Fama measured the daily and monthly serial correlations for each of the 30 securities in the Dow Jones industrials. The daily measures correlate the change

TABLE 6–1   Sample Serial Correlations on the Dow Jones Industrials

Stock	Days Lag (τ) (December 31, 1983 to December 31, 1986)					Months Lag (December 31, 1976 to December 31, 1986)		
	1	2	3	4	5	1	2	3
Alco Standard	.162	.056	− .008	.020	.019	− .030	− .069	− .073
Allied Signal	.000	.000	.000	.000	.000	.000	− .060	− .102
American Can	.105	− .074	.054	− .020	.012	.021	− .001	.009
American Express	.048	− .060	− .042	.056	− .058	.123	.043	− .060
AT&T	.040	− .045	− .047	− .035	.024	− .052	− .016	.004
Bethlehem Steel	.200	.026	− .003	− .051	− .042	− .172*	.004	− .067
Boeing	.077	− .038	− .132	− .046	− .020	.068	.077	− .037
Chevron	.114	− .090	− .106	− .041	− .002	− .070	.002	.057
Coca Cola	.014	.001	− .055	.030	.036	.017	.016	− .076
Du Pont	.091	− .049	− .050	.008	− .008	.036	− .044	− .067
Eastman Kodak	.044	.120	− .033	− .014	− .027	.100	− .008	.098
Exxon	.039	− .093	− .098	.023	− .079	− .045	.028	.116
General Elec	.010	− .035	− .034	.013	.039	.156	− .091	− .029
General Motors	.061	− .025	.007	− .027	− .039	.028	.079	− .032
Goodyear Tire & Rubr	.049	− .009	− .004	− .008	.024	− .147	.092	− .191
IBM	.015	.018	− .012	− .006	.024	.108	− .020	.021
International Paper	− .016	− .007	− .034	− .021	.011	− .190*	.014	− .078
McDonalds	.105	− .040	− .074	.002	− .007	.106	− .010	− .068
Merck	.118	− .025	− .042	− .027	− .052	− .160	− .097	− .139
Minnesota Mng & Mfg	.020	.003	− .052	− .001	.023	− .027	.139	− .097
Navistar Intl	− .026	− .018	.021	.008	− .053	.014	.097	.119
Philip Morris	.050	.018	.001	.011	.026	− .099	− .114	.011
Procter & Gamble	.023	− .039	− .077	.031	.012	− .023	− .014	.014
Sears	.056	− .041	− .027	− .043	.010	− .085	.057	.046
Texaco	− .002	− .002	− .001	.000	.000	− .084	− .157	− .046
U S X	.073	− .049	− .025	.013	.012	− .007	− .110	− .019
Union Carbide	.067	− .013	− .066	.029	.061	− .098	− .081	.071
United Technologies	.043	.027	.020	.006	− .020	− .040	− .107	.001
Westinghouse	.011	− .016	− .021	− .035	.017	− .088	− .026	− .059
Woolworth	.130	− .022	− .064	− .055	− .014	− .072	− .010	.059
Average for all NYSE	.036	− .001	− .008	− .005	.007	− .041	− .035	− .034

*Sample correlation is two standard deviations from zero.
Source: Computed from CRSP tapes.

in price on a daily basis with the change in price on the same security with a lag of 1 day, 2 days, and so on. The monthly measure does the same thing for monthly price change intervals. Table 6–1 presents these results for daily lags of up to five days, and monthly lags of up to three months for a recent period using Fama's methodology.

The figure in the first column for AT&T indicates an estimated correlation coefficient of − .040 for returns calculated from day-to-day changes in closing prices. The figure for daily returns compared over two-day intervals is − .045. The statistically significant figures (at least two standard deviations away from zero) are indicated with an asterisk (*).

The *daily* data, for short lags at least, show a sign of slight serial dependence. Thus, there are 26 positive and only 4 negative values for one-day lags. This suggests that for some securities there is a greater tendency for positive daily returns to be followed by positive daily returns than would be expected from an independent or truly random series of returns.

Interestingly, however, only 8 of the 30 correlations for the two day lag are positive. The general tendency for sign changes between the 1 day and 2 day lag indicates a tendency for high and low returns to be clustered at two-day intervals. Moreover, the tendencies that seem apparent from the first two columns of the daily results dissipate quickly as the lag period is increased. Finally, from a statistical perspective, *none* of the 60 values in the first two columns are statistically significantly different from zero. Overall, the average serial correlation of daily returns for all NYSE securities during this period was .036, leading to the conclusion that there is only nominal short-term dependency in some common stock prices.[5]

The serial correlations of monthly returns are not different from the "daily" results. The two significant values found in the monthly lag section of the table would occur by change from the sample of 30 firms. The *average* correlation for all NYSE stocks for the one-month lag was − .041, and for the two-month lag was − .035.

The existence of some nominal dependency in stock returns does not imply that the structure of returns is *materially* nonrandom. One might question the economic, rather than the statistical, importance of the serial correlations. To make our point, take the highest figure in the table—about .19 for International Paper for the one month lag. Since this is a correlation coefficient, squaring it—a figure of .036—indicates the proportion of the total variance of returns that can be attributed to the return generated on the prior day. Stated another way, of the total variance of daily returns on *IP,* 3.6 percent is accounted for by the variation in yesterday's return. The other 96.4 percent is attributable to other factors (earnings announcements and economic events, we hope). These figures are so remarkably small that it's doubtful that one should devote any time to attempting to take advantage of knowledge of the dependency. Sales commissions, time, and other transactions costs would almost immediately wipe out profits that could be gained from a trading strategy based on short-term correlations.

Of course these results were derived mostly from observing 30 of the largest securities where trading is active and continuous. The results may not easily generalize to other stocks or other financial instruments. However, serial correlation coefficients also have been estimated for a number of commodity futures contracts or financial futures contracts (an investment in a contract to purchase a specified commodity or financial opportunity at some future date). These results are summarized in Table 6–2 by using the averages of the correlations estimated separately for a number of futures contracts. Thus, the .06 correlation for soybeans in row three is an average of five individual correlations estimated for five different futures contracts. Only one of these five estimates was significantly different from zero, and this is indicated in the last column of the table.

Only the futures market for wheat gives a hint of a statistically significant degree of

---

[5]The degree of dependence varies considerably from security to security, suggesting that the cause of the dependence may have something to do with the firm itself, or the way it's traded on the market. One possible explanation would be that the dependence is induced by the methods adopted by the specialist unit that is in charge of trading the security on the floor of the NYSE.

TABLE 6–2   Serial Correlations for Commodity and Financial Futures

	Period of Lag				Ratio of Individually Significant Correlation to Total Correlations for One-Day Lag
	1	2	3	5	
Semi–Monthly					
Wheat*	.13	.03	− .05	—	4/5
Corn*	.03	.05	− .01	—	0/5
Soybeans*	.06	.12	.01	—	1/5
Daily					
Corn†	− .01	− .06	—	.05	1/12
Soybeans†	− .02	− .06	—	.03	0/12
Daily					
British pound‡	.01	− .03	.02	—	0/2
Canadian dollar‡	.07	− .01	.03	—	0/2
German mark‡	.01	− .09	.05	—	0/2
Japanese yen‡	.03	.00	.02	—	0/2
Swiss franc‡	− .02	− .07	− .02	—	0/2

*Numbers are averages of correlations measured for a set of different contracts, Dusak [1973].
†Numbers are averages of correlations measured for each of a number of different years, Stevenson and Bear [1970].
‡Numbers are averages of correlations measured for spot and futures contract prices, Cornell and Dietrich [1978].

dependence in price changes. Even here, however, only between 2 and 4 percent of the variation in the price change on day t can be attributed to the price change on day $t - 1$. In the other cases, no argument can be made that there are important dependencies in these investment markets (at least, of a form that can be picked up with the computation of serial correlations). The evidence seems to suggest that these market price changes follow a random walk to a good approximation. Clearly, it seems to be the case that the values are low enough to ensure that investors could not use the estimates as a basis for developing a strategy that would generate above-normal returns.

Dependencies from Transaction to Transaction.   In an efficient stock market the price change that occurs between transactions should be unrelated to the price changes that occurred between prior transactions. In other words, if there is a $1/4$ point price change at one point during the course of the day's trading, it should hold no implications for the next change in price as the next transaction is consumated. At least one study suggests that this is not the case, and, as a consequence, leads us to conclude that there are some important (but perhaps not profitable) very short-term dependencies in the market for securities.

For example, Neiderhoffer and Osborne [1966] found that for five actively traded stocks (and 10,500 transactions) the probability of a price change in a given direction in a given amount depended on the prior price change. Part (a) of Figure 6–3 indicates the probability distribution of price changes for the five securities studied. In about 52 percent of the cases there was no price change, in about 20 percent of the cases the price change was plus $1/8$, in another 20 percent the price change was minus $1/8$, and so on. However,

FIGURE 6–3   Probability of Price Changes Conditioned on Prior Price Change

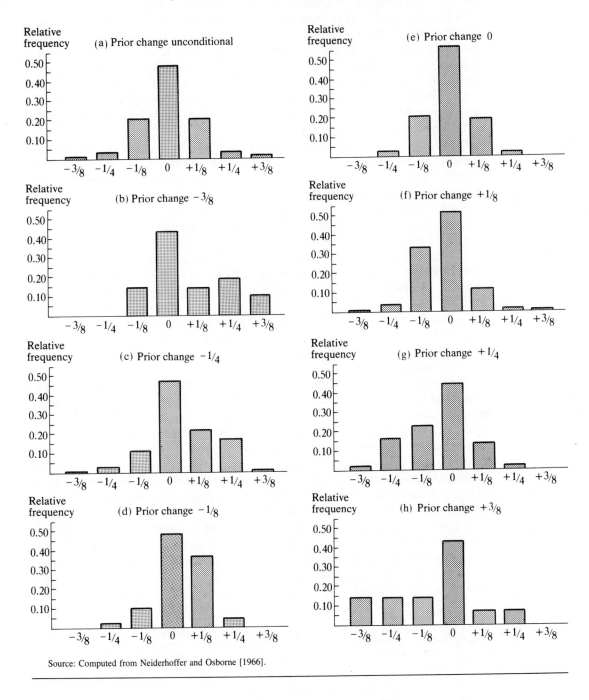

Source: Computed from Neiderhoffer and Osborne [1966].

when the immediately prior price change was $-\frac{3}{8}$, the distribution looks much different (part (b)). The chance of a *positive* price change is much greater.

In fact, the tendency is for the distributions to be above zero when any negative price change occurs on the prior trade, and for the distribution to be below zero when the immediate prior price change is positive. The evidence, in other words, points to a tendency for stock prices to reverse themselves over very short intervals (from one transaction to the next). This is what gives rise to the leftward shift of the distributions as we move from part (b) of the table, where the distribution is conditioned on the prior price change being $-\frac{3}{8}$; to part (h) of the table, where the distribution is conditioned on the prior price change being $+\frac{3}{8}$.

In addition, Neiderhoffer and Osborne found some more-complex dependencies. For example, the probability of a fall in price differs as a function of whether the two prior changes were *rise-rise* or *fall-rise*. There also was a tendency for transactions to take place at even eighths (even dollars, $\frac{1}{4}$, $\frac{1}{2}$, $\frac{3}{4}$).

No statistical study is very convincing without some logic to back up the results and this study is no exception. Neiderhoffer and Osborne attribute their results to the combination of two factors that relate to the established trading practices on the NYSE.

The first is the specialist who has the capacity to trade for his own account. Without substantially violating the performance standards set up by the NYSE, the specialist is able to fill **market buy orders** by selling from inventory at a price that is an eighth to a quarter of a point greater than the price he can sell at to fill **market sell orders.** Competition from floor brokers may prevent him from doing this, but as long as competition is not perfect and as long as market buy and sell orders occur randomly, there will be more price reversals from transaction to transaction than would be expected to occur by chance.[6]

The second factor contributing to reversals is the widespread use of the **limit order** (explained in Chapter 4). As random market buy and sell orders come to the specialist position, they will either be crossed or executed according to the limit orders on the specialist's book. A market buy order will be matched with a limit order to sell at a price above market. A market sell order will be matched with a limit order to buy at a price below market. This sequence of transactions will create a *nonrandom* pattern of reversals from the *random* occurrence of buy and sell orders. Moreover, if limit orders tend to be placed at even eighths, the orders will tend to be executed at even eights, thus explaining Neiderhoffer and Osborne's second observation.

It's not clear how knowledge of this dependency could be used to the investor's advantage. Conceivably your brokerage representative on the floor of the exchange could use this information to improve on how or when your orders are executed. Moreover, it seems as if these observations would argue for using limit orders instead of market orders when buying or selling common stock, and for placing orders at *odd* eighths of a point.[7]

---

[6]In fact, this tendency for reversal will exist in any market where the market maker (the dealer) has the capacity to buy or sell for his own account, and has the sole or major market-making function. Pure brokerage markets, such as residential home markets where no inventory is maintained by the broker, do not exhibit this same tendency.

[7]Generalizing from these points, it appears that there are a number of ways that the reversal tendency could be reduced. Among these are competitive specialist systems, a computer-based market-making function, and different evaluation techniques for rating the performance of specialist firms.

To be complete, we should not fail to alert the reader that such tendencies exist in most secondary markets to a greater or lesser degree. Perhaps more important than being able to profit from these short-run dependencies is that knowledge of the dependencies in any financial market seems to be a prerequisite to shielding oneself from the profit-seeking actions of other market participants (e.g., large traders, floor brokers, or specialists).

Finally, another sort of transaction-to-transaction dependency seems to exist that relates to the pressure on price from the sale of a large block of a security. The efficient-market hypothesis relies, in part, on the assumption of **perfect marketability** of securities. This implies that prices do not reflect temporary imbalances between supply and demand, and that investors trading large blocks of stock do so at the same prices at which small traders execute transactions. The real question is whether large transitory changes in supply and demand affect observed market prices. If they do, this would suggest that markets are not perfectly marketable and, thus, are not perfectly efficient. Evidence from analysis of large-block transactions on securities listed on the NYSE suggests that there *is* temporary downward pressure on the price of the security when a large block is sold. The amount of this pressure may be as much as 1 percent of the market price of the security. The recovery of its price occurs almost immediately after the block trade is completed. There appears to be no such temporary effect on price when the block transaction is initiated as an order to *buy* the security. Once again, there is some evidence of very short-term dependencies in security prices. In this case, some investors attempt to do something about it. Specifically, large institutional investors spend a good deal of time and effort searching for brokers who can handle large-block transactions with less of an adverse effect on the price at which the transaction is completed. Indeed, the liquidity of the market is a matter of primary concern for the investor and the broker.

Seasonality. Two studies of monthly seasonality are presented in Figure 6–4. One of the studies covered the period between 1904 and 1974, and found that a large proportion of the annual return on a broad-based stock market index was generated in the months of January, July, and August. January's return, on average over the 70-year period, was nearly as large as all other months combined. The other study covered a more recent period, 1963 to 1982. Approximately the same finding was in evidence. January returns were significantly higher than those in other months. This study (which was based on the calculation of returns from daily data) found only January to be different from the other months, and January returns made up almost 40 percent of the total yearly returns.

Finding a pattern of seasonality in returns is not sufficient to argue that excess returns can be earned with the use of that knowledge. After all, you have to wait 11 months before you can once again secure the larger January return. One investigator (Pettengill [1985]), however, attempted to see if higher than average returns could be generated by buying T-bills in those months when returns historically have been low in stocks, and by buying stocks in all other months (January, July, and August at least). He found that returns were 1.7 percent higher with the seasonal strategy, when transactions costs were ignored, and 1.9 percent lower when transactions costs were accounted for. In both cases, the standard deviation of the seasonal portfolio was less (due to the investment in T-bills in some months). Thus, it appears that the average investor cannot profit from knowledge

FIGURE 6–4 **Seasonality in Stock Market Returns**

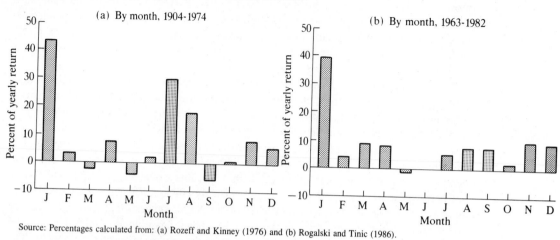

Source: Percentages calculated from: (a) Rozeff and Kinney (1976) and (b) Rogalski and Tinic (1986).

of the seasonal component in stock returns, though large institutional investors with exceptionally low transactions costs may be able to benefit to some extent.

Evidence of a strong **January effect,** as it has come to be called, brought forth a host of hypotheses regarding its cause. Blame for the higher return in January was placed on taxes, transactions costs, increased risk in January when corporations begin to issue their annual reports, trading by institutions that are bent on "cleaning up" their portfolios, and so on. Some of these hypotheses are *inconsistent* with the existence of market efficiency, and none of the hypotheses seemed to be able to entirely explain the phenomenon. There are three pieces to the puzzle that lend us some understanding of the January effect, however:

- A study of the Australian stock market found significantly higher January returns, even though the fiscal year end for Australian companies is in June. Thus, taxes don't explain everything. (Officer [1975])
- The largest returns in January are generated by the smallest firms, and these returns were concentrated in the first few days of the month. Thus, large and actively traded securities may not experience nearly as large a level of seasonality. (Keim [1983])
- The standard deviation of returns on smaller firms (those generating the larger returns) during the month of January is substantially larger than that found in other months. Thus, there is some evidence that the larger January returns, generated by smaller firms, are accompanied by a larger level of risk, as might be expected in a risk-averse market.

If it turns out that much of the January effect can be attributed to smaller-sized, larger-risk firms, then the apparent seasonality is associated with risk, and does not lead to the conclusion that stock markets are inefficient. A complete resolution of this perplexing empirical anomaly awaits further examination, however.

FIGURE 6–5   S&P Returns by Day of the Week, 1962–1978

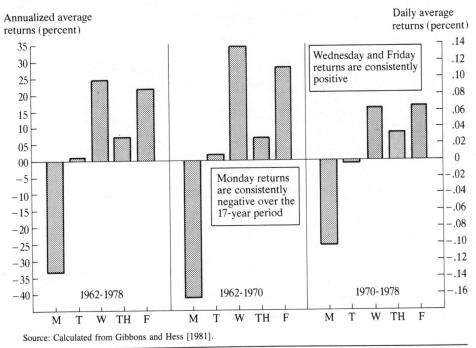

Source: Calculated from Gibbons and Hess [1981].

Another form of seasonality also is evident in securities markets. Monday returns are different from those generated in other days of the week in both stocks markets and foreign exchange markets.[8] Monday returns on the New York Stock Exchange tend to be negative, and Figure 6–5 shows the extent of this seasonality. This study by Gibbons and Hess [1981], describes the different returns generated on different days of the week over a 17-year period from 1962 to 1978—a total of over 4,000 observations of daily returns. Moreover, these differences seem to persist in each period when the data are divided in two subperiods. Monday offered negative returns consistently and Wednesday and Friday offered the most positive daily returns. The differential return figures are not small either. The negative Monday effect corresponds to an annualized return of −33.5 percent (though you could capture only one fifth of this number since Mondays occur only one fifth of the time)!

A more recent study of intradaily and day of the weeks effects by Harris [1986a], over 14 months between December 1981 and January 1983, found Monday returns continued to be negative. The other four days of the week supplied returns that were positive and of about the same magnitude. Moreover, he found that about half of the negative returns between Friday's market close and Monday's market close occurred

---

[8]French [1980] and Gibbons and Hess [1981] found this form of seasonal dependence. McFarland, Pettit and Sung [1982] also found foreign exchange prices exhibited a daily effect—on Mondays and Thursdays. Jaffee and Westerfield [1985] also found seasonals in foreign exchange prices.

FIGURE 6–6   **Cumulative Returns Generated within the Day**

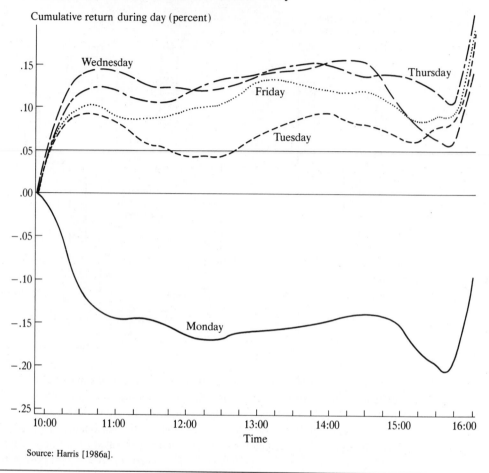

Source: Harris [1986a].

"over the weekend." That is, one half of the Monday effect could be attributed to a decline in prices between Friday's close and Monday's open. .

Within the day, the pattern of returns is *not* constant, as you can see in Figure 6–6. Returns are high in the first 45 minutes of the day, except on Mondays, and high again in the last 30 minutes. Returns were close to zero during the rest of the day, on average, over the period studied. On Monday most of the decline in price during the course of the day took place in the first 45 minutes of trading. After that initial decline Monday's returns look much like those on any other day. There are some strategic implications in these numbers. Other things constant, it pays to buy at the opening bell on all days but Monday, or buy at least 30 minutes before the closing bell on all days including Monday. Of course the usual caveats must be mentioned: (1) the numbers reflect the experience over a short 14-month period, (2) the market already may have adjusted so as to negate the pattern summarized by Harris, and (3) measurement problems may have lead to some of the estimated intradaily seasonality.

Seasonals have been found in other financial markets as well. Jaffee and Westerfield [1985] found Monday returns were lower than those on other days in Canadian and United Kingdom stock markets. However, *Tuesday* returns were the lowest of the week in the stock markets of Japan and Australia (though Monday returns still were negative). Finally, a number of studies have found Monday returns to be lower than other days in the market for U.S. Treasury bills. What could cause an effect like that observed in these two markets? Some hypotheses have been put forth (such as the settlement practices used in the markets, or biases that are created by some securities not actively trading), but the result still stands as anomalous evidence on the efficiency of the securities market.

Direct Tests for Dependencies

Direct exploration for market dependencies concentrates on (1) measuring the success or failure of particular trading strategies, or (2) measuring the market response to information signals that are *expected* to cause a change in the supply of and demand for a security.

Trading Strategies. If markets are efficient, the set of information used by market participants, ϕ_t, surely ought to include all past price information, if for no other reason than that such information is among the most readily available. Thus, the use of past price information as a basis for making investment decisions should not yield returns that exceed returns secured, on average, from any other naive investment strategy. Consequently, "technicians" who rely on an analysis of past prices should generate only normal returns.

Perhaps the simplest way to introduce this idea is to consider whether securities that have supplied higher than normal returns last year are more or less likely to repeat that this year. Beaver and Landsman [1981] did just this. Each year between 1932 and 1977 securities were classified as "winners" if, in the prior 20 months, they had supplied higher than normal returns; or "losers" if, in the prior 20 months, they had supplied lower than normal returns. On average the "winners" supplied above normal returns of 33.3 percent over that 20-month period. The "losers" supplied below normal returns of -31.3 percent. The figures, of course, suggest the extent of the differences that can exist on security returns over a relatively short 20-month period.

If markets are efficient, however, there should be no differences between the winner and loser portfolios over the 12 months *subsequent* to their classification. Past results don't portend the future, in other words, if market efficiency holds. The authors found that in 23 of the 46 years winner portfolio returns were higher than normal; in the other 23 years returns were lower than normal. For the loser portfolios the results were almost identical, with losers supplying higher than normal returns in 22 of the 46 years. A summary of their results is presented graphically in Figure 6–7. The conclusion is that knowledge of past returns doesn't help the investor determine which securities are likely to outperform the market in the future.

Other investigations that have attempted to address this issue have measured the success or failure of a few of the infinite number of technical trading rules available. The one we discuss here is the "filter rule."

A **filter rule** is a mathematical rule that can be applied to produce buy and sell signals. For example, it may dictate that the stock should be purchased when a security moves up in price by X percent or sold (with the investor going short) when the security falls

FIGURE 6–7 **Returns to "Winner" and "Loser" Portfolios**

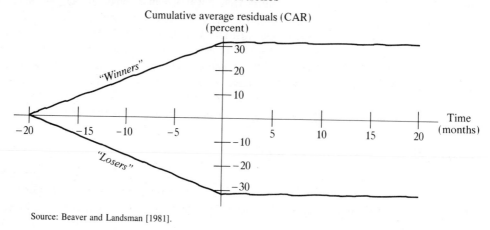

Source: Beaver and Landsman [1981].

from its previous high by *X* percent. Clearly, the presumption on the part of those who advocate such a rule is that security prices trend in such a way that it is relatively likely a security, if increasing in price, will move up by another *X* percent before it falls by *X* percent, or if falling, will fall by another *X* percent before it rises by *X* percent. In other words, the rule counts on security prices exhibiting trends over intervals of time are that sufficiently long to allow the investor to capture a portion of the gain from the trend.

The rates of return earned from applying such a trading rule, compared with the rates of return earned from a policy of buying and holding the common stock, are presented for each of the 30 Dow Jones Industrial securities in Table 6–3. There are some obviously disconcerting figures for those who think that competition should eliminate price dependencies. For example, the return from the 1 percent filter applied to Alcoa returned 30.8 percent per year, whereas the buy and hold policy as an alternative returned only 2.3 percent. Alternatively, the 1 percent filter applied to Goodyear returned − 19.5 percent, and buy and hold 8.3 percent—which suggests that the inverse application of the filter (go short instead of long when security rises and long instead of short when security falls) also would have proved a useful investment policy. Individually, however, it's difficult to interpret these apparent dependencies (in opposite directions) for Alcoa and Goodyear. Are the returns to the filter *statistically* different from the buy and hold strategy? Or are they merely chance occurrences caused by the randomly generated price changes over the period of investigation? Is there any reason to expect the sign of the return dependency to vary between securities? To develop specific answers to these questions requires more information than is available.

The average return comparisons over all 30 stocks are given in Table 6–4. Only the .5 percent filter, with its 11.5 percent return, is higher than the 10.4 percent return to the buy and hold strategy. This clearly does not bode well for filters of moderate or large size. Can the .5 percent filter be profitably applied? Two forms of transaction costs suggest not. First, to monitor this small filter would require almost constant attention to the market. Second, as summarized in Table 6-4, transaction costs (even of those holding seats on the floor of the NYSE) would be excessive to carry out the 12,514 *transactions* required for the 30 securities over the period of this investigation. Returns after com-

TABLE 6–3   Annual Rates of Return to Filter Rules Applied to 30 Dow Jones Common Stocks (1956–1962)

Size of Filter

Security	.5% F	.5% B	1% F	1% B	5% F	5% B	10% F	10% B
Allied Chemical	15.5%	6.8%	8.7%	6.9%	−3.8%	5.2%	5.5%	5.6%
Alcoa	40.1	2.5	30.8	2.3	3.7	2.5	−15.7	.5
American Can	12.1	8.5	−6.5	7.5	−12.5	5.9	9.0	5.9
AT&T	15.0	18.9	14.6	18.9	13.5	17.4	8.3	19.5
American Tobacco	16.5	17.0	1.9	16.8	−2.0	15.7	19.7	16.4
Anaconda	28.8	4.7	10.1	4.9	−2.7	5.0	−4.5	3.1
Bethlehem Steel	8.2	3.2	5.1	3.3	−15.3	3.8	−4.2	1.0
Chrysler	3.1	.4	−9.0	−.2	−6.0	2.0	9.0	−2.5
Dupont	15.2	10.7	12.5	10.6	7.6	9.6	7.1	7.4
Eastman Kodak	7.8	19.4	2.5	19.5	9.9	17.0	7.4	16.4
General Elec.	8.0	7.8	4.6	7.5	5.4	6.0	−11.6	5.1
General Foods	12.2	25.7	12.2	25.6	6.1	26.5	22.6	25.2
General Motors	10.7	8.8	10.8	9.1	−11.7	9.9	2.5	10.0
Goodyear	−22.9	8.6	−19.5	8.3	−34.1	12.5	1.8	7.8
International Harvester	−8.8	18.0	−8.2	17.7	5.4	16.3	−2.4	16.9
International Nickel	21.8	14.8	17.0	13.6	4.7	15.4	1.9	13.6
International Paper	20.5	1.0	15.6	.7	−2.6	1.4	.1	7.0
Johns Manville	2.1	9.4	−1.6	9.3	−6.5	6.9	−7.4	8.2
Owens Illinois	.8	11.3	−3.6	11.6	4.3	9.6	6.2	8.9
Procter & Gamble	31.5	21.0	29.0	21.2	13.3	22.6	15.6	22.6
Sears	33.7	25.8	24.9	25.6	20.0	24.7	16.3	22.9
Standard Oil (Calif.)	7.6	9.3	5.2	9.0	−13.4	8.9	−11.3	8.1
Standard Oil (N.J.)	3.6	7.7	−7.2	6.7	−16.4	6.1	−7.7	4.3
Swift & Co.	1.0	4.7	.2	4.2	−4.9	3.8	−12.1	4.8
Texaco	17.2	18.8	16.5	19.2	.5	16.2	6.1	15.8
Union Carbide	29.0	5.2	12.4	5.2	1.7	3.5	9.8	4.2
United Aircraft	−2.5	5.4	−2.0	5.2	−5.0	4.7	−1.7	1.7
U.S. Steel (USX)	10.1	1.4	−3.9	1.0	−2.3	1.3	8.4	1.4
Westinghouse	.8	3.8	−10.3	4.0	−8.3	4.8	−2.5	3.6
Woolworth	6.8	12.8	1.2	13.2	−4.9	14.5	9.1	15.0
Average	11.5	10.4	5.5	10.3	−1.9	10.0	3.0	9.3

F = Filter.
B = Buy and hold.

Source: Fama and Blume [1966]. © 1966 *Journal of Business*. By permission of The University of Chicago Press.

TABLE 6-4   Annual Rates of Returns to Filter Rules before and after Commissions on 30 Dow Jones Stocks (1956–1962)

Buy and Hold Filter	*(1)* Average Annual Return before Commissions	*(2)* Total Transactions	*(3)* Average Annual Return after Commissions
0.5%	11.5%	12,514	− 103.5%
1.0	5.5	8,660	− 74.9
1.5	2.8	6,270	− 56.1
2.0	.2	4,784	− 45.1
2.5	− 1.6	3,750	− 37.3
3.0	− 1.7	2,894	− 30.5
3.5	− .8	2,438	− 24.4
4.0	.1	2,013	− 19.5
4.5	− 1.2	1,720	− 18.1
5.0	− 1.9	1,484	− 16.6
6.0	1.3	1,071	9.4
7.0	.8	828	− 7.4
8.0	1.7	653	− 4.9
9.0	1.9	539	− 3.6
10.0	2.9	435	− 1.4
12.0	5.2	289	2.3
14.0	3.9	224	1.4
16.0	4.2	172	2.3
18.0	3.6	139	1.9
20.0	4.3	110	3.0
25.0	2.7	73	1.7
30.0	− .5	51	− 1.4
40.0	− 2.7	21	− 3.4
50.0	− 21.4	4	− 22.9

*Columns (1) and (3) show the average returns per security provided by each of the different filters. The figures in column (3) are adjusted for both dividends and commissions, while those in column (1) are adjusted only for dividends.

Source: Fama and Blume [1966]. © 1966 *Journal of Business*. By permission of The University of Chicago Press.

missions for each of the filters are given in the third column of the table. Note, you would have *used up all your money on commissions* by employing the .5 percent filter.

In similar studies of commodity futures markets, some dependencies have been noted. One study[9] of corn and soybean futures found a tendency for moderate-sized filters (3 and 5 percent) to generate profits that exceed the profits from buy and hold policies over a 12-year period. These results suggest some positive dependence over reasonably long periods of time (i.e., a tendency for prices to cycle). Characteristically, however, the profitability of filter techniques applied to futures markets vacillates. Profits do not seem to accrue consistently. Rather, profits and losses vary with the commodity, the period, and the size of filter. Sometimes profits accrue to the application of a filter of 5 percent to the corn futures; at other times to a 1 percent filter on wheat. From an investment policy perspective, this suggests that past commodity price changes may contain useful information, but not without some greater knowledge of the factors affecting the structure of prices.

___
[9]Stevenson and Bear[1970].

Price Reactions to Information Signals. Since information provides the stimulus for a change in supply or demand leading to a change in share price; observing how prices change as information is conveyed to the market should tell us much about market efficiency. Suppose information is communicated to the market at the time $t = 0$. According to the efficient-market hypothesis the price reaction to that information ought to occur at that time and only at that time. Any delayed reaction, say at $t = 1$, would be evidence that markets are not completely efficient. The five graphs in Figure 6–8 show five different patterns of market reaction to a hypothetical piece of information that causes the market to increase its assessment of the value of the firm by $5 (from $80 to $85 on the vertical axis). In each of the graphs the $5 per share reaction is a supplement to other pieces of information that are being delivered to the market and are the cause of the smaller, more or less random, "blips" in the price of the security that are continuously recorded throughout the time period.

The first two graphs represent cases where the market takes some time to digest the impact of the information. Graph (a) is a case where the market has overreacted to the information, and it takes an additional five periods until that overreaction is eliminated. This would be a biased and not instantaneous reaction to the information, which is not consistent with the price reaction we would expect in an efficient market. Graph (b) represents a biased and delayed underreaction. Graph (c) is a biased but instantaneous reaction in the sense that the first transaction after the announcement is $5 higher than the $85 new equilibrium price for the security. Clearly, if there was a general tendency in security markets for initial price reactions to be upward or downward biased, the market could not be considered efficient.

Graph (d) is different in that the market's reaction begins 5 periods prior to the publication of the information. Two scenerios are consistent with this pattern. One is that the pattern of price changes reflects the fact that some investors have prior knowledge of the information to be published at $t = 0$. This violates the free and equal access to information doctrine of the efficient-market hypothesis, and so violates the principles of market efficiency. The other is that the pattern simply reflects the public release of information that is correlated with the information released at time 0. Thus, if the announcement at $t = 0$ was that the firm's reported earnings were much greater than expected, the positive price change five days before could have been a reaction to the manager's announcement on that day that "this year's earnings will be up substantially above last year's." Nothing in this set of events suggests that the market is reacting in a manner that is inefficient.

Only graph (e) represents a case where the market reaction is unbiased and instantaneous and is, therefore, without question consistent with the reactions you would observe in an efficient market.

In general, if prices adjust instantaneously and unbiasedly to new information, then historical returns should be higher than normal during the time of dissemination of favorable information, and lower than normal when unfavorable information is conveyed to the market. Empirically, to represent this "abnormal" return generated during the time that information is released to the market and the market is reacting, most studies calculate,

(8–3) $$u_{it} = \tilde{R}_{it} - E(\tilde{R}_{it}|R_{mt})$$

where $E(\tilde{R}_{it}|R_{mt})$ is the return the security normally would have achieved had no new firm-specific piece of news been published, conditional on the overall market return

FIGURE 6–8 Efficient and Inefficient Market Reactions to Information

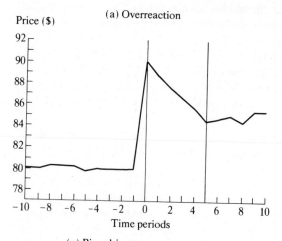

(a) Overreaction

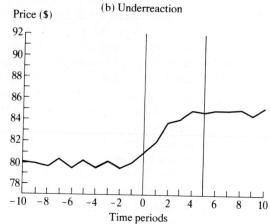

(b) Underreaction

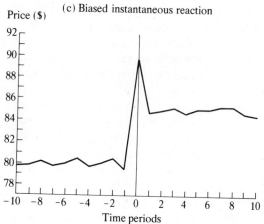

(c) Biased instantaneous reaction

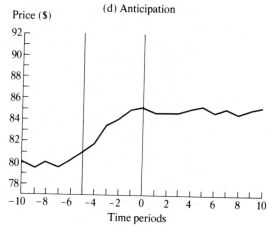

(d) Anticipation

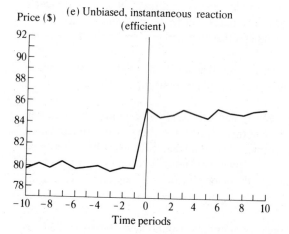

(e) Unbiased, instantaneous reaction (efficient)

during period t, R_{mt}.[10] The value u_{it} is the **excess return** or **abnormal return** during period t.

In efficient markets, u_{it} would tend on average to be different from zero only at the point in time the information is released to the market. At all other points before or after the announcement the expected value of u_{it} would be zero.

The classic study of whether the market responds efficiently to new information is an investigation of the price changes accompanying stock splits. As you know, stock splits, by changing only the number of shares outstanding, have no consequences for the value of the shareholder's claim. There should be no "news" effect at the point in time the intention to split is announced by the firm, nor, in an efficient market, should there be any tendency for price responses to be positive or negative after the announcement. That this is so is illustrated in Figure 6–9(a). Here the abnormal returns are positive and vary between zero and 4 percent in periods before the announcement for a broad cross section of firms announcing splits. Apparently, firms that choose to split their stock have generated high returns in the recent past. However, there is no tendency for the returns to be abnormally high in the month of the split announcement or in the months after. The

FIGURE 6–9   The Behavior of Stock Prices during Periods Surrounding Stock Splits

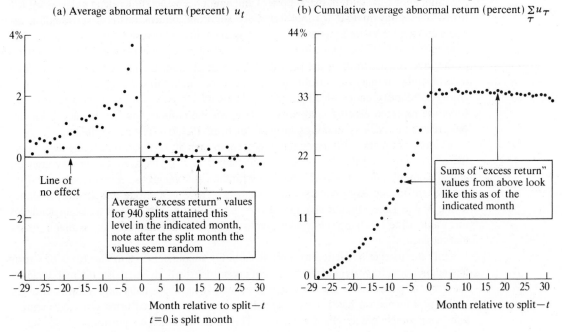

(a) Average abnormal return (percent) u_t

(b) Cumulative average abnormal return (percent) $\sum_\tau u_\tau$

Line of no effect

Average "excess return" values for 940 splits attained this level in the indicated month, note after the split month the values seem random

Sums of "excess return" values from above look like this as of the indicated month

Month relative to split — t
$t = 0$ is split month

Month relative to split — t

Source: Fama, Fisher, Jensen, and Roll [1969].

[10]The form of the conditional expectation is left unspecified. It will suffice, at this point, to simply note that it is based on how the individual security returns tend to react to the multitude of other influences that tend to affect the returns on all other securities, which are contained in R_m. That is, it simply answers the question: How does this security's price change when the prices of all securities change?

reaction of the market to this "signal" is entirely consistent with market efficiency. Part (b) of the figure sums those abnormal returns over time to generate **cumulative abnormal returns** or **cumulative excess returns,** otherwise known as **CARs.**

Clearly, it would be possible to look at each and every possible type of corporate announcement, use this methodology to see if important news was communicated to the market with the announcement, and measure if the price changes or returns generated correspond to an efficient market reaction. Indeed, empirical studies have looked at most conceivable types of announcements to try and develop an understanding of whether market reactions are efficient or not. Thus, researchers have investigated announcements of earnings, dividends, mergers, stock splits and dividends, reverse stock splits, corporate spin-offs, management proposals to change the firm's articles of incorporation, corporate refinancing plans, corporate capital budgeting plans, and many others. Moreover, most of these announcements have been investigated using monthly, weekly, and daily time intervals; a few have looked at changes in price *within* the day of the announcement.

Four of these studies are summarized in Figure 6–10. In each case the time period (in "days" for these studies) relative to the announcement date is shown on the horizontal axis. The vertical axis gives the cumulative abnormal returns up to and including the specified dates. The studies in Parts (a) and (b) investigate returns 10 days before to 10 days after announcements of share repurchases by 140 firms through a tender offer (at a premium above the current market price) and announcements of dividend changes by 135 firms. The study in Part (c) looks at daily abnormal returns on days surrounding announcements by Value Line of changes it has made in the "investment performance rank" of securities it follows. Thus, in this case, the announcement is by Value Line but relates to the investment worth of the security. The highest rank is 1 and the lowest is 5. This recommendation may be valuable to the extent the market thinks highly of Value Line's ability to identify undervalued securities. The study in Part (d) investigates returns surrounding reported earnings surprises. The higher the number attached to each CAR line the greater the positive earnings surprise for firms included in that portfolio.

Evidence of market efficiency seems present in each of the first three graphs. In general, there is an effect on the day of the announcement and, perhaps, up to one day after the announcement, but no noticeable tendency for the CAR values to continue rising or falling subsequent to one day after the announcement. There is a strong anticipation tendency in the Value Line ranking changes. However, this probably reflects a strong tendency for Value Line to change its ranking after other evidence has become available to the marketplace.

Only the market's reaction to surprise earnings announcements in Part (d) is of a form that suggests an important and pervasive market imperfection. There is a distinct tendency for firms in portfolios 9 and 10 to continue supplying abnormally high returns after the earnings information has been presented to the market. These firms reported earnings that were much greater than expected. The firms included in portfolios 1, 2, and 3 continued to experience abnormally low returns after their very negative earnings were reported.

In general, most of the empirical evidence on the reaction of the market to specific information signals is in support of the hypothesis of a reasonable level of market efficiency. The studies suggest that the market reacts very quickly to new information of any kind, and reacts in a manner that is not systemically wrong or biased. When daily prices are used the results usually show a *complete* market reaction within a two day-

FIGURE 6–10   **Market Price Reactions to Four Different Informational Events**

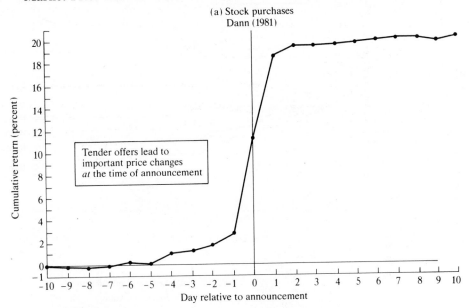

Source: Dann [1981].

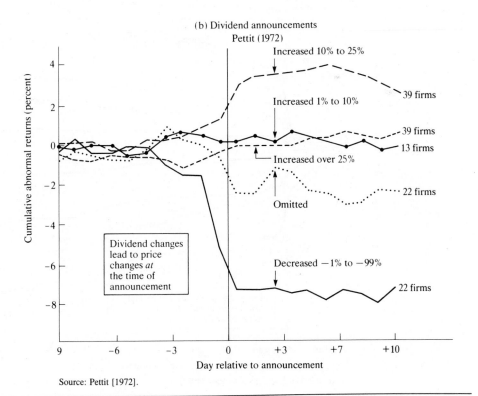

Source: Pettit [1972].

FIGURE 6–10 *(Concluded)*

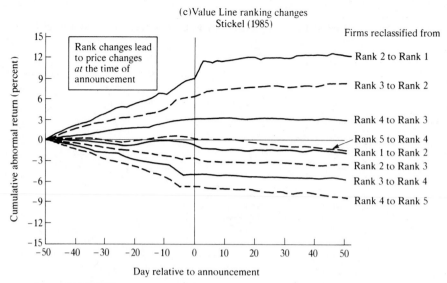

**(c)Value Line ranking changes
Stickel (1985)**

Source: Stickel [1985].

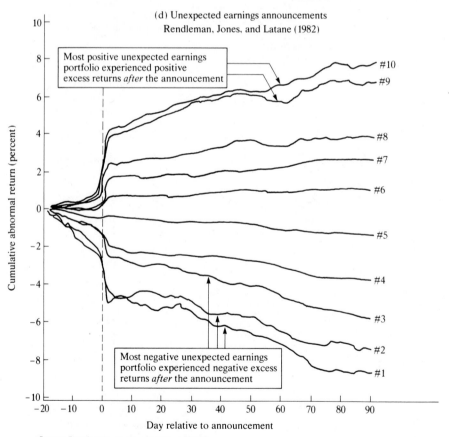

**(d) Unexpected earnings announcements
Rendleman, Jones, and Latane (1982)**

Source: Rendleman, Jones, and Latane [1982].

window surrounding the announcement. Considering the problems of measuring when a specific piece of information becomes "public," the two-day maximum reaction time found cannot be used to strongly reject the notion of market efficiency.

There is some "anomalous" evidence, however (like that presented in Part (d) of Figure 6–10). Some of this evidence can be cast aside because of an inability by researchers to specify precisely when publication of the information occurs, or an inability to specify precisely the magnitude of the "normal" return, $E(\tilde{R}_{it})$, that is subtracted from the observed return to measure the abnormal return, u_{it}. Indeed, though we cannot tell for sure, the results in Part (d) of the figure could be caused by biases created in the construction of the abnormal return figures. Only time and further investigation will reveal whether the market reacts efficiently or inefficiently to earnings surprises.

The studies we mention here are but a sampling, of course, and they are presented as an initial indication of the dynamic behavior of security returns. Whether these studies are at all useful to the development of an investment strategy will await our discussions in Part IV of the book.

The Use of Technical and Fundamental Analyses

Ever since transactions prices for securities have been recorded, a significant number of market participants have attempted to squeeze useful information out of analyses of *past price series*. The rationale underlying such an approach is as follows:

> There are people in the market who have knowledge of the operation of firms and the economy that is superior to the knowledge held by the vast majority. Their operations will affect the market gradually and in well-defined ways. Observing past prices, which slowly reflect the actions of the knowledgeable, thus provides an indirect tap on the kind of information held by this group. Thus, those technicians that understand how prices behave over time can use this information to reap superior profits.

Clearly, for one to adopt this mode of analysis requires one to assume that the market is inefficient in reacting to information. For, if there was relevant information in the past price series, the attempts of technical analysts to capture it will adjust the price to reflect such information. The consequence would be a price series that reveals no dependencies.

This raises an interesting question. If we have a good deal of documented evidence to suggest prices respond quickly to information, then why would not technical analyses tend to disappear from the market? There are two possible responses for which we have strong opinions but little proof. One is that studies of the sort just investigated do not test for the existence of the actual kinds of complex dependencies that exist in the securities markets. In fact, many of the dependencies technicians believe exist, including "support levels," "breakouts," "resistance points," "head and shoulders," "necklines," "triple bottoms," and so on, are so complex that they cannot be easily modeled (in part, because of their ambiguity). Consequently, investors adopting these methods convince themselves that academic investigations have not proved their approach to be fruitless.

The second possible response, and the one we hold dear, is that security markets *tend* to be efficient with respect to past prices, but the technicians for the most part are wasting their labor services. Of course, this leads to a final question. If technical activity is not productive (in the sense that a bank teller, business executive, or mechanic are productive), how do they come to do it? A potential response comes form psychologist B. F. Skinner [1948]. He argues persuasively, "To say that a reinforcement is contingent upon a response may mean nothing more than that it follows the response." He demonstrated that purely unrelated actions of pigeons tended to be reinforced by the temporal proximity of a reward. The bird behaved as if there were a connection between the bird's actions (flapping a wing, turning around) and the delivery of a morsel of food even though the food was randomly delivered. The analogy to the stock market is quite close. Technicians observing a pattern in close prior proximity to a price increase may have their beliefs "reinforced," even though the relationship is purely an accident. The pattern preceding a price increase may occur frequently (though randomly) enough to continuously reinforce the relationship in the searcher's mind.

Of course, we hope that systematic empirical investigations will prove, once and for always, that technical analysis of the market does or does not lead to a way to generate higher returns. As of now the weight of evidence strongly supports the conclusion that technical analysis of past price changes will not give any clue as to future price changes.

To be complete and fair, we do want to point out that most complex technical trading rules (i.e., those more complex than filter rules) have not been tested directly—and perhaps they can't be. Nevertheless, we believe it's most important for you to be skeptical about the purported success of any technical trading rule.[11]

The analysis of more fundamental kinds of information related to a security's value and the ability to use it to outperform the market is an issue to be addressed in later chapters. At this point, it's sufficient to note the possibility that the analysis of other information may bear the fruits of the resources expended. That is, the profitably of other methods of analysis is not ruled out by the lack of usefulness of technical analysis. This issue, being much more involved, is considered in depth later in the book. It's not that technical analysis is prima facie worthless, but that it's unlikely, from what we know of financial markets, that it will be profitable.

Oh, Yes. What about the Top 20?

Now we take you back to the 20 best performers of the Fortune 500 presented at the introduction to this chapter. Their performance over the period from the end of 1981 through the end to 1985 is presented in Figure 6–11. As nearly as we can judge, there is no relationship between the returns generated by these firms over the more recent period and the returns they generated over the prior decade. In fact, as a point estimate, the return on these 20 firms in the recent period, on average, was *less* than that on the S&P 500. However, there is no statistically significant difference (based on this small sample) between their performance and the S&P index between 1981 and 1985, which is exactly what you would expect in an efficient market.

---

[11]If technical analysis doesn't work, then why don't technicians learn there is no payoff to their labors? It could be that some technicians will randomly outperform the rest of the market (and some will underperform). The success exhibited by these randomly selected market participants may provide sufficient reinforcement to cause new analysts to take the place of those old analysts who have quit the strategy because they haven't done well.

FIGURE 6–11   Top 20 from 1981 through 1985 (Fortune 500 common stocks)

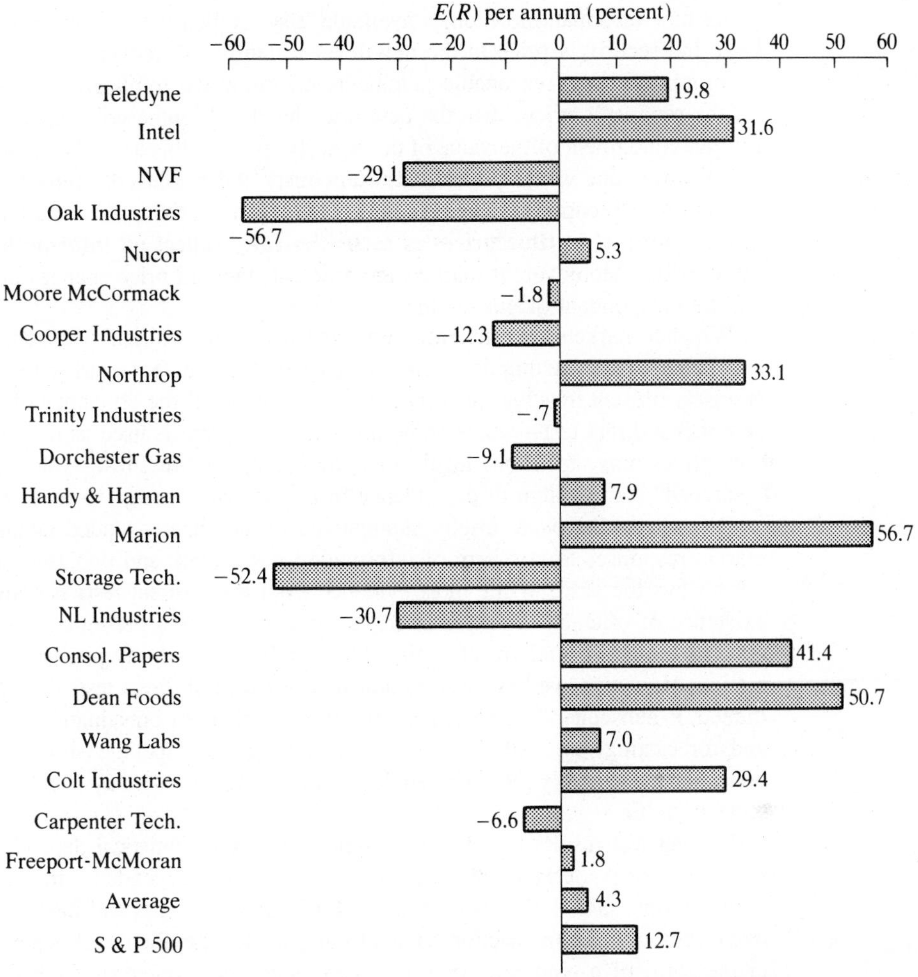

$E(R)$ per annum (percent)

Company	Value
Teledyne	19.8
Intel	31.6
NVF	−29.1
Oak Industries	−56.7
Nucor	5.3
Moore McCormack	−1.8
Cooper Industries	−12.3
Northrop	33.1
Trinity Industries	−.7
Dorchester Gas	−9.1
Handy & Harman	7.9
Marion	56.7
Storage Tech.	−52.4
NL Industries	−30.7
Consol. Papers	41.4
Dean Foods	50.7
Wang Labs	7.0
Colt Industries	29.4
Carpenter Tech.	−6.6
Freeport-McMoran	1.8
Average	4.3
S & P 500	12.7

Summary

The purpose of this chapter has been to introduce you to how security prices tend to move over time. The approach was to summarize how markets would operate if a number of simplifying assumptions were present. These assumptions, which characterize an **ideal market,** include perfect market liquidity, price continuity, fairness, and equal access to freely available information regarding security values. In such a market, individual investors acting in their own self-interest use all available information in an attempt to secure the best portfolio position (highest return after taking risk into account). Any potential profits from trading in securities will quickly be acted upon by a large number of investors, which will tend to move the security from one equilibrium price to a new equilibrium price. The new price will reflect all information that may be available regarding the value of the security.

As new information becomes available, the competitive pressure from investors will force the security's price to the new level instantly. Moreover, as long as everyone is attempting to draw reasonable judgments regarding the implications of the information for the security's price, then the new price level will unbiasedly represent the market's summary judgment of the value of the security. It is via this logic that an **efficient market** is defined as one where prices **instantaneously** and **unbiasedly** reflect any information relevant to a security's value. Another way of summarizing the concept is to say that, **at any moment in time prices of securities fully reflect all information available in the market.** Moreover, if markets are efficient, then all price changes or rates of return will be independent of one another over time.

Whether markets are efficient or not is basically an empirical question, since we know that some of the assumptions that are part of the efficient market hypothesis are not precisely present in actual security markets. Any test of the efficiency of the market may be either a direct test—where some informational event is used as a basis for observing how prices move from one level to another—or an indirect test—where price series are "searched" for any sign of dependence from one price change to another.

Direct tests that were briefly summarized in the chapter tended to suggest that most market responses to any item of information were quick and unbiased, although this is not always the case. While most evidence from these direct tests is consistent with the existence of efficient capital markets, some evidence was presented that suggested that markets tended to underreact to the value implications of any published piece of information. However, we have just scratched the surface of direct tests of market efficiency. Indeed, in subsequent chapters, particularly in the chapters on valuation, security analysis, and forecasting, we will be much more thorough and specific about whether security prices have accurately incorporated items of information that may be relevant to assessing security value.

Indirect test results found little evidence of simple statistical dependence in security returns or prices. Serial correlation tests or other tests of dependence found positive results only for very short-term price changes. Daily price changes and intraday price changes from transaction to transaction tended to display some evidence of dependence—usually in the form of a tendency for price changes to show reversals from one to the next, although the economic importance of these dependencies was questionable. There was also some evidence to suggest that security price changes and returns exhibited a calendar effect. Returns in different months and in different days of the week may tend to have different values. Of course, this does not necessarily indicate that markets are not efficient since there may be valid economic reasons for month-to-month or day-to-day discrepancies.

References

Alexander, S. [1961] "Price Movements in Speculative Markets: Trends or Random Walks." *Industrial Management Reivew* (May).

Ball, Ray, and Brown, Philip. [1968] "An Empirical Evaluation of Accounting Income Numbers." *Journal of Accounting Research* 6 (Autumn).

Beaver, William H., and Landsman, Wayne R. [1981] "Note on the Behavior of Residual Security Returns for Winner and Loser Portfolios." *Journal of Accounting and Economics* (July).

Berry, M., and Grant, D. [1986] "Pre-Event Trading: Exception or Rule?" Working Paper, University of New Mexico.

Charest, Guy. [1978] "Split Information, Stock Returns and Market Efficiency—I." *Journal of Financial Economics* (June–September).

Copeland, Thomas E., and Mayers, David. [1982] "The Value Line Engima (1965–1978): A Case Study of Performance Evaluation Issues." *Journal of Financial Economics* (November).

Cornell, Brad, and Dietrich, J. Kimball. [1978] "The Efficiency of the Market from Foreign Exchange under Floating Rates." *Review of Economics and Statistics* (February).

Dann, Larry. [1981] "Common Stock Repurchases: An Analysis of Returns to Bondholders and Stockholders." *Journal of Financial Economics* (June).

Dann, Larry; Mayers, David; and Raab, Robert., [1977] "Trading Rules, Large Blocks and the Speed of Price Adjustment." *Journal of Financial Economics* (January).

Dusak, Katherine. [1973] "Trading and Investor Returns: An Investigation of Commodity Market Risk Premiums." *Journal of Political Economy* (November–December).

Dyckman, Thomas; Downes, David; and Magee, Robert. [1975] *Efficient Capital Markets and Accounting: A Critical Analysis.* Englewood Cliffs, N.J.: Prentice-Hall.

Fama, Eugene F. [1965] "Random Walks in Stock Market Prices." *Financial Analysts Journal* 21.

Fama, Eugene F. [1965a] "The Behavior of Stock Market Prices." *Journal of Business* (January).

Fama, Eugene F. [1970] "Efficient Capital Markets: A Review of Theory and Empirical Work." *Journal of Finance*.

Fama, Eugene F. [1976] *Foundations of Finance.* New York: Basic Books.

Fama, Eugene F., and Blume, Marshall. [1966] "Filter Rules and Stock Market Trading Profits." *Journal of Business* (Supplement, January).

Fama, Eugene F., and French, Kenneth R. [1986] "Permanent and Temporary Components of Stock Prices." Working Paper, University of Chicago (July).

Fama, Eugene F.; Fisher, Lawrence; Jensen, Michael; and Roll, Richard. [1969] "The Adjustment of Stock Prices to New Information." *International Economic Review* (February).

French, Kenneth K. [1980] "Stock Returns and the Weekend Effect." *Journal of Financial Economics* (November).

Gibbons, Michael R., and Hess, Patrick. [1981] "Day-of-the-Week Effects and Asset Returns." *Journal of Business* (October).

Granger, Clive W. T., and Morgenstern, Oskar. [1963] "Spectral Analysis of New York Stock Market Prices." *Kyklos* 16.

Harris, Lawrence. [1986a] "A Transaction Data Study of Weekly and Intradaily Patterns in Stock Returns." *Journal of Financial Economics* (May).

Harris, Lawrence., [1986b] "How to Profit from Intradaily Stock Returns." *Journal of Portfolio Management* (Winter).

Holthausen, Robert; Leftwich, Richard; and Mayers, David [1986] "The Effect of Large Block Transactions of Security Prices: A Cross-Sectional Analysis." Working Paper, University of Chicago (May).

Jaffee, Jeffery, and Westerfield, Randolph. [1985] "The Week-End Effect in Common Stock Returns: The International Evidence." *Journal of Finance* (June).

Jensen, Michael C. [1978] "Some Anomalous Evidence Regarding Market Efficiency." *Journal of Financial Economics* (June–September).

Jensen, Michael E., and Benington, George. [1970] "Random Walks and Technical Theories: Some Additional Evidence." *Journal of Finance* (May).

Keim, Donald. [1983] "Size-Related Anomalies and Stock Return Seasonality." *Journal of Financial Economics* (June 1983).

Larson, Arnold. [1964] "Measurement of a Random Process in Futures Prices." In *The Random Character of Stock Market Prices,* ed. P. H. Cootner. Cambridge, Mass.: The M.I.T. Press.

McFarland, James; Pettit, R. Richardson; and Sung, Sam K. [1982] "The Distribution of Foreign Exchange Price Changes: Trading Day Effects and Risk Measurement." *Journal of Finance* (June).

Niederhoffer, Victor, and Osborne, M. F. M. [1966]

"Market Making and Reversal on the Stock Exchange." *Journal of American Statistical Association* (December).

Officer, R. R. [1975] "Seasonality in Australian Capital Markets: Market Efficiency and Empirical Issues." *Journal of Financial Economics* (March).

O'Hanlon, John, and Ward, Charles W. R. [1986] "How to Lose at Winning Strategies." *The Journal of Portfolio Management* (Spring).

Pettengil, Glen N. [1985] "Persistent Seasonal Return Patterns." *The Financial Review* (November).

Pettit, R. Richardson. [1972] "Dividend Announcements, Security Performance, and Capital Market Efficiency." *Journal of Finance* (December).

Pinches, George. [1970] "The Random Walk Hypothesis and Technical Analysis." *Financial Analysts Journal* 26.

Praetz, Peter. [1976] "Rates of Return on Filter Tests." *Journal of Finance* (March).

Reilly, Frank K., and Drzycimski, Eugene F. [1973] "Tests of Stock Market Efficiency Following Major World Events." *Journal of Business Research* 1.

Rendleman, Richard; Jones, Charles D.; and Latane, Henry A. [1982] "Empirical Anomalies Based on Unexpected Earnings and the Importance of Risk Adjustments." *Journal of Financial Economics* (November).

Rogalski, Richard J., and Tinic, Seha M. [1985] "The January Size Effect: Anomaly or Risk Mismeasurement?" Working Paper, The Amos Tuck School of Business Administration, Dartmouth College (October).

Rosenberg, Barr; Reid, Kenneth; and Lanstein, Ronald. [1985] "Persuasive Evidence of Market Inefficiency." *Journal of Portfolio Management* (Spring).

Rozeff, Michael S., and Kinney, William R. [1976] "Capital Market Seasonability: The Case of Stock Market Returns." *Journal of Financial Economics* (October).

Schwartz, R. A., and Whitcomb, D. K. [1977] "The Time-Variance Relationship: Evidence of Autocorrelation in Common Stock Returns." *Journal of Finance* (March).

Skinner, B. F. [1948] "Superstition in the Pigeon." *Journal of Experimental Psychology* 38.

Solt, Michael E., and Swanson, Paul J. [1981] "On the Efficiency of the Markets for Gold and Silver." *The Journal of Business* (July).

Stevenson, Richard, and Bear, Robert. [1970] "Commodity Futures: Trends on Random Walks." *Journal of Finance* (March).

Stickel, Scott E. [1985] "The Effect of Value Line Investment Survey Rank Changes on Common Stock Prices." *Journal of Financial Economics* (May).

Taylor, Stephen, and Kingsman, Brian. [1977] "Comment: An Autoregressive Forecast of the World Sugar Future Option Market." *Journal of Financial and Quantitative Analysis* (December).

Theobald, Michael, and Price, Vera. [1984] "Seasonality Estimation in Thin Markets." *Journal of Finance* (June).

Tinic, Seha M., and West, Richard R. [1984] "Risk and Return: January vs. the Rest of the Year." *Journal of Financial Economics* (December).

Watts, Ross L. [1978] "Systematic 'Abnormal' Returns after Quarterly Earning Announcements." *Journal of Financial Economics* (June–September).

Questions and Problems

1. The efficient market hypothesis asserts that:
   a. The stock market is not a random walk.
   b. Stock prices rise as inflation rises.
   c. Technical analysis is superior to fundamental analysis.
   d. Stock prices fully reflect all publicly available information.

   CFA

2. A recent study concluded: "Excess or abnormal returns observed from 60 days before the announcement of tender offers for firms' shares to 60 days after the announcement followed a pattern that is consistent with price efficiency in the marketplace." Considering the period both before and after the announcements, what is implied about the pattern of excess or abnormal returns?

3. What assumptions underlie the efficient market hypothesis? We are asking you to: discriminate between the assumptions that underlie the theory, the process or logic that is part of the development of the conclusions of the theory, and the implications and conclusions of the theory.

4. Suppose the market for NYSE common stocks and bonds is efficient. What characteristics of prices, price changes, and/or rates of return result from market efficiency?

5. The Securities and Exchange Commission is very concerned with setting policy that contributes to market price efficiency. The SEC does so by establishing standards to encourage the publication of important information and to discourage the use of private information in making investment decisions. Write a paragraph suggesting what the SEC must consider in establishing a specific policy statement about how managers should handle information they receive concerning their firm being the target of a merger proposal by another firm.

6. One Wall Street enthusiast observing the fact that Union Carbide doubled in price in 1986 argues: "Markets obviously are not efficient. The market ignored the real value of Union Carbide for three or four years and finally woke up only when Carbide's management decided to sell some of its assets. How can you argue the efficiency of markets when prices turn out to be wrong so often?" What is wrong with this critique?

7. One of the assumptions that leads to the efficient market hypothesis is that information is disseminated on a free and equal basis to all market participants. How closely does this assumption match the realities of the financial marketplace? Are there some kinds of information that are less likely to be revealed at the same time to all investors?

8. Suppose investors draw different implications from an important piece of information. Does this have implications for the efficiency of financial markets?

9. The price of Long Island Lighting bonds recently fell as the firm announced more problems with one of its nuclear power generating plants. Assuming that the market's response to the information was consistent with the efficient market hypothesis, what levels of return would be experienced by investors in the period before the announcement, at the point of announcement, and after the announcement?

10. The following announcement was published recently in *The Wall Street Journal.*

Westinghouse Is Downgraded as Uncertainty Follows in Wake of Revamping and Rebound

BY RANDALL SMITH

Just as Westinghouse Electric stock hit an all-time high to cap a four-year comeback culminating in its centennial year, Wall Street analysts came down on the company like a ton of bricks.

Three brokerages—Goldman Sachs, Salomon Brothers and Smith Barney, Harris Upham—downgraded the stock just as Westinghouse reported a 26% gain in 1986 per-share net income Jan. 19. The price rose $2^3/_8$ that day, only to tumble $3^1/_4$ the next. Since then, the stock has weakened a bit further, closing yesterday at $63^1/_4$.

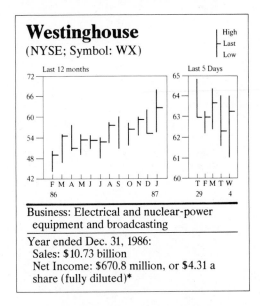

Westinghouse
(NYSE; Symbol: WX)

Business: Electrical and nuclear-power equipment and broadcasting

Year ended Dec. 31, 1986:
Sales: $10.73 billion
Net Income: $670.8 million, or $4.31 a share (fully diluted)*

To the extent that it is possible to generalize from the particular, does this situation seem to correspond to an efficient market reaction to the two public announcements summarized in this article?

11. Suppose, in addition to the information in question 10, you know a Westinghouse employee who believes that the firm's common stock is worth only $50. Is this evidence inconsistent with market efficiency?

P A R T

III

PORTFOLIO CHOICE AND EQUILIBRIUM MARKET RETURNS

Portfolio Choice

Risk Management

Investors dislike taking unnecessary risks. Those with diminishing marginal utility for wealth would choose to pay less for risky opportunities than they would for opportunities offering certain outcomes and possessing identical expected values. Chapter 5 discussed the effect of this on actual security returns. We found that corporate bonds, for example, supplied ex post arithmetic mean returns of 3.9 percent per year, while stocks supplied mean returns of approximately 12.1 percent per year over the 60-year period from 1926 through 1985.

In this chapter, we explicitly consider the problem of dealing with investment risks. The chapter might be alternatively titled "Risk and Return Management." It is a prescriptive chapter because it deals with the problem of what can be done to mitigate the effects of uncertainty.

Two aspects of risk management will be considered. These are:

1. The selection of a combination of risk and return that reflects the investor's tolerance for risk and desire for return; i.e., **preferences.**
2. The management of investment alternatives to improve the set of opportunities available; i.e., **opportunities.**

Chapter 2 dealt with the first of these issues. In it, we derived for the investor a set of indifference curves defined in terms of expected returns and standard deviation of returns. A straightforward application of these preferences might lead a very risk-averse investor to choose U.S. Treasury bills or very conservative certificates of deposit. The more risk-tolerant investor might choose common stocks or call options if they offered higher returns.

However, much more can be done to help the investor secure the most desirable (utility-maximizing) opportunities. Investment opportunites can be packaged together by forming **portfolios.** This markedly increases the number of investment opportunities available at any specified risk level. The potential for creating portfolios changes the whole problem of investment choice. Risk-averse investors may be able to find a way to invest in common stocks or real estate to earn the higher returns these opportunities seem to offer without a significant increase in risk exposure.

How can this expansion of opportunities be accomplished? The simplest way to do this is by diversifying, or spreading the uncertainty over a portfolio of a number of securities. How does diversification work to achieve the benefit of higher returns without an increase in risk? The answer emanates from the so-called **Law of Large Numbers,** which (roughly translated) states the following:

> The observed frequency of an event in the population more closely approaches the true underlying probability of that event in the population as the sample size grows larger.

It is this law which predicts, for example, that if you were to toss a fair coin 10,000 times, the observed frequency of "heads" will tend more closely to approach $\frac{1}{2}$ than it would in a typical sample of 10 tosses. In the latter sample, it would not be terribly unusual to observe, for example, that 70 percent of the tosses came up "heads," whereas if this occurred in a sample of 10,000 tosses it would be sufficient evidence to conclude beyond a reasonable doubt that the coin was not fair. The probability of 7,000 heads in 10,000 tosses of a fair coin is astronomically low, and much lower than the probability of 7 heads in 10 tosses.

Just how does the law of large numbers apply to diversifying a portfolio? To illustrate the general concepts, we discuss the manner in which insurance companies diversify their portfolios.

The Insurance Principle

Suppose a property and liability insurance company offers fire insurance to individual residential property owners. Currently the company has 150,000 policies in force. The company's actuaries estimate, based on historical figures, that the probability of the average house in an average city burning in any given year, for example, is 0.001, or one in a thousand. And, when the average house does burn, it results in a loss of $35,000 for the insurance company.

Because of the nature and causes of residential house fires, and the diversification of the company's policies on a geographic basis, it is assumed that the chance of fire to an individual policyholder is *independent* of the chance of fire to any other policyholder. In statistical terms, this means that the fact that my house may burn tomorrow in no way affects the probability of your house burning. The two events are statistically unrelated.

Now, the company in this situation expects to experience casualty losses in an average year which total $5.25 million, a figure based on the expectation of 150 houses burning, each incurring a loss of $35,000. There is some year-to-year variation in actual losses, however. Last year, for example, the company experienced only 142 residential fires, while the year before there were 167 fires. The company estimates that the distribution of actual residential fires each year per 150,000 homes is approximately normally distributed with a mean of 150 and a standard deviation of 12.25. Seen in this light, recent experience is not unusual. In a normal distribution, approximately 68 percent of observations will lie within one standard deviation on either side of the mean. Thus, in slightly over two thirds of the years, the company expects to experience between 137.75 and 162.25 fires, assuming that it keeps a constant base of 150,000 homes insured.

In contrast, consider the problem of a much-smaller insurance company with only 1,500 residential fire insurance policies outstanding. Assuming these are houses similar in every way to those insured by the larger company, the smaller firm can expect to experience casualty losses in a typical year which equal $52,500, a figure based on the expectation of 1.5 houses burning down. The standard deviation is 1.224 houses based on the .001 loss ratio and 1,500 homes, so that in two thirds of the years the smaller firm can expect to experience losses between .276 houses and 2.724 houses. The variation relative to the expected loss for the small firm is much greater (1.224/1.5 for the small firm and 12.25/150 for the large firm).

The larger insurer's losses are obviously more predictable on a per-policy basis because of the larger population of houses it insures. The law of large numbers states that the larger the sample size, the more probable it is that the sample mean—in this case, the proportion of insured houses which actually burn down in a given year—comes closer to the population expected value, which is the proportion of *all* houses which burn. The result holds whenever the probability of a given event occurring in the population—a house burning—is statistically independent from one member of the population to the next.[1]

Risk, to an insurance company, is obviously incurred whenever the possibility exists that its predictions will not be realized. Insurance premiums are based on expectations, or predictions, and not on how the actual results come out. Therefore, insurance companies, to offer competitive premiums, have an incentive to "manage" their loss experience (i.e., their risks). This can be done by improving the company's forecasting ability, but it can also be done through diversification among a large number of independent risks.[2]

---

[1]A more formal way of stating this result is that the standard error of the sample mean is given by $\sigma_M = \sigma/\sqrt{N}$, where N is the number of observations in the sample and σ is the population standard deviation. Thus the standard error (the standard deviation of the sample mean) is inversely proportional to the square root of the sample size. In a sample of 1,500 homes, for example, the proportion of houses burning in a given year may vary from year to year with a standard deviation of $\sigma/\sqrt{1,500}$, whereas the proportion of houses burning in a sample of 150,000 houses has a standard deviation which is only 1/10th that for 1,500 houses, or $\sigma/\sqrt{150,000}$.

[2]And this also explains why one finds insurance companies frequently "pooling" risks among themselves. It is always better to have a proportionate share of a much larger pool of independent risks than to have the whole of a smaller group of risks as long as there is some perceived reason to be averse to risk (either the insurance companies are risk-averse, the stockholders who own the companies are risk-averse, or there are some costs to maintaining a risky portfolio of policies, e.g., some bankruptcy cost).

Risk Reduction in Stock Portfolios

The insurance example can readily be applied to diversifying a portfolio of financial securities. We will assume, for expository purposes at this point, that returns on individual securities are statistically independent. Consider a hypothetical situation involving a common stock universe in which all stocks are identical in their risk and return characteristics. Suppose there are 100 stocks, each of which offers an expected rate of return of 10 percent per annum ($E(\tilde{R}) = .10$) with a standard deviation of 20 percent ($\sigma(\tilde{R}) = .20$). By assumption, their rates of return are independent. Thus, any given stock's rate of return is unaffected by any other stock's rate of return.

In this situation there is *no* decision problem concerning which of these stocks is to be included in a portfolio, since they are identical. However, it can make a big difference *how many* of these stocks are held! It is easy to show that the risk the portfolio offers—in terms of the standard deviation of the portfolio's return—is a function of the number of stocks in the portfolio, which we shall label N. Assuming all stocks in the portfolio are purchased in equal dollar amounts, the proportion of the investor's funds that are placed in each stock will be $1/N$. Then, it follows that the standard deviation of the portfolio's return will be given by:

$$\sigma(\tilde{R}_p) = \frac{\sigma(\tilde{R})}{\sqrt{N}}$$

If the investor holds just one stock in the portfolio, the portfolio risk will be 20 percent per annum, since $\sigma(\tilde{R}_p) = (.20)/1 = .20$. However, with two stocks, it will be only $\sigma(\tilde{R}_p) = (.20)/1.41 = .1418$. And with three stocks, the risk is further reduced to $\sigma(\tilde{R}_p) = (.20)/1.73 = .1156$. This reduction in portfolio risk as more firms' stocks are added continues until all 100 stocks are included. This can be seen in Figure 7–1, which graphs the portfolio standard deviation as a function of N. Notice that when only four stocks are held, the riskiness of the portfolio is exactly half of the risk associated with holding only one stock. And when 16 stocks are included, portfolio risks drops to only one fourth of the one-stock level. A little diversification goes a long way toward risk reduction, at least when independence of returns is assumed.

A happy consequence of diversification in this example is that portfolio risk is reduced without sacrificing expected return. Recall that each stock in the universe is expected to earn a 10 percent return per annum. Since a portfolio's expected return is just a weighted average of the component stock's returns, where the weights are the proportion of the investor's funds devoted to each stock, it follows that:

Portfolio
expected $= E(\tilde{R}_p) = (1/N)(.10) + (1/N)(.10) + \cdots + (1/N)(.10) = .10$
return

Thus, no matter how many stocks are added, the investor still expects a 10 percent return from his portfolio.

Empirics of Risk Reduction

In the real world our assumptions about the independence of individual stocks are unrealistic. In the first place, most stocks have been found empirically to have positive

FIGURE 7–1   **Rewards to Diversification among Hypothetical Stocks Having Independent Returns**

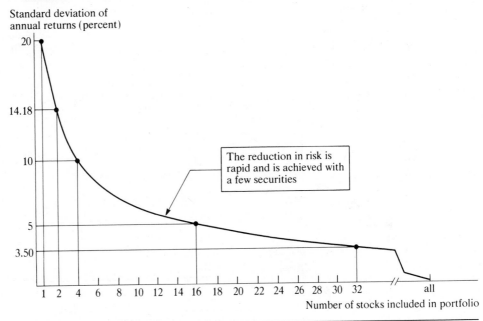

comovement or to offer returns which are correlated with one another in a statistical sense. The average common stock price, in part, reflects the expectations that are held by investors for the economy and the entire business sector. Expectations of corporate profits tend to rise as the economy expands, and, in response, firms' common stocks tend to increase in value together. When expectations tend to become negative, these same firms find their successes withering and their stock values falling together. Some firms' successes and failures tend to magnify economic expectations, however, while others are relatively immune to alterations in expectations of the economy. Common stocks such as Deere & Co., General Electric, and Merrill Lynch tend to have a high level of covariability with general market trends. Other stocks, such as Anheuser Busch and R. J. Reynolds, tend to be affected less by such movements. In fact, the vast majority of stocks' returns are positively correlated with the movements of major stock market indexes, such as the Standard & Poor's 500 or the Dow Jones Industrial Average (the average correlation is .4 to .5). Moreover, there also are differences in the individual variability offered by different stocks. Some, including most public utilities, have returns which do not vary a great deal over time. Returns on other stocks, such as U. S. Home and Mattel Inc., are much more variable (airlines, construction, and natural resource companies—along with some high-tech firms—tend to be the most variable).

To shed some light on the risk-reducing effect of diversification among stocks, suppose we begin constructing portfolios consisting of one security, then portfolios of two randomly selected securities with an equal investment in each, then eight randomly selected securities, and so on until we have one portfolio made up of the entire market. Then, we calculate the expected annual return and standard deviation of return for each portfolio.

FIGURE 7–2   The Reduction in Standard Deviation of Annual Returns from Portfolios Containing Different Numbers of Stocks Listed on the NYSE (1926–1965 and 1960–1981)

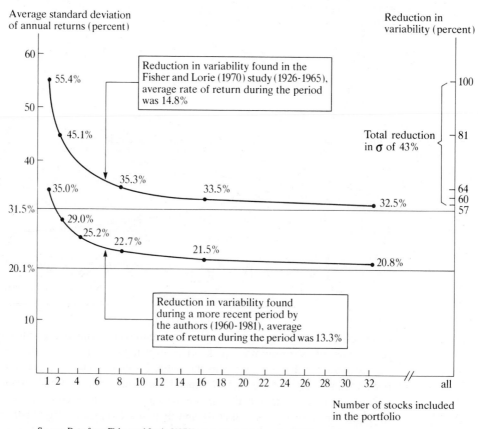

Source: Data from Fisher and Lorie [1970], and calculated from the CRSP tapes.

These calculations were performed twice, once over the 40-year period 1926 to 1965 and once for the 22-year period 1960 to 1981. The results of this simulated portfolio management process are summarized by the two curves in Figure 7–2. This figure plots the *average* of the calculated standard deviations for all one-security portfolios, all two-security portfolios, all eight-security portfolios, and so on. The resulting standard deviation suggests the remaining risk the investor would have been subject to, on average, if a randomly selected portfolio of the size indicated was held for one year. The average returns don't change with portfolio size, of course.

Obviously, both curves indicate that risk cannot be reduced to zero even if the entire market portfolio is held. Yet, it is not hard to see from Figure 7–2 that, even when individual stocks have a tendency for positive comovement, there are still substantial benefits to diversification. The comedian who once remarked that a diversified portfolio

FIGURE 7–3   **Reduction in Variability from Random Diversification in Eight National Stock Markets**

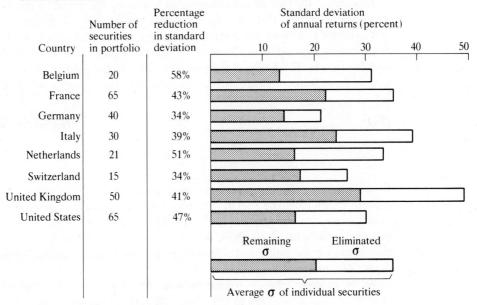

Country	Number of securities in portfolio	Percentage reduction in standard deviation	Standard deviation of annual returns (percent)
Belgium	20	58%	
France	65	43%	
Germany	40	34%	
Italy	30	39%	
Netherlands	21	51%	
Switzerland	15	34%	
United Kingdom	50	41%	
United States	65	47%	

Source: Estimated from Solnik [1974] and *Capital International Perspective*.

is one in which "your money goes down the drain in several different sinks at once" was neither very funny nor accurate. A person who held a typical one-stock portfolio during the 1926–65 period experienced an average annual rate of return of 14.8 percent with a standard deviation of 55.4 percent. Approximately two thirds of the time a single, randomly selected stock's return would have ranged between − 40.6 percent and 70.2 percent.

The year-to-year fluctuations, as you can see, are much smaller when just one additional stock is added to the investor's holdings—the standard deviation falls to 45.1 percent. And the same is true when you go from 2 stocks to 8 (35.3 percent), from 8 to 16 (33.5 percent), and so on. Ultimately, by holding a portfolio of the entire market, 43 percent of the variability was eliminated. Note, however, the marginal risk reduction from further diversification is smaller as the portfolio grows in size. The same tendency exists when more recent data are used. The ultimate reduction in standard deviation in the more recent period was from 35 percent to 20.1 percent—the same 43 percent reduction in risk.[3]

The effect of diversification holds for other stock markets as well. Studies of stock markets in European countries show a similar reduction in standard deviation. Figure 7–3 shows the percentage reduction for seven European stock markets and a U.S. market. The figures summarizing the reduction in risk are quite close to the reductions shown in Figure 7–2.

---

[3]All these figures assume there are no costs to diversifying. Even though it is clear that dramatic risk reduction can be achieved with a few stocks, the additional brokerage commissions and information costs associated with diversification must be reckoned with.

Measures of the Comovement of Returns

Obviously, the lack of independence of returns or the degree of comovement among securities is an important consideration in the risk-reducing attributes of portfolios. The comovement influences the portfolio's risk, or its standard deviation. The measure of comovement developed in Chapter 2 is the covariance. The covariance between two security returns, R_i and R_j, is the expected value of the product of the way the returns deviate from their own expected values. The calculation from a set of observed values is:[4]

(7–1)   *Calculation of Covariance*

$$Cov(\tilde{R}_i, \tilde{R}_j) = \frac{1}{T} \sum_{t=1}^{T} [R_{it} - E(\tilde{R}_i)][R_{jt} - E(\tilde{R}_j)]$$

In this expression R_{it} and R_{jt} are the decimal returns on our two securities for period t; perhaps the tth month of a set of T months used to measure the covariance. The expected values of the random variables are denoted $E(\tilde{R}_i)$ and $E(\tilde{R}_j)$. If R_{it} tends to be above its expected value when R_{jt} is above its expected value and below it when R_{jt} is below, the calculation on the right-hand side will be a large positive number—indicating a high degree of comovement.

As an example, the covariance between Chevron and Exxon, calculated using 60 monthly returns from 1980 to 1984, was .052. The monthly return pairs are plotted in Figure 7–4 to supply a picture of the degree of positive comovement in this case.

The correlation, as indicated previously, is the covariance divided by the product of the standard deviations of the two variates. It normalizes the covariance to values between minus and plus 1.0. For Exxon and Chevron:

(7–2)   *Calculation of Correlation Coefficient*

$$\rho_{ij} = = \frac{Cov(\tilde{R}_i, \tilde{R}_j)}{\sigma(\tilde{R}_i)\sigma(\tilde{R}_j)} = \frac{Cov(\tilde{R}_{XON}, \tilde{R}_{CHV})}{\sigma(\tilde{R}_{XON})\sigma(\tilde{R}_{CHV})} = \frac{.052}{(.210)(.346)}$$

Since the standard deviation of returns for Chevron and Exxon are 34.6 percent and 21.0 percent, respectively, the correlation is a very high .72. More generally, the comovement between pairs of securities may be very high—as that between two mutual funds that have adopted similar investment strategies—or very low—as that between two relatively specialized firms in different industries.

As a practical matter, relatively few pairs of securities tend to show complete independence, since most firms are affected by the same set of underlying events (though they may be affected in different degrees). Actions of the Federal Reserve that may change interest rates would tend to have an impact on all firms. It's doubtful that any firm can completely insulate itself from the variety of market forces that influence overall economic well-being.

---

[4]An example was presented in Table 2–1 in Chapter 2 showing the calculation of the covariance and its related correlation coefficient.

FIGURE 7–4   **Covariability with Positive Dependence of Returns**

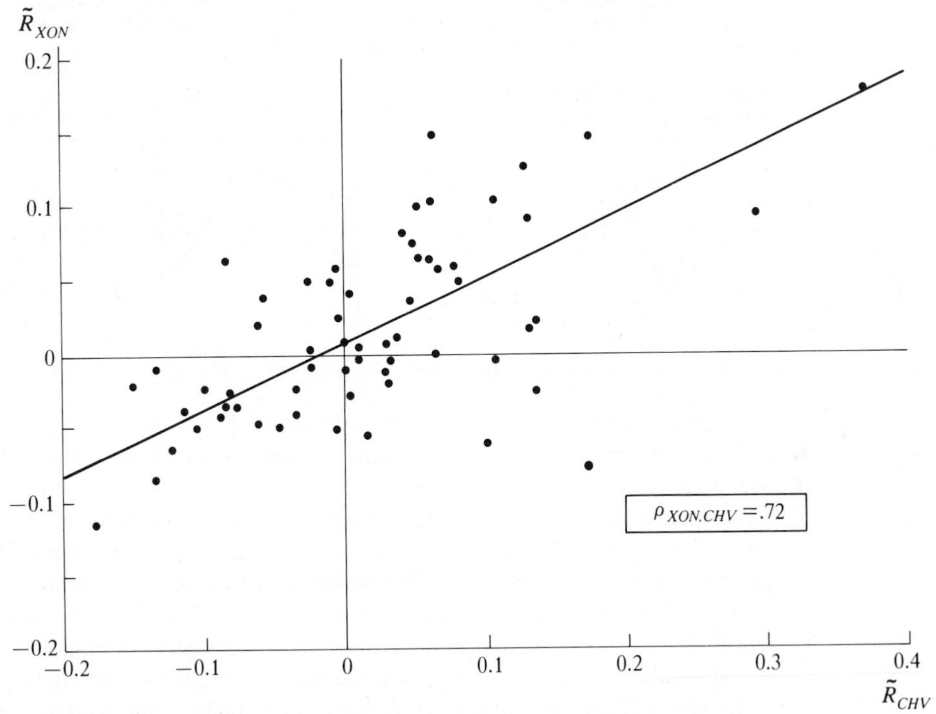

$\rho_{XON.CHV} = .72$

When Diversification Pays

Since we are measuring risk reduction through diversification, a key question at this point is: How does the degree of comovement between two stocks affect the benefits of diversification? More simply: When does it pay to diversify?

A hypothetical series of returns is shown for two stocks, *i* and *j*, in Figure 7–5(a). As can be seen, the two stocks are perfectly positively correlated and move in tandem over time.

Consider holding a portfolio in which half of your funds are invested in *j* and half in *i*. The dashed line in the figure shows this portfolio's returns over time. Notice that the portfolio returns fluctuate to the same degree as do the returns for the two stocks on average taken individually. The standard deviation of the portfolio's returns can be shown to be halfway between the standard deviations of each of the two stocks' returns. This result implies there is no gain to diversifying. Less risk could be obtained simply by holding the stock with the lower standard deviation, which in this case is stock *j* (though it may have a lower return as well).

To take the opposite extreme, assume the different hypothetical series given in Figure 7–5(b). This is the same sort of relationship, except that the two stocks are now perfectly negatively correlated. When stock *j*'s returns rise, *i*'s fall in exact counterpoint.

FIGURE 7–5   Correlation or Covariance Over Time

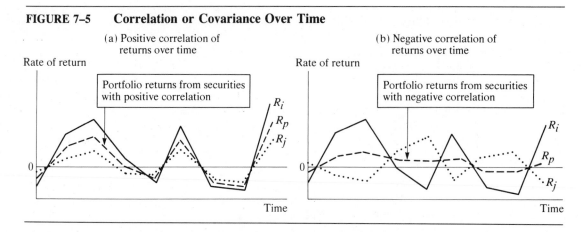

Once again we can construct a portfolio in which half the funds are invested in *i* and half in *j*. Notice, however, that this time the dashed line showing the portfolio's returns over time is almost completely flat. This is because, when *i*'s returns are negative, *j*'s are positive and vice-versa, causing the portfolios' performance to "net out" most of these fluctuations. Clearly, if one could find two stocks like this, there would be considerable gain to diversifying among them. The variability of the return from the portfolio of *i* and *j* is lower than the variability of each of the securities held individually without sacrificing return. In fact, there is one portfolio (not involving equal holdings in each stock) that would reduce variability to zero given the perfect negative comovement.

By now it should be obvious to you that risk reduction is enhanced by finding securities whose returns are relatively independent.[5] The lower the (positive) correlation between two securities, the greater the potential benefits accruing to the investor who diversifies. The portfolio's returns tend to "net out" or wash out some of the return fluctuations. Thus, for example, if airline stocks tend to gain whenever railroad stocks lose, diversifying among both airline and railroad issues will reduce risk. Alternatively, if tire manufacturers and automobile companies tend to prosper and suffer together, it may not reduce one's portfolio standard deviation to hold both types of stock in one portfolio.[6]

The Effect of Diversification on Risks and Returns

Each security's return is a random variable that contributes a probability distribution to the portfolio. To specify the precise effect of diversifying with particular securities, we

---

[5]The press is full of examples of cases where nondiversified portfolio positions have resulted in remarkable gains or, alternatively, remarkable losses from specialized positions—Nelson Bunker Hunt and his family invested a significant portion of their substantial wealth in the silver market in 1979 and early 1980. In part this buying pressure seems to have been responsible for the price of an ounce of silver rising from $6 to $55. By 1981 the price had fallen below $10. Their losses were enormous.

[6]Thus, for example, it may not be wise to devote a significant portion of your portfolio to investments in a call option on GM stock if you already hold some GM stock in your portfolio. But note that you could hold the call option and "sell short" GM stock to create a portfolio where the component parts would have *negative* covariability.

need only know how to calculate portfolio expected return, $E(\tilde{R}_P)$, and portfolio risk, $\sigma(\tilde{R}_P)$, that results from the combination of individual securities. Rules were developed near the end of Chapter 2 to solve this problem.

To begin, we define a **feasible portfolio** as a collection of individual securities, such that the sum over all securities of the fraction of the investor's wealth devoted to each totals 1.0. Mathematically, letting x_i represent the fraction of the investor's wealth invested in the ith security and N represent the number of different securities available, we have:

$$\sum_{i=1}^{N} x_i = x_1 + x_2 + \cdots + x_N = 1.0$$

Thus, suppose $N = 3$, so that there are three stocks under consideration. If an investor has \$10,000 to invest, of which \$5,000 is invested in security 1, \$2,500 in security 2, and \$2,500 in security 3, then the x's are:

$$x_1 = \$5,000/\$10,000 = 0.50$$
$$x_2 = \$2,500/\$10,000 = 0.25$$
$$x_3 = \$2,500/\$10,000 = 0.25$$
$$\text{Total} = 1.00$$

This portfolio is clearly feasible since the sum of the proportionate holdings equals 1.0, indicating that the investor's funds are fully committed and do not lie idle. A feasible portfolio may contain one or many stocks, e.g. if the investor places all his money in security 1, $x_1 = \$10,000/\$10,000 = 1.0$ is a feasible portfolio.

Two-Security Diversification

Consider the arbitrary selection of two stocks for a portfolio: say Eastman Kodak (*EK* is the ticker symbol) and Texaco (*TX*). If the expected return on Kodak is 20 percent ($E(\tilde{R}_{EK}) = .20$) and on Texaco is 15 percent ($E(\tilde{R}_{TX}) = .15$), then any selected portfolio specifying the proportion of the portfolio invested in each, x_{EK} and x_{TX}, will have an expected return of

(7–3)   ***Portfolio Expected Return***

$$E(\tilde{R}_p) = x_{EK}E(\tilde{R}_{EK}) + x_{TX}E(\tilde{R}_{TX})$$

Each security's weight in the portfolio
Portfolio expected return = times the security's expected return
summed over the included securities.

The expected return on the portfolio is a linear combination of the expected returns on the component securities. Since the values x_{EK} and x_{TX} must sum to 1.0 to be feasible in the two-security case, the investor must choose only the proportionate holding in one of the stocks, say *EK*. Once the value of x_{EK} has been chosen, the value of x_{TX} is set equal to $1 - x_{EK}$.

By varying the value of x_{EK}, the investor can vary the expected return of the portfolio. Obviously, the higher x_{EK}, the higher that expected return will be since:

(7–4) $$E(\tilde{R}_p) = x_{EK}(.20) + (1 - x_{EK})(.15)$$

FIGURE 7–6 **Portfolio Expected Return as a Function of the Proportionate Holding in Kodak**

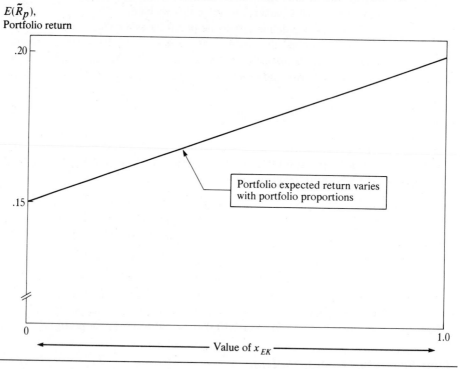

Figure 7–6 shows this effect. The vertical axis of this graph shows portfolio expected return while the horizontal axis shows the value of x_{EK}. As x_{EK} approaches the value of 1.0, $E(\tilde{R}_p)$ approaches .20, or 20 percent. And as x_{EK} approaches 0.0, $E(\tilde{R}_p)$ goes to .15, or 15 percent.

On the basis of Figure 7–6, one could not draw any conclusions regarding the best portfolio since portfolio risk has not yet been considered. Hence, we must next look at the effect of varying x_{EK} on the portfolio's standard deviation.

The standard deviation of any arbitrary portfolio of Kodak and Texaco is a quadratic function of the proportionate holdings in each stock, and depends on both the standard deviations of the two stocks taken individually and the degree of comovement between them. According to the definitions for mathematical operations on random variables given in Chapter 2, the risk of a two-stock portfolio consisting of *EK* and *TX* is given by:

(7–5)

$$\sigma(\tilde{R}_p) = [x_{EK}^2[\sigma(\tilde{R}_{EK})]^2 + x_{TX}^2[\sigma(\tilde{R}_{TX})]^2 + 2x_{EK}x_{TX}Cov(\tilde{R}_{EK}, \tilde{R}_{TK})]^{1/2}$$

Portfolio Risk

Portfolio standard = deviation
Each security's squared weight times the security's squared standard deviation summed over the included securities plus covariance terms weighted by the proportion in each security to measure the comovement of each security with the other.

The third term, or covariance term, measures the effect on portfolio risk of the comovement of the two security's returns. There are two equal covariance terms. One for *EK*'s comovement with *TX*, and one for *TX*'s comovement with *EK*.

This expression has a very simple message. It says that the riskiness of a portfolio of two securities depends on (*a*) the proportionate holdings in each security, (*b*) the variability of the securities held, and (*c*) the degree to which the securities held have correlated returns. By choosing the proportionate holdings, then, the investor can affect the degree of risk undertaken.

If the standard deviations of returns on Kodak and Texaco are 28.7 percent and 20.5 percent, respectively, then the degree of risk in a portfolio formed from these two will depend on the investment proportions (the *x*'s) and the covariance between the two returns. Consider a number of alternative values for the covariance between the two securities: .0588, .0230, 0.0, and − .0588. The first number, .0588, is a value for the covariance which implies a perfect positive degree of comovement—a correlation of 1.0.[7] Now if the proportion invested in Kodak is varied from 1.0 to 0.0 (i.e., $x_{EK} = 1.0$, then $x_{EK} = .99$, then $x_{EK} = .98 \ldots x_{EK} = 0.0$), the standard deviation of the portfolio will linearly decline from .287 (Kodak's standard deviation) to .205.

For example, if x_{EK} is set at .5 the portfolio's risk is:

$$\sigma(\tilde{R}_p) = [x_{EK}^2(.287)^2 + x_{TK}^2(.205)^2 + 2(x_{EK})(x_{TX})(.0588)]^{1/2}$$

$$= [.5^2(.287)^2 + .5^2(.205)^2 + 2(.5)(.5)(.0588)]^{1/2} = .246$$

In Figure 7–7, portfolio standard deviation is shown on the vertical axis, and the value of x_{EK} is shown on the horizontal. When x_{EK} equals 0.0, all the investor's money is in Texaco and $\sigma(\tilde{R}_p)$ therefore just equals the standard deviation of .205. Conversely, when $x_{EK} = 1.0$, the investor has invested everything in Kodak and portfolio risk is .287, the level of Kodak's standard deviation. The .246 portfolio standard deviation lies on a straight line between the two standard deviations. There is no diversification benefit because this case was constructed under the assumption that the comovement of the two was perfect.

With the covariance of − .0588 there is perfect negative comovement and the proper selection of x_{EK} can drive the portfolio risk to zero. For example at $x_{EK} = .40$ diversification is perfect, and risk is zero, as shown in Figure 7–7. Note also that if this portfolio could be constructed it would be very valuable. More than likely this would tend to drive up the prices of Kodak and Texaco—until the portfolio offered the same return as available on other *riskless* securities.

At the covariance of zero the third term in Equation (7–5) vanishes, leaving only the standard deviation terms:

$$\sigma(\tilde{R}_p) = [x_{EK}^2(.287)^2 + x_{TX}^2(.205)^2]^{1/2}$$

In this case, the most dramatic effect on portfolio risk comes with intermediate values of x_{EK}. There is a significant drop in $\sigma(\tilde{R}_p)$ when the portfolio is diversified. And there is one portfolio for which $\sigma(\tilde{R}_p)$ is minimized. This portfolio, called the minimum variance or **minimum standard deviation portfolio, MSDP,** occurs when investing 38.4 percent

---

[7]This value has been calculated using Equation (7–2), by setting $\rho_{EK,TX} = 1$ and solving for $Cov(\tilde{R}_{EK}, \tilde{R}_{TX})$.

FIGURE 7–7   Portfolio Standard Deviation as a Function of the Proportionate Holding in Kodak

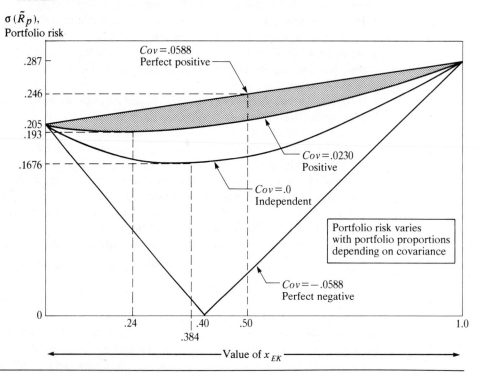

of the investor's funds in Kodak and 61.6 percent in Texaco.[8] If this is done, portfolio risk will equal:

$$\sigma(\tilde{R}_p) = [.384^2(.287)^2 + .616^2(.205)^2]^{1/2} = .1676$$

It might be tempting to conclude that the MSDP is the best portfolio because it has the least risk. Yet such a conclusion is not warranted since a higher expected return must be given up to achieve this level of risk.

In fact, the covariance that Kodak and Texaco have experienced in the recent past is .0230 (a correlation of about .40). With this perhaps more realistic covariance the change in the portfolio's standard deviation as x_{EK} is changed is still dramatic, as indicated in

---

[8]The minimum standard deviation portfolio can be found by taking the partial derivative of $\sigma(\tilde{R}_p)$ with respect to x_1, setting the result equal to zero and solving for x_1. For the two-stock case, x_1 and $1 - x_1$ can be calculated by

$$\frac{\partial\sigma(\tilde{R}_p)}{\partial x_1} = \frac{2[x_1[\sigma(\tilde{R}_1)]^2 - [\sigma(\tilde{R}_2)]^2 + x_1[\sigma(\tilde{R}_2)]^2 + (1 - 2x_1)Cov(\tilde{R}_1, \tilde{R}_2)]}{^1/_2\sigma(\tilde{R}_p)} = 0$$

which yields the solution

$$x_1 = \frac{[\sigma(\tilde{R}_2)]^2 - Cov(\tilde{R}_1, \tilde{R}_2)}{[\sigma(\tilde{R}_1)]^2 + [[\sigma(\tilde{R}_2)]^2 - 2Cov(\tilde{R}_1, \tilde{R}_2)]}$$

FIGURE 7–8   The Opportunity Set in the Two-Stock Case

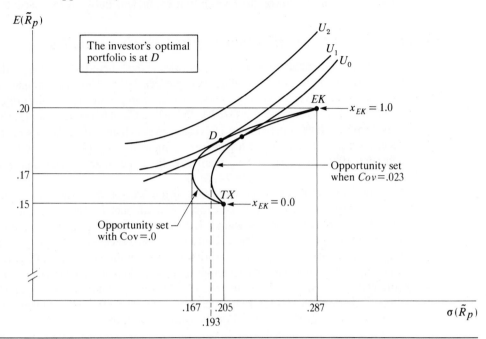

the shaded area of Figure 7–7, reflecting the benefit of diversifying among the two securities that make up the portfolio. Yet it is less than the substantial benefit that accrues if the securities move completely independent of one another, i.e., a covariance of zero. The MSDP when the covariance is .0230 is achieved when 24 percent is invested in Kodak and 76 percent in Texaco.

We can combine into one graph the resulting figures for $E(\tilde{R}_p)$ and $\sigma(\tilde{R}_p)$ for any portfolio of the two stocks. The reason for doing so should be obvious from Figure 7–8. It allows us to consider feasible portfolio positions in expected return and risk space, in order to isolate the effect of these new opportunities on investor preferences.

If the investor's indifference curves are given as shown in Figure 7–8, portfolio D will be held. By reading D's expected return and standard deviation off the graph, the proportionate holdings in Kodak and Texaco that are required can be determined. The opportunity set in Figure 7–8 (the curve EK-D-TX) is a loci of points defined by allowing x_{EK} to vary from 1.0 to zero, given values for the standard deviations *and* the covariance.

The convexity of the efficient frontier is, strictly speaking, due to the fact that the expected return on the portfolio is a linear combination of the expected returns on the two securities (Figure 7–6), while the standard deviation on the portfolio is a nonlinear combination of the standard deviations of the two securities (Figure 7–7). In fact, a portfolio of any two securities will have a standard deviation that is less than the weighted average of the standard deviations of the component securities—unless the securities are perfectly positively correlated. The greater the gain to diversification, that is, the lower the covariance, the greater the "bulge" in the opportunity set. The result is just what we would expect: **The potential rewards to diversification are greater the lower the covariance or the lower the correlation coefficient between two securities.**

Risk Reduction and Diversification Applied to Six Securities

Arbitrary computations for two securities show where the benefits of diversification come from, but a more revealing example can be used to make pointed observations regarding the diversification process. In this example we use six securities: American Express (*AXP*), Merck & Co (*MRK*), Procter & Gamble (*PG*), Sears (*S*), Texaco (*TX*), and Navistar Int'l (International Harvester; *NAV*). Standard deviations for each security and covariances between each pair were computed using 193 weekly returns from 1982 through 1986. The estimated standard deviations, covariances, and expected returns, all annualized, are given in Table 7–1.

The numbers reveal some important differences between these firms that will affect their contribution to a portfolio's expected return and risk. For example, the low correlations and relatively low standard deviation of Texaco give it a low covariance with each of the other five securities. Thus, in any two-security portfolio, the "bulge" in the opportunity set will be greater and risk will, accordingly, be less. Potentially, at least, the reduction in the standard deviation of a portfolio that includes Texaco will more than offset the relatively low return it offers (14.8 percent). Obviously the high returns expected from American Express and Navistar will make them valuable additions, but their high variances and, in some cases, high covariances will detract from their "worth."

Note that the numbers are consistent with our intuition about the comovement of different firms. During this period Texaco's returns were governed, in large part, by large changes in the price of oil and the inability of OPEC to operate effectively as a cartel. Since these factors did not directly influence Sears or Procter & Gamble, it's not surprising to find the return series of these firms moving independently from that of Texaco. Moreover, since American Express, Sears, and Procter & Gamble all generate a large portion of their profits from consumer purchases you might expect their returns to be highly correlated.

The returns on these securities were those generated on average over four years in the mid 1980s. There is no guarantee, of course, that these returns are the ones that an investor might logically expect for the future. We have used them only for illustrative purposes. In fact, the very high return on Navistar was due to its emergence from virtual bankruptcy in 1980. Since those same circumstances do not exist today we would not expect the same level of returns. The problem of estimating returns is considered in great depth in later chapters (those on valuation).

Unlike returns, the standard deviations and covariances between one firm and another exhibit more stability over time. Thus, as a first pass, it is not unrealistic to suppose that the historically estimated values in Table 7–1 are those that are useful and relevant to the current portfolio choice problem. These numbers, like expected returns, do change over time, but the nature and rate of change is such that history provides a reasonable first approximation. Changes in these values, and their causes are also discussed in subsequent chapters. For now, it's appropriate to think of the numbers in Table 7–1 as forecasts relevant to the current investment decision.

If we apply Equations 7–3 and 7–5 to pairs of these securities we can identify a number

TABLE 7–1   **Covariances, Standard Deviations and Expected Returns for Six Securities**

		(AXP)	(MRK)	(PG)	(S)	(TX)	(NAV)
						covariances	
American Express	(AXP)	**.32**	.029	.025	.047	.007	.055
Merck & Co.	(MRK)	.26	**.35**	.024	.030	.008	.015
Proctor & Gamble	(PG)	.39	.34	**.20**	.021	.004	.031
Sears	(S)	.52	.31	.37	**.28**	.012	.068
Texaco	(TX)	.08	.09	.08	.16	**.26**	.011
Navistar Int'l	(NAV)	.31	.08	.28	.44	.08	**.55**
		correlations coefficients				standard deviations	
Expected return		.26	.19	.135	.193	.148	.316

of different sets of two-security portfolios—like the one constructed in Figure 7–8 for Kodak and Texaco. A number of these two-security opportunity sets are pictured in Figure 7–9.

When three securities are included in the portfolio the possibilities for additional benefits from diversification are enhanced. The three-security portfolio with

$$x_{AXP} = .4 \qquad x_S = .4 \qquad x_{PG} = .2$$

has an expected return of 20.8 percent and a standard deviation of 22.9 percent (located at point "P_3" in Figure 7–9). The values were calculated by applying the formulas in Chapter 2 to the combination of *three* random variables. Thus,

(7–6) $\qquad E(\tilde{R}_p) = x_{AXP}[E(\tilde{R}_{AXP})] + x_S[E(\tilde{R}_S)] + x_{PG}[E(\tilde{R}_{PG})]$

$$= .4(.26) + .4(.193) + .2(.135) = .208$$

and

(7–7) $\qquad \sigma(\tilde{R}_p) = [x_{AXP}^2[\sigma(\tilde{R}_{AXP})]^2 + x_S^2[\sigma(\tilde{R}_S)]^2 + x_{PG}^2[\sigma(\tilde{R}_{PG})]^2$

$$+ 2 x_{AXP} x_S Cov(\tilde{R}_{AXP}, \tilde{R}_S) + 2x_{AXP} x_{PG} Cov(\tilde{R}_{AXP}, \tilde{R}_{PG})$$

$$+ 2x_S x_{PG} Cov(\tilde{R}_S, \tilde{R}_{PG}]^{1/2}$$

$$= [.4^2(.32)^2 + .4^2(.28)^2 + .2^2(.2)^2$$

$$+ 2(.4)(.4)(.047) + 2(.4)(.2)(.025) + 2(.4)(.2)(.021)]^{1/2}$$

$$= .229$$

This portfolio offers an expected return and risk package that dominates that of many of the two-security opportunity sets in Figure 7–9. The diversification benefits delivered with this combination are substantial, even though they all are in the consumer goods and services sector, and have correlations that average above .4.

It should now be clear that by adding more and more securities to the portfolio further benefits from diversification may be created. With all six securities, equally weighted in the portfolio (one sixth in each security), the return and risk combination is $E(\tilde{R}_p) = .206$ and $\sigma(\tilde{R}_p) = .203$. These coordinates locate the portfolio slightly below and well to the left of the three-security portfolio, at P_6.

FIGURE 7–9   **Risk-Return Opportunities from Portfolios of Two Securities**

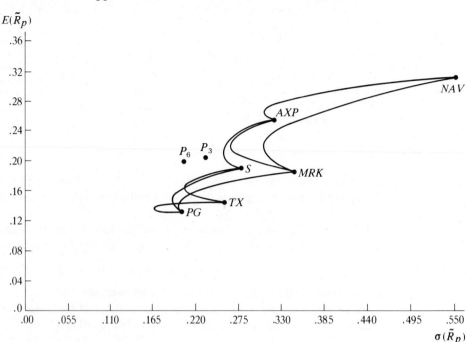

Interestingly, for this particular six-security portfolio, the magnitude of the 30 covariance terms that have to be accounted for, collectively, is over twice the size of the six standard deviation terms included. Thus, with just six securities, the influence of each security's own variability has come to be dominated by the magnitude of the covariance that each has with the others in the portfolio. A security's own variability becomes less important in a well-diversified portfolio, and the strength of its covariance takes on a more and more important role.

The N Security Case

In the general case where any combination of available securities may be held in the portfolio, the formulas determining portfolio expected return and standard deviation are simple extrapolations of Equations (7–3) and (7–5). For an arbitrary list of N securities the terms are:

(7–8)   ***Portfolio Expected Return***

$$E(\tilde{R}_p) = x_1 E(\tilde{R}_1) + x_2 E(\tilde{R}_2) + \cdots + x_N E(\tilde{R}_N)$$

$$= \sum_{i=1}^{N} x_i E(\tilde{R}_i)$$

> *Portfolio expected = return*   *The sum of the weighted expected returns from the securities included in the portfolio.*

and

(7–9)   *Portfolio Risk*

$$\sigma(\tilde{R}_p) = [x_1^2[\sigma(\tilde{R}_1)]^2 + x_2^2[\sigma(\tilde{R}_2)]^2 + \cdots + x_N^2[\sigma(\tilde{R}_N)]^2$$
$$+ x_1 x_2 Cov(\tilde{R}_1, \tilde{R}_2) + x_1 x_3 Cov(\tilde{R}_1, \tilde{R}_3)$$
$$+ \ldots x_2 x_1 Cov(\tilde{R}_1, \tilde{R}_2) + \cdots + x_N x_{N-1} Cov(\tilde{R}_N, \tilde{R}_{N-1})]^{1/2}$$

Equation 7–9 can be summed and rewritten as:

$$\sigma(\tilde{R}_p) = \left[\sum_{i=1}^{N} x_i^2[\sigma(\tilde{R}_i)]^2 + \sum_{i=1}^{N} \sum_{\substack{j=1 \\ i \neq j}}^{N} x_i x_j Cov(\tilde{R}_i, \tilde{R}_j) \right]^{1/2}$$

$$= \left[\sum_{i=1}^{N} \sum_{j=1}^{N} x_i x_j Cov(\tilde{R}_i, \tilde{R}_j) \right]^{1/2}$$

since

$$Cov(\tilde{R}_i, \tilde{R}_i) = [\sigma(\tilde{R}_i)]^2:$$

> *Portfolio risk =*   *Square root of the sum of all variances and covariances weighted by the proportions invested in each i and j security (there are N^2 terms to be summed, thus the double summation, $\Sigma\Sigma$).*

The latter definition is complex only because it contains a lot of terms (N^2, to be exact). Yet there are only two *types* of terms present in Equation 7–9. There are N variance terms (one for each security) and $N^2 - N$ covariance terms. One covariance term is included for each pair of securities in the portfolio. Thus, there is a covariance of each *i*th security with all *j*th securities, and a covariance of each *j*th security with all *i*th securities.

Varying the weights will influence the portfolio's expected return and standard deviation in the *N*-security case. The magnitude and direction of the effect is quite complicated, however, even when relatively few individual securities are available. Reducing the weight of a security with a high standard deviation may tend to either decrease or increase the standard deviation of the portfolio, depending on (1) how large a proportion of the portfolio is committed to that security, (2) how large its standard deviation is, (3) how that security comoves with all other securities in the portfolio, and (4) how *all* other securities terms would be influenced by their own increased x_i (since the portfolio weights must sum to 1.0). Obviously, the task of sorting out and keeping straight these separate terms would be staggering. Even investors with substantial number sense would be unable to keep track of the influence of one security on portfolio standard deviation unless computer aid was available, or unless summary measures that simplify the calculation can be developed (they *will* be developed in the next two chapters).

Efficient Portfolios and Optimal Diversification

The prior examples show that arbitrarily selected portfolios offer some diversification benefits. Even the random selection of stocks and weights enables us to significantly reduce portfolio risk. No forecasting of future returns is necessary, nor is any knowledge about the stock market or about the individual stocks in it. In spite of these advantages, random diversification is not an approach most investors would seriously consider. It does not make use of information on the riskiness of individual securities or on the apparent covariability of security returns. In short, the method is inefficient.

An alternative means of diversifying which does take such information into account is based on **Portfolio Theory.** This theory is, in fact, a normative model which tells the investor **how to diversify optimally,** given certain assumptions about the nature of the investor's preferences and the set of securities available. The theory was first developed in the mid 1950s and has since formed the basis for fundamental applications to investment management made by Wall Street firms and professional money managers.[9]

As is true of all theories, portfolio theory begins with a set of assumptions. These include the three assumptions that we previously labeled the **operating efficiency** assumptions:

1. **Liquidity**—no transactions costs, and all investors are price takers.
2. **Price continuity**—underlying supply and demand determine price.
3. **Fairness**—only price and time are used to discriminate between different prospective buyers and sellers.

To which we add three more:

4. **Divisibility**—securities can be traded in infinitely small units.
5. **Expected return and standard deviation**—investor's preferences are influenced only by the portfolio's expected return and standard deviation of return.
6. **Single investment period**—of any given length.

Assumption 4 allows for securities to be traded in infinitely small units. Thus, there is nothing to keep the investor from devoting $10 of his wealth to a particular security.

Assumption 5 involves no change from the way we represented preferences in Chapter 2. There we were able to summarize an individual's preferences down to consideration of the trade-offs between expected return and uncertainty measured by the standard deviation. With this "approximation" we are able consider the investor's choice in two dimensions.[10]

Assumption 6 states that the investor makes investment decisions for one investment period only. The length of the period could be long or short, but investment choices are made *once* in an effort to maximize utility.

---

[9]Two studies form the basis for modern portfolio theory. They are by James Tobin in a 1958 *Review of Economic Studies* article entitled "Liquidity Preference as Behavior Toward Risk" and by Harry Markowitz in his pioneering 1952 article "Portfolio Selection" (later expanded on in a 1959 book).

[10]Of course, if probability distributions of returns are "normal," the expected value and standard deviation of returns will completely define the distribution. That is, nothing else could be important to the investor since nothing else helps to describe the distribution.

To make decisions in this environment we can think of our utility-maximizing investor as employing the following logic: **Find the set of portfolios of securities that results in the lowest possible level of risk at each and every available level of return.** We would consider these portfolios to be the ones that offer the greatest level of diversification available from all the portfolios that could be constructed. This is the set of efficiently diversified portfolios. Then, from this set, select the single portfolio that gives rise to the greatest level of utility (places the individual on the highest indifference curve).

It should be clear that an efficiently diversified portfolio (an **efficient portfolio**) is a feasible portfolio, which also possesses the following two (not independent) properties:

1. No other feasible portfolio has the same expected rate of return with lower risk (standard deviation).
2. No other feasible portfolio has the same risk level with a higher expected rate of return.

Since the investor views additional expected return as desirable but views additional risk as undesirable, an efficient portfolio will always dominate all other feasible portfolios. All inefficient portfolios can be ignored. Therefore, the objective of portfolio theory is to aid the investor in identifying efficient portfolios and in selecting from among the possible efficient portfolios the one which possesses a risk–return level that is optimal in view of the investor's preferences.

The Efficient Frontier

Figure 7–10 shows a graph with portfolio expected return, $E(\tilde{R}_p)$, on the vertical axis and portfolio standard deviation, $\sigma(\tilde{R}_p)$, on the horizontal. The shaded region, consisting of an infinite number of individual points, represents all of the feasible portfolios which can be constructed from a given universe of N securities. The risk–return combination offered by each portfolio can be determined by reading off the coordinates of any point in $E(\tilde{R}_p) - \sigma(\tilde{R}_p)$ space.

As can be seen, some portfolios in the figure have more desirable combinations of risk and expected return than do others. In particular, the set of dots which makes up the curved line on the west and northwest portion of the feasible (shaded) region represents the set of most desirable risk–return combinations. This is the **efficient frontier,** on which all efficient portfolios lie. It extends from point T through point Q to point V on the curve.

Notice that portfolios lying along the efficient frontier actually do dominate all interior points. Consider portfolio S, for example. It does not lie on the efficient frontier, even though it is a feasible portfolio. No one who wants to achieve the maximum expected return for a given amount of risk would hold this portfolio, since at least two other efficient portfolios clearly dominate it. Efficient portfolio Q, for example, has the same risk level as S, but considerably higher return. And portfolio V has lower risk than S, with the same expected return. Hence, S would not be considered for purchase.

In the two-security case the efficient frontier is nothing but a portion of the loci of points created by changing the proportion invested in each security, i.e., from $x_1 = 1.0$ to $x_1 = .99$ and so on. Thus, the cruve *EK-D-TX* in Figure 7–8 is an efficient set.

FIGURE 7–10   **The Feasible Region of Portfolios**

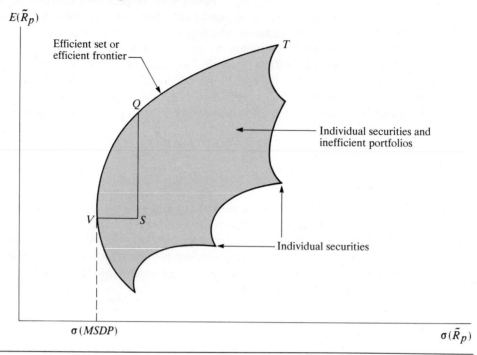

In the case of three or more securities, the efficient frontier is the result of a maximization that is apparent from the definition of the **efficient set:**

> The efficient set consists of those portfolios that offer the highest return for each and every level of risk, or the lowest risk for each and every level of return.

Thus, there are a series of maximization problems of the form: **maximize return, subject to a standard deviation constraint.** The efficient set will be traced out by solving this maximization problem for many different, arbitrarily set constraints on portfolio standard deviation. The form of the maximization problem is:

(7–10)
$$\underset{\{x_i\}}{MAX} \; E(\tilde{R}_p) = \sum_{i=1}^{N} x_i E(\tilde{R}_i)$$

Subject to

$$\sigma(\tilde{R}_p) = \left[\sum_{i}^{N} \sum_{j}^{N} x_i x_j Cov(\tilde{R}_i, \tilde{R}_j) \right]^{1/2} = \text{a constant}$$

and

$$\sum_{i=1}^{N} x_i = 1.0, \quad x_i \geq 0 \text{ all } i.$$

Thus, the constant might be set at .20 and the problem is to maximize portfolio expected return by choosing the x_is with the restriction that portfolio risk cannot exceed .20. The solution gives one point on the efficient set. A second problem is then solved with the constant at .19, then at .18, and so on until a set of points on the efficient set is identified.

After all risk levels are exhausted, the efficient set will consist of a loci of points much like those pictured in Figure 7–10. Equivalently, the same problem could be solved (the dual problem) by arbitrarily setting a return value and finding that combination of x_i values which minimizes the standard deviation of return.

Two other constraints also are part of the maximization: **the weights must sum to 1.0,** and **individual weights must exceed or be equal to zero.** The latter is consistent with not permitting the investor to sell securities short, or to hold negative amounts of any security. We will relax this constriant toward the end of this chapter.

The actual efficient set for our six-security example has been constructed with the use of a computer algorithm developed by Modern Portfolio Strategies, Inc., and called MPS. It is presented graphically in Figure 7–11 superimposed over the original Figure 7–9.

FIGURE 7–11   The Six-Security Efficient Set

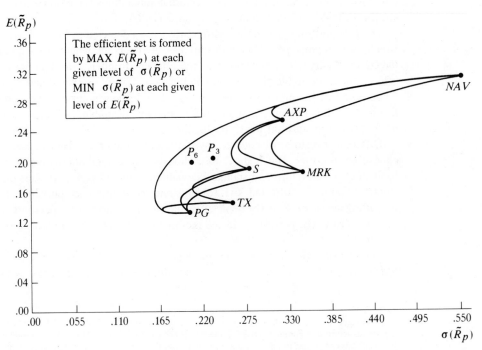

This set constitutes the *best* set of portfolios that can be constructed from these six securities. No lower risk or higher return portfolios are available.[11]

No matter how many securities are considered for inclusion in the portfolio the efficient set will have the convex shape suggested by Figures 7–10 or 7–11. The precise slope and location will depend on the expected returns, standard deviations, and covariances that make up the calculations. In general, the larger the returns and the smaller the standard deviations and covariances the more to the left and higher will be the efficient set.

Portfolio Choice

How would the investor choose from among the available portfolios on the efficient set? We know these portfolios differ from each other, not just in the number and type of securities held, but also in the combination of risk and return they offer. Consequently, all we need to know to represent the investor's choice is to consider the investor's willingness to exchange expected return and standard deviation. That is, we need to consider the effect on the investor's utility of $E(\tilde{R}_p)$ and $\sigma(\tilde{R}_p)$. That issue has already been answered by construction of the investor's indifference set (in Chapter 2).

These indifference curves are superimposed over the six-security efficient set in Figure 7–12. Each point on the indifference curves in part (a) represents a potential risk-return combination. Points which lie on the same curve are viewed by the investor as equally desirable, and points on higher indifference curves are uniformly preferred to points on lower indifference curves. Thus, risk–return combinations lying on indifference curve U_0 are less desirable than are points lying on curve U_1.

The best portfolio, given the indifference curves depicted in Figure 7–12(a) is the one which lies at point p^*. This portfolio lies at the point where the highest attainable indifference curve, U_1, is tangent to the efficient frontier. No other feasible portfolio offers a more desirable risk–return combination. Portfolios like T and V, for instance, while efficient, lie on a lower (less preferred) indifference curve. And portfolios which lie on curves higher than U_1, and therefore are more desirable, are not feasible. Therefore p^* is the best or **optimal portfolio** for this investor.

Different investors, of course, have different preferences. Hence, not everyone will choose portfolio p^*. But if they, too, choose from among alternative portfolios on the basis of expected return and standard deviation, they will pick portfolios on the efficient frontier. Figure 7–12(b) and 7–12(c) illustrate the indifference curves of two other hypothetical investors. Part (b) depicts the indifference curves of a person with an intense dislike for risk. The portfolio selected is close to the MSDP—minimum standard deviation portfolio.

The investor whose preferences are depicted in part (c) of the figure, by contrast, has little aversion to $\sigma(R_p)$ and chooses a portfolio made up of securities with the highest returns. This individual is almost risk-neutral.

---

[11]We have noticed a tendency of many students to verbalize the efficient set as "the set of portfolios that maximizes return *and* minimizes risk." Note this is *not* a correct interpretation of the problem or its solution. You can't maximize one thing and minimize another at the same time. Either you maximize return at a given risk, or minimize risk at a given return.

FIGURE 7–12   Optimal Portfolios for Different Investors

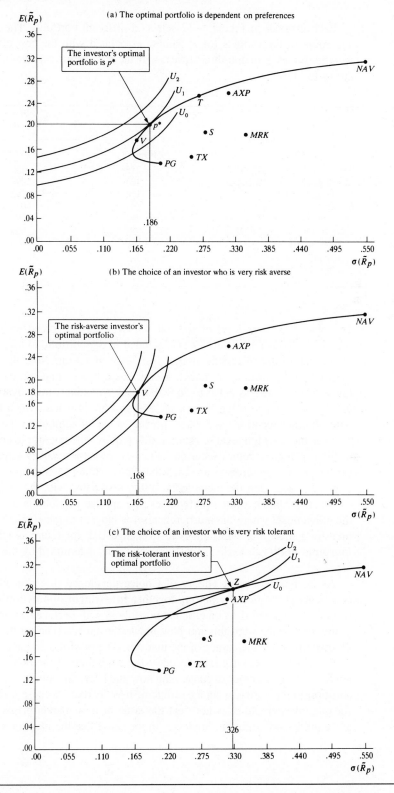

Each investor in Figure 7–12 selects a different portfolio. The securities are chosen according to the weights (or x_i values) associated with the best efficient portfolio. The weights for each of the three cases, and the risk-return characteristics of the portfolios are as follows:

			Weights	
Security		*(a) at p**	*(b) at V*	*(c) at Z*
American Express	*(AXP)*	.285	.187	.646
Merck & Co.	*(MRK)*	.125	.097	—
Procter & Gamble	*(PG)*	.165	.293	—
Sears	*(S)*	.041	.070	—
Texaco	*(TX)*	.292	.305	—
Navistar Int'l	*(NAV)*	.092	.048	.354
Total		1.000	1.000	1.000
$E(\tilde{R}_p)$		.20	.18	.28
$\sigma(\tilde{R}_p)$		.186	.168	.326

To achieve a lower level of risk (at V) investors are forced to invest in lower-return securities, though all securities are included in the portfolio to take maximum advantage of the gains from diversification at this level of return. Note that more is invested in Merck than in Sears even though Merck has a higher standard deviation and a slightly lower return. The reason has to do with Merck's relatively low covariance with the returns on Navistar (which offers a very high return) and Texaco (which has a low covariance with all other securities and is, as a result, a useful addition to the portfolio).

To achieve a high level of return (at Z) requires the investor to concentrate his holding in the two highest return securities. Such an investor receives some benefit of diversification, but his preferences are such that he is willing to give up some of the benefits of reduced risk to gain the incremental utility associated with the higher return.

Whatever the investor's preferences, the optimal portfolio is specified as that point on the efficient set where the indifference set is tangent to the efficient set. At this point the investor's **marginal willingness** to exchange risk for return is equal to the investor's **marginal ability** to exchange risk for return, as determined by the slope of the efficient set.

As in the two-period Theory of Choice developed in earlier chapters, this solution comes about by properly putting together **investment opportunities** and **prices** (in the form of returns and risks on efficient portfolios) with **preferences** and **wealth** (how much is invested in the portfolio and how much consumed). The result is a defined portfolio $p*$ that represents the choice of the investor. The portfolio problem then is an application of the Theory of Choice introduced at the beginning of the book. And like that earlier application to the choice of consuming now and later, this solution is a **partial equilibrium solution** to the portfolio choice problem. It is "partial" because it represents the solution for one investor and does not treat the issue of how market prices are determined. It is an "equilibrium" solution, however, in the sense that the investor's choice is determined and will not change unless the input values—the risks and returns and preferences—change.[12]

What is the practical gain from an application of this principle of diversification from portfolio theory? In fact the gains are realistic and can be directly applied to the practical aspects of investor decision making! For example, the portfolio p^* in Figure 7–12(a) offers an expected return of 20 percent with a standard deviation of 18.6 percent. This is a slightly higher return than that available from Sears alone (19.3 percent) with a much lower standard deviation (28 percent). Or, looked at another way, the risk of p^* is slightly lower than that of Procter & Gamble, but offers an expected return that is $6^1/_2$ percentage points greater. The effect of an additional $6^1/_2$ percent per year return on accumulated wealth over a few years (even accounting for the year to year variability) is extremely great.

---

[12]We have represented the investor's solution to portfolio choice as a two-step solution: (1) the efficient set is traced out and (2) the preference set is superimposed over the efficient set to determine the optimal portfolio. However, the whole problem of the investor choosing the best portfolio can be treated in one step. The whole efficient set does not need to be identified—only the optimal portfolio needs to be designated. This goal can be accomplished by setting up a different maximization problem—one where the solution forms the portfolio that achieves the greatest utility.

The task of the investor is to choose values of $x_1, x_2, \ldots, x_N$, in order to maximize utility (rather than maximizing return at a given risk level), or

$$\underset{\{x_1, x_2, \ldots, x_N\}}{MAX} \quad E\{U[E(\tilde{R}_p), \sigma(\tilde{R}_p)]\}$$

where

$$E(\tilde{R}_p) = \sum_{i=1}^{N} x_i E(\tilde{R}_i), \text{ and } \sigma(\tilde{R}_p) = \left[\sum_{i=1}^{N} \sum_{j=1}^{N} x_i x_j Cov(\tilde{R}_i, \tilde{R}_j)\right]^{1/2}$$

Subject to:

$$\sum_{i=1}^{N} x_i = 1.0$$

The solution to this maximization problem takes four things into account: (1) the impact of the portfolio's return on utility, (2) the impact of individual security return on the portfolio's return, (3) the impact of the portfolio's risk on utility, and (4) the impact of the individual security standard deviation and covariances on portfolio risk.

Once this problem is solved and the best portfolio determined, a characteristic of the solution or a condition for the solution to be an optimum is that for all securities included in the portfolio:

Condition for Optimum

$$\left(\frac{\partial U(\tilde{R})}{\partial E(\tilde{R}_p)}\right) \left(\frac{\partial E(\tilde{R}_p)}{\partial x_i}\right) + \left(\frac{\partial U(\tilde{R})}{\partial \sigma(\tilde{R}_p)}\right) \left(\frac{\partial \sigma(\tilde{R}_p)}{\partial x_i}\right) = 0$$

$$\begin{pmatrix} \text{marginal} \\ \text{utility of} \\ \text{portfolio} \\ \text{return} \end{pmatrix} \begin{pmatrix} \text{effect of} \\ \text{security } i \\ \text{on portfolio} \\ \text{return} \end{pmatrix} + \begin{pmatrix} \text{marginal} \\ \text{disutility} \\ \text{of portfolio} \\ \text{risk} \end{pmatrix} \begin{pmatrix} \text{effect of} \\ \text{security } i \\ \text{on portfolio} \\ \text{risk} \end{pmatrix} = 0$$

Each of these four terms corresponds to the four points mentioned above. Terms 1 and 3 identify how the portfolio's characteristics influence overall satisfaction, while terms 2 and 4 identify how the securities in the portfolio interact to determine the characteristics of the portfolio. *Portfolio theory* concentrates on understanding terms 2 and 4 while *portfolio choice* must also consider the influence on utility, terms 1 and 3.

Finally, while the expected-return figures used in the six-security portfolios are those generated historically, and may not be indicative of the returns that normally might be expected from these securities in the future, the returns are greater for the higher-risk securities. In fact, the returns correspond fairly closely to those that might be expected based solely on each security's contribution to the portfolio's risk. More, much more, will be said about this in the following chapters.

Risk-Free Borrowing and Lending

In addition to choosing from among a universe of risky stocks, an investor may have the option of placing funds in a riskless asset, such as a government-insured savings account or a T-bill with a maturity corresponding to the desired holding period. If so, "risk-free lending" may be viewed as an additional security in the process of optimal diversification.[13]

Further, the investor may be able to borrow funds at a risk-free rate of interest. To be truly risk-free, this interest rate must be known in advance. It must also contain no risk premium; that is, there must be no discrepancy between it and the rate at which, say, the federal government can borrow money. Although it is probably unrealistic to assume that individuals can borrow at the same rate as the government can, it is one of those initial abstractions we choose to make to get to the core of the diversification issue. Thus, assumption 7:

7. **A risk-free security exists**—that can be invested in or issued,

also is part of the portfolio choice model, and needs to be added to the list of assumptions presented earlier.

By definition, a risk-free asset has a zero standard deviation of return. And its expected return—which we continue to denote R_f—is a constant. Consider creating a portfolio consisting of an investment in Merck (MRK) and in the risk-free asset. The expected return of such a portfolio would be:

(7–11)
$$E(\tilde{R}_p) = x_{MRK}(E(\tilde{R}_{MRK})) + (1 - x_{MRK})R_f$$

letting R_f be .08, and $E(\tilde{R}_{MRK})$ be .19, this reduces to:

$$E(\tilde{R}_p) = x_{MRK}(.19) + (1 - x_{MRK})(.08)$$

which says that the portfolio's expected return is equal to a weighted average of 19 percent and 8 percent, where the weights are the proportionate holdings in the stock and the risk-free asset, respectively.

The standard deviation of such a portfolio is especially simple to calculate, since the risk-free asset has a zero standard deviation, and the covariance of a constant, R_f, with a random variable, R_{MRK}, is zero. Consequently,

(7–12)
$$\sigma(\tilde{R}_p) = x_{MRK}\,\sigma(\tilde{R}_{MRK})$$

---

[13]In fact, a security like a T-bill is only *nominally* risk-free for the investment period. If inflation is uncertain, then the *real* risk-free rate is not given by T-bills. It would be given by a security that pays off in a representative basket of goods and services, but no such security currently exists.

FIGURE 7–13   **Portfolio Combinations of a Risk-Free Asset and a Risky Stock (*MRK*)**

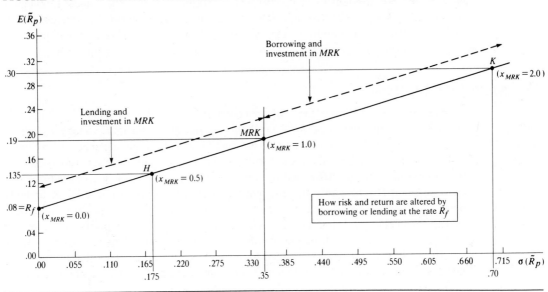

Thus, the standard deviation equals the proportionate holding in the security times the security's standard deviation.

Using the two formulas above, we can calculate the expected return and risk of any portfolio of *MRK* and the risk-free asset. Suppose for instance, we wish to place 50 percent of our funds in *MRK* and 50 percent in a savings account. The expected return is $(.5)(.19) + (.5)(.08) = .135$. If $\sigma(\tilde{R}_{EK})$ is 35 percent, the standard deviation of the portfolio is $(.5)(.35) = .175$.

The feasible portfolio combinations are depicted in Figure 7–13. As can be seen, combinations of the risk-free asset and Merck lie on a straight line in a graph of $E(\tilde{R}_p)$ and $\sigma(\tilde{R}_p)$ space. Points lying on the line between R_f and *MRK* are attained by some combination of lending and investment in Merck. Point *H*, for instance, corresponds to a 50–50 combination.

If risk-free borrowing is also allowed, points on the line which lie above and to the right of *MRK* are also feasible. These are attained by short-selling the risk-free asset, which is the equivalent of holding negative sums of money in the savings account, or simply, borrowing.

Risk-free borrowing is very much like buying stocks on *margin*. Suppose an investor with $10,000 to invest decides to borrow another $10,000 and invest the entire $20,000 in Merck. His proportionnate holdings, when viewed as a percentage of his own funds equal:

$$x_{MRK} = \$20,000/\$10,000 \quad = \quad 2.0$$
$$1 - x_{MRK} = -\$10,000/\$10,000 = -1.0$$
$$\text{Total} = \overline{\quad 1.0 \quad}$$

Thus, the proportionate holding in the risk-free asset is a negative 1.0. This portfolio has an expected return equal to $(2.0)(.19) + (-1.0)(.08) = .30$. The standard deviation equals $(2.0)(.35) = .70$. Risk-free borrowing, whenever the borrowing interest rate is lower than the expected return of the risky stock, has the effect of raising both portfolio expected return and risk. This is shown graphically in Figure 7–13 as point K.

The Separation Theorem

While Figure 7–13 shows the investment opportunities that are available by combining an inefficient individual stock (MRK) with the risk-free asset, the figure changes markedly when we reintroduce other stocks or the efficient frontier itself into the analysis. In Figure 7–14, once again we have the six-security efficient frontier, this time superimposed over the straight line between MRK and R_f. Our investor, who found the highest indifference curve at point D when only the efficient frontier of portfolios was available, or finds point G is optimal when considering only Merck and the risk-free security, may now find an even better portfolio. You might recognize that the best risky portfolio to combine with the risk-free asset will be the one that gives the greatest tilt to the ray drawn from R_f. That will be the portfolio specified by the point on the efficient set that is tangent to that ray. This is portfolio p^* in Figure 7–14, with a return of 23.4 percent and a risk of 23 percent.

FIGURE 7–14   **The Optimal Portfolio with the Efficient Set and with Risk-Free Borrowing and Lending**

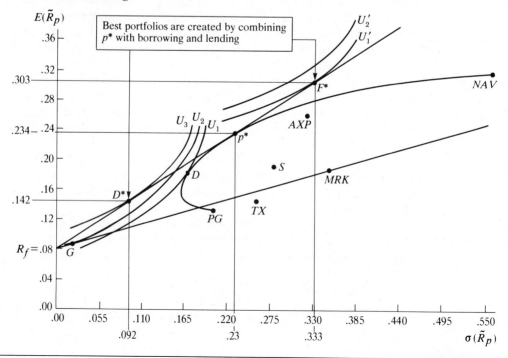

A 40 percent investment in this risky portfolio with 60 percent in the risk-free asset positions the individual on the highest attainable indifference curve (designated U_3) at point D^*. (We know the proportions are 40 percent and 60 percent because D^* is 40 percent of the distance from R_f to p^*.) This portfolio would have the risk $.4\sigma(\tilde{R}_{p^*})$, or 9.2 percent, and return of $.6(R_f) + .4(E(\tilde{R}_{p^*}))$, or 14.2 percent.

The implications of this are important for actual decision making. The investor who may choose to hold a well-diversified portfolio of corporate bonds located at point D on the efficient set in Figure 7–14 could benefit substantially from changing security weights to move his risky portfolio to p^*. Then his invested wealth could be allocated between p^* and R_f to achieve position D^* and greater expected utility.

In this case the investor would select proportions: $x_{AXP} = .183$, $x_{MRK} = .06$, $x_{TX} = .088$, $x_{NAV} = .069$, and .6 in the risk-free asset.

Interestingly, a second investor with different preferences, having the same forecasts of returns available and, thus, the same view of the efficient set, would choose to hold the same risky portfolio p^*, but would combine it with the risk-free asset in different proportions. Thus, the individual with the preference set U_1' and U_2' in Figure 7–14 would choose to locate at point F^* by borrowing (in this case by borrowing about 45 percent of his invested wealth to move return to 30.3 percent and risk to 33.3 percent).

There are two components to selecting the best possible (expected utility maximizing) portfolio. First, the optimal portfolio of risky assets is determined (i.e., p^*). Second, the investor selects the optimal proportion of his invested wealth to devote to the risky portfolio, and the optimal proportion to devote to the riskless asset (i.e., D^* or F^* by using R_f and p^*).

This logic leads to a very important theorem in finance, first stated by James Tobin [1958]. The theorem results directly from including a risk-free asset in the opportunity set of investors. It says the following:

> If an investor may borrow or lend freely at a risk-free rate of interest, there is only one optimal efficient portfolio of risky securities, and this portfolio's composition is completely independent of the shape of the investor's indifference curves. This is the portfolio **separation theorem.**

This **separation theorem** suggests that two investors with very different risk-return indifference curves but with identical forecasts concerning security returns and standard deviations would select the same optimal portfolio of risky securities. The two would differ only in their borrowing/lending activities. The choice of the optimal risky portfolio can be *separated* from a consideration of the investor's preferences.

This theorem has immensely important practical implications. For example, it is often believed by professional money managers and others that portfolios of stocks must be "tailored" to the preferences of the investor. Thus, the proverbial "little old lady" who must live off the cash flow generated by her portfolio would be steered in the direction of stocks possessing low risk. Conversely, a young independent investor whose consumption would not be disastrously affected by losses if they occur, can afford to purchase stocks having considerable risk (and possibly higher expected rewards). The separation theorem suggests this is inappropriate, at least in the presence of agreement about the future prospects for securities. The theorem implies that, in fact, both types of investors will wish to hold identical portfolios of risky stocks. However, the conservative investor would be advised to avoid placing all funds in such a portfolio; perhaps a large portion should be invested in risk-free securities such as T-bills. The more risk-tolerant individual on the other hand, will perhaps wish to margin his stock purchases to effectively lever risk and return. Risk is optimally adjusted, according to the theorem, by varying the extent of one's commitment to the risk-free asset.

When considering the direct applicability of portfolio theory, it is, of course, important to consider the departures from reality inherent in the assumptions. In developing the theory we have assumed no transaction costs and equal borrowing and lending rates. Transaction costs do exist and they may affect one's ability to secure the optimal risky portfolio. For example, T-bills are difficult to purchase in small quantities, and savings accounts have traditionally been prevented from paying market interest rates by Federal Reserve Regulation Q (though that is not now the case).

Moreover, it may be more expensive to borrow than to lend, though this is not as obvious a conclusion as it may seem. Rather, when investors borrow they are actually issuing a security that is not really risk-free, in which case it would carry a higher rate than that available on T-bills.

There are three reasons why the possible violation of assumptions does not detract from the model's usefulness, however. First, fundamental relationships and underlying tendencies have been uncovered that provide a framework for both improving decisions and for understanding the investment policies of other market participants. The theory predicts basic behavior if not all the nuisances of practical decisions. Thus we can understand and predict at least some of the events of the real world, e.g., diversification, risk-return trade-offs, and investor concern for comovement of security returns.

Second, many of the conclusions drawn from portfolio theory are robust to a relaxation of the assumptions. Only slight alterations are needed for taxes and transaction costs or security returns that are not described by expected return and standard deviation of return. Many of these adjustments are made in later chapters when applications are directly considered.

Third, our financial markets fortunately have been moving in the direction of the assumptionns. Some taxes have been simplified (e.g., capital gains and dividends are now taxed at the same rate). Transaction costs have been substantially reduced and divisibility of investments have been enhanced by the creation of money market mutual funds. There are now fewer restrictions on the kinds of accounts that financial institutions can offer and the rate they can pay than was the case a few years ago. Morever, at the instigation of the Securities and Exchange Commission, a competitively determined bro-kerage commission structure has been installed. In fact, it is our belief that the implications of portfolio theory hold up well to a relaxation of the assumptions on which the theory is based.

Short Selling and the Efficient Set

Investors also may be able to benefit from selling securities short. At first glance it may seem that such an action would be advisable only if the security is expected to have a *negative* return. That is not necessarily the case, however. To consider the effect of short

FIGURE 7–15   The Efficient Set with Short Selling and Free Use of the Proceeds

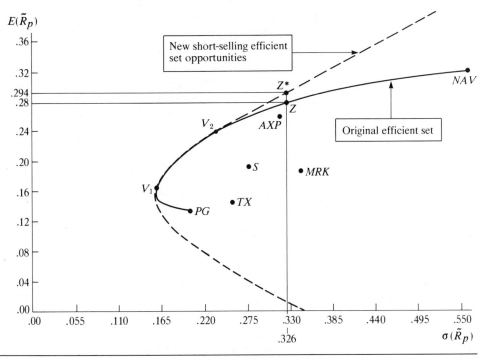

selling on portfolio choice, assume the following: the investor can sell securities short and receive the full proceeds from the sale for use in purchasing other securities (going "long"). This significantly expands the individual opportunities available by allowing the investor an option that is equivalent to *issuing* securities.

In terms of the maximization problem that permits us to trace out the efficient set, the investor can maximize return without being constrained to set x_i at a value that is greater than or equal to zero. As might be expected, these new opportunities can be used to create a new efficient set that, at some return levels, dominates the efficient set that can be constructed when x_i is constrained. The new efficient set for the six-security portfolio is presented in Figure 7–15. On the frontier from V_1 and V_2 the curve is the same as it was when short selling was not permitted. Beyond V_2, however, higher returns are achieved. For example, at point Z^* (with the same level of risk, 32.6 percent, as at Z in Figure 7–12(c)) the return is 29.4 percent. The weights for this portfolio are much different than for portfolio Z, and are:

$$x_{AXP} = .748 \qquad\qquad x_s = -.091$$

$$x_{MRK} = .254 \qquad\qquad x_{TX} = .230$$

$$x_{PG} = -.440 \qquad\qquad x_{NAV} = .297$$

This portfolio requires that Procter & Gamble be sold short in an amount equal to 44 percent of the investor's wealth. The proceeds from this sale and that of Sears are used to finance supplementary purchases of the other four stocks. The net result is a 1.4

percentage point increase in return. Of course, those investors not wanting to accept this degree of risk can hold Z^* as their risky portfolio, and invest in the risk-free asset to move to a lower risk level, for example.

The effect of short selling on portfolio opportunities is more beneficial the lower the returns expected on some individual securities. Short selling will be less beneficial if there are constraints placed on the use of the sale proceeds. In fact, for many investors, **margin requirements** are established to prevent the seller from receiving the proceeds. Oddly enough, in this case, it is the brokerage firm that gains the benefit of this transaction by retaining funds in an (escrow) account—paying no interest to you—until the short sale is *covered* by a reversing purchase in the customer's account.

An Efficient Set for the Dow Jones Securities

Finally, Figure 7–16 shows the efficient set that was constructed using historical standard deviations and covariances for the 30 securities included in the Dow Jones Industrial Average. The return figures were established on an ad hoc basis to reflect the risk of these securities rather than simply their historical returns. The efficient set gives you a practical look at the reduction in risk that can be achieved with a diversified portfolio of the largest and best-known securities on the New York Stock Exchange.

With a 7 percent risk-free rate of interest the optimal risky portfolio is shown at point p^* in the figure. This particular portfolio includes 25 out of the 30 Dow securities. The

FIGURE 7–16 Efficient Set Constructed from the 30 Dow Jones Industrial Stocks

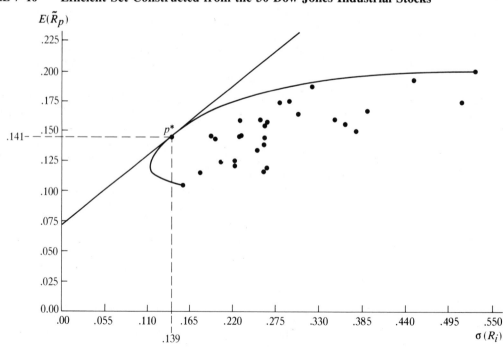

weights vary from a low of .2 percent in Aluminum Co. of America to 12.4 percent in Exxon. The portfolio itself has an expected return of 14.1 percent and a standard deviation of 13.9 percent. Clearly, the portfolio dominates by a good deal the risk/return opportunities available from any single security. **Diversification pays.**

The probability distribution that is associated with portfolio p^* is summarized as follows:

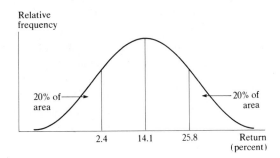

This distribution represents the return outcomes and their chance of occuring. Essentially, it summarizes what you have *bought* with an investment in portfolio p^*.

Portfolio Revision

How frequently should the portfolio selection problem be addressed? If there were no transactions costs the answer is obvious: portfolio choice ought to be reconsidered whenever information is available to the investor that would cause a change in any of the expected returns, standard deviations, or covariances.

However, given that it takes time and effort to evaluate the input parameters and explicit transactions costs to change portfolio weights, investors rationally would set a threshold level of information below which it would not make economic sense to revise. This level would vary from investor to investor, of course, reflecting the size and nature of costs faced. Professional money managers ordinarily would find the costs to be small relative to the potential costs of carrying a less-than-optimal portfolio of millions of dollars of securities. A small individual investor facing transactions costs of 1 or 2 percent of the value of the transaction perhaps would need a substantial change in expected return or covariance before wishing to make a revision.

The level of the threshold also would depend on the sensitivity of the change in optimal portfolio weights to changes in the data available. A portfolio of many securities may not be too sensitive to a change in the level of the standard deviation of one security, but may be very sensitive to a change in the covariance of one security with many others.

Needless to say, this is a complex problem. It takes portfolio choice in all its intrinsic complexity and adds another consideration: how the shape and position of the efficient set would change with changes in the data. The investor must consider whether the change in the efficient set is rewarding enough to overcome the transactions costs associated with changes in the portfolio weights. As yet there are no general solutions to this problem, and investors are forced to rely on a simple comparison of benefits and costs.

Errors in Estimation

A related problem concerns the confidence the investor has in the parameter input values. The expected returns, standard deviations, and covariances all are estimated values. We do not know precisely the nature of the probability distribution that represents an investment opportunity. In a sense we aren't sure of the probabilities of the game we are playing when we invest (perhaps unlike some games of chance where the outcomes and their probabilities are known for sure).

How does this potential error in estimation affect the portfolio choice problem? Oddly enough, the optimal portfolio has been shown to be insensitive to this **estimation risk** when the parameter input values are randomly different from the true underlying parameter values. In practical applications of the portfolio choice model, however, money managers often place upper bounds on the weights to hedge against a major investment position in a security based on incorrect forecasts of returns and risks.

Summary

The message of this chapter is that diversification among securities having imperfectly correlated returns is an effective means for reducing portfolio risk without impairing the portfolio's expected return. The results of empirical studies reveal that even random diversification among NYSE stocks yields dramatic reduction in portfolio risk with no effect on the return obtained by the investor.

Optimal portfolio diversification, using portfolio theory, is superior to random diversification because it makes use of knowledge about individual securities' expected returns, standard deviations, and degree of comovement. That knowledge can be used to generate an efficient portfolio frontier in which portfolios lying on the frontier dominate all other investment opportunities. For these portfolios, it is true that no other feasible portfolios possess higher expected returns for the same degree of risk (as measured by standard deviation) or possess the same expected return with a lower degree of risk. Investors who choose between alternative portfolios based on expected return and risk will prefer efficient portfolios to inefficient ones.

The set of efficient portfolios is expanded with the introduction of a risk-free investment opportunity. Moreover, the existence of a risk-free asset that can be used as a borrowing or lending mechanism leads to a two-step decision process for the investor: first, to find the optimal portfolio of risky assets and then to find the optimal proportion of wealth to invest in the risky portfolio. This leads to a separation theorem that suggests that individuals with the same expectations but different preferences would hold the same risky portfolio.

References

Alexander, Gordon J., and Resnick, Bruce. [1985] "More on Estimation Risk and Simple Rules for Optimal Portfolio Selection." *Journal of Finance* (March).

Bawa, V. S. [1978] "Safety-First, Stochastic Dominance, and Optimal Portfolio Choice." *Journal of Financial and Quantitative Analysis* (June).

Benninga, Simon, and Blume, Marshall. [1986] "Decision Intervals and Portfolio Strategy." Working Paper, University of Pennsylvania.

Blume, Marshall. [1970] "Portfolio Theory: A Step toward Its Practical Application." *Journal of Business* (April).

Brealey, R. A., and Hodges, S. D. [1974] "Playing with Portfolios." *Financial Analysts Journal* (March).

Brennan, J. J. [1975] "The Optimal Number of Securities in a Risky Asset Portfolio Where There Are Fixed Costs of Transacting: Theory and Some Empirical Results." *Journal of Financial and Quantitative Analysis* (September).

Brito, Ney. [1978] "Portfolio Selection in an Economy with Marketability and Short Sale Restrictions." *Journal of Finance* (May).

Chen, Andrew H. Y.; Jen, Frank C.; and Zionts, Stanley. [1974] "The Joint Determination of Portfolio and Transaction Demands for Money." *Journal of Finance* (March).

Cohen, Kalman, and Pogue, Jerry. [1967] "An Empirical Evaluation of Alternative Portfolio-Selection Models." *Journal of Business* (April).

Conine, Thomas E., Jr., and Tamarkin, Maurry J. [1981] "On Diversification Given Asymmetry in Returns." *Journal of Finance* (December).

Elton, Edwin, and Gruber, Martin. [1973] "Estimating the Dependence Structure of Share Prices—Implications for Portfolio Selection." *Journal of Finance* (December).

Elton, E. J., and Gruber, M. J. [1981] *Modern Portfolio Theory and Investment Analysis.* New York: John Wiley & Sons.

Elton, E. J., and Gruber, Martin J. [1974] "On the Optimality of Some Multi-Period Portfolio Selection Criteria." *The Journal of Business* (April).

Elton, E. J., and Gruber, Martin. [1974] "Portfolio Theory When Investment Relatives Are Lognormally Distributed." *Journal of Finance* (September).

Elton, E. J.; Gruber, M. J.; and Padberg, M. W. [1976] "Simple Criteria for Optimal Portfolio Selection." *Journal of Finance* (December).

Elton, E. J.; Gruber, M. J.; and Padberg, M. W. [1978] "Simple Criteria for Optimal Portfolio Selection: Tracing out the Efficient Frontier." *Journal of Finance* (March).

Fama, Eugene R. [1965] "Portfolio Analysis in a Stable Paretian Market." *Management Science* ser. A (January).

Fisher, L., and Lorie, J. H. [1970] "Some Studies of the Variability of Returns on Investments in Common Stocks." *Journal of Business* (April).

Gennotte, Gerard. [1986]. "Optimal Portfolio Choice under Incomplete Information." *Journal of Finance* (July).

Goldsmith, D. [1976] "Transactions Costs and the Theory of Portfolio Selection." *Journal of Finance* (September).

Gressis, N.; Philippatos, George; and Hayya, J. [1976] "Multiperiod Portfolio Analysis and the Inefficiencies of the Market Portfolio." *Journal of Finance* (September).

Harrington, Diana R. [1983] *Modern Portfolio Theory and the Capital: A User's Guide.* Englewood Cliffs, N.J.: Prentice-Hall.

Jacob, Nancy, L. [1974] "A Limited Diversification Portfolio Selection Model for the Small Investor." *Journal of Finance* (June).

Kose, John. [1981] "Efficient Funds in a Financial Market with Options: A New Irrelevance Proposition." *Journal of Finance* (June).

Lintner, John. [1965b] "Security Prices, Risk and Maximal Gains from Diversification." *Journal of Finance* (December).

Long, John. [1977] "Efficient Portfolio Choice with Differential Taxation of Dividends and Capital Gains." *Journal of Financial Economics* (August).

Markowitz, Harry. [1952] "Portfolio Selection." *Journal of Finance* (March).

Markowitz, Harry. [1959] *Portfolio Selection.* New York: John Wiley & Sons.

Mossin, Jan. [1968] "Optimal Multiperiod Portfolio Policies." *Journal of Business* (April).

Sharpe, William. [1963] "A Simplified Model for Portfolio Analysis." *Management Science* (January).

Sharpe, William. [1972] "Risk Market Sensitivity and Diversification." *Financial Analysts Journal* (January–February).

Solnik, B. H. [1978] "Inflation and Optimal Portfolio Choices." *Journal of Financial and Quantitative Analysis* (December).

Solnik, Bruno. [1974] "Why Not Diversify Internationally?" *Financial Analysts Journal* (July–August).

Tobin, James. [1958] "Liquidity Preference as Behavior towards Risk." *Review of Economic Studies* 25 (February).

Wagner, W. and Lau, S. [1971] "The Effect of Diversification on Risk." *Financial Analysts Journal* (November–December).

Ziemba, W. T.; Parkan, C.; and Brooks-Hill, R. [1974] "Calculation of Investment Portfolios with Risk-Free Borrowing and Lending." *Management Science* (October).

Questions and Problems

1. Which statement about portfolio diversification is correct?
   a. Proper diversification can reduce or eliminate the risk of marketwide variation in returns.
   b. The risk-reducing benefits of diversification do not occur meaningfully until at least 10–15 individual securities have been purchased.
   c. Because diversification reduces a portfolio's total risk, it necessarily reduces its expected return.
   d. Typically, as more securities are added to a portfolio, total risk would be expected to fall at a decreasing rate.

   CFA

2. Define and describe the efficient set of risky securities. As part of your answer show how investors with varying risk-aversion select different optimal portfolios.

3. Which portfolio *cannot* lie on the efficient frontier?

Portfolio	Expected Return	Standard Deviation
W	10%	20%
X	5	7
Y	15	36
Z	12	15

   CFA

4. Portfolio theory is *most* concerned with:
   a. The elimination of systematic risk.
   b. The effect of diversification on portfolio risk.
   c. The identification of unsystematic risk.
   d. Active portfolio management to enhance returns.

   CFA

5. Diversification can reduce portfolio risk only if security return correlation is:
   a. More than 1.0.
   b. Less than 1.0.
   c. Less than zero.
   d. Equal to 1.0.

   CFA

6. If two stocks have positive standard deviations, but can be combined to form a completely riskless portfolio, what must be the correlation between the two securities?

   CFA

7. Detail how the opportunities available to an investor change when the efficient set of risky opportunities is supplemented by the introduction of a risk-free security that can be bought. How does the set of opportunities change further when the investor is allowed the option of selling or issuing this risk-free security?

8. Describe in general terms how the composition of portfolios on the efficient set changes as one moves from the highest return point on the set to the lowest risk point on the set. In other words, how do the x_i values change from the highest-return efficient portfolio to the lowest-risk efficient portfolio.

9. Assume that you hold a well-diversified portfolio of securities on the efficient set. Ten percent of that portfolio is made up of an investment in Symbolics, a maker of specialized computers and computer programs. Upon attending a public meeting with the management of the firm you revise downward your estimate of the management of the firm's ability to penetrate the com-

puter market and, as a result, reduce your return estimate from 20 percent to 15 percent. How would this change affect the return on your existing portfolio? If nothing else changes how would this estimate likely affect the optimal amount to invest in Symbolics? If less is optimally invested in Symbolics is it likely that the funds freed up from the sale will be devoted to securities that comove closely with Symbolics, or securities that move relatively independently of Symbolics?

10. In the Symbolics case in Problem 9, assume that you increase your estimate of the covariance of Symbolics return with other securities available to you, but your estimate of the return is unchanged. In this case, how would the optimal proportionate investment in Symbolics change?

11. Assume IBM and General Electric have the same expected returns, the same standard deviations, but different covariances with other securities. Would the demand for these securities be the same? That is, would you expect the prices of these securities to be the same, other things constant?

For Problems 12 through 16 consider the following information on four securities that have been suggested to you. The returns, standard deviations, and covariances, similar to those presented in Table 7–1 in the chapter, have been presented to you by a reputable security analyst.

	a	*b*	*c*	*d*	
a	.22	.033	.026	.018	
b	.6	.25	.038	.050	← covariances
c	.4	.5	.30	.036	
d	.2	.5	.3	.40	← standard deviations
E($\bar{R}_i$)	.15	.12	.15	.21	← correlations

12. Describe formally a systematic approach that will achieve the maximum benefits from diversification with the use of these four securities?

13. The analyst also suggested to you that an equal investment in each security would achieve nearly

the maximum benefit of diversification with these four securities. Compute the portfolio return and standard deviation that would be created with this combination. Now compute the portfolio return and the standard deviation created with a portfolio (one on the efficient set, by the way) that consists of 56 percent in security 1, 0 percent in security 2, 9 percent in security 3, and 35 percent in security 4, and comment on the accuracy of the analyst's suggestion.

14. Suppose that a risk-free security exists that can be used for both borrowing and lending. How could the efficient set constructed with these four risky securities be expanded to create new investment opportunities? Which optimal risky portfolio on the efficient set should be used for this expansion?

15. Suppose the optimal risky portfolio to combine with borrowing and lending at a 7 percent rate is one that has an expected return of 17 percent and a standard deviation of 21.4 percent. Identify the risk-return properties of the following two portfolios:

    a. 75 percent in the optimal risky portfolio and 25 percent in the risk-free security.

    b. 150 percent in the optimal risky portfolio financed by borrowing 50 percent at the risk-free interest rate.

16. If more and more securities were considered along with these four for investment purposes, would there be any improvement in the efficient set? Could there be some securities that, if considered for inclusion, would result in an efficient set that was less favorable than that constructed from these four?

17. Lloyd's of London specializes in insuring unique and specialized assets such as satellites, oil tankers, and the hands of a famous pianist. Recently, Lloyd's has experienced a substantial number of major losses that have cut heavily into its profitability. Given the assets they insure, summarize their diversification problem, and the relationship this has to the insurance premium rates they set.

18. Stocks A, B, and C each have the same expected return and standard deviation. Given the following correlation matrix, which portfolio constructed from two of these stocks has the lowest risk?

Correlation Matrix

Stock	A	B	C
A	+1.0		
B	+0.8	+1.0	
C	+0.1	−0.3	+1.0

a. A portfolio equally invested in A and B.
b. A portfolio equally invested in A and C.
c. A portfolio equally invested in B and C.
d. A portfolio totally invested in C.

CFA

19. Describe and explain the return and risk trade-offs expected to be present in the marketplace across the three asset classes, given the capital market expectations in the table:

Capital Market Expectations Assuming Horizon of 5 Years

	Bills	Bonds	Common Stocks
After-Tax Expected Annual Returns	4.5%	6.0%	8.0
Standard Deviation of Annual Returns	1.5	3.0	10.0
Correlation Matrix			
Bills	1.00		
Bonds	.70	1.0	
Stocks	.30	.50	1.0

CFA

CHAPTER

8

Capital Asset Pricing

Market Equilibrium

In Chapter 7 a model in which individual investors chose optimally diversified portfolios from among available financial securities was presented. Investors who employ this model must possess forecasts of security expected returns, risks, and covariances. The composition of the optimal portfolio chosen by an investor depends on the nature of those forecasts. In detailing the portfolio choice model in Chapter 7 we did not consider explicitly where these forecasts came from. In fact, all of our examples used numbers that were estimated from past rate of return data or were drawn from the air to represent forecasts. In this chapter we urge you to begin to think of these returns, standard deviations, and covariances as ex ante values that must be forecast. The chapter following this one, and all of the valuation chapters, have as one of their prime objectives the identification and formulation of ex ante estimates of these variables.

We turn now to the question of how optimal portfolio diversification—if pursued by every investor in the market—will in turn affect the prevailing market prices of securities. If every investor chose a portfolio in accordance with portfolio theory, the aggregate demand for different securities in the market would reflect "consensus," or average, expectations concerning expected returns, standard deviations, and covariances. Further, since aggregate demand will influence a security's price, how will expected returns, standard deviations, and covariances change with price? Finally, what will be the market clearing price, or equilibrium price, for the security and its corresponding package of equilibrium return and risk?

The Complexity of the Problem

Market equilibrium is a difficult issue to deal with primarily because of the great degree of interdependence in the demand for securities by the investor. Suppose that all individual investors establish their demands for securities by finding the optimal tangency portfolio. Simultaneously, they all take their demands to the market. In the marketplace the market maker (the specialist, say) adds up the demands and supplies to see if the market will clear at the current market price. If there is any excess demand the market maker will be forced to raise the price to attempt to clear the market. With an excess supply (from investors trying to liquidate their positions) the market maker will be forced to reduce the price.

Unfortunately, as the price of one security is changed, investors will have to change their expectations of returns (and perhaps standard deviations and covariance). As a result, all investors will be forced to "re-solve" for *new* optimal portfolio proportions. Because a change in the input values will change the optimal proportions of other securities demanded, the change in the price of one security, potentially, brings about a change in the demand for all securities.

In other words, as the price of General Motors' common stock increases due to the excess demand for it, investors will form new, lower expectations of return. With this revision investors, naturally, will want to determine again the optimal proportions (the x_i values) invested in all securities. Investors will find that the reduction in $E(\bar{R}_{GM})$ will change their demands for *GM* and for other securities as well. There are two reasons for this. First, for the portfolio to be fully invested, the lower x_{GM} selected due to the lower expected return will have to be made up through increasing the weights on at least some other securities. Second, the reduction in x_{GM} makes it less desirable than it was before to include securities that have low covariances with *GM*, and more desirable than before to include securities that have low covariances with the securities whose weights are increased. Effectively, the reduction in x_{GM} would not be expected to lead to anything close to a proportional increase in the x_i values for all other securities.

Basically, the problem is that the change in the price of one security can have immediate consequences for the demand for other securities. The result is that identifying the set of prices that simultaneously would clear the market in all securities is a complex mess. This problem is not unique to financial markets. It exists in commodity markets whenever there is substitutability or complementarity between goods and services. The demand for cars influences the demand for steel and tires, for example. The difference in the market for securities is that the interdependence of demand is pervasive. In the General Motors example the x_i values of securities that are substitutes for *GM*'s effect on the portfolio (Chrysler or Ford, perhaps) would be expected to increase, while the x_i values for securities that are complements to *GM*'s effect (those with low covariance) would increase less or decrease. More generally, the substitutability in terms of return, standard deviation, and covariance is exceptionally high in security markets, and we need to find a way of summarizing the equilibrium prices that result from the complex selections of securities by all investors.

A Definition of Equilibrium

Since the concept of **market equilibrium** plays such a key role, we need a precise definition of the term. We use the term to mean:

> A state of the world in which the quantity of every individual security in the capital market which is demanded by fully informed investors equals the quantity of each of those securities which is supplied to the market, either by other investors wishing to liquidate their positions, by issuing firms, or by governments who seek capital for financing asset acquisitions. The price at which such an equilibrium is achieved is referred to as the **equilibrium price.**

Recall from our earlier discussions in Chapters 1 and 6 that the price at which demand and supply schedules intersect in a market is the price at which that market is said to "clear." At this price, supply exactly equals demand. At any price higher than the equilibrium price, there will be **excess supply.** Sellers will be willing to supply a greater quantity of that security than buyers are willing to purchase at that price. The inevitable tendency in this situation is for price to drop, since to find willing buyers, sellers must lower their asking prices. Similarly, at any price lower than the equilibrium price, there will be **excess demand** for the security in question. The tendency here is for price to rise, since buyers will have to raise their bids to attract willing sellers. Only when the price is that for which the supply and demand schedules intersect will the market *clear*. At this point, and only at this point, excess supply and excess demand are both simultaneously zero. In *equilibrium* this must hold for each and every security.

Consistent with our earlier discussion of the efficient markets hypothesis, it's perfectly reasonable to suppose that, in establishing their demands, investors make full use of the available information set, ϕ_t, at the time decisions are made. Each investor employs the contents of ϕ_t in forecasting the expected returns, risk, and covariances between all available securities.

In such a market we would not expect the prices of securities to be formed from irrational or erratic responses of investors, but to tend to reflect the underlying value of the security. Prices that did not reflect this value would not tend to persist over time. Explanations or theories of value that do not rest on these assumptions are not likely to offer many useful insights. In fact, therefore, all of our discussions of bond, stock, and other security valuation in the remaining chapters are derived from the idea that prices in an efficient market tend to move toward their equilibrium levels.

The Capital-Asset Pricing Model

The **capital-asset pricing model (CAPM)** is the name given to a set of principles describing how people behave in the market. These principles lead to an explicit statement of what equilibrium prices, returns, and risks will be for securities. There are other theories that attempt to do this, but the CAPM is particularly useful for two reasons.

First, it is relatively simple and intuitive and can be developed through a direct application of portfolio theory as presented in Chapter 7. Second, its implications have been widely explored with actual data and found to be substantially consistent with most of the theory's predictions. While the theory does not always predict correctly, its implications generally conform to what we observe on security markets. Thus, at the very least, it can be used as an appropriate basis for further adjustments and refinements—which is exactly how it is used by many corporate financial officers, investment bankers, and professional money managers.[1]

The key assumptions that underlie the development of the model are those we have used to describe operating efficiency and those used as a basis for the portfolio choice model.

As a reminder, these are:

1. **Liquidity**.
2. **Price continuity**.
3. **Fairness**.
4. **Divisibility**.
5. **Preferences are a function of $E(\tilde{R}_p)$ and $\sigma(\tilde{R}_p)$.**
6. **A single investment period**.
7. **There is a risk-free security**.

One more assumption is necessary as an abstraction to relate to you our method of describing how equilibrium is established in the financial markets. This is,

8. **Homogeneous expectations**—investors have identical expectations of the returns, standard deviations, and covariances.

This latter assumption is a simplifying assumption that eases the description of the process that leads to a set of prices for securities that will clear the market.[2]

The Market Portfolio

The assumptions just presented have a direct implication for equilibrium prices, expected returns, and risks of individual securities. We illustrate this implication graphically in Figure 8–1.

Note first that since all investors possess identical expectations for the prospects offered by individual securities, **every investor will face the same efficient frontier of risky**

---

[1]The intuition underlying the CAPM was developed by Jack Treynor [1961] with the formal model developed by William F. Sharpe [1964] and independently by John Lintner [1965]. Many generalizations of the theory were made in ensuing years but the most significant was by Jan Mossin in 1966. All of these general equilibrium concepts drew heavily from suggestions made originally by Harry Markowitz. The theory often carries the name of the Sharpe-Lintner-Mossin CAPM.

[2]Obviously, the assumption that investors have homogeneous expectations is not accurate. The assumption's inaccuracy does not necessarily invalidate the model or its conclusions. It is a trick that is employed to avoid some of the messy problems that occur if we were to try to aggregate over all investor's choices with differing expectations. The mathematics would quickly become cumbersome, and at this stage we think that would blur rather than clarify the central relationships. In the appendix we will generalize the model in a subjective and nonmathematical way to account for heterogeneous forecasts of investors.

FIGURE 8–1   **The Efficient Frontier and Optimal Portfolio Held by All Investors with Homogeneous Expectations**

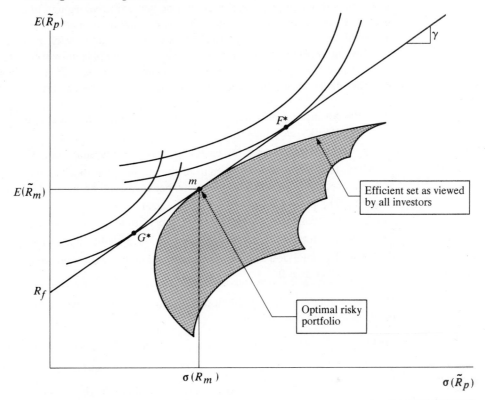

assets. The composition of each portfolio on the frontier will be identical for all investors. And, since the risk-free interest rate is also the same for all, the optimal tangency portfolio—denoted m in the figure—will contain the same securities in identical proportions for all investors. Everyone will look at this picture and conclude that m is the optimal risky portfolio. Some, depending upon their preferences, may choose to combine this portfolio with lending so as to achieve a portfolio such as at point G^* in the figure. Others, however, will combine m with borrowing at the risk-free rate so as to achieve a portfolio like F^* in the figure. All, however, will hold m in some combination with the risk-free asset.

This raises an interesting possibility. Any risky security not included in m will be held by no one. This violates the basic market-clearing condition necessary to achieve equilibrium. Suppose, for instance, that a given firm uses its cash account to build a widget factory costing $1 million. To replenish the cash account the firm issues stock offering a given combination of expected return and risk. If, at the offering price, these securities are not included in portfolio m, the firm will not be able to raise a dime in the capital market. The stock price would have to fall in order to raise the return expected from the stock. The higher return may be sufficient to persuade investors to include it in *m*. That is, the attractiveness of the stock to investors will be inversely related to its market price. At a sufficiently low price, the stock will be just attractive enough to enter portfolio *m*. In fact, at a low enough price, the stock issue may be oversubscribed. Eventually, the price will attain a level at which investors desire to hold exactly the number of shares issued by the firm. The market will then clear and equilibrium will be attained.

What does this price adjustment mechanism have to say about the composition of portfolio *m*? To answer this question, we use the following notation:

i = An index representing each different security; there are *N* different kinds of risky securities (i.e., $i = 1, \ldots N$)

k = An index representing each of *K* different investors (i.e., $k = 1, \ldots K$)

W^k = The dollar invested wealth of the *k*th investor allocated to risky securities in portfolio *m* (remember investors' preferences differ)

x_i^m = The proportion of W^k devoted by each investor (remember they have identical expectations) to risky security *i*

s_i = The total dollar amount of security *i* supplied to the capital market

$d_i(P_{i0})$ = The total dollar amount of security *i* demanded by investors at price P_i at time 0.

Using this notation, the **equilibrium price** of stock *i*, P_{i0}^e, would be that which would result in demand equaling supply, or,

(8–1)   ***In Equilibrium Demand = Supply***

$$d_i(P_{i0}^e) = S_i \quad \text{(for all } i = 1, 2, \ldots N)$$

$$\frac{\textit{Quantity of i demanded}}{\textit{at price } P_{i0}^e} = \frac{\textit{Quantity of i supplied}}{\textit{at price } P_{i0}^e}$$

Either side of this expression is simply the total market value of security *i*, in equilibrium. Thus, if the price for a security is \$50 and at that price 10 million shares are both demanded and supplied, equilibrium is achieved and $d_i(P_{i0}^e)$ or s_i is \$50 million. The aggregate demand for a security is the sum of all investors individual demands so it also must be that

(8–2) $$d_i(P_{i0}^e) = \sum_{k=1}^{K} (x_i^m W^k) = s_i \quad \text{(for all } i = 1, 2, \ldots N)$$

$$\frac{\textit{Aggregate investment}}{\textit{in security i}} = \frac{\textit{Aggregate value of}}{\textit{security i}}$$

Moreover, aggregate invested wealth in all securities (i.e., sum (8–2) over all *N* securities) is

(8–3) $$\sum_{i=1}^{N} \left(\sum_{k=1}^{K} (x_i^m W^k) \right) = \sum_{i=1}^{N} s_i$$

$$\frac{\textit{Aggregate investments in all}}{\textit{securities by all investors}} = \frac{\textit{Aggregate value of}}{\textit{all securities}}$$

But since X_i^m sums to 1.0 for the portfolios to be fully invested the ratio of (8–2) to (8–3) is simply

$$(8\text{–}4) \qquad \frac{x_i^m \sum\limits_{k=1}^{K} W^k}{\sum\limits_{k=1}^{K} W^k} = x_i^m = \frac{s_i}{\sum\limits_{i=1}^{N} s_i} = \quad \begin{array}{l} \textit{Ratio of total market} \\ \textit{value of security i} \\ \textit{to total market} \\ \textit{values of all securities} \end{array}$$

In other words, in equilibrium, x_i^m selected by all investors (i.e., the proportionate investment in security i) will be in proportion to each security's total aggregate market value. Thus, portfolio m is a unique portfolio that requires an investment in each security in proportion to its value in financial markets. In other words, we should think of m as the **market portfolio** because it reflects proportionate equilibrium market values. If all investors (with homogeneous expectations) did not choose x_i^m as defined above, supply wouldn't equal demand, and equilibrium market prices wouldn't exist.

Suppose the capital market consists of just two securities. Security A has an equilibrium aggregate market value of $10 million; security B has an equilibrium aggregate market value of $20 million. Thus, the market value of all securities is $30 million. One third of each investor's wealth devoted to risky securities will be held in the shares of security A, and .667, therefore, in security B.[3] Holdings other than these would imply that the market values of one or both of these firms were not equilibrium values where supply and demand are equal.

To summarize, the implications of this discussion are:

> The equilibrium prices for individual securities will result in all investors holding some portion of their wealth in the market portfolio, which is the optimal portfolio of risky securities for every investor.

This is the single implication of the capital-asset pricing model from which all statements about equilibrium prices, expected returns, and risks of all individual securities—including common stocks, corporate bonds, and any other financial securities representing claims to future, uncertain income—are derived. In the sections which follow we discuss some of these derivative statements.

---

[3]The existing proportions of the Standard & Poor's Index of 500 stocks is given for some of the largest securities below. These are market proportions relative to the 500 stocks, of course, and so exclude thousands of other securities: stocks and bonds alike. However, this 500 includes an estimated 40 percent to 50 percent of the market value of all publicly traded stocks and bonds, so the figures do suggest something of the values of x_i^m for the existing market portfolio. As of late 1986 the proportions were:

Du Pont	1.18%	Exxon	2.97%
General Motors	1.23	AT&T	1.57
IBM	4.29	Church's Fried Chicken	.02

The Capital Market Line

Since all investors hold the same risky portfolio, *m,* and differ only in terms of the amount of their wealth devoted to *m* and R_f, each investor's optimal portfolio (G^* or F^* in Figure 8–1) will plot along the same straight line that connects R_f and *m.* This is the **opportunity set**. It is called the **capital market line (CML),** and is summarized in Figure 8–2.

Mathematically, the CML is written as follows:

(8–5)   *The Capital Market Line*

$$E(\tilde{R}_p) = R_f + \gamma\sigma(\tilde{R}_p)$$

where *p* is any portfolio that combines *m* and R_f. The slope of the line, $\gamma > 0$, represents the trade-off between risk and return in equilibrium which the capital market offers to investors.

The intercept of the capital market line, R_f, may be thought of as the **reward per unit of time** which investors earn for deferring consumption.[4] The slope may be viewed as the **reward per unit of risk** undertaken. Since investors dislike risk, each additional unit of standard deviation in an efficient portfolio must be rewarded in the marketplace if equilibrium is to be attained. If risk were not so rewarded, everyone would seek to hold the risk-free asset and would spurn all risky securities. Obviously, this situation is not consistent with a positive supply of risky securities existing. Hence, as long as individual firms' production plans are subject to uncertainty, some risky securities will exist. To induce investors to hold these securities, γ will be positive.

What does the value of γ equal? Since it represents the slope of the capital market line it also must be defined as

(8–6)   *Slope of the CML*

$$\gamma \equiv \frac{(E(\tilde{R}_m) - R_f)}{\sigma(\tilde{R}_m)}$$

The numerator of this relationship is just the excess return, over and above the risk-free rate, offered by the market portfolio. The denominator is the standard deviation of the market portfolio's return. Hence, γ is literally the reward for bearing risk, per unit of such risk, offered by the market portfolio. All efficient portfolios are expected in equilibrium to earn a risk premium (that is, a return above R_f) equal to γ per unit of risk undertaken.

Putting these definitions together and restating equation (8–5) verbally, we see that:

$$\begin{matrix} \textit{Expected return of} \\ \textit{an efficient portfolio} \end{matrix} = \left(\begin{matrix}\textit{Reward per unit} \\ \textit{of time}\end{matrix}\right) + \left(\begin{matrix}\textit{Reward per} \\ \textit{unit of risk}\end{matrix}\right)\left(\begin{matrix}\textit{Risk of the} \\ \textit{portfolio}\end{matrix}\right).$$

---

[4]The risk-free rate is usually assumed to be positive. This is because most of the time most economies have expectations of expanding—in the long run if not in the short run. This implies that future consumption is likely to be larger than current consumption for most individuals. If most individuals wish to transfer some of their future wealth to the present, say to even out their consumption, then rates of return, and R_f in particular, will be positive. Decaying economies isolated from the rest of the world's financial markets may offer negative risk-free rates however.

FIGURE 8–2   The Capital Market Line and Capital Market Equilibrium

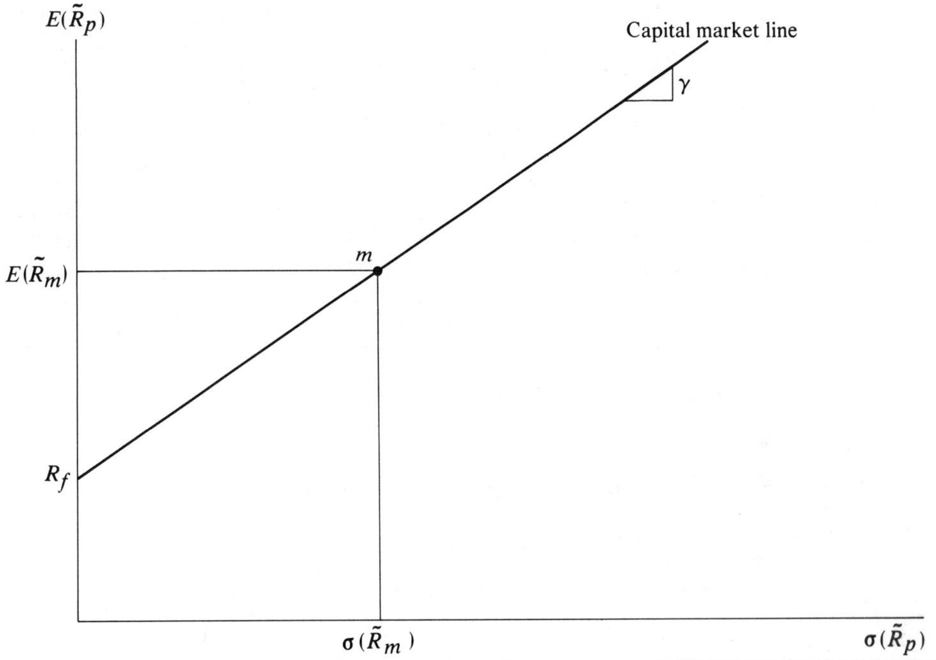

An efficient portfolio's expected return depends on its riskiness. The greater (or lower) the risk, the higher (or lower) the expected return. And the relevant measure of risk for such efficient portfolios is—not surprisingly—the standard deviation of returns. It represents the total variability—as perceived and disliked by investors at the beginning of the period—of returns to be realized during the investment period.

An analogy may be useful at this point. Suppose the wholesale market for diamonds is such that a unit or portfolio of diamonds consists of 1,000 carats. These portfolios are rated by quality, and higher quality portfolios sell for higher prices. If we could observe the two dimensions of quality and price we might expect, given equilibrium in the market for diamonds, a curve that would look very much like the capital market line (though it may not be linear for diamonds). In the case of securities the *price* is denominated in terms of an expected return, and the *quality* is denominated in terms of the standard deviation of the portfolio.

Security Risk and Return

The capital market line indicates the risk-return trade-off in the financial markets in equilibrium. The market portfolio lying on the line is valued according to its expected return, $E(\tilde{R}_m)$, and risk, $\sigma(\tilde{R}_m)$. Moreover, we know that all securities must be valued so that they are included in the market portfolio, otherwise excess supply or demand would exist and we would be in disequilibrium. But, as yet, we don't have a great deal of information on the characteristics of individual securities that will make them highly valued (in which case the dollar value of the security supplied, s_i, is large relative to the total value of all securities). We can get to the heart of this issue by asking two questions:

1. How does an individual security contribute to the expected return on the market portfolio?
2. How does an individual security contribute to the risk or standard deviation of the return on the market portfolio?

Only by answering these two questions can we state categorically what it is that would make one security worth more than another. Thus, of two securities that offer the same contribution to portfolio return, the one that contributes the least to portfolio risk will be more highly demanded by investors. Moreover, by answering these two questions we can answer a third:

3. What is the equilibrium relationship between individual security risk and individual security expected return?

The initial steps in answering these questions were considered in Chapter 7. We found that the security's standard deviation did not necessarily play the most important role in determining the choice portfolio's risk, but, rather, it was the security's comovement with others in the portfolio. We must now address the questions fully, since the answers are the basis for understanding how security values are determined.

Security A's Contribution to Market Portfolio Return

How does security A contribute to portfolio return? The expected return on portfolio m, $E(\tilde{R}_m)$, is simply the sum of the expected returns, $E(\tilde{R}_i)$, on all assets included in the portfolio, weighted by their relative importance in the market portfolio x_i^m. Thus,

(8–7)   ***Market Portfolio Return***

$$E(\tilde{R}_m) = \sum_{i=1}^{N} x_i^m E(\tilde{R}_i) = x_1^m E(\tilde{R}_1) + x_2^m E(\tilde{R}_2) + \cdots$$
$$+ x_A^m E(\tilde{R}_A) + \cdots + x_N^m E(\tilde{R}_N)$$

For a particular security, say security A, the only term including A is $x_A^m E(\tilde{R}_A)$. Thus, **an individual security contributes to portfolio return in proportion to its own expected return.** The factor of proportionality is its weight x_A^m. Thus, if security A's weight in the portfolio is lifted from 5 percent to 10 percent, portfolio expected return will be lifted by .05 $E(\tilde{R}_A)$.[5]

Consequently,

---

[5] The partial derivative of $E(\tilde{R}_m)$ taken with respect to x_A is simply

$$\frac{\partial E(\tilde{R}_m)}{\partial x_A} = E(\tilde{R}_A)$$

This calculation determines how much $E(\tilde{R}_m)$ increases with an increase in x_A. The answer is a constant equal to $E(\tilde{R}_A)$.

> The contribution of an individual security to the market portfolio expected return is in direct proportion to that security's return. Thus $E(\tilde{R}_i)$ must be *one* characteristic of the individual security of direct concern to investors.

Security A's Contribution to Market Portfolio Standard Deviation of Return

The equation for portfolio standard deviation, as we learned in Chapter 7, is made up of many variance and covariance terms. For portfolio $\dot{m}$ the definition is[6]

(8–8)   ***Market Portfolio Risk***

$$\sigma(\tilde{R}_m) = \left[\sum_{i=1}^{N} x_i^2 [\sigma(\tilde{R}_i)]^2 + \sum_{i=1}^{N} \sum_{\substack{j=1 \\ i \neq j}}^{N} x_i x_j Cov(\tilde{R}_i, \tilde{R}_j) \right]^{1/2}$$

where N includes all risky securities. Which terms include some characteristic of any arbitrary security? For example, for security A the terms within the brackets are

(8–9)   ***The Terms in $\sigma(\tilde{R}_m)$ that Include Security A***

$$x_A^2 [\sigma(\tilde{R}_A)]^2 + x_A x_1 Cov(\tilde{R}_A, \tilde{R}_1) + x_A x_2 Cov(\tilde{R}_A, \tilde{R}_2)$$
$$+ x_A x_3 Cov(\tilde{R}_A, \tilde{R}_3) + \cdots + x_1 x_A Cov(\tilde{R}_1, \tilde{R}_A) + x_2 x_A Cov(\tilde{R}_2, \tilde{R}_A) + \cdots$$

There is one variance term and two times $(N - 1)$ covariance terms, so the security's contribution to portfolio m's risk depends on the comovement of this security with the other securities in the market weighted by the proportionate investment in them. This should come as no surprise, since in Chapter 7 the individual took account of these covariances when selecting x_i to construct the optimal portfolio.

Fortunately, while expression 8–9 contains a large number of terms, it can be vastly simplified by making use of some manipulations that were presented in Chapter 2. In particular, covariance terms can be summed.

The result of the summation is that the complex variance and covariance relationships with other securities can be packaged into a single term equal to $x_A Cov(\tilde{R}_A, \tilde{R}_m)$. The total market portfolio standard deviation is made up of a series of like covariance terms (one for each security) that summarize how each security contributes to the portfolio's variance, $[\sigma(\tilde{R}_m)]^2$. Thus,

(8–10)
$$\sigma(\tilde{R}_m) = [x_1 Cov(\tilde{R}_1, \tilde{R}_m) + x_2 Cov(\tilde{R}_2, \tilde{R}_m)$$
$$+ \cdots + x_A Cov(\tilde{R}_A, \tilde{R}_m) + \cdots]^{1/2}$$

$$= \left[\begin{array}{cccc} \text{Security 1's} & \text{Security 2's} & & \text{Security A's} \\ \text{contribution} + & \text{contribution} + \cdots + & & \text{contribution} + \cdots \\ \text{to } [\sigma(\tilde{R}_m)]^2 & \text{to } [\sigma(\tilde{R}_m)]^2 & & \text{to } [\sigma(\tilde{R}_m)]^2 \end{array} \right]^{1/2}$$

---

[6]Here we have dropped x_i^m and substituted the simpler x_i to indicate the portfolio weight. The x's still represent market portfolio weights.

Thus, the portfolio's variance is the sum of the contributions of each security, as measured by their weighted covariance with the portfolio. To see exactly how security A affects $\sigma(\tilde{R}_m)$ we simply need to evaluate the way $\sigma(\tilde{R}_m)$ is changed as x_A is changed. This derivative is

(8–11)   *Individual Security Risk*

$$\frac{\partial \sigma(\tilde{R}_m)}{\partial x_A} = \frac{Cov(\tilde{R}_A, \tilde{R}_m)}{\sigma(\tilde{R}_m)}$$

In words, and in general for any security:

> The contribution of an individual security to the market portfolio risk is measured by the ratio of that security's covariance with the market portfolio in relation to the market portfolio's risk. Thus, $Cov(\tilde{R}_i, \tilde{R}_m)/\sigma(\tilde{R}_m)$ must be the *second* characteristic of the individual security of direct concern to investors.

We conclude that $Cov(\tilde{R}_i, \tilde{R}_m)/\sigma(\tilde{R}_m)$ is the relevant measure of risk for any individual security. By "relevant," we mean that **this measure of risk is the one and only one which determines a security's equilibrium price.** Imagine for a moment holding the standard deviation of portfolio m constant. Then, the higher security i's covariance with m, the higher the ratio $Cov(\tilde{R}_i, \tilde{R}_m)/\sigma(\tilde{R}_m)$, and the greater the risk added to m when additional amounts of security i are included. Since all investors are assumed to hold portfolio m, the risk associated with security i to such investors is *not* measured by the standard deviation of i's returns, $\sigma(\tilde{R}_i)$, but rather more properly by the **contribution of a marginal unit of i to the risk of the overall portfolio, m.** That is the risk that *really* counts to an investor, and that amount is given by Equation 8–11.

If individual securities affect portfolio return in proportion to $E(R_i)$, and affect portfolio risk in proportion to $Cov(\tilde{R}_i, \tilde{R}_m)/\sigma(\tilde{R}_m)$, these are the characteristics that investors use in deciding which individual securities to purchase. Clearly, for securities to be priced in equilibrium (so that the quantity demanded equals the quantity supplied) their contributions to portfolio risk, $Cov(\tilde{R}_i, \tilde{R}_m)/\sigma(\tilde{R}_m)$, must be matched in some way with their expected return, $E(\tilde{R}_i)$. If two securities offer the same covariance (since this is the only term in $\sigma(\tilde{R}_m)$ including i) they must not offer different returns. Otherwise, the portfolio could be improved upon by shifting some of the invested funds from the lower-returning one to the higher-returning one. But what if two securities offer different risks (covariance terms)? How much higher must the return be on the one security with greater risk to ensure that both securities will be held in equilibrium? In other words, what is the risk–return trade-off for individual securities comparable to that for the efficient market portfolio described by the **capital market line** in Figure 8–2 and Equation (8–5)?

Security Market Line

The answer, fortunately, is a simple one. In equilibrium a security's risk in relation to its return is *exactly the same* as that for the efficient market portfolio. For if that were not true then one could purchase or sell an individual firm's securities and construct a

FIGURE 8–3   Individual Security Risk and Expected Return

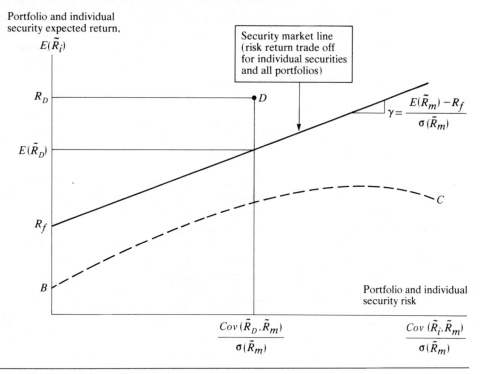

well-diversified portfolio that offered higher returns than that offered by market portfolio *m*—in which case this portfolio could no longer be considered to be the best available, and it would not depict equilibrium in the marketplace. Thus, if the capital market line, from Equation (8–5), is

$$E(\tilde{R}_p) = R_f + \gamma\sigma(\tilde{R}_p)$$

the **security market line (SML),** or **risk-return trade-off** for individual (inefficient) securities in equilibrium must be,

(8–12)   *Security Market Line*

$$E(\tilde{R}_i) = R_f + \gamma\left(\frac{Cov(\tilde{R}_i,\tilde{R}_m)}{\sigma(\tilde{R}_m)}\right)$$

$$= R_f + \left(\frac{E(\tilde{R}_m) - R_f}{\sigma(\tilde{R}_m)}\right)\left(\frac{Cov(\tilde{R}_i,\tilde{R}_m)}{\sigma(\tilde{R}_m)}\right)$$

Any other relationship would imply that the market portfolio was not efficient, and would not therefore be an equilibrium. Equation (8–12) is presented graphically in Figure 8–3. Any security that lies above the line would be in great demand because its high return (for its risk) would serve to increase the return on the market portfolio, making the current market portfolio inefficient. As the price of this security rises in face of the high demand, its return drops—and will keep dropping until excess demand is satiated. That would be the point at which it offered a level of return no greater or no less than that offered by other securities with the same level of risk. Indeed, this is the sense in which equilibrium is established. Market pressures of excess demand and supply force the security to a price such that its return and risk are comparable to all other securities—that is, on the line. Any other configuration, such as point D or line BC, would be a disequilibrium situation. Verbally, this equilibrium relationship is

$$\begin{pmatrix} \text{Equilibrium} \\ \text{expected return for} \\ \text{individual risky} \\ \text{securities} \end{pmatrix} = \begin{pmatrix} \text{Reward per} \\ \text{unit of time} \end{pmatrix} + \begin{pmatrix} \text{Reward per} \\ \text{unit of risk} \end{pmatrix} \begin{pmatrix} \text{Contribution of} \\ \text{individual security} \\ \text{to risk of market portfolio} \end{pmatrix}$$

As before, investors are rewarded for their patience. They are also rewarded for assuming risk. The relevant measure of risk is each individual security's contribution to the risk of portfolio m. For this reason, some securities have higher equilibrium expected returns than others. Those with the highest covariance with the market portfolio in equilibrium will offer the highest expected returns. Those with little or no covariance with the market portfolio will offer expected returns very close to the risk-free interest rate.

Now let's reintroduce our diamond analogy. Just as it was possible to represent equilibrium in the market for portfolios of diamonds, it is possible to represent equilibrium in the market for individual diamonds. The curve representing this would have the price of an individual diamond (per carat price, perhaps) on the vertical axis and the quality of the individual diamonds on the horizontal axis. In the market for diamonds the dimension of quality may be the same for individual diamonds as it is for portfolios of diamonds, in which case the definition of the horizontal axis would be the same for both portfolios of diamonds and individual diamonds. In the case of individual securities, however, the "quality" dimension changes in moving from portfolios to individual securities because the quality of the portfolio ($\sigma(\tilde{R}_m)$) is not the sum of the "qualities" of the individual securities—at least not as measured by the standard deviation. Rather, the quality dimension must change to reflect the interaction among securities in determining the "quality" of the portfolio. This is what the term $Cov(\tilde{R}_i,\tilde{R}_m)/\sigma(\tilde{R}_m)$ does for us.

The concepts and implications contained in the capital market line and security market line are part of what is termed the **capital-asset pricing model**—or the **CAPM**. It is a model that describes equilibrium relationships in financial markets under uncertainty.

Beta and the Security Market Line

It is often convenient to translate mathematical relationships into graphic ones, as we did with the capital market line. Let the ith security possess what is termed a **beta** value, or β, given by:

(8–13) *Security Beta*

$$\beta_i \equiv \frac{Cov(\tilde{R}_i,\tilde{R}_m)}{[\sigma(\tilde{R}_m)]^2}$$

for $i = 1, \ldots, N$. Note that beta is the ratio of security i's covariance with m to m's variance, *not* m's standard deviation. With this definition we can make a minor change

FIGURE 8–4   The Security Market Line

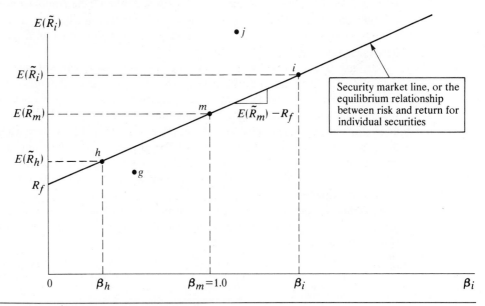

in the form in which we write the security market line—somewhat more simply than before—using (8–12) and (8–13), or,

(8–12)   *Security Market Line Again*

$$E(\tilde{R}_i) = R_f + \gamma \left(\frac{Cov(\tilde{R}_i, \tilde{R}_m)}{\sigma(\tilde{R}_m)} \right)$$

$$= R_f + \left(\frac{E(\tilde{R}_m) - R_f}{\sigma(\tilde{R}_m)} \right) \left(\frac{Cov(\tilde{R}_i, \tilde{R}_m)}{\sigma(\tilde{R}_m)} \right)$$

$$E(\tilde{R}_i) = R_f + \beta_i [E(\tilde{R}_m) - R_f]$$

This is still a relationship between expected return and risk; however, the relevant measure of risk has now been "defined" to be security i's β. Since the variance and standard deviation of m's returns are the same, respectively, for all securities, β_i ranks risk for different risky assets in the same order as does its marginal contribution to the risk of portfolio m, which is given by $Cov(\tilde{R}_i, \tilde{R}_m)/\sigma(\tilde{R}_m)$. Beta is just stated in different units. Since the two measures provide the same relative risk rankings for different securities, no substantive change is introduced by this. It is like switching from Celsius to Fahrenheit scales in temperature measurement. It doesn't matter which risk scale we use, as long as one scale is just a linear transformation of the other.

Using the last equation above, we obtain a graph like that shown in Figure 8–4. Note that the vertical axis measures expected return. The horizontal axis measures beta. The slope, which can be inferred from the definition of β and the security market line, is $\gamma\sigma(\tilde{R}_m)$ or $E(\tilde{R}_m) - R_f$. Each point in this space represents a particular combination of expected return and beta. Only points that plot on the security market line, such as h and *i,* represent equilibrium combinations of risk and return. Conversely, points off the line, such as *j* and *g,* represent securities with expected return–beta combinations that do not exist *in equilibrium.* Exactly the same information regarding equilibrium is contained in Figures 8–3 and 8–4. The only difference is the way the information is packaged in the horizontal axis and the slope coefficient.

Any risk-free asset has a zero beta, since its covariance with *m* (and with any other risky asset for that matter) must be zero. The security market line also implies that any security which has a standard deviation of return but also has a zero beta will earn the risk-free interest rate. One might think this strange, since it implies that some assets with uncertain returns will earn *risk-free* returns. Does this imply there is no reward for bearing the uncertainty contained in these assets? The answer is yes, since any security which has a zero covariance with the market portfolio contributes *nothing* to the variability of that portfolio's return. Hence, investors will be willing to hold it even if they earn only the risk-free interest rate.

In addition, note that point *m* plots on the security market line with a beta of 1.0. This beta, β_m, may be interpreted as the beta of the market portfolio with respect to itself. Note from our definition of covariance,

(8–14)   ***Beta of the Market***

$$\beta_m = \frac{Cov(\tilde{R}_m, \tilde{R}_m)}{\sigma^2(\tilde{R}_m)} = \frac{\sigma^2(\tilde{R}_m)}{\sigma^2(\tilde{R}_m)} = 1.0,$$

or the market portfolio beta is 1.0. In fact, any risky security having a beta equal to 1.0 is expected, in equilibrium, to earn the same return as does the market portfolio. Such an asset is viewed as equally risky as *m;* hence, it is priced to earn the same expected return as *m.*

What about other risky securities? Those with beta values greater than 1.0 (like security *i* in the figure) will have expected returns that exceed *m*'s expected return. These securities contribute more to the risk of an efficiently diversified portfolio than the average security does; hence, they are priced to earn higher returns. Similarly, securities possessing beta values less than 1.0 will earn expected returns somewhere between the risk-free interest rate and the expected return on *m.* In short, the higher a security's beta, the higher its expected return.

There could possibly be securities with negative beta values in the market. These are securities for which the returns are negatively correlated with those on the market portfolio. Although the line in Figure 8–3 has not been extended to cover the range of negative beta securities, they will earn returns less than the risk-free rate. Who would hold such securities? Many would have the incentive to because they *reduce* the risk of an efficiently diversified portfolio (i.e., *m*) to such an extent that investors are willing to sacrifice part or all of their reward for time. These securities are like insurance policies; their expected returns may even be negative (as is the case with insurance). They are demanded in spite of this, however, because of their ability to reduce portfolio risk.

Over- and Undervalued Securities

It is frequently useful to view the significance of the security market line in terms of potential departures from equilibrium. We have asserted that, in equilibrium, all risky securities have expected return–beta combinations that plot exactly on the line. What if, however, points like *j* and *g* in Figure 8–4 exist?

Consider point *j*, which represents a hypothetical risky security. It offers a higher expected return than other risky securities offer at the same beta level in equilibrium. As a result, *j* will appear to be extremely attractive as an investment. Since *j* plots above the line:

(8–15a)   *Undervalued Security*

$$j\text{'s return} > R_f + \beta_j[E(\tilde{R}_m) - R_f]$$

But this situation cannot persist. Investors will seek to hold more of *j* than is present in *m*. Excess aggregate demand will force *j*'s price to rise. This will reduce the expected return *j* offers, driving *j*'s position in Figure 8–4 toward the security market line. Thus, as long as *j*'s expected return–beta combination lies above the line, one can say that it is **undervalued** by the capital market.

Consider point *g*. It offers a lower expected return than other risky securities with the same beta. For security *g*, then:

(8–15b)   *Overvalued Security*

$$g\text{'s return} < R_f + \beta_g[E(\tilde{R}_m) - R_f]$$

and investors will view *g* as relatively unattractive or **overvalued** by the market. Everyone will seek to divest themselves of the shares of *g* they hold. This will force *g*'s price to fall, raising its expected return, and driving its position toward the security market line in Figure 8–4. Points such as *j* and *g* can exist but cannot persist.

Portfolios

We have stated throughout that the security market line shows the expected return–risk trade-off for individual securities. Actually, the security market line shows the expected return–risk trade-off for all risky assets in the market, including: *(a)* individual securities, *(b)* efficient portfolios, and *(c)* inefficient portfolios. Every security and feasible portfolio—whether or not efficient—if priced in equilibrium will plot on this line. It is thus a more general relationship than we have described. Moreover, any individual security can be thought of as an (inefficient) portfolio. Indeed, corporations are portfolios—of managerial and labor talent, cash, inventories, and productive plant and equipment.

Equilibrium Prices

The relationships derived thus far have been stated in terms of expected return and risk for individual securities and portfolios. Although the theory is termed the capital-asset pricing model, or CAPM, actual equilibrium prices have been mentioned only indirectly. It is, of course, the movement of security prices to equilibrium values that propels the risk–return positions to the depicted relationships. It is important not to lose sight of this fact. Any statement about equilibrium in any market is a statement about the structure of relative prices. All other relationships (e.g., that between expected returns and beta) are of necessity derived from such a statement.

An interesting perspective can be gleaned from examining security prices that prevail in CAPM equilibrium. To do this, we need only recognize that security i's equilibrium expected rate of return, $E(\tilde{R}_i)$, over the single investment period is related to its beginning-of-period *equilibrium* share price, P_{i0}^e, as follows:

(8–16) *Equilibrium Return*

$$E(\tilde{R}_i) = \frac{E(\tilde{P}_{i1}^e) + E(\tilde{D}_{i1}) - P_{i0}^e}{P_{i0}^e}$$

$$\begin{array}{c} \text{Security's} \\ \text{expected return} \end{array} = \begin{array}{l} \text{The investor's expected end-of-period} \\ \text{dollar payoff per share, divided by the beginning-of-period cost.} \end{array}$$

where:

$P_{i0}^e = i$'s beginning-of-period (time 0) share price

$P_{i1}^e = i$'s end-of-period (time 1) share price, which is unknown at the beginning of the period

$D_{i1} = i$'s end-of-period dividend per share, which is unknown at the beginning of the period.

Note that the end-of-period dollar payoff has two components, both of which are subject to uncertainty: the future share price of i, and i's future cash flow (interest or dividend payment). Since these are random variables, the computation of the expected return on i involves finding the expected value of the future price plus the expected value of the future dividend. We can solve this expression for the current market price to have a model for the price of a security based on the risk–return concepts already developed. In particular,

(8–17) *Equilibrium Value of the Security*

$$P_{i0}^e = \frac{E(\tilde{P}_{i1}^e) + E(\tilde{D}_{i1})}{1 + E(\tilde{R}_i)}$$

$$\begin{array}{c} \text{Beginning-of-period} \\ \text{share price} \end{array} = \begin{array}{l} \text{The present value of the} \\ \text{expected future payoff.} \end{array}$$

The present-value discount rate is the risky discount rate appropriate to security i, $E(\tilde{R}_i)$. Since we are concerned with equilibrium prices and returns, we know that for P_{i0}^e in Equation (8–17) to represent an equilibrium price, i must offer investors an expected rate of return equal to that available from other securities with the same risk given by the security market line. Hence, if $E(\tilde{R}_i)$ is equal to $R_f + \beta_i[E(\tilde{R}_m) - R_f]$ as indicated by the SML, P_{i0}^e will be the equilibrium price per share. By paying this price, no more-no less, investors expect to earn exactly the return they require.

Equivalently, investors analyze the prospects offered by i in terms of its expected future dollar payoff and discount this back to time 0 at a rate of return that reflects the risk-free rate, the security's risk, and the premium per unit of risk in the market. Investors will offer to pay no more than P_{i0}^e per share. At that price, and only at that price, the market for i will clear.

A brief example will illustrate this. Suppose the risk-free interest rate equals 10 percent, the expected return on portfolio m is 20 percent, security i's beta is 1.5, the expected future dividend on i is $1.00, and i's future price is expected to be $10. What should i be selling for today? We first compute i's equilibrium expected return, using the security market line, or,

$$E(\tilde{R}_i) = .10 + 1.5(.20 - .10)$$

which equals .25. Then, with Equation (8–17) we find that $P^e_{i0} = (\$10 + \$1)/$ $(1.25) = \$8.80$. To be priced in equilibrium, i's current price must be $8.80 per share. At that price, investors can expect to earn a 25 percent return on their investment—a return equal to that available on other securities of equal risk.

Summary

The capital-asset pricing model is a model of security price formation in a world characterized by uncertainty and competitive, frictionless capital markets. The key assumptions are that: there are no transaction costs or taxes; all market participants are atomistic competitors; investment decisions are made in a single-period framework; investors make these decisions on the basis of portfolio-expected returns and standard deviations; expectations regarding the future prospects of all securities are homogeneous; and a risk-free asset exists that may be borrowed or lent freely at a single rate of interest.

Using these assumptions one can derive a key implication:

> The market portfolio, in which all securities are held in proportion to their aggregate market values in equilibrium, is the optimal portfolio of risky securities for every investor.

From this, we know that all investors will hold identical risky portfolios. Other implications of the theory are derived from this implication. Among these are relationships between equilibrium-expected returns and risks which can be summarized by: *(a)* the capital market line, and *(b)* the security market line.

The capital market line is a relationship between expected return and risk for **efficient** portfolios. It states that the equilibrium-expected return on such portfolios is given by

$$E(\tilde{R}_p) = R_f + \left[\frac{E(\tilde{R}_m) - R_f}{\sigma(\tilde{R}_m)}\right] \sigma(\tilde{R}_p)$$

Thus, for efficiently diversified portfolios the expected return consists of two components: a reward for time (waiting or deferring consumption), and a reward for bearing risk. The relevant measure of risk in this relationship is the efficient portfolio's standard deviation of returns.

The security market line is a relationship between expected return and risk for all individual securities and portfolios in the market. It states that

$$E(\tilde{R}_i) = R_f + \beta_i[E(\tilde{R}_m) - R_f]$$

As before, the return expected has two components: a reward per unit of time, and a reward for each unit of risk borne. The relevant measure of risk here is the β_i, or beta of such assets. The beta for a risky security or portfolio measures the contribution of i to the risk of the market portfolio. The larger the beta is for security i, the greater the contribution to $\sigma(\tilde{R}_m)$, the greater the risk, and the larger its equilibrium expected return.

APPENDIX: Relaxing the Assumptions of the Capital-Asset Pricing Model

Since the CAPM's introduction in 1965, students of academic finance literature have made a number of valid criticisms of the theory. Most criticisms relate to the restrictive nature of the theory's assumptions. Think about it. Do markets really offer risk-free borrowing and lending opportunities at a single, common interest rate equally accessible by all participants? Is there even such a thing as a truly risk-free asset? Do all investors agree on the prospects of every security? Is the world free of transactions costs and taxes? If you answered no to most or all of these questions, you have an instant appreciation of the theory's potential weaknesses.

Fortunately, however, we do not have to throw out the theory in order to relax many of the restrictive assumptions. It turns out that the theory is very robust with respect to some—but not all—of the key assumptions. Hence, we can still make statements about the nature of capital-market equilibrium, or the shape of the security market line, when these assumptions are relaxed. We turn next to doing precisely this.

Risk-Free Borrowing and Lending

One of the first reactions students in an investments course have to the CAPM, is that the theory is unrealistic because it assumes investors can borrow money at the same interest rate they can lend it. Everyone knows, they point out, that this is not possible for the average investor. The borrowing rate is invariably higher than the lending rate. Can this important fact about the real world be incorporated into the theory? The answer is yes.

Suppose the risk-free borrowing rate is denoted R_B, and the risk-free lending rate denoted R_L, where $R_B > R_L$. Then consider Figure 8A–1. This graph shows the feasible region of risky securities and the new opportunity set composed of combinations of riskless and risky assets, given the divergence between borrowing and lending rates. The solid line extending from R_L to Q represents combinations of lending at rate R_L and investment in risky portfolio Q. As you can see, Q happens to be the optimal combination of risky securities for those individuals who find it optimal to lend. Such individuals will choose to hold portfolios like T, where an indifference curve is tangent to the "lending line." They will invest a portion of their funds in Q and lend the remaining portion at rate R_L. Borrowers, on the other hand, will choose to invest in risky portfolio S and borrow funds at rate R_B in order to do so. They will hold portfolios like V in the graph, where an indifference curve is tangent to the "borrowing line." Notice that the dashed portions of the lending and borrowing lines are infeasible. For example, the dashed portion of the borrowing line which lies between R_B and S could be attained only if an investor could

FIGURE 8A–1   The Efficient Frontier with Divergent Borrowing/Lending Rates

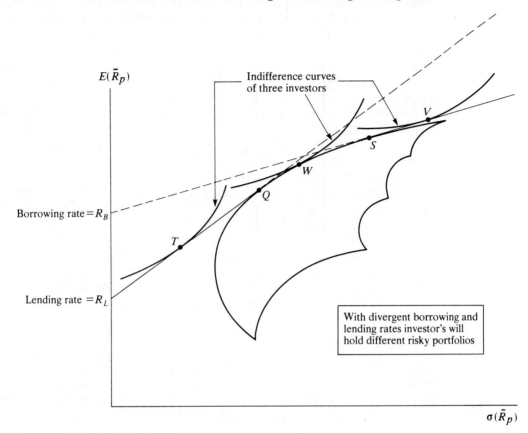

lend at the borrowing rate. This is not allowed. Similarly, the dashed portion of the lending line, which lies above portfolio Q, is not feasible for it is attainable only by borrowing at the rate R_L.

Some individuals in the market will choose to neither borrow nor lend. Their indifference curves lie tangent to the frontier of risky assets at points like W. They will simply hold risky securities, finding it optimal neither to leverage their portfolios nor to reduce portfolio risk with lending.

It is clear that there is no longer a uniquely optimal risky portfolio which all investors seek. Some see Q as the optimal portfolio. Others see S as optimal. Still others find an infinite number of risky portfolios, lying between S and Q on the curved portion of the frontier as optimal. What can be said about equilibrium?

To answer this question definitively, it is necessary for us to relax one other assumption. That assumption concerns an investor's ability to sell short any risky security. Recall from Chapter 7 that if no short sales are allowed, the x_i value for the ith security included in a portfolio must be nonnegative. We now allow x_i to assume negative values; the sum of the x_is, however, must still equal 1.0. Under these conditions, it can be shown (though we will not derive it) that all portfolios lying on the curved segment between Q and S

in Figure 8A–1 are just feasible portfolios constructed by combining Q and S in different proportions. (In mathematical terms, this means they are linear combinations of Q and S.) A portfolio like W, for example, involves investing in some specified proportion, say x_Q of the investor's wealth in Q and $(1 - x_Q)$ in S. Since every investor will choose a portfolio along this curved segment of the frontier, every investor's portfolio will be some specific linear combination of Q and S. It follows from this that, if all securities in the market are to be held by someone (i.e., that the market reaches equilibrium), portfolio m—the market portfolio—must *also* be a linear combination of Q and S.

This Two–Mutual Funds Theorem states that any portfolio lying on the curved portion of the frontier, even those points lying above and to the right of S or below Q, can be represented as linear combinations of any two arbitrarily selected portfolios also on the curved portion of the frontier. Thus, we needn't pick Q and S to represent the contents of m—we could pick *any* two portfolios!

One portfolio lying on the curved portion of the frontier has particularly interesting properties. Because of those properties, it is ideally suited to be picked as one of our two "mutual funds." Due to the two–mutual funds theorem and the assumption that investors can sell short any risky security it is possible to construct a portfolio lying on the curved frontier which has a beta of zero with respect to the market portfolio. (For example, suppose Q's beta is 1.3 and S's beta is 2.5. We can construct a zero-beta portfolio by selling an amount of S short equal to 108 percent of our wealth and investing the proceeds, along with our original wealth, in Q. That gives a beta equal to $(-1.08)(2.5) + (2.08)(1.3) = 0.0$. We call this portfolio (not surprisingly) the **zero-beta portfolio,** and use the letter z to denote it. Portfolios Q, S, m, and z are shown in Figure 8A–2. As you can see, z is inefficient (no one would hold it by itself) and is risky, even though it has zero covariance with the market portfolio. Thus, though its returns vary, they do so in a fashion which is unrelated to the variation in returns on m. The other "mutual fund" we will pick is m itself. Given m and z, Fischer Black [1972] showed that the security market line can be stated as

(8A–1)   ***The Zero-Beta Form of the Security Market Line***

$$E(\tilde{R}_i) = E(\tilde{R}_z) + \beta_i[E(\tilde{R}_m) - E(\tilde{R}_z)]$$

This relationship, given divergent borrowing and lending rates, holds true for all risky securities and portfolios composed of risky securities only.

Observe that portfolio z in Equation (8A–1) plays a role analogous to that of the risk-free asset in the CAPM developed earlier. Each risky asset in the market—as reflected in both equations—is priced to earn an expected return which is the sum of: *(a)* a reward per unit of time or the return expected on an asset possessing zero correlation (zero beta) with the market portfolio, and *(b)* a reward for risk, which is the market risk premium over and above the zero-beta asset's return times the risky asset's beta. Thus, the only difference between the CAPM's implications under a single risk-free borrowing–lending rate and divergent borrowing–lending rates is that in the former case the zero-beta asset is risk-free; in the latter it is not.

The zero-beta CAPM holds even in a world in which there is no risk-free asset at all. Indeed, no R_f value is included in the zero-beta CAPM or in Figure 8A–2. Here, the relevance of the two–mutual funds theorem is once again apparent. Any portfolio an

FIGURE 8A–2   The Market Portfolio and the Zero-Beta Portfolio

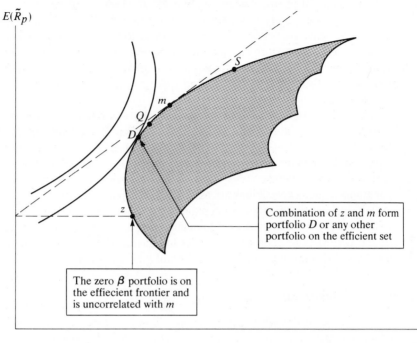

investor chooses may be viewed as a linear combination of portfolios m and z. The optimal choice lies at a point of tangency between the risky asset frontier and the investor's indifference curves, such as at point D in the figure. While individuals will never choose portfolio z itself because it is inefficient, they will choose some combination of z and m. In equilibrium, Equation (8A–1) will hold for all securities and portfolios, including efficient ones.

It is also possible to derive the CAPM's implications under the assumption that investors may lend at some risk-free interest rate, but they cannot borrow at the risk-free asset at all. That assumption makes intuitive sense to some people (though we show below that it isn't realistic). We won't go through the logic to show it; however, once again Equation (8A–1) turns out to be the relevant security market line. Only risky securities and portfolios not involving positive holdings of the risk-free asset will plot on the security market line given by (8A–1), however. In short, Equation (8A–1) is *the* governing general security market line for risky securities when risk-free borrowing lending activities are restricted.

Several questions are raised by relaxing the risk-free borrowing/lending assumptions of the CAPM. First, in the case in which we introduced divergent borrowing and lending rates, if borrowers must pay, say 10 percent (R_B) per annum in interest payments, and lenders receive only 8 percent (R_L), who is pocketing the 2 percent spread? Normally, one thinks of a financial intermediary doing this as compensation for bringing borrowers and lenders together. But why would borrowers and lenders in a competitive and frictionless market pay an intermediary to do this? There are no transaction costs; hence, it is costless for borrowers and lenders to get together and bypass such middlemen. In the CAPM, financial intermediaries simply have no reason to exist.

Second, look closely at the situation in which it was assumed there was no risk-free asset at all. Investors, however, were assumed to be able to sell short any risky asset without cost. If investors are not allowed to sell short the risk-free asset due to some market imperfection, why doesn't this same imperfection prevent them from selling short risky assets? In the real world, we find some practical restrictions on the short sales of virtually *all* financial securities.

Third, the case in which risk-free lending, but not risk-free borrowing, was allowed is even less satisfactory than the first two. To whom is the lender of the risk-free asset lending? If the lender is lending a risk-free asset, it means that that person perceives no possibility of default or unexpected price changes which would cause the loan's real return to vary randomly. Why, then, is the borrower not also perceiving these same conditions, since expectations are assumed to be homogeneous?

To conclude, relaxing the assumption of risk-free borrowing and lending tends to raise more questions than it answers. Although we have shown the basic relationships posited by the CAPM to be robust with respect to relaxing this assumption, it is not clear that the revised relationships are any more useful than the original ones.

Heterogeneous Expectations

We now consider what happens if we allow investors to possess different forecasts concerning the future prospects of individual securities. To do this, we retain all the other assumptions of the CAPM and focus only on the effect of heterogeneous expectations.

Under heterogeneous expectations, each investor in the market views himself as facing an efficient frontier, like that shown in Figure 8A–3, which is possibly very unlike the efficient frontiers faced by other investors. Assuming all investors can borrow and lend freely at a common rate R_f, each investor will possess an optimal tangency portfolio of risky securities which is unique to the investor's own forecasts. For investor k, we have denoted this optimal tangency portfolio as m^k in Figure 8A–3. It may or may not contain every asset in the market; hence, it need not be the market portfolio. We do know two things, however. The first is that, if the market for all risky assets is to clear, the true market portfolio must be held *in the aggregate* by all investors. Thus, the market portfolio must be a combination of all individual investors' optimal tangency portfolios. Prices will adjust until this condition holds. Second, every investor will face his own personal security market line, along which all securities will plot in equilibrium. For each investor:

(8A–2) $$E^k(\tilde{R}_i) = R_f + \beta_i^k[E^k(\tilde{R}_m) - R_f]$$

where the superscript k denotes an expectation held by investor k and which may or may not be shared by anyone else. Every asset will be priced in equilibrium according to k's own personal version of the security market line. Investors will generally disagree among themselves concerning the values of security-expected returns, standard deviations, covariances, and betas. They will agree, however, that the market is in equilibrium whenever Equation (8A–2) holds.

To conclude, we see that the CAPM is robust with respect to heterogeneous expec-

FIGURE 8A–3 **The Efficient Frontier as Seen by Investor k in a World of Heterogeneous Beliefs**

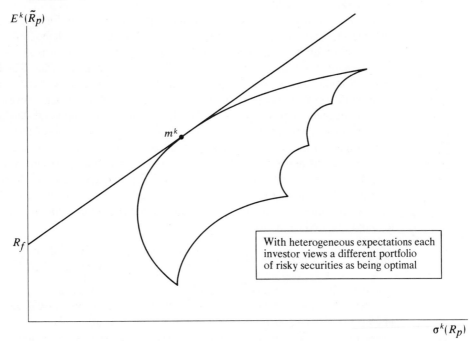

With heterogeneous expectations each investor views a different portfolio of risky securities as being optimal

tations. Expectations are heterogeneous in the real world. Hence, this relaxed version of the theory is potentially more useful than the original except for one aspect. The security market line is no longer an objective property of a single "market expectation." There are potentially as many security market lines as investors in existence. Even though it is possible to construct, mathematically, a "market" security market line reflecting the weighted average of all investors' expectations, one must be aware that it reflects only security market participants' aggregate expectations. It will nevertheless represent a market equilibrium trade-off between risk and return that determines the opportunities available in the market.

Taxes

As you now might suspect, it is possible to relax the no-taxes assumption of the CAPM without damage to the essence of the theory that equilibrium returns on securities will be a linear function of their betas. If investors face different marginal tax rates, the expected returns, standard deviations, and covariances used as inputs for the formation of the efficient set will differ. The inevitable conclusion is that each investor with a different tax rate will perceive a different (after-tax) efficient set. The investor in a higher tax bracket will see the efficient set as being compressed, or offering lower returns and lower standard deviations than available if taxes were nonexistent. Essentially, taxation of returns causes the investor to share the returns and risks of investment pursuits with the federal government.

The net result is a security market line that will be unique for investors in different tax brackets, and can be described in exactly the manner in which the SML was described for a world with heterogeneous expectations, i.e., in Equation (8A–2).

Differential effective tax rates on dividends and capital gains, caused by the investor's ability to delay paying taxes until the capital gain is realized, will cause the shape and position of the efficient set to change further. For a high-tax-bracket investor, dividend-paying stocks or interest-bearing bonds will have after-tax returns and standard deviations that are lower than offered by securities having a major portion of their returns in the form of capital gains. If the dislike for dividend and interest return and the preference for capital gains return were universal, investors would bid up the prices of securities of firms that offer their return in the form of capital gains, and bid down the prices of other securities. This would lead to a higher equilibrium return on dividend- and interest-bearing securities, and an after-tax SML describing risk/return opportunities for the investor might be defined as follows:

$$(8A–3) \qquad E(\tilde{R}_i^\tau) = R_f^\tau + \beta_i^\tau[E(\tilde{R}_m^\tau) - R_f^\tau] + \gamma_i \begin{pmatrix} \text{dividend or} \\ \text{interest yield} \end{pmatrix}$$

where τ refers to the after-tax values of each variable for tax rate τ.

This expression includes a *premium* for the additional burden the investor faces by having to pay taxes at a higher rate on securities that offer their return in the form of interest or dividends. It is an empirical question whether γ is an economically important coefficient. An answer is given in the next chapter.

Transaction Costs

The term **transaction costs** refers to a multitude of types of costs associated with investing in financial securities. The costs may be cash, non-cash, or both. Included are such things as information and search costs associated with acquiring data about individual securities' expected returns and β's, and even finding a buyer or a seller with whom to transact. Also included are brokerage commissions associated with executing an order to buy or sell, and the spread between bid and ask prices in the marketplace. In the real world all of these costs exist to some extent. The question is what effect their recognition has on the implications of the capital-asset pricing model.

The treatment of transaction costs is analytically very complex, depending on their nature—whether they are proportional to the dollar value invested or whether they are fixed, for example—and on whether they differ among investors. We shall not attempt to provide a full treatment here. Suffice it to say that incorporating transaction costs into the model suggests that, as with the introduction of taxes, individual investors will face different efficient frontiers—to the extent that they face different dollar transaction costs. Obviously, in such a world the logic of everyone seeking to hold the market portfolio is questionable. One would suspect that individuals will hold portfolios which are less well diversified than the market portfolio, if only from the standpoint of trading off the benefits of additional diversification with the additional transaction costs.

The result is that the relevant measure of risk for individual securities will incorporate more than just their contributions to the risk of the market portfolio. Since investors will not be perfectly efficiently diversified in the sense of holding portfolio *m*, they may tend to give more emphasis to each security's own standard deviation (or variance) of returns. Hence, in some versions of the CAPM with transaction costs, one cannot derive a risk–return relationship that is precisely the same as the security market line. If transactions costs are small it will come close, but things are just not as simple as we described earlier.

Nonmarketable Assets

Some researchers have raised legitimate concerns about the CAPM because it ignores the existence of certain nonmarketable assets which every individual possesses and which may influence portfolio choice in subtle ways. The best example of a truly nonmarketable asset is one's human capital. Human capital produces future income for most of us through our gainful employment (or that of family members). This future income is uncertain and, most important, it is likely to be correlated with the returns on risky securities. If so, these researchers argue, such correlation should affect the security portfolios each of us holds. The maximization of expected utility means being concerned about *total* portfolio risk and return, not just the risk and return on the marketable portion of our assets.

An example illustrates the point nicely. Suppose an architect wishes to select a portfolio of risky securities. The architect's future income is dependent upon the fortunes of the building construction industry, which also affects the returns on financial securities issued by firms operating in this industry. Thus, the architect's principal nonmarketable asset has returns which are likely to be highly correlated with the returns on certain marketable financial assets. To construct an efficient portfolio containing both nonmarketable assets and marketable ones, this correlation must be taken into account. If not, as has been the case so far in this chapter, the individual will end up with a needlessly risky pattern of future consumption. But, if this correlation is taken into account, then conceivably each investor in the market will hold a different marketable-security portfolio, since each of us has human capital possessing different degrees of correlation with various financial securities.

If we take a simple case where nonmarketable assets possess a distribution of future, uncertain returns denoted $\tilde{R}_h$, David Mayers [1972] showed that in equilibrium the expected return on the *i*th risky security is given by:

(8A–4)   ***CAPM with Nonmarketable Assets***

$$E(\tilde{R}_i) = R_f + \beta_i'[E(\tilde{R}_m) - R_f]$$

where β_i' is the "revised" beta of asset *i* with respect to the total portfolio consisting of both marketable and nonmarketable assets. It is defined as follows:

(8A–5)   ***Risk with Nonmarketable Assets in the Portfolio***

$$\beta_i' \equiv \frac{Cov(\tilde{R}_i,\tilde{R}_m) + \left(\dfrac{V_h}{V_m}\right) Cov(\tilde{R}_i,\tilde{R}_h)}{[\sigma(\tilde{R}_m)]^2 + (V_h/V_m)Cov(\tilde{R}_m,\tilde{R}_h)}$$

In this definition, V_h is the total value of nonmarketable assets, and V_m the total value of marketable assets.

As you can see, if nonmarketable assets have returns correlated with those of marketable ones $(Cov(\tilde{R}_m, \tilde{R}_h) \neq 0)$, each risky, marketable security's beta will be different from that value implied by Equation (8–13). Indeed, if security i has returns more highly correlated with nonmarketable asset returns than with marketable financial securities, its beta will be larger—signifying appropriately greater risk—than the beta would be if it were measured relative to marketable assets only. This is just what you'd expect—the common stock issued by an employment agency may be riskier if viewed in the context of its covariance with human capital returns as well as financial asset returns than if viewed solely in terms of its covariance with the latter.

You can also see from (8A–5) that the larger a fraction of the total value of all assets accounted for by nonmarketable assets (V_h/V_m), the more each security's "revised" beta, β_i', will differ from its beta in the conventional CAPM. This makes sense. The more important the nonmarketable assets are, the more attention investors should pay to the covariance of their financial asset portfolios with their nonmarketable asset returns.

All in all, the basic implications of the CAPM are preserved when the presence of nonmarketable assets is explicitly introduced. The expected return on each risky asset continues to be a linear function of the expected return on the market portfolio of marketable assets. The only change is, essentially, that each asset's risk must now be measured more broadly to include its covariance with nonmarketable asset returns.

Consumption-Based Asset Pricing Models

Ultimately, what is important for the investor is not portfolio return and risk, but how that return and risk impact on the investor's underlying goal of future consumption. Essentially, we ought to be able to tie security return and risk to this ultimate goal by seeing how securities *contribute* to future consumption. One model of asset prices has done this. That model measures how an individual investment opportunity contributes to the expected consumption value of national output (analogous to an aggregate national dividend) and to the expected growth of national output (analogous to aggregate national capital gains), as well as how it contributes to the risk that those expectations will not be met.

Not surprisingly, the model is called the **consumption-based capital-asset pricing model.** By assessing how individual securities contribute to expected consumption and the standard deviation of consumption, it provides a way to define equilibrium-expected returns and prices for securities. In this model,

(8A–6)
$$E(\tilde{R}_i) = R_f + \beta_i^c [E(\tilde{R}_c) - R_f]$$
and

$$\beta_i^c = \frac{Cov(\tilde{R}_i, \tilde{R}_c)}{[\sigma(\tilde{R}_c)]^2}$$

where

R_i = the security's return

R_c = the consumption return on national wealth.

This model will give you different measures of risk and different equilibrium-expected returns than the standard CAPM if, as would be expected, R_c is not the same as R_m.

References

Black, Fischer. [1972] "Capital Market Equilibrium with Restricted Borrowing." *Journal of Business* (July).

Brealey, Richard A. [1969] *An Introduction to Risk and Return from Common Stocks*. Cambridge, Mass.: M.I.T. Press.

Breeden, D. T. [1979] "An Intertemporal Asset Pricing Model with Stochastic Consumption and Investment Opportunities." *Journal of Financial Economics* (June).

Brennan, Michael. [1971] "Capital Market Equilibrium with Divergent Borrowing and Lending Rates." *Journal of Financial and Quantitative Analysis* (December).

Brennan, Michael. [1970] "Taxes, Market Valuation and Corporate Financial Policy." *National Tax Journal* 23 (December).

Brito, N. O. [1977] "Marketability Restrictions and the Valuation of Capital Assets under Uncertainty." *Journal of Finance* (September).

Constantinides, George M. [1982] "Intertemporal Asset Pricing with Heterogeneous Consumers and without Demand Aggregation." *Journal of Business* (April).

Donaldson, John B., and Mehra, Rajnish. [1984] "Comparative Dynamics of an Equilibrium Intertemporal Asset Pricing Model." *Review of Economic Studies*.

Elton, Edwin, and Gruber, Martin J. [1984] "Nonstandard C.A.P.M's and the Market Portfolio." *Journal of Finance* (July).

Fama, Eugene F. [1968] "Risk, Return, and Equilibrium: Some Clarifying Comments." *Journal of Finance* (March).

Fama, Eugene. [1971] "Risk, Return, and Equilibrium." *Journal of Political Economy* (January–February).

Fama, Eugene F., and Schwert, G. William. [1977] "Human Capital and Capital Market Equilibrium," *Journal of Financial Economics* (December).

Friend, I.; Landskroner, Y.; and Losq, E. [1976] "The Demand for Risky Assets under Uncertain Inflation." *Journal of Finance* (December).

Friend, Irwin, and Westerfield, Randolph. [1980] "Co-Skewedness and Capital Asset Pricing." *Journal of Finance* (September).

Gonedes, Nicholas. [1976] "Capital Market Equilibrium for a Class of Heterogeneous Expectations in a Two-Parameter World." *Journal of Finance* (March).

Hagerman, R. L., and Kim, E. H. [1976] "Capital Asset Pricing with Price Level Changes." *Journal of Financial and Quantitative Analysis* (September).

Hess, A. C. [1975] "The Riskless Rate of Interest and the Market Price of Risk." *Quarterly Journal of Economics* (August).

Jarrow, Robert. [1980] "Heterogeneous Expectations, Restrictions on Short Sales, and Equilibrium Asset Prices." *Journal of Finance* (December).

Jensen, Michael. [1972] "Capital Markets, Theory and Evidence." *Bell Journal of Economics and Management Science* 3 (Autumn).

Jensen, Michael D. (Ed.). [1972] *Studies in the Theory of Capital Markets*. New York: Praeger Publishers.

Klemkosky, R. C., and Martin, John D. [1975] "The Effect of Market Risk on Portfolio Diversification." *Journal of Finance* (March).

Landskroner, Y. [1977] "Intertemporal Determination of Time-Varying Systematic Risk." *Journal of Finance* (December).

Levy, H. [1980] "The CAPM and Beta in an Imperfect Market." *Journal of Portfolio Management* (Winter).

Lintner, John. [1969] "The Aggregation of Investors' Diverse Judgments and Preferences in Purely Competitive Security Markets." *Journal of Financial and Quantitative Analysis* (December).

Lintner, John. [1965] "The Valuation of Risk Assets and the Selection of Risky Investments in Stock Portfolios and Capital Budgets." *Review of Economics and Statistics* (February).

Litzenberger, Robert, and Ramaswamy, Krishna. [1979] "The Effect of Personal Taxes and Dividends on Capital Asset Prices." *Journal of Financial Economics* (June).

Mayers, David. [1972] "Nonmarketable Assets and Capital Market Equilibrium under Uncertainty." In *Studies in the Theory of Capital Markets,* ed. Michael Jensen. New York: Praeger Publishers.

Mayshar, Joram. [1981] "Transaction Costs and the Pricing of Assets." *Journal of Finance* (June).

Modigliani, Franco, and Pogue, Gerald A. [1974] "An Introduction to Risk and Return." *Financial Analysts Journal* (March–April; Part II, May–June).

Mossin, Jan. [1966] "Equilibrium in a Capital Asset Market." *Econometrica* 34 (October).

Owen, Joel, and Rabinovitch, Ramon. [1980] "The Cost of Information and Equilibrium in the Capital Asset Market." *Journal of Financial and Quantitative Analysis* (September).

Rabinovitch, R., and Owen, J. [1979] "Nonhomogeneous Expectations and Information in the Capital Asset Market." *Journal of Finance* (May).

Roll, Richard. [1977] "A Critique of Asset Pricing Theory's Tests." *Journal of Financial Economics* (March).

Ross, S. A. [1977] "The Capital Asset Pricing Model (CAPM), Short-Sale Restrictions and Related Issues," *Journal of Finance* (March).

Ross, S. A. [1978] "The Current Status of the Capital Asset Pricing Model (CAPM)." *Journal of Finance* (June).

Schipper, Katherine, and Thompson, Rex. [1981] "Common Stocks as Hedges against Shifts in the Consumption or Investment Opportunity Set." *Journal of Business* (April).

Seppi, Duane J. [1986] "Asset Market Equilibrium with Block Trading." Working Paper, University of Chicago (January).

Sharpe, William F. [1964] "Capital Asset Prices: A Theory of Market Equilibrium under Conditions of Risk." *Journal of Finance*.

Sharpe, William F. [1970] *Portfolio Theory and Capital Markets.* New York: McGraw-Hill.

Stulz, Rene M. [1985] "Asset Pricing and Expected Inflation." Working Paper, M.I.T. Press (September).

Sundaresan, Suresh M. [1985] "Portfolio Selection and Equilibrium Asset Pricing with Intertemporally Dependent Preferences." Working Paper, Columbia University (October).

Treynor, Jack. [1961] "Toward a Theory of the Market Value of Risky Assets." Unpublished manuscript.

Williams, J. T. [1977] "Capital Asset Prices with Heterogeneous Beliefs." *Journal of Financial Economics* (November).

Questions and Problems

1. Which of the following is not required in calculating a portfolio's expected rate of return using the capital-asset pricing model? (The portfolio is not the market portfolio.)
   a. Expected return of the market.
   b. Standard deviation of return.
   c. Portfolio beta.
   d. Risk-free rate.

   CFA

2. The portfolio risk that cannot be reduced through diversification is that inherent in:
   a. Individual securities.
   b. Each asset class.
   c. The overall market.
   d. Common industry factors.

   CFA

3. Market risk (the variability of R_m) can accurately be described by which of these statements:
   a. It is one important source of an investor's total variability of return.
   b. It causes price fluctuations which can be diversified away.
   c. It affects virtually all stocks in the same way and to the same degree.
   d. It is less important during rising markets.

   CFA

4. A Wall Street analyst once criticized the capital-asset pricing model by noting: "Look, during the period between 1976 and 1981 the stocks that had high betas also had very low returns. The theory simply can't explain that. Something is wrong with the theory." Critique the criticism.

5. The capital market line indicates the relationship between the standard deviation of returns on the optimal risky efficient market portfolio and the returns expected from that portfolio. Explain why this line identifies the best set of risk and return opportunities available to each investor, regardless of that investor's preferences.

6. The security market line indicates the relationship between individual security risk and individual security equilibrium-expected returns. What does "individual security risk" consist of and why does beta measure this determinant of return?

7. Construct a graph showing the security market line, and calculate the required equilibrium rates of return on the securities listed.

Per Common Share

	TMC	KRN
Current price	$39.00	$27.75
Annual dividend	1.10	.62
1986 earnings per share	2.90	1.80
1987 earnings per share	3.30	2.15
Value Line beta	1.05	.95
Risk-free rate of return	10%	
Expected market return	15%	

CFA

8. Suppose the return available on each security in Question 7, when purchased at their current market price, is 15 percent. Are these securities overvalued, undervalued, or priced in equilibrium according to the CAPM?

CFA (rephrased)

9. Interpret the meaning of each of the values that make up the definition of the security market line, including: $E(\tilde{R}_i)$, R_f, β_i, and $E(\tilde{R}_m) - R_f$.

10. Suppose you invested in the bonds of LTV corporation some time ago. They were originally issued at $1,000 per bond and promised a $110 payment per year for 20 years. LTV entered bankruptcy proceedings in 1986 as a result of poor performance of the economy and of the management. In one year, however, they are expected to exit from bankruptcy. The liquidation and reorganization of the firm is expected to result in a payment to bondholders of $250 per bond in one year. There is a good deal of risk to this arrangement though, and the market believes a beta of 1.5 is appropriate for this investment. If the risk-free rate now is 6 percent, and the expected return on the market portfolio is 12 per-

cent, what would the bonds sell for in equilibrium? Does the fact that you invested in these bonds at a much higher price than they are expected to sell for now affect either your calculation or your willingness to continue to hold them as part of your portfolio?

11. How would the slope or intercept of the security market line, or the importance of other variables in determining equilibrium-expected returns on securities change if:

    a. There is no risk-free security but investors could sell short securities and use the proceeds to buy more of the market portfolio.

    b. Human capital or other nonmarketable assets are an important part of investor wealth.

    c. Investors have different expectations of security returns, standard deviations, and covariances.

    d. There are differential tax rates applied to dividends, capital gains, and tax "shelters."

12. Why is it that the standard deviation of a security's return is deficient in measuring the contribution of the security to the risk of a diversified portfolio?

13. How do securities contribute to a portfolio's return?

14. How do securities contribute to a portfolio's standard deviation?

15. The returns of a security are perfectly correlated with the returns of the market portfolio. Which of the following statements is correct?

    a. The security's beta always equals one.

    b. The security has no unsystematic risk.

    c. The security's variance is always the same as that of the market portfolio.

    d. The security's expected return will plot below the security market line.

16. Which of the following statements is true?

    a. Portfolios that plot on the security market line (SML) are *all* efficient.

    b. Portfolios that plot on the SML are all inefficient.

    c. *Both* efficient and inefficient portfolios plot on the SML.

    d. *Only* securities plot on the SML.

17. The equilibrium-expected return for an individual risky security must account for:

    a. The reward per unit of time.

    b. The reward per unit of risk.

c. The contribution of the individual security to the risk of the market portfolio.

d. All of the above.

18. Consider these investment opportunities:

a. One security with beta equal 1.5.

b. A portfolio of securities with a weighted average beta of 1.5.

c. Borrow 50 percent of your equity (your own investment) at the risk-free rate and invest all the money in the market portfolio.

Which of the following statements about the three investment opportunities are incorrect?

a. All have the same systematic risk.

b. All have the same total risk (i.e., variance of return).

c. All will have the same equilibrium-expected return according to the CAPM.

d. In equilibrium, all three will lie on the security market line.

e. Investment C will lie on the capital market line.

Capital Asset Pricing: Evidence

According to the capital-asset pricing model, a security's beta determines its equilibrium-expected return. Specifically, the CAPM says that the return we expect to earn if a security is priced in equilibrium is a positive linear function of its beta. Moreover, if a security has no comovement with the market, it has no risk when included in a well-diversified portfolio, and its return should equal the risk-free rate of interest. In other words, equilibrium-expected returns are defined by the security market line (SML).

This concept is an important key to understanding the demand for securities and how they are priced. Therefore, it behooves us to examine whether or not actual securities markets conform to this simple description. We first need to have a solid basis for measuring security betas and expected returns. Second, we need to estimate the empirical relationship between betas and expected returns to see if it conforms to the SML. In a sense, the issue is as simple as plotting return/beta combinations for securities, and comparing the plot to the theoretically correct SML. In actual (nonlaboratory) financial markets, however, the task is complicated by an inability to directly observe betas and expected returns, and by the evolution of the market which is constantly changing as new information changes expectations.

In the first part of this chapter we concentrate on developing further our understanding of beta and the problems that play havoc with our measurement of it. In the last part of the chapter we discuss the measurement of expected returns and betas and estimation of the SML. The chapter closes with our evaluation of whether or not the numbers fit the theory.

The Market Model

Let's start by proposing a very simple model that describes the return on a security, i, in a given time period, t, as a function of the returns generated in that time period on some broad-based market index, I. One way to summarize this relationship is with the expression:

(9–1)   ***The Market Model***

$$\tilde{R}_{it} = \hat{\alpha}_i + \hat{\beta}_i \tilde{R}_{It} + \tilde{e}_{it}$$

$$\frac{Security}{returns} = \frac{A \; linear \; function \; of \; returns}{on \; an \; index \; of \; all \; securities}$$

This description, called the **market model,** says that the return on security i during time period t is a linear function of the return on market index I during that same time period, and a function of other factors that are summarized in the added term e for that security during that time period. Thus, we are attempting to "explain" the security's return over an interval of time with two *factors.* One of these factors is the return on a market index, with the coefficient β_i measuring how the security return moves with the index return. The other is a conglomeration of everything else that determines the security's return that is not captured in $\tilde{R}_{It}$.

It might seem like this process is so unrealistic that it could not possibly capture the complexities of the market sufficiently well to explain actual returns. But this is not the case. Empirical estimates of this relationship with the use of regression analysis (treating R_I as the independent variable and e_i as the error term) have determined that between 10 percent and 50 percent of the variability of individual stock returns over time can be explained by the return on market indexes like the S&P 500 or the NYSE Composite index, i.e., the coefficient of determination, or R^2 is between .1 and .5 for most stocks. The explanatory power of this relationship is higher for larger firms and firms that have productive operations in sectors of the economy that move closely with overall economic trends and expectations, and lower for smaller enterprises and those that are operating in unique business environments.

There is, of course, a logical explanation for the relatively close connection between a security's return and that of a market index. All stocks are affected to some degree by general economic expectations regarding unemployment and economic growth. Moreover, because the present value of any future cash flow is inversely related to changes in the rate at which the cash flows are discounted, changes in interest rates will tend to affect the returns generated during the time period when the interest rates change. The return on the market index, R_I, captures these aggregate effects, at least if it is a "representative" market index.

Security Characteristic Lines

The "explanatory" equation above also can be used as a predictive equation. Thus:

(9–2)   ***Security Characteristic Line***

$$E(\tilde{R}_{it} \mid R_{It}) = \hat{\alpha}_i + \hat{\beta}_i R_{It}$$

FIGURE 9–1   The Characteristic Line for Security *i*

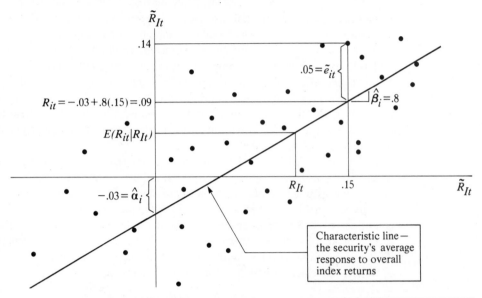

says that the expected return on security *i* at time *t*, given the index's return equals constant, $\hat{\alpha}_i$, plus another constant, $\hat{\beta}_i$, times the index's return. The actual return on security *i*, R_{it}, may not be equal to the expected value because of the random error $\tilde{e}_{it}$. The straight-line relationship in Equation (9–2) is depicted graphically in Figure 9–1. The vertical axis in the figure shows the various returns, R_{it}, which might possibly be earned by security *i* at time *t*; the horizontal axis shows the same thing for the index. By varying the *actual* return on the index in Equation (9–2), we vary our conditional prediction, $E(\tilde{R}_{it})$, for the returns on *i*. As we do this, we trace out the straight line in the figure. The line thus traced is called security *i*'s **market model characteristic line.**

To illustrate the use of a security's characteristic line, suppose we want to *predict i*'s period *t* return if the market index earns a return of 15 percent in that period. Assume *i*'s $\hat{\alpha}_i$ value equals − 3 percent, and its $\hat{\beta}_i$ value equals 0.8. Inserting these into (9–2), we see that $E(\tilde{R}_{it}|R_{It}) = -.03 + (.08)(.15) = .09$. We therefore predict security *i* would earn a return of 9 percent in *t*, *conditional* on the index earning a return of 15 percent. However, if the index earns only a 12 percent return, *i*'s return will fall to $.066 = -.03 + (.08)(.12)$. Of course, when the index's return is zero, *i*'s return will be $-.03 = -.03 + (0.8)(0)$. And so on. By varying the index's returns, we vary *i*'s returns along the straight line in the figure. Thus, the slope, $\hat{\beta}_i$, is also called the response coefficient.

It should be pointed out that unless security *i* has returns which are *perfectly correlated* with the market index the conditional predictions generated by equation (9–2)—the characteristic line—will often be wrong ex post. There are likely to be a great many other variables which affect security *i*'s returns over time, such as whether the company's chief executive officer dies or resigns or whether management makes a major new technological advance. These variables would not ordinarily be captured by the factors which are common to other securities' returns. They may be thought of as, in some sense, unique to security i. When Prudential Insurance Company faces a loss of $180 million in government contracts, the returns on other common stocks—especially those not in the life insurance business—will probably be unaffected. Similarly, when the United Auto Workers strike against Ford Motor Company, the major impact will be on Ford and its suppliers. Minor ripple effects may hit other industries but for the most part the effect will be concentrated in unique impacts on Ford. Finally, when USX receives a takeover offer, it is only USX stockholders that gain the benefits. The impacts of these unique events on the individual stocks in question will not be captured by their characteristic lines. Rather, they will be included in $\tilde{e}_{it}$.

If the conditional expected return, or the characteristic line itself (and its coefficients $\hat{\alpha}_i$ and $\hat{\beta}_i$), is estimated by regressing R_i on R_I, the e_i term will have an expected value of zero (an assumption on which the regression is based). Thus, we can think of the security's return in any period as the characteristic line plus an error term, e_{it}. If the conditions exist for consistent and unbiased estimation of the characteristic line with regression analysis, the error term will capture the effect of period t's events that *uniquely* influence i's return. In other words, we can summarize the return on a security in a period of time as the characteristic line plus the error term, or

(9–3)
$$\tilde{R}_{it} = E(\tilde{R}_{it} \mid R_{It}) + \tilde{e}_{it}$$

Sometimes the observed return on i will be below or above the level expected, but on average it will equal our predicted level.

This description of returns also is tied into the efficient market hypothesis. If price efficiency exists, new information that uniquely influences the value of security i will be fully reflected in i's price. Thus, e_{it} will be different from zero when the information is released to the market and only when it is released to the market. As a result of the efficiency of the market e_{it} will be positive when good information is delivered to the market, and negative when bad information is delivered. Over time the e_{it} values will be independent of one another, reflecting only the impact of new information that is released in t.

The two equations (9–2) and (9–3) which define the characteristic line for a security are together equivalent to Equation (9–1), which we earlier used to define the market model:

$$\underset{\substack{\text{Actual} \\ \text{return} \\ \text{on } i \text{ in} \\ \text{period } t}}{\tilde{R}_{it}} = \underset{\substack{\text{Conditional} \\ \text{prediction of} \\ i\text{'s return in} \\ \text{period } t}}{\underbrace{\hat{\alpha}_i + \hat{\beta}_i\tilde{R}_{It}}} + \underset{\substack{i\text{'s return} \\ \text{in period } t \\ \text{due to} \\ \text{unique} \\ \text{factors}}}{\underbrace{\tilde{e}_{it}}}$$

To summarize, the actual return observed on security i at time t can be expressed as the sum of two components: *(a)* a prediction of security i's return conditional on the index's return in period t, or its characteristic line, and *(b)* a random error due to factors uniquely affecting security i's returns and unrelated to the index's returns.

Note in Figure 9–1 that there is a scatter of dots around the characteristic line. The vertical distance from any one of these points to the characteristic line measures the value of e_{it} for time period t and given R_{It}. For example, consider our prediction that security i's return will be 9 percent at time t if the index's return is 15 percent. Although our conditional forecast for R_i is unbiased on average, in any given period the actual return might be different from the 9 percent expected return. How far off depends on the importance of unique factors in that time period. Suppose i's actual return at time t turns out to be 14 percent. Then, the random error $e_{it} = +.05$, as shown in Figure 9–1.

The Market Portfolio Revisited

As you might suspect, the concepts presented above have some important ties to the CAPM. First, and perhaps most obvious, $\hat{\beta}_i$ refers to the slope of the market model characteristic line. Is this the same β_i we introduced as a theoretical risk measure in the CAPM? The answer to this question is a qualified "yes."

The β defined in the context of our CAPM discussion in Chapter 8 (Equation 8-14) is,

(8-14)   ***CAPM β***

$$\beta_i = \frac{Cov(\tilde{R}_i, \tilde{R}_m)}{[\sigma(\tilde{R}_m)]^2}$$

The $\hat{\beta}$ defined by the slope of a plot of points in R_i, R_I space, in Figure 9–1 or Equation (9–1), is[1]

(9–4)   ***Market Model β***

$$\hat{\beta}_i = \frac{Cov(\tilde{R}_i, \tilde{R}_I)}{[\sigma(\tilde{R}_I)]^2}$$

The two β's are the same if the index of market returns, R_{It}, and the market portfolio, R_m, are the same.

To make a long story short, if the index, I, contains all risky securities in proportion to their aggregate equilibrium values, a security's market model beta will equal its CAPM beta. In this sense, the market model is consistent with the CAPM. In addition, the model also allows us to gain some important insights concerning the economic interpretation of beta. Since the CAPM implies that beta is the relevant measure of risk for individual securities, it must be that the slope of a security's market model characteristic line says something about the security's risk. The higher a security's beta, the steeper the slope of its characteristic line, and, we would think, the higher its equilibrium-expected return.

In the discussions which follow, we interpret the parameters of the market model characteristic line in light of the CAPM's implications.

---

[1] If you view Equation 9–1 as a simple regression equation where the constant and slope ($\hat{\alpha}_i$ and $\hat{\beta}_i$) are determined by minimizing the sum of the squared error terms, $\tilde{e}_{it}$, then the market model β is simply the covariance divided by the variance of the independent variable, R_I.

Beta and the Components of Risk

The greater the slope of the security's characteristic line, or $\hat{\beta}$, the greater its risk. Why is this? The reasoning is as follows:

> On average, and in a well-diversified portfolio made up of a number of securities, each with the same slope, the deviations of portfolio return from a point on the characteristic line will be small—close to zero—because the error terms, $\tilde{e}_{it}$, being unique to i and t, are independent from one security to another. As a result, any variation in the rate of return on the market portfolio then will be matched by variations on this portfolio of like β firms. Thus, as R_I varies from time period to time period, R_i will also vary—and on average will vary in proportion to security i's $\hat{\beta}$.
>
> For example, if a security's $\hat{\beta}$ is .8, for every unit change in R_I, the security's return on average will change by .8. If $\hat{\beta}$ is 1.2 for every unit change in R_I the value of R_i will change by 1.2. Risk for this second security is 50 percent greater 1.2/8 = 150 percent) than the risk of the first security.

Another way to view the security's β is to take total security variance $[\sigma(\tilde{R}_{it})]^2$ and break it down into its component parts. One term will be related to variability that can be traced to β and R_I. A second term will be related to variability associated with that security's random error or unique factors. This can be written algebraically as:

$$
\begin{array}{cccc}
(9\text{--}5) & [\sigma(\tilde{R}_{it})]^2 & = & \hat{\beta}_i^2[\sigma(\tilde{R}_{It})]^2 & + & [\sigma(\tilde{e}_{it})]^2 \\
& \textit{Total variance} & & \textit{Systematic} & & \textit{Unsystematic} \\
& \textit{of security i's} \; = & & \textit{variance} & + & \textit{variance} \\
& \textit{returns} & & \textit{(risk)} & & \\
& & & \| & & \| \\
& & & \textit{Variance} & & \textit{Variance due} \\
& & = & \textit{explained by} & & \textit{to factors} \\
& & & \textit{index's} & & \textit{unique to} \\
& & & \textit{movements} & & \textit{security i.}
\end{array}
$$

The first term in (9–5), $\hat{\beta}_i^2[\sigma(\tilde{R}_{It})]^2$, is termed **systematic,** *or* **market-related variance.** It is the covariance of security i's returns with the points which lie exactly on the characteristic line for security i in Figure 9–1.

The second term is $[\sigma(\tilde{e}_{it})]^2$, which is termed security i's **unsystematic, nonmarket,** *or* **residual variability.** It is the variability of the error terms about the characteristic line. It measures, intuitively, the extent to which components of i's returns are unique to i and are not explained by movements in the index's returns.

Examples of Calculated βs

We can use the calculation in Equation (9–4) to compute actual $\hat{\beta}$s. However, actual empirical estimation of these relationships requires the use of time series data. Conse-

TABLE 9–1   **Calculation of a β Coefficient**

Month End, t	$\bar{R}_{XONt}$ Return on Exxon	$\bar{R}_{It}$ Return on S&P Index	Calculated Covariance $Cov(\bar{R}_{XON}, \bar{R}_I)$	Calculated Variance $\sigma(\bar{R}_I)$
1/81	−.035	−.046	(−.035 − .005)(−.046 − .008) = .0021	.0014
2/81	−.056	.013	−.0003	.0000
3/81	−.047	.036	−.0014	.0008
.	.	.	.	.
.	.	.	.	.
.	.	.	.	.
9/85	−.017	−.035	.0009	.0018
10/85	.060	.043	.0019	.0012
11/85	−.014	.065	−.0001	.0032
12/85	.032	.040	.0009	.0010
Sum	.300	.480	.0811	.0965
Mean return	.005	.008	$Cov\,(R_{XON}, R_I) = .00135$	$\sigma(R_I)^2 = .00161$

$$\hat{\beta}_{XON} = \frac{Cov(\bar{R}_{XON}, \bar{R}_I)}{[\sigma(\bar{R}_I)]^2} = \frac{.00135}{.00161} = .84$$

quently, expected value, covariance, and standard deviation calculations using time series data have to be written as $E(\bar{R}_i)$, $Cov(\bar{R}_i,\bar{R}_j)$, $\sigma(\bar{R}_i)$, and $Cov(\bar{e}_i,\bar{e}_j)$ without the subscript t. Only the actual value of returns will be written with the subscript t to indicate which particular data point they measure; i.e., R_{it} and R_{It}. For example, using the Standard & Poor's Index to calculate R_{It} and price and dividend data for Exxon Corporation as R_{it}, we can compute Exxon's $\hat{\beta}$. In this case, monthly data for a five-year period is used, and the calculations are shown in Table 9–1. Thus, t is a one-month interval and there are 60 observations used in the calculation. In the first month (January 1981) the return on Exxon was −3.5 percent; the S&P index returned −4.6 percent. The arithmetic mean return over the entire period was .5 percent per month for Exxon and .8 percent for the index. For the covariance the first number to calculate is (−.035 − .005) times (−.046 − .008), or .0021. The first number for the calculation of the variance is (−.046 − .008)², or .0014. Given the covariance calculation and a calculation for the variance of the index, the estimated $\hat{\beta}$ for Exxon is .84.

Alternatively, the $\hat{\beta}$ could be determined by using Equation (9–1) as a simple regression model. The slope of a least-squares regression is calculated as in Equation (9–4), so the approaches yield the same number, .84. We can also measure the correlation between $\bar{R}_{XON}$ and $\bar{R}_I$. In this case it is .42, so that about 18 percent of the month-to-month variability of Exxon's stock value can be traced to the month-to-month movement of all stocks ($.42^2 \approx .18$).

A second example is presented graphically in Figure 9–2. This is a plot of Weyerhauser's returns with the returns on S&P's index. The slope is 1.14, indicating a $\hat{\beta}$ that is somewhat greater than the market average. The correlation is .7, so that 50 percent of the variance in Weyerhauser returns is accounted for by the variation in market returns.

As you might expect, computers, canned programs, and data tapes with returns on securities make the computation of βs, αs, variances, covariances, and correlations a

FIGURE 9–2   Plot of Weyerhauser and the S&P 500 Index

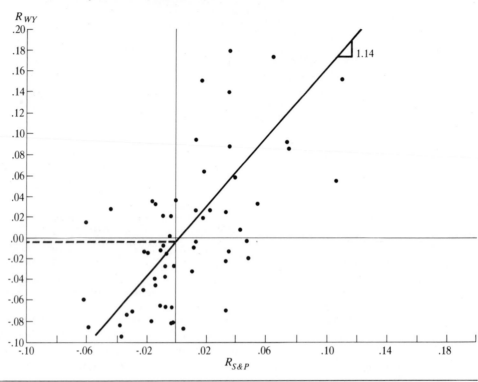

simple matter. Many brokerage houses compute these statistics and offer them to their clients as information regarding the characteristics of a given security's risk and return. Others take the simple calculations and try to improve on them in much the same way as banks might compete for business by offering economic forecasts. The hope, of course, is to build better betas; a subject we treat in depth in the following chapters on security valuation.

Alpha and Equilibrium Valuation

There is also a relationship between the intercept of the market model, $\hat{\alpha}_i$, and the capital-asset pricing model. To see this relation we will move into the world of expectations, and act as if we are analyzing securities for possible portfolio choice for the next investment period. Suppose there are three securities whose ex ante characteristic lines have the same slope, but different intercepts as Figure 9–3. Assume also that the return on the market index, R_I, represents the market portfolio return, R_m. If these relationships exist ex ante, then the investors would not be indifferent between holding A, B, or C. Since, for any given value for the return on the market index, the return on security A is higher, A would be preferred by all. There would be excess demand for A relative to B and C, and the relative price of A would rise. This would reduce A's return (since investors must pay more). The shifting would continue until A offered the same as B.

FIGURE 9–3 Characteristic Lines in Disequilibrium

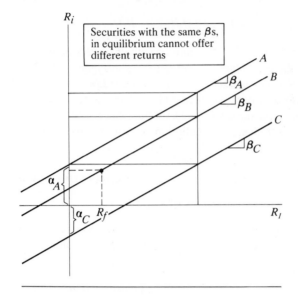

FIGURE 9–4 Characteristic Lines and Market Equilibrium

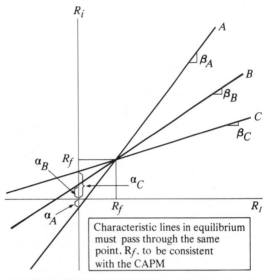

For C there would be an excess supply of the security, reducing its price and shifting its characteristic line upward. Equilibrium would be achieved only when all securities with the same slope (risk or $\hat{\beta}$) have the same intercept. This is exactly the interpretation given to security market equilibrium with the security market line (SML), but it is represented in terms of characteristic lines.

Moreover, regardless of the slope, the line would have to pass through the point R_f. Otherwise we could use the risk-free asset and the market index in a portfolio that (held long or short) could dominate any given individual security. Consequently, while the ex ante relationship in Figure 9–3 could not continue to hold given the pressures of competition to move markets toward equilibrium, in equilibrium the relationship in Figure 9–4 would have to hold. Thus:

> For the market model to be consistent with the CAPM in equilibrium, each risky security must possess an α such that the characteristic line passes through the coordinates R_f, R_f. The value of α that fulfills this requirement is $\hat{\alpha}_i = (1 - \hat{\beta}_i)R_f$.

This conclusion ties the market model directly to the CAPM. If R_I represents R_m, then the *market model* in equilibrium would be (note the lack of ^s over the coefficients),

Market Model

$$\tilde{R}_{it} = \alpha_i + \beta_i\tilde{R}_{mt} + \varepsilon_{it} = (1 - \beta_i)R_{ft} + \beta_i(\tilde{R}_{mt}) + \tilde{\varepsilon}_{it}$$

In the form of expected returns in equilibrium,

CAPM

$$E(\tilde{R}_i) = \alpha_i + \beta_i E(\tilde{R}_m) = R_f + \beta_i[E(\tilde{R}_m) - R_f]$$

because $\alpha_i = (1 - \beta_i)R_f$. This condition forces all securities with characteristic lines in equilibrium to have those lines positioned so that they all cross at R_f as in Figure 9–4. *Only in this case will they all lie on the security market line, which relates $E(\tilde{R}_i)$ to β_i.*

But what about securities whose α_i values are below $(1 - \beta_i)R_f$ as security C in Figure 9–3? This security must plot *below* the security market line, since such a security offers an expected return which is less than the equilibrium return investors require. Therefore:

Security Is Overvalued

$$\alpha_i < (1 - \beta_i)R_f$$

In contrast, securities like A whose α_i values exceed $(1 - \beta_i)R_f$ must plot *above* the security market line. They offer expected returns which are greater than their equilibrium levels. For these securities:

Security Is Undervalued

$$\alpha_i > (1 - \beta_i)R_f$$

For the sake of completion, then:

Security Is Priced in Equilibrium

$$\alpha_i = (1 - \beta_i)R_f$$

Such securities plot *on* the security market line and earn just the equilibrium-expected return.

Note that if the market's return is above R_f, the higher a security's beta, the higher its return conditional on the market's return. However, when the market's return is below R_f, the reverse situation holds. That is why high-beta securities are viewed as riskier than low-beta securities; their returns vary to a greater degree. While they are outstanding performers in market upturns, they can be disasters in market downturns.

Of course, ex post, these relationships do not need to hold. A security may do so poorly over a given period that $\hat{\alpha}$ is well below $(1 - \hat{\beta}_i)R_f$. Yet if it is priced in *equilibrium* for *this* investment period, α_i equals $(1 - \tilde{\beta}_i)R_f$ as long as the CAPM governs the way *expected* returns are established.

Portfolio Characteristic Lines

Like individual securities, portfolios of securities also have market model characteristic lines. In fact these intercepts and slope coefficients, or αs and βs, are variables that can be added and subtracted like returns and covariances (but not like standard deviations).

Thus, a portfolio's alpha and beta would be simply a weighted average of the αs and βs of the securities that make up the portfolio, or

(9–6)   ***The Portfolio's Alpha***

$$\hat{\alpha}_p \equiv \sum_{i=1}^{N} x_i \hat{\alpha}_i$$

The Portfolio's Beta

$$\hat{\beta}_p \equiv \sum_{i=1}^{N} x_i \hat{\beta}_i$$

Moreover, the portfolio's error term in any period is simply the weighted average of the error terms of the individual securities, or

(9–7)   ***The Portfolio's***
Error Term

$$\tilde{e}_{pt} = \sum_{i=1}^{N} x_i \tilde{e}_{it}$$

Suppose we now construct a two-security portfolio. The first security has an alpha of .008 and a β of .6. Thus, its relationship with the index is given by:

$$E(\tilde{R}_{1t}) = +.008 + (0.6)(R_{It})$$

Its characteristic line is graphed in Figure 9–5. In contrast, security 2—the second security in the portfolio—has a relationship with the index that is given by:

$$E(R_{2t}) = -.05 + (2.0)(R_{It})$$

Its characteristic line is also depicted in Figure 9–5. Note that we have assumed—for the sake of illustration—that security 1 is overpriced relative to CAPM equilibrium (its alpha is .02 too small), while 2 is underpriced (its alpha is .02 too large). We have assumed also that the index to which we refer is the true market portfolio.

The *portfolio's* characteristic line is a simple weighted average of the characteristic lines of individual securities. The weights are determined by the portfolio proportions, x_i. For instance, a 50–50 investment in the two will yield a portfolio whose alpha is $(0.5)(.008) + (0.5)(-.05) = -.021$, or -2.1 percent. The beta is $(0.5)(0.6) + (0.5)(2.0) = 1.3$. The portfolio's characteristic line is thus:

$$E(\tilde{R}_{pt}) = -.021 + (1.3)(R_{It})$$

By varying the proportionate holdings, it is easy to achieve a portfolio with any target beta desired. Suppose you want a beta equal to 1.0. In what proportions must you hold the two securities? To answer this, you need only solve the following equation for x_1:

$$x_1 \hat{\beta}_1 + (1 - x_1)\hat{\beta}_2 = 1.0. = x_1(0.6) + (1 - x_1)(2.0)$$

The solution is $x_1 = .714$. Hence 71.4 percent of your funds should be devoted to security 1; the remaining 28.6 percent to security 2. The resulting portfolio will have an alpha

FIGURE 9–5   Portfolio Characteristic Lines

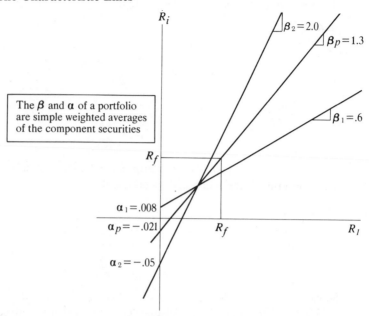

equal to $(.714)(.008) + (.286)(-.05) = -.009$. This example illustrates the following general principle:

> The characteristic line for a portfolio of securities is just a weighted average of the characteristic lines of the component securities, where the weights are the proportionate holdings in each security.

Now, an important practical aspect of portfolio construction is that the portfolio's error terms tend to be much smaller on average than those of the component securities. This phenomenon is directly related to the value of diversification. The intuitive explanation is related to a key statistical assumption that the error terms for individual securities are independent of one another. If, in a given period t, security i experiences a positive random error, this says nothing about whether security j's error will be positive, negative, or zero. Essentially, then, a portfolio which consists of both securities will have an error term which averages out these individual error terms. To the extent that these error terms are uncorrelated, the portfolio error term will be considerably smaller in absolute value than those of the two securities taken individually (by application of the law of large numbers, once again).[2]

---

[2]That is, as in Equation (9–5) for individual securities, a portfolio's variance when security returns are generated by the market model is: *(continued on next page)*

What we argued above is essentially that if the portfolio is sufficiently well diversified, the unsystematic risk approaches zero. That is because the "unique" factors peculiar to individual stocks tend to wash out in their effect on portfolio returns if enough individual stocks are held. Hence, as the number of different securities held grows, the unsystematic risk component of portfolio risk goes to zero. Graphically, we expect to see that the scatter of individual points around a portfolio's characteristic line should be concentrated closer to the line than is the case for individual securities.

For example, the Manhattan Fund for Income (a large mutual fund) has a correlation with the NYSE Index of about .9. Indeed, many mutual funds, which often hold 100 or more common stocks, frequently have correlation coefficients with market indexes like the S&P 500 that approach 0.95. This indicates that almost 90 percent of their returns are potentially explainable by so-called common factors measured by the market index.

If we carry this argument to an extreme and assume that the portfolio in question is the market portfolio, in which all stocks are held, the result immediately becomes obvious. The market portfolio, by definition, contains no unsystematic risk. Its returns are completely explained by overall market factors captured in the market index.

One of the morals of this tale is that predicting a *portfolio's* return in any future period conditional on the market's return is perhaps an easier task than making conditional predictions for *individual* securities. We expect that portfolios which are well diversified have correlations with the market index that are considerably higher than those for individual securities.

Application to the Value Line Contest

As an interesting application of the principles inherent in the CAPM and the market model, consider the case of the Value Line Investment Contest. From among 1,400 stocks rated by Value Line, individuals were permitted to pick 25 securities to be combined into an equally-weighted portfolio. The "winner" was the portfolio that generated the highest return.

Two perceptive academics theorized that, according to the market model and the CAPM, the most likely winning portfolios would come from the extremes of the range of βs. If the market goes up it is most likely that high βs will provide the highest return. On the other hand, if the market falls, the best performers will be those securities with low βs. Consequently, they selected two portfolios: one formed from the lowest 25 $\hat{\beta}$ securities, and one with the 25 highest $\hat{\beta}$ securities. During the August 18, 1972, to February 16, 1973, period of the contest the S&P index fell substantially. Not surprisingly, the low $\hat{\beta}$ portfolio outperformed the high $\hat{\beta}$ portfolio by a considerable margin. Further, of more than 90,000 contest entries, the low $\hat{\beta}$ portfolio ranked in the top 2.3 percent. The high $\hat{\beta}$ portfolio ranked in the bottom .6 percent. As an ex post proxy

$$[\sigma(\tilde{R}_{pt})]^2 = \hat{\beta}_p^2[\sigma(\tilde{R}_{It})]^2 + \sum_{i=1}^{N} x_i^2 [\sigma(\tilde{e}_{it})]^2$$

The first term on the right-hand side is the portion of the portfolio's total variance of returns that is explained by, or associated with, its comovement with the market index. The second term is the portfolio's unsystematic variability, or uncertainty that is not associated with marketwide factors. This variance is unique to the securities making up the portfolio, and approaches zero as N increases.

for return, portfolio $\hat{\beta}$ (for groups of 25 securities at least) was indeed an accurate discriminator.[3]

The Market Model and Empirical Estimates of the CAPM

The capital-asset pricing model as a description of the ex ante relationship between risks and returns of securities, must have some empirical support before we can begin to use it for valuing securities or for describing how security-expected returns are established. The market model was introduced for two reasons. First it provides some additional insight into the CAPM and the proper interpretation of security risk—the beta. Second, however, the market model provides an **empirical link** that allows us to test the theoretical relationships that are contained in the CAPM. It is to these empirical issues that we now turn.

Testing the Accuracy of the CAPM

The CAPM postulates a number of relationships for investment returns and risks. Each of these postulates is potentially testable. That is, the conclusions that are derived from the theory about markets and how people behave can be investigated to see if they conform to the principles established with our conceptual rationale.

However, there are all sorts of problems associated with testing economic theories such as the CAPM. In most cases there is no laboratory environment where the actions of individuals can be observed without influence from the confounding effects of other relationships or simply the passage of time. Moreover, it is almost impossible to observe directly the decision processes of consumers and investors to see if they conform with the processes we assume they follow. Instead, we often are forced to rely on what we can *observe* about the *result* of people's actions. Specifically, for example, we are unable to observe directly whether any individual investor has diminishing marginal utility for wealth. But we may be able to infer this result from an analysis of the portfolio the individual has selected.

And so it is with tests of the CAPM and the security market line. It is not possible to see if equilibrium-expected returns on securities and the betas of those securities line up in the way the theory prescribes. **We can't directly observe the *expected returns* and *perceived risks*** that investors have in mind when they make their decisions. Rather, **we have to use actual returns** that have been generated in past years through investment decisions, and attempt to infer whether the numbers are consistent with the CAPM. There is nothing wrong with this approach, of course, though the data may be contaminated by other unobservable influences. Empirical tests must be carefully formulated and inter-

---

[3]As a side note, the winning portfolio included 25 oil stocks. During 1973 this happened to be the approach that capitalized on a particular factor (the oil embargo) affecting a large number of firms (but not the market factor R_m). The importance of these widely influential factors, such as the oil embargo, interest rate changes, military spending, or other somewhat specific elements affecting some securities returns, is discussed in Chapter 10 when the arbitrage pricing model approach to valuation is considered. See Robert Kaplan and Roman Weil [1973].

pretations of any empirical results subjected to critical examination for effects of other influences. As an example, it has been found that smaller firms are continually "undervalued." Is this due to a problem with the theory, or due simply to problems associated with estimating the expected returns or betas of small and large firms? You will find out in the next few pages.

Implications of the CAPM

The following summarizes the basic tenets of the CAPM which are derived from the implication of the model that the market portfolio will be held by all investors as the best risky, efficient portfolio available in equilibrium.

(9–9) *CAPM*

$$E(\tilde{R}_i) = R_f + \beta_i[E(\tilde{R}_m) - R_f]$$

1. The expected return on any $\beta_i = 0$ asset is the risk-free return R_f, i.e., the intercept is R_f.
2. The greater is β_i the greater is the security expected return over and above R_f, i.e., the slope is positive, constant, and equal to the difference between the expected return on the market portfolio and the risk-free rate.
3. Only β_i is important in differentiating among security returns, i.e., there are no terms other than the risk-free rate and the premium for β that determine expected returns.

Testing the Model's Postulates

Ex Ante and Ex Post Data Problems

The largest problem associated with testing occurs because the model is an ex ante relationship. Both β and $E(\tilde{R}_i)$ are forecasted variables in the framework of the CAPM. *Expected* market returns are related to *expected* security returns via the security's ex ante β. Yet, expected returns and βs normally can't be observed (one exception is short-term riskless U.S. Treasury securities where expected returns match *current yields*). No one really knows whether the market expects the return on IBM's common stock to be 12 percent or 20 percent or its β to be .8 or 1.0. The market expectation is simply the aggregate of each individual investor's expectation, and the market does not reveal its expectations directly.

How can we overcome this problem? One way is to count on individuals behaving rationally. If individuals form their own expectations by making use of all readily available information (e.g., earnings forecasts or an understanding of macroeconomic relationships) and form rational forecasts as a basis for their decisions to invest or not, then actual returns will tend to reveal these expectations. Clearly, because of the uncertainty of random shocks to the economic system, actual returns will not always reveal expectations. They will only *tend* to reveal them, and will do so only over relatively long periods, or only on average. This is part of the data contamination problem alluded to earlier.

Suppose, for example, a drilling firm taps three wells per year. On average one out of every six wells produces harvestable oil worth $10 million. On the basis of this information, rational investors form expectations of cash flows (and their risk) and attempt to value the security. In any given year no productive wells may be struck and the returns to common stock may be lower than expected because of it. Some years, more than one may prove productive and the windfall would push ex post returns higher. Still expected returns may not change—they are based on the fundamentals which do not differ from year to year. On average over the long run, one would expect that ex post returns would tend to reflect what investors have determined is necessary or expected in view of the worth of a well and the long-run probability of successful exploration.

There are two potential problems that seem to arise in the application of these arguments to permit investigations using ex post returns to proceed. One, obviously, is that we don't know what a **sufficiently long-run period** is. The decade from 1968 to 1978 seemed to be one where there were constant shocks to the system in the form of increased inflationary expectations. These tended to have a dampening effect on stock prices so that ex post stock returns were below what one reasonably might have expected. Perhaps 10 years isn't long enough for averages to be borne out.

The second problem is that **expectations change.** Suppose the expected return on Consolidated Edison common stock was 11 percent in the 1960s, but rose to 15 percent in the 1970s. The change may have been due to increased perceived riskiness resulting from the uncertainty surrounding fuel prices, nuclear power, or even the willingness of Consolidated Edison's customers to pay their bills. Estimates using one segment of data may not conform to estimates from the other segment of data, thus limiting the conclusions that can be drawn.

In spite of these potential drawbacks, a good deal of information regarding investor behavior and the CAPM can be gleaned from ex post rates of return.

Estimating Betas and Returns

The first step in testing any of the CAPM postulates is to measure historical returns and βs. Returns, of course, can be calculated from the expression,

$$(9\text{--}10) \qquad R_{it} = \frac{P_{it} + D_{it} - P_{it-1}}{P_{it-1}}$$

for each security, i, over the time period $t - 1$ to t. The interval length between the initial assumed purchase price, P_{it-1}, and the sale price, P_{it}, may be from a few minutes to several years. Most often, for testing the CAPM postulates, returns have been calculated for daily, weekly, or monthly intervals.

Along with the returns on a set of individual securities, the estimation requires returns on the market portfolio. As noted, we cannot know for sure what this market portfolio is (since it is an ex ante value formed from investor expectations), but broad-based stock and bond market indexes have been used as a proxy for the unobservable, R_m. We have called this proxy R_I to differentiate between the CAPM and the market model. Most often, empirical work has used the Standard & Poor's Index, but the NYSE index and indexes computed from all stocks on the NYSE (both value-weighted and equal-weighted) have also been used.

The returns on these two series are then computed over many intervals of length t to form the basis for our estimates of $\hat{\beta}_i$, as we did for Exxon and Weyerhauser earlier. In the form of a simple linear time series regression of R_i on R_I,

(9–11)
$$R_{it} = \hat{\alpha}_i + \hat{\beta}_i R_{It} + \hat{e}_{it}$$

the security's characteristic line, or its $\hat{\alpha}_i$ and $\hat{\beta}_i$ are estimated. Table 9–2 shows the betas for a number of different common stocks estimated (1) at two different points in time, (2) for both weekly and monthly intervals, and (3) using the S&P 500 and NYSE indexes. The stocks' standard deviation of return and the goodness of fit of the regression equation are presented as well.

Thus, Procter & Gamble's risk level was estimated to be .41, based on monthly historical returns over the five years ending in 1985 and using the NYSE index for R_I. This would make P&G about 60 percent less risky than the average NYSE security. Based on the same data, the risks of Weyerhauser, Amax, Boeing, and UAL are greater than average, while the risks of Merck, MMM, and Texaco are estimated to be less than average. Boeing is about twice as risky as MMM and IBM. Merrill Lynch's beta is about 150 percent greater than that of the average security.

Many of these estimates may align with your intuitive understanding of security risk. It's not surprising that a firm like Merrill Lynch would be very risky, since its profitability is so closely tied to investment banking and brokerage activities that would swing with the movement of the stock market itself. Moreover, it's reasonable to expect IBM to be less risky than average since its share of the computer market seems to be effectively insulated from some of the volatility that has been experienced by other producers. Undoubtedly, UAL is more risky than the average security in the market (even though it owns the most stable airline route structure) because of the enormous fixed costs associated with this industry. Merrill Lynch, Navistar, UAL, and Amax have the highest standard deviation of returns. Procter & Gamble, Cascade Natural Gas, and Exxon have a low $\sigma(R_i)$. Not surprisingly, Merrill Lynch has the largest R^2 with the market index return.

A glance at other columns in the table, though, reveals an obvious problem. These different historical risk estimates vary, depending on how and when they are computed. The beta for 3M seems to have fallen from 1.19, based on data ending in 1979, to .76, based on the data ending in 1985. Navistar, on the other hand, saw its beta move in the opposite direction. Differences also exist between estimates based on weekly and monthly data, and, to a lesser extent, if based on the use of the S&P 500 index rather than the NYSE index. What faith can be placed in these estimates, and how can they provide a guide for understanding a company's risk? More to the point, which one is correct?

The answer, unfortunately, is not an easy one. However, it does serve to emphasize a point often overlooked by students and market practioners: risk *estimates* are just that! Risk, like expected return, is not directly observable for most securities. Investors are forced to forecast risk for the relevant investment period. Historically generated estimates of the true, but unobservable, level of risk may prove useful, but each contains errors that can cause the analyst to miss the mark. Each of the estimates in Table 9–2 contains errors of unknown magnitude. Our problem is to reduce the error as much as possible. And the existence of the errors should cause you to be cautious in the use of historical $\hat{\beta}$s for establishing the risk associated with a current investment in a security.

TABLE 9–2 Different Historical Estimates of Betas, β̂

Estimates of Beta, Using

Security	Industry	S&P Index Monthly (1985)	NYSE Index and R_t, R_t Interval			Standard Deviation of Annualized Return			Goodness of Fit R^2		
			Monthly 5 years		Weekly	Monthly 5 years		Weekly	Monthly 5 years		Weekly
		(1985)	(1985)	(1979)	(1985)	(1985)	(1979)	(1985)	(1985)	(1979)	(1985)
Cascade Nat Gas	Gas supplier	0.33	0.31	0.25	0.21	19.4%	22.0%	23.6%	5%	3%	1%
American Express	Cons. finance	1.24	1.16	n.a.	1.58	30.3	n.a.	24.2	30	n.a	46
Exxon	Oil	0.85	0.80	0.80	0.41	19.6	17.4	16.7	34	58	7
IBM	Computers	0.75	0.71	0.96	1.19	18.4	20.9	17.0	30	57	52
Navistar	Farm equip.	1.84	1.78	1.06	1.70	61.3	29.3	49.8	17	35	12
Johnson & Johnson	Medical prod.	0.76	0.70	0.88	1.18	22.6	22.6	20.8	19	40	34
Weyerhauser	Forest prod.	1.10	1.14	1.33	1.71	25.0	29.0	25.5	43	56	48
M.M.M.	Diversified	0.81	0.76	1.19	0.89	18.0	28.5	13.9	37	47	44
Merck	Drug	0.58	0.63	1.10	0.87	18.6	28.0	15.0	23	41	36
Merrill Lynch	Brokerage	2.47	2.51	2.33	2.45	49.1	49.2	34.5	54	60	54
Procter & Gamble	Household prod.	0.44	0.41	0.85	0.44	16.6	18.8	15.1	13	54	9
Sears	Retailing	1.17	1.15	0.96	1.26	28.5	24.7	20.1	34	40	41
UAL	Airlines	1.34	1.38	1.18	1.08	43.0	37.4	30.4	21	27	14
Texaco	Oil	0.90	0.85	0.90	0.33	27.9	20.0	15.9	19	54	5
Warner Comm.	Entertainment	1.17	1.12	1.34	1.30	46.6	33.7	30.1	12	43	20
Boeing	Airline mfg.	1.62	1.52	1.04	1.60	39.1	35.0	24.7	31	24	45
AMAX Inc	Metals mfg.	1.72	1.78	1.06	0.85	46.7	29.6	26.3	30	35	11
Bethelhem Steel	Steel	1.30	1.27	1.27	1.66	32.5	32.6	34.3	31	41	25
Campbell Soup	Food	0.26	0.18	0.61	0.64	23.6	19.2	21.8	1	31	9
Chase Manhatten	Banking	1.13	1.05	0.95	1.89	30.6	26.7	26.4	24	34	55
Average		1.09	1.06	1.06	1.16	30.9%	26.2%	24.3%	25%	41%	28%

n.a. = not available.
Source: Wharton School. University of Pennsylvania, and computed with MPS.

Specifically, commonly used beta estimates like those just presented suffer from a variety of potential problems. Some of these are **statistical** in nature, while others are caused by changes in underlying **economic** relationships. We will summarize the nature of these problems, and suggest what appears to be the best approach to dealing with them.

Statistical Problems.

(1) The Index Used.   If R_I, the index return used in the computation, is a poor proxy for R_m (the true but unobservable market return), the estimated β will not represent the security's risk. Clearly, if equilibrium security returns are established in view of the security's comovement with all investment opportunities, the use of an index that picks up only part of the market return will misrepresent the security's risk. The Dow Jones Industrial Average, made up of 30 of the largest NYSE securities, would not be representative of the overall market portfolio. The Standard & Poor's 500 and the NYSE indexes are both value-weighted and are more representative, but don't include over-the-counter securities, bonds, real estate, or foreign securities. Chances are they are relatively highly correlated with R_m and they may serve either as a reasonable proxy, or at least, the best proxy available. The use of an equally-weighted index, or an index that was specifically targeted to a narrow subset of the market would be inappropriate, because it would not accurately represent the makeup of *m*.

In fact, the estimates in Table 9–2 that are based on the S&P 500 are quite close to those based on the NYSE. The figures tend to be slightly higher when the S&P index is used, but this merely reflects that index's being made up of 500 firms that on the whole are larger and more stable than the 2200 in the NYSE index. The correlation between the two indexes is on the order of .95.

(2) The Return Measurement Interval.   Sometimes the length of *t,* the interval over which return is measured, affects the estimates. Monthly, weekly, and daily returns calculated using end-of-period prices are being used in the marketplace to compute betas. Theoretically, the use of daily data would be better since it includes more observations and improves the efficiency of the estimate. The numbers in Table 9–2 include monthly and weekly differencing interval estimates. The monthly values use five years of data. The weekly values use only one year of data.

Unfortunately, daily betas to a large extent, and weekly betas to a lesser extent are affected by problems that relate to the end-of-day price used to compute the security returns. One is that the last trade of the day in a thinly traded security can occur long before the close of trading on the market. Thus, the price used for the security is not *concurrent* with the price used for the market-index return calculation. For some very actively traded securities the last price of the day may be even later than that for the index, since the index is calculated from the most recent price available for all securities included in it. Monthly-return interval estimates are less subject to this **nonsynchronous trading** problem.

A second problem is that prices of some securities at the end of daily, weekly, or monthly intervals may reflect imperfections in the market price-setting process. To the extent that some prices may be temporarily affected by the actions of specialists or other market makers attempting to act for their own interests or to maintain "price continuity," the estimates of betas may be affected. (For example, the effect of traders closing out arbitrage positions in stocks and stock index futures when the future contracts mature four times a year, the so-called triple witching Fridays, may cause some prices to be temporarily distorted.)

The two problems seem to beset β estimates for smaller firms and more thinly traded firms. As a result, the historical β estimates for these firms are downward biased, or are below what they otherwise should be.

Scholes and Williams [1977] found a way of estimating this bias, and a means for attempting to correct for it. They estimate *three* slope coefficients by regressing security returns on the market index lagged one period, concurrent with the security returns, and leading one period. This gives three beta coefficients (the first and third normally will be quite small) that are summed to *reveal* a new beta estimate. Some of their estimates are given below:

	Beta Estimates*	
	Ordinary Regression	*Scholes-Williams*
Merck	1.13	1.03
Kodak	.73	.71
General Motors	1.06	.99
Owens-Illinois	1.13	1.45
IBM	1.05	1.24
Bethlehem Steel	1.75	1.98

*These estimates are for a set of rather actively traded securities, where, of course, substantial differences on average would not exist.

(3) Random Outliers.   Outliers also can be a problem. If we could secure a large enough sample of return observations we could effectively eliminate the chance that the slope of the regression would be affected by unique influences of an individual return. In reality, with 60 monthly or 100 weekly observations, the chance that a very high or low return occurs when the return on the index is high or low can influence the $\hat{\beta}$. For example, using 60 monthly observations from the beginning of 1981 through 1986, AMAX Inc. had an estimated beta coefficient of 1.78. However, when the first three observations of 1981 are dropped, the estimated risk level drops to 1.64. The reason in this case is clear; AMAX shareholders had received a tender offer than led to an immediate increase in share price from $38 to $58. During this three-month period the market return was positive, which apparently had the effect of tilting upward the slope of the line of best fit.

(4) Biases.   Given the above possibilities, historical estimates below 1.0 are more likely to be biased downward, and estimates above 1.0 are more likely to be biased upward. This will lead to a tendency for estimated βs to gravitate toward 1.0 over time. *Statistically,* in other words, if an estimated beta in one period is .6, it is more likely that this number

was subject to downward biases than to upward ones. Consequently, on average across all securities, it's more likely that the next period's estimate will be greater than .6. Knowledge of the biases on average could allow us to "update" the beta of .6 to a "more current one" equal, say, to .7.

Economic Problems. To a certain extent, the risk level of a firm and its securities can be managed. Certain decisions, such as additional reliance on the use of financial leverage or on factors of production that create fixed rather than variable costs, will affect the risk of the firm's securities. For some firms, the changes over some time periods can be so significant as to make historical estimates of β irrelevant. A merger or a major recapitalization of the firm would tend to have this sort of effect. In other cases the firm may more gradually evolve and move from one risk level to another over time. The auto industry's increasing reliance on the use of robots on assembly lines might slowly change the βs of Ford, Chrysler, and GM. Depending on the rate of change, the use of 5- or 10-year-old data can lead to historically estimated βs that significantly miss the mark.

Certainly one of the reasons for the 70 percent increase in the estimated risk of Navistar (formerly International Harvester) between 1979 and 1985 was the increasingly volatile market for farm equipment, particularly in international markets that Navistar depended on. Moreover, Merck and P&G reduced their reliance on debt financing over this period, which might help to explain the reduction in the estimated risk levels of these two securities. The reduction in risk experienced by Warner Communications probably was the result of Warner's purchase of a number of less risky corporations in 1980 and 1981 (e.g., Franklin Mint) and of the increasing maturity of the cable television business in which Warner has a big stake.

Historically estimated betas also can be influenced by the particular factor that is driving the market return during a given period. The consensus of opinion would be that the high returns generated during the decade of the 1950s were caused by increasingly favorable forecasts of the profitability of the corporate sector. Of the period between 1981 and 1986, however, the consensus is that the high returns were caused by declines in the general level of interest rates, i.e., declines in the rate at which future cash flow would be discounted. Some firms might be more sensitive or more volatile to one of these factors than to the other. Thus, it would not be unusual that a firm showing great volatility in returns in response to changes in interest rates and displaying a large beta between 1981 and 1986, might be less volatile in a different time period when profitability factors were more important.

Impact of Estimation Problems. What is the impact of all these potential problems? In essence, these estimation problems suggest that:

1. $\hat{\beta}$s estimated with monthly data over a period of five years or so are more reliable than those estimated:
    a. Over longer periods where the structural relationships may have changed.
    b. Over shorter periods where there are too few observations.
    c. Over shorter (daily or weekly) intervals where nonsynchronous trading affects the numbers.

2. The estimated βs of smaller firms are more subject to error, and more in need of correction; such as that suggested by Scholes and Williams.
3. Since many errors are random, portfolio betas are likely to be more precise than those of individual firms.
4. Because of the estimation problems it behooves both researchers and market analysts to find ways to arrive at more precise and reliable estimates. It is likely that a good deal can be gained by finding other variables (called instrumental variables) that can help in the prediction of the security's risk level. We will do this more extensively when we look at the problem of valuing securities in Section IV of the book.

With these caveats in mind we can begin to look at the extent to which the CAPM and the SML effectively describe how expected returns are formed in equilibrium.

Time Series Tests of the CAPM

The CAPM predicts that the security's expected return will be related to the overall market portfolio return. One direct way to test the CAPM, then, is with a time series regression in the form of the market model,

(9–12)
$$R_{it} = \alpha_i + \beta_i R_{It} + \varepsilon_{it} \qquad i = 1,n$$

This relation would hold (with different values of α_i and β_i) for all securities. Estimates of the coefficients α and β would be used to interpret whether the returns offered on securities on average conformed to the description offered by the CAPM.

Actual tests of this relationship were carried out in a study by Black, Jensen and Scholes [1972]. Their methodology was as follows:

1. Calculate rates of return monthly for all securities on the NYSE and for a market index.
2. Subtract an estimate of the risk-free rate of return from each of these returns and restate the model as

Time Series Regression

$$R_{it} - R_{ft} = \delta_i + \beta_i(R_{It} - R_{ft}) + e_{it}$$

where

$$\delta_i = \alpha_i - (1 - \beta_i)R_f$$

3. Estimate $\hat{\beta}$ coefficients for each firm by regressing these excess individual security returns (that is, $R_{it} - R_{ft}$ and $R_{It} - R_{ft}$), using monthly data over a five-year period (60 observations) on the market excess return over this period.
4. Rank each security by its $\hat{\beta}$ and form the securities into 10 portfolios based on their ranking. Thus, the highest 10 percent of the $\hat{\beta}$ estimates went into portfolio 1, the next highest in portfolio 2, etc.
5. Regress the monthly returns over and above R_F on *each* of these portfolios on the return on the market index for periods beyond the initial five-year period to estimate δ and $\hat{\beta}$ for each portfolio.

TABLE 9–3   Summary of Time Series Tests of the CAPM

	Portfolio	(1) Arithmetic Mean Portfolio Return	(2) $\hat{\beta}_p$	(3) δ_p	(4) $t(\delta_p)$	(5) ρ
1	Highest risk	.0213	1.56	−.0008	−0.4	.96
2		.0177	1.38	−.0019	−2.0	.99
3		.0171	1.25	−.0006	−0.8	.99
4		.0163	1.16	−.0002	−0.2	.99
5		.0145	1.06	−.0005	−0.9	.99
6		.0137	.93	.0006	0.8	.98
7		.0126	.85	.0005	0.7	.98
8		.0115	.75	.0008	1.2	.98
9		.0109	.63	.0019	2.3	.96
10	Lowest risk	.0091	.50	.0020	1.9	.90
	The market	.0142	1.00	.0000	—	1.00

$\hat{\beta}_p$ = estimated slope

δ_p = estimated intercept

$t(\delta_p)$ = t value of the intercept

ρ = correlation coefficient

Source: Black, Jensen, and Scholes [1972].

The two-step procedure of estimating individual $\hat{\beta}$s, then ranking them to form portfolios and reestimating the models' δ and $\hat{\beta}$ coefficients eliminates two statistical problems, thus providing for more efficient estimates. The results are summarized in Table 9–3. If the CAPM accurately depicts the way markets operate, the intercept, δ_p in column 3 should be zero for each of the 10 portfolios (since the risk-free rate was subtracted from R_i).

The estimated relationship does indicate larger returns for greater risks, and the increment in return for each increment of risk is about the same for low-risk as for high-risk portfolios. Thus, the relationship is approximately linear. However, while the average value for δ_p across all portfolios is close to zero, it is distinctly different from one portfolio to another. High $\hat{\beta}$ portfolios have a negative intercept and low $\hat{\beta}$ portfolios have a positive intercept. A graph summarizing the characteristic lines for these portfolios is in Figure 9–6. As can be seen, not all lines cross at the origin, which is *theoretically* what the graph should look like. While these results don't precisely confirm the CAPM, we can make an economic assessment of the divergence. For example, the value δ_{10} is .0020, which indicates an annual return of more than that predicted by the CAPM of .002 × 12, or about 2.4 percent per year. Compared to the average return on this portfolio of 10 or 11 percent over this period (1931 to 1965) this is not an insignificant amount, although of course it is the largest absolute figure from among the 10 portfolios. The tentative conclusion from this result is that low $\hat{\beta}$ securities offer somewhat higher returns than predicted by the CAPM, and high $\hat{\beta}$ securities offer somewhat lower returns than predicted by the model (though not as low as offered by low $\hat{\beta}$s). A graph of this is given in Figure 9–7. The divergence from one of the postulates of the CAPM is present, though it is certainly not an exaggerated one (the two lines in the figure are not a *great deal* different).

FIGURE 9–6   The Slope and Intercept of Annualized Values of R_p on R_I for Black, Jensen, Scholes Results

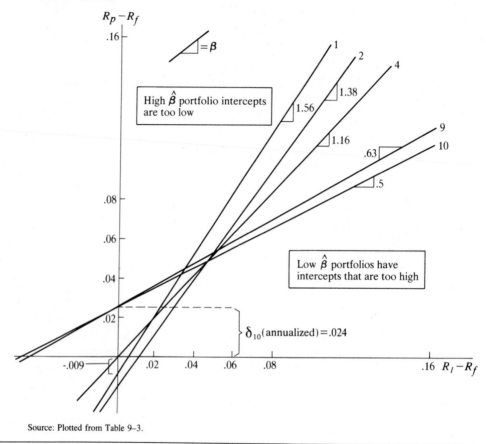

Source: Plotted from Table 9–3.

Cross-Sectional Tests of the CAPM

While time series tests do provide tests of some aspects of the CAPM (in particular, the intercept is equal to the risk-free rate), cross-sectional tests allow determination of how closely the data meet other CAPM postulates. Black, Jensen, and Scholes also perform cross-sectional tests. Their methodology is as follows:

1. Calculate rates of return monthly for all securities on the NYSE and for a market index.
2. Estimate $\hat{\beta}$ coefficients for each firm by regressing "excess" individual security returns, using monthly data over a five-year period.
3. Rank each security by its $\hat{\beta}$ and form them into 10 portfolios based on their ranking.

FIGURE 9–7   The Theoretical CAPM and B-J-S Estimates of the Risk-Return Trade-Off (from Table 9–3)

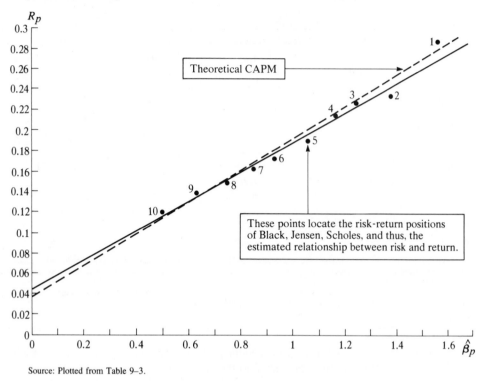

Source: Plotted from Table 9–3.

4. Calculate average returns on the 10 portfolios over the period T subsequent to the $\hat{\beta}$ estimation period and regress these average returns on the $\hat{\beta}$s of these portfolios. Thus, the regression is:

Cross-Sectional Regression

$$\tilde{R}_p - R_f = \gamma_0 + \gamma_1 \hat{\beta}_p + u_p$$

where

$$\tilde{R}_p = \frac{1}{T} \sum_{t=1}^{T} R_{pt} = Arithmetic\ mean\ portfolio\ return.$$

$$u_p = Cross\text{-}sectional\ error\ term.$$

5. Redefine the estimation period by changing T and rerun the regression. Thus, T might cover the interval 1931 to 1965, or T might cover only the 12-month interval of 1931. New βs would be estimated by going back through step 1 when estimating the cross-sectional relationship later in the period of study.

TABLE 9–4   Summary of Cross-Sectional Tests of CAPM

(a) Black, Jensen, and Scholes

Intercept		Subperiods			
	1931–1965	*1/31–9/39*	*10/39–6/48*	*7/48–3/57*	*4/57–12/65*
γ_0	.043	− .096	.053	.094	.122
$\gamma = 0$?	No	No	No	No	No
γ_1	.130	.365	.128	.040	− .014
$R_I - R_f$	.170	.264	.179	.134	.106

(b) Stambaugh

Intercept		Subperiods		
	2/53–3/59	*4/59–5/65*	*6/65–7/71*	*8/71–12/76*
γ_0	.009	.008	.012	.008
$\gamma = 0$?	No	No	No	Yes
γ_1	.166	.070	.039	.064
$R_I - R_f$	.152	.084	.059	.071
R_f	.019	.029	.049	.057

Source: Black, Jensen, and Scholes [1972] and Stambaugh [1982]. The figures are annualized values of figures in Black, Jensen, and Scholes and are annualized nominal values of *real* returns in Stambaugh. As a result, these values must be understood as an approximate annualized interpretation of these two studies.

Note: Stambaugh's estimating equation was set up so that the intercept would equal R_f if the CAPM was valid. The numbers have been adjusted to allow consistent reporting of his results with Black, Jensen, and Scholes.

If the CAPM is correct and the postulates hold up empirically, then the intercept should be zero and the slope equal to the average market return over the interval period, or

$$\gamma_0 = 0; \qquad \gamma_1 = \tilde{R}_m - R_f = \begin{array}{l} \textit{Arithmetic mean return} \\ \textit{on the market portfolio} \\ \textit{less } R_f \textit{ over interval } T. \end{array}$$

The results of their investigation, along with those of Stambaugh [1982], who performed a similar study using somewhat different statistical techniques, are presented in Table 9–4. The results can be summarized as follows:

1. Beta helps to explain the cross-sectional differences in the returns on securities.
2. The slope, γ_1, or the market-risk premium is estimated to be positive in all but one time period.
3. The intercept, γ_0, is not equal to zero, but is generally above it. The extent to which it exceeds zero is substantial and varies considerably in the Black, Jensen, and Scholes case, but is fairly constant in the Stambaugh study and is equal to about one percentage point.

Overall, the results seem to mirror the time-series figures given before. The model fits the data in all respects except that it does not imply a SML intercept equal to R_f as CAPM theory would suggest.

A picture of Stambaugh's four security-market lines is given in Figure 9–8. In each

FIGURE 9–8   **Ex Post Risk-Return Trade-Off for Four Periods**

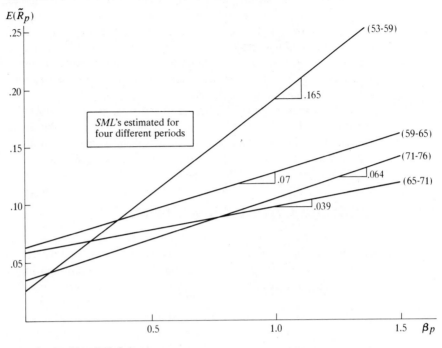

Source: Computed from Table 9–4.

case the observed T-bill rate is included to give you an idea of the difference between the theoretical line with R_f as the intercept and the intercept estimated by Stambaugh.

Stambaugh also attempted to determine if results like those presented in Table 9–4 depended on which assets were studied and which market index was used. Considering the possibility of an index that includes corporate bonds, government bonds and T-bills, real estate, automobiles, and house furnishings in addition to stocks, Stambaugh found little difference in the results. That is, the intercept and the slope coefficients, γ_0 and γ_1, were approximately the same regardless of which assets are included in defining R_I. Thus, inferences about the CAPM's empirical validity are not sensitive to how R_I is defined, as long as it consists of a broad set of securities or other investment opportunities. Basically, this outcome significantly reduced the importance of one of the complaints that had been lodged about the possibility of ever empirically verifying the CAPM.

In a separate cross-sectional investigation, Fama and MacBeth [1973] extended these results by directly investigating for (1) nonlinearities and (2) omitted variables in the determination of prices.

Thus, they ran the regression

$$R_p = \gamma_0 + \gamma_1 \hat{\beta}_p + \gamma_2 \hat{\beta}_p^2 + \gamma_3 \sigma_{up}$$

The $\hat{\beta}_p^2$ term tests for a **nonlinear relationship** between risk and return. If γ_2 is negative, it would imply the security market line bends backward to give the impression of lower and lower *increases* in returns demanded as risk is increased.

The σ_{up} term, estimated from the regression in Equation (9–12), measures the portfolio's **diversifiable variability** that, according to theory, should not play a role in valuing securities. If γ_3 is positive, it would indicate that the market thinks residual variability or diversifiable variability is important and would be counter to the diversification arguments that provide the basic tenets of the CAPM. Of course, since the actual return (instead of excess return) is on the left-hand side, γ_0 should correspond to the risk-free interest rate. They found γ_2 and γ_3 to be near zero, and, like Stambaugh and Black, Jensen, and Scholes, found γ_0 to be greater than the rate on T-bills.

In general, these studies find many of the basic CAPM postulates hold up well under empirical examination, while a few don't.

Problems with the CAPM: How Serious?

The CAPM relationship that holds up least well under empirical scrutiny is the one predicting an intercept equal to the risk-free rate. This finding has led to considerable theorizing and search for an explanation. Basically, three propositions are available for understanding this result when everything else in the model seems to fit the data fairly well.

The *first* proposition is that the model itself is deficient. It just does not do an adequate job of describing equilibrium-expected returns, and that we ought to spend time and effort in the development of a different approach to the valuation of investment opportunities. One alternative approach is called the **arbitrage pricing model** and is the subject of our investigation in Chapter 10. Conceivably, the data is more consistent with this alternative model, and we may want to consider replacing the CAPM with the APT (for arbitrage pricing theory) if that turns out to be the case.

The *second* proposition is that some of the postulates do not hold because there is still so much error in measuring the variables used in the empirical tests. In particular,

1. The estimated beta, $\hat{\beta}$, is not the true β, and an historically estimated $\hat{\beta}$ may not be that close to the current true β that actually governs expected returns (as in the CAPM).
2. The market return estimated with the use of a stock and bond market index, R_I, is not the true market index, R_m, that the theory specifies.[4]

Each of these "measurement" problems compounds the difficulty of using ex post data to test the CAPM's postulates. Each, therefore, adds a degree of confusion to the empirical tests of the model.

For example, Banz [1981] estimated the CAPM relationship in the same way as the

---

[4]Moreover, if it were the true market portfolio and also were the efficient risky portfolio, the risk–return relationship would hold by definition. Thus, perhaps the use of actual data would not lead to any definitive conclusion regarding the appropriateness of the CAPM. These arguments have been put forth by Roll (1977) in a formidable attack on empirical testing of the CAPM.

Black, Jensen, and Scholes cross-sectional tests with one added term. The added term is the relative size of the market value of the security. Thus, his regression is,

$$R_i = \gamma_0 + \gamma_1 \hat{\beta}_i + \gamma_2 \left(\frac{n_i P_i - \overline{n_m P_m}}{\overline{n_m P_m}} \right) + u_i$$

where $n_i P_i$ is the market value of firm i (that is, the number of shares times the price per share), and $\overline{n_m P_m}$ is the average market value of all firms. Obviously, according CAPM, γ_2 should be zero. Why, after adjusting for risk, would larger firms have to offer higher (if γ_2 is positive) or lower (if γ_2 is negative) returns to persuade investors to hold their securities? After placing securities into one of 25 portfolios, Banz found γ_2 to be *significantly negative*. Moreover, with further exploration he found that it was the smallest (publicly traded) firms in his sample that were responsible for the size effect. The results indicate that the CAPM may not hold for small firms; i.e., small firms have to offer a significant premium—over and above their risk to persuade investors to hold their shares.

A similar study by Reinganum [1981] found that security returns were related to $\hat{\beta}$ (as in the CAPM) as well as to the ratio of the firm's earnings per share to its price per share. The latter finding is counter to the contentions of the CAPM (which hypothesizes that only β_i is important). His estimates were economically important as well. For example, over the 15-year period 1963 to 1977, two portfolios with approximately equal βs but different earnings/price ratios offered different returns. One with a ratio of .14 offered 9 percent more per year in return than a second portfolio with a ratio of only .07. The difference is clearly substantial and suggests that either the CAPM or the data must come under close scrutiny.

In fact, the results of the Banz and Reinganum studies, in part, may be blamed on problems with the estimates of the risk of small firms that tend to have both low market value and high earnings/price ratios. Thus, one might think of the firm's size or its earnings/price ratio as a simple proxy for risk, which is difficult to measure accurately. Small firms' estimates of β, being downward-biased, are supplemented by including in the CAPM relationship a size or earnings/price variable. True risk is better estimated by the package of these variables (a proposition we will make use of in forecasting βs later in the text).

The *third* proposition is that the standard form of the CAPM, with the intercept being equal to the risk-free interest rate, doesn't capture the exact relationship between risk and return, but a variant of the standard model might. Specifically, it has been argued that one of the forms of the CAPM that results from doing away with some of the restrictive assumptions of the standard model may fit the data better. This makes sense. If the standard form of the CAPM requires a restrictive assumption that doesn't seem to fit the real world, a version of the same basic model that is less restrictive may fit the data better. It seems to be the case that the zero-beta CAPM discussed in the last chapter, or

$$E(\tilde{R}_i) = E(\tilde{R}_z) + \beta_i [E(\tilde{R}_m) - E(\tilde{R}_z)]$$

where the intercept is the return on a portfolio on the efficient set that is uncorrelated with the market portfolio (and thus has a zero β), fits the data better. This was true of the Black, Jensen, and Scholes and the Stambaugh studies, in any case.

Other variants of the basic CAPM have been proposed as substitutes, and are currently undergoing testing. As yet only limited evidence exists on these alternatives, as they, too, suffer from problems associated with measuring returns and risks.

Is the Theory Testable at All?

The most basic implication of the CAPM is that the market portfolio is a portfolio that (by definition) is on the efficient set. As we have seen, the fact that all investors seek to hold the market portfolio in equilibrium leads to the pricing relationship described by the security market line. It is this pricing relationship which empirical researchers have attempted to test. Recently, however, empirical tests of the model have been questioned. In particular Richard Roll [1977] has suggested that the CAPM is inherently not testable.

Roll observes that, for all practical purposes, the implication that the market portfolio, *m*, is efficient cannot be tested, simply because no one can really observe and measure what is contained in it. In theory, the market portfolio contains every marketable real or financial asset in the world—every stock, every bond, every share of preferred stock, every plot of real estate, every Treasury bill, etc. Roll argues that, in reality, this portfolio can't be observed. Indeed this is the reason we used separate notation for the true market portfolio, *m*, and for the index used as a proxy for it, *I*. And, since all other implications of the CAPM follow from the efficiency of the market portfolio, tests of those implications cannot be performed. For example, estimation of β depends on being able to measure the contents of the market portfolio, since it requires an assessment of each asset's covariance with the true market portfolio. But, in fact only $\hat{\beta}$ can be estimated, and it is wrong because R_I instead of R_m was used to derive it.

The real question is whether the ability to observe R_m renders all tests using R_I fruitless. The answer, we believe, is that it is still reasonable to try to find evidence generally consistent or inconsistent with the model's implications, *while keeping in mind Roll's* point that R_m and β can never be observed, and, therefore, that all tests must be subject to close scrutiny and examination from many different directions.

In effect, all tests of the theory are also tests of the reliability of the data. Thus, the CAPM could be accepted when it is wrong because of errors caused by the difference between R_I and R_m, or the CAPM could be rejected when it is right because of these errors. Yet if you are convinced that R_I is close to R_m, then you can be more sure of the validity of the empirical test undertaken. For this reason we believe evidence can be brought to bear on the CAPM issue (perhaps much like the "big bang" theory of the formation of the universe) by making predictions and seeing if the accumulated evidence is consistent with the predictions. This was the aim of the study by Stambaugh mentioned earlier. We show why this conclusion is warranted in the appendix to the chapter.

How Far Off Is the CAPM?

We have noted a number of anomalies with empirical attempts to determine the precision of the CAPM as a description of capital market equilibrium. Basically, the controversy centers on whether these anomalies can be traced to fundamental problems with the model or with the data. Many of the anomalies that seemed to indicate that the model may be wrong have subsequently been shown to be related to errors in the measurement of the key variables, R_i, β_i, R_f, and R_m. Thus, the appropriate conclusion seems to be that most of the model's postulates hold up fairly well as generalizations of what risk is and how it is related to expected security return. The problems that cannot be so easily put aside (the higher than expected intercept and the difficulty of estimating β) deserve further attention. This attention will come in the form of more-refined statistical tests and, undoubtedly, different proposed models of the equilibrium relationship (as in arbitrage pricing theory). But, until a better model comes along, it is appropriate to continue to make use of the CAPM and its postulates as a model useful for both theoretical conclusions and practical applications.

Summary

The market model is a relationship which attempts to relate the rate of return on individual securities to the contemporaneous return on an index of overall capital market performance. Verbally, it states that:

$$
\begin{pmatrix} \text{Return} \\ \text{on security } i \\ \text{at time } t \\ (R_{it}) \end{pmatrix} = \begin{pmatrix} \text{A constant} \\ (\alpha_i) \end{pmatrix} + \begin{pmatrix} \text{A constant} \\ (\beta_i) \end{pmatrix} \begin{pmatrix} \text{Market index's} \\ \text{return} \\ \text{at time } t \\ (R_{It}) \end{pmatrix} + \begin{pmatrix} \text{A random} \\ \text{error term} \\ (\varepsilon_{it}) \end{pmatrix}
$$

In this model, each security has two parameters. The constant, α_i, positions the security's characteristic line. In equilibrium α_i will equal $(1 - \beta_i)R_f$ if the security is priced according to the CAPM. Ex post, α reflects the past performance of the security assuming the market index used in the relationship is the market portfolio of the CAPM. The beta parameter represents the slope of the security's characteristic line and is equivalent to the "CAPM beta" when the market index is in fact the market portfolio, m. Beta measures systematic risk, or the tendency of the security to covary with an aggregate measure of financial market returns. The variance of the random error term represents the security's unsystematic risk, or variance not explained by factors common to all securities.

It is also shown that individual securities' total risk can be broken into two components: systematic and unsystematic risk. When portfolios are constructed, the portfolio alpha and beta are simply weighted averages of the alphas and betas of the component securities. However, the unsystematic risk of the portfolio tends to approach zero as more and more securities are included.

In summary, the market model provides a framework within which the CAPM can be better understood. That is its primary purpose. It should not be considered an alternative to the CAPM. Rather, the market model—as a description of how security or portfolio returns are generated— is useful for connecting actual return data to the conceptual relationship of equilibrium and disequilibrium wrapped up in the capital-asset pricing model.

There are a large number of empirical tests of the CAPM that have been performed with data spanning more than 60 years, using the market model to secure estimates of R_i, R_m, and β. While some postulates of the model do not hold exactly, the model's linearly positive slope and reliance on β to summarize risk hold up fairly well.

Nevertheless, the debate on the model's empirical validity and attempts to determine if alternative models fit the data better will continue. Adjustments to or generalizations of the model will be necessary. However, the model's current usefulness and applicability for understanding security markets and investment decisions is a positive force in its continued use.

APPENDIX: The Difference between m and I—Resolving the Roll Controversy

This appendix summarizes a resolution to the controversy that plagues both the professional investment community and students of markets over the testability of the capital-asset pricing model. In developing these arguments it should be kept in mind that arguments that suggest why the model cannot be tested (Roll [1977]) are not indictments of the theory or the principles contained in the CAPM. They are directed only toward whether the theory can be tested with data secured by observing ex post security returns.

Suppose the CAPM's implications are true, and security prices actually conform to their equilibrium values, so that the security market line, given in Equation (9–9), holds for all risky securities. However, since we can't observe the true market portfolio, m, we use a market index, say I, for the purposes of testing the theory. The portfolio I might be positioned relative to m as shown in Figure 9A–1. In that figure, I lies close to m in terms of its expected return and standard deviation, but it happens to be inefficient. It is likely that some assets included in m aren't contained in I; however, we should like I to lie somewhere close to m if it is to serve as a reasonable surrogate for the true market portfolio.

Using Equation (9–9) for the security market line, we know that for any risky security i the following holds:

(9A–1)   *The Security Market Line: Stated Relative to the Market Portfolio*

$$E(\tilde{R}_i) = R_f + \beta_i[E(\tilde{R}_m) - R_f]$$

We also know that a similar relationship holds for index I; namely that:

(9A–2) $$E(\tilde{R}_I) = R_f + \beta_I[E(\tilde{R}_m) - R_f]$$

as long as I is really a broad-based portfolio of securities, as may be included in a market index. Combining Equations (9A–1) and (9A–2), we find that i's expected return is actually linearly related to the expected return of the market index as follows:

(9A–3)   *The Security Market Line Stated Relative to a Market Index*

$$E(\tilde{R}_i) = R_f + \hat{\beta}_i[E(\tilde{R}_I) - R_f]$$

where

$$\hat{\beta}_i \equiv \frac{\beta_i}{\beta_I} = \frac{(the\ beta\ of\ security\ i)}{(the\ beta\ of\ market\ index\ I).}$$

Unfortunately, $\hat{\beta}_i$ is the ratio of two unobservable beta values. The numerator of $\hat{\beta}_i$ is the beta of security i with respect to the true market portfolio, m, and the denominator

FIGURE 9A–1   **Market Index Portfolio I as a Surrogate for the Market Portfolio m**

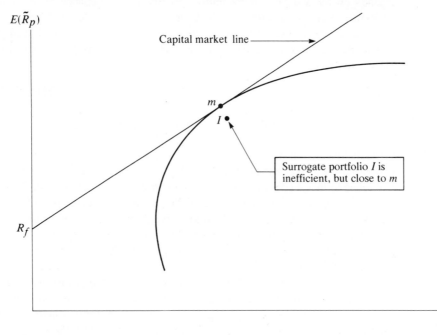

is the beta of the market index I with respect to m. Since we can't calculate the precise value of β_i without knowing the composition of m, researchers have (incorrectly) substituted the beta value of each asset with respect to the index, $\hat{\beta}_i$, in their tests of the equilibrium CAPM relationship (Equation 9–9). The real question, then, is how $\hat{\beta}_i$ in Equation (9A–3) is related to β_i.

The answer depends on the process which governs security returns over time and on the covariance (or beta) of the index, I, with respect to the true market portfolio. Let us suppose that the returns on the market index, R_I, are related to those on the true market portfolio, R_m, in terms of the market model; i.e.,

$$\tilde{R}_{It} = \alpha_I + \beta_I\tilde{R}_{mt} + \tilde{e}_{It}$$

Similarly, imagine that the returns on each security i are also related to the true market portfolio m in terms of the market model. That is,

$$\tilde{R}_{it} = \alpha_i + \beta_i\tilde{R}_{mt} + \tilde{e}_{it}$$

Under these conditions, and given the assumptions of the market model (stated earlier), we can show that:

(9A–4) $$\hat{\beta} = \beta_i\left[\frac{\beta_I(\sigma(\tilde{R}_m))^2 + Cov(\tilde{e}_{It},\tilde{R}_m)}{(\sigma(\tilde{R}_I))^2}\right] \equiv \beta_i[\gamma_{I,m}]$$

This states that the beta of security i with respect to the index is equal to the beta of i with respect to m (the true β) times a constant (in brackets) that depends only on the properties of I and m. Hence, the constant $\gamma_{I,m}$ is the same for all securities.[5] Its value depends on the variance of I's returns relative to the variance of m's returns, on the covariance between $\tilde{e}_{I,t}$ and $\tilde{R}_m$, and on the beta of the index with respect to m (which is, again, unobservable). The answer to the question, then, of how $\hat{\beta}_i$ in Equation (9A–3) is related to the beta of index I, is clear. Using Equations (9A–3) and (9A–4), we see that in equilibrium:

(9A–5)   ***Security Market Line as Tested***

$$E(\tilde{R}_i) = R_f + \hat{\beta}_i \left(\frac{1}{\gamma_{I,m}\beta_I}\right) [E(\tilde{R}_I) - R_f]$$

This relationship illustrates what happens when the CAPM is tested with the "wrong" market portfolio. When the expected returns of individual securities are tested to see how they relate to their betas with respect to the surrogate market portfolio, $\hat{\beta}_i$, as in Equation (9A–5), we think that the slope of the SML *ought* to be equal to $E(\tilde{R}_I) - R_f$. This is because we have acted as if I is the true market portfolio. But, in actuality, the slope we will observe approximates $(1/\gamma_{I,m}\beta_I)[E(\tilde{R}_I) - R_f]$. Thus, we might tend to reject the theory (even though it is true). However, if the factor $(1/\gamma_{I,m}\beta_I)$ is close to 1.0, we would tend (correctly) to accept the theory. That factor will tend to be close to 1.0 if the variance of I is close in magnitude to the variance of m, and if the covariance of $\tilde{e}_{I,t}$ with $\tilde{R}_m$ is close to zero (which it will tend toward, the more highly correlated are I and m). In other words, the "better" the surrogate I is for m, the less distortion there is in the observed slope of the security market line, as it is estimated in testing the theory, relative to its true value.

The point we have made is this: Even if we have the wrong market portfolio, one can expect the linear relationship predicted by the theory to hold up, though it will not be perfect and its slope may deviate somewhat from the theoretically predicted value. That is not such a bad result. However, Roll is clearly right that this is, strictly speaking, no longer a straight test of the theory. It is a test of whether, *if* the theory is true, we have chosen a "good" surrogate for the market portfolio as a basis for our test. *If* we are convinced that I is a good proxy for m then the tests *can* divulge whether the CAPM is *empirically* valid. The most recent test of what happens with different surrogates, by Stambaugh [1982], lends further credence to our point here that empirical tests can be used to support or deny the CAPM.

References

Alexander, G. N., and Chervany, N. L. [1980] "On The Estimation and Stability of Beta." *Journal of Financial and Quantitative Analysis* (March).

Banz, R. [1981] "The Relationship between Return and Market Value of Common Stocks." *Journal of Financial Economics* (March).

---

[5]The relationship in 9A–4 holds only as an approximation to the extent that one or more market model assumptions are violated for security i. In particular, if $Cov(\tilde{e}_{i,t}, \tilde{R}_{m,t}) \neq 0$, then $\gamma_{I,m}$ will depend on factors unique to security i as well as on I and m.

Black, Fisher; Jensen, Michael; and Scholes, Myron. [1972] "The Capital Asset Pricing Model: Some Empirical Tests." In *Studies in the Theory of Capital Markets,* ed. Michael C. Jensen, New York: Praeger Publishers.

Blume, Marshall. [1971] "On the Assessment of Risk." *Journal of Finance* (March).

Blume, Marshall. [1975] "Betas and Their Regression Tendencies." *Journal of Finance* (June).

Blume, Marshall E., and Friend, Irwin. [1974] "Risk, Investment Strategy and the Long-Run Rates of Return." *Review of Economics and Statistics* (August).

Blume, Marshall E., and Stambaugh, Robert F. [1983], "Biases in Computed Returns: An Application to the Size Effect." *Journal of Financial Economics* (November).

Breeden, Douglas T. [1979] "An Intertemporal Asset Pricing Model with Stochastic Consumption and Investment Opportunities." *Journal of Financial Economics* (September).

Chan, K. C., and Chen, Nai-Fu. [1986] "Estimation Error of Stock Betas and the Role of Firm Size as an Instrumental Variable for Risk." Working Paper No. 179, University of Chicago.

Cheng, Pao L., and Grauer, Robert R. [1980] "An Alternative Test of the Capital Asset Pricing Model." *American Economic Review* (September).

Cohen, K. J.; Hawawini, G. A.; Maier, S. F.; Schwartz, R. A.; and Whitcomb, D. K. [1983] "Estimating and Adjusting for the Intervaling Effect Bias in Beta." *Management Science* (January).

Cohen, K. J.; Hawawini, G. A.; Maier, S. F.; Schwartz, R. A.; Whitcomb, D. K. [1983] "Friction in the Trading Process and the Estimation of Systematic Risk." *Journal of Financial Economics* (August).

Dimson, E. [1979] "Risk Measurement when Shares are Subject to Infrequent Trading." *Journal of Financial Economics* (June).

Dimson, E.; and Marsh, P. R. [1983] "The Stability of U.K. Risk Measures and the Problem of Thin Trading." *Journal of Finance* (June).

Fama, Eugene, and MacBeth, James. [1973] "Risk, Return and Equilibrium: Empirical Tests." *Journal of Political Economy* (May–June).

Foster, G. [1978] "Asset Pricing Models: Further Tests." *Journal of Financial and Quantitative Analysis* (March).

Fowler, David J., and Rorke, C. H. [1983] "Risk Measurement When Shares Are Subject to Infrequent Trading." *Journal of Financial Economics* (August).

Friend, I.; Westerfield, R.; and Granito, M. [1978] "New Evidence on the Capital Asset Pricing Model." *Journal of Finance* (June).

Gibbons, Michael R. [1982] "Multivariate Tests of Financial Models: A New Approach." *Journal of Financial Economics* (March).

Gibbons, Michael R., and Ferson, Wayne. [1985] "Testing Asset Pricing Models with Changing Expectations and an Unobservable Market Portfolio." *Journal of Financial Economics* (June).

Jacob, Nancy. [1971] "The Measurement of Systematic Risk for Securities and Portfolios: Some Empirical Results." *Journal of Financial and Quantitative Analysis* (March).

Jensen, Michael [1972] "Capital Markets: Theory and Evidence." *Bell Journal of Economics and Management Science* (Autumn).

Kaplan, Robert, and Weil, Roman [1973] "Risk and the Value Line Contest," *Financial Analysts Journal* (July–August).

Klemkosky, R. C., and Martin, J. D. [1975] "The Adjustment of Beta Forecasts." *Journal of Finance* (September).

Lee, C. F., and Jen, F. C. [1978] "Effects of Measurement Errors on Systematic Risk and Performance Measure of a Portfolio." *Journal of Finance and Quantitative Analysis* (June).

Litzenberger, R. H., and Ramaswamy, K. [1979] "The Effect of Personal Taxes and Dividends on Capital Asset Prices: Theory and Empirical Evidence." *Journal of Financial Economics* (June).

Miller, Merton, and Scholes, Myron. [1972] "Rates of Return in Relation to Risk: A Reexamination of Some Recent Findings." In *Studies in the Theory of Capital Markets,* ed. Michael C. Jensen, New York: Praeger Publishers.

Pogue, G. A., and Solnik, B. H. [1974] "The Market Model Applied to European Stocks: Some Empirical Results." *Journal of Financial and Quantitative Analysis* (December).

Price, Kelly; Price, Barbara; and Nantell, Timothy. [1982] "Variance and Lower Partial Moment Measures of Systematic Risk: Some Analytical and Empirical Results." *Journal of Finance* (June).

Reinganam, M. [1981] "Misspecification of Capital Asset Pricing: Empirical Anomalies Based on Earnings Yields and Market Values." *Journal of Financial Economics* (March).

Roll, Richard. [1977] "A Critique of the Asset Pricing Theory's Tests; Part I: On Past and Potential Testability of the Theory." *Journal of Financial Economics* (March).

Roll, Richard. [1980] "A Possible Explanation of the Small Firm Effect." Working Paper, University of California (November).

Roll, Richard. [1983] "On Computing Mean Returns and the Small Firm Premium." *Journal of Financial Economics* (November).

Rosenberg, Barr. [1984] "Prediction of Common Stock Investment Risk." *Journal of Portfolio Management* (Fall).

Rosenberg, B. A., and Rudd, A. [1982] "Factor-Related and Specific Returns of Common Stocks: Serial Correlation and Market Inefficiency." *Journal of Finance* (May).

Scholes, M., and Williams, J. [1977] "Estimating Betas from Nonsynchronous Data." *Journal of Financial Economics* (December).

Schwert, G. William. [1983] "Size and Stock Returns, and Other Empirical Regularities." *Journal of Financial Economics* (June).

Scott, E., and Brown, S. [1980] "Biased Estimators and Unstable Betas." *Journal of Finance* (March).

Shanken, Jay. [1985] "Multivariate Tests of the Zero-beta CAPM." *Journal of Financial Economics* (September).

Sharpe, William F., and Cooper, Guy M. [1972] "Risk Return Classes of New York Stock Exchange Common Stocks, 1931–67." *Financial Analysts Journal* (March–April).

Simonds, Richard R.; LaMotte, Lynn Roy; and McWhorter, Archer, Jr. [1986] "Testing for Non-stationarity of Market Risk: An Exact Test and Power Considerations." *Journal of Financial and Quantitative Analysis* (June).

Smith, K. V. [1978] "The Effect of Intervaling on Estimating Parameters of the Capital Asset Pricing Model." *Journal of Financial and Quantitative Analysis* (June).

Stambaugh, Robert F. [1982] "On the Exclusion of Assets from Tests of the Two-Parameter Model: A Sensitivity Analysis." *Journal of Financial Economics* (November).

Theobald, M. [1980] "An Analysis of the Market Model and Beta Factors Using U.K. Equity Share Data," *Journal of Business Finance and Accounting* (Spring).

Vasicek, O. A. [1973] "A Note On Using Cross-Sectional Information in Bayesian Estimation of Security Betas." *Journal of Finance* 28 (December).

Wheatly, Simon. [1986] "Some Tests of the Consumption-Based Asset Pricing Model." Working Paper, University of Washington.

Wood, Robert, and McInish, Thomas. [1982] "Nonsynchronous Trading and the Behavior of Beta over Short Differencing Intervals." Working Paper, University Park: Pennsylvania State University.

Questions and Problems

1. The concept of beta most clearly is associated with:

   a. The capital-asset pricing model.
   b. Diversifiable risk theory.
   c. Mean/variance analysis.
   d. Correlation coefficients.

   CFA

2. Ex post, the intercept of security *i*'s characteristic line (the intercept of the market model), α_i, depends on how well the firm performed over the period of measurement. Ex ante, what will the value of α_i be if securities are priced in equilibrium according to the CAPM?

3. Suppose the CAPM holds. Three securities have betas of 1.4, .8, and 1.7; and expected returns of .16, .14, and .20, respectively. Are these securities priced to be consistent with the CAPM? Describe why or why not.

4. Dow Chemical, Ford, and Southern California Edison have beta coefficients of .9, 1.2, and .7, respectively. What would be the beta coefficient of a portfolio made up of equal proportions of each security?

5. General Electric is priced in equilibrium and is offering an expected return of 13 percent on its β of .9. If the risk-free interest rate is 7 percent, what is the slope of the security market line, and the expected rate of return on the market portfolio?

6. During the 1982–87 period the characteristic line of Bethlehem Steel had an intercept of − .014 and a slope of 1.2. The characteristic line of USX had an intercept of zero and a slope of .95. Using this information, show how the slope of the characteristic lines can be used to explain the relative risks of these two securities.

7. Use Figure 9–1 to discuss the differences between diversifiable and nondiversifiable variability of security return.

8. Warner Communications is a firm that rapidly expanded its operations into a number of lines of business in the first half of the 1980s. These lines of business included toys, entertainment, computers, communication transmission, and specialized consumer items. What would be the effect of this expansion on the firm's beta coefficient, and the relative proportion of diversifiable and nondiversifiable variability of the common stock of the firm?

9. In your opinion, two firms have the same beta coefficients. However, your expectation is that one of the firms is seriously underpriced in the market. The other firm is priced in equilibrium according to the capital-asset pricing model. Draw a picture of the ex ante characteristic lines for these two securities.

10. On Wall Street and in statistical studies of common stocks, analysts use recent historical returns for the estimation of a security's beta. Summarize the potential deficiencies associated with this approach.

11. Pick five firms from those listed in Table 9–2 that you are familiar with. Summarize the types of business these firms conduct, and how each type would affect the firm's beta coefficient (as you interpret how the success of their operations would move more or less than proportionally with the overall market return).

12. Find two firms in Table 9–2 that experienced a substantial change in beta between the 1979 estimates and the 1985 estimates. Using Value Line or Standard & Poor's Stock Reports from your library, identify changes that have occurred between the two periods that might explain the change in beta.

13. Pick two firms from those in Table 9–2. Search through Value Line, Standard & Poor's Stock Reports, and *The Wall Street Journal Index* for recent changes in the firms' operating or financial structure that would lead you to believe that the common stock betas have changed since the 1985 estimates.

14. How you go about investing in securities is, in large part, dependent on the "structure" of security returns. The CAPM, and the SML in particular, specifies one structural possibility. What are the model's main postulates? What have empirical studies suggested about the accuracy of the postulates in representing the structure of the security returns?

15. Why would you care about the equilibrium-expected return on a security, $E(R_i)$, if the return you actually achieve depends on the current market price, and not the equilibrium value of the security?

16. The beta coefficient on a portfolio of securities is equal to (which of the following):
   a. The slope of a characteristic line that defines the relationship between the return on that portfolio and the return on the market portfolio.
   b. A weighted average of the beta coefficients of the securities included in the portfolio.
   c. A value that is less than 1 due to the benefits of diversification.
   d. a and b above,
   e. All of the above.

17. Which is *not* a characteristic of the results of empirical tests of the validity of the CAPM?
   a. The relationship between risk and return is linear.
   b. The intercept appears to be the same as the risk-free interest rate.
   c. The slope of the relationship between risk and return is positive.
   d. The individual security standard deviation plays no part in explaining security returns.

CHAPTER

10

Arbitrage Pricing

The Law of One Price

There is an economic principle (perhaps the *only* economic principle) that says that two equivalent goods selling in the same competitive market must have the same price. This is the **law of one price.** Two bushels of wheat in Kansas City should sell at the same price if they are perfect substitutes, and two shares of IBM common stock should be priced the same.[1] If they aren't the same, the simultaneous action of selling the higher priced of the two and buying the lower priced (to deliver against the sale) would allow an investor to capture a profit with no risk and with no expenditure or investment. Profits thus generated are called **arbitrage profits,** and the individual seeking such anomalies is an **arbitrager.** Arbitrage actions are the enforcement vehicle to ensure that the law of one price holds.

In fact, we have already invoked the law of one price in developing the CAPM by showing that two securities that have the same level of risk (β) would have to offer the same return; i.e., they would be priced in the same way. A violation of this equilibrium condition would provide investor incentive for increasing the demand (or supply) for that

---

[1]The two have to be equivalent. Because of transaction costs or quality differences, the two wheat deals may not be considered as perfect substitutes. Moreover, everyone knows that a grocery store across town may be a poor substitute for one nearby. Clearly though, one share of IBM purchased on the floor of the NYSE is equivalent to a second share with only a different serial number.

firm's securities, presumably leading eventually to a reattainment of equilibrium. The assumption that we made in coming to this conclusion was that investors are concerned only with the expected return and the standard deviation of return on their portfolios. Thus, all securities with the same risk were considered perfect substitutes in terms of expected return.

The law of one price can be expanded to view capital-market equilibrium in a more complex world, leading to a somewhat different approach to understanding how securities are priced. In doing so, we develop what has come to be known as the **arbitrage pricing model** (or **arbitrage pricing theory**). The central tenet of the model is that prices will adjust until portfolios cannot be formed so as to achieve any arbitrage profit.

Multiple Factors Affecting Returns

.

In the development of the market model in Chapter 9, we assumed that security returns were a function of a market index and factors unique to the individual security. Given that returns were generated by this simple mechanism, we showed that the market model with some of the CAPM assumptions was the same as the CAPM. In other words, market equilibrium for individual securities could be described by a simple expression

(10–1)   *CAPM*

$$E(\tilde{R}_i) = R_f + \beta_i[E(\tilde{R}_m) - R_f]$$

which is the security market line.

Now, however, suppose the world is a more complex one where security returns are affected by a number of macro factors. These factors, while they affect the return on the market portfolio, may affect the returns on different securities differently. Thus, for security i in period t the return can be represented as the **combined** effect of that security's **equilibrium expected return and the impact of other influences,**

(10–2)   *Security Return*

$$R_{it} = E(\tilde{R}_i) \quad + \beta_{i1}\tilde{F}_{1t} + \beta_{i2}\tilde{F}_{2t} + \cdots + \beta_{ih}\tilde{F}_{ht} + \tilde{\varepsilon}_{it}$$

$$\frac{Actual}{return} = \frac{Expected}{return} + \frac{Effect\ on\ return\ of}{factors\ 1\ through\ h} + \frac{Unique\ effect}{on\ return.}$$

This expression simply says that the actual return on the security in period t is composed of its expected return $E(\tilde{R}_i)$ and the positive or negative influences associated with the factors, $\tilde{F}_h$, which are common to many securities, and $\tilde{\varepsilon}_{it}$ which is unique to security i. Thus, the deviations of actual returns from those expected are blamed on other influences that may affect securities in different ways. Factor one, F_1, may be related in some way to Federal Reserve announcements of the money supply, F_2 to industrial productivity, and F_3 to technological developments in micro circuits. Each of the β_hs measures the return sensitivity of firm i to that factor (or the systematic movement of R_i with F_h). Thus, firm i's return may be higher than that of other firms in a period because of a large positive value for factor 3, say, given that β_{i3} is very large.

Portfolios of Securities

Any portfolio of N individual securities, each of which has a return that is described by these factors, will have a return:

(10–3)   *Portfolio Return*

$$R_{pt} = \sum_{i=1}^{N} x_i \tilde{R}_{it}$$

$$= \sum_{i=1}^{N} x_i E(\tilde{R}_i) + \sum_{i} x_i \beta_{i1} \tilde{F}_{1t} + \sum_{i=1}^{N} x_i \beta_{i2} \tilde{F}_{2t} + \cdots \sum_{i=1}^{N} x_i \beta_{ih} \tilde{F}_{ht} + \sum_{i=1}^{N} x_i \tilde{\varepsilon}_{it}$$

$$= \sum_{i=1}^{N} x_i E(\tilde{R}_i) + \tilde{F}_{1t} \sum_{i} x_i \beta_{i1} + \tilde{F}_{2t} \sum_{i=1}^{N} x_i \beta_{i2} + \cdots + \tilde{F}_{ht} \sum_{i=1}^{N} x_i \beta_{ih} + \sum_{i=1}^{N} x_i \tilde{\varepsilon}_{it}.$$

The portfolio, in other words, is influenced by these same factors.

By selecting portfolio weights in a particular way, the portfolio can emphasize one or more of the factors. For example, it may be possible to construct a portfolio that is diversified relative to the unique influences $\tilde{\varepsilon}_i$ (that is, any x_i is small), yet has its influence concentrated in, say, factor 3.

An example is constructed for 11 securities and for two factors in Table 10–1. Thus security 1 has a high level of sensitivity to factor 2, but no sensitivity to factor 1. Suppose a portfolio is constructed by investing 40 percent of the invested wealth in security 1; security 2 is sold short in an amount equal to 10 percent of the invested wealth; and the remaining weights are as follow:

$$x_3 = \quad .4 \qquad x_6 = -.1 \qquad x_9 = \quad .2$$

$$x_4 = -.1 \qquad x_7 = \quad .3 \qquad x_{10} = -.2$$

$$x_5 = \quad .3 \qquad x_8 = -.2 \qquad x_{11} = \quad .1$$

TABLE 10–1   Sample Securities, Standard Deviations, and Betas for Two Factors, F_1 and F_2

Security i	β_{i1}	β_{i2}	$\sigma(\bar{R}_i)$
1	.0	2.0	.20
2	.0	.5	.10
3	.4	2.0	.15
4	.4	.5	.20
5	.8	2.0	.30
6	.8	.5	.05
7	1.2	2.0	.15
8	1.2	.5	.10
9	1.6	2.0	.20
10	1.6	.5	.15
11	2.0	2.0	.10

Notice the negative weights indicate the amount by which the security is held short. Thus, for every dollar of the investor's equity $.40 is invested in securities 1 and 3, $.30 in securities 5 and 7, $.20 in security 9, and $.10 in security 11. The total investment per dollar of equity is $1.70 (which is .40 + .40 + .30 + .30 + .20 + .10) of which $.70 is financed by selling short securities 2, 4, 6, 8, and 10. The proceeds from the short sale are used to finance the investment in positive amounts of securities 1, 3, 5, 7, 9, and 11. This portfolio would have a β_1 on factor 1 of .5 [i.e., (.4)(0) + (−.1)(0) + (.4)(.4) + ⋯ + (−.2)(1.6) + (.1)(2.0)], and a β_2 on factor 2 of 3.05.[2] Note that the portfolio is constructed to emphasize investment in those securities that have a high sensitivity to the second factor and a low sensitivity to the first factor. Why an investor would adopt this strategy is not really relevant at this point (it will be extremely important for investment analysis which we cover in Chapters 11–17), although an investor's forecasts of a high value for factor 2 would provide a sufficient incentive for forming the portfolio in this manner.

This portfolio is reasonably well diversified in that the influence of the unique factors, because they are independent from firm to firm, is quite a bit smaller than the average standard deviation of the individual securities. Obviously, with a larger number of securities the unique factor variability could be reduced even further, perhaps close to zero in a large portfolio.

The Arbitrage Pricing Model

The arbitrage pricing model was developed by Stephen Ross [1976] as a means of identifying the equilibrium returns that would be offered by securities that are influenced by a number of macro factors like those we used to describe returns in the prior section. In effect, Ross decided that the CAPM began with some tenets that were difficult to support, and as a consequence the model was suspect. He posited a more complex world, such as that depicted in Equation (10–2), and began investigating to determine if a set of *equilibrium returns* could be deduced from this picture of the way security returns are generated. Ross' logic proceeds with the assumption that there are a limited number of market factors, *F*, that influence security returns, as in Equation (10–2). It also assumes, as in the CAPM, that markets are operating efficiently, and that investors are risk-averse (in the sense of expressing diminishing marginal utility for wealth). It does not assume homogeneous expectations of returns, nor that investors select their portfolios according to portfolio mean and standard deviation.

---

[2]These values simply calculate

$$\sum_{i=1}^{11} x_i\beta_{i1} \text{ and } \sum_{i=1}^{11} x_i\beta_{i2}$$

An implicit part of this model's development is that investors receive the proceeds from the short sale. As we discussed in Chapter 4, investors in general cannot use these funds to expand their investment level. There are ways to effect a sale to generate approximately these portfolio weights (with the use of options, for example), and some investors have the flexibility to use short-sale proceeds (brokerage houses) so the assumption—and thus the model—may still hold in principle.

The model proceeds by forming a portfolio by selecting weights so that there is:

1. No systematic risk due to factor h on the portfolio.

(10–4)
$$\beta_{ph} = \sum_{i=1}^{N} x_i \beta_{ih} = 0, \text{ for all } h$$

2. No net investment, $\Sigma_i^N x_i = 0$.
3. Enough securities so that $\Sigma_i^N x_i \tilde{e}_i \approx 0$.

That is, the βs for each factor for the portfolio are all zero, and the weights are also constructed so that the proceeds from short sales just offset the positive investment amounts in the securities that make up the portfolios. Moreover, the portfolio is made up of enough securities so that the effect of any unique influence would be unimportant.

The key economic observation of arbitrage pricing theory (the APT) is only to note that any portfolio that (1) has no systematic risk, (2) has no net investment, and (3) has no unsystematic or residual variability *must, in equilibrium, offer no return.* If such a portfolio did offer a positive return, investors would flock to the portfolio, thereby altering the prices of the securities it contained, thereby proving that the initial prices were not equilibrium prices.

It is easy to see why this is called the **arbitrage pricing model.** We defined arbitrage as early as Chapter 2 as a term that has been used for centuries to denote **actions that are risk-free and require no investment to capitalize on a market imperfection.**[3] In this case, a portfolio is formed that is long in some securities and short in others to provide a no-net investment, no-risk portfolio.

The APT then goes one step further and with the use of some subtler rationale (and higher mathematics) is able to show that the individual security's expected return, in equilibrium, is equal to the summed products of its β coefficients with premiums per unit of risk associated with each factor, 1 through h. Thus,

(10–5)   *Arbitrage Pricing Model*

$$E(\tilde{R}_i) = \lambda_0 + \beta_{i1}\lambda_1 + \beta_{i2}\lambda_2 + \cdots + \beta_{ih}\lambda_h$$

$$\begin{array}{ccc} \textit{Equilibrium} \\ \textit{expected return} \end{array} = \begin{array}{c} \textit{Risk-free} \\ \textit{rate} \end{array} + \begin{array}{l} \textit{Sum of a series of risks (βs)} \\ \textit{each times the price of} \\ \textit{each unit of risk (λ).} \end{array}$$

The value of λ_h is the market price for the hth type of risk, β_{ih}, contained in security i. Thus, λ_0 would be the risk-free rate. The other λs would be positive or negative (a negative price for that risk) and would add to or subtract from the security's equilibrium expected return. An equilibrium return, over and above the risk-free rate, is created by the market's dislike for having to accept the risk of these factors. Thus, if λ_3 is positive, it indicates an aversion by the market to the risk contained in that factor, F_3.

Suppose F_3 is associated with labor productivity. As labor productivity unexpectedly

---

[3]Arbitragers in the foreign exchange market, for example, attempt to profit by simultaneously selling one currency in, say, London and buying the same currency in New York. Or they may simultaneously buy marks with pounds, francs with marks, and pounds with francs to capture imperfections of another sort.

increases, F_3 is positive, and firms with high β_3 would find their actual returns very high. As F_3 is negative with β_3 high, actual returns would be very low. Such would be the nature of risk associated with holding firms with high values of β_3. How would investors be persuaded to hold such a risky firm in their portfolio? Clearly, investors would hold such firms only if they offer a sufficient premium. The equilibrium expected return, $E(\tilde{R}_i)$, would have to be high enough or else the security would not be held. Thus, λ_3 must be positive.

How could we find out how much the market charges for bearing this risk? The answer is: (1) to form a well-diversified portfolio with zero risk on all factors but the one of interest and an arbitrary level of positive risk (say $\beta_3 = 1.0$) on the factor of interest, and (2) see how much the expected return on this portfolio exceeds the risk-free rate. That is, compute

(10–6) $$\lambda_3 = E(\tilde{R}_{p3}) - \lambda_0$$

where the portfolio has $\beta_{p3} = 1.0$ and $\beta_{ph} = 0.0$ for all other factors.

As in the CAPM, this is not easy to accomplish because of the difficulty of directly observing *expected* returns. However, we may be able to measure $E(\tilde{R}_{p3})$ using ex post data and by so doing determine if the APT conforms to market realities.

Similarities between the APT and the CAPM

If there were only one factor, F_1, the APT can be stated as:

(10–7) $$E(\tilde{R}_i) = \lambda_0 + \beta_i \lambda_1$$

and its similarity with the CAPM security market line is obvious. The value of λ_0 corresponds to R_f and λ_1 corresponds to $E(\tilde{R}_m) - R_f$. Thus, it is useful to think of the APT as more general and less restrictive than the CAPM. It doesn't require that all investors hold *the* market portfolio since it does not make use of the market portfolio concept at all, only that portfolios are constructed based on the factors to eliminate arbitrage profits.[4] The APT, in other words, forces equilibrium by requiring the *law of one price* to hold for all possible portfolio combinations. Two securities with the same package of βs would be forced to offer the same expected return.

The model is also more general by being able explicitly to account for the impact of numerous factors on security returns. Thus, it starts from a view of the world that is undoubtedly closer to reality.

The major disadvantage of the model is that the factors are not well specified a priori. Consequently, we have a much more difficult time saying what it is that specifically is important in establishing equilibrium relationships. The model doesn't define what factor 1 is, what factor 2 is, and so on. We are left to find out by exploring actual markets. This is not a problem with the CAPM, since the only "factor" that is priced is the expected return on the market portfolio ($E(\tilde{R}_m)$). And, the **market portfolio is well defined conceptually** (though it may be rather hard to assess empirically). This is a significant

---

[4]The model does implicitly assume that investors hold the same beliefs regarding the βs, for if it didn't, investors would flock to different arbitrage portfolios, each attempting to capture an arbitrage profit. But a lack of agreement on the βs would limit the market ability to force a stable equilibrium.

advantage for the CAPM over the APT and is the reason for the more widespread use of the CAPM in applications to actual security markets.[5]

Of course, theory can help us specify the APT factors. To do this, however, we may have to know more about the things that influence the cash flows and discount rates that form the basis for the returns and risks of securities. This is much like the problem we have with the CAPM. For the capital-asset pricing model we need to know the theoretical specification of the market portfolio, whereas for the APT we need to know what things account for the possible differences among security returns.

Some of the influences that might seem to be the most important are those things which are most likely to affect investor expectations for the entire market. Examples of these can be extracted from the daily financial pages. Some (or all) security prices seem to be affected by surprises relating to changes in interest rates, inflation rates, the level of national output, or productivity. Others might be related to capacity utilization in the industrial sector or the skills of the labor force.

Not all of these influences are independent of each other, of course. It may be difficult to identify the one influence that corresponds exactly to factor 1, say. More likely the estimated factors reflect the influence of the market's "packaging" of the information to specify an influence on a security or group of securities. Moreover, not all of the variables that might play a part in defining a factor need be measurable. Political trends to the left or right might contribute to one of the factors identified in the APT.

Let us now give some attention to tests of the arbitrage pricing model to see if it serves as an alternative or supplement to the CAPM.

Tests of Arbitrage Pricing Theory

The most basic theoretical difference between the CAPM and the APT is that the APT **allows for more than one market factor to explain expected returns.** Sole reliance on the market portfolio, as in the CAPM, is not necessary.

Empirical tests of the APT rely on a "hunt" for several **general market factors** that seem to govern security returns. The hunt proceeds as follows:

1. Form a matrix of historical returns for a large number of securities over many different consecutive (monthly) time periods:

$$
\begin{bmatrix}
R_{11}R_{21} \ldots R_{N1} \\
R_{12}R_{22} \ldots R_{N2} \\
R_{13}R_{23} \ldots R_{N3} \\
\quad \cdot \quad \cdot \qquad \cdot \\
\quad \cdot \quad \cdot \qquad \cdot \\
\quad \cdot \quad \cdot \qquad \cdot \\
R_{1T}R_{2T} \ldots R_{NT}
\end{bmatrix}
$$

R_{it} is the return on security i in period t.

---

[5]By *applications* we mean not only in empirical studies of return relationships, but also applications to decision making, such as might be required by investors engaging in security analysis or by brokerage firms attempting to locate under- or overvalued securities.

2. Use a statistical technique called factor analysis to reduce this matrix to a smaller number of variables which over time explains a sizable portion of the variability of the original matrix. These new variables are called factors and their values are called **factor scores:**

$$\begin{bmatrix} F_{11}F_{21} \ldots F_{h1} \\ F_{12}F_{22} \ldots F_{h2} \\ \cdot \quad \cdot \qquad \cdot \\ \cdot \quad \cdot \qquad \cdot \\ \cdot \quad \cdot \qquad \cdot \\ F_{1T}F_{2T} \ldots F_{hT} \end{bmatrix}$$

F_{ht} is the factor score of factor h in period t.

3. Regress each firm's returns R_{it} on these factor scores to get a set of h different β coefficients. Thus, each security might have three β coefficients if three factors were present:

$$\tilde{R}_{it} = \alpha_i + \beta_{i1}\tilde{F}_{1t} + \beta_{i2}\tilde{F}_{2t} + \beta_{i3}\tilde{F}_{3t} + \tilde{\varepsilon}_{it}$$

Each β would measure how this security's return responds to that factor. A higher β would correspond to more covariability, just as in the CAPM case. This expression would be the multiple-factor or equivalent of the market model.

4. Form portfolios (arbitrage portfolios) in a way that sets one of the β coefficients equal to 1.0 for the portfolio, sets all other β coefficients to zero, and find the portfolio (subject to these conditions) that has the minimum variance for each level of return. This is equivalent to tracing out the *efficient set* subject to additional restrictions.

5. See if the return on that portfolio is different from the risk-free interest rate. If it is, then that factor is important in the pricing of securities. If it is not, then that factor is not something that investors wish to avoid even though the factor influences ex post returns.

6. Redo step 4, setting the next β equal to 1.0 and all others to zero while forming the portfolio. Then, redo step 5 to see if that factor is priced in the market.

Tests of the APT have found the following:

1. For relatively small groups of common stocks (Hughes [1982] used 110) studies have found that a *number* of factors were important in summarizing the return matrix.

2. Between three and five of the factors were important enough to affect the relative returns offered on the securities.

These two conclusions together tend to suggest the APT might do a better job of describing reality than does the CAPM. However, the results also indicate:

3. The most important factor accounted for a much greater proportion of the variability than all other factors combined (30 percent for factor 1 relative to 21 percent for all other factors). Is this the market portfolio factor? Another study found the correlation between this first factor and the S&P 500 was in the neighborhood of .95.

4. The factors that were important for one group of securities were not always closely related to the factors that were estimated to be important for another group of securities in the same time period. Thus, consistency in the measurement of the factors seems to be somewhat lacking.

Do the Coefficients on the Factors Explain the Differences between Securities' Returns?

Finding that certain factors, F_{ht}, explain the time series of security returns is analogous to finding, in the market model, that the returns on individual securities over time can be explained by the returns on a market index, R_{It}. The β_{ih} coefficients measure the volatility of the returns to the hth factor. That does not mean that those factors are important elements determining equilibrium returns and the prices of securities. Thus, to *prove* the APT we are required to investigate possible relationships between long-run security returns and the estimated β_{ih} coefficients. This would be analogous to the cross-sectional studies of the CAPM that were reported in Table 9–4.

Unfortunately, statistical problems prevent very direct estimation of the relation between the security returns and the β_{ih} coefficients. Consequently, there has been a rather heated argument in the literature regarding whether any of the procedures accomplish what they are supposed to. Nevertheless, keeping in mind the different opinions about the validity of the statistical approaches, the cross-sectional regressions suggest that two or three of these factors are "priced." That is, they are of sufficient concern (either liked or disliked) to investors that they affect equilibrium security returns.

What Are These Factors?

Ultimately, the proof of the APT, and its usefulness for describing the differences in expected returns on securities, depends on our ability to summarize the nature of the factors. Is one factor related to interest rates and another to changes in the level of productivity in the economy? The inability of the theory to give us much intuition about the factors is one of the drawbacks to its applicability. Wall Street is not likely to make much use of a theory that cannot be tied into something that's both understood and observable. Consequently, a good deal of effort is now being devoted to investigations of the statistical relationship between the estimated factor time series and other macroeconomic variables.

Work by Chen, Roll, and Ross [1983] has found that a statistical association exists between the two or three most important factors and a number of macroeconomic variables that one would expect to influence security prices. The macroeconomic variables that were found to be important included ones that measured the unanticipated change in the term structure of interest rates, the yearly growth rate of industrial production, the change in the growth rate of industrial production, and unanticipated changes in the difference in returns on lower-grade and higher-grade bonds.

There also was an indication that some of these macroeconomic variables were able to explain the cross-sectional differences among security returns depending on the volatility of the security's return to that variable. In other words, the macro-variables seemed able to explain the different returns generated by securities, much like beta is able to explain the differences between security returns in cross-sectional studies of the CAPM. This is evidence, consistent with the APT, that these factors are "priced" in the marketplace.

The APT and a Multifactor CAPM

In theory, the APT is more general, and might be expected to describe equilibrium security returns better. Thus, the facts, to some extent, point to the APT being able to capture additional information on the determinants of equilibrium returns. Nevertheless, the empirical effort thus far seems unable to discriminate strongly between the APT and the CAPM. Tests of the CAPM against the APT as an alternative hypothesis haven't led to a rejection of the CAPM, and tests of the APT against the CAPM as an alternative hypothesis haven't led to a rejection of the APT.

Indeed, the real question centers on whether the two models lead to substantially different predictions about the behavior of security returns (though, of course, they do have different logical roots). One can think of the CAPM beta coefficient as measuring the security's volatility in response to R_m, where R_m itself summarizes the impact of a number of factors present in the market and explicitly priced as suggested by the APT. This would lead to a near equality between the right-hand sides of the APT and the CAPM, or

(10–8) *A Multifactor CAPM*

$$\beta_i(E(R_m) - R_f) = \beta_{i1}\lambda_1 + \beta_{i2}\lambda_2 + \cdots + \beta_{ih}\lambda_h$$

$$\frac{CAPM\ risk}{premium} = \frac{APT\ risk\ premiums\ based\ on\ a}{a\ number\ of\ factors}$$

The right-hand side of this expression is specified in a more detailed manner. As a result, it may be more useful in understanding how securities are priced and in developing portfolio selection strategies. Nevertheless, the left-hand-side will be quite adequate for summary statements about security returns, especially when one factor tends to dominate (and is closely correlated with R_m) or if the risk premiums on all but one of the factors are small. Moreover, we know that R_m will reflect changes in underlying economically important events (such as changes in the structure of interest rates). Yet, as we gain more information on the connection between these underlying economic events and the returns established for securities, there will be an effort to describe security returns more precisely. This will allow us to take advantage of the detail expressed by the right-hand side of the expression above. In other words, there will be a natural tendency for financial practice to make use of models that begin to look like the APT. In fact, as we begin our discussion of the valuation of securities in Chapter 11, we discuss the kinds of factors that affect security returns and the response of returns to these factors (i.e., we discuss F_{ht} and security $\beta_h s$), though it's done within the context of the CAPM and the SML.

Summary

The objective of the arbitrage pricing model is to identify equilibrium asset prices or, equivalently, expected security returns and risks. The approach begins with the very practical and applied observation that securities are influenced more by some marketwide factors than by others (e.g., interest-sensitive stocks). Then, the model uses the economic rule that all equivalent portfolios ought to offer the same returns (to prevent arbitrage) to derive the prices the market attaches to the various factors that affect security returns. Securities, then, offer equilibrium returns according to their reaction or sensitivity to the factors and the market prices for the factors. This compares with the capital-asset pricing model where there is but one factor, the market portfolio, one sensitivity coefficient, the security's β_i, and one market price for the factor, $E(R_m) - R_f$.

Empirically there is some support for the existence of between three and five common-market factors that influence security returns and that are priced in the market. However, empirical testing is in its infancy in this area, and concrete results proving the APT or disproving the CAPM do not exist. For this reason it's useful to think of the CAPM and APT as different variants of the true, but perhaps unknown, equilibrium pricing model. Both are, therefore, useful in supplying intuition into the way security prices and equilibrium returns are established.

References

Banz, R. [1981] "The Relationship between Return and Market Value of Common Stocks," *Journal of Financial Economics* (March).

Blume, Marshall E.; Gultekin, Mustafa N.; and Gultekin, N. Bulent. [1986] "On the Assessment of Return Generating Models." Rodney L. White Center for Financial Research, The Wharton School, University of Pennsylvania.

Brown, Keith C.; Harlow, W. Van, III; and Smith, Stephen D. [1986] "Assessing the Impact of Structural Change in Security Pricing Models and Tests for Abnormal Performance." Working Paper, University of Texas.

Brown, Stephen J., and Weinstein, Mark I. [1983] "A New Approach to Testing Asset Pricing Models: The Bilinear Paradigm." *Journal of Finance* (June).

Chen, Nai-Fu. [1983] "Some Empirical Tests of the Theory of Arbitrage Pricing." *Journal of Finance* (December).

Chen, Nai-Fu; Roll, Richard; and Ross, Stephen A. [1983] "Economic Forces and the Stock Market: Testing the APT and Alternative Asset Pricing The-

ories." Working Paper, University of Chicago (December).

Cho, D. Chinhyung; Elton, Edwin J.; and Gruber, Martin J. [1984] "On the Robustness of the Roll and Ross Arbitrage Pricing Theory." *Journal of Financial and Quantitative Analysis* (March).

Dhrymes, Phoebus J.; Friend, Irwin; and Gultekin, N. Bulent. [1984] "A Critical Reexamination of the Empirical Evidence on the Arbitrage Pricing Theory." *Journal of Finance* (June).

Dybvig, Philip H., and Ross, Stephen A. [1985] "Yes, The APT is Testable." *Journal of Finance* (September).

Gibbons, Michael R. [1982] "Multivariate Tests of Financial Models: A New Approach." *Journal of Financial Economics* (March).

Grinblatt, Mark, and Titman, Sheridan. [1983] "Factor Pricing in a Finite Economy." *Journal of Financial Economics* (December).

Hughes, Patricia. [1982] "A Test of the Arbitrage Pricing Theory." Working Paper, University of British Columbia, (June).

King, Benjamin. [1966] "Market and Industry Factors in Stock Price Behavior." *Journal of Business* (Supplement, January).

MacKinlay, Craig. [1985] "On Multivariate Tests of the CAPM." Working Paper (No. 25-85). University of Pennsylvania.

Perry, Philip R. [1982] "The Time-Variance Relationship of Security Returns: Implications for the Returns-Generating Stochastic Process." *Journal of Finance* (June).

Pettit, R. Richardson, and Westerfield, Randolph. [1972] "A Model of Capital Asset Risk." *Journal of Financial and Quantitative Analysis* (March).

Reinganam, M. [1981] "Misspecification of Capital Asset Pricing: Empirical Anomalies Based on Earnings Yields and Market Values." *Journal of Financial Economics* (March).

Roll, R., and Ross, S. [1980] "An Empirical Investigation of the Arbitrage Pricing Theory." *Journal of Finance* (December).

Roll, Richard, and Ross, Stephen A. [1984] "A Critical Reexamination of the Empirical Evidence on the Arbitrage Pricing Theory: A Replay." *Journal of Finance* (June).

Rosenberg, Barr. [1974] "Extra Market Components of Covariance among Security Returns." *Journal of Financial and Quantitative Analysis* (March).

Ross, Stephen. [1976] "The Arbitrage Theory of Capital Asset Pricing." *Journal of Economic Theory* 13 (December).

Ross, Stephen. [1978] "The Current Status of the Capital Asset Pricing Model (CAPM)." *Journal of Finance* (June).

Shanken, J. [1982] "The Arbitrage Pricing Theory: Is It Testable?" *Journal of Finance* (December).

Shanken, Jay. [1985] "Multi-Beta CAPM or Equilibrium-APT?: A Reply." *Journal of Finance* (September).

Shanken, Jay. [1986] "Multivariate Proxies and Asset Pricing Relations." *Journal of Financial Economics*.

Sharpe, William. [1973] "The Capital Asset Pricing Model: A Multi-Beta Interpretation." Research Paper No. 183. Stanford, Calif.: Stanford Graduate School of Business (September).

Sharpe, William F. [1984] "Factor Models, CAPMs, and the APT." *Journal of Portfolio Management* (Fall).

Questions and Problems

1. Multifactor models of security returns have received increased attention. The arbitrage pricing theory (APT) probably has drawn the most attention and has been proposed as a replacement for the capital-asset pricing model (CAPM). Briefly explain the primary differences between APT and CAPM.

   CFA

2. Define what is meant by an arbitrage profit.

3. Assume that the return-generating process is described by two factors, A and B, and that the constant component of return is zero. A's factor value is .04 while B's factor value is −.12. XYZ Corporation's factor loading on A is 1.0 while its factor loading on B is 0.7. Its total return is .06. Calculate its idiosyncratic (nonsystematic) return.

   CFA

4. The arbitrage pricing theory (APT) differs from the capital-asset pricing model because the APT:

   a. Recognizes and prices unsystematic risk factors.
   b. Recognizes more than one systematic risk factor.
   c. Places more emphasis on market risk.
   d. Minimizes the importance of diversification.

   CFA

5. Suppose that there were three market factors that affect security returns: an interest-rate factor, a productivity factor, and a technology factor. Identify three firms or kinds of firms in each category that would tend to have high-factor βs (e.g., a savings and loan might have a high-interest-rate factor β) and explain your choice.

6. Suppose one firm has a beta coefficient on factor 1 of 1.5 and on factor 2 of .6. A second firm has a beta on factor 1 of −.2 and on factor 2 of

1.2. Form a portfolio with these two securities with a zero value for β_1. What is the beta on factor 2 in this case? Form a portfolio with a zero value for β_2. What is the beta on factor 1 in this case?

7. Recently, an analyst used historical return data to estimate the market-model beta coefficients of Boeing and Weyerhauser, and found them to be 1.5 and .75, respectively. However, the analyst believes that returns normally are generated by a two-factor model of the form:

$$R_i = \gamma_{i0} + \beta_{i1} \text{ (interest-rate factor)} + \beta_{i2} \text{ (productivity factor)} + \varepsilon_i$$

which for Boeing and Weyerhauser would take the form:

$$R_{BA} = \gamma_{BA0} + 1.75 \text{ (interest-rate factor)} + .5 \text{ (productivity factor)} + \varepsilon_{BA}$$

$$R_{WY} = \gamma_{WY0} + .55 \text{ (interest-rate factor)} + 1.5 \text{ (productivity factor)} + \varepsilon_{WY}$$

Explain to the analyst how he was able to come up with historically estimated *market-model betas* of 1.5 and .75 for these two firms. Suppose, in reality the two factors ordinarily are *equally* likely to impact security returns. If this is the case, what would be a reasonable forecast of the market-model betas for the future?

P A R T

IV

VALUATION

11

Introduction to Valuation

The Basic Concept

> Capital, in the sense of capital *value,* is simply future income discounted or, in other words, capitalized. The value of any property, or rights to wealth, is its value *as a source of income* and is found by discounting that expected income. . . .
>
> Not until we know how much income an item of capital will probably bring us can we set any valuation on that capital at all. . . .
>
> The present worth of any article is what buyers are willing to give for it and sellers are ready to take for it. In order that each man may logically decide what he is willing to give or take, he must have: (1) some idea of the value of the future benefits which that article will yield, and (2) some idea of the rate of interest by which these future values may be translated into present values by discounting.

These words, written in 1906 by the eminent economist, Irving Fisher, marked the inception of a revolution in economic thought; a revolution which gave birth to the field of finance. The ideas he expressed in this brief excerpt from his seminal book *The Theory of Interest* have since been universally embraced by financial economists and finance practitioners as defining the factors which govern the value of both real and financial assets. Prior to Fisher's writings it was widely believed, for example, that the value of an agricultural crop depended on the value of the land it was grown on. No one possessed, however, a workable method of determining the value of the land except for the usual, but empty, reference to "supply and demand." Fisher realized that the value of the land depended on the expected value of its crops, and not vice versa. This conclusion, and his further development of it, led to the development of today's concepts of valuation.

There are two reasons for studying the valuation of financial securities. First, the study can help us understand how other investors determine how much they are willing to pay for different securities, and how their collective actions determine market prices. If we understand what factors influence those investors' assessments of value, we can better understand how changes in those factors will influence the future course of market prices. Second, we can apply valuation concepts to detect securities that appear to be "mispriced"; that is, to find securities which offer returns that exceed or fall short of those available on other securities with equivalent risk (if any exist). If successful in this endeavor, we can expect to reap financial rewards in the form of above-equilibrium investment returns. After all, that is ultimately the strongest reason for studying finance in the first place.

Fisher's views on valuation sound simple. However, they raise a good many questions which must be answered if we plan to apply them. He speaks, for example, of "discounting" future income. But what is the appropriate discount rate? And how is the future "income" on a financial security generated? If future income is uncertain, and investors disagree about its magnitude, whose forecasts should be used in assessing value?

This chapter, and the four following it, are devoted to an in-depth analysis of the answers to these questions and others. We would like you to know at the outset that the issues covered in these next few chapters provide the basis for applied investment analysis, or what is more commonly referred to as **security analysis.** Throughout our discussion we use examples to illustrate how concepts of valuation are applied as a prerequisite for success in financial markets.

Three Concepts of Value

"A person who owns one clock always knows what time it is, but a person with two clocks can never be sure." Fortunately or unfortunately, the concept of security valuation is a "three-clock" subject. Three separate concepts of value populate the finance literature. All are highly important. But each is appropriate in a different context, and unless the context of a particular discussion of "value" is made clear, we will be unsure of what is meant. The three definitions—discussed below—are: (1) **personal value, or personal worth,** (2) **market value or price,** and (3) **underlying equilibrium value,** or **intrinsic worth.**

Personal Value

In the financial marketplace, each investor attempts to assess the future cash flows or income from a financial security, and each discounts this future income to reflect the expected rewards for time and risk-bearing. If those future cash flows are uncertain, the investor must forecast them. Moreover, if the investor does not know with absolute certainty what the expected rewards for time and risk-bearing are (since they may not be directly observable), estimates must be substituted. For these two reasons, investors could disagree on a security's value. Whenever this happens, my subjective estimate of a security's "worth," or my personal value, may differ from yours. Thus, while I may calculate the value of a share of Allied Corporation to be "worth" $72.87, based on my assessment of its future cash flows and the appropriate discount rate, you may calculate the same share to be worth only $41.50. The concept of **personal value,** then—as its name implies—is an estimate of value that can vary from investor to investor, even though it is based on a common attempt to measure the present worth of a stream of future benefits. In financial markets the common term for the activity leading to a personal value is **fundamental analysis.**

Market Value (Price)

Market value, unlike personal value, is a readily observable, same-for-all investors concept. On a given day, Allied Corporation's common stock may sell for $50.25, regardless of whether or not I am willing to pay up to $72.87 for it. This happens because, in the collective judgments of all other investors in the market (i.e., the interaction of supply and demand), the current value of the stock is $50.25. **Market price** in a very real sense represents the prevailing "consensus" expectations in the marketplace at a single point in time. This concensus is based on information currently available to, and used by, investors. If securities markets operate in a manner consistent with the efficient market hypothesis, as discussed in Chapter 6, all information contained in the publicly available information set, ϕ_t, at time t and which is relevant to assessing the future cash flows and discount rate for a given security will be taken into account in its current market price. On the other hand, if the market is inefficient, then some piece of relevant public information is not fully reflected in the security's market price. In any event, however, it is clear that current market price is one estimate of a security's worth—it is the estimate that reflects the current market consensus.

Underlying Equilibrium Value

We use the term **underlying equilibrium value** to represent the intrinsic value of a security. This is the value that would be placed on the investment opportunity if full information were available to market participants regarding the prospects for the security's future cash flows and discount rate. Full information, however, is a nebulous concept in securities markets. Interpreting full information to mean perfect foresight would so trivialize the idea as to make it useless. At the other extreme, if full information is used to describe what is available to the marketplace, there would be no difference between the market price of a security and its intrinsic value.

In our view, **full information** means the **set of facts, figures, and opinions that exist and that, if made available to the marketplace, would tend to affect the security's market price.** This normally is a more complete set of information than that actually available to the market, and differences between this information set and ϕ_t give rise to the possibility that market price and intrinsic value (or equilibrium value) might differ.

An example may help to clarify the difference. In merger negotiations it is fairly common for each of the firms to make available detailed information on operations, marketing, and financial arrangements to the staff experts of the other firm for their analysis and valuation. Each firm would request this as a means for assessing whether the merger is a "good fit." Some of this information is proprietary and would not be disclosed to the investing public. With this information the staff could come closer to determining the intrinsic value or underlying worth of the security. Certainly, then, the staff might arrive at a different estimate of value than the market price. This assessment of equilibrium value is important. It represents the best estimate available (at least given the information known to the staff, and the staff's expertise) of the value toward which market price will tend to move as time passes and the firm's operating results are revealed to the investing public.

Of course, it's possible that sufficient information is delivered to the market to ensure that the market price of the security is the same as (or very close to) the intrinsic value. In such a case we argue that the security is in equilibrium (thus the term *equilibrium value*). In this case the market price reflects the more complete set of information relevant to the valuation of the security, and there would be no excess supply or demand for the security created with the use of that (public) information.

In the narrower context of the capital-asset pricing model (CAPM), for this state of affairs to prevail, all securities must have market prices which exactly compensate investors for their systematic risk, β_i. At such prices each security would offer an equilibrium return that is the same as all other securities with the same risk, or all securities would plot exactly on the security market line. No securities will offer returns in excess of these market-determined rewards for time and risk, nor will any securities offer lower returns.

If actual markets depart from this ideal, and certainly they must sometimes, since some information is kept from the market, then a security's market price can differ from its CAPM equilibrium value (its CAPM intrinsic value). If that happens, the security's price is in disequilibrium. Of course, as more and more information is delivered to the market, investors will note the discrepancy between the market price and the equilibrium value of the security, change their demands, and affect market price. As a result, **market price will move toward the equilibrium value of the security.** If that is the case, and the CAPM representation of equilibrium value is a powerful, rather than a weak, force, those with skills at detecting the differences between intrinsic value and market price will possess very useful talents.

"If the rest of the market saw things as I do, the price would soar," is a familiar attitude on Wall Street, and one that is not inconsistent with our concepts of value. The comment reflects the investor's personal assessment of value. Whether the price of the security soars or not depends on whether equilibrium value exceeds the current market price. If our investor's personal view of the value of the security is close to the equilibrium value, then he will profit from his forecast as market price moves toward equilibrium. In our view, for the investor to be "right" we think it is necessary for him or her to understand the manner in which market prices are established and the basis for the security's intrinsic value. It is to these subjects that we now turn.

Single-Period Valuation

The three definitions of "value" can be quantified in the context of a single-period model. Suppose at time 0, the current moment in time, the *market price* of security i equals P_{i0}^m. Investors in the marketplace, in evaluating all information to which they have access, on average expect security i's time 1 market price to equal $E^m(\tilde{P}_{i1})$; its time 1 dividend (cash income) to equal $E^m(\tilde{D}_{i1})$; and the discount rate over the period to equal $E^m(\tilde{R}_{i1})$.

Both $\tilde{P}_{i1}$ and $\tilde{D}_{i1}$ are random variables. For the sake of clarity, we have used the superscript m here to highlight the fact that these are the market's currently prevailing consensus judgments at time 0. Given these forecasts, the market price of the security is represented by the valuation expression,

(11–1) *Market Price*

$$P_{i0}^m = \frac{E^m(\tilde{P}_{i1}) + E^m(\tilde{D}_{i1})}{1 + E^m(\tilde{R}_{i1})}$$

$$\frac{Market}{price} = \begin{array}{l} \textit{The market's consensus expectations of cash} \\ \textit{flows discounted at the market's consensus} \\ \textit{return demanded from this security.} \end{array}$$

Thus, Equation (11–1) suggests that, at time 0, the beliefs and forecasts of investors are aggregated (through investors' supplies and demands) and are summarized in its market price, P_{i0}^m. This price—at the instant in time it exists—reflects the market's "collective" judgment of worth. Moreover, if the security is purchased at that market price, the *consensus* opinion suggests one can expect to earn the required return, $E^m(\tilde{R}_{i1})$.

Two subtleties in this explanation are worth noting. First, since $\tilde{P}_{i1}$ and $\tilde{D}_{i1}$ are random variables, their *actual* values—not their *expectations*—at time 1 will determine the *actual* one-period rate of return that investors will earn. This actual, or ex post return, R_i, may differ from $E^m(\tilde{R}_{i1})$, the market's ex ante expectation. Second, if we allow market prices ever to exist at (temporarily) disequilibrium values, the market price, P_{i0}^m, may not be the underlying equilibrium price. Let us now show why this is the case.

In equilibrium, i's price, denoted as P_{i0}^e, reflects the "true" expectations of the random variables $\tilde{P}_{i1}$ and $\tilde{D}_{i1}$, given "full information" at time 0. We use the notation $E(\tilde{P}_{i1})$ and $E(\tilde{D}_{i1})$ to refer to this set of expectations, to emphasize the point that they can differ, at a particular time, from $E^m(\tilde{P}_{i1})$ and $E^m(\tilde{D}_{i1})$. With this in mind, the equilibrium value, or intrinsic value, is

(11–2) *Equilibrium Price*

$$P_{i0}^e = \frac{E(\tilde{P}_{i1}^e) + E(\tilde{D}_{i1})}{1 + E(\tilde{R}_{i1})}$$

$$\frac{\textit{CAPM equilibrium}}{price} = \begin{array}{l} \textit{The expected cash flows, given all information,} \\ \textit{discounted at a rate that reflects the true} \\ \textit{existing equilibrium-expected return.} \end{array}$$

Equation (11–2) states that security i's equilibrium price equals the discounted value of i's expected future value and cash income, given all information knowable at time 0. At this price, investors can expect to earn a return which compensates them for time and security i's risk. Of course, if the CAPM governs equilibrium returns, the discount rate would compensate the investor for the security's systematic risk, or β_i.

Where does the individual investor's *personal value* fit into this? Suppose investor k estimates security i's worth differently from other investors. This might happen because k has access to a different set of information than others have, or can develop insights with the information that are unavailable to others, i.e., k has greater skills in valuing securities. Whatever the reason, we represent k's expectations for i's future market price and cash income as $E^k(\tilde{P}_{i1})$ and $E^k(\tilde{D}_{i1})$, and k's required return on i as $E^k(\tilde{R}_{i1})$. Using these forecasts, judgment, and knowledge, k arrives at a personal value estimate as follows:

(11–3)   *Personal Worth to Investor k*

$$P_{i0}^k = \frac{E^k(\tilde{P}_{i1}) + E^k(\tilde{D}_{i1})}{1 + E^k(\tilde{R}_{i1})}$$

$$\begin{matrix} k\text{'s personal} \\ \text{estimate of} \\ \text{the value or} \\ \text{price} \end{matrix} = \begin{matrix} k\text{'s expectations of cash flows, given } k\text{'s information set} \\ \text{and method of analysis, discounted at a rate that} \\ \text{reflects } k\text{'s perceptions of the risk-return opportunities} \\ \text{available in the market.} \end{matrix}$$

Thus, in k's judgment (i.e., given all information available to k and with k's skills), the future expected cash income and market price of security i warrant a value for i of P_{i0}^k. At this price, which represents the maximum amount k will be willing to pay, k expects to earn sufficient compensation for risk and for the time value of money.

Comparing (11–3) to (11–1) and (11–2), it seems clear that P_{i0}^k (security i's personal value to any arbitrary investor) can differ from both P_{i0}^m and P_{i0}^e at any time. We take comfort only in the fact that if real markets are reasonably efficient, if all publicly available information is used by at least some investors in estimating security values, and if the CAPM is a roughly accurate portrayal of the real market, we should observe that over time P_{i0}^m will tend to approach P_{i0}^e. Whether or not P_{i0}^k—your or my subjective assessment of worth—will be close enough to P_{i0}^e to capture the gain from the movement of P_{i0}^m, however, will depend on how smart, motivated, and well informed we are.

Much of the discussion in this and succeeding chapters is concerned with these three concepts of valuation. We next proceed to examine them in greater detail. This examination is necessary if we are to apply that equation successfully in practical situations.

Evaluating the Cash Flows

The numerator of the equilibrium valuation model in Equation (11–2) represents the expected value of the probability distribution of i's future cash flows, given everything knowable at time 0. Although actual cash flows depend on events occurring between time 0 and time 1, the cash flow to be discounted is just the expected value of the probability distribution.

Suppose, for example, the level of uncertainty regarding two different securities' cash flows, $\tilde{D}_{i1}$ and $\tilde{D}_{j1}$, (with $E(\tilde{P}_{i1}) = 0$ for now) is characterized by the distributions shown in Figures 11–1(a) and 11–1(b). The amounts $E(\tilde{D}_{i1}) = \$100$ and $E(\tilde{D}_{j1}) = \$120$ are those to be discounted to calculate the present values of each of the securities generating the distributions. The discounting of any other numbers, say, to be on the conservative side, could introduce biases that confound the valuation process and make it internally inconsistent. The use of **expected values** for cash flows leads to a valuation equation that is consistent with the investor's desire to maximize expected utility. Thus, valuation models constructed in this way provide information to the investor that is necessary for determining optimal portfolio weights. The use of the median value or any other value from the probability distribution of outcomes would not yield this result.

FIGURE 11–1   **Sample Probability Distributions of Future Cash Flows for Two Hypothetical Securities**

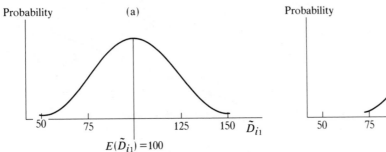

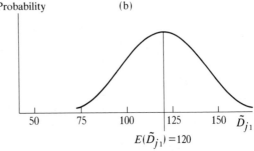

Evaluating the Discount Rate

The discount (capitalization) rate in the denominator of (11–2) measures the expected returns available *in equilibrium* on equivalent risks. This is the **market's opportunity cost** concept of the discount rate. In the capital-asset pricing model the security market line (SML) represents the equilibrium risk-return opportunities offered by all financial assets. Consequently, the equation for the security market line is the one that defines the proper discount rate for determining the present value of future cash flows. It is, as a reminder:

(11–4)   *Security Market Line: The CAPM Expected Return*

$$E(\tilde{R}_{i1}) = R_{f1} + \beta_i[E(\tilde{R}_{m1}) - R_{f1}]$$

Let's assume that Ford Motor Company issued bonds several years ago that are due to mature one year from today. These bonds carry a 14.75 percent coupon rate, which means that a bond with a $1,000 par value promises the payment of $147.50 in interest each year. The next interest payment occurs one year from today, at which time the company also will pay back the principal ($1,000 per bond). If the company defaults on the debt (an eventuality with a 10 percent chance of occurring), the bonds will pay no interest and only $500 in principal. The expected time 1 price is thus $950 = (0.9) ($1,000) + (0.1) ($500), and the expected time 1 interest payment is $132.75 = (0.9)($147.50) + (0.1)($0). The beta of the bonds is 0.2, say, and the risk-free interest rate is 8 percent. The expected return on the market portfolio, $E(\tilde{R}_m)$, is 15 percent, so that $E(\tilde{R}_{m1}) - R_{f1}$, is .07. (This corresponds roughly to the risk premia we have seen for securities over the last 60 years.) What is the equilibrium price of the bonds?

This question can be answered by plugging the appropriate values into Equation (11–2). This gives:

$$P_{F0}^e = \frac{\$950 + \$132.75}{1 + [.08 + (.2)(.07)]} = \frac{\$1,082.75}{1.094} = \$989.72$$

Thus, Ford bonds should sell in equilibrium for $989.72 in order to provide an expected return of 9.4 percent.

FIGURE 11–2   The Security Market Line: Equilibrium

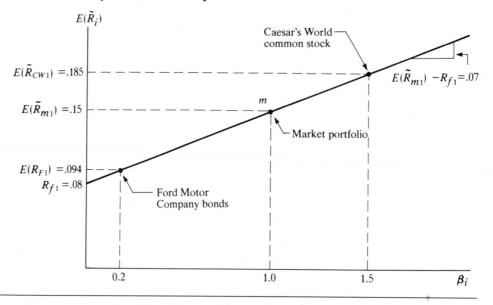

Now suppose a share of Caesar's World common stock is expected to sell for $40 one year from today, and its expected dividend at that time will be zero. The stock's beta is 1.5. What is a share of Caesar's World worth in equilibrium?

Assuming the same risk-free interest rate and market-expected return as before, we can compute the equilibrium price of the stock from Equation (11–2) as follows:

$$P_{CW0}^e = \frac{\$40 + \$0}{1 + [.08 + (1.5)(.07)]} = \frac{\$40}{1.185} = \$33.75$$

Figure 11–2 shows both the Ford bonds and the Caesar's World stock as they plot on the security market line. Notice that the slope of the security market line is .07, so that for each unit increase in β_i, a security's equilibrium expected return increases by 7 percent.

Equilibrium and Disequilibrium

Though we found that the hypothetical equilibrium price, P_{CW0}^e, of a share of Caesar's World common stock should be $33.75 and that a single Ford Motor Company bond should sell for $989.72, it is not necessarily true that their market prices will reflect those values. In fact, in picking up today's *Wall Street Journal,* you may discover that Caesar's World closed yesterday at $30.50, and a Ford Motor Company 14.75 percent bond maturing in one year is selling for $1,010. This means that if you buy the stock at its current price, assuming the forecast of its equilibrium price next year remains the same, you can expect to earn a *higher* rate of return than the 18.5 percent reflected in Figure 11–2. On the other hand, a purchase of the bond at a price of $1,010 implies a *lower* return than the 9.4 percent the market requires in equilibrium, again assuming the expected cash flows are unchanged.

In short, the current market prices of these two securities are in **disequilibrium** relative to the CAPM. If differences of opinion give rise to horse races, the apparent existence of disequilibrium gives rise to an incentive to seek and find securities with disequilibrium prices. And here is why. Any investor would like to capture the difference between the current market price, P_{i0}^m, and the equilibrium price P_{i0}^e. Because there is always a tendency for market prices to move toward equilibrium prices, the investor has the incentive to form *personal value* estimates that best represent P_{i0}^e. If the investor *knew* what P_{i0}^e is, it would be a simple matter to capture the windfall gain from a security as P_{i0}^m moves to P_{i0}^e. Of course P_{i0}^e, the equilibrium price, is a concept of how prices should be set and is not observable. Yet the investor's knowledge that the market tends to push P_{i0}^m toward P_{i0}^e is what provides the incentive for the investor to form a **personal value estimate,** P_{i0}^k. The closer the investor can come to developing a personal value estimate that reflects P_{i0}^e, the better the chance of capturing that profit.

To see how we can apply this, consider the cases of Caesar's World and Ford and their current market prices: P_{CW0}^m at \$30.50 and P_{F0}^m at \$1,010. In the case of Caesar's World the market price is below the equilibrium value:

(11–5a)   *Undervalued Security*

$$\$30.50 = P_{CW0}^m < P_{CW0}^e = \$33.75$$

Consequently, the security is undervalued by the market. In the case of Ford's bond the opposite is true and the market price is above equilibrium value:

(11–5b)   *Overvalued Security*

$$\$1,010 = P_{F0}^m > P_{F0}^e = 989.72$$

Thus Ford's bonds are overpriced by the market. However, the individual investor cannot observe the equilibrium price and consequently must estimate it. This is where the investor's personal value, P_{i0}^k comes in. This value is the investor's best guess of the true equilibrium price. Because P_{i0}^k is formed by the investor to represent P_{i0}^e, the *investor's* concept of over- and undervaluation would result in a comparison,

(11–6a)   *Investor's View of Undervalued Security*

$$P_{i0}^m < P_{i0}^k \text{ (formed as an estimate of } P_{i0}^e)$$

(11–6b)   *Investor's View of Overvalued Security*

$$P_{j0}^m > P_{j0}^k \text{ (formed as an estimate of } P_{j0}^e)$$

Thus, personal value, as we introduced it at the beginning of this chapter, is simply an attempt by the individual to determine the security's equilibrium price and whether the actual market price is above or below it. Obviously a better understanding of what determines equilibrium price, even if it can't be observed, will improve the individual's chances of determining through P_{i0}^k if P_{i0}^m exceeds or falls short of P_{i0}^e.

This whole discussion of equilibrium and disequilibrium can be tied directly to the security market line relationship shown in Figure 11–2. To illustrate the relationship between investor k's concept of over- and undervalued securities relative to the SML, we first define k's perception of security i's expected return if i is purchased *at the current market price*. We will call this k's **return forecast** or (potential) **disequilibrium return,** and denote it as R_i, or,

(11–7) *Investor k's Return Forecast*

$$\hat{R}_{i1} = \frac{E^k(\tilde{P}_{i1}) + E^k(\tilde{D}_{i1}) - P_{i0}^m}{P_{i0}^m}$$

This represents the return the investor would earn if the security is purchased at the current market price and the investor's forecasts of cash flows are actually generated.

As defined, $\hat{R}_{i1}$ differs from $E^m(\tilde{R}_{i1})$ if investor k's forecasts of the security's future cash flows differ from the market's consensus forecast of those flows. $\hat{R}_{i1}$ also differs from $E^k(\tilde{R}_{i1})$ whenever $P_{i0}^k \neq P_{i0}^m$; that is, whenever k's personal estimate of value differs from the market's.

Applying this concept of return to the current example, when k forecasts end-of-period cash flows of \$1,082.75 and \$40 for Ford Motor Bonds and Caesar's World Stock, respectively, we find:

(11–8a) $\hat{R}_{F1} =$ *Disequilibrium-expected return on Ford Motor Company bonds if purchased at the prevailing market price*

$$= \frac{\$1,082.75 - \$1,010.00}{\$1,010.00} = .072, \text{ or } 7.2\%$$

(11–8b) $\hat{R}_{CW1} =$ *Disequilibrium-expected return on Caesar's World common stock if purchased at the prevailing market price*

$$= \frac{\$40 - \$30.50}{\$30.50} = .311, \text{ or } 31.1\%$$

Plotting k's estimate of return relative to the security market line produces a picture like that shown in Figure 11–3.[1]

To investor k, Caesar's World offers a higher than equilibrium return *because* its market price is *less* than the equilibrium price (\$30.50 < \$33.75). Similarly, k expects Ford's bond to offer a lower than equilibrium return *because* its market price is *more* than the equilibrium price (\$1,010 > \$989.72). In fact, a comparison of the equilibrium

---

[1]There could be a variety of reasons for the discrepancies between the rates of return on these two securities and their equilibrium returns (i.e., between the equilibrium value and the current market value). We have already mentioned some of the reasons, but they bear repeating. First, investors in the aggregate may be forecasting expected future cash flows which differ systematically from their equilibrium expectations. This could happen if information is incomplete or very costly, so that investors do not have access to the relevant data. Alternatively, the market could be assessing the betas of these securities incorrectly, so that investors may be overestimating the beta of Caesar's World and underestimating the beta of Ford Motor Company's bonds. Finally, the discrepancies could be due to a disagreement among investors as to the expected return on the market portfolio. Any one, or a combination, of all these things can explain why the market appears to be in disequilibrium.

FIGURE 11–3   The Security Market Line: Disequilibrium

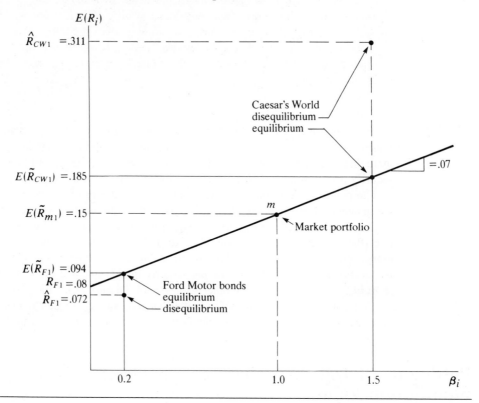

expected return and k's return calculation gives exactly the same information with regard to under- or overvaluation as we obtained from an analysis of market price and equilibrium value summarized in Equations (11–6a) and (11–6b). To be explicit, for Caesar's World stock,

(11–9a)   *Undervalued Security*

$$.311 = \hat{R}_{CW1} > E(\tilde{R}_{CW1}) = .185$$

and for Ford's bonds,

(11–9b)   *Overvalued Security*

$$.072 = \hat{R}_{F1} < E(\tilde{R}_{F1}) = .094$$

The $\hat{R}_{F1}$ and $\hat{R}_{CW1}$ numbers are the investor's best guess of the rate of return from holding each security for one period. Thus, either the price comparison in Equation (11–6) or the return comparison in (11–9) will tell the investor what is necessary.

In this simple, one-period world, the object of security analysis is to find securities whose market prices are temporarily out-of-line with their equilibrium values, or

> Security analysis is predicated on the belief that market forces are powerful enough eventually to draw market prices toward equilibrium prices. Thus, if one finds a security whose market price is *below* (*above*) equilibrium value (so that it plots above (below) the security market line), a return in excess of equilibrium returns can be expected from its purchase (sale) as market price rises (falls) toward equilibrium price.

It may be worth expending time and money engaging in this activity because of the extra return involved! If enough investors do this and equilibrium is attained, all securities, including Caesar's World and Ford eventually (perhaps quickly) will plot *exactly on* the security market line. Figure 11–4 portrays these relationships graphically.

The points made in the figure are central to our theory of valuation: **It suggests the congruence between investment analysis and valuation** (the subject of this and following chapters) **and capital market equilibrium** as represented by the security market line (the market risk-return trade-off). An undervalued security lies above the security market line and offers a return that exceeds the returns on other risk-equivalent securities. An overvalued security lies below the security market line and offers a return that falls short of the return available on other securities of the same risk.[2] Each situation will give rise to a change in price in response to the change in supply and demand when the market becomes aware of the divergence between the equilibrium price and the current market price.

Putting It All Together: The Components of Equilibrium Value

In our simple, one-period world, four components determine a security's equilibrium value. These are:

1. **The magnitude of the expected cash flows, $E(\tilde{P}_{i1}) + E(\tilde{D}_{i1})$.**
2. **The market's reward for time, R_{f1}.**
3. **The riskiness of the future cash flows, β_i.**
4. **The market's reward for risk bearing, $[E(\tilde{R}_{m1}) - \tilde{R}_{f1}]$.**

Any approach to equilibrium valuation must reflect these four components. We have chosen to incorporate the four directly through the use of the CAPM. The investor would use the CAPM form if he believes that equilibrium prices. P_{i0}^e, are set in accordance with the capital-asset pricing model. Doing so would make sense, since the investor hopes to use P_{i0}^k as an estimate of P_{i0}^e to capture the gain generated from the movement of the market price toward P_{i0}^e. Thus, if market prices are established in a way that is generally

---

[2]To say a security is over- or undervalued also is to say that the market is either wrong or is working with a different information set. Clearly, then, the conclusion that a security is in a disequilibrium position places the analyst as a member of the minority—since it's the (financial) majority that sets the market price. The price will change from P_{i0}^m to P_{i0}^k only as the majority of market participants come to concur with the evaluator's expectations.

FIGURE 11–4   Security Market Line: Equilibrium and Disequilibrium

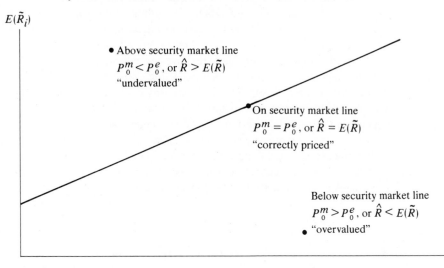

---

consistent with the CAPM, the investor's assessment of value should also. Although we assume throughout the book that the CAPM provides a good workable guide to security valuation, an investor with a different view of the world can adjust the valuation model in Equation (11–3) to suit his or her beliefs.[3]

To this point we have not suggested how the **timing**—as opposed to the **magnitude**—of expected cash flows might influence a security's equilibrium value. A single-period model does not lend itself to such analysis. We next turn to extending the basic single-period model to many periods in order to examine the issue of timing more fully.

Multiperiod Valuation

Bonds and common stocks, of course, are multiperiod securities. Cash flows from these securities are expected over many future periods of time. Consequently, it is necessary to extend our valuation model to allow for this fact.

The Problem

This constitutes something of a problem since, as we presented it, the CAPM is a one-period model. Precisely how it can be extended to two, three, or more periods into

---

[3]One approach to valuation—termed the *certainty equivalent approach*—has not been discussed here, primarily because it is not in widespread use. It has some devotees, however, because it provides a means of incorporating the influence of a security's risk into the numerator of the valuation equation rather than into the denominator, as we have done. If correctly applied, it yields the same equilibrium value as Equation (11–2) yields; however, because its derivation is rather lengthy, we confine our discussion of it to the appendix at the end of this chapter.

the future is not clear. After all, the risk-free interest rate, R_f, and the risk-return trade-off represented by the slope of the security market line, $[E(\bar{R}_m) - R_f]$, may change from one date to the next. This uncertainty regarding future parameters of the CAPM itself creates some uncertainty, namely, about how those future-period cash flows will be valued next year and the year after.

To see the importance of this to the investor, consider a case where an individual faces two investment opportunities, each expecting cash flows for only one period, and each having different risk levels. The first—security i—is an investment in a risk-free Treasury bill paying no interest and maturing one year from today at a value of $10,000. It is expected to offer an equilibrium (risk-free) interest rate of .08, or 8 percent. The other—security j—is a unit of risky commercial paper which also matures in one year and which, at that time, is expected to pay $9,359 in return of principal plus $900 in interest. Security j's beta is 0.4. The equilibrium one-year return on the market portfolio is .15, or 15 percent. Applying Equation (11–2) to the valuation of both securities, we see that:

$$P_{i0}^e = \frac{\$10,000 + \$0}{1 + [.08 + (.0)(.15 - .08)]} = \frac{\$10,000}{1.08} = \$9,259$$

$$P_{j0}^e = \frac{\$9,359 + \$900}{1 + [.08 + (.4)(.15 - .08)]} = \frac{\$10,259}{1.108} = \$9,259$$

This means they should each sell for $9,259 in equilibrium.

It would seem from this that any investor might be indifferent between the two. If we introduce a second period (year) into the analysis, however, with a new investment opportunity available only in the second period, we find this needn't be the case.

Suppose security h will become available at time 1 (that is, at the start of the next period) and represents a new issue of risky commercial paper maturing at time 2. At maturity, it is expected to pay $9,600 in return of principal and $876 in interest. Its beta, like that of security j, is 0.4. However, over the course of the year the general level of interest rates has risen by 4 percentage points. At the beginning of the second year the risk-free rate is 12 percent rather than 8 percent, and the equilibrium return on the market portfolio is 19 percent rather than 15 percent. With this new SML, h's equilibrium price when it is issued at the end of period 1 will be

$$P_{h1}^e = \frac{\$9,600 + \$876}{1 + [.12 + (.4)(.19 - .12)]} = \frac{\$10,476}{1.148} = \$9,125$$

and h's time 1 equilibrium value is expected to be $9,125. The point we make is that the investor's first-period decision (between i and j) will be influenced by the availability of h at time 1. In particular, if h is available at time 1, then the selection of the risky opportunity j at time 0 will supply a greater level of expected cash at time 1. (Recall that j is expected to pay a total of $10,259 at time 1, while i is expected to pay only $10,000.) Actually, j supplies enough extra expected cash that the investor may be able to purchase 1.124 units ($10,259/$9,125) of h when the risk-return opportunities are better at time 1. Only 1.096 units ($10,000/$9,125) can be purchased if i is selected at time 0. Given some assumptions about the investor's utility of consumption in periods 1 and 2, it can be demonstrated that choosing j may be the preferred alternative when next period's opportunities are explicitly considered.

The Multiperiod Solution

The extension of the single-period model of valuation to a multiperiod world is not easy, as this example has illustrated. The valuation of securities now available may depend on the set of opportunities available later. (To a financial economist, this is another way of saying that valuation is *conditional* on future states of the world.) And because new opportunities almost certainly become available as technology changes and new entrepreneurs are born, the market's reward for risk bearing, the risk-free interest rate, and individual security expected returns and betas will probably change, too.

To account explicitly for this, consider the equilibrium-expected return on security i for investment period t as given by:

(11–10) $$E(\tilde{R}_{it}) = R_{ft} + \beta_{it} [E(\tilde{R}_{mt}) - R_{ft}]$$

for $t = 1, 2, \ldots \infty,$

$R_{ft} =$ The risk-free interest rate for period t,

where $\quad \beta_{it} =$ Security i's beta for period t, and

$E(\tilde{R}_{mt}) =$ The equilibrium return for period t on the market portfolio

Security i's equilibrium price at the beginning of that period, or at the end of $t - 1$, can be stated as:

(11–11) $$P^e_{it-1} = \frac{E(\tilde{D}_{it}) + E(\tilde{P}^e_{it})}{1 + E(\tilde{R}_{it})}$$

where $E(\tilde{R}_{it})$ is defined in (11–10). Note that we have now explicitly introduced time as a factor, through the use throughout of the additional subscript t in the discount rate. Thus these expressions implicitly allow for equilibrium returns, or the intercept and slope of the SML to be different at time $t = 5$ than they are at time $t = 328$ or at time $t = 77$. Thus at time 4 (i.e., at the start of the 5th period) investors evaluate all information contained in ϕ_4 and use this to forecast expected security cash flows at time 5, security betas, and the expected equilibrium return on the market between time 4 and 5. The end result is

$$E(\tilde{R}_{i5}) = R_{f5} + \beta_{i5} [E(\tilde{R}_{m5}) - R_{f5}]$$

and

$$P^e_{i4} = \frac{E(\tilde{D}_{i5}) + E(\tilde{P}^e_{i5})}{1 + E(\tilde{R}_{i5})}$$

With this we can view the price in period 4 as period 5's expected cash flows discounted back one period at the equilibrium-expected return available during period 5. In effect, we view the multiperiod valuation problem as a series of one-period problems. P^e_{i4} results from discounting P_{i5}^e and $E(\tilde{D}_{i5})$ at the rate $E(\tilde{R}_{i5})$, and so on. The basic structure to the series of one-period valuations is, then,

$$P_{i0}^e = \frac{E(\tilde{D}_{i1}) + E(\tilde{P}_{i1}^e)}{[1 + E(\tilde{R}_{i1})]} \qquad P_{i3}^e = \frac{E(\tilde{D}_{i4}) + E(\tilde{P}_{i4}^e)}{[1 + E(\tilde{R}_{i4})]}$$

$$P_{i1}^e = \frac{E(\tilde{D}_{i2}) + E(\tilde{P}_{i2}^e)}{[1 + E(\tilde{R}_{i2})]} \qquad P_{i4}^e = \frac{E(\tilde{D}_{i5}) + E(\tilde{P}_{i5}^e)}{[1 + E(\tilde{R}_{i5})]}$$

$$P_{i2}^e = \frac{E(\tilde{D}_{i3}) + E(\tilde{P}_{i3}^e)}{[1 + E(\tilde{R}_{i3})]} \qquad P_{it-1}^e = \frac{E(\tilde{D}_{it}) + E(\tilde{P}_{it}^e)}{[1 + E(\tilde{R}_{it})]}$$

If we substitute for P_{it}^e in each case, starting with the most distant price, the current price of a multiperiod security at time period 0 is

(11–12)   *Multiperiod Equilibrium Value*

$$P_{i0}^e = \frac{E(\tilde{D}_{i1})}{[1 + E(\tilde{R}_{i1})]} + \frac{E(\tilde{D}_{i2})}{[1 + E(\tilde{R}_{i1})][1 + E(\tilde{R}_{i2})]} + \dots$$
$$+ \frac{E(\tilde{D}_{it}) + E(P_{it}^e)}{[1 + E(\tilde{R}_{i1})][1 + E(\tilde{R}_{i2})] \dots [1 + E(\tilde{R}_{it})]}$$

> Equilibrium
> price of a
> multiperiod =
> security
>
> Sum of the discounted values of each of
> the cash flows, where the discount rate
> applied is the SML in each period t
> given the risk of the cash flow.

$E(\tilde{P}_{it}^e)$ is the anticipated sale price of the security in period t in the future. In this framework, the 5th period's cash flow is discounted back through time at the rates $E(\tilde{R}_{i5})$, $E(\tilde{R}_{i4})$, $E(\tilde{R}_{i3})$, $E(\tilde{R}_{i2})$, and $E(\tilde{R}_{i1})$ to account for the returns available on equal-risk investment opportunities in each future period.

Of course there are some assumptions that underly this "derivation." The main one is that $E(\tilde{P}_{it}^e)$ is the same as P_{it}^e for each future t. Thus, we have assumed an equality between expected future equilibrium price and the actual equilibrium price. Since these values are not identical, the above expression for multiperiod value should be viewed only as an approximation to multiperiod equilibrium valuation in a CAPM context. They are guides as to how successive, one-period equilibria tie together into a multiperiod valuation relationship within the CAPM, and not precisely a statement of multiperiod CAPM equilibrium values.

In Equations (11–11) and (11–12) each discount rate reflects the expected risk and risk-return trade-off that exists in that future period. The concept is directly analogous to the single-period equilibrium valuation formula. However, we now see that the *timing*— as well as the *magnitude*—of future cash flows has an important impact on valuation.

The concept of different discount rates for different periods, as implied by these equations, can be depicted graphically, as in Figure 11–5. Here, three security market lines are shown, one applicable to the first investment period, one applicable to the second, and one applicable to the third. Security i's equilibrium-expected return in each

FIGURE 11–5   Multiple Period Risk-Return Trade-Offs

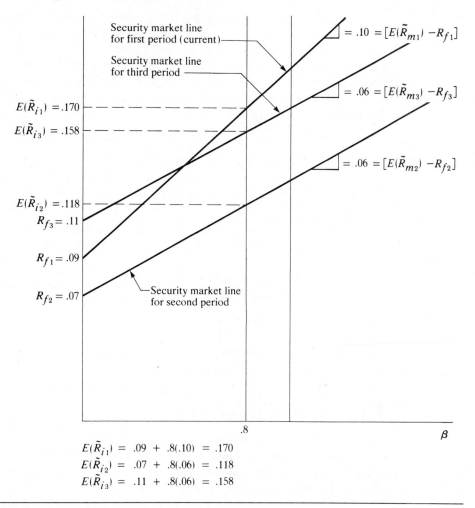

$$E(\tilde{R}_{i_1}) = .09 + .8(.10) = .170$$
$$E(\tilde{R}_{i_2}) = .07 + .8(.06) = .118$$
$$E(\tilde{R}_{i_3}) = .11 + .8(.06) = .158$$

period can be read off the appropriate SML. Thus, with a constant beta of 0.8 in each period, its period 1 expected return is 0.17, or 17 percent, while its date 2 and date 3 expected returns are 11.8 percent and 15.8 percent, respectively. Therefore, if i's expected dividend (cash flow) in each period is $100, the first three terms in its multiperiod valuation equation are given by:

$$P_{i0}^e = \frac{\$100}{(1 + .17)} + \frac{\$100}{(1 + .17)(1 + .118)}$$

$$+ \frac{\$100}{(1 + .17)(1 + .118)(1 + .158)} + \cdots$$

Stability Over Time

In practical situations, Equation (11–12) is extremely difficult to apply and in many cases unnecessarily complex. The fact is that future market equilibrium parameters are difficult to forecast accurately. (Though some do attempt to forecast future interest rates.) A solution to this problem lies in assuming that those parameters are unchanging over time, giving rise to constant values of $E(\tilde{R}_m)$, R_f, and β_i in each future period. That is, we might assume in each period a constant security market line, given by the single-period CAPM relationship,

$$E(\tilde{R}_i) = R_f + \beta_i[E(\tilde{R}_m) - R_f]$$

This allows us to reduce Equation (11–12) to a much simpler form; namely,

(11–13) $P^e_{i0} = \dfrac{E(\tilde{D}_{i1})}{[1 + E(\tilde{R}_i)]^1} + \dfrac{E(\tilde{D}_{i2})}{[1 + E(\tilde{R}_i)]^2} + \ldots + \dfrac{E(\tilde{D}_{iT}) + E(\tilde{P}^e_{iT})}{[1 + E(\tilde{R}_i)]^T}$

The last term, at period T, includes the sale price of the security in that period. If we use Σ to represent the summation of those terms, the multiperiod equilibrium value is summarized as

(11–14)   *Simplified Multiperiod Equilibrium Value*

$$P^e_{i0} = \sum_{t=1}^{T} \frac{E(\tilde{D}_{it})}{[1 + E(\tilde{R}_i)]^t} + \frac{E(\tilde{P}^e_{iT})}{[1 + E(\tilde{R}_i)]^T}$$

Because this simplification is so convenient, it is commonly made by market participants, other practitioners (i.e., those making capital investment decisions for firms), and students of finance. Indeed, we refer to it frequently in the chapters to come.

Personal Value: The Multiperiod Case

In a fashion analogous to our one-period analysis of personal value or worth of a security, a multiperiod concept of personal value can be easily stated. Assuming that investor k applies a constant, unchanging discount rate to security i in each future period, we can write this personal worth assessment as:

(11–15)   *Multiperiod Personal Value*

$$P^k_{i0} = \sum_{t=1}^{T} \frac{E^k(\tilde{D}_{it})}{[1 + E^k(\tilde{R}_i)]^t} + \frac{E(\tilde{P}^k_{iT})}{[1 + E^k(\tilde{R}_i)]^T}$$

The beauty (but *not* the utility) of this relationship lies in its generality. It is based on no particular assumptions about the return-generating process going on in the marketplace. The investor applying this model can estimate security i's expected return in accordance with personal beliefs about the factors on which that expected return is based. These beliefs may, or may not, be in accordance with the CAPM.

Suppose the investor in question has in mind a very general model of return generation; namely that:

$$E^k(\tilde{R}_i) = \begin{array}{l} \textit{A function of the risk-free interest rate and security i's} \\ \textit{risk relative to other securities.} \end{array}$$

Risk, to this hypothetical investor, may include systematic risk but also may encompass many other things. Whatever it does encompass, the investor who applies Equation (11–15) must tacitly believe that, somehow, actual market prices will adjust toward this personal estimate of value.

Market prices, of course, will tend to adjust toward a particular investor's assessment of worth only if that happens to approximate the security's true equilibrium value. But that happy situation can occur only if the investor is able to forecast future cash flows accurately, receives access to a variety of relevant information in a timely manner, and evaluates this information in the way that will disclose whether the market price will rise to the equilibrium price P_{i0}^e (i.e., it's undervalued) or fall to the equilibrium price (i.e., it's overvalued).

Thus, all of the inequality comparisons that formed the basis for conclusions as to whether a security is under- or overvalued in a one-period model hold for a multiperiod model. That is:

(11–6a)   *Undervalued*

$$P_{i0}^m < P_{i0}^k \text{ (formed as an estimate of } P_{i0}^e)$$

(11–6b)   *Overvalued*

$$P_{i0}^m > P_{i0}^k \text{ (formed as an estimate of } P_{i0}^e)$$

or

(11–9a′)   *Undervalued*

$$\hat{R}_i > E^k(\tilde{R}_i)$$

(11–9b′)   *Overvalued*

$$\hat{R}_i < E^k(\tilde{R}_i)$$

supplies the conditions necessary for the investor to determine whether or not the security is priced in equilibrium or disequilibrium relative to the investor's view of the security market line.

What is $\hat{R}_i$ in the multiperiod case? It's still k's expected return on the security—given k's expectations of cash flows and the current market price. Thus, the multiperiod analog for the investor is the solution to $\hat{R}_i$ in the expression,

(11–1b)   *k's Expected Return*

$$P_{i0}^m = \sum_{t=1}^{T} \frac{E^k(\tilde{D}_{it})}{(1 + \hat{R}_i)^t} + \frac{E(\tilde{P}_{iT}^k)}{(1 + \hat{R}_i)^T}$$

which is the rate that would set the present values of the investor's expectations of cash flows equal to the current market price. If the cash flows that are expected are actually received, the actual average return earned by an investor purchasing the stock at P_{i0}^m will be $\hat{R}_i$ in each period between 0 and T. The question is simply whether this value exceeds or falls short of the equilibrium return, $E(\tilde{R}_i)$.

Suppose, for example, an investor forecasts dividends of $4 per share for 10 years, and a sale price at the end of the 10th year of $100 (based perhaps on the present value of dividends from year 11 on). With a current market price for the security of $50 the value of $\hat{R}_i$ is derived from the equation

$$P_{i0}^m = \$50 = \frac{\$4}{(1 + \hat{R}_i)^1} + \frac{\$4}{(1 + \hat{R}_i)^2} + \ldots \frac{\$4}{(1 + \hat{R}_i)^{10}} + \frac{\$50}{(1 + \hat{R}_i)^{10}}$$

In this case the value is 13.35 percent. If the investor views the equilibrium-expected return on securities with the same risk as this one as being 15 percent, the investor would view this security as overvalued—since $\hat{R}_i < E(\tilde{R}_i)$.

In the following chapters these concepts of value are applied to fixed-income securities, common stocks, and international securities, and indirectly to the valuation of options and futures contracts.

Risk and Value

To this point we have indicated that value will be influenced by expected cash flows and the equilibrium-expected return via β_i. We all have some intuitive grasp of what determines cash flows in the form of interest, dividends, or end-of-period share value, but the intuition behind the firm's β is more elusive to most students. Thus, while we will explore β_i in depth for special types of securities as they are covered, it's useful to begin a discussion of things that contribute to β_i for a security. You can think of this as a slight digression on a subject that must be mastered before concepts of valuation can be applied.

We will do this by introducing here the terms that are often used to describe several risk components: (1) **business (operating) risk,** (2) **financial (capital structure) risk,** and (3) **interest rate risk.**

Business Risk

When, in the mid-1950s, Ford Motor Company made a major investment in producing the Edsel, it took on considerable business risk. Similarly, when Edwin Land made a decision to invest in the production of Polaroid cameras, he took a business gamble. Every firm, in fact, assumes business risk in the process of conducting its everyday operations. What is the likelihood that Boeing will lose market share to Airbus? What is the possibility that energy prices will continue to fall and depress Exxon's earnings? And, can USX compete successfully with Japanese or Korean steel producers in world markets?

Business risk, to many analysts, represents the portion of a firm's future earnings variability that could be explained *solely* by the outcomes of the firm's investment decisions (i.e., the assets they carry) and the way they interact with the performance of the economy. Some firms have greater business risk than others because their investment decisions are made in markets characterized by considerable uncertainty. That explains why Genentech (a genetic engineering firm) probably has greater business risk, in a subjective sense, than does Coca Cola. And, since earnings variability will obviously influence the level and timing of future cash flows on a firm's securities, Genentech's securities are, for this component at least, riskier than Coca Cola's. Business risk refers to the inherent instability of the firm's earning power before interest and other fixed security obligations are considered.

Financial Risk

In addition to influencing risk through its investment decisions, management also can alter security risk through financing (capital structure) decisions. For example, how a major investment decision is financed—e.g., through bonds or stock—can have a major influence on the variability of future earnings available to the firm's existing security holders. If G.E. issues $1 billion in new debt to finance the purchase of RCA stock, the value of my G.E. common stock could suffer, since the new debt increases the required fixed future interest obligations of the firm and will increase the uncertainty surrounding dividend payments on G.E.'s stock. This *may,* but not necessarily will, make the stock riskier and depress its equilibrium value (it may not if the accompanying investment decision more than makes up for the increase in risk). Financial risk refers to the added instability of after-interest earnings that comes from larger and larger fixed financial structure obligations.

Interest Rate Risk

This concept of risk relates to the sensitivity of a security's market price to a small change in the level of prevailing interest rates (a shift up or down in the security market line). As interest rates (or the SML) go down or up, the expected return on securities goes down or up, and security prices—other things constant—will go up or down. Interest rate risk is greatest when the price fluctuations due to a given change in interest rates are large. Long-term securities, then, have the greatest interest rate risk. Long-term bonds and common stocks have a good deal of interest rate risk, but, of course, for common stocks other factors may simultaneously offset the interest rate effect (e.g., if higher interest rates mean more business income for the firm).

Analysts who apply these ad hoc concepts of security risk essentially may factor them all together in some alchemist's brew in order to estimate $E(\bar{R}_i)$ in the valuation equation. But others may determine how these risk concepts ought to be quantified or how they should relate to β_i and thus to equilibrium-expected returns. Either approach may be accurate and useful, but we will suggest in following chapters the close tie that exists between a proper interpretation and integration of these ad hoc risk measures and β_i.

Summary

The theory of valuation is at the core of an understanding of investment markets. With this understanding it is possible to appreciate how other investors value securities, how market prices are determined, and how mispriced securities can be detected (if any exist) in the context of the CAPM.

There are three fundamental concepts of security value: (1) personal value, or worth; (2) market value, or price; and (3) equilibrium value, or intrinsic value. The first of these defines a particular investor's forecasts of future cash flows as well as personal estimates of the riskiness of those flows to determine a security's present value.

Market price, on the other hand, is the market's consensus valuation at a point in time of the present worth of a security's expected future cash flows, as seen through the eyes of one who has access to the information used by the average investor. Finally, equilibrium price is an ideal price that would be set in the marketplace if everything knowable is used in forecasting a security's future cash flows, and if the market behaves precisely as the CAPM implies that it should.

The three concepts of value differ with respect to *whose* forecasts are employed, and on *what information* those forecasts are based. Common to all three, however, are four basic components of value. These are:

1. The timing and magnitude of future expected cash flows.
2. The reward for time.
3. The riskiness of the future cash flows.
4. The reward for risk bearing.

If security expected returns are generated by the single-period CAPM, then the equilibrium price of any security i is:

$$P_{i0}^e = \frac{E(\tilde{P}_{i1}) + E(\tilde{D}_{i1})}{1 + R_f + \beta_i(E(\tilde{R}_m) - R_f)}$$

When our time horizon is expanded to more than one period, a general equilibrium pricing equation can only be approximated. Such an approximation, however, takes the same form as the single-period equation, though it requires more assumptions. Its general form—assuming a constant risk-return trade-off over time is this:

$$P_{i0}^e = \sum_{t=1}^{T} \frac{E(\tilde{D}_{it})}{[1 + R_f + \beta_i(E(\tilde{R}_m) - R_f)]^t} + \frac{E(\tilde{P}_{iT})}{[1 + R_f + \beta_i(E(\tilde{R}_m) - R_f)]^T}$$

The objective of security analysis is to detect securities whose market prices are different from their estimated equilibrium prices. Thus, investors form personal estimates of value, P_{i0}^k, in an attempt to uncover the true equilibrium price P_{i0}^e. If P_{i0}^k as an estimate of P_{i0}^e is above the current market price P_{i0}^m, the security has been undervalued by the market in the view of the investor.

APPENDIX: The Certainty Equivalent Approach to Valuation

As mentioned in the chapter, one approach to valuation attempts to account for a security's risk in the numerator of a valuation equation (11–2). It is called the *certainty equivalent approach,* and in a single-period framework, it arrives at security i's equilibrium value like this:

(11A–1) $$P_{i0}^e = \frac{E(\tilde{P}_{i1}) + E(\tilde{D}_{i1}) - \alpha_{i1}}{(1 + R_f)}$$

The entire numerator of (11A–1) is the certainty equivalent of the expected cash flow at time 1. In essence, the future cash flow is reduced to account for the nondiversifiable (systematic) risk of security i and for the equilibrium market reward for risk bearing. To be consistent with our formulation in terms of the CAPM, in this relationship α_{i1} would have to be defined by:

(11A–2)
$$\alpha_{i1} = \frac{[\beta_i(E(\tilde{R}_m) - R_f)][E(\tilde{P}_{i1}) + E(\tilde{D}_{i1})]}{[1 + R_f + \beta_i(E(\tilde{R}_m) - R_f)]}$$

Thus, plugging (11A–2) into (11A–1), we have:

(11A–3)
$$P_{i0}^e = \frac{(E(\tilde{P}_{i1}) + E(\tilde{D}_{i1}))\left[1 - \dfrac{\beta_i(E(\tilde{R}_m) - R_f)}{(1 + R_f + \beta_i(E(\tilde{R}_m) - R_f))}\right]}{(1 + R_f)}$$

which is just exactly equivalent to (11–2).

Equation (11A–3) *adjusts* for nondiversifiable risk and the risk premium in the second term in the numerator to generate a certainty equivalent cash flow to be discounted at the risk-free interest rate. Equation (11–2) adjusts for risk and the price of risk through the discount rate. It is often referred to as the **risk-adjusted discount rate valuation** method. Note that α_i is unique to security i, however, so the certainty equivalent approach requires use of a different discount factor in the numerator each time it is applied.

References

Brealy, Richard, and Myers, Stuart. [1981] *Principles of Corporate Finance*. New York: McGraw-Hill, chaps. 5 and 9.

Everett, James E., and Schwab, Bernhard. [1979] "On the Proper Adjustment for Risk through Discount Rates in a Mean-Variance Framework." *Financial Management* (Summer).

Fisher, Irving. [1965] "The Theory of Interest," *Reprints of Economics Classics*. New York: Augustus M. Kelley.

Gordon, Myron J. [1962] *The Investment, Financing, and Valuation of the Corporation*. Homewood, Ill.: Richard D. Irwin.

Graham, Benjamin; Dodd, David L.; and Cottle, Sidney. [1962] *Security Analysis, Principles and Technique*. 4th ed. New York: McGraw-Hill.

Merton, R. C. [1973] "An Inter-temporal Capital Asset Pricing Model." *Econometrica*.

Myers, S. C., and Turnbull, S. M. [1977] "Capital Budgeting and the Capital Asset Pricing Model: Good News and Bad News." *Journal of Finance* (May).

Stapleton, Richard, and Subrahmanyam, Marti. [1978] "Multi-Period Equilibrium Asset Pricing Model." *Econometrica* (September).

Williams, J. B. [1938] *The Theory of Investment Value*. Cambridge, Mass.: Harvard University Press.

Questions and Problems

1. Define equilibrium value and equilibrium-expected return. Why would you care about equilibrium-expected returns on a security, $E(\tilde{R}_i)$, if the return you actually achieve from an investment in the security depends on the current market price rather than the equilibrium value?

2. Houston Oil Royalty Trust is a security that is expected to offer year-end payments to security holders of $1.50, $1.75, $2.20, $1.90, $1.40, and $.90 at the end of each of the next six years. If the rates of return offered on other securities with the same risk as HORT are 14 percent, calculate the current equilibrium value of the trust unit. Calculate P_{e1}, P_{e2}, P_{e3}, P_{e4}, P_{e5}, and P_{e6}, in each case just after the dividend payment for that period.

3. In Problem 2, assume that you plan to hold the security for three years, until just after the third year's dividend payment. Calculate the security's current value based on the three intermediate dividend payments and the sale price at the end of the third year. Compare your answer with that for the current value of the security in Problem 2. What does the comparison suggest regarding the relevance of the perceived holding period to the valuation of a security?

4. An analyst for a large New York brokerage house generated the following graph for eight firms in the pharmaceutical industry she follows. Which securities are underpriced, and which are overpriced? If the analyst is correct, in which direction would you expect the prices of each to move?

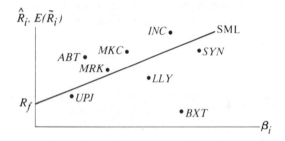

5. The risk-free interest rate is 7 percent and the equilibrium-expected return on the market portfolio is 15 percent. If you estimate that a return of 12 percent is available on an investment in the stock of Procter & Gamble, given its current market price, is P&G undervalued or overvalued? P&G's beta coefficient is .6.

6. The comparison of a personal value estimate, P_{i0}^k, with market price, P_{i0}^m, is sufficient for determining if a security is priced in disequilibrium or not. What is the equivalent return comparison?

7. The equilibrium value of any asset depends upon four things. That is, there are four components or determinants of value. What are they?

8. Cooper Industries common stock currently pays a dividend of $1.00. The stream of dividends is expected to grow at the rate of 10 percent for 10 years, at which time you plan on selling the security. You estimate the market price of the security at that time at $25. What is the current price of the security if it has a beta coefficient of 1.3, and the security market line is that given in Figure 11–2?

9. Currently, the set of risk/return opportunities available in the market can be described with a 7 percent risk-free rate and a 6 percent premium per unit of risk when risk is defined by the securities' beta. For the following opportunities determine if the market has underpriced or overpriced them:

| | | Current | Next Year's | |
Name	Beta	Price	Dividend	Expected Price
Dow Chemical	.9	$80	$2.50	$89
General Instrument	1.3	27	.35	36
Avon	.7	30	2.25	33
Armco	1.1	7	0	11
Adams Exp.	1.0	22	3.50	21

10. Ms. Fall prepared the data in the table below to assist her in evaluating the relative attractiveness of Rockwell's common stock. Having recently reviewed Martin Marietta, another diversified aerospace contractor, she decided to compare the common stocks of the two companies.

	S&P 500	Rockwell	Martin Marietta
Current price	$161.67	$32.50	$34.88
Est. 1984 EPS	18.50	2.90	5.15
Current dividend	7.10	0.88	1.34
Dividend yield	4.39%	2.71%	3.84%
Est. annual EPS and div. growth for next 3 years	9.00%	15.00%	16.00%
Est. price at end of year 3 (after dividend)	228.00	55.50	60.60
Beta	1.00	1.40	1.69

Note: Assume that the real risk-free rate of return is 3 percent and that the market's required rate of return is 15 percent.

a. Before examining the two stocks more closely, Ms. Fall reviewed The Third National Bank's latest statement on economic policy and noted that the chief economist was expecting inflation to average 6 percent over the long term. She also felt that it was necessary to understand what the risk premium was for owning equities generally.

Based on this information and the data given in the table, calculate this equity risk premium and identify the components that make up the required rate of return of the market.

b. State the formula for the required rate of return for a common stock as determined by the security market line. Calculate the required rate of return for both Rockwell and Martin Marietta. Draw a graph of the security market line.

c. Based on the data in the table, calculate expected rates of return for Rockwell and Martin Marietta, using a dividend model approach. Compare these expected returns to the required returns for the two stocks. Show computations.

d. Plot the expected rates of return for Rockwell and Martin Marietta on the security market line drawn for part *b*. Based on the graph, briefly comment on the relative attractiveness of the two stocks.

CFA

11. Next year's dividend for Oasis Inc. is expected to be $2 per share. This dividend will grow for four years (through the end of year 5) at the rate of 25 percent. The end-of-year-5 price is expected to be $60. Find the current value of this security if the intercept and slope of the security market line are .07 and .07, and the beta of Oasis is 1.1. Determine how the price of the security will change with the following changes in input values:

a. Growth is 10 percent instead of 25 percent, and year 5 price is $35 instead of $60.

b. The risk-free interest rate changes to .09.

c. The slope of the SML changes to .09.

d. The beta of Oasis changes to 1.4.

12. Currently the structure of rates of return on default-free U.S. Treasury securities is:

1 year to maturity	6%
2 years to maturity	6.5%
3 years to maturity	7.0%

Assuming that these current rates reflect differences in expected future one-year interest rates, and assuming the slope of the SML is .07 in each year, what would be the appropriate discount rates to apply in each of the next three years? What is the present value of a security with cash flow expectations of $5, $7, and $53 in each of the next three years? (As a hint you should remember that the 6.5 percent figure above refers to the rate of interest that exists as a geometric average over the two-year period between now and the end of year 2.)

CHAPTER

12

Valuation of Fixed-Income
Securities

Contracts and Claims

In our society, a variety of individuals and groups typically share in the income from a firm's productive operations. Employees and customers, for example, have certain claims against this income. These claims take the form of implicit or explicit contractual obligations which can vary considerably in their complexity. In the case of employees, for example, piece work and bonus pay agreements may hinge on few or many conditions. More ambiguous but still exceedingly complex are the firm's obligations to respect such things as right-to-work laws, occupational health and safety regulations, and nondiscrimination statutes. Customers, too, possess potential claims to the firm's income, which are enforced through warranty agreements and product safety laws.[1]

In spite of the considerable complexity that *can* exist with respect to employee and customer claims on the firm, the rules for dividing the income from production among those who hold the firm's financial securities are—in theory—quite simple. The **holders of equity** (i.e., sole owners or partners, common stockholders, and/or limited partners) have an ownership claim that entitles them to share in the net income or net assets of

---

[1]Think how significantly firms have been affected by the National Labor Relations Act, the actions of the Occupational Safety and Health Administration, and the actions of the Federal Trade Commission (in attempting to eliminate unsafe products and misrepresentation of the worth of some goods and services).

the firm after all other claims have been satisfied. Their share is in proportion to their ownership interest. Thus, if you hold 1 percent of the outstanding common stock of a firm, you own (but are not necessarily able to manage or consume) 1 percent of the net income created through the firm's operations, after all expenses, senior contractual obligations, and government claims (usually in the form of taxes owed) are met.

The **holders of fixed-income, or creditorship claims** (e.g., bonds, loans, trade credit, leases, and preferred stock)—in contrast to stockholders— are entitled to receive a pre-specified, fixed payment, or set of payments, prior to any payments to owners. This means that if the firm is to pay dividends on its stock, it must first pay the required interest on its debt.

All this sounds simple. But the simplicity can be deceptive for a number of reasons. For example, there can be a variety of fixed-income securities issued by the firm—each with different rights. Because the firm's managers can initiate investment and financing decisions which affect not only the amount of income available for distribution between the various security holders, but also affect the distribution rules themselves, the creditor position may be ambiguous. Thus, a firm's leasing arrangements may affect the firm's ability to meet the periodic interest payments it has contracted to pay on its bonds. And, some firms may issue new bonds which have prior claim over already-outstanding bonds, thus affecting the distribution of income to those existing creditors. Further, the complexities of bankruptcy and reorganization laws often make it unclear which security holders will be paid off, and to what extent, in the event the firm is unable to pay all of its contractual obligations.

This chapter discusses the basic characteristics of fixed-income securities, shows methods for valuing them, and points out the determinants of the cash flows and the risk of these securities. Chapter 13 discusses specific types of fixed-income securities and the markets in which they are traded. Chapter 14 deals with the characteristics of equity securities, their valuation, and their risk.

Definition of Fixed-Income Securities

Fixed-income claims entitle the owner of a financial security to a specific, contractually agreed-upon series of cash flows, usually in the form of periodic interest payments and the return of principal. These claims include the following: corporate bonds; term loans; negotiable certificates of deposit; passbook savings accounts; financial leases; mortgages; Treasury bills, bonds, and notes; Federal Home Loan Bank bonds; preferred stock; municipal bonds; and many others. The term *fixed income* is something of a misnomer, for while the contract between owner and issuer (the firm, individual borrower, or government agency) calls for a specified, fixed, periodic payment, in some economic situations the issuer may not be able to meet the payment. When this happens the issuer is in default. The consequence of such a situation, in terms of the security holder's ability to enforce payment, depends primarily on the nature of the security and the financial condition and legal status of the issuer.

Mortgages are the most familiar type of fixed-income security to many of us. These securities are typically issued by individuals or firms as a means of financing real estate acquisitions, and are purchased by thrift institutions, insurance companies, and pension funds for their portfolio holdings. Until a few years ago, the typical mortgage promised a fixed, monthly interest and principal payment over the life of the mortgage. In such a standard mortgage, the interest—or **coupon rate**—on such securities is fixed as a percentage of the amount borrowed—the **principal, face, or par value**. The **maturity date**—on which the final mortgage payment is promised—is also fixed in advance, although in some cases the borrower can transfer the mortgage to someone else upon sale of the real estate prior to maturity. Thus, a standard 12 percent, 30-year, fixed rate $100,000 mortgage is one in which the borrower agrees to pay the lender a fixed 12 percent annual interest rate on a loan of $100,000, to be paid back in equal monthly installments (each of which includes interest and principal repayments) over a 30-year period.

In recent years, of course, this standard mortgage has been partially supplanted by more complicated financial instruments, including the variable-rate mortgage, in which the applicable interest (coupon) rate varies over time with the general level of interest rates. Balloon-payment mortgages require the borrower to pay monthly interest and principal payments for a period of say, five years, after which time the entire loaned amount becomes due. This is the standard mortgage instrument in Canada, and recently has become widely used in the United States.

Bonds, like standard mortgages, have fixed maturity dates and coupon rates. A bond's coupon rate is stated as a percentage of its principal amount, or par value. Most corporate bonds are issued in $1,000 or $5,000 par values. Thus, a 12.75 percent annual coupon rate implies that annual interest payments of $(.1275)($1,000) = 127.50 are promised by the issuer of a $1,000 par value bond. Coupon rates are set in accordance with the rates of return that are available in the marketplace at the time of issue on bonds with equivalent risks and contract characteristics. Unlike mortgages, bonds normally do not offer the investor equal periodic cash flows over time. A typical 10-year, 14 percent coupon corporate bond having a par value of $1,000 promises the investor equal semi-annual interest payments of $70 apiece on prespecified dates over the bond's 10-year life, but on the last interest payment date the entire principal, or par value, of $1,000 plus the final interest payment is promised. After that maturity date, the bond ceases to exist.

A rich variety of bond types is traded in the marketplace. Maturities on government and corporate issues range between 1 year and over 30, and some allow for the possibility that the issuer may *call* or redeem the bonds prior to maturity at a certain, prespecified minimum price, called the **call price**. Typical maturities for newly issued corporate bonds range between 10 and 30 years, with the borrower agreeing not to call the bonds for a period of 3 to 10 years after issuance. Coupon rates on such bonds will be somewhat higher than on equivalent noncallable bonds. Some bonds are backed by specific collateral—such is the case with **equipment trust bonds**—which can be seized by the bondholders in the event of default. Others—such as **debentures**—carry only the company's statement of "good faith" and financial resources to meet its obligations.

Preferred stock is also typically thought of as a type of fixed-income security. Unlike common stockholders who receive dividend payments which can vary over time according to the judgment of management, a corporation's preferred stockholders have a contractually agreed-upon periodic dividend payment promised to them. This dividend payment, like the coupon rate on a bond, is normally specified as a percentage of the stock's par value. An 8.5 percent $100 par-value share of preferred stock promises $8.50 in annual dividends over the life of the stock, which are typically paid in quarterly installments. Some preferred stocks have a fixed maturity, while others do not and thus continue to exist indefinitely. Some preferred stocks are cumulative, which means that if the contractually specified dividend payment is omitted in any quarter, the issuing firm cannot ignore the omitted payment, but must accumulate it and promise to pay it at the next opportunity and in all cases prior to the payment of dividends on common stock.

Preferred stocks also offer the investor a great deal of variety—some are convertible at prespecified exchange rates into common stock, some offer variable dividend payment rates over time, some include voting rights, and so forth. But like other fixed-income securities, the maximum periodic income payment to the investor is generally specified at the time of issuance. Unlike common stockholders, preferred stockholders do not share in the increased profits that come from good years for the firm, nor in the decreased profits that come from bad years, unless earnings drop far enough to prohibit the preferred dividend payment.

Passbook savings accounts also promise fixed, maximum periodic interest payments. If you place $10,000 in a 5.25 percent annually compounded passbook savings account at your local commercial bank, you can expect to be paid exactly 5.25 percent interest each year on the current balance in the account. Since such accounts are federally guaranteed through deposit insurance (at least for deposits of $100,000 or less), there is no risk of receiving less than the promised interest payment or of losing your principal. Such a security is termed **default-free**.

Distribution of Cash Flows

Because of the possibility (however remote) of default on some fixed-income securities, there is a probability distribution of future cash flows payable to a fixed-income security holder at a specified future date. Such a distribution might assume a general shape like that given in Figure 12–1(a). The "promised payment" of $95 at date t shown for the hypothetical security represented in the figure is just the interest and principal which the issuer is "required" to pay on that date. The actual payment will not exceed this amount and may, as noted, fall short of it, depending on the financial circumstances. It could even fall to zero in the worst case.

The precise shape of the probability distribution depends on the issuer's **ability to pay.** For the hypothetical security in Figure 12–1(a), even though the promised payment at date t is $95, the expected payment is $86.40, or 92 percent of the promised payment. Obviously, the shape and position of the distribution will affect the current value of the security.

In contrast to the risky security depicted in Figure 12–1(a), the government's ability to issue money and to tax the population ensures that U.S. Treasury securities will always return their promised payments (short of a complete social revolution). The probability distribution in this case for any date t would look like a single point on the right-hand vertical axis, as in Figure 12–1(b). On the other hand, the probability distribution for the future cash flows on some bonds of firms in bankruptcy proceedings might look more

FIGURE 12–1   Probability Distributions of Cash Flows at Date *t* from Three Hypothetical Fixed-Income Securities

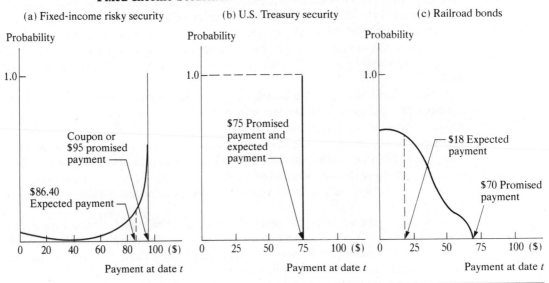

(a) Fixed-income risky security

(b) U.S. Treasury security

(c) Railroad bonds

like that in Figure 12–1(c).[2] Naturally, most fixed-income securities issued by business firms and other governmental units tend to fall somewhere between these extremes. Moreover, the gentle smooth shape given in Figure 12–1(a) and 12–1(c) may be transformed in rather unique ways by such things as collateral and bankruptcy law. Nevertheless, if we are to place a value on a fixed-income security, we must first be able to represent the distributions of possible cash flows at each future date on which they are promised up to the maturity of the security.

For a particular security, the probability distribution of cash flows is likely to be different from one date to the next. Perhaps, due to the asset base and security of short-term operations of the firm, the chance of default is very low in the near future, but will grow, given the uncertainty associated with the firm's long-run competitive position in its industry and with economic conditions generally. Figure 12–2 graphically represents this situation. In this case the expected cash flows at each future due date are different.

It is the firm's **ability to pay** that determines the location of the distribution of future cash flows, and thus the expected value of the probability distribution of cash flows. But the phrase

---

[2]To give an example, White Motor Corporation filed for protection under federal bankruptcy laws in 1980. In 1983 a settlement was reached that called for the following payoffs per dollar of par value of fixed claims previously issued by the firm: senior debt—53¢ for every $1 owed; the company retirement system—49¢ for every $1 of obligations; general unsecured creditors—49¢ per $1 owed; subordinated debentures—13.8¢ per $1 owed; and, finally, White Motor common stockholders—1 share of the reorganized company for every 10 shares held at the time the firm filed for bankruptcy. We think it is especially interesting to note that the company retirement system is only as safe as other creditors, and that stockholders' positions were not reduced to zero even though all senior claims were not fully paid off. The company retirement system, being less than fully funded, constituted a risky, nondiversified investment for those workers covered by it. See: "White Motor Owes Creditors $300 Million," *The Wall Street Journal,* August 4, 1983, p. 7.

FIGURE 12–2 **Probability Distributions of Cash Flows over Time from a Hypothetical Fixed-Income Security**

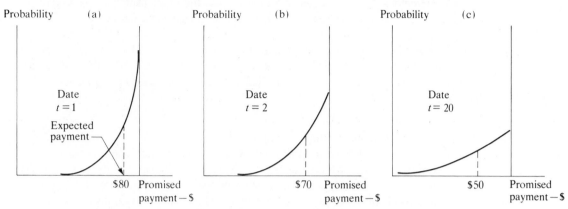

"ability to pay" encompasses many facets of a firm's operations. Three major factors, however, represent the most crucial elements in determining whether or not a firm can meet its fixed-income cash-flow obligations. They are (1) the firm's **earning power**, (2) the **market value of its assets**, and (3) the **nature of the applicable debt covenants**. Let's examine each.

Earning Power. A firm's ability to generate a level of income from its ongoing operations sufficient to meet its periodic fixed-income payments is the main avenue by which its ability to pay can be assured. If income is sufficiently high, the bondholders can expect to receive their promised payments. If income falls short of the promised payments, however, then the firm has three options: (*a*) **liquidate assets** to raise the necessary cash to meet these payments, (*b*) **issue new securities** (e.g., new bonds or stock) to raise cash, or (*c*) **default on its obligations**. If new securities are issued, potential investors will inevitably look to the firm's future earnings power in assessing the likelihood of receiving future income on those securities, because such income payments will be paid out of available earnings. Thus, earnings power determines not only the firm's ability to pay the promised income on its current obligations, it ultimately determines the amount investors are willing to pay for all the firm's securities. If, alternatively, the firm chooses to liquidate assets as a means of raising cash, the second of the three ability factors—the market value of those assets—becomes immediately relevant to the firm's ability to pay.

Market Value of Assets. Assuming the firm cannot meet its fixed-income payments, then payment may depend on the ability of the firm's shareholders (acting through management) to liquidate a portion of the firm's investment in cash, inventories, accounts receivable, or plant and equipment. Clearly, the firm's ability to acquire cash in this manner depends on the market value of the assets. The market value, in turn, depends upon the usefulness of the assets in other production processes, the transportability and accessibility of the assets, and the existence of secondary markets for them. Generally, accounts receivable and inventories are readily salable, while certain types of fixed plant and equipment may be virtually impossible to dispose of. It would be difficult, for example, to sell a set of five partially completed, but mothballed nuclear reactors located in isolated regions of the state of Washington. On the other hand, selling a general-purpose warehouse or restaurant equipment may be considerably easier.

Debt Covenants.   The third component that influences the issuer's ability to pay is disclosed in the set of rights and restrictions that are included as part of the contractural arrangement that created a security. Called *covenants,* or *indenture provisions,* they include:

1.   Specification of collateral, if any.
2.   Statement of sinking fund or repayment provisions.
3.   Definition of default and the bondholders' rights should default occur.
4.   Enumeration of any restrictions on the firm's ability to pay dividends, salary increases, issue other securities or stock options, or to invest in capital equipment, and specification of the conditions under which such restrictions apply.

In short, these provisions are set up between the firm and its bondholders to assure the bondholders that no attempt will be made by management or the stockholders to confiscate assets, to give priority to other claims, or to cause any other form of wealth transfer from bondholders to stockholders or managers. In other words, the provisions help ensure that bondholder wealth will not be adversely affected by the actions of stockholders or managers who are attempting to achieve their own, sometimes conflicting, goals. Indeed, it is in the best interests of *all* concerned to develop a set of rules that defines the obligations and behavior of each group. Otherwise, few investors would wish to hold the bonds.

In sum, the three factors—earning power, market value of assets, and debt convenants—by influencing ability to pay define the shape of the probability distribution of the cash flows to fixed-income security holders.

Valuation of Fixed-Income Securities

As was discussed in Chapter 11, the value of any security can be alternatively expressed in terms of its **personal value to individual k** (P_{i0}^k), its **current market price** (P_{i0}^m), or its **CAPM equilibrium value** (P_{i0}^e). In each case, expected future cash flows must be discounted to the present at a specified expected (required) equilibrium rate of return which compensates the investor for time and risk. Thus, if we wish to assess the equilibrium value of fixed-income security *i,* promising fixed interest payments on each of *T* future dates, on the last of which the principal (face value) will be repaid, we would apply Equation (11-14) as follows:

$$(12\text{-}1) \qquad P_{i0}^e = \frac{E(\tilde{D}_{i1})}{[1 + E(\tilde{R}_i)]} + \frac{E(\tilde{D}_{i2})}{[1 + E(\tilde{R}_i)]^2} + \cdots + \frac{E(\tilde{D}_{iT}) + E(\tilde{P}_{iT})}{[1 + E(\tilde{R}_i)]^T}$$

where $E(\tilde{R}_i)$ is the equilibrium return demand on security *i.* According to the CAPM it equals $R_f + \beta_i[E(\tilde{R}_m) - R_f]$. $E(\tilde{D}_{it})$ is the expected interest payment at date *t;* and $E(\tilde{P}_{iT})$ is the market value of the security at time *T* (maturity). The payments $E(\tilde{D}_{it})$ and $E(\tilde{P}_{iT})$ will be equal to or less than the contract amount, depending on the probability of default. For simplicity, the examples in this chapter define "periods" in terms of annual intervals and assume, therefore, that interest payments are made in annual installments (rather than in semiannual or quarterly installments as is the case with some securities). In the appendix, we illustrate refinements in the valuation equation which account for the effects of semiannual and quarterly payments, and for the fact that some fixed-income securities may be called (redeemed by the issuer) prior to maturity.

In sum,

(12–2)   ***Equilibrium Valuation for Fixed-Income Securities***

$$P_{i0}^e = \sum_{t=1}^{T}\left(\frac{E(\tilde{D}_{it})}{[1 + E(\tilde{R}_i)]^t}\right) + \frac{E(\tilde{P}_{iT})}{[1 + E(\tilde{R}_i)]^T}$$

This particular statement of security i's value assumes the equilibrium-expected return is not expected to vary from future period to period. We will return to this issue later. It is worth noting that, if principal payments are due in every period instead of only when the security matures at date T, then $E(\tilde{D}_{it})$ in each period will reflect not only the periodic interest payment but also a portion of the principal.[3] Obviously, the interpretation of $E(\tilde{D}_{it})$ depends on the payment characteristics of the particular fixed-income security being evaluated.

Take as an example the equilibrium price of a hypothetical Treasury note issued in 1981 and maturing exactly two years from now. This security promises coupon payments of $85 per $1,000 par (face) value of bond. If the expected return, as given by the security market line (SML) is now 9 percent for securities with the same risk as this one, the note's current equilibrium value is:

(12–3) $P_{i0}^e = \dfrac{\$85}{(1 + .09)} + \dfrac{\$85}{(1 + .09)^2} + \dfrac{\$1,000}{(1 + .09)^2} = \$991.20$

In this particular case, the **expected** interest and principal payments in each year are equal to the promised payments in each year, because there is no possibility of default or delay in payment on Treasury issues.

For a risky corporate security, such as the hypothetical one pictured in Figure 12–1(*a*), assuming 10 years remain until maturity, a promised annual (coupon) payment of $95 per $1,000 of par value, an expected equilibrium return of 11 percent, and **expected cash flows** of $86.40 in each of the 10 years and $920 of expected principal repayment in year 10, the equilibrium value is:

(12–4) $P_{i0}^e = \sum_{t=1}^{10}\left(\dfrac{\$86.40}{(1 + .11)^t}\right) + \dfrac{\$920}{(1 + .11)^{10}} = \$832.84$

It is important to understand that the use of **expected** cash flows in lieu of **promised** cash flows in the numerator is not a risk adjustment, but simply identifies the mean of the probability distribution. Risk, which should be determined by the size of the covariance of returns with the market portfolio's returns (i.e., the security's beta) is, in part, determined by the nondiversifiable variation from this expected value of $86.40.

---

[3] Note that for some fixed-income securities (e.g., some types of preferred stock), T could equal infinity (∞). There is even one corporate bond traded on the New York Bond Exchange with a perpetual life.

TABLE 12–1 **A Specific Example of Equilibrium Valuation Formula for Fixed-Income Securities**

A term loan of $10,000 with four balloon payments equal to $1/4$ of the original amount of the loan paid at the end of the 2nd, 4th, 6th, and 8th years, and interest on the balance outstanding at the rate of 8 percent—paid annually with no risk of default.

$$P_{i0}^e = \frac{\$800}{(1 + E(\tilde{R}_i))^1} + \frac{\$800}{(1 + E(\tilde{R}_i))^2} + \frac{\$2,500}{(1 + E(\tilde{R}_i))^2} + \frac{.75(\$800)}{(1 + E(\tilde{R}_i))^3} +$$

$$\frac{.75(\$800)}{(1 + E(\tilde{R}_i))^4} + \frac{\$2,500}{(1 + E(\tilde{R}_i))^4} + \frac{.50(\$800)}{(1 + E(\tilde{R}_i))^5} + \frac{.50(\$800)}{(1 + E(\tilde{R}_i))^6} +$$

$$\frac{\$2,500}{(1 + E(\tilde{R}_i))^6} + \frac{.25(\$800)}{(1 + E(\tilde{R}_i))^7} + \frac{.25(\$800)}{(1 + E(\tilde{R}_i))^8} + \frac{\$2,500}{(1 + E(\tilde{R}_i))^8}$$

Adjustments to the equilibrium valuation model can be made easily for any expected cash flow stream. You can test your understanding of this by formulating specific models to value home mortgages (for which the sum of periodic cash flows remain constant, but the division between interest and principal repayment in each cash flow varies), bonds with sinking funds or call options (where the security may be repurchased by the issuer prior to maturity), or income bonds (where the total periodic payment depends on the firm's earnings). One example of the valuation of a relatively complex cash flow stream is given in Table 12–1.

A second example is that of LTV's 11 percent coupon bond due in 2007. These bonds pose an interesting valuation problem because LTV filed for protection under Chapter 11 of the Federal Bankruptcy Code in 1986. While there were certainly questions about LTV's ability to pay prior to its bankruptcy, the announcement verified that there was little chance of investors in these securities receiving the promised coupon amount. The bonds sold at about 600 per $1,000 par value bond before the bankruptcy, and fell (instantaneously, as in an efficient market) to 150 shortly after the announcement.

Suppose we anticipate that nothing will be paid to bondholders until LTV exits from bankruptcy in two years. At that point new debt instruments will be issued to replace the existing 11 percent issue that will have coupon cash flows equal to 25 percent of those originally promised. Of course, some risk still remains at this point so we anticipate future cash flows equal to 80 percent of those promised. At a 14 percent discount rate (reflecting the β of these bonds) the value is $141 per $1,000 par value bond:

Year	Original Coupon	Revised "Coupon"	Original Par	Revised "Par"	Expected Cash Flow	Value at 14%
1	$110	None			$ 0	$ 0
2	110	$27.50			22.00	16.90
.	.	.			.	.
.	.	.			.	.
.	.	.			.	.
21	110	27.50	$1,000	$250	222.00	16.15
					Value =	$141.00

Rates of Return on Fixed-Income Securities

Over the past 60 years the average historical rate of return from long-term corporate and government bond portfolios has been less than 5 percent. The historical returns vary over time, of course, as the economy experiences different business conditions, inflationary pressures, or interest rates. Since 1970 the actual returns per year from corporate bonds has averaged 9.1 percent, and for government bonds has averaged 8.3 percent. Bond returns, in fact, were quite low during the period from 1977 to 1981, primarily as a result of increasing interest rates. This upward shift in the security market line led to higher demanded returns, forcing the prices of bonds down. Long-term government bonds generated a negative return of 4 percent in 1980, for example. More recently, as interest rates have fallen, bond returns have been quite high. In 1982 and 1985 both government and corporate bond portfolios supplied returns in excess of 30 percent.

The kinds of returns that might be anticipated from investments in fixed-income securities, and the risk that those returns may not be realized, are subjects investigated in the following sections.

Securities Free of Default Risk

In Chapter 11 it was noted that the investor's measure of a security's rate of return could be computed by solving one of the security's valuation equations for the discount rate that equated the present value of expected future cash flows to the security's current *market* price. If there is no chance that the issuer of a fixed-income security will fail to pay all promised income and principal repayments on or before their due dates, the security is said to have no default risk. Thus, the return forecast for the Treasury note described in Equation (12–3) is given by $\hat{R}_i$ in:

(12–5)   ***Return Forecast for a Default-Free Security***

$$P_{i0}^m = \sum_{t=1}^{T}\left(\frac{D_{it}}{(1 + \hat{R}_i)^t}\right) + \frac{F_{iT}}{(1 + \hat{R}_i)^T}$$

where D_{it} is the promised interest payment in period t and F_{iT} is the promised principal amount, or face value, of the security to be paid at maturity in T periods.

If this Treasury note could actually be purchased in the market for its equilibrium value, P_{i0}^e, of \$991.20, the security is priced in equilibrium and the return that is forecast is given by the solution to $\hat{R}_i$ below.

$$\$991.20 = \frac{\$85}{(1 + \hat{R}_i)} + \frac{\$85}{(1 + \hat{R}_i)^2} + \frac{\$1,000}{(1 + \hat{R}_i)^2}$$

which, because P_{i0}^m and P_{i0}^e are equal, is the same 9 percent as the equilibrium-expected return on the security. The correct interpretation of this expected return is this: An investor who purchases this security for \$991.20 and plans to hold it until maturity can expect, on average, to earn a rate of return of 9 percent per period over its remaining life, provided the cash flows in year 1 can be reinvested at 9 percent.

If, in the view of the investor, the market price of the security differed from the investor's view of the equilibrium value of the security (i.e., P_{i0}^k is not P_{i0}^m), $\hat{R}_i$ would not be equal to 9 percent and the security would be considered to be in disequilibrium, and off the security market line.

In fact, the actual holding-period return will be 9 percent only if the investor holds the security until maturity and if interest income can be reinvested at a rate equal to $E(\tilde{R}_i)$ itself. Let's see why this is true.

Suppose the investor expects the equilibrium return on the Treasury note to remain constant at 9 percent over the note's two-year life. If this turns out to be the case, the note will be priced at $995.40 at time 1 (one year from today), since:

$$\$995.40 = \frac{\$85}{(1.09)} + \frac{\$1,000}{(1.09)}$$

At that price, the following series of actual ex post one-year **holding-period returns** will be earned

(12–6)
$$R_{i1} = \frac{\$995.40 + \$85 - \$991.20}{\$991.20} = .09$$

$$R_{i2} = \frac{\$1,000 + \$85 - \$995.40}{\$995.40} = .09$$

which are, in each case, just equal to the forecast return and equilibrium expected return. The **average annual geometric rate of return** from these holding-period returns in periods 1 and 2 also is 9 percent, of course.

Next, we examine the situation which prevails if the investor does not hold the security until its maturity date. In this case the actual holding-period return will be determined by the market price of the bond at the time of sale. Suppose, for example, the investor sells the Treasury note at time 1 just after receiving the $85 interest payment. If the market's expected return for the security at that time is still 9 percent, we know from the preceding discussion that the bond will be priced at $995.40. In the absence of any change in the economic environment or, more specifically, in the absence of any information that would cause the security's price to change, the pattern of observed market prices of the note would be from its current $991.20 to $995.40 after one year, rising to $1,000 at maturity.[4] With information flowing into the market (e.g., regarding expectations of inflation or the general level of interest rates as influenced by Federal Reserve monetary policy), however, the value of the security would change because the demanded return, $E(\tilde{R}_i)$ would change, thereby affecting the actual holding-period return. An increase in interest rates would lead to a fall in price and a lower generated return. A fall in interest rates would raise price, providing a higher eventual return to the bondholder. For example, if after one year interest rates fell to 7 percent, the Treasury note would be priced in the market at:

$$\$1,014.02 = \frac{\$85}{(1.07)} + \frac{\$1,000}{(1.07)}$$

---

[4]That is, it would trade at an even $1,000 the instant after the interest payment is received and the instant before the principal is returned to the owner.

If the investor sold it at that price, instead of holding it until maturity, the actual holding-period return in the first period would be 10.9 percent instead of the market expected return of 9 percent,

$$R_{i1} = \frac{\$1,014.02 + \$85 - \$991.20}{\$991.20} = .109 \text{ or } 10.9\%$$

Alternatively, if interest rates fall to 7 percent and the investor holds the note until maturity, the actual holding-period return will depend on the **reinvestment rate** for the $85 received at time 1. If this sum is reinvested at the 7 percent return prevailing in period 2, the investor will accumulate the following sum of money by time 2:

$$\$1,175.95 = \$85(1.07) + \$85 + \$1,000$$

and this implies a holding-period return over the two periods, on average, of:

$$\left(\frac{\$1,175.95}{\$991.20}\right)^{1/2} - 1.0 = .0892 \text{ or } 8.92\%$$

The difference between 8.92 percent and the forecast 9 percent is accounted for by the lower (than expected) interest rate on year 1 cash flows. The moral is that if interest rates change over the holding period the return you earn in each period will be different as the market price of the security changes in response to the change in discount rates. Your average return generated over the life of your investment also will change due to the change in the rate at which you can reinvest the cash flows generated by the opportunity. The risk of this happening is called **interest rate risk**, and will be the subject for further discussion later in the chapter.

Securities with Default Risk

For securities in which cash flows are not absolutely guaranteed, the preceding discussion concerning the calculation of returns still holds. Two things, however, distinguish the case of fixed-income securities with default risk from those which are default-free. The first, and most obvious, is that the expected cash flows which are discounted will generally be less than the promised cash flows because of the possibility of default. This means that expected returns either in equilibrium or disequilibrium ($E(\bar{R}_i)$ or $\hat{R}_i$) can differ from actual holding-period returns not just because of changing interest rates but also because actual cash flows can *differ* from their expected values. The second distinguishing feature of securities with default risk is that new information flowing into the market over time can affect the expectation of cash flows, as in the LTV case summarized earlier, in addition to affecting the market's equilibrium return demand of the security. Let's examine both of these features.

Using the example of the 9.5 percent coupon bond described in Equation (12–4), suppose the current market price is at its equilibrium value of $832.84 (thus, P_{i0}^m is equal to P_{i0}^e). Then, with expected cash flows of $86.40 and $920.00 the return is found by solving:

(12–7)
$$\$832.84 = \sum_{t=1}^{10}\left(\frac{\$86.40}{(1 + \hat{R}_i)^t}\right) + \frac{\$920.00}{(1 + \hat{R}_i)^{10}}$$

This yields 11 percent, of course, equal to the *equilibrium*-expected return of 11 percent assumed earlier. Imagine, however, that the security's issuer does not default on any principal or interest payment over the entire 10-year period, that the investor holds the security until maturity and reinvests each $95 income payment in something which earns exactly 11 percent interest per year. By time 10, the following sum of money will have been accumulated:

$$\$2,588.60 = \sum_{t=0}^{9} \$95(1.11)^t + \$1,000$$

The average annual return per year achieved over 10 years is 12 percent, or:

$$\left(\frac{\$2,588.60}{\$832.84}\right)^{1/10} - 1.0 = .12, \text{ or 12 percent.}$$

In this case, the actual return earned departs from the forecast return because the cash flows actually received departed from their expected values.

Next, suppose one year from today the market consensus is that, in view of new information received, the expected cash flows are $90 in interest and $950 in principal (i.e., there has been a decrease in the probability of default leading to a rightward shift in the probability distribution of cash flows), and the market's new expected return for the security (given its reduced risk and changes in the SML) is 9.0 percent. Reflecting this market consensus, the new market price after the passage of the year will be:

$$\$976.98 = \sum_{t=1}^{9} \frac{\$90}{(1.09)^t} + \frac{\$950}{(1.09)^9}$$

The investor purchasing the security for its $832.84 price one year earlier could now sell it for $976.98 with the $95 coupon payment, the actual return for the one-year holding period would be:

$$\textbf{(12–8)} \qquad R_{i1} = \frac{\$976.98 + \$95 - \$832.84}{\$832.84} = .287, \text{ or 28.7\%}$$

This bond's price has increased for two reasons. First, the discount rate has dropped from 11 percent to 9 percent. Second, the bond has benefited from a substantial shift in the probability distribution of cash flows. The net result of these two effects was a very large return.

In summary, for fixed-income securities, $E(\tilde{R}_i)$ in equilibrium or $\hat{R}_i$ in disequilibrium are useful measures of an investor's actual expected return under certain conditions. These are that: (*a*) periodic income flows can be reinvested at the same annually compounded interest rate; (*b*) the security will be held until maturity (or if not, no new information received at future dates will change the market's demanded returns or anticipated cash flows); and (*c*) actual cash flows will always equal their expected values. In the case of default-free securities, we saw that the last of these conditions is automatically met. For securities possessing default risk, however, the violation of any one of the three conditions will cause actual returns *ex post* to depart from their expected values. Of course, for risky bonds, like other risky securities, the actual cash flows will seldom be exactly equal to those expected.

Yield to Maturity

A security's yield to maturity is defined as the **rate of return that sets the current market price equal to the present value of the security's contractually promised—rather than expected—cash income**. It is defined by:

(12–9)   *Yield to Maturity*

$$P_{i0}^m = \sum_{t=1}^{T}\left(\frac{D_{it}}{(1 + R_Y)^t}\right) + \frac{F_{iT}}{(1 + R_Y)^T}$$

where R_Y is the yield to maturity and D_{it} and F_{iT} are the **promised** cash flows. The value R_Y measures the rate of return expected if all promised cash flows *are paid* when due, if all interest income *can be reinvested* at rate R_Y per period, and if the security *is held* to maturity.

It should be obvious from the preceding discussion that for default-free securities, R_Y just equals $E^m(\tilde{R}_i)$. For securities possessing default risk, however, they are not equal, and the yield to maturity will always be larger than $E^m(\tilde{R}_i)$. The difference between them will be larger the greater are the differences between the security's expected and promised cash flows.

Let's look at the risky corporate security examined above. Its yield to maturity is given by the solution to:

$$\$832.84 = \sum_{t=1}^{10}\left(\frac{\$95}{(1 + R_Y)^t}\right) + \frac{\$1,000}{(1 + R_Y)^{10}}$$

Notice that the promised interest payments of $95 in years 1 through 10 and the promised return of principal, $F_{iT} = \$1,000$, appear in the numerator, and that market price (not equilibrium price) again appears on the left-hand side. The interest rate that solves this equation is: $R_Y = 12.52$ percent. If the issuing firm does not default on any interest or principal payments (i.e., it pays the full promised amount when due), the investor who pays the market price for this security can earn a holding-period return of 12.52 percent per year over the security's 10-year life, provided, of course, that all income can be reinvested at the yield to maturity. This is 1.52 percentage points above $\hat{R}_i$ and $E(\tilde{R}_i)$.

The indirect implication of this is that the yield to maturity is not a particularly useful measure of expected return whenever there is material risk of default. Nor should it be used for making return comparisons among fixed-income securities where those securities differ in their degree of default risk. For instance, suppose the 6.5 percent coupon bonds of Exxon Corporation (*XON*) which mature in 1998 are now selling for $910 per $1,000 par value of bond. At the same time, the 6.25 percent coupon bonds of Navistar (*NAV*) which also mature in 1998 are selling for $650 per $1,000 bond. Assuming both have 10 years of life remaining, the yields to maturity on these bonds (assuming interest income is received once per year) can be calculated from the following equations:

(12–10)   *Exxon (XON) Yield to Maturity*

$$\$910 = \sum_{t=1}^{10}\left(\frac{\$65.00}{(1 + R_Y)^t}\right) + \frac{\$1,000}{(1 + R_Y)^{10}}$$

Navistar (NAV) Yield to Maturity

$$\$650 = \sum_{t=1}^{10}\left(\frac{\$62.50}{(1 + R_Y)^t}\right) + \frac{\$1,000}{(1 + R_Y)^{10}}$$

This gives a value of $R_Y = 7.8$ percent for Exxon bonds and a value of $R_Y = 12.6$ percent for the Navistar bonds. It would appear, from a strict comparison of R_Y values, that the Navistar securities are the more attractive. The investor can obtain a substantially higher yield to maturity from purchasing those bonds. However, the ex ante difference in yield will be realized in ex post returns only if all cash flows are paid on the bonds when due. Because some investors perceive greater risk of default with Navistar, it is likely that the yield to maturity overstates the market's expected return on *NAV*'s bonds more than on *XON*'s bond.

In equilibrium we expect the yields to maturity on these and other securities to reflect differences in their nondiversifiable risk. A part of this nondiversifiable risk may reflect default risk, to the extent that default risk covaries with the returns on the market portfolio. If equilibrium prevails, investors will be indifferent between holding Navistar bonds with a yield to maturity of 12.6 percent or holding Exxon bonds with a yield to maturity of 7.8 percent. However, neither bonds' yield to maturity is an accurate measure of expected return if the probability of default by either issuer is greater than zero.

For low-risk bonds, the differences between R_Y and $E(\tilde{R}_i)$ will generally be quite small. But for moderate- or high-risk issues the yield to maturity loses much of its economic significance. Moreover, the true risk premium of a corporate bond is not represented by the difference between its yield to maturity and the yield to maturity on a default-free security. The use of R_Y for securities with default risk will confuse, rather than clarify, the set of return alternatives available to the investor.

Current Yield

Security traders and brokers often use the concept of **current yield** when referring to a fixed-income security's expected return. Indeed, this measure of expected return is the only one commonly reported in daily newspaper listings of corporate bond prices. As it is popularly defined, the current yield, *y*, is computed as:

(12–11)   *Current Yield*

$$y = \frac{D_{i1}}{P_{i0}^m} = \frac{\left(\begin{array}{c}\text{Security } i's \text{ promised} \\ \text{annual interest income}\end{array}\right)}{\left(\begin{array}{c}\text{Security } i's \text{ current} \\ \text{market price}\end{array}\right)}$$

The virtue of this computation is its simplicity. It is generally not a good measure of the expected return from purchasing the security because—as you can see—it ignores the effect of capital gains and losses, the reinvestment over time of interest income, and default risk.

One day not long ago, an issue of Xerox Corporation bonds having an 10.625 percent coupon rate and maturing in 1993 was traded on the New York Bond Exchange at a price of $1,080 per $1,000 of par value. The current yield was $y = 106.25/\$1,080 = .098$, or 9.8 percent. The yield to maturity, with a remaining life of 7 years, was 9.03 percent.

On the other hand, if we expect the bond's periodic interest income to equal $100 in each of the next 7 years and the amount of principal actually repaid at maturity to equal $970, then the expected return was just 8.1 percent. Which of the three most closely measures the expected holding-period return?

As we have discussed, the investor's actual holding-period return depends on whether or not the bond is held until maturity, at what interest rate(s) future coupon income can be reinvested, and whether or not new information flows into the market which changes investor's forecasts in some way. However, it is possible to make some fairly general statements about the relationship between the three return calculations. First, current yield always equals yield to maturity for bonds which are selling precisely at par value. Had the Xerox bonds been selling at a price of $1,000, their current yield would have been $y = \$106.25/\$1000 = .10625$, and their yield to maturity would have been identical to that figure. For bonds selling below par, the yield to maturity will be higher than current yield. This is because of the assumption in the latter calculation that periodic interest income can be reinvested at rate R_Y and the fact that there will be a capital gain at maturity. (The Xerox bonds, for example, though purchased for $1,080, may be "sold" at maturity for $1,000.)

The relationship between y and $E(\tilde{R}_i)$ is somewhat harder to characterize than the relationship between y and R_Y. For default-free securities, $E(\tilde{R}_i)$ and R_Y are identical, and so the statements of the previous paragraph also apply to the relationship between y and $E(\tilde{R}_i)$. For securities with default risk, however, yield to maturity overstates expected return, and for these securities there can be no general statement of the relative magnitudes of y and $E(\tilde{R}_i)$. This discussion implies that, **for most purposes, a security's current yield is not a particularly useful number to know**, newspaper bond listings to the contrary.

Risk of Fixed-Income Securities

We have already alluded to the possibility that some issuers of fixed-income securities may default on their obligations. We have also discussed the fact that changes in the level of future interest rates (expected returns demanded by the market) have a bearing on both the prices of and holding-period returns on fixed-income securities.

In the past these factors have given rise to material variations in returns on many fixed-income securities. For example, the historical standard deviation of return of a well-diversified portfolio of long-term corporate bonds, measured over the last 60 years, has been approximately 5 percent. This is about one quarter to one third the level of variability experienced by the S&P 500 stock index. Between 1970 and 1985 the standard deviation of yearly returns was more than 12 percent, or well over half of the variability of the S&P index.

Clearly, fixed-income security returns are uncertain. This uncertainty may affect the rate of return demanded of these securities by investors. If we continue with our assumption that the capital-asset pricing model is a good working summary of the manner in which securities are priced in the market, the uncertainty will affect price through its effect on the security's beta coefficient.[5] Another way of saying this is that nondiversifiable un-

---

[5]Here it is important to realize that it is the security's and not the firm's beta coefficient that is relevant; different securities of the same firm face different risks that result from the sharing rules that have been employed for dividing up the firm's wealth.

certainty created from the possibility of changes in interest rates and default will affect the security's beta, and through beta will affect the securities' price. Concerning the security market line, this section concentrates on identifying where bonds are located on the horizontal, or beta, axis, and why.

For a particular bond, say the *i*th one, the beta is defined as

(12–12) $$\beta_i = \frac{Cov(\tilde{R}_i, \tilde{R}_m)}{\sigma^2(\tilde{R}_m)}$$

The actual return, $\tilde{R}_i$, on the bond in any period will be the result of interest payments received plus any change in price. The change in price depends on changes in the general level of interest rates (i.e., any shifts in the security market line, SML) and on changes in expectations of future cash flows from holding the security. The greater is the degree of comovement between changes in cash flow expectations on this security and changes in the cash flow expectations that will drive the return on the market portfolio, R_m, the greater will be the beta. This is nondiversifiable default risk. In addition, the greater is the degree of comovement between changes in the expected equilibrium return used to discount future cash flows on the security, and changes in the expected equilibrium return used to discount future cash flows on the market portfolio, the greater will be the beta coefficient. This is nondiversifiable interest rate risk. Thus, we can highlight a bond's risk, or beta, as being the sum of two general components:

Bond Beta

Bond risk = Nondiversifiable default risk
+ Nondiversifiable interest rate risk.

It is the covariance of the uncertain interest payments with the return on the market portfolio which measures the nondiversifiable default risk and which, therefore, "counts" in the pricing of the security. If there is no risk of default, this covariance will be zero. It will also equal zero if the uncertainty surrounding the future payments is unrelated to the uncertainty surrounding the returns on the other securities represented in the market portfolio.

The second term in the definition of bond risk measures the extent to which the uncertainty surrounding security *i*'s *price* is related, or unrelated, to the return on the market portfolio. Its price will vary, as we saw earlier, depending on whether new information arrives in the market causing investors' demanded equilibrium returns on the security to change. If this information also affects the demanded returns on other securities, the covariance term representing *i*'s nondiversifiable interest rate risk will be nonzero.

Nondiversifiable Default Risk

As noted, if changes in cash flow expectations for the bond in question move completely independently of changes in cash flow expectations for the entire market, the covariance term is zero. Alternatively, if the firm's ability to pay its interest and principal improves with the general economic climate and gets worse as economic activity slows, then we might expect the covariance to be quite high. For example, the bonds of some airlines and construction companies might be expected to have fairly high nondiversifiable default risk. This is true because the revenues received in those industries and the profits generated by those revenues seem to follow closely movements of the overall economy which also affects the overall market portfolio return. Thus, there is comovement between $\tilde{D}_{it}$ and $\tilde{D}_{mt}$.

Consider these four situations:

1. "Bad news" flows into the market regarding the future prospects for the economy; e.g., news that the national unemployment rate is up, capital spending has fallen, and inventories are up makes the front-page headlines. As a result, investors revise downward their expectations for many firms' future earnings. Firm i, along with many other firms, is expected to find it more difficult to meet its current interest obligations.

2. "Good news" flows into the market regarding the prospects for the economy; e.g., news arrives that the national unemployment rate has been falling, capital spending is up, and inventories are being liquidated. The improving profits of firm i, along with those of other firms, relieves the pressure from the firm's current debt obligations.

3. Firm i makes a significant mistake in marketing a new product. Cash flows from existing operations are used up in financing the new product, leaving little for the payment of interest on debt. Other firms are not influenced by i's mistake and carry on business as usual.

4. A managerial change substantially improves the prospects for firm i. The earnings outlook is brightened by altered management policy. Concern that the firm may not meet its interest payments on debt is alleviated. However, this good news is unique to this firm, and is unrelated to the performance of other firms in the market.

The first two situations characterize scenarios in which nondiversifiable default risk is present—the implication of these situations is that the covariance of cash flows on firm i's debt with the market portfolio's returns is quite high. The last two situations characterize scenarios in which nondiversifiable default risk is absent (even though the possibility of default is present), since there is no covariance with the market portfolio's returns. All changes in expectations are unique to that security and are not reflected in security i's risk in a market where investors hold well-diversified portfolios.

It is important to note that the effect of default possibilities on a security's risk is different from the effect of default possibilities on a security's expected cash flows. A firm facing a suddenly increased probability of default on its debt due to factors totally unrelated to the returns on other securities will not necessarily experience an increase in the beta of its bonds. However, the expected cash flows may be reduced relative to their promised level. This will reduce the price of the bonds, not because they are suddenly (nondiversifiably) "riskier," but because the expected cash flows (in the numerator) have been revised downward. The bond's β would not change.

Suppose a pharmaceutical company issues bonds with an expected return of 14 percent, a figure which is equal to the equilibrium expected return for all other securities with the same beta. Shortly after the company issues these securities, the Food and Drug Administration forces the company to remove from the market a drug that has been generating half of the firm's total profits. The possibility of default on the bonds will be increased by this action, and this will cause investors to reduce their estimates of the interest payments and principal to be received at maturity. The increased chance of default, however, is totally unrelated to overall market returns. Thus, the security's beta is not changed (though expected cash flows are) and the discount rate, $E(\tilde{R}_i)$, will not be raised. If this result sounds counterintuitive, it is only because investors can diversify away the company's increased risk of default, and so do not feel inclined to demand higher returns in compensation for it.

Nondiversifiable Interest Rate Risk

If changes in the rates of return demanded of the fixed-income security move independently of changes in the rates of return demanded of the market portfolio, there will be no interest rate risk. Obviously, however, interest rates tend to move up and down together. As the market demands a higher rate of return on high-risk equity securities, it is also likely to demand higher returns on fixed-income securities because of the potential substitutability of these financial securities for one another.

Before we can discuss the role of nondiversifiable interest rate risk in the pricing of fixed-income securities, it is necessary to examine the relationship between changes in the market prices of those securities and changes in the level of interest rates; i.e., between price and interest rate variability.

The Maturity Effect.   Consider two different bonds and their prices. The first is a U.S. Treasury note bearing a 10 percent coupon rate and maturing two years from now. The second is a U.S. Treasury note bearing the same coupon rate as the first, but maturing in 20 years. If the 2-year note currently sells for $1,035 per $1,000 of par value and the 20-year note for $1,195, the expected return are both 8 percent per annum as given by the application of Equation (12–7):

(12–13)
$$\$1,035 = \sum_{t=1}^{2} \frac{\$100}{(1.08)^t} + \frac{\$1,000}{(1.08)^2}$$

$$\$1,195 = \sum_{t=1}^{20} \frac{\$100}{(1.08)^t} + \frac{\$1,000}{(1.08)^{20}}$$

Eight percent represents the current level of the rate of interest. Now imagine what happens if new information arrives in the market which suggests that there has been a shift in the demand for credit, causing interest rates to increase by one percentage point. This would be reflected in a parallel shift upward in the security market line, and in a 9 percent demanded return on the two U.S. Treasury notes. What does this mean for their respective prices? Using Equation (12–7) again, we discover that

(12–14)
$$\$1,018 = \sum_{t=1}^{2} \frac{\$100}{(1.09)^t} + \frac{\$1,000}{(1.09)^2}$$

$$\$1,091 = \sum_{t=1}^{20} \frac{\$100}{(1.09)^t} + \frac{\$1,000}{(1.09)^{20}}$$

or, that the 2-year note should now sell for $1,018 and the 20-year note for $1,091. Thus, there will be a drop of $17 (or 1.6 percent) in the short-term security's value, and a drop of $104 (or 8.7 percent) in the price of the longer-term security. Why the disparity in price changes?

The answer is that the longer the maturity of a bond, all other things being equal, the greater the variation in its price resulting from a one percentage point change in the market's required return. Thus, as a result,

> When interest rates or equilibrium-expected returns rise (fall), bond prices fall (rise), and the change in price and percentage change in price is greater the longer the maturity.

The Coupon Effect.   In the example above, we have intentionally held coupon rates constant in order to examine only the "maturity effect." Now, however, consider two U.S. Treasury notes both maturing in five years, one of which has a 20 percent coupon rate and the other which has a 5 percent coupon rate. If the market currently requires a return of 8 percent on securities with no nondiversifiable default risk, the two bonds will sell for $1,479 and $880, respectively, or

$$\$1,479 = \sum_{t=1}^{5} \frac{\$200}{(1.08)^t} + \frac{\$1,000}{(1.08)^5}$$

(12–15)

$$\$880 = \sum_{t=1}^{5} \frac{\$50}{(1.08)^t} + \frac{\$1,000}{(1.08)^5}$$

If the expected return rises to 9 percent, however, the two bonds will sell for:

$$\$1,427 = \sum_{t=1}^{5} \frac{\$200}{(1.09)^t} + \frac{\$1,000}{(1.09)^5}$$

(12–16)

$$\$844 = \sum_{t=1}^{5} \frac{\$50}{(1.09)^t} + \frac{\$1,000}{(1.09)^5}$$

or $1,427 and $844, respectively. The 20 percent coupon note has suffered a decline in price of $52, or 3.5 percent, while the 5 percent coupon note has declined by $36, or 4.1 percent.

Thus, there is a "coupon effect" as well as a maturity effect on bond prices associated with any change in the general level of interest rates.

> When interest rates or equilibrium-expected returns rise (fall), bond prices fall (rise) by a greater percent the smaller the level of the bond's coupon (or expected periodic cash flows if there is default risk present).

Thus, the larger coupon serves to mitigate the effect of the longer maturity. The larger coupon can be reinvested to earn the now higher interest rate. All coupon-paying bonds would have lower interest rate risk than equivalent maturity zero-coupon bonds.

The Interest-Rate Level Effect.   Suppose a U.S. Treasury note matures in five years, has an 8 percent coupon rate, and is selling at a price of $1,000 per $1,000 of par value. (That is, it is priced at par.) This implies that the market's current expected return is exactly 8 percent. If the expected return rises to 10 percent, it will sell for $924.

$$\text{(12–17)} \qquad \$924 = \sum_{t=1}^{5} \frac{\$80}{(1.10)^t} + \frac{\$1,000}{(1.10)^5}$$

which implies a drop in price of $76 (or 7.6 percent). If, later, the market's expected return rises from 10 percent to 12 percent, the bonds should sell for $856:

$$\text{(12–18)} \qquad \$856 = \sum_{t=1}^{5} \frac{\$80}{(1.12)^t} + \frac{\$1,000}{(1.12)^5}$$

which implies a drop of only $68 (or 7.4 percent). The reason the drop in price is less the second time is the market's expected return is at a higher starting point (10 percent). A one percentage point rise in required returns when interest rates are already "high" is less significant to a bondholder than the same rise when interest rates are lower.

> The higher the current level of interest rates or equlibrium-expected returns the smaller the decrease (increase) in the security's market price and percentage decrease in price resulting from a one percentage point increase (decrease) in the expected equilibrium return.

Duration

The **duration** of a fixed income security is a measure of the average life of the cash flows the security offers to its owners. A 10-year Treasury bond with a coupon interest rate of 8 percent selling at par of $1,000 has a duration of 7.25 years. The calculation of duration for bond i, using D_{it} to represent the flow of interest *and* principal, is given by:

(12–19)   *Duration*

$$Duration_i = \sum_{t=1}^{T} \left(t \cdot \frac{\left(\dfrac{E(\tilde{D}_{it})}{1 + E(\tilde{R}_i)^t} \right)}{P_{io}^m} \right)$$

or, assuming annual interest payments, for the 10-year T-bond duration is:

$$Duration_i = \frac{1 \left(\dfrac{80}{(1.08)^1} \right)}{1,000} + \frac{2 \left(\dfrac{80}{(1.08)^2} \right)}{1,000} + \ldots + \frac{10 \left(\dfrac{1,080}{(1.08)^{10}} \right)}{1,000} = 7.25 \text{ years}$$

The calculation is derived from an evaluation of the sensitivity of bond value in Equation (12–2) to changes in the discount rate applied to future cash flows. Duration is greater: (*a*) the longer the period to maturity, *T;* (*b*) the lower the expected cash flows before maturity, or the lower the coupon payment, $E(\tilde{D}_t)$; and (*c*) the lower the discount rate, or the rate of interest applied to the future cash flows, $E(\tilde{R})$. Thus, duration is a measure that summarizes a security's exposure to interest rate risk through the securities maturity and coupon, and through the market's discount rate.

Five different Treasury securities with different maturities and coupons are presented with their associated durations below:

Maturity	Coupon	Price	Yield to Maturity	Duration (years)
2 years	14 5/8	$1160	6.3%	1.9
3	6 5/8	1000	6.6	2.8
9	9 1/2	1160	7.1	6.6
18	12 3/8	1440	7.7	9.5
10	zero	463	8.0	10.0

Because duration is derived from the sensitivity of bond value to a change in the discount rate applied to future cash flows, the percentage change in bond price, or the bond's return, can be linked to duration. The expression is:

(12–20)   ***Duration and Return***

$$R_i = \frac{\Delta P_i}{P_i} = -Duration \left(\frac{\Delta E(\tilde{R}_i)}{1 + E(\tilde{R}_i)} \right)$$

The percentage change   *Minus duration times*
in the price of a bond   *the change in the*
in response to a change   =   *interest rate in relation*
in interest rates   *to 1 + the original rate*

As you can see, if interest rates rise by 1 percent from an 8 percent base, the price of the above Treasury bond with a duration of 7.25 years will fall by .067, or 6.7 percent.

Bond Betas

If measure of duration summarize how fixed-income security prices vary with variations in the general level of interest rates, then duration also must be related to nondiversifiable interest rate risk. In fact, as information is conveyed to the financial marketplace regarding the general level of interest rates, all security prices will be affected (though, as we have just seen, not all will be affected to the same extent). As interest rates rise the security market line shifts up. This leads to the adoption of higher discount rates for the valuation of future cash flows, and a general decline in the prices of all securities offering future cash flows.

As you might expect, this means that much of a typical fixed-income security's interest rate risk is nondiversifiable; i.e., the returns on such securities tend to covary with market portfolio returns. With this in mind we can consider the relationships among a security's duration, its comovement with the return on the market portfolio, and its beta. Specifically, if any security's β is given by,

$$\beta_i = \frac{Cov(\tilde{R}_i, \tilde{R}_m)}{[\sigma(\tilde{R}_m)]^2}$$

then, with equation (12–20), it must also be given by

(12–21)   *Duration and Beta*

$$\beta_i = \frac{- Duration \left[Cov\left(\left(\frac{\Delta\, E(\tilde{R}_i)}{1 + E(\tilde{R}_i)}\right), \tilde{R}_m\right) \right]}{[\sigma(\tilde{R}_m)]^2}$$

This, then, is a more detailed specification of the second component of bond beta coefficients, or the nondiversifiable interest rate risk component. Note that the covariance term would be negative, for as $E(\tilde{R}_i)$ increases (an upward shift in the security market line), the rate of return generated on the market would be low. Thus, the numerator would be positive, and an increase in duration will lead to a proportional increase in beta. If the duration of one treasury bond is twice as great as another, the beta coefficient will be twice as great as well. Of course, for securities with default risk, the nondiversifiable cash flow risk component must be added to determine accurately the bond's overall risk level.

Estimating Bond Betas

In principle, we can estimate the risk levels of bonds in much the same way that they are estimated for common stocks. Thus, historical holding-period return data on each fixed-income security can be regressed on the returns on a market index to determine the security's beta. Unfortunately, the estimation process is complicated by two characteristics of bonds. First, the duration of a bond declines over time as the security approaches maturity. Second, many bonds are traded less frequently than the common stock of the firms that issued them. They would, naturally, be more subject to the nonsynchronous trading bias we discussed in Chapter 11. This would tend to bias downward estimates of a given bond's beta.

In spite of these limitations some general statements can be made about bond risk (and, no doubt, more sophisticated statistical procedures can provide better risk estimates). During the period between 1980 and 1985 we regressed holding-period returns on an index of "high grade," long-term corporate bonds on the S&P index of 500 common stocks. We did the same thing with an index of long term government bonds. Both of the estimated betas were about .4. This indicates, of course, that bond risk is about 40 percent of the risk of common stocks.

In effect both stock and bond prices were affected by the general variation in the level of interest rates during the early to mid 1980s. As interest rates went up, the holding-period returns on both stocks and long-term bonds were low. As interest rates declined, the returns on both security types was high. This led to the covariance between bond and stock returns, and a β of .4 for these bond indexes. The corporate bond estimates include default as well as interest rate risk. But the bonds included in this index faced little risk of default. Betas on lower-grade long-term bonds would be expected to be somewhat higher.

Risk Management

By now it should be obvious to you that fixed-income security risk is a significant consideration in the management of a portfolio. Both default risk and interest rate risk affect the overall risk of a portfolio that includes these securities. Moreover, the use of beta to summarize bond risk is appropriate, though bond betas are sometimes difficult to measure with the use of historical data. The decrease in the time to maturity as time elapses ensures that historical estimates are somewhat "out of date."

Now consider a problem in risk management. Suppose an individual investor, insurance company, or pension fund has specific cash requirements at some point in time in the future. This is a common problem for insurance companies and pension funds that have actuarially defined obligations to their clients, and a common problem for individuals that may need the money for consumption after retirement or to fund a college education. In these cases investors might wish to ensure that a portion of their portfolio is devoted to opportunities that **guarantee** the need will be satisfied.

The purchase of default-free government bonds will insulate the investor from the risk of lower returns due to changes in the issuer's ability to pay, but will not insulate him from the variation in returns that comes from changes in the general level of interest rates. However, it is possible to establish a portfolio position that effectively immunizes his need from the effects of interest rate risk. In fact, there are two ways of doing this: cash flow matching, and duration immunization.

Immunizing with Matched Cash Flows. Investors with defined cash needs over a period of time can purchase a set of default-free government securities that offer cash flows that match the investor's needs. In the simplest case an investor requiring $25,000 per year for four years beginning five years from now can buy four different zero-coupon bonds maturing in years 5 through 8. Depending on the current level of interest rates it would be a simple matter to determine the current investment in each that would fulfill that need. While the bonds may vary in price over time as interest rates change, the investor's position is one that immunizes him from those effects. The same investor purchasing a 20-year T-bond would have to worry about the risk of increases in interest rates that may depress the bond's price in the years when the bond is to be sold. Similarly, if the investor purchases shorter-term bonds, he faces the risk that interest rates may fall, leaving him with a lower reinvestment rate when these short-term bonds mature.

More complex needs also can be matched. The financial markets are complete enough to ensure that securities are available to balance the cash flows from those securities with the needs of the investor. Of course, at some point the transactions cost of assembling such a portfolio may outweigh the gains from ever more precisely matched positions.

Immunizing with Matched Durations. Effectively, a portfolio position is immunized if its value at the end of the holding period, or at the time of the investor's need, is independent of the level of and course of interest rates during the investment period. Immunization can be accomplished by purchasing a default-free security with a duration that is the same as the need for the money. In fact, duration is defined to ensure that this is the case. However, since the duration of the investment changes as time passes, it is necessary to "rebalance" the portfolio at intermediate points in time (prior to the point in time the cash is needed) to ensure that the portfolio is immunized over the entire span between the point of investment and the need for the cash.

For example, suppose an investor has a specific need for $1,860 in three years. He wishes to purchase a security in an amount sufficient to cover this need, without the possibility of any variation in amount at the investment horizon. If current interest rates are 23 percent (a high value selected for illustrative purposes; interest rates don't have to be at a particular level for duration immunization to work) the investor can purchase for $1,000 a 4-year T-bond with a coupon rate of 23 percent. This bond has a duration of three years. After one year interest rates have dropped to 10 percent. As a result the price of the bond has risen to $1,323. However, the duration of the bond is now 3.4 years, which doesn't satisfy the investor's remaining needs. Thus, our investor sells the bond for $1,323, and, with this money the coupon of $230, buys a second T-bond with a 14 percent coupon and a remaining life of two years. This bond can be purchased for $1,070, so 1.45 of the bonds must be purchased ([$230 + $1,323]/$1,070 = 1.45) to keep the portfolio fully invested.

One year later, interest rates have risen to 15 percent. The T-bond, with one year remaining to maturity, will sell at $980. The value of the investor's position will be 1.45 times the value of the bond plus the coupon of 14 percent paid at the end of the year, or 1.45 ($140 + $980) = $1,625. This same bond now has a one year duration, matching the investor's final year prior to the need for cash. Since the T-bond will return the market rate of 15 percent over this year, the investor's horizon period value will be $1,625 (1.15) or $1,869. This is the same amount of money that would be available to the investor if interest rates did not change during the three-year horizon, or $230 (1.23)^2 + $230(1.23) + $1,230 = $1,861. The $8 difference occurs due to approximations in the calculation of duration on these securities for this example.

Maturity and Returns: The Term Structure of Interest Rates

Returns offered by a selection of fixed-income securities possessing identical default risks (but having different maturities) can differ. The relation between the yields offered by these securities and their maturities is called *the term structure of interest rates* or, sometimes more simply, the *yield curve.*

The term structure is often displayed visually as a chart of the yields to maturity, R_Y, offered by different, *default-free* U.S. Treasury securities in relation to the number of years until maturity. Thus defined, the term structure is a "snapshot" of the expected returns available at a single point in time to an investor who can choose from among securities with different maturity dates. Understanding the factors that underlie the term structure and determine its shape is important if we are to understand better the market's risk–return trade-off for fixed-income securities.

Figure 12–3 shows four different shapes for the term structure. Each of these shapes has existed at some time in the past for U.S. Treasury securities. Each of the four graphs in the figure was drawn by calculating the yields to maturity on various U.S. Treasury

FIGURE 12–3   Historical Term Structure Relationships

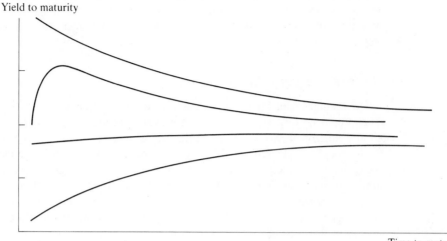

Yield to maturity

Time to maturity

securities offering different maturities, based on the market prices that actually existed as of a particular date. As you can see, sometimes the term structure has reflected a low-level and upward-sloping relationship between R_Y and time to maturity, a medium level of rates that has displayed no relationship between R_Y and time to maturity, a high level of rates with a downward sloping relationship between R_Y and maturity, or a humpbacked relationship.

Why are these functions characteristic of term structure relations? To answer this question requires an understanding of two factors that have been previously introduced: (*a*) market risk preferences and (*b*) the supply of, and demand for, securities in future time periods. We discuss each of these factors below.

Market Risk Preferences

To see the effect of market risk preferences on the term structure, consider first a horizontal term structure for default-free Treasury securities, as it is shown in the figure. If investors generally have a short-term investment horizon (say one year), changes in the level of interest rates during the investment period will cause the value of their portfolios at the end of the investment period to be higher or lower than their ex ante expected returns, as the discussions in previous sections of this chapter have shown. The exposure to this interest rate risk is larger the longer the maturity of the bonds held in the portfolio. These investors, viewing the nondiversifiable interest rate risk of investing in long-term bonds as being larger than that of short-term bonds, will be reluctant to hold them in their portfolios. This lack of demand for long-term bonds will tend to force the returns offered on these instruments upward, thereby making them more attractive. This creates a term structure that is generally upward sloping. The resulting premium for the risk of nondiversifiable interest rate fluctuations, which is caused by the possibility of changes in the general level of interest rates, is termed the **liquidity premium,** and the conceptual logic that leads to it is called the **liquidity preference theory.** It is based on the premise that investment horizons are short term, so that long-term bonds—facing greater nondiversifiable interest rate risk and having higher β's—would offer higher returns.

Anticipated Future Supply and Demand

The second factor affecting the shape of the term structure is the anticipated supply of, and demand for, fixed-income securities *in the future*. Suppose the term structure is initially horizontal. Securities of all maturities with the same risk of default are priced to have roughly equal returns. Then suppose new information arrives in the market which causes market participants to forecast lower interest rates on short-term bonds in the future. In that case, long-term bonds currently need not offer as high a return as they would otherwise have to in order to be attractive to investors. The term structure will tend to become downward sloping as a result. If the new information suggests that higher short-term interest rates will prevail in the future, however, long-term bonds will have to offer higher returns than are currently being offered on short-term bonds. This will cause the term structure to have a positive slope.[6]

To be more precise, let us construct a simple world in which only two bond maturities exist. There are one-year bonds and two-year bonds. At the present time, one-year, default-free bonds are offering expected returns (or yields to maturity) of 10 percent, while next year investors forecast that the one-year bonds *then* available will offer expected returns of 15 percent. Someone who purchases this year's one-year bond and then, when it matures, purchases another one-year bond and holds it until maturity can expect to earn the following rate of return on average over the two years,

$$.1247 = [(1.10)(1.15)]^{1/2} - 1$$

In the absence of a liquidity premium and with no arbitrage possibilities, the rate of return available from purchasing a two-year bond now and holding it for two years should be the same. That is, two-year bonds must be priced now to earn expected returns of precisely 12.47 percent.

In more general terms, if the expected return on a one-period bond at time 0 is given by $_0E(\tilde{R}_1)$, the forecasted expected return on a one-period bond at time 1 is given by $_1E(\tilde{R}_2)$, and the expected return on a two-period bond at time 0 is given by $_0E(\tilde{R}_2)$, then it should be the case that

(12–22) $$[1 + {_0E(\tilde{R}_1)}][1 + {_1E(\tilde{R}_2)}] = [1 + {_0E(\tilde{R}_2)}]^2$$

Expected two-period return from a series of two one-period bonds = *Expected two-period return from one two-period bond.*

---

[6]With certain assumptions, especially regarding the size of the liquidity premium, it is possible to work backward to determine the market's expectations of inflation from the current term structure. For example, ignoring empirical complexities, a falling term structure would indicate that expectations of future inflation are more moderate than expectations of near-term inflation. For an in-depth discussion of the inflationary implications of the term structure, see Fama [1976].

Clearly, if interest rates are forecast to be higher in the second period, $_1E(\tilde{R}_2)$ will exceed $_0E(\tilde{R}_1)$. This implies, from Equation (12–25) that the annualized rate of return currently offered on the two-period bond, $_0E(\tilde{R}_2)$ exceeds the one-period bond return at time 0. The term structure thus has a positive slope. However, the existence of a positive slope does not suggest that the two-period offers a higher return in period 1 than does the one-period bond. In fact, it all goes according to expectations, the two-period rate, $_0E(\tilde{R}_2)$, will be returned over time according to the one-period returns offered; i.e., in the first year, the investor in the two-period bond will earn $_0E(\tilde{R}_1)$, and in the second he will earn $_1E(\tilde{R}_2)$.

If the investment horizon and the expectations of future interest rates are two forces at work in financial markets, there are a number of hypotheses about the extent of their relative strength. Three alternative hypotheses in particular tend to have widespread support. They differ only with regard to the influence of the two factors we have discussed—market risk preferences, and the anticipated future supply and demand for different maturities. The three hypotheses are: (*a*) **the pure expectations theory,** (*b*) **the liquidity preference theory,** and (*c*) **the market segmentation** (or preferred habitat) **theory**.

Pure Expectations Theory.   This theory holds that the term structure is determined entirely by expectations of future short-term rates. There is no liquidity premium since there is no reason to expect either investors or the issuers of securities to prefer certain maturities. The term structure may be upward-sloping (if future short-term rates are expected to be higher than they are currently), downward sloping (if future short-term rates are expected to be lower than they are currently), or horizontal. Thus, in traditionally higher interest rate periods, the term structure would tend to be downward sloping and in lower interest rate periods, it would tend to rise.

Liquidity Preference Theory.   This theory holds that longer-term bonds must offer higher equilibrium-expected returns because of their greater level of nondiversifiable interest rate risk. Thus, the theory holds that the normal term structure should be upward sloping. This normal relationship occasionally could be offset, however, by expectations of lower future short-term interest rates in a high interest rate period, generating a moderately negatively sloped structure. In this sense, the liquidity preference theory is often employed as a modification to the pure expectations theory, rather than as a substitute for it.

Market Segmentation Theory.   This theory holds that both issuers of securities and investors in those securities tend to specialize in, or exhibit preferences for, particular ranges of maturities. It might be supposed, for example, that the U.S. Treasury tends to borrow "short" (meaning it prefers to issue securities with maturities of, say, under 5 years), whereas life insurers and pension funds seek to lend "long" (meaning they prefer to hold securities with maturities of say, over 15 years). Consequently, the rates of return offered on each maturity are set rather independently of the rates of return offered on other maturities, depending as they do on the supply and demand interaction of their own rather limited set of market participants. Under this theory, the term structure could take on any shape (including the humpback structure, for example). The major forces creating the actual term structure include the borrowing practices of the U.S. Treasury, the open market operations of the Federal Reserve, the investment behavior of private financial institutions and the borrowing practices of private corporations. The net result of these forces is a "typical" term structure which tends to have a positive slope, but which can assume any shape at all.

Empirically, attempts to test these various theories and/or to estimate the magnitude of liquidity premiums or market segmentation effects are fraught with problems. These problems stem from an inability of researchers to observe *expected* future short-term interest rates, and from the fact that a variety of factors influencing market risk preferences and the supply of, and demand for, fixed-income securities are unstable (e.g., inflation). Recent attempts to test the theories have suggested that there is, in reality, little effective market segmentation but that the liquidity premium tends to be positive. This is consistent with the idea of longer-term bonds with greater interest rate risk having higher betas and higher equilibrium returns.

Inflation and Fixed-Income Securities

In this section, we discuss the relationship between **nominal** rates of returns on fixed-income securities and their **real**, or inflation-adjusted, returns; as well as the impact of inflation on securities both with and without default risk.

Real and Nominal Returns

During 1981, the Consumer Price Index rose by 8.9 percent. In that same year, an investor who held the Standard & Poor's Composite 500 Stock Index would have experienced a total return on that investment of -4.9 percent. Adjusted for inflation, however, the **real** return was -13.8 percent. The effect of inflation on ex post investment returns is straightforward. The real return on security i is approximately equal to the difference between i's nominal return and the rate of actual, observed inflation, or;

(12–23)   *Ex Post Returns and Inflation*

$$R_{i,\text{real}} = R_i - \Omega$$

where Ω is the observed inflation rate and $R_{i,\text{real}}$ is the real rate of increase in wealth.

Because of the effect of inflation on real investment returns, and because each investor's ultimate goal is the consumption of goods and services, the anticipation of inflation is likely to affect the investor's decision as to how much to save, and in which assets to invest. These decisions, in turn, have an effect on the demanded return on securities of all risk levels. Economists theorize that well-informed investors will factor their expectations about future inflation rates into their investment decision processes, and that by their collective decisions, they will cause equilibrium expected returns (on both real capital assets and financial assets) to reflect those expectations in a manner which compensates investors for anticipated (though uncertain) inflation. This theory implies the existence of the **Fisher Effect**, which for security i states that:

(12–24)   *The Fisher Effect*

$$E(\tilde{R}_i) = E(\tilde{R}_{i,\text{real}}) + E(\tilde{\Omega})$$

FIGURE 12–4   Comparisons of T-Bill Rates and Rate of Change in the Consumer Price Index

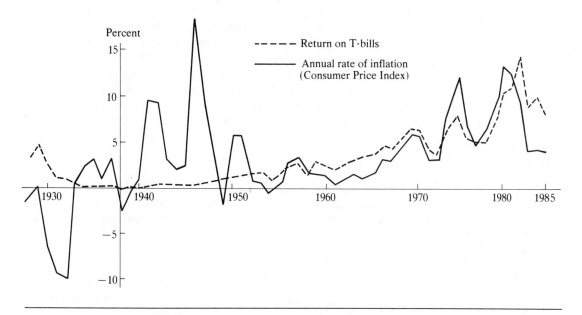

where $E(\tilde{\Omega})$ is the expected rate of inflation; $E(\tilde{R}_i)$, as before, is the nominal equilibrium rate of return that investors require on security i, given its risk relative to the market portfolio; and $E(\tilde{R}_{i,\mathrm{real}})$ is the real, inflation-adjusted required rate of return on security i.

The Fisher Effect implies that if investors in the aggregate require a 15 percent equilibrium-expected return on security i, the nominal return expected must be 20 percent when consensus anticipations are for a 5 percent rate of inflation. In other words, the Fisher Effect implies that demanded (ex ante) nominal and real returns exhibit a relationship to inflation that is precisely the same as the ex post relation given in Equation (12–23) above. The only difference is that the equilibrium-expected return, $E(\tilde{R}_i)$, is substituted for the realized (observed) return, R_i.

The Fisher Effect has been studied by Fama [1976] and Nelson and Schwert [1977], among others. Fama's results suggest that Equation (12–24) holds very closely.[7] Consequently, at any particular point in time, the security market line itself fully reflects the market's inflationary expectations. Expected rates of return to bonds, stocks, and other opportunities would compensate for the loss of purchasing power that is created by expected inflation.

These and other results have led to the conclusion that increases in expectations of inflation are the primary cause of the increases in coupon interest rates on newly issued bonds over the past two decades. Figure 12–4 compares the change in the consumer price

---

[7]One should be aware of the difficulties of measuring something like Equation (12–23). Both demanded real return and anticipated inflation cannot be observed directly, and nominal returns can be observed directly only for short-term, default-free instruments.

index with the coupon rate on newly issued U.S. Treasury bills. There is little evidence that there has been any substantive, cyclical, or secular change in the real rate of interest over this period.

For outstanding fixed-income securities, however, a consensus change in the expected inflation rate in future periods affects the discount rate (demanded return), because as interest rates change the security market lines would shift. A change in the demanded return will impact directly on the bond's price and on the ex post return earned. Moreover, for those bonds not completely free of default risk, a change in inflationary expectations could alter the issuer's ability to pay, which would influence both the expected cash flow and its covariability with other marketwide factors.

Inflation and Default-Free Securities

Consider a 30-year, 6 percent coupon, U.S. Treasury bond with 20 years remaining to maturity, with an equilibrium *real* expected return of 4 percent, and an equilibrium *nominal* expected return, $E(\bar{R}_i)$, of 8 percent, given inflationary expectations of 4 percent per year. The bond's equilibrium value would be given as:

$$(12\text{--}25) \qquad P_{i0}^e = \sum_{t=1}^{20} \frac{\$60}{(1.08)^t} + \frac{\$1000}{(1.08)^{20}} = \$803.64$$

A one-time revision of investors' inflationary expectations to 6 percent per annum (from 4 percent) over the next 20 years would tend to increase investors' nominal equilibrium-expected returns, thus reducing the securitys' price. If the equilibrium-demanded return now rises to 10 percent over the course of a year as the Fisher Effect implies it should— the price of the security would fall to:

$$(12\text{--}26) \qquad P_{i1}^e = \sum_{i=1}^{19} \frac{\$60}{(1.10)^t} + \frac{\$1,000}{(1.10)^{19}} = \$665.40$$

For those who purchased the security after the point in time the new expectations were reflected in share price, the equilibrium return they expect to earn is now 10 percent per annum. For those who held the security during the period in which expectations were changing, the ex post return generated would be highly negative in this case, since the end-of-period price would reflect the new equilibrium nominal return and the existing coupon payment. If the security were held for the year expectations of inflation were revised, the ex post return actually earned over that year is:

$$R_{i1} = \frac{\$665.40 - \$803.64 + \$60}{\$803.64} = -.0974, \text{ or } -9.74\%$$

This negative return reflects the positive coupon payment and the fall in equilibrium bond price created by the revision of inflationary expectations.

If the change in expectations is for a nonpermanent change in the inflation rate, the effect on demanded return will span only those periods over which the higher level of inflation is forecast.[8] Thus, if the higher 6 percent inflation rate is expected to last only

---

[8]The decade of the 1970s was a period of time reflecting upward revisions of inflationary expectations. Actual inflation in 1977 and 1978 reached 10 percent; at the same time, the yields to maturity on long-term high-grade bonds and mortgages were in the range of $9\frac{1}{2}$ percent to $10\frac{1}{2}$ percent. Unless the real rate of

three years, at which time inflation is expected to subside to the more "normal" 4 percent rate, and if these expectations were fully reflected in equilibrium nominal expected returns, the appropriate equilibrium valuation model would be:

$$\textbf{(12–27)} \qquad P^e_{i0} = \sum_{t=1}^{3} \frac{\$60}{(1.10)^t} + \frac{1}{(1.10)^3} \sum_{t=1}^{17} \frac{\$60}{(1.08)^t} + \frac{\$1{,}000}{(1.10)^3(1.08)^{17}}$$

$$= \$763.46$$

The decline in value is much less than when there is a more permanent change in expectations.

Inflation and Securities with Default Risk

The effect of changes in anticipated inflation on equilibrium nominal expected returns is the same for securities with default risk as it is for default-free securities. Yet, if changes in inflationary expectations cause revisions of either (*a*) the expected cash flow from the security, or (*b*) the covariance of those cash flows with market cash flows, the effect on the equilibrium price of a security with default risk is not as straightforward.

With inflation, the average firm will find its profits rising.[9] Since coupon interest costs for existing debt remain constant, the additional interest coverage may cause investors to revise upward their cash flow expectations for risky corporate debt. As this revision takes place, the expected cash flow will be revised upward with the equilibrium nominal expected return. The effect will be to mute the decline in equilibrium value caused by the upward revision of interest rates. The size of this effect depends on the unique characteristics of the firm and the way it is influenced by inflation.

Imagine a firm with low long-term variable costs of production, which has relatively new and efficient productive equipment (and therefore high fixed costs of production) that is only marginally profitable. Investors in the bond market may rationally form expectations over future cash flows that represent a substantial discount from the "promised" coupon payment. An increasing inflation rate that carries with it an increase in the price of this firm's output would cause profits to rise, also producing greater coverage for interest payments on debt and a decreased likelihood of the firm being unable to meet its interest obligations. That is, the expected cash flow from the security will rise.

The covariance of a bond's cash flows with returns on the market portfolio also may change if the increased expectations of inflation in the market cause a revision of the covariance of the firm's earnings with the returns on the market portfolio. This might happen if the increased inflationary expectations caused the firm's management to make real investment decisions which effectively alter the firm's overall beta.

Inflation and the Value of Other Economic Variables

All of the effects pointed to in this discussion must be tempered by the fact that inflation, and inflationary expectations, are the effect of—and have an effect on—an uncountable number of other factors that also influence security value. Inflation may

---

interest were close to zero, these figures suggest the expectation, prevalent at the time, that the longer-run rate of inflation would decline from its unusually high 1977–78 level.

[9] We say the average firm because some firms will fare better during an inflationary economy than others.

reflect excess demand, which would have a direct impact on a firm's cash flows. Monetary policy reactions to an inflationary economy may by themselves force up interest rates. Such a policy would interact simultaneously with inflation to create a new set of equilibrium expected returns—a new security market line. Precisely what the resulting risk-return relationship would look like would be difficult to anticipate and may depend on specific characteristics of the economy. Consequently, while any attempts to describe the specific effects of inflation on a security's value are difficult to determine, they clearly depend on the way inflation alters: (*a*) the probability distribution of interest and principal payments, (*b*) the covariance of the firm's ability to pay, and (*c*) the effect of inflation on the level and shape of the security market line.

Inflation and After-Tax Returns

Though, in theory, the Fisher Effect protects investors from the deleterious effects of anticipated inflation on real returns, the existence of the federal income tax removes this protection from the ex post returns earned by most taxable investors. The tax effect on ex post investment returns is two-fold: (*a*) nominal returns are taxed as though they are real, and (*b*) tax bracket creep causes higher marginal tax rates to apply to investment returns over time in a inflationary period, even though the investor's real income may not have risen at all. Let's see how these two factors work together to reduce investors' real investment returns.

Consider an investor who earns $50,000 in taxable income a year and is currently in the 28 percent marginal tax bracket. Suppose this individual's investment portfolio experiences a total yearly investment return of 15 percent, while the rate of inflation is 12 percent. If the investor were to liquidate the portfolio, realizing both dividends or interest payments and capital gains, she would generate a net after-tax investment return of (15 percent)—(.28)(15 percent) = 10.8 percent. After adjustment for both taxes and inflation, however, the investor has earned, effectively, a −1.2 percent return on the funds invested. The government has taxed the full, nominal increase in wealth, even though twelve fifteenths of that increase merely restored a decline in the investor's purchasing power.

Clearly, if all investors were taxed at 28 percent on their nominal income they would refuse to invest in taxable bonds unless the nominal interest rate on those bonds was "boosted up" to compensate for both inflation and the taxation of nominal returns. This would imply that interest rates and equilibrium-expected returns on taxable securities would fluctuate more than the level of expected inflation. There is some evidence that this is the case. In the inflationary period between 1978 and 1981 interest rates tended to rise by more than the level of inflation, bringing howls of protest from borrowers and calls for more regulation of financial markets. But the more rapid rise of interest rates is exactly what you would expect when lenders are taxed on their nominal returns.

The moral is that investors should and will take specific tax considerations into account when choosing from among a set of different investment alternatives. If many investors do this it is likely to affect the structure of equilibrium-expected returns. In the case of this example, the "after tax" Fisher Effect will cause larger shifts in the position of the security market line than the change in expected inflation that cause the shift.

Summary

Fixed-income securities entitle their owner to a specific, contractually agreed-upon series of cash flows, usually in the form of periodic interest payments and the return of principal. These claims include corporate bonds; term loans; negotiable certificates of deposit; passbook savings accounts; financial leases; mortgages; Treasury bills, bonds, and notes; Federal Home Loan Bank bonds; preferred stock; municipal bonds; and many others. Many fixed-income securities have a specified maturity date. The par, or face, value of a fixed-income security generally equals the amount borrowed, and the coupon rate (if any) specifies the annual, promised interest payment as a percentage of this value.

Some fixed-income securities, by their nature, expose their owner to the risk that the issuer of the security will default on the promised, or contractually specified, cash flows. The borrower's ability to pay those promised flows generally depends on three factors: (*a*) the issuer's earning power, (*b*) the market value of its assets, and (*c*) the nature of the applicable debt covenants which describe the agreement between the issuer and investors. Because the federal government has the power to tax and to print money, securities issued by the U.S. government are considered to be free of default risk. All others have some default probability.

The equilibrium value of a fixed-income security is given by the expected value of its future cash flows, discounted at the appropriate equilibrium-expected return, given the security's risk relative to the market portfolio, i.e., its β. In the case of default-free securities, the expected cash flows equal the promised cash flows. In the case of securities possessing default risk, however, the expected cash flows will be smaller than the promised cash flows, to allow for the probability that some (or all) of the promised amounts will not be paid; hence, all other things equal, the value of a security possessing default risk is less than that of a default-free security.

Three concepts of ex ante rates of return on fixed-income securities are important and frequently referred to in the financial literature and in financial markets. These are: (*a*) the expected rate of return (or internal rate), which is found by discounting the *expected* future cash flows and setting the result equal to the security's current market price, (*b*) the yield to maturity, found by discounting the *promised* future cash flows and setting the result equal to current market price, and (*c*) the current yield, which is the ratio of annual, *promised* income to current market price. Only the first of these corresponds to the returns offered in the context of the capital-asset pricing model. None of the three values necessarily will equal the investor's ex post holding-period return, but this depends on the actual reinvestment interest rate applicable to periodic income flows, whether or not the security is held to maturity, whether or not the issuer defaults, or whether or not new information arrives in the market which changes investors' required returns or cash flow expectations.

In the context of the CAPM, fixed-income securities should be priced in equilibrium to reflect their nondiversifiable default risk and their nondiversifiable interest rate risk. The former component of risk measures the extent to which the probability of default by a particular firm is related to, or affected by, the probability of default by other firms included in the market portfolio. The latter component of risk measures the extent to which a particular security's price change—due to a change in the returns investors require from that security—is related to similar changes in the required returns on other securities.

Since fixed-income securities tend to be close substitutes for one another, changes in the required returns on one security generally are accompanied by changes in the required returns on others, thus suggesting that most interest rate risk is nondiversifiable. Nevertheless, strategies exist to allow investors to immunize a portfolio from the effects of interest rate risk.

To the extent that interest rate risk is nondiversifiable and that it affects securities with longer maturities more than those with shorter maturities, it is useful to examine the relationship between the maturity and yields of a variety of fixed-income securities. This relationship is called the *term structure of interest rates*.

Inflation can affect both the ex ante (expected) returns and the ex post (observed) returns on fixed-income securities. If investors anticipate inflation, equilibrium-expected nominal returns will reflect the expected real returns that investors require, plus an adjustment for expected inflation. This hypothesis is called the Fisher Effect and, if it holds, suggests that the *security market line* should fully reflect the market's inflationary expectations.

APPENDIX: Improving the Precision of Rate of Return Calculations

Throughout this chapter, we assumed that interest payments on fixed-income securities are paid annually, and that those securities cannot be called (removed from the market) prior to maturity by the issuer. We now examine the effects on estimated bond returns from relaxing those assumptions.

Semiannual Interest Payments

Most corporate bonds pay the annual, promised interest in semiannual installments. Use of this method in calculating bonds' expected returns and yields to maturity can improve the accuracy of those estimated values. Professional bond tables generally provide yields to maturity based on the following formulation:

(12A–1)   *Yield to Maturity for η Cash Flows per Year*

$$P_{i0}^m = \sum_{t=1}^{\eta \cdot T} \left(\frac{D_{it}/\eta}{\left(1 + \dfrac{R_Y}{\eta}\right)^t} \right) + \left(\frac{F_{iT}}{\left(1 + \dfrac{R_Y}{\eta}\right)^{\eta T}} \right)$$

Notice in this equation that each year has been subdivided into η equal periods. During each period a cash flow of D_{it}/η is promised. If $\eta = 2$, then semiannual income payments are expected; if $\eta = 4$, the payments are quarterly; and so forth.

To see how this works, consider the Exxon bonds examined earlier. At a price of $910, a coupon rate of 6.5 percent, and 10 years to maturity, we calculated that the yield to maturity of the Exxon bonds was 7.83 percent, based on the assumption that interest was paid annually. Using Equation (12A–1) and assuming that the next semiannual coupon payment will be received in six months, we find that:

(12A–2)
$$\$910 = \sum_{t=1}^{20} \frac{\$32.50}{\left(1 + \dfrac{R_Y}{\eta}\right)^t} + \frac{\$1,000}{\left(1 + \dfrac{R_Y}{\eta}\right)^{20}}$$

which, when evaluated, produces a value of $R_Y = .0781$ or about 7.8 percent. This figure is a more precise measure of this security's true yield to maturity, since interest payments are made twice a year.

A formulation analogous to (12A–1) applies to the calculation of a fixed-income security's *expected return* (rather than yield to maturity), given its market price. Using Equation (12–2)—the basic equilibrium valuation equation for fixed-income securities—we can write:

(12A–3)   *Value with η Cash Flows per Year*

$$P_{i0}^e = \sum_{t=1}^{\eta \cdot T} \frac{E\,(\tilde{D}_{it}/\eta)}{\left(1 + \dfrac{E\,(\tilde{R}_i)}{\eta}\right)^t} + \frac{E\,(\tilde{P}_{iT})}{\left(1 + \dfrac{E\,(\tilde{R}_i)}{\eta}\right)^{\eta T}}$$

As noted earlier, most preferred stocks—unlike bonds—offer quarterly dividend payments. It should be clear to you how that fact can be incorporated into Equations (12A–1) and (12A–3) for obtaining estimates of those securities' yields to maturity and expected returns. In fact, you should be able to apply these equations to suit the payment characteristics of any fixed-income security offering monthly, bimonthly, quarterly, semiannually, or any other pattern of interest and principal payments.

Call Provisions

One other refinement to our basic expected return and yield formulations is worth noting. It pertains to the effect of a security's call provisions on the investor's rate of return. Some bonds and preferred stocks are callable by the issuer on or after a prespecified future date or dates at a specific minimum price or prices. For instance, a recent issue of Puget Sound Power & Light Company's preferred stock has no specified maturity date. It may, however, be called (redeemed) by the company at any time after November 15, 1992, but prior to November 15, 1997, at a price of 103 percent of par value. After that date, the company may—at its option—call the shares at par value (plus any accrued dividends). What is the investor's expected return (or yield) if the stock is called on some future date?

The answer depends on the actual call date. Suppose a fixed-income security can be called on or after a date T_c years away. T_c may be the number of years to any particular call date in which the investor is interested; the expected return or yield which assumes the security is called on that date can be found by substituting date T_c for T (the time until maturity) in Equations (12A–1) and (12A–3). Thus, if the investor in the Puget Sound Power & Light Company preferred stock is interested in knowing the yield to a call date equal to November 16, 1992, the following general equation would be evaluated:

(12A–4)   *Yield to Call Date*

$$P_{i0} = \sum_{t=1}^{\eta \cdot T_c} \frac{D_{it}/\eta}{\left(1 + \dfrac{R_Y}{\eta}\right)^{T_c}} + \frac{F_{iT_c}}{(1 + R_Y)^{\eta \cdot T_c}}$$

where F_{iT_c} is the minimum call price applicable to T_c. Assuming the stock is now selling for $95 a share, that it promises a 12 percent annual dividend payable quarterly and that date T_c is exactly 4 years (16 quarters) away, evaluation of (12A–4) produces:

(12A–5) $$\$95 = \sum_{t=1}^{16} \frac{\$3}{\left(1 + \dfrac{R_Y}{4}\right)^{t}} + \frac{\$103}{\left(1 + \dfrac{R_Y}{4}\right)^{16}}$$

The solution to R_Y is 13.6 percent.

The result states that, given the security is purchased at its current price of $95 and held, with reinvestment of all promised dividend payments at the annual interest rate of 15 percent, until November 16, 1992, when it is called by the company at a price of $103, the investor will earn a return of 15 percent per year. Note that this measure of yield-to-call has all the weaknesses of the yield-to-maturity calculation, in that it does not allow for default risk, but it is also arbitrary in the sense that the security need not be called at all, or it may be called on some other date than was assumed in the calculation. Nevertheless, it serves to notify investors that many callable fixed-income securities are in fact called prior to maturity by the issuer, and this can have a substantial effect on an investor's holding-period return.

References

Arak, Marcelle, and McCurdy, Christopher. [1979–80] "Interest Rate Futures." Federal Bank of New York *Quarterly Review* 4 (Winter).

Bierwag, G. O., and Kaufman, George. [1977] "Coping with the Risk of Interest Rate Fluctuations: A Note." *Journal of Business* (July).

Bierwag, G. O. [1977] "Immunization, Duration, and the Term Structure of Interest Rates." *Journal of Financial and Quantitative Analysis* (December).

Bomberger, W. A., and Makinen, G. E. [1977] "The Fisher Effect: Graphical Treatment and Some Econometric Implications." *Journal of Finance* (June).

Brennan, Michael J., and Schwartz, Eduardo S. [1980] "Conditional Predictions of Bond Prices and Return." *Journal of Finance* (May).

Cooper, Ian. [1977] "Asset Values, Interest-Rate Changes, and Duration." *Journal of Financial and Quantitative Analysis* (December).

Cornell, W. B. [1977] "Which Inflation Rate Affects Interest Rates?" *Business Economics* (May).

Cox, J. C.,; Ingersoll, J. E., Jr.; and Ross, S. A. [1979] "Duration and the Measurement of Basic Risk." *Journal of Business* (January).

Dietrich-Campbell, Bruce, and Schwartz, Eduardo. [1986] "Valuing Debt Options: Empirical Evidence." *Journal of Financial Economics* (July).

Eddy, A. R. [1978] "Interest Rate Risk and Systematic Risk: An Interpretation." *Journal of Finance* (May).

Fama, E. F. [1976] "Inflation Uncertainty and Expected Returns on Treasury Bills." *Journal of Political Economy* (June).

Fama, Eugene F. [1984] "The Information in the Term Structure." *Journal of Financial Economics* (December).

Fama, Eugene F. [1984] "Term Premiums in Bond Returns." *Journal of Financial Economics* (December).

Fisher, Lawrence, and Weil, Roman. [1971] "Coping with the Risk of Interest-Rate Fluctuations: Returns to Bondholders from Naive and Optimal Strategies." *Journal of Business* (October).

Hessel, Christopher, A., and Huffman, Lucy. [1981] "The Effect of Taxation on Immunization Rules and Duration Estimation." *Journal of Finance* (December).

Jaffe, J. F., and Mandelker, G. [1979] "Inflation and the Holding Period Returns on Bonds." *Journal of Financial and Quantitative Analysis* (December).

Kidwell, David S., and Trzcinka, Charles A. [1982] "Municipal Bond Pricing and the New York City Fiscal Crisis." *Journal of Finance* (December).

Mason, Scott P., and Bhattacharya, Sudipto. [1981] "Risky Debt, Jump Processes, and Safety Covenants." *Journal of Financial Economics* (September).

Nam, Sangkoo, and Pettit, R. Richardson. [1980] "The Specification of Factors Affecting the Risk of Fixed Income Securities." University of Houston, Working Paper no. 58.

Nelson, C. R., and Schwert, G. W. [1977] "Short-Term Interest Rates as Predictors of Inflation: On Testing the Hypothesis that the Real Rate of Interest is Constant." *American Economic Review* (June).

Vu, Joseph D. [1986] "An Empirical Investigation of Calls of Non-Convertible Bonds." *Journal of Financial Economics* (June).

Weinstein, Mark I. [1983] "Bond Systematic Risk and the Option Pricing Model." *Journal of Finance* (December).

Questions and Problems

1. Using the second section of *The Wall Street Journal,* identify the different kinds of fixed-income securities whose bid and ask prices, transactions' prices, or yields are quoted on a daily basis.

2. A T-bond with seven years remaining to maturity pays a coupon of 13 percent. If the market demands a return $E(\tilde{R}_i)$ of 7 percent on this security what is its current market price? Another T-bond with the same period to maturity and demanded return was issued during periods of low market interest rates and has a coupon of 4 percent. What is its current market price?

3. Recalculate the values of the two bonds in Problem 2 on the assumption that each has 25 years remaining to maturity.

4. A bond issued by the World Bank (guaranteed by an agency of the U.S. government) has a coupon interest rate of $12^3/_8$ percent and is due to mature in 15 years. If its current price 134.28 (where the price is quoted in 32nds of a $) what is the return expected by an investor in these bonds?

5. The bonds of Avnet Corp. have a par value of $1,000, a coupon rate of 12 percent, and are due to mature in exactly 20 years. It can reasonably be assumed that the intercept and slope of the security market line are .08 and .06, respectively. Moreover, one analyst thinks that in view of the default risk accompanying the bond, the bond's beta should be about .4, and on average over the long run, the expected value of each year's interest and principal will be equal to 95 percent of that promised. Based on the analyst's beliefs, what is the estimated value of the security? If the current market price of the security is $110, has the security been over-priced or underpriced by the market?

6. Calculate the return an investor logically might expect to earn on the bonds in Problem 5. Compare this return with the yield to maturity, and explain why the yield to maturity does not adequately indicate the return the investor could get from Avnet's bonds.

7. As an analyst you have just completed work that led you to estimate that the debentures listed be-

low have beta coefficients that range between .2 and .6, as follows:

	Beta	Years to Maturity
Athlone Industries	.5	15
Sterling Drug	.3	8
Philadelphia Electric	.2	20
Hughes Tool	.6	12
Dow Chemical	.3	10

Unfortunately, in today's *Journal,* articles appeared about each of these firms, and you are faced with the task of updating your estimates. Indicate the direction of the effect of these announcements on each bond's beta.

Athlone revealed it is being sued by a number of former employees for past discrimination in wage rates. As a result, Athlone is taking a substantial charge against earnings.

Sterling announced that it is entering markets in the Middle and Far east for the first time.

Phil. Elec. announced that it was getting out of the nuclear power business.

Hughes tool announced that it was buying Baker Intl. and that Baker has a number of very risky but profitable lines of business that Hughes will try to exploit.

Dow just experienced a big management shakeup that is likely to cause the firm to be more profit oriented in the future.

8. Regardless of their effect on betas, how would each of the above changes likely impact the bond-holder's expected future cash flows?

9. A portfolio manager anticipates a major *increase* in market interest rates. Which trading strategy would be most likely to generate above-average returns in a bond investment:
    a. Purchasing long-maturity bonds with low coupon rates.
    b. Purchasing speculative-grade bonds with high coupon rates.
    c. Purchasing short-maturity bonds with high coupon rates.
    d. Purchasing bonds that will increase the average duration of the investment portfolio.

    CFA

10. These variables have been suggested as risk measures for evaluating the performance of fixed-income portfolios:
    a. Standard deviation.
    b. Beta, and
    c. Duration.
    Discuss the limitations of *each* of these risk measures.

    CFA

11. The interest rate risk of a bond is normally:
    a. Greater for shorter maturities.
    b. Lower for higher coupons.
    c. Lower for longer duration.
    d. All of the above.

    CFA

12. At the moment, Union Carbide's 13-1/4% (coupon) debenture due to mature in seven years is selling at 103. A 13-1/4% Treasury issue, also due in seven years, is selling at 130. In terms of a well-defined valuation model (e.g., CAPM) explain the factors that would account for the difference in prices.

13. All other things equal, which one of these bonds will have the greatest price volatility?
    a. 15-year, 15% coupon bond.
    b. 5-year, 10% coupon bond.
    c. 15-year, 10% coupon bond.
    d. 5-year, 15% coupon bond.

    CFA

14. Assume a $10,000 par value zero-coupon bond with a term-to-maturity at issue of 10 years and a market yield of 8 percent.
    a. Determine the duration of the bond.
    b. Calculate the initial issue price of the bond at a market yield of 8 percent, assuming semiannual compounding.
    c. Twelve months after issue, this bond is selling to yield 12 percent. Calculate its then-current market price. Calculate your pre-tax rate of return assuming you owned this bond during the 12–month period.

    CFA

15. Rank the following bonds in order of *descending* duration. Explain your reasoning. (No calculations required).
    a. 15% coupon, 20-year, yield-to-maturity at 10%.

b. 15% coupon, 15-year, yield-to-maturity at 10%.

c. Zero-coupon, 20-year, yield-to-maturity at 10%.

d. 8% coupon, 20-year, yield-to-maturity at 10%.

e. 15% coupon, 15-year, yield-to-maturity at 15%.

CFA

16. Assume the following average yields on U.S. Treasury bonds at the present time:

Years to Maturity	Yield
1	8.50%
2	8.90
5	9.25
9	9.75
10	10.00
15	11.25
20	11.75
25	12.25

Compute the forward rate for year 2 based upon the yields specified, assuming a pure expectations hypothesis of the term structure of interest rates. *Three* major hypotheses of the term structure of interest rates are:

a. Market segmentation, preferred habitat or hedging pressure hypothesis.

b. Unbiased, or pure expectations hypothesis.

c. Liquidity, or interest rate risk hypothesis.

Given the yield curve implied by the above data, discuss how *each* of these hypotheses would explain the shape of the curve.

CFA

17. Briefly explain why bonds of different maturities have different yields in terms of the expectations, liquidity, and segmentation hypotheses. Briefly describe the implications of each of the three hypotheses when the yield curve is

a. upward sloping, and

b. downward sloping.

CFA

CHAPTER

13

Fixed-Income Securities Markets

Chapter 12 discussed the broad characteristics of fixed-income securities and their valuation. In this chapter, we supply detail on the vast variety of types of fixed-income securities available in the marketplace and the manner in which they are traded. This information is essential to investors who must consider how these securities differ in investment attractiveness. We discuss securities issued by the federal government and its agencies, state and local governments, corporations, and individuals.

Federal Government Securities

The U.S. Treasury sells financial securities to investors for the purpose of financing the deficits that arise between tax receipts and government expenditures. Some deficits arise in the budgeting process and can be foreseen. The federal government has, for example, during the past 25 years from the early 60s regularly incurred annual deficits which cumulatively total over $1 trillion. There are also timing problems that arise in the annual cycle of tax payments and the expenditures of federal agencies. These cash-flow problems must be financed by issuing securities.

The market for U.S. Treasury securities—due to the sheer volume of them issued each year—occupies a central position in the financial markets in the United States. The total face value of all outstanding debt of the Treasury currently is about $1.5 trillion. This sum includes marketable and nonmarketable securities.

The nonmarketable issues sold by the U.S. Treasury are largely U.S. savings bonds.

These securities were first issued in 1935 in small denominations as a means of encouraging consumer savings. During recent years the Treasury has promoted Series EE and Series HH bonds. With a maturity of five years (some can be extended beyond that) these securities are sold as discount bonds, meaning that there are no periodic interest payments. The original sale price is set by the Treasury as a discount from the maturity value to supply the investor with a competitive return. Tax on the interest income is not due until the security matures. The bonds are not marketable, but may be redeemed early at a prespecified interest penalty. In recent years the return set by the Treasury on these securities has been more stable than the returns offered on competitive marketable securities. As a result, series EE and HH bonds, at times, have offered higher returns than those available from other, risk-equivalent, market opportunities.

The U.S. Treasury also sells marketable securities, which are actively traded in the secondary securities markets. In fact, the market is so large that on any given day, over $100 billion worth of these securities changes hands. These issues include Treasury bills, Treasury bonds, and Treasury notes.

Treasury Bills

A Treasury bill is a short-term obligation of the U.S. government. By definition, no bill has a maturity at issue that is in excess of one year. Thirteen- and 26-week bills are auctioned each week by the Treasury, and 52-week bills are auctioned once each month. Bills of all these maturities are sold on a discount basis in minimum $10,000 denominations. All interest accrues and is paid at maturity and is taxed at ordinary income rates.

Figure 13–1 shows a listing of Treasury bill price quotations as it appeared in *The Wall Street Journal,* January 7, 1987, for market activity which took place on the prior day. Looking at the Treasury bill which matures on October 1, we see that the "bid" is 5.57, the "ask" is 5.55, and the "yield" is 5.81. What do these numbers mean?

Treasury bill prices and yields are quoted somewhat uniquely among fixed-income securities, as a percentage discount from face value. That is, the price is quoted in terms of a rate of return instead of a $ price for the issue. The larger the percentage price quote the larger the discount from face value. To compute the actual bid price from the quoted bid discount of 5.57, the following formula is used:

$$(13\text{--}1) \quad \begin{array}{l} \textit{Bid price as a} \\ \textit{percentage of} \\ \textit{par value} \end{array} = 100 - \left(\frac{\textit{No. days to maturity}}{360} \right) \left(\begin{array}{l} \textit{Quoted} \\ \textit{bid} \\ \textit{discount} \end{array} \right)$$

Plugging in the numbers, we see that the bid price of the bill, assuming it matures in 236 days, is $100 - ((236/360)(5.57))$, or $96.349 per $100 of par value. Similarly, the ask price can be computed from the quoted ask discount.

$$(13\text{--}2) \quad \begin{array}{l} \textit{Ask price as a} \\ \textit{percentage of} \\ \textit{par value} \end{array} = 100 - \left(\frac{\textit{No. days to maturity}}{360} \right) \left(\begin{array}{l} \textit{Quoted} \\ \textit{ask} \\ \textit{discount} \end{array} \right)$$

Thus, the ask price of the same bill is $96.362 since the dollar ask price is above the dollar bid price, the "yield" bid will be above the yield ask.

FIGURE 13–1

TREASURY BONDS, NOTES & BILLS

Tuesday, January 6, 1987

Representative mid-afternoon Over-the-Counter quotations supplied by the Federal Reserve Bank of New York City, based on transactions of $1 million or more.

Decimals in bid-and-asked and bid changes represent 32nds; 101.1 means 101 1/32. a-Plus 1/64. b-Yield to call date. d-Minus 1/64. k-Nonresident aliens exempt from withholding taxes. n-Treasury notes. p-Treasury note; nonresident aliens exempt from withholding taxes.

Treasury Bonds and Notes

Rate	Mat.	Date	Bid	Asked	Bid Chg.	Yld.
9¾s,	1987	Jan p	100.6	100.10	.....	4.54
9s,	1987	Feb n	100.8	100.12	.....	5.16
10s,	1987	Feb p	100.16	100.20	.....	5.34
10⅞s,	1987	Feb n	100.15	100.19	.....	4.89
7¼s,	1990	Mar p	102.2	102.6	− .2	6.49
10½s,	1990	Apr n	111.6	111.10	+ .1	6.60
8¼s,	1990	May	105.6	105.14	+ .1	6.42
11⅜s,	1990	May p	114.1	114.5	− .3	6.60
7¼s,	1990	Jun p	102.3	102.7	− .1	6.53
10¾s,	1990	Jul n	112.18	112.22	− .2	6.65
9⅞s,	1990	Aug p	110.3	110.7	− .1	6.64
10¾s,	1990	Aug n	112.28	113	+ .3	6.64
6¾s,	1990	Sep p	100.14	100.18	.....	6.58
11½s,	1990	Oct n	115.21	115.25	− .2	6.69
9⅝s,	1990	Nov k	109.26	109.30	− .1	6.66
13s,	1990	Nov n	121.1	121.5	− .2	6.68
6⅝s,	1990	Dec p	100.3	100.5	.....	6.58
11¾s,	1991	Jan n	117.13	117.17	.....	6.70
9⅛s,	1991	Feb k	108.16	108.20	.....	6.69
12⅜s,	1991	Apr	120.17	120.21	− .1	6.73
8⅛s,	1991	May p	105.6	105.10	+ .1	6.70
14½s,	1991	May n	128.30	129.6	+ .1	6.66
13¾s,	1991	Jul n	126.22	126.26	.....	6.77
7½s,	1991	Aug p	103	103.4	− .1	6.70
14⅞s,	1991	Aug n	131.27	132.2	.....	6.69
12¼s,	1991	Oct p	121.26	121.30	− .1	6.79
6½s,	1991	Nov p	99.3	99.7	+ .1	6.69
14¼s,	1991	Nov n	130.9	130.17	− .2	6.76
11⅝s,	1992	Jan p	119.28	120.4	.....	6.82
6⅝s,	1992	Feb p	99.24	99.26	.....	6.65
14⅝s,	1992	Feb n	133.10	133.14	− .2	6.77
11¾s,	1992	Apr	121.3	121.11	− .2	6.86
13¾s,	1992	May n	130.5	130.9	+ .1	6.89
10⅜s,	1992	Jul p	115.21	115.25	.....	6.86
4¼s,	1987-92	Aug	95.9	96.9	− .1	5.02
7¼s,	1992	Aug	102.11	102.27	.....	6.63
9¾s,	1992	Oct p	113.6	113.14	+ .2	6.89
10½s,	1992	Nov n	117	117.4	+ .3	6.89
8¾s,	1993	Jan p	108.22	108.30	+ .1	6.91
4s,	1988-93	Feb	95.14	96.14	− .2	4.68
6¾s,	1993	Feb	100.1	100.17	.....	6.64
7⅞s,	1993	Feb	104.17	105.1	+ .7	6.85
10⅞s,	1993	Feb n	119.2	119.6	.....	6.96

U.S. Treas. Bills

Mat. date -1987-	Bid	Asked (Discount)	Yield
1- 8	4.08	3.94	0.00
1-15	3.11	2.87	2.91
1-22	5.41	5.37	5.46
1-29	4.71	4.67	4.75
2- 5	4.30	4.24	4.31
2-12	5.02	4.98	5.07
2-19	5.29	5.25	5.36
2-26	5.26	5.22	5.33
3- 5	5.43	5.39	5.51
3-12	5.52	5.50	5.63
3-19	5.56	5.54	5.68
3-26	5.50	5.46	5.60
4- 2	5.54	5.50	5.65
4- 9	5.51	5.49	5.64
4-16	5.54	5.50	5.66
4-23	5.54	5.50	5.67
4-30	5.49	5.47	5.64
5- 7	5.53	5.49	5.67
5-14	5.54	5.50	5.69
5-21	5.52	5.48	5.67
5-28	5.47	5.43	5.62
6- 4	5.53	5.49	5.69
6-11	5.51	5.47	5.68
6-18	5.53	5.49	5.71
6-25	5.51	5.47	5.69
7- 2	5.54	5.50	5.73
7- 9	5.53	5.51	5.75
8- 6	5.57	5.53	5.77
9- 3	5.54	5.52	5.77
10- 1	5.57	5.55	5.81
10-29	5.57	5.55	5.83
11-27	5.56	5.54	5.84
12-24	5.53	5.51	5.82

Source: Reprinted from *The Wall Street Journal,* Wednesday, January 7, 1987. Reprinted by permission.

The "yield" calculation shown in the newspaper listing is an estimate of the annualized return from purchasing a Treasury bill at the stated ask discount and holding it until maturity. However, since most of the bills listed mature prior to one full year from the date of the listed price quotation, this yield estimate is an "as if" estimate of holding-period return. It treats the bill in question "as if" it would be held for a year. In the example, the yield is shown as 5.81 percent. This number is called the **bond equivalent yield,** and is found this way:

(13–3) ***Bond Equivalent Yield***

$$\begin{array}{l}\textit{Annualized}\\ \textit{treasury}\\ \textit{bill yield}\end{array} = \left[\left(100 - \begin{array}{c}\textit{\$ Ask price}\\ \textit{relative to}\\ \textit{\$100 of}\\ \textit{par value}\end{array}\right)\left(\frac{365}{\begin{array}{c}\textit{No.}\\ \textit{days to}\\ \textit{maturity}\end{array}}\right)\right] \Bigg/ \left(\begin{array}{c}\textit{\$ Ask price}\\ \textit{relative to}\\ \textit{\$100 of}\\ \textit{par value}\end{array}\right)$$

$$= [(100 - 96.362)(365/236)]/96.362 = .0583$$

The effect of this calculation is to convert the quoted ask discount to an annualized discount figure, and then to express the result as a percentage of the asking price. The numbers are not exactly the same, due to *The Wall Street Journal* rounding of the ask discount of 5.55.

To start each week's auction, the Treasury publishes an advance notice of the offering and invites both competitive and noncompetitive bids. Anyone may submit a bid. Competitive bids state a maximum price as a percentage of par value that the bidder is willing to pay. Noncompetitive bids may also be submitted. These are stated without an associated maximum price, and they are actually filled at a price which represents the average price of all successful competitive bids. Though, as mentioned, anyone may submit a bid, by far the largest number of bills sold at these auctions is purchased by a small group of security dealers who deal directly with the trading desk of the Federal Reserve Bank of New York, which is the account manager for issues of all U.S. government securities. Currently, there are about 40 security dealers actively dealing with the Federal Reserve Bank of New York trading desk.[1] Commercial banks, nonbank dealers, and broker dealers (like Merrill Lynch) make up this group.

The dealers who purchase these securities sell them in an open market to those desiring to hold short-term money market instruments. In this dealer market all trading is transacted by telephone by the small group of dealers and others who stand ready to buy and sell Treasury securities at quoted prices. By custom there are no commissions associated with the acquisition or sale of Treasury securities in the market. The dealers themselves attempt to make profits through the maintenance of a positive spread between their quoted bid and ask prices. Dealers generally have highly levered operations with typically more than 95 percent of the value of their holdings at any point in time being financed with borrowed money. Delivery of securities (and funds used to purchase the securities) typically takes place on the same business day. The delivery and safekeeping of securities is in large part handled by an explicit book entry system that is provided by the Federal Reserve bank.

The market for these short-term U.S. Treasury bills is extremely large. The average **daily** value of transactions in Treasury bills exceeds $50 billion. The size of this market makes it undoubtedly the most liquid of all investment opportunities in world financial markets. Financial positions of market participants can be changed virtually instantaneously through transactions on these markets. A firm that finds itself with $50 million cash that cannot be effectively used for, say, 25 days is easily able to find a Treasury bill that approximately meets its maturity requirements, and in which there is no concern for the marketability of the securities purchased.

The primary holders of Treasury bills include the Federal Reserve System, commercial banks, foreign and international investors, state and local governments, and private corporations, most of whom tend to hold these securities as investment outlets for relatively short-term excess cash. Many individual investors do not hold Treasury bills directly because of the relatively large par values ($10,000, $50,000, $100,000, $500,000 and $1 million) involved; however, a large number of individuals have in recent years held Treasury bills indirectly through their purchase of shares in money market mutual funds.

---

[1] Recently, concern has been expressed that this group is so small and inbred that "understandings" or outright collusion is possible in this market.

Treasury Bonds and Notes

Treasury bonds and notes, unlike Treasury bills, are coupon-paying issues whose maturities at issuance exceed one year. These bonds and notes, like bills, are free of default risk. Nevertheless, there are some major differences in the investment and trading characteristics of the securities.

By law, notes have an original maturity of from 1 to 10 years. Bonds are permitted to have any maturity longer than one year, but Congress has placed restrictions on the amount of these long-term bonds that can be outstanding at any one time. Currently, there are over $200 billion in par value of outstanding bonds, and about $800 billion in par value of outstanding notes. Both bonds and notes tend to be issued with minimum denominations of $1,000. Semiannual interest payments are promised by the Treasury during the life of each.

Treasury notes and bonds are offered periodically to the public, either through an auction or though subscription. In either case, advance notices of the offering are published between one and three weeks prior to the event. In the case of an auction, potential buyers submit bids for the yield, rather than the price, of the notes or bonds. That is, a potential buyer offers a particular annual yield, such as 8.325 percent, rather than a price expressed as a percentage of par. The Treasury then allocates the securities it wishes to issue among the bidders by filling the lowest bids first. With this system, as with Treasury bills, some dealers or individuals wind up paying more than other dealers or individuals do. With the subscription offering, on the other hand, the Treasury sets the offering price (and associated yield), and potential buyers indicate their interest in advance by "subscribing" to a specified quantity of the notes or bonds at the stated price. In this system, all buyers pay the same price and receive the same yield to maturity. If an offering is oversubscribed, allocations are made on a percentage basis, with some small initial portion of the subscription (say $100,000) being allocated in full to each buyer.

Price quotations on notes and bills in the secondary market are expressed in 32nds of a "point," where par value equals 100 points. Sample quotations are displayed in Figure 13–1. In this figure, notice that bonds and notes are listed together. Notes are distinguished from bonds by the small "n" after the entry for the security's maturity date. A "p" indicates a note that is exempt from nonresident withholding tax. Consider the note which matures in October 1992 and has a stated coupon rate of $9\,^3/_4$ percent. The "bid" for this security on January 6 was 113.6, and the "ask" was 113.14. The "yield" shown is 6.89. This listing tells that the dealers' bid price for the note was 113 and 6/32nds, or 113.1875 per $100 of par value, while dealers' ask price was 113 and 14/32nds, or 113.4375 per $100 of par value. The yield shown is yield to maturity if the note is purchased at the dealers' ask price. The price quoted does not include interest accrued on the security since the last semiannual coupon payment date. It is added to the quoted price the buyer agrees to pay the seller.

Some Treasury bonds shown in Figure 13–1 list a series of maturity dates. Consider, for example, the Treasury bonds with a "maturity" of August 1987–92, and a coupon rate of $4^1/_2$ percent. The normal maturity of these bonds is August 1992, but the Treasury has indicated in the bond indenture that it may call, or redeem, all or some of these bonds in August 1987. Bonds having this feature are known as **term bonds** and are callable only five years prior to maturity. Their yields to maturity, as shown, are reported only to the call date. Typically, T-bond maturities extend as long as 30 years, though these are not shown in the partial listing in Figure 13–1.

The average daily dollar trading volume for Treasury bonds and notes in the secondary market is about the same as that for Treasury bills, or $50 billion each day.

A "flower bond" is a special Treasury bond that has been designated as acceptable at par value for payment of Federal estate taxes under certain conditions. Thus, a flower bond that promises a low coupon payment may still be valuable to individuals who believe they (or their heirs) will have to pay estate taxes at some time relatively soon. Such a bond will generally sell for a market value lower than its par value. Thus, the government essentially subsidizes the payment of estate taxes through use of flower bonds. Another attractive feature is that these bonds are taxed to the estate at their market, rather than their par, value.

Finally, the interest income on all U.S. Treasury securities is exempt from state and local income and property taxes. This is a very attractive feature for taxable investors who are domiciled in states with high marginal income tax rates.

Federal Agency Securities

In addition to U.S. Treasury bills, notes, and bonds, federal agencies and government-sponsored enterprises issue bonds. The debt of federal agencies, such as the Tennessee Valley Authority, the Export-Import Bank, and the Small Business Administration, are guaranteed by the full faith and credit of the U.S. government and so are free of default risk. The debt of government-sponsored enterprises, such as the United States Postal Service, the Federal Home Loan Banks, and the Federal Home Loan Mortgage Corporation, however, is not explicitly backed by the government. Instead, all are fully backed by the assets and/or revenues of the issuer. Because of the history of support and concern for the operation of these agencies by the federal government, however, the securities of these government-sponsored enterprises are widely considered to have little or no default risk.

For the most part, federal agency securities are similar to U.S. Treasury securities. Except for a few short-term discount notes issued by such agencies as the Government National Mortgage Association (GNMA), agency securities are coupon issues promising interest payments semiannually. The interest income on all these issues is subject to federal income and estate taxes; however, the interest on some issues is exempt from state and local income and property taxes.[2]

Call features on these securities vary considerably. Some agency issues are not callable at all; others tend to be callable by the issuer after a specified period of time and at a specified premium above par value.

---

[2]The exemption of interest income on agency securities rests on whether or not such securities are deemed to be "obligations of the United States." Generally speaking, obligations which are merely guaranteed by the United States—such as the securities issued by the Export-Import Bank—are not considered obligations of the United States, and thus their purchasers do not enjoy exemption from state and local taxes. On the other hand, securities issued by government-sponsored enterprises—such as by the United States Postal Service—generally enjoy such exemption, even though they are not direct obligations of the United States nor are they backed or guaranteed by the government.

FIGURE 13–2

GOVERNMENT AGENCY ISSUES

Tuesday, January 6, 1987
Mid-afternoon Over-the-Counter quotations usually based on large transactions, sometimes $1 million or more. Sources on request.
Decimals in bid-and-asked represent 32nds; 101.1 means 101 1/32. a-Plus 1/64. b-Yield to call date. d-Minus 1/64.

FNMA Issues

Rate	Mat	Bid	Asked	Yld
10.70	1-87	99.30	100.4	1.61
11.15	1-87	99.30	100.4	2.04
9.90	2-87	100.8	100.14	4.91
11.05	2-87	100.10	100.17	5.00
5.45	3-87	NL		0.00
7.75	3-87	100.3	100.9	5.98
10.75	5-93	116.12	116.28	7.37
7.75	11-93	NL		0.00
7.38	12-93	100.6	100.8	7.33
11.95	1-95	125.8	125.24	7.60
11.50	2-95	122.27	123.2	7.63
11.70	5-95	124.8	124.24	7.63
11.15	6-95	121.6	121.18	7.63
10.50	9-95	117.18	118.2	7.61
10.60	11-95	118.16	118.28	7.62
9.20	1-96	109.24	110.4	7.63
9.35	2-96	110.16	111	7.65
8.75	6-96	106.28	107.12	7.64
8.00	7-96	NL		0.00
8.15	8-96	NL		0.00
7.70	12-96	100.14	100.18	7.62
7.10	12-97	94.4	96.28	7.52
12.35	12-13	124.20	125.20	9.66
12.65	3-14	126.30	127.30	9.71
10.35	12-15	120.30	121.30	8.33
8.20	3-16	98.26	99.14	8.25

Federal Farm credit

Rate	Mat	Bid	Asked	Yld
9.90	1-87	100	100.6	4.49

Rate	Mat	Bid	Asked	Yld
13.20	1-87	100.1	100.10	4.27
14.63	1-87	100.1	100.13	3.15
5.75	2-87	NL		0 00
5.70	3-87	NL		0.00
11.45	3-87	100.18	100.26	5.85
14.10	4-91	124.18	125.2	7.20
9.10	7-91	106.28	107.12	7.17
14.70	7-91	128	128.16	7.22
10.60	10-91	113	113.16	7.21
13.65	12-91	125.16	126	7.25
11.50	1-92	117.6	117.22	7.24
15.20	1-92	132.2	132.18	7.35
13.75	7-92	127.24	128.8	7.43
10.65	1-93	114.10	114.26	7.55
11.80	10-93	121.14	121.30	7.60
12.35	3-94	124.30	125.14	7.66
14.25	4-94	135.18	136.2	7.69
13.00	9-94	129.20	130.4	7.71
11.45	12-94	121.12	121.24	7.72
11.90	10-97	128.14	129.6	7.84

Student Loan Marketing

Rate	Mat	Bid	Asked	Yld
11.25	10-87	103.8	103.20	6.09
10.10	1-88	103.16	103.24	6.16
9.63	5-88	104.5	104.9	6.33
11.70	7-88	107.4	107.16	6.36
7.90	7-89	102.17	102.25	6.67
12.85	9-89	114.20	115.4	6.53
10.90	2-90	111.4	111.20	6.73
10.50	4-93	115	115.16	7.37
7.75	12-96	99.30	100.2	7.74

Fed. Home Loan Bank

Rate	Mat	Bid	Asked	Yld
10.10	2-87	100.14	100.20	5.19
10.45	2-87	100.14	100.21	5.29
11.05	2-87	100.15	100.23	5.40
11.05	3-87	100.29	101.1	6.04
11.10	3-87	100.28	101.3	5.81
11.25	3-87	100.30	101.4	5.81
7.75	7-93	NL		0.00
11.70	7-93	121.12	121.28	7.42
11.95	8-93	122.26	123.10	7.43
7.95	9-93	NL		0.00
7.88	10-93	NL		0.00
7.38	11-93	100	100.16	7.28
12.15	12-93	NL		0.00
12.00	2-94	NL		0.00
10.00	6-95	NL		0.00
10.30	7-95	NL		0.00
8.10	3-96	NL		0.00
7.75	4-96	NL		0.00
7.70	8-96	NL		0.00
8.25	9-96	NL		0.00
7.88	2-97	NL		0.00

World Bank Bonds

Rate	Mat	Bid	Asked	Yld
7.65	5-87	100	100.12	4.65
7.75	8-87	100.24	101.4	5.64
14.63	8-87	105.20	106	3.56
13.45	9-87	104.22	105.2	4.17
10.38	3-88	104.24	105.4	5.79

10.00	5-88	104.24	105.4	5.96
15.00	12-88	115.20	116	6.06
11.00	10-89	109.23	110.3	6.58
4.50	2-90	93.26	94.6	6.63
5.38	7-91	93.24	94.4	6.92

GNMA Issues

Rate	Mat	Bid	Asked	Yld
8.00		99	99.8	8.09
8.50		100.17	100.25	8.37
9.00		102.10	102.18	8.62
9.50		104.15	104.23	8.81
10.00		106.24	107	8.98
10.50		107.27	108.3	9.31
11.00		107.23	107.30	9.81
11.50		107.19	107.27	10.29
12.00		108	108.8	10.71
12.50		108.13	108.21	11.12
13.00		109	109.8	11.50
13.50		109.19	109.27	11.88
14.00		110.2	110.10	12.27
15.00		114.2	114.10	12.59
16.00		114.8	114.16	13.42

Private Expl. Fndg. Corp.

Rate	Mat	Bid	Asked	Yld
7.30W	1-92	100¼	100½	7.25
14.125P	6-91	105½	106	12.39
12.35Q	11-90	104½	105	10.81
10.75R	11-89	105¼	105¾	8.53
11.25S	2-92	107¾	108¼	9.25
11.25T	10-95	108	108½	9.80

Source: The Wall Street Journal, Wednesday, January 7, 1987. Reprinted by permission. © Dow Jones & Company, Inc., 1987. All rights reserved.

Trading in the secondary market for agency securities is quite active for some issues and inactive for others. Consequently, the liquidity associated with agency securities is highly variable. Often, for longer-term maturities which are issued and traded in small amounts, the spread between dealers' bid and ask prices can be quite large. Thus, transactions costs can be significant, and the investor's ability to buy or sell a particular security without influence on its market price can be limited. As for Treasury securities, trading in the secondary market is effected through a telephone network linking the various securities dealers. The average daily dealer sales of agency securities is about $15 billion per day; much of it concentrated in short-term issues.

Figure 13–2 displays price quotations for various government agency bonds as they appeared in *The Wall Street Journal* for trading which took place on January 6, 1987. The prices of government agency securities—like those for Treasury notes and bonds—are quoted in 32nds of a point. Thus, the Federal Home Loan Bank 11.7 percent coupon issue maturing in July 1993 displayed in this figure shows a "bid" price of 121.12, or 121 and 12/32nds. Given the ask price of $121.28 the "spread," in this case, is 16/32nds, or $5 per $100 of par value, or about .4 percent of the value of the transaction.

For the most part, agency securities have desirable investment characteristics, including very low default risk and a level of liquidity that makes them close substitutes for U.S. government securities. Commercial banks are the largest holders of agency securities, followed by the U.S. government itself and the various Federal Reserve banks. The yield differentials between agency and U.S. Treasury securities varies considerably over time and for particular agency issues, but currently the yield differential on equivalent maturity instruments is about 50 basis points, or one half of 1 percent of yield. This yield differential is due largely to two effects: (1) the difference in the liquidity offered between U.S. Treasury obligations and those of various federal agencies, and (2) the difference in state and local income and property tax exemptions applicable to different agency issues.

Some agency securities have attributes that give them very different investment characteristics. An important example is GNMA issues. These are mortgage-backed bonds, where the agency guarantees that the interest and principal on the bonds will be paid. The agency does not guarantee that the principal on the mortgages that back the bonds will not be paid off early, however. As interest rates fall, homeowners that have issued the mortgages tend to pay them off and refinance their loans with lower interest mortgages. As this happens, holders of GNMA securities will find their investment being liquidated. Further, since interest rates have fallen, the liquidation portion can only be reinvested to earn a lower return. When mortgage interest rates are low relative to the GNMA coupon rate the **liquidation risk** is quite high. Thus, such GNMA issues have a higher risk and higher return than most agency securities.

State and Local Government Securities

State and local governments and various local government agencies and authorities also sell debt issues in securities markets. They do so for a variety of reasons, ranging from the financing of temporary imbalances between tax receipts and expenditures to the financing of major construction projects. All these issues are called **municipal securities.** Two general types exist: *(a)* general obligation bonds, and *(b)* revenue bonds.

General Obligation Bonds

General obligation bonds are backed by the "full faith and credit" of the issuer and carry with them the ability of the issuing municipality to levy taxes on its citizenry to meet its interest and principal repayment obligations. Some general obligation bonds are **unlimited tax bonds,** which means the issuing municipality has the ability—generally specified in the bond indenture—to raise taxes of whatever type it is empowered to levy as high as necessary to avoid default on the debt. Other general obligation bonds are called **limited-tax bonds;** the borrower is limited in its ability to raise additional taxes to pay off the debt. Obviously, unlimited-tax general obligation bonds carry a lower risk of default than do limited-tax issues. Generally speaking, however, municipal debt issues have moderate to low default risk, and defaults have tended to be infrequent during the past 50 years. Though investors have experienced more than 6,200 municipal bond defaults since the first such default occurred in 1939, most issuers who have defaulted have eventually repaid all the principal, if not the full, promised interest.[3]

---

[3]*The Wall Street Journal,* Wednesday, July 13, 1983, p. 27.

One of the more famous municipal bond defaults occurred in 1975 when New York City failed to pay the principal on $2.4 billion of its short-term notes. The bondholders in that situation received periodic interest payments which were considerably less than the promised amounts and didn't receive repayment of the principal on the notes until several years after the notes matured. In a more recent example, the Washington Public Power Supply System, a consortium of public utilities formed to construct five nuclear power plants, had issued $2.25 billion in outstanding debt to finance construction of two of the five plants. Construction on these two plants has now been halted, and the resulting default is the biggest in the history of the municipal bond market. (WPPSS bonds recently have sold for as little as 10–15 percent of their par value.) Nevertheless, major defaults have been infrequent and are highly atypical of the vast majority of the thousands of municipal bonds that have been issued over the years.

General obligation bonds are issued by state governments, state government agencies, cities, water and sewer commissions, school districts, and a variety of other government entities. They are issued to raise funds for a variety of purposes, including improving and maintaining highways, constructing refuse collection facilities, building schools and dams, and refunding existing debt as it matures.

One example of a general obligation issue announcement is reproduced in Figure 13–3. In that announcement, Tigard, Oregon, issued 2.1 million of general obligation municipal bonds to refinance another issue. The interest and principal repayments would be supported by future property taxes paid by residents of that city. Some bonds are also insured by the Municipal Bond Insurance Association, which—in return for fees paid by the issuer—stands ready to meet the promised interest and principal payments should the issuer be unable to do so. This provision may help lower investors' required returns on the bonds (if the insurer can cover some nondiversifiable risk), and so may wind up saving interest costs (though it must pay the additional fee).

Note that the bond issue advertised is being sold in several maturities. The issuance of a variety of maturities with different coupon rates is a common practice among municipal bond issuers and reflects a desire to spread fixed principal repayment obligations over a number of years to correspond to the flow of tax receipts and also to avoid having to refund large amounts of debt on some single date in the future when interest rates might be high.

Revenue Bonds

Unlike general obligation bonds, revenue bonds are backed by the revenues generated by the particular project financed by the issue. If the issuer uses the bonds to finance the construction of a toll bridge or a sports stadium, for example, the revenues generated through the subsequent use of these facilities are pledged to ensure the repayment of principal and interest. Because of this revenue bonds are generally considered to possess higher default risk than general obligation bonds, all other things being equal. Often the issuer doesn't have the authority or the obligation to levy additional taxes on its constituents in order to avoid a default. Consistent with this the defaults with the longest waits by investors have involved revenue bonds. West Virginia Turnpike bonds, which were issued in 1952, for example, remained in default for more than 20 years before the roadway

FIGURE 13–3   **General Obligation Bond**

NEW ISSUE — COMPETITIVE   SALE DATE: JANUARY 27, 1987
                                    RATING: MOODY'S _____

In the opinion of Bond Counsel, under existing law, assuming compliance with the Issuer's covenants relating to the Tax Exemption, interest on the Bonds is exempt from all federal income taxes, except for: (i) alternative minimum taxes on the book income of corporations; and, (ii) taxes on corporate alternative minimum taxable income imposed under the Superfund Amendments and Reauthorization Act of 1986, and state of Oregon personal income taxes.

CITY OF TIGARD
WASHINGTON COUNTY, OREGON

$2,115,000*
GENERAL OBLIGATION REFUNDING BONDS
SERIES 1987

DATED: January 1, 1987   **DUE: June 1, 1987-2004**

The Bonds are registered bonds in $5,000 denominations or integral multiples thereof. Interest is payable semiannually beginning June 1, 1987 through the principal trust offices of the registrar and paying agent of the City, currently United States National Bank of Oregon, Portland, Oregon.

Bond proceeds will be used to advance refund the callable portion of the City's General Obligation City Building Bonds, Series 1984, which are dated June 1, 1984. The City is obligated to levy on all taxable property within the City a direct annual ad valorem tax, in addition to all other taxes, sufficient to pay bond principal and interest promptly when and as they become due.

MATURITY SCHEDULE

Due June 1	Principal Amount*	Interest Rate	Yield	Due June 1	Principal Amount*	Interest Rate	Yield
1987	$ 10,000			1996	$145,000		
1988	25,000			1997	160,000		
1989	30,000			1998	170,000		
1990	30,000			1999	180,000		
1991	30,000			2000	190,000		
1992	30,000			2001	205,000		
1993	35,000			2002	215,000		
1994	35,000			2003	235,000		
1995	140,000			2004	250,000		

Redemption Provision — The bonds are subject to redemption prior to maturity.

Legal Opinion — The Bonds are offered for sale to the original purchaser pursuant to the official Notice of Sale of the District, subject to the final approving opinion of Lindsay, Hart, Neil & Weigler, Bond Counsel. It is expected that the Bonds in definitive form will be available for delivery in Portland, Oregon on or before February 27, 1987.

*Subject to change

which was constructed with the proceeds of these bonds generated sufficient toll revenues to meet the promised principal and interest payments.[4] Moreover, because payments depend on revenues from some venture, nondiversifiable risk seems higher (in addition to simply the possibility of default), thus enlarging revenue bond βs relative to those of general obligation bonds.

A recent study of revenue bonds suggested their risk and return characteristics were quite similar to those of corporate bonds. The standard deviation of the revenue bond portfolio was less than half that of the S&P 500. Individual bond betas, relative to the S&P 500 stock index varied between .1 and .4, with an average of about .25. Of course, these values include both default and interest rate risk components.

The typical municipal bond issue has a maturity of 10 to 20 years at issuance, although the particular maturity selected by the issuer reflects the type of asset to be financed through the sale of the debt. In the case of revenue bonds, in particular, where the interest and principal repayments are generated through the operation of the facility constructed or acquired, the maturity of the revenue bonds tends to equal, or be less than, the expected useful life of the facility (for obvious reasons).

Figure 13–4 displays a notice for a new issue of the Utah Municipal Power Agency. These bonds also have been issued with a variety of maturity dates and coupon rates. All are revenue bonds, however, since the issuer "has no taxing power." The advertisement also mentions the fact that the bonds do not carry an implicit guarantee of any other tax authority.

Municipal bonds have many of the same characteristics as the securities of the federal government and its agencies. However, most municipal bonds—unlike many federal government and agency securities—are somewhat illiquid. Many of the securities traded in this market have not been issued in large amounts; hence, trading activity is light and intermittent. For this reason, the typical spread between bid and ask prices in this market is considerably larger than for comparable federal government and agency securities.

Municipal bonds possess another distinguishing feature as well. Their interest income is exempt from federal income taxes. In many cases it is also exempt from state and local income taxes, but usually only in the issuing state. These tax features are attractive to taxable investors, including commercial banks, corporations, and individuals. This causes the observed yields on these securities to be lower than the *before-tax yields* on taxable securities, such as corporate bonds. The individuals who tend to purchase municipals, therefore, are those who face relatively high marginal income tax rates.

Figure 13–5 shows quotations on municipal ("tax exempt") securities appearing recently in *The Wall Street Journal*. The dealer price quotations are expressed as a price per $100 of par value.

Figure 13–5 lists only a small fraction of the thousands of municipal securities that have been issued and are still outstanding. Obtaining regular price quotations on many municipal securities is a significant problem for investors because of the illiquidity in some sectors of this market. Reliance on newspaper quotations for these issues is not advisable; rather, the investor needs to consult regularly with municipal bond dealers to obtain reliable quotations.

---

[4]*The Wall Street Journal*, Wednesday, July 13, 1983, p. 27. "Possible Effects of a WPPSS Bond Failure Are Visible in Past U.S. Municipal Bond Defaults."

FIGURE 13–4 **Revenue Bond**

NEW ISSUE

In the opinion of Bond Counsel, interest on the 1986 Series A Bonds is exempt from regular Federal income tax imposed by the Internal Revenue Code of 1986, as amended, subject to the assumption described under "Tax Exemption" herein; the 1986 Series A Bonds are not private activity bonds; and under the Utah Municipal Bond Act, as amended, interest is exempt from taxation in the State of Utah except for the corporate franchise tax.

$47,360,000*
Utah Municipal Power Agency
Electric System Revenue Refunding Bonds
1986 Series A

Interest from: December 1, 1986   Due: July 1, as shown below

Interest is payable on July 1, 1987, and semiannually thereafter on each January 1 and July 1, and principal is payable on July 1 in each of the years and in the amounts set forth below. The 1986 Series A Bonds are issued as fully registered bonds in denominations of $5,000 or any integral multiple thereof.

The 1986 Series A Bonds are subject to redemption prior to maturity as described herein.

The Agency is issuing the 1986 Series A Bonds to refund a portion of the outstanding 1985 Series A Bonds of the Agency.

The Agency is obligated to make payment on the 1986 Series A Bonds solely from the Revenues of the Agency's electric system and certain funds pledged under the Indenture, subject to the payment of Operating Expenses. Such Revenues are anticipated to be derived principally from payments made to the Agency pursuant to Power Sale Agreements with the Members as described herein.

The 1986 Series A Bonds do ot constitute a general indebtedness or a pledge of the full faith and credit of the Agency and are ι ot obligations of the State of Utah or any city, town or other political subdivision or entity of Utah other than the Agency as provided in the Indenture. The Agency has no taxing power.

$10,710,000 Serial Bonds*

Due	Principal Amount	Rate	Price	Due	Principal Amount	Rate	Price
1991	$ 70,000	%	%	1997	$ 980,000	%	%
1992	290,000			1998	1,045,000		
1993	770,000			1999	1,120,000		
1994	815,000			2000	1,195,000		
1995	865,000			2001	1,275,000		
1996	925,000			2002	1,360,000		

$ 6,520,000*   % Term Bonds Due 2006—Price   %
$30,130,000*   % Term Bonds Due 2017—Price   %

(Accrued interest from December 1, 1986 to be added)

The 1986 Series A Bonds are offered when, as and if issued and accepted by the Underwriters, subject to the approval of validity of the Bonds by Dewey, Ballantine, Bushby, Palmer & Wood, New York, New York, Bond Counsel, and the approval of certain legal matters by Duncan, Allen and Mitchell, Washington, D. C., General Counsel to the Agency, and by Fox, Edwards, Gardiner & Brown, Salt Lake City, Utah, Counsel for the Underwriters. It is expected that delivery of the Bonds will be made in New York, New York, on or about December 30, 1986.

PaineWebber
Incorporated

The First Boston Corporation

Prudential-Bache Securities Inc.

The date of this Official Statement is December   , 1986.

FIGURE 13–5 **Tax-Exempt Bonds**

TAX-EXEMPT BONDS

Tuesday, Jan. 6, 1987

Here are representative current prices for several active tax-exempt revenue and refunding bonds, based on large institutional trades. Changes are rounded to the nearest one-eighth. Yield is to maturity.

Issue	Coupon	Mat.	Price	Chg.	Yld.
Austin Util Sys Rev	7.300	05-15-17	99⅜	+ ⅛	7.35
Brazos Rv Tx PCR Tex Ut	8.250	12-01-16	102¼	+ ¾	8.05
Cal Hou Fin Home Mtg Ref	6.900	08-01-16	100⅜	+ ⅛	6.87
Cal Vets Home Pur Rev	7.375	08-01-12	102⅛	+ ⅛	7.19
Cobb Co Ga Watrsew Impr	6.800	07-01-08	98¼	. . .	6.96
Fla Bd Ed Cap Out Ser C	7.125	06-01-17	101½	+ ⅛	7.01
Ga Muni El Au Gn Pw	7.875	01-01-18	104¼	+ ⅛	7.52
Ga Muni El Ref	7.750	01-01-18	103⅜	+ ⅛	7.47
Gwinnett Wtr Swr Ref	6.500	08-01-06	97⅜	+ ¼	6.74

Source: Reprinted from *The Wall Street Journal,* Thursday, January 8, 1987. Reprinted by permission, © Dow Jones & Company, Inc., 1983. All rights reserved.

In addition to the municipal securities of state and local governments in the United States, foreign governments often issue securities which are held for investment by individuals and corporations within the United States. The market for these securities is relatively volatile for two reasons. First, there may be considerable uncertainty about the future rate of exchange of U.S. dollars for the currency in which the issue is denominated.[5] Second, some of the issuers of these securities have relatively unstable economies, or face relatively unstable political situations, which implies a considerable possibility of default. If the possibility of default is related to world economic conditions it may imply a higher β as well.

Deposits at Financial Institutions

Most individual investors have some funds on deposit with one or more financial institutions as part of their investment portfolios. Institutions accepting such deposits include commercial banks, savings and loan associations, mutual savings banks, credit unions, and cooperative banks. Each of these institutions acts as an intermediary in the financial markets, collecting the deposits of individual investors, aggregating them, and lending larger pools of money to various borrowers, including (sometimes) other financial institutions. In the process they provide the following services to investors:

- **Divisibility and liquidity**—relatively large and illiquid business loans, consumer loans, mortgages, and construction loans are converted into highly divisible savings accounts of small denomination that have immediate liquidity.

---

[5]To overcome some of the hesitancy of U.S. investors to purchase foreign securities because of the exchange risk associated with their acquisition, governments of foreign countries have begun issuing dollar-denominated bonds or other money market instruments. Such a financial arrangement places all of the foreign exchange risk on the issuing government, but makes it easier for them to tap dollar financial markets.

- **Default risk reduction through diversification**—by pooling a number of individually uncertain loans and investments, the bank or thrift institution can virtually eliminate diversifiable variability associated with borrower default, and, with federal or state deposit insurance, offer investors a nearly risk-free investment opportunity.[6]
- **Interest rate risk management through maturity selection**—by offering deposit accounts with a variety of maturities they allow investors to match their future cash obligations to deposit account maturities.

Typically, deposit accounts at most institutions span the range of maturities up to 10 years. The particular maturity structure offered by any given bank will depend on the maturity structure of its assets.

To a considerable degree, the deposits offered by these institutions are substitutes for investments in Treasury securities. They are quite appealing to smaller investors due to the low transactions costs associated with relatively small and continuous transactions. That is, they offer a "convenience return," which is an important part of the investment decision process for some investors. During the last decade competition from brokerage firms and mutual funds (through money market funds and cash management accounts) has forced financial institutions to offer even better investment opportunities.

Corporate Securities

Private corporations are the remaining large issuers of both long- and short-term fixed-income securities. Those securities issued by the larger, more well-established firms are available for purchase in the secondary markets by individuals, institutional investors, and other corporations. Financial intermediaries also issue corporate securities that are distinguished from the savings and time deposits just discussed.

Money Market Securities of Corporations

The term *money market security* refers to a short-term, low default risk, highly liquid fixed-income security. The money market includes, in addition to Treasury bills and other short-term U.S. government and agency securities, some of the short-term securities issued by large corporations in need of cash for short-term uses. The short-term securities issued by General Electric, General Motors Acceptance Corporation, or the Metropolitan Life Insurance Company fall into this category. They tend to be good substitutes for one another and for short-term government securities. Any dissimilarities between these corporate money market securities are attributable to differences in maturity (some may mature tomorrow; others may mature in a year), marketability (some are not traded at all in secondary markets but are sold privately to investors by dealers), and the default risk of the issuer. The major security types are: *(a)* commercial paper, *(b)* negotiable

---

[6]They are not absolutely default-free because no one is sure what would happen in the event that the insuring organization—such as the FDIC—could not satisfy all the claims presented to it. The U.S. government might, in that eventuality, rescue the insuring organization. On the other hand, it might not. In a catastrophic collapse of a number of large institutions, the insurance fund itself would be clearly inadequate. And, there is also the fact that in the event that it must pay claims presented to it, the insuring organization can take considerable time in doing so. This can effectively cause the investor to lose a portion of the expected investment return, which is tantamount to a partial default.

certificates of deposit, *(c)* banker's acceptances, *(d)* federal funds, and *(e)* Eurodollar deposits.

Commercial Paper.   Commercial paper refers to a short-term, unsecured general obligation of a particular firm. It is backed by the "full faith and credit of the firm," but not by any specific assets. Maturities of commercial paper vary from 30 to 270 days, and the denominations (par values) range from a minimum of $1,000 to over $1 million. Bank holding companies, large manufacturing companies, retailers, and many other types of firms may issue commercial paper. The security, like Treasury bills, is sold on a discount basis and carries no coupon rate. The prices quoted for specific commercial paper issues by secondary market dealers (mainly commercial banks) are not listed in the newspapers; they must be obtained directly from the dealers. Commercial paper is typically issued by corporations to finance their needs for cash on a short-term basis, particularly to finance the time gap between the cycle of cash revenues and cash expenses.[7] There is about $350 billion of commercial paper outstanding. About 75 percent is issued by financial institutions.

Negotiable Certificates of Deposit.   These securities are large-denomination, short-term fixed-income securities issued by large commercial banks to attract depositors (and funds) during periods of active bank lending. Denominations and maturity are negotiable, but such deposits typically have maturities of from one month to one year, and are issued in units of $25,000 to $10 million. Until 1970, the interest rates paid on negotiable certificates of deposit (called **CDs**) were limited by Federal Reserve Regulation Q. Currently, however, rates are set competitively and CDs are highly substitutable for other money market instruments. As their name implies, they can be traded by the investor at any time prior to the maturity of the deposit.

Banker's Acceptances.   These securities are really drafts which a particular customer of a bank draws on that bank and which the bank agrees to pay at a particular date in the future. The term *acceptance* means that the bank has accepted this obligation, and that allows the security to be traded in the secondary market thereafter. These securities, like commercial paper, are traded on a discount basis and carry no coupon rate. Their maturities vary from 30 to 180 days. Because the agreement is generally drawn on a large commercial bank, banker's acceptances are safe and liquid. Yet, because they are often created as a result of international trade, they are issued in very larage denominations unsuitable for investment by most individual investors. Foreign investors hold the majority of banker's acceptances. As is the case for commercial paper, current price quotes must be obtained directly from a dealer, such as a commercial bank. The yields and quoted prices for individual issues are not listed in the newspapers.

Federal Funds.   These securities are very short-term (usually maturing overnight) financial arrangements among financial institutions and sometimes between a financial

---

[7]The commercial paper market was severely affected by the collapse of Penn Central in 1970, which had $82 million in commercial paper outstanding at the time. Shortly after, the commercial paper market declined in volume by almost $15 billion (or by about 30 percent) over the ensuing 12 months, as investors became much more wary of the creditworthiness of potential issuers.

institution and a nonfinancial corporation for the immediate acquisition of cash, usually to allow a bank to cover its reserve requirements. Mechanically, the security consists of two checks, one drawn on the lender immediately and one drawn on the borrower at the maturity date. The length of maturity and the difference in the value of the two checks implies the associated interest rate. These securities are not available to individual investors and cannot be bought and sold in secondary markets in the normal sense.

Eurodollar Deposits. Eurodollar deposits and dollar-denominated deposits existing in foreign financial institutions and in foreign branches of U.S. commercial banks. Because they involve fairly large transactions, the interest rates on such money market instruments are negotiable and competitively determined. Holders of these securities can be either U.S. or foreign investors, and either corporations or individuals. The recent rapid growth of the Eurodollar market is attributable to the widespread use of the dollar in international transactions in the 1960s and 1970s. The stability of the currency value made it a relatively safe investment, even for investors who eventually converted to a currency other than the dollar and, as a result, were exposed to exchange risk. Since the dollar historically has been widely used as the international unit of account in a large number of foreign transactions, many foreign and international investors found the Eurodollar market to be a safe, convenient, and exchange risk-free medium for investing short-term excess funds. There is nearly $300 billion in Eurodeposits outstanding, though this figure is deceptively large due to substantial "redeposit" activities that pyramid up the amounts held.[8]

Representative rates on money market instruments are presented on a daily basis in many papers. An example is given in Figure 13–6. The interest rates on the various instruments are different, depending primarily on liquidity considerations and on maturity. Default risk, because it is so low for the widely traded securities, tends not to be the most significant factor affecting the yield differentials among these securities.

Table 13–1 shows historical patterns of yields among various money market securities and a few longer-term securities from 1976 through 1986. The historical closeness of these rates to each other at a given point in time, and the similarity of the changes over time suggests the high degree to which these securities are substitutes for one another. The substitutability, of course, reflects the fact that default risk is very low and interest rate risks are similar because of like maturities.

Corporate Bonds and Preferred Stock

Corporate bonds and preferred stock are issued by a variety of firms, both large and small, in virtually every industrial and commercial sector of the U.S. economy. Over the past decade rapid growth has taken place in the amount of these issues outstanding.

There is a substantial variability in the form of corporate bonds and preferred stock, but the bulk of it can be characterized by the presence or absence of a number of standard features, including: **callability, convertibility, sinking fund provisions, degree of sub-**

---

[8]Redeposit activities increase the amount of Eurodollar deposits when one bank accepts a deposit and lends it out to another bank. Both transactions are included in the total of Eurodollar deposits in existence.

FIGURE 13–6   Money Market Interest Rates

MONEY RATES

Monday, December 29, 1986

The key U.S. and foreign annual interest rates below are a guide to general levels but don't always represent actual transactions.

PRIME RATE: 7½%. The base rate on corporate loans at large U.S. money center commercial banks.

FEDERAL FUNDS: 9¼% high, 7% low, 9% near closing bid, 9¼% offered. Reserves traded among commercial banks for overnight use in amounts of $1 million or more. Source: Prebon Money Brokers Inc., N.Y.

DISCOUNT RATE: 5½%. The charge on loans to depository institutions by the New York Federal Reserve Bank.

CALL MONEY: 8¼% to 9%. The charge on loans to brokers on stock exchange collateral.

COMMERCIAL PAPER placed directly by General Motors Acceptance Corp.: 7.10% 30 to 44 days; 6.25% 45 to 59 days; 6% 60 to 89 days; 5.90% 90 to 270 days.

COMMERCIAL PAPER: High-grade unsecured notes sold through dealers by major corporations in multiples of $1,000: 7.50% 30 days; 6.75% 60 days; 6⅜% 90 days.

CERTIFICATES OF DEPOSIT: 7½% one month; 6½% two months; 6¼% three months; 6.10% six months; 6.10% one year. Typical rates paid by major banks on new issues of negotiable C.D.s, usually on amounts of $1 million and

more. The minimum unit is $100,000.

BANKERS ACCEPTANCES: 7.45% 30 days; 6.50% 60 days; 6.17% 90 days; 6% 120 days; 5.95% 150 days; 5.87% 180 days. Negotiable, bank-backed business credit instruments typically financing an import order.

LONDON LATE EURODOLLARS: 7¾% to 7⅝% one month; 7% to 6⅞% two months; 6 11/16% to 6 9/16% three months; 6½% to 6⅜% four months; 6⅜% to 6¼% five months; 6⅜% to 6¼% six months.

LONDON INTERBANK OFFERED RATES (LIBOR): 6¾% three months; 6⅜% six months; 6 5/16% one year. The average of interbank offered rates for dollar deposits in the London market based on quotations at five major banks.

FOREIGN PRIME RATES: Canada 9.75%; Germany 6.75%; Japan 5.243%; Switzerland 5.75%; Britain 11%. These rate indications aren't directly comparable; lending practices vary widely by location. Source: Morgan Guaranty Trust Co.

TREASURY BILLS: Results of the Monday, December 29, 1986, auction of short-term U.S. government bills, sold at a discount from face value in units of $10,000 to $1 million: 5.68%, 13 weeks; 5.68%, 26 weeks.

Source: Reprinted from *The Wall Street Journal.* Tuesday, December 30, 1986. Reprinted by permission © Dow Jones & Company, Inc., 1983. All rights reserved.

ordination, **indenture restrictions,** the **existence of secondary market trading,** and most importantly, **investment risk.** The first five of these features are specified in the indenture, which is the agreement between the bond's issuer and the investors. The last two features reflect the market's assessment of the security as an investment opportunity and, of course, are in turn influenced by the first five features. These features are discussed below with particular attention paid to the effect each has on risk and equilibrium-expected return.

To provide a basis for our discussion of these features, Table 13–2 gives pertinent facts for a sample of corporate bonds.

Callability.   Many bond indentures contain provisions whereby the issuing corporation retains the option to retire or "call" all (or a portion of) the outstanding issues at a fixed price for a specified period of time. This feature enables the corporation to call bonds with a high coupon rate after market interest rates have dropped, for example. Reissuing new bonds at the lower rate saves the firm the differential interest cost.

While this feature has obvious value to the corporation when there is a chance that interest rates may drop below the coupon rate of a particular outstanding issue, there is an obvious disadvantage, and associated cost, to the bondholders. Their high-return investment may be liquidated at the "call price" during a time of generally low returns on other opportunities. If the call price is not high enough (it usually represents a slight premium over par value), the liquidation value when the bond is called will not provide the investor with sufficient funds to generate the same promised cash flows as were anticipated on the existing bonds before they were called. Consequently, the existence of a call feature lowers the price investors are willing to pay for a bond; all other things

TABLE 13–1   **Interest Rates on Financial Instruments** (year-end annualized rates)

Percent

	1976	1977	1978	1979	1980	1981	1982	1983	1984	1985	1986
Money market:											
Federal funds (overnight)	4.47	6.65	10.25	13.82	19.44	12.54	8.79	9.62	7.95	8.02	5.87
Prime commercial paper (3-month)	4.63	6.66	10.55	13.04	17.51	12.66	8.52	9.43	8.11	7.73	5.57
Banker's acceptances (3-month)	4.70	6.71	10.93	13.11	16.84	12.63	8.54	9.51	8.14	7.67	5.44
Negotiable certificates of deposit (3-month)	4.70	6.78	10.96	13.36	17.60	13.03	8.57	9.69	8.25	7.80	5.57
Eurodollar deposits (3-month)	5.03	7.33	11.95	14.41	19.29	13.14	9.36	10.09	8.63	7.98	5.79
U.S. Treasury bills (3-month)	4.49	6.16	9.25	12.00	14.62	11.69	8.01	9.18	7.67	7.02	5.27
Capital market:											
U.S. Treasury bonds (10-year)	6.42	7.79	9.14	10.65	12.29	14.07	10.26	11.65	11.13	9.38	7.59
Corporate bonds (all industries, average maturities)	8.37	8.61	9.62	12.06	13.91	15.69	12.98	13.09	12.68	10.70	9.35
Prime rates	6.35	7.75	11.55	15.30	20.35	15.75	11.50	10.75	12.00	9.90	7.90

Source: *Federal Reserve Bulletin*, various issues.

TABLE 13–2   **Examples of Outstanding Corporate Bonds and Notes**

Company Name	Issue Date	Coupon	Maturity	Callable after	Callable at	Yield to Maturity at Issue	Amount of Issue ($ millions)	Convertible into	Rating
Bell Telephone Co. of Pennsylvania (debentures)	1/16/79	9.25	2019	1/15/84	$106.86 (−$.23/yr)	9.37%	$150		AAA
Chris Craft Industries (subordinated sinking fund debentures)	1/23/79	13	1999	2/01/89	par	13.0	25		B
Electro Audio Dynamics (senior subordinated debenture)	2/1/79	12.875	1999	immediate	$112.875 (−$1.2875 per year)	12.875	13		B
Citicorp (convertible subordinated note)	6/30/75	5.75	2000	8/31/82	$105.750 (−$.30 per year)	5.75	350	24.39 shares common	NR
Computervision (convertible subordinated debenture)	4/4/84	8.00	2009	12/1/86	108	8.00	110	22.22 shares common	NR
Interfirst Corp. (Eurobonds)	5/14/85	11.625	1992	noncallable		11.625	200		AAA

equal, they prefer bonds which cannot be called. The yield on callable bonds, therefore, tends to be higher than that on noncallable issues.

The market-determined price for the callable bond will reflect its value as a straight bond *less* the value of the option retained by the firm to call the bonds. This "call option" will have a higher value to the issuing firm, the greater is the chance that interest rates will fall below the coupon rate during the life of the bond, and the lower is the call price. Characteristically, the call price is set at par ($1,000) plus one annual coupon payment initially. Thus on a 5 percent coupon bond, the call price would be $1,050. The call price generally declines toward par at maturity. Sometimes a moratorium on calling the issue exists for the first 5 or 10 years of the bond's life. This reduces the value of the call option to the issuer.

As an example, the Bell Telephone Co. of Pennsylvania bonds listed in Table 13–2 are callable at $106.86 per $100 par value of bond. But the bond indenture agreement specifies that they may not be called for five years from the date of issuance. This is termed a "five-year call deferment." Thus, on January 16, 1984, the bonds may be called at $106.86. A year later they may be called at $106.63—since the call price declines $.23 per year to maturity. The Chris Craft issue is callable at par, but not until 10 years after issue. When each of these bonds becomes callable, the existence of the option will preclude the bond's price from rising above the call price.[9] In effect, the firm has captured from the bondholder the upper end of the probability distribution on price (created by falling interest rates).

The callability feature is an important one. In the mid-1980s when interest rates dropped rapidly the prices of many bonds rose sharply. In a number of cases the prices of callable bonds rose well past their call price. Either investors were not aware of the call provision, or did not feel the firms would exercise their call option. In any case, many firms did take advantage of the lower interest rates to refinance their operations, and many investors in callable bonds faced a substantial capital loss when this happened.

Convertibility.   A conversion privilege gives the holder of a bond the right to exchange the bond for a given number of shares of the common stock of the firm for a period of time that is usually as long as the maturity of the bond. As in the case of the call feature, the conversion feature is an option. In this case, however, it's an option issued by the firm and held by the bondholder.

As an example, each Computervision debenture (see Table 13–2) is convertible into 22.22 shares of common stock anytime until maturity in 2009. Equivalently, the "exercise price" at which the common stock can be "purchased" using the bond is $45, given as

$$\frac{Conversion}{price} = \frac{Exercise}{price} = \frac{Par\ value}{Number\ of\ shares\ into\ which\ each\ bond\ can\ be\ converted}$$

$$\$45.00 = \$1,000/22.22$$

Early in 1986, the common stock of Computervision was selling around $18 per share; the option to purchase the shares at $45.00 has little value. Reflecting this, the convertible

---

[9]Actually, the price could rise slightly above the call price due to flotation costs which prevent the firm from refinancing the issue at only slight reductions in market interest rates.

bond traded at $88 during this period, well below its par value, and near to its value as a straight bond.

A different case is that of Citicorp's convertible issue, which had an exercise price of $41 per share (24.39 shares per bond), well below the $56 early 1986 market price of the common. As a consequence of the high value of the option to convert, even given the low coupon interest rate, the bond traded in the $140 range at that time.

As these examples suggest, a convertible bond's market price is a function of its value as a bond as well as its value as an option to purchase the shares of common stock of the issuer. These instruments are discussed in detail in Chapter 19. However, it should be clear at this point that convertible bonds will be priced higher in the market the higher the price of the common stock into which they can be converted, the larger the number of shares that the bondholder gets in exchange, and the greater the coupon interest rate on the bond.

As a reflection of the value of the conversion option, the interest rates on such instruments are considerably below otherwise equivalent nonconvertible issues: often more than one percentage point (100 basis points) lower, depending, of course, on where the exercise price is set with respect to the common stock price.[10]

In addition to the lower interest rate, firms often point out that another advantage of issuing convertibles is that it allows them to issue common stock at a higher than current market price when the exercise price is above the market price of the common at the time of issue. This is offset by two disadvantages: (1) there is some uncertainty as to whether the firm is issuing debt or equity, and (2) when the bond is converted by investors the effective sale price (exercise price) is *below* the price at which new common stock could be issued in the market. The latter effect, of course, dilutes the ownership claims to cash flows generated by the firm.

Sinking Fund Provisions.   Part of many bond indentures is a provision for serial reductions in the firm's principal obligations. Often at the insistence of the bondholders, sometimes at the insistence of the issuer, such provisions are introduced to increase the likelihood of the eventual, complete repayment of principal. Sinking funds may take one (or more) of three forms:

1. The firm is obligated at some point (usually yearly, some number of years after the issue is outstanding) to deposit into an interest-bearing escrow account an amount to be used to retire the issue at maturity.
2. The firm, through either a random or preselected process, specifies a portion of the issue for retirement—liquidating an investor's position.
3. The firm is proscribed or allowed to buy through open market purchases an amount of the outstanding issue.

In general, if one of these provisions exists the effective duration of the bond is different than it otherwise would be. With a sinking fund provision that requires the firm to purchase and retire or serially retire a portion of the bonds each year, the maturity of the issue, on average, is reduced. The reduction in maturity serves to reduce the duration of the

---

[10]Typically, the exercise price is set 10 to 20 percent above the price of the common stock at the time of the issue. The option's value then depends on the probability that at some point the stock price will exceed the exercise price.

issue. In addition, bondholders may not appreciate the possibility of their particular bonds being called for early retirement according to the provision. On net, whether bondholders are affected favorably or adversely by such an arrangement is uncertain. Empirically, studies have not been able to find any strong relationship between sinking fund provisions and bond value that cannot be explained by other factors, such as the business risk of the firm.

Subordination Level.   Explicit in the indenture statement, or implicit in securities laws, is the ranking of creditor claims for receipt of funds in the event of bankruptcy or liquidation of the firm. Essentially, more senior issues are paid interest and principal first. Subordinated debt is paid only prior to payments on preferred and common stock. The general level of subordination is usually incorporated into the title of the issue as in Chris Craft's issue of "Subordinated Sinking Fund Debentures."

The level of subordination, and the potential for the firm to issue securities with more senior ranking, has important effects on the value of a bond. If greater fixed charges created by issuing additional senior debt can be undertaken by the firm, the subordinated bondholder faces lower expected cash flows and an increase in the bond's risk. The result is a lower price for the subordinated bonds to pay for this possible cost, or an indenture agreement that helps protect the value of the bondholder's position. Evidence on the extent of the protection or lack thereof is incomplete, but it seems quite certain that firm stockholders have an incentive to affect adversely the bondholders' positions, and that many bond issues are not adequately protected against some stockholder actions. However, it seems clear that we will see more and more indenture agreements that include statements limiting the firm's ability to unexpectedly issue more senior debt subsequent to an issue of more subordinated debt.

Indenture Restrictions.   The $150 million debenture issue of Bell Telephone Co. of Pennsylvania includes very few restrictions that limit the operations of the company. However, the issue of Electro-Audio Dynamics includes the following restrictions:

> Company may not declare dividends or make distributions on its capital stock or redeem, purchase or otherwise acquire or permit any subsidiary to purchase or acquire any capital stock of the company if after giving effect thereto the aggregate of all such dividends, distributions and acquisitions after November 1, 1978, would exceed the sum of (1) 50 percent of consolidated net income after July 29, 1978, plus (2) the net cash proceeds to the company from the issuance or sale of capital stock after November 3, 1978, or from the issuance or sale of any indebtedness or debt securities which are converted into capital stock after February 1, 1978, plus (3) $4 million. [Subject to certain provisions.]

And,

> Trustee for 25 percent of the ventures outstanding may declare principal due and payable (30 days grace for payment of interest).

And,

> Indenture may be modified, except as provided, with consent of $66 \, ^2/_3$ percent of debentures outstanding.

Other provisions may further limit the firm's financial transactions, or even its productive operations.

Collateral.   Some bonds are tied to specific assets. In the event of the failure and liquidation of the firm, the asset itself becomes (at least part of) the property of the bondholders. The bondholder trustee normally would sell the asset with the proceeds being used to compensate the bondholders. The collateral may be anything of value, but usually tends to be a marketable asset that is mobile and can be used in a variety of production processes. More often than not the funds acquired with the collateralized bond are used to purchase the asset that is the collateral. Equipment Trust Certificates, for example, are often issued by railroads to finance the purchase of rolling stock. Airline companies also issue securities using specific aircraft as collateral. As a counter example, a paper machine, being essentially immobile and available for use in only one process, would seldom be used as collateral for a bond issued by a paper company.

Secondary Markets.   Many bonds are traded in secondary markets. Trading activity varies widely and generally in proportion to the size of the issue and the size of other issues of the same corporation. Trading typically takes place in units as small as one bond on both listed bond markets (New York Exchange Bonds and American Exchange Bonds) and the over-the-counter markets. By far the largest trading volume takes place in the over-the-counter market in much the same way as in the over-the-counter stock market, and in the markets for U.S. Treasury and federal agency securities.

Fig. 13–7 shows a section of the listing of price quotations for New York Stock Exchange Bonds. The prices quoted in this listing, unlike other bond price quotations we have discussed, are not dealer bid and ask prices, but rather actual transaction prices

---

FIGURE 13–7   Corporate Bond Price Quotations

Source: The Wall Street Journal, Tuesday, January 20, 1987. Reprinted by permission. © Dow Jones & Co., Inc., 1987. All rights reserved.

for trades which took place on the previous day. Thus, the Exxon bonds with a 6 percent coupon maturing in 1997 were last traded on January 19, 1987, at a price of 98 $\frac{1}{4}$, or 98.25 per $100 of par value, and throughout that day traded in a range of from $89 to 89 $\frac{1}{4}$. The current yield (*not* the yield to maturity) for those bonds was 6.7 percent at the last trade, and the volume of bonds traded was $23,000.

Some bonds are also placed privately. Typically such bonds are sold to insurance companies, mutual and pension funds, and other large investors. Because their issue does not require as extensive a documentation with the Securities and Exchange Commission, there is a saving of flotation costs. Often this means that issuers are willing to pay a slightly higher coupon rate to purchasers than they would otherwise. Such a higher rate is necessary due to the lack of marketability.

Risk

Bond risk was thoroughly covered earlier in Chapter 12, though not in the context of these specific features. Yet it is possible to specify, in general, the impact of these features on risk. With the definition of bond risk,

$$\beta_i = \frac{Cov\ (\tilde{R}_i, \tilde{R}_m)}{[\sigma(\tilde{R}_m)]^2}$$

all we need do is observe how the *covariance* of bond returns with market returns differs with each of these features. Some observations generally can be made, including:

1. **Callability.** Since the call feature narrows the range of prices the bond can take on by eliminating the top end of the distribution of prices, any change in R_m will be accompanied by less movement in R_i than when the bond is not callable. Call features will reduce bond risk (but not so much as to compensate for the decline in expected cash flows).

2. **Convertibility.** The option feature of the convertible bond will expand the set of prices the bond can take on (upward, as the option takes on value with an increase in stock price) and increase its covariability with movements of the market return. Convertible features will increase bond risk (but not so much as to offset the increase in expected cash flows granted by the conversion option).

3. **Sinking funds.** Since a sinking fund reduces the duration of the bond it would be expected to have a negative effect on bond risk. This is partly offset by a common provision in most sinking fund arrangements that provides the firm with the option of buying the bond in the open market if its current market price is below the par value, or buying the bond at its par value from selected holders if the market price exceeds the par value. This option, granted to the firm by the bondholders, serves to increase risk to the bondholders over that which exists for a bond with a set fixed serial retirement and the same duration.

4. **Indenture restrictions.** The impact of indenture restrictions on risk, of course, cannot be generalized. Normally, however, such restrictions are introduced with the idea of assuring creditors of an ability to meet required payments in spite of what may happen with the firm's operations. If properly constructed,

many restrictions would serve to reduce the covariance and thereby reduce bond risk.

5. **Collateral.** By securing a bond issue with specific assets, bond risk *may* be reduced. But clearly the amount of reduction would depend on how the market value of the collateralized asset would tend to comove with market returns. If an airline company fails to meet its interest and principal obligations due to a downturn in the industry that is associated with a widespread decline in the economy, the market value of an airplane used as collateral is likely to be quite low as well, since the productivity of all alternative uses of the aircraft (by other companies) is likely to be low.

   Contrarily, if the value of real estate tends to move relatively independently of the economy, then the airline company's Manhattan office building is likely to retain most of its value even in the event of the economic downturn. Clearly, the risk-reducing effect of collateral needs to be analyzed on a case-by-case basis. Some kinds of collateral will insulate the bondholder from covariance much better than will other kinds.

6. **Secondary markets.** The fact that the security is actively traded in secondary markets means the investor is less likely to exert any upward pressure on price when purchasing the security, or downward pressure on price when selling it. While this obviously has a beneficial effect on cash flows and the value of the instrument, it's doubtful that this effect is associated with variation in R_m. Thus, we think there is little relation between the secondary market activity of a bond and bond risk.

Specialized Corporate Debt Securities

In recent years a variety of new types of fixed-income securities have been developed. Many of these have been created by investment banking firms as an outgrowth of the competition for the control of corporations we have seen in the 1980s. Some of those that are widely used and some that have unique characteristics are summarized here.

Eurobonds. These are bonds issued overseas by U.S.-based corporations. The incentive for corporations to issue securities in European financial centers stems from IRS and SEC regulations. Foreign investors ordinarily were subject to a withholding tax on their purchases of securities issued in the United States. By issuing securities "offshore" the tax on foreign investors could be avoided. Without the tax, corporations found the supply of foreign financial capital to be larger, and the costs of acquiring it to be less. The corporation also could avoid the costs of registering the securities with the SEC, if the securities were not to be traded on U.S. financial markets.

The size of the Eurobond market has grown enormously in the last few years due to its increasing efficiency. It is now easy for IBM, Exxon, or many smaller firms to tap this market. Moreover, while the market originally catered to dollar-denominated securities, and thus appealed mostly to U.S. firms, it has expanded to allow large firms and governments to issue securities in most major trading currencies. Thus, IBM can issue securities denominated in French francs to finance its operations in France, and Renault can raise dollars to finance its American Motors division in the United States.

Floating Rate Notes.   These are intermediate or long-term securities whose coupon interest rate varies with the general level of interest rates. Thus, these notes are similar to variable rate mortgages. The incentive for their issuance is that they usually carry a lower expected long-run interest cost, since interest rate risk is placed on the issuer rather than the holder of the security.

Collateralized Mortgage Obligations.   A CMO is a bond-like security that is backed by a pool of mortgages whose cash flows are repackaged to create securities of different maturities. Essentially, a large number of individual mortgages are pooled and then split up into different obligations with expected maturities that appeal to specific investment horizons. Because the securities offer some protection against early repayment on the mortgage loan, the market has grown rapidly. About $30 billion of these securities were offered to the market in 1986—triple the volume offered just a year earlier.

Junk Bonds.   The only thing that makes these securities different from other long-term corporate bonds is the default risk of the issuer. Prior to the late 1970s corporations with a substantial risk of default were encouraged by the investment banking community to find nondebt sources of financing. High risk bonds were not issued, but became high risk through a decline in the issuer's creditworthiness after issue. Today, however, due primarily to the efforts of a few investment bankers, high-risk, high-return bonds are issued. Some are issued by corporations in very risky lines of business. Others are issued by firms with a very high level of financial leverage. They have frequently been used to finance leveraged buyouts, leveraged acquisitions, and takeovers.

The expected equilibrium return on these securities should be equal to the return on other risk-equivalent securities. Thus, the return demanded, in a CAPM world, should be a function of the junk bond's beta. While the history of these securities is relatively brief, and summary figures on their performance should be viewed with caution, one study has found that over a nine-year period junk bond portfolios offered about the same returns and the same betas as portfolios of high-grade bonds. We would not normally expect this to persist into the future.

Puttable Bonds.   These securities allow the holder to sell the bond to the owners of the firm at a very high price if certain conditions exist—particularly a hostile takeover of the firm by another group. The bonds, in other words, have been issued to attempt to make it very expensive for a hostile suitor to take over the firm that has issued the puttable bond. The holders of the bond have been given a put option that is very valuable only under a limited set of conditions. The bond usually is seen as a means of entrenching the current management of the firm.

Stock-Paying Bonds.   As a recent innovation, at least one firm has found its niche in financial markets by offering buyers the option of receiving their interest payments in the form of cash or stock of the issuing firm. For example, United Water issued bonds through its Hakensack Water division with a coupon of 7 percent payable in cash or an equivalent number of shares of United Water (at a 5 percent discount).[11]

---

[11]There also are a few bonds still outstanding, issued early in the century, that require interest to be paid in gold coin. The courts decided the contract was unenforceable when the government restricted individual

Bond Ratings

It is difficult for most investors to assess directly the risk of default on particular corporate bonds, municipal securities, or federal agency securities. This is because most investors do not have ready access to copies of the bond indentures which govern investors' rights in the event of a default, nor do they take the time to scrutinize the details of the periodic, published financial statements of the issuers of these debt instruments. Bond rating services are designed to provide bond market investors with a convenient means of assessing default risk, and thus to lower the costs to an investor of obtaining information relevant to assessing this risk. These services scrutinize issuer financial strength and the details of the indenture agreement.

Two bond rating services in the United States are the most widely known. These are Moody's *Bond Record* and in Standard & Poor's *Bond Guide*. Both these services rate individual security issues of a large number of municipal securities, commercial paper, corporate bonds, and U.S. government and federal agency securities. Not all outstanding, publicly traded issues are rated, however. Sometimes both rating services refuse to rate the safety of a particular fixed-income security, either because the issuer did not apply for a rating, the issue or issuer belongs to a group of companies or securities that the rating service does not rate as a matter of policy, the financial data with which to rate the issue is not available, or the issue has been privately placed and therefore is not traded on secondary markets.

Fig. 13–8 describes the various rating categories and their interpretations which have been established by Standard & Poor's. The very highest ratings (AAA for S&P and Aaa for Moody's) are given only to those issuers and the particular securities of those issuers that are considered to have very little default risk. American Telephone & Telegraph, Minnesota Mining and Manufacturing Corporation, IBM Credit Corporation, and General Electric Corporation fall in this category. The next highest rating category (AA in S&P and Aa in Moody's) applies to issues which also have very low default risk, but whose issuer's ability to pay is judged slightly lower than that for the very top-rated issues. Bonds rated in this category have included Phillips Petroleum debentures, Northwest Bancorporation debentures, and Missouri Pacific Railroad equipment trust bonds.

Bond ratings for a security issue are valid as of a particular point in time, given all financial information the rating service has currently available on the borrower. From time to time, the rating agencies reevaluate their ratings, based on new information. This can result in the downgrading of an issue—if the financial condition of the borrower has deteriorated since the last review; and upgrading—if the borrower has strengthened its financial condition. The rating assigned to a firm or other issuer by one of these two widely followed services directly affects the coupon rate that must be offered if the issuer is to succeed in marketing the bonds. The lower the rating, the higher the promised coupon rate which generally must be offered. For that reason rating changes are significant to both issuers and investors. They directly affect the returns investors require on those issues, and so affect the issuer's cost of funds. Securities whose ratings are downgraded invariably find their price falling as the market reacts to this new information.

---

holdings of gold beginning in the 1930s. Recently, courts have been asked to consider that the contract be enforced as stated, since the government is again issuing gold coin.

FIGURE 13–8   Standard & Poor's Corporate and Municipal Debt Rating Definitions

A Standard & Poor's corporate or municipal debt rating is a current assessment of the creditworthiness of an obligor with respect to a specific obligation. This assessment may take into consideration obligors such as guarantors, insurers, or lessees.

The debt rating is not a recommendation to purchase, sell or hold a security, inasmuch as it does not comment as to market price or suitability for a particular investor.

The ratings are based on current information furnished by the issuer or obtained by Standard & Poor's from other sources it considers reliable. Standard & Poor's does not perform any audit in connection with any rating and may, on occasion, rely on unaudited financial information. The ratings may be changed, suspended or withdrawn as a result of changes in, or unavailability of, such information, or for other circumstances.

The ratings are based, in varying degrees, on the following considerations:

I. Likelihood of default-capacity and willingness of the obligor as to the timely payment of interest and repayment of principal in accordance with the terms of the obligation;

II. Nature of and provisions of the obligation;

III. Protection afforded by, and relative position of, the obligation in the event of bankruptcy, reorganization or other arrangement under the laws of bankruptcy and other laws affecting creditors' rights.

AAA: Debt rated AAA has the highest rating assigned by Standard & Poor's. Capacity to pay interest and repay principal is extremely strong.

AA: Debt rated AA has a very strong capacity to pay interest and repay principal and differs from the higher rated issues only in small degree.

A: Debt rated A has a strong capacity to pay interest and repay principal although it is somewhat more susceptible to the adverse effects of changes in circumstances and economic conditions than debt in higher rated categories.

BBB: Debt rated BBB is regarded as having an adequate capacity to pay interest and repay principal. Whereas it normally exhibits adequate protection parameters, adverse economic conditions or changing circumstances are more likely to lead to a weakened capacity to pay interest and repay principal for debt in this category than in higher rated categories.

BB, B, CCC, CC: Debt rated BB, B, CCC and CC is regarded, on balance, as predominantly speculative with respect to capacity to pay interest and repay principal in accordance with the terms of the obligation. BB indicates the lowest degree of speculation and CC the highest degree of speculation. While such debt will likely have some quality and protective characteristics, these are outweighed by large uncertainties or major risk exposures to adverse conditions.

C: The rating C is reserved for income bonds on which no interest is being paid.

D: Debt rated D is in default, and payment of interest and/or repayment of principal is in arrears.

Plus (+) or Minus (−): The ratings from "AA" to "B" may be modified by the addition of a plus or minus sign to show relative standing within the major rating categories.

Provisional Ratings: The letter "p" indicates that the rating is provisional. A provisional rating assumes the successful completion of the project being financed by the debt being rated and indicates that payment of debt service requirements is largely or entirely dependent upon the successful and timely completion of the project. This rating, however, while addressing credit quality subsequent to completion of the project, makes no comment on the likelihood of, or the risk of default upon failure of such completion. The investor should exercise his own judgment with respect to such likelihood and risk.

NR: Indicates that no rating has been requested, that there is insufficient information on which to base a rating, or that S&P does not rate a particular type of obligation as a matter of policy.

Debt Obligations of issuers outside the United States and its territories are rated on the same basis as domestic corporate and municipal issues. The ratings measure the creditworthiness of the obligor but do not take into account currency exchange and related uncertainties.

Bond Investment Quality Standards: Under present commercial bank regulations issued by the Comptroller of the Currency, bonds rated in the top four categories (AAA, AA, A, BBB, commonly known as "Investment Grade" ratings) are generally regarded as eligible for bank investment. In addition, the Legal Investment Laws of various states impose certain rating or other standards for obligations eligible for investment by savings banks, trust companies, insurance companies and fiduciaries generally.

Standard & Poor's publication "CreditWeek" contains a section entitled "CreditWatch" indicating whether certain events have positive or negative implications with respect to the ratings of the debt of certain issuers.

Standard & Poor's does not act as a financial advisor to any issuer in connection with any corporate or municipal debt financing. Standard & Poor's receives compensation for rating debt obligations. Such compensation is based on the time and effort to determine the rating and is normally paid either by the issuers of such securities or by the underwriters participating in the distribution thereof. The fees generally vary from $1,000 to $10,000 for municipal securities, and from $1,500 to $20,000 for corporate securities. While Standard & Poor's reserves the right to disseminate the rating, it receives no payment for doing so, except for subscriptions to its publications.

Source: Standard & Poor's *Bond Guide*, October 1982.

Private Individual Issues

Individuals, too, issue securities, including mortgages, consumer debt, and revolving credit agreements. While these borrowing capabilities provide an efficient means for the individual to allocate wealth over time to achieve a desired consumption pattern, they also provide viable investment outlets for those with more wealth than they wish to consume in the current period. Some of these instruments, because of their small size and lack of uniformity, are not generally marketable. Revolving credit agreements and consumer loans, for example, are set up through individual negotiation with financial intermediaries, and, because risk, return, and repayment patterns vary from loan to loan, such agreements and loans usually are not sold directly in secondary markets.

By far the largest component of the set of marketable financial instruments issued by individuals are **mortgages.** Mortgages are fixed-income securities that characteristically have promised a series of equal monthly or annual payments that include both interest and principal. Mortgages are collateralized by real property and tend to have a long maturity, though not exceeding the life of the property serving as collateral. The obvious advantage to consumers of housing services is that mortgages provide an efficient mechanism for the consumer to acquire the use of property well before his monetary wealth would permit it.

Individual investors may hold mortgages directly, but more typically, investments in mortgages are indirect, through investments in the common securities of financial institutions, pension funds or mutual funds that funnel resources to the mortgage market, or the common stock of real estate investment trusts. The risks and returns from these alternatives differ substantially, primarily because they vary in terms of equity or debt participation.

In the past few years, two important developments have taken place that have served to broaden the availability of the mortgage market to both consumers of housing services and investors. One is the creation of **mortgage-backed securities.** These securities, issued by the Federal National Mortgage Association (FNMA, or Fannie Mae, a quasi-governmental agency) and the Federal Home Loan Mortgage Corporation (FHLMC, or Freddie Mac) are backed by purchases of packages of mortgages originally written by savings and loans and others involved in mortgage origination. The originator of the mortgage usually continues to service the instrument by collecting payments, but Fannie Mae receives the interest and principal and uses the funds to pay interest on the mortgage-backed securities it has issued. An explicit set of mortgages is used as collateral for the securities issued by Fannie Mae.[12] Any investor can purchase these mortgage-backed securities, much like a corporate bond can be purchased.

The second new development directly affecting the consumer of housing services and, thereby, the opportunities available to the investor, is the invention of "**alternative mortgage instruments.**" These instruments do **not** provide for a steady periodic payment. **Graduated payment mortgages** (GPMs) have interest and (if any) principal payments that are low in early years and increase during part of the life of the mortgage. Such an instrument allows individuals with low current income and expectations of higher income in the future to consume housing services more in line with their long-run income stream.

---

[12]This development has been greatly facilitated by the invention of an insurance policy on a part of the mortgage that has the effect of standardizing the instrument so it can be included in the mortgage pool.

Variable rate mortgages (VRMs) allow the interest rate on the instrument to vary with the general level of interest rates. This shifts interest rate risk from the holder of the mortgage to the issuer (the homeowner). The theory behind this security is that households may be better able to accept this risk than can depository institutions, because household income is more likely to vary with the business conditions that bring about changes in interest rates. This theory is questionable. However, it appears that at least some consumers are willing to accept the risk inherent in VRMs in hopes of incurring lower overall expected interest charges.

Even more recently, a growing market for **home equity loans** has developed. If these loans can be effectively "pooled" they, like other mortgage-backed securities, will provide investors with an additional investment outlet.

Summary

The markets for fixed-income securities reflect a broad range of levels of marketability and liquidity. Some are not marketable at all. Others, such as U.S. Treasury bills and most Treasury bonds and Treasury notes, are traded in such large quantities in so many places that complete liquidity is assured.

Municipal securities and corporate bonds vary in their marketability according to the size of the issue, the quantity of other similar securities of the same issuer, and general market interest in the security type. Nonstandard types of securities would generally be less easily marketed. For this reason most corporations that choose to issue securities with unusual covenants, maturity structure, or sinking fund provisions are forced to issue the security on the private placement market with one or a few large institutional buyers.

The marketing process for most fixed-income securities differs from that for stocks traded on exchanges. Transactions are arranged through an over-the-counter network of dealers. There may be relatively few very large dealers, as in the Treasury bill market, or many dealers attempting to make markets for transactions—much like exists in the over-the-counter stock market. Only the bonds of large corporations are traded on organized bond exchanges that operate like the NYSE. These are the New York Bond Exchange and the American Bond Exchange, which are affiliated with their respective stock exchanges.

Unfortunately, perhaps, the price quote process for fixed-income securities is not standardized. Some are provided through a yield quote that implies the price to be paid for one unit of the security. Others are priced in dollar amounts, but without accrued interest that would be added into the final transaction price to complete the exchange.

Corporate issues vary considerably among themselves in terms of the provisions in the indenture contract. Many of these provisions are established to constrain the activities of one group or another (the managers or stockholders) so as to protect bondholders from having a firm's wealth expropriated. Indenture restrictions, sinking fund arrangements, specification of the degree of subordination of the issue, collateral, and convertibility are all partially directed to solving this problem. The firm, by placing these provisions in the contract prior to the security offer, assures itself of a lower interest rate than it would have to pay without them. Other provisions (such as the option to call the bonds) force the firm to pay a higher equilibrium interest rate in return for added flexibility. These provisions also have an effect on the beta of the security, depending, of course, on the way the provision is likely to affect comovement of holding-period returns with the returns on the market portfolio.

References

Ang, James, and Patel, Kiritkumar. [1975] "Bond Rating Methods: Comparison and Validation." *Journal of Finance* (May).

Black, Fischer, and Cox, John. [1976] "Valuing Corporate Securities: Some Effects of Bond Indenture Provisions." *Journal of Finance* (May).

Blume, Marshall E., and Keim, Donald B. [1986] "Risk and Return Characteristics of Lower-Grade Bonds." Working Paper, University of Pennsylvania.

Bodie, Zvi, and Friedman, Benjamin. [1978] "Interest Rate Uncertainty and the Value of Bond Call Protection." *Journal of Political Economy* (February).

Connelly, Julie. [1978] "The Irrepressible Growth of Commercial Paper." *Institutional Investor* (March).

Cox, John C.; Ingersoll, Jonathan E., Jr.; and Ross, Stephen. [1980] "An Analysis of Variable Rate Loan Contracts." *Journal of Finance* (May).

Emanuel, David. [1983] "A Theoretical Model for Valuing Preferred Stock." *Journal of Finance* (September).

Feder, Gershon, and Ross, Knud. [1982] "Risk Assessments and Risk Premiums in the Eurodollar Market." *Journal of Finance* (June).

Fisher, Lawrence. [1959] "Determinants of Risk Premiums on Corporate Bonds." *Journal of Political Economy* (June).

Garbade, Kenneth, and Hunt, Joseph. [1978] "Risk Premiums on Federal Agency Debt." *Journal of Finance* (March).

Handbook of Securities of the United States Government and Federal Agencies. First Boston, published biennially.

Ho, Thomas S. Y., and Singer, Ronald F. [1982] "Bond Indenture Provisions and the Risk of Corporate Debt." *Journal of Financial Economics* (December).

Jen, Frank, and Wert, James. [1967] "The Effect of Call Risk on Corporate Bond Yields." *Journal of Finance* (December).

Lucas, Charles; Jones, Marcos; and Thurston, Thom. [1977] "Federal Funds and Repurchase Agreements." Federal Reserve Bank of New York *Quarterly Review* (Summer).

Melton, William. [1977–78] "The Market for Large Negotiable CDs." Federal Reserve Bank of New York *Quarterly Review* (Winter).

Ott, Robert A. [1986] "The Duration of an Adjustable-Rate Mortgage and the Impact of the Index." *Journal of Finance* (September).

Pinches, George, and Mingo, Kent. [1973] "A Multivariate Analysis of Industrial Bond Ratings." *Journal of Finance* (March).

Pinches, George, and Singleton, J. Clay. [1978] "The Adjustment of Stock Prices to Bond Rating Changes." *Journal of Finance*.

Pye, Gordon. [1967] "The Value of Call Deferment on a Bond: Some Empirical Results." *Journal of Finance* (December).

Pye, Gordon. [1966] "The Value of the Call Option on a Bond." *Journal of Political Economy* (April).

Resengren, Eric, and Rzepczynski, Mark S. [1986] "The Effect of Dealer Failures on the Government Securities Market." Working Paper, University of Houston.

Skelton, Jeffery L. [1983] "Relative Risk in Municipal and Corporate Debt." *Journal of Finance* (May).

Smith, Clifford, and Warner, Jerold. [1979] "On Financial Contracting: An Analysis of Bond Convenants." *Journal of Financial Economics* (June).

Smith, Wayne. [1968]. "Repurchase Agreements and Federal Funds." *Federal Reserve Bulletin* (May).

Questions and Problems

1. Calculate the bond equivalent yield on the following two T-bills:

	Bid Price	Ask Price	Days to Maturity
(1)	94.36	94.48	300
(2)	98.22	98.32	62

2. How do Treasury bills differ from Treasury notes and bonds?
   a. They are issued at a discount from par rather than bearing coupons.
   b. Investors do not pay state or local taxes on interest.
   c. Lending institutions always accept them as collateral at par value.
   d. They offer higher promised yields during the period of investment.

   CFA

3. It is true that bonds issued by all agencies of the United States government:
   a. Are exempt from federal income tax.
   b. Become direct obligations of the United States Treasury.
   c. Are secured bonds backed by government holdings.
   d. None of the above.

   CFA

4. The price stability of investment-grade bonds is a function of:
   a. credit (or default) risk.
   b. interest rate risk.
   c. secondary market liquidity.
   d. all of the above.

   CFA

5. The *best* measure of marketability of a preferred stock is the:
   a. number of stock exchanges on which it is traded.
   b. total number of shares outstanding.
   c. price volatility of the shares.
   d. size of the spread between the bid and offer price.

   CFA

6. Suppose the marginal income tax rate is 25 percent and that a *tax-free* municipal bond is purchased with a yield of 11 percent. This yield would be equivalent to that received on a *taxable* bond with a yield of:
   a. 12.15%.
   b. 13.53%.
   c. 14.67%.
   d. 15.53%.

   CFA

7. When can a bond with a "deferred call" be retired?
   a. At any time prior to maturity if the issuer gives reasonable notice.
   b. After a specified period following the date of issue.
   c. At any time, but the issuer will have to pay all accrued interest.
   d. Before its maturity date by issuing a similar term bond carrying a higher promised yield.

   CFA

8. How do serial bonds differ from other bonds?
   a. They are secured by the assets and taxing power of the issuer.
   b. Their par value is usually well below $1,000.
   c. They possess a succession of maturity dates, each maturity date being a small bond issue in itself.
   d. They are exempt from federal, local, and state income taxes.

   CFA

9. The trustees of a large pension plan have asked you, as investment manager, for suggestions for investing in money market securities. Any purchase would be in the $1–$5 million range. You submit the following issues:

Description	Yield
Three-month U.S. Treasury bill	8.65%
Three-month General Motors Acceptance Corporation commercial paper	8.90
Three-month Citibank Bankers Acceptance (B/A)	9.15
Three-month Citibank Domestic Certificate of Deposit (CD)	9.25

   The trustees have asked you to give several illustrations explaining in nonmathematical terms why each security provides a different yield.

a. Briefly compare the important characteristics of the Treasury bill and the General Motors Acceptance Corporation commercial paper that explain why the GMAC commercial paper provides a higher yield.

b. Briefly compare the important characteristics of the Citibank B/A with those of the Citibank CD that explain why the CD provides a higher yield than the B/A.

CFA

10. Lone Star Industries, a major producer of concrete products, plans to acquire a number of smaller currently distressed producers. Financing will require the issue of $200 million of debt. They currently have a senior issue of debt outstanding that includes indenture provisions preventing them from issuing debt equal to or above the seniority of that debt. As their investment banker, you are to advise them how the money can be raised at the least cost. They want your comments on the effect on the bonds' risk and the cost of financing of each of the following proposals:

a. The inclusion, in the new debt issue, of a sinking fund provision giving them the option of buying bonds back from investors on a random basis, or in the open market at the current market price.

b. The use of the plants to be purchased as collateral for the debt to be issued.

c. The inclusion of a call option allowing Lone Star to retire the debt after five years at par value. The call option would last until maturity.

d. The inclusion of a convertibility option allowing bondholders to "buy" the firm's stock at a set price until maturity, using the bonds' par value for the purchase.

e. The sale of the issue privately to a large insurance company.

f. The inclusion of a provision in the agreement prohibiting the firm from selling a major portion of the firm's assets to pay a large dividend to stockholders.

11. A clipping from *Barron's* summary of transactions of the New York Bond Exchange is shown below. Answer questions (*a*) through (*d*) below.

a. What does the heading "Cur Yld" refer to, and what does it measure?

b. Why would there be more than one entry for any one firm?

c. What does the "cv" refer to and why is no yield figure given for this entry?

d. Describe the first two Duquesne Light ("DuqL") entries.

***BARRON'S* / MARKET WEEK**

BONDS NEW YORK

D-E-F

52-Weeks High	52-Weeks Low	Name and Coupon		Cur Yld	Sales $1,000	Weekly High	Weekly Low	Last	Net Chg.
103	94⅝	Dana	9s2000	8.7	30	103	102⅝	103	+ 1¾
101	94	Dana	8⅞08	8.8	1	101	101	101	+ 1¾
99½	78	Dana	dc5⅞06	cv	159	98½	97	97½	− ½
97½	82½	DatGen	8⅜02	8.7	11	96½	96½	96½	− ½
75¼	48	Datpnt	8⅞06	cv	227	61½	60½	61⅛	+ ⅝
96	85	DaytP	8⅛01	8.5	5	96	95½	95½	− ½
96	85⅝	DaytP	8½07	8.9	15	96	96	96	+ 1⅞
99½	92½	Deere	8.45s	8.6	50	97¾	97¾	97¾	+ 1⅜
108½	90	Deere	5½01	cv	5	108½	108½	108½	+ 3¼
104¾	102	Deere	11½89	11.	35	103½	102½	102½	− 1
110¾	98½	Deere	9s08	cv	344	107¾	106¼	107¼	− ⅝
102	93	DeereCr	9.35s03	9.2	31	102	100⅛	102	+ 2
97⅛	89¾	DelPw	3⅞88	4.0	10	97⅛	97⅛	97⅛	+ 1
85¾	73½	DetEd	6s96	7.1	32	85	84⅞	84⅞	+ ¼

52-Weeks High	52-Weeks Low	Name and Coupon		Cur Yld	Sales $1,000	Weekly High	Weekly Low	Last	Net Chg.
60	50	DuqL	5s2010	8.5	5	59	59	59	+ ⅝
100	87½	DuqL	8¾00	8.9	8	98¼	98⅛	98¼	− ¾
100	89⅛	DuqL	9s06	9.1	146	99⅜	98¼	99⅜	+ ⅝
106½	96½	DuqL	10⅛09	9.7	3	104⅝	104⅝	104⅝	− 1⅞
111	105	DuqL	12¼10	11.	29	110	109½	110	+ 2
90	57⅝	ECL	9s89f		1	90	90	90	+ ⅛
106	95	EKod	8⅝16	8.5	5	101½	101½	101½	+ ¾
130	100	EKod	4½88	cv	1	130	130	130	+ 3
99	86	Eaton	7.6s96	7.7	15	99	99	99	+ 1
99	95½	Ekco	4.60s87	4.6	20	99	99	99	+ 2⅛
109	103¾	ElPas	12.45s97	11.	20	109	108	109	+ 1
120⅛	108	ElPaso	15s00	13.	34	113	111½	113	+ 2
105	97⅝	Ens	9¾s95	9.6	5	102	102	102	+ ¾
98½	82½	Ens	8¾01	8.9	22	98⅜	98⅜	98⅜	+ ⅝
109⅜	97½	Ens	10s01	cv	185	109⅜	108	109	+ ⅛
110	91	EnvSys	6¾11	cv	346	106½	102½	102½	− 2

Source: *Barron's*, March 9, 1987. Reprinted by permission.

12. Using the bond table given in Problem 11, answer the following:

    a. Why are some of these issues selling above $100 and some below?

    b. What explanation can you give for the low price of the first Duquesne Light issue? Why is the Datapoint ("Datpnt") issue selling at such a low price?

    c. The four Deere issues are selling within a $10 range despite vastly different coupon interest rates. What explanations can there be?

    d. The issue of ECL has varied in price between 57 and 90 over the past year. What could account for so much price variability in a "fixed-income" security?

CHAPTER

14

Valuation of Equity Securities

Stockholder Claims

Common stockholders have a residual claim on the firm's wealth. They own the firm. The value of their claim is determined by assessing the value of the firm's assets net of its outstanding obligations to creditors, employees, and customers, and it is realized over time in the form of cash flows paid out as dividends or through the repurchase of common stock. Dividends may be paid regularly on a quarterly, semiannual, or annual basis, from funds generated through the normal course of a firm's productive operations. Dividends may also be paid for special and unique occurrences, as is the case with a liquidating dividend. Regular dividends, however, constitute the major portion of the distributions made by firms to their stockholders. In recent years the repurchase of common stock by firms has significantly augmented dividend payments. The value of the firm's common stock rests on these payments or anticipation of these payments. For convenience in this chapter we will use the term *dividends* to include all cash distributions to stockholders regardless of their form. This chapter is devoted to specifying how the anticipation of dividend payments is valued in the marketplace.

Though stockholders are, collectively, the owners of the firm, they do not have the unilateral right to make decisions for the firm regarding the payment of any kind of dividend. Nor do they have the right to remove their ownership portions from the firm's operations; i.e., as a shareholder you cannot remove your investment by confiscating a filing cabinet or a unit from the firm's finished goods inventory. In fact, stockholder rights are generally limited to voting for directors of the firm in proportion to ownership interest, approving mergers and/or acquisitions, and voting on other substantial changes in the nature of the ownership interest itself.[1] The alternative for any shareholder, of course, is ultimately to sell the ownership shares.

The board of directors is charged with hiring top management and, in cooperation with management, authorizes dividend payments to stockholders. Stockholder recourse to decisions of the board, as noted, is limited to attempts to unseat them, to sue them individually or collectively in the courts, and to sell their shares in the secondary market.[2]

In spite of these special traits, the valuation of the common stock of a firm proceeds in much the same way as for fixed-income securities. The numerator of each term in the valuation equation must correctly specify each expected future cash flow. The denominator of each term must discount that cash flow to reflect accurately its current value. The discounting process involved in the determination of equilibrium value accounts for the equilibrium compensation for time and for risk, given the amount of risk.

Distribution of Cash Flows

Like their fixed-income counterparts, the cash flows from the firm to the stockholder in the form of dividend payments are subject to uncertainty. The amount and nature of the uncertainty depends on a myriad of factors to be discussed in this chapter, but in general this uncertainty in the dividends received can be represented by a frequency distribution, (two are shown in Figure 14–1). The distributions themselves may take on any shape. Indeed, they may be highly skewed to the right or left, or even discontinuous. Yet, because of the limited liability provisions of corporate common stock, the possible cash flows cannot fall below zero.[3]

Regardless of the shape of the distribution, however, the value to be used in specifying cash flows for the purpose of assessing the present worth of the common stock is the **expected value** of the cash flow distribution; i.e., its mean. In Figure 14–1(b) the expected value of the dividend at time 1 is $0.15 per share. This may reflect the investor's perception that this firm does not now pay a dividend, but may do so next year. Thus, there is a relatively high probability that no dividend will be paid next year, and some probability

---

[1]Substantial changes normally include, besides mergers and acquisitions, the issuance of new securities—such as bonds, preferred stock, or additional common stock—or a complete recapitalization of the firm. The shareholders normally must also approve the choice of the firm's auditors, any proposed change in the authorized number of directors, and any change in the firm's name.

[2]The limited nature of the actions that can be taken by stockholders does not imply that boards and managers can and do act as they wish. Even these limited actions may be sufficient to ensure that managers act in the best interests of all stockholders. This is an important topic—vitally important, in fact—to investors. Treatment of the manager-owner decision nexus must await the development of a valuation model and is taken up at various points throughout the next four chapters.

[3]For some investment opportunities, including commodity futures contracts, unincorporated equity in real estate, and certain kinds of options, the investor's potential loss is not limited to the money committed initially to the investment. One is obliged, for example, to cover a short position on a commodity futures contract regardless of whether or not the cost exceeds the money put up to participate in the transaction in the first place. The owners of common stock, however, are protected from being asked to put up additional capital should the firm incur losses, default on its debt, or lose a major lawsuit. However, short positions in common stock *can* potentially result in virtually unlimited losses to the investor, if the short remains "uncovered" while the stock's price rises over time.

FIGURE 14–1   The Distribution of Cash Flows from Common Stocks (dividends per share)

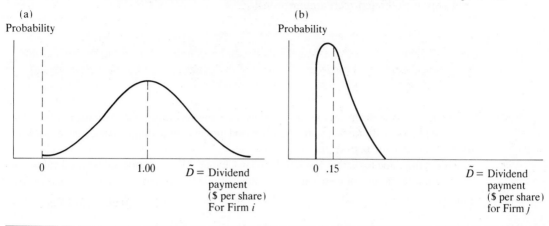

(a)
Probability

0   1.00 $\tilde{D}$ = Dividend
                                    payment
                                    ($ per share)
                                    For Firm i

(b)
Probability

0 .15 $\tilde{D}$ = Dividend
                                    payment
                                    ($ per share)
                                    for Firm j

that dividends will be greater than zero. We will not know the actual dividend until next year's value is announced by the firm. The nature and extent of the deviation of actual dividends from their expected value may be important, but to the extent that the dispersion of the distribution influences the stock's value, its influence will be accounted for in the determination of the stock's risk, β_i.[4]

Valuation of Common Stock

In a one-period world, the equilibrium time 0 (current) value of a share of common stock whose expected dividend at time 1 (a year from now) is $E(\tilde{D}_{i1})$, is simply:

(14–1)   ***Single Period Valuation***

$$P_{i0}^e = \frac{E(\tilde{D}_{i1})}{1 + E(\tilde{R}_{i1})} + \frac{E(\tilde{P}_{i1}^e)}{1 + E(\tilde{R}_{i1})}$$

where, as in Chapter 11, $E(\tilde{R}_{i1})$ is the current equilibrium-expected rate of return on i, given the market risk-return trade-off, i.e., $E(\tilde{R}_{i1}) = R_{f1} + \beta_i[E(\tilde{R}_{m1}) - R_{f1}]$ according to the CAPM; P_{i0}^e is the current equilibrium value; and $E(\tilde{P}_{i1}^e)$ is the expected time 1 equilibrium price.

---

[4]Because, in the CAPM, individuals hold well-diversified portfolios in which the influence of unique random factors "washes out" across all the securities held, a portion of the deviation of actual cash flows from the expected value of the distribution of cash flows (those caused by factors unique to the particular firm) are not relevant to the determination of beta and thus to the determination of the stock's equilibrium expected return, $E(\tilde{R}_i)$. In fact, only the nondiversifiable portion of the variability from expected value given in Figure 14–1 is relevant to the determination of $E(\tilde{R}_i)$. Unique factors influencing the firm may change the shape of the probability distribution of future dividends, but they are important to common-stock valuation only insofar as they affect either the expected dividend payment or the stock's beta.

To answer the question of what governs the expected time 1 price, $E(\tilde{P}^e_{i1})$, we need only appeal to the (correct) argument that:

> The only legal way in which wealth can be transferred from the corporation to its stockholders is through the payment of dividends (including share repurchases).

It directly follows from this argument that the expected price one year from now must be dependent on dividends and end-of-period price in the future—discounted back to time 1 (the start of period 2).

This is the same logic that was employed in Chapter 11 to describe multiperiod valuation as the sum of the discounted values of future dividends to period T. The expression is,

(14–2)   *Multiperiod Valuation*

$$P^e_{i0} = \sum_{t=1}^{T} \frac{E(\tilde{D}_{it})}{[1 + E(\tilde{R}_i)]^t} + \frac{E(\tilde{P}^e_{iT})}{[1 + E(\tilde{R}_i)]^T}$$

Equation (14–2) relates the current equilibrium value of the stock to its expected future dividends in periods 1 through T, plus its period T equilibrium-expected price. Importantly, the stock's current equilibrium value is independent of the date of anticipated sale of the security. There is no reason why the current value of the security should depend on different assumptions about when the security is to be sold if there is a readily available secondary market whose participants see the security's value as depending on the expectation of dividends from that time forward. Essentially, at any future point, the security's value depends on future dividends from that time forward.

Finally, since T may be any arbitrary date—including one infinitely far into the future—Equation (14–2) may be restated as the present value of all future expected dividends:

(14–3)   *Dividend Capitalization Model*

$$P^e_{i0} = \sum_{t=1}^{\infty} \frac{E(\tilde{D}_{it})}{[1 + E(\tilde{R}_i)]^t}$$

$$\frac{\textit{Equilibrium}}{\textit{value of a stock}} = \frac{\textit{The sum of the expected future dividends each}}{\textit{discounted at the equilibrium-expected return.}}$$

This is the general expression for the equilibrium value of a share of common stock. On Wall Street and in finance classrooms it is called the **dividend capitalization model**.[5]

Logical and often-asked questions which arise in response to the presentation of the dividend capitalization model are: "Where are earnings? Aren't they important to val-

---

[5]As noted in Chapter 11, this multiperiod formulation has been derived from the series of single-period valuation equations by recursively substituting for values of expected future equilibrium price. Mathematically speaking, this procedure is only an approximate method. However, the resulting present value formulation in (14–3) represents the prevailing, accepted theory concerning the present value of a share of common stock. One other point: The dividends discounted in Equation (14–3) represent only those dividends to be received by the firm's current shareholders. If, in future periods, the firm issues new shares of stock and pays dividends on those shares, anticipation of the "new share" dividends will not affect the time 0 equilibrium value of the old shares of stock because they do not appear in (14–3).

uation, too?" Analysts, brokers, and even tipsters seem to base many of their recommendations on earnings, and yet earnings do not even appear in Equation (14–3). Obviously this requires an explanation.

The Role of Earnings in Valuation

As one steps behind dividends—back into their determinants within the firm—it is apparent that dividends in any period are just the earnings available for the payment of dividends less any funds retained by the firm for investment purposes, or

(14–4)   ***Total Dividends Paid at Time t***

$$n_{it}D_{it} = Y_{it} - I_{it} \quad \text{for } t = 1, 2, 3, \ldots, \infty$$

Total $ dividends = Earnings less retained funds.

The left-hand side of this equation represents the total value of dividends paid by the firm at time t and equals the product of the number of shares outstanding at t, n_{it}, and the dividends per share at t, D_{it}; Y_{it} is firm i's accounting net income after interest, preferred dividend payments, and taxes (i.e., its net earnings available for common dividends); I_{it} is firm i's net investment outlays financed by its retained earnings.

A diagram of this process is presented in Figure 14–2. It represents the production process of the firm in each of four operating periods. Revenues and costs from operations—as affected by the factors of production employed, competitors, and economic conditions—generate earnings available for common stockholders. The level of earnings is divided by the firm's management in consultation with the board of directors into retained funds and dividends. Retained earnings are used for the acquisition of factors of production to support investment opportunities the firm is undertaking. These new productive operations then, it is hoped, increase the level of earnings in future periods to provide a base for the payment of a larger level of dividends in the future. In this way the firm can grow, and provide a stream of expected dividends for stockholders. The current price of the common stock is based on the expectation of dividends generated from future earnings through these future operations.

With this representation it is easy to see how we could restate the value of the common stock as a function of earnings and retained earnings. First, write expected earnings on a per share basis as

$$E(\tilde{y}_{it}) = E(\tilde{Y}_{it}/n_{it})$$

Then, solving (14–4) for D_{it} and substituting into the dividend capitalization model yields:

(14–5)   ***Earnings Capitalization Model***

$$P_{i0}^e = \sum_{t=1}^{\infty} \frac{E(\tilde{y}_{it}) - E(\tilde{I}_{it}/n_{it})}{[1 + E(\tilde{R}_i)]^t}$$

where $E(\tilde{y}_{it})$ is the expected value of i's **earnings per share** at time t, and $E(\tilde{I}_{it}/n_{it})$ is the expected value of **net investment outlays per share** at t. Simply stated, Equation (14–5) says that the value of a share of common stock is equal to the *discounted value of the*

FIGURE 14-2   The Dividend Generating Process

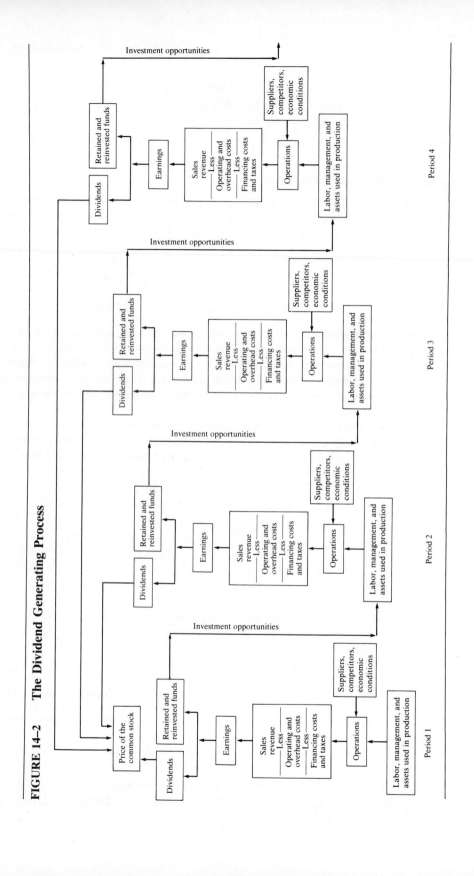

difference between expected future earnings per share and net investment per share. Equation (14–5), the **earnings capitalization model,** *is exactly equivalent—both mathematically and financially*—to the dividend capitalization model.

Clearly, the earnings capitalization model does not simply capitalize, or discount, earnings per share. To discount earnings, one would write:

(14–6)   *The Wrong Model*

$$P_{i0}^e = \sum_{t=1}^{\infty} \frac{E(\tilde{y}_{it})}{[1 + E(\tilde{R}_i)]^t}$$

But this model double-counts future cash flows. It includes not only future earnings per share which are in part generated by the reinvestment of current earnings, it also counts those current earnings per share directly *as though* they were available to the shareholders and not reinvested. Thus, the funds retained are counted twice; once when they are originally generated and retained within the firm, and a second time when the investments undertaken eventually generate cash flows to be paid out in the form of dividends. To eliminate the double-counting, the dividend capitalization model counts the earnings only when they are received by the stockholders in the form of dividends. The earnings capitalization model does the same thing by **subtracting** from earnings the funds required to be retained, I_{it}, to generate those future earnings.

Analysts also often speak in terms of a firm's cash-flow-generating ability. Cash flows can be incorporated into the equilibrium valuation model by accounting explicitly for depreciation (which is a noncash expense). The model would be stated as:

(14–7)   *Cash Flow Capitalization Model*

$$P_{i0}^e = \sum_{t=1}^{\infty} \frac{E(\tilde{y}_{it}) + E(\tilde{N}_{it}/n_{it}) - E(\tilde{Z}_{it}/n_{it})}{[1 + E(\tilde{R}_i)]^t}$$

where N_{it} is the dollar amount of accounting depreciation for firm i at time t, and $Z_{it} = N_{it} + I_{it}$ is firm i's gross investment outlays, including funds reinvested to replace depreciated capital (i.e., including funds counted as part of N_{it}). Note that $E(\tilde{N}_{it}/n_{it})$ equals the expected accounting depreciation per share, and $E(\tilde{Z}_{it}/n_{it})$ is the expected gross investment per share.

Of course, because:

$$Z_{it} \equiv N_{it} + I_{it},$$

Equation (14–7), which is termed the **cash flow capitalization model,** is precisely *equivalent* to the earnings and dividend capitalization models. If Z_{it} were very large in some future period, so that it exceeded the cash flows available in that period for retention, the numerator of (14–7) for that period would be negative. Since limited liability prevents the firm from requiring existing shareholders to commit additional funds, the firm would have to obtain the money by issuing new securities. Assuming it issued new stock, for instance, the negative term in the numerator of (14–7) for period t would represent the old shareholders' portion of the dividend dilution brought on by the newly issued shares. Such funds normally would be forthcoming as long as earnings generated in future periods were expected to be sufficient to compensate for the negative flow during period *t;* i.e., as long as the present value of the invested funds (properly evaluated) was positive.

An Application.   The dividend capitalization model or its equivalents, the earnings and cash flow capitalization models, are completely general in allowing for different patterns of expected dividends over time. The model equally well represents the value of the stock of a firm that is growing or stagnating. To illustrate, we will use it to value the shares of Houston Oil Trust when they were originally issued in 1981. This is a useful example because management's expectations of the dividends to be paid were given in the prospectus. This allows us to ignore, for the moment, the problem of estimating the future dividends.

Houston Oil Trust Securities actually are not common stock but trust certificates. The trust was created by Tenneco in 1981, and included a number of oil-producing properties. Thus, the valuation problem is simply one of trying to assess the per share value of the revenues received by the trust from the sale of oil from these specified properties. The prospectus presented a set of net cash flows, or dividends per share, from this ownership interest. We have calculated the present value of these flows, assuming a beta of 1.0, a risk-free rate of 11.5 percent (its value in 1981), and a risk premium of 7 percent. This leads to an expected equilibrium return, or a discount rate, of 18.5 percent, and the following valuation for the security.

Year	Expected Dividends	Present Value of Dividends
1981	$6.09	$5.14
1982	7.37	5.25
1983	6.76	4.06
1984	5.50	2.79
1985	3.94	1.69
1986	2.93	1.06
1987	2.32	.71
1988	1.93	.50
1989	1.53	.33
1990	7.26	1.33
1991	1.15	.18
Present value of future cash flows		$23.03

Thus, we would expect the security to be worth $23. In fact, at the time it was issued its market price was $34. The difference may be accounted for by the market's adjustment of the cash flows given in the prospectus to reflect what it thought were more realistic assumptions, or by the use of a different risk level for the security or risk premium for the market. It turns out, for whatever reasons, that the dividends that could be paid by the trust were much lower than those forecast. Dividends in each year between 1981 and 1986 averaged less than $2.00 per share. By 1987 the units were selling for about 2 $^1/_4$, reflecting the market's expectations of cash flows from 1987 and beyond.

The Role of the Firm's Investment Opportunities in Valuation

Figure 14–2 shows the link between the firm's retention of earnings, its investment opportunities, and future periods' earnings. This link can be formalized in terms of a valuation model that is equivalent to the dividend capitalization model and to those just outlined. The model is presented below—without the formal derivation, which is rather tedious and obtuse

(14–8) *Investment Opportunities Capitalization Model*

$$P_{i0}^e = \frac{E(\tilde{y}_{i0})}{E(\tilde{R}_i)} + \sum_{t=1}^{\infty} \frac{E\left[\left(\frac{I_t^*}{n_{i0}}\right)[\tilde{R}_t^* - E(\tilde{R}_i)]\right]}{E(\tilde{R}_i)} \left[\frac{1}{1 + E(\tilde{R}_i)}\right]^t$$

All these variables have been previously defined except $\tilde{R}_t^*$, which is the rate of return the firm earns after interest and taxes on its investment opportunities undertaken in period t in the future.

The first term in (14–8) is the present value of the firm's earnings derived from its current asset base. The particular form of this term is due to an assumption in the model that the current level of earnings per share of the firm, $E(\tilde{y}_{i0})$, will continue to be generated without growth or decline in the future. Of course, without growth, all of the earnings from current operations can be paid out in the form of dividends. The present value of these constant future dividends is simply the ratio of the dividends expected each year to the discount rate. This is the value of the dividend perpetuity.

The terms within the summation sign represent the present value of expected future earnings per share generated through all future investment opportunities available to the firm. This model is termed the **investment opportunities capitalization model,** and it is an alternative way of expressing the basic determinants of value.

The investment opportunities capitalization model has some useful interpretive qualities. A reading of Equation (14–8) suggests the following:

a. The firm's share value will be increased by investment only if the rate of return on investment opportunities, R^*, exceeds the market's equilibrium return $E(\tilde{R}_i)$, which directly supplies an investment decision rule equivalent to the "internal rate of return rule" used by corporations and presented in corporate finance textbooks.

b. The contribution of an investment opportunity to the firm's share value will be higher the greater is R^* compared to $E(\tilde{R}_i)$, holding the amount invested in the opportunity constant.

c. The contribution of an investment opportunity to the firm's share value will be higher the greater is I^*, holding $R^* > E(\tilde{R}_i)$ constant.

d. The contribution of an investment opportunity to the firm's share value will be greater the nearer it is to the present.

e. A given change in the firm's equilibrium return, $E(\tilde{R}_i)$, will have a greater effect on the firm, the greater the portion of the firm's value which is concentrated in yet-to-be-realized investment opportunities. That is, a given change in $E(\tilde{R}_i)$ has more effect on the terms within the summation sign than it has on the first term in the expression.

For an application of this approach to value, suppose a firm is generating $5.00 per share now and expects to generate the same amount from current operation into the forseeable future. In addition the firm has a single investment opportunity that will be purchased in year 5. The investment will cost $100 per share, has a 20 percent return, and the equilibrium return for the firm and its opportunities is 13 percent. The firm's value would be

$$P_{i0}^e = \frac{E(\tilde{y}_{i0})}{E(\tilde{R}_i)} + I_5^* \left(\frac{R_5^* - E(\tilde{R}_i)}{E(\tilde{R}_i)} \right) \left(\frac{1}{[1 + E(R_i)]^5} \right)$$

$$= \frac{5}{.13} + \frac{100(.20 - .13)}{.13} \left(\frac{1}{(1 + .13)^5} \right)$$

$$= \$38.46 + \$29.22 = \$67.68$$

In this case the single, very profitable, very large investment opportunity contributes about 40 percent to the value of the firm.

It should be obvious at this point that a limitless supply of valuation models can be constructed, all consistent with one another and with the fundamental dividend capitalization model. Each model may help to reveal the factors or characteristics of a firm and the environment in which it operates that affect its value. For these models to supply correct information to the analyst, however, it is essential they be derived from the basic concepts of valuation presented to this point. They cannot simply suggest an ad hoc connection between the factor of interest (be it earnings, management talent, or the book value of assets) and the dividend capitalization model.

Growth and the Dividend Capitalization Model

The stock market has always been infatuated with growth. So-called "growth stocks" have been and continue to be praised as a way for the investor to participate in the (expected) growth of our economy. Yet, definitions of growth are characteristically ambiguous, and the relation between growth and return is often not precisely specified. Generally, growth has related to how earnings have moved over time. One popular definition has been to include as a "growth stock" any firm whose earnings are "growing about twice as much as a broad index of common stocks over a period of 5 to 10 years."[6]

Whatever the explicit definition of a growth stock, it should be clear that the growth is important only if it can be tied into valuation. Expectations of increasing earnings may bring about increasing expectations of dividends and, therefore, high value, but this depends on how much it costs to generate those earnings. Referring back to the earnings capitalization model or to Figure 14–2, if higher future earnings can be generated only at the expense of a large outlay for capital, I^*, there is little reason to expect the firm's share value to be high. Yet, if those higher earnings can be generated with only a moderate

---

[6]Sauvain [1959, p. 404]. Reprinted by permission. Other views are, "A growth company's sales and earnings should be expected to show a rising trend, and the trend should climb more steeply than the average," excerpt from Peter L. Bernstein [September-October 1956, p. 91]. Reprinted by permission from Harvard Business Review, © 1956 by the President and Fellows of Harvard College, all rights reserved. And from Graham, Dodd, and Cottle [1962], growth stocks are referred to as "those issues whose per-share earnings have increased at an average annual rate of at least 7.2 percent."

outlay for the cost of the investment, the contribution of growth to value may be quite substantial.

The use of a valuation expression such as the earnings capitalization or investment opportunities model has the advantage of putting growth in its proper perspective. Expensive growth can be detrimental to value. In the content of capital budgeting decision rules, investment opportunities that supply a return of greater than zero but less than the demanded return, $E(\tilde{R}_i)$, will contribute positively to future earnings, but negatively to value. A firm that shows earnings growth at a high rate, but has required an extremely large volume of funds to be invested, may very well have a low incremental value. Equivalently, a firm that has a large volume of marginally profitable investment opportunities [R^* only slightly exceeds $E(\tilde{R}_i)$] will find earnings growth to be rapid, dividend growth slow, and stock price increments close to zero.

Constant Growth and Value.   In the same way that earnings and investment opportunities can be incorporated into the dividend capitalization model, particular characteristics of the stream of cash flows can be incorporated. These more specialized models describe the growth characteristics of the dividend stream. They emphasize precisely how the growth (and changes in expectations of it) influence value.

For example, a security that has a constant rate of growth of g per annum from now on could be described by the valuation model,

(14–9) $$P^e_{i0} = \frac{E(\tilde{D}_{i1})}{[1 + E(\tilde{R}_i)]} + \frac{E(\tilde{D}_{i1})(1 + g)}{[1 + E(\tilde{R}_i)]^2} + \frac{E(\tilde{D}_{i1})(1 + g)^2}{[1 + E(\tilde{R}_i)]^3} +$$

$$\cdots + \frac{E(\tilde{D}_{i1})(1 + g)^{t-1}}{[1 + E(\tilde{R})]^t}$$

If this expression is reduced by summing its terms [provided $E(\tilde{R}_i)$ exceeds g], the resulting value is given by the simple expression:

(14–10)   *Constant Growth Valuation Model*

$$P^e_{i0} = \frac{E(\tilde{D}_{i1})}{E(\tilde{R}_i) - g}$$

This is termed the **constant growth valuation model.**[7] The obvious advantage of this model is its simplicity. If expected dividends are \$2 next year (at time 1), the equilibrium-expected return is 15 percent, and the expected rate of growth, g, is 5 percent, the estimated value of a share is:

$$P^e_{i0} = \frac{\$2}{.15 - .05} = \$20$$

The obvious disadvantage of the constant growth valuation model is that it is not likely to hold precisely for any firm, and will not hold even approximately for the vast majority

---

[7]If earnings grow at a constant rate of zero, the valuation of a stock is simply $P^e_{i0} = E(\tilde{D}_{i1})/E(\tilde{R}_i)$. This might be an appropriate valuation model that might work well for perpetually outstanding preferred stock that doesn't share in the firm's growth.

of firms that experience secular or cyclical growth behavior. Nevertheless, the model serves as a useful investigatory tool because of its ease of application. It also holds approximately for so-called mature firms—say, perhaps, U.S. Steel or Consolidated Edison—whose future average earnings growth is expected to be slow, but rather steady. Inspection of Equation (14–10) shows that, for a given demanded return and dividend level, a firm that has twice the growth rate of another firm will typically not have twice the current share price—the actual relationship between the two prices depends on the level of g as compared to $E(\tilde{R}_i)$.

It may not be too far off the mark to use the model to value a broad-based index of many common stocks, at least on the assumption that the stocks in the index as a group are likely to grow at about the same level as the entire economy. If long-run economic growth is relatively constant, the model may supply us with some interesting insights. Take the S&P 500 index, for example. In early 1987 the earnings per share of the index were reported by Standard & Poor's to be about $16.50. Estimated earnings for the year-end 1987 were about $18.75. Over the past 20 years the firms included in the index had paid out between 55 and 65 percent of their earnings in the form of dividends. Based on this, we forecast next year's dividend to be $11.25.

In early 1987 the risk-free rate, based on the yield on one-year T-bills, was 5.75 percent. With a 6 percent risk premium (and a beta of 1.0, of course) the discount rate to apply is 11.75 percent. During this time period economists' expectations for the growth of the economy averaged between 6.5 and 7 percent per annum (reflecting real growth expectations of 2.5 to 3 percent and expectations of inflation of 4 percent). If we use these numbers, the value of the index should be,

$$\textbf{(14–11)} \qquad P^e_{S\&P,1987} = \frac{\$11.25}{.1175 - .0675} = \$225.$$

Of course other investors might argue with our numbers, and come up with a different value. Apparently this was the case because the value of the index at this time was closer to 275. A growth rate of 7.7 percent would justify this value. Of course if growth expectations are much greater we would begin to wonder if the discount rate, which increases with inflation, is high enough.

Two Stages of Growth and Value.   Perhaps a more realistic growth model for many individual firms would have dividends growing at rate g_s for a number of years—reflecting, say, a period of subnormal or supernormal growth—followed by a more normal growth rate g_n subsequent to the initial growth period. If g_s begins at time 1 and lasts for $T - 1$ years (until time T) after which g_n takes over, the model would be:

(14–12)   *Two-Stage Growth Model*

$$P^e_{i0} = \sum_{t=1}^{T} \frac{E(\tilde{D}_{i1})(1 + g_s)^{t-1}}{[1 + E(\tilde{R}_i)]^t} + \left[\frac{E(\tilde{D}_{i1})(1 + g_s)^{T-1}(1 + g_n)}{E(\tilde{R}_i) - g_n} \right] \left[\frac{1}{1 + E(\tilde{R}_i)} \right]^T$$

The first term reflects the present value of dividends generated during the first predicted growth stage, culminating at date T. The second term is the present value of a stream of dividends with an initial value at date $T + 1$ of $E(\tilde{D}_{i1})(1 + g_s)^{T-1}(1 + g_n)$, and growing from that time onward at the annual rate of g_n. The last discount rate term $[1/(1 + E(\tilde{R}_i))]^T$, brings the value back from time T to time 0.

There is a good deal of commonsense logic to representing the growth of the firm over two stages. In many cases firms will have a competitive edge in their markets that allows them to rapidly increase profits for a few years. Eventually, however, other firms are able to construct productive capacity, enter these same markets, and reduce profits to a more normal level. As this process of maturation develops, the growth of profits and dividends is reduced to a "normal" level—perhaps equal to the rate of growth of the economy as a whole. Note also that each year's term can be easily modeled through the use of readily available computer spreadsheet programs, such as Lotus 1-2-3 or Multiplan, making it less necessary to "memorize" specific valuation equations.

The period of rapid growth may be quite different for different firms or firms in different industries. It is also affected by patents (that allow the firm to exclude competitors for a period of time) and by specialized skills or assets that cannot be easily reproduced. This might justify a relatively long anticipated period of growth for a firm such as Genentech (with highly specialized skills in molecular biology) or INC Pharmaceutical (with a patent on a potential curative for AIDS). On the other hand, an airline company that has a very profitable and high-growth route structure might find competition affecting its profitability next year.

For example, suppose the common stock of Hexel (a maker of high-tech plastics, e.g., skis) has an expected equilibrium return of 20 percent based on its β, an expected dividend at time 1 of \$1 on an earnings base next year of \$2.50, and expects to enjoy a period of supernormal growth at 30 percent for nine years (until year 10), followed by normal growth at a rate of 7 percent per year indefinitely. The expected dividend stream associated with these assumptions is shown in Table 14–1. Using Equation (14–12) we find Hexel's equilibrium share price, or intrinsic value, is estimated as

$$P^e_{HX,0} = \sum_{t=1}^{10} \frac{(\$1)(1.30)^{t-1}}{(1.20)^t} + \left[\frac{(\$1)(\$10.604)(1.07)}{(.20 - .07)} \right] \left[\frac{1}{1.20} \right]^{10}$$

$$P^e_{HX,0} = \$12.26 + \frac{\$87.28}{(1.20)^{10}} = \$26.36$$

Notice that about half the value of the firm is associated with dividends expected during the high-growth period.

It is also easy to see how value would change with any change in inputs. For example:

- If supernormal growth drops to 15 percent, value = \$19.40.
- If the supernormal growth period is only five years, value = \$16.40.
- If the discount rate drops to 15 percent, value = \$51.06.
- If the normal growth rate drops to 5 percent, value = \$24.25.

It is important for you to understand that only gross generalizations can be made about the effect of growth on value. The sensitivity of a firm's value to a change in one of the inputs depends on the values of the other inputs. The sensitivity of value to a change in the growth rate depends on the discount rate and the period of growth, for example.

TABLE 14–1   Valuation of Hexel with $g_s = 30\%$ for Nine Years until Year 10, Followed by $g_n = 7\%$ Indefinitely, $E(\bar{R}_i) = 20\%$

Time	Expected Dividend	Present Value	
1	$ 1.000	$ .83	↑
2	1.300	.90	
3	1.690	.98	
4	2.197	1.06	Period
5	2.856	1.15	of
6	3.712	1.24	Supernormal
7	4.827	1.35	Growth
8	6.275	1.46	
9	8.157	1.58	
10	10.604	1.71	↓
11	11.34	1.53	↑
12	12.14	1.36	
13	12.99	1.21	Period
14	13.90	1.08	of
15	14.87	.97	Normal
.	.	.	Growth
.	.	.	
.	.	.	↓

$$P^e_{HX,0} = \$26.36$$

The Growth of Earnings and Dividends

Unlike the constant growth model, there is nothing in the two-stage growth model to suggest that earnings and dividends grow at the same rate during the high-growth period. Firms with a high rate of growth typically maintain a relatively low dividend payout ratio. The retention of earnings helps finance the growth. The payout ratio is increased as the growth declines to g_n. This will create a level of growth in dividends that exceeds the growth in earnings, though dividends start from a much lower level.

GAF is a firm that currently is paying a very low dividend of $.10 per share, relative to its current earnings level of $2.25. It is doing so because it has the opportunity to invest funds in a modernization program that is expected to generate a high rate of return. Next year's earnings per share are expected to be $2.75. Analysts believe earnings will increase at the rate of 22 percent for five years after that (through year 6). Beyond year 6 the firm is expected to grow at 7 percent—equal to the general growth of the economy. During this time period GAF's dividend payout rate will increase from its current value of 4 percent to the industry average of 65 percent by the end of year 6. This objective is reasonable since its need for internally generated funds will decline as it approaches the end of its supergrowth period. This provides the basis for our expectations of dividends of $.30, $.75, $1.25, $2.00, $3.00, and $3.75 for the next 6 years. The rate of growth implicit in these numbers is about 66 percent per year. Table 14–2 (developed using Lotus 123, in fact) shows the future expectations for earnings per share, dividends per share, payout, and share price for each of the next 20 years. Each future share price reflects the discounted value of future dividends from that point in time forward. The discount rate used was 14.15 percent, as given in the table. Based on these assumptions,

TABLE 14–2   Valuation of GAF

Period of Growth .... 6 Years
Supernormal Growth 22.00%
Normal Growth 7.00%
β_{GAF} 1.2
R_f 5.75%
$E(\tilde{R}_m) - R_f$ 7.00%
$E(\tilde{R}_{GAF})$ .... 14.15% = $R_f + \beta_{GAF}(E(\tilde{R}_m) - R_f)$

Year	Earnings per Share	Payout	Dividend	Value $P^e_{GAF,t}$	Dividend Growth
0	$ 2.25	4%	$ 0.10	**$35.38**	200.0%
1	2.75	11	0.30	$40.08	150.0
2	3.36	22	0.75	$45.00	66.7
3	4.09	31	1.25	$50.12	60.0
4	4.99	40	2.00	$55.22	50.0
5	6.09	49	3.00	$60.03	36.3
6	7.43	55	4.09	$64.43	16.7
7	7.95	60	4.77	$68.78	15.9
8	8.51	65	5.53	$72.98	7.0
9	9.11	65	5.92	$77.39	7.0
10	9.74	65	6.33	$82.01	7.0
11	10.42	65	6.78	$86.84	7.0
12	11.15	65	7.25	$91.87	7.0
13	11.93	65	7.76	$97.12	7.0
14	12.77	65	8.30	$102.56	7.0
15	13.66	65	8.88	$108.19	7.0
16	14.62	65	9.50	$113.99	7.0
17	15.64	65	10.17	$119.95	7.0
18	16.74	65	10.88	$126.05	7.0
19	17.91	65	11.64	$132.24	7.0
20	19.16	65	12.46	$138.50	7.0

the underlying *current equilibrium value* for the stock is 35.38 per share (the first entry in the "Value" column).

Nondividend-Paying Growth Stocks and Value

The fact that a firm may not currently be paying dividends is no real impediment to applying the "growth stage" models to valuation. We can show this by valuing Digital Equipment Corporation (DEC), which is currently attempting to increase its share of the small mainframe and personal computer market. To do so requires a substantial investment in research and development and marketing. For this reason it now pays no dividend. Of course, if it is able to achieve its objective (basically to be a close second to IBM in these markets) its profits will grow very rapidly. In fact, in the past five years its profits increased by about 30 percent per year, as it began to see the returns from its prior investments. The firm just reported earnings for last year of $5.50 per share, and analysts expect next year's earnings per share to be $8.00.

TABLE 14–3   **Valuation of Digital Equipment Corporation**

		Period of Growth	8 Years	
		Supernormal Growth	24.00%	
		Normal Growth	7.00%	
		β_{DEC}	1.1	
		R_f	5.75%	
		$E(\bar{R}_m) - R_f$	7.00%	
		$E(\bar{R}_{DEC})$	13.45% $= R_f + \beta_{DEC}(E(\bar{R}_m) - R_f)$	
		Market Price	.00	

Year	Earnings per Share	Payout	Dividend	Value $P^e_{Dec,t}$	Dividend Growth
0	$ 5.50	0%	$ 0.00	$125.85	
1	8.00	0	0.00	142.78	—
2	9.92	0	0.00	161.98	—
3	12.30	8	1.00	182.77	—
4	15.25	13	2.00	205.35	100.0%
5	18.91	19	3.50	229.47	75.0
6	23.45	23	5.50	254.84	57.1
7	29.08	28	8.00	281.11	45.5
8	36.06	33	12.00	306.92	50.0
9	38.59	60	23.15	325.05	92.9
10	41.29	60	24.77	344.00	7.0
11	44.18	60	26.51	363.76	7.0
12	47.27	60	28.36	384.32	7.0
13	50.58	60	30.35	405.67	7.0
14	54.12	60	32.47	427.76	7.0
15	57.91	60	34.74	450.55	7.0
16	61.96	60	37.18	473.97	7.0
17	66.30	60	39.78	497.94	7.0
18	70.94	60	42.56	522.35	7.0
19	75.90	60	45.54	547.07	7.0
20	81.22	60	48.73	571.92	7.0
21	86.90	60	52.14	596.70	7.0
22	92.99	60	55.79	621.16	7.0
23	99.49	60	59.70	645.01	7.0
24	106.46	60	63.88	667.89	7.0
25	113.91	60	68.35	689.38	7.0
26	121.88	60	73.13	708.97	7.0
27	130.42	60	78.25	726.07	7.0
28	139.55	60	83.73	740.00	7.0
.	.	.	.	.	.
.	.	.	.	.	.
.	.	.	.	.	.

Using these figures, and an in-depth analysis of the firm and the industry, we estimate that earnings will grow at a 24 percent rate for the next eight years, followed by a normal growth rate of 7 percent from then on. The figures in Table 14–3 indicate that DEC will begin paying dividends in three years at the rate of about 8 percent of earnings. Dividends will rise rapidly thereafter as the profitable level of operations, and the reduced need for cash for reinvestment, allows larger and larger annual payments. By the ninth year DEC will be growing more slowly, and establish a payout ratio of about 60 percent. The 8-year supernormal growth period reflects our estimate of the increasingly competitive nature of the industry, and the chance that supernormal investment opportunities will be eliminated rather quickly. Based on these inputs the estimated intrinsic value of DEC's stock is $126. Once again, this number may differ from the market value to the extent that the market adopts different expectations for the future of the firm.

Growth and Stockholder Returns

While it is obvious from the preceding discussion that the expected growth of dividends and value are closely related, there is *no relation* between growth and stockholder returns *if the expected growth has been properly reflected in the current share price.* This counterintuitive statement can be demonstrated with an example.

Assume that two investor-owned utilities, Baltimore Gas & Electric and Houston Natural Gas, are valued according to the constant growth valuation model of Equation (14–10). Both have initial expected dividends of $2.00 a share at time 1, both have equilibrium-expected returns of 12 percent, but Baltimore Gas & Electric (security i) expects a constant growth rate of $g = 4$ percent, while Houston Natural Gas (security j) expects a constant growth rate of $g = 8$ percent. Their equilibrium share values are:

$$P_{i0}^e = \frac{E(\tilde{D}_{i1})}{E(\tilde{R}_i) - g} = \frac{\$2.00}{.12 - .04} = \$25$$

$$P_{j0}^e = \frac{E(\tilde{D}_{j1})}{E(\tilde{R}_j) - g} = \frac{\$2.00}{.12 - .08} = \$50$$

Clearly, Houston Natural Gas is more highly valued than Baltimore Gas & Electric because it has a higher growth rate. After one year, the respective values of the two securities are:

$$P_{i1}^e = \frac{\$2.00(1.04)}{.12 - .04} = \$26$$

$$P_{j1}^e = \frac{\$2.00(1.08)}{.12 - .08} = \$54$$

Houston Natural Gas has appreciated more in value, but the total return earned by each firm's shareholders over the time interval is exactly the same! That is,

$$R_{i1} = \frac{P_{i1}^e - P_{i0}^e + D_{i1}}{P_{i0}^e} = \frac{\$26 - \$25 + \$2}{\$25} = .12$$

$$R_{j1} = \frac{P_{j1}^e - P_{j0}^e + D_{j1}}{P_{j0}^e} = \frac{\$54 - \$50 + \$2}{\$50} = .12$$

The reason the returns are the same is that all of the anticipated growth is reflected in share price. Essentially, higher growth securities, when the growth is anticipated by the market, do not offer higher returns. This conclusion is consistent with stock market efficiency. The price already reflects the growth which is expected. It is only if high growth is *unanticipated* that higher growth firms will produce higher returns for their shareholders.

In the cases of DEC and GAF, market prices of 126 and 35 $^1/_2$ would mean that market expectations properly incorporated growth. With these market prices DEC's shareholders would earn a return of 13.45 percent over time, while GAF's shareholders would earn a return of 14.15 percent. The returns are the same as the expected equilibrium returns in each case, of course, since each security has been priced according to its own expected growth.

Rates of Return on Common Stock

As is the case with fixed-income securities, the rate of return that is generated *ex post* from holding a common stock depends on how expectations of future cash flows and the discount rate change and the extent to which the stock's market price deviates from its equilibrium level. If the expectations of $\tilde{D}_{i1}, \tilde{D}_{i2}, \tilde{D}_{i3} \ldots$ do not change over the holding period, and if market price P_{i0}^m, always equals P_{i0}^e—the equilibrium price—the ex post holding-period return the security generates is just equal to ex ante equilibrium-expected return. For example, if a stock's expected dividend and end-of-period equilibrium price were $5 and $25, respectively, with a 15 percent demanded return, the initial time 0 equilibrium value would be:

$$P_{i0}^e = \frac{\$25 + \$5}{1.15} = \$26.09$$

Assuming the stock is actually selling for $26.09 at time 0, an investor purchasing the security and then receiving the time 1 dividend of $5 and selling the stock for a time 1 equilibrium price of $25 would secure the ex post holding-period return:

$$R_{i1} = \frac{\$25 + \$5 - \$26.09}{\$26.09} = .15$$

However, suppose either the market price at time 1 is not equal to its equilibrium level, or the equilibrium price itself has changed from $25 due to revised expectations of future dividends. If, for example, the stock is priced at the end of period 1 at $22, the investor's holding-period return is only:

$$R_{i1} = \frac{\$22 + \$5 - \$26.09}{\$26.09} = .035$$

This 3.5 percent return, obviously, is well below the expected equilibrium return of 15 percent due to the revision of expectations regarding end of period 1 value.

As expectations change, as a stock's market price sometimes deviates from its equilibrium value, and as realized dividends or end of period prices depart from their expected levels, ex post returns can—and usually do—deviate from their ex ante equilibrium levels. These factors are sources of uncertainty associated with holding securities and lead naturally to our discussion of common-stock risk.

Risk of Common Stocks

Common stock returns, of course, are risky. Like any security, the contribution of a stock to the market portfolio's standard deviation is proportional to the stock's beta coefficient, or

(14–13) ***Risk Again***

$$\beta_{it} = \frac{Cov(\tilde{R}_{it},\tilde{R}_{mt})}{[\sigma(\tilde{R}_{mt})]^2}$$

The factors that give rise to this level of risk are those that cause the security's price to change in ways that covary with changes in the value of the market portfolio. These nondiversifiable elements of uncertainty are the same for common stocks as they are for fixed-income securities—interest rate risk and default risk.

Interest rate risk is related to uncertainty surrounding the rate at which future cash flow expectations are discounted in the marketplace. As the security market line shifts upward, the prices of all securities will tend to fall. And, since common stocks are long-term securities (hence, they have a long duration) they will tend to have a relatively high level of interest rate risk.

Default risk is related to uncertainty surrounding the cash flows themselves. For fixed-income securities this type of risk was described in terms of the possibility that promised coupon payments and principal repayments would be less than or more than expected. For common stocks the cash flows are dividend payments paid to stockholders after all other contractual claims have been satisfied. The payments are not promised in any amount, but are paid to shareholders in the long run in the amount of "what's left over." For common stocks this component is labeled **nondiversifiable cash flow risk**, rather than default risk, to emphasize the differences between fixed-income and common-stock contracts.

Thus, the risk of a common stock, or its beta coefficient, can be decomposed into two parts, or

Components of Risk

$$\frac{Stock}{risk} = \frac{Nondiversifiable\ cash\ flow\ risk}{+\ nondiversifiable\ interest\ rate\ risk}$$

Nondiversifiable Cash Flow Risk

For all firms, the cash flow risk on the firm's common stock exceeds the default risk on the firm's bonds. This is inherent in the common stockholder's *claim* to dividends paid from the *residual* value of the firm, after bondholders and others have been paid according to their contracts. This factor accounts for much of the difference between bond and stock risk.

Since dividend payments in the long run are governed by the earnings generated from a firm's operations, the nondiversifiable cash flow risk hinges on how the firm's earnings covary with earnings of the entire market.[8] If, when overall earnings (and returns) in the

---

[8]The actual level of dividends paid by the firm is affected by the managers' willingness to pay them. The willingness does not follow immediately from the ability for two reasons. First, managers may feel that in times of improving cash flows and generally good business conditions, the return from reinvesting funds in the firm are high, and that the high cash flows can be best put to use within the firm to generate higher future dividends—rather than paying them out to shareholders in the form of higher current dividends. Such an effect will tend to hold down the measured covariance between actual dividends and market returns. Second, dividend policy seems to have developed within the objective that stable dividends are beneficial. As explained in detail

(continued on page 424)

economy are high (low) relative to expected levels, the firm's earnings are very high (very low), the covariance term is high and, therefore, so is risk. Alternatively, a firm whose earnings are well insulated from changes in the economic environment and from changes in the earnings of most other firms would not find its ability to pay dividends in any period very greatly affected by the rest of the economy. Consequently, the firm would have a lower covariance of earnings and would tend as a result to have a lower beta than other firms might. In other words, if cash flow expectations for firm i change more than proportionately with the cash flows generated by all firms, this component of firm risk is greater than most securities. If cash flow expectations change less than proportionately, the component is less risky than average.

A couple of hypothetical examples can be used to illustrate this. Suppose people generally purchase yachts only when the economy is near its peak level of activity and salaries and corporate profits are high. Yacht sales, however, plummet when the economy is in a downturn and most firms are experiencing declining earnings and lower compensation levels for employees. One might therefore expect that shares of common stock in a yacht manufacturer (such as Uniflite) would have high nondiversifiable cash flow risk, since the earnings on which dividends are based in the long run are fluctuating widely with, and relative to, earnings of other firms.

At the other extreme, consider the fate of an electric utility firm. The demand for its services may fluctuate modestly with the general level of business activity. Certainly business consumption of electricity is likely to go up somewhat when firms are at or near capacity. But for the most part the demand is fairly stable and fluctuates much less than the demand for most goods and services. Consequently, the cash flow risk of a utility is likely to be quite small.

Conceivably, there may be a few firms whose cash flows move inversely with economic conditions. The case most often cited is that of firms that produce gold. As the economy grows weak, and there is concern about the ability of dollar-denominated investments supplying adequate returns, the demand for gold increases, supplying high returns to those firms producing gold. As the economy grows strong the opposite is the case. Thus, it is the flight from and to the U.S. dollar that creates the negative relation between a gold firm's cash flows and the cash flows of the entire market. Whether this relationship is strong enough to lead to a negative beta coefficient for these firms is debatable.

In reality, the magnitude of nondiversifiable cash flow risk may be influenced by many factors. Some will be generally beyond the control of the firm, such as relative consumer demand for the goods and services the firm produces, and some will be well within the control of the firm, such as the firm's financial leverage or operating leverage. While it would be impossible to enumerate all of the factors that could influence cash flow risk, some of the more important will be discussed to provide you with means for seeing how

---

in Chapter 17, firms are reluctant either to increase or reduce dividend payments in the short run. Firms experiencing much higher or lower cash flows seldom are willing to change the current dividend in response unless they are quite sure that the higher or lower levels of cash flows are "permanent," and will enable them to sustain the new level in subsequent periods. This effect also contributes to a relatively low covariance of current dividends with market returns—even though, in the long run, the covariance may be quite high. Effectively, it takes a number of time periods before the effect of higher or lower real earnings are reflected in the dividend payment pattern.

a given factor influences risk. Extensions made in the next three chapters suggest how you can analyze the likely effect of any specific factor on an individual firm's risk.[9]

In general, the relationship can be derived from a detailed microeconomic analysis of the relationship between beta and the production (supply) and demand functions faced by the firm. In particular:

Beta will be higher,

a. the greater the proportional comovement of firm *i*'s revenues with the revenues of other firms in the market portfolio; i.e., the more sales fluctuate with the economy.

b. the greater the proportional comovements of firm *i*'s product prices with the prices of all goods and services in the economy.

c. the greater the proportional comovement of the demand for the firm's output with aggregate economic demand.

Beta will be lower, on the other hand,

a. the greater the proportional comovement of the firm's cost of labor inputs (or the less the proportional comovement of the firm's labor productivity).

b. the greater the proportional comovement of the cost of real capital equipment employed in the production process (or the less the proportional comovement of the firm's capital productivity).

Summarized another way, anything that *increases* the comovement of *cash inflows* to the firm with market flows will *increase* the firm's beta. Anything that *increases* the comovement of the firm's *cash outflows* with market flows will *decrease* its beta. A brief example will help to clarify this summary.

Firms in the airline industry are often thought to be subject to the pressures of changes in the economic climate. As economic conditions slow and personal income drops, both business and recreational travel drop off. The reduced plane load factor in the presence of high fixed costs brings about much reduced profits. Alternatively, as conditions improve, revenues rise and profits rise even faster (due to fixed costs). The covariance of cash flow (and therefore dividend) expectations of firms in the airline industry with overall market returns is large. Other things held equal, this would tend to suggest high beta coefficients for firms in this industry. (Note that if their costs fluctuated *with* the economy, and thus *with* their revenues, the β would be lower.)

---

[9]For example, you could analyze how stock dividends of a company influence its beta (they don't), how a shift from a labor-intensive production technology to a more capital-intensive technology would affect risk (it probably increases it), or how a change in the way rates are set by a public utility commission would affect risk (it could, in either direction).

Nondiversifiable Interest Rate Risk

Common stock exists for the life of the firm. And, since much of the expected flow of cash will come in the form of dividends far into the future, common stock will have **interest rate risk** that is conceptually equivalent to that of long-term fixed-income securities such as Treasury and corporate bonds. As the security market line (SML) shifts up, stock prices will drop. As the SML shifts down, stock prices will rise.

Whether stocks have a level of interest rate risk that is less than or greater than that of the bonds issued by the firm depends on the duration of the securities. If expected cash flows to stockholders are concentrated in periods relatively near to the current one then the stock's duration is low, and so is its interest rate risk. If expected cash flows are far in the future (certainly a situation that would describe GAF or DEC analyzed earlier) the duration is large, and so is interest rate risk. Even a small change in the discount rate applied to these distant cash flows brings a large change in value. For example, a stock with a constant level of expected dividends in perpetuity and a 15 percent discount rate has a duration of just under 8 years. However, if that same stock is growing at a rate of 7 percent the duration jumps to almost 27 years. For comparative purposes the duration of a 20-year 10 percent coupon bond with a discount rate of 10 percent has a duration of 10 years. Remember, as duration doubles, the interest rate risk of the security doubles.

Empirical Estimates of the Relationship between β_i and Firms' Characteristics

Obviously, there may be characteristics of a firm or a particular common stock that can illustrate the relationships we have hypothesized. Table 14–4 is made up of correlation coefficients between betas estimated for a sample of actual firms and certain of their characteristics. The table reports on two studies done over a 20-year period. The first was conducted by Beaver, Kettler, and Scholes. They looked at data for selected NYSE-listed firms over 1947–56 and 1957–65. The second study, by Pettit and Westerfield, examined data for a different group of NYSE-listed firms over two periods, 1947–56 and 1957–68.

In Table 14–4 each of the variables in the left-hand column for all the firms in the sample has been cross-sectionally correlated with the estimated betas from the market model for the same period. The variable "earnings beta" listed on the left-hand side is a different measure of beta. It closely corresponds to the "nondiversifiable cash flow risk" discussed above, because it measures the covariance of the changes in a firm's accounting earnings over time with changes in the accounting earnings imputed to a representative, broadly based stock market index. Some of the other measures in the table—such as size, liquidity, growth, leverage, and dividend payout are more traditional measures of risk exposure. Their formal relationship to the firm's beta will be discussed in Chapter 17. Suffice it to say that some of these measures (e.g., dividend payout and earnings growth) do seem to correlate with the observed market risk level. Others may be related to risk determination (e.g., leverage and liquidity) but do not show in this simple paired com-

TABLE 14–4   Correlations between Risk (β) and Variables that Characterize the Nature of the Firms' Operations

Variable	Individual Securities	Five-Security Portfolios	Individual Securities	Five-Security Portfolios
Beaver, Kettler, Scholes	*1947–56*		*1957–65*	
Payout (dividends/earnings)	− .50	− .77	− .24	− .45
Earnings growth	.23	.51	.03	.07
Leverage (debt/equity)	.23	.45	.25	.56
Liquidity	− .13	− .44	− .01	− .01
Firm size (assets)	− .07	− .13	− .16	− .30
Earnings variance	.58	.77	.36	.62
Earnings beta	.39	.67	.23	.46
Beta on earnings/Price ratio	—	—	—	—
Number of observations	305	61	—	—
Pettit and Westerfield	*1947–56*		*1957–68*	
Payout (dividends/earnings)	− .48	− .77	− .39	− .72
Earnings growth	.22	.41	.25	.48
Leverage (debt/equity)	.05	.09	.07	.15
Liquidity	− .07	− .20	.01	.03
Firm size (assets)	− .07	− .16	− .18	− .40
Earnings variance	—	—	—	—
Earnings beta	.26	.45	.18	.26
Beta on earnings/Price ratio	.33	.63	.29	.40
Number of observations	338	67	543	108

Source: Beaver, Kettler, Scholes [1970] and Pettit and Westerfield [1972].

parison because they may be self-selected by the firm's management in recognition of other factors influencing the firm's risk.[10]

The Price/Earnings Ratio

Market analysts and experienced investors often speak in terms of the level of the price/earnings ratio of the firm. This ratio measures nothing more than the price of a share of common stock per dollar of earnings generated. As such, it is often used as a

---

[10]Thus, for example, high leverage may be adopted only by those firms having low risk from other sources. This effect, in a cross-sectional study like that shown in Table 14–4, would tend to offset the apparent fact that as a firm increases its financial leverage it increases its risk.

basis for comparing one stock to another. A price/earnings ratio of 20 implies the security is twice as expensive (per dollar of earnings) as a security with a price/earnings ratio of 10. Why would these ratios vary among firms? Insights into the price/earnings ratio and its relationship to the concepts of valuation introduced earlier can connect the subject of valuation with the practice of security evaluation and analysis.

As a starting point, let us consider the two-stage growth model of valuation given in Equation (14–12). This is the model that incorporates supernormal (or subnormal) growth at rate g_s for T-1 years (until time T), after which normal growth at rate g_n is sustained indefinitely. The equation is:

(14–12 repeated)

$$P^e_{i0} = \sum_{t=1}^{T} \frac{E(\tilde{D}_{i1})(1 + g_s)^{t-1}}{[1 + E(\tilde{R}_i)]^t} + \left[\frac{E(\tilde{D}_{i1})(1 + g_s)^{T-1}(1 + g_n)}{E(\tilde{R}_i) - g_n} \right] \left[\frac{1}{1 + E(\tilde{R}_i)} \right]^T$$

If both sides of (14-12) are divided by earnings per share expected at time 1, $E(y_{i1})$, the left-hand side will be a price/earnings ratio, or P/E, given by:

(14–14)   *Price/Earnings Ratio*

$$\frac{P}{E} = \frac{P^e_{i0}}{E(\tilde{y}_{i1})} = \sum_{t=1}^{T} \frac{\left(\dfrac{E(\tilde{D}_{i1})}{E(\tilde{y}_{i1})} \right) (1 + g_s)^{t-1}}{[1 + E(\tilde{R}_i)]^t}$$

$$+ \left[\frac{E(\tilde{D}_{i1})}{E(\tilde{y}_{i1})} \frac{(1 + g_s)^{T-1}(1 + g_n)}{E(\tilde{R}_i) - g_n} \right] \left[\frac{1}{1 + E(\tilde{R}_i)} \right]^T$$

If we take this rather specific equation and generalize from it, the price/earnings ratio will be a positive function of both growth rates and the period of supernormal growth (if $g_s > g_n$), a negative function of the demanded return $E(\tilde{R}_i)$, and a positive function of the ratio of expected dividends per share to expected earnings per share—which is just the dividend payout rate.[11]

A general summary statement of the determinants of the price/earnings ratio and the direction of their influence would be:

$$(+) \, (+)(+)(+)(-)$$

(14–15) $P/E =$ a function of: $\left[\dfrac{E(\tilde{D}_{i1})}{E(\tilde{y}_{i1})}, \, g_s, \, g_n, \, T, \, E(\tilde{R}_i) \right]$

Moreover, since the equilibrium-expected return is a positive function of the stock's beta coefficient, it is also true that beta would have a negative influence on the P/E ratio. Thus, price/earnings ratios are a function of the expectations of the growth of dividends

---

[11]Price/earnings ratios often are calculated by dividing price by the immediate past reported annual earnings. The conceptual differences in the calculations are small. One can compare price/earnings ratios based on historical earnings or expected earnings. The historical-earnings calculation has one flaw the expected-earnings calculation does not have: It incorporates nonrecurring factors that affected earnings in that historical period. Clearly, this could be adjusted for, however.

and earnings, the percentage of expected earnings paid out in the form of dividends, the period of abnormal growth and risk (which is compensated through $E(\tilde{R}_i)$).

For comparative purposes, based on next year's earnings, the price/earnings ratios of the sample firms we have valued thus far are,

	g_s	T	g_n	Payout	$E(R_i)$	P/E
S&P 500 Index	6.75%	∞	6.75%	.6	11.75%	13.3
Hexel Corp.	30.00	10	7.00	.4	20.00	10.5
GAF	67.00	6	7.00	.04*	14.15	12.9
DEC	†	8	7.00	.00*	13.45	15.6

*Variable and increasing payout ratios.
†Technically, growth is infinite since current dividends are zero.

Valuation of Common Stock: Empirical Evidence

The theoretical relationships regarding valuation presented in the first half of this chapter have their basis in (and are derived from) the doctrines of consumer-investor choice and capital market theory developed in Parts I and II. Few would argue with these general conclusions, *given agreement on the assumptions* underlying the behavior of individuals and markets. In this sense, then, it was demonstrated that the anticipation of earnings and dividend growth, dividend payout, and risk as measured by a stock's beta determine current equilibrium value.

Yet, as was discussed in Chapter 11, a security's market price can deviate—at least in the short run—from its theoretically derived equilibrium price. Not all information is available to investors, hence the market's prevailing forecasts of future dividends and its required returns in the marketplace may differ from what those values and forecasts would be in a market with complete information. Consequently, it is necessary to test the theory to see if it actually holds, or holds approximately, in the real world. Final validation of any theory about real markets must be based on observed empirical relationships.

Solving these remaining issues sounds easy. It seems simple enough to take one stock valuation model, say the cash flow capitalization model,

(14–7 repeated) $$P^e_{i0} = \sum_{t=1}^{\infty} \frac{E(\tilde{y}_{it}) + E(\tilde{N}_{it}/n_{it}) - E(\tilde{Z}_{it}/n_{it})}{[1 + E(\tilde{R}_i)]^t}$$

and compare the implied value of equilibrium price, P^e_{i0}, to the stock's actual market price, P^m_{i0}, at the current point in time. If we repeated this at several different times, we could simply determine the degree of association that exists between the theoretical equilibrium price and the actual market price of the stock. In that way, the part that expected earnings or risk actually plays in real-world valuation can be established.

There are problems that make this task more difficult than it seems. The three major problems are:

1. The variables that influence CAPM equilibrium value—such as expected future earnings per share—are forecasts that are not directly observable. Even the market's "consensus" forecasts of these variables are not observable. Conse-

quently, substitute or proxy variables must be found if the theory is to be tested at all. These proxy variables will contain an unknown degree of measurement error.

2. Equation (14–7) is nonlinear, and the most powerful statistical tools available for testing purposes assume relationships are linear.

3. Some of the proxy variables may be determined by the security's actual market price, thus confusing cause and effect and possibly affecting the measured relationship's magnitude and statistical significance.

Keeping in mind that the existence of these problems can affect the degree of faith one has in any empirical observation, we now attend empirically to confirming the basic concepts of valuation.

Hypotheses to Be Tested

The theory of value suggests the following hypotheses:

1. Price/earnings ratios are a function of the expected future growth in dividends, the dividend payout rate, and the equilibrium-demanded return (which is related to risk).

2. Dividends are dependent upon the earnings generated by the firm and the volume of funds that are retained to maintain the production process or provide for its growth.

3. Risk is measured by the security's beta coefficient (β).

4. Because of the discounting process involved in valuation, future expected dividends are worth less than current dividends.

5. Growth is of value only if it creates expectations of higher future dividends, not just higher expected future earnings.

Subsidiary questions that arise out of these general hypotheses include:

1. How important are expectations of future earnings and dividends relative to dividend payout and risk in determining value?

2. To what extend can differences among stock prices be explained by observable proxy variables?

3. What association exists between β and the firm's accounting or operating characteristics?

4. How stable is risk over time?

A Regression Study of Price/Earnings Ratios

The degree of association or goodness of fit among financial relationships can be assessed with standard multiple regression analysis. In regression analysis a linear equation of the form

(14–16)   ***Valuation Regression***

$$\left(\frac{P}{E}\right)_i = a_0 + a_1\,(\text{payout}_i) + a_2\,(\text{growth}_i) + a_3\,(\text{risk}_i) + e_i$$

is estimated to find the coefficients that best "explain" the cross-sectional variability among firms' price/earnings ratios. If the variables on the right-hand side of the expression explain a good deal of the observed variability in price/earnings ratios of firms, the result is evidence in support of valuation theory.[12]

A number of regression studies of stock value have been undertaken. Among the most interesting were two that attempted a comparison between a set of right-hand-side variables constructed from an historical base and a set constructed from the expectations of a group of professional security analysts. This approach is intriguing because it comes to grips with the issue of whether the market is overly reliant on historical numbers in its valuation of securities.

The two sets of numbers (historical and expectational) are compared with two sets of regressions. The historical regressions use the explanatory variables: recent past payout ratio, 5 to 10-year average historical growth of the firm, a number of historical risk variables—including the historical beta coefficient. The expectational regressions use the explanatory variables: average of analysts' expected payout next year based on next year's earnings, average of analysts' five-year growth expectations for the firm's earnings, a number of risk variables—including Value Line's estimate of beta. In each case the regression equations are estimated for a number of different points in time.

The results of these regressions can be summarized in the following way:

1. The payout ratio and growth are important determinants of value. In all equations for all years payout and growth positively affected P/E ratio, and the relationship was always statistically significant.

2. The explanatory power of the expectational regressions is substantially greater than that of the historical regressions. The R^2 values average about .5 for the historical explanatory variables and .75 for the expectational variables. Thus, the market does not simply rely on the past to predict the future.

3. Risk, as measured by the beta coefficient usually had a negative effect on the P/E ratio, as theory indicates it should. However, the coefficient was not always statistically different from zero, and occasionally had the wrong sign. In addition, sometimes other risk variables did a better job of explaining the cross-sectional variation in the P/E ratio. The most probable explanation of this goes back to our discussion of beta in Chapter 11—there is a good deal of error associated with attempts to estimate a firm's nondiversifiable risk.

4. The coefficients change over time as different market-wide factors affect the

---

[12]For this empirical procedure to give efficient, consistent, and unbiased estimates, however, these conditions must be met:

   (1) The direction of association must run from the right-hand side variables (independent variables) to the left-hand side variable (no "simultaneity").

   (2) The variables must have probability distributions that result in e_i being normally distributed with a *constant* variance irrespective of the value of any of the independent variables (no "heteroskedasticity").

   (3) There must be no omitted variables that are related to one or more of the other independent variables (no "equation misspecification").

   (4) The variables must be properly measured (no "variable misspecification").

To the extent that one or more of these conditions is not met, the regression equation may be unable to confirm or deny the hypothesis being tested.

overall value of the market portfolio. For instance, the coefficients are much different in periods when interest rates are high than when they are low.

The regressions give something of a global look at the things that influence value. They allow us to draw broad generalizations regarding how security prices are formed— that payout, growth, and risk are influential in setting stock market prices. Unfortunately, they don't allow us to describe the finer points of the market's valuation process. However, there are empirical techniques that have been widely used in finance to look at the specifics of market valuation. These techniques go by the name of event studies, and we discuss them next.

Event Studies of Security Value

Managers periodically supply information to the market, or signal the market, regarding the operations of the firms they manage. Information also comes from analysts who have investigated the firm, and from other individuals or agents who publish information that may be relevant to the firm's success or failure (e.g., regarding general economic conditions). If this information does not change the expectations of investors regarding the dividends to be received in the future or the rate at which those dividends are discounted, investors will simply earn the equilibrium-expected return, $E(\tilde{R}_i)$.

However, if the information causes a change in expectations, the price of the security will change accordingly. In this case, the actual return that an investor receives during the period in which the market reacts to the information would be different from the equilibrium-expected return. We can use this knowledge to test the validity of theoretical valuation models if we can establish a link between the information published and the resulting market price.

For example, there is a natural link between reported earnings, the expectations of future profitability, and future dividends. So, if firms that announce substantial increases in earnings per share supply higher actual returns than expected in the period surrounding the announcement, there is support for the notion that future dividend expectations affect firm value.

Measuring the importance of the information conveyed can be accomplished simply by observing the difference between actual returns and those that might logically have been expected in the absence of the information.[13] This number is,

(14–17)   ***Excess, Abnormal, or Residual Return***

$$u_{it} = R_{it} - E(\tilde{R}_i)$$

where R_{it} is the actual return on security i during time period t, and u_{it} is the excess, abnormal, or residual return on the same security during that time period. If information that changes expectations is released during t, the value of u_{it} will be different from zero.

---

[13]Different studies have used different values for the expected equilibrium return. The most widely used measures of $E(\tilde{R}_i)$ include

$$R_{ft} + \beta_i [R_{mt} - R_{ft}] \qquad \text{Ex Post CAPM}$$

$$\alpha_i + \beta_i R_{mt} \qquad \text{Market Model}$$

A number of informational events or signals have been studied, using the abnormal return measure. Usually, these studies identify a sample of firms with similar signals. The abnormal return values are calculated for each firm in the sample and averaged, or

Average Residual

$$u_t = \frac{1}{J} \sum_{i=1}^{J} u_{it}$$

Where u_t measures the average abnormal return on the sample of J firms in period t, and $t = 0$ represents the point in time at which the signal is delivered to the market. Sometimes the average residual is accumulated over time for periods from well before the signal, at τ say, to well after it. Thus, the cumulative abnormal return is,

Cumulative Average Residual

$$CAR_T = \sum_{t=\tau}^{T} u_\tau$$

These **cumulative average residuals** (CAR's) are presented in Table 14–5 for two studies of earnings and dividend announcements, which illustrate the connection between such announcements and the performance of the firms making them. The results suggest that both earnings and dividend signals convey information to the market that the market considers useful to the estimation of value. We would argue that the linkage most consistent with the results is as shown in Figure 14–3. To see that the results confirm this hypothesis, note the 16.8 percentage point differential (7.3 percent and −9.5 percent) between the two columns of the first study. The major difference between the firms in these two columns is the nature of the signal regarding the firms' annual earnings in time period 0. The other columns in the table show better performance for firms reporting higher earnings, and firms that announced changes in dividends (the vast majority of which were positive changes). Firms reporting high earnings that increased dividends in the few months prior to the earnings report performed the best. Low-earnings-performing firms did the worst. All of these numbers suggest that reported earnings cause significant revisions in expectations, and, thereby, the value of the security.

Finally, Neiderhoffer and Regan [1972] found a strong association between actual reported earnings changes and changes in stock price over both a one-year and five-year period. They compared the earnings-per-share figures for the 50 stocks that had the largest increase and the largest decrease (percentages) in stock price in 1970 and in the 1966–

$\gamma_0 + \gamma_1 \beta_i$	Ex Post Security Market Line
$\dfrac{1}{N} \sum_{t=1}^{N} R_{it}$	Average Historical Return

All of the measures estimate β_i in periods other than t. The first two measures are simply ex post versions of models we have previously discussed. The third expression arrives at the parameters γ_0 and γ_1 by estimating the relationship between risk and return in the market in period t. The fourth expression simply says the best estimate of the expected return on a security is the return it has generated in the past.

TABLE 14–5   Cumulative Excess Return Values, CAR

Earnings per Share Performance

Month relative to announcement month	(1) Ball and Brown		(2) Pettit							
	Positive	Negative	High Quartile		Moderately High Quartile		Moderately Low Quartile		Low Quartile	
			A*	B*	A	B	A	B	A	B
−11	.7	−.8	−.1	.7	−.2	.3	−.5	.2	−.7	.1
−10	1.5	−1.8	−.2	1.5	−.7	.6	−1.1	.4	−1.4	.3
−9	1.7	−2.3	−.5	2.3	−1.2	1.1	−1.5	.6	−2.1	.5
−8	2.2	−2.9	−.9	2.8	−1.9	1.5	−2.0	.8	−2.7	1.0
−7	2.7	−4.0	−1.1	3.5	−2.4	1.7	−2.4	1.0	−3.6	1.4
−6	3.4	−5.2	−1.2	4.0	−3.2	2.0	−3.1	1.3	−4.4	1.6
−5	3.9	−5.9	−1.4	4.6	−4.0	2.3	−3.6	1.6	−5.3	1.5
−4	6.0	−7.0	−1.9	5.0	−4.6	2.9	−4.2	1.8	−6.0	1.4
−3	6.0	−7.8	−2.4	5.2	−5.2	3.3	−4.5	1.9	−6.8	1.4
−2	5.8	−8.1	−2.8	5.4	−5.7	3.6	−4.7	2.0	−7.5	1.1
−1	6.2	−8.7	−2.7	5.3	−6.2	3.8	−5.2	2.0	−8.1	.8
0	7.3	−9.5	−2.6	5.3	−6.6	3.6	−5.6	2.1	−8.7	.8
+1	7.6	−10.1	−2.7	5.3	−7.1	3.3	−6.0	1.9	−9.0	.7
+2	7.8	−10.3	−3.1	4.7	−7.4	3.0	−6.3	1.8	−9.1	.9
+3	7.9	−10.5	−3.4	4.1	−7.9	2.9	−6.6	1.5	−9.0	1.1
+4	7.9	−10.8	−3.8	3.1	−4.3	2.8	−6.8	1.4	−9.0	1.2
+5	7.7	−10.9	−4.4	2.3	−8.6	2.7	−6.8	1.2	−8.9	1.2
+6	7.4	−11.1	−5.0	1.6	−8.9	2.5	−6.9	1.3	−9.0	.9

*Column A for each quartile includes those firm months in which no change in dividend has been made for at least 12 months. Column B includes those firm months in which a change in dividends had occurred in the prior 12 months. For those firms that changed dividends, by far the largest portion were dividend increases.
Source: Ball and Brown [1968], and Pettit [1972].

FIGURE 14–3

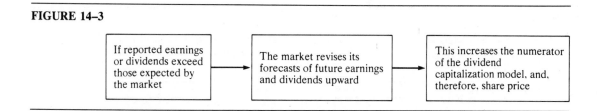

70 period. These comparisons are shown graphically in Figure 14–4(a) and (b). For comparison, figures are also shown for a set of 50 randomly selected stocks.

The top 50 performers in 1970 had a median increase in stock price of 48.4 percent and a median increase in earnings per share of 21.4 percent. These figures compare with the bottom 50 performers that had a median decrease in share price of 56.7 percent and a decrease in earnings of 83 percent! The close correspondence between earnings and share price is even more apparent for the five-year period where a 200 percent median increase in earnings was matched by a 182 percent increase in share price. On the lower side the bottom 50 price performers (62 percent decrease in share price) had earnings decreases averaging 61 percent. In the long run, earnings exert considerable control over stock prices.

Are Stock Prices Too Volatile to Be Explained by Earnings or Dividend Expectations?

Whether stock prices rationally reflect intrinsic value or underlying worth is an empirical question. That is, as investors revise their estimates of future dividends and earnings, stock prices rationally would reflect these revisions; at least that is what theory would predict. This contention has been questioned by some who feel that stock prices are much more volatile than either dividend or earnings valuation models would predict. This "observation" has led some to ask if the stock market may be subject to waves of speculative optimism or pessimism that are not consistent with valuation theory as we have presented it.

Of course we would expect that for some firms in some situations, there is a good deal of stock price volatility. A firm that announces a surprise 10 percent positive increase in earnings would not necessarily anticipate a 10 percent increase in stock price. That would depend on how expectations of future earnings and dividends are altered by the announcement, whether those revisions in expectations are on earnings in the near term or farther out in the future, and what the discount rate is.

Nevertheless, we would expect that the volatility of stock prices, on average in the long run and over many securities, would reflect the volatility of earnings, dividends and the discount rate. The question is, does it? The answer is subject to heated debate these days in financial markets. Some empirical studies have suggested that stock prices are many times more volatile than the pattern of dividend payments would predict. Other studies have suggested that these empirical tests are deficient by not properly incorporating the tendency that managers have to "smooth" dividends and reported earnings. Still others have suggested that the empirics are deficient by assuming that the rate at which the

FIGURE 14–4

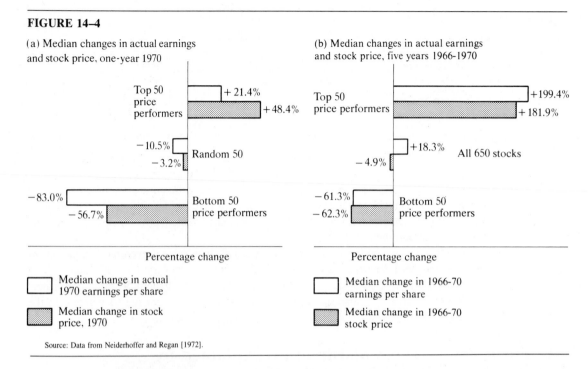

(a) Median changes in actual earnings
and stock price, one-year 1970

(b) Median changes in actual earnings
and stock price, five years 1966-1970

Top 50 price performers: + 21.4% / + 48.4%

Random 50: − 10.5% / − 3.2%

Bottom 50 price performers: − 83.0% / − 56.7%

Percentage change

Top 50 price performers: +199.4% / + 181.9%

All 650 stocks: +18.3% / − 4.9%

Bottom 50 price performers: − 61.3% / − 62.3%

Percentage change

☐ Median change in actual 1970 earnings per share

▨ Median change in stock price, 1970

☐ Median change in 1966-70 earnings per share

▨ Median change in 1966-70 stock price

Source: Data from Neiderhoffer and Regan [1972].

dividends are discounted is constant. In other words, a significant portion of the variability of stock prices over some periods can be traced to shifts in the security market line.

Exactly where this debate will end is not clear. It is clear that earnings, dividends, the discount rate, and information relating to these variables does affect stock prices in the predicted direction with little elapsed time. What is not clear is whether stock market prices are more volatile than can be explained by changes in expectations of these variables. This issue is an important one for understanding the basis from which security values are determined. If excessive optimism and pessimism characterize the marketplace (which implies that even a number of rational investors can't correct things by attempting to take advantage of the "disequilibrium"), we've got more work to do.

Integration of Valuation Theory with Portfolio Choice

Where do we go from here? Ultimately, of course, we not only want to supply you with an understanding of how prices are established, which has been the major theme of the last few chapters, but also with an ability to use your knowledge of the process to make better investment choices. That is our next goal.

In particular, we now turn our attention to two closely related topics that are the purview of security analysts. The first is concerned with the use of concepts of valuation to assess whether there are differences between the underlying equilibrium value of a security and its current market price. The second topic is concerned with estimating the parameters that are required for identifying the efficient set and the optimal risky portfolio. To do this, you remember, requires estimates of each security's return (in equilibrium or disequilibrium), standard deviation of return, and each pair of security covariances (or correlations) of return. Collectively, these topics make up the subject of security analysis, and professional analysts are charged with the responsibility of supplying a body of knowledge that is useful to achieving these ends. The next two chapters address these subjects.

Summary

In this chapter we have attempted to lay out the basic ingredients of common-stock valuation. All valuation forms—whether they concentrate on earnings, growth, or investment opportunities—are derived from the same dividend capitalization model of equilibrium valuation,

$$P_{i0}^e = \sum_{t=1}^{\infty} \frac{E(\tilde{D}_{it})}{[1 + E(\tilde{R}_i)]^t}$$

This model and all of its derivatives attempt properly to incorporate expectations in a way that represents how securities should be valued in the market.

The variation in the value of common stock over time is caused by the revision of expectations accompanying information that may flow into the market. Ex post returns earned on stock investments will differ from those expected if there is any revision of expectations.

Anticipated growth will be reflected in share price so that growth stocks will not earn larger returns than other stocks with the same risk. Unanticipated growth (or decline) when realized in the market will lead to returns that are above (below) the equilibrium level.

Empirical support for the hypothesis that value is a function of dividend payout, growth, and risk is strong. Moreover, it appears that a substantial portion of the firm's value can ultimately be traced to its earning power.

References

Aharony, Joseph, and Swary, Itzhak. [1980] "Quarterly Dividend and Earnings Announcements and Stockholders Returns: An Empirical Analysis." *Journal of Finance* (March).

Ball, Ray, and Brown, Philip. [1968] "An Empirical Evaluation of Accounting Income Numbers." *Journal of Accounting Research* (Autumn).

Basu, S. [1977] "Investment Performance of Common Stocks in Relation to Their Price-Earnings Ratios: A Test of the Efficient Market Hypothesis." *Journal of Finance* (June).

Beaver, William. [1968] "The Information Content of Annual Earnings Announcements." *Journal of Accounting Research* 6 (Supplement).

Beaver, William H.; Kettler, Paul; and Scholes, Myron. [1970] "The Association between Market-Determined and Accounting-Determined Risk Measures." *Accounting Review* (October).

Beaver, William, and Manegold, James. [1975] "The Association between Market-Determined and Accounting-Determined Measures of Systematic Risk." *Jounal of Financial and Quantitative Analysis* (June).

Beck, Paul J., and Zorn, Thomas S. [1982] "Managerial Incentives in a Stock Market Economy." *Journal of Finance* (December).

Brown, Stephen J. and Warner, Jerold B. [1985] "Using Daily Stock Returns: The Case of Event Studies." *Journal of Financial Economics* (March).

Brown, Stephen J., and Weinstein, Mark I. [1985] "Derived Factors in Event Studies." *Journal of Financial Economics* (September).

Collins, D., and Dent, W. [1984] "A Comparison of Alternative Testing Methodologies Used in Capital Market Research." *Journal of Accounting Research* (Spring).

Eades, Kenneth M.; Hess, Patrick J.; and Kim, E. Han. [1985] "Market Rationality and Dividend Announcements." *Journal of Financial Economics* (December).

Fama, E. F., and Schwert, G. A. [1977] "Asset Returns and Inflation." *Journal of Financial Economics* (November).

Feldstein, Martin. [1980] "Inflation and the Stock Market." *American Economic Review* (December).

Flavin, Marjorie A. [1983] "Excess Volatility in the Financial Markets: A Reassessment of the Empirical Evidence." *Journal of Political Economy* (December).

Flood, Robert P., Hodrick, Robert J., and Kaplan, Paul. [1986] "An Evaluation of Recent Evidence on Stock Market Bubbles." Working Paper, National Bureau of Economic Research (July).

Graham, B., Dodd, R. and Cottle, S. [1962] *Security Analysis*. New York: McGraw-Hill.

Grinblatt, Mark S.; Masulis, Ronald W., and Titman, Sheridan. [1984] "The Valuation Effects of Stock Splits and Stock Dividends." *Journal of Financial Economics* (December).

Holt, C. C. [1962] "The Influence of Growth Duration on Share Prices." *Journal of Finance* (September).

Jaffe, J. F., and Mandelker, G. [1976] "The 'Fisher Effect' for Risky Assets: An Empirical Investigation." *Journal of Finance* (May).

Jones, Charles P.; Rendleman, Richard, J. Jr., and Latane, Henry A. [1985] "Earnings Announcements: Pre-and-Post Responses." *The Journal of Portfolio Management* (Spring).

Kalay, Avner, and Loewenstein, Uri. [1986] "The Informational Content of the Timing of Dividend Announcements." *Journal of Financial Economics* (July).

Kleidon, Allan W. [1986] "Variance Bounds Tests and Stock Price Valuation Models." *Journal of Political Economy* (forthcoming).

LeRoy, Stephen F., and Porter, Richard D. [1981] "The Present-Value Relation: Tests Based on Implied Variance Bounds." *Econometrica* (May).

Malatesta, Paul H. [1986] "Measuring Abnormal Performance: The Event Parameter Approach, Using Joint Generalized Least Squares." *Journal of Financial and Quantitative Analysis* (March).

Malatesta, Paul H., and Thompson, Rex. [1985] "Partially Anticipated Events: A Model of Stock Price Reactions with an Application to Corporate Acquisition." *Journal of Financial Economics* (June).

Malkiel, Burton, and Cragg, John. [1970] "Expectations and the Structure of Share Price," *American Economic Review* (September).

Mankiw, N. Gregory, Romer, David, and Shapiro, Matthew D. [1985] "An Unbiased Reexamination of Stock Market Volatility." *The Journal of Finance* (July).

Marsh, Terry A., and Merton, Robert C. [1986] "Dividend Variability and Variance Bounds Tests for the Rationality of Stock Market Prices." *The American Economic Review* (June).

Nerlove, Marc. [1968] "Factors Affecting Differences among Rates of Return of Investments in Individual Common Stocks." *Review of Economics and Statistics* 50.

Niederhoffer, Victor, and Regan, Patrick. [1972] "Earnings Changes, Analysts' Forecasts, and Stock Prices." *Financial Analysts Journal* (May–June).

Pettit, R. [1972] "Dividend Announcements, Security Performance, and Capital Market Efficiency." *Journal of Finance* (December).

Pettit. R. Richardson, and Westerfield, Randolph. [1972] "A Model of Capital Asset Risk." *Journal of Financial and Quantitative Analysis* (December).

Poterba, James M. [1986] "The Market Valuation of Cash Dividends: The Citizens Utilities Case Reconsidered." *Journal of Financial Economics* (March).

Rosenberg, Barr, and Guy, James. [1976] "Beta and Investment Fundamentals—II." *Financial Analysts Journal* (July–August).

Sauvain, Harry. [1959] *Investment Management.* 2nd ed. Englewood Cliffs, N.J.: Prentice-Hall.

Scholund, John Douglas. [1977] "An Investigation of Investor Expectations and Security Valuation." Ph.D. dissertation, Purdue University (August).

Schwendiman, Carl J., and Pinches, George E. [1975] "An Analysis of Alternative Measures of Investment Risk." *Journal of Finance* (March).

Shiller, Robert. [1981] "Do Stock Prices Move too Much to be Justified by Subsequent Changes in Dividends." *American Economic Review* (June).

Shiller, Robert J. [1986] "Fashions, Fads and Bubbles in Financial Markets." *Takeovers and Contests for Corporate Control* (forthcoming).

Summers, Lawrence. [1986] "Do Market Prices Accurately Reflect Fundamental Values?" *Journal of Finance* (July).

Vander Weide, James H., and Carleton, Williard T. [1985] "Investor Growth Expectations and Stock Prices." Working Paper, University of Arizona (December).

West, Kenneth D. [1984] "Speculative Bubbles and Stock Price Volatility." Financial Research Center, Memo (December).

Questions and Problems

1. Wall Street often seems to be preoccupied with a firm's earnings per share. This emphasis neglects the dividends of the firm, which, according to the dividend capitalization model, are the source of its value. What are the reasons for this concentration on the firm's earnings? How valid are earnings as an indicator of the firm's future dividend-paying ability?

2. Wall Street often seems preoccupied with the *growth* of earnings as an indicator of the firm's ability to pay future dividends, and of its value. Discuss (using Figure 14–2, perhaps) the problems associated with excessive concentration on earnings growth to determine value.

3. Detroit Edison is a public utility operating in a stable market and is expected to experience earnings growth at the rate of 6 percent. Next year's earnings are expected to be $2.40, and the firm in the long run expects to pay out 65 percent of all earnings as dividends. If the slope and intercept of the security market line are .08 and .08, respectively, and the firm's beta is .5, find the stock's value.

4. Using recent-past reported earnings and dividends for the S&P 500 index (available in S&P's Statistical Service—Security Price Index Record in your library), estimate the current underlying value of the index, $P_{S\&P0}$. (You are to derive a number of input values, including future dividends and a discount rate. Explain how you arrived at these estimates. You may choose to use any of the valuation models introduced in the chapter.)

5. GTE has an outstanding issue of preferred stock paying a $2.48 dividend annually. The stock also is callable at a price of $30 per share. If its risk-free rate is .06, the slope of its SML is .07, and its beta is .5, what is your estimate of its value?

6. Microsmooth is just going public, and you are asked by the firm's investment banker for your opinion of the security's value. The numbers you report are to help set a price at which the security will be offered. Microsmooth does not anticipate paying a dividend for three years, because its cash needs for investment opportunities will be great. During that time earnings are expected to grow rapidly and reach $4.50 per share by the end of year 3. The firm then plans on paying out 10 percent of earnings as an initial dividend. Dividends are expected to grow at a rate of 55 percent for the next seven years as the firm becomes profitable and cash is freed up. By year 11 you believe the market for the firm's products will have matured, and earnings and dividends will grow at the more normal rate of 9 percent from then on. Microsmooth's beta is estimated at 2.0,

and other publicly traded securities with the same risk currently offer equilibrium-expected returns of 17 percent. The current risk-free rate is 7 percent.

a. What is your estimate of the value of the security?

b. If you are correct and have precisely identified its true underlying value and that price is used as the offering price, what return will stockholders realize over time? Will that return vary depending on whether it is generated in the company's high-growth or normal-growth phase?

7. From a discussion with Microsmooth's chief executive officer (refer to problem 6) about product development plans, you have the impression that the new stock's beta would be higher than you originally thought. You revise your estimate of beta to 2.4. How does this change your estimate of the stock's value?

8. At the present time the price/earnings ratio of General Motors (based on next year's expected earnings) is 13, Data General's is 18, and USX's is 9. Identify the factors that, in general, account for cross-sectional differences in P/E ratios.

9. Although General Motors' price/earnings ratio now is 13, three years ago, computed in the same way, it was 17, and six years ago it was 5. How can you explain this great variation? Does it indicate that firms like General Motors often are severely underpriced or overpriced, i.e., in disequilibrium?

10. Price/earnings ratios are sometimes computed using the most recent past earnings of the firm. How can this computation lead to unwarranted conclusions about the market's expectations for the firm's future?

11. Ted Broome prepared the data in the table below to assist in evaluating Delta's common stock as a possible investment.

a. Calculate the required rate of return on Delta's stock, using the capital-asset pricing model.

b. List and briefly describe the specific variables that determine the nominal required rate of return for a stock.

c. Ted is considering investing in Delta stock with a two-year investment horizon. He forecasted next year's dividend at $.80 per share and the second year's dividend at $1.00 per share. Using the P/E ratio approach, Ted forecasted the price of Delta two years hence at $45^1/4$. Calculate the current value of Delta's stock, using a dividend valuation model and the required rate of return you calculated in answering part (a) above. Show all calculations.

d. Ted also is considering the purchase of People Express stock, which pays no dividend. Does this mean that the value of People Express stock is not the present value of all future dividends? Explain your answer.

e. Discuss the applicability of the constant-growth valuation model to true-growth companies.

CFA

Selected Stock Data

	Delta	*People Express*
Dividend (last 12-months)	$.60	None
P/E ratio (last 12-months earnings)	6.4X	14.6X
Current price	$40	$8 1/4
Forecasted dividend growth rate	25%	40%
Forecasted dividend payout ratio	18.0% (constant)	0.0% (for 5 years) 20.0% (after 5 years)
Stock beta	1.15	1.40
Risk-free rate of return	8%	
Expected return on market	14%	

12. Metabolic Business Automaton (otherwise known as MBA) is a company specializing in the production of decision-making aids for corporations. MBA's market is large and growing rapidly. One analyst privately has predicted that past and future investment opportunities available to the firm (new markets, etc.) will allow it to generate a 25 percent growth in earnings over the next eight years.

To finance this growth, the firm will have to retain all of its earnings for two years, after which it can pay out 25 percent of its earnings until the end of year 8. After that time it will pay out 60 percent of its earnings and grow at the economy-wide rate of 8 percent to infinity. Current earnings are $.80 per share.

a. Assuming the analyst believes the security market line has an intercept and slope of .09 and .08, and that the firm's beta is 1.5, set up an equation and find this analyst's estimate of the underlying value of MBA.

b. Suddenly, the analyst is affected by the winds of change. He receives information from the FTC suggesting that the firm's major product is a hoax with little real value. Discuss how input parameters to the analyst's valuation model might change with this information.

CHAPTER

15

Security Analysis

The quantity of money that changes hands in the normal course of a day's trading on financial markets is large. The gains and losses recorded are enormous. The attendant wealth changes potentially recorded by these fluctuations serve as a constant incentive to those who hope to secure financial power and independence by anticipating price changes. Samuelson [1957] best describes this incentive.

> Suppose my reactions are not better than those of other speculators, but rather one second quicker . . . in a world of uncertainty, I note the consequences of each changing event one second faster than anyone else. I make my fortune not once, but every day that important events happen.

Can those who try to predict price changes really be successful, or is there so much competition for profits that the average returns go to zero?[1]

One of the primary purposes of security analysis is to predict these price changes by using the principles of valuation to determine if the underlying value of the security exceeds or falls short of the current market price.

The Production of Private Information

In earlier chapters we discussed the free flow of publicly available information and the impact of this information on security prices and capital market efficiency. Here we begin

---

[1]The *perfect competition* solution to this question implies that individuals would be compensated, depending on the skill and time they employ in the endeavor. That is, as in other labor markets, analysts, on average, would be paid according to their productivity.

a discussion of the *production of private information,* and the potential for such production to increase the wealth of those producing it.

The production of private information that may be useful in security selection is very similar to the production of any other service. An individual with talent views a perceived need for the service and enters the market (for information) in hopes of being adequately rewarded for his effort. Those with the greatest talent receive the greatest reward. There are a few respects, however, in which the production of information that may help identify undervalued or overvalued securities is different from other types of information. First, any information service about financial securities contains a great deal of uncertainty regarding its worth. An analyst who concludes that Standard Oil of California's offshore drilling efforts are likely to be highly profitable may be wrong or may be right, yet will not gain or lose if the market consensus (unbeknownst to the analyst) already incorporated this information into SD's share price. Thus, the incentive to produce information emerges, in part, from possible *differences* in beliefs as to what the future will bring. There is no point in searching for information already known to the market.

A second way in which information about financial securities differs from other types of information is in terms of possible rewards from its use. Valuable private information used to construct a portfolio of undervalued securities is worth more to the individual the larger his portfolio. Does this reduce the incentive for small investors to produce private information, putting them at a disadvantage in the securities markets? Not at all, because the information produced by a small investor can be sold to others to secure the reward (though it cannot be sold to all investors—else it becomes useless). For example, Joe Granville's *Market Report* is sold to a limited number of clients at a fairly high price. *Value Line,* on the other hand, is sold to a wider audience at a lower price.[2] Price and demand for the information will depend on the believability of the information and the ability of the producer to convince the customer of the quality of the service (perhaps much like an auto mechanic's services).

Whether an individual chooses to "market" the private information directly by using it as the basis for constructing portfolios (as a money manager would do), or indirectly by offering labor services to others (as a security analyst for a brokerage house or a mutual fund does) depends on things like the cost of production and the elasticity of demand for the service. Essentially, the producer of research and information has the same sort of production and pricing decisions to make as the producer of cars or textbooks.[3]

The third way financial information differs is that the value of most private information to the investor depends on its eventually being made public.[4] Standard Oil's price would

---

[2]Brokerage houses (both retail and institutional) typically choose either to sell research and analysis along with executions of customer orders (full service brokers) or to sell the two services separately (discount brokers and financial services firms). Those who choose to market the two services together are offering a tie-in sale. Research and analysis is given away to those who buy the firm's execution services. Unfortunately, this method of selling brokerage services provides the firm with the incentive to produce the kind of analysis that is (1) likely to result in an excess of transactions (too many buy and sell recommendations) or (2) likely to foster heterogeneous expectations among market participants. These incentives, if effective, would lead to a greater output of research and analysis and more executions than is optimal.

[3]This may be an appropriate point to bring up a topic dear to the heart of many of our students; namely: "If we know so much about securities markets why aren't we out there putting our knowledge to work?" Of course, what we have chosen to do is to sell (through a university salary) our expertise to others who may then choose to "apply" the knowledge. The selection of this method of production was based upon the nature of the analysis in which we have expertise, our wealth levels, and the elasticity of demand for the service.

move up only as the analyst released the private information to the securities market. The analyst has the incentive to publish the information just after taking the appropriate position in the security.

Moreover, the production and eventual publication of private information can aid in an optimal allocation of resources by causing security prices to be "better," in the sense of being based on a larger information set, or closer to underlying intrinsic value.[5]

Security Analysis and the Production of Private Information

In 1934 Benjamin Graham and David Dodd, in their book *Security Analysis,* specified the ingredients necessary for the successful analysis of individual securities. In their words,

> In that portion of the analyst's activities which relates to the discovery of undervalued, and possibly of overvalued securities, he is more directly concerned with market prices. For here the vindication of his judgment must be found largely in the ultimate market action of the issue. This field of work may be said to rest upon a two-fold assumption: first, that the market price is frequently out of line with the true value; and, second, that there is an inherent tendency for these disparities to correct themselves.

To emphasize the continued relevance of these points, the *Financial Analysts Journal* presented this quote on the front cover of its September 1984 issue. The same concepts are emphasized here with the attention to detail and precision required for successful analysis in complex securities markets.

Security analysis is concerned with two things:

1. Determining whether a given security is undervalued, correctly valued, or overvalued in the market.
2. Estimating the expected return and risk measures necessary for making portfolio choices.

The two activities are not independent, of course, but for clarity we discuss them separately.

In Chapter 11, by way of introduction, we identified three concepts of valuation—**personal value, market price,** and **equilibrium value.** Personal value is the investor's assessment of the true underlying value of the security. Market price is the equivalent assessment by the rest of the market. That is, the market price of the security reflects the aggregate of all investors' assessments of underlying value. Equilibrium value is the price that would prevail if full information were available to all market participants in an efficient

---

[4]The exception is private information that gives a more accurate figure for portfolio risk. An investor, using this information, can construct a portfolio more suitable to his preferences with better estimates. This information does not need to become common knowledge to allow the investor to be better off.

[5]That is, the production of information may help eliminate mispriced securities. This doesn't mean that all information will better the whole of society. Some may simply lead to arbitrary wealth transfers between security holders. For a discussion of this and other issues related to information production see: Grossman (1976); Hirshleifer (1971); and Rabinovitch and Owen (1978).

market. With which of these concepts of value is security analysis concerned? Security analysis attempts to **determine if differences exist between the equilibrium value and market price.** Not surprisingly, many attempts to identify this difference concentrate on future earnings, dividends, interest payments, risk, and the discount rate, as we discussed in earlier chapters.

Moreover, portfolio choice requires that the investor arrive at estimates of security returns, standard deviations, and covariances (or correlations) with other securities. With these numbers the portfolio choice problem can be solved, leading to a set of weights that gives the investor an explicit guide for investing. Thus, estimating these parameters is also part of the function of security analysis.

Analyst's Valuation

The value estimated for security i by analyst k was defined in Chapter 11 (Equation 11–3) as,

(11–3)   *Analyst's Valuation*

$$P_{i0}^k = \sum_{t=1}^{\infty} \frac{E^k(\tilde{D}_{it})}{[1 + E^k(\tilde{R}_i)]^t}$$

This is a multiperiod dividend capitalization model using the inputs (or forecasts) of the analyst. The numerator includes estimates of the cash flows the security will deliver in the future. The denominator is the investor's calculation of the rate at which those cash flows should be discounted to reflect the security's risk, the risk-free rate, and the premium per unit of risk in the market. If the market price of the security is equal to this assessment of value, the investor would conclude that the security is correctly priced by the market, or that the market price is an accurate estimate of the true underlying (intrinsic) value. In this case, the rate of return the analyst would expect to earn from holding the security is equal to the discount rate $E^k(\tilde{R}_i)$ that has been applied to the cash flow estimates.

Analyst's Expected (Disequilibrium) Return

If there is a difference between the analyst's estimate of value and the market price, then the return that can be earned by investing in the security, which we have labeled $\hat{R}_i$, will be different than $E^k(\tilde{R}_i)$. The actual value of $\hat{R}_i$ depends on how quickly the market recognizes that the current market price is incorrect, or how quickly it adjusts to reflect more closely the values that have been applied by our analyst. Thus, the return earned by the investor depends on (1) the difference, if any, between his assessment of value and the market's, and (2) the point in time the market recognizes the error that it has made, which leads to an adjustment in the market price of the security. The windfall gain accrues to the investor when this second step takes place, and not before.

The best illustration of this important element of security analysis can be made by considering the limits of the point at which the market reacts. In doing this we assume the investor is correct regarding his future expectations, for if he is incorrect the market price will not adjust as expected and no excess return will be earned.

First, suppose the market price adjusts as early as tomorrow to reflect the analyst's expectations. If so, a one-time capital gain in the amount of the percentage change in price is generated, or,

$$P_{i0}^m = \frac{P_{i,\text{Day } 1}^k}{(1 + \hat{R}_i)} \quad \text{or}$$

$$\hat{R}_i = \frac{P_{i \text{ Day } 1}^k - P_{i0}^m}{P_{i0}^m} = \frac{53 - 50}{50} = .06$$

Suppose you estimate the security's value to be $53 and the market price is $50. If the market comes to agree with your estimates tomorrow (perhaps because the information you correctly anticipated was announced), the price will jump to $53. The one-day return is 6 percent—a sizable excess return for a day's investing.

At the other extreme, suppose the market comes to agree with your assessment only slowly over many years as the firm publishes its earnings and announces its dividends. The market continually underestimates the value of the security, but by a smaller amount each period as the firm's results are made public.

In this case, the return the investor would expect to earn, per annum, can be reasonably represented by the solution to $\hat{R}_i$ in the model where the discounted value of future dividends is set equal to the current *market price*. That is, $\hat{R}_i$ is the internal rate of return in the model,

(15–1)
$$P_{i0}^m = \sum_{t=1}^{\infty} \frac{E^k(\tilde{D}_{it})}{(1 + \hat{R}_i)^t}$$

As an example, suppose an analyst estimates that USX is undervalued because foreign competition for USX's products has been overstated. Rather than expecting the market's misperception to be corrected in the next year or two, the analyst believes the true level of competition will be revealed slowly over the next 30 or 40 years as USX reports its results from operations. The rate of return for the next investment period is less than it would be if the market recognized its error in a period relatively close to the present.

In essence, the return per annum earned by the investor depends on *how* and *when* the market price adjusts to reflect the analyst's forecasts. In the general case, where that realization occurs at period T in the future, the value of $\hat{R}_i$ is given by

(15–2)
$$P_{i0}^m = \sum_{t=1}^{T} \frac{E^k(\tilde{D}_{it})}{(1 + \hat{R}_i)^t} + \frac{E^k(\tilde{P}_{iT})}{(1 + \hat{R}_i)^T}$$

The second term reflects the analyst's estimate of the present value of expected future dividends after T. $\hat{R}_i$ is the return earned on the assumption that the market agrees with the investor as of, but not before, T.

It is the value of $\hat{R}_i$ that is required as an input into the portfolio choice model. It should be substituted for $E(\tilde{R}_i)$ in the set of inputs used for calculation of the optimal portfolio weights when the investor identifies a difference between market price and his estimate of value. Now to some applications.

GAF Illustration

Let's refer back to the GAF illustration in the Chapter 14. There we represented (Table 14–2) the equilibrium value, or intrinsic value, of GAF to be $35^1/_2$. Now suppose that analyst k's investigation leads to the same inputs and the same $35^1/_2$ value (i.e., k has come up with the "correct" estimate of equilibrium value). In addition, suppose the current market price is $32. Thus, our analyst believes the security is undervalued, and should provide a higher return than could be expected from other securities with the same risk. How much higher, as we just indicated, depends on when the market "corrects" itself. If k believes that correction will take five years to complete (perhaps it will take five years of operating results to convince the market that a 22 percent supernormal growth rate for six years is reasonable), the return is given by solving

$$(15\text{–}3) \quad \$32 = \frac{\$.30}{(1 + \hat{R}_{GAF})^1} + \frac{\$.75}{(1 + \hat{R}_{GAF})^2} + \frac{\$1.25}{(1 + \hat{R}_{GAF})^3}$$
$$+ \frac{\$2.00}{(1 + \hat{R}_{GAF})^4} + \frac{\$3.00 + \$60.}{(1 + \hat{R}_{GAF})^5}$$

for $\hat{R}_{GAF}$, which is 16.53 percent. Note that the expected dividends are those given in Table 14–2, and the value of $P^k_{GAF}{}^5$ is the discounted value of expected dividends from that time forward (and is given in the "Value" column of the table). This return is larger than the discount rate of 14.15 percent, based on GAF's beta of 1.2, but not by much because of the relatively long period estimated for the correction to take place and the small difference between the estimate of value, $35^1/_2$, and the current market price, $32.

DEC Illustration

The Digital Equipment example in Table 14–3 can be used for a second illustration. Once again, suppose the analyst estimates the value to be $126 ($P^k_{DEC,0} = 126$). DEC's current market price is $110. In this case, however, k thinks the market will come to form the same expectations he has when the *next fiscal year's results* are published in 12 months. $\hat{R}_{DEC}$ is

$$\$110.00 = \frac{E^k(\tilde{D}_{DEC,1}) + E^k(\tilde{P}_{DEC,1})}{(1 + \hat{R}_{DEC})^1} = \frac{\$.00 + \$142.78}{(1 + \hat{R}_{DEC})^1}$$

$$\hat{R}_{DEC} = \frac{\$142.78 - \$110}{\$110} = .298 \text{ or } 29.8\%$$

which is way above the discount rate of 13.45 percent. Stated another way, given DEC's β, it plots well above the security market line.

In both the GAF and DEC cases, of course, the return figures, $\hat{R}_{GAF}$ and $\hat{R}_{DEC}$, are part of the private information set produced by the analyst.

How Large Can the $\hat{R}_i$ Values Be?

This discussion brings to light three questions that ought to be asked by each and every investor (three questions that play a part in the decision to engage in security analysis): (1) whether and how far market prices depart from the underlying, or full information equilibrium, value, (2) how long it takes before the market adjusts price to correspond to the underlying value, and (3) whether the investor has sufficient skill, ingenuity, and inclination to recognize when and by how much market price has departed from equilibrium value. The first two questions address the issue of how different are $\hat{R}_i$ and $E(\hat{R}_i)$.

In a very general sense, at least, we have access to data relevant to the first question. We know there are major differences in the returns actually generated on securities within a given time period. During the period between 1960 and 1985, for example, the difference in annual returns between the worst-performing 10 percent of NYSE securities, and the best-performing 10 percent of NYSE securities averaged about *80 percentage points* (e.g., -35 percent to $+45$ percent). The figures for over-the-counter securities are even more disperse. Thus, the potential reward for the production of private information that can capture even a small portion of the real differences between actual returns and expected returns is enormous. The second and third questions are considered in the rest of the chapter and are resolved eventually by what happens when an investor attempts to determine security values.

Security Analysis

To make the concepts of valuation practical, we only need to consider those things that account for the differences between the analyst's estimate of value and the market price [or between $\hat{R}_i$ and the analyst's estimate of the expected equilibrium return, $E^k(\hat{R}_i)$]. To see those differences, consider the dividend capitalization model from the perspectives of both the market and analyst k, or

$$(15\text{--}4) \qquad P_{i0}^m = \sum_{t=1}^{\infty} \frac{E^m (\tilde{D}_{it})}{(1 + R_f^m + \beta_i^m [E^m (\tilde{R}_m) - R_f^m])^t}$$

$$(15\text{--}5) \qquad P_{i0}^k = \sum_{t=1}^{\infty} \frac{E^k (\tilde{D}_{it})}{(1 + R_f^k + \beta_i^k [E^k (\tilde{R}_m) - R_f^k])^t}$$

Of course, the two can differ if investor k and the rest of the market hold different views regarding any of these:

1. Expected future dividends.
2. The risk-free interest rate (applied in some future period), or the intercept of the SML.
3. Beta.
4. The compensation required per unit of risk by the market, or the slope of the SML.

Each of these factors will be discussed in the pages that follow. Differences between the market and the analyst with regard to them determines how much a security is over- or undervalued. In addition to $\hat{R}_i$, we discuss the standard deviation and correlation with other securities, which are necessary inputs for portfolio choice.

Dividends and Earnings

Dividends are the key cash flow affecting the value of a stock, and interest payments are the key cash flow affecting the value of a bond. This means that earnings, which determine a firm's dividend and interest distributions, are central to valuation. Of course, this message should have come through loud and clear in our prior discussion.

A summary of the empirical relationship between earnings and market prices is presented in Figure 15–1. We have drawn two lines parallel to a hypothetical security market line. The top line is about 7 percentage points above the SML and represents the average level of excess returns over a 12-month period on firms that announced positive earnings surprises. The bottom line, 9.5 percentage points below the SML, indicates the negative excess returns on firms that announced negative earnings surprises.

Alternatively, suppose you calculated the actual, observed relationship between reported earnings and stock prices. Then, if you could *perfectly forecast* earnings, how much would you benefit from this knowledge? Brealey [1969] answered this question, in part, with a study of 48 firms that showed an average return over a 14-year period of

---

FIGURE 15–1   **Differences in Annual Returns for Firms with Positive and Negative Earnings Surprises**

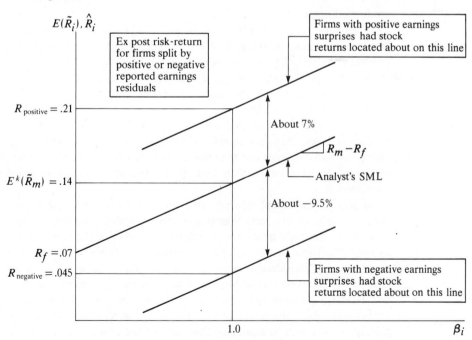

12 percent. He selected, at the beginning of each year, the eight stocks that subsequently (at the end of that year) reported the top percentage increase in earnings. With this "perfect knowledge" he earned an average annual return of 30 percent! Earnings, in sum, are very important to stock analysis and valuation, and this is appropriately emphasized by Wall Street analysts and security brokers.

We next consider the determinants of earnings, the difference between *reported* earnings and *normalized* earnings or earning *power,* the time series behavior of earnings, and the extent of the comovement (or correlation) of one firm's earnings with another's.

Determinants of Earnings

Operating Revenues and Costs.   The major determinants of a firm's earnings are the nature of the firm's operations. This fact was emphasized in Figure 14–2. Production, sales, and the costs of factors of production all directly affect pretax earnings. A new method of production that cuts operating costs by $100,000 (with no other changes) will result in an increase in pretax earnings of a like amount. Similarly, a sales increase of 10 percent at the same unit price will result in a 10 percent increase in profits if per unit costs are constant.

In fact, firm i's total earnings, Y_i, can be expressed as

$$Y_i = (\text{Price}_i)(\text{units sold}_i) - (\text{cost of units produced}_i).$$

Thus, net income before tax and interest is given by price times quantity sold less production costs.

In general, a firm's revenues will be governed by its share of the market, by changes that may take place in the size of the market, and by the elasticity of demand for the product produced. The costs of operation will be influenced by the same considerations in the market for the firm's factors of production. Moreover, since earnings are determined by the difference between revenues and costs, the importance of these factors to the firm's level of profitability is clear.

If the firm has some control over the cost of factors of production as demand for its product changes, then profits will not be so variable (as revenues change, costs tend to change in a like manner and magnitude). On the other hand, if costs are fixed or do not rise as rapidly as revenues, then dollar profit fluctuations will be as exaggerated as dollar sales change.

In general, the extent to which costs of operations rise less than proportionally, rise proportionally, or rise more than proportionally with any increase in quantity demanded depends on the basic processes required to manufacture the goods or services produced by the firm. These factors will create costs which are essentially fixed and do not vary, or which vary considerably with changes in output. For example, a public utility that produces electric power with nuclear or water energy sources will have less variable costs and greater fixed costs than one using oil or natural gas. Ignoring the response of rate-setting authorities, the profits of the nuclear and water users will be more variable. The principle is no more complicated than the volume-cost-profit relationships discussed in the most basic finance, accounting, and economics books, though its application to understanding the profits of a particular firm could get very complex, of course.

TABLE 15–1

ELI LILLY & COMPANY
Balance Sheet Position
1985 ($000)

Assets		*Liabilities*	
Current assets	$1,940	Current liabilities	$1,046
Fixed assets	2,014	Long-term debt	239
		Equity	2,669
Total assets	$3,954	Total liabilities	$3,954

DELTA AIRLINES
Balance Sheet Position
1985 ($000)

Assets		*Liabilities*	
Current assets	$ 614	Current liabilities	$ 941
Fixed assets	3,013	Long-term debt	535
		Equity	2,151
Total assets	$3,627	Total liabilities	$3,627

As an example consider the (abbreviated) balance sheet and income statements of Delta Airlines and Eli Lilly and Company in Table 15–1. Both offer consumer goods in competitive industries. Both have reasonably unstable sales due mostly to revenue growth over the years. However, Delta Air Lines technology is such that most costs (airplane depreciation, repairs, landing fees, labor costs and fuel) are fixed and independent of the number of passengers flying on any given route in the short run. Lilly can more easily vary its expenditures on factors of production as demand changes. Essentially Lilly's **per unit** cost is fixed while Delta's **total costs** are fixed. Delta's operating profit margin varied between 3 and 21 percent over the decade while Eli Lilly's varied only from 24 to 29 percent. The effect on profit fluctuations is enormous, as seen in Figure 15–2 that plots index values for the two firms' earnings (with 1976 values at 100). In effect, the profit fluctuations are exaggerated at Delta because of fluctuating revenues and the low level of correlation between the firm's revenues and costs. In contrast, profit fluctuations at Lilly are dampened by their close correlation.

General statements regarding the standard deviation of earnings follow directly from this. The standard deviation will be greater: (1) the more variable are total revenues, (2) the more variable are total costs, and (3) the smaller the covariance between revenues and costs (since the term is *subtracted* by the rules for subtracting random variables).

Interest Charges. Interest charges are determined by the extent of a firm's borrowing. Especially in recent years, interest-rate fluctuations have caused some firms' earnings after interest to fluctuate much more than earnings before interest. Consider the case of Gibraltar Financial, for example, described in Figure 15–3. During the mid to late 1970s the heavily debt-laden Gibraltar's borrowing was mostly short term. As interest rates rose throughout the decade, total interest charges rose rapidly and after-interest profits fluctuated wildly—dependent almost totally on short-term interest rates. As interest rates have dropped in the mid-1980s the profits of Gibraltar have recovered.

The variability of the firm's earnings is attributable to the interest rate risk that is

FIGURE 15–2   Indexes of Earnings Levels (for Delta Airlines and Eli Lilly, 1976 = 100)

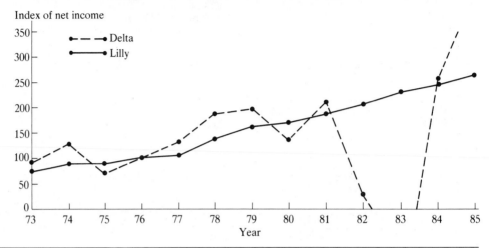

inherent in their extensive use of debt to finance the purchase of longer-term interest-bearing loans and investments. As more and more debt is used in financing the firm's operations, the variability and level of earnings per share will increase. Firms with more debt, other things constant, tend to have a greater level of earnings per share, and more variability in the level of earnings per share over time.

Taxes.   Between 1950 and 1986 the marginal statutory income tax rate for all but the smallest corporations has varied between 46 percent and 52 percent. The actual tax rate during the period varied substantially from firm to firm and industry to industry as a result of special tax and subsidy legislation built up over the 35-year-period. For example, Kaiser Aluminum paid 26 percent of its income in the form of taxes in 1975. By 1981 their average tax rate was a mere 5 percent. Merrill Lynch, on the other hand paid 51 percent and 43 percent in the same two periods. Partly in response to the different *incidence* of corporate taxation, the 1986 Tax Reform Act changed the corporate tax rate to a flat 34 percent and eliminated a number of major corporate tax shelters (e.g., the investment tax credit). This should result in a somewhat more uniform rate of taxation. As a result it should ease, somewhat, the problem analysts and other investors have in trying to measure corporate profitability. That is, as ambiguities regarding the long-term level of taxation of a firm diminish, after-tax reported profits will be less variable, and it should become easier to measure a firm's underlying earning power.

Normalized Earnings

During any fiscal period *there are differences between a firm's reported earnings and the firm's earning power*. The earning power of a firm is difficult to measure. Generally accepted accounting principles (GAAP) attempt to enforce consistency onto firms' reporting procedures, but are not specifically directed at providing financial statements that give an *accurate* picture of the underlying profitability of the firm during that period.

FIGURE 15–3   **Revenues, Interest Expense, and Earnings** (Gibralter Financial, 1985 = 100)

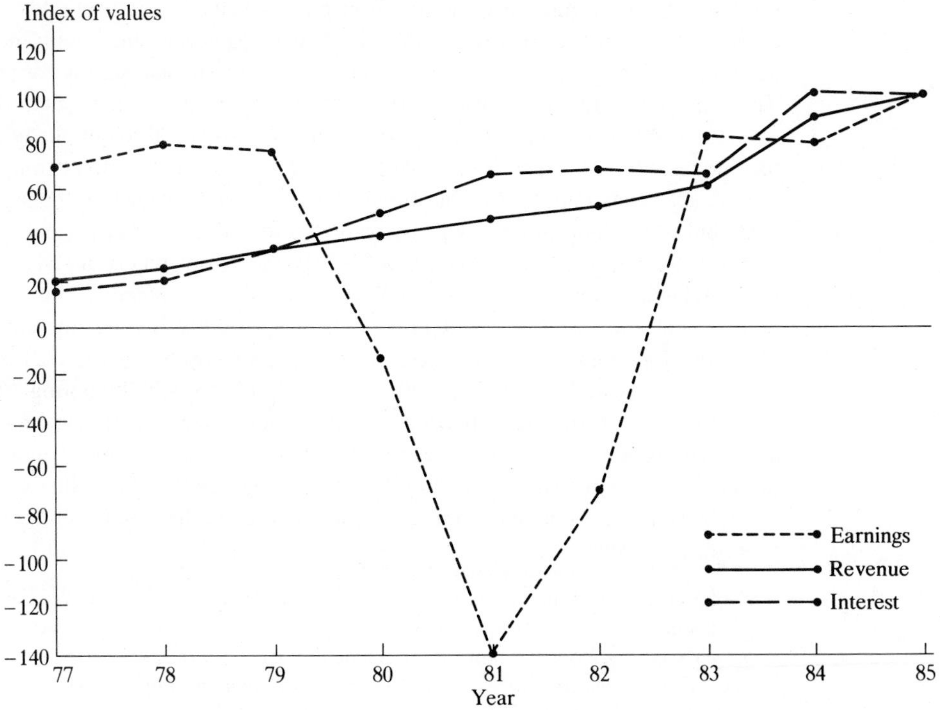

Moreover, it is unlikely that *any* auditing or monitoring system could accurately reveal a firm's true level of earnings.

Security analysts, on the other hand, are interested only in the *earning power* of the firm during the period, because that value has implications for future profitability and future dividends. Consequently, analysts spend time and effort with reported financial statements in their attempt to estimate the **normalized earnings** of the firm. Normalized earnings give the analyst a better picture of the current earning power of the firm than do unadjusted earnings.

The methods by which analysts transform reported earnings into normalized earnings differ substantially. Nominal adjustments include eliminating one-time charges or benefits, such as greater-than-normal investment tax credits. Other approaches involve estimating the extent to which some components of income have been "unearned." For example, it has been a characteristic of many firms that sell time-sharing units in campgrounds or condominiums to include all the proceeds from the sale of the unit into this period's revenues, even though the cash from the sale will be received and expenses will be incurred only over a 10-year period. In this case, the calculation of normalized earnings is uncertain because neither the revenues from this source, nor the costs to be incurred from this activity, are known. Estimating earning power, in other words, is itself a process accompanied by uncertainty.

None of this is meant to suggest that accounting methods are unimportant. Accounting for earnings serves as a basic and necessary step in the creation of useful valuation information. Moreover, accounting convention, properly applied, is an effective tool used by management to minimize the long-run present value of the firm's taxes.

However, noneconomic decisions with respect to accounting should not, and do not seem to, fool the market. There appears to be little or no "accounting for profit illusion." Thus, managing reported earnings so that they appear more stable than they really are over time or "manufacturing" temporary earning's growth through changing accounting techniques will not affect share price permanently. Temporary effects may be present as the market reacts initially to what (mis)information is conveyed by the accounting numbers, but in the long run this will be corrected for in the market price.

For example, one study (Archibald [1972]) of 69 firms that changed from accelerated to straight-line depreciation for reporting purposes concluded, "The switch-back announcement and resultant profit improvement apparently had no immediate substantial effect on stock market performance." Moreover, a study by Ball [1972] of 267 changes in *non-value related* accounting methods sums up his research by noting "that the market is not fooled by income reports which contain changes in accounting techniques." Finally, a study by Kaplan and Roll [1972] of 275 firms that switched from handling investment tax credits from deferral accounting to flow through and 57 firms that continued to use the deferral method concluded there were no important effects of the change in accounting procedures. They note:

> Earnings manipulation may be fun, but its profitability is doubtful. We have had difficulty discerning any statistically significant effect that it has had on security prices. Relying strictly on averages, however, one can conclude that *security prices increase around the date when a firm announces earnings inflated by an accounting change*. The effect appears to be temporary.

In spite of this evidence, many managers seem reluctant to take actions that negatively affect *reported earnings* while leaving unchanged *earning power*, taxes, and other variables that may have real effects on value. Many firms refused to adopt LIFO inventory reporting (not for tax purposes) fearing the one-time effect of such a change on reported earnings. Other studies have looked at oil and gas reporting methods and methods of accounting for mergers. No adverse or favorable accounting effect could be documented.[6]

It is even possible that increases in earnings generated by selective accounting practices may have a negative effect on a stock's price if the firm is perceived to be taking actions in an attempt to cover up or fool the market.

Of course, the analyst is required to investigate the impact of these accounting methods on reported earnings in order to have a sound basis for measuring the firm's normalized earnings.

---

[6]Kaplan [1975] cites the case of a *Business Week* (July 28, 1975) article regarding the use of deferred tax accounts for oil firms given that depletion allowances were changed by Congress. The tax account would artificially allow the effect of the reduction of depletion allowances to be written off over time—thus reducing the immediate effect on reported earnings and on retained earnings. One oil executive was quoted, "This is going to make oil stocks a lot less attractive because many investors do not look beyond the net income figure," and the story's conclusion, in part, noted that the *reduction* in retained earnings on the balance sheet through a direct restatement of retained earnings for the change will cause an increase in debt/equity ratios (by reducing book equity) which will make borrowing more difficult. Only if the market ignores easily available information, and if banks and other lenders ignore everything but book values, could such conclusions ever be drawn.

Properties of Earnings and Dividends

The earnings and dividends of a firm vary over time in at least two respects. First, earnings and dividends may experience growth or decline. Second, they may vary a little or a good deal from the time trend of growth or decline. Figure 15–4 pictures these two

FIGURE 15–4   Time Series of Earnings and Dividends, 1976–1985 (1976 = 100)

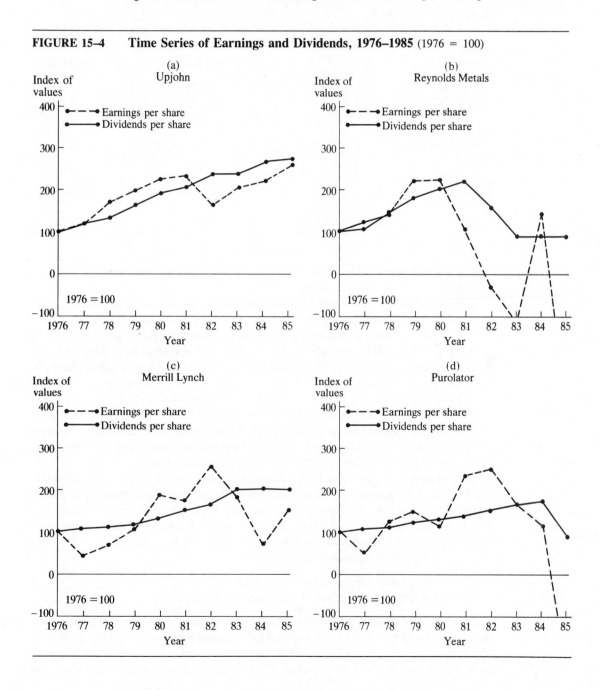

TABLE 15–2 Growth Rates of Revenues, Net Income, and Earnings (1976–1985)

	Revenue	*Net Income*	*Earnings per Share*
		Growth Rates	
Airlines			
Delta Airlines	11.8%	14.0%	17.0%
Piedmont Aviation	23.4	31.2	10.3
Security			
Purolator	9.3	1985 deficit	1985 deficit
Food			
Southland	19.3	18.2	13.2
Philip Morris	14.5	16.8	16.7
Railroad			
Burlington Northern	19.1	27.0	18.8
Brokerage			
Merrill Lynch	13.5	7.7	4.1
Drugs			
Eli Lilly	9.3	10.0	9.8
Chemical			
Monsanto	4.7	1985 deficit	1985 deficit
Oil			
Amoco	10.5	10.7	9.3

effects for four firms, using an index constructed from earnings per share and dividend per share figures with 1976 equaling 100.

Upjohn seems to have been able to maintain a steady growth of earnings and dividends over the decade. Merrill Lynch and Purolator both have paid steadily higher dividends over the years in spite of fluctuating earnings (at least until Purolator experienced a substantial loss in 1985). Reynolds Metals earnings and dividends have fluctuated considerably over the period, with dividends being flat or reduced when profits dropped off. Reynolds reduced dividends when a loss was generated from operations in 1983, but maintained that dividend level through another significant loss in 1985.

Table 15–2 compares revenue and earnings growth rates for a number of different firms in different industries. In general, there is a reasonably close association between the growth rates. Nevertheless, this is not a representative sample and only illustrates, rather than explains, the connection between revenues and earnings.

In more general terms, the reported earnings of a firm and its ability to pay dividends are influenced by a myriad of factors such as revenues, costs, and interest charges. In addition, these factors, and *thus* earnings, are affected by elements that are unique to a firm (e.g., management decisions) as well as by others that represent happenings in the macroeconomy. Is it possible to develop simple representations of the behavior of a firm's earnings? Two specific questions come to mind:

1. How do the earnings behave over time?
2. How are earnings related to macroeconomic events?

The first question clearly is relevant to forecasting future earnings. If the time series behavior of earnings is known, the analyst's job is made easier, but perhaps less profitable. The second question clearly is relevant to understanding what influences the profitability of a firm during a given time period. If earnings are down during a recession, the

TABLE 15–3   Serial Correlations between Changes in Net Income

	Net Income		Earnings per Share	
	Lag 1 Year	*Lag 2 Years*	*Lag 1 Year*	*Lag 2 Years*
Average over all firms	− .001	− .023	− .135	− .068
10 percent of firms with highest correlation	.406	.292	.152	.180
10 percent of firms with lowest correlation	− .418	− .307	− .416	− .304

implications are different from those of a decline caused by some poor management choices.

Time Series Behavior of Reported Earnings and Dividends.   If reported earnings of a firm fluctuate randomly about the overall trend of earnings, then the changes in earnings from period to period follow a **random walk.** Alternative descriptions would be that large positive changes in earnings in one year tend to be followed by large positive changes in the next (high profitability tends to follow high profitability), or that large positive changes in earnings tend to be followed by small or negative changes in the next.

Studies of the earnings behavior of individual firms strongly suggest that for most firms earnings changes closely follow some form of a random walk. For example, Foster [1986] reports correlations between the change in net income in one year and the change in the next year. This correlation, on average, over all firms, was − .001! Table 15–3 shows more detail of Foster's figures. These figures imply that neither this period's change in net income nor this period's change in earnings per share explain next period's value very well. Even for selected firms with the highest and lowest correlations (some created by chance alone) less than 20 percent of next year's changes could be explained by this year's changes ($-.418^2$ is only .174).

In effect, there simply is no strong evidence that the earnings, on average, behave in specific identifiable patterns. If this is true, then simple extrapolations from past trends ought to do just as well in forecasting future earnings as more "statistically sophisticated" models. We will see more evidence of this in Chapter 16.

On the other hand, *dividend changes over time do not seem to follow a random walk.* In fact, managers seem intent on smoothing the dividend pattern by increasing dividends slowly over time and only when profitability can justify the higher level. An equation that does a reasonable job of describing the actual changes in dividends for most firms, on average, is,

(15–6)   *Predicted Dividends*

$$\begin{matrix} \text{Dividend} \\ \text{change} \end{matrix} = 1.0 + .15 \begin{bmatrix} \text{This} \\ \text{period's} \\ \text{earnings} \end{bmatrix} - .30 \begin{bmatrix} \text{Last} \\ \text{period's} \\ \text{dividend} \\ \text{level} \end{bmatrix}$$

Thus, this period's change in dividends is equal to a constant plus the effect of the change in earnings less the effect of the level of dividends in the prior period. Moreover, unless the incentive for changing the dividend is fairly large (the prediction from the above equation is quite different from zero) there is a tendency for managers not to change dividends at all. By far the largest observed dividend "change" is zero.

In summary,

> *For Earnings.* Earnings per share and net income figures seem to follow a random walk with a trend. Thus, deviations about a trend line of earnings are random. Positive deviations do not tend to follow positive deviations any more than they follow negative deviations.[7]
>
> *For Dividends.* Dividend per share values seem to be inflexible downward and depend very much on earnings changes. Moreover, if the dividend level is already high (relative to earnings) the tendency is for firms to adopt smaller (perhaps zero) changes in dividends.

Earnings and Macroeconomic Activity.   We can think of a firm's earnings as consisting of one or more *common* (macro) elements and a *unique* (micro) element. Do a firm's earnings fluctuate because of the overall movement of the economy or industry or because of factors unique to that firm? One way of answering is to think of an index of a firm's earnings, an index of industry earnings, and an index of overall market earnings (such as the earnings of the S&P index or perhaps aggregate personal income). Then a simple time series regression of the firm's earnings index change (Δ) on the change in index values for the industry and economy will identify the importance of industrywide, marketwide, and unique components of earnings changes. For example, considering only marketwide influences, where Y_i is earnings of the firm, and Y_m is the market earnings,

(15–7)   *Market Model of a Firm's Earnings*

$$\Delta \text{ (index of } Y_i) = a_i + b_i \Delta \text{ (index of } Y_m) + \varepsilon_i$$

Change in the value of the firm's index of earnings	=	*A linear function of the change in value of a market index of earnings*	+	*The unique change in earnings of the firm.*

The coefficient b_i indicates the reaction of firm i's change in earnings to a similar value for the market. This is referred to as the security's **earnings beta.** The value ε_i represents the component of a firm's earnings not related to economywide factors. Of course, on average, over all securities b_i would be 1.0 and a_i would be zero. If, for a particular security, b_i was greater than 1.0, it would indicate that earnings changes tend to respond more than proportionally to a change in overall market earnings. If a_i is greater than zero, it indicates a higher-than-average growth of earnings. In a particular period, if ε_i is

---

[7]The best known of these studies are by Ball and Watts [1972], Little [1962], Raynor and Little [1966], Brealey [1969], and Lintner and Glauber [1972].

FIGURE 15–5   **The Relationship between Firms' Earnings and Market Earnings**

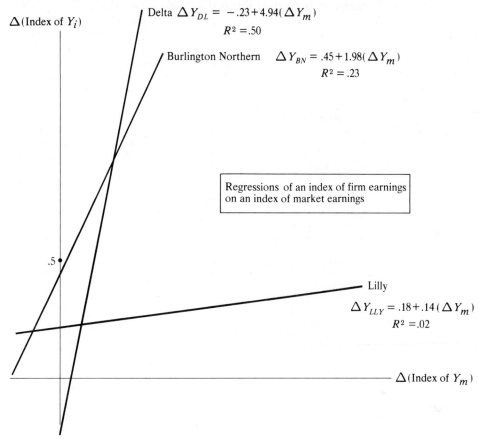

Delta $\Delta Y_{DL} = -.23 + 4.94(\Delta Y_m)$
$R^2 = .50$

Burlington Northern $\Delta Y_{BN} = .45 + 1.98(\Delta Y_m)$
$R^2 = .23$

Δ(Index of Y_i)

Regressions of an index of firm earnings on an index of market earnings

Lilly
$\Delta Y_{LLY} = .18 + .14(\Delta Y_m)$
$R^2 = .02$

Δ(Index of Y_m)

positive, it indicates a unique positive effect on the firm's earnings (one unrelated to factors that affect all firms). The b_i term in (15–7) represents the macro effect and ε_i represents the micro effect on the earnings of the firm.

This regression is performed for Eli Lilly Co., Burlington Northern, and Delta Airlines, using 13 years of annual earnings data (Figure 15–5). The market earnings values used were those of Standard & Poor's Composite Index of 500 Stocks. Delta's and Burlington Northern's earnings are very volatile relative to all corporate earnings, moving up and down about two to five times as much as any up or down movement of the S&P earnings index. Lilly's earnings are much more stable, changing less than 15 percent as much as the average corporation. In fact, there is little correlation ($R^2 = .02$) between Lilly's earnings and those of most other corporations (could it be due to its profits from the drugs it has developed and marketed?).

In more detail, the influence of industry earnings and aggregate U.S. corporate earnings on individual firms earnings is summarized in Table 15–4. These figures show the total explanatory power of industry and aggregate corporate net income on the income of 315

TABLE 15–4   **Influence of Aggregate U.S. Corporate Earnings and Industry Earnings on the Earnings of Individual Firms** (Coefficients of determination)

		Average R^2 Values			
	Industry	*Industry Earnings*	*Aggregate Corporate Earnings*	*Industry and Corporate Earnings*	*Number of Firms*
1.	Crude petroleum and natural gas	.23	.14	.35	18
2.	Paper and allied products	.60	.49	.61	15
3.	Drugs	.26	.14	.40	16
4.	Petroleum refining	.54	.37	.60	28
5.	Steel and blast furnaces	.53	.35	.58	17
6.	General industrial machinery and equipment	.29	.23	.44	12
7.	Radio and T.V. transmitting equipment	.17	.14	.29	14
8.	Electronic components	.37	.32	.44	10
9.	Trucking	.42	.21	.48	12
10.	Air transportation	.15	.12	.25	16
11.	Electric services	.39	.08	.47	61
12.	Natural gas distribution	.11	.13	.21	17
13.	Electric and other service combinations	.45	.06	.51	47
14.	Retail, grocery stores	.17	.09	.26	10
15.	State banks, Federal Reserve System	.25	.05	.30	22
	Totals	.36	.17	.43	315

Source: Foster [1986], p. 199.

large firms in 15 industries. The figures are average squared correlations generated through regressions similar to that presented above. There is a relatively close correlation between the profitability of individual firms and the larger economy. The inescapable conclusion is that comovement of firms' earnings is fairly strong, and probably helps to create the comovement evident in the returns on securities.

Risk or Beta

A firm's beta coefficient is the second factor (after $\tilde{R}_i$) an analyst must have knowledge of to determine the value of a security (or to calculate $E^k(\tilde{R}_i)$ for comparison with $\hat{R}_i$ to find if the security is under- or overvalued). Risk, or β_i, can change over time in much the same way as earnings and dividends change. While such changes in βs, or errors in estimating them, may frustrate academicians who are attempting to sort out one theory from another, the existence of errors in estimating risk helps the analyst make money. By inventing a better predictive model of β, the analyst can more precisely measure if a security offers a return that exceeds, is equal to, or falls short of the security market line. Any method that allows the analyst to come closer to the true β during the investment period would be extremely useful. Because there may be a difference between the true β and the analyst's forecasts of it, we use the notation $\hat{\beta}_i$ to denote an estimate of beta for security i. Thus, $\hat{\beta}_i^k$ would be the kth analyst's forecast of the true but unobservable risk level, β_i.

Here we restrict ourselves to summarizing the magnitude of observed changes in β values and whether those changes tend to be positive or negative. In Chapter 16 we deal with *forecasts* of security risk to determine if the market's error in forecasting risk can be profitably exploited.

Empirically, researchers have noticed the following tendencies, some of which were pointed out in Chapter 11:

1. From one five-year period to the next, the $\hat{\beta}$'s of individual firms vary substantially. For portfolios of securities the changes are of much smaller magnitude.
2. There is a tendency for $\hat{\beta}$ to change in a specific direction. On average, firms with $\hat{\beta}$ estimated at below 1.0 in one period tend to have somewhat higher $\hat{\beta}$ in the following period. The effect is in the opposite direction for those with a $\hat{\beta}$ that exceeds 1.0.
3. Betas are different, though not systematically so, when returns are observed over daily, weekly, monthly, or annual periods.[8]
4. Betas are different when different market indexes are used for R_m. However, the differences are close to being proportional for most individual securities. Thus, if ATT's β using the NYSE index as the market index is 90 percent of what it is using the S&P index, beta will be about 90 percent for most other stocks as well.
5. Betas on fixed-income securities, especially those of short duration, are difficult to measure using historical data. The problem is that the continuously shorter period to maturity implies a continuously changing true β.

Evidence on the first two points comes from studies by Blume [1975, 1979]. Using two seven-year historical periods he found the correlation between sample stock $\hat{\beta}$'s in one period and those of the next to be only .6 for individual securities. For 10-firm portfolios, the correlation was a much higher .9. Blume also found in a regression of the more recent estimated $\hat{\beta}_i^k$ on the earlier $\hat{\beta}_i^k$ that there was a significant tendency for a security's $\hat{\beta}_i^k$ to gravitate toward 1.0. His regression equation was

(15–8)   *Blume's Risk Adjustment*

$$\text{New } \hat{\beta}_i^k = .2 + .8 \,(\text{Old } \hat{\beta}_i^k)$$

Thus, firms with $\hat{\beta}$'s of .75 in the earlier period, on average, tended to have $\hat{\beta}$'s of .8 in the later period. This "regression tendency," as it has come to be known in the investment field, may be caused by real factors (e.g., changes in financial structure to move the firm closer to an average level of risk) or may be the result of random or nonrandom error in measuring the β coefficient.

---

[8]The dearth of observations for annual data makes this a highly suspect method for risk estimation.

The random measurement error works like this: Firms that show low $\hat{\beta}^k$ coefficients in one estimating period are more likely (than high $\hat{\beta}^k$ firms) to have had measurement error in estimating β that reduced the value of $\hat{\beta}^k$. The next period, that measurement error will be different and will likely increase $\hat{\beta}^k$. The opposite effect occurs for those firms that show high $\hat{\beta}^k$ (i.e., are more likely to have been subject to positive measurement error).

The next chapter pays special attention to methods of forecasting $\hat{\beta}^k$ values with sophisticated statistical techniques.

Security Market Line

The third component of the analyst's valuation is the intercept and slope of the security market line. The SML identifies the risk/return opportunities available in equilibrium in the market. Thus, with the security's beta the SML indicates the return demanded by the analyst. A graph of this function is given in Figure 15–6, along with an illustration of $\hat{R}_{GAF}$ and $\hat{R}_{DEC}$ for the two securities analyzed earlier. Thus, the intercept and slope represent the SML that was presumed to exist when these two securities were analyzed.

In general, the vertical intercept of the security market line is the existing risk-free interest rate. A good approximation of this rate is given by the yield to maturity on a U.S. Treasury bill with a maturity that matches the investor's horizon. Thus, if you tend to invest for a horizon of one year, use the 1-year T-bill as the risk-free rate.

A term structure of interest rates that is markedly increasing or decreasing suggests the possibility of different risk-free rates for different future periods. This implies different SMLs for different periods, and different discount rates attached to future cash flows. To "back out" the future risk-free rates from the term structure requires some strong assumptions about how those rates are established (e.g., pure expectations theory); hence, we will not cover the subject in detail here.

The slope of the SML depends on the level of risk aversion of the investing public, and the standard deviation of the return on the market portfolio. These two together establish the equilibrium-expected return on the market portfolio, and, thus, $E(\tilde{R}_m) - R_f$. The investor's *estimate* of the true underlying values are $E^k(\tilde{R}_m) - R_f$. On average, over long spans of time in the last 60 years this figure has varied in the relatively narrow range of .05 to .08 when estimated with the use of Standard and Poor's Index of 500 stocks— this being the average difference between the index and the risk-free rate.[9]

We believe that the risk-aversion propensities of investors are rather constant over long spans of time. To the extent there are changes in the slope of the SML, they can be attributed to changes in the anticipated variance of the return on the market portfolio. At a time when there is great uncertainty about the level of economic activity, the slope of the line surely will increase to reflect the increased compensation demanded for that risk.

---

[9]This naive estimate of the risk premium in financial markets can be argued with. Indeed, more sophisticated econometric procedures give different numbers, and suggest the possibility of substantial variations in the value from one decade to the next. As the period of the estimate gets shorter and shorter the estimated value gets more variable. But this is what would be expected if it takes a long period of time before "expectations" of the market are borne out.

FIGURE 15–6   The Security Market Line of the Analyst

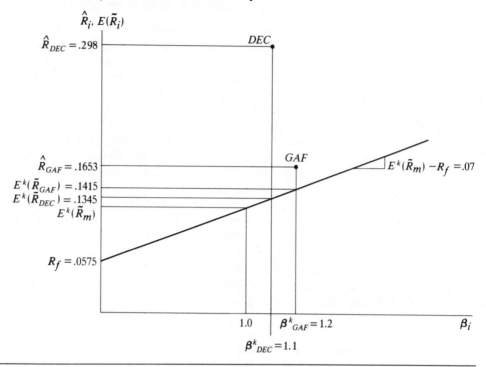

Standard Deviations and Covariances

Finally, to complete our analysis, we need to estimate the standard deviations of the security and the security's covariance with other securities. A number of approaches to this problem have been suggested, including the following methods:

1. We might use historically estimated values—in the belief that variances and covariances, unlike returns, are relatively stable over time. Note however, that covariances cannot be more stable than betas, since each security's beta is proportional to the sum of the covariances of that security with all others.

2. We might, alternatively, use values constructed from each security's estimated beta coefficient; i.e., assuming

$$\text{Cov}(\tilde{R}_i, \tilde{R}_j) = \hat{\beta}_i \hat{\beta}_j \, [\sigma(\tilde{R}_m)]^2$$

This approach traces the covariance between two firms through their relationship with the market portfolio.

3. We could use $\sigma_{ij}\sigma(\tilde{R}_i)\sigma(\tilde{R}_j)$ where the correlation, σ_{ij}, between all i and j securities is the same. This model assumes that we have little knowledge of the ex ante covariance between two securities. Therefore, it makes sense to use the average level of correlation (probably between .3 and .5) to represent the best estimate of the comovement of security returns.

4. We could use historical estimates as a basis, but revise the numbers for both standard deviations and covariances where forecasts are more likely to be accurate.

Which of these approaches should be adopted? It depends on the trade-off between the benefits of increased precision and the costs of acquiring and analyzing more and more data. Indeed many Wall Street analysts cut the process to its bare bones and simply suggest that investors not concentrate a significant portion of their wealth in any one industry. Effectively, they may employ a very naive diversification strategy based on the idea that industry classification is a good proxy for determining which firms will have low covariances with each other.

Any of the approaches listed above generally would substantially improve on the "different industry" approach. The first three approaches are relatively inexpensive to employ, and will become less and less expensive as historical security return data becomes more available. The fourth approach, obviously, is more expensive, but may allow the investor to capture significant gains from diversification that come either from finding securities with low comovement or avoiding securities with high comovement.

To give you an indication of the differences that can exist, Figure 15–7 computes two efficient sets using 17 securities. In both cases the same standard deviations (historical) and returns [CAPM $E(\tilde{R}_i)$s with historical betas] are used. Case 1 uses historical correlations, or method 1, above. Case 3 uses the average of all of the historical correlations of this set of securities: a value of .4. This latter approach corresponds to method 3, above. Obviously, the two efficient sets are different. At a 13 percent return level the case 1 optimal portfolio includes 16 of the 17 securities and has a standard deviation of 14.1 percent. At that same expected return the case 3 optimal portfolio includes 9 securities and has a standard deviation of 15.7 percent. The difference in the structure of each optimal portfolio is due to case 3 emphasizing more the standard deviation of each security, since there is little to choose from when all correlations are the same. More importantly, if case 1 represents the "true" correlations then selecting the portfolio using method 3 correlations leads to a portfolio that is not on the efficient set. In particular, using the weights for the case 3 optimal portfolio and the method 1 correlations generates a standard deviation of 15.5 percent. This is a level of portfolio risk that is 1.4 percentage points above that which could be achieved using the "true" correlations.

In summary, it is worthwhile to attempt to forecast future standard deviations and covariances. Consider the significant changes in American Telephone and Telegraph that took place when it was broken up into six different units. As this transformation took place there is no doubt that what was left of AT&T after the divestiture was a common stock that had a higher standard deviation than before, a greater level of correlation with firms in the computer and technology areas, and a lower level of correlation with firms in the service and communications sector (since these were the functions that AT&T divested itself of). These changes undoubtedly affect how AT&T should optimally be used with other securities to form an *efficient portfolio*.

Analysis of Aggregate Market Returns: Timing

A careful reading of this chapter shows a concentration on the *analysis of individual securities*. Thus, each security's $\hat{R}_i$ and $E^k(\tilde{R}_i)$ is determined to indicate under- or over-valuation, which—along with standard deviations and covariances—provides inputs to

FIGURE 15–7   **Efficient Sets Using Historical Correlations and All Correlations Equal to .4**

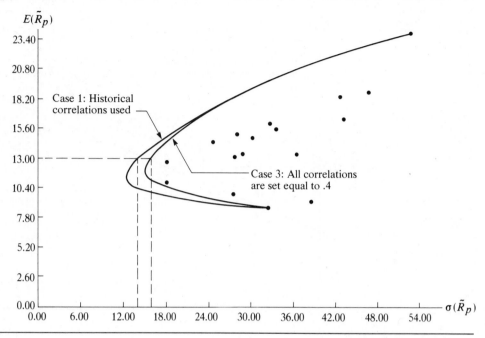

solve for optimal portfolio weights. Yet some analysts concentrate their efforts toward *timing* their entry into, or exit from, the market. Is that consistent or not with the approach we have taken thus far?

In general, **market timing analysis** can be consistent with the framework we presented. Specifically, *market timing* is an attempt to determine if the *preponderance* of securities in the market are undervalued or overvalued. Stated differently,

> **Market timing** asks if there are factors, neither anticipated by the market nor incorporated into overall market prices, which generate a return to a broad portfolio of securities that is likely above the equilibrium return?

An attempt to time the market is simply an attempt to acquire sufficient information, or employ a means of analysis that would indicate if

(15–9)   *Overall Market Disequilibrium Returns*

$$\hat{R}_m \gtreqless E^k(\tilde{R}_m)$$

where $\hat{R}_m$ is the potential disequilibrium return earned on the broad-based portfolio when it is purchased at the current market price. Figure 15–8 represents the relationship between

---

FIGURE 15–8 **Differences in Expectations of Overall Market Returns**

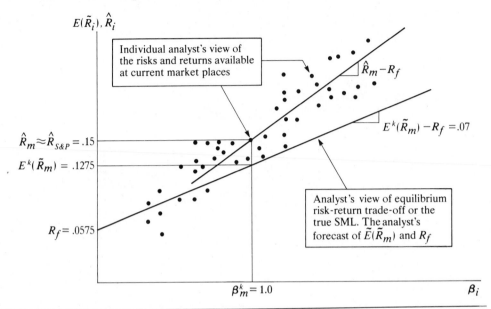

the analyst's view of the returns that would be supplied by securities in equilibrium, and the disequilibrium returns they are offering when incorrectly priced. Of course, since any broad-based portfolio is made up of a large number of individual securities, the existence of such a relationship implies that a large number of individual securities are undervalued as well. In this sense, market timing analysis is no more than an aggregation of individual security analyses.

Consider the application of the dividend capitalization model to an analyst's valuation of the Standard & Poor's 500 Index. Suppose the nominal rate of growth of overall corporate earnings and dividends is expected to be 9 percent (reflecting inflation and the real growth of the economy) for 8 years. After that the growth is expected to remain at the level of 7 percent for the foreseeable future. Moreover, next year's earnings "per share" on the S&P index is expected to be \$22.00, if 65 percent of the earnings are expected to be paid out as dividends, on average, in the future, and if the discount rate applied by the analyst to the market portfolio is 12.75 percent ($R_f = 0.575$, and $E^k(\tilde{R}_m) - R_f = .07$) the analyst's estimate of the S&P's value is about 275. The numbers relevant to this calculation are given in Table 15–5.

If this estimate of the underlying value is above the current market value of the S&P index, the "market" is undervalued, and the return that could be earned on an "index fund" that attempted to match the S&P index would be higher than the 12.75 percent equilibrium-expected return. How much higher, of course, depends on when and if the market makes the adjustment that causes it to value the index in a manner that is similar to the way the analyst has valued it.

Suppose the *market value* of the index is 260, and the analyst has every reason to

TABLE 15–5   **Valuation of the Standard & Poor's 500 Index**

Growth Period .... 8 Years
Supernormal Growth 9.00%
Normal Growth 7.00%
Beta 1
R_f 5.75%
$E^k(\tilde{R}_m) - R_f$ 7.00%
$E(\tilde{R}_m)$ .... $12.75\% = R_f + 1.0[E^k(\tilde{R}_m) - R_f]$
Market Price $260.00

Year	Earnings per Share	Payout	Dividend	Value $P^k_{S\&P,t}$	Dividend Growth
0	$20.00	65%	$13.00	$274.37	
1	22.00	65	14.30	295.17	10.0%
2	23.98	65	15.59	317.35	9.0
3	26.14	65	16.99	340.96	9.0
4	28.49	65	18.52	366.06	9.0
5	31.05	65	20.19	392.71	9.0
6	33.85	65	22.00	420.95	9.0
.	.	.	.	.	.
.	.	.	.	.	.
.	.	.	.	.	.

believe that the market will adjust within the next year (as overall corporate profit, GNP, and money supply figures are released), then $\hat{R}_{S\&P}$ would be,

$$260 = \frac{E^k(\tilde{D}_{S\&P,1}) + E^k(\tilde{P}_{S\&P,1})}{(1 + \hat{R}_{S\&P})} = \frac{\$14.30 + \$295.17}{(1 + \hat{R}_{S\&P})}, \text{ or}$$

$$\hat{R}_{S\&P} = .19, \text{ or } 19 \text{ percent}$$

On the other hand, if the analyst expects that it will take three years for the correction, the relevant disequilibrium-return forecast for the index fund would be:

$$260 = \frac{\$14.30}{(1 + \hat{R}_{S\&P})} + \frac{\$15.59}{(1 + \hat{R}_{S\&P})^2}$$
$$+ \frac{\$16.99 + \$340.96}{(1 + \hat{R}_{S\&P})^3}, \text{ or } \hat{R}_{S\&P} = .15, \text{ or } 15 \text{ percent}$$

This figure is used in Figure 15–8 to represent the (disequilibrium) returns available in the market, on average, when the preponderance of securities is underpriced.

Of course, within the framework of the valuation model we can specify those things that might cause a broad-based portfolio of securities to be mispriced. These factors are attributable to different expectations regarding:

1. Expected future dividends.
2. The risk-free interest rate (applied in some future period), or the intercept of the SML.
3. Market risk, or, for a well-diversified broad-based portfolio, the portfolio's beta (1.0 for the S&P 500 index).

4. The compensation required per unit of risk by the market, or the slope of the SML.

The factors are the same ones we mentioned earlier in the chapter that provided a basis for the discussion of analyses of individual securities.

To generalize, market timing analysis is fundamentally no different than the analysis of individual securities. Substantive differences relate only to the fact that successful market timing is based more on an understanding of the causes and consequences of *overall* corporate revenues, costs, and profitability, rather than those that affect the individual security. As is the case with individual securities, shifts in the intercept (as interest rates change) or slope (as risk aversion or the standard deviation of the market portfolio changes) of the security market line to conform to the analyst's view of equilibrium-expected returns brings windfall gains or losses to the broad-based portfolio, in the same way it did to an individual security.

Two relevant questions remain. First, how much benefit is likely to accrue from one's ability to forecast the movement of the market? And second, what evidence exists to suggest that such forecasting is profitable? This latter question is addressed in Chapter 16. We close out this chapter with a look at the former question.

How Valuable Is a Good Forecasting Technique?

How useful is it to have information on what returns the market will offer? First, having such knowledge will allow you to shift from one aggregate investment mechanism to another (e.g., from savings accounts or T-bills to bonds or stocks) to take advantage of higher returns or avoid lower ones. The question is "How valuable is it if you could *time* your entrance into one market or another to take advantage of market mispricing?" Thus, if you could shift from stocks to a savings account when market returns on stocks are low and shift back again when returns are high, how much would you benefit?

The best answer is supplied in a simulation performed by Sharpe [1975] using the period between 1929 and 1972. Sharpe posited a strategy of investing in Standard & Poor's index if its return was above the rate on Treasury bills, and investing in Treasury bills if the return was lower. During the period studied there were 17 years when the S&P index offered returns less than T-bills and 27 years when the S&P offered higher returns. The S&P return, on average, over all periods was 10.6 percent; on T-bills the return was 2.4 percent. The commensurate standard deviations were 21.1 percent and 2.0 percent.

With "perfect knowledge" of whether the stock return exceeded or fell short of the T-bills, the strategy generated an annual rate of return of 14.9 percent and a standard deviation of 14.6 percent. The improvement with perfect foresight seems substantial. The policy has not only generated a higher return but has also reduced the variance of return (Sharpe used standard deviation as a measure of risk since the constructed portfolios are well diversified).

No one can be expected to have perfect foresight, of course, so Sharpe's analysis also considered what would happen if the analyst could predict a good year 75 or 80 percent of the time or more. In this case, the analyst would make some errors, but have a forecasting ability that is better than would be available from chance alone. The performance of these levels of predictive ability after adjusting for the transactions costs of employing the strategy is summarized as follows:

Predictive Ability	Return	Standard Deviation
Stocks only	10.6%	21.1
T-bills only	2.4	2.0
75% right	12.0	14.5
80% right	12.8	14.4
85% right	13.7	14.3
90% right	14.6	14.2
Perfect foresight	14.9	14.6

These figures indicate that there may be some gain that results from a partial ability to predict overall market movements. Nevertheless, the potential gain is not extraordinarily large if predictive ability is good but not great. This is true because the peaks and declines in the stock market are not that pronounced. Some gain may accrue to the analyst, but as Sharpe suggests, you need a high level of predictive ability to gain very much.

There is another strategy available to allow an investor to capitalize on some predictive ability. That strategy is to buy higher β securities when the market return is predicted to exceed the T-bill return. This strategy would increase both the return and risk from those available in the above figures.

Summary

Security analysis is an attempt to determine the equilibrium value of a security. Through the process of valuation the analyst attempts to determine if the equilibrium value of the security exceeds, is equal to, or falls below the current market price. With the estimated value and an estimate of when the market is likely to revise its expectations to conform to the analyst's, a (disequilibrium) return can be earned by purchasing or selling the security at its current market price.

Success at security analysis, then, depends on: whether and how far market prices deviate from their equilibrium values, how long it takes before the market price moves to the equilibrium price, and whether the analyst has the skills and ingenuity to determine if the market price differs from the intrinsic value.

In this chapter we have suggested that valuation can and should proceed from the CAPM form of the dividend capitalization model. Within this model, differences between the analyst's estimate of value and that of the market depend upon: expectations for future dividends, the security's risk level or beta coefficient, and the slope and intercept of the security market line.

In addition to the return that can be anticipated from the security, analysts must come up with estimates of the standard deviation of return and the covariance, or correlation, of the returns with other securities that might be considered for inclusion in the portfolio.

Is it possible to value the market portfolio *m;* i.e., to try to *time* your entrance or exit from the market? In theory, of course, the same models of valuation that are relevant to valuing individual securities can be applied to the valuation of a major stock market index. In practice, it seems as if your analytical abilities would be useful in such an endeavor only if you have an unusual degree of forecasting accuracy.

The next chapter specifically considers the success or failure of a variety of different forecasting models, and a variety of different market professionals.

References

Archibald, R. Ross. [1972] "Stock Market Reaction to the Depreciation Switchback." *The Accounting Review* (January).

Baesel, Jerome B., and Stern, Garry R. [1979] "The Value of Information: Inferences from the Profitability of Insider Trading." *Journal of Financial and Quantitative Analysis* (September).

Ball, Ray. [1972] "Changes in Accounting Techniques and Stock Prices." *Empirical Research in Accounting: Selected Studies, 1972*. Supplement to *Journal of Accounting Research* 10.

Ball, Ray, and Ball, Philip. [1968] "An Empirical Evaluation of Accounting Numbers." *Journal of Accounting Research* (November).

Ball, Ray, and Watts, Ross. [1972] "Some Time-Series Properties of Accounting Income Numbers." *Journal of Finance*.

Beaver, William. [1970] "The Time Series Behavior of Earnings." *Empirical Research in Accounting: 1970*. Supplement to *Journal of Accounting Research* 8.

Blume, Marshall. [1975] "Betas and Their Regression Tendencies." *Journal of Finance* (June).

Blume, Marshall. [1979] "Betas and Their Regression Tendencies: Some Further Evidence." *Journal of Finance* (March).

Bodie, Z. [1976] "Common Stocks as a Hedge Against Inflation." *Journal of Finance* (May).

Bosch, Jean-Claude. [1983] "Speculation and the Market for Recommendations." *Journal of Financial Research* (Summer).

Brealy, Richard. [1969] *An Introduction to Risk and Return from Common Stocks*. Cambridge, Mass.: MIT Press.

Cassidy, David B. [1976] "Investor Evaluation of Accounting Information: Some Additional Empirical Evidence." *Journal of Accounting Research* (Autumn).

Christie, Andrew A. [1982] "The Stochastic Behavior of Common Stock Variances: Value, Leverage and Interest Rate Effects." *Journal of Financial Economics* (December).

Cornell, Bradford. [1983] "Money Supply Announcements and Interest Rates: Another View." *Journal of Business* (January).

Demsetz, Harold. [1970] "The Private Production of Public Goods." *Journal of Law and Economics* (October).

Elgers, P. T.; Haltiner, J. R.; and Hawthorne, W. H. [1979] "Beta Regression Tendencies: Statistical and Real Causes." *Journal of Finance* (March).

Fama, Eugene. [1972] "Components of Investment Performance." *Journal of Finance* (June).

Fama, Eugene, and Babiak, Harvey. [1968] "Dividend Policy: An Empirical Analysis." *Journal of the American Statistical Association* (December).

Foster, George. [1977] "Quarterly Accounting Data: Time-Series Properties and Predictive-Ability Results. *Accounting Review* 52.

Foster, George. [1973] "Stock Market Reactions to Estimates of Earnings Per Share by Company Officials." *Journal of Accounting Research* 11.

Foster, George. [1986] *Financial Statement Analysis*. 2nd ed. Englewood Cliffs, N.J.: Prentice-Hall.

Gonedes, N. [1973] "Properties of Accounting Numbers: Models and Tests." *Journal of Accounting Research* (Autumn).

Grauer, Robert R. [1981] "Investment Policy Implications of the Capital Asset Pricing Model." *Journal of Finance* (May).

Griffin, P. [1977] "The Time-Series Behavior of Quarterly Earnings: Preliminary Evidence." *Journal of Accounting Research* 15.

Grossman, S. [1976] "On the Efficiency of Competitive Stock Markets Where Traders Have Diverse Information." *Journal of Finance1 (May).*

Grossman, Sanford, and Stiglitz, Joseph. [1976] "Information and Competitive Price Systems." *American Economic Review* (May).

Hakansson, Nils H.; Kunkel, J. Gregory; and Ohlson, James A. [1982] "Sufficient and Necessary Conditions for Information to Have Social Value in Pure Exchange." *Journal of Finance* (December).

Hirshleifer, Jack. [1971] "The Private and Social Value of Information and the Reward to Inventive Activity." *American Economic Review* (September).

Kalay, Avner, and Loewenstein, Uri. [1985] "Predictable Events and Excess Returns: The Case of Dividend Announcements." *Journal of Financial Economics* (September).

Kane, Alex, and Marcus, Alan J. [1986] "The Valuation of Security Analysis." Working Paper series, *National Bureau of Economic Research, Inc.* (June).

Kane, Alex; Lee, Young ki; and Marcus, Alan. [1984] "Earnings and Dividend Announcements: Is There a Corroboration Effect?" *Journal of Finance* (September).

Kaplan, Robert S., and Roll, Richard. [1972] "Investor Evaluation of Accounting Information: Some Empirical Evidence." *Journal of Business* (April).

Kaplan, Robert S. [1975] "The Information Content of Financial Accounting Numbers: A Survey of Empirical Evidence." Carnegie-Mellon University, unpublished working paper (November).

Lintner, John, and Glauber, Robert. [1972] "Higgledy Piggledy Growth in America." In *Modern Developments in Investment Management,* ed. James Lorie and Richard Brealey. New York: Praeger.

Little, I. M. D. [1962] "Higgledy Piggledy Growth." Oxford, England: Institute of Statistics (November).

McDonald, Bill [1985] "Making Sense Out of Unstable Alphas and Betas." *Journal of Portfolio Management* (Winter).

Malkeil, Burton G., and Gragg, John G. [1982] *Expectations and the Structure of Share Prices.* Chicago: University of Chicago Press.

Merton, Robert C. [1981] "On Market Timing and Investment Performance. I. An Equilibrium Theory of Value for Market Forecasts." *Journal of Business* (July).

Nichols, William D., and Brown, Stewart L. [1981] "Assimilating Earnings and Split Information: Is the Capital Market Becoming More Efficient?" *Journal of Financial Economics* (September).

Ohlson, James A., and Penman, Stephen H. [1985] "Volatility Increases Subsequent to Stock Splits: An Empirical Abberation." *Journal of Financial Economics* (June).

Pettit, R. Richardson, and Westerfield, Randolph. [1972] "A Model of Capital Asset Risk." *Journal of Financial and Quantitative Analysis* (December).

Rabinovitch, R., and Owen, J. [1978] "Nonhomogeneous Expectations and Information in the Capital Asset Market." *Journal of Finance* (May).

Rayner, A. C., and Little, I. M. D. [1966] "Higgledy Piggledy Growth Again." Oxford: Basic Blackwood.

Rudd, Andrew, and Rosenberg, Barr. [1980] "The 'Market Model' in Investment Management." *Journal of Finance* (May).

Samuelson, P. A. [1957] "Intertemporal Price Equilibrium: A Prologue to the Theory of Speculation." Weltwirtschaftliches Archiv. (December). Reprinted in *The Collected Scientific Papers of Paul A. Samuelson,* ed. J. E. Stiglitz. Cambridge, Mass.: MIT Press, 1966.

Scholes, M., and Williams, J. [1977] "Estimating Betas from Nonsynchronous Data." *Journal of Financial Economics* (December).

Sharpe, William F. [1975] "Likely Gains from Market Timing." *Financial Analysts Journal* (March–April).

Stern, Joel M. [1974] "Earnings per Share Don't Count." *Financial Analysts Journal* (July–August).

Stickel, Scott E. [1985] "The Effect of Value Line Investment Survey Rank Changes on Common Stock Prices." *Journal of Financial Economics* (March).

Sunder, Shyam. [1973] "Relationships between Accounting Changes and Stock Prices: Problems of Measurement and Some Empirical Evidence." *Empirical Research in Accounting: 1973.* Supplement to *Journal of Accounting Research* 11.

Treynor, Jack. [1972] "The Trouble with Earnings." *Financial Analysts Journal* (September–October).

Treynor, Jack L., and Ferguson, Robert. [1985] "In Defense of Technical Analysis." *Journal of Finance* (July).

Urich, Thomas, and Wachtel, Paul. [1981] "Market Response to the Weekly Money Supply Announcements in the 1970s." *Journal of Finance* (December).

Questions and Problems

1. What part does security analysis play in the investor's objective of selecting an optimal -risky portfolio? If all securities were viewed as being positioned on the security market line (i.e., priced according to their equilibrium value) would security analysis still be helpful in forming an optimal risky portfolio?

2. You are applying for a job as a security analyst with a major brokerage house. You would analyze individual securities and would have some input into the development of policy regarding the department's functions. What would you tell the vice-president interviewing you that an analyst does and the way he should go about doing it?

3. You've arrived at an estimate of $80 for the value of Kodak's common stock, using the dividend capitalization model with dividend expectations formed far into the future. The current market price of Kodak is $70. What information do you need to project an estimate of the return, $\hat{R}$, for evaluating whether Kodak ought to be included in your portfolio?

4. For the GAF illustration in the chapter, a 5-year period was used for calculating $\hat{R}_{GAF}$. That is, it was assumed that it would take 5 years before the market realizes the true underlying value of GAF, and establishes a price for the security equal to the analyst's expectation. How would this number change if, alternatively, 4, 3, 2, or 1 years was used as the basis for the calculation?

5. As a portfolio manager for a pension fund with a long time horizon, you are considering either KC (Coca Cola) or PEP (Pepsico) as an addition to the portfolio.

   a. Calculate the implied one-year return for both KO and PEP.

   b. Calculate the SML-based expected return for both KO and PEP, using the security market line data below.

   c. Select either KO or PEP for the portfolio. Give well-supported reasons for your choice.

	Return per Common Share	
	KO	*PEP*
Stock price (Jan. 16, 1984)	$51³/₄	$36⁷/₈
1984 estimated earnings	4.80	3.55
Indicated dividend	2.90	1.71
Price range (1983) High	57¹/₂	40¹/₄
Low	45¹/₂	32⁵/₈
Book value	23.85	20.95
Expected stock price (Jan. 16, 1985)	56³/₄	40¹/₂
Value Line beta	.80	.95

Other Market Data

Risk-free return	9.0%
Expected market return	14.0%

CFA

6. You are Paul R. Overlook, CFA, an investment adviser for a large endowment fund, and have recently read of a basic valuation model which values an asset according to the present value of the asset's expected cash flows. You now are using this valuation framework to explain to the fund's trustees how inflation affects the rates of return on various asset types. After your presentation the trustees ask:

   a. If common stocks are attractive for hedging inflation, why did stocks perform so poorly in the 1970s when the inflation rate was increasing?

   b. Historical results indicate that over the long run Treasury bill returns and the inflation rate have been approximately the same. Because the current Treasury bill rate considerably exceeds the inflation rate, does this indicate that Treasury bills now are unusually attractive?

   c. If stocks are attractive inflation hedges, it seems that stock prices should rise the most when inflation increases. Why then did stock prices appreciate so much from 1982–1986 when the inflation rate was declining?

   Prepare and briefly explain your response to *each* of these *three* questions in the context of the valuation model referred to above.

CFA

7. Using the information in the table below, carry out the following tasks:

   a. Construct a graph showing the security market line (SML) and the position of stocks KRN and TMC relative to the SML.

   b. Calculate the required rates of return on the two securities. Identify which security is more attractive. Justify your selection.

   c. Using the available information, list and briefly comment on additional factors to be considered in selecting either KRN or TMC as the more attractive investment opportunity.

		Return per Common Share	
		TMC	*KRN*
Current price		$39.00	$27.75
Annual dividend		$ 1.10	$ 0.62
1983 E.P.S.		$ 2.90	$ 1.80
1984 E.P.S.		$ 3.30	$ 2.15
1979–83 average P/E	High	13.0	13.6
	Low	8.3	8.8
Value line beta		1.05	0.95
Expected rate of return		14.9%	12.8%
Other Market Data			
Risk-free rate of return		10.0%	
Expected market return		15.0%	

CFA

8. Weyerhauser's stock has risen rapidly due to changing expectations of the firm's near-term profitability. In fact, one analyst believes the firm's current earnings of $3 per share are likely to grow to $4 by the end of next year; to $5 by the end of the following year; and reach $6 at the end of year 3. After that high-growth period, the analyst expects earnings to grow at the economy's overall rate of 7 percent. Dividends now are 50 percent of earnings and are expected to remain so for the foreseeable future. If the intercept and slope of the SML, according to the analyst, are .06 and .07, respectively, and Weyerhauser's beta is 1.2, what is the analyst's estimate of the value of the stock?

9. Using the results from Problem 8, what is the analyst's expected ex-dividend price at the end of the third year? If Weyerhauser's current market price is $55, and the analyst expects that market price will be similar to the analyst's by

the end of the third year, what return might be expected from the stock?

10. The current market price of Lucky Stores is $28. Mr. Adelman believes the value (with some minor changes in operations) is $40. The firm's current management team thinks the underlying value is closer to $50. Within the context of the dividend capitalization model, what factors might help account for the substantial differences between Mr. Adelman, Lucky's management, and the market?

11. It is true that there is more effort devoted to forming expectations of betas and (disequilibrium) returns from securities than there is to forming expectations of their standard deviations and covariances. Is this emphasis misplaced? Consider in the discussion the possible improvement in portfolio positions with better estimates of *each* of the variables.

12. An analyst valuing each of the following securities is in a quandary regarding the time period to use to establish his $\hat{R}$ values. From the brief explanation given for each case, offer your opinion on whether 1 year, 3 years, 10 years, or the life of the firm ought to be the basis for calculating the disequilibrium return:

   a. General Electric—overvalued, due to GE's long-run inability to run the RCA division profitability.

   b. Symbolics—overvalued, due to disappointment over the quality of this year's new products.

   c. Hughes Tool—undervalued, due to an expected rebound in the price of oil.

   d. Datapoint—undervalued, due to the expectation of a takeover attempt in the next few months.

   e. Rochester Savings Bank—overvalued, due to an expected increase in longer-term interest rates within the next 2 or 3 years.

   f. USX—undervalued, due to their better-than-anticipated ability to increase labor productivity enabling them to compete with foreign imports.

13. As director of research for a medium-sized investment firm, Jeff Cheney was concerned about

the mediocre investment results experienced by the firm in recent years. He met with his two senior equity analysts to consider alternatives to the stock selection techniques employed in the past.

One of the analysts suggested that the current literature has examined the relationship between price/earnings ratios (P/E) and securities' returns. A number of studies had concluded that high P/E stocks tended to have higher betas and lower risk-adjusted returns than stocks with low P/E ratios.

The analyst also referred to recent studies analyzing the relationship between security returns and company size as measured by equity capitalization. The studies concluded that when compared to the S&P 500 Index, small capitalization stocks tended to provide above-average risk-adjusted returns while large capitalization stocks tended to provide below-average risk-adjusted returns. It was further noted that little correlation was found to exist between a company's P/E ratio and the size of its equity capitalization.

Jeff's firm has employed a strategy of complete diversification and the use of beta as a measure of portfolio risk. He and his analysts were intrigued as to how these recent studies might be applied to their stock selection techniques and thereby improve their performance. Given the results of the studies indicated above:

a.   Explain how the results of these studies might be used in the stock selection and portfolio management process. Briefly discuss the effects on the objectives of diversification and on the measurement of portfolio risk.

b.   List and briefly discuss why this firm might *not* want to adopt a new strategy based on these studies in place of their current strategy of complete diversification and the use of beta as a measure of portfolio risk.

CFA

CHAPTER

16

Forecasting Returns

Myths and Realities

> And men still grope t'anticipate
> The cabinet designs of Fate
> Apply to wizards to foresee
> What shall and what shall never be.
>
> *Hudibras,* part iii, canto 3

Prophetic statements have always enjoyed wide appreciation and, for some at least, have been sufficiently well received to supply the prophets with a reasonable standard of living. There are thousands of SEC-registered investment advisers, many of whom apply their talents to forecasting the future of the economy or an individual firm. Is it possible that such forecasts can be used to develop a better estimate of the underlying worth of a security, or does competition among analysts and other forecasters make such efforts, at the margin, worthless? This chapter looks at that issue.

Valuation, Analysis, and Forecasting

Differences between an analyst's estimate of value, P_{i0}^k, and the current market price of a security, P_{i0}^m, depend on differences in estimates of future cash flows (like dividends), risk, and the slope and intercept of the security market line (SML). **Valuation** is the study of the relationships between these variables and the price of the security. **Security analysis** is concerned with investor application of the concepts of valuation to assessing

475

whether the security is currently underpriced or overpriced in the market. Somewhat more generally, we pointed out in Chapter 15 that the job of the analyst is to come up with estimates of the return that can be earned from an investment in a security relative to the SML, and estimates of the security's standard deviation and correlation with other securities. These sets of numbers provide the proper inputs for determining the optimal composition of an investor's portfolio.

The formation of these estimates, however, depends on the analyst's willingness and ability to **forecast** into the future. The analyst who has a solid understanding of the factors that influence security value cannot hope to directly capture the rewards from that knowledge unless he or she also has the ability to forecast the factors. In this chapter we investigate the accuracy and usefulness of a number of forecasting models and methods for identifying underpriced investment opportunities. We will consider not only some statistical forecasting techniques but also the ability of some groups of market professionals to forecast factors affecting security price.

Of course, the forecasting efforts of analysts ultimately must lead to better estimates of future dividends, beta, the intercept and slope of the SML, and the firm's standard deviation and correlations. To this end we concentrate on forecasts of a firm's earnings per share, the firm's risk, market interest rates, and the rate of return on the market portfolio, in that order. In addition, issues pertaining to the use and misuse of inside information and to technical analysis (which attempts to forecast future stock prices with past prices and volume) also are discussed.

Requirements of a Forecasting Model

The accuracy and worth of any forecasting method should be questioned thoroughly before using it. In general, three conditions must hold:

1. The values of the variables used in the forecast must be available at the time the forecast is made.
2. The selection of those variables must occur before the success or failure of the approach is measured.
3. The measurement of success or failure must be for a different period than the one used to estimate the relationships; in general, the measurement period should not *exist* prior to constructing the model.

The first point suggests that you must know exactly when values of the variables used as a basis for the forecast (the "predictor variables") will become available. Finding that corporate earnings for the period ending December 31 are significantly positively related to stock market returns in January is not useful if earnings reports are not available until February. Data used to summarize the level of economic activity over a "period of time" are not useful for forecasting until the *reporting* date. For most macroeconomic and many microeconomic variables this means a few weeks or even months after the end of the period being measured.

The second requirement points out that you must estimate the magnitude of one variable's effect on another prior to the period used to measure the success of the scheme. You could not estimate relationships between earnings and stock market returns, for example, using 10 years of data for the period 1970 to 1979 and also use that period's data to test whether the forecasting scheme works.

The third condition states that the *selection* of predictor variables should not be made with the same data used to test the model's predictive ability. Thus, if you use 1970 to 1980 data to determine that the money supply was a better predictor of stock prices than the Index of Industrial Production you would be precluded from using *any* of the 1970 to 1980 period for testing whether the model had predictive ability. This is true even if the model coefficients were estimated with only part of the data (say 1970 to 1975), with the rest of it used for testing.

If any of these requirements is violated, then we are forced to conclude the model's predictive ability *was not tested*. Therefore, no conclusion on the usefulness of the forecasting method can be reached.

Forecasting Earnings

The numbers below represent the immediate past level of earnings per share and year-to-year growth rates of earnings for Digital Equipment Corporation (DEC).

	1977	*1978*	*1979*	*1980*	*1981*	*1982*	*1983*	*1984*	*1985*	*1986*
Earnings per share	$1.39	$1.70	$2.05	$2.73	$3.35	$3.77	$2.50	$2.87	$3.71	$4.81
Year-to-year growth		22.3%	20.6%	33.2%	22.7%	12.5%	−34.0%	14.8%	29.3%	29.6%

These increases over time represent an average rate of growth per year of 16.8 percent, and an average annual geometric growth rate of 14.8 percent. An obvious question is: Is any information in these numbers useful for forecasting future earnings? Alternative approaches to using these past values include, for example, forecasts based on: (1) last year's earnings, (2) last year's earnings growth, (3) the arithmetic average yearly growth of earnings over the entire 10-year period, and (4) the geometric growth over the entire 10-year-period. Let's consider how well different earnings forecasting techniques perform. The techniques range from simple historical extrapolations, such as those just mentioned, to complex forecasts undertaken by professional securities analysts based on an in-depth look at the firm, its management, and the markets in which it operates.

Statistical Extrapolations

A number of commonly used statistical models for predicting near-term earnings are presented in Table 16–1. They all are based on extrapolations from the recent past earnings history of the firm. All of these methods are designed to forecast firm i's earnings per share in period t, y_{it}, but similar designs using net income, operating income, or even revenue could be constructed, and may prove useful. The figures in Table 16–2 are forecasts of DEC's 1987 earnings per share using some of the models from Table 16–1.

How well do these models forecast earnings over a broad range of securities and time periods? The answer is found in the summarized results of a number of studies in Table

TABLE 16–1   Models to Forecast Earnings

Random walk

$$\hat{y}_{it} = y_{it-1}$$

Average growth

$$\hat{y}_{it} = y_{it-1} + \frac{y_{it-1} - y_{it-\tau}}{\tau - 1}$$

Average percentage growth

$$\hat{y}_{it} = y_{it-1}\left[1 + \frac{1}{\tau}\sum_{\delta=t-\tau}^{t-1}\left(\frac{y_{i\delta} - y_{i\delta-1}}{y_{i\delta-1}}\right)\right]$$

Average geometric growth

$$\hat{y}_{it} = y_{it-1}\left[1 + \left(\frac{y_{it-1}}{y_{it-\tau}}\right)^{1/_{\tau}-1}\right]$$

Exponential smoothing

$$\hat{y}_{it} = ay_{it-1} + (1 - \alpha)\hat{y}_{t-1}$$

$\hat{y}_{it}$ is forecasted earnings of the firm.
$y_{it-\tau}$ is actual earnings τ periods prior to the forecast.
a is an estimated coefficient.

16–3 part (a). *Forecasting ability* is measured here using the average absolute percentage forecast error of the earnings prediction. This measure of forecasting error is compiled by calculating the difference between actual earnings and predicted earnings, and then dividing the absolute value of this difference by the actual level of earnings.

The figures in Table 16–3(a) suggest an error of between 20 and 40 percent in predicting earnings one year ahead, depending on the firms and the years included in the analysis. The study that found the lowest prediction error, 20 percent, used the arithmetic average growth of earnings in the most recent 5-year period as the basis for its extrapolation (moreover, percentage increases or decreases in earnings that exceeded 100 percent were set equal to 100 percent to reduce the effect of extreme fluctuations on the predictions). To be generous, these results suggest that mechanical extrapolations of past earnings can do no better than an absolute percentage forecast error of 20 to 25 percent. Since this figure is quite large (if applied to the DEC figures it would suggest a range for actual earnings, on average, of $5.61 plus or minus $1.10), it's not surprising that analysts spend time and effort trying to improve on these models.[1]

Forecasts Using Other Predictor Variables

While it may be difficult to achieve accurate forecasts using extrapolations of past earnings, improvements may occur by making use of the values of other predictor variables. Some firms' earnings at time t may be highly sensitive to changes in the money

---

[1]As authors of a book on investments we feel we understand a great deal about the operation of security markets. That does not necessarily mean we have exceptional talents for either forecasting earnings and dividends or imputing the market consensus forecast. On the other hand, we may have such talents yet never present them in this book. Our decision would depend on the marginal revenues secured from the sale of additional books containing the forecasting methodology, compared with the marginal revenues from sales to a more limited audience ("our clients") or the risk-adjusted marginal profit from employing the methodology using our own portfolios. Because the first means of disclosure is not likely to be the most profitable, you don't see many *published* highly successful schemes. The corollary is that any widely published scheme for getting rich quick is not likely to work for anyone but the author.

TABLE 16–2   Forecast of DEC's 1987 Earnings per Share

Models	Period Based on	Calculation	Forecast
Random walk	1986	$4.81	$4.81
Average growth	1977–86	$4.81 + ($4.81 − 1.39)/9	5.19
Average percent growth	1977–86	$4.81(1 + .168)	5.61
Average geometric growth	1977–86	$4.81(1 + .148)	5.52

supply in period $t - 1$, for example. Chant [1980] employed three models to predict earnings based on the money supply, banks loans, and Standard & Poor's Stock Price Index. His contention is that since these values have been shown to be so-called "leading indicators" of economic activity, they may successfully predict firms' earnings. Specifically the models are:

TABLE 16–3   Accuracy of Earnings Prediction Models

		Number of Firms Studied per Year	Forecast Period	Absolute Percentage Forecast Error
(a)	*Naive or Statistical Models*			
	Random walk	50	1971–74	35%
	Random walk	218	1968–77	31
	Random walk	519	1963–65	23
	Random walk	517	1963–72	28
	Random walk	50	1968	28
	Average growth	517	1963–72	37
	Average growth	50	1968	40
	Average growth	218	1968–77	31
	Average percentage growth	410	1969–79	20
	Exponential smoothing	218	1968–77	32
	Box Jenkins	50	1971–74	35
(b)	*Models Using Other Economic Measures*			
	Money supply predictor	218	1968–77	30%
	Stock index predictor	218	1968–77	31
	Bank loan index predictor	218	1968–77	33
(c)	*Professional Forecasts*			
	Managers' forecasts	50	1968	20%
	Managers' forecasts	12	1968	14
	Managers' forecasts	88	1970–71	10
	Analysts' forecasts:			
	Value line	50	1971–74	29
	S&P Forecaster	213	1973	23
	S&P Forecaster	50	1969–72	18
	S&P Forecaster	92	1972–76	24
	S&P Forecaster	88	1970–71	14
	S&P Forecaster	410	1969–79	16

Sources: Carey [1978]; Basi, Carey and Twark [1976]; Brown and Neiderhoffer [1968]; Chant [1980]; Brown and Rozeff [1978]; Richards and Fraser [1977]; Richards, Benjamin, and Strawser [1977]; Green and Segall [1967]; Copeland and Marioni [1972]; Givoly and Lakonishok [1979, 1984].

Money Supply Predictor

$$\hat{y}_{it} = y_{it-1}(M1_{t-1}/M1_{t-2})$$

Stock Index Predictor

$$\hat{y}_{it} = y_{it-1}(S\&P_{t-1}/S\&P_{t-2})$$

Bank Loan Index Predictor

$$\hat{y}_{it} = y_{it-1}(BL_{t-1}/BL_{t-2})$$

Each model predicts next year's earnings by multiplying last year's earnings by that year's percentage change in the indicated variable (plus one).

These models perform only slightly better than the naive extrapolations, as shown in part (b) of Table 16–3. That is, the percentage forecast error is reduced only slightly over those values for comparable time periods indicated in part (a).

Managers' Forecasts

Managers of firms, having access to private information within the firm, should be able to forecast earnings fairly accurately. How accurate these forecasts are is an empirical question. The answer is presented in Table 16–3(c). The results can be compared with the naive prediction models of 16–3 part (a).

One study by Copeland and Marioni [1972] of forecasts of 1968 earnings (made at various times during 1968) for 50 different firms found an absolute forecast error of 20 percent of actual earnings during the period. This was an improvement over naive forecasting models. The absolute forecast error was 28 percent and 40 percent for the same set of firms for the naive models. This improvement over naive models should come as no great surprise, though it should be pointed out that in some cases these forecasts were made well into the fiscal year (that is, they are not "one-year-ahead" forecasts).

Other studies (part (c) of Table 16–3) also have found that executive forecasts improve on naively constructed forecasts of earnings, though with considerable error. Viewed in the perspective of the security market, it seems as if manager forecasts are improvement enough to supply new, relevant information to the market when they are published.

If managers' forecasts are more accurate than the forecasts of other models, does the market respond to them? The market would not if it were already cognizant of the earning power of the firm. And, if expectations do change in response to the managers' forecasts, is the response immediate and unbiased as we would expect in an efficient market, or could one use the managers' forecasts to select undervalued securities?

The answer to both questions is suggested by a number of studies on the market's reaction to managers' forecasts. These results can be summarized most easily by graphing the price movement of a typical $30 stock having a standard deviation of about $.50 per day (about average for a NYSE security). Figure 16–1 plots these figures for a period surrounding the forecast announcement for two studies. In each study, managers' forecasts of earnings were divided into two groups. The first group contained forecasts which seemed to supply positive information about the firm's future earnings, while the second contained forecasts implying negative information. The magnitude of the changes found in these two studies, while not unduly large, are statistically significant and economically

FIGURE 16–1   **Price Changes around Management Forecasts from Eight Weeks before to Eight Weeks after the Announcement**

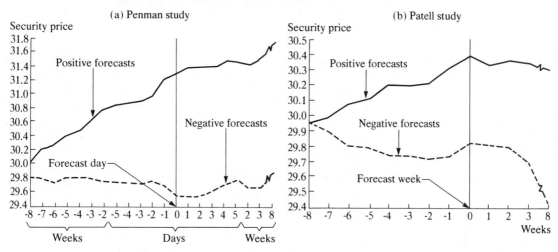

important. Nevertheless, it is obvious that the market uses other information besides managers' forecasts. Patell [1976] sums up the results, noting:

> The anticipatory price changes prior to management forecast disclosure are consistent with investor processing of alternative information sources concerning earnings prospects. It is important to note that this preannouncement behavior may not imply prior leakage of the forecast to insiders, but rather the market's efficient use of publicly available indicators, many of which may be embodied in the management forecast itself. (pp. 272–73)

Analysts' Forecasts

Forecasts of an individual firm's earnings are made by professional analysts employed by brokerage houses and others who provide investment services. These forecasts are important for at least three reasons. First, they may improve on the accuracy of more mechanical forecasting techniques by incorporating more recent and relevant information about the firm's operations. Second, they provide independent confirmation or denial of the forecasts of managers (who may be either too conservative in their estimates or too optimistic, depending on their incentives). Third, investors may make use of the information contained in the forecast for their investment decisions.

Analysts' forecasts are published in a number of places. For example, Value Line publishes its internally generated forecasts for the 1800 firms it follows in the *Value Line Investment Survey*. These forecasts are for the next two fiscal years, and for earnings approximately three to five years into the future.

Lynch, Jones, & Ryan, an institutional brokerage firm, sells the I/B/E/S database, which includes earnings estimates formed by most major brokerage firms for each of the next two fiscal years the next four quarters, and for five year growth rates for over 7,500 firms worldwide. They form a consensus forecast by averaging the forecasts of the

TABLE 16—4 I/B/E/S Database

Sector/Industry/Company	Actual				Estimates—Fiscal Year One							Estimates—Fiscal Year Two						Estimated 5 Year Growth Rate	
	Price	Fiscal Year	EPS	Mean	Percent Change Actual	Relative	6 mo.	Revisions % Up	% Down	Coeff. of Var.	Mean	Percent Change Actual	Relative	6 mo.	Revisions % Up	% Down	Coeff. of Var.	Median	S.D.
Paper																			
ALCO STANDARD	49-1	9/86	2.97	3.97	33.8	0.85	6.4	14	17	6.8	4.98	67.8	0.91	1.7	8	9	6.3	11	4
BOWATER INC	35-0	12/86	2.67	3.44	28.8	0.82	-2.3			2.2	4.23	58.6	0.86	NA		30	4.3	12	1
			1.51	2.20	46.0	0.93	-5.7	7	47	9.9	3.14	108.3	1.13	NA			10.0	12	3
CENTURY PAPERS	11-0	3/86	0.46	0.85	85.9	1.18	0.0				1.25	173.4	1.48	0.0					
CHESAPEAKE CORP	44-0	12/86	1.36	3.11	129.0	1.45	22.6	33	25	15.8	4.06	198.8	1.62	NA	29	14	14.6	12	5
CONSOL PAPERS	66-6	12/86	4.02	3.92	-2.5	0.62	-7.0	36	29	4.8	4.83	20.2	0.65	NA	25	13	13.5	10	7
DUPLEX PROD	19-1	10/86	1.53	1.57	2.4	0.65	-14.5			7.4	2.00	30.7	0.71	NA				10	1
FT HOWARD PAPER	53-4	12/86	2.18	2.72	24.9	0.79	-8.7		17	6.5	3.31	51.8	0.82	NA	8	8	6.7	13	3
GLATFELTER, PH	32-6	12/86	1.66	2.07	24.5	0.79	11.0	17		7.8	2.95	77.7	0.96	NA	50		7.2	10	0
GRT N NEKOOSA	83-2	12/86	4.00	6.46	61.6	1.03	31.5	25	10	13.6	8.28	107.0	1.12	NA	9	9	6.5	10	5
INTL PAPER CO	93-2	12/86	4.73	6.78	43.4	0.91	20.7	24	10	8.0	8.79	85.8	1.01	NA	9	27	4.6	11	7
JAMES RIVER CORP	36-1	4/86	1.69D	2.27	34.0	0.85	1.5	11	11	9.9	2.83	67.6	0.91	1.7	11		8.0	14	2
KIMBERLY CLARK	107-6	12/86	5.87	6.97	18.7	0.75	4.3	14	10	2.7	8.14	38.8	0.75	NA			3.6	12	3
LONGVIEW FIBRE	59-4	10/86	3.20	5.63	76.0	1.12	80.3			12.6	6.85	114.1	1.16	NA			7.2	20	
MEAD CORP	68-0	12/86	3.03	5.02	65.8	1.05	5.8	10	5	7.5	6.43	112.2	1.15	NA	10		7.2	10	3
MOSINEE PAPER	11-7	12/86	0.60	0.66	10.0	0.70	-42.6	50		8.6	1.03	71.7	0.93	NA			9.6	8	4
PENTAIR CORP	26-5	12/86	1.76	2.15	22.1	0.77	-9.4		57	4.2	2.58	46.6	0.80	NA		40	4.1	12	1
SCOTT PAPER	69-6	12/86	4.96	5.91	19.2	0.76	1.6	14	5	4.6	6.90	39.2	0.76	NA			4.6	10	
SUNOCO PRODS	53-2	12/86	2.50	2.89	15.7	0.73	0.0	14	29	2.5	3.49	39.5	0.76	NA	25		1.4	12	2
UNION CAMP	61-2	12/86	2.65	4.21	59.0	1.01	6.0	10	10	5.2	5.37	102.7	1.10	NA			6.1	12	4
WAUSAU PAPER MLS	30-6	8/86	2.52	2.57	2.3	0.65	-5.6		100	1.4	3.20	27.1	0.69	NA		50	4.4	8	4
WESTVACO CP	44-3	10/86	2.50	3.15	26.1	0.80	2.5	10	30	5.8	4.15	65.8	0.90	NA	8	8	8.9	10	3

Steel

	Code	FY																	
Steel			−6.51	0.67	NM	NM	−23.8	14	12	118.2	1.65	NM	NM	−10.5	9	5	43.7	10	6
MAJOR STEEL PROD			−9.51	0.54	NM	NM	−28.3	19	8	203.4	1.67	NM	NM	NA	12	7	55.2	7	6
ARMCO INC	12-1	12/86	−0.50	0.75	NM	NM	40.6	23	8	87.6	1.65	NM	NM	NA	20	20	69.3	5	1
BETHLEHEM STEEL	15-5	12/86	−3.37	0.26	NM	NM	−66.1	27		812.9	0.70	NM	NM	NA			221.7	5	3
INLAND STEEL IND	32-4	12/86	0.37	1.83	393.7	3.13	13.0	19	19	78.4	2.62	609.0	3.85	NA		17	57.6	6	6
LTV CORP	5-6	12/86	−35.41	0.04	NM	NM	NM	NM	19	999.9	0.13	NM	NM	NA	17	17	141.4	5	2
NATL INTERGROUP	15-7	3/86	−2.71	−0.28	89.6	0.07	NM	NM	9	628.0	0.99	NM	NM	NA	14		63.5	10	2
USX CORP	31-7	12/86	−5.36	0.64	NM	NM	−46.6	21	8	120.1	2.39	NM	NM	NA	13	6	40.5	8	5
OTHER STEEL PROD			−3.88	1.53	NM	NM	−13.9	15	15	8.8	2.88	24.7	0.68	NA	13	13	6.8	13	3
ACME STL CO DEL	13-1	12/86	−3.66	0.75	NM	NM	NA					NM	NM						
FOSTER L B CO	3-0	12/86	−5.74	−0.50	91.3	0.06	NM												
INTERLAKE INC	45-0	12/86	2.85	3.19	11.8	0.71	3.0		14	4.2	3.80	33.3	0.72	NA			7.4	12	2
NUCOR CORP	39-6	12/86	2.17	2.46	13.4	0.72	−20.8	31	15	10.0	2.57	18.3	0.64	NA	33		4.5	14	3
ROANOKE ELEC STL	18-0	10/86	1.46	1.85	26.7	0.80	10.4		33	30.5	1.85	26.7	0.69	NA	33	33	19.5		
VALLEY INDS	1-5	11/86	−1.46	−0.35	76.0	0.15	0.0												
WHEEL PITTS ST	10-1	12/86	−49.10	1.80	NM	NM	38.5					NM	NM						
STAINLESS STEEL			−6.82	1.81	NM	NM	−8.4	7	7	33.5	3.75	240.9	1.85	−16.7			28.3	8	6
ALLEGHENY INTL	19-0	12/86	−17.97	−0.53	97.0	0.02	NM			155.3							28.3	8	0
CARPENTER TECH	46-1	6/86	1.10	1.39	26.8	0.80	−7.1	10	10	44.0	3.75	240.9	1.85	−16.7			28.3	8	6
CYCLOPS CORP	93-7	12/86	5.26	9.00	71.1	1.09	12.5											27	

Source: I/B/E/S Data Set 1987, p. 184. Lynch, Jones, & Ryan.

individual analysts, and also calculate the standard deviation of analysts' forecasts. An example of the data they make available is presented in Table 16–4.

It would be surprising to find that analysts could not improve on naive statistical forecasting models, and the evidence suggests that they do—though the improvement is not as substantial as you might expect. The results of some studies were compared in Table 16–3. The study of Value Line's predictions showed a 29 percent absolute prediction error, which is less than the prediction error of 35 percent using naive statistical forecasts for the same set of firms. S&P forecast errors from studies of different firms over different time periods vary between 14 and 23 percent. In all, these investigations suggest a reduction in absolute percentage error with analysts' forecasts of about 5 to 10 percentage points from error present in naive statistical forecasts. Moreover, when we consider that these forecasts are not always a full year ahead of the last reported earnings, the results seem to *question whether analysts have great accuracy* in forecasting.

The most extensive study of analysts' earnings forecasts and their relationship to reported earnings was undertaken by Brown, Foster, and Noreen [1985] on behalf of the American Accounting Association. Their results are detailed and extensive and cover an analysis of both I/B/E/S consensus forecasts, and forecasts of a large money manager— Wells Fargo Investment Advisors. One of their most significant findings relates the absolute percentage error in analysts' forecasts, on average, to the number of months before the earnings actually are reported. Their calculations, from 22 months before the reported earnings were published to 2 months before, are based on the overall *mean forecast* and on the mean of the forecasts after eliminating the 10 percent most extreme overestimates and underestimates (the truncated mean). By eliminating the most extreme forecast errors the authors hoped to eliminate biases in the figures resulting from: (1) the forecasts of a few firms whose earnings just are not at all predictable, (2) analysts who may have made a prediction without a serious investigation of the firm, and (3) situations in which the reported earnings are near zero (so that the denominator controls the forecast error ratio). These are the absolute percentage forecast error values they calculated:

	Number of months before earnings reported										
	22	*20*	*18*	*16*	*14*	*12*	*10*	*8*	*6*	*4*	*2*
Average absolute percentage error (%)	39.0	41.1	42.8	39.1	32.9	28.5	23.1	20.3	18.3	15.6	10.2
Truncated average absolute percentage error (%)	25.6	26.7	26.9	25.3	22.3	21.3	18.3	15.6	13.3	11.0	7.6

The numbers clearly reveal a tendency for the estimates to be more accurate as the reporting date approaches. The large drops in forecast errors around the period 10 to 12 months before publication is associated with the additional information available to the analyst as that year's earnings are reported. Approximately, the 10- to 12-month figures correspond to those generated in other investigations that were summarized in Table 16–3. Of course, the continuing decline in error rates between months 10 and 2 reflects the use of quarterly earnings reports and other information used by analysts in their forecasts. There is some information presented separately by the authors that suggests analysts revise

TABLE 16–5 **Correlations for One- and Five-Year-Ahead Forecasts**

	One-Year Ahead Forecasts		Five-Year-Ahead Forecasts	
	Average Correlation of Forecasts with Actual Earnings	*Average Number of Firms Where Forecast Was Made by the Analyst*	*Average Correlation of Forecasts with Actual Earnings*	*Average Number of Firms Where Forecast Was Made by the Analyst*
1	.31	111	.32	165
2	.48	64	.32	163
3	.32	124	.53	75
4	.22	159	.60	90
5	.58	33	.49	148
6	.48	75	.52	91
7	.26	157	.47	114
8	.38	51	.55	56
9	.34	190	.46	42
10	.44	52	.16	111
11	.38	88	.12	143
12	.10	108	.23	157
13	.09	154		
14	.27	152		

their forecasts in response to price changes in the security. In other words, analysts' forecasts may not be completely exogenously determined. If this is so, it detracts from their usefulness to investor attempts to value the security.

Another way to assess earnings predictability is to measure the accuracy of analysts' forecasts by correlating them with the earnings eventually reported. In an interesting study, Malkiel and Cragg [1982] looked at the earnings projections of 14 individual analysts. A correlation was estimated for each analyst, giving us the opportunity to see if there is any difference in the accuracy of different analysts. The correlations are shown in Table 16–5.

While there is quite a difference among the various analysts, the most accurate among them experienced correlations at a level of .6, implying that about 36 percent of the variation in reported earning could be explained by the analyst's forecasts. In fairness, it should be pointed out that Malkiel and Cragg's request that these analysts supply them with forecasts on up to 190 firms biases against finding a stronger correlation. No professional analyst would ordinarily be charged with making nearly this many forecasts. Most analysts concentrate their efforts on a few firms or in an industry.

Another way of approaching this is to correlate actual earnings with forecasted earnings, after all information in naive statistical forecasts is accounted for. That is, to attribute as much forecasting ability as possible to statistical extrapolations such as the average historical growth and see if analysts' forecasts provide additional power to explain actual earnings. A study by Givoly and Lakonishok [1984] did this by looking at the *partial* correlation of reported earnings with analysts' forecasts. Over 11 years and some 400 firms, the average partial correlation was .51. When the relationship is turned around and the authors consider the correlation of actual earnings with naive forecasts, given the forecasts of analysts, the figure is −.04. In other words, the addition of analysts' forecasts helps to explain next year's reported earnings over and above the information contained in naive forecasts.

Clearly, the ultimate test of the value of the forecasts of analysts is not how accurately

FIGURE 16–2   Excess Returns (on high versus low predicted earnings)

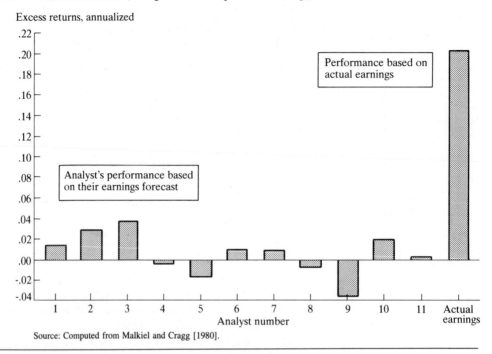

Source: Computed from Malkiel and Cragg [1980].

they predict earnings, but whether their predictions make money for investors. Both the studies by Malkiel and Cragg and Givoly and Lakonishok looked at this issue by measuring *excess* or *abnormal* returns on portfolios formed on the basis of the forecasts. Thus, for each of the analysts studied by Malkiel and Cragg, the difference between the returns on a portfolio of firms with *predicted* earnings growth greater than average and a portfolio of firms with *predicted* earnings growth less than average was calculated. These results were compared with the difference in returns based on whether *actual* earnings were greater or less than average. The results are presented in Figure 16–2. These figures suggest, first and foremost, that knowledge of the *actual* earnings "next year" would provide a sizable excess return of about 23 percent! Alternatively, formation of the portfolio based on the forecasts of 11 of the 14 analysts they studied generates less than a 1 percent excess return, on average. The result strongly indicates that use of the analysts' forecasts, even if you had them before the rest of the market, would be of marginal benefit only.

However, the study of Givoly and Lakonishok provides more optimistic results. They found that a trading rule based on the analysts' forecasts generated positive excess returns, even when transactions costs are accounted for. Their results are summarized in Table 16–6. These excess returns are based on a strategy of buying the security when there is a given sized revision in the forecast. The numbers are large, and do not seem to depend on your having knowledge of the analysts' revision before the rest of the market.

The 12.29 percent figure is meant to indicate the excess annual returns that accumulate

TABLE 16–6

		Strategy	
	Round Trip Transaction Cost	*Buy at End of Revision Month and Sell One Month Later*	*Buy at End of Revison Month and Sell Upon First Downward Revision*
5% upward revision of earnings forecast	2%	9.55%	12.20%
10% upward revision of earnings forecast	2	12.29	14.92

to investors that buy the security at the end of the month in which there was at least a 10 percent upward revision of forecasts, after accounting for the costs of transacting (at 2 percent) and the "idle" time during which there were no 10 percent upward revisions to invest in. The idle time was significant, in this case, being in excess of 80 percent of the months studied by the authors (which suggests that there are not too many cases in which there are large forecast revisions).

On the whole, the results of empirical investigations of the accuracy of analysts' forecasts lead to the conclusion that:

Knowledge of future earnings is valuable information for the formation of expectations of returns from investments in securities. Professional analysts' forecasts of these earnings provide modest improvements in accuracy over the use of naive statistical extrapolations. Moreover, the market seems to move in conjunction with revisions in analysts' forecasts, if not in response to them. Nevertheless, there are substantial errors in analysts' forecasts, which undoubtedly fuels continuing efforts to come up with better forecasting procedures.

Forecasting $\hat{\beta}$

Fundamentally, the prediction of risk is no different than the prediction of earnings or dividends. One might begin with a historically calculated estimate of risk, $\hat{\beta}$, and see how well that value predicts the *future risk* which, like future earnings, will be revealed only as time passes. From what we know about studies of $\hat{\beta}$ coefficients, a variety of prediction models have been employed to forecast risk, and are summarized below:

Historical

Using five years of past monthly observations, estimate the coefficients of the following model, using simple linear regression

(16–1)   ***Market Model***

$$R_{it} = \hat{\alpha} + \hat{\beta}_i R_{mt} + u_{it}$$

Blume Adjusted

Blume found that, for NYSE firms, the relation between one five-year historical β estimate and the next five-year β estimate was (approximately)

(16–2)   *Blume Adjusted β*

$$\text{New } \hat{\beta}_i = .2 + .8 \text{ (old } \hat{\beta}_i)$$

Thus, the historical estimate above can be used to get a new adjusted $\hat{\beta}_i$ as follows:

$$\text{Adjusted } \hat{\beta}_i = .2 + .8 (\hat{\beta}_i)$$

Then the adjusted $\hat{\beta}_i$ is the figure to use for the current investment period. If Computer Science Corp. has an estimated $\hat{\beta}$ of 1.83, using 1981–86 data, the current relevant $\hat{\beta}$ might be

$$\text{Adjusted } \hat{\beta}_i = .2 + .8(1.83) = 1.66$$

Merrill-Lynch Adjusted

Merrill Lynch computes and publishes both historical and adjusted $\hat{\beta}$s. Their method of adjusting $\hat{\beta}$s is derived from the use of Baysian statistics that gives some weight to the historical β and some weight to the fact that the average β of all securities is 1.0. Thus, their adjusted $\hat{\beta}$ is

(16–3)   *Merrill-Lynch Adjusted β*

$$\text{Adjusted } \hat{\beta}_i = \omega(\hat{\beta}_i) + (1 - \omega)(1.0)$$

where ω is the weight used to measure the relative impact of the statistically and historically estimated $\hat{\beta}$, with the average of all firms being 1.0.

Both of these latter approaches were based on the kind of observations summarized in Figure 16–3. Here security $\hat{\beta}$s were estimated for 1947–54 and were placed into one of eight portfolios based on their $\hat{\beta}$ rank. The $\hat{\beta}$s were reestimated for 1955–61 and 1961–68. The dispersion of $\hat{\beta}$s for each of the eight portfolios is substantially less for the most recent period. The $\hat{\beta}$s seem to have tended to change and move toward the average of all $\hat{\beta}$s, 1.0—i.e., there is a regression tendency toward 1.0.

BARRA Adjusted

As mentioned in Chapter 15, the consulting firm BARRA adjusts historical risk estimates using a set of "fundamental" variables that attempt to reduce the estimation errors in historical betas and allow for changes in the operation of the firm that have affected its underlying risk posture. A number of the variables used by BARRA for their predictions are listed in Table 16–7 with coefficients that, at the time they were formed, identified the effect of each variable on the prediction of $\hat{\beta}$.

Note that some of these variables are closely related to the risk factors discussed in the chapter on equity valuation. Other variables are important for predictive purposes because they provide a *signal* to the market regarding the management's perception of

FIGURE 16–3 **The Movement of Betas over Time** (three periods from 1947 to 1968)

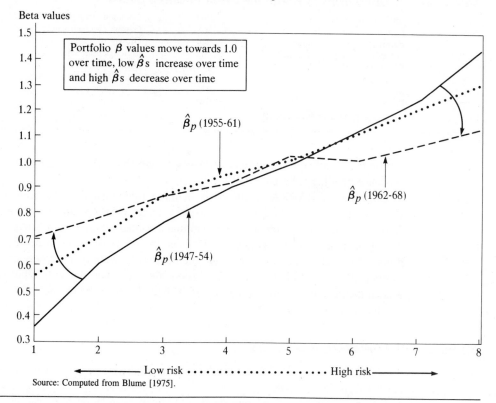

Beta values

> Portfolio β values move towards 1.0 over time, low $\hat{\beta}$s increase over time and high $\hat{\beta}$s decrease over time

$\hat{\beta}_p$ (1955-61)

$\hat{\beta}_p$ (1962-68)

$\hat{\beta}_p$ (1947-54)

←———— Low risk · High risk ————→

Source: Computed from Blume [1975].

the firm's risk (and, perhaps, the return). Dividend policy items such as "payout" and "dividend cuts" would fall into this category. These values were found to be significantly statistically related (at the 95 percent level) to future $\hat{\beta}$ after the total effect of the historical $\hat{\beta}$ was incorporated.[2] All these values are standardized by the variability of the values. Thus, the value of $-.02$ for payout indicates that a firm whose payout ratio was one standard deviation above the mean of all payout ratios would have a risk lowered by .02. For a security with an estimated historical $\hat{\beta}$ of 1.00, the adjusted (for payout) $\hat{\beta}$ would be .98. A one standard deviation *below* the mean ratio of debt to assets would decrease $\hat{\beta}$ by an additional .017 to .963.

We need to mention one caveat regarding the use of these figures. Since many of the variables in the table are closely related to one another (e.g., dividend yield and payout are closely correlated), *all* would have to be used in forming the adjusted $\hat{\beta}$ estimate. This makes the technique cumbersome, to say the least, and involves the use of a rather

---

[2]Actually, the results incorporate a number of other "market type" variables as well, e.g., β^2, price level, price range. However, these factors appear to have an influence that is independent of the financial statement figures. Consequently, the coefficients in the text are unaffected.

TABLE 16–7   Adjustments to $\hat{\beta}$ with the Use of Financial Data

Variance of cash flows	.007	Common stock price	.034
Earnings covariability	.008	Current dividend yield	−.022
Earnings/price covariability	.024	Growth of assets	.043
Growth in earnings per share	−.065	Earnings/price ratio	.017
Dividend cuts	.011	Debt/assets	.017
Total assets	.026	Potential dilution of shares	−.010
Market value equity	−.042		
Payout	−.020		

Source: Rudd and Clasing [1982].

complex computer routine and a larger data set—which provides a reason for the continued existence of a firm like BARRA.

Estimates by BARRA on the basis of these fundamentals have been formed since 1975, so the opportunity exists to measure whether BARRA adjustments lead to a prediction of beta that is more accurate than that afforded by other techniques—particularly the use of simple historically generated values. In fact, BARRA-estimated betas for 1,000 firms, while still containing some measurement error, were more closely correlated with subsequent estimated betas than were historically estimated betas. In other words, there was an increase in accuracy when historical beta estimates were updated to reflect more current operations of the firm.

Summary of Forecasting Schemes

A number of agencies that publish, sell, or otherwise produce betas for their clients are listed in Table 16–8.

Common sense, and an understanding of financial relationships, can go a long way toward supplying you with information useful for forecasting the risk level of a bond or common stock (or any other asset). Knowledge of the current structure of the firm's operations, summarized by the extent to which the firm employs fixed-cost factors of production or financial leverage, also helps.[3] Even for firms issuing stock for the first time, it is possible to get some idea of the extent that earnings or cash flows are likely to comove with the economy. Many of the same variables that affect future returns also will determine the security's beta.

Can Analysts Forecast Individual Security Returns?

Brokerage houses and investment advisors often recommend whether a particular security should or should not be bought. By doing so, these advisers are offering their opinion

---

[3]Consider the case of financial leverage, for example. Given that $Cov(\tilde{Y}_i, \tilde{Y}_m)$ is positive, $Cov(a\tilde{Y}_i, \tilde{Y}_m)$ is greater if $a > 1.0$. In Chapter 17 we showed that a would be equal to $1 +$ (debt/equity) which exceeds 1.0 as a function of the debt employed in financing the firm. Operating leverage also would cause an increase in a, and an increase in comovement of the firm's earnings with the earnings of all other firms.

TABLE 16–8

	Market Index	Length of Period Used for Historical β	Interval for Return Observations	Adjustment Method
Merrill Lynch	S&P	5 years	Monthly	$\omega(\beta_i) + (1 - \omega)(1.0)$
Value-Line	NYSE	5 years	Weekly	Similar to above
Wharton School	NYSE	5 years	Monthly	None
Wharton School	NYSE	1 year	Weekly	None
Weisenbergers (Mutual Fund βs)	NYSE	Estimated over each market cycle	Monthly	None
BARRA		5 years	Monthly	Regression to account for fundamental variables

regarding the risk–return position of the security relative to the equilibrium risk–return trade-off they believe exists in the market. For example,

> Jamesway's current share price is undervalued relative to the general market and to the discount retail group as a whole. The shares are volatile because of the company's 1986 jagged EPS gains. While we expect EPS of $1.70 for the current year, and $2.15 next year (versus 1985's $1.30), the EPS improvement is coming in the second and fourth quarters while first and third quarters show flattish results.[4]

Other recommendations may be more or less ambiguous. For those cases in which unambiguous recommendations are made we can determine analysts' track records by measuring the ex post performance of the securities recommended. If, on average over the long run, recommended securities perform better than other securities with the same risk, we can say the analysts are successful.

One study by Growth, Lewellen, Schlarbaum, and Lease [1979] looked at 6,000 recommendations made by one brokerage firm over a seven-year period. Of the total recommendations, 77 percent advocated purchase of a particular security and 13 percent suggested sale. The rest merely provided information or were ambiguous. Overall, the excess returns were positive, indicating an ability to select undervalued securities. This is shown in Figure 16–4. Returns were high before the recommendation month, during the month of recommendation, and even after the month of recommendation.

These excess returns are significant. For example, the excess returns earned in the recommendation month were almost 21 percent per year (i.e., 1.018 to the 12th power is 1.21). These figures are strong enough to be somewhat surprising and should not be accepted without further analysis. For example, it may be (1) that the recommendation itself sparks interest in the security and becomes self-fulfilling, (2) that this security firm tends to make its buy recommendations *after* a period of price increase (explaining away all but the returns from month + 1 and after), and (3) that some quirk exists in the measurement technique that caused past recommendation returns to be overstated. The evidence, however, seems to document an ability to forecast which securities will offer

---

[4]Prudential Bache Securities [1986] *Research,* Jamesway Corporation (September 11).

FIGURE 16–4   Monthly Investment Return Residuals on Recommended Securities

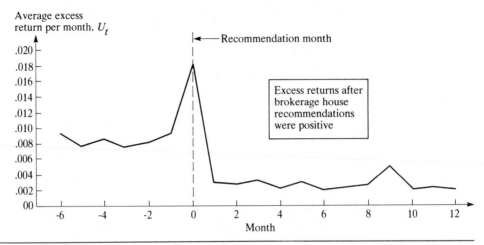

---

superior returns. From month 1 after the public announcement of the recommendation to month 12, the excess returns accumulate to almost $3^1/_2$ percent.

In addition to estimating earnings, the *Value Line Investment Survey* provides *performance predictions,* or forecasts of security returns, on approximately 1,700 common stocks. Employing some 200 analysts, Value Line places each of the 1,700 firms it follows in one of five "anticipated performance" portfolios each week. Portfolio 1 consists of the securities ranked during that week for highest in expected performance for the next 12 months. Portfolio 5 is made up of those securities ranked lowest. The assignment to portfolios is made by Value Line according to a set of criteria that are heavily weighted by earning power and current relative price. Thus, firms that have substantial earning power per unit of price, as measured by Value Line, would tend to be placed in portfolio 1. On average, about 52 percent of the securities are placed in portfolio 3, with 18 percent each in portfolios 2 and 4 and about 6 percent in portfolios 1 and 5. How these portfolios perform is summarized in two graphs prepared in a study by Copeland and Mayers [1982].

The first graph, part (a) of Figure 16–5, gives the cumulative performance measured by calculating market model excess returns. These cumulative excess returns, or *CAR* values, are plotted for the period from publication of the *Investment Survey* to 26 weeks after its publication.

Interestingly, the performance of each portfolio corresponds exactly to the Value Line ranking, indicating some ability of Value Line to predict returns. The difference in excess returns is about 4.5 percentage points over the six-month period. Some predictive ability seems to be apparent in the figures.

The second graph, part (b) of Figure 16–5, plots the same measure for securities that were shifted up by Value Line from a lower portfolio to a higher one (e.g., from portfolio 3 to 2), or shifted from a higher to a lower one. The figure suggests the shifts were appropriate, because performance after the shift was positive for the "up" securities and negative for the "down" securities. Both of these values differed from the set of securities that did not change classes.

FIGURE 16–5   Value Line Ranking and Cumulative Excess Returns

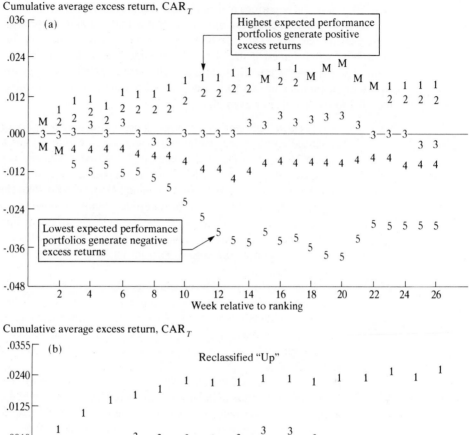

Source: Copeland and Mayers [1982].

While the excess return figures form a convincing case for Value Line's methods of analysis, there is one caveat we should mention. Since Value Line is a widely published and widely used service, can the Value Line forecast itself be the cause of the differential portfolio performance? We don't have an answer to this, and it may not matter: the differential performance seems to be present in any case.

Insider Information and Return Predictions

Rule 10.b.5. of the Securities and Exchange Act prevents insiders from acting on private information regarding company operations that is material and not generally available to those outside the firm. The rule helps ensure equity and fairness in the market. Few "outsiders" would invest if they knew knowledgeable insiders could take advantage of them. The purpose of the rule is to help achieve market efficiency. However, as is the case with many rules of this sort, a number of questions arise concerning the ability of the SEC to enforce it. For example,

1.   *What is inside information and what is publicly available information?* Clearly, announced earnings are public and unannounced earnings figures are not. But suppose McDonnell-Douglas Corporation incurred substantial cost overruns in manufacturing military aircraft. Further, suppose these cost overruns involve a hefty penalty. An employee of McDonnell-Douglas who sells shares based on this knowledge would seem to be an insider. Suppose, however, that with a lot of hard work the same data could have been gleaned from Air Force documents received under the Freedom of Information Act. Since anyone could acquire the same information as the employee from publicly available sources, is the information really private?

2.   *Who is an insider?* Employees and directors are, of course, but are customers of the firm (think of firm A canceling an arrangement with firm B; can A's employees trade B's securities)? What about the firm's bankers or accountants, friends of employees, or friends of friends? Actually, the SEC calls anyone with material nonpublic information, who has reason to expect the information is not public, an insider.

3.   *If everyone is potentially an insider, doesn't enforcement discourage the production of information about firms by analysts?* The answer, we suppose, depends on the penalties—since the rewards for the use of nonpublic information may be substantial. Moreover, isn't it likely that such a rule may be inconsistent with other rules binding managers of funds held in fiduciary accounts? Take the case of Ray Dirks. He received some correct information from an employee of Equity Funding regarding bogus insurance policies written by the firm. As an investment adviser and manager, Dirks acted on behalf of his clients, as any good fiduciary should, and sold the stock out of their portfolios. The SEC through the Department of Justice prosecuted him as an insider for trading on inside information.

4.   *Wouldn't failure to act on relevant inside information mean that the market price is set without considering data that are necessary to assess the security's true value?* If so, isn't there a greater chance that the market price is wrong and that markets are less "informationally efficient"? Equity Funding's true value was close to zero. Yet the "misinformation" supplied by management had created a value of $24 per share. Is it better to have mispriced securities, or to tolerate a bit of unfairness by permitting some use of inside information?

Doonesbury

5. *How can the SEC know if certain traders are acting on inside information?* It is difficult, of course, to know the basis for anyone's action. SEC enforcement operates on the assumption that if an insider sells or buys the security and subsequently an important piece of information is released, the case must be investigated. For example, the recent Santa Fe Industries case, where Middle Eastern interests were proposing to buy the firm, attracted the attention of the SEC because of a huge increase in the security's volume and price prior to the public announcement.[5]

6. *How can we resolve these issues in a manner that will not drive those without inside information from the market, yet will provide a mechanism that leads to more informationally correct prices?* In theory, the answer is easy. All we have to do is to motivate managers and others to reveal their inside information. In practice, the realities of the world are such that motivation may be a difficult thing to instill. Managers, for example, are reluctant to reveal too much of their knowledge for two reasons. First, some of the information may be used by competitors to the disadvantage of the firm. Forecasts relating to new markets or new products would seem to fall in this category. Second, as long as everything in the future is not known with complete certainty, information regarding manager expectations that is announced and does not come true subjects the manager to possible litigation. Moreover, it's not precisely clear what kind of SEC policy would come closest to instilling proper incentives. Some have argued that complete prohibition on managers trading the stock means they have little to lose by revealing inside information. Others have argued that an extensive set of regulations covering how all situations (say a merger offer) should be handled by insiders is the answer.

---

[5]In this case the insiders who are accused of illegally buying the security were a Santa Fe director, another director's accountant, a Kuwaiti businessman, and a few employees and their friends. The accountant, by the way, seems to have deduced that favorable news was forthcoming simply from the directors' request for information on his tax obligations on a sudden capital gain. Is he an insider? See Hudson [1982], p. 31.

These are difficult questions. The issues have been made all the more important with recent "insider trading" cases brought by the Department of Justice against Ivan Boesky, Timothy Tabor, and others. Moreover, The Institute of Chartered Financial Analysts, one of the main educational and certification bodies for investment brokers, advisers, and analysts, emphasizes the need for the people they certify being aware of all laws and regulations, and what constitutes ethical behavior with respect to inside information.

Evidence on Returns and Insider Trading.   There are a few other questions that are relevant to an understanding of financial markets and inside information. First, do insiders earn higher investment returns than do outsiders? Second, does information regarding the *purchase* and *sale* transactions of corporate managers and directors allow outsiders to capture excess profits? Both of these questions can be addressed empirically because managers and directors are required to report any transactions they make within 10 days of the trade. This information is made publicly available a few days after the end of the trading month.

Regarding the first of these issues, studies have shown that insiders do make moderately higher returns on their firm's shares than do outsiders. The risk-adjusted excess return from portfolios formed when an insider bought a security was around 3 percent in the month of purchase (i.e., had one bought at the beginning and sold at the end of the month), 1 percent the month after, and perhaps 2 additional percentage points over the next 10 months. For portfolios formed when an insider sold, the month of sale return was a -1 percent, with the next 11 months showing a -3 percent return (from Finnerty [1976]).

Another study of Canadian firms listed on the Toronto Stock Exchange (Baesel and Stein [1979]) found that transactions by directors of the banks the firms dealt with, and ordinary insiders, both earned superior returns. The cumulative excess returns on stock purchases are shown and compared with a control portfolio in Figure 16–6.

Penman [1982] also found evidence of profitable insider trading. He investigated 550 firms that published manager forecasts of annual earnings. He observed the three-day excess return around the announcement, and ranked all 550 firms based on their calculated three-day return. The ranked securities were formed into one of 20 portfolios. The five portfolios with the highest three-day returns surrounding the announcement of the forecasts tended to be made up of firms where insiders had *purchased more* or *sold less* before the forecast than after it. For the five portfolios with the worst three-day returns, the insiders *purchased less* or *sold more* before the forecast was made. In the two months before the announcement the big gainers sold on net only 1,800 shares (22 firms), while during the two months after the announcement 22,000 shares were sold. For the five portfolios that performed the worst over the three-day period, shares sold net of purchases were 63,000 before the (negative) forecast announcement while afterward the sales on net amounted to only 6,000 shares. Of course, these sales and purchases may have been planned all along. Yet the figures suggest the timing of insider transactions are set to conform to periods when the insider can benefit from the stock price movement. The results clearly tie insider transactions to announcements that have a major effect on security prices. The SEC's goal of preventing insider activity is not totally successful—to say the least.

If insiders seem to generate excess profits in the aggregate, can investors using published information on the transactions of insiders generate profits? Jaffe [1974] suggests

FIGURE 16–6   **Cumulative Excess Returns on Insider Purchases of 111 Canadian Stocks**

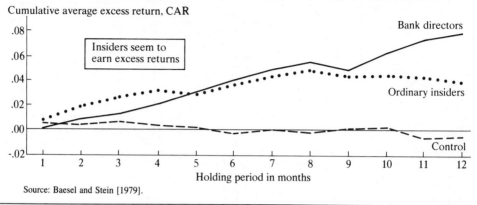

Source: Baesel and Stein [1979].

that they may be able to. He simulated transactions in excess returns from simulated investments in stocks *after* reports of insider transactions were filed with the SEC, and found that his strategy produced excess returns.

The Levine Insider Trading Case.   In May 1986 the SEC, through the Department of Justice, charged that Dennis Levine, in his capacity as an investment banker, engaged in insider trading in 54 securities involved in mergers or other takeovers over a six-year period. In some of these cases Levine and the firm he worked for had direct involvement as an investment banker with the firm in question. In other cases Levine received the information from a third party. In each case cited by the SEC there was a corresponding date on which Levine executed a trade either in the security itself or in the options on the security. Trades occurred as early as 49 days before the eventual announcement and as late as one day before the announcement. A study of these cases by Berry and Grant (1986) reveals positive excess returns, on average, on the days when Levine traded, and for each day subsequent to that initial trade until, approximately, the information on which Levine was acting was made public. There was no indication of excess returns prior to Levine's trading in the security. In effect, there was a gradual increase in security price that corresponds rather closely to the point in time in which Levine entered the market, through the point in time that the information was revealed to the public. **In some cases, at least, inside information *is used* and *does affect* the price of the security.**

Forecasting Returns on the Market Portfolio

Look at Figure 16–7. Here our investor has identified his estimate of the relationship between security risk and equilibrium security returns. This is the investor's view of the security market line, or the risk–return opportunities available if the market is in equilibrium. From this line the investor finds the discount rate to apply in determining the present value of the securities' expected future cash flows, or $E^k(\tilde{R}_i)$. The line represents the standard from which to assess over- or undervaluation by the market. Our question

FIGURE 16–7   Differences in Expectations of Overall Market Returns

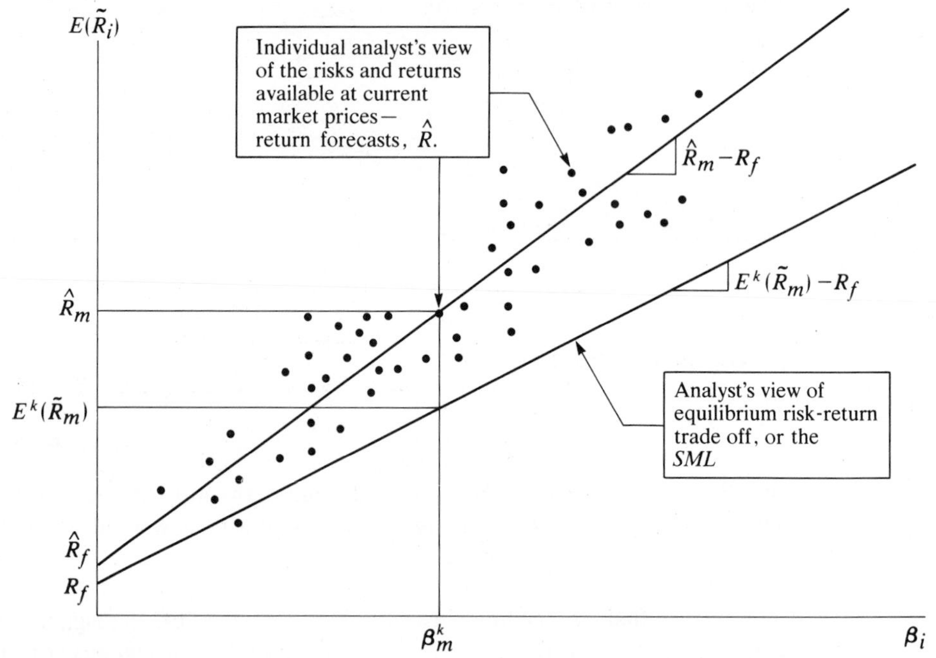

now is whether it's possible at some point in time, given market prices, for most securities to lie above the line (as represented in the figure) and offer returns that are greater than those that should be available in equilibrium. In other words, is it possible for the entire market to be in disequilibrium, offering a return, $\hat{R}_m$, that exceeds the equilibrium return, $E^k(\tilde{R}_m)$?

To arrive at this conclusion (or its opposite but equivalent, the market is overvalued) means that our investor must have future earnings and dividend expectations that differ from the market's, or must have applied a discount rate to those future expected cash flows that is different than the market applied. Different dividend expectations may occur with different expectations about the growth or efficiency of the economy. Different discount rates may occur if the investor forecasts a future path for interest rates or the slope of the security market line that is different from the market's. We will discuss these issues under the headings *Forecasting Interest Rates* and *Forecasting Aggregate Market Earnings*.

Forecasting Interest Rates

"Interest rates are the stuff of which nightmares are made. No one—not bull nor bear—can claim a respectable short-term forecasting performance for the past two years. One should therefore view with considerable skepticism today's consensus forecast that the bottom has been reached in the interest rate cycle. Given the extreme volatility of interest rates in recent years, anything can happen."[6] Indeed, shortly after this observation was made, interest rates dropped substantially, and continued to do so for most of the next four years. In general, the quotation reflects the opinion of many regarding models that predict interest rates. While we know something about many of the factors that *determine* interest rates (money supply, the demand for loanable funds, etc.) little evidence exists to suggest these factors can be predicted with enough accuracy to successfully *predict* the rates.

Yet, the potential reward from correct anticipation of an interest-rate change is sufficient to persuade many to keep searching for a technique to predict rates. For a security growing at a constant rate of 7 percent, a decline in the discount rate from 14 percent to 12 percent that may accompany a 2 percentage point decline in interest rates, leads to a 40 percent increase in share price!

It should not be surprising to you that it is difficult to predict interest rates. If you find yourself hesitant to predict stock market returns since the prices of stocks are set to reflect consensus expectations, then you should also be hesitant about forecasting interest rates (the risk-free rate is the intercept of the security market line that, in part, determines expectations of stock market returns). Current interest rates are set by the interaction of the supply of and demand for loanable funds. But the supply of and demand for loanable funds reflects many things—including investor forecasts of the *future* supply of and demand for loanable funds. If many borrowers and lenders feel the future supply of funds will be low—thus raising future rates—lenders will remove current funds from the market and borrowers will demand more, leading to an increase in *current* interest rates. Thus, current rates will reflect expectations of the future.

This theme is entirely consistent with our earlier discussion of the efficient market hypothesis. We suggested that if financial markets are efficient, security prices and rates of return (including T-bills, commercial paper, CDs, etc.) will move independently over time. They will have no memory. Thus, interest rates, being the return on low- or zero-risk securities, also will change randomly over time.

It is possible, of course, for a small number of investors to have a valid predictive model of interest rates. The large econometric models, such as the Wharton-FRB model, attempt to predict rates two to three years into the future. Yet they have not been very successful at predicting any monetary variables—particularly those relating to interest rates and security returns.

Simpler models also exist. One large bank, for example, uses a simple one-equation model that allows the analyst to plug in forecasted real and monetary values and the model develops a forecast. A great deal of reliance is not placed on the result, however.

In fact, Argus Research may have the best answer. It's a self-made model (see Figure 16–8) that simply requires the investor to provide answers to four questions. The total numerical score provides the answer of rising, constant, or falling rates. Does the model work for some investors? Of course we don't know, but it may be as useful a guide as anything else available.

---

[6]Argus Research Corporation [1982].

FIGURE 16–8

TAKE THE INTEREST RATE QUIZ

Given the current controversy among economists concerning the future path of interest rates, the reader is asked to join the forecasting game by taking the following test. Just circle your answer to each of the four questions, then follow the scoring guide to arrive at your interest rate forecast that will be consistent with your own assumptions about the key economic variables.

A. A recession or downturn in business activity:
1. Will resume in the second quarter.
2. Is over, but the recovery will begin slowly.
3. Is over, and will be replaced by a relatively strong recovery.

B. In the course of the next few months, the overall rate of inflation will:
1. Decline.
2. Stay about the same.
3. Increase.

C. Again for the next few months, the U.S. dollar's value in the foreign exchange markets will:
1. Appreciate.
2. Remain stable or decline slightly.
3. Depreciate rapidly.

D. Money growth in the next three months will:
1. Continue to be de-emphasized by the Fed.
2. Be moderate, consistent with long-term Fed goals.
3. Be too rapid for the Fed to ignore.

Scoring guide: Add up the numbers corresponding to the selected answers. If your total score is 6 or less, you must forecast declining interest rates. If you score 7–8, your forecast calls for stable interest rates. And a score of 9 or higher means you think interest rates will soon be rising.

Source: Argus Research Corporation [1983].

Forecasting Aggregate Market Earnings

Forecasting the general level of economic activity is big business itself. There are hundreds of firms and consultants that pride themselves on being able to predict things such as GNP, personal income, corporate profits, and other national income account figures. Almost all large banks and all brokerage houses have research divisions that attempt to do the same thing. Some of the prediction models are large and extensive, encompassing hundreds of equations and elaborate estimation techniques.

On the whole these models have been somewhat successful in predicting the level of overall economic activity. For example, one study of the major existing econometric models found that during economic expansions the typical error in estimating the level of real GNP was 1.2 percent; in the level of inflation it was 1.1 percent. During economic contractions, however, these error rates grew to 3 percent and 2.5 percent, respectively. In effect, these models tend to miss the big moves of the economy.

The success of macro forecasting models diminishes rapidly as special sectors of the economy are considered. Thus, the error rates in predicting corporate profits would probably be substantially greater than those in predicting GNP.

Whether some forecasters are significantly better than others at predicting the successes and failures of the corporate sector is an open question. One analyst may be able to predict important values better than another, but it's very difficult to determine in fact whether the analyst was good at predictions, or just lucky.

Forecasting Market Returns

Some analysts attempt to put their forecasts of future cash flows and discount rates together to predict overall market returns, $\hat{R}_m$. This is the equivalent of predicting whether the market currently is overpriced or underpriced. Of course, this prediction is closely related to attempts by the investor to time an entrance or exit from the stock market. Investors who are willing to act on their belief that the market is overvalued, would shift out of stocks and other risky securities into bonds and bills, or would hedge their positions in stocks with strategies that use options or futures market transactions.

In reality, most brokerage house analysts offer "quasi" forecasts of market returns, rather than unambiguous suggestions about how to invest. Recommendations of the form "the market may go up if. . . ." are common. Given the typical ambiguity of the recommendation it is very difficult to determine if anybody can predict overall market returns. An example of such a forecast will illustrate this problem:

> The recent rally in the fixed-income market has restored equities to a position of fair relative value. The implied 16 percent total rate of return for equities compares favorably with our forecasts of long-term inflation and interest rates. In the short run, however, equities may be vulnerable to a correction. There is a risk that the initial benefits of declining interest rates on equity prices may be superceded by poor corporate earnings reports. . . . Nevertheless, we believe the 1981 outlook for both fixed-income and equity securities is positive, even though their interim performance is likely to remain volatile.[7]

Note the ambiguity in the forecast.

Alternatively, unambiguous, mechanical forecasting models of stock market returns don't work well at all. For example, one study attempted to develop a forecasting model by regressing stock market returns on variables like the level of unemployment, money supply growth, inflation, and the balance of payments. When these variables could be observed with perfect foresight (in the month in which the stock market return was measured) an excess return per annum of almost 2 percent was generated. However, using predetermined values of the variables (without perfect foresight, and using the last available figure for the variable before the month of the market return was measured) resulted in virtually no excess return. Of course, in an efficient securities market this is exactly what you would expect. Publicly available information on unemployment, to the extent it is important in valuing securities, would tend to be fully reflected in the prices of securities at the point in time it is released.

In summary, while it is true that at any time the market may be undervalued or overvalued (perhaps we can see evidence of this, ex post, when unusually large or small returns are generated on the S&P index), little evidence exists to suggest that future excess returns can be easily forecast. Excess returns on the market portfolio seem to follow a pattern over time that approximates a random walk, and few seem to be able to anticipate when those returns will be positive or negative with sufficient consistency to profit from their analysis.

---

[7]Merrill Lynch [1981], p. 6.

Forecasting with "Technical Analysis"

Technical analysis refers to any and all attempts on the part of market participants to determine the future movement of security prices, using only past data that measures market facts and figures; i.e., past stock or bond price data, volume of trading data, short interest, and other characteristics of the trading process. Technical analysis may be applied to individual securities or to aggregate stock prices. The rationale that underlies the application of technical analysis to security prices is as follows:

> Market participants, in general, do not have access to appropriate fundamental information as soon as do "inside" analysts. These inside analysts, acting on the basis of their fundamental information, affect the demand and, therefore, the price of the security. The "insiders," however, constitute a very small proportion of the total set of market participants. Consequently, the impact of these individuals, with knowledge unavailable to other market participants, causes the prices of a security to form particular patterns as they change over time. That is, there are trends or structures to past prices caused by the actions of a few knowledgeable individuals. One way that those investors who are not privy to the information can take advantage of it is to understand how prices are changing in response to the actions of these select few. In other words, technical analysts attempt to use past prices in order to capture effects that can be attributed to information that is not generally available to them. They expect to *read* from past price changes whether the next price change will be positive, zero, or negative. The justification for technical analysis hinges on an assumption that the true value of securities will be revealed only slowly over time. A particular twist to price changes offers some evidence about the kind of information available to those "in the know."

In fact, much of technical analysis seems to have neglected the above justification and has concentrated solely on attempting to generalize from particular historical price or volume patterns. Observing that a "head and shoulders" pattern (a particular shape to past prices) precedes a downward or upward movement in security prices is cause enough for the analyst to act. Justifications that relate to demand for the security tend to be ignored. The problem with this applied approach to technical analysis is that the analyst too often generalizes from the particular when no such generalization may be appropriate, given the actual process by which security prices are determined. Indeed, most of the evidence presented in Chapter 6 suggests that price changes in these securities markets are independent from one to the next. Independence itself is sufficient to imply that any analysis of past price movement would be useless for purposes of identifying under- or overvalued securities.

Why does technical analysis exist? The answer may have something to do with human behavior, as we discussed the issue with reference to market efficiency in Chapter 6. There is a tendency for all of us to generalize from the particular. Technical analysts, who observe that for three different securities the same pattern (at least in their perception) of historical price changes has been associated with a subsequent positive price change, and who use this information to develop an investment strategy, may simply be exhibiting behavioral tendencies to generalize, when no such generalizations can be justified on economic and statistical grounds. So much for "empirical observations" without a theory.

If it is true that price changes are indeed independent from one to the next, then why would anyone use technical analysis? Wouldn't analysts applying technical methodologies to security markets ultimately realize that they were not securing additional returns and find alternative methods for the formation of their portfolios? The answer to the question lies in random performance and turnover. During any given investment period, half the technical analysts will do better than average and half will do worse than average. The half that does worse than average will leave. However, knowing that some technical analysts performed well without knowing of those who performed poorly may be enough to induce new analysts into the field, thus perpetuating technical analysis as a useless artifact.

Not all technical analysis necessarily falls into this category. Our initial discussion suggested a rationale for the success of some technical analysis. However, such success must hinge upon a sound justification for the pattern of price movement used in the analysis. The potential technician must critique the rationale that leads to the use of that technique. It is not obvious what signal may be conveyed through an analysis which identifies a "head and shoulders" price pattern, or a "resistance level," or a "support level."

In one study, by Arditti and McCollough [1978], technicians were asked to differentiate between price series generated by random simulation and actual price series for individual securities. The technicians were unable to tell which price series was simulated and which was real, suggesting that "reading" the observed price change pattern may be a difficult task indeed.

Summary

Forecasting concentrates on developing models or methods to improve on the prediction of future earnings and dividends and the components of risk. Because of the obvious rewards from successful forecasts, a good deal of time and effort is devoted to the process by thousands of market professionals.

Most studies of the accuracy of earnings forecasts imply that managers and professional analysts improve on mechanical forecasting techniques only moderately. In general, the average absolute percentage forecast error from naive mechanical models averages about 30 percent, while that from professionals averages about 20 percent. The accuracy of the forecasts seem to vary considerably with the firm whose earnings are being forecast, and over time with business fluctuations.

Evidence is ambiguous on the question of whether it's possible to use professional forecasts as the basis for identifying undervalued securities to include in a portfolio. Conclusions from studies span the range from "absolutely no benefit" to "substantial excess returns from investment strategies based on the publication of the earnings forecast."

Forecasting the components of a security's risk—beta, standard deviation of returns, and correlation of returns between securities—is no less important. In fact, in recent years, a number of brokerage houses and other investment service firms have concentrated more effort on the prediction of security risk. Much of this has been devoted to improving on purely historical estimates of security beta coefficients.

There is quite a bit of evidence suggesting that firms' insiders have information that allows them to form better predictions than outsiders, and we presented some of the philosophical points on insider *use* of this information.

Regarding the ability to forecast overall trends in the market we are relatively negative. Neither interest rates nor the rate of return on the market portfolio appears to be easy to forecast. Simply, there is little evidence to suggest that professional forecastors can predict on a consistent basis, over long periods of time, overall market returns.

References

Alexander, Gordon J., and Chervany, Norman L. [1980] "On the Estimation and Stability of Beta." *Journal of Financial and Quantitative Analysis* (March).

Altman, Edward. [1968] "Financial Ratios, Discriminant Analysis, and the Prediction of Corporate Bankruptcy." *Journal of Finance* (September).

Arditti, Fred D., and McCollough, W. Andrew. [1978] "Can Analysts Distinguish between Real and Randomly Generated Stock Prices?" *Financial Analysts Journal* (November–December).

Argus Research Corporation. [1982] "The Interest Rate Outlook: Expect Surprises." *Argus Weekly Economic Review* (January 18).

Argus Research Corporation. [1983] "Argus Economics: The Interest Rate Outlook: Confusion Reigns." New York: Argus Research Corporation (February 14).

Baesel, Jerome B., and Stein, Garry R. [1979] "The Value of Information: Inferences from the Profitability of Insider Trading." *Journal of Financial and Quantitative Analysis* (September).

Basi, B. A.; Carey, K. J.; and Twark, R. [1976] "A Comparison of the Accuracy of Corporate and Security Analysts Forecasts of Earnings." *Accounting Review* (April).

Beaver, William; Lambert, Richard; and Morse, Dale. [1980] "The Information Content of Security Prices." *Journal of Accounting and Economics* (January).

Beckers, Stan. [1983] "Variances of Security Price Returns Based on High, Low, and Closing Prices." *Journal of Business* (January).

Berry, M.; and Grant, D. [1986] "Pre-Event Trading: Exception or Rule?" Working Paper, University of New Mexico.

Bjerring, James H.; Lakonishok, Josef; and Vermaelen, Theo. [1983] "Stock Prices and Financial Analysts' Recommendations." *Journal of Finance* (March).

Black, Fischer. [1971a] "Implications of the Random Walk Hypothesis for Portfolio Management." *Financial Analysts Journal* (March–April).

Black, Fischer. [1973] "Yes Virginia, There Is Hope: Tests of the Value Line Ranking System." *Financial Analysts Journal* (September–October).

Blume, Marshall. [1975] "Betas and Their Regression Tendencies." *Journal of Finance* (June).

Brown, Lawrence D., and Rozeff, Michael. [1978] "The Superiority of Analysts Forecasts as Measures of Expectations: Evidence from Earnings." *Journal of Finance* (March).

Brown, Philip; Foster, G.; and Noreen, E. [1985] "Security Analyst Multi-Year Earnings Forecasts and the Capital Market." *Studies in Accounting Research #21,* American Accounting Association.

Brown, Phillip, and Kennelly, John W. [1972] "The Information Content of Quarterly Earnings: An Extension and Some Further Evidence." *Journal of Business* (July).

Brown, Philip, and Niederhoffer, Victor. [1968] "The Predictive Content of Quarterly Earnings." *Journal of Business* (October).

Carey, Kenneth J. [1978]. "The Accuracy of Estimates of Earnings from Naive Models." *Journal of Economics and Business* (Spring–Summer).

Chant, Peter D. [1980] "On the Predictability of Corporate Earnings per Share Behavior." *Journal of Finance* (March).

Copeland, Ronald, and Marioni, Robert. [1972] "Executives' Forecasts of Earnings per Share versus Forecasts of Naive Models." *Journal of Business* (October).

Copeland, Thomas E., and Mayers, David. [1982] "The Value Line Enigma (1965–1978): A Case Study of Performance Evaluation Issues." *Journal of Financial Economics* (November).

Cornell, B., and Dietrick, J. K. [1978] "Mean-Absolute-Deviation versus Least-Squares Regression Estimation of Beta Coefficients." *Journal of Financial and Quantitative Analysis* (March).

Elton, E. J., and Gruber, M. J. [1972] "Earnings Estimates and the Accuracy of Expectational Data." *Management Science* (April).

Elton, Edwin J.; Gruber, Martin J.; and Gultekin, Mustafa N. [1984] "Professional Expectations: Accuracy and Diagnosis of Errors." *Journal of Financial and Quantitative Analysis* (December).

Finnerty, Joseph. [1976] "Insiders Activity and Inside Information: A Multivariate Analysis." *Journal of Financial and Quantitative Analysis* (June).

Finnerty, Joseph. [1979] "Insiders and Market Efficiency." *Journal of Finance* (September).

Foster, G. [1973] "Stock Market Reaction to Estimates of Earnings per Share by Company Officials." *Journal of Accounting Research* (Spring).

Fried, Dov, and Givoly, Dan. [1982] "Financial Analysts' Forecasts of Earnings." *Journal of Accounting and Economics* (June).

Givoly, Dan, and Lakonishok, Josef. [1979] "The Information Content of Financial Analysts' Forecasts of Earnings." *Journal of Accounting and Economics* (August).

Givoly, Dan, and Lakonishok, Josef. [1984] "The Quality of Analysts' Forecasts of Earnings." *Financial Analysts Journal* (October).

Green, David, Jr., and Segall, Joel. [1967] "The Predictive Power of First-Quarter Earnings Reports." *Journal of Business* (January).

Growth, John C.; Lewellen, Wilbur; Schlarbaum, Gary; and Lease, Ronald. [1979] "An Analysis of Brokerage House Securities Recommendations." *Financial Analysts Journal* (January–February).

Henriksson, Roy D., and Merton, Robert C. [1981] "On Market Timing and Investment Performance.

II. Statistical Procedures for Evaluating Forecasting Skills." *Journal of Business* (October).

Holloway, Clark. [1981] "A Note on Testing and Aggressive Investment Strategy Using Value Line Ranks," *Journal of Finance* (June).

Hopewell, Michael H., and Schwartz, Arthur L. [1978] "Temporary Trading Suspensions in Individual NYSE Securities." *Journal of Finance* (September).

Huberman, Gur, and Kandel, Shmuel. [1986] "Autoregressive State Variables Explain the Value Line Enigma." Unpublished working paper, University of Chicago (June).

Huberman, Gur, and Kandel, Shmuel. [1986] "Value Line and Firm Size." Unpublished working paper, University of Chicago (May).

Hudson, Richard L. [1982] "SEC Goes after Santa Fe Insiders but Light Penalties Draw Criticism." *The Wall Street Journal*, November 22, 1982.

Jaffee, Jeffrey. [1974] "Special Information and Insider Trading." *Journal of Business* (July).

Jones, Charles P., and Litzenberger, Robert H. [1970] "Quarterly Earnings Reports and Intermediate Stock Price Trends." *Journal of Finance* (March).

Joy, M. O.; Litzenberger, R. H.; and McEnally, R. W. [1977] "The Adjustment of Stock Prices to Announcements of Unanticipated Changes in Quarterly Earnings." *Journal of Accounting Research* 15 (Autumn).

Latane, H. A.; Tuttle, D. L.; and Jones, C. P. [1969] "Quarterly Data: E/P Ratios vs. Changes in Earnings in Forecasting Future Price Changes." *Financial Analysts Journal*.

Latane, Henry; Joy, O. Maurice; and Jones, Charles. [1970] "Quarterly Data, Sort-Rank Routines and Security Evaluation." *Journal of Business* (October).

Lloyd-Davies, Peter, and Canes, Michael. [1978] "Stock Prices and the Publication of Second-Hand Information." *Journal of Business* (January).

Malkiel, Burton, and Cragg, John G. [1982] *Expectations and the Valuation of Shares*. Chicago: University of Chicago Press.

Merrill Lynch, Pierce, Fenner and Smith, Inc. [1981] *Investment Strategy: A Bi-Monthly Perspective* (February).

Merton, Robert C. [1981] "On Market Timing and Investment Performance. I. An Equilibrium Theory of Value for Market Forecasts." *Journal of Business* (July).

Nelson, C. R. [1975] "Rational Expectations and the Predictive Efficiency of Economic Models." *Journal of Business* (July).

Nicholson, S. Francis. [1968] "Price-Earnings in Relation to Investment Results." *Financial Analysts Journal* (January-February).

Patell, James. [1976] "Corporate Forecasts of Earnings per Share and Stock Price Behavior: Empirical Tests." *Journal of Accounting Research* (Autumn).

Penman, Stephen H. [1980] "An Empirical Investigation of the Voluntary Disclosure of Corporate Earnings Forecasts." *Journal of Accounting Research* (Spring).

Penman, Stephen H. [1982] "Insider Trading and the Dissemination of Firms' Forecast Information." *Journal of Business* (October).

Penman, Stephen H. [1983] "The Predictive Content of Earnings Forecasts and Dividends." *Journal of Finance* (September).

Penman, Stephen H. [1985] "A Comparison of the Information Content of Insider Trading and Management Earnings Forecasts." *Journal of Financial and Quantitative Analysis* (March).

Rendleman, Richard; Jones, Charles P.; and Latane, Henry A. [1982] "Empirical Anomalies Based on Unexpected Earnings and the Importance of the Risk Adjustments." *Journal of Financial Economics* (November).

Richards, R. Malcolm; Benjamin, James J.; and Strawser, Robert H. [1977] "An Examination of the Accuracy of Earnings Forecasts." *Financial Management* (Fall).

Richards, R. Malcolm, and Fraser, Donald R. [1977] "Further Evidence on the Accuracy of Analysts' Earnings Forecasts: A Comparison Among Ana-

lysts." *Journal of Economics and Business* (Spring–Summer).

Rosenberg, Barr, and Guy, James. [1976] "Prediction of Beta from Investment Fundamentals." *Financial Analysts Journal* (July–August).

Rosenberg, Barr, and Marathe, Vinay. [1975] "The Prediction of Investment Risk: Systematic and Residual Risk." Chicago: University of Chicago, Seminar on the Analysis of Security Prices, CRSP (November).

Rosenberg, Barr, and McKibben, Walt. [1973] "The Prediction of Systematic and Specific Risk in Common Stocks." *Journal of Financial and Quantitative Analysis* (March).

Rudd, Andrew, and Clasing, Henry K. [1982] *Modern Portfolio Theory: The Principles of Investment Management*. Homewood, Ill.: Richard D. Irwin.

Skinner, B. F. [1948] "Superstition in the Pigeon." *Journal of Experimental Psychology* (no. 38).

Stanley, Kenneth; Schlarbaum, Gary; and Lewellen, Wilbur. [1980] "Actual Investor Performance with Brokerage Recommendations." Purdue University.

Stickel, Scott E. [1985] "The Effect of Value Line Investment Survey Rank Changes on Common Stock Prices." *Journal of Financial Economics* (September).

Treynor, J., and Black, F. [1973] "How to Use Security Analysis to Improve Portfolio Selection" *Journal of Business* (January).

Trueman, Brett. [1983] "Motivating Management to Reveal Inside Information." *Journal of Finance* (September).

von Furstenberg, G. M., and Malkiel, B. G. [1977] "Financial Analysis in an Inflationary Environment." *Journal of Finance* (May).

Watts, R. [1978] "Systematic 'Abnormal' Returns after Quarterly Earnings Announcements." *Journal of Financial Economics* (June–September).

Questions and Problems

1. Studies have suggested that professional stock market analysts' forecasts of earnings per share improve only moderately on naive historical extrapolations. What reasons can you give for this surprising outcome?

2. The SEC suggests that one reason professional analysts have not accurately forecast earnings is

that many firms tend to mislead the public. They make public announcements understating management's expectations when positive results are expected and overstating (i.e., they are less pessimistic than they should be) management's expectations when negative results are expected. Regardless of the managers' tendency, what rules could the SEC make that would encourage managers to make public statements reflecting their true expectations? Would any of these rules have costly side effects?

3. Use the efficient market hypothesis to suggest why analysts find it difficult (not impossible, necessarily) to predict:

   a. Changes in the general level of interest rates.

   b. The returns on an index of stock prices.

4. Recently it has become easier to assemble information on the forecasts of earnings per share made by professional analysts. Is this trend likely to lead to a set of market prices for securities that are closer to the underlying equilibrium, or intrinsic, values of the securities?

5. For each of the following changes, identify the direction of the effect of the change on the common stock's beta coefficient:

   a. United Airlines parent, Allegis, decides to sell its extensive hotel business.

   b. Citibank raises new capital with a $700 million issue of new common stock.

   c. Digital Equipment decides to bring out a new (very expensive) system to allow its computers to work directly with those of IBM and other major producers.

   d. Your parent's small business decides to co-sign on a loan for your sister's education.

6. The second page of the second section of *The Wall Street Journal* includes an index to businesses that are the subject of an article in that day's *Journal*. Pick five firms from this list that also are covered by Value Line. Using Value Line betas and the news article for each firm, indicate how the "information" in the article would be expected to

change the security's beta. Make sure to explain the magnitude and direction of the effect you forecast.

7. Suppose you are a money manager with primary responsibility for making decisions on 10 large trust accounts. A business acquaintance, who works for a rapidly growing genetic technology firm, confides that many of their "new products" may take two more years' of intensive research and development before they are ready to be marketed. You are surprised to learn this. Should you sell shares of this company on behalf of your clients? What other actions should be taken, either before or after the sale, if that is the action you choose? Would your answer differ if the information came from an employee of another firm in the same industry, who based his expectation on information gathered from customers and others?

8. Describe how each of the following would be expected to affect a firm's common stock beta coefficient:

   a. An increase in the degree of financial leverage.

   b. An increase in the degree of operating leverage.

   c. An increase in the standard deviation of the return on the market portfolio.

   d. An increase in the covariance of the firm's revenues with the growth of the national economy.

   e. An increase in the covariance of the firm's costs of operations with the growth of the national economy.

   f. The purchase of an asset with a large standard deviation of return but with no covariance with the market return.

17

Management Decisions and Value

The Managerial Decision Nexus

Management decisions have a direct impact on the value of the firm's debt and equity securities. For example, a decision to increase productive capacity can play a major role in the determination of value. So, too, might a decision to enter into a labor contract calling for a wage increase for hourly employees. To evaluate the consequences of such decisions requires a solid understanding of the managerial decision process, and how that process affects value. In fact, some analysts view managerial talent as *the* primary influence determining security values.

In aggregate terms, **financial managers** are charged with managing the size and structure of the firm's assets and liabilities, as they are reflected in the balance sheet. The major categories of decisions they make are: the investment decision, the financing decision, and the dividend payment decision. By their decisions managers may influence current and expected future returns and the risk of the firm's shares. Of course, a manager who acts solely *on behalf of shareholders* of a publicly traded common stock will attempt to maximize value through decisions in these areas. Schematically, the corporate financial decision process can be represented as,

(17–1)   *Management's Goal*

$$\text{Max } (P_{i0}^e) \quad = \sum_{t=1}^{\infty} \frac{E(\tilde{D}_{it})}{[1 + E(\tilde{R}_i)]^t}$$

$$\left\{ \begin{array}{l} \text{Investment decisions} \\ \text{Financing decisions} \\ \text{Dividend decisions} \end{array} \right\}$$

> Maximization of value
> by choice of investment,
> financing, and dividend
> decisions

=

> A function of how those decisions
> impact upon expected future
> cash flows, risk, and thus
> the equilibrium expected return.

The market analyst must ascertain how the firm's decisions impact upon expected future dividends and the discount rate. Without this knowledge shareholders cannot evaluate the effect of an announced decision (an increase in dividends, or an issue of new common stock, say), and cannot, therefore, anticipate the effect on return and risk.

In this chapter we summarize the impact on share value, if any, of these management decisions. As you will see, some decisions have a direct and substantial effect on share price. Others that are widely thought to have an effect (e.g., cash dividend policy, and stock dividends) actually do not influence share price under most conditions.

Investment Decisions and Value

In the early 1980s Outboard Marine decided to meet increasing foreign competition by eliminating outdated production facilities and building smaller specialized plants. This decision was primarily responsible for the increase in stock price from a low of $5 at the end of 1980 to $30 just five years later. In general, productive investments undertaken by the firm affect its cash flows, risk, and the ability to pay dividends. The key to correct decision making from a financial perspective is to evaluate available opportunities in a framework consistent with maximizing the firm's value. This is the capital budgeting decision, or project evaluation decision. In corporate finance or accounting courses the decision-making process is correctly described as:

> Accept all capital budgeting opportunities that provide positive net present values, and reject all those that generate negative net present values.

To illustrate its application, suppose a firm has an opportunity to invest $400,000 in the production of a new product (the project). Management expectations are that the project will generate net cash flows of $100,000 per year beginning next year and lasting into the foreseeable future. If other equivalent risk opportunities in the marketplace offer returns of 20 percent, the project's net present value is

$$NPV_{j0} = -\frac{400,000}{(1 + .20)^0} + \sum_{t=1}^{\infty} \frac{100,000}{(1 + .20)^t} = -400,000 + 500,000 = \$100,000$$

In this case, management's acceptance of the project would be expected to add value to the firm.

More generally, the net present value decision rule can be stated as,

$$(17\text{--}2) \qquad NPV_{j0} = \sum_{t=0}^{\infty} \frac{E(\tilde{Y}_{jt})}{[1 + E(\tilde{R}_j)]^t} - \sum_{t=0}^{\infty} \frac{E(\tilde{I}_{jt})}{[1 + E(\tilde{R}_j)]^t}$$

Rule: if $NPV_{j0} > 0$ Accept

$NPV_{j0} < 0$ Reject

where NPV_{j0} = Net present value of the jth investment opportunity.

I_{jt} = Incremental net cash outflows from shareholders generated by the jth opportunity in t.

Y_{jt} = Incremental net cash inflows to shareholders generated by the jth opportunity in t.

$E(\tilde{R}_j)$ = The demanded return on securities with risk equal to the jth investment opportunity.

If the manager rejects a good investment opportunity ($NPV > 0$), or accepts a bad one ($NPV < 0$), the value of the firm will be lower than it otherwise could be.

The entire process can be represented graphically within the context of the security market line by setting NPV equal to zero, solving the above expression for the internal rate of return, and comparing the internal rate with the project's required return, $E(\tilde{R}_j)$. For example, the internal rate of return on the project in the prior example is 25 percent. This value is compared with the required return from the security market line of 20 percent in Figure 17–1. Simply put, as long as the project is located above the SML, the firm will benefit through acceptance of the project. Importantly, the appropriate $E(\tilde{R}_j)$ to be used as the "cutoff" rate, or minimum required rate, is the SML rate for the project's risk level, β_j.

Anticipated and Unanticipated Investment Opportunities

The rules for making investment decisions hold regardless of the market's knowledge of the project. However, the state of the market's knowledge of the project and its NPV together determine whether there will be a *price reaction* to a public announcement of the firm's capital spending plans.

If the project is unknown to the market at the time it is being evaluated, then publication of the acceptance of the project will provide new information to the market. In this case the price of the stock of the firm will change. If the market agrees with the management's assessment of the project's value, the management can anticipate a positive price reaction to a positive NPV project. The process is depicted graphically in Figure 17–1 for the firm choosing project j. Essentially, a new portfolio is formed, F^*, by combining the original firm, F, with the project, j. This "new" firm lies above the SML.[1]

The market, observing that the acceptance of the project will move the firm to a position above the line, increases its demand for shares of the firm. The excess demand, as always, will be eliminated by an increase in the price of the shares. Through this process the value of the project is embedded into share price. Of course, the effect on share price is governed by expectations of the worth of the project, and may affect share price well before investment in the project begins. Indeed, "growth" stocks, for the most part, are those where the market has expectations that the firm has extraordinary opportunities for future investment, i.e., lots of projects above the SML.

If the project under consideration already has been anticipated by the market, then

---

[1]Because the new, larger firm can be thought of as simply a portfolio of the original firm and the project, and because portfolio risk is a linear combination of component βs, the new temporary disequilibrium risk-return relation, F^*, will lie on the ray between the project j and original firm position, F. How far along the vector it is temporarily located depends on how large the project is relative to the market value of the firm.

FIGURE 17–1   Investment Opportunities and Market Values

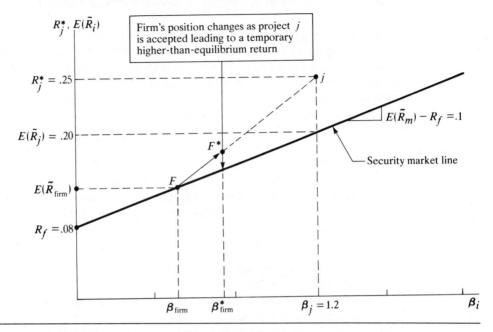

publication of the firm's acceptance of the project will not affect share price. In terms of Figure 17–1, the market already has recognized the firm as F^*, rather than F, and share price has adjusted to reflect the value of the project. For example, growth stocks have high prices relative to current earnings partly because the market has incorporated the expected value of anticipated future projects.

In general, the change in market price depends on the *NPV* of the project, management's decision regarding acceptance or rejection, and the extent to which the market has anticipated the project. Of course, the market is continuously reassessing the value of the firm's portfolio of projects. Complete enumeration of the possible effects on market price is summarized below:

	Positive NPV		Negative NPV	
	Anticipated	*Not Anticipated*	*Anticipated*	*Not Anticipated*
Accept	No change	Price up	No change	Price down
Reject	Price down	No change	Price up	No change

A few examples will help to clarify these relationships. On February 21, 1986, Compaq unveiled a new line of faster and lighter personal computers. Its stock price rose 10 percent on that day and another 4 percent the next day. Apparently the market viewed the new products as having positive *NPV*s. Some years before, RCA Corporation announced its decision to get out of the computer business. The price of the stock rose considerably on that day, apparently reflecting the rejection of a project that had been under consideration by RCA's management, and had been viewed by the market as a negative *NPV* opportunity.

More complex examples exist, of course. In early 1986, Symbolics held a meeting with a large group of security analysts to publicly announce a new line of products for development in the near future. Symbolics' stock price fell by almost 15 percent within two days. Either the market viewed management as getting into negative *NPV* projects, or the market revised downward its estimate of the value of previously anticipated positive *NPV* projects.

The Real Effects on Price

It's hard to measure how close the connection is between the firm's capital investment plans, the expectations of the market, and share price. Companies are naturally reluctant to give much information to the market (or to researchers studying the subject) on the success or failure of individual projects. The information is considered proprietary.

What we know about the process can be summarized as follows:

1. Firms that discover superior investment opportunities ultimately find a positive effect on their stock's price.
2. The market is not completely and perfectly able, as of the time of the announcement of a project, to discriminate between firms whose investments ultimately prove successful and those whose investments prove unsuccessful.

Because of this, security analysts spend considerable time and effort attempting to gather information on a firm's capital investment plans, both those that have been undertaken recently and those to be undertaken in the near future. Information on new products and new markets is particularly sought after.[2]

Mergers and Value

Recently RCA Corporation was acquired by General Electric for securities valued at $6.4 billion. From the announcement of the merger agreement to the completion of the merger (a period of six months) RCA stockholders' values increased by 22 percentage points more than the market. GE's stockholders gained about 4 percentage points more than the market.

Technically, a merger is a combination of two or more firms. It represents the formation of a portfolio of assets and liabilities of firms that formerly operated separately. As is the case in any applied portfolio problem, the justification for the merger would rest on the ability to generate either higher returns or lower risk. If one or the other of these is

---

[2]To this point our discussion has treated the investment decision rather narrowly, as if the problem always involves the acquisition of a piece of real-capital equipment. Actually, investment decisions include a much broader set of problems. Any time a decision influences the size and/or efficiency of the production processes, it is an investment decision, and should be evaluated by measuring the net present value of cash inflows and outflows as influenced by the action taken. For example, the institution of a retirement program that influences the costs of production directly through hourly wage costs and indirectly through greater productivity associated with a more stable labor force is an investment decision.

accomplished the shareholders benefit from the merger. This seems to have been the case for the GE/RCA combination.

Of course, since investors can include the securities of the two merging firms in their own portfolio, there are *no standard deviation reducing benefits* conferred through the merger. Diversification by the firm that occurs from combining operations that are not perfectly correlated is superfluous. Nothing is gained over and above that which is available from the separate inclusion of the firms in the investor's portfolio.

On the other hand, if the merger affords management the opportunity to change operations in a way that would reduce the beta coefficient, then stockholders would benefit. Whether this can be accomplished or not depends on the particular situation. Normally, since the combination is similar to the formation of a portfolio, we would expect the beta of the combined firm to be a weighted average of the betas of the two firms operating independently. In the case of the GE/RCA merger the new risk level would be a weighted average of $\beta_{GE} = .9$ and $\beta_{RCA} = 1.0$, for a new $\beta_{GE} = .93$.

The net effect of these propositions is that mergers can be analyzed in the same context that other capital budgeting decisions are considered. That is, the net present value of the merger from the perspective of either firm can be calculated. Equivalently, they can be evaluated by comparing the return and risk of the combined post-merger firm with the weighted average of the returns and risks of the buying and selling firms operating individually. This amounts to nothing more than determining whether the merger will (temporarily) move the firm above the SML.

For example, if the beta of the combined firm is equal to the weighted average of the betas of the buyer and seller, and the expected (disequilibrium) return of the combined firm is greater than the weighted average of the equilibrium returns of the buyer and seller, due to cost savings programs, the merger should contribute to value. If the market expects this to occur, a windfall gain will be captured for shareholders who held the securities at the time of the announcement (or later if the market does not initially form such expectations). The common term for this windfall is **synergy.** Of course, a merger will be harmful to one or both of the shareholder groups if these conditions do not exist.

Mergers and Valuation: An Example

A way to approach the valuation consequence of a merger is to consider the value of each firm separately—and then together. Suppose two firms, the Buyer, B, and the Seller, S, are valued currently at $20,000 each. The characteristics that give rise to the value are listed in columns 1 and 2 of Table 17–1. Each firm is growing at a constant, though different, rate in perpetuity and each firm has a different current level of earnings and dividends. Firm value in each case would be given by the constant growth valuation model (developed in Chapter 14), or,

(17–3)   *Buyer's Value*

$$V_{B0} = n_B P_{B0}^e = \frac{n_B E(\tilde{D}_B)}{E(\tilde{R}_B) - g_B} = \frac{1,000(\$.50)}{.10 - .075} = \$20,000$$

(17–4)   *Seller's Value*

$$V_{S0} = n_S P_{S0}^e = \frac{n_S E(\tilde{D}_S)}{E(\tilde{R}_S) - g_S} = \frac{1,000(\$1.00)}{.10 - .05} = \$20,000$$

TABLE 17–1   Characteristics and Value of Firms before and after a Merger: No Synergy

	(1)	(2)	(3)	(4)
				Combined C,
	Buyer, B	Seller, C	Combined, C	(with 25% premium)
Earnings $E(\tilde{Y})$	$1,000	$2,000	$3,000	$3,000
Number of shares, n	1,000	1,000	2,000	2,250
Earnings per share	$1.00	$2.00	$1.50	$1.33
Share price, P_0^s	$20	$20	$20	$17.8
Total firm value	$20,000	$20,000	$40,000	$40,000
Price/earnings	20	10	13.3	13.3
Dividend, $E(\tilde{D})$	$ .50	$1.00	$ .75	$ .667
Growth of dividends, g	7.5%	5.0%	*	*
Equilibrium return, $E(\tilde{R})$	.10	.10	.10	.10

*Growth will vary over time.

With no synergy, a combination, C, of the two firms consummated by the buyer issuing one of its shares for each share of the seller would mean

Combined Value

$$V_{CO} = V_{BO} + V_{SO}$$

$$= \$40,000$$

The characteristics of this new firm are indicated in column 3 of Table 17–1. The combined earnings per share are larger than the buyer's earnings per share, but this growth occurs only as a result of the higher level of earnings of the seller relative to its total value (due to its lower growth rate). Importantly, since the value, in the absence of synergy, is only the sum of the values of the two firms, the price/earnings ratio has fallen from 20 to 13.3. Can this be justified? Indeed, it could not be otherwise, since the growth rate of dividends of the combined firm will now be lower than 7.5 percent. Actually, the growth rate will now vary as the years go by, starting out at 5.83 percent and increasing over time as the size of the buyer grows to dominate the size of the seller (the merged firm's growth is 6.9 percent after 10 years).[3]

The last column of the table indicates what would happen if the buyer paid a premium of 25 percent over the current market price for the selling firm (or $25), by issuing 1.25 shares of the buying firm for each share of the selling firm. The market price per share is calculated by dividing the total market value of $40,000 by the number of shares outstanding. In this case there has been a wealth transfer of $2.20 (or $20 − $17.80) per share from the buying firm's shareholders to the selling firm's shareholders. Obviously, the merger will be detrimental to the buyer's shareholders unless sufficient "synergy" exists to offset the premium paid to the buyers. In this case an increase in earnings of $382.50, if all paid out as dividends, would offset the premium cost of buying the firm.

---

[3]Implicit in some statements accompanying merger announcements is the suggestion that the increase in earnings "created" out of the merger of a high P/E ratio firm with a low P/E ratio firm, such as in the example in the text, itself created the illusion of growth that would be valued by the market. However, because analysts can separate illusory growth (the change in e.p.s. from 1.00 to 1.50) from the real growth (7.5 percent and 5 percent) there is no reason to expect a rational market to be fooled by the merger. There is some evidence that the market was not fully adjusting for merger-created growth brought about by the substantial number of conglomerate mergers occurring during the 1960s. There are alternative explanations for the very high (in the 1960s) and then very low (in the 1970s) prices for these firms, however.

Mergers and Valuation: The Empirics

There have been a large number of studies of mergers. These studies have concentrated on measuring whether there have been any net gains from the combination of two firms (i.e., synergy) or any significant wealth transfers between security holders. Most of the studies have attempted to measure the excess returns (cumulative abnormal returns) to stock- and bondholders of buying and selling firms in periods before, during, and after the merger announcement.

We will briefly look at acquisitions made through **tender offers** and through cooperative **merger agreements** between the managements of the two firms. In tender offers the buying firm offers to purchase the common stock of the "seller" directly from shareholders at a premium over its current market price. The actual merger is consummated some time after the successful completion of the tender offer. If the tender offer does not enable the buyer to acquire a sufficient number of shares to affect the merger it is termed unsuccessful. In cooperative merger agreements the details of the combination are negotiated directly by the managements (the approval of the seller's board of directors and stockholders may be required).

In both of these cases there typically is an identifiable announcement date when the terms of the transaction are communicated to the market. Studies of these announcements are summarized in Table 17–2. These figures, along with others not included in the table, suggest:

- Both buyers and sellers tend to be high performers before successfully completed mergers, generating excess returns as high as 20 percent in the year prior to the tender offer or merger announcement.
- Buyers offer significant premiums for seller's shares (that's why the returns to sellers is high), and as a result, windfall returns are captured by the seller.
- The total gain from the merger is, at best, only slightly positive, i.e., the level of synergy appears to be small. In fact, figures not included in the table indicate that the dollar level of synergy is insignificantly different from zero.
- Since unsuccessful attempts to combine result in much lower returns to seller's stockholders, there appears to be little reason for the seller's management to take any action to thwart the combination, i.e., the typical seller reaction that "the merger terms don't offer our shareholders fair value" is, on average, nonsense!

Other issues relating to the control of corporate assets also have been widely studied.

TABLE 17–2   Cumulative Abnormal Returns from Mergers

	Percent CAR from Announcement through Outcome	
	Buyer	*Seller*
Successful		
Merger agreement	−2%	20%
Tender offer	1	28
Unsuccessful		
Merger agreement	−5%	−3%
Tender offer	−1	16

The results of these investigations suggest that the stockholding public is quite sensitive to management actions that potentially affect their well-being. For example, most anti-takeover charter amendments, that make it more difficult or more expensive to buy a target firm, have a negative effect on share price. Thus, it seems that changes in the corporate charter to permit staggered elections for boards of directors, super majority votes for mergers, "poison pills" or "shark repellants," and "greenmail" or "standstill" arrangements to selectively bargain with major stockholders are taken by stockholders as being not in their best interests. For example, when GAF, a firm heavily involved in takeovers as both a buyer and a seller, adopted a number of anti-takeover provisions its stock price fell by 8 percent over the two-day period around the announcement. The only anti-takeover provision that seems to be beneficial to shareholders is one that ensures that any offer must apply to all shareholders (this prevents minority shareholders from being squeezed and forced to accept a lower offer).

Another anti-takeover provision, the issuance of two classes of common stock—with the publicly held issue being identical to the "privately" held issue except that it is nonvoting—is currently in vogue. Dow Jones & Co., for example, recently adopted this technique for the avowed purpose of consolidating control of voting shares in the hands of the family trust. The widespread use of this provision is too recent to allow us to offer opinions as to how the market reacts to it. *Our* reaction, however, is that such a provision puts the value of nonvoting shares at risk by making the value dependent on the actions of voting shareholders.

Financing Decisions and Value

Managers are called upon to make many decisions regarding the financial structure of their firms. Among them are the proportion of debt and equity to use in financing the firm's operations, the kinds of fixed-income and equity securities to issue, and the nature of the specific covenants (maturity, collateral, callability, etc.) to include as part of the financial arrangement. As is the case with any decision, there is the possibility that the selection of any one financial structure will result in a lower or higher value for the firm than an alternative structure. Indeed, it has long been presumed that there is an optimal structure—one that creates the greatest value for the firm. In this section we will outline the basic relationship that exists between financial structure and value. As you will see, relationships that may seem intuitive on their face (e.g., leverage increases returns and, therefore, value) do not always hold in financial markets.

According to the dividend capitalization model, risk and expected future dividends determine security value. Thus, the obvious questions that arise regarding financial structure and valuation are: (1) how does a change in financial structure influence the dividend received by shareholders, and (2) how does a change in financial structure influence β?

Debt and Returns to Shareholders

The basic relationship between the proportion of debt used and the dividend flows to shareholders is best described by assuming a simple no-growth situation where the firm is expected to generate cash flows in perpetuity. A set of hypothetical figures for an arbitrary year for this situation is given in Table 17–3. The firm's total size is $100 of assets. Income before interest is $17 (a 17 percent return). The debt/equity ratio is varied

TABLE 17–3	Returns to Shareholders under Alternative Financial Structures				
Assets	$100	$100	$100	$100	$100
Debt	10	25	50	75	90
Equity	90	75	50	25	10
Income before interest	17	17	17	17	17
Interest (8%)	.8	2.0	4.0	6.0	7.2
Profit	$ 16.2	$ 15.0	$ 13.0	$ 11.0	$ 9.8
Return to shareholders	18%	20%	26%	44%	98%

from 10 percent debt to 90 percent debt. As it does so, of course, the investment of equity and the flows to equity holders change. For example, for the 10 percent debt case, the income after interest is $16.20, which (since it's a perpetuity) would all flow to shareholders as dividends. On a $90 investment by shareholders this is a return (expected to be received in perpetuity) of 18 percent. As debt is increased relative to equity, income available for paying dividends decreases (due to increasing interest charges), but the necessary commitment of funds by shareholders decreases at a faster rate—creating an increasing expected return per dollar invested, as shown in the last row of the table.

Not surprisingly, there is an exact expression for how the rate of return to stockholders changes as debt is substituted for equity. The expression for the stockholder's new return, $\hat{R}_i^{new}$, with debt issued and equity purchased at equilibrium rates, is[4]

(17–5)   *Return and Leverage*

$$\hat{R}_i^{new} = E(\tilde{R}_i)\left(1 + \frac{\text{Market value of new debt}}{\text{Market value of remaining equity}}\right) - E(\tilde{R}_d)\left(\frac{\text{Market value of new debt}}{\text{Market value of remaining equity}}\right)$$

Thus, for the firm moving from the 25/75 structure to the 50/50 structure, and debt issued at 8 percent, we would calculate

$$\text{New return to stockholders} = \hat{R}_i^{new} = .20\left(1 + \frac{25}{50}\right) - .08\left(\frac{25}{50}\right) = .26,$$

or 26 percent, as can be seen in Table 17–3.

The formula is correct even if interest rates change with leverage. If the interest rate on the new $25 of debt were a higher 11 percent (to compensate for the greater risk to lenders with the increasingly debt-laden structure) the new return would be 24.5 percent, given by[5]

$$\hat{R}_i^{new} = .20\left(1 + \frac{25}{50}\right) - .11\left(\frac{25}{50}\right) = .245$$

---

[4]The expression is derived assuming perpetuity flows and a permanent level of debt financing, with the equilibrium return on debt and equity being defined by the security market line.

[5]The equation will work for any financial structure change. Use it, for example, to determine the sensitivity of the expected rate of return on your residence, assuming different mortgage loan-to-value ratios, different mortgage interest rates, or the effect of taking out a second mortgage on a home you already own.

Debt and Risk

Risk, or β, also changes with leverage. Interest costs are fixed, so variations in before-interest income with greater leverage gives rise to greater relative fluctuations in after-interest income. Since β is defined by

$$(17\text{--}6) \qquad\qquad \beta_i = \frac{Cov(\tilde{R}_i,\tilde{R}_m)}{[\sigma(\tilde{R}_m)]^2}$$

the new β, with the new leverage is

$$(17\text{--}7) \qquad\qquad \beta_i^{new} = \frac{Cov(\tilde{R}_i^{new},\tilde{R}_m)}{[\sigma(\tilde{R}_m)]^2}$$

Substituting for $\tilde{R}_i^{new}$, this can be written as a function of the original risk level, β_i, as follows:

$(17\text{--}8)$ **Risk and Leverage**

$$\beta_i^{new} = \beta_i \left(1 + \frac{\text{Market value of new debt}}{\text{Market value of remaining equity}} \right) - \beta_d \left(\frac{\text{Market value of new debt}}{\text{Market value of remaining equity}} \right)$$

New
stock = A weighted average of the equity risk
risk   and debt risk, with debt having a
          negative weight since it was issued.

The analogy with the new return in Equation (17–5) is obvious. Essentially, the first term adjusts risk for the increased leverage. The second term subtracts some of the leverage effect since the bondholders are absorbing a portion of the firm's risk (β_d exceeds zero).[6]

For the firm shifting from 25 percent debt to 50 percent debt, where the β on the equity before the new debt is issued is 1.2 and on the debt is .3, the new β will be

$$\beta_i^{new} = 1.2\,(1\,+\,25/50)\,-\,.3(25/50)$$

$$= 1.8\,-\,.15\,=\,1.65$$

If the firm was able to issue risk-free debt, the new risk level for equity would be 1.8. When *risky* debt is issued, some of the firm's risk is shifted to the bondholders.

Given the way that return and risk have changed, the question regarding the effect of any proposed change in financial structure on value can now be answered. Suppose the firm is beginning from an *equilibrium* position on the security market line (point F in Figure 17–2) with a financial structure of 25 percent debt and a β of 1.2. The equilibrium

---

[6]Remember the portfolio βs are weighted averages of the component securities. Here the stock of the firm is a portfolio of the firm, held long, and debt issued (or held short). Thus, Equation (17–8) is not new [nor is (17–5)]. It's just our portfolio formula applied to a firm.

FIGURE 17–2   Changes in Risk and Return with Changes in Financial Structure

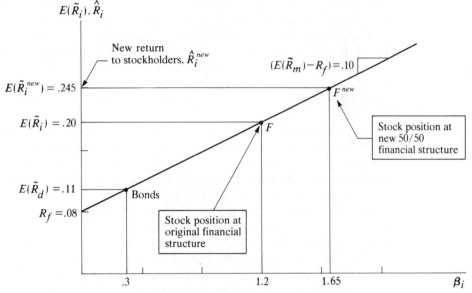

$E(\tilde{R}_i) = .08 + .10(1.2) = .20$ from SML.

New return to stockholders $= \hat{R}_i^{new} = .20(1 + \dfrac{25}{50}) - .11(\dfrac{25}{50}) = .245$ from equation (17-5).

But $E(\tilde{R}_i^{new}) = .08 + .10(1.65) = .245$ from the SML given β_i^{new} of 1.65

Since new return to stockholders, $\hat{R}_i^{new} = E(\tilde{R}_i^{new})$ no price change occurs.

rate of return is 20 percent. In other words, the firm is now correctly valued by the market and is starting from an equilibrium position where there is no excess supply of or demand for the security, and thus no tendency for any price change to take place.

Moving to a 50/50 debt ratio will change risk, according to Equation (17–8), to 1.65. At the same time, return generated to stockholders will change, using Equation (17–5), to 24.5 percent. Note the new risky debt offers an equilibrium 11 percent return, given its β of .3.

Debt and Value

As can be seen in Figure 17–2, **this new combination of risk and return generated still leaves the stock on the security market line.** The stock has moved from point *F* on the line to another point *F^{new}*, but there has been no excess demand or supply created, no temporary disequilibrium and, therefore, no change in value. The increase in return generated for shareholders has been precisely offset by the increase in risk—and, therefore, in the equilibrium return $E(\tilde{R}_i)$. The conclusion is that the firm cannot manipulate itself off the capital market line by changing its debt/equity ratio. Financial structure and value are unrelated. Importantly, the only assumption that has been made in the analysis so far is that the debt issued by the firm offered an equilibrium return, $E(\tilde{R}_d)$. In other words the debt was *correctly priced,* given its risk, when it was issued.

Obviously, the absence of a relationship does not seem consistent with the considerable attention that managers and market analysts seem to give to the financial structure. But these relationships provide us with the means to identify situations in which the corporation and its shareholders are likely to gain from any financial structure decision. Basically the shareholders will gain anytime the firm is able to issue debt at an effective *cost* that is less than the equilibrium rate required of that debt consistent with its risk and the SML. There are two obvious cases where this may be possible, that are represented in Figure 17–3.

Case A represents a situation where the firm's investment bankers are able to issue long-term debt at a disequilibrium rate of 10.5 percent when the current market rate is 11 percent. The issuance of such "cheap" debt obviously benefits the firm's stockholders, by allowing the return they earn to exceed the SML equilibrium return at the new risk level. The increase in return to 24.75 percent for stockholders more than offsets the increase in risk to 1.65. The new bondholders, of course, bear the brunt of this cost by accepting a rate of return that is lower than they otherwise could have earned in the market. The amount of the potential wealth transfer from under- or overpriced debt can be large. The present value of the .5 percent interest differential on a 25-year bond issued in the amount of $100 million (a fairly standard issue size), using a discount rate of 11 percent is approximately $4.5 million.

Case B represents the contribution the U.S. Treasury makes to the whole process by allowing corporations to deduct interest payments on debt as a cost of doing business for the calculation of corporate income taxes. In this case the effective cost of the debt is reduced by the corporation's marginal income tax rate, T_C, to $(1 - T_C)E(R_d)$, or in the example in Figure 17–3 to 7.26 percent $((1 - .34)(.11) = .0726)$.

Note that beta also changes as a result of the tax deductibility of interest payments. Only $(1 - T_C)$ of the bond risk is shifted to bondholders, since the tax shelter that is gained by the firm from interest deductibility is itself as risky as the debt that was issued to create it. The new beta for the stockholders is 1.7.

The total aggregate value of this tax shelter is equal to the discounted present value of all of the taxes saved as a result of the deductibility of interest payments on the outstanding debt. If the debt is assumed to be permanently issued, the present value is simply T_C times the value of the debt that is issued and outstanding. In other words, the issuance of a $1 of debt brings an immediate increment of $.34 to shareholders if the corporation's marginal tax rate is 34 percent. On a $100 million issue the present value is $34 million.

Case B doesn't necessarily represent the final answer to the net benefits of the use of debt. Merton Miller has argued that as long as the *after-tax cost* of debt is perceived to be below the SML (below 11 percent in the example), firms will continue to issue debt and forego the issuance of "high" cost equity. As more and more firms issue debt however, the rate charged on debt will increase—essentially forcing the SML for debt instruments to separate from and rise above the SML for other securities. The net effect is that, at the margin, the after-tax cost of debt $((1 - .34)E(R_d)$ for most corporations) will be located on the original SML. If debt is priced in this manner, and if corporations attempt to issue debt to capture the shelter associated with it, individual corporations (and their

FIGURE 17–3   Case A: The Effect of Issuing Debt at Less Than the Equilibrium Rate

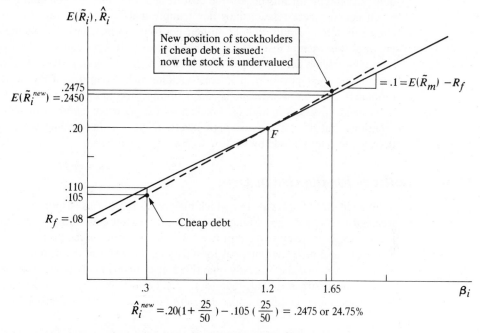

$$\hat{R}_i^{new} = .20(1 + \frac{25}{50}) - .105\,(\frac{25}{50}) = .2475 \text{ or } 24.75\%$$

Case B: The Effect of Issuing Tax-Sheltered Debt

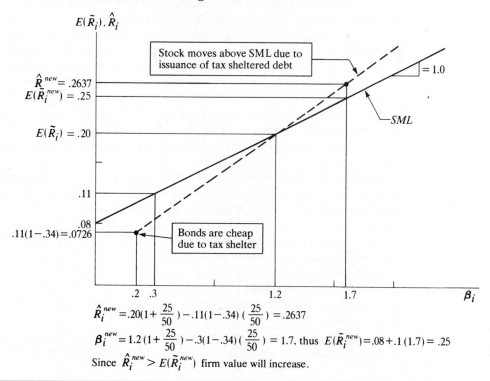

$$\hat{R}_i^{new} = .20(1 + \frac{25}{50}) - .11(1 - .34)\,(\frac{25}{50}) = .2637$$

$$\beta_i^{new} = 1.2\,(1 + \frac{25}{50}) - .3(1 - .34)\,(\frac{25}{50}) = 1.7, \text{ thus } E(\tilde{R}_i^{new}) = .08 + .1\,(1.7) = .25$$

Since $\hat{R}_i^{new} > E(\tilde{R}_i^{new})$ firm value will increase.

shareholders) will not benefit from the tax deductibility of the interest payments on the debt. In bidding for this benefit the cost of debt rises and the potential gain disappears.

Of course, these relationships don't imply that investors are neutral regarding their choice of debt or equity to hold in their portfolio. In fact, investors facing low personal tax rates (tax-exempt institutions, or investments in IRA accounts, for example) will find the high-yielding debt to be perfect for them. Other things constant, they will choose to concentrate their portfolio in interest-yielding debt securities. They are the ones that ultimately gain the benefit of the deductibility of corporate interest payments. On the other hand, investors in high tax brackets will lean toward investing their funds in equity securities that do not provide high levels of current income and where taxes can be deferred to later periods by waiting to realize capital gains.

Other Incentives for the Use of Debt

In addition to the tax shelter which may result from firms issuing debt, and the wealth transfer associated with issuing debt at below market equilibrium rates, there are other incentives for the employment of fixed-income securities in the firm's financial structure. Some of these have the potential for changing the value of the firm to the shareholders. While these cannot be as easily quantified, they undoubtedly play a role in the selection of a financial structure and, therefore, affect value. In very general terms, these other incentives can be included under the rubric of agency costs and incentive signaling.

Agency Costs.   In a large corporation (and many small ones), the ownership interest is typically heavily weighted in favor of nonmanager owners. The managerial team either directly or indirectly owns only a small portion of the total outstanding shares of common stock. While their total monetary compensation, through stock ownership options, bonuses, or salary may be heavily tied to the success of the firm, they undoubtedly receive utility from perquisites such as a large office, use of the company plane, power and political clout, etc. Because the cost of these nonpecuniary rewards is split among *all* shareholders and is not paid for solely by the individuals consuming them, the managers have an incentive to consume them at a relatively more rapid rate or in greater quantity than they would otherwise. They become *almost* "free goods" to the manager. Their consumption, however, represents a cost to the firm that will result in a lower value for the firm's equity.

Obviously nonmanager owners (the outside shareholders) have an incentive to restrict managers' consumption of these items, and do so in a variety of ways by monitoring the firm's activities. Monitoring includes the use of outside auditors and boards of directors, creating specific managerial job definitions, and the potential for firing the manager. The obvious benefit of monitoring to the stockholders is the reduced consumption of perks by managers. However, at some point this benefit will be offset by the cost of monitoring.

The relevant aspect of these two agency costs (the consumption of the perks and the monitoring costs incurred to avoid them) to the capital structure problem is that the level of debt influences the costs incurred. In turn, the agency costs incurred will, in part, determine firm value.

In particular, the agency costs to the firm of stockholders' monitoring activities increase as the proportion of equity relative to debt increases. This is due to the greater incentive

FIGURE 17–4   Agency Costs, Financial Leverage, and Valuation

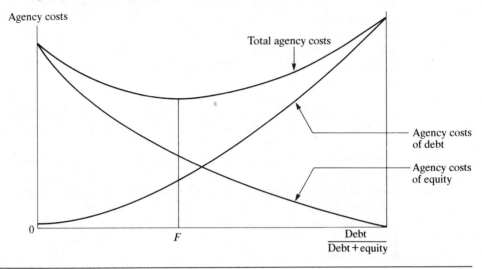

(and consequently greater cost) manager-owners have to consume nonpecuniary rewards when outside shareholders hold a larger portion of the firm. Stated another way, this **agency cost of *equity*** falls as the proportion of debt financing to equity financing increases (there is less equity) and this is shown in the curve labeled "Agency costs of equity" in Figure 17–4. Because managers would be accused by owners of incurring these agency costs—and their salary and other compensation lowered to adjust for these costs—the managers would find ways of persuading owners of their willingness to forego these perks. One way is to increase debt, for that places a larger proportionate cost of the perks on the managers. When managers face a larger potential cost, they will restrict perk consumption; for the betterment of nonmanager owners. As a result, the firm's value will increase with debt as debt ensures the avoidance of these costs.

This effect alone would suggest that managers could avoid agency costs by increasing debt toward 100 percent of all external financing. Yet fixed-income obligations also engender some agency costs that prevent this from happening. These **agency costs of *debt*** include: (1) incentive effects in levered firms, (2) monitoring costs to reduce the incentives, and (3) bankruptcy costs, which we now discuss.

A highly levered firm creates an incentive for the owner-manager to take actions that will tend to transfer wealth from the bondholders to the equity owners. As Jensen and Meckling [1976] so aptly put it:

> Potential creditors will not loan $100,000,000 to a firm in which the entrepreneur has an investment of $10,000. With that financial structure the owner-manager will have a strong incentive to engage in activities (investments) which promise very high payoffs if successful even if they have a very low probability of success. If they turn out well, he captures most of the gains, if they turn out badly, the creditors bear most of the costs.

One way manager-owners can transfer wealth is to issue debt, using the proceeds to purchase assets that contain more risk than that anticipated by the bondholders. Another way is to issue additional debt that has an equivalent or superior claim in the event of firm default. Both tactics tend to push risk onto the existing bondholders in a form that the firm's equity holders don't have to pay for since interest on the existing debt is fixed. Realizing this possibility may exist, potential bondholders may either demand higher interest payments to compensate for the potential wealth transfer, or they may demand monitoring or bonding procedures be set up by the owners to protect themselves against such transfers.

Stockholders, through the managers, observing that they may be "charged" for these incentives beforehand, will set up monitoring procedures on their own; i.e., they will guarantee to the potential bondholders that they will not expropriate bondholder wealth. All these monitoring activities cost money, of course.

Procedures commonly used include rather complex indenture restrictions or covenants, such as limitations on additional debt issues, or limitations on officer salaries and dividends. But whatever their form, these monitoring and bonding costs *increase* as the proportion of debt in the firm's financial structure increases.

The final agency costs of debt are termed bankruptcy costs. Bankruptcy is a legal concept that is difficult to define precisely. In general, however, bankruptcy occurs whenever the firm fails to meet interest payments on debt, or fails to meet some other obligation specified in the indenture agreement. If there were no special costs associated with the event of bankruptcy or its probability of occurrence, the value of the firm would be unaffected by the increasing probability of bankruptcy that occurs with a more and more levered financial structure. But such is not the case. The possibility of bankruptcy, in practice, gives rise to the demand for certain indenture restrictions that limit the firm's freedom to attempt to increase the wealth of owners and gives rise to a process for the adjudication of claims of creditors, suppliers, employees, and customers that may arise from bankruptcy. The possible incurrence of these costs will be of concern to both potential bondholders and equity holders, since they will tend to reduce the amount of the firm's wealth available for the payment of interest and dividends. These costs also will increase with an increase in the amount of financial leverage.

The net result is that the monitoring and bonding costs and the bankruptcy costs of debt will increase as the proportion of debt in the financial structure increases. These costs are included in Figure 17–4 as "Agency costs of debt."

While the particular functional relationship between the agency costs of debt and equity and the firm's financial leverage may depend on the characteristics of the firm, the industry, and its managers, the general shapes are as indicated in the figure. "Total agency costs" are simply the sum of the agency costs of debt and equity. Since the value of the firm is reduced by the amount of these agency costs, its value would be highest where the "total agency cost" curve is the lowest—that is, at F.

Incentive Signaling.   If a manager's rewards are closely tied to changes in the value of the firm, the manager has the incentive to *correct* any perceptions by market participants that cause the firm to be under-valued in the market.[7] The incorrect perceptions may be

---

[7]Undervalued in this context is relative to the value perceived by the manager.

the result of the market viewing the firm's risk as being higher than it actually is or viewing its possible future cash flows as being lower than their "true" expected levels. The perceptions clearly may be changed by the actions of the manager. Corporate public relations campaigns are one method that has been actively used. But such methods may have little impact because the market may view the manager as having nothing to lose by such tactics.

Increasing the debt in the firm's financial structure, however, is a potentially more effective signal. If the manager increases the amount of debt in the firm's capital structure, and the firm subsequently does poorly, the consequences on the ex post monetary package received by the manager may be quite serious—diastrous—if the firm faces default and bankruptcy. Looked at in this light, the market is likely to perceive an increase in debt as *evidence* of the favorable perceptions of the manager regarding cash flows and risk. The response to this managerial signal may be an increase in the demand for the firm's shares and a resulting rise in stock price.[8]

Dividend Policy and Value

The levels of current and future expected dividends are basic determinants of the value of common stock. Yet managers have considerable latitude regarding *when* cash flows generated by the firm are paid out in the form of dividends. Dividend policy refers to the management's decision as to how cash flows are to be paid out over time. Implicit in the solution to this problem is the solution to the related problem of whether funds should be generated by issuing new shares of common stock. In studying the dividend policy problem, it's important not to confuse the discussion by introducing any investment or financing change into the analysis. In particular, our discussion assumes that the firm's investment and financing levels have already been established.[9]

When the problem is put in this perspective, the dividend policy issue is simply one of specifying a low level of dividends (high retained earnings) and a low level of funds raised by issuing new equity, or a high level of dividends (low retained earnings) and a high level of funds acquired by issuing new common stock. Moreover, since this kind of decision must be made each period,[10] the firm's dividend policy also will exhibit some stability or instability over time. **Dividend policy,** in other words, **refers to the manager's choice of the level and stability of the firm's dividend payments to shareholders**—given the firm's investment and financing policies.[11]

---

[8]Signals are continuously given by managers to the market. Incentive-signaling theory holds that only those signals that reveal something of the manager's true beliefs are going to have an impact, and that true beliefs are only going to be recognized if they are tied to the managerial incentive scheme—i.e., the manager's pecuniary and nonpecuniary compensation package. Sale of the company plane, or an attempt to change the compensation package to straight salary from bonus arrangements, are likely to be received as negative signals, for example.

[9]If, in fact, the firm lets its dividend decision influence its capital budget it is making an incorrect investment decision which will clearly have an effect on firm value, as discussed in the first part of this chapter.

[10]Most firms determine their basic need for funds for investment purposes only once a year, though obviously changes may be made as required by events taking place during intervening months.

[11]In an exceptionally thorough empirical study, Fama has shown that firms *do* tend to treat investment policy independently of dividend policy. See Eugene Fama [1974].

TABLE 17–4   Dividend Policy Examples

	Murphy Oil	National Distillers	Western Airlines	Xerox	General Mills	General Tele&Elect	B.F. Goodrich
			Dividend per Share (dollars)				
1985	$1.00	$2.20	Nil	$3.00	$2.24	$3.12	$1.56
1984	1.00	2.20	Nil	3.00	2.04	3.04	1.56
1983	1.00	2.20	Nil	3.00	1.84	2.96	1.56
1982	1.00	2.20	Nil	3.00	1.64	2.88	1.56
1981	.75	2.20	Nil	3.00	1.44	2.78	1.56
1980	.50	2.00	$0.25	2.80	1.28	2.72	1.56
1979	.33$^3/_8$	1.80	.40	2.40	1.12	2.60	1.44
1978	.26$^3/_4$	1.70	.40	2.00	.97	2.36	1.32
1977	.26$^3/_4$	1.60	.40	1.50	.79	2.12	1.22
1976	.20	1.40	.40	1.10	.66	1.90	1.12
1975	.20	1.20	.47	1.00	.50$^1/_2$	1.80	1.12
1974	.20	1.02$^1/_2$	.38	1.00	.53	1.76	1.12
1973	.10$^1/_2$	.90	.23$^1/_2$	.90	.50	1.66	1.03
1972	.10	.90	.08$^1/_8$	.84	.48	1.56	1.00
1971	.10	.90	Nil	.80	.45	1.52	1.00

	Murphy Oil	National Distillers	Western Airlines	Xerox	General Mills	General Tele&Elect	B.F. Goodrich
			Dividend Payout Ratios (percent)				
1985	43%	97%	0%	87%	55%	NL%	NL%
1984	31	108	NL	88	86	57	59
1983	28	123	NL	68	40	58	250
1982	23	102	NL	69	36	61	NL
1981	17	55	NL	43	37	67	33
1980	12	63	NL	38	38	96	45
1979	12	45	13	36	38	62	29
1978	21	51	14	35	31	55	30
1977	21	44	37	54	34	54	31
1976	15	40	34	24	32	58	118
1975	19	41	138	23	37	63	68
1974	11	28	24	37	33	58	31
1973	8	49	17	24	33	58	25
1972	26	71	11	27	39	60	30
1971	32	76	0	30	43	65	44

NL = Net loss.

Examples of the policies that have been followed by some firms are included in Table 17–4. The top section of the table gives **annual dividend payments** by year. The bottom section contains the percentage of earnings paid out in the form of dividends, or the **payout ratio.** Clearly there is substantial variation in both the proportion of earnings paid out and in the frequency with which dividends are adjusted on a year-to-year basis. The fact that some of the values exceed 100 percent is evidence of the reluctance of some firms to reduce dividends when earnings fall. B.F. Goodrich maintained a relatively stable, slowly growing dividend in spite of some rather wild gyrations in earnings. Xerox, on the other hand, has a very stable and constant payout ratio and steady dividend growth. The quarterly payment of dividends is by far the most common means of payment to shareholders, but most firms change the quarterly dividend rate only once a year—if that often.

The Ex-Dividend Behavior of Stocks

A firm whose value is defined by the present value of expected dividends, with the first dividend to be received 365 days from now, is[12]

(17–9)
$$P^e_{i0} = \sum_{t=1}^{\infty} \frac{E(\tilde{D}_{it})}{[1 + E(\tilde{R}_i)]^t}$$

As the year proceeds and the expected payment gets closer to the present, ignoring other things that may change value, the price will rise until on the 364th day it will be

(17–10)   *Pre-Dividend Value*

$$\text{Pre-dividend } P^e_{i1} = D_1 + \sum_{t=2}^{\infty} \frac{E(\tilde{D}_{it})}{[1 + E(\tilde{R}_i)]^{t-1}}$$

On day 365 the dividend of D_1 will be paid, and simultaneously the security will begin to trade without the dividend. In other words, the security goes "ex-dividend", and price will fall by the amount of the dividend paid to

(17–11)   *Ex-Dividend Value*

$$\text{Ex-dividend } P^e_{i1} = \sum_{t=2}^{\infty} \frac{E(\tilde{D}_{it})}{[(1 + E(\tilde{R}_i)]^{t-1}}$$

This expression reflects the present value of expected dividends from the end of the first period on. The process continues year after year, giving rise to a price sequence that would look like an elongated sawtooth if no changes in expectations were to take place.

As an example, consider a stock with an expected dividend payment of $2 in perpetuity and a demanded return of 20 percent. Its initial value will be

$$P^e_{i0} = \sum_{t=1}^{\infty} \frac{\$2}{(1 + .20)^t} = \$10$$

As the year goes by, its value will rise to

$$P^e_{i1} = \$2 + \sum_{t=2}^{\infty} \frac{\$2}{(1 + .20)^{t-1}} = \$12$$

the day before going ex-dividend. On the ex-dividend day the prices drops to $10.[13]

In ideal financial markets, where there are no transactions costs, taxes, or other impediments, the dividend policy the firm follows is irrelevant. Anything the firm might

---

[12]The analysis here assumes an annual dividend payment. It can be directly generalized to monthly, quarterly, or semiannual payment periods, however.

[13]The individual who purchased it on the 364th day and sold it on the 365th would have spent $12 and received $10, plus the $2 dividend sent to him as the owner of the security at the point in time the stock went ex-dividend—for no gain or loss. Thus, except for taxes, or transactions costs, the investor would be indifferent between purchasing the security for $12 and simultaneously receiving a $2 check from the company, or waiting a day until the security goes ex-dividend and buying it for $10.

do regarding the payment of dividends can be *costlessly* undone by those shareholders who are inconvenienced by the firm's actions. The firm, with an equilibrium-expected return of $E(\tilde{R_i})$, that pays out cash in the form of dividends to the shareholder who currently does not wish to consume imposes no cost on the shareholder. The firm has forced the liquidation of a portion of the shareholder's portfolio, but this effect can be offset by simply reinvesting the funds to earn $E(\tilde{R_i})$ again. The reinvestment may be in the same firm or in another (with same β_i). In any case, the individual's portfolio position post-dividend is the same as it was pre-dividend.

If the payment of dividends means the firm must go to the capital market to raise new funds, those funds will be acquired at a "cost" of $E(\tilde{R_i})$—the same as demanded by our shareholder—so the value of existing shareholders' positions will not be changed. The firm has simply substituted one form of financing (new equity) for another (retention of earnings). The net effect is zero.

If the firm does not pay out dividends this year, an investor who wishes to consume this year simply sells shares in a voluntary liquidation of a portion of the portfolio. This investor takes the capital gain that occurs from the retention of funds (the *non*payment of dividends) and liquidates it to *create* his own cash flow consistent with his preferences for consumption. The capital gain that occurs is exactly equal to the amount the security would drop, ex-dividend, if the dividend were paid. Thus, the firm that decides *not* to pay a $2 dividend finds its stock price *not* dropping by $2 because it never goes ex-dividend.

Whatever may be done by the firm regarding the payment of dividends can be easily undone by the shareholder. Thus, the policy of paying or not paying a dividend this year or next cannot matter, and the value of shareholder positions is not affected.

In other words, in an ideal market, with an ability to exchange dollars of dividends for dollars of capital gain (by liquidating a portion of security holdings), different prices could not exist for two firms differing *only* with respect to dividend policy. Their values would have to be identical.

Preferences for Dividends

In real world financial markets the actions taken to "undo" a firm's dividend policy may involve important costs. If so, individual stockholders may have a preference for receiving their return in the form of dividends or capital gains. This preference may translate into a demand for shares of firms that have a policy that meets the stockholders' objective. The most important of these costs are taxes paid on dividends and capital gains.

Before 1986 many investors had a strong preference for securities offering returns in the form of capital gains. Sixty percent of such long-term gains were not taxed. However, with passage of the 1986 Tax Reform Act, and an equalization of the tax rates on realized capital gains and dividends, much of the reason for investor preference for low-dividend-paying securities disappeared. Now, it seems, there is little reason to prefer one form of income over another and the sticky question of whether stock prices might be influenced by the dividend policy followed by the firm has become less important.

One part of the argument remains, however. Capital gains on securities are taxed only when they are realized through the sale of the security. Thus, at the margin, capital gains still might be preferred by some to the extent they offer flexibility regarding when taxes are paid. Of course, they would be preferred to dividend income by investors in higher tax brackets. Concomitantly, tax-exempt entities and low-tax-rate individuals are likely to hold higher-dividend-yielding securities. However, it's doubtful that this preference is strong with equal tax rates applied to dividends and realized capital gains, and it would be very surprising to find that high- and low-dividend-yielding securities are priced differently in the marketplace.

Dividend Signaling: The Informational Content of Dividend Announcements

Empirical studies of corporate behavior indicate a very strong tendency for firms to stabilize dividend payments over time. Firms seem reluctant to decrease their dividends unless the management's cash flow expectations are so low that they cannot support the current dividend stream. Penn Central maintained a dividend of $.60 per share per quarter until six months prior to filing for bankruptcy. Perhaps because of this reluctance to decrease dividends, there is an accompanying reticence on the part of managers to increase dividends until the managers are assured that the higher level can be maintained in future periods.

To the extent this behavior is part of the corporate scene, changes in the dividend paid provide a **signal** to the investing public about management's expectations of future earning power (and the ability to pay future dividends) or risk. Receipt of the information (conveyed via an increase or decrease in dividends) and its incorporation into investor expectations will result in a change in demand for the security and a change in market price.

Precisely why dividend payments are chosen as a means for conveying information is not clear. Partially, it seems to have grown out of precedents set by market participants long ago. More importantly, however, dividends seem to have been chosen as an important means for transmitting information because it's one of the few ways that can be used by managers that is *believed* by the market. It's believable because there is a real cost to management of being wrong. The real costs are those transaction costs incurred in making up a cash "shortfall" in the event cash flows after dividend payments are not sufficient for the firm's normal operations. The cost of these shortfalls lands on both the stockholders and managers.[14]

While this **signaling hypothesis** is admittedly somewhat nebulous, it is still consistent with dividend policy irrelevancy. That is, it does not matter whether the firm adopts a low payout policy or a high payout policy. What may matter, however, is whether dividends are changed as a means of conveying information to the market. That is, dividend policy is not important *per se,* but changes in dividend payments may be important because of the value of the information conveyed to the market regarding the firm's earning power.

As always, such contentions as the signaling effect of dividend announcements must be subjected to empirical investigation. Such investigations are difficult, however, primarily because there are a variety of other signals conveyed at the same time dividend

---

[14]This argument is developed more completely in Bhattacharya [1979].

FIGURE 17–5   Cumulative Excess Returns Surrounding Changes in Dividends

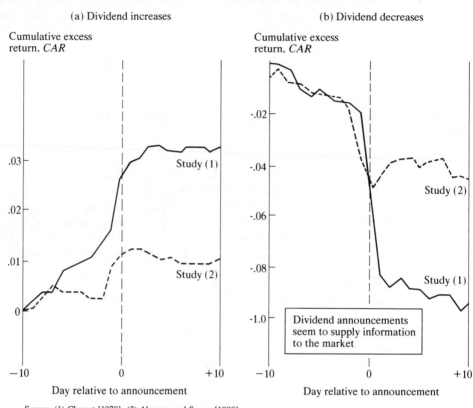

Source: (1) Charest [1978], (2) Aharony and Swary [1980].

changes are announced that may also contain information on the firm's future earning power or risk. Firms that announce higher reported earnings are also more likely to be those firms that announce higher dividend payments. Obviously, attempting to separate the influence on share price of information contained in reported earnings and in announced dividend changes requires some care in measuring the informational impact.

Two studies of daily performance around dividend announcement dates seem to have successfully dealt with this problem. The results are summarized in Figure 17–5. Consistent with signaling theory, there seems to be an effect associated with the dividend announcement. Firms that reduced or omitted their dividends fared poorly (i.e., had negative cumulative average residuals) at the time of the announcement. Also, the results indicate a rapid incorporation of whatever information is conveyed into share price. This is, of course, a process that is consistent with an efficient financial market.

In sum, it appears that the level of dividends set by management is relatively unimportant to the security's price, while *changes* in dividends seem to signal to the market some information on the firm's long-run earnings prospects.

Share Repurchase and Value

Instead of paying cash dividends, firms can use the funds to repurchase their own shares. Such a purchase can be consumated either through an **open market purchase** at the existing market price or through the mechanism of a **tender offer purchase.**

Open Market Purchases

On September 22, 1986, M/A Com announced that it would be purchasing up to 2 million shares in the open market (NYSE) "in the near future." If the shares are purchased through normal market channels, the effect on the firm's per share value would be expected to be zero. A firm with an equilibrium value, P_{i0}^e, repurchasing m_i of its n_i shares outstanding would have a "post" repurchase price,

(17–12)   *Post-Repurchase Price*

$$\text{"post" } P_{i0}^e = \frac{n_i P_{i0}^e - m_i P_{i0}^e}{n_i - m_i} = \text{"pre" } P_{i0}^e$$

$$\begin{array}{l} \textit{New equilibrium} \\ \textit{price} \end{array} = \begin{array}{l} \textit{Total value of the equity less the expendi-} \\ \textit{ture for shares divided by the new} \\ \textit{number of shares.} \end{array}$$

The firm has reduced the number of shares outstanding, which will increase per share value. But it has also reduced the total value of the firm by expending $m_i P_{i0}^e$ dollars to purchase the shares. In essence it has purchased an investment (its own stock) with a net present value of zero. For a firm with 1.1 million shares, priced currently at \$40/share, planning to repurchase 100,000 shares, the new price would be,

$$\text{"post" } P_{i0}^e = \frac{1,100,000(\$40) - 100,000(\$40)}{1,100,000 - 100,000} = \$40$$

There is one condition under which open market purchases benefit the shareholders. That condition is if the security is not currently priced in equilibrium in the market. If the firm is undervalued, the firm is buying an investment with a positive *NPV*. In this case those shareholders who did not sell their shares would benefit at the expense of those who sold their shares to the firm.[15]

Since the management cannot pull the firm up by its own bootstraps, the relevant question is whether the manager's action is a signal to the market that causes concensus

---

[15]Exactly why management would choose to take this action, which is detrimental to one group of shareholders, when they are supposed to be operating for the benefit of all shareholders is not clear, but it can happen. Moreover, if the management takes the action based on information not readily available to all market participants, then it would seem to violate Rule 10/b5 of the Securities and Exchange Act. This section of the Act makes it illegal for anyone classified as an insider (which is anyone with inside information) to trade on the basis of inside information. Nevertheless, the incentive system works in the manager's favor, since only those who remain shareholders would have a vote to elect the board that controls management, and those who remain as shareholders are the ones who have gained.

expectations of the value of the firm to change. That is, market participants may form revised expectations on the value of the firm solely from the fact that: (1) managers have a superior ability to estimate the value of the shares of firms they manage, and (2) the action of repurchasing shares conveys the manager's value assessment.[16] Repurchasing, as a signal or an information-conveying event, then is much like the announcement effect of cash dividend changes. For example, M/A COM's intention to repurchase shares resulted in a jump in price from $13^1/_4$ to $14^5/_8$ on the day of the announcement. If the repurchase is announced, as it often is, then all shareholders will participate in the price increase. Thus, only the intention to repurchase matters. All of this effect is conditional on the market believing the signal, of course.

Tender Offer Repurchases

A tender offer is an offer by the firm to all stockholders to purchase from them a specified number of shares at a specified price that is above the current market price. For example, in 1985 Holiday Corp. announced a tender offer for the purchase of 10 million of their shares. The purchase was financed with the sale of hotel properties.[17]

In general, the offer to buy may last for a few days or a few weeks. All stockholders have the option to tender any and all shares they own to the firm (in fact, the shareholder owns a *put option* to sell to the firm). Participation in the actual sale is apportioned equally on the basis of the number of shares tendered. The **tender offer price** is set above the current price to encourage shareholders to tender their shares.

There are two components to the typical tender offer that introduce some uncertainty into the value of the option. First, the number of shares that will actually be tendered is unknown. It depends on the response of the shareholders.

Second, the number of shares to be purchased may vary, at the will of the firm, from the number indicated in the offer itself. In the typical tender offer, the firm will retain the option of purchasing (1) more than the number indicated if more are tendered, (2) less than the number indicated if fewer than that are tendered, or (3) none of the shares if less than the number indicated are tendered.

The net effect on a shareholder's wealth of the tender offer depends on these two considerations. In general, if all shareholders tender their shares there will be *no* changes in wealth, and the per share price after the repurchase takes place will be *lower* (the ex-dividend effect of the repurchase). All shareholders have sold some shares at the tender offer price (above the current equilibrium price) and still hold the remaining shares at the lower price that exists after the tender is completed. If fewer than 100% of all shareholders tender their shares there will be a wealth transfer from the nontendering shareholders to those tendering their shares.

These wealth transfer relationships raise a number of important questions. What is to be gained by the offer itself if it does not increase the value of the firm? Why would

---

[16]Equivalently, the action of issuing new shares, without information on the use of the funds raised with the issue, possibly would convey negative information to the market.

[17]Interestingly, in this case, the tendering stockholders could "request" a price of between $46 and $49 per share. The stockholder, in submitting a higher price within this range, risks the possibility of being excluded by lower-priced offers. This "Dutch auction" process is not typical of most tender offers.

managers take actions that would seem to harm one group of stockholders (those not tendering) and benefit another group? And, finally, do most shareholders tender, and if not, why not?

The answer to the first question may be the same as that which rationalized the price effect of dividend announcements—the offer signals favorable information to the market. If so, the stock price would rise by the value of the information at the time the tender offer was announced. Holiday Corp. stock price, for example, rose by 8 percent in the two days surrounding the offer announcement. However, the second question raises an issue regarding whether the tender offer is a satisfactory way to signal the market. Studies (Masulis [1980]) have shown that only 15 to 25 percent of all shares outstanding are tendered. Thus, even if the tender price was at a small premium, the wealth transfer would be significant.

Why would investors choose not to tender their shares? Obviously, if everyone thought the security was priced in equilibrium all would tender their shares. But if some investors felt the security was undervalued at the tender offer price would they be rational in holding back their stock? Financial theory says they still should tender, thus capturing the gain that occurs if not everybody tenders. If they are convinced that the security is undervalued they may want to hedge against the chance that the price will rise past the tender offer price while their already tendered shares sit at the corporate office. This can be done by trading in the options market or by buying more of the security on the open market. The point is that the tender offer suplies an expectation of superior profits relative to doing nothing even if the security is undervalued. The prescription for investors in this situation is to tender their shares.

Masulis' [1980] study of daily returns around the date of announcement of tender offerings found the combined "information effect" and "less than complete tendering effect" to be roughly 16 to 18 percent of the value of the stock—a very sizable amount. Prior knowledge of the forthcoming tender offer would prove very valuable, and, it seems, the information contained in a tender offer announcement is substantial.

Stock Dividends, Stock Splits, and Value

Stock dividends and splits effect a change in the number of shares outstanding. But because no new funds are acquired with this change, and because all new shares are apportioned on an equal basis to all shareholders, there is no valuation effect. A stock dividend of 5 percent results in each shareholder receiving notification that he or she is now the proud owner of 5 percent more shares. In a stock split each shareholder receives new shares according to the split ratio. In a 3–1 split the original shares technically would be exchanged for new shares on a three-for-one basis. The owner of 100 shares would own 300 shares after the split.

As you would expect, this bookkeeping entry would neither improve nor be detrimental to the shareholder's wealth. A larger number of shares will be owned but per share price will decline to offset exactly the change in the number of shares outstanding. If S is the stock dividend or split ratio, e.g., 1.05 or 3/1, the ex-split or ex-dividend price, is,

$$\text{(17–13)} \qquad \text{Post-split } P_{i0}^e = \frac{P_{i0}^e}{S} = \frac{\$75}{3/1} = \$25$$

The total value of the firm before the split, $n_iP_{i0}^e$, and after the split, $n_i(S)$(post-split P_{i0}^e), are the same.

Can we guarantee that the price will fall exactly to the post split P_{i0}^e so that shareholders are not affected? Of course not. As always, such a theoretical contention (though a rather straightforward one in this case) is subject to verification. Moreover, perhaps other factors that are part of the split or stock dividend may affect the market's assessment of firm value. Information conveyed through the split announcement may provide a positive (or negative in the case of a reverse stock split) signal regarding the manager's assessment of the firm's long-run earnings potential. However, the connection between the two does not seem very direct, and this means of conveying information is unlikely to be very important.

If nothing is to be gained through stock dividends or splits, then why do managements use them? The answer seems to lie in the market lore that an absolute stock price of between $25 and $50 is most appealing to market participants. Why this should be, if true, must have something to do with "affordable" round lot transactions, and the necessity for investors to hold diversified portfolios. This would suggest that firms offering stock dividends or splits are relatively high priced, possibly firms that have generated high ex post returns in the recent past.

Studies of stock dividends and splits tend to conform to the hypothesis formulated here. In particular,

- There seems to be no valuation effect of the split other than can be explained by a cash dividend effect.
- On the ex-dividend or ex-split date, share price falls as hypothesized.
- Those firms that announce stock dividends and splits have generated excess returns in periods *prior* to the date of announcement.

Summary

Management impacts on a firm's value by the decisions it makes on asset selection, financing structure, and dividend policy. Some decisions have a greater potential to affect share price, of course, and others have an effect only if financial markets contain imperfections such as transaction costs or taxes.

As the firm undertakes new real investment projects, its position relative to the security market line will be affected. As long as the firm accepts all changes in its asset structure or operations that, in management's view, will cause the firm to be positioned in a temporary disequilibrium position above the SML, then the firm will be acting to maximize share value. All projects that, if accepted, would move the firm below the SML should be rejected by the management. Only those decisions not previously anticipated correctly will cause a change in share price.

Financing decisions will have an effect on firm value only if there is some cost or benefit that allows the firm to issue debt as if the debt were mispriced in the market. If the debt were not mispriced, the firm could not move itself off of the security market line simply by issuing debt. The cost and benefits that seem to play a part in the financing decisions of most firms include: (1) the tax deductability of corporate interest payments on the debt (thus forcing the U.S. Treasury to share in the cost and risk of the debt), (2) bankruptcy costs, monitoring costs, and other agency costs of debt and equity.

Dividend policy, like financial policy, rests on the existence of some costs that arise in real-world markets due to transactions, taxes, and imperfect information about the firm that management can rectify. Without these costs, dividend policy is irrelevant, and for much the same reason as in the case of debt—everything the firm can do can be duplicated by individual investors (or stated another way, can be done or undone by them). Therefore, if investors can do everything that the firm can do with respect to dividend policy it is not likely that potential shareholders would pay more for a firm adopting one policy or the other.

Share repurchase and stock splits and dividends are aspects of the dividend policy issue, and their relevance hinges upon the same arguments as those that suggested the relevance of cash dividends—taxes, transaction costs, and informational effects. In these cases the net effect seems to be less, and some of these policies do not affect share price under existing circumstances in U.S. financial markets.

References

Aharony, Joseph, and Swary, Itzhak. [1980] "Quarterly Dividend and Earnings Announcements and Stockholder Returns: An Empirical Analysis." *Journal of Finance* (March).

Asquith, Paul. [1983] "Merger Bids, Uncertainty, and Stockholder Returns." *Journal of Financial Economics* (April).

Asquith, Paul; Bruner, Robert F.; and Mullins, David W., Jr. [1983] "The Gains to Bidding Firms from Merger." *Journal of Financial Economics* (April).

Asquith, Paul, and Kim, E. Han. [1982] "The Impact of Merger Bids on the Participating Firms' Security Holders." *Journal of Finance* (December).

Baron, D. P. [1974] "Default Risk, Homemade Leverage, and the Modigliani-Miller Theorem." *American Economic Review* (March).

Bhattacharya, Sudipto. [1979] "Imperfect Information, Dividend Policy and 'The Bird in the Hand' Fallacy." *Bell Journal of Economics* (Spring).

Black, Fischer. [1976] "The Dividend Puzzle." *Journal of Portfolio Management* (Winter).

Black, Fischer, and Scholes, Myron. [1974b] "The Effects of Dividend Yield and Dividend Policy on Common Stock Prices and Returns." *Journal of Financial Economics* (May).

Bradley, Michael; Desai, Anand; and Kim, E. Han. [1983] "The Rationale behind Interfirm Tender Of-

fers: Information or Synergy?" *Journal of Financial Economics* (April).

Charest, G. [1978] "Dividend Information, Stock Returns and Market Efficiency—I and II." *Journal of Financial Economics* (June–September).

Dann, Larry Y. [1981] "Common Stock Repurchases: An Analysis of Returns to Bondholders and Stockholders." *Journal of Financial Economics* (June).

DeAngelo, Harry, and Masulis, Ronald W. [1980] "Leverage and Dividend Irrelevancy under Corporate and Personal Taxation." *Journal of Finance* (May).

DeAngelo, Harry, and DeAngelo, Linda. [1985] "Managerial Ownership of Voting Rights: A Study of Public Corporations with Dual Classes of Common Stock." *Journal of Financial Economics* (March).

DeAngelo, Harry, and Rice, Edward M. [1983] "Antitakeover Charter Amendments and Stockholder Wealth." *Journal of Financial Economics* (April).

DeJong, Douglas V., and Collins, Daniel W. [1985] "Explanations for the Instability of Equity Beta: Risk-Free Rate Changes and Leverage Effects." *Journal of Financial and Quantitative Analysis* (March).

Dielman, Terry E., and Oppenheimer, Henry R. [1984] "An Examination of Investor Behavior During Periods of Large Dividend Changes." *Journal of Financial and Quantitative Analysis* (June).

Divecha, Arjun, and Morse, Dale. [1983] "Market Responses to Dividend Increases and Changes in Payout Ratios." *Journal of Financial and Quantitative Analysis* (June).

Dodd, Peter, and Ruback, Richard. [1977] "Tender Offers and Stockholder Returns: An Empirical Analysis." *Journal of Financial Economics* (December).

Eades, Kenneth, M.; Hess, Patrick J.; and Kim, E. Han. [1984] "On Interpreting Security Returns during the Ex-Dividend Period." *Journal of Financial Economics* (March).

Elton, Edwin J., and Gruber, Martin J. [1970] "Marginal Stockholder Tax Rates and the Clientele Effect." *Review of Economics and Statistics* (February).

Fama, Eugene. [1974] "The Empirical Relationship between the Dividend and Investment Decisions of Firms." *American Economic Review* (June).

Fama, Eugene; Fisher, Lawrence; Jensen, Michael; and Roll, Richard. [1969] "The Adjustment of Stock Prices to New Information." *International Economic Review* (February).

Feenberg, Daniel. [1981] "Does the Investment Interest Limitation Explain the Existence of Dividends?" *Journal of Financial Economics* (September).

Gonedes, Nicholas J. [1977] "Corporate Signaling, External Accounting, and Capital Market Equilibrium Evidence on Dividends, Income, and Extraordinary Stems." Working Paper, University of Chicago, Center Research in Security Prices.

Hamada, R. S. [1969] "Portfolio Analysis, Market Equilibrium and Corporation Finance." *Journal of Finance* (March).

Hamada, Robert. [1972] "The Effect of the Firm's Capital Structure on the Systematic Risk of Common Stocks." *Journal of Finance* (May).

Haugen, R. S., and Senbet, L. W. [1978] "The Insignificance of Bankruptcy Costs to the Theory of Optimal Capital Structure." *Journal of Finance* (May).

Hite, Gailen L., and Owers, James E. [1983] "Security Price Reactions around Corporate Spin-off Announcements." *Journal of Financial Economics* (December).

Holderness, Clifford G., and Sheehan, Dennis P. [1985] "Raiders or Saviors? The Evidence on Six Controversial Investors." *Journal of Financial Economics* (December).

Jarrell, Gregg A., and Pound, John. [1986] "The Economics of Poison Pills." Working Paper, Office of the Chief Economist, Securities and Exchange Commission (March).

Jensen, M. C., and Meckling, W. H. [1976] "Theory of the Firm: Managerial Behavior, Agency Costs and Ownership Structure." *Journal of Financial Economics* (October).

Jensen, Michael C., and Ruback, Richard S. [1983] "The Market for Corporate Control: The Scientific Evidence." *Journal of Financial Economics* (April).

Kalay, Avner. [1982] "Stockholder-Bondholder Conflict and Dividend Constraints." *Journal of Financial Economics* (July).

Kim, E. H. [1978] "A Mean-Variance Theory of Optimal Capital Structure and Corporate Debt Capacity." *Journal of Finance* (March).

Kim, E. H.; McConnell, J. J.; and Greenwood, P. R. [1977] "Capital Structure Rearrangements and Me-First Rules in an Efficient Capital Market." *Journal of Finance* (June).

Langetieg, T. C. [1978] "An Application of a Three Factor Performance Index to Measure Stockholder Gains from a Merger." *Journal of Financial Economics* (December).

Laub, Michael P. [1976] "On the Informational Content of Dividends." *Journal of Business* (January).

Lease, Ronald C.; McConnell, John J.; and Mikkelson, Wayne H. [1983] "The Market Value of Control in Publicly-Traded Corporations." *Journal of Financial Economics* (April).

Linn, Scott, C., and McConnell, John J. [1983] "An Empirical Investigation of the Impact of 'Antitakeover' Amendments on Common Stock Prices." *Journal of Financial Economics* (April).

Lintner, J. [1956] "Distribution of Incomes of Corporations among Dividends, Retained Earnings and Taxes." *American Economic Review* (May).

Litzenberger, R. H., and Ramaswamy, K. [1969] "The Effect of Personal Taxes and Dividends on Capital Asset Prices: Theory and Empirical Evidence." *Journal of Financial Economics* (June).

Long, J. B., Jr. [1978] "The Market Valuation of Cash Dividends: A Case to Consider." *Journal of Financial Economics* (June–September).

Malatesta, Paul H. [1983] "The Wealth Effect of Merger Activity and the Objective Functions of Merging Firms." *Journal of Financial Economics* (April).

McConnell, John J., and Schlarbaum, Gary G. [1981] "Evidence on the Impact of Exchange Offers on Security Prices: The Case of Income Bonds." *Journal of Business* (January).

Masulis, Ronald W. [1983] "The Impact of Capital Structure Change on Firm Value: Some Estimates." *Journal of Finance* (March).

Masulis, Ronald W. [1980] "Stock Repurchase by Tender Offer: An Analysis of the Causes of Common Stock Price Changes." *Journal of Finance* (May).

McConnell, John J., and Muscarella, Chris J. [1985] "Corporate Capital Expenditure Decisions and the Market Value of the Firm." *Journal of Financial Economics* (September).

Miller, M. H. [1977] "Debt and Taxes." *Journal of Finance* (May).

Miller, Merton H., and Modigliani, Franco. [1961] "Dividend Policy, Growth and the Valuation of Shares." *Journal of Business* (October).

Miller, Merton, and Scholes, Myron. [1978] "Dividends and Taxes." *Journal of Financial Economics* (December).

Modigliani, Franco, and Miller, Merton H. [1958] "The Cost of Capital, Corporation Finance and the Theory of Investment." *American Economic Review* (June).

Myers, S. C. [1977] "Determinants of Corporate Borrowing." *Journal of Financial Economics* (November).

Myers, Stewart C., and Majluf, Nicholas S. [1984] "Corporate Financing and Investment Decisions When Firms Have Information that Investors Do Not Have." *Journal of Financial Economics* (June).

Pettit, R. Richardson. [1976] "The Impact of Dividend and Earnings Announcements: A Reconciliation." *Journal of Business* (January).

Pettit, R. Richardson. [1977] "Taxes, Transactions, Costs and the Clientele Effect of Dividends." *Journal of Financial Economics* (December).

Reilly, Frank K., and Drzycimski, Eugene F. [1981] "Short-Run Profits from Stock Splits." *Financial Management* 10.

Rosenberg, Barr. [1985] "Prediction of Common Stock Betas." *Journal of Portfolio Management* (Winter).

Ross, S. A. [1977] "The Determination of Financial Structure: The Incentive-Signaling Approach." *Bell Journal of Economics* (Spring).

Ruback, Richard S. [1983] "Assessing Competition in the Market for Corporate Acquisitions." *Journal of Financial Economics* (April).

Schipper, Katherine, and Thompson, Rex. [1983] "Evidence on the Capitalized Value of Merger Activity for Acquiring Firms." *Journal of Financial Economics* (April).

Schipper, Katherine, and Smith, Abbie. [1983] "Effects of Recontracting On Shareholder Wealth: The Case of Voluntary Spin-Offs." *Journal of Financial Economics* (December).

Scholes, Myron. [1972] "The Market for Securities: Substitution versus Price Pressure and the Effects of Information of Share Prices." *Journal of Business* (April).

van Horne, James C., and McDonald, John G. [1971] "Dividend Policy and New Equity Financing." *Journal of Finance* (May).

Vermaelen, Theo. [1981] "Common Stock Repurchases and Market Signaling: An Empirical Study." *Journal of Financial Economics* (June).

Warner, J. B. [1977] "Bankruptcy Costs: Some Evidence." *Journal of Finance* (May).

Waud, R. [1970] "Public Interpretation of Federal Reserve Discount Rate Changes: Evidence on the Announcement Effect." *Econometrica* (March).

Westerfield, Randolph, and Keeley, Robert. [1970] "An Empirical Analysis of the Value Effects of Merging Firms." Working Paper, Philadelphia: University of Pennsylvania.

Questions and Problems

1. CLS is a firm with substantial future investment opportunities. Currently it's believed that the market anticipates a 17 percent growth of earnings and dividends over the next few years. Partly because the market's become aware of these opportunities the price of the stock has risen sharply over the past five years. In a recent discussion with a number of security analysts, the management of CLS made public its plans for a new product line. You're sure the new opportunity offers a very high net present value. Identify the necessary and sufficient conditions for you to be

able to earn a greater than normal return from an investment in CLS's common stock.

2. It has been argued that one of the reasons why mergers and other corporate combinations result in large excess returns when they are announced is that, unlike most firms' investment opportunities or divestment plans, mergers are not anticipated. Does this argument make sense? Would the situation for a firm change if it announced that it either

   a. Would follow a strategy of attempting to buy what it felt were other undervalued firms?

   b. Would seek another firm to buy it out?

3. Suppose a firm announces publicly that, "henceforth it will not issue any announcement of its business plans and strategy, but will limit itself to the publication of three quarterly and one annual report according to SEC reporting requirements." How would the price of this security tend to vary over time between reporting dates? How would the price tend to vary during those few periods when the firm publishes its quarterly or annual reports.

4. What can account for the empirical observation that in most mergers the buying firm's value doesn't increase, on average, while there is an instant appreciation in the value of the target firm by about 15–20 percent?

5. As an analyst, you expect a merger between GAF and NCB will create about $50 million of synergy. GAF plans on offering one share of its stock for each share of NCB's stock outstanding. At the time of the merger announcement the market price of GAF's stock was $115 and UCB's was $100. Each firm has 10 million shares outstanding. If the market agrees with your assessment of the synergistic gain from the merger, what windfall gain or loss would you expect at the time of the announcement as an investor in the shares of GAF. (You may assume markets are price efficient.)

6. The SML risk-free rate is 8 percent, and the risk premium is 6 percent. Safeway's beta coefficient is .85, its total market value is $2.5 billion, and it has virtually no debt outstanding. However, Safeway is going through a buyout which will increase its debt ratio from near zero to 80 percent of the value of the firm. To do this it will issue $2 billion of debt with a beta coefficient of .7.

Assuming the common stock is priced in equilibrium before the buyout is announced, the new debt offers an equilibrium-expected return, and the proceeds of the debt issue is used to buy back the common stock at current market prices (this implies that there are no information signals in the buyout announcement itself), what new rate of return will be offered on the stock? What new beta coefficient will be associated with this new more highly levered position? Will this new return give rise to any excess supply or demand leading to a change in the price of the common stock?

7. Suppose, in Problem 6, that the buyout is being organized by the Sultan of Brunei, the world's wealthiest individual. Moreover, the Sultan feels that he might be able to reduce the risk and the return on the debt by offering his personal guarantee on the debt, in return for total ownership of the firm. With this guarantee the debt beta is reduced to .3. Now determine the new return on common stock with the 80/20 leverage ratio, and the new beta coefficient on the common stock held by his highness. Would the value of the common stock be greater than that in Problem 6.

8. Verbally describe how some firms might be able to benefit from the use of debt financing if interest is a tax-deductible expense, and if the market's capacity to demand taxable debt at interest rates consistent with the security market line has not been exceeded.

9. The agency costs of debt refer to the higher risks or lower returns that may be created for debtholders from certain actions that benefit shareholders or managers. An example would be when the firm issues debt that is senior to the outstanding debt of the firm without a change in the original debt contract to compensate the bondholders for their more risky position. Agency costs of equity refer to actions that benefit bondholders or managers at the expense of shareholders. These concepts, of course, are more completely described in the chapter. Using a recent *Wall Street Journal*, describe and briefly analyze situations in two news articles that suggest the possibility of any agency cost, who it might be imposed on, and whether there appears to be adequate protection for the relevant security holder.

10. At the same time we argue for the use of the dividend capitalization model we suggest that dividend policy is irrelevant. How can you rationalize this seemingly incongruous set of conclusions?

11. Suppose ABC and CBS, unbeknownst to each other, both are looking at the possibility of developing an all-sports cable channel. ABC's beta coefficient is 1.6, and CBS's is .9. Both view the investment opportunity as having a beta of 2.2 (due to the risky reliance on subscriber fees), and offering a disequilibrium return of 32 percent (an excess return over and above the SML of 10 percent). Is one of these firms more likely than the other to invest in the project, or would they have equivalent views on the capital budgeting opportunity?

12. General Motors just announced a plan to buy back up to 20 percent of the value of their common stock in the open market. Explain to GM why such an action is not likely to benefit shareholders if GM's common stock is already priced in equilibrium. Now explain to GM why there may be an instantaneous jump in stock price when the announcement is made.

13. Suppose in Problem 12, that GM chose to buy back the common stock from shareholders through a tender offer at a 10 percent premium over the current market price. Would this affect shareholder value differently if all shareholders tendered their shares for the buyback? Would it affect shareholder value differently if only half of the shareholders tendered their shares?

Futures and Forward Markets

Futures and Forward Contracts

Futures contracts and forward contracts are instruments created by two parties who promise now to exchange a specified amount of money for goods or services at a future "delivery" date and place. Thus, a farmer may agree *now* to deliver 10,000 bushels of wheat in nine months to the miller. If the price for the exchange is set forth in the contract along with the goods to be delivered, the farmer and miller have constructed a *forward contract*. No money need change hands at the initialization of the contract, though many such contracts will require a sum of money to serve as a bonding requirement to ensure compliance.

Obviously, the farmer will be better off with the contract than without it if the price of wheat falls during the term of the contract. The benefit he reaps is the difference between the then current (or spot) price of wheat at the delivery date and the price specified in the contract. Alternatively, the miller is worse off by the same amount, since if he had waited he could have purchased the commodity for less than his obligation under the forward contract.

In one sense this example relates a type of investment that is fundamentally different from those we have studied thus far: There is no commitment of funds required now, when the contract is invented. One might even argue that it is not an investment at all, but speculation on the price movements of the goods or service contracted for. In another sense, however, these contracts very much influence (in desirable ways) the expected future wealth of the parties to the contract and the risk that the expected wealth may not be achieved. Of course, following our definition, the fact that these contracts affect the probability distribution of future wealth makes them investments. As such, they can be considered as alternatives to stocks, bonds, or other securities that optimally might be included in one's portfolio.

Definitions of Important Terms

Futures and forward markets are enough different from other securities markets that some new terms are used to describe their important characteristics. Refer back to these terms as we present the arguments for investing in and valuing these instruments.

- **Commodity:** any good or service (including money itself) that may be part of a futures or forward contract.
- **Delivery date or maturity:** the date the exchange is to be consummated, either in terms of a calendar date or in terms of a number of days from the contract date.
- **Contract amount:** the number of units of the good or service to be delivered.
- **Spot price:** the current price of the commodity if purchased in the open market.
- **Forward price:** the price of a forward contract or the *current* price of the "commodity to be delivered at the forward contract delivery date." (Just like present value, the price of a commodity to be received in the future is different from the price of that commodity if exchanged for money now.)
- **Futures price:** the price of a futures contract or the *current* price of the "commodity to be delivered at the futures contract delivery date."
- **Delivery point:** the place of delivery.
- **Margin:** the bonding fee to ensure the investor will be able to follow through with his side of the transaction.
- **Hedger:** an operator in the market who has, or will have, a spot position in the commodity and who attempts to eliminate or reduce risk exposure by taking an offsetting position in the futures or forward market.
- **Speculator:** an operator in the market willing (for a price) to take on the risk the hedger wishes to eliminate. Hedgers and speculators may be the same investors, taking different positions at different points in time.
- **Long position:** the position held by the individual who expects to receive the commodity. He gains if the spot price of the commodity goes up.
- **Short, or sold, position:** the position of the individual who will deliver the commodity and receive the money.
- **Commodity specification:** the precise definition of the goods or service to be delivered.

Forward Contracts

A forward contract specifies the precise requirements for the commodity, and its price, quantity, and delivery date. Normally no money changes hands until delivery. Thus, our farmer may hold a forward contract detailing the exact price per bushel at which 10,000 bushels of No. 2 hard winter wheat will exchange hands on the day and place specified.

Since all facts and figures relating to the transaction are specified, each participant in the contract knows everything but the future spot price of the commodity. Having a forward contract that specifies the price at which the commodity will be exchanged at the delivery date is useful for planning production and marketing activities, and permits each individual or firm to make better decisions than could be made if the price risk was still present. The farmer can be reasonably accurate in calculating expected revenue and can use this to make decisions regarding the purchase of capital equipment or land without fearing the effects of adverse price moves in the wheat market.

Some forward contracts allow for leeway in the obligations of one or both of the parties. As a result, not all of the risk is shifted with the use of the forward contract. For example, mortgage bankers often contract with builders to purchase mortgages created as part of their sales activities. While the price is specified in advance, the dollar value of mortgages to be delivered to the mortgage banker is left to be determined at a later point. The delivery date is also left imprecise since it depends on the builder's ability to sell houses. As you might imagine, the mortgage banker, being uncertain about whether and when the builder will deliver the mortgages, attempts to extract a fee from the builder (a commitment fee) to cover the remaining risk.

Situations such as that faced by the mortgage banker are not going to be of great concern to us here. Unique forward contracts are often invented to satisfy particular requirements of one party to the contract, and, therefore seldom become a standard instrument that you and I might include in our investment portfolios. Nevertheless, you should be aware that forward contracts often constitute an important part of many business transactions in many industries. Some examples include:

- Import-export business: where a U.S. exporter contracts for the delivery of a foreign currency in 60 days.
- Apparel or toy manufacturer firms: where stores would contract for the delivery of the "new fall line" in early spring.
- Savings and loan associations: where a thrift institution would contract to deliver a pool of mortgages to another thrift in 90 days.
- Public utilities: that engage in fairly long-term continuous forward contracts for the delivery of coal or natural gas.

Clearly, an understanding of the basics of the valuation of such forward contracts is useful for corporate planning, as well as for evaluating the risk–return trade-offs available to these firms. In this section of the book we will deal only with those forward contracts that precisely indicate the commodity, price, quantity, and delivery date.

Futures Contracts

Futures contracts also are contracts calling for an exchange of money for a commodity at some future date. Like forward contracts, price, quantity, and delivery date are specified. There are two differences, however, that are caused by the institutional arrangements that have been set up for trading in futures contracts. First, futures trading takes place on organized exchanges that are similar to those for trading in listed bonds and stocks. Here potential buyers and sellers (actually their member representatives) get together and through a double auction system specify the contract price. This contract will have standard features and will vary only with regard to its price. All organized futures exchanges restrict trading to contracts which specify precisely the commodity, the number of units of the commodity making up one contract, the delivery point, and which offer a limited number of alternative delivery times, each of which constitutes a separate contract. Thus the Chicago Board of Trade is a marketplace where futures contracts for 60,000 pounds of soybean oil for delivery in March or May can be conceived.

The second difference between futures and forward contracts has to do with the way the parties "settle up" for the gains and losses that occur. In the forward contract market the farmer realizes the "profit" as the difference between the sale price indicated in the contract and the spot price of wheat at the time delivery is required. The gain or loss (the forward contract price less the spot price) is realized at maturity. In a futures contract the profit or loss is counted up and transferred on a daily basis. The basis for the transfer is the "settlement price," which is closely related to the closing price on that day. Thus, the farmer who held a short position in wheat futures would have to pay 1 cent per bushel for every 1 cent rise in the price of the futures contract. The payment would occur at the close of the trading day. For a wheat contract specifying delivery of 5,000 bushels this would amount to a $50 transfer. As wheat falls by 1 cent the transfer would be made in the opposite direction—to the farmer.

Obviously, throughout the life of the futures contract there will be as many possible transfers as there are trading days until maturity. These differences are illustrated in Figure 18–1 for a case where the forward and futures **contract price** is 350 cents per bushel and the eventual **spot price at maturity** is 360 cents per bushel. For the forward contract the profit on the long position in this case is the difference between 360 and 350. The settlement takes place at the close of trading in that commodity in May 1988. For the futures contract the short position would settle up by paying 3 cents ($365 - 362$) at the close on day $t + 1$. The following day ($t + 2$), the long position would settle up by paying 2 cents ($363 - 365$). Effectively, then, the futures contract is a series of one-day-forward contracts, each struck at the settlement price on that day. The action of settling up itself is called "marking-to-market." The total dollar profit is the same in both cases, but the flow of cash over time on a futures contract is different from that on a forward contract.

Practically, of course, it would be impossible for the long and short position in the commodity to get together day by day to settle accounts. For this reason, all futures market transactions are consummated on a commodity exchange through commodity brokers. Each day the exchange and the member firms settle up according to the price movements in that commodity. It is then up to the broker to get back to the investor to make up the amount. Thus, the first difference between futures and forward contracts is really attributable to the second. The settlement procedures indicate that futures transactions can take place only on organized security exchanges to provide safeguards for investors and brokers.

The brokers protect themselves against adverse price movements and against having to contact customers daily by requiring an amount that serves as a guarantee bond—called margin, or **initial margin**, but not be confused with margining a stock (borrowing to invest). Buyers and sellers then may be required to put up additional funds to satisfy minimum margin requirements if the account balance falls below the **maintenance margin**. The net result of this daily settlement procedure is that the final payment in exchange

FIGURE 18–1   Example for Forward and Futures Profit Realizations for the May Wheat Contract

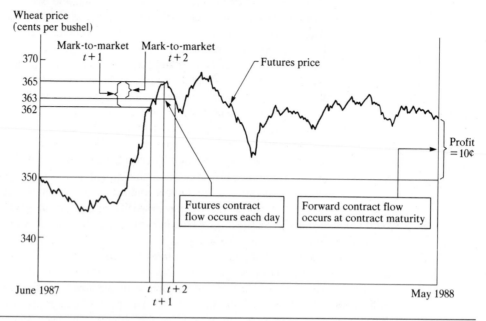

for the commodity at delivery is just equal to the spot price at the maturity of the contract (the profit of 10 cents, in the example, when subtracted from the spot price of 360 cents leaves the contract price of 350 cents).

Profits and Losses

Profits are generated from a long position if the price of the futures contract goes up, and from a short position if the price goes down. Thus, suppose you purchase a futures contract on the Chicago Board of Trade calling for the delivery of 60,000 lbs of soybean oil in July of next year at 19.10 cents/lb. If the price of that contract rises tomorrow to 19.14 cents/lb, your profit is .04 cents/lb (60,000), or $24. The individual holding the short, or sold, side of this contract has lost $24.

If at the maturity of the contract next july the spot price of soybean oil is 23.30 cents/lb, your gain is 23.30 cents less 19.14 cents times 60,000 lbs, or $2,496. This will be your profit because you can accept delivery of 60,000 lbs (paying 19.14 cents/lb) and immediately resell the oil in the spot market for 23.30 cents/lb. Thus, at the moment of maturity of the futures contract its value *must* be equal to the then-current spot price. If this were not so, arbitrage profits would be available.

Note the profit from the futures market transaction is not dependent on the spot price of the commodity at the time the contract is purchased. In particular, the futures price is based on anticipated supply and demand for oil next July when the contract matures, and differs from the current spot price, which depends on the current supply and demand

FIGURE 18–2   Profits on Long and Short Futures Position

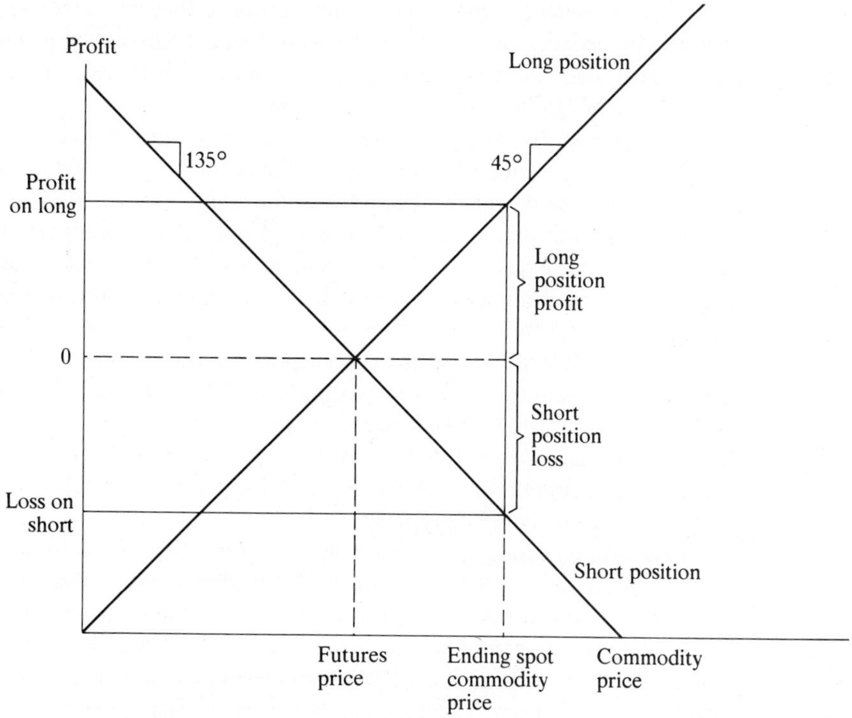

Profit

Long position

135°   45°

Profit
on long

Long
position
profit

0

Short
position
loss

Loss on
short

Short position

Futures   Ending spot   Commodity
price   commodity   price
                 price

configuration. Moreover, since today's demand or supply will more than likely be different than next year's, the futures price can vary a good deal from the current spot price, and it is likely to differ more the longer the maturity of the contract.

Figure 18–2 graphs the profit or loss from a futures market transaction relative to the spot price of the commodity at the delivery point. If the commodity price rises, the profit from the long position increases dollar for dollar. The loss from the short position just equals the dollar profit on the long position. Notice the profit from the long position and the commensurate loss on the short position are theoretically unlimited.

The Purpose of Futures and Forward Contracts

The farmer who expects to be producing and selling wheat next year can lock in the price of next year's wheat now by selling in the futures market. Similarly, the miller who expects to require wheat for next year's production can lock in the cost of next year's wheat by buying in the futures market. Transacting with each other, they can both reduce their price risk in desired directions. The only remaining source of uncertainty faced by each party is in the quantity of wheat that will be produced for sale or needed for milling. Indeed, the purpose of both forward and futures markets is to allow individuals to select desired risk positions. By being able to manage risk in a way that is more consistent with overall well-being each individual is better off with futures markets than without them. In this example both the farmer and miller are considered to be **hedgers.**

In markets such as these, there is no guarantee that the natural demand for futures contracts by hedgers on one side of the market equals the supply of contracts by hedgers on the other side. More farmers than millers may wish to hedge or more users of gold may wish to hedge than do producers of gold.

If the demand for hedging on the long side of the market does not equal the supply of hedging on the short side of the market, the futures price may differ from the market's consensus expectations of the spot price of the commodity at delivery. If, in this configuration, the futures price exceeds the expected spot price, a profit can be made by selling contracts with the expectation of being able to buy the commodity at maturity for a price below the futures contract price and deliver it against the short, or sold, position in the contract. If, for example, the December futures contract price of wheat is 350 cents/bu and the market's expectation of the spot price of wheat in December is 345 cents/bu, then investors would expect to reap a profit of 5 cents/bu by selling December futures contracts for wheat now and expecting to cover their short position at 345 cents/bu when the contract matures in December. Such potential profits will encourage individuals to step into the market and meet the demand for hedging activities whether or not they produce or use the commodity itself.

Those with no productive interest in the commodity who help meet the demand for hedge positions are labeled **speculators.** The pejorative use of this term to describe these individuals is unfortunate, since without them the desired volume of hedging would not be met and hedgers would be unable to secure optimal risk positions.

It is also important to note that while speculative activity is not inherently evil or unwelcome, neither are speculators philanthropists. They charge for taking the opposite side of the contract from the hedgers by the profits they earn from the price difference.

Which Commodities Will Have Forward or Futures Markets?

Forward or futures contracts can be useful to individuals or corporations any time they desire to eliminate or reduce the price risk inherent in a good or service to be sold or bought in the future. Thus, forward or futures markets will exist at the demand of those with a desire to hedge their positions. Since most goods and services are needed in the future as well as the present, it would seem that forward and futures contracts would be available on a wide range of commodities where price risk is present. Indeed they are. In fact, there are really only two economic prerequisites for the development of these markets: that the commodity can be graded and standardized, and that the commodity is sufficiently widely used to ensure competitive price determination.

This restriction constitutes no problem in the establishment of a futures market for No. 2 Hard Red or Hard Yellow winter wheat delivered in Kansas City, since wheat can be graded and specified to ensure a high level of substitutability. Moreover, standardization is not *too much* of a problem in U.S. Treasury bonds. The bonds will differ in terms of coupon and maturity, but they can be made close substitutes by computing the value of the bond if it were based on a standard coupon and maturity to ensure an equivalent value. Maine and Idaho potatoes are considered substitutes; as are feeder cattle—as long as they are a minimum 80 percent "choice." Equivalence may be more difficult for a house painter, a financial consultant, or an RCA television set, however, since substitution would not ensure that precisely the same commodity was delivered as was contracted for. In that case, forward or futures markets would not exist—or would not exist in a form that would lead to active daily market activity.[1]

Institutional Arrangements and Trading Procedures

Forward and futures markets tend to differ most in terms of the institutional arrangements within which trading takes place. Because of the daily settlement procedures in futures markets, trading takes place only on organized security exchanges.

Commodity Exchanges: Futures Trading

A sample of some of the most active futures markets and pertinent facts regarding the contracts traded on these markets are outlined in Table 18–1. It would be impossible to indicate each and every commodity in which futures trading takes place—there are active markets in the U.S. and Canada alone in over 70 different commodities. Some of these differ only with regard to the delivery point. For example, there are grain markets for delivery in Chicago, Kansas City, Minneapolis, and Winnipeg. Futures trading in the U.S. and Canada takes place on 12 reasonably active exchanges listed at the bottom of Table 18–1 and a few smaller ones. Other futures markets exist around the world.

As an example of the reporting of futures transactions, a recent day's trading in three commodities is given below.

	Open	High	Low	Settle	Change	Lifetime High	Low	Open Interest
–GRAINS AND OILSEEDS–								
CORN (CBT) 5,000 bu.; cents per bu.								
Mar	160½	162¾	158¼	158¾	− 2¼	242½	152¾	52,478
May	166¾	168¼	164½	165¼	− 1¼	242	160¼	25,309
July	170	171¾	168½	169	− 1¼	227	164½	26,762
Sept	172¼	173½	171	171½	− ¼	201½	168¼	5,971
Dec	175¼	176½	173½	174¼	− ½	197	171¼	17,240
Mr88	182½	183¾	181¼	182	− ½	203¾	179½	2,452
May	185¼	186¼	183¾	184¼	− ¾	195½	183	333
Est vol 45,000; vol Mon 19,024; open int 130,545, −969.								

	Open	High	Low	Settle	Change	Lifetime High	Low	Open Interest
SILVER (CBT)–1,000 troy oz.; cents per troy oz.								
Jan	553.0	553.0	545.0	545.0	− 21.0	571.0	523.0	35
Fb87	559.0	559.0	545.0	546.5	− 20.5	725.0	510.0	2,061
Apr	568.0	568.0	551.0	553.0	− 20.5	660.0	519.0	4,513
June	575.0	575.0	557.0	559.5	− 21.0	694.0	525.0	3,004
Aug	577.0	578.0	566.0	566.0	− 21.0	638.0	535.0	298
Oct	585.0	585.0	572.5	572.5	− 21.0	650.0	542.0	107
Dec	595.0	595.0	578.0	579.0	− 21.0	650.0	542.0	2,511
Fb88	595.0	595.0	585.5	585.5	− 21.0	625.0	569.5	227
Est vol 2,000; vol Mon 657; open int 12,793, −7.								

	Open	High	Low	Settle	Change	Lifetime High	Low	Open Interest
–WOOD–								
LUMBER (CME)–130,000 bd. ft.; $ per 1,000 bd. ft.								
Mr87	172.20	176.50	172.20	175.80	+ 4.20	180.50	153.00	3,215
May	166.00	168.40	166.00	168.10	+ 2.50	179.00	155.50	1,283
July	163.10	165.20	163.10	164.00	+ .90	177.80	155.10	728
Sept	161.00	161.90	160.30	161.70	+ 1.20	177.90	159.50	390
Est vol 1,284; vol Mon 1,413; open int 5,760, −240.								

Source: The Wall Street Journal, Wednesday, January 21, 1987. Reprinted by permission of *The Wall Street Journal* © Dow Jones & Company, Inc., 1987. All rights reserved.

The range of trading is given in cents per bushel for corn, cents per troy ounce for silver, and dollars per 1,000 board feet for lumber.

Also indicated is the trading unit. Corn trades in units of 5,000 bushels for a total

---

[1]Clearly, it would be possible to contract with either of the authors to perform some financial service a year from now. Such a forward contract would contain many of the same characteristics as the ones we have been discussing but would not be generally marketable. The nature of the consulting service is tied to the individual and hence is neither completely prespecified in terms of quality nor substitutable, since the nature of the service is unique and dependent on the individual.

TABLE 18–1   Futures Markets: A Sample of Their Characteristics

Commodity	Exchange*	Units	Quote Basis	Number of Different Contract Months	Most Distant Month	Approx. Dollar Value of Contract	Dollar Value of a 1 Cent Move	Maximum Move Permitted Daily
Corn	CBT	5,000 bu	$/bu	7	16	$ 11,000	$50	20¢/bu
Soybean oil	CBT	60,000 lbs	¢/lbs	9	13	$ 10,000	$600	1¢/lb
Wheat	MPLS	5,000 bu	$/bu	5	11	$ 15,000	$50	25¢/bu
Cattle, live	CME	40,000 lbs	¢/lb	6	12	$ 24,400	$400	1.5¢/lb
Pork bellies	CME	38,000 lbs	¢/lb	5	12	$ 27,000	$380	1.5¢/lb
Coffee	CSCE	37,500 lbs	¢/lb	6	13	$ 70,000	$375	2¢/lb
Orange juice	CTN	15,000 lbs	¢/lb	9	17	$ 16,000	$150	3¢/lb
Potatoes	NYM	50,000 lbs	¢/lb	4	8	$ 3,200	$500	0.5¢/lb
Sugar	CSCE	112,000 lbs	¢/lb	7	14	$ 7,000	$1,120	1¢/lb
Copper	CMX	25,000 lbs	¢/lb	13	23	$ 16,000	$250	5¢/lb
Gold	CMX	100 troy oz	$/troy oz	13	22	$ 40,000	$1.00	
Platinum	NYM	50 troy oz	$/troy oz	6	14	$ 22,000	$0.50	1000¢/troy oz
Silver	CBT	1,000 troy oz	$/troy oz	13	23	$ 6,000	$10	20¢/troy oz
Lumber	CME	130,000 bd ft	$/1,000 bd ft	8	15	$ 17,500	$1.30	500¢/1000 bd ft
British pound	IMM	25,000 pounds	$/pound	4	10	$ 38,000	$250	
Swiss franc	IMM	125,000 francs	$/francs	4	10	$ 70,000	$1,250	
Eurodollar	IMM	$1 million	($/$ principal)	4	10	$885,000	$100	
T-bonds	CBT	$100,000	64ths of $/$100 par	12	30	$ 93,000	$10	64/32nds
GNMA (8%)	CBT	$100,000	64ths of $/$100 par	12	34	$ 66,500	$10	64/32nds
T-bills	IMM	$1 million	¢/$100 par	8	22	$945,000	$25	
Bank CDs	IMM	$1 million	¢/$100 par	4	10	$940,000	$100	
NYSE Composite	NYFE	500 (Index)	$ value	6	16	$ 75,000	$5	
S&P 500	CME	500 (Index)	$ value	4	12	$125,000	$5	
Value Line	KC	500 (Index)	$ value	5	14	$120,000	$5	

*CBT—Chicago Board of Trade; MPLS—Minneapolis Grain Exchange; CME—Chicago Mercantile Exchange; CSCE—Cotton, Sugar & Cocoa Exchange; CTN—New York Cotton Exchange; NYM—New York Mercantile Exchange; CMX—Commodity Exchange, New York: IMM—International Monetary Market at CME, Chicago; NYFE—New York Futures Exchange; KC—Kansas City Board of Trade; NOCE—New Orleans Commodity Exchange; WPG—Winnipeg Commodity Exchange.

contract value of about $8,000. Silver trades in units of 1,000 troy ounces and lumber in units of 130,000 board feet. The lumber contract value is about $22,000. Also indicated is the change in price from the previous day, the settlement price (for marking-to-market at the close of the day), and the high and low prices for the life of the contract indicated in each row. The "MAR" contract for corn has a wide historical price range because it has existed since it was initially traded approximately 14 months before (in January of the prior year). **Open interest** indicates the number of contracts outstanding as of that day. The figure changes daily as new traders enter the market or existing traders close out their positions.

Transactions on Futures Markets

In many ways the act of purchasing or selling a futures contract is similar to that of purchasing or selling a common stock. The customer's initial contact would be with a brokerage house that has a membership or affiliate membership on the exchange in which the transaction will be processed. This may be a general-line brokerage house willing to transact in a broad variety of financial instruments, or a specialized brokerage house that may deal in only a few commodities. Moreover, the types of orders that can be placed on commodity exchanges are similar to those that can be placed on an organized stock exchange. Both limit and market orders can be placed by the investor as well as the stop and stop limit orders we discussed in Chapter 4.[2]

Unlike the New York and American Stock Exchanges there is no specialist through which all market transactions take place. Instead, transactions take place among floor traders physically located near the trading "pit." One might characterize the trading as an auction process where bid and ask prices are constantly (and in many cases simultaneously) exchanged between those who stand ready to buy or sell the futures contracts. In established commodities the process comes close to a competitive specialist system where market makers compete with each other for trades while attempting to make a profit by selling contracts at a higher price than they buy them, i.e., they hope to gain by the difference between their bid and ask prices.

Because there are multiple (but geographically very close) markets, it's possible for traders to "miss the market." Thus, while the system has the advantage of competition in market making, it is possible for trades to take place below (above) unexecuted buy (sell) orders in the hands of a floor broker acting as a representative for your transaction.

Transactions in futures contracts also differ from stock markets in terms of the relationship between the buyer and the seller of the contract. In the stock market, if individual A purchases from individual B 100 shares of a security, the exchange simply acts as an intermediary with the exchange of cash for securities taking place five days later as the buyer and the seller settle up. In the futures markets, the mechanism is substantially more complex. If you go the the market and purchase a contract, you will hold a long position in that commodity. The individual that sold you the contract through an exchange floor representative holds a short position in that commodity. As soon as that transaction is completed on the floor between the individuals representing the buyer and seller, the futures exchange **clearing corporation** becomes the seller of the contract for your long position and the purchaser of the contract for the other individual's short position. Thus, two transactions appear to be created out of one. The futures exchange takes over the short position and becomes the seller as the buyer of the contract perceives it. The exchange also takes over the long position and becomes the buyer from the perspective of the original seller's position. Both the long and short positions are registered on the exchange's books and **open interest** is increased by one unit.

When the exchange is the effective seller and purchaser of the contract, costs that would be incurred if each trader had to be screened for his creditworthiness can be eliminated. In effect, the exchange serves as the guaranteeing agent. As a result, each investor only needs to be concerned with whether the exchange can follow through with its contractural obligation. Not all risks are eliminated through this process, of course, since the exchanges themselves may at some point be unable to follow through with their side of the transaction.

Moreover, by severing the contractual relationship between the original buyer and

---

[2]Thus, an individual that places a limit order for purchase of a contract at a price equal to or below the limit has the advantage of being able to ensure that the execution of the transaction will not be at a price higher than expected. For this restriction, the investor faces the possibility that his order will not be executed at all.

seller, each may act independently of the other subsequent to the initial transaction. For example, if you now have a long position in a contract which you wish to close out, you would go to the market and offer it for sale. The exchange would then net out your prior long position with the new short position, reducing your net position in the futures contract to zero. If the other party to that sale happens to be an individual who is engaging in a purchase transaction (long position) to cover a prior short position, then open interest on the exchange would fall by one unit. That is, the exchange would not only net out your position in the futures contract but also the position of the individual on the other side of this most recent transaction. If, on the other hand, your sale transaction happens to be with an individual who has no prior short position in that futures, then open interest would remain the same—that is, the contract remains in existence.

Typically, futures trading in a contract begins when a new contract month is originated by the exchange. Initially, open interest, or the net number of contracts outstanding, will increase at a relatively steady rate as hedgers and speculators enter the market. Then, as the contract comes closer to maturity (perhaps a month or two prior to the delivery date), the open interest will begin to fall as both speculators and hedgers eliminate their prior positions.

Of course, an individual holding a long or short position has the option of not closing out that position. If this option is selected, then the investor must either accept delivery or deliver the commodity. While it is true that all speculators in the commodities markets would tend to liquidate their positions prior to the delivery date to avoid having to accept or deliver the commodity itself, it is also true that most hedgers net out their positions. In other words, the volume of deliveries associated with transactions in futures—that is, the consummation of the transaction with actual delivery of the commodity—is relatively small. By some estimates only about 2 percent of all contracts result in delivery.

Contrary to market mythology, the likelihood of an investor receiving notice that a carload full of frozen hog bellies is sitting in a railroad care on a siding in the Chicago stockyards just waiting for delivery to him is very, very small. Most people involved in futures market trading are aware that the market exists primarily for purposes of shifting risk rather than for purposes of gaining access to a delivery.

The last day of trading prior to the possibility of a delivery actually being required varies widely from commodity to commodity. For example, the last trading day for cattle is the 20th calendar day of the delivery month while for coffee it is the last business day of the delivery month.

Commodity Futures Trading Commission

Many of the rules and restrictions associated with trading in commodities are set up by the relevant exchange and by the Commodities Futures Trading Commission. The CFTC is a federal government agency that has some of the same functions as has the Securities and Exchange Commission regarding securities transactions. Regulations and requirements range from such innocuous items as capital requirements and bookkeeping procedures to be used by member firms, to the Commission's ruling on whether new futures markets in particular commodities should be authorized.

One of the CFTC's requirements is that large traders file reports which can be compared to determine whether speculators and/or hedgers seem to be one side of the market or the other. In other words, such information collected from these large traders allows the CFTC to make a rough judgment about whether hedgers tend to be on one side of the market and speculators on the other, or whether they tend to be intermixed and not clearly discernable. For example, anyone with over 25 contracts in orange juice futures is required to report transactions and positions to the CFTC.

The CFTC has also established limits on the positions that may be held and the quantity of daily transactions in some commodities by some types of traders. For example, the maximum position limit in potato futures is 350 contracts. That also happens to be the maximum number of trades an individual can engage in during the course of a given day.

Price Limits

An unusual aspect of transactions in futures market is that there are daily trading limits above or below which the price of a commodity is not allowed to vary. For example, no transactions can be made in corn that are more than 20 cents above or below the previous market close. Thus, if during the course of a day the equilibrium price of corn were to fall by more than 20 cents, trading would not continue. There could be no further transactions in corn unless and until the equilibrium price rose back to within the 20 cent barrier. Table 18–1 gives the limits for the commodities listed there.

It is not unusual for these limits to be reached in some commodities, and such limits constitute an obvious risk to transactors since they would tend to reduce market liquidity. Simply, if the price falls by more than the prescribed limit, the individual has no choice but to wait for the next day to determine if trading might be possible on that day. It is not clear why daily price change limits exist or how their existence affects the operation of these financial markets.[3]

Margin

While no money need change hands when a contract is originated, brokerage houses, as a result of regulations that emanate from the exchanges, have to require that an amount of money be deposited in the customer's account to bond the customer and ensure his ability to follow through with the transaction. In other words, the brokerage house will require the individual to put up an amount of money which will cover possible losses associated with buy/sell or sell/buy transactions in the market. This deposit of money is called a margin, and it serves as a guarantee to ensure compliance. In most commodities the initial margin amount is between 2 percent and 10 percent of the value of the commodity. Thus, the margin is about $5,000 for a $100,000 principal amount of bank CD futures, but may be lower on some commodities and higher on others.

As the commodity's price varies, additional "maintenance margin" may be required to account for the payments that are made on a daily basis to settle accounts. An individual with a short position may be required to deposit additional funds if the price of the commodity rises, while an individual with a long position potentially could withdraw

---

[3]The limits can be changed by the exchange under some circumstances. For example, if a commodity is "down" or "up" limit for a few days in a row, the limit can be eliminated. Moreover, no price limit moves exist in the delivery month.

funds. The process affects the investor in much the same way as maintenance margin on stocks discussed in Chapter 4.

Valuing Futures and Forward Contracts

Like any financial instrument, the price of a futures contract results from the interaction of supply and demand. And, as in other securities, individual participants may be on one side of the market at one point and the other side of the market somewhat later. Fortunately, however, the pricing of commodity futures contracts is relatively straightforward if we employ a simple arbitrage argument to set limits on the futures price.

The arbitrage argument is as follows: At the instant before the futures contract matures on the delivery date, its price must be equal to the spot or cash price of the commodity at that point in time. If it isn't, any individual would be able to take a long position in the lower of the two prices and a short position in the other and lock in a profit equal to the difference between the two prices.

Arbitrage and the Expected Future Spot Price

As long as there are no impediments or costs to the movement of commodities between periods of time and as long as the net supply of the commodity is fixed, the current spot price and the futures price would be the same. Arbitrage actions of investors would ensure this. Any time the futures price exceeds the current spot price, arbitragers would enter the market and buy the commodity in the current spot market while simultaneously selling the futures contract. When the futures contract matures, they would then deliver the inventoried commodity to cover their short position in the futures market.

If the spot price of wheat is 350 cent/bu currently and the futures price is 400 cent/bu, there is an obvious incentive to store wheat. The net profit is the difference between the futures price, $F_{t,T}$, due to mature at point T and the current spot price, S_t, or,

(18–1)   *Arbitrager's Profit*

$$F_{t,T} - S_t$$

Similarly, if the futures price is below the current spot price, arbitragers would hope to buy the futures contract while simultaneously selling on the spot market (out of inventories), securing the profit

(18–2) $$S_t - F_{t,T}$$

Obviously, these arbitrage actions will tend to reduce profits to zero so that

(18–3) $$F_{t,T} = S_t$$

The two will be equal because the commodity can be shifted between t and T without any cost. Arbitrage would ensure this.

We know, of course, that in actual markets the futures price differs from the spot price and different maturity futures prices differ from each other. We can resolve this, in part, by recognizing the existence of some costs to the arbitrage activity.

Specifically, in the above example, the arbitrager lost a current sale by inventorying the commodity—by taking it off the spot market. The cost of this is R_f per dollar of lost sales revenue per unit of time, since interest income at the rate R_f could have been earned on the funds received if the sale had been made in the spot market. Another way of thinking about this amount is that by buying the futures contract you can save your money and invest it to earn $R_{f,T-t}$ where $T - t$ is the period to maturity. Thus, with a positive interest rate, the futures contract price in Equation (18–3) must be adjusted to reflect interest that could be earned over the interval t to T, or,

(18–4)   **Equilibrium Futures Price with Interest Costs**

$$F_{t,T} = S_t(1 + R_{f,T-t})$$

Futures price at t $=$ *Spot price at t times an adjustment to reflect the opportunity cost of the delay in selling the commodity, or the benefit to the futures contract buyer of not having to buy the commodity.*

While the simplicity of Equation (18–4) is alluring, it has three shortcomings that must be dealt with. First, it does not allow for any carrying costs associated with holding the commodity. Second, it doesn't allow for the possibility of *future* production affecting supply, or future consumption affecting demand (and thus the net future supply of the commodity). Third, it doesn't address the issue of the *demand* for the hedging service itself (or speculators' supply of the service).

Carrying Costs

Futures prices are influenced by the carrying costs of holding the commodity. These refer to the noninterest costs that result from moving the commodity from period t to period T or from period T to t. They may differ in amount and kind from commodity to commodity. For example, the major carrying costs for precious metals are for physical storage and insurance. The main costs for cattle and hogs are in feeding, and in stock index futures it is the opportunity costs of not receiving the dividends paid on the securities that make up the index if the index is held. Wheat is expensive to store because of spoilage and the physical risks to people and equipment inherent to grain-storage silos. The costs for carrying T-bills is near zero (since R_f has already been accounted for).

Because futures contracts allow the holder of the long position to avoid these storage costs, the futures price will be bid up relative to the spot price so that

(18–5)   **Equilibrium Futures Price with Carrying Costs**

$$F_{t,T} = S_t(1 + R_{f,T-t}) + \text{Carrying costs}$$

The Expectations Hypothesis

This analysis is correct as far as it goes. But it has not allowed for the possibility that future supplies of a commodity may be different from current supplies. You may remember that it was based on an assumption that the aggregate supply of the commodity was fixed. This may be a reasonable approximation for gold, but clearly not for most agricultural commodities and all financial commodities. This means that we need to incorporate *expectations* of future supply and demand—since they will affect the perceived profit, and, thus, the futures contract price.

Suppose, in fact, that there is *no* current supply of the commodity. In this case there is no current spot market. Yet at maturity investors know that the futures price would have to reflect the spot price at maturity when the spot market exists. Prior to maturity, of course, investors would anticipate that this condition will hold at maturity. To make sure that they don't pay too much now, they would begin to anticipate what the spot price will be at maturity. If the current (at point t) market consensus of the *expected* spot price of the commodity at delivery is $E_t(\tilde{S}_T)$, then the market would establish the futures contract price at the same amount. Thus, the current futures price must equal the expected spot price at delivery. Algebraically, the price of a futures contract, F, at point in time t before delivery at point T would be,

(18–6)   *Unbiased Expectations Hypothesis*

$$F_{t,T} = E_t(\tilde{S}_T)$$

The market forms unbiased expectation at t of the future spot price at time T, $E_t(\tilde{S}_T)$, and sets the future price equal to it. This hypothesis about how prices are formed in this market is called, not surprisingly, the **unbiased expectations hypothesis.**

If the unbiased expectations hypothesis holds when there is no current supply (and thus a complete inability to shift the commodity between periods to capture arbitrage profits) and the **arbitrage pricing relationship** (Equation 18–5) holds when supplies can be shifted with some costs, what relationship will tend to govern $F_{t,T}$ in actual markets? The answer is that:

> The market price of the futures contract will reflect the minimum of: (1) the expected future spot price, or (2) the current spot price adjusted for interest and carrying costs of "moving" the commodity to the maturity date of the contract.

Two extremes might help to explain this pricing relationship. Fresh strawberries cannot be inventoried for more than a few days or spoilage rates approach 100 percent. The carrying costs are infinite. Thus, a strawberry futures contract price would be governed exclusively by the market's expectations of future supply and demand, i.e., the expected future spot price, $E_t(\tilde{S}_T)$. On the other hand, lumber (at least in an immature forest) is easily stored at perhaps no carrying cost (growth might even offset $R_{f,T-t}$). Thus, the current spot price might provide an upper bound on the futures price.

The final factor that we need to introduce is the demand for hedging.

Normal Backwardation and Contango: The Demand for Hedging and Futures Prices

One of John Maynard Keynes' many areas of expertise was in the futures market, where he made a considerable fortune. His belief was that in some commodities there was a natural tendency for hedgers to be concentrated on the short side of the futures market: they would normally *sell* futures contracts. This large supply would drive down the price of futures contracts below the expected spot price at delivery. This lower price would provide an expected profit of

$$\textbf{(18–7)} \qquad E(\widetilde{Profit}) = E_t(\tilde{S}_T) - F_{t,T}$$

Thus, an incentive would exist for individuals to enter the market for the profit and accept the price risk the hedgers are attempting to eliminate. In equilibrium the size of the expected profit would depend upon the concentration of hedgers on the short side of the market and the amount of price risk inherent in the commodity itself. Since the futures price must be below the expected spot price to supply the profit to those accepting the risk, Keynes gave the name **normal backwardation** to the phenomenon.

Contango is the name given to the opposite price relationship that occurs when hedgers are concentrated on the long side of the market. In this case the futures price will be above the expected spot prices at delivery.

The effect of normal backwardation or contango on the equilibrium price of the futures contract is simply to change the terms in the pricing equation to reflect the profit that may be demanded by those catering to the hedgers' needs. The profit figure would flow to the speculator (be paid by the hedger) and would increase or decrease the futures price, depending on whether the hedgers tend to be concentrated on the short side or long side of the market. If hedgers are on the short side, creating normal backwardation, $E(\widetilde{Profit})$ reduces the futures price. If hedgers are on the long side of the futures market, creating contango, $E(\widetilde{Profit})$ increases the futures price.

Whether normal backwardation or contango is the prevalent relationship in futures markets seems to be an empirical question. There is no reason a priori to suspect that hedging activity will be concentrated on one side of the market or the other. For every seller of a commodity there is a buyer; for every farmer a miller; for every producer of gold a consumer. Indeed one would have to investigate the preferences or risk-averting proclivities of producers and users to determine who may be the least willing to tolerate the price risk.

Note that none of the pricing relationships suggested here precludes a futures market from developing when the commodity to be delivered does not now exist (e.g., when storage costs are infinite). Left to their own development, futures markets would exist for many goods and services solely on the basis of *anticipated* supply and demand. In fact, in many farm commodities, futures extend out to a maturity of at least two years, well before planting. In this case the risk-shifting attributes of futures are in anticipation of the commodities' existence.

Obviously, since commodity futures can predate the commodity itself, it is possible that the total supply of the commodity spoken for through futures contracts may exceed the total available supply at maturity. Indeed, it would be impossible to control futures trading to prevent this from happening since the "future" supply of a good is unknown by definition.

As a practical matter this has not constituted a serious problem. The outstanding market value is usually small relative to total supplies. There have been only a few cases in the history of organized futures markets where supplies were squeezed.[4]

Fortunately, because organized futures exchanges become the effective buyer from the seller and seller to the buyer, the investor is not dependent on the individual transactor, but rather on the exchange. Nevertheless, since these exchanges do not have unlimited resources, it is theoretically possible that the exchange could default and the contract would be worth less to the individual holder than is implied by the then-current spot price.

Supply and Demand

Spot prices and futures prices (since they are closely related to future spot expectations) are governed by the fundamental forces of supply and demand. The influences on supply and demand vary considerably from one commodity to another, of course, so a special understanding of factors relevant to a particular commodity may be necessary to explain price movements. Farm prices tend to be affected by acreage allotments, weather, and the demand by foreign governments, to name a few.[5] Most metals, which tend to have a rather stable underlying supply (the rate of production of gold and silver do not vary much over short intervals) are influenced mostly by variations in the net demand for these commodities as a "store of value."[6] Yet some generalizations can be made that will tend to indicate the magnitude of any price change that would occur with the presence of any given special factor.

Price changes in commodity spot and futures will be influenced by (1) the expected elasticity of the supply or demand for the commodity, and (2) the magnitude of the shift in supply or demand caused by any event that occurs. In general, large price changes

---

[4]One important case occurred in the May 1976 potato futures when 997 futures contracts matured that were not closed out prior to the close of trading and were not delivered. As a result these contracts to deliver 50 million lbs of Maine potatoes were in default. What seems to have happened is this: A large Idaho producer took a speculative short position by selling more contracts than his firm could deliver. Those holding the long side of the contract (Maine processors) decided to accept delivery rather than close out their positions involving about 1,900 contracts. Delivery was made on 900 of the contracts, but supplies were not available on the spot market to meet the others. The New York Mercantile Exchange, being the effective seller to the long position, could not deliver since the Idaho producer could not clear his contract with the exchange. Extensive litigation followed that has not clarified the position of hedgers and speculators relative to the exchange.

[5]In 1986 the price of wheat fell following a report that the production of wheat in the U.S.S.R. was at an eight-year high. A major factor in the fall in price seemed to relate to the difficulty U.S. producers would have in competing internationally with "subsidized" production in Russia. In 1982, the price of corn and corn futures fell as supplies increased with the 1982 harvest. It appeared that a major factor in the increased market supply was that storage facilities were already loaded with corn from prior harvests. You begin to get an idea of the special factors that may affect commodity prices. The question for investors, of course, is whether they have a sufficient understanding of these factors to operate effectively in this market.

[6]Gold and silver are reputedly held by investors fearing a decline in the value of the "currency" they could hold as an alternative. Thus, an investor who wishes to avoid a 20 percent decline in the monetary value of the French franc, for example, when French bonds yield 10 percent may choose to hold gold as a store of value. However, it is not clear why gold is a store of value. Its industrial uses are limited, and clearly, society could get along without it. While it is true, unlike bonds and stocks, that its value is not dependent on a country's currency, its value is still dependent on the willingness of others to buy it.

are most likely to occur where supply and demand are inelastic or where either supply or demand are elastic and the shift in supply or demand is large. Because the major functions of futures and forward markets are to allow individuals to shift the risk of price changes, such markets are likely to be more active in commodities that are characterized in these ways.

Supply, Demand, and Commodity Spreads

In some commodities, due to carrying costs, seasonal factors affecting expectations, or some other factor, a particular structure of future prices may exist that is related to the futures delivery date. For example, the lumber market structure may look like that in Figure 18–3 when observed on a particular day. The **basis** is the difference between the current futures price and the current spot price, or,

(18–8) $$\text{Basis} = F_{t,T} - S_t$$

Changes in the basis provide profits or losses to those holding both short and long positions in different maturities. Thus, an investor who is short in the three-month contract and holds the spot commodity long will gain if the basis narrows, and will lose if the basis widens.

Sometimes speculators or arbitragers will attempt to profit from what they view as an unusual structure to the basis. Suppose, for example, the seven-month contract is priced

FIGURE 18–3   Commodity Price-Maturity Relationships: Lumber

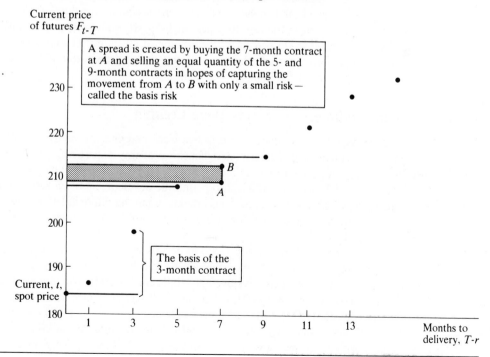

at *A* dollars per unit instead of *B*. Some market participants assessing this to be *unusual* may create an *almost* riskless transaction called a *spread* by purchasing (going long in) the seven-month contract in expectation of its increasing in price, and selling (going short in) an equal dollar amount of the five- and nine-month contracts to ensure against a negative movement in the price of all lumber futures contracts.

If the price of the seven-month contract rises as expected, it will move to *B* without any change in price for the five- and nine-month contracts. If all contract prices fall, but the seven-month contract regains its normal relationship with other contracts, the loss on the seven-month contract will be less than the gain on the short positions on the five- and nine-month contracts.

One does need to be concerned with what is normal, of course, since special economic circumstances may be responsible for the apparent market anomaly rather than a temporary mispricing of the seven-month contract. **Spread transactions** are a common part of commodities trading and are an imperfect form of arbitrage transaction in which the investor hopes to gain from temporary market distortion. Reflecting the low risk of spread transactions (because long and short positions of near maturities are held), the margin required is often half or less of the ordinary trading margin for a long or short position. The risk is that the basis will change in an unexpected direction.

Financial Futures Markets

Financial futures are futures contracts written on securities or money. Thus, financial futures include contracts for the delivery of T-bills, the Standard & Poor's Composite Index of 500 common stocks, and German marks. Some of these contracts are relatively new to the financial marketplace, and, by some accounts, constitute the most important financial innovation in the last 40 years. In 1980, 16 million financial futures contracts constituting less than 20 percent of the volume of all futures contracts were traded. By 1985 the number of financial futures contracts traded grew to 90 million, and made up almost 60 percent of the trading in all contracts.

Why Futures in Financial Securities Were Created

Initially, futures contracts on securities were introduced to allow investors to hedge against fluctuations in interest rates that the economy experienced in the early 1970s. Prior to this time interest rate fluctuations were rather limited, and the need to hedge against this risk was not sufficient to permit the development of an active market in this "commodity." But with increasing uncertainty regarding future inflation, and the resulting increase in interest rate volatility, there was a need for an instrument that would serve to transfer this risk.

The first futures contract developed to do this was for GNMA securities, which, we hope you remember, are "bonds" that are backed by pools of mortgages. Shortly after this, active futures markets developed in T-bills and T-bonds. The original T-bill contract was for an 8 percent 90-day U.S. Treasury bill having a face value at maturity of $1 million with deliveries in March, June, September, or December. These, and the newer futures contracts introduced since then, provide the opportunity for investors to perfectly hedge positions in these instruments, and to partially hedge price risks on investments in other bonds or money market securities, since all interest rates tend to move together.

Hedging and Speculating with Interest Rate Futures

An individual receiving funds in three months could use the three-month T-bill future to lock in an interest rate now and avoid the risk of a decline in rates before the funds are received. If the T-bill future currently is priced to yield 10 percent, then the purpose of the future will guarantee that in three months the individual will have an investment in T-bills with a 10 percent yield. Without the futures contract, the investor may find a lower (or higher) rate available in three months when the funds actually become available for investment. An investor forecasting lower rates in three months thus has a means for capturing the expected benefit of his forecasts as well as for eliminating risk.

As interest rates change with the passage of time, the value of the futures contract will also change. If interest rates fall, the price of the futures contract guaranteeing delivery of a 10 percent T-bill must rise. If interest rates rise, the contract's worth is less, of course, and its price would fall. If the investor chooses to close out his position just before delivery, he can take the gain (loss) and use that to offset the opportunity loss (gain) that exists because interest rates have fallen (risen). If the investor chooses to allow the contract to mature and accepts delivery of the T-bill, his position is the same. He will have received the profit (loss) on the futures contract through the daily settlement procedures and will have a T-bill with the then current interest rate.

Table 18–2 illustrates the profit and loss on these transactions. For convenience only two intermediate settlement dates are indicated. The initial transaction involves buying a three-month T-bill future yielding 10 percent[7] ($R_{TB} = .10$) that will require a payment of $975,610 upon execution in three months [$.10/4 = .025$ is the three-month rate and $975,610 (1 + .025) = $1,000,000]. If interest rates rise to 11%, the value of a 10 percent T-bill will fall, since this instrument would pay below market rates. Thus, at the first settlement date the futures exchange clearing mechanism must be paid $2,374, which equals the fall in the price of the futures contract from $975,610 to $973,236. One month later rates rise to 12 percent and a second loss is incurred requiring a $2,362 settling payment. If the position is closed out just before maturity for $970,874 (the value of a 10 percent T-bill when market rates are 12 percent), a 12 percent T-bill can be purchased in the open market to yield an interest payment of $29,126. Subtracting the settlement payments incurred as losses on the futures yields a net flow of $24,390. This figure is exactly .025 percent of the amount originally devoted to the T-bill purchase, $975,610.

---

[7]You should note that the 10 percent yield indicated in this problem is not the rate that would be quoted on T-bills. T-bills are quoted on a discount basis. Thus,

$$\text{Price} = 100 - 100(\text{days to maturity}/360)(\text{discount basis})$$

If the discount basis is 9.626 percent, the price of a 90-day T-bill is

$$\$100 - \$100(90/360)(.09626) = \$97.59$$

At this price the annualized return over 90 days is

$$[(\$100 - \$97.59)/\$97.59](365 \text{ days}/90 \text{ days}) = .100$$

or 10 percent. We have simplified the example in the text by assuming a 360-day year and a rate of return on the bond of 10 percent. The "discount basis" or quote on this bond would be

$$97.561 = 100 - 100(90/360)(\text{discount basis})$$
$$\text{discount basis} = 9.756\%$$

Thus, the price of the bond will be $975,610 per $1 million with face value.

TABLE 18–2   Hedging against Interest Rate Changes with T-Bill Futures

$t = 0\text{-Month}$ Purchase $R_{TB} = 10\%$	$t = 1\text{-Month}$ Settlement	$t = 2\text{-Month}$ Settlement	$t = 3$ Months, Just before Maturity	$t = 3$ Months at Maturity
	Rates Rise:			
	$R_{TB} = 11\%$	$R_{TB} = 12\%$	$R_{TB} = 12\%$ Action: Close position out; buy T-bill at market yielding 12%	$R_{TB} = 12\%$ Action: Accept delivery of T-bill yielding current rate of 12%
Action: Buy 3-month future to yield 10% for a price of $975,610*	Price: $973,236 Loss: 2,374	Price: $970,874 Loss: 2,362	Price: $970,874 Interest: 29,126 Less: Loss on futures 4,736 Net flow $ 24,390	Interest: 29,126 Less: Loss on futures 4,736 Net flow $ 24,390
	Rates Fall:			
	$R_{TB} = 9\%$	$R_{TB} = 8\%$	$R_{TB} = 8\%$ Action: Close position out; buy T-bill at market yielding 8%	$R_{TB} = 8\%$ Action: Accept delivery of T-bill yielding current rate of 8%
	Price: $977,995 Gain: 2,385	Price: $980,392 Gain: 2,397	Price: $980,392 Interest: 19,608 Add: Gain on futures 4,782 Net flow $ 24,390	Interest: 19,608 Add: Gain on futures 4,782 Net flow $ 24,390

*Three-month interest is .025, so the bill's price is $1,000,000/(1 + .025) = $975,610.

If interest rates fell during the contract life to 8 percent, the holder of the future would gain $4,782 through settlement transactions, would close this position just before maturity, receiving $980,392, and purchase an 8 percent T-bill. This instrument would yield $19,608 [(.08/4)($980,392)]. With the gain on the futures the net income is $24,390, or exactly the same as the income for the case in which interest rates rose, and it amounts to a 10 percent annual return on the planned investment of $975,610.

The last column in the table indicates what would happen if the investor accepted delivery instead of closing out the position. Because of the intervening settlements the gain or loss has been accounted for and the commodity to be delivered will be a T-bill, whatever its coupon (either 12 percent or 8 percent). Yet in either case the individual is in exactly the same position.[8]

Now, in fact, the current value of the futures contract for delivery in three months may not be equal to the value of the T-bill in the spot market at that moment. It will be different, for example, if market expectations are for rising or falling rates over the three-month period. If at time 0 the market interest rate was 10 percent but the futures price was set to yield 9.7 percent, then only the 9.7 percent rate could be locked in by the futures market transaction.

In theory, if there are a larger number of investors who wish to hedge by guaranteeing themselves a T-bill rate in three months, then the demand for long contracts (by hedgers) will exceed the supply of short contracts at the 10 percent rate. This will force the futures

---

[8]Note that if a forward contract was involved instead of a futures contract, there would be no before-maturity settlements and the equivalent of a 10 percent T-bill would be delivered (not the 12 percent or 8 percent current market rate T-bill). Its value would be simply $975,610 which at maturity would yield the same $24,390.

price up and yield down to compensate speculators who may enter the market to meet the demand for hedging. However, money may be so fungible between periods of time (as is consistent with the expectations hypothesis of the term structure) that arbitrage will prevent compensation to speculators in the financial futures market. The futures price will equal the current spot price plus the implied opportunity benefit of R_f. If it does not, arbitragers will enter the market and force the futures price back into this structure. Consequently, the price of a financial futures contract will be governed by the $S_t(1 + R_{f,T-t})$ term in the valuation Equation (18–4). There are no other carrying costs, and the current spot price, S_t, will already reflect the "unbiased expectations" of the future value of the financial investment, $E_t(\tilde{S}_T)$. The end result is that arbitrage will force financial futures to be priced by the expression,

(18–9)   ***Equilibrium Price of Financial Futures***

$$F_{t,F} = S_t(1 + R_{f,T-t})$$

Hedging Transactions with Interest Rate Futures

Conceivably, the U.S. Treasury may wish to enter the futures markets on the short side to hedge against movements in the rates they have to pay in the future when borrowing by issuing T-bills. They don't do this, of course, but could engage in such a short hedge to lock in their future borrowing rate. However, other short-term borrowers do use the T-bill futures market to attempt to hedge against changes in their borrowing rates.

Since other short-term interest rates tend to move very closely with T-bills, an approximate hedge, or **cross hedge** as it is called, can be formed to shift the risk normally associated with any future short-term borrowing or lending opportunity. A bank, knowing it will have to borrow in the "large 180-day certificate of deposit" market in five months to meet the obligations it has made to its customers, can hedge by selling CD futures or by selling T-bill futures. If interest rates rise on CDs in the same proportion as they rise on T-bills, either hedge will be perfect. If not, the T-bill hedge will be imperfect, with the bank effectively eliminating the risk of yield changes on T-bills and retaining the risk of some separate movement in CD yields.

The T-bill futures will provide a better hedge the closer is the instrument a substitute for a T-bill. Thus, the three-month T-bill futures market will serve as a good hedge for transactions in financial instruments that have a maturity of close to three months and are close to being risk-free. Prime rate loans to large corporations, CDs, and banker's acceptances all could be effectively hedged with T-bill futures, while long-term corporate borrowing, term loans, or mortgage loans could not. An example of a firm forming an approximate hedge to insulate itself from variations in the cost of borrowing in six months is described in Table 18–3. Here the current interest rates are 10 percent on T-bills and 12 percent on six-month term loans. But the funds are not needed for another six months. By selling a six-month futures the firm can insulate itself from variations in the three-month T-bill rate over the next six months. It still retains the risk that the rate on its borrowing arrangements may vary differently from the T-bill rate. In this example, where interest rates rise from 10 to 12 percent on T-bills and from 12 to 14.25 percent on term loans, its net cost is much less than if it had not hedged: $30,889 compared to $35,625. The net interest cost is 12.36 percent, or 1.9 percentage points below the 14.25 percent borrowing rate at the time the funds are needed. Note that because the firm is borrowing

TABLE 18–3   Hedging Transactions for a Firm Issuing (Borrowing) a Six-Month Term Loan Six Months from Now

	$t = 1$ *First Settlement* $R_{TB} = 11\%$	$t = 2$ *Maturity and* *Second Settlement* $R_{TB} = 12\%$
$t = 0$ $R_{TB} = 10\%$		
Action: Sells $1,000,000 T-bill futures for a price of $975,610		Action: Buys $1,000,000 T-bills futures to close out position
	Price: $973,236 Loss: 2,374	Price: $970,874 Loss: 2,362 Action: Issues $500,000 six-month term loan at 14.25%

Cost: $35,625
Less profit
on futures: 4,736
Net cost $30,889

$$\frac{\$\,30,889}{\$500,000} = .06178$$

$.06178 \times 2 = .1236$
or 12.36% annual
interest

for six months and paying six months interest, it has to sell twice as many three-month T-bills to hedge the same dollar value of interest payments. Another example is constructed in Table 18–4.

Expanding Interest Rate Futures

Because of the instant success of GNMA and T-bill futures and the inability to use them to hedge perfectly against other types of loan arrangements, alternative financial futures contracts were created. Contracts now exist for Treasury bonds (long term), Treasury notes (intermediate term), and bank certificates of deposit (short term). These instruments tend to span most debt-instrument maturities. Thus, a corporation that plans to issue long-term bonds a year from now could hedge its position by selling Treasury bond futures. A savings and loan might enter the other side of the market (long) in Treasury notes to insulate itself from variations in the rate it receives as it expands its mortgage portfolio.

Existing contract arrangements allow a given hedge to be maintained for a maximum of two years. An investor desiring to hedge for a greater length of time could not do it directly (though he could "roll over" the contract whenever it matures). This constraint tends to limit the risk-shifting capabilities of futures markets. For the most part the relatively short life of futures contracts reflects the demand for these instruments rather than an inherent problem unique to long-term futures. Thus, while it should be easy to operate a futures market for T-bills that extends out five years, it doesn't appear as if the demand warrants this.

Just as in other commodity futures, only a small portion of the futures positions results

---

TABLE 18–4   A Hedging Example

Situation:
   The management of Tandy Corportion knows the firm will need to borrow in one year to finance a $1 million expansion of inventories for a six-month period (until sold). It believes it can finance the expansion at 1 percent above the T-bill rate (currently 10 percent). Consequently, the firm can use the one-year maturity futures contract as a hedge against having to borrow funds at a much higher rate one year from now.

Transaction:
   The firm goes short in the 90-day T-bill futures market by selling a $2 million contract for delivery of a 90-day T-bill in one year. If the interest is 9.42 percent on this future, the future's price is

$$\frac{\$2,000,000}{1 \ + \ .0942(3/12)} \ = \ \$1,953,983$$

At maturity the firm issues its term loan and has one of two options. It can close out its short position by buying the futures contract just before maturity. If the spot T-bill rate is now 13 percent the transactions net out to:

$$
\begin{aligned}
\text{T-bill future sale price (10\%)} &= \$1,953,983 \\
\text{T-bill future purchase price (13\%)} &= -\$2,000,000/[1 \ + \ .13(3/12)] \\
&= -\$1,937,046 \\
\text{Six-month interest cost on term loan (14\%)} &= -\$1,000,000[1 \ + \ .14(6/12)] \\
&= -\$70,000 \\
\text{Net cost} &= \$53,063
\end{aligned}
$$

The second option (theoretically) available is to issue the term loan and raise the proceeds to buy a T-bill to deliver against the short position in the futures market. This transaction nets out to

$$
\begin{aligned}
\text{T-bill future sale price (10\%)} &= \$1,953,983 \\
\text{T-bill spot purchase price (13\%)} &= -\$1,937,046 \\
\text{Six-month interest cost on term loan (14\%)} &= -\$70,000 \\
\text{Net cost} &= \$53,063
\end{aligned}
$$

The net cost of the arrangement per dollar of needed cash is

$$\frac{\$53,063}{\$1,000,000} \ = \ .053063$$

for six-months, or an annual rate of 10.61 percent. The figure is slightly different from the *current* term loan borrowing cost of 11 percent, for two reasons:
   a. The one-year futures price of the 90-day T-bill, $1.954 million, implied an interest rate of 9.42 percent. Adding the one percent premium, the term loan "future" (if one existed) would be priced to yield 10.42 percent.
   b. Since T-bills are sold at about a discount, not quite $1,000,000 was hedged. The loss on this amount was the cost of not hedging about $45,000 of the 1,000,000 actually needed.

---

in delivery (T-bills have a 20 to 30 percent delivery rate, however). In the case of financial futures, delivery cannot be made in exactly the same instrument in which the futures trading takes place. Treasury bond futures specify an 8 percent interest rate. Obviously, at delivery, an 8 percent instrument may not exist. To adjust for this the existing instrument (say a 10 percent T-bond) is adjusted in value so that it will yield 8 percent. Similar adjustments can be made for small differences in the maturity of the futures versus the existing contract if delivery actually occurs.

Stock Market Futures

Financial futures exist for other types of financial instruments as well. There are currently a number of **stock market index futures,** each with a maximum delivery point of about one year and most for 500 units of the index. For example, a long position in the S&P 500 futures index entitles you to receive the value of the index times 500 at the maturity of the contract in exchange for the dollar amount of the futures contract. If the price of the futures is \$240 and the S&P 500 rises to \$260, your gain is simply the difference between the two, times 500. Because the current futures price (\$240) can be different from the current spot price, the purchase of a futures contract does not necessarily supply the same expected reward as a direct investment in the index. The expected cash flow per unit of index, if the index itself is held, is

(18–10)   *Expected Profit from Holding the Index*

$$E_t(\tilde{S}_T) - S_t$$

or the difference between the expected spot price of the index in T and its current spot price in t. The cash flow from the futures is

(18–11)   *Expected Profit from Holding the Futures*

$$E_t(\tilde{S}_T) - F_{t,T}$$

where $F_{t,T}$ is the price of the futures contract now, at time t, for delivery in T.

In this case there are two factors that will affect the relation of $F_{t,T}$ to S_t:

- The opportunity benefit of funds *not* committed to the index *increases* the price of the futures relative to the spot index price at t at the rate $R_{f,T-t}$ (the term is the same as on T-bill futures).
- The opportunity cost of the dividends (or interest payments, if the financial futures contract is a coupon-paying bond) that will be received if the index is held (and not received if the futures contract is held). This decreases the futures price relative to the current spot price at the rate $E(\tilde{D}_{T-t})$. The value $E(\tilde{D}_{T-t})$ is the expected dividend stream paid to the holder of the index that is not part of the futures contract (making the futures contract worth less by that amount). The price of the foregone dividends per dollar of the index is $E(\tilde{D}_{T-t})/S_t$.

The net effect of these two (one a benefit, increasing the value of the futures; the other a cost, decreasing the value) is the valuation equation,

(18–12)   *Price of a Stock Market Futures Contract*

$$F_{t,T} = S_t[1 + R_{f,T-t} - E(\tilde{D}_{T-t})/S_t]$$

$$\begin{array}{ll}
\text{Futures} \\
\text{price} \quad = \\
\text{at } t
\end{array}
\quad
\begin{array}{l}
\textit{The current spot index value} \\
\textit{at t times 1 plus the} \\
\textit{risk-free return net of the} \\
\textit{dividend yield on the index.}
\end{array}$$

FIGURE 18–4 **Differences between Actual and Theoretical Prices** (September 1983 S&P 500 contract)

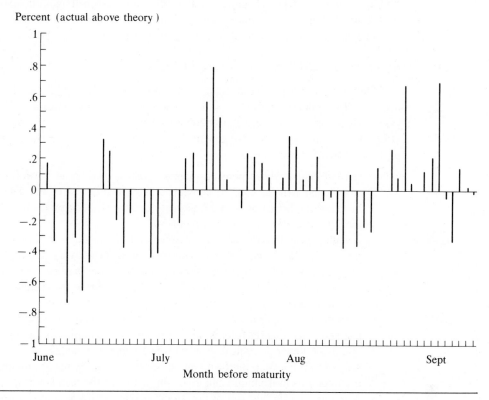

Percent (actual above theory)

Month before maturity

If the index is priced at $240, the risk-free rate is 10 percent and the dividend yield is 4 percent, the six-month futures contract price is,[9]

$$\$247.20 = \$240[1 + .10(^1/_2) - .04(^1/_2)]$$

The clear-cut nature of Equation (18–12) makes it seem as if the price of the contract cannot deviate from this value. In fact, empirical researchers found that there were some differences between the actual contract price and the "theoretically correct" price in (18–12). One example of this is presented in Figure 18–4 for the contract on the S&P 500 that matured in September 1983. The graph gives the percentage difference between the actual and theoretical price. The average difference is close to zero over the period of measurement, but the differences frequently exceed .2 percent, and occasionally exceed .5 percent. Someone with a small cost of transacting in the futures market and the stock

---

[9]Interestingly, the stock index itself supplies an equilibrium-expected return, $E(\tilde{R}_I)$, that exceeds the risk-free rate, but $E(\tilde{R}_I)$ does not enter directly into the valuation of the stock market futures contract. It does enter indirectly, however, since the spot index value, S_t, is lower the greater is the rate at which future anticipated cash flows from the index are discounted. And the discount rate is $E(\tilde{R}_I)$. Thus, since $F_{t,T}$ is an explicit function of S_t the effect of $E(\tilde{R}_I)$ is present.

market may be able to take advantage of the differential. Not surprisingly, in more recent years, some large arbitrage traders have done just this by "programming" computerized trading systems to take advantage of the differential when it is sufficiently large and persistent enough to be profitable. The pressure of these trades should move the price of the futures contract toward its theoretically correct value.

Hedging Transactions with Stock Index Futures

Who might wish to hedge using a stock market futures index? After all, the index is never really produced by anyone—it is just a collection of securities. The answer is essentially the same as that given for other financial futures. Anyone who may be adversely affected by a fall or rise in the general level of stock prices may choose to hedge his position. Thus, for example,

- An individual whose pension plan is invested in a broad portfolio of common stocks that will be used to compute a fixed annuity as of the date of his 65th birthday can hedge against an untimely decline in stock prices by going short in the futures market when he is 63 or 64.
- A mutual fund that experiences seasonal outflows of funds in November and large inflows in March can sell stock market futures for delivery in November to lock in sales of securities that will be needed at that time, and can buy March futures to assure itself of the price it will pay when investing those funds it expects to receive at that time.
- A manufacturing firm wishing to sell stock in a year to finance capital expenditures can sell stock market futures now to avoid the possibility of having to sell stock at a much lower price next year. This is an imperfect hedge, of course, since the relationship between the firm's price per share and the market index depends on the importance of unique and common factors in the firm's return.
- A mutual fund might sell or buy stock market futures as a means of temporarily increasing or decreasing its β coefficient. This is faster and less costly than selling or buying the securities themselves.

As you can see, anyone who is to receive money to be funneled to the stock market may have reason to hedge on the long side of the futures market, and anyone obligated in the future to pay money by liquidating a stock market position may have reason to hedge on the short side of the market.

One interesting characteristic of stock market futures is that delivery is never made. On the last day of trading in this futures contract a final settlement payment is made as a means of closing out the long and short positions. Anyone actually interested in holding this portfolio of securities would have to construct it after receiving his cash from settlement on the closing day. This doesn't affect the contract's ability to serve as a hedge since the commodity is available for purchase—even though it is not exchanged through contract delivery.

Foreign Exchange Futures

Active financial futures and forward markets exist for foreign currencies. These markets allow individuals who are temporarily invested in a foreign currency (that is, not their "home currency") to eliminate the risk of changes in the value of the foreign currency relative to the home currency. A U.S. exporter due to receive 10 million French francs in three months faces the risk of fluctuations in the value of the franc relative to the dollar over this period. That risk can be eliminated either by selling forward francs (per U.S. dollar) for delivery in three months or by buying U.S. dollars (per French franc) for delivery in three months.

Ordinarily the opportunity to convert U.S. dollars to francs is provided by the U.S. foreign exchange markets. The franc to U.S. dollar transaction alternatively is available in French foreign exchange markets. Arbitrage, of course, ensures that prices in the two markets are the same.

U.S. consumer-investors may also take advantage of foreign exchange markets to eliminate risk. For example, an investor with a sizable investment in a firm that derives a major portion of its cash flows from foreign operations may offset the risk of a decrease in the value of that foreign currency by selling it on the forward market (of course, the firm could do it for him). The forward sale effectively (though imperfectly if the cash flows are not certain) transfers the investment back into dollars.

As another example, consider the individual who plans to purchase a Mercedes-Benz in six months and who does not want to risk the possibility of the price of the car being higher as a result of a decline in the value of the dollar relative to the German mark. This consumer buys marks now for future delivery so that any increase in the car's price due to a decline in the dollar is offset by an increase in the value of his forward position in marks.

Active foreign exchange **forward markets** exist for many currencies and less active forward markets exist for almost all currencies. Active **futures markets** exist for the major trading currencies including: marks, Swiss francs, British pounds, Japanese yen, Eurodollars, and Canadian dollars.

Valuation of Foreign Exchange Futures

The argument has been made in the foreign exchange market that because money is so fungible, with its current value incorporating anticipations of its future value, spot or cash prices for foreign exchange behave as if they follow a random walk. Thus, estimates of the value of currency next period will directly affect the current value of that currency in a manner very similar to the way future stock price or dividend estimates are reflected in today's stock price. As a result, the futures price will reflect the current spot price after adjusting for interest costs (there are no significant noninterest costs, of course). However, the interest cost is not simply R_f in this case. While the purchase of the foreign currency requires you to forego interest you could have earned with your domestic currency, the opportunity lost will be offset by the interest you can earn on the foreign currency. Thus, the interest cost depends on the relative level of interest rates in the two currencies.

Suppose, for example, that the British pound spot and one-year futures price were $1.70 and $1.75, respectively. A U.S. investor who bought pounds on the spot market now could invest in an interest-bearing instrument issued by the British government yielding 10 percent. In addition, the investor sells future pounds to return his wealth to dollars and eliminate the risk of currency fluctuations. If he originally invested $1.7 million, his transaction would return $1,925,000 or $225,000 net, as follows

Buy $1.7 million worth of pounds	£1,000,000
Interest at 10%	100,000
Total	£1,100,000
Sell £1.1 million futures to yield	
£1,100,000 (1.75 $/£) =	$1,925,000

This is a 13.2 percent return on the $1.7 million transaction. The return is composed of the interest earned as well as the change in the value of the $1.1 million due to the difference of $.05 between the spot and futures price of pounds.

This transaction will be profitable if U.S. interest rates are below 13.2 percent, and unprofitable (relative to the alternative of holding dollars) if U.S. rates are above 13.2 percent. If the transaction is profitable, of course, many arbitragers will enter the market, increasing the demand for spot pounds and increasing the supply of futures pounds. This will tend to close the gap between the two prices, $F_{i,T}$ and S_t, and reduce the profitability of the transaction. At the same time there is less invested at the U.S. interest rates and more at the UK rate, perhaps altering somewhat relative interest rates in the two economies. All these pressures will cause S_t and $F_{t,T}$ as well as the two countries' interest rates, $R_f^£$ and $R_f^\$$, to change. Nevertheless, the search for arbitrage profits will continue to put pressure on these prices until no arbitrage profits are available. That point will be attained when the futures price is

(18–13)   ***Interest-Rate Parity: Equilibrium Price of Foreign Exchange Futures***

$$F_{t,T} = S_t \frac{(1 + R_f^d)}{(1 + R_f^f)}$$

where R_f^d and R_f^f are the domestic and foreign interest rates, respectively. This relationship is called **interest-rate parity** for obvious reasons, and adequately seems to describe the structure of foreign exchange futures and forward prices.

In the example, if the pound interest rate ($R_f^£$) is 11 percent and the dollar interest rate ($R_f^\$$) is 13 percent, the futures price will be

(18–14) $$F_{t,T} = S_t \frac{(1 + .13)}{(1 + .11)} = \$1.70(1.018) = \$1.7306$$

Empirically, the relationship described by interest-rate parity holds very closely in foreign exchange futures markets. For example, at 2:00 P.M. on April 18, 1981, the pound could be bought for $2.2710. In the six-month futures market (on the IMM exchange) the price at the same time was $2.2903. The respective interest rates for six months were 6.235 percent for the pound and 7.125 percent for the dollar. Thus applying these numbers to the right-hand side of equation (18–13):[10]

$$\$2.2900 = \$2.2710 \, (1.07125/1.06235)$$

---

[10]Broad cross-sectional and time series studies of interest-rate parity relationships for describing the relation between spot and forward market prices for foreign exchange have suggested close conformity to (18–13).

The actual price, $2.2903, is about $.0003 from this mark. Since transaction costs in making the arbitrage transaction are greater than $.0003, the current price configuration conforms to the hypothesis put forth by interest-rate parity.

Summary

Futures contracts and forward contracts are financial arrangements where two parties agree now to exchange a commodity for a specified sum at a specified future date. The purpose of these financial arrangements is to allow individuals to manage the risks of commodity price fluctuations they are exposed to. Through the use of short or long positions in contracts for a particular commodity, producers or users of the goods can shift their risk to others to improve their own overall level of utility. They may be able to do so only at some cost, of course, so there is a risk–return trade-off that must be considered in the process of evaluating the portfolio impact of a position in the market.

Futures markets are exchange markets where numerous traders compete in making a market in the commodity. Forward markets tend to be over-the-counter markets where price is determined by individual negotiation. The prime difference between the two, however, involves the way profits or losses arising from price changes are settled up. In futures markets explicit transactions are made to transfer profits to the short or long position on a daily basis—called "marking-to-market." In the forward market profits are not transferred until the contract matures.

A wide variety of futures markets exist in many different types of commodities, including agricultural commodities, metals, currencies, fixed-income financial securities, and even in stock market indexes. Because the commodities traded in futures markets are so different, there are different forces governing the prices established for the contracts. Yet all are determined by supply and demand, and the supply and demand tend to be influenced or constrained by two related forces. The weak force is that of the future expectation for the value of the commodity itself. That is, the market consensus expectation for the future spot price of the commodity will control, in part, the current price of a futures contract that will mature at that future point. The second, or strong force, is a no-arbitrage condition that we have used on occasion before (and will use again in Chapter 19) to define the price limits of certain securities.

In some commodities, those where commodities can be shifted between time periods, the no-arbitrage condition will establish a link between the current spot prices and the futures price. The link may involve storage or carrying costs, or the costs of foregone interest, but the force of the market to capture an arbitrage profit will help establish the price of the futures contract. Most financial contracts and currency contracts fall into this category, along with easily stored metals.

Most agricultural commodities have some storage capabilities that allow them to be transferred over time, but the seasonal and production characteristics make future expectations more important in the pricing process. Those commodities where arbitrage possibilities are limited also will be affected by the demand for risk-shifting, or hedging. When the demand for hedging tends to be from the producers of the commodity, the structure of prices will give rise to futures selling below the expected spot price (and, therefore, probably the current spot price). This situation is described as normal backwardation. The opposite situation, where the demand for hedging is from the users of the commodity, the price relationship will be turned around and contango exists.

Futures contracts have expanded rapidly in the past few years and now constitute an important market for investors attempting to manage their portfolio positions to secure the highest risk-adjusted return consistent with their preferences.

References

Bacon, P. W., and Williams, R. E. [1976] "Interest Rate Futures: New Tool for the Financial Manager." *Financial Management* (Spring).

Black, Fischer. [1976] "The Pricing of Commodity Contracts." *Journal of Financial Economics* (January).

Bodie, Zvi, and Rosansky, Victor. [1980] "Risk and Return in Commodity Futures." *Financial Analysts Journal* (May).

Capozza, Dennis, and Cornell, Bradford. [1979] "Treasury Bill Pricing in the Spot and Futures Markets." *Review of Economics and Statistics* (November).

Cornell, Bradford, and French, Kenneth R. [1983] "Taxes and the Pricing of Stock Index Futures." *Journal of Finance* (June).

Cornell, Bradford, and Reinganum, Marc R. [1981] "Forward and Future Prices: Evidence from the Foreign Exchange Markets." *Journal of Finance* (December).

Cox, John C.; Ingersoll, Jonathan E., Jr.; and Ross, Stephen A. [1981] "The Relation between Forward Prices and Futures Prices." *Journal of Financial Economics* (1981).

Dusak, Katherine. [1973] "Futures Trading and Investor Returns: An Investigation of Commodity Market Risk Premiums." *Journal of Political Economy* (November–December).

Ederington, Louis. [1981] "Living with Inflation: A Proposal for New Futures and Options Markets." *Financial Analysts Journal* (January–February).

Ederington, Louis. [1979] "The Hedging Performance of the New Futures Markets." *Journal of Finance* (March).

Fabozzi, Frank J., and Kipnis, Gregory M. [1985] *Stock Index Futures.* Homewood, Ill: Dow Jones-Irwin.

Fama, Eugene. [1976] "Forward Rates as Predictors of Future Spot Rates." *Journal of Financial Economics* (October).

Figlewski, Stephen. [1981] "Futures Trading and Volatility in the GNMA Market." *Journal of Finance* (May).

Figlewski, Stephen. [1984] "Hedging Performance and Basis Risk in Stock Index Futures." *Journal of Finance* (July).

Figlewski, Stephen; Kose, John; and Merrick, John. [1985] *Hedging with Interest Rate Futures: From Theory to Practice.* Cambridge, Mass.: Ballinger Publishing.

French, Kenneth R. [1983] "A Comparison of Futures and Forward Prices." *Journal of Financial Economics* (November).

Froewiss, Kenneth. [1978] "GNMA Futures: Stabilizing or Destabilizing?" Federal Reserve Bank of San Francisco, *Economic Review* (Spring).

Gay, Gerald D., and Manaster, Steven. [1982] "Hedging against Commodity Price Inflation: Stocks and Bills as Substitutes for Futures Contracts." *Journal of Business* (July).

Holthausen, D. M., and Hughes, J. S. [1978] "Commodity Returns and Capital Asset Pricing." *Financial Management* (Summer).

Jarrow, Robert A., and Oldfield, George S. [1981] "Forward Contracts and Futures Contracts." *Journal of Financial Economics* (December).

Johnson, L. L. [1960] "The Theory of Hedging and Speculation in Commodity Futures." *Review of Economic Studies* (June).

Makin, John H. [1978] "Portfolio Theory and the Problem of Foreign Exchange Risk." *Journal of Finance* (May).

McFarland, J. W.; Pettit, R. R.; and Sung, Sam. [1982] "Distribution of Foreign Exchange Price Changes:

Trading Day Effects and Risk Measurement." *Journal of Finance* (June).

Modest, David A. [1984] "On the Pricing of Stock Index Futures." *Journal of Portfolio Management* (Summer).

Park, Soo-Bin. [1982] "Spot and Forward Rates in the Canadian Treasury Bill Market." *Journal of Financial Economics* (March).

Peters, Ed. [1985] "The Growing Efficiency of Index Futures Markets." *Journal of Portfolio Management* (Summer).

Poole, William. [1978] "Using T-Bill Futures to Gauge Interest-Rate Expectations." Federal Reserve Bank of San Francisco, *Economic Review* (Spring).

Puglisi, D. J. [1978] "Is the Futures Market for Treasury Bills Efficient?" *Journal of Portfolio Management* (Winter).

Rendleman, Richard, and Carabini, Christopher. [1979] "The Efficiency of the Treasury Bill Futures Market." *Journal of Finance* (September).

Richard, Scott F., and Sundaresan, M. [1981] "A Continuous Time Equilibrium Model of Forward Prices and Futures Prices in a Multigood Economy." *Journal of Financial Economics* (December).

Rutledge, D. J. S. [1972] "Hedgers' Demand for Futures Contracts: A Theoretical Framework with Applications to the U.S. Soybean Complex." *Food Research Institute*.

Stevens, Neil. [1976] "A Mortgage Futures Market: Its Development, Uses, Benefits, and Costs." Federal Reserve Bank of St. Louis, *Review* (April).

Telser, Lester, and Higinbotham, Harlow. [1977] "Organized Futures Markets: Costs and Benefits." *Journal of Political Economy* (October).

Questions and Problems

1. What is a futures contract, and what expected benefits does it create for the buyer and seller?

2. What do normal backwardation and contango in agriculture futures markets refer to? What are the pressures that give rise to either of them?

3. In recent years the value of the U.S. dollar has fallen relative to that of the Japanese yen. In that period Japanese investors would have been better off staying away from U.S. securities markets, and U. S. investors better off by investing in Japanese markets. You are concerned about what you feel is an unjustifiably high level for the yen, but are interested in developing an internationally diversified portfolio that includes Japanese securities. Develop a strategy using foreign exchange futures that will meet these objectives if you are:

   a. A U.S.-domiciled investor.

   b. An investor domiciled in Japan.

4. Banks and other financial institutions are major participants in the futures markets for financial instruments. How do they use futures contracts to help manage exposure to risk?

5. The futures market for July wheat currently is at 275 cents per bushel. The current spot price for a bushel of wheat is 285. If the price on the spot market in July when this contract matures is 278, what gain or loss will the holder of a long position have in the futures contract? What gain or loss will the holder of the short, or sold, position have? If the holder of the short position in the futures contract also produces wheat for sale in July what gain or loss will be sustained?

6. On November 7, in about six months, you plan on buying a large house in the suburbs, using a $300,000 mortgage to help finance the purchase. Currently, interest rates on mortgages are 9 percent, but they may rise substantially before the closing date. How can you hedge against adverse changes in the rate with the use of interest rate futures? Is this a perfect hedge—i.e., have you been able to entirely eliminate the risk of changes in the rate you will be charged?

7. Your mother plans on retiring from her job as an executive with a large oil company in 18 months. Currently, her defined-contribution pension fund has a value of $2 million, consists mostly of investments in common stocks of the sort included in the S&P 500 Index, and cannot be cashed in prior to her retirement. The market is at an all-time high, and you, as her financial adviser, fear her standard of living will be ad-

versely affected if there is a substantial drop in the market. How can she avoid this potential drop? Define a specific strategy that will alleviate some of the risk she faces. What risks will yet remain?

8. Using today's *Wall Street Journal,* determine the expected equilibrium price for the S&P 500 futures contract, using the latest contract delivery month available. The spot price for the S&P 500 is given on the next to last page of the *Journal,* the dividend yield on the index (we will assume) is 3.2 percent per year, and the risk-free interest rate for the term of the futures contract is given in the section of the *Journal* titled "Treasury Bonds, Notes, and Bills." Is this equilibrium value greater or less than the current futures contract price?

9. You have just been put in charge of the Soy Sauce division of General Foods. The previous manager was fired because of extreme fluctuations in the division's quarter-to-quarter profitability. You have determined that most of the variability in profits was attributable to variations in the price of soybeans, the sauce's principal ingredient. Set forth a strategy that will help preserve your job. Is it likely that this strategy will have an effect on the division's overall long-run profit level? Why?

10. Recently, we proposed that a futures market be established for an index of residential home prices.

The index itself would be created through statistical sampling of actual transaction prices for homes across the country. Much like stock market futures contracts, settlement in the futures market for residential housing would be on a cash basis—no one would ever have to "deliver" the houses contained in the index. What would be the advantages of futures contract like this? What obstacles or difficulties would exist that might prevent the market from developing to its full potential?

11. As the manager of a large pension fund you have just received $10 million in additional contributions to invest. Currently the S&P 500 is at 275. The six-month futures contract on the index is at 285. The six-month T-bill rate is 8 percent per year, and the dividend yield on the index is 3 percent per year. If you wish to commit $10 million to the market are you better off doing it directly by purchasing the securities that make up the index, or doing it though a long position in the futures contract? (Differential transactions cost on these two arrangements can be ignored.)

12. Assume the same set of circumstances as those presented in Problem 11. Now, however, you are searching for arbitrage opportunities in the securities market. Does one exist? Define a strategy that creates an arbitrage profit for the pension fund.

CHAPTER

19

Options

Introduction

Trading volume in stock options has grown remarkably in recent years, beginning with the creation of standardized option contracts in the 1970s. On any given day, for example, the number of shares of IBM common stock involved in options trading approaches (and often exceeds) the number of shares of IBM traded on the NYSE exchange floor. Collectively, the number of shares involved in options trading on organized exchanges has frequently exceeded the number of shares traded on the NYSE—even though options trading exists for only about 450 different firms! On a more average day, trading in options on the major options exchanges involves shares equal to 50 to 60 percent of the volume trading on the NYSE.

This level of trading activity in options has been a blessing to some, a concern to others, and a surprise to just about everyone. In this chapter we will try to explain the characteristics of the basic option instruments, describe why their popularity should come as no surprise, and set forth the rudiments of the valuation of these financial claims. As an introduction, however, the New York Institute of Finance securities manual proposes trading in options for many purposes including,

1. Protection against substantial (stock market) losses.
2. Preservation of 'paper' profits.
3. Deferment of tax liabilities.

4. Speculation at minimal dollar cost.
5. Improvement of capital return.[1]

The Option as a Financial Instrument

An option is any contract that provides to its holder (the buyer) **the right to purchase from or sell to the issuer** (the writer) **a specified piece of property, at a designated price** called the exercise price or striking price, **for a given period of time.** All options contracts are characterized by these three conditions. In all cases, the *right* contained in the contract must specify:

1. The property to be delivered: ordinarily a security or other good or service that is designated so specifically that there is no uncertainty regarding what is to be delivered, e.g., a specific piece of land or 100 shares of General Motors common stock.
2. The price of the property set for purposes of the exchange, e.g., for a cash purchase price of $100,000, or for $150 per share.
3. The period of time or point in time during which the right held by the buyer can be exercised. The right to exercise may last for one day or many years, or may exist only on May 26, 1988.

Importantly, the individual who may be called upon to deliver the property is not required currently to possess it, though for some options the lack of possession may substantially reduce the option's value.[2] Moreover, neither the owner of the property nor other claimants to the property nor the issuer of the security need to be informed of the option's existence. General Motors, in other words, has no control over the nature or number of options written on its stock.

In fact, as you can probably see, an option has many of the characteristics of a forward contract. The exchange of money for goods occurs later, and the time, price, and property are all indicated. However, options differ from forward contracts in two important respects. First, the holder of the option has the *right,* not the obligation, to purchase or sell the underlying property. Second, in most option contracts the right exists for a period of time—typically from the time the contract is formed until the **maturity** or **expiration date.** For this right the writer of the option extracts a payment from the purchaser at the time the contract is formed. It is this payment, called a **premium,** that represents the value of the option contract.

Because the value of the property that underlies the option may vary, so may the value of the option vary and affect the future wealth positions of both the buyer and writer. Consequently, options are investments in the traditional sense and constitute alternatives for other financial instruments we have already covered.

---

[1]"Securities Options," New York Institute of Finance Manual [1978], p. 3.

[2]The writer of an option to purchase a building in Manhattan may find it difficult to sell if he does not now own the building. His ability to follow through may be questioned. The concern would not be as great if the option were for the purchase of 100 shares of GM stock.

Kinds of Options

Call Options

A call option is a right to buy a common stock (or any other security) from the option writer at a specified price for a specified period of time. Most of the trading in call options takes place for options on the common stocks of most of the 500 or so largest publicly traded corporations. Trading also is very active in call options on indexes of common stocks that have been developed for the purpose. Thus, active markets exist for trading options on the New York Stock Exchange index, the S&P 500 Index, and the S&P 100 Index, for example. The purchase price set forth in the option contract, or **exercise price,** is usually set near to the current market price for the stock, and the life of the option at origination is typically between three months and one year. Almost all options are written for 100 shares of the stock.

Calls are actively traded on organized options markets and in the over-the-counter market. (See Table 19–1 for an example of closing price quotes from the Chicago Board Options Exchange for both stock options and index options as presented in *The Wall*

TABLE 19–1

CHICAGO BOARD

Option & NY Close	Strike Price	Calls—Last			Puts—Last		
		Mar	Apr	Jul	Mar	Apr	Jul
Am Exp	70	r	9	r	r	r	r
78⅞	75	r	5¾	r	r	r	r
AGreet	30	r	1 11/16	2½	r	r	r
Amrtch	85	r	r	r	¼	1	r
88¾	90	⅝	1⅝	r	r	r	r
88¾	95	r	5/16	1¼	r	r	r
Amrtc o	80	s	r	r	s	r	⅝
88¾	83⅜	s	r	6¼	s	r	r
88¾	90	r	2	r	r	r	r
88¾	93⅜	r	1	r	r	r	r
Atl R	55	s	r	r	s	1/16	r
70⅛	60	r	r	r	r	⅛	r
70⅛	65	r	6½	7⅜	⅛	9/16	r
70⅛	70	1¼	2⅝	4	r	2	4
70⅛	75	r	13/16	r	r	r	r
BankAm	10	r	r	3	r	⅛	5/16
12⅜	12½	5/16	⅝	1¼	½	¾	1⅛
12⅜	15	r	⅛	7/16	2⅞	2 13/16	r
12⅜	17½	r	1/16	r	r	r	r
BellAtl	65	r	r	6¾	r	3/16	1
70¾	70	1⅜	2	r	⅝	r	r
70¾	75	r	½	1½	r	r	5¾
Chryslr	35	19¾	r	s	r	r	s
54⅞	40	14¾	14⅞	14½	r	1/16	¼
54⅞	45	9½	9¾	10¾	r	⅛	⅞
54⅞	50	4¾	5½	7¼	⅛	13/16	2⅛
54⅞	55	1⅛	2 7/16	4½	1⅝	2¾	4⅜
Citicp	45	s	r	r	s	1/16	⅝
53⅛	50	2⅞	4	5⅜	⅛	11/16	1¾
53⅛	55	¼	1⅜	2¾	2	2⅞	r
53⅛	60	1/16	3/16	1⅜	r	r	r
53⅛	65	r	1/16	r	r	r	r
Cullin	7½	r	3⅜	r	r	r	r
11⅛	10	r	1⅜	2	r	⅝	r
11⅛	12½	1/16	7/16	1	r	r	r
Delta	55	8	8⅜	9¾	1/16	3/16	1
63¼	60	3⅝	4⅜	6⅜	r	r	2 5/16
63¼	65	⅝	2	3¾	2¾	3⅞	r
63¼	70	1/16	½	2⅛	r	r	r

INDEX OPTIONS

Tuesday, March 10, 1987

Chicago Board

S&P 100 INDEX

Strike Price	Calls—Last Mar	Calls—Last Apr	Calls—Last May	Puts—Last Mar	Puts—Last Apr	Puts—Last May
220	59¾	....	....	1/16	....	....
225	56	56½	....	1/16	1/16	....
230	....	51	....	....	1/16	....
235	46	....	....	....	1/16	¼
240	40	41½	....	1/16	⅛	⅜
245	37	36¼	....	1/16	1/8	9/16
250	31	30½	31¼	1/16	5/16	¾
255	26½	27	27½	1/16	½	1 5/16
260	21½	22⅛	24	1/16	⅞	1 15/16
265	16¼	18	18¼	⅛	1 9/16	3
270	11¼	13¾	15	½	2 9/16	4½
275	7	10⅛	12	1¼	4⅛	6⅛
280	3⅝	7¼	9⅜	2 15/16	6⅛	8½
285	1⅜	4⅝	7¼	6	8¾	12
290	5/16	2 13/16	5	9½	11⅞	15¼
295	1/16	1 9/16	3¾	15½	....	....

Total call volume 177,836 Total call open int. 513,009
Total put volume 149,330 Total put open int. 908,261
The index: High 280.99; Low 277.63; Close 280.93, +2.77

S&P 500 INDEX

Strike Price	Calls—Last Mar	Calls—Last Apr	Calls—Last Jun	Puts—Last Mar	Puts—Last Apr	Puts—Last Jun
215	74⅞	....	....	....	....	....
220	....	....	....	1/16	....	....
225	65¼	....	....	....	....	⅛
230	58½	....	....	1/16	....	3/16
240	48½	....	....	1/16	....	....
250	40	....	....	1/16	....	....
255	34⅞	....	....	....	....	1¼
260	30½	....	32⅛	1/16	....	1⅝
265	25¼	....	....	1/16	....	2⅜
270	19⅝	....	24¼	1/16	1	3⅜
275	15	....	....	5/16	1 9/16	4⅝
280	11½	13¼	18¼	½	3	5⅞
285	7¼	10⅛	14½	1 5/16	4	8
290	3½	6¾	11⅝	2¾	6½	10⅛
295	1 9/16	4⅝	8⅝	5½	8½	....
300	7/16	3	7⅝	10⅛	11⅞	....
305	⅛	1 9/16	5¾	....	....	18

Total call volume 27,725 Total call open int. 150,979
Total put volume 21,982 Total put open int. 146,284
The index: High 290.87; Low 287.89; Close 290.86, +

American Exchange

MAJOR MARKET INDEX

Strike Price	Calls—Last Mar	Calls—Last Apr	Calls—Last May	Puts—Last Mar	Puts—Last Apr	Puts—Last May
380	....	....	....	....	1/16	....
385	54	....	....	....	....	....
390	50½	....	....	....	3/16	....
395	....	....	....	1/16	5/16	....
400	42	....	....	1/16	½	1½
405	38	....	....	⅛	¾	....
410	31⅝	37¼	....	⅛	1	2 11/16
415	30	30½	....	⅛	1⅝	3¼
420	25	28½	29½	¼	2	5½
425	21½	25	....	½	3⅛	5⅞
430	16⅛	19½	....	15/16	4¼	7
435	12⅜	17	19⅝	1 13/16	5¾	....
440	8⅜	14	14⅝	3	7½	12¾
445	5¼	11	14½	5	10	....
450	3	8¾	9¾	7¾	13¾	....
455	1 7/16	6⅛	9	....	....	....
460	⅝	4⅜	6	....	19	....
465	3/16	2⅞	6¼	2⅞	....	....

Total call volume 34,347 Total call open int. 63,718
Total put volume 28,518 Total put open int. 96,574
The index: High 445.70; Low 438.48; Close 445.09, +4.78

COMPUTER TECHNOLOGY INDEX

Strike Price	Calls—Last Mar	Calls—Last Apr	Calls—Last May	Puts—Last Mar	Puts—Last Apr	Puts—Last May
125	9	....	....	....	....	....
130	4¾	6	7⅝	9/16	....	....
135	1⅛	3½	4⅝	....	3¾	....

Total call volume 427 Total call open int. 928
Total put volume 4 Total put open int. 187
The index: High 134.46; Low 131.99; Close 134.33, +2.31

OIL INDEX

Strike Price	Calls—Last Mar	Calls—Last Apr	Calls—Last May	Puts—Last Mar	Puts—Last Apr	Puts—Last May
155	....	....	....	1/16	....	....
160	11⅛	....	....	....	13/16	....
165	....	....	....	½	1¾	....
170	2¾	....	....	1⅞	....	....
175	1	2¾	....	5	....	....
180	....	1 3/16	....	....	....	....

Total call volume 162 Total call open int. 2,199
Total put volume 131 Total put open int. 2,563
The index: High 171.77; Low 170.52; Close 171.74, +1.06

Source: *The Wall Street Journal,* March 11, 1987. Reprinted by permission.

Street Journal.) Option exchanges normally establish between 6 and 18 standard call options having differing maturities and exercise prices for each stock represented. For example, during a recent time period there were 18 different calls on Eastman Kodak traded on the Chicago Board Options Exchange as follows:

Exercise Price	Date of Expiration and Last Price per Share		
	Oct.	Jan.	Apr.
$65	$19^3/_4$	$20^1/_4$	s*
70	$15^1/_4$	$15^3/_4$	17
75	$10^3/_8$	$11^1/_2$	$13^1/_8$
80	$5^7/_8$	$8^3/_8$	10
85	$2^9/_{16}$	$5^1/_2$	7
90	s*	$3^3/_8$	5

*Call option has not been offered.

The first call, which last traded at a price per share of $19^3/_4$, specifies an exercise price of 65 and an October expiration date. To purchase this call option to buy 100 shares would cost a total of $1,975 plus a brokerage commission. Of course, this call will have value only if the price of Kodak is above $65 at the point when the call is to be exercised. If the price of the stock is below $65 the option is worthless. If the price is above $65 the option's value will be equal to the difference between the price at which the stock is selling at the time it is exercised and the exercise price indicated in the option contract. Prior to the point when the call must be exercised, it can be worth more if there is some *possibility* of the stock price exceeding the exercise price or exceeding it more than it currently does. Exchange-traded calls can be bought and sold at any time. It is not necessary to hold them to maturity and then decide to exercise or abrogate your right. The price at time of sale will be set, as always, by supply and demand.

Over-the-counter calls may be written on Kodak or any other security. The advantage of over-the-counter calls is that they can be tailored to an individual investor's particular needs. Thus, an exercise price of $87 or a February maturity could be constructed with an option contract for someone who expects to receive cash in February but does not want to wait until then to invest in Kodak.

The obvious disadvantage of over-the-counter calls is that the lack of standardization often results in a loss of liquidity because of the difficulty of reselling the security. Someone with needs similar to our investor's may be difficult to find. The net result of this constraint on over-the-counter calls has been an enormous increase in trading exchange-listed calls due to their better liquidity, and the virtual elimination of the over-the-counter market for all but those securities whose calls are not traded on options exchanges.

A **European call** is the name given to a call option that can be exercised only on the exercise or expiration date and not before. **American calls** can be exercised any time before that date as well, though we shall see that in most cases they would not be exercised before expiration.

Put Options

A put option is an option to sell a security to the option writer at a specified price for a specified period of time. While a call may be purchased in anticipation of an increase in the security's price, a put would be purchased in anticipation of a decline in price. Puts are traded much like calls, and the put options available for Eastman Kodak, for example, have the same expiration dates and exercise prices as for call options. For the same date as the Kodak calls, the Kodak puts are:

Exercise Price	Date of Expiration and Last Price per Share		
	Oct.	Jan.	Apr.
$65	$^1/_{16}$	$^5/_{16}$	s*
70	$^1/_{16}$	$^7/_8$	$1^3/_8$
75	$^3/_{16}$	$1^5/_8$	$2^1/_2$
80	$^{11}/_{16}$	$2^7/_8$	$4^3/_8$
85	$2^5/_{16}$	5	6
90	s*	$8^1/_4$	$9^1/_4$

*s means that put option has not been offered.

The right to sell 100 shares of Kodak at a price of $80 before the closing date in January can be purchased for $287.50. Obviously, the put is worth nothing at expiration unless the price of Kodak is below $80 per share at that time. The market price of the stock on the date of these option quotes was approximately $85. The October option to sell at $65 is virtually worthless since the chance of Kodak's stock dropping to that level before expiration is (as assessed by the market) very small.

Puts also may be traded over-the-counter with the same advantages and disadvantages as the call options. Table 19–1 also presents closing price data from *The Wall Street Journal* for a sample of put options on individual securities and market indexes.

Warrants

A warrant is a call option that has been issued by the firm for the purchase of the firm's own securities. Most often warrants are issued by a firm as part of another security issue (a new issue of bonds or stock). This is done either as a "sweetener" to compensate potential security holders to encourage them to purchase the new issue, or as a means of compensating investment bankers for the marketing services they perform.

Often, warrants are attached to a new bond with the provision that they not be *detached* for individual trading until a few months or years after the issue. Warrants typically have a life that is substantially longer than that of call options. Perpetual warrants even exist that have a life as long as the corporation's.

A number of warrants and their characteristics are listed in Table 19–2. The Wickes warrant, for example, which recently traded at a price of $3 per warrant, can be tendered to the firm with $4.43 to acquire one share of common stock. This warrant was originally issued as part of Wickes bankruptcy and reorganization in 1985. Unlike call options,

TABLE 19–2   Warrants

	Warrants Issued		Expiration Date	Initial Life	Exercise Price	Conversion Ratio	1981		1986	
							Price of Common Stock	Price of Warrant	Price of Common Stock	Price of Warrant
	In	As Part of								
Atlas Corp.	—	—	perpetual	—	$31.25	1.00	20	$8^{1}/_{2}$	$12^{1}/_{8}$	$3^{1}/_{2}$
Eastern Airlines	1980	pfd.	10/15/87	7 yrs	10.00	1.00	$6^{1}/_{4}$	$2^{7}/_{8}$	$8^{3}/_{4}$	$^{13}/_{32}$
US Air	1967	Sub. deb.	4/01/87	20 yrs	18.00	1.04	$11^{3}/_{8}$	$5^{1}/_{2}$	$31^{1}/_{8}$	$14^{3}/_{8}$
Wickes	1985	Bankruptcy reorganization	1/26/92	7 yrs	($17.31/ share) 4.43	1.00	12	n.a.	$5^{7}/_{8}$	3
Pier 1	1983	Sub. deb.	7/15/88	5 yrs	14.67	2.85	3	n.a.	$16^{7}/_{8}$	$23^{1}/_{2}$
US Home	1985	Notes	4/15/90	5 yrs	9.25	1.00	10	n.a.	$6^{1}/_{2}$	
Eastern Airlines	1983	Common	10/15/87	4 yrs	16.00	1.00	$6^{1}/_{4}$	n.a.	$8^{3}/_{4}$	$^{5}/_{32}$

n.a. = Not available.

warrants are not priced in terms of the standard round lot of 100 shares. For example, the warrants of US Air are for the purchase of 1.04 shares of stock (or .96 warrants plus $18 will permit purchase of the stock). Sometimes the warrant entitles the holder to use another security as a means of paying for the common stock that can be acquired with the warrant. Thus, the bonds of firm A may have 10 attached warrants that together allow the holder to purchase 10 shares of common stock at a price of $100 per share, or to purchase 10 shares by tendering the warrants *and* a $1,000 *par* value bond of that firm. If the bond is selling below par, this means of purchase would effectively reduce the warrant's exercise price.

Because warrants result in a flow of cash to the issuing firm when the warrant is exercised, the firm is directly affected by the transaction. This, you may remember, is different from a call option where there was no effect upon the firm's operations. This is not to imply that the firm is either better off or worse off as a result of the warrants being exercised. As they are exercised the firm collects cash and issues securities. If the warrant is exercised when the market price of the common stock exceeds the exercise price, then the flow of funds into the corporation will not be quite sufficient to offset some dilution of the existing equity holder's position. This occurs as a result of the firm issuing those new shares of common stock at a price (the exercise price) that is below the then current market value of the stock.

Rights

Rights are an option issued by the corporation to existing shareholders, in proportion to their ownership interest, for the purchase of a specified amount of *new* common stock that the corporation was planning to issue. The purchase price (exercise price) is set forth in the right, as is the period of time during which the shareholder may acquire new shares of stock. The corporation issues these rights in hopes of persuading existing shareholders to increase their demand for the firm's new shares of common stock.

The right has some immediate exercise value as long as the exercise price is below the market value of the existing and outstanding common stock of the firm. Typically, firms set the exercise price about 5 percent below the existing market price. Therefore, the right is expected to have some value to the shareholders. Normally, when rights are issued they are immediately available for trading in a secondary market. Thus, shareholders who do not wish to take advantage of the opportunity to purchase new shares of that firm can receive the value of the rights offering by selling those rights in the secondary market.

Rights are normally issued for a very short duration. The average rights option has a life of between two weeks and a month.

Because there is usually only a small difference between the exercise price contained in the rights offering and the current price of the common stock, and because of its short life, the value of an individual right is usually quite small. In some cases the rights sent to a stockholder involve such a small amount of money that they are often ignored. The shareholders choose neither to exercise their option nor to sell the right in the secondary market. Practically then, this makes rights offerings a rather cumbersome and often expensive (collectively for the shareholders) means of issuing new common stock.

Rights offerings originally were prescribed by corporate charters as a means of protecting against the dilution of ownership control of a corporation. But as the corporation grows and the issue of control becomes less important, the rights offering simply complicates the rather simple process associated with corporate equity issues. Rights offerings have become less and less important over the past few years.

There are no gainers or losers from an issuance of stock rights. The existing shareholders receive a right which has some value, but it is exactly matched by the smaller quantity of funds that is delivered to the firm since the shares are sold at the exercise price rather than the current market price of the stock. In effect, the rights offering is a liquidation of a small portion of the firm's assets to those shareholders who choose to sell their rights in the secondary market rather than exercise them. If the market is working properly, there should be no wealth transfers associated with this financial arrangement.

Options on Futures Contracts

Options on futures contracts are relatively new financial instruments. Each contract supplies the buyer with the right to purchase a futures contract at a specified price for a specified period of time. Of course, the particular futures contract (e.g., the June contract for Japanese yen) needs to be specified also. Moreover, the term of the option contract must be for a period of time that is no longer than the life of the futures contract it's written on.

Currently, options on futures exist for most of the widely traded foreign currencies and financial futures, and on futures for some metals and agricultural commodities. Because of the nature of the leverage supplied by the futures contract, the risks associated with "futures options" are quite large.

Employee Stock Purchase Options

Employee-held options are similar to call options and warrants with the singular exception that there may be limitations on their sale in the secondary market. Thus, like some warrants, they are not exercisable for some specified period of time after their receipt, and may not be exercisable at all if the employee leaves the firm.

Most employee stock options tend to be long-term and are "given" to the employees as part of a labor contract in order to provide them with the incentives to act in ways consistent with the objectives of the stockholders. In fact, firms have been developing innovative stock option plans as a means of overcoming some of the agency costs that arise from the manager-stockholder-bondholder conflicts that are part of the modern firm.

Corporate Call on Bonds

In issuing bonds, corporations often retain the option of calling and retiring the bonds. The bondholders thus become option writers. This bond indenture provision was discussed in Chapter 13. Typically, the exercise price is slightly above the par value of the bond. Usually this option is written to exist between some future date (5 years or 10 years from issue) and the maturity of the bond. In these cases the call option's existence is delayed for a number of years. The premium paid by the corporation for retaining this option is a higher interest rate than it would otherwise pay. Retention of this call option provides greater financial flexibility for the firm's operations by allowing the firm to retire the bond issue if that is in the firm's best interest (e.g., after a significant drop in bond interest rates).

Convertible Bonds and Convertible Preferred Stock

Convertible financial instruments were introduced in Chapter 12. The conversion feature is an option which is held by the owner of the bond and is written by the issuing firm. The option is similar to a call option except that it is generally for a long term—usually for the life of the security—and cannot be separated from the bond or preferred stock itself. Thus, the convertible bond or preferred stock would be valued as a combination of a straight debt instrument and an option on the stock. As an example, the bonds of Compaq Corporation are convertible into shares of common stock at a price of $39.65 per share. The exercise price in this case is equal to the par value of the bond divided by the number of shares into which the bond is convertible. These bonds in late 1986 were selling at a price of about $132 per $100 par value. The bond was selling above its par value even though the interest rate on the bond was somewhat below market rates (a $9\frac{1}{2}$ percent coupon rate) because of the value of the conversion option. In other words, the sum of the value of the interest payments, if the instrument were a straight bond, and the value of the option itself dictated a total market value of $132. At the same time the 10 percent coupon convertibles of Ramada Inns were selling at $76 (reflecting the close to zero value of the convertible feature).

Typically, the initial exercise price on a convertible is set about 20 percent above the current stock price. Thus, to the extent that the conversion option has value as of the issue date of the bonds, it is attributable to an *expectation* that over the life of the option the market price of the common stock would rise above the exercise price.

Extendable and Redeemable Bonds

Some financial instruments contain an option whereby they can be *extended* by increasing the maturity date or (at a price) redeemed early, prior to maturity. Extendable bonds, in other words, provide the bondholder with the option to continue receiving interest payments past the originally specified maturity date of the bond itself. This then is not an option to buy but rather an option to continue an existing contractual arrangement.

Most certificates of deposit, or CDs, and time deposits are *redeemable* prior to maturity at some penalty (e.g., the holder foregoes three months' interest). The holder of this instrument then holds a put option to "sell" the CD back to the issuer. The holder would "put" the CD when the current value of the CD was below the "with penalty" price at which the holder could redeem the deposit. The current value of the CD may be low, for example, if interest rates have risen since the CD was originally issued.

The Equity Option

It is possible to view almost any asset in an option framework. In some cases this helps us to understand the major characteristics of basic financial instruments, whereas in other cases it may amount to nothing more than semantics. For example, it is possible to think of the equity position in a firm as simply being an option that is held by the firm's owners. In other words, one might argue that the owners of the firm have an option to rebuy the firm each and every period by whatever steps are necessary to avoid bankruptcy. This may involve the payment of interest on existing debt instruments or by meeting obligations to the firm's customers. For example, since the firm has the option not to pay the interest on debt when it is due and face the possibility of seeing action being taken by bondholders, the equity position in the firm can measure its position and determine if it wants to exercise its option to remain in business. It does so by meeting those prespecified obligations to customers (in the form of warranties) or debtholders (in the form of interest payments and principal repayments). We suppose that it is even possible to think of a professor of finance with tenure having the option to retain that position for an additional year. Not to exercise the option to report for work—that is, to quit—is exactly like not exercising a call option. The decision at that time would depend upon the value of the employment (the work being the exercise price) and has most of the attributes of the ordinary call option (except that it does not have secondary market liquidity).

Profits in Options

Options are called **contingent claims** or **derived financial instruments** because their value is contingent on and derived expressly from the value of the underlying security—the security that can be purchased or sold with the use of the option. If you purchased a call option that gives you the right to buy NCR at $80 per share, that option will have value as long as NCR's market price exceeds $80 at the time the option must be exercised. If NCR is at $90 you can simultaneously exercise your option at 80 and sell in the market at $90 to gain the $10 difference. The shares received from exercising your option can be used to deliver against your sold position in the market.

FIGURE 19–1   Profits to Buyers of Call Options

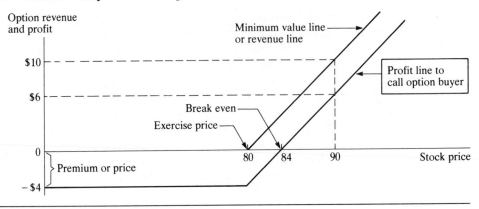

Figure 19–1 describes the relationship between the price of the common stock, the exercise price, and the revenue from the call option at the maturity of the option contract.[3] The revenue line is a 45-degree line since for each dollar increase in share price there is a one-dollar gain in cash flows from exercising the option at the higher price. There is no cash flow if the stock price is below the exercise price, since the owner of the option would simply exercise the right not to buy the security, and the option would expire without action. The revenue line is also called the **minimum-value line,** since the market value of an option would never be below the values indicated by the line. If, at the point of expiration, the stock price *is* $90 and the exercise price *is* $80, the "minimum" value of the option must be $10. If it were not, someone could buy the option for less than $10, exercise it to buy the stock at $80, and sell the stock in the open market at $90 to secure a riskless instantaneous gain.

Of course, it is this revenue potential (the potential that the stock price exceeds the exercise price) that forms the basis for option valuation. To gain this potential the buyer pays and the writer receives a *premium* at the time the contract is initiated. This premium is the potential capital loss for the buyer (and the potential profit for the writer). That loss will be incurred *if the stock price is below the exercise price at the exercise date.* The *profit line,* then, is the difference between the revenues and the amount paid as a premium for the option.

Recently, for example, a six-month option to buy the common stock of NCR at $80 would have cost $4 per share. The buyer would exercise the option if, at the exercise date, the stock price exceeded $80. However, the buyer would not make a profit unless the stock price rose above $84 by the exercise date, since $4 was paid to acquire the option ($84 is the breakeven stock price, ignoring brokerage commissions).

Clearly, since revenues depend on the chances that the stock price will exceed $80,

---

[3]Figure 19–1 and the similar figures following it have been drawn showing option revenue and profit on a per share basis; i.e., assuming an option is the right to buy or sell one share of stock. Thus, for example, in Figure 19–1, the call option premium of $4 is the price of the option stated on a per share basis (as it is reported in the newspaper). To find the actual market price, one would multiply the premium by 100.

FIGURE 19–2   Call Option Premiums and Profit Lines Depend on Current Stock Price and on Exercise Price

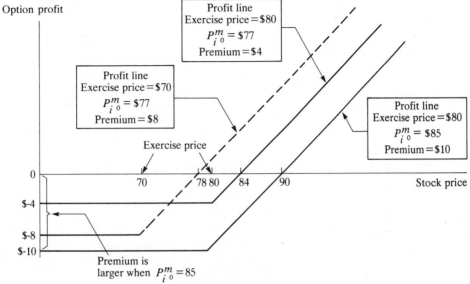

the current market price of the stock will play a major role in establishing the size of the premium. The greater the current market price, P_{i0}^m, relative to the exercise price, the greater the premium. This relationship is established in Figure 19–2. The premium on the option to purchase at $80 is $4 when current market is $77, and $10 when the price is $85. Investors apparently are willing to pay a larger premium if stock price is higher because the chance of ending up on the sloping line segment (i.e., the chance that exercising will prove to be valuable) is greater.

Revenues are also a function of the exercise price. The lower the exercise price the higher the revenue line for any given stock price, simply because you pay less to acquire the share. However, this greater revenue will extract a larger premium, so the profit figure is reduced. This is shown by the dashed line in Figure 19–2 where the premium is $8 when the exercise price is $70.

Ignoring commission costs, the profit line for the writer of the option is equal to *minus* the profit line for the buyer. Remember that the transaction is simply between the buyer and writer. No productive operations take place within this transaction to expand the cash flow to both. If the stock price rises by a dollar, the writer loses exactly what the buyer has gained. The profit function for the writer of a call option is in Figure 19–3. If the price rises to $86, say, the writer will be forced to sell at $80, whereas he could have sold in the market at 86. The $6 loss is only partially offset by the $4 premium.[4] The

---

[4]In measuring the profit, it doesn't matter whether the writer currently holds the stock or must purchase it in the open market. If the stock is held, the $6 is an opportunity loss. If the writer has to venture to the market to buy it at $86, the loss is still $6, since only $80 is received when the holder of the option demands delivery.

FIGURE 19–3   Profits to Writers of Call Options

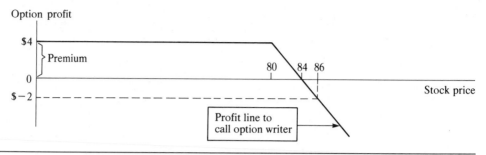

writer's potential loss is limited only by the maximum possible price the stock might attain.

To summarize:

> *Call Options:* The profits to the call option buyer increase with a rise in stock price, while the option writer's profits decrease with a rise in stock price. The sum of cash flows to both parties is always zero.

The profits to the buyer of a put option, conveying the right to sell, will be a dollar-for-dollar function of the decline in stock price. Thus when the current stock price is $77, the buyer of the put pays a premium (equal to $7 in Figure 19–4), which represents the maximum possible loss to the put owner. As stock price falls below the exercise price of 80, the put buyer gains from the ability to sell at the exercise price. Figure 19–4 shows this relationship. The zero profit point is at a stock price of $73, since $80 less the premium is $73. As the price falls beyond $73, the holder of the put accumulates profits.

As in the case of call options, the writer of the put option receives minus the cash flows to the buyer. The writer's position is described in Figure 19–5. Note the put option writer's losses are potentially limited only by a stock price of zero. Of course, the price of the put or call, or the premium, will be set by the interaction of supply and demand. The $7 price of the put in the above example was set in the market as a function of the current market price ($77), the exercise price ($80), and the market's estimate of the possible gains or losses from holding the put.

> *Put Options:* The profits to the put option buyer rise with a fall in stock price, while the put option writer's profits fall with a fall in share price. The sum of the cash flows to both parties is always zero.

These profit functions are markedly different from those for stocks or commodity futures where gains and losses are proportional. From the view of the buyer of the put or call option they provide ways to limit losses to a specified amount (the premium).

FIGURE 19–4	**Profits to Buyers of Put Options**

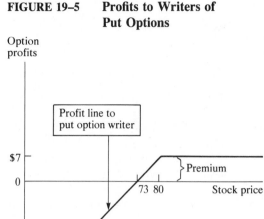

FIGURE 19–5	**Profits to Writers of Put Options**

Interestingly, combinations of different kinds of options on the same stock will yield the sum of these profit figures, with correspondingly different profit functions. For example, a **straddle** is a combination of a put and a call and results in a profit function that is V-shaped with the point of the V at the exercise price and below the zero profit point by an amount equal to the sum of the premiums on the put and call. A combined put and call at different exercise prices would generate a V-shaped profit line with a flat bottom. Both of these relationships are shown in Figure 19–6, parts (a) and (b), assuming a current stock price of $77, along with the combination of a put at higher exercise price and the call at the lower exercise price, shown in Figure 19–6, part (c). In this latter case, you will recoup some of your $17 premium regardless of the stock price. If the stock price ends at $75 in this example, the call is worthless. However, the put pays off $10. The premium less the profit on the put is a $7 loss, which is shown as point A. If the stock price ends up at $80, both the call at 75 and the put at 85 would be exercised for a total loss of,

$$\text{Revenue on call } + \text{ Revenue on put } - \text{ Premium}$$
$$\$5 + \$5 \qquad\qquad -\ \$17 \qquad = -\$7$$

Note that the put and call premium of $17 is the same here as the premium on the combined put and call (in Figure 19–6(b)) at the $75 exercise price for the put and $85 exercise price for the call. Indeed, they would have to be the same, since if the two amounts varied arbitrage profits could be made by writing the higher-priced of the two and using the premium to purchase the lower-priced of the combined instruments. Market forces would ensure that this parity is maintained so equivalent investments yield the same rewards.

It is also possible to combine options by buying and writing options (either puts or calls) on the same security with different exercise prices. Thus, buying a call with an exercise price of 85 (premium $2) and writing one with an exercise price of 80 (premium $4) would lead to a different profit function. At all prices at or below $80 the option combination gains $2 (the premium difference). At all prices $85 or above the combination loses $3. Between $80 and $85, the profits vary, because of the different exercise prices.

FIGURE 19–6   Profits from Combined Options

(a) From a straddle

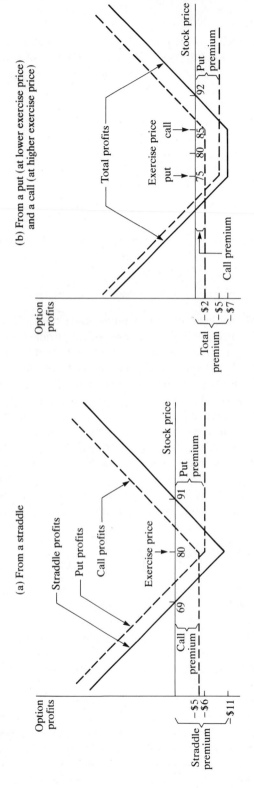

(b) From a put (at lower exercise price) and a call (at higher exercise price)

(c) From a call (at lower exercise price) and a put (at higher exercise price)

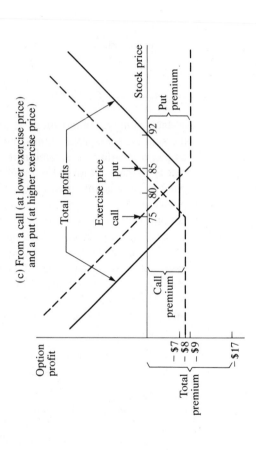

FIGURE 19–7 **Probability Distribution of Stock Price and Return, ADS Consolidated at $t = 1$**

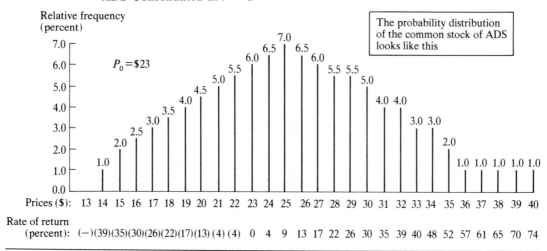

This combination of buying and selling options with different exercise prices is called a **money spread.** Obviously, there is very little risk (and perhaps little reward) to the strategy.[5]

Options Returns: An Illustration

According to our estimates, the common stock of ADS Consolidated has a probability distribution for its price in one year as indicated in Figure 19–7. The current price is $23. With the expected price of $25.66 and no forthcoming dividends, the analyst expects a return of

$$\hat{R}_{ADS} = \frac{\$25.66 - \$23}{\$23} = .1157 \text{ or } 11.57\%$$

A one-year call option written on this stock for an exercise price of $23 and costing $3 per share ($300 total) supplies the probability distribution in Figure 19–8. Of course, if the stock price after one year is below $23 the option will not be exercised. There is a 37 percent chance of this happening. At a price of $24 the option will be exercised, recouping $1 of the $3 premium for a return of −67 percent. If the price goes to $30, the option is worth $7 less the premium of $3, for a $4 net gain and a net return of 133 percent.

A comparison of the rate-of-return outcomes suggests that the option is riskier than the stock. And this would be the case if an equal dollar investment were considered for either the stock or the stock's option. But remember that the option that can be purchased

---

[5]A "calendar spread" involves buying and writing options with different maturity dates. An investor holding a "butterfly spread" writes or buys an option and buys or writes two options on either side of the maturity or striking price. Such tactics are used when one suspects an unnatural price relationship exists.

FIGURE 19–8   **Probability Distribution of Call Option Return on ADS Consolidated at** $t = 1$

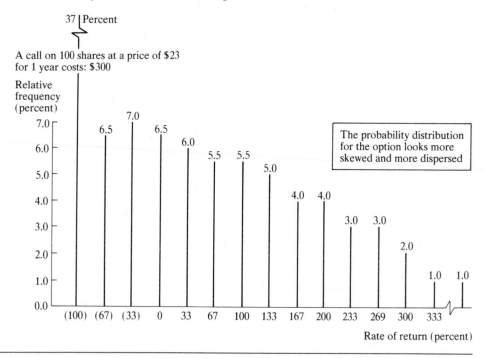

for $3 entitles you to participate in a portion of the probability distribution of a stock selling at $23. The comparison is not so direct as it might at first seem. In fact, consider the return distributions from these four different strategies:

1. $2,300 invested in 100 shares of the stock.
2. $2,300 invested in $7^2/_3$ options to buy 767 shares of stock (i.e., with $2,300 you can buy $7^2/_3$ options for $300 each).
3. $300 invested in one option, and $2,000 invested in a savings account at 8 percent.
4. $300 invested in one option, and $2,000 of the stock sold short at $23 per share.

The probability distributions of end-of-period wealth are compared in Figure 19–9, parts (a)–(d). In strategy (b) there is a 37 percent chance of losing all $2,300. In strategies (c) and (d) the maximum loss is only $300. Clearly, much of the risk of an option as it contributes to portfolio variability depends on how it is packaged in the portfolio. Options can be risky, as in (b), or can be used to hedge against unexpected or unwanted risks, as in (d).

Why Do Options Exist?

Options and commodity futures have often been denigrated by those who feel such instruments are blatantly speculative devices. It's often pointed out by the detractors that,

**FIGURE 19–9   Relative Frequency of Wealth from $2,300 Investment,
Using Different Strategies**

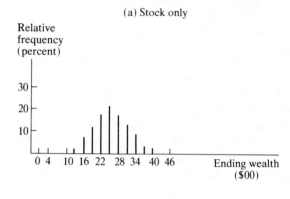

(a) Stock only

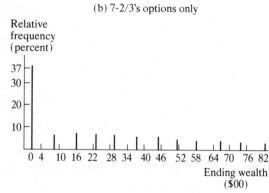

(b) 7-2/3's options only

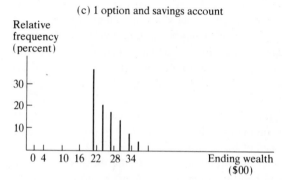

(c) 1 option and savings account

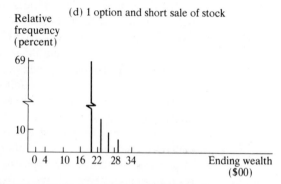

(d) 1 option and short sale of stock

like futures, few options are exercised. Moreover, some have argued that investing in options as a substitute for stocks or bonds results in no new net corporate investments and no increase in economic output. The money, it is argued, never gets to the corporation.[6]

Others have argued that options encourage savings and investment by providing alternatives that are appealing and, depending on how they are packaged, serve to decrease the inherent risk in holding stocks and bonds. Also, it has been suggested that hedges that can be formed from options to limit losses keep people from panic selling, and, on net, encourage savings and investment to the benefit of all.

In what sense are investors better off with options as investment alternatives? In what sense is society as a whole better off? The bases for answers to these questions were formed in earlier chapters. Options provide a mechanism for purchasing a probability distribution of returns that allows the investor to take advantage of his forecasts or to develop a portfolio more consistent with his preferences than would otherwise be possible.

Suppose, for example, that you believe an increase in the price of oil is likely (more

---

[6]Every option transaction is a *net* transaction in the sense that a dollar invested by the buyer is received by the writer—who then may purchase stocks or bonds. The funds never really disappear.

likely than the views held by the rest of the market), and that it will substantially benefit firms in the oil field service industry. You could act on your beliefs by buying securities issued by these firms or by buying call options on these securities. Given the need to retain a relatively diversified portfolio position, you might find it undesirable to risk the 40 percent or 50 percent of your portfolio wealth required to purchase 1,000 shares of Reading and Bates (an oil field service firm). Alternatively, 1,000 shares of the firm can be *controlled* with the purchase of 10 options on the firm's common stock, perhaps (depending on the price of the options) by devoting less than 10 percent of your portfolio's value to the purchase. Which of the alternatives actually turns out to be the best for you will depend on the alternative probability distributions available from the two strategies. But there is, at least, the distinct possibility that the option would be preferable. Thus, different probability assessments lead to a demand for options and a better portfolio for the individual. Society may benefit as well if the potential gain from using options encourages the investment of time and effort in the development of better forecasting methods.

As a second example, consider the situation faced by a professor of finance who is obliged in the near future to send an only daughter to four years of college at an expected cost of $100,000. With a $110,000 portfolio what might be done to "ensure" a large portion of the portfolio from the ravages of a decline in the stock market? One answer is to buy enough put options (perhaps on a stock market index or perhaps on the securities included in the professor's portfolio) to "lock in" $100,000 of wealth. Certainly this should be considered as an alternative to the obvious strategy of liquidating the vast majority of the portfolio and investing the proceeds in T-bills. Which of the alternatives might be preferred in this case depends on the probability distribution of portfolio returns generated, and the risk-return preferences of the family. Thus, options are a useful way to position the portfolio to appeal to investor preferences. (Note that in this case there is no apparent difference between the probability beliefs of the investor and the market.) Society benefits if investors are more willing to save when options can be created and traded than when they cannot.

While more formal proofs exist, we can generalize from these examples and suggest that,

> Options serve individuals and society by increasing the number of possible probability distributions of investment returns available to investors. This increases their welfare and enhances their willingness to save.

Trading Options on Exchanges

Trading in options on option exchanges is similar to trading on stock and commodity exchanges. However, there are a few important differences that we outline here.

As in the case of stocks and commodities, potential buyers, sellers, and writers of options get together on the exchange in a central location called a **trading pit**. Then, through a **double-auction process**, traders come to an agreement regarding the price for the option. If the transaction is between a buyer and a writer, a new option is brought into existence. At this point the Options Clearing Corporation, an exchange clearinghouse, steps in and becomes the writer of the option from the viewpoint of the buyer, and the buyer of the option from the viewpoint of the writer:

Thus, a new set of books is created and the actual transaction results in a charge to the buyer's account in the amount of the premium and the delivery of notification of ownership of that option. In turn, the writer receives the premium through the clearinghouse and a notification of an obligation under the terms of the option. All credit investigations of writers and their ability to discharge their obligations to deliver can be centralized and carried out by the exchange.[7] The only default risk, then, is whether the exchange can follow through to meet its side of the bargain.

Once an option has been created the owner of the instrument has two ways of disposing of his investment. The option can be returned to the exchange floor for sale to another buyer, or the option holder can contact the clearing corporation and demand delivery. Obviously, which of these routes is selected depends on which is most beneficial to the holder. At the exact point of the option's maturity the two methods should yield the same cash flows. Since having the option to buy is always worth something at any time before maturity, the option price for a call in the market will never be below the value that can be derived from exercising the option. Thus, most all call options are held until maturity or until sold in the open market.

As an existing option is resold on the exchange floor, the exchange clearinghouse simply assigns the option to the new owner, with that new owner holding the right to exercise at the same striking price and date.

When and if an owner decides to exercise the option to purchase (call) or sell (put), the clearinghouse assigns a delivery order to a member firm chosen randomly from all firms. The firm then assigns the delivery order to one of its customers who has written that particular option.

One other difference between option exchanges and stock exchanges is that trading is not necessarily continuous during the course of the trading day. Since in active markets there may be well over 30 separate put and call option arrangements per security that differ by exercise price and expiration date, there is often a rotation process for trading in particular options. Thus, the option to "exercise at 40 due in April" may trade only once in the first hour, depending on the activity and interest in that option.

---

[7]In many ways this process is similar to the process followed by other financial institutions. For example, banks or savings and loans serve the same function by investigating potential borrowers. Investors can then invest indirectly in term loans or mortgages without being concerned about the individual creditworthiness of the borrower. Obviously, the exchange has the incentive to investigate the writer, and may even require a performance bond to be put up as a guarantee.

There are a number of active options exchanges currently authorized to trade in options. These include, with their approximate number of optionable securities,

	Stocks	Indexes
Chicago Board Options Exchange (CBOE)	150	2
American Stock Exchange	120	4
Philadelphia Stock Exchange	90	3
Pacific Coast Stock Exchange	80	2
New York Stock Exchange	10	2

As in the case with common stocks, trading for most of us would take place through exchange members. These may be large general-line brokerage houses, smaller regional brokerage houses, or specialized option houses. The process for buying and selling options is also very similar to buying and selling other securities. Orders are submitted through exchange member firms. These orders may be limit or market orders. Your firm's floor representative would attempt to secure the highest bid price for a sell order or the lowest ask price for a buy.

Writers of options may be anyone operating through the same network. Thus, it is possible for any of us to write options in essentially the same way stocks can be sold short. In fact, most options are written by independent floor traders and their limited set of customers who hope to gain, on average, from the premium charged.

Because of the special obligation of writers, the exchange and their members set up additional financial requirements for writing options when the stock is not held in the writer's portfolio (naked writing). These capital requirements are established to prevent the possibility of default that might impair the ability of either the exchange or the member from following through on their obligations. The requirements are not rigid, however, and anyone with sufficient incentive can buy or write options almost at will.

Finally, just as the exchange attempts to ensure against any default by its membership or their customers, it also attempts to ensure against actions by the firm on which the option is written that may affect option values. For example, exchange-traded options are protected against dilution that may come from a stock split or stock dividend. Thus, if a company splits its stock two-for-one, the exercise price automatically is cut in half. If a 10 percent stock dividend is paid, the original exercise price is cut by dividing by 1.1.

Listed options are not protected against cash dividends or stock repurchases, however. As a stock goes ex-dividend and its price falls, the stockholder receives the cash dividend to just offset the fall in share price. The option holder, on the other hand, receives nothing, yet experiences a decline in call option value due to the drop in the price of the common stock.

Trading Over-the-Counter

Over-the-counter options also can be constructed in stocks either (1) to set exercise prices or dates not available from standardized exchange listed options, or (2) to develop options in securities where options trading does not exist on exchanges. Any option can be written—for a price. Normally, over-the-counter options are written through a brokerage house in much the same way as over-the-counter trading in securities takes place—that is, shopping by phone for a potential writer.

TABLE 19–3   Comparison of Listed and Over-the-Counter Options and Markets

	Over-the-Counter	Listed
Types of options traded	Calls, puts, combination options.	Calls, puts, combination orders permitted.
Striking price	Any price buyer and writer negotiate.	Standardized price ending in $5, $2.50, or $0.
Expiration date	Any date buyer and writer negotiate.	Saturday after third Friday in designated expiration month.
Expiration time	3:15 P.M. eastern time.	5 P.M. eastern time.
Last date and time option can be sold	Same as expiration date and time.	2 P.M. central time. 3 P.M. eastern time on business day immediately prior to expiration date.
Adjustment for cash dividend	Striking price reduced on ex-dividend date.	No change in striking price.
Adjustment for stock dividends, stock splits, and reverse splits	Both striking price and number of shares covered by options are adjusted to reflect capital change.	
Adjustment for rights or warrants issued to common shareholders	Striking price reduced by value of rights or warrants.	
Limitation on purchase or sale of options on one stock	None, but limits have been proposed.	1,000 contracts on same side of the market (e.g., long calls *and* short puts); limit applies to all expiration dates.
Unit of trading	One contract is an option on 100 shares of the underlying stock before any adjustments	
Method of option price determination	Buyer and writer negotiate through put and call broker.	Central auction market.
Secondary market	Limited; special options advertised in newspaper.	Very active secondary market.
Buyer's recourse to obtain performance on option contract	Primary responsibility for performance belongs to endorsing broker who may be any member of the NYSE.	The Options Clearing Corporation is primary obligor guaranteeing writer's performance.
Evidence of ownership	Bearer certificate.	Broker's confirmation slip.
Method of closing out transaction when stock sells above striking price	Option may be exercised by buyer or sold to put and call broker who exercises the option and sells the stock.	Exercise is rare; contract is usually closed out in a closing purchase-sale transaction.
Transaction costs	High.	Moderate.
Commission structure	Basic charge is negotiated by put and call broker as a spread between premium paid by buyer and premium paid to writer.	Negotiated commission rates since May 1, 1975.
Stocks on which options are available	Almost any stock.	About 500 selected stocks 15 Indexes in the United States and a growing list of stocks elsewhere in the world.
Pricing information	Brokers publish indicated premiums to buyers or writers	Actual transaction prices published daily.
Procedure for exercise	Buyer exercises by notifying endorsing broker.	Buyer's broker notifies The Options Clearing Corporation, which selects writers essentially at random.
Extensions	Available if writer agrees.	Not available.
Tax treatment	Identical.	
Margin requirement: call buyer	100% of the option premium.	
Margin requirement: covered writer	No margin required beyond that needed to carry stock position.	
Margin requirement: uncovered writer	Minimum requirement is related to price of stock with adjustment for amount of premium received and amount by which option is in or out of the money. Margin requirements should be checked in detail with each brokerage firm.	

Source: Gastineau [1979].

FIGURE 19–10   In-the-Money and Out-of-the-Money Call Options

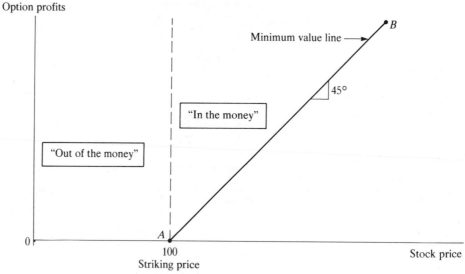

In over-the-counter options the brokerage house serves the function of investigating the writer and, in fact, will usually require the writer to deposit shares of the firm on which the option is written. Because of this, most call option writers in over-the-counter securities (and many in listed options) are investors who already own the shares, yet wish to earn their profit from the option premium rather than an increase in share price. Obviously, they also retain the risk of share price decreasing.

Over-the-counter option buyers face substantial liquidity constraints since the marketability of these options is rather limited relative to over-the-counter stocks or exchange-listed options. In most cases they should be constructed on the assumption that they will be held to maturity. Characteristics of listed and over-the-counter options are compared in Table 19–3.

Option Valuation: Calls

Earlier in this chapter we introduced (Figure 19–1) the options "minimum-value line" as the maximum of (1) zero, or (2) the value secured if the option is exercised at the striking price and the shares sold at their market price; i.e., the difference between the stock price and the exercise price. Graphically, the call option's value would have to be *on* or *above* line OAB (the minimum-value line) in Figure 19–10. Thus at the instant prior to maturity, the minimum value of an option to purchase at $100 when the stock price is $100 is zero. At any lower price for the stock the value of the right to purchase at $100 is zero. This option is "out of the money." However, at a stock price of $105, the option to purchase at $100 is worth $5. This option is "in the money." In fact, the value of the option at the instant before maturity will be higher—on a dollar-for-dollar basis—the higher is the stock's price.

At any time prior to maturity, investors will observe that the minimum-value line will hold at maturity and, thus, are willing to pay at least this amount. Yet, they will pay an added premium as well that will depend on their assessment of the likelihood that the stock price (1) may exceed the exercise price even if it does not exceed it now, or (2) may exceed the exercise price by more than it does now. Thus, the probability distribution of the future stock price at maturity plays a major role in option valuation.

To examine this *potential* more closely, we will consider a simple case where there is an equal probability of the stock price being $130 or $90 in six months. With the current stock price and exercise price at $100, this option holds value simply because there is a one half chance that *at maturity* the stock price will be $130, implying that the right to purchase is worth $30.

How much the option is now worth (six months before maturity) is an issue we can deal with rather explicitly by using a simple application of a no-arbitrage or law-of-one-price condition. Using P_0^m to indicate the current stock price, P_1^m the stock price at maturity, and C_0 and C_1 the call option prices before and at maturity, respectively, note that:

(19–1)   *Call Payoffs*

$$\text{if } P_1^m = \$130 \rightarrow C_1 = \$30$$

$$\text{if } P_1^m = \$90 \rightarrow C_1 = \$0$$

The dollar difference in the outcomes from holding the stock is $40, while for the option it is $30. We can duplicate the stock price "risk" by holding $1^1/_3$ options. Now consider the following transactions:

- Buy one share of stock at its current price of $100 and write $1^1/_3$ options at the exercise price of $100. The investment is $100 *less* the premium received on $1^1/_3$ options, at a price C_0, for a net investment of $P_0^m - 1^1/_3 C_0$.
- If the stock price at maturity is $130, each option is worth $30, and $1^1/_3$ options are worth $40. Cash flows are

$$P_1^m - 1^1/_3 C_1 = \$130 - \$40 = \$90$$

  since the option has been written (like a short position).
- If the stock price at maturity is $90, the options are worthless, and cash flows are

$$P_1^m - 1^1/_3 C_1 = \$90 - \$0 = \$90$$

The outcome from the investment is $90 regardless of what happens to stock price. By buying the stock and selling the option, a portfolio has been created that has eliminated all risk at maturity.

As is always the case in equilibrium (here is where the arbitrage argument is used), any investment with no risk must offer the riskless interest rate as its return. This means that the portfolio originally constructed must have an equilibrium value of $90/

$[1 + R_f(^6/_{12})]$. Thus, if the risk-free rate is 10 percent (or 5 percent for six months), the no-arbitrage condition requires that,

(19–2)   *Hedge Portfolio of Stock and Calls*

$$P_0^m - 1^1/_3 C_0 = \$90/(1 + .05)$$

If the current stock price is $100, C_0 must be

(19–3)   *Price of Six-Month Call*

$$(1^1/_3)C_0 = P_0^m - \$90/(1 + .05)$$

$$C_0 = [\$100 - \$90/(1 + .05)]/1^1/_3$$

$$C_0 = \$10.73$$

If the market price of the stock is an equilibrium price, then C_0 is an equilibrium price also. Even if P_0^m is not an equilibrium price, we can still label the call price—contingent on the stock price—to be priced in equilibrium with respect to P_0^m (though not necessarily with respect to the rest of the market). Of course, if the length of the option contract is different, the discount rate will change and C_0 will also. For example, if in one year the stock price will be either $150 or $80 and the interest rate is 10 percent, the call option's value is as follows:

$$\text{if } P_1^m = \$150 \rightarrow C_1 = \$50$$

$$\text{if } P_1^m = \$80 \rightarrow C_1 = \$0$$

• Buy one share of stock and write $1^2/_5$ options. The net investment is

$$P_0^m - 1^2/_5 C_0$$

• If the stock price reaches $150 the cash flows are

$$P_1^m - 1^2/_5 C_1 = \$150 - 1^2/_5(\$50) = \$80$$

• If the stock price falls to $80 the flow is

$$P_1^m - 1^2/_5 C_1 = \$80 - \$0 = \$80$$

Thus, the riskless investment must yield

(19–4)   *Price of a One-Year Call*

$$P_0^m - 1^2/_5 C_0 = \$80/(1 + .10)$$

$$C_0 = [\$100 - \$80/(1 + .10)]/1^2/_5$$

$$C_0 = \$19.48$$

The ratio of options sold (written) to a share of stock held long ($1^1/_3$ or $1^2/_5$ in the above cases) in the riskless portfolio, or the **hedge ratio** as it is called, did not occur by chance. The perfect hedge was enabled by the perfect correlation between the stock value and option value. If the stock price reaches $130 the option value is $30—always. If the stock price falls to $90 the option value is zero—without exception. The hedge ratio value is dependent only on the range of values of the stock and option. Thus, if the range of values of the stock price is allowed to vary, the hedge ratio will vary. Consider the possibility of different pairs of stock price outcomes from our simple example (giving the maximum and minimum values for stock price and the option value):

$P_{1,max}^m - P_{1,min}^m$	$C_{1,max} - C_{1,min}$	Hedge Ratio	Option Value (6-month 5% rate)
$110 - \$ 95 = \$15$	$\$10 - \$0 = \$10$	$1\frac{1}{2}$	$6.35
$115 - 95 = 20$	$15 - 0 = 15$	$1\frac{1}{3}$	7.16
$105 - 95 = 10$	$5 - 0 = 5$	2	4.76
$110 - 100 = 10$	$10 - 0 = 10$	1	4.50

As you can see, the hedge ratio, defined as the number of options to sell per share of stock, is simply

(19–5)   *Hedge Ratio*

$$H = \frac{P_{1,max}^m - P_{1,min}^m}{C_{1,max} - C_{1,min}}$$

The value $1/H$ would indicate the proportion of a share of stock to hold long for each option written.

In summary,

> Because an option is valued solely on the basis of the outcomes of the common stock that can be purchased with it, the options value is totally dependent on (1) the possible future stock values, (2) the exercise price, (3) the current stock price, and (4) the risk-free interest rate. The first two points allow one to specify the hedge ratio. Thus, the value of the option is given by C_0 in the expression

$$P_0^m - (H)C_0 = \frac{\text{Hedge portfolio outcome}}{[1 + R_f(\text{for the maturity})]}$$

In applications, of course, all values of the above expression are known once the hedge ratio is known. The hedge ratio itself is known once the range of the stock price is known. These values must be forecast, obviously, but these are the same values that must be forecast to value the common stock itself (to identify the expected future stock price and risk).

Option Pricing: Black, Scholes, and Merton

In reality, no stocks follow a distribution in which there are two possible outcomes, $P_{1,max}^m$ and $P_{1,min}^m$. An even and continuous distribution provides a more realistic view of future stock prices. How can a hedge ratio be formed to value the option in this case? The answer is that it can't, since a hedge that would ensure the same portfolio cash flows for an individual pair of stock price outcomes would not be the same for all pairs.

Thus, while the analysis of the two-outcome stock was revealing in that it suggested what is important in valuing an option, it does not allow us to handle completely all option valuation problems.

Fortunately, however, the hedge portfolio concept has been extended through some ingenious sleight-of-hand by Fischer Black and Myron Scholes [1973], and by Robert Merton [1973]. Through their work, and extensions of it by another group of researchers, new insights into the option valuation problem are possible. In a few words, the insight of Black, Scholes, and Merton was that over a short-enough interval the idea that a stock could move up or down by only one very small, incremental amount was not so outlandish an assumption as it might at first seem. As these short intervals are accumulated, successive stock prices reflect the sum of these small price changes and take on distributional characteristics much like those we observe for stocks over daily, monthly, or annual intervals. The only problem with this was that it would necessitate setting a hedge ratio and then revising it as the price (and, therefore, the possible outcomes of the next small interval) changes up or down. The hedge ratio would have to be revised in each new short interval!

In the limit, the interval over which the stock's price is allowed to vary is *instantaneous,* and the stock price change very small. This means the hedge ratio must be constantly revised, a significant problem if and when the valuation model is to be applied to the real world. Nevertheless, the mathematics of the problem are complex enough that solutions are possible only if events are assumed to unfold in "continuous time."[8]

While the assumption of continuous trading seemingly would detract from the applicability of the model, the model is, in fact, used by a broad array of options market participants. We choose to make note of this prior to letting you view the model for fear that the equation itself and the abstract assumptions on which it is based may lead you to conclude that it is only a theory with no apparent use.

The Black-Scholes call option valuation model is:

(19–6)   ***Black-Scholes Option Value***

$$C_0 = P_0^m N(d_1) - X(e^{-R_f \cdot t})N(d_2)$$

where

C_0 = The call option's current market value

P_0^m = The stock's current market value

X = The option's exercise, or striking, price

t = Years to maturity

e = Base of natural logarithm, 2.71828

R_f = The continuously compounded riskless interest rate

---

[8]In other words, the techniques for solving the valuation problem mathematically require the use of certain principles of calculus that are defined only in continuous spaces. Subsequent extensions, by Cox, Ross, and Rubinstein [1979], in particular, have allowed discrete time options to be valued, but at the cost of some additional assumptions.

$N(d_i)$ = The *probability* that a value of d_i or less will be drawn from a standard normal distribution, where:

(19–7a)
$$d_1 = \frac{\ln(P_0^m/X) + (R_f + \frac{1}{2}[\sigma(\tilde{R})]^2)t}{\sigma(\tilde{R})\sqrt{t}}$$

(19–7b)
$$d_2 = \frac{\ln(P_0^m/X) + (R_f - \frac{1}{2}[\sigma(\tilde{R})]^2)t}{\sigma(\tilde{R})\sqrt{t}}$$

In Equations (19–7a) and (19–7b) we used the notation:

$\ln(\cdot)$ = The natural logarithm of $(\cdot)$
$\sigma(\tilde{R})$ = The standard deviation of the continuously compounded annual rate of return on the stock

Two examples of the use of the Black-Scholes model are shown in Table 19–4.[9] In that table, two call options are evaluated. The first (call A) is a right to purchase one share of stock for $95 at a time six months from now. The second (call B) is a right to purchase one share of a different stock for $35 at a time nine months from now. The risk-free interest rate is assumed to be 10 percent per annum in the case of call A, and 15 percent per annum in the case of call B. The underlying stock's current share price and its standard deviation differ between the two options. As you can see from the table, call A is valued by the model at $18.64, while B is valued at $3.64.

The $N(d_1)$ value of .678 and $N(d_2)$ of .544 in example A are values taken from a table listing the probability that a random variable which is normally distributed will assume a value which is less than or equal to a specified number. Thus, $N(.463)$ corresponds to

TABLE 19–4   Sample Black-Scholes Call Valuation

	Call A	Call B
Stock price, P_0^m	100	32
Exercise price, X	95	35
Years to maturity, t	$\frac{1}{2}$	$\frac{9}{12}$
Risk-free rate, R_f	.10	.15
Standard deviation, $\sigma(\tilde{R})$	.5	.3
d_1	$\dfrac{\ln(^{100}/_{95}) + [.10 + \frac{1}{2}(.5)^2]\frac{1}{2}}{.5\sqrt{^1/_2}}$ $= .463$	$\dfrac{\ln(^{32}/_{35}) + [.15 + \frac{1}{2}(.3)^2]\frac{9}{12}}{.3\sqrt{^9/_{12}}}$ $= .218$
d_2	$\dfrac{\ln(^{100}/_{95}) + [.10 - \frac{1}{2}(.5)^2]\frac{1}{2}}{.5\sqrt{^1/_2}}$ $= .110$	$\dfrac{\ln(^{32}/_{35}) + [.15 - \frac{1}{2}(.3)^2]\frac{9}{12}}{.3\sqrt{^9/_{12}}}$ $= -.042$
$N(d_1)$	.5 + .178 = .678	.5 + .086 = .586
$N(d_2)$	.5 + .044 = .544	.5 - .017 = .483
$e^{-R_f t}$	.9512	.8936
C_0	$100(.678) - $95(.9512)(.544) = $18.64	$32(.586) - 35(.8936)(.483) = $3.64

---

[9]Robert Merton developed a similar option valuation model but, for some reason, the model has generally been referred to in the literature as the Black-Scholes model.

a value of .678 and means that the probability of a standard normal variate having a value .463 or less is 67.8 percent; i.e., $N(.463)$ is .678. For $N(d_2)$, a d_2 value of .110 corresponds to a value of .544, which means that the probability of a standard normal variate being equal to or less than .110 is 54.4 percent.

Interpretation of the Black-Scholes model is rather straightforward. The first term in Equation (19–6) is the value of a right to that portion of the probability distribution of the stock's price that lies above the call option's exercise price. This is the mean of the cross-hatched area in Figure 19–11, discounted to its present value by R_f.

The second term in Equation (19–6) equals the present value of the exercise price times the probability that the exercise price will have to be paid; i.e., the probability that the option will be exercised at maturity, which is represented by $N(d_2)$. In the formula the expected stock price at maturity of the option does not appear explicitly. Rather, it has been incorporated into the determination of the current stock price. In any case, the call price as determined by Equation (19–6) is an equilibrium price with respect to the price of the underlying stock into which it can be converted.

The formula can be made equivalent to a present-value formula by discounting at a risk-adjusted rate the expected future value of the call option (at maturity). In this sense the Black-Scholes formula is consistent with other discounted cash flow valuation models presented earlier for stocks, bonds, and other securities.

Example: How Does Price Vary as Terms Change?

With the Black-Scholes formula the option value is written as an explicit and known function of its exercise price, stock price, maturity, standard deviation of stock price, and the risk-free interest rate. Since the relationship is explicit we can draw any one of a number of relationships between the value of the option and its different characteristics. For example, given the exercise price, the relation between stock price and option value is as shown in Figure 19–12. The maximum-value line is a 45-degree line drawn from the present value of the exercise price $X/(1 + R_f)^t$. This line will be further to the left of X, of course, the longer the maturity. If the maturity is six months, $t = \frac{1}{2}$. If the maturity is three months, $t = \frac{1}{4}$. Thus, longer-term options have greater value than otherwise equivalent shorter-term options (assuming R_f is positive).

In addition to the "present value of the exercise price," there is an additional maturity effect that works through the security's variance. For a given degree of variability in the underlying stock, the longer the option's maturity the greater the chance that the eventual stock price will exceed the exercise price. This effect is easy to see when comparing a one-day option to a six-month option. For a given standard deviation in the daily price of the underlying stock, say $.50, the chance that the stock selling at $48 would exceed an exercise price of $50 by tomorrow would be very small. The one-day option on that day would be virtually worthless. However, a six-month option to buy at $50 would be worth considerably more since the six-month standard deviation would be much greater—more than 12 times greater in fact.[10] This chance of the stock price exceeding the exercise

---

[10]If the daily standard deviation is indeed $.50, the six-month standard deviation is $.50\sqrt{180} = \$6.71$. Thus, the chance that the stock price, now at $48, might exceed $50 in six months is about 40 percent even if the expected future stock price is $48. This probability is clearly enough to impute some *current* value to the option.

FIGURE 19–11

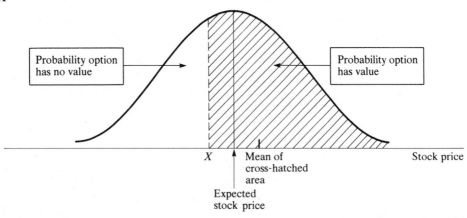

price gives rise to a greater premium (or current value) to the longer maturity option. In other words, distance *a* in Figure 19–12 is longer than distance *b*.

If two options are alike in all respects except for the standard deviation of the continuously compounded annual rate of return in the price of the underlying security, the one with the higher $\sigma(\tilde{R})$ will be more highly valued. This is due to the higher variance positively affecting the probability with which the stock price exceeds the exercise price. Thus, in Figure 19–13, if the current stock price and exercise price are the same, the expected value of the cross-hatched area in the higher variance stock (*B*) is greater than the mean of the area for the lower variance stock (*A*).[11]

The standard deviation of the stock's return must be estimated. If a stock's variance did not change over time, all we would need to do is look at the past. In fact, like equilibrium returns and betas, $\sigma(\tilde{R}_i)$ will change over time and should be predicted. If an important event is impending, or if the firm's performance is likely to depend on highly uncertain factors (e.g., its ability to compete in a market or its vulnerability to technological obsolescence) the variance is likely to rise, and the prices of options on the stock will be higher in response.

Dividends and Value

On American call options that can be exercised at any time prior to maturity (remember European calls can only be exercised at maturity), there is always some value to the remaining life of the option. Hence, in theory, without transaction costs no call options

---

[11]This statement may be confusing, given all the time we have spent discussing the market's required compensation for risk. But the above description is not inconsistent with the concept of risk aversion. For example, two stocks that offer identical future expected dollar payoffs, with one being more risky, will not be priced the same. The more risky stock will have a lower P_0^m. However, given the same price, for two stocks with different variance (the higher variance stock obviously offering higher future cash flows) and alike in all other respects, the option on the higher-variance stock will be priced higher than that on the lower-variance stock.

FIGURE 19–12   Black-Scholes Option Price as It Varies with Maturity

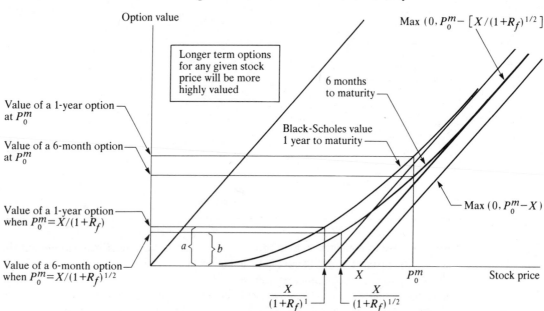

would be exercised prior to the maturity date. Because of this, American calls (which won't be exercised early) and European calls (which can't be exercised early) will sell at the same price.

However, it's a different story for options on stocks that pay dividends. On a listed option no adjustments are made to the exercise price when the stock goes ex-dividend. Thus, call options lose value and put options gain value when the dividend is paid. For this reason it may pay the investor in an exchange-traded American call to exercise his option "early"—just before the dividend ex-date.

Whether or not the option is exercised early depends on the market's evaluation of the value of the dividend or the value of the option, given the stock price will be lower by the amount of the dividend paid. Investors, anticipating the dividend payment, would value the option at the maximum of its conversion value to receive the dividend or its value as an option on the stock that will trade at the ex-dividend price.

Valuing Puts: Put–Call Parity

The value of a put option will be different than that of a call since with a put you buy the right to a different portion of the probability distribution of the rate of return. However, since the put option is a derived asset just like the call, the call option itself can be used to value the put.

Suppose you purchase a share of common stock, purchase a put option, and write a call option. The call and put are written at the same exercise price, X, which may or

FIGURE 19–13   Higher $\sigma(\tilde{R})$ Stock Has More Potential for Profitable Exercise of Option

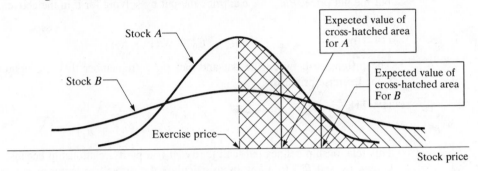

may not be equal to the current stock price. For options on one share (ignoring transaction costs) the cash outflow to form this portfolio is:

(19–8)   *Put, Call, Stock Portfolio*

$$Portfolio = +C_0 - Put_0 - P_0^m$$
$$cost$$

$$\begin{array}{llll} Portfolio & Call & Put & Cost\ of \\ cost & = premium - & premium - & stock \\ & received & paid & paid. \end{array}$$

where C_0, Put_0, and P_0^m represent the per-share call premium, put premium, and stock price. The cash inflows depend on what happens to stock price. The table below indicates the cash flows per share at maturity on each instrument:

Stock Price	On Call	On Put	On Stock	On Portfolio (sum)
Rises	$-(P_1^m - X)$	0	$+ P_1^m =$	X
Falls	0	$+(X - P_1^m)$	$+ P_1^m =$	X

If the stock price rises you lose on the call (you have written it) but gain on the stock. If the stock price falls you lose on the stock but gain on your put ownership.

This situation defines a portfolio that is fully hedged against any movement of P_0^m. Since a cash flow equal to the value of X is received with certainty after t periods, and the portfolio initially required an investment of $-P_0^m - Put_0 + C_0$, the relationship

(19–9)   *A Risk-Free Investment Must Offer a Risk-Free Return*

$$0 = \underbrace{-P_0^m - Put_0 + C_0}_{\text{Investment}} + \underbrace{X/(1 + R_f)^t}_{\text{PV of Cash Inflows}}$$

must hold (i.e., a risk-free portfolio must earn a return of R_f). Since everything is known but the put price, Put_0, we can price the put by solving for it in the above equation. The result is

(19–10)
$$Put_0 = C_0 + X/(1 + R_f)^t - P_0^m$$

The difference between the put and call price (remember they are options having the same exercise price) is

(19–11)   *Put–Call Parity*

$$C_0 - Put_0 = P_0^m - X/(1 + R_f)^t$$

This relationship defines put–call parity. It is a parity relationship because everything is known (X and P_0^m) to allow us to calculate the difference between put prices and call prices. Note that if the exercise price is equal to the current stock price the formula is even simpler—it is just the time-adjusted difference $1 - 1/(1 + R_f)^t$.

The call option in our prior example (call A) was worth $18.64. The value of the put then would be

$$Put_0 = \$18.64 + \$95/(1 + .10)^{1/2} - \$100$$

$$= \$18.64 - \$10.24 = \$8.40$$

Does the parity relationship hold up in actual markets? One day recently, Kodak closed at $70\frac{1}{4}$ per share. A nine-month call at $70 was priced at $7\frac{1}{4}$ at the close of trading on that day, and nine-month T-bills were yielding 9.9 percent. Thus, the implied put price would be

Kodak's Put Price

$$7\frac{1}{4} - Put_0 = 70\frac{1}{4} - (\$70/[1 + (.099)(270/360)])$$

$$Put_0 = 7\frac{1}{4} - 70\frac{1}{4} + (\$70/1.07425)$$

$$Put_0 = \$2.16$$

The actual price was $4\frac{3}{8}$—$2.20 higher than the put-call parity suggested. Is there a profit opportunity here?

Unfortunately not. Kodak paid a $3 per year dividend during this period. Over nine months this dividend amounted to $2.25, an amount that comes very close to offsetting the $2.20 differential. Since the stock would normally go ex-dividend in the amount of $2.25 (if we pretend the amount of the dividend is known in advance), the call was priced lower than it would have been if no dividends were paid. Thus, we can approximate the put–call parity relationship with dividends as follows:

Put–Call Parity with Dividends

$$\left(C_0 + \frac{Dividend}{over\ t}\right) - Put_0 = P_0^m - X/(1 + R_f)^t$$

$$\begin{array}{cccc}
\textit{Price of call} & & & \\
\textit{if no dividends} & - & \textit{Price} & = & \textit{Price} & - & \textit{Present value of} \\
\textit{paid} & & \textit{of put} & & \textit{of stock} & & \textit{exercise price.}
\end{array}$$

We can rearrange this to

$$C_0 - Put_0 = \left(P_0^m - \frac{\text{Dividend}}{\text{over } t} \right) - X/(1 + R_f)^t$$

$$\begin{array}{ccc} \textit{Price} & \textit{Price} & \text{``Ex-dividend''} & \textit{Present value of} \\ \textit{of call} & - & \textit{of put} & = & \textit{current stock} & - & \textit{exercise price.} \\ & & & & \textit{price} & & \end{array}$$

In summary,

> Just as the concept of a hedge portfolio allows us to derive the value of a call option from the characteristics of the security, the value of a put option can be derived from the call price, stock price, and risk-free interest rate (and, perhaps the dividend).

Strategies for Using Options to Affect Portfolio Characteristics

The existence of options is justified because they may give the investor an asset whose probability distribution of returns cannot be duplicated with other financial instruments. Indeed, this is obvious from the profit and loss diagrams presented earlier. A call option allows the buyer to participate in the higher-valued end of the probability distribution of stock returns, and for a fixed premium, the investor is able to ensure against any downside risk of a fall in stock price below the exercise price. The downside risk is eliminated, in other words, at an obvious cost.

The put buyer attains the opposite effect. By holding an option to sell the stock at a fixed price, the investor gains from downside variations in stock price while avoiding the variability of upside fluctuations that could not be avoided if the stock was sold short. For this, the put buyer pays a premium.

Both of these examples illustrate the basic insurance principle at work with puts and calls. These options allow an investor to "participate" only in that portion of the stock price probability distribution that is desired. And as in any insurance, there is a fee for avoiding this risk—a premium.

In this section we endeavor to compare the nature of the risks associated with different strategies for including puts and calls in a portfolio. We will also indicate the returns to these strategies with the usual caveat:

> Historical rate of return distributions for any risky security are unreliable guides to future return distributions unless the observations and the time period studied are lengthy, and the probability distribution stationary.

The numbers we summarize here are for a short historical period and so are not a very useful basis for forming expectations of future returns from the strategy. The figures will aid us in characterizing the risk of alternative strategies, however. The strategies used are:

Most Effective Market	Strategy
Bearish	1. Uncovered (naked) call option writing: Under this strategy you simply write a call and hold an investment in the risk-free security to ensure that you have the funds to comply with your obligation. If price falls, the call is unexercised. If price rises, you lose and pay for your loss with the funds invested in the risk-free security.
Bullish	2. Uncovered (naked) put option writing: Write a put and hold a risk-free security to ensure your compliance. If price falls, put is exercised and you use the risk-free investment to cover your obligation to purchase.
Neutral	3. Covered call option writing: Write a call and hold the stock to be used to deliver against the obligation. If price falls you lose on the stock but receive the option premium. If price increases you don't gain since the holder would require delivery.
Bullish	4. Protective put option investment: Buy a put and purchase the stock to be "put" to the writer if price drops below the exercise price. If price falls, you exercise your right to sell at price higher than current market. If price rises your put is worthless but you gain on stock held long. The put is an insurance policy against stock price declines.
Neutral	5. Put/call conversions: Buy a put, buy the stock, and write a call. If stock price falls you exercise your put and deliver (call is worth nothing). If stock price rises holder of call will exercise his right and you deliver the stock held (put is worth nothing). This strategy is almost riskless and is neither bullish or bearish.

Simulated investments in all of these strategies have been performed using actual stock prices and "manufactured" option prices with the Black-Scholes model and a put/call parity theorem similar to that described earlier. The prices of the stocks were observed from 1963 to 1977, and all manufactured options were six-month instruments. In all, 136 stocks were used. The results are summarized with the expected return and standard deviation plotted in Figure 19–14. Each number represents one of the specific strategies listed above. Two other strategies are included for comparison. *CP* represents investment in commercial paper, and *m* indicates the risk–return values for an equally weighted common-stock portfolio formed from all 136 firms. For all these strategies the dollar investment is identical, so direct comparisons using $E(\tilde{R}_p)$ and $\sigma(\tilde{R}_p)$ can be used.

The figures suggest that these option strategies reduce risk compared to a direct investment in common stock. The put and call strategy (No. 5) produces an almost risk-free portfolio. The combination produces offsetting gains and losses that eliminate both the top and bottom end of the probability distribution of stock returns. It is almost a hedge portfolio.

Uncovered call (No. 1) and put (No. 2) strategies reduce the risk inherent in stock portfolios. It is difficult to make return comparisons, of course, but the returns seem to be about the same (No. 1) or somewhat lower (No. 2) than the direct investment route.

In all, these strategies suggest that options can be used to create a level of risk exposure that is consistent with the risk-aversion propensities of any investor. This, of course, is the justification for the creation of options in the first place.

FIGURE 19–14   **Risks and Returns from Option Strategies, and the Market**

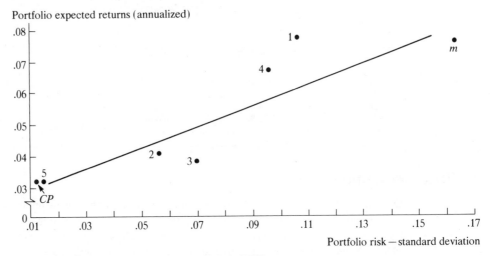

Source: Computed from Merton, Scholes, and Gladstein [1982].

Options Have Betas

One of the alternatives available to investors is to include options in the portfolio along with other securities. The inclusion of options affects portfolio risk, and the effect on risk is proportional to the option's beta. Thus, options, like any other security included in a well-diversified portfolio, have beta coefficients that summarize their individual contribution to the portfolio's risk. And, because the option's price is an *explicit function* of the underlying security and the terms of the option contract, the option's beta is also. That is, the option's beta depends on the price of the security, the exercise price, the interest rate, time to maturity, the variance of the stock, *and* the stock's beta.

The calculation of option betas is mechanically simple, but tedious. Fortunately it can be computerized. We will limit our discussion to the examples in Table 19–5. For these examples the beta of the underlying stock is 1.0. (For stock betas that are different from 1.0, the option beta numbers would be multiplied by the stock's beta.)

Options with lower exercise prices have lower betas, all other things equal, and this relationship always holds. For the examples in the table it seems that increases in the time to maturity and in the standard deviation also serve to reduce the call option's risk. These latter relationships do not necessarily hold for options of very short duration, or for options that are way "out of the money."

Put option betas, representing something of a negative position in the security, have negative betas. Since the beta of a portfolio is equal to the weighted average beta of the component securities, put options can be used to reduce the nondiversifiable risk of a portfolio, perhaps to position it more in line with the investor's preferred risk level.

TABLE 19–5   **Option Betas (stock price = $50 and R_f = .10)**

	Standard Deviation of Underlying Stock							
	= .20				= .40			
Exercise Price	Months Remaining to Maturity of the Option							
	3	6	9	12	3	6	9	12
$60	27.1	15.1	10.9	8.7	10.0	6.3	4.9	4.1
$55	18.1	11.0	8.3	6.9	8.0	5.4	4.3	3.7
$50	11.7	8.0	6.4	5.5	6.4	4.6	3.8	3.3
$45	7.5	5.9	5.0	4.4	5.2	4.0	3.4	3.0
$40	5.2	4.6	4.0	3.7	4.3	3.5	3.1	2.8

Valuing Warrants

Earlier, Table 19–2 supplied some information on a number of different warrants that were issued by firms in connection with another security issue. For example, Wickes issued warrants in 1985 permitting each warrant holder to purchase one share of stock at $4.43 (the striking price) until the option expires in 1992. its current value of $3 reflects the length of time remaining to maturity as well as the exercise price, stock price, R_f, and the variance of the stock's price. It will, in fact, be valued in exactly the same way as call options were valued in the prior section. The warrant differs from a call option only by the length of its life (and in the manner in which it is created, which is irrelevant to its valuation).

Valuing Convertible Securities

Convertible bonds and convertible preferred stocks are compound securities that include a fixed-income claim and a warrant (or call option) to purchase the common stock of the firm. In the absence of any particular constraint on what can be done with this security, its value can be represented as just the sum of the value of its component parts,

(19–12)   ***Convertible Bond Value***

$$\begin{matrix}\text{Convertible} \\ \text{bond} \\ \text{value}\end{matrix} = \begin{matrix}\text{Straight} \\ \text{bond} \\ \text{value}\end{matrix} + \begin{matrix}\text{Value of} \\ \text{the option} \\ \text{to convert}\end{matrix}$$

Thus, the value of the convertible bond is equal to the sum of the security's value as a straight debt instrument and the value of the call option attached to it.[12] If it were not, then an investor could buy or sell an equivalent bond or call option to capture the profit inherent in the under- or overpriced convertible.[13]

The relationship between the value of the underlying common stock and the convertible

---

[12]The principle of "Value additivity" (Schall [1972]) would indicate this conclusion. Thus, just as the value of a portfolio of A and B is equal to the sum of their independent values, the value of the convertible is equal to the sum of the values as if each component is traded separately.

[13]In practice it may be difficult to duplicate a convertible bond with a call option and a straight bond. There may be no equivalent call options traded separately that could be used. Near substitutes undoubtedly exist, however.

FIGURE 19–15   Valuing Convertible Securities

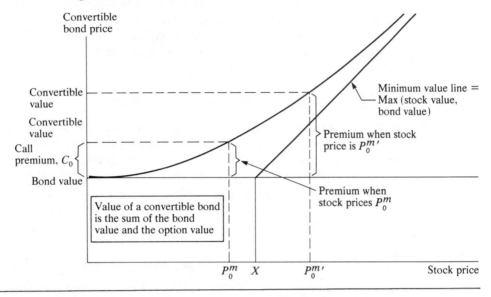

bond will look very similar to that between the common stock and a call option to purchase the common stock, as we have discussed. This is shown in Figure 19–15.

The minimum-value line is the maximum of the bond value or the value, in terms of the firm's stock, of the conversion privilege. The value of the conversion privilege equals the number of shares the conversion option allows the holder to buy at the exercise price times the current stock price. The value of the convertible will be greater than the minimum value for exactly those reasons that were specified earlier for call option valuation. In Figure 19–15, at a stock price of P_0^m, the conversion option has value C_0. When the stock price rises, the convertible's price rises also, but by a smaller percent.

Valuing Other Option-Type Instruments

As we said in the introduction to this chapter, there are a wide variety of options that are part of many financial investments: employee stock options, lease-purchase options, real estate options, extendability (of a bond or life insurance contract) options, call and retirement options, and forward commitment options, to name but a few. Theoretically, all these options can be valued, and some have been explicitly valued as extensions of the Black-Scholes valuation model.[14] The major practical problem with the extension of this model to some of these instruments is the requirement of Black and Scholes that trading in the instrument is more or less continuous. Only if this is the case can the hedge portfolio be formed and arbitrage principles employed to develop an explicit valuation model.

---

[14]For example, Brennan and Schwartz [1977] have valued Canadian government bonds where the holder has the option to extend the life of the bond.

Obviously, valuing employee stock options that cannot be traded, or valuing the option to purchase a unique piece of real estate that cannot be duplicated in the financial market, prohibits a direct application of the Black-Scholes model. Qualitative relationships can be inferred (e.g., the longer the option's life, the greater the value), but explicit numerical formulas have yet to be developed, and will quite likely depend heavily on particular assumptions made in solving for the value.

Empirical Evidence on the Pricing of Options

Evidence on options valuation has concentrated on whether actual option prices seem to follow the Black-Scholes model. That is, given the risk-free rate, stock price, exercise price, and the variance of stock price, empirical studies determined how close the Black-Scholes price predictions are to the real thing. For example, with the following inputs

$$P_0^m = \$48$$
$$X = \$50$$
$$\sigma(\tilde{R}) = .4$$
$$R_f = .1$$
$$\text{life} = t = 1/2 \text{ year (or 6 months)} = 6/12$$

an application of the Black-Scholes Equation 19–6 would imply a call option price of $5.81, or

(19–13) *Call Price Calculated*

$$d_1 = \frac{\ln(\$48/\$50) + [.10 + 1/2(.4^2)]6/12}{.4\sqrt{6/12}} = .1739$$

$$d_2 = \frac{\ln(\$48/\$50) + [.10 - 1/2(.4^2)]6/12}{.4\sqrt{6/12}} = .1205$$

$$C_0 = P_0^m N(d_1) - X(e^{-Rf^t})N(d_2)$$
$$C_0 = \$48N(.1739) - \$50e^{-.05}N(-.1205)$$
$$C_0 = \$48(.5690) - \$50(.9513)(.452) = \$5.81$$

With put-call parity the price of a put at the $50 striking price is (from Equation 19–11)

(19–14) *Put Price Calculated*

$$Put_0 = C_0 - P_0^m + X/(1 + R_f)^t$$
$$Put_0 = C_0 - \$48 + \$50/(1 + .10)^{1/2}$$
$$\$3.58 = \$5.81 - \$2.23$$

Calculated values such as these can be compared with actual option prices to see if, in fact, option prices closely follow the model's dictates.

There are two problems in applying this empirical methodology. The first is that the variance of the stock's return must be estimated—it is not directly observable. The second is that it may be difficult to get exactly contemporaneous stock prices, i.e., those that exist at the same moment the option trade is observed.[15]

---

[15]For example, if you look at the closing option price and closing stock price you will not in general find exact conformance with the model since the last option trade may not occur at the same time as the last stock trade on a given day.

FIGURE 19–16 **How Well Do Theoretical Models Price Actual Options**

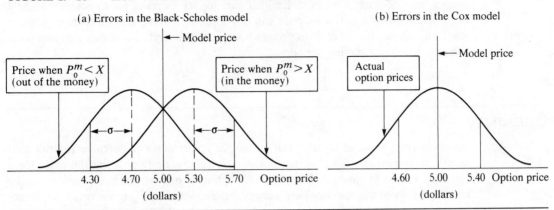

(a) Errors in the Black-Scholes model

(b) Errors in the Cox model

In spite of these difficulties the model quite accurately predicts actual option prices. The average percentage error for six actively traded options was about 6 percent and standard deviation of the error about 8 percent (from MacBeth and Merville [1979, 1980]). Moreover, the error for options when the stock market price was below the exercise price ("out of the money" options) tended to give a market price *above* the Black-Scholes model price, and when stock market price was above the exercise price ("in the money" options) the error seemed to be in the opposite direction. These results are summarized in Figure 19–16(a) for a fictional option priced by the model at $5. As you can see, these theoretical model prices are fairly accurate descriptions of reality, given the two estimation problems addressed.

One way to improve the model's prediction is to get better estimates of the stock return variance. A new model was developed by Cox [1975] which allows variance to change over time in a particular manner.[16] Estimates of the consistency of this new model with actual option prices do not seem to be related to whether the stock price exceeds or is below the striking price. The errors in this model are summarized in Figure 19–16(b).

In summary, it appears that option prices very closely follow the Black-Scholes option pricing model or a similar and slightly more complex model developed by Cox. Thus, options markets can be accurately characterized by the theoretical model presented here. Conformity with the theory is very close. As a result the Black-Scholes model is used extensively on Wall Street.

Taxation of Options

Taxes on options' gains and losses were significantly simplified with the passage of the 1986 Revenue Act which eliminated differential taxation of short- and long-term gains and losses. Now all income (or loss) from options will be taxed at the investor's marginal income tax rate. Options do have a particular tax advantage however, in that they can

---

[16]Stock return variances do change, of course, due to factors within or beyond the control of the firm. Debt structure changes or changes in credit markets or the economy would all effect $\sigma(\bar{R})$ just as they may have an effect on $E(\bar{R})$.

be effectively used to delay tax impacts. An individual with a large short-term gain on a stock who does not want to realize that gain for tax purposes nor to continue to hold the stock and risk a fall in its price can buy a *put* to insulate himself from a potential loss. This allows the investor to protect his capital gain and also to delay paying taxes until the next tax reporting period.

Summary

An option is a financial security that allows the holder either to purchase from (a call) or sell to (a put) the writer of the option a specific security at a specific price for a specified period of time. A European call option is one in which the option can be exercised only at the maturity date and not before. Some lease contracts are so characterized, as are many real estate options. An American call option can be exercised at any time prior to the maturity date.

An option is a contingent claim that, in theory, can be valued with knowledge of: (1) the current interest rate, (2) the market price of the security to be purchased with the option, (3) the standard deviation of the stock, (4) the exercise price of the option, and (5) the time to maturity. The result is the Black-Scholes option pricing model. In practice, the prices of call and put options traded on securities exchanges conform very closely to this pricing model.

Options markets have become so popular recently because they offer individuals a means of altering the probability distribution of portfolio returns in ways that conform more closely to preferences, and afford those with particular probability beliefs a chance to act on those beliefs. By offering these two services, the expansion of the options markets has helped to make the market more complete and, therefore, more appealing to investors. How options contribute to this market-completing function is easily seen by comparing the profit functions for different option strategies with the (different) profit functions for stocks, bonds, futures, or other financial opportunities. In fact, combinations of options, or options and other securities, can create a portfolio that is free from risk or very risky, depending on the strategy used to form the portfolio.

Organized options exchanges are active markets, and, from what we have been able to observe thus far, efficient. One need not fear trading in options any more than in the markets for other securities, if the nature of the risks these investment opportunities offer is fully understood.

References

Ball, Clifford A., and Torous, Walter N. [1986] "Futures Options and the Volatility of Futures Prices." *Journal of Finance* (September).

Black, Fischer. [1974] "Fact and Fantasy in the Use of Options." *Financial Analysts Journal* (July–August).

Black, F., and Scholes, M. [1973] "The Pricing of Options and Corporate Liabilities." *Journal of Political Economy* (May–June).

Black, Fischer, and Scholes, Myron. [1972] "The Valuation of Option Contracts and a Test of Market Efficiency." *Journal of Finance* (May).

Bokron, Nicholas. [1975] *How to Use Put and Call Options*. Springfield, Mass.: John Magee.

Bookstaber, Richard M. [1981] "Observed Option Mispricing and the Nonsimultaneity of Stock and Option Quotations." *Journal of Business* (January).

Bookstaber, Richard M. [1984] *Option Pricing and Strategies in Investing*. Reading, Mass.: Addison-Wesley.

Brennan, Michael, and Schwartz, Eduardo. [1977] "The Valuation of American Put Options." *Journal of Finance* (May).

Brennan, Michael, and Schwartz, Eduardo. [1977] "Convertible Bonds: Valuation and Optimal Strategies for Call and Conversion." *Journal of Finance* (December).

Chiraas, D. P., and Manaster, S. [1978] "The Information Content of Option Prices and a Test of Market Efficiency." *Journal of Financial Economics* (June–September).

Cox, John, and Ross, Stephen, [1976] "The Valuation of Options for Alternative Stochastic Processes." *Journal of Financial Economics* (January).

Cox, John; Ross, Stephen; and Rubinstein, Mark. [1979] "Option Pricing: A Simplified Approach." *Journal of Financial Economics* (September).

Dawson, Frederic S. [1979] "Risks and Returns in Continuous Option Writing." *Journal of Portfolio Management* (Winter).

Dothan, Uri, and Williams, Joseph. [1981] "Education as an Option." *Journal of Business* (January).

Evnine, Jeremy, and Rudd, Andrew. [1985] "Index Options: The Early Evidence. *Journal of Finance* (July).

Eytan, T. Hanan, and Harpaz, Giora. [1986] "The Pricing of Futures and Options Contracts on the Value Line Index." *Journal of Finance* (September).

Finnerty, Joseph. [1978] "The Chicago Board Options Exchange and Market Efficiency." *Journal of Financial and Quantitative Analysis* (March).

French, Dan W. [1984] "The Weekend Effect on the Distribution of Stock Prices: Implications for Option Pricing." *Journal of Financial Economics* (December).

Galai, Dan. [1978] "Empirical Tests of Boundary Conditions for CBOE Options." *Journal of Financial Economics* (June–September).

Galai, Dan. [1977] "Tests of Market Efficiency of the Chicago Board of Options Exchange." *Journal of Business* (April).

Galai, Dan. [1983] "The Components of the Return from Hedging Options against Stocks." *Journal of Business* (January).

Galai, Dan, and Mausulis, Ronald W. [1976] "The Option Pricing Model and the Risk Factor of Stock." *Journal of Financial Economics*.

Gastineau, Gary. [1979] "Options Risk and Reward." *The Stock Options Manual*, 2nd ed. New York: McGraw-Hill.

Geske, Robert, and Roll, Richard. [1984] "On Valuing American Call Options with the Black-Scholes European Formula." *Journal of Finance* (June).

Geske, Robert; Roll, Richard; and Shastri, Kuldeep. [1983] "Over-the-Counter Option Market Dividend Protection and 'Biases' in the Black-Scholes Model: A Note." *Journal of Finance* (September).

Gould, J. P., and Galai, Dan. [1974] "Transactions Costs and the Relationship between Put and Call Prices." *Journal of Financial Economics* (July).

Grube, R. Corwin; Panton, Don B.; and Terrel, J. Michael. [1979] "Risks and Rewards in Covered Call Position." *Journal of Portfolio Management* 5.

Jennings, Robert, and Starks, Laura. [1986] "Earnings Announcements, Stock Price Adjustment, and the Existence of Option Markets." *Journal of Finance* (March).

Latane, Henry A., and Rendleman, Richard J., Jr. [1976] "Standard Deviations of Stock Price Ratios Implied in Option Prices." *Journal of Finance* (May).

MacBeth, James, and Merville, Larry. [1979] "An Empirical Evaluation of the Black-Scholes Call Option Pricing Model." *Journal of Finance* (December).

MacBeth, James, and Merville, Larry. [1980] "Tests of the Black-Scholes and Cox Option Valuation Models." *Journal of Finance* (May).

Malkiel, Burton, and Quandt, Richard. [1969] *Strategies and Rational Decisions in the Securities Options Market*. Cambridge, Mass.: MIT Press.

Merton, Robert C. [1973a] "Theory of Rational Option Pricing." *Bell Journal of Economics and Management Science* (Spring).

Merton, Robert C. [1973b] "The Relationship between Put and Call Prices: Comment." *Journal of Finance* (March).

Merton, Robert; Scholes, Myron; and Gladstein, Matthew. [1978] "The Returns and Risk of Alternative Call Option Portfolio Investment Strategies." *Journal of Business* (April).

Merton, Robert C.; Scholes, Myron S.; and Gladstein, Matthew L. [1982] "The Returns and Risks of Alternative Put Option Portfolio Investment Strategies." *Journal of Business* (January).

Parkinson, Michael. [1977] "Option Pricing: The American Put." *Journal of Business* (January).

Phillips, S. M., and Smith, C. W. [1980] "Trading Costs for Listed Options: The Implications for Market Efficiency." *Journal of Financial Economics* (June).

Pozen, Robert C. [1978] "The Purchase of Protective Puts by Financial Institutions." *Financial Analysts Journal* (July).

Reback, Robert. [1975] "Risk and Return in CBOE and AMEX Option Trading." *Financial Analysts Journal* (July/August).

Rogalski, Richard J. [1978] "Variances in Option Prices in Theory and Practice." *Journal of Portfolio Management* (Winter).

Ross, Stephen A. [1975] "Options and Efficiency." *Quarterly Journal of Economics* (February).

Rubinstein, Mark (assisted by John C. Cox). [1980] *Option Markets.* Englewood Cliffs, N.J.: Prentice-Hall.

Schall, Lawrence. [1972] "Valuation, Firm Investment, and Firm Diversification." *Journal of Business* (January).

Schwartz, Eduardo. [1977] "The Valuation of Warrants: Implementing a New Approach." *Journal of Financial Economics* (January).

Smith, Clifford W., Jr. [1976] "Option Pricing; A Review." *Journal of Financial Economics* (January–March).

Sterk, W. [1982] "Tests of Two Models for Valuing Call Options on Stocks with Dividends." *Journal of Finance* (December).

Sterk, William E. [1983] "Comparative Performance of the Black-Scholes and Roll-Geske-Whaley Option Pricing Models." *Journal of Financial and Quantitative Analysis* (September).

Stoll, Hans R. [1969] "The Relationship between Put and Call Option Prices." *Journal of Finance* (December).

Whaley, Robert E. [1982] "Valuation of American Call Options on Dividend-Paying Stocks: Empirical Tests." *Journal of Financial Economics* (March).

Questions and Problems

1. Define a call option contract.

2. Woolworth's common stock just closed the day at a price of 53 $\frac{1}{2}$. A call option with an exercise price of 50, due to mature in exactly four months has a price of 7 $\frac{1}{8}$, while the put option with the same maturity and exercise price sells at 3 $\frac{1}{8}$. If the four-month (annualized) risk-free interest rate is 7 percent, and Woolworth expects to pay a dividend of $.30 sometime before maturity, does put/call parity hold? Explain.

3. You have been asked to provide information concerning the use of the following option strategies to modify portfolio risk/return relationships:

    a. Writing covered calls.

    b. Purchasing protective puts (the long-stock, long-put strategy).

    c. Selling stock market futures.

    Briefly describe each of these three strategies. Draw a graph for each strategy which shows the manner in which the risk/return relationship is modified (i.e., draw a graph of the stock price/profit relationship and interpret the relationship in view of its effect on portfolio risk and return).

    CFA

4. On May 1 an investor purchased a call option on Boeing common stock with an expiration date the following December and an exercise price of $60. The premium for the option was $8. The stock price at the moment he purchased the option was $65.

    a. Why would the call option sell for more than $5, which is its mathematical value, if the investor chose to exercise his option to convert on May 1?

b. The price of an equivalent call option on Boeing that matures the following March is 10 ¹/₄. Why would this option sell for more?

c. On the same day the investor had the chance to buy a call option on General Foods with the same exercise price, period to maturity, and underlying stock price as the Boeing call. However, the options market price was $7. What could account for the price difference?

d, If the interest rate (annualized) is 8 percent, there are 220 days to maturity, Boeing plans on paying a $1 dividend during the period before maturity, and put/call parity holds, what is the price of the equivalent put option?

5. Warrants tend to sell at a premium over minimum value. (1) Briefly explain the term "minimum value," and discuss the reasons for the existence of a "premium" over minimum value. (2) Briefly discuss each of the following factors affecting the value of the warrant:

a. The anticipated appreciation of the underlying stock.

b. Trading over the counter versus trading on a national exchange.

c. The length of the remaining life of the warrant.

CFA

6. An investor who owns 100 shares of a common stock and writes a call option on that stock has:

a. Reduced the effect of a price decline.

b. Written a naked call option.

c. Diversified his position.

d. Eliminated market risk.

7. Listed option prices follow the Black-Scholes formula reasonably closely when the historically estimated standard deviation is used. How would the following changes affect the value of put and call options of each firm (assume the prices of the underlying stock do not change):

a Texaco finally resolves its litigation with Pennzoil by paying $1.5 billion, thus averting further court rulings on damages.

b Apple Computer gets mad at analysts, and says it isn't going to make any further public statements regarding operations until its annual report is filed with the SEC in four months.

c Hershey Foods decides it will no longer speculate in the futures market for cocoa, but will enter the market only to hedge against price variations in the supply of cocoa it needs for its product.

d Safeway decides to refinance a good portion of the debt it issued in connection with its recent leveraged buyout. It will do so by issuing common stock.

8. You have the option of holding the common stock of Storer Broadcasting with its current price of $44, or purchasing a call option on the stock for a premium of $7 and an exercise price of $40. Calculate the breakeven future common stock price, i.e., the price that gives the same profit at maturity with either strategy.

9. You have established that the probability distribution for the price of Datapoint common stock in one year (it pays no dividend) is as follows:

Price	Probability	Price	Probability
$7	.1	$10	.25
8	.15	11	.15
9	.25	12	.1

Datapoint's current stock price is $8. If a one-year option is available at an exercise price of $8, and costs $2, calculate the probability distributions for outcomes from these strategies:

a. $8,000 invested in the stock (this one is trivial, of course).

b. $8,000 invested in the option.

c. $2,000 invested in the option and $6,000 in a savings account paying 10 percent interest.

d. $2,000 invested in the option, $4,000 deposited in your account at the brokers office to cover an $8,000 short sale of the security, and $2,000 invested in the savings account earning 10 percent.

10. IMB's common stock is selling at $150. You can buy a six-month call option to exercise at 150 for $12, and a put option for the same maturity and exercise price for $9. Plot the option profit function for each option separately, and for an investment in one call and one put held simultaneously (a straddle).

11. Identify the profits and losses from the following transactions:

Type of Option Transaction	Premium	Exercise Price	Stock Price at Beginning	Stock Price at Maturity
Buy call	$ 5	$ 50	$48	$ 52
Buy call	7	80	81	95
Write call	3	15	16	12
Write call	15	50	60	75
Buy put	6	30	27	22
Buy put	12	85	81	90
Write put	4	15	13	12
Write put	14	100	95	125
Buy call and stock	7	50	50	60
Buy put and stock	8	50	48	45

Type of Option Transaction	Premium	Exercise Price	Stock Price at Beginning	Stock Price at Maturity
Sell call and buy stock	7	50	50	60
Sell put and buy stock	8	50	48	45

12. If options have value to the holder of the option, why does the presence of a call option on a corporate bond serve to increase the rate of interest (or reduce the price, other things constant) that that bond must pay to get investors to hold the bonds in their portfolio? Why does the presence of a convertibility option on a corporate bond have the opposite effect?

CHAPTER

20

International Securities

International Investing

Most of the financial instruments we have discussed thus far have been dollar-denominated investments. Some, of course, have international aspects to them. Ford, for example, derives about 20 percent of its sales from its non-U.S. operations, and in some recent years profits from foreign sources have served to offset losses from domestic operations. As another example, Citicorp has offices in most countries and all money market centers around the world. In this sense, U.S. investors holding the securities of U.S.-domiciled firms have an important stake in foreign investments; and the returns and risks of U.S. securities has a significant international component.

In this chapter, we investigate the structure, opportunities, and benefits that may be available to an individual who invests part of his portfolio in financial claims denominated in other currencies. In studying these **international or foreign national** investments we will determine how the opportunity set may be expanded and will simultaneously supply some insights into the valuation of U.S. firms' foreign-investment interests.

The Size and Nature of Foreign Investment Opportunities

It has been estimated that the current aggregate market value of all *publicly* held equity of firms domiciled outside the United States is approximately equal to the value of the outstanding equity of all United States firms.[1] This would imply a value for each of the

---

[1]Computed from figures given in *Capital International Perspective* (1985:IV).

markets of approximately $2 trillion. Moreover, while the six or seven largest publicly held firms are domiciled in the United States, there are at least 150 firms outside of the United States and Canada with equity market values exceeding $2 billion. For comparison, the United States and Canada house more than 200 such firms.[2]

Comparable figures for international bond markets are not so readily available due mostly to over-the-counter trading in these securities. Nevertheless, estimates place the total of all governmental and corporate issues at well over $4 trillion, with the foreign component being about 30 percent larger than that of U.S. issuers (though an important percentage of the foreign issues are denominated in U.S. dollars).[3]

With some exceptions, foreign securities tend to correspond to those types of securities we have discussed in prior chapters. Foreign firms issue common stock. Most issue bonds that have similar provisions to those issued by U.S. and Canadian firms, and some convertible and callable issues exist. Preferred stock is also available. Foreign firms and foreign banks also issue short-term money market instruments comparable in almost every way with certificates of deposit, commercial paper, and bankers' acceptances except, of course, the unit of payment is a different currency.[4] Foreign governments issue both short-term and long-term debt instruments—some in extensive quantities—that are often held by investors residing outside of the issuing country.[5]

Foreign stock exchanges are active in equity transactions, and all industrialized countries have organized exchanges. Besides a number of exchanges in Germany, Canada, and Hong Kong, there is also the Sydney Stock Exchange, the Tokyo Stock Exchange, Paris Bourse, the Singapore Exchange, and so on. Trading on these exchanges, in some cases, is a simple task. It's no problem to get your U.S. or Canadian broker to buy or sell a security on the Tokyo Exchange. It's a somewhat more difficult task to trade in Lagos or Calcutta. Some of these exchanges are set up differently than the NYSE— without specialists. Trading in these markets compares more with futures market transactions on U.S. commodities markets, where multiple market makers create a competitive specialist system.

The volume of activity in most of these markets is large. Annual turnover in 1984, or the value of transactions in that year as a percent of total value, was 50 percent in the

---

[2]The figures are from *Capital International Perspective*. Moreover, there are some very large privately held foreign firms. In fact, public ownership of major producers is not as common in many countries as it is in the U.S., Canada, and Japan.

[3]The values are taken from Ibbotson, Siegel, and Love [1985].

[4]More and more large firms, such as international oil companies and other well-known firms, are issuing debt securities that are denominated in other currencies than the *home* currency of their common stock. They do this, of course, when they perceive the cost of borrowing to be less in that foreign currency. Whether the cost turns out to be less depends on a number of things, including changes in the value of that foreign currency relative to the home currency. Governments are beginning to do this as well. Such actions by firms and governments will change the relative structure of interest rates in different countries so that no country's currency has an obvious advantage in the borrowing market over any other currency.

[5]In recent years many Third World countries have issued debt instruments on foreign markets. For example, in 1983 Brazil had $66 billion of outstanding short-term debt on a GNP base of $265 billion, and Mexico's debt burden was $85 billion with GNP at $247 billion. Most of this debt was issued to, and continues to be held by, European and U.S. banks. By 1986 secondary markets for many issues had developed, but with prices at substantial discounts from par. To illustrate, bid prices ranged from 8 percent of par value for Bolivian debt to 75 percent of par for debt issued by Venezuela. Most issues (those of Chile, Argentina, Ecuador, Mexico, The Philippines, Poland, and Nigeria) were trading in the range of 50 percent to 70 percent of par value. (*The Wall Street Journal*, October 7, 1986.)

United States (NYSE), 46 percent in Japan (Tokyo Exchange), 37 percent in Germany, 33 percent in Hong Kong, 25 percent in France and the United Kingdom, 21 percent in Canada, and 11 percent in Singapore. Virtually all of these figures represent increased turnover levels from 10 years earlier, suggesting that the increased volume of trading in U.S. stocks discussed in Chapters 3 and 4 is a universal phenomena.

As in the United States and Canada, most bond trading, as well as some stock trading, is performed over-the-counter. Bond markets for issues of major European companies or countries are quite active. Smaller issues suffer from the same thinness and lack of liquidity as in the smaller U.S. issues. Obviously, such issues may hold less appeal for international investors.

Historical Returns on Foreign Financial Opportunities

At this point it is useful to develop some definitions, since foreign investments add a layer of confusion to concepts of risk, return, and security value.

Price of a Currency: the domestic price of a foreign currency, or the quantity of the domestic currency which must be given up to buy a unit of another currency, $S_0^{d/f}$ is the exchange rate per domestic unit of foreign currency at time 0, e.g., $S_0^{d/f}$ for U.S. dollars and British pounds may be $1.75/£.

Forward Price of a Currency: the currency price contracted for now for future exchange. $F_{0,T}^{d/f}$ is the *current* forward rate for the exchange of domestic currency per unit of foreign currency at period T, e.g., $1.73/£ may be the current price for a pound delivered in three months.

Foreign Interest Rate: the rate on a riskless investment denominated in a foreign currency. R_f^f may be the interest rate for pounds. The subscript still refers to the risk-free rate, the superscript to the foreign currency that pays that rate. R_f^d is the equivalent domestic rate.

Foreign Inflation Rate: Ω^f is the foreign inflation rate. Ω^d is the equivalent domestic rate.

Column (1) of Table 20–1 indicates the average annual geometric returns that have been generated on investments in equity markets in a variety of countries by U.S. investors between 1970 and 1985. The figures take into account the changes in exchange rates that occurred during the period. Column (2) gives equivalent values from the perspective of Canadian investors. The returns are larger for Canadian investors over this period due to the fall in the value of the Canadian $ relative to the U.S.$, making it (relatively) more advantageous for Canadian investors to have been "out of" Canadian dollar investments over the period. Column (3) gives returns in the local currency (without taking into account changes in the value of each currency).

Note that very high local returns on Mexican equities was more than offset by a decline in the value of the peso. Both Canadian and U.S. investors would have lost money, on average, on direct investments in peso-denominated common stocks. EAFE is an index constructed of European, Australian, and Far East companies, and reflects the performance of equities in developed, non-U.S., countries.

The next three columns of the table give: (4) aggregate market values, (5) price/earnings ratios, and (6) dividend yields on each of these national portfolios and the two international

TABLE 20–1 **Foreign Stock Market Returns (1970–1985)**

	Average Annual Geometric Returns (January 1970 to September 1985)			Estimated 1985		
	(1) To United States Investors	(2) To Canadian Investors	(3) In the Local Currency	(4) Value of Equity (billions)	(5) Price/ Earnings Ratio	(6) Dividend Yield
Australia	4.6%	6.2%	7.7%	$ 63	12	3.8%
Austria	10.1	11.9	7.9	3	56.5	1.8
Belgium	9.2	10.9	9.8	16	8.4	9.8
Canada	7.2	8.9	8.9	134	14	3.4
Denmark	11.5	13.3	13.4	11	14.1	2.3
France	6.2	7.9	8.9	56	11.9	4.3
Germany	9.5	11.2	7.3	133	14.7	3.1
Hong Kong	6.8	8.8	12.1	33	13.5	4.1
Italy	2.6	4.2	9.7	50	21.6	2.4
Japan	17.3	19.1	13.6	817	25.6	1.0
Mexico	− 25.3	− 5.3	56.8	3	4.7	4.1
Netherlands	10.6	12.3	9.3	42	6.8	5.0
Norway	12.5	14.2	13.2	8	5.7	3.6
Singapore	13.9	15.9	11.4	26	23	2.7
Spain	0.5	2.1	6.1	16	10	8.6
Sweden	10.3	12.1	13.5	22	7 9	3.1
Switzerland	9.8	11.5	5.1	63	10.7	2.5
U.K.	9.6	11.4	13.4	290	11.1	4.6
U.S.A.	7.3	9.0	7.3	1,710	11.3	4.4
EAFE	8.6	10.5	8.6	1,650	15.6	2.6
World	8.0	9.7	8.0	3,515	13	3.5

Source: Constructed from information presented in *Capital International Perspective,* various years.

portfolios, EAFE and World. It's interesting to note the unexpected diversity of price/earnings ratios and dividend yields among the countries. The dividend yield of 1 percent and the price/earnings of 25 make Japanese stocks look fundamentally different from those issued in other countries. In part this is a reflection of differences in methods used to measure reported profits, i.e., generally accepted accounting principles are not the same in all countries. The ratio of price to cash flow (with cash flow including accounting depreciation) for Japanese companies is much closer to the world norm.

Foreign Exchange Markets and Exchange Risk

The purchase of a foreign-denominated security requires the prior "purchase" of the currency in which the security is denominated. A U.S. investor buying 100 shares of Unilever or British Petroleum is first required to purchase British pounds, £. Concomitantly, the sale of the security involves the sale of pounds, or the repurchase of dollars. These currency transactions take place on foreign exchange markets, thus requiring the investor to operate in two speculative markets for one investment.

Obviously, the purchase of Unilever's common stock involves some risk (Unilever's β) and, therefore, presumably some expected return. But the purchase of pounds also may involve some risk since a non-British consumer would have to reacquire the currency as the investment position in the stock is closed out. Foreign exchange prices—the rate at which dollars can be exchanged for pounds—do vary, and there is uncertainty regarding this rate of exchange.

Fortunately, foreign exchange markets tend to be broad and resilient for most currency transactions, making this part of the purchase particularly easy to perform. Spot markets for foreign exchange are handled by major money market banks (perhaps handled for you by your broker) and can be performed almost instantly at the request of the trader. These foreign currency transactions involve small transaction costs, even for small investors, undoubtedly because of the enormous size of the overall foreign exchange market. There are some natural limitations, of course, that are dictated by the extent of the exchange of goods and services internationally. It is easy to change British pounds into Australian dollars, but a somewhat more difficult task to transform Malagary francs into Peruvian soles (one may have to go through the dollar market). For some securities the task is made even easier by the creation of American Depository Receipts.

American Depository Receipts

American depository receipts (ADRs) remove many of the problems of trading and custodial services that are associated with owning some foreign equities. An ADR is a negotiable receipt issued by an American depository in lieu of the underlying shares it holds in custody overseas. Morgan Guaranty Trust Company is the principal issuer of ADRs. Normally such ADRs are issued only for shares of stock that are traded on relatively well-functioning foreign security exchanges. The ADRs are then traded and transferred in exactly the same way as stock certificates of a U.S. firm listed on an exchange. Dividends are received and transmitted to owners by the depository, which also performs other custodial services as may be required by capital changes, mergers, tender offers, or stock dividends. For this service the depository charges a small fee. The net effect is that ADRs serve as essentially perfect substitutes for the shares of the foreign firm issuing the securities.

Foreign Exchange Risk

How much risk is involved in the foreign exchange transaction depends on the situation. At first glance it might seem that the transaction into and out of the foreign currency involves substantial risk. Foreign exchange prices vary, sometimes considerably. Take the example of the U.S. investor buying shares of Unilever. The foreign exchange price of the pound is quoted as $1.45. This indicates that an individual can buy one pound for $1.45. At the same time an individual buying dollars with pounds would find the cost of each dollar to be 1/1.45 or £.69.[6] Thus, the foreign currency exchange rate is simply a ratio that indicates the value of one currency relative to another.[7]

---

[6]Following the no-arbitrage condition, this relationship between the dollar price of pounds ($1.45) and the pound price of dollars (£.69) would have to hold. If it didn't, you could make a very large sum by simultaneously buying one currency and selling the other. No investment would be required since you could use the purchase in one market to deliver against the sale in the other.

[7]Similarly, the price of anything quoted in terms of dollars is simply the ratio of the number of dollars relative to one unit of the good or service being purchased.

Suppose that the purchase of 100 shares of Unilever requires £3,400. The U.S. investor would be required to purchase £3,400 at a total cost of ($1.45/£)(£3,400), or $4,930, in order to make the acquisition. After six months the value of 100 shares of Unilever rises to £3,800. In addition, the value of the British pound has dropped so that it is now worth only $1.42/£. The U.S. investor who sells his shares in Unilever for £3,800 would then exchange those pounds for ($1.42/£)(£3,800), or $5,396. While the percentage price increase of Unilever over the six-month holding period is £400/£3,400, or 11.8 percent, the net return including transactions in the foreign exchange market is

$$\frac{£3,800(\$1.42/£)}{£3,400(\$1.45/£)} - 1.0 = .095$$

or 9.5 percent per six months. It is important to note that the effect of the change in exchange rates to $1.42/£ at the time of the sale has affected the *total quantity of funds invested* in Unilever, £3800 at the point of sale, and not just the profits generated. A general expression for the calculation of the rate of return on an investment opportunity which accounts for possible changes in the rate at which the currencies can be exchanged is:

(20–1)   *Rate of Return Including the Change in Value of the Foreign Currency*

$$R_1 = \frac{(D_1^f + P_1^f)(S^{df})}{P_0^f(S_0^{df})} - 1$$

$$= \left(\frac{D_1^f + P_1^f}{P_0^f}\right)\left(\frac{S_1^{df}}{S_0^{df}}\right) - 1$$

$$\begin{matrix} \textit{Rate of return on} \\ \textit{foreign investment} \end{matrix} = \begin{matrix} (1 + local \\ security\ return)(1 + currency \\ "return") - 1 \end{matrix}$$

In this expression P_1^f and P_0^f are the ending and beginning prices of the *foreign security,* D_1^f is the *interest,* or *dividend,* paid in the foreign currency, and S_1^{df} and S_0^{df} are the ending and beginning prices of the *foreign currency* in terms of the domestic currency (i.e., $1.42 and $1.45, respectively). This is the calculation that was used to construct Table 20–1 when the domestic currency was, alternatively, the U.S. dollar and the Canadian dollar.

In sum, unlike domestic investments, there are two components to foreign investment returns: (1) the change in value and cash flows of the foreign security in its own currency, and (2) the change in the value of the foreign currency relative to the domestic currency of the investor. This expression holds true no matter what the domestic currency is.

Clearly, it is important for the investor to determine the risks of changes in *both* the price of the foreign security and the foreign currency. Figure 20–1 gives a few clues regarding standard deviations of these values for some foreign countries. The left bar in each case indicates the (annualized) standard deviation of the foreign currency price from a $ investor's perspective, while the right section of the bar indicates the standard deviation of annual returns calculated for a well-diversified portfolio of common stocks domiciled in those countries (the local market portfolio). The figures indicate that both components

FIGURE 20–1   Standard Deviations of Returns: Stock Returns and Currency Price Changes

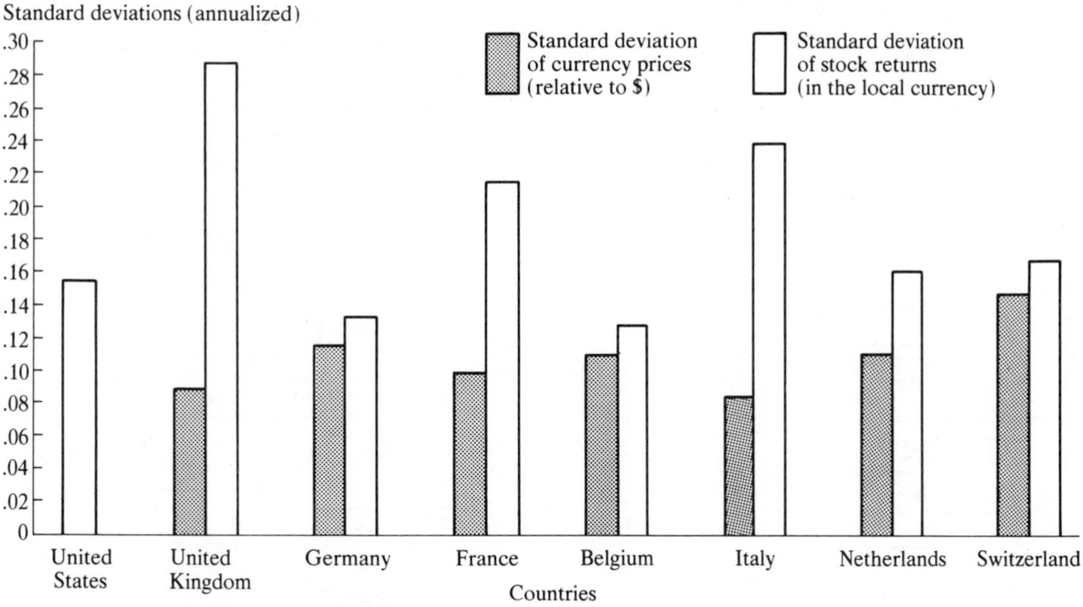

Source: Calculated from Solnik and Nemeth [1982].

of Equation 20–1 are variable. If changes in foreign exchange prices relative to the dollar (S_1^{df}/S_0^{df}) are positively related to the price change of the foreign security (P_1^f/P_0^f), the holding-period return figure, R_1, will vary wildly. If they tend to move in opposite directions, the ratios will have a dampening effect on one another, and R_1 will have less variability. Some perspectives on this effect can be gained by adjusting the figures given in Table 20–1 on U.S. dollar and Canadian dollar returns from 1970 to 1985 for the exchange-rate changes that took place over this period. These values are given in Figure 20–2. The numbers represent the component figures for the total return achieved by a U.S. or Canadian investor. Thus, of the total return of 9.8 percent per year from investments in Swiss securities, 4.7 percent was due to an appreciation of the Swiss currency relative to the $, and 5.1 percent represented the increase in stock prices inside Switzerland. In the case of Spain, the devaluation of their currency at the rate of 5.6 percent per year almost completely offset the domestic stock price increase of 6.1 percent leaving only .5 percent (see Table 20–1) for the U.S. investor.

While the data given in Figures 20–1 and 20–2 suggest that the two components of foreign investment returns are both subject to variability, there are two reasons why the foreign currency risk component may not have as *much* of an effect of an investor's well-being as seems apparent from the figures.

First, the risk may be moderated by the pattern of consumption of the investor. Second, some of the variability in foreign exchange prices may be diversifiable, and international portfolio diversification may reduce the impact of foreign currency price fluctuations. These are discussed in the next two subsections.

FIGURE 20–2   Currency Returns and Stock Return by Country: To U.S. Investors and Canadian Investors

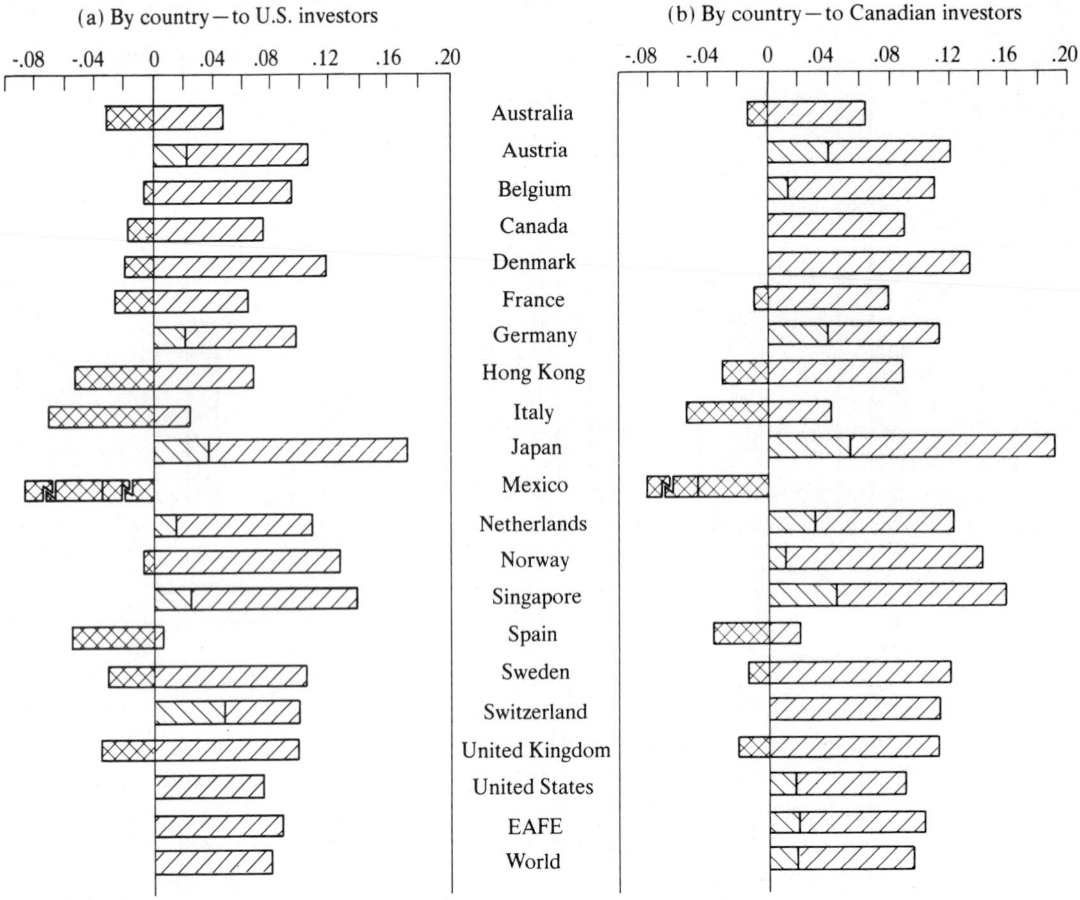

(a) By country — to U.S. investors   (b) By country — to Canadian investors

Source: Calculated from Table 20–1 and foreign currency prices.

Foreign Exchange Prices, Inflation, and Interest Rates

There is an explicit set of relationships that tie together interest rates, inflation rates, and currency prices. If expected inflation is higher in the foreign country than in the domestic country the effect will be to raise interest rates on investments in the foreign country (remember the Fisher effect described in Chapter 12). This will be offset by an expected decline in the value of that country's currency which will tend to offset the benefit of the higher interest rate. Foreign currency risk exists because the actual decline in the foreign currency's price may be different than the expected decline. At least part of this risk can be offset if the investor is a consumer of that country's goods and services. Essentially, the unexpected loss (gain) incurred when the investor converts back into the

TABLE 20–2   **Correlations among Countries' Changes in Exchange Rates**
(quarterly, 1970–1983 in U.S. dollars)

	United Kingdom	France	Germany	Italy	Japan
United States	.12	−.41	−.34	−.04	−.17
United Kingdom		.14	.22	.15	.05
France			.69	.48	.09
Germany				.25	.15
Italy					.02

Source: Computed by Institute of International Business, University of Houston.

domestic currency is offset by the gain (loss) associated with the cheaper (more expensive) foreign goods.

A recent example clearly demonstrates these relationships. In 1986 a number of investment bankers began marketing portfolios of Australian bonds. These bond portfolios had negligible default risk and offered a yield to maturity of 13 percent at the same time equivalent U.S. bonds were offering yields of 7 percent. Australia had been experiencing an inflation rate of 10 percent while the U.S. rate was about 4 percent, and these expectations were reflected in the interest rate differential. The spot rate for the Australian dollar at this time was $.60/A$. Of course, the investor attempting to take advantage of the 6 percent higher Australian interest rate would find the "apparent" benefit negated by an expected decline in the value of the Australian currency during the period of the investment. But, more to the subject of foreign exchange risk, the investor is exposed to the possibility that the value of the Australian dollar may fall to a level (approximately, a level below $.566/A$) that would imply a net return that is less than the 7 percent rate available in the United States. This risk is moderated to the extent that the investor is a consumer of Australian goods and services. If the $A falls more than expected, the goods and services effectively are cheaper to the U.S. investor, offsetting the greater decline in the value of his portfolio. To carry the generalization to its logical conclusion, if the relationships between inflation, currency exchange rates, and interest rates hold precisely, and if the investor's consumption package consists of 5 percent Australian goods and services, the investor who places 5 percent of his wealth in Australian bonds does not actually face any foreign exchange risk. Of course, with a different proportion of his wealth committed to this foreign economy some risk remains.

Foreign Exchange Prices and Diversification

How much foreign exchange risk remains after accounting for international consumption depends on the correlations between the foreign exchange rates. Table 20–2 presents correlation coefficients between six different countries' currency values. Because the figures are all relative to U.S. dollars, the correlations with the United States are mostly negative. However, other correlations are far less than perfect and imply that some portion of the variability of exchange rate changes can be diversified by "holding" a mix of currencies that are not closely related to each other or to the dollar. Thus, a U.S. investor's exposure to exchange risk can be softened by the somewhat independent price movements of the different currencies the investor may hold as part of his international portfolio. However, because of generally positive correlations, not all the variability can be eliminated with international diversification.

In practice, in other words, foreign exchange risk is something an investor must be aware of. Moreover, management of this risk is possible through the use of forward or futures markets for foreign exchange—our next subject.

Forward Markets for Foreign Exchange

Interest Rate Parity

If you buy a foreign currency, purchase the riskless bonds of that country, and sell the amount to be realized from your investment in their forward foreign exchange market at maturity T for a price $F_{0,T}^{dif}$, you have a riskless investment (since you buy riskless bonds and have covered your foreign currency risk). Such a transaction ought to yield you exactly the same return as a riskless bond in your home currency. If it doesn't, a riskless arbitrage opportunity is available, indicating that the market was wrong—someplace. The transaction says that

(20–2)   *Interest-Rate Parity or Covered Interest Arbitrage*

$$(1 + R_f^d) = (1 + R_f^f)\frac{F_{0,T}^{dif}}{S_0^{dif}}$$

$$\frac{(1 + R_f^d)}{(1 + R_f^f)} = \frac{F_0^{dif}}{S_0^{dif}}$$

The ratio of 1 plus the domestic interest rate relative to the foreign interest rate $=$ *The ratio of the current forward rate to the current spot rate.*

Suppose interest rates in the United Kingdom were 10 percent and in the United States were 8.48 percent. If the forward rate for the pound is $1.43 and the spot rate for the pound is $1.45, then no arbitrage opportunities are available, and foreign exchange prices and interest rates are correctly priced relative to each other, since

$$\frac{1.0848}{1.10} = \frac{\$1.43}{\$1.45}$$

However, if interest rates in the United States were 8 percent, an investor could, without risk, buy pounds at $1.45, earn a return of 10 percent, and sell pounds at $1.43, netting

$$\frac{\$1.43(1.10)}{\$1.45} = 1.0848$$

The 8.48 percent return is greater than that available in his domestic currency, and is a rate structure that cannot be maintained.

Eliminating Foreign Exchange Risk

The interest rate parity relationship suggests a means by which the foreign exchange risk can be *reduced* on foreign-denominated investments. The reduction can be accomplished by *covering* all transactions in forward or futures foreign exchange markets. The process is very similar to that followed by an individual hedging in commodity or financial futures markets.

There are two available mechanisms for such hedging transactions. The first is the use of the so-called **Interbank Foreign Exchange Market.** Actually, the Interbank Foreign Exchange Market is made up of two foreign exchange markets: the spot market and the forward market. The spot market is available for those individuals who wish to exchange one currency for another at this time. The forward market is for the exchange of currencies at some future point in time. Thus, considering the Unilever example again, through the use of the Interbank Market it is possible for you to arrange to exchange pounds for dollars six months from now in order to reconvert your investment in the pound-denominated Unilever stock back into dollars. The price of the forward transaction will be determined by interest rate parity. The transaction using the forward foreign exchange market to hedge your position in the foreign currency would take place as follows:

- Purchase British pounds for $1.45 each and use the proceeds from that transaction to buy 100 shares of Unilever at £3,400; total outlay is $4,930.
- Simultaneously, anticipating a six-month holding period, sell British pounds in the Interbank Forward Market at a rate of, say $1.43 (reflecting the interest rate differential between the two countries).
- After the six-month holding period liquidate the position in Unilever for £3,800 and use these proceeds to deliver against the sold position in the foreign exchange forward market at the specified price of $1.43. This yields the investor £3,800, each worth $1.43 for a dollar inflow of $5,434. The net return on the investment in foreign securities is given by:

$$(20\text{--}3) \qquad R_1 = \frac{P_1^f F_{0,1}^{\$/£}}{P_0^f S_0^{\$/£}} - 1 = \frac{£3800\ (\$1.43£)}{£3400\ (\$1.45/£)} - 1 = .102$$

The return is different from the uncovered 9.5 percent return using Equation (20-1) because the current forward rate for delivery in period 1, $F_{0,1}^{\$/£}$, was different ($1.43 in this example) from the future (period 1) spot rate, $S_1^{\$/£}$ (assumed to be $1.42 in that earlier example), which will vary and is uncertain. The forward market transaction has simply substituted a currently known rate of exchange for an unknown future spot rate. This eliminates the source of uncertainty due to variations in the spot rate. If, in the Unilever example, it turns out that the spot rate in six months is $1.42, you not only eliminated this source of risk, but are better off (selling at $1.43) than if you had waited and sold pounds on the spot market at $1.42. Of course, if the spot rate remained at $1.45 during the six-month investment period, with hindsight, you would have been better off not hedging the currency risk. In any case, the use of the forward market shifted the variability to someone else (a speculator in the forward foreign exchange market).

In fact, the actual transaction as set forth in this example cannot be completed in exactly the way set forth in Equation (20–3) because the return on Unilever's common stock is uncertain. We do not know for sure that £3,800 pounds will be received upon sale in six months. The hedge can be based on the anticipated end-of-period sale price, but, of course, the actual end-of-period price may differ substantially from that anticipated. Suppose, for example, that you expect a change in value from £3,400 to £3,600. In view of this expectation you sell £3,600 in the forward Interbank Market. Of the £3,800 you actually receive, £3,600 would be delivered against the sale price in the forward contract at $1.43. The remaining £200 would be subject to the variation in the exchange rate from $1.45 to the actual exchange rate that exists in the spot foreign exchange market at the close of the transaction six months after it was initiated.

The second method by which an investor can hedge the foreign exchange portion of his foreign investment is through an organized exchange called the International Monetary Market (IMM). This market was opened as a subsidiary of the Chicago Mercantile Exchange in 1972. Its sole purpose is to maintain active futures markets to exchange dollars for a number of foreign currencies. Thus, as is the case with any futures market, the specified delivery date for the foreign currency would be indicated in the futures contract. The September contract for pounds might require closure according to the contract on a specific date in September.[8] The size of each of these futures contracts for active currencies is summarized below:

		Recent Dollar Value
British pound	25,000 pounds	$40,000
German mark	125,000 marks	60,000
Canadian dollar	100,000 dollars	70,000
Swiss franc	125,000 francs	75,000
Japanese yen	12.5 million yen	80,000

These are fairly large quantities, of course, which makes it difficult for small investors to use this mechanism as a hedge against small dollar-value risks.

Efficiency of Foreign Exchange Markets

If foreign exchange markets are speculative or uncertain markets, then it is natural to ask whether these markets are efficient. Do foreign currency prices "fully reflect available information?" Or can profits be made from trading rules based on past prices or from the use of current public information?

Investigations of the issue seem to suggest that there are small dependencies from day to day, but that it is doubtful that anyone could gain by trying to capitalize on them. Three methods in particular have been used to test for efficiency in both spot and forward markets. These are (1) tests for independence—random walk tests, (2) tests of trading strategy, and (3) tests of interest rate parity.

---

[8] As we pointed out in Chapter 18, there are some differences between futures and forward markets. The difference in this case is that active markets in forward foreign exchange, as take place in the Interbank Market, are for delivery in some round number of days, such as 30 days, 60 days, 90 days, six months, or one year. The transactions in the futures market are for particular calendar-date transaction settlements. Thus, for IMM in the British pound the closure takes place in March, June, September, and December. Of course, you also have daily "marking-to-market" in futures contracts.

Random Walk Tests. These tests suggest some serial correlation in foreign exchange prices. However, critiques of these tests suggest that, particularly in foreign exchange markets, this test does a poor job of measuring efficiency. For one thing, the daily prices of foreign exchange are influenced by settlement procedures in foreign exchange markets. Thus, returns on Wednesdays and Thursdays are influenced by the fact that on Wednesday transactions the cash settlement takes place on Friday, but for the Thursday transactions the settlement doesn't take place until the following Monday, leaving one transactor with two extra days interest income.[9]

Trading Strategies. These tests seem to infer that one can earn slightly positive returns before transaction costs, but once the costs of trading in foreign exchange are considered, the profits from most naive trading strategies disappear.[10]

Interest Rate Parity. Studies of interest rate parity (IRP) are looking for a slightly different kind of market efficiency. Instead of questioning if prices fully reflect information and are thus a fair game with respect to the information available, IRP studies check to see if any arbitrage possibilities exist between spot and forward foreign exchange prices, given the exchange rates and the interest rates that exist in the two countries. Thus, they test the empirical validity of Equation (20–2) by asking if:

(20–4)
$$\frac{1 + R_f^d}{1 + R_f^f} - \frac{F_{0,T}^{dif}}{S_0^{dif}} = 0$$

In other words, these studies check to see if the forward rate matches the domestic interest rate (plus 1) relative to the foreign interest rate (plus 1). A variety of studies have suggested that this relationship holds precisely enough, even on a daily basis, that it would be very difficult for anyone to capture arbitrage profits.[11]

International Portfolios and Diversification

Given the possible costs associated with transacting in foreign currency markets and the attendant risks of not hedging one's currency position, one might begin to wonder whether international investment opportunities are worth it. Indeed, it seems as if most U.S. investors have concluded that they may not be. Best estimates place the level of foreign investment by U.S. investors at less than 10 percent. In fact, there are some major potential benefits associated with international investing. Obviously, there is always the possibility that individual investment opportunities in foreign countries will yield larger returns or smaller risks than are available domestically. In fact, this has been the case in the last two decades!

More than this, however, is the possible benefit from the improvement in diversification through holding foreign securities. In other words, are there important gains to be made in reducing portfolio risk by including foreign securities? This question simply addresses

[9]See Levi [1978] and McFarland, Pettit and Sung [1982].
[10]Cornell and Dietrich [1978]; Logue, Sweeny, and Willet [1978].
[11]See Bilson [1981].

TABLE 20–3   Correlations among Countries' Changes in Industrial Production
(annually, 1948–1982)

	United Kingdom	France	Germany	Italy	Japan
United States	.46	−.17	.07	.47	.45
United Kingdom		.21	.21	.50	.39
France			.28	.20	.02
Germany				.38	.42
Italy					.63

Source: Computed by Institute of International Business, University of Houston.

the issue of whether the efficient set might be pushed farther to the left as foreign securities are added to the available set from which the efficient frontier is constructed.

Countries differ substantially in the natural resources they have available to them, their technological expertise, their labor force, and the type of government that may affect the economic output of the nation. As a consequence of these differences, one would expect that the economies of different countries, to some extent, operate independently of one another. This is not to say that there are not substantial ties between the economic success of one country and that of another. Yet, it seems clear from any casual perusal of world events that there is a *degree* of independence that exists among countries' economies. While the automobile industry in the United States is doing relatively poorly, it may be that the automobile industry in Japan is doing rather well. Political problems in Eastern Europe that affect the economic output of those countries and their trading partners might have a substantially larger effect upon the value of equities in some closely related countries than in countries such as the United States and Canada that can operate relatively independently of the happenings in that part of the world.

Of course, if some independence among foreign economies exists, then there is a potential for investors to capture some additional benefits from an internationally diversified portfolio. Thus, the lack of perfect comovement of returns on equities in one country with the returns on equities in another country would suggest that investors in both of these countries could attain a reduction in the standard deviation of portfolio returns by making use of equities traded in both countries. Evidence has accumulated that suggests that substantial benefits may be available from international diversification. Table 20–3 shows the correlations between changes in countries' indexes of industrial production. There is a relatively strong degree of comovement in the growth of industrial production between the United Kingdom and the United States, for example, and a much smaller degree of comovement in the growth of GNP between Japan and France.

Additionally, the benefit from diversification might be stronger if there appear to be low correlations among common stocks of different countries. Estimates of these correlations are in Figure 20–3. The correlations are with reference to the U.S. market index and the Canadian market index. The markets in Hong Kong and Singapore and Australia, have been combined into "Other Asia," and Denmark, Spain, and Norway into "Other Europe", because of the very small size of those equity markets. Two points are clear from these figures. The first is that the values are low enough that international diversification is likely to give rise to significantly reduced portfolio standard deviations.

FIGURE 20–3 **Correlation of U.S. and Canadian Stock Market Returns with Those of Other Countries**

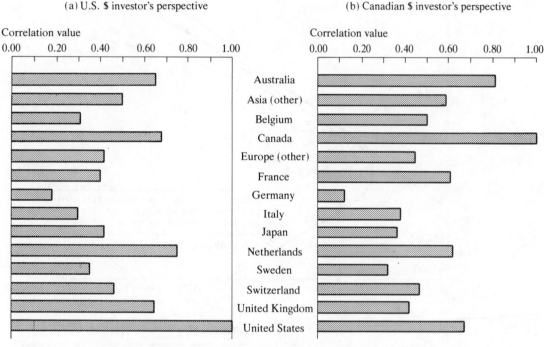

(a) U.S. $ investor's perspective   (b) Canadian $ investor's perspective

Source: Computed using data from 1970 to 1985 collected from *Capital International Perspective*, various issues.

Second, the correlations vary widely. Consequently, optimal portfolio construction is likely to provide benefits that exceed those available from a random selection of country equities.

Interestingly, in comparing these numbers with ones from other published estimates, the correlations of returns between countries generally has been increasing over time. This seems to be a natural extension of the integration of world markets for goods and services, and reflects a more closely associated international economic community.

Using historical estimates for standard deviations and correlations, two efficient sets are constructed in Figure 20–4. In both cases the expected returns are based on each equity market's beta coefficient in order to reflect equilibrium pricing of these national market portfolios. The first efficient set is calculated with the assumption that investors cannot sell the securities short. The second assumes costless short selling with free use of the proceeds of the sale.

In both cases the benefits of diversification seem substantial, though the U.S. portfolio is relatively close to the efficient set due to the degree of diversification it offers investors. Nevertheless, the reduction in variability accompanying international diversification at most return levels is important to the investor. At the 15.6 percent return level (the optimal risky portfolio with a lending rate of 7 percent), the standard deviation of the portfolio

FIGURE 20–4   Efficient Sets of National Equity Portfolios

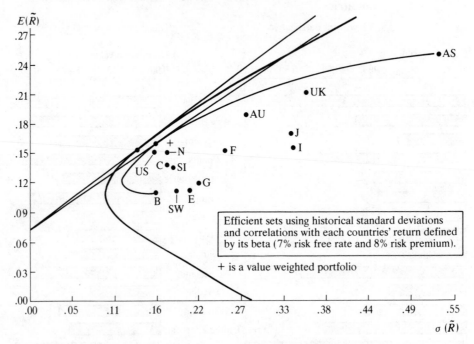

Efficient sets using historical standard deviations and correlations with each countries' return defined by its beta (7% risk free rate and 8% risk premium).

+ is a value weighted portfolio

		Optimal Risky Portfolio Proportions	
Country	*Code*	*No Short Sales*	*Short Sales Allowed*
Australia	AU	.035	− .635
Asia (Other)	AS	—	− .242
Belgium	B	—	− .486
Canada	C	—	1.450
Europe (Other)	E	—	− .542
France	F	.047	− .005
Germany	G	.054	.850
Italy	I	.043	.364
Japan	J	.074	.401
Netherlands	N	—	− .679
Sweden	SW	—	− .293
Switzerland	SI	—	− .219
United Kingdom	UK	.075	.428
USA	US	.672	.609
		1.000	1.000
$E(\tilde{R}_p)$		15.6%	15.1%
$\sigma(\tilde{R}_p)$		16.4	14.0

Source: Computed by MPS.

is 16.4 percent, or about 4 percentage points lower than the *average* standard deviation of the securities included in that particular portfolio. This portfolio offers a return that is .5 percent above that on the U.S. portfolio. With higher expected returns (say 18 percent in the figure) the benefits of a diversified portfolio over specialized investments in Japan, Other Asia, or the U.K. are much greater.

The efficient set with the short selling option is, of course, above and to the left of the curve when no short selling is allowed. A value-weighted portfolio also is shown in the figure to gain some perspective on the location of "international index funds" relative to the efficient set itself. The actual portfolio proportions for the best risky portfolio with and without short selling (at a 7 percent risk-free rate) are tabulated just below the figure.

While these results are computed from standard deviations and correlations relevant to a $ investor, the picture would look much the same for investors around the world. It is quite clear that diversification beyond any investor's national boundary is beneficial. The reduction in risk is essential for investors from countries with high variance stock markets. It is substantial for U.S. investors in spite of the fact that the U.S. market is a diversified one that includes almost half of the world's publicly held equities.

Diversification and Transaction Costs

A number of factors are cited as explanations for the low level of international diversification. Most pertain to the perceived illiquidity of many foreign national equity markets. They include:

1. Withholding taxes on foreign dividends.[12]
2. Unfamiliar and peculiar methods of making a market in a security.
3. High transaction costs due to the monopolistic nature of the market-making function in some foreign markets.
4. Barriers to the free movement of capital, or the possibility that such barriers may be established.
5. Trading hours are different from the home market.
6. Differences in accounting and reporting methods in foreign countries.

There is no doubt that these factors play a part in reducing the incentives investors have to internationalize their portfolios. Nevertheless, developments in the last five years have greatly reduced the importance of these factors. The London Stock exchange, in cooperation with NASDAQ, currently is engaging in an experimental dual-listing arrangement that makes trading in some securities open for 16 hours a day. Moreover, in late 1986 London substantially changed its operations to eliminate cumbersome trading practices (that had developed over centuries) and introduced systems that will enhance competition.

Japanese investment banking firms are buying seats on the NYSE to make it easier for them buy U.S. securities for their clients. Similarly, Merrill Lynch and other U.S. brokers hold memberships on the Tokyo Exchange to serve their U.S. clients and to attempt to garner a share of the flow of investment dollars from the large number of Japanese investors. Even governments now are realizing that restrictions on the flow of capital (particularly foreign capital) put their economies at a competitive disadvantage.

On the whole, the liquidity of the international equity market is substantial and is expanding very rapidly. The magnitude of the change has been fostered by the demands of the marketplace, and enabled by the efforts of the securities industry to meet the needs

---

[12]Taxation of foreign-held security dividends takes the form of a withholding tax. This rate depends on the investor's country and the country of the security. Typically, the rates do not vary widely. For example, a U.S. investor is subject to a 15 percent withholding tax on an investment in most countries.

of their clients. In many respects it's now as easy and beneficial to buy foreign securities as it is to buy over-the-counter stocks and bonds.

Beta Coefficients on Foreign Securities

If it is optimal to hold an internationally diversified portfolio, then it is necessary to identify the risk of a foreign security to determine which securities should be included in the portfolio. Are βs relevant and, if so, how should they be calculated?

An answer to the question depends in part on the extent of the segmentation of foreign security markets. If there were a perfectly free flow of capital internationally, it would be easy to construct the world-market portfolio (*w*) and determine the risk of individual securities by relating the return on the individual security over time with the rate of return on the world-market index. On the other hand, if an investor in the United States, say, is restricted primarily to investments in the U.S. stock market with only an occasional foray into a foreign security holding, then the risk of that foreign security could be determined by relating its return over time to the rate of return on the U.S. market index.

As mentioned in the prior section, the realistic situation is undoubtedly somewhere in between these two extremes but is leaning in the direction of integration of separate national markets.

The type of risk levels that one might get from an application of these approaches are presented in Table 20–4. There column (1) indicates the standard deviation of annual returns from a stock market index for each of the indicated domestic equity markets from the perspective of U.S. investors. Thus, an index of Australian common stocks shows a standard deviation of annual returns over the study period of 28.3 percent. The standard deviation of the world market portfolio as calculated was 15.4 percent. If, using historical returns, the rate of return on the Australian stock market index is regressed on the world index, the resulting beta coefficient is estimated to be 1.44 [column (3)]. Thus, the average Australian stock is 40 to 50 percent more risky than the average security in the entire world.

You should note that the U.S. equity market picks up about 50 percent of the total world equity market, so its relationship would have to be fairly close to the world index, since the world index is in large part determined by U.S. index. Thus, the β on the U.S. stock market is .99.

Column (2) in Table 20–4 gives comparable beta coefficients estimated from a regression of the country index returns on the U.S. market index. These values would be relevant to that investor with only an occasional foray into the international securities market.

Diversification, Using Multinational Firms

Given some of the costs of diversifying internationally, it may be possible to achieve some of the benefits of international diversification through the purchase of large firms that have their real-asset and liability structure spread among many countries. Their income flows come from all over the world, so they are by their nature diversified internationally.

Unfortunately, the stock market rates of return on multinational firms seem to track the U.S. stock market quite closely. A diversified portfolio of multinationals acts very

TABLE 20–4   Risk Levels of Indexes, *I*, of Stocks in Different Countries

Country	(1) Standard Deviation of Annual Returns $\sigma(\tilde{R})_1$	(2) β of Country Index Relative to U.S. Market Portfolio $\hat{\beta}_1^{US}$	(3) β of Country Index Relative to World Market Portfolio β_1^{w}
Australia	28.3%	1.13	1.44
Asia (Other)	52.0	1.92	2.20
Belgium	16.1	0.31	0.47
Canada	18.2	0.75	0.84
Europe (Other)	21.0	0.71	0.50
France	25.6	0.62	1.01
Germany	22.2	0.25	0.60
Italy	34.2	0.63	1.04
Japan	33.9	0.85	1.24
Netherlands	18.0	0.83	1.00
Sweden	19.4	0.42	0.50
Switzerland	18.8	0.53	0.80
U.K.	35.9	1.40	1.74
U.S.A.	16.3	1.00	0.99
EAFE	18.5	0.70	1.01
World	15.4	0.88	1.00

Source: Estimated from 16 years of annual returns (1970–85) except for Hong Kong (13 years) and Singapore and EAFE (14 years). Too few observations existed to compute a β on Mexican securities, though we can assure you it is quite high.

much like the U.S. stock market and not very much like the world stock market. For example, for 23 U.S.-based multinationals, Jacquillat and Solnik [1978] found that when the returns on a portfolio of these firms were regressed on the U.S. market index and other indexes of Germany, Switzerland, etc., the dominating explanatory variable was the U.S. market. No other market was statistically related to the portfolio of multinational firms. Apparently direct international diversification is much more rewarding than indirect diversification through dollar-based international companies.

Valuation of Foreign Securities

How are equilibrium prices established for foreign securities? The process is approximately the same as suggested in Chapters 12 to 16. Investors form expectations of cash flows derived from holding those securities and calculate an equilibrium-expected return that reflects the risk and risk–return trade-off associated with such an investment. But how are expected returns generated internationally?

If international financial markets were completely integrated, then the equivalent of an international capital-asset pricing model or arbitrage pricing model exists that governs the way in which equilibrium returns are set. In other words, securities' expected returns depend upon their beta coefficient (or coefficients, in the case of the arbitrage pricing model), and the international security market line (along which all securities would tend to fall in equilibrium) could be stated as:

(20–5)
$$E(\tilde{R}_i) = R_f + \beta_i^{w}[E(\tilde{R}_w) - R_f]$$

FIGURE 20–5   **The International Capital Asset Pricing Model**

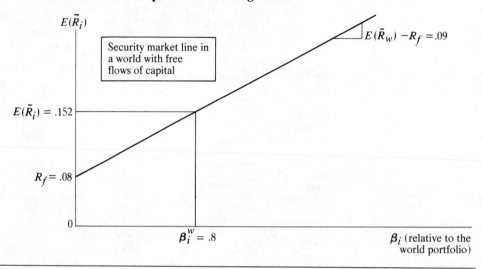

with β_i^w being the beta with reference to the world portfolio w. This is shown in Figure 20–5. The risk–return trade-off would have a slope that was given by the difference between the equilibrium-expected world-market portfolio return, $E(\tilde{R}_w)$, and the world risk-free rate of return, R_f. These figures might suggest an expected return of 15.2 percent on a security with a world β of .8, a world risk-free rate of 8 percent, and a market risk premium of .09, or 9 percent.

The equilibrium valuation of the ith (foreign or domestic) security then would be

(20–6)   *Valuation of a Foreign Security*

$$P_{i0}^e = \sum_{t=1}^{\infty} \frac{E(\tilde{D}_{it})}{(1 + E(\tilde{R}_i))^t}$$

with the discount rate as indicated in Equation (20–5). The numerator and denominator may be defined in terms of any currency; e.g., the U.S. dollar. The view of the Canadian investor would differ from this only to reflect the possibly different expected rate of change in the value of the currency. In real terms, the international CAPM or international arbitrage pricing model would be identical for all investors regardless of their domicile.

If capital markets are not *perfectly* integrated then there is a possibility that other factors may need to be incorporated in the expected-return configuration. For example, a Canadian investor in German securities faces a higher tax rate on dividends than does an Australian investor. The Canadian investor would then seem to require a higher pretax return in order to adjust for the rate at which he is taxed. The net result of this effect may be that fewer Canadian investors would find it optimal to invest in the German securities market. This would be a factor which could be incorporated into the international capital-asset pricing model that would determine expected returns, but would quickly make the model much more complex and beyond the scope of our initial discussion here.

FIGURE 20–6   **CREF's Performance from Foreign Investments in Equities during One Historical Period**

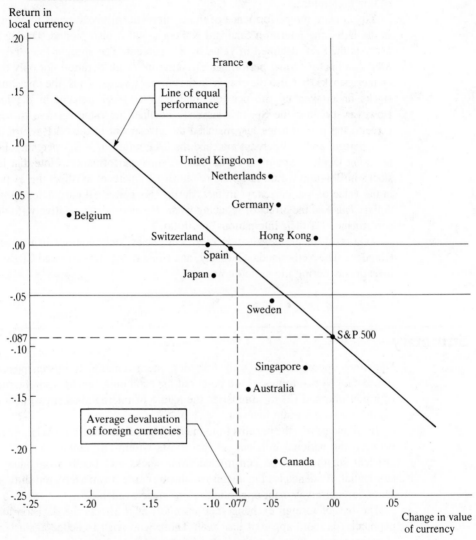

Success at Investing Internationally: An Example

College Retirement Equities Fund, a large New York–based pension fund, invests about 10 percent of its portfolio in international equities. CREF measures its performance in these endeavors by graphing the net returns in terms of the local currency against the extent of appreciation or depreciation of the currency value (relative to the dollar). An example of their calculation is displayed in Figure 20–6 with each point representing the portfolio of that country's equities. Thus, French equities increased in value by about 18 percent over the period but the franc declined in value by about 6 percent to offset part of this high return.

To compare the performance of these international investments to equity investments in the U.S., the return on Standard & Poor's 500 is also plotted. During this period of analysis the S&P declined in value by 8.7 percent. The straight line drawn through the S&P is a line of "equal performance" taking into consideration not only the local return on these stocks, but also the change in the currency value. Thus, the investment in Spanish stocks undertaken by the pension fund returned − .7 percent in the local currency. However, because the Spanish currency declined in value relative to the dollar by 8 percent, the performance just matched the investment in the S&P return index (that is, − .7 percent and −8 percent matched the S&P return of −8.7 percent). For that reason the point labeled "Spain" is *on* the line of equal performance. Note that investments in stocks in Belgium would have had to return 12.3 percent to offset the 21 percent decline in the value of that currency. In fact, during this period all currencies fell relative to the dollar. This had the effect of reducing what was otherwise a relatively (to the S&P) good performance for their international portfolio.

As a result of the devaluation of all currencies, only equities in France, The United Kingdom, The Netherlands, Germany, and Hong Kong outperformed CREF's U.S. equity investments during the period covered.

Summary

Numerous opportunities exist for investing internationally. In this chapter we have tried to accomplish two things: (1) to point out the economic benefit from internationalization of a portfolio and (2) to summarize the nature of international investment opportunities available to a domestic investor.

By all measures, the benefits from international diversification are large. The difference between the national efficient set that exists within any country and the international efficient set that can be constructed from stocks and bonds from many countries is substantial. Evidence leading to this conclusion comes from a leftward shift of the efficient set as foreign investment opportunities are made available.

The risk of foreign exchange-rate changes, as it affects the decision to invest internationally, is more apparent than real. Those who wish to hedge against exchange-rate changes can do so with little cost. Moreover, foreign exchange prices seem to move somewhat independently of each other, so the systematic risk associated with exposure to changes in currency prices is lower than the total variability of the price changes. Finally, to the extent that the investor is also a consumer, what is lost in the decline of the value of a foreign currency may be made up for in an increased level of purchasing power for goods and services produced in the country whose currency lost value.

The range of foreign national investment opportunities is at least as great as it is for U.S. and Canadian domestic investors. Firms in other countries issue stock, short-term commercial paper, and fixed-income securities that are, in many cases, traded on active exchanges. In addition, new securities have developed that allow firms and governments to issue bonds and notes denominated in currencies other than the home currency of the issuer.

Valuing international investment opportunities is done in a way that compares closely with the capital-asset pricing model. In the absence of any restrictions on investing, the equilibrium return on any security would be a linear function of the world-market portfolio. This would give rise to a world security market line with betas estimated with respect to the world portfolio. With restrictions on international capital market transactions (e.g., capital flow restrictions) the equilibrium structure of security prices could be more complicated.

References

Adler, Michael, and Dumas, Bernard. [1983] "International Portfolio Choice and Corporate Finance: A Synthesis." *Journal of Finance* (June).

Adler, Michael, and Simon, David [1986] "Exchange Risk Surprises in International Portfolios." *Journal of Portfolio Management* (Winter).

Agmon, T. [1972] "The Relations among Equity Markets: A Study of Share Price Comovements in the United States, United Kingdom, Germany and Japan." *Journal of Finance* (September).

Aliber, Robert Z. [1973] "The Interest Rate Parity Theorem: A Reinterpretation." *Journal of Political Economy* (November–December).

Bergstrom, Gary L. [1975] "A New Route to Higher Returns and Lower Risks." *Journal of Portfolio Management* (Fall).

Bergstrom, Gary L.; Koeneman, John K.; and Siegel, Martin J. [1982] "International Securities Markets." In *Readings in Investment Magement,* ed. Frank Fabozzi, Homewood, Ill.: Richard D. Irwin.

Bilson, John F. O. [1981] "The 'Speculative Efficiency' Hypothesis." *Journal of Business* (July).

Black, Fischer. [1974] "International Capital Market Equilibrium with Investment Barriers." *Journal of Financial Economics* (December).

Black, Fischer. [1978] "The Ins and Outs of Foreign Investment." *Financial Analysts Journal* (May–June).

Chance, Don M., and Ferris, Stephen P. [1985] "A Hedge Strategy for International Portfolios." *Journal of Portfolio Management* (Fall).

Cornell, Bradford. [1977] "Spot Rates, Forward Rates, and Market Efficiency." *Journal of Financial Economics* (August).

Cornell, W. Bradford, and Dietrich, J. Kimball. [1978] "The Efficiency of the Market for Foreign Exchange under Floating Exchange Rates." *Review of Economics and Statistics* (February).

Dornbusch, Rudiger. [1976] "Expectations and Exchange Rate Dynamics." *Journal of Political Economics* (December).

Errunza, Vihang, and Losq, Etienne. [1985] "International Asset Pricing under Mild Segmentation: Theory and Test." *Journal of Finance* (March).

Eun, Cheol, S., and Janakiramanan S. [1986] "A Model of International Asset Pricing with a Constraint on the Foreign Equity Ownership." *Journal of Finance* (September).

Giddy, Ian H. [1976] "An Integrated Theory of Exchange Rate Equilibrium." *Journal of Financial and Quantitative Analysis* (December).

Giddy, Ian H., and Dufey, Gunter. [1975] "The Random Behavior of Flexible Exchange Rates." *Journal of International Business Studies* (Spring).

Grauer, Frederick L. A.; Litzenberger, Robert H.; and Stehle, Richard E. [1976] "Sharing Rules and Equilibrium in an International Capital Market under Uncertainty." *Journal of Financial Economics* (June).

Grauer, Robert R., and Hakansson, Nils H. [1986] "Gains from International Diversification: 1968–85 Returns on Portfolios of Stocks and Bonds." Working Paper, Simon Fraser University (May).

Grubel, H. G. [1968] "Internationally Diversified Portfolios: Welfare Gains and Capital Flows." *American Economic Review* (December).

Heckerman, Donald. [1973] "On the Effects of Exchange Risk." *Journal of International Economics* (November).

Hodrick, R. [1981] "International Asset Pricing with Time-Varying Risk Premia." *Journal of International Economics* (November).

Ibbotson, Roger G.; Siegel, Lawrence B.; and Love, Kathryn S. [1985] "World Wealth: Market Values and Returns," *Journal of Portfolio Management* (Fall).

Isard, Peter. [1978] "Exchange Rate Determination: A Survey of Popular Views and Recent Models." *Princeton Studies in International Finance*.

Jacquillat, Bertrand, and Solnik, Bruno H. [1978] "Multinationals Are Poor Tools for Diversification." *Journal of Portfolio Management* (Winter).

Jorion, Philippe, and Schwartz, Eduardo. [1986] "Integration vs. Segmentation in the Canadian Stock Market." *Journal of Finance* (July).

Lee, W. Y., and Sachdeva, K. S. [1977] "The Role of the Multinational Firm in the Integration of Segmented Capital Markets." *Journal of Finance* (May).

Lessard, Donald R. [1976] "World, Country, and Industry Relationships in Equity Returns: Implications for Risk Reduction Through International Diversification." *Financial Analysts Journal* (January–February).

Levi, Maurice. [1978] "The Weekend Game: Clearing House vs. Federal Funds." *Canadian Journal of Economics* (November).

Levy, H., and Sarnat, M. [1970] "International Diversification of Investment Portfolios." *American Economic Review* (September).

Logue, Dennis; Sweeny, R. J.; and Willett, T. D. [1978] "Speculative Behavior of Foreign Exchange Rates during the Current Float." *Journal of Business Research* (December).

Magee, Stephen P. [1978] "Contracting and Spurious Deviations from Purchasing Power Parity." In *The Economics of Exchange Rates*, ed., Jacob Frenkel and Harry G. Johnson. Reading, Mass.: Addison-Wesley.

Makin, J. H. [1978] "Portfolio Theory and the Problem of Foreign Exchange Risk." *Journal of Finance* (May).

McCormick, Frank. [1979] "Covered Interest Arbitrage: Exploited Profits? Comment." *Journal of Economy* (April).

McDonald, John. [1973] "French Mutual Fund Performance: Evaluation of Internationally Diversified Portfolios." *Journal of Finance* (December).

McFarland, James; Pettit, R. R.; and Sung, S. [1982] "The Distribution of Foreign Exchange Price Changes: Trading Day Effects and Risk Measurement." *Journal of Finance* (June).

Papadia, F. [1981] "Forward Exchange Rates as Predictors of Future Spot Rates and the Efficiency of the Foreign Exchange Market." *Journal of Banking and Finance* (June).

Roll, R., and Solnik, B. [1977] "A Pure Foreign Exchange Asset Pricing Model." *Journal of International Economics* (May).

Senschak, A. J., and Beedles, W. L. [1980] "Is Indirect International Diversification Desirable?" *Journal of Portfolio Management*.

Solnik, Bruno. [1974] "An Equilibrium Model of the International Capital Market." *Journal of Economic Theory* (August).

Solnik, Bruno H. [1974] "Why Not Diversify Internationally?" *Financial Analysts Journal* (July–August).

Solnik, Bruno. [1982] "The Relation between Stock Prices and Inflationary Expectations: The International Evidence." CESA, Working Paper (August).

Solnik, B. [1983] "International Arbitrage Pricing Theory." *Journal of Finance* (May).

Solnik, Bruno H., and Nemeth, Eric. [1982] "Asset Returns and Currency Fluctuations." *CESA Working Paper (April)*.

Stapleton, R. C., and Subrahmanyam, M. G. [1977] "Market Imperfections, Capital Market Equilibrium, and Corporation Finance." *Journal of Finance* (May).

Stehle, Richard. [1977] "An Empirical Test of the Alternative Hypotheses of National and International Pricing of Risky Assets." *Journal of Finance* (May).

Stoll, H. R. [1972] "Causes of Deviations from Interest Rate Parity." *Journal of Money, Credit and Banking* (February).

Stulz, R. M. [1981] "A Model of International Asset Pricing." *Journal of Financial Economics* (December).

Stulz, R. M. [1981] "On the Effects of Barriers to International Investment." *Journal of Finance* (September).

Questions and Problems

1. The XYZ Company asks an independent investments consultant about international equities and whether or not the company's Investment Committee should consider them as an additional asset for the pension fund.

    a. Explain the rationale for including international equities in the equity portfolio.

    b. List arguments that can be made against international equity investment and briefly discuss their significance.

    CFA

2. Many have argued that foreign exchange risk constitutes the primary roadblock to international diversification of investment portfolios. Most often this is a reference to the "additional risk" inherent in investing in another country's currency. What three arguments can you offer that foreign exchange risk is not as serious an impediment as has been portrayed?

3. You are a U.S.-domiciled investor. Over the past year your West German investments have gone up by 17.4 percent. During that period however the mark/dollar exchange rate has changed from $.55 per mark to $.57 per mark. Allowing for the change in currency value, what has been your net ($-based) return?

4. The current spot rate for Japanese yen is 170 yen per U.S. dollar. The futures rate for a one-year contract is 165 yen per U.S. dollar. If the one-year risk-free interest rate in the United States is 6.4 percent, find the interest rate in Japan that implies interest rate parity.

5. The current spot rate for U.S. dollars in Japan is $.00588 per Japanese yen. The futures rate for a one-year contract is $.00606 per yen. If the one-year risk-free interest rate in the United States is 6.4 percent, find the interest rate in Japan that implies interest rate parity.

6. The formation of the European Economic Community has resulted in greater integration of the economies of European countries. What does this fact suggest about portfolio strategies that ought to be employed by:

    a. European investors.

    b. Non-European investors.

7. A perceptive money market fund portfolio manager on Wall Street notes that the annualized interest rate on six-month U.S. dollar deposits in London is $6^7/_{16}$ percent, while the rate for British sterling deposits is $8^1/_2$ percent. Explain why this interest rate differential may not present a profitable investment opportunity for the fund. Suppose the manager investigates the issue further, and finds that the spot price of sterling is $1.60 and the six-month forward rate is $158.5. Is one of these deposit accounts better than the other?

8. In 1985 and 1986 a market for Australian bonds grew rapidly in the United States. In part this may have been the result of brokers marketing thee bonds as "high interest rate secured" investment opportunities. In a sense these advertisements were correct since the bonds offered yields to maturity of 12 percent and more when comparable U.S. bonds were yielding 8 percent. On the other hand, it was not reasonable to suppose that U.S. investors would earn returns that were even close to 12 percent. Why do you think that was the case? If, at the time of these offerings, the spot price was $.71 for each Australian dollar, identify the lowest futures price for Australian dollars that would still imply the Australian bonds were a "good" investment opportunity for U.S. investors.

9. Cite a number of factors that would help to explain the relatively low level of international diversification, even in the presence of the significant level of risk reduction afforded by including foreign securities in a portfolio.

10. By the mid-1980s most U.S.-based portfolios that invested a portion of their funds internationally, did so by edict. That is, they simply decided that international investing was appropriate, and allocated 5 or 10 percent of the portfolio to the endeavor. Indicate why this allocation scheme is almost certain to be less than optimal. Briefly trace out a strategy for allocating the portfolio's funds that will serve to increase the portfolio's return or reduce its risk.

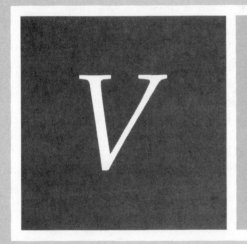

P A R T

V

MANAGING THE
INVESTMENT
PROCESS

CHAPTER

21

Investment Portfolio Management

Everyone with money to invest is faced with the problem of forming and managing a portfolio of financial assets. This is as true for an individual investor as it is for a large pension fund. Financial planning involves specifying goals and objectives, considering alternative strategies for accomplishing those objectives, and choosing a strategy for implementation. Indeed, these points have been covered throughout the book. In this chapter, we attempt to refine the analysis to take into account the complexities associated with "actual" securities markets (such as transactions costs) and "real" investors (who may have special requirements). In part, this requires us to reconsider how the investment process should be handled if some of the assumptions we have made don't hold perfectly.

The "Financial Planning Model" Developed So Far

A brief synopsis of the "financial plan" we have developed would be as follows: (1) estimate **security returns, standard deviations,** and **covariances** with the use of appropriate valuation models; (2) estimate the **efficient set of portfolios** that can be formed from the individual securities, and find the weights for the "optimal-risky portfolio"; (3) with the investor's preferences, or relative willingness to exchange risk for return, find the **utility-maximizing proportions** of invested wealth that should be allocated to the (*a*) risk-free security and (*b*) to each security in the optimal-risky portfolio.

This model was based on a number of assumptions and conclusions about the behavior of investors and the nature of the financial marketplace, including:

1. **Liquidity:** no transactions costs and all investors are price takers.
2. **Price continuity:** underlying supply and demand determine price.

645

3. **Fairness:** only price and time are used to descriminate between buyers and sellers.
4. **Divisibility:** securities can be traded in infinitely small units.
5. **Investor preferences:** are defined through expected return and standard deviation of return.
6. **A single investment period.**
7. **A risk-free security exists (or perfect short selling).**
8. **Competitive pressures move security prices toward underlying equilibrium values:** where markets are reasonably efficient, market prices tend to reflect public information, and there always is a tendency for security market prices to move toward their underlying equilibrium values (though, at any point in time, these market prices may not be equal to underlying values).

To some extent the validity or practicality of these assumptions has been addressed as the issue arose in the development of our approach to investing. For the most part the approach holds up quite well in practice. However, we will now consider further how certain realities of the marketplace might best be handled by practicing portfolio managers—large and small.

Applying the Model

Not all possible questions will be considered. In fact we concentrate on five questions, which are related to the above assumptions, as follows.

1. *The Active/Passive Management Question.* Should the portfolio be actively managed to attempt to "beat the market," or passively managed to attempt to duplicate the risk and return available on the market portfolio?
   Assumption at issue: **Are there really identifiable differences between market prices and underlying equilibrium values?**

2. *The Portfolio Revision Questions.* How frequently should the contents of the portfolio be examined for possible changes?
   Assumption at issue: **Is it sufficient to think of the portfolio choice problem as a one-period problem?**

3. *The Transactions Costs/Diversification Question.* In the presence of transactions costs, how diversified should the portfolio be?
   Assumption at issue: **Are transactions costs close enough to zero to buy what the investor views as the optimal-risky portfolio?**

4. *The Constraints Question.* Are investors only concerned about expected portfolio return and portfolio standard deviation, or are there other goals or objectives that need to be met?
   Assumption at issue: **Is the expected return/standard deviation of return model adequate?**

5. *The Manager Question.* Does it make sense for an investor to manage his or her own portfolio, or should a professional manager be used, and what kinds of professional managers are available?

Assumption at issue: **Do some investors have better access to information or a better means of using the available information than others?**

The Active/Passive Management Question

Investors have the opportunity to participate in securities markets with varying degrees of activity. Each must make choices regarding the time and effort to be devoted to portfolio management, the degree and nature of analysis of individual securities or groups of securities, and the process of portfolio choice based on the results of this analysis. For simplicity, we can think of the degree of active participation in terms of two opposite extremes: (*a*) purely **active,** and (*b*) purely **passive** portfolio management strategies. As you might guess, the choice of one or the other of these extreme strategies depends on the investor's beliefs about the pricing of securities and about one's comparative advantage in transacting in such markets.

Passive Management

For investors who believe that market prices so closely reflect underlying values that it is not possible to profit from the hunt for over- or underpriced securities, passive portfolio management is appropriate. This also would hold true for those investors who believe that, though under- and overpriced securities certainly exist, it is not possible to differentiate, ex ante, between the eventual "winners" and "losers."

Passive management refers to any attempt to construct a portfolio that mimics overall market returns. In the framework of the capital-asset pricing model, that means attempting to construct a portfolio that includes all marketable assets in proportion to their value in the marketplace. While this might seem like a trivial thing to accomplish, there are a number of practical impediments to the creation of this market portfolio.

First, it is not clear what assets should be included. As we discussed earlier in the book, assets have different degrees of marketability. Should the portfolio include real estate and closed (privately held) corporations? Even if theory helps to answer these questions, practical issues pertaining to the marketability of the asset create problems for someone attempting to assemble such a portfolio.

Second, to purchase a very broad portfolio sometimes requires a very small proportionate investment in many firms. With transactions costs this precludes an investor from assembling such a portfolio unless the investor has an enormous level of wealth to commit to the market.

Generally these problems are solved through the creation of mutual funds or other commingled funds (such as might be assembled by a professional money manager). With hundreds of millions and sometimes billions of dollars, these managers attempt to develop a portfolio that mimics a well-known stock market index. Two groups of "indexers" are very active and popular in today's market environment: index funds, and index managers.

Index Managers. Wells Fargo Investment Advisors (WFIA) manages over $60 billion for large pension funds and other groups with large amounts of money to invest. In the past decade or so they have adopted a strategy that attempts to duplicate as closely as possible the "performance" of the S&P 500. In their efforts to do this, for example, they now hold more than 10 million shares of IBM—equal to about 1.7 percent of the shares of IBM outstanding. Much of their trading is mechanical in nature (to track the weights of the index) and is done at a very low cost due to the large size of their transactions. In fact, costs are so low that they are able to charge some clients as little as $1/10$ of 1 percent of the amount of money managed. Most of the charge, it can be inferred, goes to cover expenses associated with accounting for client funds.

A number of other professional money managers have adopted this basic philosophy. Many of them, like WFIA, offer other services as well. Many of these other services, such as "portfolio insurance," allow clients to adjust the risk of the indexed portfolio to match their risk-aversion propensities. In other words, they provide a mechanism that allows investors to select their "borrowing or lending" proportions simultaneously with their investment in the market index.

The common characterstic of these managers, of course, is that they do not try to pick stocks that are likely to outperform others. Moreover, they do not attempt to time their entrance or exit from the market by holding cash positions for clients, or select a beta for the portfolio in view of their expectations for the performance of the market as a whole. In fact, by definition, the beta is identically 1.0, at least with respect to the index they are matching.

Index Funds.   An index fund is an open-end mutual fund that, like the index managers discussed above, attempts to match the performance of one or another closely followed stock market index. These funds are available to small investors with limited capital. A number of fund groups offer an index fund, along with their more traditional offerings of growth, income, balanced, or special situation funds. Vanguard First Index Investment Fund is one of the more well known of these.

As you might expect, the operating expenses, transactions costs, and management fees of index funds generally are less than those of other mutual funds that spend time and effort selecting individual securities or timing their movements into and out of the market.

To achieve its primary objective, an index fund does not need to "slavishly" replicate the precise composition of the index it seeks to follow. For one, the S&P 500 or the NYSE Index can be tracked quite accurately with the prudent use of 150 or 200 securities. For another, since we don't know exactly the makeup of the theoretical market portfolio, attempting to match the S&P 500 to within .01 percent seems to be a waste of time and, possibly, resources.

Active Management

Active management makes sense when an investor believes securities may be mispriced, and when someone (not necessarily the investor) can profit from the movement of market price toward the securities' underlying equilibrium value. The chapters on security analysis, of course, set forth the circumstances under which these conditions may exist. Of course, any strategy that attempts to capture benefits from market mispricing must rely upon a proportionally greater investment in the "undervalued" set of securities, and thus the investor is exposed to the possibility of investing in a portfolio that will perform worse than a passively managed portfolio. A reasonable way to represent this trade-off is shown in Figure 21–1.

FIGURE 21–1   **Two Basic Portfolio Management Styles**

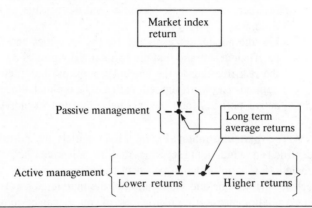

The successful active investor over the long run is able to generate greater-than-average returns, essentially in compensation for the manager's skills and efforts at selecting securities and timing market entry. Of course, only time will tell whether a given strategy for active portfolio management will pay off. Suffice it to say that there are a large number of actively managed portfolios in the marketplace, many with different strategies, and quite a few, of course, with a strategy based on approaches to valuation that are consistent with the principles of valuation presented in this book. Moreover, there is a large and active attempt to measure active management performance. Indeed, there are a number of "consulting" firms whose sole purpose is to periodically measure the ex post performance of active managers. The **measurement of performance** is the subject we treat in the last chapter of the book.

Active/Passive Combinations

It is not uncommon for professional money managers to allocate some of the funds they manage to a passive portfolio, with the rest being allocated to an actively managed portfolio. In the absence of being able analyze all available investment alternatives, it makes sense for the manager to specialize in analyzing a smaller subset of securities. As in any production process, specialization very well might lead to better results: in this case better estimates of the returns and risks on a limited number of individual securities. Unfortunately, the construction of portfolios formed from these specialized estimates has important costs in the form of *less diversification*. The "active/passive combination" provides a reasonable approach to handling the trade-off between the need for diversification and the desire to develop accurate estimates of security risk and return.

Application of the active/passive approach involves three steps—each of which, individually, has been discussed before:

1. Identify the expected return and standard deviation of the portfolio that the passive portion of wealth is to be invested in. Ordinarily the return would correspond to the equilibrium-expected return on the portfolio, since no attempt is made to value this portfolio independently of the market's valuation of it.

2. Identify the equilibrium or disequilibrium-expected returns, standard deviations, and correlations among the securities that are individually analyzed. Correlations between each of these securities and the passive portfolio also would have to be estimated.

3. Use the parameters estimates for the securities and the passive portfolio to form an efficient set, and find the optimal-risky portfolio to hold by drawing a ray from the risk-free rate to the tangency point on the efficient set. The weights for this optimal-risky portfolio will indicate the optimal allocation between the passive and active portions, and the optimal allocation to individual securities in the active component.

A four-part illustration (Figure 21–2) depicts the portfolio of an investor who has identified eight individual securities that are "mispriced" to go along with a passive portion, labeled *M*. The information pertinent to the analysis is presented in the form of: (*a*) the security market line and the location of the individual securities relative to the SML; (*b*) the correlation matrix (the covariances, of course, can be computed from the correlations), the standard deviations, and returns; (*c*) the efficient set (calculated with the parameter values using the **Modern Portfolio Strategies** program) along with the optimal-risky portfolio; and (*d*) the optimal weights consistent with point *p**.

In this case the optimal portfolio consists of a 27 percent investment in the passive portfolio. Note that, given the standard deviations and correlations, the optimal-risky portfolio has a somewhat higher standard deviation than the passive portfolio alone, but a substantially higher return. This ordinarily is the type of trade-off one might expect. The beta of this portfolio is .998, so it duplicates the market risk of the passive portfolio. It is also of interest that the optimal portfolio includes security *G,* which offers the same return as the passive component but with a larger standard deviation. Its value to the portfolio is due to *G*'s low correlation with the other securities, including *M*. Security *D,* which is *underpriced* given its return, is not included in the optimal-risk portfolio.

Of course, the success of this portfolio strategy depends on the analyst's ability to forecast, more accurately than the rest of the market, the returns and risks of these eight securities. If this can be accomplished, the benefits to the portfolio from better performance may be enough to distinguish this portfolio manager from all others.

Variants of the Active/Passive Strategy

There are two strategies used in practice that are closely related to that outlined above. One strategy decides upon the allocation to the active component of the portfolio before the individual securities are analyzed. Obviously, this approach must yield results that are less than optimal since the allocation between the two components does not depend upon the estimated risks and returns of the individual securities analyzed. On the other hand, because this strategy does not require estimates of the return and standard deviation of the passive portfolio component, the management problem can be broken into two completely separate parts. There may be valid management reasons for adopting this approach. A pension fund, for example, can allocate 75 percent of its portfolio to a passive manager, such as Wells Fargo Investment Advisors, and the rest to a different manager whose speciality is finding a limited number of undervalued individual securities.

The other strategy is more complex in that it allows the manager leeway to form

FIGURE 21–2 Optimal Active/Passive Portfolio Strategies

(a) Risk and return and the security market

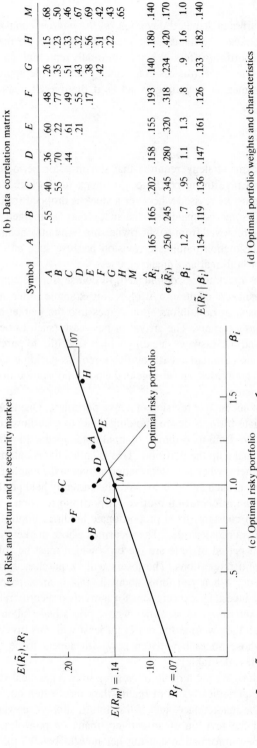

(b) Data correlation matrix

Symbol	A	B	C	D	E	F	G	H	M
A		.55	.40	.36	.60	.48	.26	.15	.68
B			.55	.70	.22	.77	.35	.23	.50
C				.44	.61	.49	.51	.33	.46
D					.21	.55	.43	.32	.67
E						.17	.38	.56	.69
F							.42	.31	.42
G								.22	.43
H									.65
M									
$\hat{R}_i$	.165	.165	.202	.158	.155	.193	.140	.180	.140
$\sigma(\tilde{R}_i)$	.250	.245	.345	.280	.320	.318	.234	.420	.170
β_i	1.2	.7	.95	1.1	1.3	.8	.9	1.6	1.0
$E(\tilde{R}_i\mid\beta_i)$	.154	.119	.136	.147	.161	.126	.133	.182	.140

(c) Optimal risky portfolio

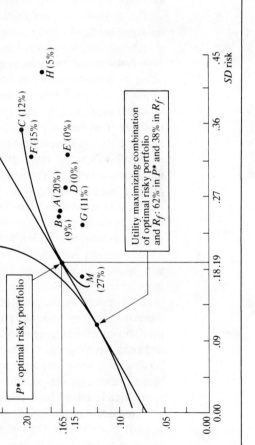

(d) Optimal portfolio weights and characteristics

Investment weights		Portfolio characteristics
A	.203	$\hat{R}_p = .165$
B	.091	$\sigma(\tilde{R}_p) = .190$
C	.124	
D	.000	$\beta_p = 1.00$
E	.000	
F	.145	$E(\tilde{R}_p\mid\beta_p) = .14$
G	.114	
H	.052	
M	.271	
	1.000	

disequilibrium estimates of the return and standard deviation *on the passive component as well*. Such attempts, of course, mean the manager is attempting to time the market by forecasting the returns the market portfolio offers. Whether this really represents passive management or not is disputable, but it nevertheless constitutes a reasonable approach to portfolio management when the manger is willing to act as if the overall market is under- or overpriced.

The Revision Question

Even a passive portfolio management strategy requires that the investor periodically consider revising the contents of an investment portfolio. An index fund which tracks the S&P 500 Index, for example, must be revised whenever a stock is dropped from the index and a new one added. Also, some companies in the index may be merged with other companies, go bankrupt, or be removed from public ownership. And major changes in the investor's personal financial situation requires a revision because such an event alters the investor's overall level of both real and financial assets.

The portfolio revision problem is much more complicated, of course, for the actively managed portfolio. Professional managers of these portfolios, for example, often make investment decisions on a daily basis, as new information comes into the market or as cash flows to and from the portfolio's owners. The arrival of new cash (such as occurs when dividend payments are received) necessitates deciding which securities to purchase to maintain a fully invested portfolio. Similarly, cash outflows require deciding which securities to sell to generate cash. In both cases, any change in the portfolio's proportionate holdings constitutes a portfolio revision.

There are two developments that necessitate revision of active portfolios. One is when the portfolio's actual holdings deviate from its desired holdings, due to cash flows or to the portfolio having "wandered away" from its original, optimal holdings due to relative price changes in the securities that make up the portfolio. This is called the **rebalancing motive** for portfolio revision. The other is when new information arrives in the marketplace and alters the investor's expectations in such a way as to make the currently held portfolio no longer desirable. This is called the **information motive** for portfolio revision.

Rebalancing portfolios to reattain constant, fixed proportionate holdings implies that you should "Cut your gains, but let your losses ride." The securities whose market values have increased the most in a given period of time are the ones which must be sold in order to restore the original portfolio proportions. The losers will be purchased in additional quantities with the proceeds. When you think about it, this is an appropriate portfolio revision rule, provided the investor's expectations for individual security returns and risks have not changed in the interim. The securities whose prices have fallen will now be even more undervalued than they were at the outset (at least with *this* investor's perceptions), and the securities whose prices have risen now will appear to be more appropriately priced (and thus are less desirable).

Pure portfolio rebalancing revisions are not terribly interesting from a practical standpoint if one's expectations change periodically, as in reality they most often do. New information constantly arrives in the marketplace, and if this information is relevant to security valuation, it may warrant the revision of an actively managed portfolio. For example, if an investor receives new information causing her now to believe that the expected return on a security is 40 percent per annum instead of the 25 percent she originally forecast, she should recalculate the weights of the optimal-risky portfolio.

In revising for rebalancing and information motives, both the cost of transacting and the effect of income taxes must be considered. There is no simple model that can be used to determine when to revise and when not to based on these considerations, for they differ from investor to investor. However, there are some simple ground rules that make this determination easier: (1) avoid revisions so minor that they cause the portfolio to incur transaction costs that are disproportionately high; (2) invest dividend receipts in a time deposit or money market fund until the cash accumulated allows you to purchase a reasonable amount of a security, thus controlling costs (some mutual funds offer the convenience of reinvestment of dividend income in new fractional shares at no transaction cost, and this is a big boon to the smaller investor); (3) wherever possible, time portfolio revisions so that gains and losses can be optimally liquidated for tax purposes.

In general, however, the reduction in transactions costs on large trades has been so great that portfolio managers with hundreds of millions of dollars under management normally can afford to trade whenever information flows or rebalancing calls for a revision. For these portfolios the costs of transacting have been reduced to between 5¢ and 10¢ a share, or less than 1/8 of a point of the security's price.

The Diversification Question

There are two reasons for holding a less-than-perfectly diversified portfolio. One is transaction costs. For both active and passive portfolio management strategies, a small amount of investable wealth simply cannot be feasibly applied to holding the market portfolio, m. By reducing the number of securities held, one can save transaction costs but lose some of the benefits of diversification. For very small amounts of wealth, one viable alternative is to use mutual funds to achieve inexpensive diversification. Clearly, index funds (as mentioned earlier) are an attractive means of investment for the very small investor. Alternatively, there are a number of simplified portfolio selection models based on portfolio theory, which allow the small investor to invest directly in individual securities without incurring excessive transactions costs. One such approach, discussed in Jacob [1974], involves using the market model and knowledge of individual security beta values to select the best-diversified portfolio of N securities. The investor may choose the value of N which is consistent with the level of wealth to be invested. Thus, an investor with only $5,000 to invest in securities might choose a value of N equal to 3 or 4, while an investor with $10,000 to invest might choose a value of N equal to 6 or 7.

While the evidence we discussed in Chapter 7 implied that a little diversification goes a long way—i.e., that holding 15 or 20 stocks reduced the portfolio's risk to close to that of the market portfolio—transaction costs, *especially* for small portfolios can be substantial. An obvious way to reduce transaction costs is to reduce the frequency of trading. The disadvantage to this is that new information—if not acted upon—could have deleterious effects on the portfolio's value.

The second reason for holding a less-than-perfectly diversified portfolio is to gain advantage from the selection of mispriced securities; i.e., when actively managing the portfolio. An active stock selection strategy, for example, requires the investor to give up some attainable level of diversification. For this reason, the active portfolio must be evaluated, taking into account its standard deviation of returns. Of course, other things being constant, the more the portfolio is concentrated in securities estimated to be mispriced, the less diversified it is and the larger its standard deviation of returns.

The Constraints Question

Constraints on the portfolio management activity may arise, as noted earlier, from personal considerations unique to a particular investor, or they may arise from externally imposed realities and/or laws and regualtions. Whatever, their source, it is possible to identify several types of constraints. These are constraints on: (*a*) **cash flows** and their application, (*b*) **portfolio porportionate holdings,** (*c*) **eligible securities,** (*d*) the **portfolio's time horizon.** Each of these is briefly examined below.

Cash Flows

Usually cash flow constraints involve an attempt by the investor to ensure that a certain minimum level of portfolio income will be available for consumption purposes at regular intervals. Thus, one type of cash flow constraint might require that the portfolio generate an expected flow of income equal to or greater than, say, $1,000 per month. This can be accomplished by investing in individual securities or mutual funds having expected future dividend payments adequate to meet this objective.

Cash flow constraints might also arise from tax considerations. An investor in a very high tax bracket may not wish to incur additional tax liabilities through the realization of periodic interest or dividend income, and thus might impose a constraint that the portfolio is to generate no current income at all. This could be accomplished by holding shares in common stocks paying no dividends, for example. The capital gains (if any) from such a portfolio do not incur a tax liability until realized; hence, the investor could defer the tax until such time as his marginal tax rates were reduced, or to take advantage of the delay in tax payments.

Another reason a cash flow constraint might arise is that the investor has no initial lump sum to invest in securities and so must invest small amounts on a regular basis over a number of years. In this case, the constraint is externally imposed (by a lack of funds), and applies to cash inflows (as opposed to outflows in the form of income). This constraint may limit available choices (at least at the outset) to mutual funds, passbook savings accounts, or a few shares of one or two common stocks.

Portfolio Proportionate Holdings

The most obvious reason to establish constraints on portfolio proportionate holdings is to ensure adequate diversification. An investor may decide, as was mentioned earlier, to hold no more than 10 percent (or some other percentage) of his funds in the securities of any one issuer. Alternatively, if the investor in question is employed in the auto industry, he may—for reasons that relate to his *whole* portfolio of real and financial assets—restrict himself to holding, say no more than 2 percent of his funds in the securities of auto and steel firms and their suppliers.

Constraints on proportionate holdings may also be applied to set a floor on the amounts invested in certain securities or industries. To ensure adequate liquidity, the investor might require that he hold at least 50 percent of his funds in Treasury bills (or another risk-free asset) at all times. Or, he might have a target of investing at least 10 percent of his funds in foreign stocks and bonds, in order to achieve a minimum level of international diversification.

Open-end mutual funds (discussed later in this chapter) are required under the Investment Company Act of 1940 to hold no more than 5 percent of their funds in the shares of any one firm, and to own no more than 10 percent of the shares outstanding of any firm. This constraint is imposed by federal law and is designed, ostensibly, to ensure that both minimum diversification levels are achieved and that the fund behaves as *an investor* and does not attempt to exercise *control* over the companies whose shares it holds.

Eligible Securities

Most often, institutional investors—such as bank trust departments, pension funds, and mutual funds—have what is called an "eligible securities list" or an "authorized securities list." This list, usually approved by an investment committee of top management and periodically revised, specifies which securities may be purchased or held in the portfolio. In the case of bonds, often the authorized list includes any bond with a specified rating (say, Baa in Moody's) or higher. In the case of common stocks, only those stocks that the firm's security analysts have studied and believe to offer a risk–return combination consistent with the portfolio's objectives will be included. Sometimes, too, the eligible list will exclude (for social policy reasons, say) any security issued by an organization with objectives or interests held to be offensive. The eligible securities list may also exclude certain types of securities for tax or other reasons. For example, tax-exempt institutional investors would obviously wish to exclude municipal bonds from consideration.

Individual investors might also find it desireable to establish constraints on the types of securities to be held in the portfolio. These constraints can be used in conjunction with constraints on the portfolio's proportionate holdings to ensure adequate diversification and relatively efficient portfolio management.

Portfolio Time Horizon

Strictly speaking, the selection of an appropriate time horizon within which to manage one's portfolio is less a constraint than it is a question of matching up the portfolio's objectives with the investor's unique needs. If the investor is an open-end mutual fund facing the possibility that anyone holding shares in the fund may present them to the fund for liquidation at any point in time, the mutual fund's management may seek to manage the underlying securities portfolio so that it includes securities with short maturity or high marketability. Alternatively, if the investor is a life insurance company with predictable long-run cash outflows and with no expectations of sudden withdrawals of funds from the portfolio, it can invest in such things as privately placed bonds (for which there is no organized secondary market), knowing that its time horizon is long (and its need for short-term liquidity slight).

The Manager Question

Most investors face the ultimate decision of whether to manage their own security portfolios or hire someone else to do it (e.g., a mutual fund manager or professional money manager). We have already discussed ways in which an individual might proceed to manage his own portfolio. Under what conditions will it pay to hire a manager instead? To answer this question, let's look at the types of professional money management available.

Since the 1950s, and particularly in the late 1970s and early 1980s, there has been a proliferation of professional money management organizations worldwide. Essentially, these organizations can be divided into two groups, although in practice the groups tend to blend together. The first group consists of those firms or individuals who **separately manage** the investment portfolios of individuals according to the needs and preferences of that investor. Financial planners, money managers, and bank and thrift institutions' trust departments cater to individuals who seek separately managed portfolios and have significant levels of investable funds to be able to afford the fees charged for this service. (From a practical standpoint, one generally has to have well over $100,000 in investable funds before this type of professional management is economically feasible.) The other group of managers operate with **commingled funds** (that is, they pool the funds of a number of investors into one professionally managed portfolio). These managers include mutual funds (and their various special types such as bond funds, real estate investment trusts (REITs), common-stock funds, and money market funds), pension funds, and bank and thrift institution's commingled trust funds.

Given the variety of professional management mechanisms available, it is not surprising that not all managers try to accomplish the same thing. However, there are four key services which some or all managers attempt to furnish:

- They may attempt to provide active stock selections and/or market timing services.
- They may provide portfolio diversification services.
- They may "create" new securities or engage in instrument intermediation that creates a new and desirable financial asset (i.e., mutual funds turn a portfiolio of common stocks into a mutual fund share) having greater marketability than the securities in the portfolio.
- They may manage a flow of cash or securities for the investor or perform other clerical duties that are necessary for receiving investment returns, monitoring firms' decisions for the benefit of shareholders, and otherwise protecting investor holdings.

In the remaining parts of this chapter we discuss specific types of professional managers and the funds they manage in order to offer some insights into what these managers do and why an investor might choose to invest in one or more of the portfolios they manage.

Types of Professionally Managed Funds

Open-End Mutual Funds

There are two basic types of mutual funds. **Closed-end mutual funds** (discussed later in this chapter) have a fixed number of mutual fund shares outstanding, and those shares change hands at a market-determined price. Closed-end funds constitute an investment opportunity that is, in most respects, similar to other common stocks. **Open-end mutual funds** are entities that more or less continuously issue or redeem shares at a price that reflects the net asset value of the portfolio held by the fund. Thus, as investors wish to purchase more mutual fund shares, the quantity of money flowing into the mutual fund for portfolio investment expands. Investors in the funds pay a price which precisely reflects the net asset value of the portfolio held at the point the funds are deposited in the account. Those who wish to liquidate their investment in the mutual fund do so by accepting a price equal to the net asset value on the day the shares are redeemed by the fund. In this section we look at open-end funds.

For a number of reasons, mutual funds have experienced substantial growth in the period since World War II. Total assets in mutual funds at the end of 1960 approximated $17 billion. By the early 1970s this figure rose to $60 billion and remained constant until the late 1970s and early 1980s, when there was a further substantial flow of money into these mutual funds. There are a large variety of stock and bond funds outstanding. Many of these funds tend to specialize. They provide a diversified portfolio of securities within an investment category. An example would be a specialized gold or metals fund which purchases the common stocks of firms that are involved in the basic-metals markets. Other funds may specialize in municipal bonds, growth stocks, high-yielding preferred stocks, or stocks issued by firms located in countries in Asia, for example.

Most funds are managed by a **mutual fund management organization** that creates, distributes, and manages a group of funds with a variety of characteristics. Ordinarily the management firm is a privately held company or a closed corporation. However, in recent years a few of the larger management companies have gone public or have merged with publicly held companies. As in any firm, the management company establishes a set of investment policies consistent with the goals of the funds it directs. In turn, the mutual fund shareholders benefit from the implementation of policies set up to achieve the goals of the fund. For the most part, the larger management companies offer a broad range of funds that appeal to a cross-section of investors. A number of managers offer more than 15 different types of funds, and Fidelity Investments offers more than 60.

The management company makes its profit by charging an advisory fee or management fee to the fund itself. This cost is borne by the fund's shareholders, and includes the cost of custodial services and audit fees, and decision making costs associated with management of the portfolio. Fund shareholders also pay all transactions costs incurred in buying and selling securities. There is considerable variation in the management expenses experienced by different mutual fund management companies. A fund that has relatively rapid portfolio turnover and a very active management company which attempts to find undervalued securities or to engage in market timing is a fund that, in general, could be expected to create fairly high expenses. Often the total of all expenses associated with

TABLE 21–1   Expense Ratios for Categories of Mutual Funds

Average Expense Ratios

Fund Objective	Highest 10%	Lowest 10%	All Funds
Stock funds	1.65%	0.47%	1.02%
Bond funds	1.60	0.52	0.96
Municipal bond funds	1.37	0.44	0.79
Money market funds	1.08	0.39	0.68
Size of Fund			
Less than $50 million	1.71%	0.54%	1.13%
$50–250 million	1.24	0.50	0.83
More than $250 million	0.97	0.36	0.63

Note: Sample excludes funds with expense ratios of 2 percent or more.

Source: Prepared by Vanguard Statistical Services Department, using data from Wiesenberger Investment Companies Services, *Mutual Funds Panorama*, December 31, 1980, as presented in Blume and Friedman [1982], p. 516. Reprinted by permission from *Encyclopedia of Investments*, © 1979 by Warren, Gorham & Lamont Inc. All rights reserved.

managing a fund can be as high as 1 to 2 percent or more of the market value of the fund per year. Average figures for such expenses are suggested in Table 21–1.

As mentioned above, mutual funds purport to offer the following services: (*a*) **diversification,** (*b*) **expertise in stock selection and market timing,** (*c*) **investment intermediation and liquidity,** and (*d*) **custodial care.** Let's examine each briefly.

Diversification. This is the major advantage mutual funds can offer to investors; an advantage that is particularly important to those with limited funds to invest. A well-diversified portfolio, that could not be held directly by the small investor due to excessive transactions costs, can be purchased from a mutual fund that holds 50, 100, or even 200 different securities.

Expertise in Stock Selection and Timing. Often, mutual funds convey the impression (or the fact) that their managers have analytical abilities allowing them to either time their entry into the market (or adjust their beta coefficients up and down to accomplish the same thing), or select undervalued securities in a manner that generates superior returns for fund shareholders. This is an issue we will take up explicitly in Chapter 22, but it is clear by the nature of their operations and the time and effort spent on advisory services and employing people in analysis that many funds expect to be able to generate superior returns. The exceptions are index funds, of course.

Investment Intermediation and Liquidity. Funds are also often able to take positions in investment opportunitites that create an increased level of liquidity for the fund holders. Essentially, mutual funds package a portfolio of individual securities together, some of which may be relatively illiquid and thin, and repackage that portfolio into a mutual fund share which is liquid, easily converted into cash, and always marketable.

Custodial Care. Mutual funds also offer a significant advantage of caring for the securities portfolio of the investor. In other words, they do all those things which are necessary to manage the pieces of paper that are part of security investment. They handle all cash exchanges, dividend reinvestment plans, accounting for the securities themselves, and updating the bookkeeping and tax records that each investor needs. Many make arrangements for the investor to be able to make regular (monthly) accumulations to fund shares, or regular withdrawals of money through the periodic sale of fund shares.

Differences between Funds. Because of the fact that mutual funds provide diversified portfolios of securities, many people think that each mutual fund within a given category is fairly equivalent to other mutual funds in the same category. On the contrary, within broad categories, mutual funds can differ substantially. The nature of a portfolio and the degree to which it may be relatively concentrated in a limited number of industries or investment categories are some of the ways that they differ. These differences are reflected in the level of mutual fund risk, which may also vary substantially. Mutual fund betas are computed and available to the investor from organizations that monitor the characteristics and performance of mutual funds, such as Weisenberger's Investment Company Service.

Mutual Fund Returns. The returns to holders of mutual funds come in three forms: **dividend distributions, capital gain distributions,** and **increases (decreases) in net asset value.**

1. **Dividend distributions** arise from the mutual fund passing through to its shareholders all dividend payments made by firms whose shares are included in the fund's portfolio. These distributions are taxed (subject to exclusions) at the shareholder's ordinary income tax rate.
2. **Capital gain distributions** are the result of *realized* gains and losses on security transactions arising within the portfolio. These must also be passed through to the fund's shareholders, and they are taxed in the same way as gains and losses of directly held securities.
3. **Increases (decreases) in net asset value** are the result of *unrealized* gains and losses on portfolio holdings. They are not taxed until realized.

There seems to be a tendency among most mutual fund managers to "clean up" the portfolio to even out capital gain distributions from one year to the next. Thus, a fund with sizable realized gains during a given calendar year may sell some of its losing positions at the year's end in an attempt to equalize this year's distributions with next year's. This may help the investor by reducing the number of "surprises" the investor is faced with that adversely affect tax planning.

Mutual fund shares may be easily purchased dirctly through the management company's sales force, or through a brokerage house. A loading fee is usually charged (most of which goes to the sales representative) for this initial purchase. Such a charge effectively reduces the quantity of funds invested. The fee may range from 8 percent of the amount invested to 0 percent. Those mutual funds charging nothing are called (not surprisingly) *no-load* mutual funds. Generally, no-load funds will have a somewhat higher management fee to offset the absence of the load fee. Of course, because the load fee can be a substantial porportion of the amount invested, the investor would not place funds available for a short period in a fund with a high-load fee.

Information is widely available for most mutual funds. Weisenberger's *Investment Companies Service* is a publication that does a good job of explaining the various characteristics of mutual funds; it tracks their individual record of performance and supplies the investor with information on each fund's management fees and load charges.

There are over 1400 open-end mutual funds available in the United States, of which 350 are money market funds (to be discussed in the next section). Excluding money market funds, open-end funds now manage over $300 billion worth of securities for investors. There is no doubt that open-end mutual funds have contributed significantly to the efficiency and liquidity of the market, by making it possible for small or inexperienced investors to take investment positions that otherwise would not be available to or suitable for them.

Money Market Funds

Money market funds are no-load, open-end mutual funds which invest in money market securities. They pool the assets of many investors to provide a means for participation in Treasury bills, negotiable certificates of deposit, commercial paper, and other money market securities. The primary reason such pooling of funds is an efficient mechanism for allowing investors to take part in such financial opportunities is that these securities are issued in relatively large denominations. Most are issued in denominations in excess of $10,000, and some have denominations in excess of $1 million. The pooling of funds thus allows efficient and effective purchase of such instruments by investors with limited funds.

In addition, while less important (due to the low risk of default), the pooling of funds allows for effective diversification. There have been times in the past where defaults, or at the very least, scares of defaults have occurred that have resulted in considerable loss of value on some of these instruments.[1]

Money market funds are of fairly recent origin. Prior to 1974, they did not exist. They seem to have been created in the 1970s primarily as a result of sharply increasing interest rates that placed the individual investor at a substantial disadvantage in seeking equilibrium returns in fairly safe investments (over and above the Federal Reserve Board's Regulation Q cap on interest rates paid by banks and thrift institutions). The resulting growth of money market mutual funds has been nothing short of phenomenal. Assets under management now are in excess of $250 billion.

A number of organizations issue money market mutual funds. Financial institutions, such as bank trust departments, can organize and put together a money market mutual fund. Brokerage houses have also put such funds together for their clients. In addition, some large money market mutual funds have been organized, maintained, and operated by existing equity mutual funds management groups. The particular advantages of the

---

[1]For example, Penn Central had a substantial amount of commercial paper outstanding at the time of its financial problems and ultimate bankruptcy. Some of this commercial paper declined substantially in value, as a result. Though the entire commercial paper market declined in value at roughly the same time, a diversified money market fund that would have held other types of money market securities as well would have been partially insulated from this decline in value.

money market mutual funds are that they are immediately liquid and have low operating costs. Effectively, they duplicate the advantages of the deposit accounts held by individual investors at banks and thrift institutions, without causing those investors to forego the higher interest income available on large-denomination money market securities.

Different money market funds offer different yields. The chief sources of variation in yields offered are differences in maturity and differences in the particular types of securities held. It is possible to manage a money market fund that has an average maturity which is as short as two to three weeks, for example. Other funds might have average maturities as long as three or four months. Each fund's management selects a particular average maturity and a particular mix of securities—such as Treasury bills, commercial paper, bankers' acceptances, or Eurodollar deposits—which it views as best, and then passes along to the individual shareholders the returns which are generated. Since interest rates can differ, depending on the type of instrument and its maturity, it is clearly possible for different funds to offer different returns.

Closed-End Mutual Funds

Closed-end funds, or closed-end mutual funds, differ from other funds we have discussed in that the number of share units that back the portfolio of securities held in the fund is fixed. The number of shares outstanding can be altered only through a new, formal issue of the fund's securities. Unlike open-end funds, shares of a closed-end fund must be purchased from other investors who have made the decision to sell.

The prices of closed-end fund shares reflect the relative supply of, and demand for, the shares of the closed-end fund corporation. There can be substantial differences between the estimated net asset value of the portfolio of securities held by the fund and the per share value at which the closed-end fund shares actually trade. Presumably, there is a reason for this differential. In the past, there have been many cases in which the differential has persisted for years, and frequently has been as high as 15 to 25 percent.

At the present time, there are approximately 70 closed-end funds whose shares are traded publicly on either a listed exchange or over-the-counter. In the aggregate these funds manage less than $10 billion of investor wealth, and so are small relative to their open-ended counterparts. There is a strong tendency for closed-end funds to specialize in certain types of securities. Japan Fund, which did very well by concentrating in the stocks of Japanese firms, was one of the largest and best known until its conversion into an open-end fund.

Real Estate Investment Trusts

Real Estate Investment Trusts (REITs) are closed-end mutual funds that concentrate their investment portfolios in real estate holdings. Like mutual funds, they are conduits for investing, and are not operating companies. Thus, the typical REIT would passively purchase real estate in the hope that the (separate) operation and management of the real estate venture itself would generate profits flowing to the REIT's shareholders. As long as REITs operate in this manner, they are considered to be "trusts" by the Internal Revenue Service and incur no tax liability (the taxes are paid by the REIT's shareholders).

Like mutual funds, REITs have stated objectives that define the form of real estate investments they tend to concentrate on. For the most part, REITs are either equity trusts—investing equity capital in real estate ventures—or are mortgage trusts—investing in real estate by holding a mortgage on the property.

REITs are a relatively recent entrant to the investment scene, due to a delay in the achievement of the "trust" classification. However, they grew rapidly during the boom in real estate in the 1960s and then fell in popularity just as rapidly during the rise in interest rates and subsequent decline in real estate values in the late 1970s. Many of the problems of REITs stemmed from excessive leverage of their real estate ventures, leading to substantial negative cash flows as interest rates rose. However, a second significant contributing factor was the lack of complete separation of the real estate management and operations from the fund itself. Trust managers were often able to create ancillary activities that legally could engage in real estate operations. This led to conflicts of interest (a component of "agency costs" discussed previously) that made REITs a questionable investment vehicle. A REIT is unlike a mutual fund, of course, since in the latter there is a complete separation of the fund and the company in which the fund holds shares.

In spite of these problems, some REITs continue to exist. The idea of a fund of real estate investments is a viable one. Such funds do offer diversification services into a set of opportunities—the real estate market—that is generally not open to small investors (except through holding savings deposits of thrift institutions or GNMA pass-through securities) and is available to large investors only in lumpy (nondiversifiable) and illiquid forms.

The only viable alternatives to REITs currently available are real estate limited partnerships. These contractual arrangements offer some of the services of REITs (but generally not diversification) and have some of the traditional REIT problems of conflicts of interest between owners and managers.

Bank Commingled Funds

Trust departments of banks and thrift institutions offer to individuals or corporations investment management which commingles the funds of the individuals who are party to the trust relationship. In the broadest sense, the idea of commingling the funds of many individuals can be compared with the creation of a mutual fund share. In both cases, participants share in the total return of the fund in the form of cash dividends, interest payments, and capital appreciation. Because pooled or commingled funds carry many of the characteristics of a mutual fund, they have some of the mutual funds' advantages. They can offer, for example, a diversified portfolio of investment opportunities, as well as (perhaps) expertise in the area of analysis and timing that may lead to greater returns.

Investments made by the trust departments of banks can be in both equity and fixed-income securities. By law and by nature these investment portfolios have tended to be conservatively managed. Trust departments are forced to operate in a "prudent" manner on behalf of the investors. In fact, in many states there are explicit restrictions on the kind of investments that can be undertaken by the commingled fund—in some cases, even to the extent of the construction of a list of "acceptable" investment opportunities.

As long as the commingling of the funds is done in a manner maintaining a degree of homogeneity among the investors in the fund, such commingled funds can be used to appeal to the particular traits and characteristics of the investor. This may offer a more efficient mechanism for some investors to achieve their investment objectives than would, say, a mutual fund made up of a broader set of investors having more heterogeneous interests.

The trustee (the bank) would be responsible for the valuation of the shares in the event of any additional acquisition or retirement of the share units created from the commingled fund. One of the distinct advantages of this form of investment for relatively well-off investors is that the fund trustee would provide custodial care for all of the securities and actions that would be required to keep the security accounts up-to-date. In other words, the custodian of the trust would be in charge of ensuring that correct principles were applied in accounting for dividend and split distributions, for dividend reinvestment, for subscription offerings, for purchase or exchange offers, or for tender offers for the securities held in the portfolio. They would also be required to keep current any company name changes or conversions of preferred stock and bonds, and any modification of indenture provisions. In other words, they would essentially act as the owner for any action required.

Pension Funds

Pension funds provide individuals with a series of future (perhaps uncertain) cash flows at retirement. There are two basic types of pension plans: defined benefit plans and defined contribution plans.

Defined benefit pension plans are not funds in the sense we have discussed to this point. These plans "promise" a fixed amount of retirement income, either in the form of a defined annuity or a lump sum payment. The plan's promise is backed by the employer who "funds" the required payments. Funding can come from transfers made by the firm to the assets of the pension plan, usually from profits or retained earnings. If the promised obligations of the plan are fully backed by the plan's assets (rather than by the firm's future earnings), the plan is said to be fully funded. However, if the fund's assets are not actuarially sufficient to cover all obligations, the plan (like the Social Security system) is not fully funded and must count on further firm payments to finance the plan. Obviously, the firm's future payments in a less-than-completely-funded plan may depend on the investment performance of the plan's assets, which may create the perverse incentive for the firm to invest the pension fund assets in more risky ventures, or even in the firm's own common stock.

Defined contribution plans do the opposite. In these plans the employer and/or employee contribute a regular (often fixed) amount of money at regular intervals to a fund that is then managed to provide a portfolio used to fund the employee's retirement. The fund is in all respects like a mutual fund, except that it cannot be liquidated by the investor prior to retirement. The value of the employee's accumulation (i.e., the employee's share of the total portfolio's value) at retirement will vary with the returns earned by the fund over time and, of course, the amount invested per unit of time. At retirement, the employee is typically allowed to "reinvest" the accumulated value to provide a fixed or variable annuity or a lump sum payment. The variable annuity or the investment of the lump sum payoff may create a flow of income that is subject to risk.

Technically, the defined contribution plan is more like an investment plan than a retirement plan, in the sense that funds are committed over time which, with the investment performance, give rise to future wealth. Defined benefit plans (particularly not fully funded ones) are more like deferred compensation plans. Nevertheless, both types of plans affect future consumption, and both should be considered when individuals make decisions concerning their nonpension investments.

The risks of these two types of plans can vary substantially. The risks of defined contribution plans depend on the betas of the securities included in the fund portfolio—just like for mutual funds. The risks of defined benefit plans are present—even if the benefit is promised—and more complex than those of defined contribution plans. The fully funded defined benefit plan has a risk that is the same as the beta of the portfolio held by the fund. This is in spite of the promised payments which seemingly negate risk. If the portfolio value falls substantially with a decrease in market returns due to a high beta, then someone must make up the difference. This may be the future pensioners, if the firm reduces its "promised payments"; it may be the firm, if it pays for the difference through reduced profits; or it may be current employees, through lower wages.[2] In two of the three cases, the brunt of the loss falls on the employees. Thus, risk is present, even if the plan is fully funded. That risk can be eliminated, of course, by investing fund assets in low- or no-risk securities, but the lower return on these securities must be offset by higher average employer contributions to the fund.

In underfunded plans, the pension risks are large. The ability to meet the future promised payments to retirees depends solely on the firm. The potential pensioner faces firm-unique risks as well as risks emanating from the firm's beta. The pension that is half funded and invested in a diversified portfolio faces *unique* risks on the unfunded half. Those risks expose the employee to the costs of a nondiversified portfolio. This risk would be quite large were it not for the fact that firms are required to meet some funding requirements out of profits on an annual basis before the firm can return profits to the owners in the form of dividends. Thus, while pension funding obligations are senior to stockholder payments, they are in no sense guaranteed.

Pension fund assets have risen at a rapid rate in the past three decades, reflecting three effects. First, more and more employees are covered. Second, legislation (particularly the Employee Retirement Income Security Act of 1974 (ERISA)) has forced firms to move toward full funding. Third, defined contribution plans, which are by definition fully funded, have grown faster than defined benefit plans at the insistence of employees, who have expressed concern over funding.

Summary

In this chapter, we have examined a variety of considerations that go into the planning of a successful portfolio management strategy. The most important component of such a strategy is the specification of the investor's objectives, along with any personal or

---

[2]It may seem as if the risk is reduced if the firm is able to make up the losses through allocations from its profits. But no firm is assured of being able to do this. Profits are subject to variability and to firm-unique risks.

externally imposed constraints which apply to the choice of a strategy designed to meet those objectives.

It is assumed that the ultimate aim of portfolio selection is to allocate one's wealth among available financial securities in order to achieve maximum expected utility. Although this sounds simple, these five basic questions must be answered if this objective is to be achieved:

1. Should investment in financial securities be timed to take advantage of economic cycles, and/or should mispriced securities be actively sought?
2. How frequently should the investor examine portfolio contents for possible revisions?
3. How diversified should the portfolio be?
4. What constraints should be employed to ensure that the portfolio adequately reflects the investor's preferences?
5. Should the portfolio be managed directly by the investor or by a professional manager?

The answer to the first question depends in part on the investor's beliefs about the extent of market efficiency, as well as on the aptitude of the investor in identifying whether differences exist between the current market price and the underlying value of the security.

Periodic portfolio revision may be necessary either to rebalance the portfolio's proportionate holdings if they have "wandered" from their desired levels over time as security prices have changed, or to respond to new information which alters the investor's forecasts about security expected returns. In either case, the frequency of revision depends, at least in part, on the magnitude of transactions costs and on tax effects.

The degree of diversification that is desirable depends on the level of investable wealth and on whether or not the investor is pursuing an active stock selection approach which requires concentration in a few mispriced securities. However, the pursuit of such an approach implies the inevitable trade-off between the safety of diversification and the higher returns anticipated from concentration.

Constraints may be imposed either externally or by the investor himself. Such constraints may dictate the desired level of portfolio periodic income or cash flows, the level of the portfolio's proportionate holdings in certain securities, the type of securities which may be held, or the planned holding period for the portfolio.

For most investors, it is possible to choose between managing one's own portfolio and hiring a professional manager to do it. Professional managers provide a variety of services including diversification; active portfolio management; the creation of new, liquid securities; and the performance of clerical and other duties associated with keeping track of the investor's money. Professionally managed funds include open-end mutual funds, money-market funds (which are a type of open-end fund), closed-end mutual funds, Real Estate Investment Trusts, pension funds, bank commingled funds, and others. A great variety of investment objectives, portfolio management styles, and management expense levels are present in the professional fund management industry. For this reason, investors are often able to select a fund or a set of funds well suited to their personal needs, wealth levels, and objectives.

References

Ambachtscheer, Keith P. [1976] "Can Selectivity Pay in an Efficient Market?" *Journal of Portfolio Management* (Summer).

Ambachtscheer, Keith P., and Farrell, James L. [1979] "Can Active Management Add Value?" *Financial Analysts Journal* (November–December).

Anders, George. [1987] "Using Rote and Math, Wells Fargo Succeeds as Money Manager." *The Wall Street Journal* (March 23).

Black, Fischer. [1974] "Can Portfolio Managers Outrun the Random Walkers?" *Journal of Portfolio Management* 1.

Blume, Marshall, and Friedman, Jack (eds.) [1982] *Encyclopedia of Investments.* New York: Warren, Gorham & Lamont, Inc.

Brealey, Richard A. [1986] "How to Combine Active Management with Index Funds." *Journal of Portfolio Management* (Winter).

Chen, A.; Jen, F.; and Zions, S. [1971] "The Optimal Portfolio Revision Policy." *Journal of Business* (January).

Cirino, Robert J. [1976] "Timing: Can Money Managers Deliver Their Promises?" *Institutional Investor* (June).

Fisher, Lawrence. [1975] "Using Modern Portfolio Theory to Maintain an 'Efficiently Diversified' Portfolio." *Financial Analysts Journal* (May–June).

Ferguson, Robert. [1975] "Active Portfolio Management: How to Beat the Index Funds." *Financial Analysts Journal* (May–June).

Friend, Irwin; Blume, Marshall; and Crockett, Jean. [1970] *Mutual Funds and Other Institutional Investors.* New York: McGraw-Hill.

Frost, Peter A., and Savarino, James E. [1986] "Portfolio Size and Estimation Risk." *Journal of Portfolio Management* (Summer).

Good, Walter; Ferguson, R.; and Treynor, Jack. [1976] "An Investor's Guide to the Index Fund Controversy." *Financial Analysts Journal* (November–December).

Gray, William. [1976] "Index Funds and Market Timing: Harris Trust's Approach." *Trusts & Estates* 115 (May).

Jacob, Nancy L. [1974] "A Limited Diversification Portfolio Selection Strategy for the Small Investor." *Journal of Finance* (July).

Langbein, John, and Posner, Richard [1976] "Market Funds and Trust-Investment Law." *American Bar Association Research Journal.*

Lanstein, Ronald J., and Jahnke, William W. [1979] "Applying Capital Market Theory to Investing." *Interfaces* (February).

Lyon, Andrew B. [1984] "Money Market Funds and Shareholders Dilution." *Journal of Finance* (September).

Malkiel, Burton. [1977] "The Valuation of Closed-End Investment-Company Shares." *Journal of Finance* (June).

McDonald, John G. [1975] "Investment Objectives: Diversification, Risk, and Exposure to Surprise." *Financial Analysts Journal* (March–April).

McDonald, John G. [1974] "Objectives and Performance of Mutual Funds 1960–69." *Journal of Financial and Quantitative Analysis* (June).

Pari, Robert A., and Chen, Son-Nan. [1985] "Estimation Risk and Optimal Portfolios." *Journal of Portfolio Management* (Fall).

Rudd, Andrew, and Rosenberg, Barr. [1980] "The Market Model in Investment Management." *Journal of Finance* (May).

Shapiro, Harvey. [1976] "How Do You Really Run One of Those Index Funds?" *Institutional Investor* 10 (February).

Tepper, Irwin. [1974] "Optimal Financial Strategies for Trusteed Pension Plans." *Journal of Financial and Quantitative Analysis* (June).

Tepper, Irwin. [1981] "Taxation and Corporate Pension Policy." *Journal of Finance* (March).

Treynor, Jack, and Black, Fischer. [1973] "How to Use Security Analysis to Improve Portfolio Selection." *Journal of Business* (January).

Treynor, Jack, and Mazuy, F. [1966] "Can Mutual Funds Outguess the Market?" *Harvard Business Review* (July–August).

Weisenberger [Annually] *Investment Companies Service*. New York: Warren, Gorham and Lamont.

Winkler, Robert L., and Barry, Christopher B. [1975] "A Bayesian Model for Portfolio Selection and Revision." *Journal of Finance* (March).

Questions and Problems

1. Summarize the three steps necessary for optimal management of a portfolio that contains both an active and a passive component.

2. What do index managers and index funds attempt to do?

3. Using Weisenberger's *Investment Companies Service* as your major source of information, identify five mutual funds whose objectives seem to be most consistent with your preferences. Compare the total expected costs per year as a percent of a $5,000 investment in each of these funds, with the calculations based on three-year and six-year holding periods. Include the expense ratios calculated by Weisenberger (which include management fees and transactions costs incurred in managing the funds), front-end (when you buy) or back-end (when you sell) load charges, and expected transactions costs based on the historical turnover of the fund portfolio.

4. What does the portfolio revision question refer to, and what variables need to be considered in developing an answer?

5. You are being interviewed for a position with a large money management firm ($6 billion under management). Currently under discussion by top-level management is: How much of the portfolio to devote to passive management in an attempt to duplicate the S&P 500 Index. The interviewer asks you to outline briefly:

   a. The costs and benefits of devoting a portion of the portfolio to a passive strategy.

   b. A systematic approach to solving the problem.

6. Using Weisenberger's *Investment Companies Service:*

   a. Identify the most recent 5-year and 10-year growth rates for assets under mutual fund management.

   b. The average yearly performance of these funds, using rate-of-return figures for the funds in comparison with returns on a broad-based stock market index.

CHAPTER

22

Performance Measurement

Control

An important ingredient in managing any production process is the maintenance of **control** of the process. An essential component of production control is measuring the **performance** of the process. This is as true for portfolio management as it is for any other good or service. In this chapter we describe methods for measuring performance and apply those methods to assessing the relative past performance of self-managed and professionally managed portfolios.

Of course, decisions in financial markets are made with respect to portfolio risk and return. Thus, any portfolio performance measurement technique must explicitly account for both of these characteristics.

Performance

The portfolio manager who is consistently able to spot undervalued and overvalued individual securities should be credited with superior performance. So too should the manager who is able to spot when a broad-based securities index is over- or undervalued. To the extent such superior performance exists, it must be based on knowledge held by the manager that is superior to that held by the rest of the market. The superior knowledge might come from superior forecasting abilities (of earnings, dividends, and discount rates) or from a better understanding of the things that determine security values.[1]

---

[1]Needless to say, it could also come from the manager's ability to acquire inside information. But the use of that information is illegal when the manager knows that the information has not been released to the public.

FIGURE 22–1   **Under- and Overvalued Opportunities**

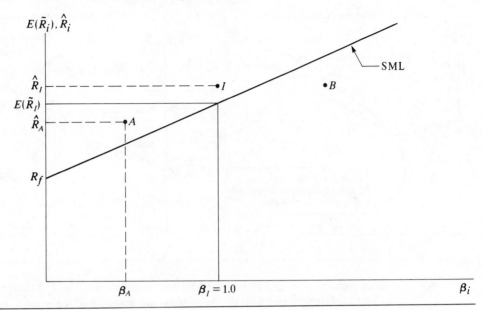

These simple statements regarding performance are represented graphically in Figure 22-1, which shows the position of certain securities relative to the security market line. Security A and market index I are undervalued and security B is overvalued. Unfortunately, perhaps, this view of the world is an ex ante one which does not guarantee to the manager that discovery of these undervalued securities leads to high returns. Thus, while the portfolio manager's explanation of the facts and forecasts may convince us that A is undervalued, the passage of time and the events that transpire during the period of the investment may eventually cause the actual return on A to deviate substantially from $\hat{R}_A$. The economy may suffer a recession, or an unanticipated negative event may overwhelm the positive, and correct, anticipations of the manager.

In the end, of course, we will only be able to assess whether the manager's expectations are correct on average, in the long run, as the results of the management of the portfolio are recorded. This effort is an imperfect one, as are most management evaluation techniques. The process requires a **standard from which performance can be measured,** and an understanding of the ways in which managers attempt to exceed the standard or "beat the market."

The Performance Standard

From the perspective of portfolio choice and the capital-asset pricing model, a reasonable theoretical standard of performance is given by the **optimal-risky portfolio,** or p^* in Figure 22–2(a). Those managers who find this portfolio, or any portfolio on the capital market line, have achieved a kind of "par." Managers who buy an inefficient portfolio or an efficient portfolio that is not the optimal-risky portfolio can be viewed as having

FIGURE 22–2

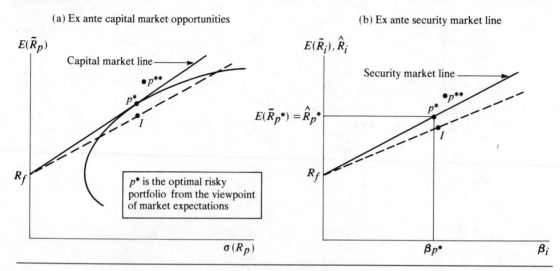

(a) Ex ante capital market opportunities

(b) Ex ante security market line

$E(\tilde{R}_p)$

Capital market line

$\bullet p^{**}$

p^*

I

$E(\tilde{R}_i), \hat{R}_i$

Security market line

$\bullet p^{**}$

p^*

$E(\tilde{R}_{p^*}) = \hat{R}_{p^*}$

I

R_f

p^* is the optimal risky portfolio from the viewpoint of market expectations

R_f

$\sigma(R_p)$

β_{p^*}

β_i

inferior performance; one of which is the market index portfolio, I. Managers who have superior knowledge, and with this knowledge are able to find a portfolio, like p^{**}, that offers greater return or less risk than p^* are superior performers. Then, if everything goes according to plan, p^* will be located on the security market line, as it is described in Figure 22–2(b); p^{**} will lie above it; and I will be below it. From this we can infer superior and inferior performance, using the security market line as the ultimate standard. The manager who is above the SML is a superior manager. All of this is consistent with our description of the purpose of valuation and security analysis in earlier chapters.

Unfortunately, there are two problems with the use of p^* as the optimal-risky portfolio and the SML as the standard by which managers can be compared. First, if the assumptions of the CAPM do not hold precisely, there may be some ambiguity in the composition of the optimal-risky portfolio. Second, even if the first problem is overcome, p^* is not directly observable. It is this second fact that has added confusion and consternation to the world of performance measurement, as we now see.

Suppose in our attempts to locate p^* we come up with a market index, I. In general, I will offer risk–return opportunities that are inefficient relative to p^*. As the "portfolio to beat" I clearly has some deficiencies. All that would not be so bad if we could be assured that p^{**} or p^* would be *rated* as having superior performance, thus giving those managers credit for their selections. Such assurance depends in part on the validity of the assumptions that underlie the CAPM. If the CAPM is a valid description of the securities' world, successful managers finding p^* or p^{**} will be rated as having superior performance when compared with the index.[2] Unfortunately, it is also true that many

---

[2]Some would argue that, strictly speaking, since the CAPM assumes homogeneous expectations, no one would find p^{**}. To us, a more reasonable statement is that there could not be very many managers who found p^{**}, or else market prices would begin changing. Thus, superior performance based on superior knowledge can exist within the *substance* of the CAPM.

inefficient portfolios will show positive performance, i.e., plot above the dashed estimated SML through I in Figure 22–2(b). Thus, performance measurement must be an imperfect game where some ambiguity remains.

Next, if these principles make some sense, we need to be concerned with how they can they be implemented to measure performance after the fact, or after the investment period has been completed.

Ex Post Security Selection Ability

Suppose the manager who spotted the portfolio p^{**} in Figure 22–2 bought that portfolio and earned a return of $R_{p^{**}t}$ over the investment period. During the same time the risk-free interest rate was R_{ft}, and the return observed for the market index (to be used as the standard of performance) was R_{It}. The last two numbers give us a basis for constructing the set of risk–return opportunities available during that period, or allow us to draw an ex post version of the SML that was available to investors. With knowledge of the risk level of the portfolio, $\beta_{p^{**}}$, we can see whether the portfolio's return was sufficient to place it above, on, or below the ex post SML.

This ex post relationship measuring performance is calculated by

(22–1) *Manager's Security Selection Ability*

$$\varepsilon_{p^{**}t} = R_{p^{**}t} - [R_{ft} + \beta_{p^{**}} (R_{It} - R_{ft})]$$

$$= R_{p^{**}t} - R_{nt}$$

$$\begin{matrix} \textit{Security} \\ \textit{selection} \\ \textit{ability in} \\ \textit{period t} \end{matrix} = \begin{matrix} \textit{Actual portfolio} \\ \textit{return in} \\ \textit{period t} \end{matrix} - \begin{matrix} \textit{Return expected on} \\ \textit{portfolio p** conditional} \\ \textit{on the portfolio's risk,} \\ \textit{and actual index return} \end{matrix}$$

and is shown in Figure 22–3 for a portfolio with a beta of 1.2. R_{nt} is the return on a naively constructed portfolio with the same risk as portfolio p^{**}. Formally, this calculation is one that measures the ability of the manager to use superior knowledge to select undervalued securities to include in the portfolio, or it measures the **security selection ability** of the manager.

In implementing this calculation in practice it's possible to come up with different representations of the general level of risk–return opportunities that were available to investors in a given period. For example, instead of using the ex post values of R_I and R_f, the intercept and slope coefficients of the cross-sectional regression,

$$R_{jt} = \gamma_{0t} + \gamma_{1t}\beta_j + \varepsilon_{jt} \qquad \text{for } j = 1, 2, \ldots J$$

can be estimated, with security selection ability calculated as,

(22–2) $$\varepsilon_{p^{**}t} = R_{p^{**}t} - [\gamma_{0t} + \gamma_{1t}\beta_{p^{**}}]$$

$$= \begin{matrix} \textit{Portfolio} \\ \textit{return} \end{matrix} - \begin{matrix} \textit{Average return} \\ \textit{on a portfolio} \\ \textit{with risk } \beta_{p^{**}} \end{matrix}$$

FIGURE 22–3   Ex Post Security Market Line and Security Selection Ability

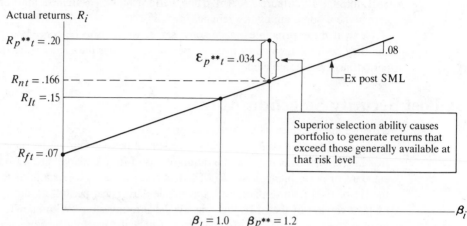

With this method, the intercept of the ex post SML would be γ_{0t} instead of R_{ft}, and the slope would be γ_{1t} instead of R_{It}. Both methods, of course, try to describe what happened to investment opportunities in the market in period t.

In the case of the illustration presented in Figure 22–3, the calculation to measure security selection ability of the manager would be,

$$\varepsilon_{p**t} = .20 - [.07 + .08(1.2)] = .034$$

Ex Post Market Timing

To take advantage of superior knowledge of the kinds of returns that might be offered on an overall market index requires that the manager select a risk level for the portfolio that is suitable to the expectations that have been formed. Doing so successfully allows the manager to capture general movements of the market. Clearly, when the market index is viewed by the manager as being undervalued, it behooves the manager to "lever up" the investment in the index, by borrowing or by buying higher beta securities that in other ways mimic the movements of the index. When the market index is viewed as being overvalued, the manager does the opposite, by buying lower beta securities; perhaps even to the point of holding a zero beta (of cash assets) or negative beta portfolio (of put options or short positions in stock market futures).

A reasonable way to measure the manager's success at **timing the market** is to compare the returns that normally would have been achieved (abstracting from security selection ability), with the risk level that was actually held during the investment period, β_{p**}, to the returns that would have been achieved, given the "normal" or "target" risk level, β^τ. The difference between the two beta coefficients reflects the manager's willingness to engage in market timing activities. The success of this venture is measured by the extent to which the manager selects a larger risk level when it pays to do so. That is, when the

FIGURE 22–4 **Ex Post Market Timing**

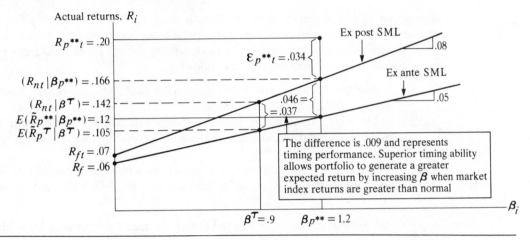

Actual returns, R_i

$R_{p**_t} = .20$

$\varepsilon_{p**_t} = .034$

Ex post SML

.08

$(R_{nt} | \beta_{p**}) = .166$

Ex ante SML

.05

$(R_{nt} | \beta^T) = .142$
$E(\tilde{R}_{p**} | \beta_{p**}) = .12$
$E(\tilde{R}_p^T | \beta^T) = .105$

$.046 = \{$
$= .037$

$R_{ft} = .07$
$R_f = .06$

The difference is .009 and represents timing performance. Superior timing ability allows portfolio to generate a greater expected return by increasing β when market index returns are greater than normal

$\beta^T = .9$ $\beta_{p**} = 1.2$ β_i

actual returns on a broad-based portfolio of securities is greater than expected. The exact measure can be written as,

(22–3)   *Manager's Market Timing Ability*

$$T_{p**_t} = (\beta_{p**} - \beta^T)([R_{It} - R_{ft}] - [E(\tilde{R}_I) - R_f])$$

Timing ability in period t = $\begin{pmatrix} \textit{Difference between} \\ \textit{actual and target beta} \end{pmatrix}$ $\begin{pmatrix} \textit{Difference between the ex post and} \\ \textit{ex ante risk premium on the} \\ \textit{market index portfolio} \end{pmatrix}$

Graphically, it measures the difference between the two bracketed quantities in Figure 22–4. Given the parameters there, the calculation of **market timing** performance for this manager is

$$(1.2 - .9)([.08] - [.05]) = .009$$

When the actual β selected is above the target, the manager will be credited with superior performance when the slope of the ex post security market line exceeds the slope of the ex ante security market line, or the expected compensation in the market for risk.

Total Performance

The manager's **total performance** sums the manager's ability to select individual mispriced securities and to time the market, or,

(22–4)   *Manager's Total Performance*

Total performance $= \varepsilon_{p**_t} + T_{p**_t}$

Total performance $= $ *Manager's security selection ability* $+$ *Manager's market timing ability.*

Performance Measurement: An Example

During one 12-month period, Keystone Growth Stock Fund shareholders enjoyed a 29 percent return. Can we estimate how well the fund was managed, and did the results reflect positive security selection ability or market timing ability? The information relevant to answering these questions includes the following:

1. During this 12-month period the return on the S&P 500 Index was 27.7 percent and on risk-free T-bills, 7.7 percent.
2. At the beginning of the investment period the expected equilibrium return on a broad-based index like the S&P 500 was 14 percent and the T-bill rate was 8 percent.
3. Over the past 10 years the fund had maintained a beta that averaged 1.3. However, during this period the fund had selected a portfolio with a beta of about .9.

Applying the expressions for selectivity and timing, the fund's performance is calculated as,

$$\varepsilon_{pt} = R_{pt} - R_{nt}$$

$$= .29 - [.077 + .9(.20)]$$

$$.033 = .29 - .257$$

$$T_{pt} = (\beta_p - \beta^\tau)([R_{It} - R_{ft}] - [E(\tilde{R}_I) - R_f])$$

$$= (.9 - 1.3)([.20] - [.06])$$

$$-.056 = (-.4)(.14)$$

These relationships are reproduced in Figure 22–5. As the numbers reveal, Keystone's management of the fund can be summarized as positive on selectivity and negative on market timing (for having reduced the funds β_p at the very time the market was supplying very high returns to securities). Overall, the fund's performance during this period was slightly negative at $-.023$, or -2.3 percent, per year.[3]

Diversification Performance

Any manager who attempts to select individual securities may have given up something in terms of diversification and, of course, diversification is an important portfolio management goal. If the portfolio is not fully diversified, then the investor is exposed to some diversifiable risk, and β_p will not precisely measure that portfolio's risk. An adjustment to β_p that accounts for this **cost of less than complete diversification** is to divide it by the correlation coefficient between the portfolio selected and the market return. Thus, the

---

[3]A critical interpretation of the use of such performance calculations is contained in a paper by Richard Roll [1977]. In this paper the whole question of performance measurement using the CAPM as the basis is questioned. Mayers and Rice [1979] provide a rebuttal to Roll's critique. More recently, Dybvig and Ross [1985] have provided further insight into the theoretical and practical issues of performance measurement.

FIGURE 22–5   **Keystone's Performance as a Money Manager**

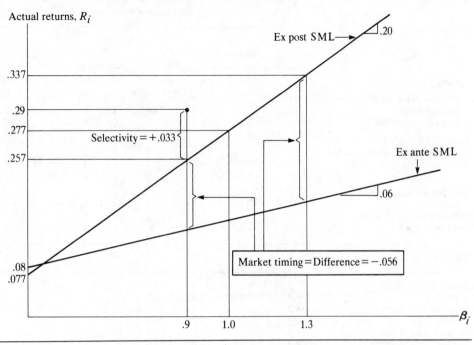

adjusted risk is β_p/ρ_{pm}. If a fund's β of 1.39 was held with a correlation of .90 with the market index, then the fund's-holders were worse off by the difference in returns on average offered by β_p and β_p/ρ_{pm}, or,

(22–5)   *Cost of Limited Diversification*

$$[R_{ft} + \beta_p/\rho_{pm}\,(R_{It} - R_{ft})] - [R_{ft} + \beta_p\,(R_{It} - R_{ft})]$$

*Average return on   Average return on
portfolio with risk adjusted   −   fully diversified
for lack of diversification   portfolio.*

Two issues related to diversification performance need to be mentioned. First, the measure assumes the market index, I, to be fully diversified. To the extent that it's not the market portfolio, it is not fully diversified, and the lack of correlation between it and the managed portfolio carries less meaning and significance. The difference between a correlation of .9 and 1.0 becomes of questionable importance—though a portfolio that correlates .5 with the index is probably much less than well diversified.

Second, mutual fund shareholders have other investments and assets. Consequently, most do not need to count on a particular mutual fund's shares to supply all of the diversification required by the investor.

As a result of these problems with assessing fund diversification performance, we prefer to emphasize "total performance," including both stock selection and market timing measures *separately* from the diversification performance of the portfolio.

TABLE 22–1   Mutual Fund Performance: Examples for Nine Funds

Percentage Performance Values

	Selection Ability				Market Timing				Overall Performance
Income	*1983*	*1984*	*1985*	*1983–85*	*1983*	*1984*	*1985*	*1983–85*	*1983–85*
Axe-Houghton Inc FD	11%	7%	−12%	2%	−2%	2%	−4%	−1%	1%
Decatur Fund	10	2	−25	−4	−1	1	−2	0	−5
Kemper Income Fund	9	−3	−2	1	0	0	−1	0	1
Long-Term Growth									
T. Rowe Price Growth and Inc	−6	−3	−5	−5	2	−2	4	1	−4
Growth Fund of America	5	−12	−5	−5	−3	4	−7	−2	−7
Fidelity Destiny	4	−1	1	1	−2	3	−6	−1	−1
Maximum Capital Gains									
Sequoia	11	11	5	9	−4	5	−9	−2	−7
Stein Roe Special Fund	3	−6	−6	−4	−1	1	−2	0	−4
44 Wall Street	−10	−42	−47	−36	−3	4	−7	−2	−38
Nine Fund Average	4	−5	−11	−4	−2	2	−4	−1	−5
Actual market return	22.5	6.3	32.2	19.8					
T-bill return	8.9	10.0	7.8	8.9					
Equil. exp. market return	14.2	16.0	15.0	15.1					
Risk-free rate	8.2	10.0	9.0	9.1					
Ex post slope of SML	13.6	−3.7	24.4	10.9					
Ex ante slope of SML	6.0	6.0	6.0	6.0					

An Application of Performance Measurement Techniques

Table 22–1 has been constructed using the selectivity and timing performance measures given in Equations (22–1) and (22–3). The return on Treasury bills and return on the S&P Index were used to calculate the ex post risk–return trade-off. The ex ante risk–return trade-off (the SML) was calculated using the beginning period rate on T-bills, and with an assumption that the expected equilibrium return on the market portfolio would be 6 percentage points above the T-bill rate (i.e., that the slope of the ex ante SML is .06). These figures are given in the bottom rows of the table.

This particular sample of mutual funds performed somewhat worse than the market, on average, during the three-year period of measurement. In large part this was due to the performance of one fund that experienced highly negative security selection ability. Undoubtedly, this reflects the fund's relative concentration in an industry sector (e.g., oil service stocks) that did not perform as well as the overall market did in this three-year period. No attempt was made to select these funds at random, so generalizations about the performance of mutual funds during this period are not possible. Nevertheless, it is apparent that security selection ability tends to be the dominant force in fund performance. In general this would be true for most funds in most time periods. Most mutual funds do not attempt to time the market to the degree that would cause their betas to

FIGURE 22–6   A Single Parameter Portfolio Performance Measure

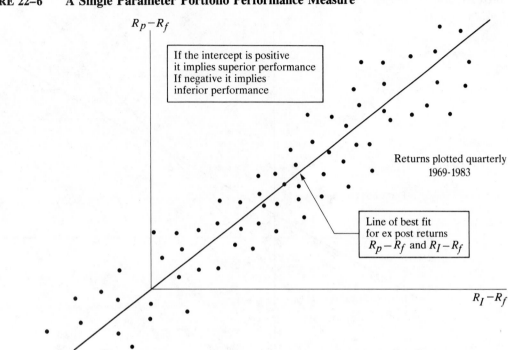

change from a very large value to a zero or negative risk level. For these funds, at least, the largest change in β was from 1.4 prior to 1983 to 1.0 during the 1983–85 period. In general, market timing efforts are less emphasized by most mutual funds, and security selection ability plays the dominant role in fund performance.

Single Parameter Performance over Many Periods

The manager's stock selection and market timing measures just presented offer a means of measuring performance in any given operating period. Yet in some respects it is important to come to an overall conclusion. Does this manager, on average over the long run, perform better than others? One way of arriving at a conclusion on this issue is to combine the aforementioned measures over time to view the total experience of the portfolio. The easiest way of doing this is to plot the returns on the portfolio, net of the risk-free rate, against the returns on a market index, R_I, net of R_f, as in Figure 22–6. Then, according to our prior discussion, each point would be composed of timing and selectivity performance, as well as the effect of the portfolio's β and the market return. According to the CAPM, a line of best fit or regression line should pass through the origin if the returns on the portfolio, on average, conform to the returns generally offered on all securities during the test period. However, if the portfolio tended to supply higher

FIGURE 22–7   Jensen's Performance Criteria

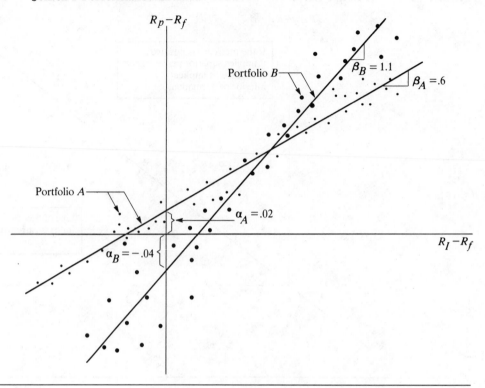

returns in most periods than other securities or portfolios with the same risk the intercept would be greater than zero. Consequently, one overall measure of performance for portfolio p would come from the simple time series regression,

(22–6)   *Jensen Performance Index*

$$R_{pt} - R_{ft} = \alpha_p + \beta_p(R_{It} - R_{ft}) + u_{pt}$$

and the intercept, α_p, will be greater than, equal to, or less than zero if the performance was positive, neutral, or negative. The coefficient β_p estimates the portfolio risk over the t periods. The error term u_{pt} may be positive or negative in period t, of course,[4] and when positive would indicate better-than-average performance that period. The value of α_p is called the **Jensen Performance Index** after its author, Michael Jensen [1968]. Figure 22–7 displays the positive performance of portfolio A and the negative performance of portfolio B. Note the fact that they have different risk levels does not impede the use of the intercept in comparing their performance.

---

[4]The sum of the squared value of u_{pt} over the t periods would be zero by construction in the least-squares regression estimates of the intercept and slope coefficients.

Two other measures of performance have been derived from Equation 22–7 and are used in evaluating portfolios. The **Treynor Performance Index** divides both sides of Equation 22–6 by β_p, (ignore the u_{pt} term and drop the t subscripts to see this relationship), leaving,

(22–7)   *Treynor Performance Index*

$$\frac{R_p - R_f}{\beta_p} = \frac{\alpha_p}{\beta_p} + R_I - R_f$$

and since,

(22–8)

$$\frac{\alpha_p}{\beta_p} = \frac{(R_p - R_f)}{\beta_p} - (R_I - R_f)$$

$$Jensen\ PI/\beta_p = Treynor\ PI - (R_I - R_f)$$

the measure is a simple transformation of the Jensen performance value. It normalizes the excess performance, α_p, by the portfolio's risk, β_p.

The **Sharpe Performance Index** divides both sides of Equation (22–6) by the portfolio's standard deviation, $\sigma(\tilde{R}_p)$. Thus,[5]

(22–9)   *Sharpe Performance Index*

$$\frac{R_p - R_f}{\sigma(\tilde{R}_p)} = \frac{\alpha_p}{\sigma(\tilde{R}_p)} + \frac{R_I - R_f}{\sigma(\tilde{R}_I)}$$

or,

$$\frac{\alpha_p}{\sigma(\tilde{R}_p)} = \frac{R_p - R_f}{\sigma(\tilde{R}_p)} - \frac{R_I - R_f}{\sigma(\tilde{R}_I)}$$

$$\frac{Jensen\ PI}{\sigma(\tilde{R}_p)} = Sharpe\ PI - \frac{R_f - R_f}{\sigma(\tilde{R}_I)}$$

This calculation normalizes excess performance by the portfolio's standard deviation— its risk if fully diversified.

Historical Performance of Professionally Managed Portfolios

With the phenomenal growth of mutual funds, pension funds, and other professional money managers has come a concentrated effort in determining if these professionals offer superior investment performance. Investors count on these estimates to help them

---

[5]This follows, since one way to write β_p is

$$\beta_p = \frac{\rho_{pI}\sigma(\tilde{R}_p)}{\sigma(\tilde{R}_I)}$$

Substituting this for β and canceling terms leaves Equation (22–9).

FIGURE 22–8   **The Timing and Selection Ability of 37 Mutual Funds (1960 to 1976)**

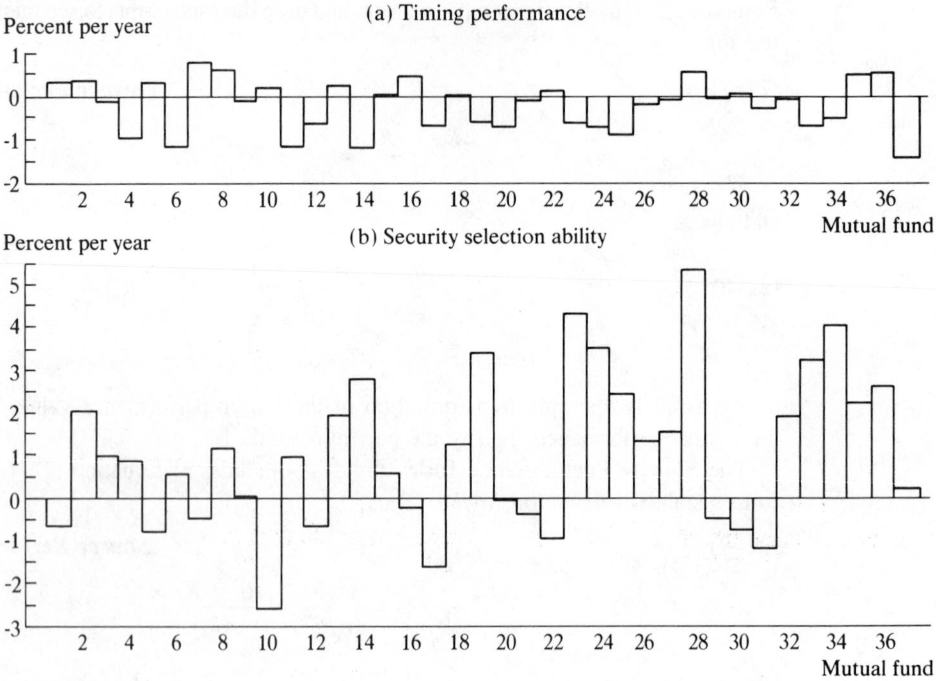

(a) Timing performance

Percent per year

(b) Security selection ability

Percent per year

Mutual fund

Source: Kon [1983].

decide between a professionally managed or self-managed portfolio, and between the use of active or passive management techniques. It's now common for investors to hire three or four professional managers, measure how each performs, and replace existing managers with new ones when performance falls below par. In fact, there are a number of consulting firms whose sole purpose is to rate managers according to specified criteria such as timing and selection ability.

Our appraisal of historical performance is limited to a study by Kon [1983], in Figure 22–8, and to a summary table of other studies of the performance of market professionals, Table 22–2.

Kon's technique uses sophisticated "switching regression" estimates of performance, with monthly data on 37 mutual funds between 1960 and 1976. His calculations of selection ability and timing are very similar to those we introduced earlier, but allow for simultaneous estimates of the extent to which the mutual funds *attempted* to time the market by changing their betas. His results indicate that 27 of the funds, at some time during the period of study, adopted beta levels that were statistically significantly different than they had adopted at other times. Thus, this sample exhibited an attempt to "time the market." The average difference in betas between these time periods for all 37 funds was in excess of .4. One fund changed from a beta of .9 to one of 3.2. Of course, some of the funds may have adopted their different betas for only a few months over the 17-

TABLE 22–2   The Performance of Professional Managers

Study Author	Type of Manager	Measure of Performance	Period of Study	Number of Managers Evaluated	Transactions Costs Included	Number with Positive Performance	Number with Negative Performance	Average Performance Entire Group Annualized (%)
Jensen	MF*	Jensen	1945–64	115	Yes	39	76	−1.1
	MF	Jensen	1945–64	115	No	48	67	−.4
	MF	Jensen	1945–64	115	No	60	61	−.1
Bogle and Twardowski	Bank-managed trust accts	$R_p - R_I$	1968–77		No	Not available		−.4
	Insurance Co. managed trust accts	$R_p - R_I$	1968–77	1551	No	Not available		−.3
	Investment counselor-managed trust accts	$R_p - R_I$	1968–77		No	Not available		−.8
	Mutual funds	$R_p - R_I$	1968–77	187	No	Not available		+.6
Sharpe	MF	Sharpe	1953–64	34	Yes	11	23	Not available
	MF	Sharpe	1953–64	34	No	19	15	Not available
McDonald	Maximum capital gain MF	Jensen	1960–69	18	Yes			+1.4
	Growth MF	Jensen	1960–69	33	Yes			+1.2
	Growth/income MF	Jensen	1960–69	36	Yes			+0.7
	Income/growth MF	Jensen	1960–69	12	Yes			0.0
	Balanced MF	Jensen	1960–69	12	Yes			−1.2
	Income MF	Jensen	1960–69	12	Yes			0.0
	All MF	Jensen	1960–69	123	Yes	67	56	+0.6

*MF is mutual fund.
Source: Jensen [1968]; Bogle and Twardowski [1966]; Sharpe [1966]; and McDonald [1974].

year period. Nevertheless, the results suggest that investors in mutual funds must look carefully at a prospective fund to determine whether they engage in attempts to time the market.

The performance results themselves indicate little or no ability to correctly time market movements. Of the 37 firms, 23 experienced negative market timing performance, though almost none of the values were statistically significantly different from zero! On average, timing performance was less than − .2 percent on an annualized basis.

Results on security selection ability are somewhat more encouraging. Twenty-four of the funds showed positive values, with about five of the funds values being significantly above zero. The average level of selection ability was on the order of 1.0 percent per year.

Overall performance is near zero. Only six funds had both positive timing and selection ability, while nine funds were negative on both scores. Twenty-two had positive total performance, but only 2 or 3 of these were statistically above zero. The best performing fund, however, did quite well—generating excess returns of almost 5 percent per year over the 17-year period. The worst performing fund lost about 3 percent per year relative to the market.

FIGURE 22-9   Mutual Fund Risk and Excess Return Performance (1960-1969)

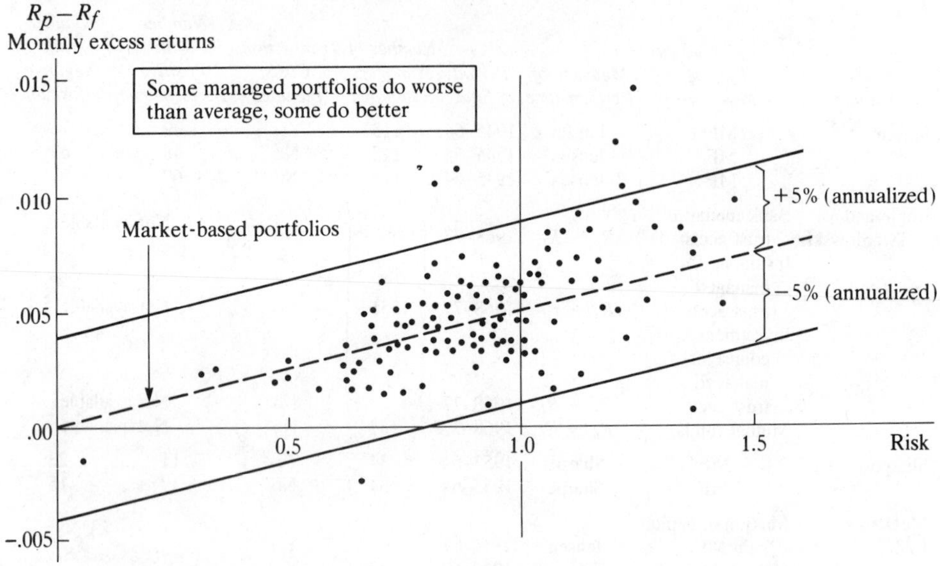

Source: McDonald [1974].

In much more general terms we have summarized the basic results of other studies in Table 22-2.

The conclusions from these studies are:

- In some periods mutual funds or other specific groups of institutional investors modestly outperform the market, while in other periods they underperform the market. In 1945-64 the performance tended to be negative. In the latter half of the 1960s, the performance was positive. In the 1970s, mutual funds had positive performance while others had negative performance values.
- Transactions costs have a negative impact on performance, perhaps as much as .5 percent or more for the average fund.
- In all periods some funds do better than average and some do worse. This point is made clearly by Figure 22-9, where fund β is plotted on excess return (monthly). Some funds are well off the line (by 5 percent or more annually) in both directions.
- Performance is not necessarily tied closely to the mutual fund's β. Some high β funds outperform the market and some underperform. The same is true for low β funds.

On the whole these results suggest that while professionally managed portfolios will sometimes beat the market, the typical fund can only duplicate similar-risk market returns. The figures suggest that perhaps these portfolios must count on the diversification, clerical services, and low cost of transacting that managers supply to customers to sell their wares. Of course, this is sufficient to justify their existence.

Can Some Funds Outperform the Market Consistently?

Some funds may outperform the market consistently in the long run, but the evidence here is not very persuasive either. Sharpe [1966] found that the variation in the performance of 34 funds in the 1944–53 period explained only about 12 percent of the variation in the 1954–63 period. Other studies have found similar results. Barrons'/Lipper Survey of Mutual Fund Performance (see Table 22–3) lists the top and bottom 25 funds in terms of total returns for 10 years, 5 years, and 1 year. Of the 10-year best performers, only seven are also 5-year best performers (even though the 10-year period *contains* the 5-year period); and there are only three 1-year best performers. In large part this is due to the existence of factors in the 5-year and 1-year results that helped some specialized (international) funds, but such is the nature of selectivity and timing performance.

One might begin to wonder, when faced with this evidence, why these professional investors would continue expending money and effort on selectivity and timing. One answer may be that these managers simply don't believe the evidence, but believe that the performance analysis is flawed. Another more cordial conclusion is that the activities of such investors are part of the competitive effort that results in market efficiency.

Other Performance Characteristics

There is other somewhat disconcerting evidence dredged up by these studies of performance. In particular:

1. Funds with higher sales charges or load fees tend to do no better on a before-cost basis than those with lower sales charges. **Avoid high-load fee funds.**
2. Funds with higher expense-to-asset ratios tend to do no better and no worse than those with lower expense ratios. **Avoid high management expense ratio funds.**
3. Larger funds tend to earn slightly higher risk-adjusted returns. Thus, it is a market fallacy that small funds are better because they have greater flexibility to manipulate their portfolio. **Don't buy a small fund just to avoid large funds.**
4. There is some correlation between the fund's stated objectives and the fund's β, but the relationship between "objective" and "risk" is not perfect. **Look into a fund's past β to estimate risk. Don't go by its stated objective.**
5. Many funds change their βs in an attempt to gain from their forecasts of the direction of market returns. **Past knowledge of a fund's β must be updated with current information on how the β may be changing.**
6. Firms with higher portfolio turnover seemed to have higher *before management fee* performance, but this was for a fairly narrow span of time. After-fee performance does not seem to be better for funds with high turnover. **In general, high turnover, very active portfolios do not do better (and some seem to do worse) than relatively more passive approaches to management.**

The Performance of Self-Managed Portfolios

One study has looked at the portfolio performance characteristics of self-managed portfolios. Not surprisingly, if we can't find superior performance for professionally managed

TABLE 22–3   The Consistency of Fund Performance (in periods from 1976–1986)

Top Funds over Time

One Year 9/30/85 to 9/30/86		Five Years 9/30/81 to 9/30/86		Ten Years 9/30/76 to 9/30/86	
Zenith Fd-Capital Growth	138.62%	Fidelity Magellan Fund	297.99%	Fidelity Magellan Fund	1616.33%
Fidelity Overseas	106.84	Vanguard Qual Dvd I x	277.65	Twentieth Century Select	1000.59
BBK International	98.00	BBK International	273.91	Evergreen Fund	910.03
GT Japan Growth	91.62	Merrill Lyn Pacific	273.43	International Investors	901.48
Benham Target 2010	86.95	Lommis-Saylies Capital x	270.57	Amer Capital Pace	894.88
Merrill Lyn Pacific	85.20	Vanguard World-Intl Gro	261.48	Quasar Associates x	894.10
Vanguard World-Intl Gro	82.67	Fidelity Sel Health	243.57	Lindner Fund x	881.16
GT Pacific Growth Fd	82.11	Oppenheimer Target	235.42	Twentieth Century Growth	865.49
GT International Growth	82.48	Phoenix Growth	233.15	Weingarten Equity	794.96
FT International	82.35	Quest for Value Fund	227.83	Loomis-Sayles Capital x	749.89
GAM International	79.62	Putnam Intl Equities	226.96	Nicholas Fund	749.33
Newport Far East	77.78	Evergreen Total Return	220.76	Franklin Gold Fund	721.35
Transatlantic Fund	77.35	Sequoia Fund x	215.24	Lindner Dividend x	693.83
Alliance International	76.05	Lindner Dividend x	214.67	Amev Growth Fd	693.48
T Rowe Price Intl Fund	74.96	United Contl Income	214.32	Sequoia Fund x	684.64
Nomura Pacific Basin	72.38	Fidelity Destiny I	214.29	US Gold Shares	681.99
Kemper International Fd	72.18	Phoenix Stock	207.86	Fidelity Destiny I	651.88
Benham Target 2005	70.64	Phoenix Balanced	207.71	Over-the-Counter Sec	646.07
IDS International	70.63	United Income	206.51	NEL Growth Fund	633.57
Keystone International	67.75	Templeton Global I x	206.48	Pennsylvania Mutual x	624.58
Oppenheimer A I M	67.63	Ivy Growth	206.09	Value Line Lvge Growth	618.78
Gt Europe Growth	65.47	Windsor Fund x	205.84	Phoenix Stock	615.98
Scudder International	64.53	Fairmont Fund	204.90	Vanguard Qual Dvd I x	603.43
Eaton Vance Total Return	63.10	Alliance International	204.65	Growth Fund of America	601.99
Financial Port-Pacific	61.73	Franklin Utilities	202.59	Mutual Shares	599.14

Bottom Funds over Time

Fund		Fund		Fund	
First Inv Ntrl Resources	−22.00%	44 Wall Street	−64.27%	First Inv Ntrl Resources	−28.43%
88 Fund	−18.35	First Inv Ntrl Resources	−38.64	44 Wall Street	8.57
American Heritage	−18.06	American Heritage	−27.63	Steadman Amer Industry	10.49
Industry Fund of America	−14.67	Steadman Oceanographic	−23.88	Steadman Oceanographic	19.04
Bowser Growth	−14.06	Interstate Cap Growth	−21.86	American Heritage	52.46
Steadman Amer Industry	−13.24	Steadman Amer Industry	−20.04	Steadman Investment	52.99
Strategic Silver	−10.29	Industry Fund of America	−18.99	Steadman Associated Fund	76.22
Fidelity Sel Electronic	−7.84	Sherman, Dean Fund	−18.17	Industry Fund of America	82.21
Lowry Market Timing	−4.25	American Investors	−16.95	American Investors	87.36
US Locap Fund	−3.59	44 Wall Street Equity	−4.30	Sherman, Dean Fund	92.21
Sherman, Dean Fund	−3.54	Strategic Investments	−3.57	Newton Income Fund	97.60
Industrial-American	−3.49	Putnam Energy Resources	1.42	Franklin U.S. Government	110.95
Eagle Growth Shares	−2.93	Golconda Investors Ltd	2.77	Lexington GNMA Income	111.57
First Inv Discovery	−2.68	Keystone Prec Metals	9.64	Div/Gro-Dividend Sr	113.33
44 Wall Street	−2.11	US Gold Shares	12.53	First Inv Fd for Growth	113.50
Div/Gro-Laser& Adv Tech	−1.96	Steadman Investment	18.36	Nicholas Income	114.26
Continental Option Inc	−1.86	Dean Witter Ntrl Res	22.49	Phoenix Total Return	115.37
Putnam Energy Resources	−0.83	Fidelity Sel Prec-Mtls	28.18	National Growth	124.09
Nautilus Fund	−0.68	First Inv Fd for Growth	29.05	Composite Income Fund	127.34
Steadman Oceanographic	−0.22	Franklin Gold Fund	31.05	Fund for U.S. Govt Sec	128.93
Explorer Fund x	−0.03	Lexington Goldfund	33.13	NEL Income Fund	129.48
Franklin Corp Cash	0.58	Fidelity SEI Energy	37.32	National Industries	132.90
Integrated Corp Investor	1.08	Afuture Fund	39.40	AMA Income Fund	133.31
Westergaard Fund	1.13	Value Line Special Sit	43.58	Liberty Fund	135.84
ISI Income Fund	1.58	Rainbow Fund	44.82	State Bond Common Stock	137.34

Source: *Barron's*, November 10, 1986.

FIGURE 22–10 **Distribution of Excess Returns ($R_i - R_m$) on 75,000 Round Trip Individual Investor Transactions** (no transactions cost included)

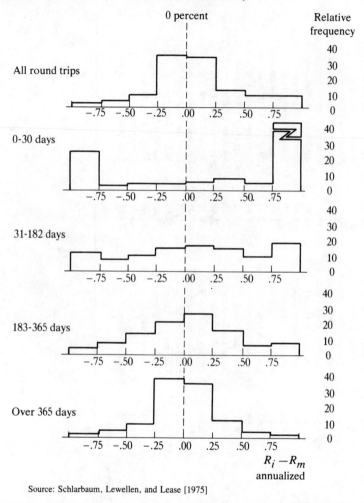

Source: Schlarbaum, Lewellen, and Lease [1975]

portfolios, we are unlikely to find inferior performance for self-managed ones. This study, by Schlarbaum, Lewellen, and Lease [1975, 1978], analyzed the returns on 75,000 round-trip transactions of a sample of 2,500 accounts of a major retail brokerage house.

The study calculated the differential return on the observed security transaction with the return on a market index held over exactly the same interval as the security was held by the investor. The transactions covered the period from 1964 to 1970. The results are summarized as annual excess rates of return in Figure 22–10. The overall average excess return is 3.2 percent per year. Also shown are the distributions of annualized return outcomes for the sample split by the length of the period over which the investment in the security was held. Shorter holding periods show up as supplying very high or very low annualized returns.

This evidence suggests the possibility of even *positive performance* for these investors. However, two things mitigate this conclusion. First, transactions costs would reduce the figures (particularly for the transactions of short duration). Second, the risk level of these securities exceeds the market average. Actually, the authors found that the 3,500 stocks held in these investor's portfolios had an average β of 1.38. If the excess returns were risk-adjusted, the 3.2 percent figure would drop—depending on the slope of the ex post security market line during this period.

In spite of these problems in interpreting the results, the figures are revealing. They argue that the average individual investor is *not* at a disadvantage with respect to institutional investors. Being in the market alongside large funds does not seem to force a significant wealth transfer from the small to the large.

Summary

Whether self-managed or professionally managed, investment portfolio performance must be assessed. This can be accomplished by measuring the security selection ability, timing, and diversification characteristics of the portfolio.

Selection ability measures the difference between actual portfolio return and the return on an average portfolio with the same risk level. Timing measures the difference in return on an average portfolio with the risk level selected for the portfolio with the expected equilibrium return on an average portfolio with the target or normal risk level typically adopted by the manager. Total performance is the sum of selectivity and timing. The diversification performance of a portfolio can be measured by the portfolio's correlation with the market index. In all three measures there are problems of measurement that dictate care in generalizing from particular calculations.

A single performance measure can be constructed to assess the performance of portfolios over many investment periods. One simple measure (the Jensen Performance Index) uses the intercept of a regression of the portfolio's return (less the risk-free rate) on the return on a stock market index (less the risk-free rate).

In general, the results of an application of performance measurement techniques suggest that neither professionally managed portfolios nor self-managed portfolios consistently outperform the other. However, in any given period some portfolios will do substantially better than others. No strong evidence exists to suggest that any mutual fund or other institutional investor is able to consistently and materially outperform the average, naively constructed portfolio.

References

Admati, Anat R.; Bhattacharya, Sudipto; Pfleiderer, Paul; and Ross, Stephen A. [1986] "On Timing and Selectivity." *Journal of Finance* (July).

Bogle, John C., and Twardowski, Jan M. [1980] "Institutional Investment Performance Compared." *Financial Analysts Journal* (January–February).

Dybvig, Philip H., and Ross, Stephen A. [1985] "Differential Information and Performance Measurement Using a Security Market Line." *Journal of Finance* (June).

Fama, Eugene. [1972] "Component Investment Performance." *Journal of Finance* (September).

Ferguson, Robert. [1986] "The Trouble with Performance Measurement." *Journal of Portfolio Management* (Spring).

French, Dan W., and Henderson, Glenn V., Jr. [1985] "How Well Does Performance Evaluation Perform?" *Journal of Portfolio Management* (Winter).

Friend, Irwin, and Blume, Marshall. [1970] "Measurement of Portfolio Performance under Uncertainty." *American Economic Review* (September).

Jensen, Michael. [1969] "Risk, the Pricing of Capital Assets, and the Evaluation of Investment Portfolios." *Journal of Business* (April).

Jensen, Michael. [1968] "The Performance of the Mutual Funds in the Period 1954–64." *Journal of Finance* (May).

Kim, Tye. [1978] "An Assessment of the Performance of Mutual Fund Management: 1969–75." *Journal of Financial and Quantitative Analysis* (September).

Kon, Stanley. [1983] "The Market-Timing Performance of Mutual Fund Managers." *Journal of Business* (July).

Kon, Stanley J., and Jen, Frank C. [1978] "Estimation of Time-Varying Systematic Risk and Performance for Mutual Fund Portfolios: An Application of Switching Regression." *Journal of Finance* (May).

Kritzman, Mark. [1986] "How to Detect Skill in Management Performance." *Journal of Portfolio Management* (Winter).

Lorie, James. [1968] *Measuring the Investment Performance of Pension Funds for the Purpose of Interfund Comparisons*. Park Ridge, Ill.: Bank Administration Institute.

Mayers, David, and Rice, Edward M. [1979] "Measuring Portfolio Performance and the Empirical Content of Asset Pricing Models." *Journal of Financial Economics* (March).

McDonald, John G. [1974] "Objectives and Performance of Mutual Funds, 1960–1969." *Journal of Financial and Quantitative Analysis* (June).

Roll, Richard. [1977] "A Critique of the Asset Pricing Theory's Tests." *Journal of Financial Economics* (March).

Roll, Richard. [1978] "Ambiguity When Performance Is Measured by the Securities Market Line." *Journal of Finance* (September).

Schlarbaum, Gary G.; Lewellen, William G.; and Lease, Ronald C. [1978] "The Common Stock-Portfolio Performance Records of Individual Investors: 1964–70." *Journal of Finance* (May).

Schlarbaum, Gary G.; Lewellen, William G.; and Lease, Ronald C. [1975] "Realized Returns on Common Stock Investments: The Experience of Individual Investors." Paper No. 511, Krannert Graduate School of Industrial Administration, Purdue University (May).

Sharpe, William. [1966] "Mutual Fund Performance." *Journal of Business* (Supplement, January).

Spigelman, Joseph. [1974] "What Basis for Superior Performance." *Financial Analysts Journal* (May–June).

Treynor, Jack. [1965] "How to Rate Management of Investment Funds." *Harvard Business Review* (January–February).

Questions and Problems

1. Identify the data needed to calculate the Sharpe, Jensen, and Treynor measures of investment performance.

2. Using the methods given in the chapter, identify the data needed to measure a manager's security selection ability performance and market timing performance.

3. Jackson's Hole Fund recently decided to shift its beta from 1.1 to .7 as a result of its forecast that the market would supply somewhat lower returns in the future. If the risk-free rate during the investment period was 6 percent and the market index return was 8 percent, comment on the fund managers' timing performance. (You will have to make some assumptions about the slope and position of the ex ante SML.)

4. Rank the following portfolios, using the Sharpe and Treynor performance measures. (Assume the risk-free interest rate over the period was 10 percent.)

Portfolio	Average Return	Std. Dev. of Return	Beta
A	25%	30%	1.0
B	10	22	0.5
C	15	11	0.7
D	30	40	1.4
E	30	25	1.0
F	20	15	0.8
G	17	20	0.9
m	25	25	1.0

5. How does the evidence on timing and selection ability of professional money managers presented in the chapter relate to the hypothesis of market efficiency?

6. During 1987 a large pension fund for university professors generated a return of 22.3 percent on a portfolio beta of .85. Normally the fund's beta is maintained at the market average. During this period the market return was 23.7 percent and the T-bill rate was 7.6 percent. If the ex ante SML had an intercept of 7 percent and a slope of 6 percent, calculate the selection ability, timing, and overall performance of the fund.

7. Based on the historical performance presented in the chapter, and considering the other services that some mutual funds offer to investors, would you recommend mutual funds to investors with between $3,000 and $30,000 to invest? Why?

8. Considering the same circumstances as in Question 7, would it normally be prudent for small investors to diversify their holdings among a number of mutual funds? In other words, does data in Tables 22–1, 22–2, or 22–3, and in the text suggest there is much diversifiable variability to be eliminated from mutual fund returns?

9. Calculate the selection ability and timing performance of these six funds:

Fund	2-Year Return	Actual Beta	Target Beta
A	17.6%	1.3	1.1
B	13.2	.5	.8
C	11.6	1.6	1.4
D	22.1	.9	1.3
E	18.4	1.4	1.2
F	8.4	.4	.4

The market index return was 17.1 percent during this period, and the T-bill rate was 8 percent.

Use ex ante SML values of 8 percent for the risk-free rate and 14 percent for the equilibrium-expected return on the market portfolio in your calculations.

10. You have been successfully handling Dr. Mason's account for five years when you receive a call from him that he has been in poor health and will bring his son Henry with him to the annual performance review.

Dr. Mason's portfolio is currently comprised of 5 percent cash or equivalents, 10 percent real estate, 50 percent tax-exempt bonds, and 35 percent "blue chip" common stocks. In the midst of the review, Henry presents you with portfolio performance data for the Essex Institute Foundation, of which he is a trustee and chairman of the Finance Committee. He claims that the Foundation's equity performance and total portfolio performance were better than Dr. Mason's. The key data for the two portfolios and for the financial markets are in the following table:

	Past 12 Months Total Return	Beta
Essex Institute Foundation (equity only)	32.2%	1.6
Essex Institute Foundation (total portfolio)	24.6	
Dr. Mason (equity only)	26.5	1.0
Dr. Mason (total portfolio)	21.6	
S&P 500	24.0	
Lehman Brothers, Kuhn Loeb Total Bond Index	14.8	
91-day Treasury bill	10.0	
Bond Buyer Index (tax exempt)	12.2	

a. Calculate the risk-adjusted performance of the two equity accounts, using the Treynor and Jensen measures.

b. Compare the two equity portfolios with each other and with the S&P 500.

c. List reasons why any comparative conclusions drawn from the performance data in the table may be misleading.

CFA

APPENDIX

Selected Investment Information Sources

General Information—Periodicals

Barron's (weekly)

A "national business and financial weekly," *Barron's* offers articles on individual companies and their earnings and dividend prospects; it offers analyses of stock market trends and forecasts; and it has detailed summaries of weekly securities prices. *Barron's* also carries many intriguing advertisements for subscriptions to private investment newsletters and forecasting services.

Note: No short list of investment information sources can possibly purport to be comprehensive, as the possible sources are virtually limitless. We have attempted to list only well-known publications that are also readily available either in public libraries or on newsstands. The authors wish to thank the librarians at the University of Washington School and Graduate School of Business Administration Library for their assistance in compiling this list.

Business Week (weekly)

Business Week contains short articles on current events in the business and financial world. It concentrates more on business news than on analysis of events or company prospects.

Forbes (semi-monthly)

Forbes is geared to the investor who seeks short, readable articles about individual companies and their prospects and about individual business executives. It has several special annual issues on such topics as banking, mutual funds, insurance, an "Annual Report on American Industry," and an "Annual Directory Issue." The latter issue ranks the 500 largest U.S. corporations by assets, sales, net profits, and other financial measures.

Fortune (semi-monthly)

An excellent source of general information about what is going on in the world of business, both nationally and internationally. Each issue of *Fortune* features a number of short, extremely well-written and extensively researched articles, each focusing on a particular company, industry, business leader, or economic issue. Several special issues are included throughout the year, including one devoted to the latest financial results for the Fortune 500 (that is, the 500 largest U.S. industrial corporations), another devoted to similar results for the second largest 500 corporations, a third listing financial results for the largest U.S. nonindustrial corporations, and a fourth for the top foreign corporations.

The Investment Dealer's Digest (monthly)

This is a journal oriented toward institutional Wall Street investors. In addition to supplying current information regarding new security issues of firms issuing securities, it has a blend of articles that attempt to treat issues of importance to Wall Street professionals. The digest concentrates much of its effort toward institutional or conceptual ideas that directly impact on the investment banking community.

New York Times (daily)

Now available the same day in most large U.S. metropolitan areas, the *New York Times* is almost as readily available nationally as *The Wall Street Journal*. In addition to its well-deserved reputation as an excellent comprehensive source of national and international news (many regional newspapers reprint *NYT* news articles several days after they appear in the *NYT*), its coverage of business and financial news nicely complements that appearing in *The WSJ*. The "Business Day" and "Business Digest" columns appearing in the second section of the *NYT* on weekdays keep the reader informed about major business events. Other columns report earnings announcements, discuss the accomplishments of prominent business people, and analyze economic events. Detailed daily listings of stock, bond, options, mutual fund, and commodity prices are also provided. The Sunday issue also contains extensive business analyses.

The Wall Street Journal (daily, except Saturday and Sunday)

The Wall Street Journal is considered by many to be the "bible" of current information about business and the economy, with special emphasis on the United States. (An international edition of *The WSJ* is also sold abroad.) The contents of *The WSJ* include current financial news; digests of company earnings reports; daily listings of stock, bond, options, mutual fund, and commodity prices; foreign exchange quotations; and analyses of recent events having an impact on securities markets. Many serious investors regularly read either *The WSJ* or the *New York Times,* and often both.

Wall Street Transcript (weekly)

This publication is a compendium of recommendations and information on individual securities. Its primary purpose is to update Wall Street on the recommendations that have been made for purchase or sale of individual securities as well as for summarizing recent information relevant to those securities. It comes in the form of a newspaper much like *Barron's.*

Guides to Information Sources—Indexes and Encyclopedias

Business Periodicals Index (monthly)

This publication is described by the publisher as "a cumulative subject index to English language business periodicals." It also contains citations to business-related book reviews. Published monthly (except August), with a bound cumulation each year, the index is useful for researching news events pertaining to particular companies, industries, and/or business topics.

Encyclopedia of Business Information Sources (4th edition, 1980)

This two-volume set contains a comprehensive listing of a wide variety of information sources on subjects ranging from finance to specific industries and foreign countries.

The National Directory of Investment Newsletters (annual)

Published by the Idea Publishing Corporation, this directory describes all major domestic information services designed to aid in investment decision making. Included are the names and addresses of the publishers of investment newsletters covering stocks, commodities, options, mutual funds, numismatics, philately, gems, real estate, bonds, and other investment opportunities.

The Wall Street Journal/Barron's Index

Published in an annual bound volume with monthly updates for *The Wall Street Journal,* this index contains brief abstracts by subject of articles that have appeared in both these national business and financial publications. *The Wall Street Journal* index is divided into two sections—"Corporate News" and "General News"; for *Barron's,* these two sections are combined.

Economic and Industry Statistics—Periodicals and Reference Volumes

Federal Reserve Bulletin (monthly)

The *Federal Reserve Bulletin* is a compendium of recent and historical U.S. economic, banking, and monetary statistics. Included are data on money market interest rates, international financial flows, the amounts recently issued and outstanding of various types of securities (with emphasis on U.S. government securities), and so on. The data contained here generally have a lag of several months behind the current date, so if very recent information is needed, this is not the best source for it. See also: *Federal Reserve CHARTBOOK* (annual) for graphic displays of a number of economic time-series data.

International Financial Statistics (monthly)

Contains information on aggregate financial and economic statistics for each country, including exchange rates, GNP figures, stock index summaries, and so forth.

Standard & Poor's Industry Surveys (quarterly)

A two-volume reference work published quarterly and divided into over 30 sections covering more than 60 major domestic industries, from aerospace to utilities. The information within each industry analysis includes a statement of the future outlook, financial data on individual companies, and composite industry statistics. Very useful in the analysis of common stocks.

Standard & Poor's Trade and Securities: Statistics (monthly)

Appearing in a looseleaf format, it contains economic statistics with special emphasis on banking and finance, production and labor, commodities prices, and the levels of activity in such industries as building and building materials, metals, and chemicals. A good source of historical economic and industrial data.

Survey of Current Business (monthly)

Contains much the same information as the *Federal Reserve Bulletin,* but leans less to financial data and more toward productivity and employment data by sector and industry.

U.S. Department of Commerce—U.S. Industrial Outlook (annual)

Similar to *Standard & Poor's Industry Surveys,* this publication contains information on recent developments, problems, and near-term prospects for about 200 individual domestic industries.

Historical Securities Prices—Periodicals and Reference Volumes

Bank and Quotation Record (monthly)

Published by the same publisher as the *Commercial and Financial Chronicle,* this newspaper contains monthly opening, closing, low, and high prices for all stocks listed on the NYSE, AMEX, Philadelphia, Toronto, Midwest, Boston, and Pacific Coast Stock exhanges, plus over-the-counter bonds and stocks, mutual funds, public utility preferred stocks, insurance stocks, and U.S. government securities. Prices of many securities not found in the more readily available papers many times can be found here.

Commercial and Financial Chronicle (weekly)

Billed by its publisher as "the only comprehensive index of the financial markets," this newspaper contains weekly summaries of prices for all New York Stock Exchange stocks and bonds, American Stock Exchange stocks and bonds, NASDAQ over-the-counter stocks, Chicago Board Options Exchange-listed options, Pacific Stock Exchange stocks, Toronto Stock Exchange stocks, and U.S. government securities.

Standard & Poor's Daily Stock Price Record (quarterly)

This publication is issued in three sets: New York Stock Exchange, American Stock Exchange, and Over the Counter. Each volume gives a daily and weekly record of the trading volume, high/low and closing prices, and dividend payments of individual listed stocks. Daily market indicators, such as Standard & Poor's Indexes and Dow Jones Averages are provided at the beginning of each volume.

Corporate Statistics: Evaluations of Individual Securities—Periodicals and Reference Works

Capital International Perspective (monthly)

Monthly issues focus on recent stock market performance for over 1,000 international stocks and industry groups. Once every quarter, an issue is published which contains 15-year graphically portrayed data on the 1,100 largest companies headquartered outside North America, arranged by industry.

Moody's Bond Record (monthly)

This publication provides details on call prices, maturity and interest payment dates, par values, and safety ratings as assessed by Moody's staff, for over 19,000 bond issues, including municipal and corporate bonds, convertible bonds, and preferred stocks.

Moody's Bond Survey (monthly)

This publication analyzes individual bonds and gives recommendations for purchase or sale. It discusses changes in ratings for particular issues, and it evaluates new issues.

Moody's Dividend Record (semi-weekly)

This publication provides details on dividend declaration dates, payments of cash and stock dividends, stock splits, and rights offerings for thousands of U.S. common stocks traded on domestic exchanges and over the counter. An annual cumulative issue is published in the first week of each year.

Moody's Handbook of Common Stocks (quarterly)

This paperback book contains price charts, investment ratings, and historical financial statistics for over 900 of the most widely held common stocks in the United States.

Moody's Manuals: Utilities, Transportation, Bank and Financial, Municipal and Government, International (annually, updated weekly)

These publications (one for each sector) summarize the financial characteristics of any corporation Moody's chooses to cover. This publication and Standard & Poor's equivalent described below constitute the most comprehensive set of information on individual firms, for a broader range of firms than is available anywhere else. In these publications, it is possible to get relatively current information on even the smallest of publicly traded issues. The manual identifies the business of the firm and summarizes its past financial statements, as well as indicating specific characteristics of its financial structure. For example, the publication will outline the nature of a particular firm's debt offerings in terms of that debt's major characteristics.

Standard & Poor's Bond Guide (monthly)

Like *Moody's Bond Record,* this publication provides a description of each included bond issue including a listing of its coupon rate, S&P's quality rating, periodic interest payment dates, the underwriter and year of underwriting, recent price ranges, current yield, and yield to maturity. Coverage is similar to that of Moody's and includes corporate and municipal bonds, federal agency securities, and utility preferred stocks.

Standard & Poor's Corporation Records (annually, updated weekly)

This publication attempts to perform the same task as that undertaken by *Moody's Industrials*. In large part, the two publications are duplicates of one another; the same information is available from either.

Standard & Poor's Security Owner's Stock Guide (updated monthly)

This publication features monthly supplements which cover about 5,250 common and preferred stocks, as well as over 400 mutual funds. Each analysis lists S&P's rating of the stock's investment prospects, as well as historical data on stock prices, cash dividends, earnings per share, and other financial information.

Standard & Poor's Stock Reports: New York Stock Exchange, American Exchange, O-T-C, and Regional Exchanges (periodically)

This periodical contains comprehensive two-page reports on more than 3,000 companies, including analyses of near-term sales, dividend and earnings prospects, plus a commentary on each stock's overall longer-term outlook.

Value Line Investment Survey (weekly)

This comprehensive publication appears in looseleaf form with weekly supplements. *Value Line* provides detailed financial and historical information on over 1,500 common stocks, with each stock analysis updated quarterly. It comes in three sections. The first, "Summary and Index," summarizes *Value Line's* forecasts for the future performance and safety of each of the stocks surveyed. The second section, "Selection and Opinion," contains an analysis of recent stock market events, individual stock highlights, and occasional economic forecasts. The third section, "Ratings and Reports," provides a 10-year history of the values of 23 key financial figures (such as sales, earnings per share, dividends per share, price/earnings ratios, net worth, cash flow per share, and annual depreciation) for each of the stocks followed, as well as analyses of the prospects for individual securities.

Value Line Options and Convertibles (weekly)

This is the "bible" for serious options investors. Evaluating about 8,000 exchange-listed options, as well as over 500 convertible bonds and approximately 75 listed warrants, this periodical provides up-to-date price and trading-volume data, information on the Black-Scholes option value, and other useful data on each security.

Weisenberger's Investment Companies (annual, with supplements)

This publication is the most comprehensive single source for information on U.S. mutual funds and investment companies. It gives historical performance information, discusses investment objectives, provides data on load charges, expense ratios, historical fund betas (both in "up" and "down" markets), and includes coverage of open-end, closed-end, dual-purpose, special, and tax-exempt bond funds.

The World Directory of Multinational Enterprises (London, June 1980)

This two-volume set profiles over 500 major multinational enterprises and provides information on their main divisional organizational structure, their products, their corporate histories, and it includes a five-year financial performance summary.

Information Available in Machine-Readable Form

Berkeley Options Data Base (University of California, Berkeley)

Through the cooperation of the Chicago Board Options Exchange, the University of California compiles and sells data tapes that contain continuous price information (both bid/ask prices and transactions prices) on options that are traded on the Chicago Board Options Exchange. Data is available from 1976.

Business and Financial Information Systems

(A number of firms now publish information either regarding articles or news releases pertaining to a particular firm or regarding financial information on the firm through continuous computer access.)

The Dow Jones News Retrieval Service, Micro Disclosure, and Data Resources Inc. all have systems that allow you to access their data banks from a remote computer. This may be a personal computer or a larger business computer. These services are available by acquisition, and many supply hardware that enables the analyst to make calculations as part of the access routine.

Center for Research and Security Prices (University of Chicago, annually)

CRSP produces and sells data tapes which contain information on security prices and volume, as well as information that pertains to individual firm dividends and earnings and the dates that they are released publicly. CRSP publishes daily price information (beginning in 1962) and monthly price information (beginning in 1926). CRSP also publishes a tape containing all stock market indexes and a bond price file.

The Chicago Board of Trade (current)

The Chicago Board of Trade publishes the prices of commodities in which it makes a market. The information is available either on a transaction-to-transaction basis or on a daily basis. The data is only available for the period of time that the CBT has been maintaining machine readable prices—that is, since about 1980.

Compustat (annually)

A division of Standard & Poor's, Compustat publishes in computer tape form information contained in financial statements of a large number of publicly held corporations. The information is broken down by the nature of the firm (industrial, utility, banking and finance, and transportation). The financial statements for each firm are included for a period of 20 years on the annual Compustat file and for a period of five years on the quarterly Compustat file. The quarterly information is much more limited in the data items included. The data is now available for use on personal computers.

Lynch, Jones, & Ryan—I/B/E/S (monthly)

Includes comprehensive data on earnings forecasts for a large number of firms by professional security analysts. Most well-known broker-dealer firms that have security analysis services contribute their forecasts to Lynch, Jones, & Ryan for summarization and processing.

Other Financial Markets

A number of other financial markets make trading data available to the public upon request. There is a strong trend in this direction, and we expect that all major world exchanges, options markets, and futures markets will make their data more and more available. They have the incentive to do so, because only in that way can investors be convinced that the market is one that is liquid, resilient, and suitable for their investment choices.

Value Line (annually)

Much like Standard & Poor's, Value Line publishes a computer tape that includes financial information on those firms that Value Line covers as part of its forecasting process.

Author Index

A

Archibald, R. Ross, 454
Arditti, Fred D., 503
Argus Research Corporation, 499
Arrow, Kenneth, 73

B

Baesel, Jerome B., 496
Ball, Ray, 454, 458 n
Banz, R., 282–83
Basi, B. A., 479 n
Bear, Robert, 156 n, 166 n
Beaver, William H., 169, 170 n, 426–27
Benjamin, James J., 479 n
Bernstein, Peter L., 414 n
Berry, M., 497
Bhattacharya, Sudipto, 529 n
Bilson, John F. O., 629 n
Black, Fisher, 244, 276–80, 282–83, 598–601
Blume, Marshall, 134 n, 165 n, 166 n, 461, 488, 489 n, 658 n
Bodie, Zvi, 136
Bogle, John C., 681 n
Brealey, Richard, 449, 458 n
Brennan, Michael, 609 n
Brown, Lawrence D., 479 n
Brown, Philip, 479 n

C

Carey, Kenneth J., 479 n
Chant, Peter D., 479
Chen, Nai-Fu, 300–301
Clasing, Henry K., 490 n
Copeland, Ronald, 479 n, 480
Copeland, Thomas E., 492, 493 n
Cornell, W. Bradford, 156 n, 629 n
Cottle, S., 414 n
Cox, John, 598 n, 611
Cragg, John G., 485–86

D

Dietrich, J., Kimball, 156 n, 629 n
Dodd, R., 414 n

Dolde, Walter, 72 n
Dusak, Katherine, 156 n
Dybvig, Philip H., 674 n

F

Fama, Eugene F., 151 n, 152 n, 153–54, 165 n, 166 n, 170 n, 281–82, 358 n, 361 n, 525 n
Finnerty, Joseph, 496
Fisher, Irving, 307
Fisher, L., 188 n
Fisher, Lawrence, 170 n
Foster, George, 457
Foster, Orline, 97 n
Fraser, Donald R., 479 n
French, Kenneth K., 161 n
Friedman, Jack, 134 n, 658 n

G

Gastineau, Gary, 593 n
Gibbons, Michael R., 161
Givoly, Dan, 479 n, 485–86
Glauber, Robert, 458 n
Graham, B., 414 n
Grant, D., 497
Green, David, Jr., 479 n
Grossman, S., 444 n
Growth, John C., 491

H

Hakansson, Nils, 73 n
Harris, Lawrence, 161, 162 n
Hess, Patrick, 161
Hirshleifer, Jack, 444 n
Hoag, James W., 135
Homer, Sidney, 71 n
Hopewell, Michael, 72 n
Hudson, Richard L., 495 n
Hughes, Patricia, 299

I–J

Ibbotson, Roger G., 136, 138–39, 140 n, 141 n, 618 n
Ibbotson Associates, 123, 132 n
Jacob, Nancy L., 653

Jacquillat, Bertrand, 635
Jaffee, Jeffrey, 161 n, 163, 496–97
Jensen, M. C., 523
Jensen, Michael, 170 n, 276–80, 282–83, 678–79, 681 n
Jones, Charles D., 172 n

K

Kaplan, Robert S., 268 n, 454, 454 n
Keim, Donald, 160
Kettler, Paul, 426–27
Kon, Stanley, 680–81

L

Lakonishok, Josef, 479 n, 485–86
Landsman, Wayne R., 163, 164 n
Latane, Henry A., 172 n
Lease, Ronald C., 491, 686
Levi, Maurice, 629 n
Lewellen, Wilbur, 491
Lewellen, William G., 686
Lintner, Jack, 226 n
Lintner, John, 485 n
Little, I. M. D., 458 n
Logue, Dennis, 629 n
Lorie, J. H., 188 n
Love, Kathryn S., 136, 138–39, 141 n, 618 n

M

MacBeth, James, 281–82, 611
McCollough, W. Andrew, 503
McDonald, John G., 681 n
McFarland, James, 167 n, 629 n
Malkiel, Burton, 485–86
Marioni, Robert, 479 n, 480
Markowitz, Harry, 202 n, 226 n
Masulis, Ronald W., 533
Mayers, David, 249–50, 492, 493 n, 674 n
Meckling, W. H., 523
Melville, Larry, 611
Merrill, Lynch, Pierce, Fenner & Smith, Inc., 501 n
Merton, Robert, 598, 599 n
Miller, Merton, 69 n
Mossin, Jan, 226 n

N

Neiderhoffer, Victor, 156–58, 433–35, 479 n
Nelson, C. R., 361
Nemeth, Eric, 623 n

O–P

Officer, R. R., 160
Osborne, M. F. M., 156–58
Owen, J., 444 n
Patell, James, 481
Penman, Stephen H., 496
Petit, R. Richardson, 167 n, 171 n, 426–27, 629 n
Pettengill, Glen N., 159

R

Rabinovitch, R., 444 n
Raiffa, Howard, 38 n
Rayner, A. C., 458 n
Regan, Patrick, 433–35
Reinganum, M., 283
Rendleman, Richard, 172 n
Rice, Edward M., 674 n

Richards, R. Malcolm, 479 n
Roll, Richard, 170 n, 282 n, 284, 286–88, 300–301, 454, 674 n
Rosansky, Victor, 136
Ross, Stephen A., 295, 300–301, 598 n, 674 n
Rozeff, Michael, 479 n
Rubinstein, Mark, 598 n
Rudd, Andrew, 490 n

S

Samuelson, P. A., 442
Sauvain, Harry, 414 n
Schall, Lawrence, 608 n
Scharlbaum, Gary G., 491, 686
Scholes, Myron, 274, 276–80, 282–83, 426–27, 598–601
Schwartz, Edwardo, 609 n
Schwert, G. W., 361
Segall, Joel, 479 n
Sharpe, William F., 226 n, 468–69, 681 n, 683
Siegel, Lawrence B., 136, 138–39, 141 n, 618 n
Sinquefeld, Rex A., 140 n
Skinner, B. F., 174

Solnik, Bruno, H., 189 n, 623 n, 635
Stambaugh, Robert F., 280–82, 284, 289
Stein, Garry R., 496
Stevenson, Richardson, 156 n, 166 n
Stickel, Scott E., 172 n
Strawser, Robert H., 479 n
Sung, Sam K., 161 n
Sweeny, R. J., 629 n

T

Tobin, James, 202 n, 213
Treynor, Jack, 226 n
Twardowski, Jan M., 681 n
Twark, R., 479 n

W–Y

Watts, Ross, 458 n
Weil, Roman, 268 n
Westerfield, Randolph, 161 n, 163, 426–27
Willet, T. D., 629 n
Williams, J., 274
Winjun, James O., 133 n
Winjun, Joanne T., 133 n
Yeoman, R. S., 134 n

Subject Index

A

Ability to pay, 335–38
Abnormal return, 167–70
Active management, 646–52, 679–80
  and diversification, 653–54
  and portfolio revision, 652
Agency costs, 62, 522–24
Aggregate world market wealth
  portfolio, 138–39
Alpha, 262–65
Alternative mortgage instruments, 399–
  400
American depository receipts (ADRs),
  96–97, 103, 621
American Stock Exchange (AMEX),
  83
  futures market compared with, 549
  history of, 85
  listing requirements of, 88
  Market Value Index, 109
  options trading on, 592
  and over-the-counter market, 100
  trading process on, 97
AMEX; see American Stock Exchange
Analysts' forecasts, 481–87, 490–93
Anti-takeover provisions, 515–16
APT; see Arbitrage pricing theory
  (APT)
Arbitrage, 21, 292, 296
  foreign exchange market, 626, 629
  futures market, 544, 552–54, 567–
  69
Arbitrage pricing theory (APT), 282,
  292–302
  and capital asset pricing model,
    similarities between, 297–98
  and foreign securities valuation,
    635–36
  and multifactor capital asset pricing
    model, 301
  nature of factors in, 300–301
  tests of, 298–300
Ask price, 93–94
Auctions, Federal government security,
  375–76; see also Double auctions
Australia, 625, 634
AutEx, 98–99
Averages, stock price, 106–8

B

β; see Beta
Balloon payment mortgages, 334
Bankers' acceptances, 82, 386, 561,
  661
Bank loans, as earnings forecast
  predictor, 480
Bankruptcy, 62, 524
BARRA risk estimates, 488–90
Barron's/Lipper Survey of Mutual Fund
  Performance, 683
Basis, 557–58
Beliefs, and probability, 27
Best efforts offering, 80
Beta, 236–38, 255, 293, 301; see also
  Capital asset pricing model
  (CAPM) and Risk
  common stock, 407, 422–27, 431
  components of, 326–27
  earnings, 458–59
  and financing decisions, 516
  of fixed-income securities, 347–56,
    382, 394–96, 461
  forecasting, 487–90
  of foreign securities, 631, 634
  historical, 270–76
  and index managers, 648
  and leverage, 518–20
  and market model, 259–68
  and mergers, 513
  mutual fund, 659, 676–77, 682–
    83
  and nonmarketable securities, 250
  options, 607
  pension fund, 664
  and performance measurement, 671–
    77
  portfolio, 264–65
  portfolio with zero, 244–45
  in security analysis, 448, 460–62,
    467
  of self-managed portfolios, 687
  and testability of capital asset pricing
    model, 284, 286–88
Bid price, 93–94
Black-Scholes option valuation model,
  597–600, 606
  empirical evidence on, 610–11

Black-Scholes option valuation
  model—Cont.
  option-type instruments valued using,
    609–10
Block transactions, 98–99
Blue chips, 88
Boesky, Ivan, 496
Bond equivalent yield, 374–75
Bond funds, 656–57
Bonds, 58–59, 68, 333–34; see also
  Corporate bonds; Federal agency
  securities; and U.S. Treasury
  bonds
  costs and benefits of, 62–65
  margin purchases of, 95–96
  NYSE listings of, 88
  and primary securities markets, 78
  in round lots, 90
British pound (£), 620–22, 627–28
Brokers, 385
  analysts' forecasts by, 481–87, 490–
    93, 501
  commission, role of, 85, 89
  commodity, 543
  and futures trading, 548–49
  money market funds of, 660
  over-the-counter market, 100–101
Business risk, 326
Business Week, 454 n
Butterfly spread, 587 n
Buttonwood Agreement, 84

C

Calendar spread, 587 n
Call options, 69, 575–76, 605
  American, 576, 601–2
  beta of, 607
  combination of put options and, 585
  European, 576, 601–2
  profit on, 581–85
  trading of, 591
  valuation of, 594–602
  valuation of put options using, 602–5
Call price, 334, 388–90
Call provisions, 68, 334
  corporate bond, 387–90, 394, 580
  federal agency security, 377
  and rate of return, 367–68

Canada, 619, 623
Capital asset pricing model (CAPM),
 223–88; *see also* Equilibrium
 value, underlying *and* Security
 market line (SML)
 and arbitrage pricing theory, 293–
  302
 assessment of, 282–85
 capital market line in, 230–31, 236
 and common stock valuation, 407–8,
  429–30
 concept of, 225–31
 consumption-based, 250–51
 equilibrium prices in, 239–41
 and fixed-income security valuation,
  338–40, 347–48
 and foreign securities valuation,
  635–36
 with heterogeneous expectations,
  246–47
 implications of, 269
 and market model, relation between,
  259–68
 multifactor, 301–2
 and multiperiod valuation, 319–28
 with nonmarketable assets, 249–50
 and passive management, 647
 and performance measurement,
  670–71
 and single-period valuation, 310–19
 testability of, 284, 286–88
 tests of, 268–82
  cross-sectional, 278–82
  estimating betas and returns in,
   270–76
  ex ante and ex post data problems
   in, 269–70
  time-series, 276–77
 with transaction costs, 248–49
 underlying equilibrium value in, 310
 zero beta, 242–46
Capital gains, 117, 659
Capital gains tax, 528–29, 654
Capitalization, and investment returns,
 129
Capital market line (CML), 230–31, 236
Capital structure risk; *see* Financial risk
CAPM; *see* Capital asset pricing model
 (CAPM)
Carrying costs, and futures prices, 553,
 557
Cash flows
 in cash flow capitalization model,
  411–12, 429
 matched, 355
 nondiversifiable, risk of, 423–28
 as portfolio management constraint,
  654
 and rate of return, 116–17
 uncertainty of, 406–7
 in valuation model, 312

Central Limit Theorem, 31 n
Certainty equivalent approach, 319 n,
 328–29
Certainty equivalent wealth, 38
Certificates, stock, 66
Certificates of deposit (CDs), 64, 78
 hedging, 561
 negotiable, 82, 386, 660
 redeemable, 581
Chicago Board of Trade, 543–44
Chicago Board Options Exchange, 84,
 575–76, 592
Chicago Mercantile Exchange, 628
Choice, theory of, 5–22, 208
 basic components of, 6–8
 and investment, 16–22
 and savings, 8–16
Clarity, contract, 61–62
Clearing corporation
 futures, 549
 options, 591
Clearing price; *see* Equilibrium price
Collateral, bond, 393, 395
Collateralized mortgage obligations
 (CMOs), 396
Collectibles, 132–35
College Retirement Equities Fund,
 637–38
Commercial banks, 78
 commingled funds of, 662–63
 deposits at, 384–85
 over-the-counter trading of securities
  of, 100
Commercial paper, 82, 386, 660–61
Commingled funds, 647, 656
 bank, 662–63
Commodities exchanges, 542–44,
 547–52
Commodity futures; *see* Futures
 contracts
Commodity Futures Trading
 Commission, 550–51
Commodity Research Bureau Futures
 Price Index, 138
Common stock, 58–59, 78; *see also*
 Dividend capitalization model *and*
 Stock market indexes
 convertibility to, 390–91
 costs and benefits of, 62–65
 eligible securities list of, 655
 foreign, 132, 617–19
 margin purchases of, 95–96
 marketability of, 72
 market value of all, 138–39
 rates of return on, 117–23, 138, 422,
  432–33
  bond returns compared with,
   123–26
  and commodity future returns
   compared, 136–37
 real, 139

Common stock—*Cont.*
 risk of, 422–23
  and firm characteristics, 426–27
  types of, 423–26
Common stock funds, 656–57; *see also*
 Index funds
Consolidated Quotations Service
 (CQS), 102
Consumer debt, 399
Consumer Price Index (CPI), 360–62
Consumption, and investment, 116; *see
 also* Choice, theory of
Consumption-based capital asset pricing
 model, 250–51
Contango, 555–56
Contracts; *see* Financial contracts
Convertible bonds, 68, 387–88, 390–
 91, 394, 580, 608–9
Convertible preferred stock, 387–88,
 580
Cooperative banks, 382–85
Corporate bonds, 333–34, 387–95
 beta of, 354–55
 call options on, 580
 foreign, 617–19
 probability distribution of interest
  payments on, 32
 quantity of, 139
 rates of return on, 138, 341
  real, 139
  stock index returns compared with,
   123–27
  Treasury bond investment returns
   compared with, 131
 ratings of, 397
 risk of, 394–95
 standard features of, 387–94
 yields on, 389, 394
Corporate securities, 385–96; *see also*
 Corporate bonds
Corporations
 open, costs and benefits of, 59–67
 public offerings of, 78
Correlation, 44, 46
Correlation coefficient; *see also*
 Covariance of security returns
 currency value, 625, 630–33
 security return, calculation of, 190
Costs, as earnings determinant, 450–
 51, 456
Coupon rate, 333–34
 and bond ratings, 397
 and interest-rate risk, 351
Covariance, 44–45, 51–52; *see also*
 Covariance of security returns
Covariance of security returns, 190,
 645
 and diversification benefits, 191–92
 and estimation error, 218
 and market equilibrium, 223–25
 for *N*-security case, 201

Covariance of security returns—*Cont.*
in security analysis, 463–64
for six-stock portfolio, 198–99
for two-stock portfolio, 195–96
Covering a short position, 90
Credit unions, 78, 384–85
Cross hedge, 561
Crossing orders, 86
Cumulative abnormal returns, 170
Cumulative average returns, 433
Cumulative excess returns; *see*
Cumulative abnormal returns
Current yield, 111, 117, 345–47, 394

D

Dealers, over-the-counter market,
99–101
Dean Witter Reynolds, Inc., 80
Debentures, 334
Debt covenants, 337–38
Debt/equity ratio, 516–17
Default-free securities, 335
and inflation, 362–63
return rates on, 341–43
and risk management, 355
Default risk, 423
on agency securities, 378
and bond ratings, 397
and deposit accounts, 385
and inflation, 363
on junk bonds, 396
on money market securities, 387
on municipal securities, 379–82
nondiversifiable, 348–50
and return rate calculation, 343–44
and Treasury securities, 376
and yield to maturity, 345
Defined benefit plans, 663–64
Defined contribution plans, 663–64
Deposits, at financial institutions,
384–85
Dirks, Ray, 494
Discount rate, in valuation
evaluation of, 313–14
multiperiod, 322–23
Dispersion, 30–31
Diversifiable variability, 282
Diversification; *see also* Optimal
portfolio
and active/passive management, 619
and divisibility, 63–64
effects of, on risk/return, 192–201
in *N*-security case, 200–201
in six-security portfolio, 198–200
in two-security portfolio, 193–98
in foreign security investment,
629–33
multinational firms used in,
634–35
and transaction costs, 633–34

Diversification—*Cont.*
with independent stock return
movements, assumption of, 186
and insurance principle, 184–85
mutual fund, 653, 658, 660
optimal, 202–5
performance measurement for,
674–75
and portfolio error term, 266–67
and portfolio proportionate holdings,
654–55
question of, 646, 653–54
in real world, 186–92
Dividend capitalization model, 407–9,
516
and cash flow, 411–12, 429
and earnings, 409–11
empirical evidence on, 429–35
and growth, 414–17
and investment opportunities,
412–14
and security analysis, 436–37, 448,
466–68
and stock price volatility, 435–36
Dividends; *see also* Dividend
capitalization model
and beta forecasts, 489
flow of, and leverage, 516–17
foreign market, 619–20
mutual fund, 659
and nondiversifiable cash flow risk,
423–25
and options valuation, 601–2, 604–5
policy on, and valuation, 508,
525–30
preferred stock, 334–35
properties of, 455–58
in security analysis, 448–60, 467
stock, 533–34
and stockholder claims, 405–7
taxation of, 654
uncertainty of cash flows from,
406–7
Divisibility
of contract units, 63–64
of deposits, 384
operating efficiency assumption of,
202, 226, 646
Dodd, Benjamin, 444
Dodd, David, 444
Double auctions
futures market, 549
options, 590–91
Dow Jones Composite Average, 106–7
Dow Jones Industrial Average (DJIA),
106–9, 128, 187, 216–17
Dow Jones Public Utility Average,
106–7
Dow Jones Transportation Average,
106–7
Dual listing, 88

Duration, 352–53
and bond betas, 353–54
and interest rate risk, 426
matched, immunization with, 355–56
and sinking-fund provisions, 391–92,
394

E

EAFE index, 132, 619–20
Earning power, and ability to pay,
337–38
Earnings; *see also* Forecasting
beta of, 458–59
in common stock valuation, 408–11
growth of, 418–21
volatility of, 435–36
determinants of, 450–52
normalized, 452–54
properties of, 455–58
in security analysis, 449–60
Economy
and cash flow risk, 423–25
earnings fluctuations and movement
in, 458–60
Efficiency, of foreign exchange
markets, 628–29
Efficient frontier, 204–5
with divergent borrowing/lending
rates, 242–45
with heterogeneous expectations,
246–47
and market portfolio, 227
and optimal portfolio selection,
205–10
Efficient market hypothesis, 151–52,
309
and interest rate forecasts, 499
and market equilibrium, 225
and market model, 258
tests of, 152–53
direct (semistrong), 153, 163–73
indirection (weak), 153–63
and use of technical and
fundamental analyses, 173–74
Efficient portfolios
and capital market line, 230–31
and optimal diversification, 202–5
Efficient set, 204–5, 284, 299, 645
and differing tax rates, 247–48
for Dow Jones securities, 216–17
for international securities, 631–35
optimal portfolio choice from,
205–10
short selling effect on, 214–16
Electronic Display Book System, 93
Eligible securities list, 655
Employee Retirement Income Security
Act (ERISA), 664
Employee stock purchase options, 579,
609–10

Energy crisis, 119 n
Equal access to information, 148–49, 167
Equal rate of return principle, 20–21
Equilibrium price, 146–47, 223–25;
see also Arbitrage pricing theory (APT); Capital asset pricing model (CAPM); and Efficient market hypothesis
in capital asset pricing model, 225, 228–29, 239–41
in efficient market hypothesis, 151–52
factors determining, 147–51
Equilibrium value, underlying, 308–10;
see also Valuation
components of, summarized, 318–19
and security analysis, 444–45
Equipment trust bonds, 334
Equipment trust certificates, 393
Equity Funding, 494
Equity option, 581
Estate taxes, 377
Estimation risk, 218
Eurobonds, 395
Eurodollar deposits, 387, 661
Event studies of security value, 432–33
Excess return, 168–69
Excess supply/demand, for securities, 225
Expected rate of return; see Rate of return
Exercise price, 390–91, 574–75
Expected value, 29–30, 39, 122; see also Rate of return
and certainty equivalent worth, 38
of combinations of variables, 49–50
expected utility versus, 35–36
and law of large numbers, 185
in normal distributions, 32
and skewness, 32–33
Expiration date, on options, 574
Export-Import Bank, 377
Extendable bonds, 581, 609

F

Face value, 334
Factor scores, 299
Fairness, 72–73, 85–86, 148, 202, 226, 646
Feasible portfolios, 193, 203
Federal agency securities, 78, 377–79;
see also Mortgage-backed securities
Federal funds, 386–87
Federal Home Loan Banks, 377
Federal Home Loan Mortgage Corporation (FHLMC), mortgage-backed securities of, 377–78, 399

Federal National Mortgage Association (FNMA), 80
mortgage-backed securities of, 399
Federal Reserve Bank of New York, 375
Federal Reserve System, 96, 190, 375
Fidelity Investments, 657
Filter rules, 163–66
Financing Analysts Journal, 444
Financial contracts, 58–61
costs and benefits of, 61–66
types of, 66–70
Financial futures contracts, 558–69
expansion of, 562–63
foreign exchange, 566–69
hedging/speculating with, 559–62
purpose of, 558
serial correlation coefficients for, 155–56
stock market index, 564–66
Financial institutions, 78–79
Financial risk, 326–27
Financing decisions, and value, 508, 516–25
Fisher Effect, 360–64, 624
Fixed-income securities, 68, 332–68;
see also Bonds
definition of, 333–35
and inflation, 360–64
privately-issued, 399–400
probability distribution of cash flows from, 335–38
rates of return on, 341–47, 366–68
for default-free securities, 341–43
real/nominal, 360–64
for securities with default risk, 343–44
and term structure of interest rates, 356–60
ratings of, 397
risk of, 347–56, 382, 387–88, 394–96
components of, 348–54
estimation of, 354–55
management of, 355–56
types of, 372–401
valuation of, 338–40
Floating rate notes, 396
Flower bonds, 377
Forecasting, 475–504
beta, 487–90
earnings, 477
aggregate market, 500
analysts' forecasts in, 481–87
leading indicators in, 478–80
managers' forecasts in, 480–81
statistical extrapolations in, 477–78
individual security returns, 490–93
insider information in, 494–97

Forecasting—*Cont.*
market portfolio returns, 497–501
requirements for, 476–77
technical analysis used in, 502–3
value of, 468–69
Foreign exchange
efficiency of market for, 628–29
forward markets for, 567, 626–28
futures on, 566–69
market for, and exchange risk, 620–26
Foreign securities; see International securities
Fortune 500, 149, 174
Forward contracts, 540
commodities for, 546–47
concept of, 541–52
foreign exchange, 567, 626–28
options compared with, 574
purpose of, 545–46
valuation of, 552–58
Forward price, 10, 541
of a currency, 619
Frequency distributions; see Probability distributions
Fundamental analysis, 173–74, 308–9
Futures contracts, 69–70, 73–74, 82, 540–70; see also Financial futures contracts
commodity, 540–58
and filter rules, 166
return rates on, 136–38
serial correlation coefficients for, 155–56
concept of, 542–44
foreign exchange, 627–28
institutions and trading of, 81–82, 547–52
options on, 579
profit/loss in, 544–45
purpose of, 545–46, 588–89
valuation of, 552–58, 567–69
types of market for, 546–47
Futures price, 10, 541

G

Gaussian distributions; see Normal distributions
General obligation bonds, 379–80
Gold, 556n
Good-till-canceled orders, 91
Government National Mortgage Association (GNMA), mortgage-backed securities, 64, 377, 379
futures on, 558, 562
Graduated payment mortgages (GPMs), 73–74, 399
Granville, Joe, 443

Greenmail, 62
Gross national product (GNP), 500
Growth, in dividend capitalization
  model, 414–15
  constant, 415–16
  of earnings/dividends, 418–19
  and stockholder returns, 421–22
  two-stage, 416–18, 428
Growth stocks, 414, 419–21, 510

H

Hedge ratio, 596–98
Hedging, 541
  foreign exchange market, 627–28
  futures contract, 545–46, 550
    demand for, and futures prices,
      555–56
    with interest rate futures, 559–62
    with stock index futures, 566
Holding period return; *see* Rate of
  return
Home equity loans, 400
Homogenious expectations assumption,
  226–27, 246–47, 295
Houston Oil Trust, 412
Human capital, and capital asset pricing
  model, 249–50
Hunt, Nelson Bunker, 192 n

I

Ideal markets, 148–51
Immunization, 355–56
Incentives for use of debt, 522–25
Income bonds, 62n, 74
Income effect, 16
Indenture provisions, 337–38
Index funds, 647–48, 652, 658
Index managers, 647–48
Indifference curves, 13–14
  and efficient portfolio choice,
    205–8
  and marginal utility, 34–35
  and minimum standard duration
    portfolio, 197
  and portfolio choice, 183–84
  risk aversion shown using, 40
  and separation theorem, 212–14
Industrial production, 630
Inflation
  and arbitrage pricing theory, 298
  and commodity future returns, 137
  and fixed-income securities, 360–64
  and foreign investment, 619, 624–25
  and investment returns, 139–40
Information motive for portfolio
  revision, 652–53
Initial margin, 543, 551
Insider information, 494–98

Instinet, 101
Institute of Chartered Financial
  Analysts, 496
Instrinsic worth; *see* Equilibrium value,
  underlying
Insurance companies, 78, 80, 100
Insurance principle, 184–85, 605
Interbank Foreign Exchange Market,
  627–28
Interest charges, as earnings
  determinant, 451–52, 456
Interest-rate futures; *see* Financial
  futures
Interest-rate parity, 568–69, 626–28
Interest-rate risk, 326–27, 343
  and deposit accounts, 385
  and financial futures, 558–63
  on floating-rate notes, 396
  nondiversifiable, 348, 350–53
    and bond beta, 353–54
    on common stock, 423, 426
    and immunization, 355–56
    and liquidity preference theory,
      358–59
Interest rates; *see also* Interest-rate
  parity; Interest-rate risk; Rate of
  return; *and* Risk-free interest rate
  and arbitrage pricing theory, 298,
    300
  and call price, 389
  forecasting, 498–99
  foreign, 619, 624–25
  level of, and fixed-income securities
    prices, 352
  and market equilibrium, 19–20
  and market model, 256
  term structure of, 356–60
  and theory of choice, 11, 15–16
Intermarket Trading System (ITS), 81,
  86, 102
International Monetary Market (IMM),
  628
International securities, 132, 617–39
  betas of, 631, 634
  diversified portfolios of, 629–35
  and exchange risk, 620–26
  foreign government, 384
  and forward exchange forward
    markets, 626–28
  historical returns on, 619–20
  investment opportunities in, 617–19
  market for, 96–97
  successful example of investment in,
    637–38
  valuation of, 635–36
In-the-money options, 594
Investment
  decisions on, and value, 508–12
  definition of, 57
  financial versus real, 70–71

Investment—*Cont.*
  opportunities for, and common stock
    valuation, 412–14
  and theory of choice, 16–22
Investment bankers, 78, 80
Investment Company Act of 1940, 655
Investment motive, 8–9

J–K

January effect, 160
Japan, 132, 620, 630
Japan Fund, 661
Jensen Performance Index, 678–79
Junk bonds, 396
Keynes, John Maynard, 555
Keystone Growth Stock Fund, 674
Kidder, Peabody & Co., 80
Kurtosis, 33

L

Large-block orders, 92, 159
Large numbers, law of, 30, 184
Leverage, and valuation, 516–25
Levine, Dennis, 497
Limited-tax bonds, 379
Limit orders, 91, 158
Liquidation risk, 379
Liquidity, 71–73, 85–86, 645
  and capital asset pricing model, 226
  of deposit accounts, 384
  in ideal markets, 148–50
  of international equity market,
    633–34
  and mutual funds, 658
  and portfolio theory, 202
Liquidity preference theory, 357–59
Liquidity premium, 357–58
Listing requirements
  NASDAQ, 102–3
  securities exchanges, 87–88
Loading fees, 659, 683
Locking the market, 86
London Stock Exchange, 102, 663
London Times, 133–35
Long position, defined, 541
Long-term securities markets, 81–82
Lynch, Jones, & Ryan I/B/E/S
  database, 481–84

M

Maintenance margin, 551–52
Making a market, 86–87
Managers' forecasts, 480–81
Manhattan Fund for Income, 267
Margin, on futures contract, 541, 543,
  551–52
Marginal rate of time preference, 13

Margin calls, 96
Margin requirements, 216
Margin transactions, 95–96, 211
Marketability, 64, 71–73, 85–86, 95
Market equilibrium, 19–20, 223–25;
    see also Capital asset pricing
    model (CAPM) *and* Equilibrium
    price
  and arbitrage, 21
  and equal rate of return, 20–21
Market model, 256–68, 300
  and capital asset pricing model,
    259–69, 293
Market model characteristic line
  individual security, 257, 259, 263
  portfolio, 264–67
Market orders, 90–91, 158
Market portfolio, 226–29; *see also*
    Capital asset pricing model
    (CAPM)
  and arbitrage pricing theory, 297–98
  forecasting returns on, 497–501
  in market model, 259
  testability of, 284, 286–88
Market price, 308–10
  of assets, and ability to pay, 337–38
  of securities listed on exchanges, 83
  and security analysis, 444–45
  in single-period valuation, 310–18
  in theory of choice, 6–7, 11
Market-related variance, 260
Market Report, 443
Market segmentation theory, 359–60
Market timing
  ability in, 672–73
  and security analysis, 464–68
Marking to market, 543
Maturity
  of contracts, 64–65
  date of, 334
  and interest-rate risk, 350–51
  and term structure of interest rates,
    356–60
Maturity date of options, 574
Mean; *see* Expected value
Mergers, and value, 309, 508,
    512–16
Merrill Lynch, Pierce, Fenner & Smith,
    Inc., 85, 488, 633
Merrill Lynch White Weld Capital
    Markets Group, 80
Minimum standard deviation portfolio
    (MSDP), 196–97
Minimum-value line, 582, 594–95
Modern Portfolio Strategies, Inc., 205,
    650
Monetary policy, 129, 364
Money market mutual funds, 73–74,
    375, 656, 660–61
Money markets, 81–82, 385

Money market securities
  of corporations, 385–87
  foreign, 618
  yields on, 387
Money spread, 585–87
Money supply, as earnings predictor,
    478–80
Monitoring costs, 63
Moody's *Bond Record,* 397
Morgan Guaranty Trust Company, 621
Mortgage-backed securities, 64, 399
  FHLMC, 377–78, 399
  FNMA, 339
  GNMA, 64, 377, 379, 558, 562
Mortgage bankers, 78, 80–81, 542
Mortgages, 353–54, 399–400
MPS, 205
Multinational firms, diversification
    using, 634–35
Multiple regression, 48
Municipal Bond Insurance Association,
    380
Municipal bonds, 78, 333, 379–84
Mutual funds, 64, 385, 647, 656–61
  closed-end, 657, 661
  diversification by, 653, 658, 660
  growth of, 657
  market index correlations of, 267
  money market, 73–74, 375, 656,
    660–61
  no-load, 659–61
  open-end, 655, 657–61
  performance of, 676–83
Mutual savings banks, 78, 80, 384–85

N

NASDAQ; *see* National Association of
    Securities Dealers Automatic
    Quotation (NASDAQ)
National Association of Securities
    Dealers (NASD), 101
National Association of Securities
    Dealers Automatic Quotation
    (NASDAQ), 101–3, 633
  National Market System (NMS),
    101–2
  OTC Composite Index, 106, 109
National exchanges, 83
Negotiable certificates of deposit
    (CDs), 82, 386, 660
Negotiated markets, 99
Net present value, 18
  of investment opportunities, 509–12
New York City, bond default by, 380
New York Curb Market Association
    (NYCMA), 85
New York Institute of Finance, 573–74
New York Stock Exchange (NYSE),
    77, 83–84, 109

New York Stock Exchange (NYSE)—
    Cont.
  bond listings on, 393–94
  futures market compared with, 549
  history of, 84–85
  international securities on, 618–19,
    633
  liquidity of stocks on, 72–73
  listing requirements of, 87–88
  option trading on, 573, 592
  and over-the-counter market, 100,
    102
  seasonality on, 161
  specialists of, 86
  trading process on, 90, 93–97
  transaction-to-transaction dependency
    and practices of, 158
New York Stock Exchange (NYSE)
    Composite Index, 106, 108–9
  in capital asset pricing model tests,
    271
  and index funds, 648
  in market model, 256
  options on, 575
No-load mutual funds, 659–61
Nonmarketable assets, capital asset
    pricing model with, 249–50
Nonmarket variance; *see* Unsystematic
    variance
Normal backwardation, 555–56
Normal distributions, 29, 31–33, 39
Normalized earnings, 452–54
NYSE; *see* New York Stock Exchange
    (NYSE)

O

Objects of art, 132–35
Obligations of the United States, 377 n
Odd-lot differential, 91
Odd lots, 90–91
One price, law of, 21, 292–93, 297
Open orders, 91
Opening Automated Report Service
    (OARS), 94
Open interest, 548–50
Open market operations, and term
    structure, 360
Open market purchases, 531–32
Operating efficiency assumptions, 71–
    73, 148, 202, 226; *see also*
    Efficient market hypothesis
Operating revenues, as earnings
    determinant, 450–51, 456
Operating risk; *see* Business risk
Opportunities, 6, 9–11, 193, 208
Opportunity cost, and discount rate, 313
Opportunity set, 15–16, 183
  in capital asset pricing model, 230
  in two-stock portfolio, 196–99

Optimal portfolio, 205–10
  and active/passive management, 650
  and capital asset pricing model, 227
  for Dow Jones securities, 216–17
  and market equilibrium, 223–25
  as performance measurement
      standard, 669–70
  with risk-free borrowing and lending,
      210–12
  and separation theorem, 212–14
  and short selling, 214–16
Options, 69, 73–74, 82, 84, 573–612;
      see also Black-Scholes option
      valuation model; Call options; *and*
      Put options
  beta of, 607
  concept of, 574
  exchange trading of, 590–94
  on futures contracts, 73–74, 579
  kinds of, 575–81
  markets for, 81–82
  over-the-counter trading of, 592–94
  profit in, 581–88
  purpose of, 588–90
  skewness of payments on, 32
  strategies for use of, 605–6
  taxation of, 611–12
  valuation of, 594–606, 608–11
Options exchanges, 573, 575–76,
      590–92
Orders, security exchange, 89–92
Out-of-the-money options, 594
Over-the-counter market
  corporate bonds, 393
  foreign securities, 618–19
  options, 575–76, 592–94

P

Pacific Coast Stock Exchange, 84, 592
Paris Bourse, 618
Partial equilibrium solution, 15, 208–9
Partnership agreements, trading of,
      68–69
Partnerships, 59
Par value, 334
Passbook savings accounts, 333, 355
Passive management, 646–52, 679–80
Past price series analyses, 173–74
Peakedness, 33
Penn Central Bank, 386 n, 660 n
Pension funds, 647–48, 656, 663–64
  active/passive strategy for, 650
  performance of, 679
  types of, 663–64
Performance measurement, 649, 668–
      87
  application of, 676–77
  diversification, 674–75
  example of, 674

Performance measurement—*Cont.*
  indexes for, 677–79
  market timing, 672–73
  for professionally managed
      portfolios, 679–83
  security selection, 671–72
  for self-managed portfolios, 683–87
  total, 673
Personal value, 308–9, 338
  and equilibrium price determination,
      311–12, 315
  multiperiod, 324–26
  and security analysis, 444
Philadelphia Stock Exchange, 84, 88,
      592
Portfolio insurance, 648
Portfolio management issues, 645–65;
      see also Professionally managed
      funds
  active/passive, 646–52
  constraints, 646, 654–56
  diversification, 646, 653–54
  manager type, 646, 656
  revision, 646, 652–53
Portfolio revision, 217, 646, 652–53
Portfolio selection, 183–218
  of Dow Jones securities, 216–17
  empirics of risk reduction in, 186–92
  and estimation risk, 218
  and insurance principle, 184–85
  optimal diversification in, 202–5
  optimal portfolio choice in, 205–14
  and portfolio revision, 217
  random diversification in, 192–201
      for *N*-security case, 200–201
      for six-security portfolio, 198–200
      for two-security portfolio, 193–98
  short selling and efficient set in,
      214–16
Portfolio theory
  applying to optimal portfolio choice,
      205–10
  assumptions of, 202–5
  and capital asset pricing model, 226
Precautionary motive, 8–9
Predictor variables, in forecasting,
      476–79
Preferences, 183, 646
  in theory of choice, 6, 7, 13–14, 208
Preferred habitat theory; *see* Market
      segmentation theory
Preferred stock, 78, 65, 333–35
  foreign, 618
  rates of return on, 367–68
  standard features of, 387–94
Premium, on options, 574
Present value, 12–13; *see also* Net
      present value
  of the exercise price, 600
  of productive investment, 18, 21–22

Price
  of a currency, 619
  law of one, 21, 292–93, 297
  and rate of return, 116–17
  in theory of choice, 208
Price continuity, 72–73, 85–86, 645
  and capital asset pricing model, 226
  in ideal markets, 148–50
  and portfolio theory, 202
Price-earnings (P/E) ratio, 427–29
  foreign market, 619–20
  relationship between stock valuation
      and, 430–32
Price limit orders, 91–92
Primary securities markets, 78–80
Prime rate loans, hedging, 561
Principal, 334
Private placements, 394
Probability, definition of, 27
Probability distributions, 29
  joint, 44–49
  and risk, 34
  summary measures of, 29–33
Productivity, in arbitrage pricing
      theory, 296–97, 300
Professionally managed funds, 646,
      656; *see also* Mutual funds *and*
      Pension funds
  performance of, 679–83
  types of, 657–64
Profit line, 582
Proprietorships, 59
Prospectus, 80, 103
Prudential-Bache Securities, Inc., 85
Public utilities, 187, 542
Pure expectations theory, 359
Put options, 577, 605
  beta of, 607
  combination of call options and,
      585
  profit on, 584–85
  valuation of, 602–5
Puttable bonds, 396

R

Random variables, 28–29
  combinations of, 49–52
  probability distributions of, 29
Random walk, 152 n
  of earnings changes, 457
  of foreign exchange prices, 628–29
  of security prices, 151, 156
Rate of return, 115–42; *see also*
      Capital asset pricing model
      (CAPM); Common stock;
      Corporate bonds; Efficient market
      hypothesis; Fixed-income
      securities; *and* Standard deviation
      of returns

Rate of return—*Cont.*
active/passive management and
identification of, 649–50
on aggregate world market wealth
portfolio, 138–39
in arbitrage pricing theory, 293–97
arithmetic average, 122, 126–27
calculation of, 116–17
in capital asset pricing model, 225,
268, 270–82
changing units from dollars to,
41–42
on collectibles and objects of art,
133–35
on commodity futures, 136–38
on common stock indexes, 117–29
and comovement of stock returns,
186–92
on corporate bond indexes, 123–27
disequilibrium, 315–16, 445–48
for Dow Jones efficient set,
216–17
in efficient market hypothesis, 151
for efficient portfolios, 202–5
equal, 20–21
and estimation error, 218
on foreign investments
and exchange rates, 622
historical, 132, 619–20
on Fortune 500, 145, 174
geometric mean, 120–23, 126–27
holding period, 116–17
on common stock indexes, 117–29
on fixed-income securities, 342–
43, 347
in ideal markets, 149–51
independent stock return movements
assumed, 186
and leverage, 516–17
and market equilibrium, 223–25
in market model, 256–68
for optimal portfolios, 205–10
option, 587–88
and pricing process, 146–48
and random diversification, 192–201
for *N*-security case, 200–201
for six-security case, 198–200
for two-security case, 193–98
real, 139–41
on real estate, 135–36
and risk, 140–41
with risk-free borrowing and lending,
210–12
seasonality of, 153, 159–62
and short selling, 214–16
and trading strategies, success of,
163–66
on U.S. Treasury securities, 129–32
Real estate, rates of return on, 135–36,
138

Real estate investment trusts (REITs),
656, 661–62
Real estate limited partnerships, 662
Rebalancing motive for portfolio
revision, 652–53
Redeemable bonds, 581
Redistribution motive, 8
Regional exchanges, 83, 88
Regression, 44, 46–48
application of, 48–49
multiple, 48
Regression tendency, 461
Regulation Q, 214, 386
Regulation T, 96
Reinvestment rate, 343
Residual variance, *see* Unsystematic
variance
Retail houses, 85
Revenue bonds, 380–84
Revenue line; *see* Minimum-value line
Revolving credit agreements, 399
Rights, 578–79
Risk, 34; *see also* Beta; Capital asset
pricing model (CAPM); Common
stock; Default risk; *and* Fixed-
income securities
and assumption of independent stock
return movements, 186
of bond index returns, 123–24
business, 326
in capital asset pricing model, 225
diminishing marginal utility and
aversion to, 33–39
effects of random diversification on,
192–201
of efficient portfolio, 202–5
estimation, 218
and financial contracts, 60, 65
foreign exchange, 620–28
and forward/futures contracts, 542,
545–46
in ideal markets, 149
independent stock returns assumed,
186
and insurance principle, 184–85
liquidation, 379
management of, 183–84
in market model, 256–68
of mutual funds, 660
of optimal portfolio, 205–14, 216–17
and options, 588–90, 605
of pension funds, 664
and pricing process, 147–48
in real world, 186–89
and return, summary of, 140–41
of stock index returns, 123–24
trade-off between wealth and, 39–42
and value, 326–27
Risk-adjusted discount rate valuation
method, 329

Risk-free borrowing/lending,
assumption of, 210–14, 226, 242–
46, 646
Risk-free interest rate, 210, 214, 216
and arbitrage pricing theory, 296,
299
in capital asset pricing model, 255,
282–83
and multiperiod valuation, 320–21
and options valuation, 596–600
in security analysis, 448, 462, 467
Risk-return trade-off; *see* Security
market line (SML)
Round-lot orders, 90

S

Salomon Brothers, 85
High Grade Long-Term Bond Index,
123
Santa Fe Industries, 495
Saving
reason for, 8–9
and theory of choice, 9–16
and uncertainty, 26–27
Savings and loan associations, 384–85,
399, 542, 562
Scalar value, 30
Seasonality of returns, 153, 159–63
Secondary markets, 81
for agency securities, 378
for corporate bonds, 387–88,
393–95
for options, 579–80
Securities, 57–111
costs and benefits of, 61–66
exchange trading of, 81–82
marketability of, 64, 71–73
purchased on margin, 95–96
purpose of, 10–11, 18–19
types of, 66–70, 73–74, 81–82
and wealth of society, 70–71
Securities Act Amendments of 1975,
104–6
Securities Act of 1933, 103
Securities and Exchange Commission
(SEC), 214, 394, 550
and insider information, 494–97
and over-the-counter market, 102
regulatory powers of, 81, 103–4
Securities Exchange Act of 1934,
103–4
Rule 10.b.5 of, 494, 531 n
Securities exchanges, 77, 83–99
history and organization of, 84–85
listing requirements of, 87–88
membership of, 85–87
trading process on, 89–90
Securities Investor Protection Act
(SIPC), 104

Securities markets, 77–111
  over-the-counter, 99–103, 109
  primary, 78–80
  regulation of, 103–6
  secondary, 81
Security analysis, 436–37, 442–70,
    648, 670
  beta in, 448, 460–62, 467
  dividends and earnings in, 449–60
  and forecasting, 475–76
  market timing analysis compatibility
    with, 464–68
  and production of private
    information, 442–47
  and security market line
    intercept/slope, 462
  and size of disequilibrium return,
    448
  standard deviations and covariances
    in, 463–64
Security Analysis (Dodd and Dodd),
    444
Security market line (SML), 234–36,
    255, 293
  and active/passive management, 650
  and beta, 236–38
  and differing tax rates, 248
  and forecasting, 475–76, 497–98
  and foreign securities valuation,
    635–36
  and interest rate risk, 426
  and investment decisions, 510
  and leverage, 519–20
  and market model, 263
  in multiperiod valuation, 319–23
  and over- or undervalued securities,
    238–39
  and performance measurement,
    669–73, 677
  and security analysis, 448, 462,
    468
  in single period valuation, 310–19
  tests of, 268, 276
  zero-beta form of, 244–45
Security prices; *see also* Arbitrage
    pricing theory (APT); Capital asset
    pricing model (CAPM); Efficient
    market hypothesis; *and*
    Equilibrium price
  factors determining, 146–52
  information signals and reactions of,
    163, 167–73
  NASDAQ quotations of, 101–3
  past series analysis of, 173–74
  serial correlations of changes in,
    153–56
  and trading process on exchanges, 89
  transaction-to-transaction
    dependencies between changes
    in, 153, 156–59

Security selection ability, 671–72; *see
    also* Performance measurement
Selection bias, 133
Separation principle, 18
Separation theorem, 212–14
Serial correlation of security prices,
    153–56
Settlement, 95
Settlement price, 543–44
Share repurchase, and value, 508,
    531–33
Sharpe Performance Index, 679
Short position, defined, 541
Short selling, 89–90
  and efficient set, 214–16
Signaling
  dividends, 529–30
  incentive, 524–25
Silver, 556 n
Singapore Stock Exchange, 618
Single investment period, assumption
    of, 202, 226, 646
Sinking fund provisions, 387–88,
    391–92, 394
Skewness, 32–33
Small Business Administration, 377
Small businesses, 65, 283
Small Order Execution System (SOES),
    102
Specialists
  books of, 92–93
  role of, 85–87, 91, 95, 105
Specialist units, 86
Special orders, 91–92
Speculation, 541, 546, 550
  with interest rate futures, 559–62
Spot price, 541, 543; *see also* Forward
    contracts *and* Futures contracts
  arbitrage and expected future,
    552–53
Spread transactions, 558
Standard deviation, 31–32, 39
  in capital asset pricing model, 295
  of combinations of variables, 50–52
  and skewness, 32–33
Standard deviation of returns, 41, 186,
    190, 645; *see also* Capital asset
    pricing model (CAPM)
  active/passive management and
    identification of, 649–50
  in capital asset pricing model, 225
  and diversification benefits, 191–92
  of efficient portfolio, 202–3
  and estimation risk, 218
  on fixed-income securities, 347
  on foreign securities, 622,
    630–32
  and market equilibrium, 223–25
  in N-security case, 200–201
  of optimal portfolio, 205–10

Standard deviation of returns—*Cont.*
  in options valuation, 600–601
  and risk-free borrowing, 210–12
  in security analysis, 463–64
  in six-security diversification,
    198–200
  in two-security diversification,
    193–98
Standard & Poor's *Bond Guide,* 397
Standard & Poor's Composite Index of
    500 Stocks, 106, 108–9, 174,
    187, 323
  and arbitrage pricing theory, 299
  in capital asset pricing model tests,
    270–71
  construction of, 127–29
  and earnings beta, 454
  in earnings forecasting, 479
  futures on, 558, 564–66
  and index funds, 648, 652
  and index managers, 647–48
  and market model, 256, 261, 267
  in market portfolio, 229 n
  options on, 575
  price-earnings ratio for, 429
  rates of return on, 117–20, 123–27
    fixed-income security returns
      compared with, 347, 354
    international investment returns
      compared with, 638
    real/nominal, 360
    Treasury security returns compared
      with, 131, 468–69
  performance measurement against,
    674, 676
  valuation of, 416, 466–67
Standard & Poor's stock market
    indexes, 108, 575; *see also*
    Standard & Poor's Composite
    Index of 500 Stocks
Stock; *see* Common stock *and*
    Preferred stock
Stock dividends, 533–34, 592
Stock market indexes, 106, 108–9; *see
    also* Index funds *and* Standard &
    Poor's Composite Index of 500
    Stocks
  in capital asset pricing model tests,
    270–71, 275
  construction of, 127–29
  futures on, 73, 564–66
  and market model, 256
  options on, 575
  and passive management, 647–48
  stock return movement correlations
    with, 187
Stock market indicators, 106–9
Stock options; *see* Options
Stock-paying bonds, 396
Stock splits, 169, 533–34, 592

Stop limit orders, 92
Stop orders, 91–92
Straddle, 585
Street names, 96
Strike price; *see* Exercise price
Submartingale, 152 n
Subordination level, 387–88, 392
Subscription sales of Treasury
    securities, 376
Substitution effect, 16
SuperDOT, 95
Supply and demand
    and equilibrium price, 224–25, 228
    in futures market, 546, 552, 556–57
    for loanable funds, and interest rates,
        499
    in pricing process, 146–50
    and term structure of interest rates,
        358–60
Sydney Stock Exchange, 618
Synergy, 513–15
Systematic (market related) variance,
    260

T

Tabor, Timothy, 496
Taxes
    and bond returns, 364
    capital gains, 528–29, 654
    and cash flow constraints, 654
    and choice of debt or equity, 522
    differing rates of, and capital asset
        pricing model, 247–48
    as earnings determinant, 452
    of options, 611–12
Tax Reform Act of 1986, 452, 528,
    611–12
Technical analysis, 173–74, 502–3
Tender offers, and valuation, 515–16,
    531–33
Tennessee Valley Authority, 377
Term bonds, 376–77
Term structure of interest rates,
    356–60
Theory of Interest, The (Fisher), 307
Third-party financial contracts, 69–70
Third World debt, 618 n
Ticker tape, 97–98, 101
Time horizon of portfolio, 655–56
Time limit orders, 91
Timing, market; *see* Market timing
Tokyo Stock Exchange, 77, 83, 86,
    102, 618–19, 633
Toronto Stock Exchange, 496
Trading pit, 549, 590
Trading strategies, and efficient
    markets, 163–66
Trading through the market, 86
Trading volume, 83

Transaction costs
    capital asset pricing model with,
        248–49
    and diversification, 646, 653
    on foreign security transactions, 621,
        633
    and ideal markets, 148–49
    mutual fund, 657, 682
    and passive management, 647, 648
    and portfolio revision, 217, 653
    and portfolio theory, 214
Treynor Performance Index, 679
Two-Mutual Funds Theorem, 244

U

Unbiased expectations hypothesis,
    553–54
Uncertainty; *see also* Random variables
    and Risk
    concept of, 26–27
    decisions under, 33–37
    and geometric mean return, 120–23
    and saving decision, 8–9
    valuation under, 42–43
Underlying equilibrium value; *see*
    Equilibrium value, underlying
Unlimited tax bonds, 379
Unlisted trading, 88
Unseasoned issues, 100
Unsystematic variance, 260, 267
U.S. Department of Justice, 494–97
U.S. Postal Service, 377
U.S. savings bonds, 372–73
U.S.S.R., 556 n
U.S. Treasury, 359–60, 561
U.S. Treasury bills, 64, 78, 82, 333,
    373–75
    futures on, 558–63
    money market fund investments in,
        660–61
    rates of return on, 129–32, 138,
        468–69, 674, 676
U.S. Treasury bonds, 78, 333,
    376–77
    durations of, 352–53
    futures on, 546, 562–63
    rates of return on, 129–32, 138,
        362–63
U.S. Treasury notes, 78, 333,
    376–77
    futures on, 562
    and nondiversifiable interest-rate risk,
        350–52
U.S. Treasury securities, 68, 333, 372–
    77; *see also* U.S. Treasury bills;
    U.S. Treasury bonds; *and* U.S.
    Treasury notes
    Consumer Price Index and rate on,
        361–62

U.S. Treasury securities—*Cont.*
    and default risk, 335
    futures on, 73
    margin requirements for purchase of,
        96
    marketability of, 72
    and primary securities market,
        78
    and term structure of interest rates,
        356–57
Utility
    comparisons of, 38–39
    diminishing marginal, 34–35
    expected, 36–38
Utility curve, 34

V

Valuation, 307–29, 670; *see also*
    Dividend capitalization model;
    Equilibrium value, underlying;
    Fixed-income securities; Forward
    contracts; Futures contracts;
    Options; *and* Security analysis
    analyst's, 445
    certainty equivalent approach to,
        319 n, 328–39
    concept of, 307–8
    equilibrium/disequilibrium in,
        314–18
    and forecasting, 475–76
    and management decisions,
        508–35
        dividend policy, 525–30
        financing, 516–25
        investment, 509–12
        mergers, 512–16
        share repurchase, 531–33
        stock dividends/splits, 533–34
    multiperiod, 319–26
    single-period, 310–14
    three types of, 308–10
    under uncertainty, 42–43
Value Line Investment Contest,
    267–68
Value Line Investment Survey,
    442, 481, 484, 492–93
Vanguard First Index Investment Fund,
    648
Variable-rate mortgages (VRMs), 73–
    74, 334, 400
Voting rights, 87–88

W

Wall Street Journal, The, 108, 109,
    373–75, 378, 382, 575–76
Warrants, 68–69, 577–78, 608

Washington Public Power Supply
    System, 380
Wealth
    accumulation of
        and common stock rates of return,
            118–23
        implied by stock and bond
            investments, 126–27
    aggregate, and financial investment,
        70–71
    certainty equivalent, 38
    diminishing marginal utility for, 34–35

Wealth—*Cont.*
    in theory of choice, 6–7, 12–13,
        208
    trade-off between risk and, 39–42
Weisenberger's Investment Company
    Service, 659–60
Wells Fargo Investment Advisors
    (WFIA), 484, 647–48,
    650
When issued basis, 95
White Motor Corporation, 336 n
Wholesale houses, 85

Wilshire 5000 Equity Index, 106, 109,
    128–29
Wilshire Total Performance Index,
    109

Y–Z

Yield curve, 356–60
Yield to call, 367–68
Yield to maturity, 345–47, 356,
    366–67
Zero coupon bonds, 73